FORT WORTH LIBRARY
3 1668 05268 1951

P9-ELR-063

Library and Book Trade Almanac™

formerly **The Bowker Annual**

2011 | 56th Edition

Library and Book Trade Almanac™

formerly **The Bowker Annual**

2011 | 56th Edition

Editor Dave Bogart
Consultant Julia C. Blixrud

Published by Information Today, Inc.

International Standard Book Number 978-1-57387-412-0
International Standard Serial Number 2150-5446
Library of Congress Catalog Card Number 55-12434

Information Today, Inc.
143 Old Marlton Pike
Medford, NJ 08055-8750
Phone: 800-300-9868 (customer service)
800-409-4929 (editorial queries)
Fax: 609-654-4309
E-mail (orders): custserv@infotoday.com
Web Site: http://www.infotoday.com

Printed and bound in the United States of America

Contents

Part 1
Reports from the Field

Special Reports

Federal Agency and Federal Library Reports

National Association and Organization Reports

International Reports

Part 2
Legislation, Funding, and Grants

Legislation

Funding Programs and Grant-Making Agencies

Part 3
Library/Information Science Education, Placement, and Salaries

Part 4
Research and Statistics

Library Research and Statistics

Book Trade Research and Statistics

Part 5
Reference Information

Bibliographies

Ready Reference

Distinguished Books

Part 6
Directory of Organizations

Directory of Library and Related Organizations

Directory of Book Trade and Related Organizations

Preface

This 56th edition of the *Library and Book Trade Almanac* once again incorporates practical information and informed analysis of interest to librarians, publishers, and others in the rapidly evolving information world.

The past year has brought continuing challenge and change. Recovery from the world financial crisis continues to be slow, and its effects are felt everywhere. Libraries are asked to do more, but with fewer resources. Meanwhile, the march of technology poses constant and growing questions for the publishing industry.

With it all, the demand for accurate and helpful information continually increases, and our aim is to help answer that demand.

This edition's Special Reports focus on three areas of interest.

- Dennis Dillon assesses the impact of electronic books on the publishing world and the challenges they present for libraries. How successfully are we coming to grips with what he terms "a seminal change in consumer behavior"?
- Jeffrey W. Seifert discusses the increasingly complex task of government information management as security becomes an ever-greater issue in light of leaks and cyberattacks.
- Jane E. Kirtley examines the plight of newspapers and what their decline may mean for other media, government, libraries, and the public.

Part 1 continues with reports on the activities of federal libraries, federal agencies, and national and international library and publishing organizations.

Recent and current legislation is covered in Part 2, along with the programs and activities of major grant-making agencies.

Part 3 offers a wealth of professional information for librarians, including salary studies, job-seeking advice, and a list of the year's library scholarship and award winners.

Part 4 contains our growing statistics and research section, which offers detailed data on many aspects of the library and publishing worlds, from trends in school library media resource funding to an examination of U.S. world trade in books.

Reference information fills Part 5, including a roster of major literary prize winners and lists of notable books and other resources for all ages.

Part 6 is our directory of library and publishing organizations at the state, national, and international levels, and also includes a calendar of major upcoming events.

The *Library and Book Trade Almanac* is the work of many hands. We are grateful to everyone who supplied reports, assembled statistics, and responded to our many requests for information. Special gratitude is due to Consultant Editor Julia C. Blixrud and Contributing Editor Catherine Barr, and to Chris McNaull for her great skill in making it all come together.

We believe you will use this reference work frequently, and, as always, we welcome your comments and suggestions for future editions.

Dave Bogart
Editor

Part 1
Reports from the Field

Special Reports

E-books Pose Major Challenge for Publishers, Libraries

Dennis Dillon

Associate Director for Research Services
University of Texas Libraries, University of Texas at Austin
P.O. Box P, Austin, TX 78713-8916
512-495-4269, fax 512-495-4347

Consumers, publishers, and libraries have all extended their embrace of e-books, although libraries and publishers have done so somewhat reluctantly, generally treating e-books as an add-on to traditional print activities while doing their best to ignore the nagging possibility that e-books represent a fundamentally disruptive technology and a seminal change in consumer behavior.

As a result, the past couple of years have been marked by a series of uneven and tentative efforts to come to grips with the e-book market, publisher by somewhat-reluctant publisher, and library by somewhat-reluctant library. Meanwhile consumer e-book sales continue to set new records, quietly heralding a multitude of changes that will alter long-standing practices of both publishers and libraries.

To recap, late in 2007 Amazon introduced the Kindle e-reader, which could wirelessly download a $9.99 book in less than a minute. The following year brought the recession and a changed publishing environment in which print magazines and newspapers struggled, and it was not unusual for venerable publishing operations to downsize, merge, go digital, or cease publishing altogether. Then 2010 brought an announcement from Amazon that its e-book sales were now greater than its hardcover sales, and Apple introduced the iPad, whose presentation of digital magazines and books delighted millions of consumers who also viewed it as an alternative to the cumbersome physicality of print. And, in December 2010, Google brought out Google eBooks, designed, in theory, to include all e-books, all the time, available to (almost) any device, delivered from a permanent worldwide digital cloud. Google eBooks will allow readers to establish an extensive personal e-book library that will be accessible wherever they go and can include all the books they have purchased from childhood to old age.

Throughout 2010, the e-book world continued to await the settlement of the authors' and publishers' curiously self-defeating suit against the original Google Books project; authors and publishers were suing (under the guise of copyright concerns) to, in effect, make it more difficult for time-strapped modern readers to discover what books (many originally digitized from library collections) readers might want to purchase or read. The ruling was finally handed down in March

2011, against Google, but Google's plans for pursuing the case were not immediately known.

Libraries continued to expand their use of e-books, but in a generally cautious manner, as if haunted by the concern that e-books might result in fewer readers needing or wanting to physically visit libraries, and thereby potentially eroding community support.

But 2010 was also a year marked by widespread library acceptance of patron-driven acquisitions, the concept of mounting records of selected e-books in the library catalog and then automatically and instantly purchasing the books that users clicked on to read.

Overall, the e-book industry continued to be marked by a search for effective business models and by an uncertainty about the best long-term approach to take for different market segments. For example, some e-books, such as bestsellers, are read intensively from beginning to end, and are usually marketed to be downloaded and read by consumers on e-readers, while other books are briefly sampled in order to gather a single fact or a relevant passage—such as many academic and professional books, which are often sold as Web-accessible online content.

In general, publishers continued to be concerned about protecting their copyrights, existing markets, and traditional revenue streams, while readers struggled to navigate their way through the e-book maze, attempting to discover what e-books were for sale, how to buy them, and wondering whether the e-books they found were compatible with their particular e-reader (whether it was a stand-alone device or software installed on a laptop or iPad).

Today's readers are bombarded with a multitude of entertainment distractions and information options. Readers have to exert considerable special effort to seek out e-books, but they continue to do so in record-breaking numbers; publishers, in contrast, remain primarily focused on protecting themselves from losing control of their content and pricing models, and have been taking only the most cautious of baby steps to develop new customers and markets. Nevertheless, what publishers fear (that the supply and marketing side of the industry is about to be changed forever) and what readers hope for (that the demand side is about to be improved to the point that it will finally be easy to buy an e-book) are both on the verge of becoming a reality.

E-Book Market Growth

Forrester Research has predicted that e-book sales will grow from just under $1 billion in 2010 to $2.8 billion by 2015, while noting that the digital publishing category increased from 3.7 million U.S. users at the end of 2009 to more than 10.3 million a year later.

The Association of American Publishers announced in December 2009 that e-book content sales in January–October 2009 reached $130.7 million compared with $46.6 million for the same period in 2008, an increase of 180.5 percent. A year later, *Time* magazine reported that 2010 e-book sales had risen 193 percent over 2009 and that e-books now accounted for almost 10 percent of U.S. consumer book sales.

A Book Industry Study Group (BISG) January 2010 report, "Consumer Attitudes Toward E-Book Reading," found that 1 in 5 people surveyed said they had stopped purchasing print books in the preceding 12 months in favor of purchasing the digital edition. Among the consumers who read e-books, 19 percent said they exclusively bought e-books, and another 25 percent said they mostly bought e-books. A follow-up study released in April 2010 reported that 23 percent of respondents said that they now bought e-books exclusively.

Barnes & Noble Chairman Len Riggio likened e-books to the debut of mass-market paperbacks, which transformed the industry by making books more widely available than they had been and at cheaper prices. Barnes & Noble predicted that e-books would grow to a $6 billion business by 2013.

In July Amazon declared that e-book sales topped print hardcover sales for the first time in the second quarter of 2010, with 143 e-books sold for every 100 print hardcover books. The *New York Times* announced that it would begin publishing e-book bestseller lists in 2011. The *Times* has spent two years creating the system that will measure e-book sales. And Random House announced that its e-book sales increased 300 percent in the first half of 2010.

From the flood of available reports, surveys, statistics, and anecdotal user experiences over the past two years, e-books appear to be consistently winning over the readers who buy them, and, as a result, publishers are slowly beginning to grasp the economic realities inherent in this surprising but growing consumer adoption of digital reading alternatives.

Formats and Devices

BISG's third 2010 study on consumer attitudes toward e-book reading, released in July 2010, found that the single device that most people used to read e-books was a desktop or laptop computer, at 37 percent. This was followed by the Kindle at 32 percent, with every other device being in the single digits (including the Sony Reader at 6 percent, the iPod iTouch at 5 percent, the iPhone at 5 percent, and the iPad, which was released in April 2010, coming in at 3 percent). The top sites for acquiring e-books were Amazon at 60 percent, Barnes & Noble at 23 percent, e-books.com at 10 percent, Google at 10 percent, iTunes at 10 percent, Borders.com at 9 percent, libraries at 9 percent, and direct from the publisher at 8 percent.

At the end of 2010 the Kindle 3 was the most popular E Ink-based e-reader, with 40 percent of users preferring the Kindle, while the iPad (along with its Apple cousins the iTouch and iPhone) was the most popular LCD screen e-reader with a total of 28 percent of respondents indicating that they had used the device. E Ink devices are less power-hungry, produce less eyestrain during extended reading, and have a longer battery life, but they do not have the color capability of LCD-based e-readers such as the iPad. Affordable color E Ink devices are still some way off.

There was some initial hope in the book industry that the iPad would be so popular that it would help push e-books beyond the 3 percent to 5 percent of the market that they now occupy. Apple's decision to enter the e-book market was an unusual reversal for Apple's chief executive, Steve Jobs, who had indicated two years before that the book market could not be salvaged, saying, "It doesn't matter how good or bad the product is, the fact is that people don't read anymore. Forty percent of the people in the U.S. read one book or less last year." However, Apple's multi-use tablet has sold well and Forrester Research predicts that by 2015 twice as many people will own tablets as own e-readers, despite most people's preference for E Ink screens over LCDs for sustained reading. But device sales are not the full story. In a November 17, 2010, BISG press release, Kelly Gallagher, Bowker's vice president of publishing services, said the latest data Bowker had captured for BISG indicated that "So far, the iPad shows only marginal impact on the popularity of the Kindle and the [Barnes & Noble] Nook. It appears that heavy to moderate book buyers want a dedicated device for reading that doesn't have a lot of distractions bundled with it. However, we do see that iPad owners may influence overall sales by bringing new and light e-book buyers into the market." On the other hand, the iPad bundles a consumer's books, movies, newspapers, games, and work and home life demands all into one device—providing consumers with a multitude of distractions that any iPad e-book will have to compete against.

Publishers' fears of e-book piracy and reliance on digital rights management (DRM) encryption for all but some academic titles continue to make life unnecessarily difficult for consumers who want to buy and use e-books. DRM has been implemented in different ways by different companies, although the main ones in current use are Adobe's Adept DRM, which is used by many third party e-readers as well as Adobe Digital Editions, and Amazon's DRM, which is an adaptation of the old Mobipocket format. Apple is using ePub formatting, but wraps it in its own DRM software called Fairplay; Barnes & Noble also uses ePub formatting but wraps it in DRM, which is a variant of the Adobe ADEPT scheme. Not to be forgotten, the new Google eBooks platform uses the now more or less standard Adobe Content Server 4, which works across a huge swath of current e-book readers, smart phones, and other devices.

All of these attempts at locking down proprietary e-book files have resulted in a mind-boggling proliferation of formats, with the iPad, the Nook, and the Sony Reader supporting the XML-based ePub format. With its flowable and easily resized text, ePub is rapidly gaining ground on the Kindle's proprietary azw format, and the venerable pdf and HTML formats. Some of the current popular file formats and the extensions that consumers must contend with include: plain text (.txt), HTML (.html), PostScript (.ps), Portable Document Format (.pdf), DJVU (.djvu), ePub (.epub), FictionBook (.fb2), Mobipocket (.prc and .mobi), Kindle (.azw), e-reader (.pdb), Broadband e-book (.lrf and .lrx), WOLF (.wol), Tome Raider (.tr2, .tr3), Arghos Reader (.aeh), Microsoft Reader (.lit), and multimedia books with .exe. Although several of today's dedicated e-readers support multiple formats, the same file can still display differently on different devices depending upon each device's implementation schemes. This can be a serious problem with text such as poetry, where the author's formatting can be destroyed by the overrides inherent in the device.

Of course, the battle over formats is not just an effort to prevent piracy, as digital rights management software can be easily circumvented even on a home computer, and as even the most unskilled can scan, digitize, or retype any printed book in existence and then quickly distribute it worldwide over the Internet with relatively little effort. Since the skills needed to convert printed text to digital text are already possessed by hundreds of millions of people, the piracy genie cannot be put back into the bottle by technology alone. More importantly, the proprietary formats and DRM schemes lie at the heart of larger corporate business strategies and the war to win market share. Vendors hope that their format and suite of services will win over consumers and eventually lock those consumers into one company for years to come, just as Microsoft was able to control the computer market for years with Windows and Microsoft Office. These corporate strategies make minor complaints about the format wars being bad for the industry and a turn-off for consumers simply irrelevant to major e-book providers, given the revenue potential at stake. Reader lock-ins to particular devices and sales channels—Amazon and Apple being the primary corporate culprits—are ideal solutions for companies that are intent on dominating the market and exercising as complete control as possible over their product line. Google eBooks has a more device-agnostic strategy for e-books in that its e-books can be purchased and read anywhere on almost any device (except Amazon's Kindle) and represent a more open and growth oriented overall approach for the industry. But Google's vision of e-books that are permanently available in the cloud for every device only works if Google is the host—although it is conceivable that other companies could also enter the cloud e-books market. Amazon, by completely controlling the e-book experience from initial sale to the e-reader device, has been able to simplify the user experience and has also been successful in sustaining customer loyalty. Amazon's reliance on E Ink e-readers is also distinctive in that E Ink maximizes the time the human eye can read an e-book without eyestrain, which is preferable for serious readers who are likely to buy multiple e-books during the year.

Libraries

E-book usage in all types of libraries continued to increase during 2010. Most library e-book purchases were of e-books viewable through Web-based e-book aggregators and publishers, although some libraries were circulating e-readers (primarily Kindles) with pre-loaded books, and public libraries were reporting positive experiences with patron-downloaded e-books from OverDrive.

In October *Library Journal* and *School Library Journal* held an e-book summit that drew more than 2,500 participants. Among the participants, the average public library offered 1,500 e-book titles, while the average academic library offered more than 30,000. Among the observations of the participants:

- Libraries expect e-book usage to increase
- Libraries and publishers are not yet on the same page in regard to what is needed to make e-books effective in libraries
- DRM is still a huge issue for library users in that it makes e-books difficult to use

- Academic librarians are embracing both patron-driven acquisitions and e-book bundles (both subscription and one-time purchases)
- Libraries of all types plan to increase their purchase of e-books

In November the *Chronicle of Higher Education* reported extensively on academic libraries' use of patron-driven acquisitions for e-books, and in October Portico announced that it would begin offering library e-book preservation services in 2011 with an initial corpus of 66,000 titles. The service will mirror the model currently in place with Portico's library e-journal preservation program. Access to archived e-book content will be available to subscribing libraries when specific trigger events occur that make the commercially vended e-book unavailable.

Libraries have also increasingly turned to traditional printed book suppliers for assistance with e-book acquisitions, and vendors including Baker & Taylor and Ingram have stepped forward with platforms that allow libraries to order both print and e-books, with the e-books typically being supplied through one of the major e-book aggregators such as ebrary, EBL, NetLibrary, or MyiLibrary. These vendors also have the ability to set up profiles for an approval plan that supplies e-books in addition to printed books. One indicator of how far e-books have come in the past two years is that several large research libraries have established approval plan profiles in which the e-book version is preferred to the print when both are published simultaneously.

In general, however, libraries have not been a factor in the planning of most publishers' e-book efforts, which tend to focus on e-book sales to the devices owned by consumers. Since libraries exist to buy a book once and share it many times, it's only common sense that publishers are not eager to undercut potential consumer sales by designing e-books that work well in a library setting. Why would a publisher sell one copy to a library when it could sell a dozen or more copies to that library's community of users?

Libraries are not a critical part of existing trade e-book distribution channels, except in the most cumbersome way, via the purchase of expensive and fragile e-reading devices, which are then loaded with a single e-book and lent to library patrons in the same manner as a printed book. The practice of lending preloaded e-readers is somewhat illogical, even nonsensical, from a library staffing, efficiency, and budgeting standpoint, but is nevertheless effective in engaging public interest.

The exception to this exclusion of libraries from general e-book market strategy lies with the publishers of academic titles, as print versions of academic books traditionally have been marketed to libraries, and have limited mass-market appeal. These e-books are intended to be Web-accessible and read without librarian intervention. In some cases many users are able to read a single e-book simultaneously; in other cases, viewing is limited to one reader at a time. Acquisitions and operating costs for online e-books are less expensive than those of e-books preloaded onto fragile e-readers (along with their hidden costs of maintenance, library staff handling, and proprietary controls), even when taking into account that libraries are sometimes willing to pay extra to allow multiple simultaneous reading of online e-books.

The libraries' problem, however, is simple. Bestsellers and mainstream trade e-books are primarily sold to be loaded on e-reader devices, and academic niche e-books are primarily sold to be accessed via the Web. At present, libraries do not have a single reliable channel through which they can purchase all types of e-books of interest to their customers. Libraries want options that will allow them to conveniently serve the growing market of library e-book users while simultaneously working with publishers in a way that is productive for everyone involved: libraries, readers, and publishers. Until this market develops, libraries will need to regularly revise their print and e-book strategies.

Publishers and Aggregators

E-Book Library (EBL), ebrary, MyiLibrary, NetLibrary, and dawsonera (United Kingdom) are vendors of Web-based e-books from the major academic publishers, selling primarily to academic libraries. There is significant content overlap. They have slightly different business models and interfaces; they all have proven track records and loyal customers; they sell books for permanent purchase; each (except for dawsonera) has a patron-driven acquisitions model; a couple have significant subscription models; they all use digital rights management software; and each (except ebrary) has some titles that can be downloaded. NetLibrary, the oldest of these vendors, was recently sold by OCLC to EBSCO, and many of its features will be upgraded in 2011. And as if to re-emphasize the continued uncertainty of the entire e-book industry, the major library vendor ProQuest announced in early January 2011 that it had acquired ebrary. Continued consolidation among e-book aggregators that sell to libraries would not be surprising given the impact of the recession on library funding and the restraints this has put on the ability of libraries to move into new areas of consumer demand.

Many academic publishers also provide Web-accessible e-books direct to libraries from their own Web sites—among them Springer, Elsevier, Wiley, Taylor & Francis, Cambridge, Palgrave Macmillan, Oxford, and Duke. Trade publishers including HarperCollins, Macmillan, Penguin, Simon & Schuster, and Random House sell directly to consumers but not to libraries. University presses have been struggling to come up with a workable approach to e-books that does not cannibalize their already thin revenue streams, and this hesitancy has left them slightly behind every curve and vulnerable to changes in the economy, changes in reader preferences, and changes in technology.

During 2010 a number of university presses announced that they were teaming up with Project Muse to distribute their e-books to academic libraries. Project Muse is a well-respected online academic journal distributor with more than 450 journal titles. By the end of the year, 18 university presses had signed up, with a product release planned for late 2011; other university presses were planning to team up with JSTOR, a similarly well-known distributor of online academic journals in the library market.

Publisher's Association

In October the Publisher's Association (United Kingdom) announced that all major British trade publishers had agreed to allow public libraries to offer e-lending, as long as the books were not downloaded outside the library premises. As the entire basis of the modern networked world is ubiquitous access to information no matter where a particular reader is located, this solution causes more problems than it solves and is the latest example of an uncertain publishing industry trying to hold off the effects of changing technology through policy or legislation rather than through adapting to circumstances, recognizing opportunities, and pursuing solutions that grow the market. British publishers argued that, in theory, a single library could purchase a single book, and that all the readers in the world could then become members of that library and download and read that single book; therefore the publishers believed they had no choice but to insist on restrictions to protect their businesses. By similar logic, a single printed book could be scanned and uploaded to the Internet and distributed worldwide by a single teenager during a single evening, but, for now, publishers are not focusing on stopping the distribution of printed books. OverDrive, which supplies most of the e-books lent by British public libraries, replied that libraries are trusted, responsible channels for publishers and authors to promote and provide access to copyrighted e-books, that all library borrowers are authenticated before downloading, and that libraries are respectful of publishers' interests and provide valuable sales and marketing support for publishers. The conflict had not been resolved at the time this article was prepared, but it further points out e-books' disruptive impact on the business models of both publishers and libraries. In theory, the British publishers' erection of barriers between the reading public and libraries could render public libraries irrelevant—or force libraries to carry e-books from non-British publishing houses.

One problem with all of these various e-book efforts is that the e-book market is being held back by an interlacing mesh of hand-wringing, worry, and hyper-concern that the print book market is such a fragile house of cards that it can be easily destroyed by any stray breeze from technology and the modern Internet. One would like to think that an industry that has been around for 500 years has proven its societal value, and that it merely needs to make adjustments to fit into this growing modern distribution channel. But caution has ruled most publishers' strategies. The pre-e-book publishing world was built on a foundation of regional and national trade restrictions and legal boundaries, combined with the formidable impracticalities involved in distributing bulky, heavy, printed books far from wherever they were printed. But that situation has changed.

Nowadays, it is possible that Indian, Australian, or U.S. e-books downloaded onto cell phones, e-readers, or laptops from countless sources could overrun the British Isles no matter what restrictions British publishers choose to implement or what British libraries choose to do, and no matter what Internet barriers are erected via trade regulation. As we've seen before, part of publishers' initial response to these challenges has been to tightly control e-books with digital rights management software and licensing restrictions in order to maintain control of their product and market. As a result, no e-books function in a manner that is entirely satisfactory to readers. E-books cannot be played on multiple devices, and there are restrictions on how they can be read, where they can be accessed, with whom they can be shared, and whether portions can be printed or pasted or the content otherwise used in a manner that people are used to. This is where Google eBooks enters into the picture.

Google eBooks

E-books from Google eBooks will be permanently housed in the digital cloud and can be accessed and read at any time by many different devices. Once a user purchases a book, he or she can read it on a laptop, Sony Reader, Barnes & Noble Nook, iPad, iPhone, Android phone, or most other devices. Google eBooks has been in the works for several years and was announced in December 2010. This service has the potential to be a game-changer for the e-book market in that an individual can now build a personal library in the online cloud where every book he or she has ever purchased will forever be accessible from almost any device. There is no room for libraries or institutional sales in this model, which is based on maximizing e-book sales to individuals over their lifetime.

Google eBooks will let publishers set prices, and Google claims that it is attempting to set up a more open e-book ecosystem, one that cannot be dominated by a single closed vendor system or format. This is a direct challenge to Amazon, which has been the dominant player in the e-book market until now. Amazon is not participating in Google eBooks and is instead ramping up its efforts to make its e-books readable on more devices, including through the Web.

Google eBooks has a global strategy, and if its more cooperative and open approach works, it could be a huge step toward setting up a single global e-book market. This strategy also unambiguously establishes Google as the location where this global virtual market would occur. There is every reason to believe that Amazon will attempt to replicate this strategy and to make Kindle e-books equally accessible while remaining outside Google's control. As currently designed, both Amazon and Google are essentially locking libraries out of the mainstream trade e-book market, thus leaving libraries to occupy other e-book niches—such as scholarly publications and older, no longer commercially viable e-books. Vendors other than Google and Amazon may be able to make a profit through selling to the smaller library and institutional market.

Publishers and Pricing

In February 2011 Macmillan and Amazon had a much-publicized dispute that resulted in Amazon pulling the publisher's titles after Macmillan changed its e-book terms from the wholesale model, in which a publisher sells books to the distributor at a set price (usually 50 percent off list), to the agency model, in which the publisher sets the prices and retailers get a fixed commission. Under the wholesale model, Amazon had been selling bestsellers for its Kindle editions at $9.99—a price point that publishers felt was too low. Amazon was losing money on the majority of sales, but by setting its own low price for customers it was treating the books themselves as loss leaders in order to fuel the growth of the Kindle e-reader and build the Amazon customer base. The fear among publishers was that Amazon's dominance of e-books and e-readers would mean that at some point Amazon would demand further price discounting from publishers, thus cutting publisher profits to the bone.

Macmillan eventually won this dispute, but in the meantime Apple opened the iPad and Apple's iBooks to the agency model, quickly exploiting this potential gap in the pricing dominance of Amazon and thus providing publishers with an alternative distributor that allowed them more control over the pricing of their e-books while increasing the inventory of Apple's iBookstore.

What all of this means is that e-books may range in price from $11.99 to $16.99 at iBookstore, while Amazon continues to sell most titles for $9.99 or less—making it obvious to consumers that higher-priced titles are a result of specific publishers setting higher prices for their books. Barnes & Noble, which offers more e-books than either Amazon or Apple, is unhappy with publishers' expectations for higher pricing and is evaluating its publisher contracts. Google eBooks is allowing publishers to set prices, and for most of its titles the prices are similar to Amazon's. All of these e-book-pricing models still leave e-book prices at roughly half those of print hardcovers. On the other hand, e-books sold in the much smaller library market tend to range from 100 percent to 150 percent of the list price of the print edition. Even at 150 percent of list price, e-books represent a savings for libraries in that the e-books do not require shelving (shelf space for a single book in newly constructed libraries exceeds $100) nor do e-books incur the other routine costs associated with circulation, maintenance, heating and cooling, and so forth. Nevertheless, the divergence in pricing between the consumer market and the library market is striking.

Traditionally, print books also had many different prices, based on where the book was being sold. Books published in the United States would be distributed in Britain or India, for instance, by another company, sometimes under a different title, and with a price that fit local conditions. The Internet is destroying these quaint and profitable arrangements. A reader waiting in an airport can download a book to his mobile reading device from many different vendors, no matter what traditional trade barriers or pricing are in place. Individuals can also bypass publishers entirely, as Steven Covey did when he sold directly to Amazon the digital rights for two of his bestsellers that were originally published by Simon & Schuster. As a result, he greatly increased his share of the income from his e-book sales, including those of his *The Seven Habits of Highly Effective People,* which was retailing for just $5.65 in the Kindle edition late in 2010.

Typically, an author's share of e-book sales is 15 percent of the list price or 25 percent of the publisher's net receipts. Since the publishers are not paying for printing and shipping costs with e-books, many authors feel that their share of net receipts for e-books should be higher than 25 percent. This has added to the concerns publishers have felt about the Amazon wholesale pricing structure and explains why they prefer the agency model, which gives them more control over setting the final price.

E-books are marketed through many different business models. They are sold to libraries by subscription, title-by-title, in large bundles, via rental, accompanied by printed editions, and through patron-driven acquisitions where an event (number of user sessions, page views, prints, time limits, and so forth) triggers a purchase or rental at a pre-set price. Depending on the business model, a library may pay anywhere from $1 per book per year for a subscription up to 150 percent of list price for a purchase. Consumer prices are much lower, although e-books are still sometimes sold bundled with a print edition or with a mobile device app. No one is sure where these different pricing plans will lead, but regardless of current pricing experiments, the primary issue remains how to make the e-book experience convenient for the reader. The reader needs to be able to discover the book, understand the pricing, view the e-book on a device of his choosing anywhere in the world, and manipulate the book in a manner that meets his needs (such as copying a passage, or lending it to a friend).

It is also important that e-books be available to buyers at the same time as the print edition. It doesn't do the publisher or author any good if the e-book is a victim of "windowing," an industry practice in which the e-book release date is delayed so that the publisher can wring maximum profit out of the print edition. All this does is prevent an e-book sale and irritate a consumer at precisely the time when the book is being reviewed and publicity is at its highest. The disappointed consumer is left with little choice but to buy a different e-book, browse the Web for free content, or rent a movie to watch on his iPad (assuming that at the moment of potential sale the consumer is not standing in a bookstore but is instead in an online environment and disappointed with the publisher).

ISBN Conflicts

The purpose of the International Standard Book Number (ISBN) is to identify a book and its format—hardcover, paperback, large print, audio CD, Kindle e-book, Barnes & Noble Nook e-book, or whatever. The ISBN has always identified one particular iteration of a book. But with the proliferation of e-books and the explosion of formats in the last two to three years, many smaller publishers are less than eager to purchase blocks of ISBNs to assign to each and every format of every book. A proposed solution has been to append the ISBN with a suffix that designates a particular e-book format. While this would be cheaper, it conflicts with the International Standard Text Code identifier (ISTC), whose purpose is to identify a single work that the book industry can then use to link to the book's many formats. The ISTC links to many ISBNs and makes it easier to find the particular format a customer needs. Concern over the best use of the ISBN has resulted in a somewhat contentious industry debate that in the long run will affect how effective the links are between a book's metadata and each ISBN, and how easy it is for a consumer to discover a book in the particular format they need. If smaller publishers opt out of the ISBN system, then their books will not be automatically picked up by Google and other discovery services and will be harder to find. At the end of 2010, this conflict was yet to be resolved.

Digital Textbooks

Student and parent protest over the price of textbooks in recent years has been heard loud and clear by legislators, college administrators, and entrepreneurs—all of whom see the traditional model as excessively priced and ripe for reconceptualizing. Traditional textbook publishers have been rushing to go digital (usually with pricing discounts from the print model that are smaller than students, administrators, and parents expect) while entrepreneurs are coming to the scene sensing that even heavily discounted digital textbooks would still leave room for a more than handsome profit.

The king of digital textbooks is Vital Source Technologies, a subsidiary of Ingram, with more than 60,000 titles from Elsevier, Pearson, Cengage, Macmillan, Wiley, McGraw-Hill, Wolters Kluwer, Oxford University Press, Taylor & Francis, and others; titles are available for download, viewing over the Web, and are accessible via mobile technologies including the iPad.

Many colleges have made tentative movements to embrace digital textbooks, and such companies as Wiley, McGraw-Hill, and Pearson are partnering with universities in pilot programs through which the university directly contracts with publishers to reduce textbook cost. Students, however, have consistently given digital textbooks mixed grades. Amazon's experiments with several well-publicized textbook alternatives on the Kindle during 2010 did not go well, with as many as 80 percent of participating MBA students at the University of Virginia saying they would not recommend the Kindle as a classroom study aid. This was similar to findings from Princeton, the University of Washington, and elsewhere. The problem: Students using textbooks like to flip back and forth between pages and e-readers are too slow for that, plus which the Kindle didn't allow students to scribble in the margins, dog-ear pages, highlight passages, or get the most out of color charts and graphs. An October 2010 study by Campus Research, a division of the National Association of College Stores, found that 74 percent of students preferred print to digital texts (though, admittedly, the sponsors of this study, college bookstores, cannot be considered an entirely disinterested party as print textbook sales are their bread and butter). The study also found that 77 percent of the students who had recently purchased an e-book indicated they had used a laptop or netbook computer to read it; 30 percent indicated a desktop computer was their preferred reading device; 19 percent read their e-books on a smart phone; and another 19 percent said they used an e-reader.

Nevertheless, online textbooks have a certain appeal to instructors because they are often accompanied by such helpful instructional materials as PowerPoints and videos, and the textbooks themselves can always be projected to a classroom screen. In some iterations, such as with Macmillan's Dynamic Books, instructors are able to customize the texts for their individual classes, reorganizing and deleting chapters and even rewriting individual paragraphs.

However, as anyone in higher education—teacher, librarian, or parent—knows all too well, a significant portion of students will do almost anything to avoid buying textbooks. They'll buy used copies on the Web, borrow and scan texts from friends, borrow a library copy, buy pirated print or e-book copy, or just do without. Students hate to spend unnecessary money and have been burned too many times by buying a textbook that was not essential to the class. The existing textbook system with its ever-escalating costs and a focus on profits for both publishers and faculty authors, can rightly be accused of overreaching, and finally exceeding, the generous parental and student zones of tolerance as well as society's ability to absorb the costs.

There are alternatives. As of September 2010 institutions of higher education must comply with what is known at the "textbook law," which is actually section 133(d) of the Higher Education Opportunity Act, mandating that the ISBN and retail price of all required and recommended texts be listed in the institution's course schedule. The point of this law is twofold: to force faculty to consider the pricing of assigned textbooks, and to give students a chance to use the Internet to seek out cheaper sources of their texts. A proposed law introduced by U.S. Sen. Richard J. Durbin (D-Ill.), called the Open College Textbook Act, would have gone one step further and created competitive grants for the writing of open (free) textbooks. This would have been similar to the effort by the California Learning Resource Network to develop open source digital textbooks. In the private sector, the growing popularity of free online textbooks from such vendors as Flat World Knowledge or low-cost textbooks from such vendors as Best Value Textbooks, as well as textbook rental plans, are challenging the existing paradigm, as are self-publishing options ranging from Lulu.com to the Espresso Book Machine (a print-on-demand device in an increasing number of college bookstores), both of which allow faculty to assemble their own textbooks. The large commercial textbook companies are well aware of this competition and have been creating their own business models that focus on cheaper digital downloads and online textbooks as well as print-on-demand supplemental material.

Another challenge on the textbook horizon is the possibility that the U.S. market could soon be flooded with the stripped-down editions that publishers have designed for the foreign market. These editions are frequently priced at half or even a quarter of U.S. editions, use different bindings and low-quality paper, and lack color images. A case currently before the U.S. Supreme Court, *Costco Wholesale Corporation* v. *Omega,* will determine whether publishers can use the "first sale doctrine" codified in the Copyright Act of 1976 to keep these cheaper editions out of the U.S. market. This case has large implications for libraries, not just textbook publishers and consumers, as it is basically about determining whether companies can set differential pricing for identical goods as they flow across borders. It will also answer questions about what rights flow with the sale of those goods. The American Library Association has filed a friend-of-the-court brief in the case because of concerns that rights to sell or lend more than 200 million books manufactured outside the United States could be jeopardized. This provides another glimpse into the complications of trade in an Internet world and is an indicator of the series of threats facing the once-dominant print textbook paradigm in which publishers enjoyed the ability to set prices and control the market while limiting student choices.

Under fire in both the print and digital realm, textbook pricing is in for a radical readjustment. At the moment, publishers and educational institutions are dragging their feet and failing to wholly embrace technology to find an effective solution. Most proposals are half steps designed to preserve profit margins and maintain existing low-effort course teaching designs. Educational institutions are failing to replace the textbook concept with freely available online content, drawn from online articles and vetted Web sites, to create their own open-source texts, to use their clout to commission authors and publish original textbooks at cost, or to partner with other institutions and make bulk purchases of texts at discounted prices. Publishers are losing a window of opportunity to change their business models and offer lower-cost alternatives, whether these are Web sites, pdfs, or e-books, before global textbook competition sets in and the U.S. market is flooded with new textbook options from India, Hong Kong, Australia, South Africa, and similar cost-conscious innovators that are not wedded to high-margin business models.

Summary

By now most publishers have accepted that e-books are going to be a critical part of their future. But the market keeps changing. The rise of self-publishing companies like XLibris and Lulu, along with the growth of print-on-demand and the rise of many small alternative publishers, has flooded the market with books. In 2005 a reported 172,000-plus titles were released, whereas by 2009—if self-published and alternative titles such as those carried by Amazon were counted—the total had climbed to more than a million. While not all of these were e-books, all of these titles are nonetheless a huge Internet-inspired disruption in what was a previously predictable and slow-to-change industry. Printed reference books, dictionaries, atlases, and titles supporting hobbies from quilting to home repair, as well as books directed at sports fans, movie fans, music fans, and so forth, all of which used to provide dependable print sales, are in the process of being replaced by heavily used Internet sites. Not only are these former categories of books no longer needed in print—they are unlikely to ever become e-books either. Those industries that used to depend on printed books—bookstores, libraries, publishers—are on the cusp of painful adjustments. E-books are one stage in this adjustment as more and more information moves to the digital realm and becomes more dispersed and available from more sources from more countries.

Last year was marked by several e-book milestones that garnered the media's attention, such as Amazon's announcement that e-book sales were now outpacing hardcover sales. These types of observations are already commonplace and no longer surprising; e-books have passed the tipping point and are the fastest-growing market in publishing. This brings with it dangers that the longstanding societal roles of publishers, authors, editors, agents, booksellers, and librarians could all change in ways that weaken societal bonds as well as respect for the well-constructed and carefully authored linear communication that has been the book. Whatever directions the industry takes, let us hope that the unique communication product that is the book survives.

Sharing and Safeguarding Government Information: Evolving Postures and Rising Challenges

Jeffrey W. Seifert
Congressional Research Service, Library of Congress

Since the September 11 terrorist attacks nearly a decade ago, the information sharing and security practices of the United States government have undergone a dramatic transformation. Numerous studies have been published (for example, *The 9/11 Commission Report; Report and Recommendations of the Presidential Task Force on Controlled Unclassified Information; Securing Cyberspace for the 44th Presidency*). Several pieces of legislation have been signed into law (among them the Homeland Security Act of 2002, the Intelligence Reform and Terrorism Prevention Act, and the Reducing Over-Classification Act). Significant portions of the government have been reorganized around a renewed interest in the idea of "homeland security." Most notable, in late 2002, was the establishment of the Department of Homeland Security (DHS)—a composite assembly of several previously existing agencies and some new ones, such as the Transportation Security Administration (TSA). Similarly, in April 2005 the Office of the Director of National Intelligence (ODNI) stood up[1]—an entity charged with, among other things, the responsibility to serve as the head of the intelligence community, and to "ensure maximum availability of and access to intelligence information within the intelligence community consistent with national security requirements."[2]

For these entities—and the many more boards, offices, fusion centers, and joint agreements that have been added to the information-sharing community—a major theme of their respective charges is to promote and implement an information-sharing culture that emphasizes a more inclusive "need to share" instead of a more restrictive "need to know." However, overturning decades of an ingrained need-to-know culture does not happen overnight. It requires clear guidance, incentives, persistent follow-through, and trust. Moreover, with the need to share also comes the need to secure. Securing information is done through physical and cyber practices, as well as by creating "rules of the road" for classifying, declassifying, and sharing information.

Arguably, the shift from a need-to-know to a need-to-share information culture remains a work in progress. While perhaps the genie cannot be put back in the bottle, the information-sharing culture is still fragile, and still susceptible to being influenced by major setbacks such as cyberattacks and leaks.

A comprehensive assessment of the current state of federal information sharing and information security would fill all the pages of this volume, and perhaps more. Instead, this report undertakes the more modest goal of highlighting some of the latest federal policy initiatives to both share and protect information—and considering the condition of the enduring challenge—to lick the leaks.

Jeffrey W. Seifert is a section research manager at the Congressional Research Service (CRS) of the Library of Congress. The views expressed here are those of the author and do not necessarily reflect the position of the Congressional Research Service or the Library of Congress.

Sharing Posture

The federal government's posture toward information sharing is perhaps reflected most clearly through its official information-handling policies. Policies regarding "classified" information, and "controlled unclassified" information, are particularly relevant as many information-sharing initiatives focus on terrorism-related information. Two recently issued executive orders and new legislation signed into law in October 2010 provide some insights.

Executive Order 13526—Classified National Security Information

A key element in the sharing and safeguarding of government information is the handling of classified national security information. While Congress has legislated on this issue from time to time, it has largely been the role of the president to determine matters such as who may classify information, who may access classified information, and how such information is marked (given a security designation) and later declassified. As a result, nearly every president since Franklin D. Roosevelt has issued at least one executive order on classified information.[3] Successive executive orders often continue many of the provisions of the previous directive, such as the use of specific classification markings—"confidential," "secret," and "top secret." However, other changes can set a tone for the types of information activities a presidential administration wants to encourage or discourage.

On December 29, 2009, President Barack Obama issued Executive Order 13526 on classified national security information.[4] As noted in a report[5] in last year's edition of the *Library and Book Trade Almanac,* significant features of E.O. 13526 include:

- Restoring the standards providing that where "there is significant doubt about the need to classify information, it shall not be classified" and that where "there is significant doubt about the appropriate level of classification, it shall be classified at the lower level"[6]
- Emphasizing the requirement that the "unauthorized disclosure could reasonably be expected to cause identifiable or describable damage to the national security"[7]
- Prescribing a new fundamental principle that "No information may remain classified indefinitely"[8]
- Prohibiting the reclassification of information after its declassification and release to the public under proper authority except when agencies can comply with specified restrictions[9]
- Requiring agency heads to "complete on a periodic basis a comprehensive review of the agency's classification guidance, particularly classification guidelines, to ensure the guidance reflects current circumstances and to identify classified information that no longer requires protection and can be declassified"[10]
- Establishing "within the National Archives a National Declassification Center to streamline declassification processes, facilitate quality-assur-

ance measures, and implement standardized training regarding the declassification of records determined to have permanent historical value"[11]

- Facilitating approved information sharing by promoting maximum possible access to classified information by persons who meet standard criteria for access[12]
- Eliminating an intelligence community veto of declassification decisions made by the Interagency Security Classification Appeals Panel that had been granted by the prior administration[13]

In a memorandum accompanying the executive order, President Obama re-emphasized a commitment to addressing two enduring issues related to the handling of classified national security information. Regarding the declassification of records, the president noted a backlog of "more than 400 million pages of accessioned Federal records previously subject to automatic declassification," and directed the National Declassification Center to address the situation "in a manner that will permit public access to all declassified records from this backlog no later than December 31, 2013."[14] Regarding the delegation of original classification authority, in addition to reiterating long-standing policy that such delegation should be "limited to the minimum necessary to carry out this order," departments and agencies were directed to carry out a review of such delegations and report their findings to the director of the Information Security Oversight Office (ISOO) within 120 days.[15]

Regarding the latter goal, ISOO cited quick progress. On April 15, 2010, ISOO released its *Report to the President for Fiscal Year 2009.* Although the annual report covered a period before the issuance of E.O. 13526, ISOO referenced the president's December 29, 2009, memorandum and reported that the number of officials with delegated original classification authority (OCA) had dropped from 4,109 in fiscal year (FY) 2008 to 2,557 in FY 2009. This drop in the aggregate total was attributed to a concerted effort by the Department of State, in which the number of delegations of OCA shrank from 2,560 to 999.[16]

ISOO Implementing Guidance

On June 28, 2010, ISOO published its implementing directive in the form of a final rule in the *Federal Register.*[17] The document gives agencies guidance for implementing and complying with various aspects of E.O. 13526, including classifying and declassifying, use of markings, safeguarding information, education and training of personnel, and reporting requirements. Reflecting the realities of working in a 21st century networked office, the guidance includes a section on "classification marking in the electronic environment." Lest the informal nature of some forms of electronic communication lead users to relax their security protocols, the guidance reminds agencies of the obvious—that national security information in an electronic form is subject to all requirements of the executive order. To that end, the marking and handling of classified content in various electronic media is addressed, including e-mail, Web pages, audio and video files, URLs, dynamic documents and relational databases, blogs, wikis, instant messages, and chat rooms.[18] Also of note, although the sharing of classified information appears to be explicitly mentioned just once in the executive order, the implementing guidance refers to the activity on at least five occasions. In the context of classifying elements of dynamic documents or relational databases that may include unclassified information or information classified at a lower level, users are instructed to "avoid unnecessary classification and/or impediments to information sharing."[19] Similarly, in the context of requesting portion marking waivers, such requests submitted to the director of ISOO must "demonstrate that the requested waiver will not create impediments to information sharing."[20] In the context of a definition of risk management principles, such principles are "applied for assessing threats and vulnerabilities and implementing security countermeasures while maximizing the sharing of information to achieve an acceptable level of risk at an acceptable cost."[21] In two other instances, minimum training requirements for personnel with either original or derivative classification responsibilities is to include, among other topics, information sharing.[22]

Reducing Over-Classification Act

Acting upon growing concerns over perceived information-sharing failures between federal, state, local, and tribal governments, Congress has held hearings and considered legislation. A particular focus has been the dilemma of sharing classified information with non-federal entities when many of their personnel do not have the security clearances required to receive or access the information. Originally introduced in 2007 during the 110th Congress and reintroduced in 2009 during the 111th Congress, the Reducing Over-Classification Act passed the House and the Senate the following year, and was signed into law by President Obama on October 7, 2010.

Cognizant of the administration's efforts on this front, the accompanying report language stated:

> The Committee wishes to emphasize that none of the provisions in this Act is intended to supplant the Executive Branch's longstanding authority to determine what information should be appropriately classified within the framework established in Executive Order 13526 and its predecessors. Indeed, the Committee believes that the provisions of the Act complement and do not conflict with Executive Order 13526, and that both the Order and the Act will promote the goals of increased transparency, information sharing, and security.[23]

Among its provisions, the law

- Directs the secretary of homeland security to designate a "classified information advisory officer" within the department. This adviser would be responsible for developing and disseminating training programs for state, local, and tribal governments, and private sector entities, relating to the sharing and use of classified information. Such training is to focus specifically on procedures for challenging classification designations of information received; and means for personnel to apply for security clearances.[24]
- Directs the director of national intelligence, in accordance with E.O. 13526, to develop guidance to standardize the formats for classified and unclassified intelligence products for the purposes of promoting sharing

of these products, and to develop policies and procedures for the increased use of portion markings.[25]

- Directs the secretary of homeland security to integrate information and analysis from both departmental and non-departmental sources into finished intelligence and information products in both classified and unclassified formats.[26]
- Directs the Interagency Threat Assessment and Coordination Group (ITACG), which is located in the National Counterterrorism Center (NCTC), to make recommendations to the secretary of homeland security to produce and disseminate intelligence products at a classification level that would best enable sharing with state, local, and tribal governments, and private sector entities.[27]
- To promote accurate classification of information, allows departments and agencies, when making cash awards to employees with classification authority, to "consider such officer's or employee's consistent and proper classification of information."[28] Also directs the inspector general of each department or agency with classifying authority to carry out a minimum of two evaluations by September 30, 2016. In coordination with ISOO, the evaluations are to "assess whether applicable classification policies, procedures, rules, and regulations have been adopted, followed, and effectively administered . . ." and "to identify policies, procedures, rules, regulations, or management practices that may be contributing to persistent misclassification of material . . ."[29]
- Requires departments and agencies, in accordance with E.O. 13526, to provide training annually to employees with original classification authority, as well as every two years for employees with derivative classification authority. The training is to include the proper use of classification markings, incentives, and penalties relating to classification of intelligence products, and guidance on the formatting of finished intelligence products.[30]

Executive Order 13556—Controlled Unclassified Information

Another issue that has frustrated information-sharing efforts is the proliferation of markings for information that is unclassified, but that agencies have deemed "sufficiently sensitive to warrant some level of protection."[31] Sometimes referred to as "sensitive but unclassified" (SBU) information, or more broadly now, "controlled unclassified information" (CUI), the use of such markings extends far beyond just terrorism-related information. In a May 27, 2009, memorandum,[32] President Obama directed the secretary of homeland security and the attorney general to lead a task force to examine the policies and procedures surrounding the categorization and sharing of SBU information, as well as the CUI Framework.[33]

In December 2009 the task force released its report, which identified "over 100 unique markings and at least 130 different labeling or handling regimes" used across the executive branch.[34] The report contained 40 recommendations intended to consolidate and bring order to this unwieldy patchwork of overlapping, and at times contradictory, markings. The recommendations included establishing a moratorium on the creation of new SBU regimes, expanding the scope of the CUI Framework beyond a focus on terrorism-related information to include all SBU information, simplifying the categories and markings used, establishing a life cycle (generally ten years) for decontrolling information, creating training for personnel, and establishing internal oversight controls within agencies. The report also recommended the adoption of a new definition of CUI—"All unclassified information for which, pursuant to statute, regulation, or departmental or agency policy, there is a compelling requirement for safeguarding and/or dissemination controls."[35]

On November 4, 2010, President Obama issued Executive Order 13556 on "controlled unclassified information."[36] Among its provisions, the executive order

- Establishes "an open and uniform program" for managing all CUI information across the executive branch[37]
- Designates the National Archives and Records Administration (NARA) to serve as the executive agent for implementing the order[38]
- Requires each agency to carry out a review of all markings used by the agency to "designate unclassified information for safeguarding or dissemination controls" and submit this catalog to the executive agent within 180 days[39]
- Directs the executive agent to "approve categories and subcategories of CUI and associated markings to be applied uniformly throughout the executive branch"; to develop and issue directives to implement the order, giving "appropriate consideration" to the CUI Task Force report; and to develop a public registry of these markings and associated procedures[40]
- Within 180 days of the executive agent issuing its policies and procedures for implementing the order, all agencies are to "provide the Executive Agent with a proposed plan for compliance with the requirements."[41]
- Authorizes the director of national intelligence to "issue policy directives and guidelines as the Director deems necessary to implement this order with respect to intelligence and intelligence-related information"[42]

Security Posture

The federal government's posture toward information security is perhaps even more fluid at this time than its posture toward information sharing. Federal information security has remained on the Government Accountability Office's (GAO's) high-risk list since 1997. In 2003 GAO enlarged the scope of this area to also include cyber critical infrastructure.[43] While federal computing and critical infrastructure have many differences, many of the cybersecurity threats to these systems are similar. More importantly, these threats continue to escalate. The complexity, speed, and global nature of these threats represent an eternal game of cat and mouse.

In addition to the seemingly regular series of data breaches, lost laptops, and Web site hacks that fill the news, there have been some especially significant attacks recently. In late 2009 and early 2010 Google experienced a sophisticated attack, reportedly directed specifically at the password system it uses to provide services to millions of users.[44] Some reports suggested that the attack may have been related to a public dispute Google was having with China regarding Internet controls. Later, in mid-2010, a multifaceted computer worm surfaced, dubbed Stuxnet. Although the Stuxnet worm appears to have been targeted specifically to affect the control systems used to operate nuclear power plants in Iran, and did not appear to have wide-reaching effects on systems to which it was spread in other countries, the Stuxnet worm represents a qualitative change in potential threats.[45] The worm was notable not only for its carefully crafted exploitation of multiple vulnerabilities, including four so-called "zero day" vulnerabilities (weaknesses that are previously unknown, and hence do not have an immediate fix), but also for the apparent care taken to minimize collateral damage to other computer systems. However, with the worm's computer code available on the Internet, concerns now turn to whether others may modify the code and deploy it to attack with wider effect. And of course, there is WikiLeaks.

While many agencies have some role in cybersecurity, it is, broadly speaking, the Department of Homeland Security, in conjunction with the Office of Management and Budget (OMB), that has been largely responsible for leading or coordinating cybersecurity efforts in the federal civilian and private sector, while the Department of Defense has focused on securing its own networks and the evolving area of cyberwarfare. While this relative separation between civilian and military may never have been absolute, the convergence of threats and the reliance on a shared national critical infrastructure appears to be driving growing interest in developing centralized mechanisms to better coordinate and integrate cybersecurity efforts between the civilian, military, and intelligence communities.

In May 2009 the White House released the *Cyberspace Policy Review*. The result of a 60-day review ordered by President Obama, the report plainly stated that "the architecture of the Nation's digital infrastructure, based largely upon the Internet, is not secure or resilient."[46] Put in terms of costs, the report continued, "Our digital infrastructure has already suffered intrusions that have allowed criminals to steal hundreds of millions of dollars and nation-states and other entities to steal intellectual property and sensitive military information."[47] Acknowledging the need to balance a complex mix of interests—including efficiency, innovation, economic prosperity, free trade, safety, security, civil liberties, and privacy[48]—the report put forward 24 recommendations. These recommendations, representing ten near-term actions plans and 14 mid-term action plans, proposed the development of various coordinating mechanisms, response plans, frameworks, and collaborations, as well as the appointment of a "cybersecurity policy official responsible for coordinating the Nation's cybersecurity policies and activities," who would be "dual-hatted to the NSC" (National Security Council).[49] In December 2009 the president appointed Howard Schmidt to serve as special assistant to the president and cybersecurity coordinator; a post in which he "leads a new Cybersecurity Directorate within the National Security Staff (NSS), works closely with the economic team, and has created a close partnership with the Office of Management and Budget (OMB) and the Office of Science and Technology Policy."[50] In an October 2010 report, GAO indicated that two of the recommendations had been fully implemented and the other 22 had been partially implemented. The two fully implemented recommendations both involved the appointment of personnel associated with NSC; the appointment of Schmidt, and the designation of a privacy and civil liberties official in the NSC Cybersecurity Directorate.[51]

In July 2010 then-Director of OMB Peter Orszag and Cybersecurity Coordinator Schmidt issued a memorandum to departments and agencies on the subject "Clarifying Cybersecurity Responsibilities and Activities of the Executive Office of the President and the Department of Homeland Security."[52] The two-page memorandum focuses on the significant but relatively bounded activity of implementing the Federal Information Security Management Act of 2002 (FISMA). As it is the primary law governing the security of federal information systems, compliance with FISMA requirements is a central feature of federal information technology planning, budgeting, and management. In summary, the responsibilities are outlined as follows:

- "OMB will be responsible for the submission of the annual FISMA report to Congress, for the development and approval of the cybersecurity portions of the President's Budget, for the traditional OMB budgetary and fiscal oversight of the agencies' use of funds, and for coordination with the Cybersecurity Coordinator on all policy issues related to the prior three responsibilities."[53]
- "The Cybersecurity Coordinator will have visibility into DHS efforts to ensure Federal agency compliance with FISMA and will serve as the principal White House official to coordinate interagency cooperation with DHS cybersecurity efforts."[54]
- ". . . DHS will exercise primary responsibility within the executive branch for the operational aspects of Federal agency cybersecurity with respect to the Federal information systems that fall within FISMA under 44 U.S.C. §3543."[55]

In October 2010 DHS and the Department of Defense (DoD) signed a memorandum of agreement regarding cybersecurity. The purpose of the agreement is to

> . . . set forth terms by which DHS and DoD will provide personnel, equipment, and facilities in order to increase interdepartmental collaboration in strategic planning for the Nation's cybersecurity, mutual support for cybersecurity capabilities development, and synchronization of current operational cybersecurity mission activities. Implementing this Agreement will focus national cybersecurity efforts, increasing the overall capacity and capability of both DHS's homeland security and DoD's national security missions, while providing integral protection for privacy, civil rights, and civil liberties.[56]

The agreement outlines a number of responsibilities on the part of DHS and DoD, including the National Security Agency (NSA) and the United States Cyber Command (USCYBERCOM),[57] regarding the assignment of personnel to a partner department to facilitate coordinative and collaborative activities.

Throughout this period, Congress was also dedicating significant attention to the development of comprehensive cybersecurity legislation. Reflecting the deliberative nature of the legislative process, several bills were introduced and many hearings were held. Representing differing perspectives and a range of policy options, the bills collectively addressed a wide range of cybersecurity-related issues, including procurement of products and services that meet security requirements, protection of critical infrastructure, development of standards and guidance, training and accreditation for federal information security personnel, scholarships to recruit more people into the cybersecurity field, information sharing and security clearances for private sector partners, civil liberties protections, and establishing regular reviews and reports going forward.

Another prominent issue was coordination of cybersecurity efforts across the federal government. Here too, a number of options were put forward. For example, the Protecting Cyberspace as a National Asset Act of 2010 (S. 3480), introduced by Sen. Joseph Lieberman (I-Conn.), included a provision that would have established an Office of Cyberspace Policy in the Executive Office of the President, with a director appointed by the president with the advice and consent of the Senate. The office's primary responsibilities would have included developing and implementing a national strategy for improving the security of cyberspace and coordinating efforts across the civilian, defense, and intelligence sectors. Another example, the Cybersecurity Act of 2010 (S. 773), introduced by Sen. Thomas Carper (D-Del.), took a slightly different approach. The bill would have directed the president to develop and implement a national cybersecurity strategy; would have established a cybersecurity advisory panel composed of private sector and public sector representatives to provide advice on cybersecurity matters; and would have required the director of national intelligence, the secretary of commerce, the secretary of homeland security, the attorney general, the secretary of defense, and the secretary of state to provide a joint assessment of cybersecurity threats and vulnerabilities to Congress. Yet another approach was taken by the International Cyberspace and Cybersecurity Coordination Act of 2010, introduced by Sen. John Kerry (D-Mass.), which focused primarily on the global aspects of cybersecurity. The bill would have created the position of coordinator for cyberspace and cybersecurity issues within the office of the secretary of state. The coordinator would have served as the primary adviser on cybersecurity issues to the secretary of state, including coordination of cybersecurity activities relating to interests overseas, and coordination with other departments on international cybersecurity issues.

Although none of these bills made it to the president's desk, a building momentum to pass legislation at the end of the 111th Congress suggested that the topic would continue to be active in the 112th. Less clear, however, is whether attempts toward compromise will ultimately coalesce into enough support for a single comprehensive bill, or even agreement on one or more bills focused on a selected set of issues.

Also unclear is whether, in toto, these policy proposals and initiatives portend larger shifts in the U.S. cybersecurity structure, or a temporary blip in the ever-evolving thinking of the policy community. Regardless, the question that arises is what impact, if any, this evolving cybersecurity posture might have on the information-sharing posture.

WikiLeaks

WikiLeaks.org first appeared on the Web in late 2006. While popularly associated with Julian Assange, who is credited with founding the site, WikiLeaks.org is operated by a loosely organized group of volunteers with no centralized headquarters and is funded through donations.

The site reportedly describes itself as a "public service designed to protect whistle-blowers, journalists, and activists who have sensitive materials to communicate to the public."[58] In its first few years of operation, the site published a variety of governmental and non-governmental content, including an operations manual associated with the U.S. detention facility at Guantanamo Bay, documents attributed to the Church of Scientology, and e-mail messages from Sarah Palin's Yahoo account.[59] The site gradually gained notice and notoriety for sensitive content, and 2010 marked a significant turning point. In March 2010 the site posted a classified video clip of a 2007 air strike targeted at journalists mistakenly believed to be combatants carrying weapons in Baghdad. In July the site posted more than 70,000 U.S. government documents relating to the war in Afghanistan, including classified field reports containing unredacted names of intelligence sources and individuals cooperating in antiterrorism efforts. In October WikiLeaks released a similar batch of 400,000 documents relating to the war in Iraq. As it would turn out, the national security implications of even these significant illegal disclosures would pale in comparison to what was to come.

In November 2010 WikiLeaks began releasing more than 250,000 State Department cables, revealing many years' worth of reporting and communications from U.S. diplomats around the world.[60] According to media reports, the cables date as far back as 1966 and include 117,000 that are marked confidential or secret.[61] As with its previous large-scale disclosures, WikiLeaks had already hinted to the world of what it was about to make public, and had tried to broker an exclusive arrangement with a few selected news media outlets to publicize and redistribute the content in an attempt to mitigate expected efforts to shut down WikiLeaks. In late November, with the "big reveal" imminent but apparently unstoppable, the State Department began damage control efforts by contacting its counterparts around the world to warn them of what they might find in the cables and try to assuage bruised egos regarding the less-than-diplomatic characterizations of individuals and countries that appeared in some of the internal communiqués.[62]

According to news reports, the alleged culprit of this data theft, taken into custody in May 2010, was Bradley Manning, an Army enlisted man stationed in Iraq. A military intelligence analyst, Pfc. Manning is said to have had access to the Secret Internet Protocol Router Network (SIPRNet), as part of his official duties.

Over time, various systems have been connected to SIPRNet, a network used for transmitting classified information, in an effort to facilitate better information sharing. Capitalizing on multiple weaknesses in cyber and physical security, and abusing the trust placed on someone in his position, Manning reportedly downloaded the data to read/writable compact discs marked as containing music, and was able to leave the facility with these discs on multiple occasions over a period of many months.[63]

Initial Response to the Leaks

In the immediate wake of the incident, OMB Director Jacob Lew sent a one-page memorandum to departments and agencies entitled "WikiLeaks—Mishandling Classified Information." In the memorandum, Lew assessed the WikiLeaks incident in very blunt terms: "The recent irresponsible disclosure by WikiLeaks has resulted in significant damage to our national security." The memorandum also reminded agencies of the role that classified information plays in protecting "our citizens, our democratic institutions, and our homeland," and of their obligations under E.O. 13526, and other laws, to safeguard classified information. To that end, agencies were given the following "immediate instructions":

- Each department or agency that handles classified information shall establish a security assessment team consisting of counterintelligence, security, and information assurance experts to review the agency's implementation of procedures for safeguarding classified information against improper disclosures. Such review should include (without limitation) evaluation of the agency's configuration of classified government systems to ensure that users do not have broader access than is necessary to do their jobs effectively, as well as implementation of restrictions on usage of, and removable media capabilities from, classified government computer networks.
- The Office of Management and Budget, the Information Security Oversight Office, and the Office of the Director of National Intelligence will stand up processes to evaluate, and to assist agencies in their review of, security practices with respect to the protection of classified information.[64]

On December 1, 2010, the White House released a fact sheet further detailing the federal government's actions.[65] While noting the "considerable improvement in information-sharing" that had occurred since the September 11, 2001, terrorist attacks, the fact sheet also underscored "the importance of the existing prohibitions, restrictions, and requirements regarding the safeguarding of classified information." Under the heading of National Security Staff Initiatives, it was announced that Russell Travers had been named to serve as the national "security staff's senior advisor for information access and security policy," and would lead "a comprehensive effort to identify and develop the structural reforms needed in light of the WikiLeaks breach." Also under this heading, it was announced that the President's Intelligence Advisory Board (PIAB) would "take an independent look at the means by which the Executive Branch as a whole shares and protects classified information."

Under the heading of "Department of State Initiatives," it was announced that the department was conducting a review of its policies and procedures "to ensure that measures taken strike the correct balance between the critical need to protect classified information and the equally compelling requirement to ensure that it is shared with those who need it in their work to advance our national security." It was also announced that the State Department had "suspended access to the Net Centric Diplomacy (NCD) database of diplomatic reporting," as well as to its ClassNet Web sites and SharePoint sites, which it had made accessible through SIPRNet.

Under the heading of "Department of Defense Initiatives," it was announced that DoD, in response to two reviews commissioned by Secretary of Defense Robert Gates in August 2010 regarding earlier concerns relating to WikiLeaks, was assessing and implementing a variety of technical, educational, and training recommendations.

Under the heading of the "Office of the Director of National Intelligence (ODNI) Initiatives," it was announced that the ODNI, in coordination with OMB, was "developing recommendations to enhance security within the Intelligence Community (IC)."

More Guidance—Don't Look at the Leaks

As departments and agencies were ramping up efforts to review the security of their systems, they were also scrambling to address a growing concern about employees and contractors using either government or personal computers to access, download, or transfer documents found at WikiLeaks and reposting them in other places.

While not officially available through the OMB Web site, various media outlets reported on a model notice, attributed to the OMB general counsel's office, that was provided to departments and agencies to use in developing guidance to their employees not to access leaked classified materials.[66] With new front-page headlines coming out around the clock, creating a wicked blend of reported information mixed with the reproduction of classified information, agencies quickly found themselves caught in the unpopular position of reminding employees that, regardless of how widely available, materials that were classified continued to remain classified, subject to all applicable laws, and should not be accessed or downloaded to nonclassified systems. While commentators critical of this guidance often ignored the legal and policy realities of the status of the classified documents, the magnitude of the situation illustrated not only the practical limitations of enforcing actions, but also how quickly an entire body of data (not just a document or two) can be transferred endlessly around the globe.

The Widening Survey

On January 3, 2011, the director of OMB sent a second memorandum to departments and agencies titled "Initial Assessments of Safeguarding and Counterintelligence Postures for Classified National Security Information in Automated Systems."[67] It served as a transmittal of an attached joint memorandum from the director of the Information Security Oversight Office (ISOO) and the National Counterintelligence Executive within the Office of the Director of National Intelligence (ONDI), elaborating on the requirements and questions to be addressed in the "initial self assessments" that departments and agencies were ordered to carry out in the November 28, 2010, OMB memorandum. With a January 28, 2011, deadline, departments and agencies were directed to:

1. Assess what your agency has done or plans to do to address any perceived vulnerabilities, weaknesses, or gaps on automated systems in the post-WikiLeaks environment.

2. Assess weakness or gaps with respect to the attached list of questions, and formulate plans to resolve the issues or to shift or acquire resources to address those weaknesses or gaps.
3. Assess your agency's plans for changes and upgrades to current classified networks, systems, applications, databases, websites, and online collaboration environments as well as for all new classified networks, systems, applications, databases, websites or online collaboration environments that are in the planning, implementation, or testing phases—in terms of the completeness and projected effectiveness of all types of security controls called for by applicable law and guidance (including but limited to those issued by the National Security Staff, the Committee on National Security Systems, the National Institute for Standards and Technology).
4. Assess all security, counterintelligence, and information assurance policy and regulatory documents that have been established by and for your department or agency.

As part of this initial self assessment, departments and agencies that handle classified information were directed to respond to several pages of questions "*with an emphasis on their application in automated systems*" (emphasis original), organized under eight categories. The eight categories and a selected sample of the questions for each category follows.

Management and Oversight

- How does your agency ensure the self-inspection programs evaluate the adherence to the principles and requirements of the Executive Order 13526 (the Order) and 32 C.F.R. Part 2001 (the Directive) relative to safeguarding of classified information in automated systems?
    - □ Do required assessments cover the certification and accreditation of automated systems with respect to classified information?
    - □ Do required assessments cover safeguarding of classified information specific to automated systems?
    - □ Are corrective actions developed as indicated in the results/lessons-learned?
    - □ Are deficiencies tracked centrally to enable trend analysis?
    - □ Are security education and training programs updated to reflect common deficiencies and lessons learned?
    - □ Are agency policies reviewed regularly to address common deficiencies and lessons learned?
- Do supervisors evaluate employee's acceptance and adherence to the security rules for physical security, counterintelligence (CI), information assurance (IA), and overall information protection? Does this evaluation consider the issues specific to the use of automated systems?

Counterintelligence

- Has your agency identified its high value information and processes that must be protected? What process is in place to update and reevaluate these?

- Describe what, if any, process your agency employs to regularly receive information to identify which of your agency's information or processes are of priority interest to adversary collectors.
- Does your agency have a process in place to evaluate its contracts, acquisitions, and procurements for foreign interest or involvement? If so, please describe the workings of that process.

Safeguarding

- How does your agency ensure access to classified information in automated systems is limited to those persons who: (a) have received a favorable determination of eligibility from the agency head or their designee, (b) have signed an approved non-disclosure agreement, and (c) have a need to know the information?
- How does your agency ensure that procedures are in place to prevent classified information in removable media and other media (back-up tapes, etc.) is not removed from official premises without proper authorization?
- How are need-to-know determinations made in your agency reflected in your management of automated systems?

Deter, Detect, and Defend Against Employee Unauthorized Disclosures

- Are there efforts to fuse together disparate data sources such as personnel security and evaluation, polygraph, where applicable, IT auditing or user activities, and foreign contact/foreign travel information to provide analysts early warning indicators of insider threats?
- What metrics do you use to measure "trustworthiness" without alienating employees?
- Do you use psychiatrist and sociologist to measure:
    - □ Relative happiness as a means to gauge trustworthiness?
    - □ Despondence and grumpiness as a means to gauge waning trustworthiness?

Information Assurance Measures

- Specific to national security systems (NSS) that process classified information: Do you perform Risk assessments and security categorizations in accordance with CNSS, NIST and FIPS standards?
- How does your agency examine NSS and evaluate their vulnerability to foreign interception and exploitation?
- How do you assess the overall security posture of systems and disseminate information on threats to and vulnerabilities?

Education and Training

- How does your agency ensure that every person who has access to classified information via automated systems has received contemporaneous training on the safeguarding of classified information?

- How does your agency ensure that persons who have access to classified information understand their responsibility to report any actual or possible compromise or disclosure of classified information to an unauthorized person(s) to an official designated for this purpose?
- Does your training address "need to know" decisions specific to automated systems?

Personnel Security

- Have you established a comprehensive personnel security program? If so, please describe your investigative, adjudicative, and continuous evaluation processes. Do you train your adjudicators to look for insider threat indicators?
- Have you conducted a trend analysis of indicators and activities of the employee population which may indicate risky habits or cultural and societal differences other than those expected for candidates (to include current employees) for security clearances?
- Are all employees required to report their contacts with the media?

Physical/Technical

- Has your agency developed annual reports of the status and welfare of the secure facilities that support the protection of classified information and mission accomplishment?
- Has your agency conducted a trend analysis for activities and events affecting information protection at any particular site or a group of sites?
- Do you look for unscheduled maintenance or unusual failures of security hardware (which might indicate end-of-life deficiencies or insider manipulation)?

Conclusion

As measured by the building of fusion centers, dedication of personnel, and money spent, it would appear that information sharing enjoys significant mindshare in the homeland security and national security communities. As measured by the guidance, legislation, and serious nature of recent security incidents, the future direction of information sharing is less clear. Information sharing is based on trust. Leaks undermine this trust, and can lead people to either hold back information or withdraw from using the system altogether, undermining its usefulness. Information sharing, then, also requires security. The tone and precision of security methods can significantly affect the level of participation, efficacy, and accountability of information sharing.

The results of the post-WikiLeaks security review were still pending at the time this report was prepared. However, it is clear from some of the questions in the review that the "need to know" perspective remains a significant organizing principle in securing and sharing at least some types of government information. Such an approach is not inherently inappropriate. Indeed, it is critical that the government take sufficient steps to secure classified and sensitive information. While it can be overstated, and the phrase is a bit outdated, there is still some truth to the World War II era slogan "Loose lips might sink ships."

At the same time, information sharing is critical to the security of the nation. In a rapidly evolving global environment, awareness may be one of our best defenses. Moreover, with difficult budget decisions ahead, such investments are not only strategically important, but also economically necessary. However, terrorism-related information sharing has been on GAO's high-risk list since 2005. In a February 2011 update, GAO stated that although some progress has been made to implement the Information Sharing Environment (ISE), as called for in the Intelligence Reform and Terrorism Prevention Act of 2004,[68] the federal government ". . . did not yet have a comprehensive approach that was guided by an overall plan and measures to help gauge progress and achieve desired results."[69]

The balance between the sharing and security postures is unsettled at this time, with many opportunities and challenges ahead. With important implications for the future of information sharing, privacy, and civil liberties, it is an area worth watching. Most immediately, the implementation of the executive orders, sharing agreements, and laws discussed earlier in this report may provide some early hints of changing directions. Likewise, the findings and reactions to WikiLeaks security reviews will likely be a major influence.

Notes

1. The ODNI was established by the Intelligence Reform and Terrorism Prevention Act of 2004 (118 Stat. 3638–3872.), which was signed into law by President George W. Bush on December 17, 2004.
2. 118 Stat. 3650.
3. Kevin R. Kosar, CRS Report for Congress, R41528 *Classified Information Policy and Executive Order 13526* (Dec. 10, 2010).
4. *Federal Register,* vol. 75, Jan. 5, 2010, pp. 705–736.
5. Harold C. Relyea and Jeffrey W. Seifert, "Access to Government Information: The Presidential Transition, 2008–2009," *Library and Book Trade Almanac,* 55th Edition, (Information Today, Inc., 2010) pp. 3–26.
6. *Federal Register,* vol. 75, Jan. 5, 2010, pp. 707, 708.
7. Ibid., p. 709.
8. Ibid.
9. Ibid., pp. 710–711.
10. Ibid., p. 712.
11. Ibid., p. 719.
12. Ibid., p. 720.
13. Ibid., pp. 724-725.
14. U.S. White House, Office of the Press Secretary, *Memorandum for the Heads of Executive Departments and Agencies,* Subject: "Implementation of the Executive Order, 'Classified National Security Information'," (Dec. 29, 2009), p. 1.
15. Ibid., p. 2.
16. National Archives and Records Administration, Information Security Oversight Office, *Report to the President for Fiscal Year 2009,* (March 31, 2010), p. 4.

17. Federal Register, vol. 75, Jan. 28, 2010, pp. 37254–37280.
18. Ibid., pp. 37260–37262.
19. Ibid., p. 37261.
20. Ibid., p. 37263.
21. Ibid., p. 37279.
22. Ibid., pp. 37275–37276.
23. U.S. Congress, Senate Committee on Homeland Security and Governmental Affairs, *Reducing Over-Classification Act,* S. Rept. 111-200, 111th Cong., May 27 (GPO, 2010) p. 4.
24. 124 Stat. 2649.
25. 124 Stat. 2650.
26. Ibid.
27. 124 Stat. 2651.
28. Ibid.
29. Ibid.
30. 124 Stat. 2652–2653.
31. U.S. Presidential Task Force on Controlled Unclassified Information, *Report and Recommendations of the Presidential Task Force on Controlled Unclassified Information,* (Washington, D.C.: Aug. 25, 2009) p. vii.
32. U.S. White House, Office of the Press Secretary, *Memorandum for the Heads of Executive Departments and Agencies,* Subject: "Classified Information and Controlled Unclassified Information," (May 27, 2009).
33. "CUI Framework refers to the single set of policies and procedures established by the Presidential Memorandum of May 7, 2008, governing the designation, marking, safeguarding, and dissemination of terrorism-related SBU information, which pursuant to that Memorandum, is renamed as 'Controlled Unclassified Information.'" U.S. Presidential Task Force on Controlled Unclassified Information, *Report and Recommendations of the Presidential Task Force on Controlled Unclassified Information,* (Washington, D.C.: Aug. 25, 2009) p. vii.
34. Ibid., p. 5.
35. Ibid., p. 9.
36. *Federal Register* vol. 75, Nov. 9, 2010, pp. 68675–68677.
37. Ibid., p. 68675.
38. Ibid.
39. Ibid.
40. Ibid., p. 68676.
41. Ibid.
42. Ibid., p. 68677.
43. U.S. Government Accountability Office, *High Risk Series: An Update,* GAO-11-278, Feb. 2011, p. 101.
44. John Markoff, "Cyberattack on Google Said to Hit Password System," *New York Times,* April 19, 2010, available at http://www.nytimes.com/2010/04/20/technology/20google.html?_r=1&sudsredirect=true, and Andrew Jacobs and Miguel Helft, "Google, Citing Attack, Threatens to Exit China," *New York Times,* Jan. 12, 2010, available at http://www.nytimes.com/2010/01/13/world/asia/13beijing.html.
45. Paul K. Kerr, John Rollins, and Catherine A. Theohary, CRS Report for Congress, R41524 *The Stuxnet Computer Worm: Harbinger of an Emerging Warfare Capability,* (Dec. 9, 2010).

46. U.S. White House, *Cyberspace Policy Review: Assuring a Trusted and Resilient Information and Communications Infrastructure,* May 2009, p. i.
47. Ibid.
48. Ibid.
49. Ibid., p. 37.
50. U.S. White House, National Security Council, "Cybersecurity Progress after President Obama's Address," July 14, 2010, at: http://www.whitehouse.gov/administration/eop/nsc/cybersecurity/progressreports/july2010. See also: http://www.whitehouse.gov/blog/2009/12/22/introducing-new-cybersecurity-coordinator.
51. U.S. Government Accountability Office, *Cyberspace Policy: Executive Branch Is Making Progress Implementing 2009 Policy Review Commendations, But Sustained Leadership Is Needed,* GAO-11-24, Oct. 2010, p. 13.
52. U.S. Office of Management and Budget, *Memorandum for the Heads of Executive Departments and Agencies,* Subject: "Clarifying Cybersecurity Responsibilities and Activities of the Executive Office of the President and the Department of Homeland Security," (July 6, 2010).
53. Ibid., p. 1.
54. Ibid.
55. Ibid.
56. U.S. Department of Homeland Security and U.S. Department of Defense, *Memorandum of Agreement Between the Department of Homeland Security and the Department of Defense Regarding Cybersecurity,* (Oct. 13, 2010), p. 1.
57. USCYBERCOM began initial operational capacity on May 21, 2010. According to its mission statement, USCYBERCOM "plans, coordinates, integrates, synchronizes, and conducts activities to: direct the operations and defense of specified Department of Defense information networks and; prepare to, and when directed, conduct full-spectrum military cyberspace operations in order to enable actions in all domains, ensure US/Allied freedom of action in cyberspace and deny the same to our adversaries." U.S. Department of Defense, *U.S. Cybercommand Fact Sheet,* (May 25, 2010), http://www.defense.gov/home/features/2010/0410_cybersec/docs/CYberFactSheet%20UPDATED%20replaces%20May%2021%20Fact%20Sheet.pdf.
58. Laurie Ure, "Soldier Accused of Leaking Classified Info," CNN, June 7, 2010, available at http://articles.cnn.com/2010-06-07/us/soldier.leak.accusation_1_leaking-crowley-computer-hacker?_s=PM:US.
59. Raffi Khatchadourian, "No Secrets," *New Yorker,* June 7, 2010, available at http://www.newyorker.com/reporting/2010/06/07/100607fa_fact_khatchadourian?printable=true.
60. Glenn Kessler, "U.S. Warns Allies About WikiLeaks," *Washington Post,* Nov. 26, 2010, p. A2.
61. Sean Reilly, "WikiLeaks Fallout: Info-Sharing Clampdown," *Federal Times,* Dec. 6, 2010, p. 1.
62. Glenn Kessler, "U.S. Warns Allies About WikiLeaks," *Washington Post,* Nov. 26, 2010, p. A2
63. Sean Reilly, "WikiLeaks Fallout: Info-Sharing Clampdown," *Federal Times,* Dec. 6, 2010, p. 1; Kevin Poulsen and Kim Zetter, "'I Can't Believe What I'm Confessing to You': The WikiLeaks Chats," *Wired,* June 10, 2010, available at http://www.wired.com/threatlevel/2010/06/wikileaks-chat.
64. U.S. Office of Management and Budget, *Memorandum for the Heads of Executive Departments and Agencies,* Subject: "WikiLeaks—Mishandling of Classified Information," (Nov. 28, 2010).

65. U.S. White House Office, Office of the Press Secretary, *FACT SHEET: U.S. Government Mitigation Efforts in Light of the Recent Unlawful Disclosure of Classified Information,* (Dec. 1, 2010).
66. Brian Kalish, "OMB: Don't Look at Leaked Documents," *NextGov,* Dec. 6, 2010, http://www.nextgov.com/nextgov/ng_20101206_5274.php#; Ed O'Keefe, "OMB: WikiLeaks Off-Limits to Federal Workers Without Clearance," *Washington Post,* Dec. 4, 2010, http://voices.washingtonpost.com/federal-eye/2010/12/wikileaks_off-limits_to_unauth.html.
67. U.S. Office of Management and Budget, *Memorandum for the Heads of Executive Departments and Agencies,* Subject: "Initial Assessments of Safeguarding and Counterintelligence Postures for Classified National Security Information in Automated Systems," (Jan. 3, 2011).
68. 118 Stat. 3665.
69. U.S. Government Accountability Office, *High Risk Series: An Update,* GAO-11-278, Feb. 2011, p. 96.

Imperiled Newspapers, WikiLeaks, and Access to Information

Jane E. Kirtley

Newspapers, it is said, are dying. The statistics are grim. In 2008 and 2009, several large daily newspapers, including the award-winning *Rocky Mountain News* in Denver, ceased operations. Other newspapers curtailed their print editions or went online only. Many others are in bankruptcy.[1]

Yet according to the Pew Research Center's Project for Excellence in Journalism study "The State of the News Media 2010," reports of the death of the newspaper are somewhat exaggerated: "Only half a dozen of any size went out of business, and most of those were second papers in their market. More papers, nearly 100, cut back at least one day a week, but most of those were very small."[2]

The National Newspaper Association, the trade industry group for weekly and community newspapers, defiantly reports that many small newspapers are doing just fine, claiming that 86 million Americans read nearly 8,000 community newspapers each week.[3]

And the Newspaper Association of America, which represents the larger dailies, claims that newspaper Web sites "saw tremendous traffic" in the fourth quarter of 2010, reaching 62 percent of all adult Internet users.[4]

The challenge that remains is how to harness that traffic and turn it into revenue. With the exception of the *Wall Street Journal,* few major U.S. newspapers have erected a pay wall requiring visitors to subscribe in order to read most online content—at least for any period of time, or with any success. The *New York Times* reported in January 2011 that Journalism Online, an experimental project run by Steven Brill that enables newspapers to charge fees to their regular visitors who read more than a specified number of articles each month, had a minimal impact on unique visits, page views, and advertising revenue. These readers, at least according to the study, may be loyal, but they are generally small in number: between 5 percent and 15 percent, according to Brill, who therefore concludes that for most visitors, the pay wall would be a "nonevent." Nevertheless, the *Times* article cautioned that extrapolating the experience of the two dozen small- to medium-sized newspapers to larger newspapers that have yet to try the experiment is difficult, quoting Tim Ruder, a news media consultant, who noted that "how well that success will translate to larger sites depends on many things, including the quality, nature and exclusivity of content."[5] And in a commentary on the online Huffington Post, Jarvis Coffin of Burst Media observed that it is probably at the least illogical to charge your best "customers" for the privilege of reading your content while permitting the casual visitor to consume the product for free, especially when "[i]t appears not to make a dent in the business model."[6]

The critical issue raised by the Pew study is that as circulations drop and advertising revenues stall, newspapers will continue to reduce not only the physi-

Jane E. Kirtley is Silha Professor of Media Ethics and Law, School of Journalism and Mass Communication, University of Minnesota.

cal size of their printed product, but also their staffs and the other resources necessary to conduct the kind of watchdog journalism that has been the life blood of American participatory democracy. Although there have long been advocacy and other special interest groups to monitor developments in their particular areas of concern, it has been primarily the role of the newspaper to provide day-to-day oversight of the more mundane aspects of government functions by checking police logs and attending city council and school board meetings.

Indeed, the federal government was sufficiently concerned about what it perceives as a national crisis in the news industry that in 2009 and 2010 two federal regulatory commissions—the Federal Trade Commission (FTC) and the Federal Communications Commission (FCC)—launched initiatives to, respectively, "reinvent journalism" and study the "future of media and information needs of communities in the digital age." In May 2010 FTC released a discussion draft of a series of proposals, including creating new antitrust exemptions for the press; liberalizing copyright law to allow news purveyors to assert broader ownership and control over their intellectual property; providing government subsidies and grants to news media and individual journalists (which would be paid for through new taxes and fees), and allowing certain news organizations to acquire tax-exempt status.[7]

Also in 2010 FCC conducted workshops and maintained interactive blogs to elicit comment from the public on how best to "ensure that all Americans have access to vibrant, diverse sources of news and information that will enable them to enrich their families, communities and democracy."[8] A final report was pending as of this writing, but many expect that public subsidies in some form to supplement dwindling statehouse coverage by the news media would be part of the plan. *U.S. News & World Report* quoted Chris Long, the head of Wisconsin's public affairs television network, as saying that, "[w]e just want to make sure we're included in the FCC report" as potential recipients of federal funding to underwrite camera coverage of state legislatures, similar to the cable industry-funded C-SPAN.[9]

But many observers are dismayed at the prospect of the news media being tempted to trade independence for financial security by feeding at the government trough. Commentators such as Jeff Jarvis of the blog "BuzzMachine" and Mark Tapscott of the (Washington) *Examiner* have warned that these proposals would undermine the "adversarial relationship" between the press and the government that is guaranteed by the First Amendment. Moreover, they claimed, the proposals focus on creating incentives to keep the struggling "legacy media" industry afloat while ignoring the burgeoning blogosphere.[10]

Both expressed particular concerns about FTC's proposal to limit the "fair use" defense to the Copyright Act and to expand the "hot news" doctrine, effectively allowing news organizations to "own" facts and prevent competitors from disseminating them for a period of time. As Jarvis wrote:

> What disturbs me most . . . is that the FTC frets about "difficult line-drawing between proprietary facts and those in the public domain." Proprietary facts? Is it starting down a road of trying to enable someone to own a fact the way the patent office lets someone own a method or our DNA? Good God, that's dangerous.[11]

In fact, the "hot news" doctrine is neither new nor novel, dating back to a 1918 U.S. Supreme Court decision, *International News Service* v. *Associated Press,*[12] which held that news organizations may claim a quasi-property right (as opposed to copyright) in commercially valuable, time-sensitive information. Although the doctrine is currently limited to a few states, the FTC report mused that a uniform, federal approach might be preferable.

In the meantime, a 2010 case brought in federal court in New York by an investment firm persuaded a judge to enjoin a financial news Web site, Theflyonthewall.com, from publishing stock information using the hot news doctrine.[13] Fourteen news organizations filed amicus (friend-of-the-court) briefs arguing that "free-riders," including news aggregators, threaten their ability to make money doing journalism. Others, including Google and Twitter, claimed that the doctrine is unconstitutional and violates other Supreme Court precedent holding that facts are not protected by copyright, regardless of how much effort is expended compiling and organizing them. "[I]n an age of instantaneous, global dissemination of factual information over the Internet, cable, and satellite, a tort of 'hot news' misappropriation is obsolete," they argued in an amicus brief.[14] At this writing, a petition for rehearing before the Second Circuit U.S. Court of Appeals was pending.

In a similar vein, a number of traditional news outlets, including the Associated Press, the *Las Vegas Review-Journal,* and several Colorado newspapers including the *Denver Post,* have pursued Web site owners and bloggers for using their content without permission. Perhaps the most notorious are the efforts by the law firm Righthaven, an affiliate of the *Review-Journal*'s parent company, Stephens Media, which reportedly has filed more than 150 lawsuits against a wide variety of online publishers since March 2010.[15] Although Mark Hinueber, vice president and general counsel of Stephens Media, has asserted that Righthaven's efforts are aimed at online business competitors, not "mom and pop" bloggers, critics contend that the lawsuits stifle free expression and could even undermine reporters' relationships with their sources. But Steve Friess, a freelance writer and blogger, defended the practice, posting the following comment on the *Las Vegas Weekly* Web site:

> The thing that's killing the media is the devaluation of its assets, something in which [the media] is a willing participant. This could be the first step toward reminding people that information may want to be free, but those who provide it have bills to pay, too.[16]

The WikiLeaks Hullabaloo

The issue of "who owns facts" was brought into sharp focus in July 2010 when the Web site WikiLeaks published tens of thousands of classified reports filed by American troops and intelligence officials in Afghanistan. WikiLeaks provided access to the reports to the *New York Times,* Britain's *Guardian,* and the German magazine *Der Spiegel* on condition that the media organizations not report the contents until the Web site posted them online. Many of the documents revealed suspected, but previously unconfirmed, information, such as that the Pakistani intelligence agency supported insurgents in Afghanistan, as well as details of the use of heat-seeking missiles by Taliban fighters. Although some in government contended that little information in the documents was actually news, advocates of openness in government expressed concern that the disclosures would prompt tighter controls on information and increased classification.

WikiLeaks' release of more documents in late November 2010—this time, the first set of purportedly more than 250,000 secret diplomatic cables sent from U.S. embassies—prompted more controversy. The Web site worked with five news organizations, including *El Pais* (Spain) and *Le Monde* (France). Rather than engaging in the "document dump" of which he had been accused in July, WikiLeaks founder Julian Assange asserted that WikiLeaks and the partner media organizations were vetting the cables for potentially sensitive information, despite the State Department's refusal to cooperate in the process.

WikiLeaks had not sought input from the U.S. government, at least prior to its initial release of the classified reports in July. However, Assange claimed that when he had approached the Pentagon for help in reviewing a second set of documents, he had been rebuffed by Defense Department lawyers. The *New York Times,* by contrast, reported that it had sought guidance from the White House, which, it claimed, had "thanked us for handling the documents with care, and asked us to urge WikiLeaks to withhold information that could cost lives."[17]

This kind of cooperation between the U.S.-based press and the government was not unusual. As Benjamin Bradlee, then executive editor of the *Washington Post,* wrote in an essay in 1986, "we do consult with government regularly about sensitive stories and we do withhold stories for national security reasons, far more often than the public might think."[18] But to some, these revelations indicated that the legacy media were not putting freedom of information and the public interest first, but were instead allowing themselves to be manipulated by the government. The fundamental disagreement was, as David Leigh, an investigative editor at the *Guardian,* told *Vanity Fair* magazine:

> Neither us [*sic*] nor *Der Spiegel* nor the *New York Times* was ever going to print names of people who were going to get reprisals, any more than we would do on any other occasion. We were starting from: "Here's a document. How much of it shall we print?" Whereas Julian's ideology was: "I shall dump everything out and then you have to try and persuade me to cross a few things out." We were coming at it from opposite poles.[19]

Not surprisingly, then, the legacy media found themselves in a complicated position. They were eager users (and in some cases, recipients) of the WikiLeaks documents, and published numerous stories based on them. On the other hand, they also took pains to distance themselves from Assange and his organization, and many suggested that what WikiLeaks was up to did not constitute "journalism" at all. For his part, Assange was reportedly enraged when the *New York Times* published a critical profile of him in October. He argued in an op-ed column published by the *Australian* in December that he was creating "a new type of journalism: scientific journalism," which consisted of not only reporting the news, but providing readers with links to the original documents. "Democratic societies need a strong media and WikiLeaks is part of that media," he contended.[20]

The "strength" of the media in the United States, at least regarding the right to publish classified information, had been established many years before.

Release of the WikiLeaks documents was equated by many with the publication of the "Pentagon Papers" by the *New York Times* and *Washington Post* after they were leaked to the newspapers by Daniel Ellsberg in 1971. The Nixon administration's attempt to enjoin the newspapers from continuing to release the documents led to one of the most significant First Amendment cases decided by the U.S. Supreme Court, *New York Times* v. *United States.*[21] In that case, the high court reasserted its previous precedent that prior restraints were presumed to be unconstitutional, and that the government had failed to meet its heavy burden of proving irreparable harm to national security, which was necessary to support an injunction on the press. But in separate opinions, several of the justices made clear that subsequent prosecution under appropriate federal statutes—assuming any existed—would not be precluded by the First Amendment.

Nevertheless, the federal government has not yet attempted to prosecute legacy media organizations that are the recipients of classified documents, although it has used espionage and theft of government property statutes successfully against a government employee who leaked classified photographs to the British-based *Jane's Defence Weekly.*[22]

Whether existing federal law would provide the means to prosecute WikiLeaks or its founder, Assange, for espionage or theft of government property (assuming that jurisdiction could be obtained) remains a subject of much debate. But the continued detention of Army Pfc. Bradley Manning, a military intelligence analyst suspected of being the source of at least some of the WikiLeaks documents and previously charged with violation of military regulations regarding the storage and transfer of classified information, suggests that the federal government is serious about pursuing government employees who leak to the media.

The government acted swiftly to discourage government employees from even gaining access to the WikiLeaks documents. Steven Aftergood reported in *Secrecy News* that access to the WikiLeaks Web site was blocked by the Library of Congress, which meant that, among other things, the library's Congressional Research Service could not provide guidance to the relevant House and Senate oversight committees.[23] Aftergood also reported that the government had "directed federal employees and contractors not to access or read the records outside of a classified network."[24] The Office of Senate Security similarly instructed employees and contractors not to visit the WikiLeaks site (although they could look at news sites that reported on the material).[25] The Air Force Materiel Command (AFMC) issued guidance in early February 2011 stating that accessing the documents "under any circumstances," whether by military members and employees or their families, could result in prosecution under the Espionage Act.[26] That guidance was later withdrawn, with the Air Force reminding its military members to refrain from downloading classified documents to unclassified networks, stating that it would defer to the Department of Justice as to "all non-military matters related to WikiLeaks."[27]

While the Justice Department considered its options, some members of Congress, including Sen. Joe Lieberman (I-Conn.) and Rep. Peter King (R-N.Y.), drafted legislation known as the SHIELD (Securing Human Intelligence and Enforcing Lawful Dissemination) Act in December 2010 to expand the authority of the government to prosecute the publication of the names of military and intelligence informants.[28] King claimed that "WikiLeaks presents a clear and present danger to the national security of the United States, and Julian Assange, an enemy of the U.S., should be prosecuted under the Espionage Act."[29]

The House of Representatives held a hearing on issues raised by the WikiLeaks releases on December 16, 2010, focusing primarily on the problem of government overclassification of information, which most of those testifying contended can actually compromise security, and whether the Espionage Act should be revamped as proposed. Constitutional scholar Geoffrey Stone claimed that applying the SHIELD Act to non-government employees would violate the First Amendment. Although Kenneth L. Wainstein, a Washington, D.C., lawyer, argued that failing to prosecute WikiLeaks would encourage the Web site to "redouble their efforts, and copycat operations will sprout up around the Internet," law professor Stephen I. Vladeck argued that any revision to the law should distinguish between "leakers" and "spies"—and should not extend to either whistleblowers or the press.[30]

Inevitably, then, the question arose: Is Julian Assange a journalist? Wainstein contended that WikiLeaks was "fundamentally different" from the legacy media because it merely collects and discloses information with no editorial review process, while Thomas Blanton of the National Security Archive claimed that, because of its ongoing redaction efforts, "They [WikiLeaks] are looking more and more like a media organization."[31]

The same debate over WikiLeaks' status as a member of "the press" continued in the mainstream media as well. Hagit Limor, president of the Society of Professional Journalists, blogged that "there is no consensus" on the question, but argued that the distinction was basically beside the point, because legislation like the SHIELD Act would target not only Assange, but anyone who publishes classified information, including reporters. What makes a journalist, she wrote, is the "decision making process," the "tool-gathering skill set," coupled with verification, providing context, recognizing potential harm, and "acting responsibly." "I don't care who you are or what you call yourself, if you're not applying these principles, you're not a journalist," she concluded.[32]

Libraries Weigh In

The controversy surrounding WikiLeaks and its methods has not been limited to the journalism community. It has also involved librarians. At its annual Midwinter Meeting in San Diego, the American Library Association (ALA) considered several resolutions calling for support for Assange, and condemning the Library of Congress for blocking access to the WikiLeaks site. The resolution, as passed on January 11, 2011, commended President Barack Obama for initiatives to reform the classification system, urged the passage of laws protecting whistleblowers, urged the government to "defend the inalienable right of the press and citizens to disseminate information to the public about national security," and affirmed "the principle that government information made public within the United States should be available through libraries and the press without restriction." The resolution mentioned WikiLeaks, almost in passing, as the vehicle for "renewed debate" about access to government information. It did not expressly "support" Assange.[33]

Bill Sleeman, a member of ALA's Google Books Task Force and associated with the Thurgood Marshall Law Library at the University of Maryland, criticized the reaction of his colleagues to what he called "the WikiLeaks dump." He blogged that the Library of Congress had no choice but to block access to WikiLeaks "because we are dealing with stolen government property, not declassified information." He also argued that librarians should question Assange's motivation. "Is he a whistleblower combating government secrecy, a journalist, an archivist? . . . Is Assange the Daniel Ellsberg of the Internet?" Sleeman wrote. Rather than unquestioningly "harvest and preserve this material," librarians should, he suggested, think long and hard about facilitating access to it. "Would we knowingly acquire stolen property for our library collections in any other situation?" he asked. "Just because we believe in open access does not mean we should embrace and encourage everything we find on the Internet."[34]

On the other hand, Al Kagan, a professor at the University of Illinois and a former member of ALA's governing Council, argued in a column in *American Libraries* magazine that ALA has an obligation to support WikiLeaks, just as most librarians had supported the *New York Times* and the *Washington Post* during the Pentagon Papers case.[35] James Jacobs, government documents librarian at Stanford University, dissected Sleeman's essay in detail, arguing, among other things, that librarians have an obligation to preserve the WikiLeaks materials for future scholars, perhaps embargoing their release until they can be authenticated and their legal status confirmed. "Preservation does not happen by accident," he wrote. "If we rely on others to preserve material that is important to our users, we may find that we are losing important information."[36]

And so we return to an important question raised by the anticipated death of newspapers. If librarians, like the general public, rely on newspapers to procure, disseminate, and maintain information, what will happen if newspapers disappear? It is a sobering prospect.

For more than 80 years, going back to the *Near* v. *Minnesota*[37] decision that first established the presumptive unconstitutionality of prior restraints on the press, the news media have been responsible for litigating the seminal Supreme Court cases guaranteeing the First Amendment right to disseminate information freely. They have forged the nearly iron-clad protection for reports on the activities of public officials and public figures[38] and for expression of even offensive opinion about matters of public concern.[39] They have thrown open the doors of the nation's courtrooms to the public, as well as the press.[40] Some were mainstream media, like the *New York Times,* the *Richmond Times-Dispatch* and the Riverside (California) *Press-Enterprise.* But many were as much "outliers" as WikiLeaks: Jay Near's *Saturday Press,* the John Birch Society's *American Opinion,* Larry Flynt's *Hustler* magazine.

In the states, the effort to keep state government open and accountable has largely been the work of newspapers, both as lobbyists seeking the adoption and strengthening of freedom of information and open meetings laws, and as litigators seeking their enforcement. In an era when public access to digitized government records is increasingly curtailed on privacy or national security grounds, it is often newspaper archives that are the only accessible repository of criminal history information.

Continuing these activities costs money. Apart from reductions in personnel, meaning that there are fewer watchdog reporters out on the beat, tighter budgets should also mean that it is harder for newspapers to continue to fulfill what many of them regard as their civic duty: to preserve freedom of expression, and to promote access to government information. Most bloggers and other online-only publications lack the financial resources to turn to the courts for relief.

The encouraging news, however, is that, at least for many of the larger newspapers and media companies, this type of litigation remains relatively robust. The *New York Times* reported in February 2010 that some companies were actually expanding their legal efforts, especially in jurisdictions where they may be awarded legal fees if they prevail. In addition to the *Times* itself, Hearst and the Associated Press claim that, if anything, they have become more aggressive in litigating, with AP reporting that it appealed more than 40 denied federal Freedom of Information Act requests in 2009.[41]

Nevertheless, the decline in the numbers and financial vitality of newspapers does portend what might be the end of an era. Unless new economic models emerge, it seems inevitable that fewer "legacy media" will remain viable. Whether their successors will undertake the kinds of battles that will be essential to protect the public's right to know remains an open question.

Notes

1. RonNell Andersen Jones, "Litigation, Legislation and Democracy in a Post-Newspaper America," *Washington and Lee Law Review* (forthcoming 2011), accessible at: http://ssrn.com/abstract=1710910.
2. Pew Research Center Project for Excellence in Journalism, "The State of the News Media: An Annual Report on American Journalism 2010" (March 15, 2010), accessible at: http://www.stateofthemedia.org/2010.
3. National Newspaper Association, "2010 Community Newspaper Readership Survey Report," accessible at: http://www.nnaweb.org/?/nnaweb/nnanews02/353.
4. Newspaper Association of America, "Trends and Numbers" 2010, accessible at: http://www.naa.org/TrendsandNumbers.aspx.
5. Jeremy W. Peters, "Under Pay Model, Little Effect Seen on Papers' Web Traffic," *New York Times,* Jan. 17, 2011, accessible at: http://www.nytimes.com/2011/01/18/business/media/18brill.html.
6. Jarvis Coffin, "So Far, Newspaper Pay Walls Are a Nonevent," *Huffington Post,* Jan. 19, 2011, accessible at: http://www.huffingtonpost.com/jarvis-coffin/so-far-newspaper-pay-wall_b_811273.html.
7. Federal Trade Commission, Potential Policy Recommendations to Support the Reinvention of Journalism (Discussion Draft dated May 24, 2010), accessible at: http://www.ftc.gov/opp/workshops/news/jun15/docs/new-staff-discussion.pdf.
8. Federal Communications Commission, "Future of Media and Information Needs of Communities in a Digital Age," accessible at: http://reboot.fcc.gov/futureofmedia.
9. Paul Bedard, "Washington Whispers: Little C-SPANs Sprout Up Across Nation," *U.S. News and World Report,* Sept. 3, 2010.

10. Mark Tapscott, "Will Journalists Wake Up in Time to Save Journalism from Obama's FTC?," *Examiner,* May 29, 2010, accessible at: http://washingtonexaminer.com/82681.
11. Jeff Jarvis, "FTC Protects Journalism's Past," BuzzMachine, May 29, 2010, accessible at: http://www.buzzmachine.com/2010/05/29/ftc-protects-journalisms-past.
12. 248 U.S. 215 (1918).
13. *Barclays Capital, Inc.* v. *Theflyonthewall.com,* 2010 U.S. Dist. LEXIS 25728 (S.D.N.Y. March 18, 2010).
14. Patrick File, "News Media Seek Legal Tools to Protect Original Content," *Silha Bulletin* at 25 (Summer 2010).
15. Patrick File, "Law Firm's Approach to Protecting News Media Copyrights Raises Eyebrows," *Silha Bulletin* at 19 (Fall 2010)
16. Ibid. at 22.
17. Patrick File, "WikiLeaks' Document Dump Sparks Debate," *Silha Bulletin* at 3 (Summer 2010).
18. Benjamin C. Bradlee, "The Post and Pelton: How the Press Looks at National Security," *Washington Post,* June 8, 1986, at F1.
19. Sarah Ellison, "The Man Who Spilled the Secrets," *Vanity Fair,* February 2011, accessible at: http://www.vanityfair.com/politics/features/2011/02/the-guardian-201102.
20. Julian Assange, "Don't Shoot the Messenger for Revealing Uncomfortable Truths," *The Australian,* Dec. 7, 2010, accessible at: http://www.themarketguardian.com/2010/12/julian-assange-op-ed-in-the-australian.
21. 403 U.S. 713 (1971).
22. *United States* v. *Morison,* 844 F.2d 1057 (4th Cir. 1988).
23. Steven Aftergood, "CRS Seeks Guidance on Using Leaked Docs," *Secrecy News*, Dec. 8, 2010, accessible at: http://www.fas.org/blog/secrecy/2010/12/crs_guidance.html.
24. Steven Aftergood, "Govt Response to WikiLeaks Said to Cause More Damage," *Secrecy News*, Dec. 10, 2010, accessible at: http://www.fas.org/blog/secrecy/2010/12/govt_response.html.
25. Steven Aftergood, "Senate Offices Told to Avoid WikiLeaks," *Secrecy News*, Jan. 24, 2011, accessible at: http://www.fas.org/blog/secrecy/2011/01/senate_wikileaks.html.
26. Steven Aftergood, "Accessing WikiLeaks Violates Espionage Act, USAF Says," *Secrecy News*, Feb. 7, 2011, accessible at: http://www.fas.org/blog/secrecy/2011/02/accessing_wikileaks.html.
27. Steven Aftergood, "Air Force Rescinds New Guidance on WikiLeaks," *Secrecy News*, Feb. 9, 2011, accessible at: http://www.fas.org/blog/secrecy/2011/02/af_rescinds_guidance.html.
28. "A bill to amend section 798 of title 18, United States Code, to provide penalties for disclosure of classified information related to certain intelligence activities of the United States, and for other purposes." Accessible at: http://homeland.house.gov/sites/homeland.house.gov/files/The%20SHIELD%20Act_0.pdf.
29. Robert Herriman, "NY Rep. Peter King Introduces the SHIELD Act to Get the Likes of Julian Assange," examiner.com, accessible at: http://www.examiner.com/foreign-policy-in-national/ny-rep-peter-king-introduces-the-shield-act-to-get-the-likes-of-julian-assange.
30. *See generally,* Chloe Albanesiu, "WikiLeaks Hearing Stresses Over-Classification More Than Assange," PCMAG.COM, Dec. 16, 2010, accessible at: http://www.pcmag.com/article2/0,2817,2374424,00.asp.
31. Ibid.

32. Hagit Limor, "The Consensus on WikiLeaks: There Is No Consensus. But Consider the Ethics," Freedom of the Prez, Dec. 2, 2010, accessible at: http://blogs.spjnetwork.org/president/?tag-julian-assange.
33. Jonathan Kelley, "ALA Council Unanimously Passes WikiLeaks-Related Resolution," OIF Blog, Jan. 11, 2011, accessible at: http://www.oif.ala.org/oif/?p=1796.
34. Bill Sleeman, "A Librarian Reacts to WikiLeaks," Jan. 24, 2011, accessible at: http://ethics.journalism.wisc.edu/2011/01/24/a-librarian-reacts-to-wikileaks.
35. Al Kagan, "Midwinter's WikiLeaks Letdown," *American Libraries,* Feb. 1, 2011, accessible at: http://americanlibrariesmagazine.org/columns.
36. James Jacobs, "A Librarian Reacts to 'A Librarian Reacts to WikiLeaks,'" Free Government Information, Feb. 13, 2011, accessible at: http://freegovinfo.info/node/3178.
37. 283 U.S. 697 (1931).
38. *New York Times Co.* v. *Sullivan,* 376 U.S. 254 (1964).
39. *Gertz* v. *Robert Welch, Inc.,* 418 U.S. 323 (1974); *Hustler Magazine* v. *Falwell,* 485 U.S. 46 (1988).
40. *Richmond Newspapers* v. *Virginia,* 448 U.S. 555 (1980); *Press Enterprise Co.* v. *Superior Court* (II), 478 U.S. 1 (1986).
41. Tim Arango, "Despite Budgets, Some Newsrooms Persist in Costly Fight for Records," *New York Times,* Feb. 14, 2010, accessible at: http://www.nytimes.com/2010/02/15/business/media/15hearst.html.

Federal Agency and Federal Library Reports

Library of Congress

10 First St. S.E., Washington, DC 20540
202-707-5000, http://www.loc.gov

James H. Billington
Librarian of Congress

Founded in 1800, the Library of Congress is the nation's oldest federal cultural institution and the largest library in the world, with more than 147 million items in various languages, disciplines, and formats. As the world's largest repository of knowledge and creativity, the library's mission is to make its resources available and useful to the U.S. Congress and the American people and to sustain and preserve a universal collection of knowledge and creativity for future generations. The library serves Congress and the nation both on-site in its reading rooms on Capitol Hill and through its award-winning Web site, http://www.loc.gov, and a "personalized" Web site at http://myLOC.gov.

Legislative Support to Congress

Serving Congress is the library's highest priority, particularly in the area of legislative support, which it provides through its Congressional Research Service (CRS), Law Library, and the U.S. Copyright Office.

During 2010 CRS delivered to Congress an array of products focused on the key public policy issues deemed likely to be on the legislative agenda. CRS provided policy analyses regarding such increasingly complex legislative domestic issues as reform of the financial regulatory system, mortgage finance, unemployment compensation, employment and training, healthcare reform, offshore oil drilling, food safety, postal reform, and aviation policy. In the area of foreign affairs, CRS supported congressional debate on U.S. relations with China and Pakistan, military engagement in Afghanistan, sanctions against Iran and North Korea relating to nuclear proliferation, and the implications of the Greek debt crisis for the U.S. economy. CRS also responded to countless congressional requests pertaining to the January 2010 earthquake in Haiti and the floods in Pakistan.

Report compiled by Audrey Fischer, Public Affairs Specialist, Library of Congress.

More than a decade after its inception, the library's Legislative Information System (LIS), developed solely for use by Congress and congressional staff members, continued to provide access to information on past and current legislation through all facets of the lawmaking process. CRS worked with other offices in the library to provide for the next generation of LIS. Enhancements to LIS included a new home page and integration with the CRS.gov site, which dramatically improved the ability to find CRS products through LIS.

The Law Library—the world's largest, comprising 2.6 million items—provided Congress with comprehensive international, comparative, and foreign law research based on the most current information available. During the year Law Library staff prepared 473 legal research reports, special studies, and memoranda in response to congressional inquiries. Foreign law specialists assisted members of Congress in researching legislative issues including oil-spill liability, mining regulations, immigration, campaign finance, corporate residency taxation, crimes against humanity, government procurement agreements, and health care.

The *Global Legal Monitor,* a continually updated online publication covering legal news and developments worldwide, remained a popular page on the Law Library's Web site. At year's end, the publication had more than 13,000 subscribers. Other online resources added to the Law Library's Web site during the year included special presentations on the nomination of Supreme Court Justice Elena Kagan.

The Global Legal Information Network (GLIN) provided Congress and other participating parliamentary bodies with more than 188,000 laws, judicial decisions, and related legal materials contributed by 34 member nations and international organizations. In 2010 more than 14,000 legal materials were added to the GLIN database. Legal information analysts at the Law Library added more than 1,700 laws to the database for 16 nations outside the network.

The U.S. Copyright Office provided policy advice and technical assistance to Congress on important copyright laws and such related issues as statutory licenses for satellite carriers, orphan works (copyrighted works whose owners are unknown or cannot be located), and public performance rights for sound recordings broadcast over the air.

The U.S. Copyright Office worked with Congress and stakeholders on legislation reauthorizing the statutory license for satellite carriers. Signed into law on May 27, 2010, the Satellite Television Extension and Localism Act of 2010 (P.L. 111-175), extends the Section 119 license for another five years and modernizes the statutory licenses governing the retransmission of distant television signals by cable and satellite television operators to address the recent transition from analog to digital television.

With input from the Register of Copyrights, the Librarian of Congress, on July 26, 2010, announced six classes of works subject to exemption from the Digital Millennium Copyright Act (DMCA), Section 1210 of the U.S. Code. The legislation prohibits the circumvention of technological measures that control access to copyrighted works. Works cited for exemption include certain uses of DVDs, cell phone programs, eBooks, and other works.

Security

Keeping the library's staff, patrons, facilities, and collections secure remains a high priority. In 2010 the focus was placed on enhancing the library's emergency preparedness program, improving security at its Capitol Hill buildings and outlying facilities, and strengthening personnel security programs.

Throughout the year the library and the U.S. Capitol Police (USCP) coordinated on policy and operational matters affecting library security, in accordance with the September 2009 merger of the Library of Congress Police with USCP.

Work continued to develop a "continuity of operations" management site from which key library personnel can operate in the event Capitol Hill facilities are compromised. The library continued to improve its electronic and physical security controls to safeguard its collections and assets in all library buildings on Capitol Hill. Important security projects were completed at the library's off-site facilities, including Modules 3 and 4 at Fort Meade, Maryland; the Landover Center Annex; and the Packard Campus for Audio Visual Conservation in Culpeper, Virginia.

The library's Information Technology Security Program ensures that its mission-critical systems are reliable and secure and that the technology infrastructure that supports these systems is uncompromised. The library's technology infrastructure includes three data centers, more than 350 servers, 250 library-wide systems and applications, 9,500 voice connections, 14,000 data network connections, 5,000 workstations, and 1,000 local printers. Library staff completed mandatory annual information technology security awareness training.

Strategic Planning

The Librarian of Congress's management agenda, issued in July 2009, called for a review and revision of the library's strategic plan. During 2010 managers and staff from all major units of the library participated in the development of a strategic plan for fiscal years (FYs) 2011–2016. The revised plan includes an update of the library's mission statement that places greater emphasis on the primacy of serving Congress as well as the library's key contributions to the American people. A specific budget and planning framework based on the new plan is scheduled for implementation on October 1, 2011. To view the revised plan, visit http://www.loc.gov/about/strategicplan/strategic_plan2011-2016.pdf.

Budget

The FY 2010 Legislative Branch appropriations bill [P.L. 111-68] was signed into law on October 1, 2009. The act provided an appropriation for the library of $684.3 million, including authority to spend up to $40.962 million in offsetting receipts. The act supported strategic goals by providing funds specifically to restore and renew the library's technological infrastructure and to make collections materials available and useful in the digital environment.

Development

During FY 2010 the library's fund-raising activities brought in a total of $16.7 million, representing 769 gifts from 590 donors. These gifts, including $4 million received through planned gifts, were made to 64 library initiatives. The library forged partnerships with 218 first-time donors who gave a total of $4.3 million, representing 26 percent of the gifts received during the year.

Private gifts supported a variety of new and continuing initiatives throughout the library, including exhibitions, acquisitions, and symposia and other scholarly programs. The Target store chain and the *Washington Post* gave more than $1.3 million to support the 2010 National Book Festival, and a $5 million gift from David M. Rubenstein will help ensure the stability of the annual festival over the next five years. The library will create a board that will advise, promote, and support the festival and assist with fund raising.

Other donors committed $3.6 million to create a Residential Scholars Center to provide a home for scholarly discourse in the nation's capital.

A $3.3 million bequest from Dina Koston and Roger Shapiro established a fund in their name to support commissions for new activities including concerts, lectures, publications, and acquisitions.

Gifts from the James Madison Council—the library's private sector advisory group—in FY 2010 totaled nearly $9 million, bringing the council's total support since 1990 to $199 million. Gifts from the council supported the World Digital Library, the National Book Festival, the Junior Fellows Program, and an exhibition featuring psychiatrist Carl Gustav Jung's *The Red Book.*

Educational Outreach

The library's Educational Outreach Office makes its online resources useful and accessible to teachers and students through a Teachers Page (http://www.loc.gov/teachers) and through its Teaching with Primary Sources Program (TPS). During the year the Teachers Page was augmented with primary sources and teaching guides centered on the NAACP, the library's Veterans History Project, and the nation's westward expansion. Special collections were developed for the study of the Wright Brothers and the Everglades National Park. New teachers' guides for primary source analysis were developed for oral histories and political cartoons.

The four-day TPS Summer Teacher Institute, held at the library annually, taught 150 educators from 31 states and three countries how best to use the library's digitized primary sources in the classroom. Participants were required to develop a primary source project plan to be implemented in their educational setting by the end of the fiscal year.

During 2010, using a train-the-trainer model, the 24 members of the TPS Educational Consortium made more than 1,000 presentations to nearly 13,000 teachers in 11 states on how the library's digitized primary sources could be used in the classroom.

At a number of forums throughout the year the Library of Congress demonstrated the potential for digital resources to enhance the curriculum and spark critical thinking in the classroom. The library's Educational Outreach Office sponsored a two-day global professional development conference in March to train teachers around the world to educate students on the importance of civic engagement. The Civic Voices Project of the American Federation of Teachers Educational Foundation is supported by a three-year grant from the U.S. Department of Education, funded by the Education for Democracy Act. The project brings together teachers to build an International Democracy Memory Bank. The project asks students to conduct oral-history interviews with people who have helped advance human rights and freedom around the world. These videos and transcripts will be available online at http://www.civicvoices.org.

Literacy Promotion

The Library of Congress promotes reading and literacy through the Center for the Book, the National Book Festival, collaborative public service advertising campaigns, the appointment of a National Ambassador for Young People's Literature, and through its popular literacy-promotion Web site, http://www.Read.gov.

With its network of affiliates in all 50 states and more than 80 organizational partners, the Center for the Book led the library's reading-promotion efforts. [For more on the center's activities, see the following article, "Center for the Book"—*Ed.*].

Read.gov is supported by an advertising campaign directed by the library's Public Affairs Office in cooperation with the private, nonprofit Advertising Council (http://www.adcouncil.org). Since 2000 the library has worked with the Ad Council on a series of national public service announcement campaigns to highlight the library's Web resources for children and families and to promote lifelong learning through reading. In August 2010 the library and the Ad Council launched a series of announcements to encourage parents to read with their children. Featuring children's book character Curious George, the campaign was created in partnership with Universal Partnerships and Licensing and Houghton Mifflin Harcourt publishing company.

To reach out to children and teens, the library opened a Young Readers Center in its Thomas Jefferson Building in October 2009. Visitors can choose to read a book from an up-to-date collection of noncirculating titles; they can browse the Web's child-friendly sites; or they can attend programs especially designed for young readers. During its first year in operation, the Young Readers Center expanded its programming, particularly during the summer months.

In March 2010 the library hosted the National Education Association's (NEA's) 13th annual Read Across America Day. First Lady Michelle Obama and U.S. Secretary of Education Arne Duncan took part in the event, which marked the 106th anniversary of the birthday of Theodor Seuss Geisel (the children's writer Dr. Seuss) and launched NEA's national reading-promotion campaign. NEA President Dennis Van Roekel addressed nearly 300 District of Columbia area elementary school students who came to the Library of Congress for the event. The First Lady read the Dr. Seuss classic *The Cat in the Hat,* and Secretary Duncan read *Horton Hears a Who!*

Collections

During 2010 the size of the library's collections grew to 147.1 million items, an increase of 2.5 million over the previous year. This figure included more than 33.9 million cataloged books and other print materials, 64.5 million manuscripts, 16.5 million microforms, 5.4 million maps, 6 million pieces of sheet music, 14.6 million visual materials (photographs, posters, moving images, prints, and drawings), 3 million audio materials, and more than 1 million items in miscellaneous formats.

Important Acquisitions

The library receives millions of items each year from copyright deposits, federal agencies, and purchases, exchanges, and gifts.

During 2010 the Copyright Office forwarded to the library more than 800,000 copies of works with a net value estimated at $32.9 million. About half were received from publishers under the mandatory-deposit provisions of the copyright law.

Significant acquisitions made possible by the Madison Council included rare maps documenting the first U.S.-British boundary dispute from the late 1700s; a star chart by William Croswell from 1810; Leonard Bernstein's autograph manuscript for "Screwed on Wrong," with lyrics by Stephen Sondheim; a rare Bible printed in Venice in 1475, and Igor Stravinsky's proof copy for the ballet "Apollo." The library also acquired the following significant items and collections by purchase and donation:

- The Twitter Archive, composed of all public "tweets" since the social network's inception in 2006
- The papers of Jack Kemp (1935–2009), covering his career as a cabinet secretary, vice presidential candidate, congressman, and professional football player
- More than 1,000 sound recordings and other items relating to jazz saxophonist Dexter Gordon (1923–1990)
- Some 15,000 letters written by listeners of Radio Azadi, the Afghan broadcasting service of Radio Free Europe/Radio Liberty
- An 80-volume set documenting the family tree of Chinese philosopher Confucius (dating back 83 generations)
- The Liljenquist Collection of nearly 700 Civil War photographs

Cataloging

The Library of Congress cataloged 361,562 new works in 2010. Production of full- and core-level original cataloging totaled 266,827 bibliographic records. The library serves as the secretariat for the international Program for Cooperative Cataloging. Together, the member institutions created 336,945 name and series authority records and 58,790 subject authorities. Of these, 103,525 name and series authority records and 54,860 subject authorities were created by the library.

Bibliographic Control and Standards

During the year the library continued to pursue several projects in response to the recommendations of its Working Group on the Future of Bibliographic Control in its report "On the Record." One project included expansion and enhanced automation of the Cataloging in Publication program. The program, which provides publishers with bibliographic data prior to publication, switched from a paper-based system to the Electronic Cataloging in Publication (ECIP) program in January 2007. Three new partners joined the program in 2010, bringing the total to 15. Along with the Library of Congress, these partner institutions collectively cataloged 55,976 titles. The library also piloted a method to generate MARC 21 records from publishers' ONIX data; this resulted in the production of 2,810 bibliographic records.

The library continued to serve as a member of the joint steering committee for development of a new descriptive cataloging standard, Resource Description and Access (RDA). The online RDA product was released in June by the American Library Association's ALA Publishing. The Library of Congress, the National Agricultural Library, and the National Library of Medicine designed a test of RDA in the United States and made preparations to begin testing. At year's end 26 institutions had signed on as RDA testers and testing was scheduled to begin in 2011. The findings of the test will inform the U.S. national libraries' joint decision on whether to implement the new code.

Reference Services

The Library of Congress provides reference services to the public in its reading rooms and through its Web site. During the year the library's staff handled more than 527,000 reference requests received in person, on the telephone, and through written and electronic correspondence. Its reference staff also responded to questions posed by patrons using the Ask a Librarian feature on the library's Web site. More than 1.1 million items were circulated for use within the library.

In its first full year of operation, a total of 44,321 new on-site patrons were registered in the Automated Reader Registration System, bringing the total to 70,918 since its inception in April 2009.

Demand for online reference services remained high. To better serve remote users, the library provided access to the Electronic Resources Management System (ERMS) online public access catalog, providing title-level access to electronic journals as well as holdings information for those titles.

Implemented in 2010, a completely redesigned search system at http://www.loc.gov/findingaids, offers 1,100 finding aids to more than 32 million archival items in the library's collections.

Online Resources

Through its National Digital Library program and digitization efforts by its various divisions, the library has been adding high-quality digital content to its award-winning Web site, http://www.loc.gov. Recognized as one of the top federal sites, it recorded more than 77 million visits and 581.1 million page views in 2010.

The Web site provides users with access to the institution's unparalleled resources, such as its online catalog, selected collections in various formats, copyright and legislative information, webcasts and podcasts of library events and exhibitions, and other resources. Special presentations are dedicated to the achievements of African Americans, Asians, Hispanics, Jews, women, and veterans.

As a portal to the library's 24.6 million online primary source files, the Wise Guide (http://www.loc.gov/wiseguide) continued to introduce new and returning users to the Web site. The site is updated monthly with a series of articles containing links to the library's online resources.

Also accessible on the Web site, the public legislative information system known as THOMAS (http://thomas.loc.gov) continued to track legislative issues. Now in its 15th year, the system was enhanced to include several new features. These include a top bills list, a tip of the week, connectivity to the Library of Congress Law Library through Web 2.0, and a state legislatures page with a map interface to highlight state-sponsored legislative information systems pages.

By subscribing to the library's RSS feeds and e-mail update service, users can stay informed about areas of the library's site that interest them. To sign up for either service, visit http:/www.loc.gov/rss.

The library continued to promote its activities by producing podcasts and making them accessible at http://www.loc.gov/podcasts. Webcasts of selected lectures, readings, conferences, and symposia held at the library were added to the Web site at http://www.loc.gov/webcasts, as were interviews with authors participating in the National Book Festival.

Web 2.0

To develop new communication channels and new relationships, to reach new audiences, and to experiment with and explore new technologies, the Library of Congress continued to participate in media-sharing and social networking sites including Twitter, YouTube, Facebook, iTunes U, and Flickr. The library continued to add content to these sites, such as a group of photographs of jazz figures taken by music columnist and photographer William P. Gottlieb from 1938 to 1948. The library's images are accessible at http://www.flickr.com/photos/library_of_congress.

Launched August 2, a new Library of Congress application for the iPhone and iPad allows users to take a virtual tour of the Thomas Jefferson Building. The free app is a useful accompaniment to an on-site tour or can accompany the online tour of the Library of Congress Experience at myLOC.gov.

The library's main blog at http://blogs.loc.gov—among the first federal blogs at the time of its launch on April 24, 2007—has since been joined by blogs generated by the library's Music Division, Science and Technology Division, and the Law Library. The blog site contains links to all Library Web 2.0 sites.

Global Access

The Library of Congress acquires and provides access to global resources through cooperative agreements and exchanges with other nations, its overseas offices, and the World Digital Library Web site.

Overseas Offices

The library's six overseas offices (in Rio de Janeiro, Cairo, New Delhi, Jakarta, Nairobi, and Islamabad) acquired, cataloged, and preserved materials from parts of the world where book and information industries are not well developed. In 2010 those offices brought in and distributed 293,402 items to the Library of Congress and, on a cost-recovery basis, provided 394,515 items to other U.S. libraries.

During the year the library awarded a contract to VTLS, Inc., for the development of a new system to manage its overseas operations. A contract was also awarded to the Council for American Overseas Research Centers (CAORC) to develop an acquisition model that would address the need to collect more aggressively in West Africa without incurring the significant costs associated with creating a new field office. The CAORC office, to be established in Dakar, Senegal, will serve as a cost-effective model for collecting that can be replicated elsewhere in the world.

World Digital Library

Launched in April 2009, the collaborative World Digital Library (WDL) Web site (http://www.wdl.org) makes significant primary materials in various formats from cultures around the world available on the Internet, free of charge, in the United Nations languages (Arabic, Chinese, English, French, Russian, and Spanish) plus Portuguese.

During 2010 work focused on recruiting new partners, establishing a project governance structure, and adding content. At year's end 101 partners from 63 countries were participating—nearly double the participation rate of the previous year.

In March 2010 the partners adopted a charter that designated the Library of Congress as the WDL Project Manager for the period 2010–2015. The charter also provides for an Executive Council elected by the partners, standing committees to advise on technical and content issues, and an annual partners meeting. The council was elected during the year and the first partners meeting took place in Washington in June 2010.

Noteworthy content added to the WDL site from partner institutions during the year included Mesoamerican codices from the 12th to the 16th centuries (National Institute of Anthropology and History, Mexico); manuscripts in Welsh and Cornish from the 13th, 14th, and early 16th centuries (National Library of Wales); rare manuscripts and prints relating to the history of medicine (Wellcome Library, London); manuscripts from the 12th through 14th centuries by the philosopher Moses Maimonides (National Library of Israel); and maps and manuscripts relating to the early history of Florida (State Library and Archives of Florida).

Preservation

Preserving its unparalleled collections—from cuneiform tablets to born-digital items—is one of the library's major activities. During the year, more than 9 million items from its collections were bound, repaired, mass-deacidified, and microfilmed or otherwise reformatted. The library's Preservation Directorate surveyed the preservation needs of nearly 490,000 items from the general and special collections, including books, photographs, maps, audiovisual materials, and other formats. Of these, nearly 360,000 items were housed in protective containers.

To meet the challenges of preserving traditional and new media, in 2010 the Preservation Directorate opened three new preservation science laboratories, the Center for the Library's Analytical Science Samples (CLASS), and a collections recovery room.

The optical properties laboratory contains a hyperspectral imaging system, an environmental scanning electron microscope and a Fourier Transform Infrared Spectroscopy system. Hyperspectral imaging, a noninvasive process of taking digital photos of an object using distinct portions of the light spectrum, can reveal what previously could not be seen by the human eye. For example, using this technology to examine Thomas Jefferson's rough draft of the Declaration of Independence, the library's scientists were able to confirm that Jefferson at first wrote "our fellow subjects" but replaced the word "subjects" with "citizens."

The renovated chemical and physical properties laboratories contain equipment that gives the library the ability to understand the chemical and physical changes that occur in materials to better preserve its collections for future generations.

The CLASS is a designated room to store scientific reference sample collections of fibers, test papers, and sample books for use by scientists and other scholars. The collections recovery room serves as an isolated space in which to stabilize and treat collection materials that have been affected by an emergency event (e.g., exposure to water, mold, or vermin) as well as to train staff to perform such preservation work.

Books

The library continued to fill modules 3 and 4 at its book-storage facility in Fort Meade, Maryland. During 2010 a total of 532,712 volumes were transferred to the facility, bringing the total to nearly 3.6 million. These modules also contain shelving designed to hold special-format materials (e.g., photographs, maps, microforms, globes, and manuscript boxes). During the year the library transferred to the facility more than 21,000 boxes of microfilm (containing 219,600 reels of microfilm masters), 600 containers of microfiche, 3,750 folders of maps, and 21,200 manuscript containers. The retrieval rate for material stored at Fort Meade—within 12 business hours or less—was 100 percent.

The Digitizing American Imprints project, which was funded by a grant of $2 million from the Alfred P. Sloan Foundation, was completed in December 2009. The focus of the project was at-risk "brittle books" from the library's general collections. All told, the library digitized more than 65,000 volumes comprising more than 12.5 million pages. The scanned materials are accessible on the Internet Archive's Web site (http://www.archive.org) with bibliographic links to the digitized books in the library's Integrated Library System. Under a set of agreements with Amazon.com, patrons can obtain copies of these public domain digital books through print-on-demand services or as Kindle e-books, both in the United States and in Europe.

In 2010 the library began serving as the sponsor for the book-digitization project, with scanning facilities shared with other federal libraries through a FEDLINK master contract. During the year 23,000 volumes from the library's public domain general collection were scanned, comprising 4.3 million pages.

Newspapers

In partnership with the National Endowment for the Humanities (NEH), the Library of Congress is participating in the National Digital Newspaper Program (NDNP), a collaborative initiative to digitize and provide free public access to historic American newspapers that are in the public domain. During 2010 the number of NDNP state projects contributing digitized content grew to 25, and 171 new newspaper titles were added to the project. Since March 2007 the library has been making this material accessible on the Chronicling America Web site (http://www.loc.gov/chroniclingamerica), a free, searchable database of American newspaper pages published between 1860 and 1922. At year's end the site contained 2.7 million newspaper pages.

Photographs

More than 1 million of the library's 12 million photographs are accessible via its Prints and Photographs Online Catalog at http://www.loc.gov/pictures. These include the photographs of Carol M. Highsmith, who began donating her images, copyright-free, to the library in 1992. In 2010 Highsmith embarked on a multi-year project to create a visual record of 21st century America, which will also be preserved in the library. The project is the first comprehensive photographic study of the entire nation since the historic Farm Security Administration work of Dorothea Lange, Walker Evans, and other photographers during the Depression and Dust-Bowl era—a collection that is also housed in the library and accessible on its Web site.

A collection of 700 rare Civil War photographs are also being preserved. A gift from the Liljenquist family, the photos will be on display at the library this year.

Maps

The library's Geography and Map Division, in collaboration with the Preservation Directorate, completed a seven-year project to rehouse, relabel, and conserve nearly 187,000 U.S. maps in the Titled Collection. The uncataloged, single-sheet maps rank among the division's most heavily used items.

Following a three-month display in the library's "Exploring the Early Americas" exhibition, the Matteo Ricci Map of the World (1602)—the first Chinese map to show the Americas—was digitally scanned by the division and is accessible on the library's American Memory Web site (http://memory.loc.gov).

Audiovisual Collections

Opened in July 2007, the library's Packard Campus for Audio Visual Conservation in Culpeper, Virginia, consolidated the library's sound, film, and video collections—the world's largest and most comprehensive—which were previously housed in library buildings in four states and the District of Columbia.

Philanthropist David Woodley Packard and the Packard Humanities Institute donated the state-of-the-art facility to the American people, making it the largest-ever private gift to the legislative branch of the U.S. government. The $155 million facility was financed jointly by the gift from Packard and appropriations from Congress totaling $82.1 million.

The library's Packard Campus consists of a collections building, where 5.7 million items (1.2 million moving images, nearly 3 million sound recordings, and 1.5 million related items such as manuscripts, posters, and screenplays) are housed under ideal conditions; a conservation building, where the collections are acquired, managed, and preserved; and a separate facility with 124 vaults where combustible nitrate films can be stored safely. Researchers in the library's related reading rooms on Capitol Hill will be able to access derivative copies of the digital files through high-speed fiber-optic connections from Culpeper.

In 2010 the Packard Campus Film Laboratory began processing operations with two of six processing machines. Nearly 600 reels of new safety preservation copies were developed on the new equipment. In addition, about the same number of reels of original nitrate film were prepared for preservation (inspected, cleaned, and hand-repaired) during the fiscal year. Of these, approximately 250 reels were transferred to new safety preservation copies.

The facility's 200-seat theater resumed its popular film screenings in 2010. The Art Deco-style theater is one of only five in the United States equipped to show original classic film prints on nitrate film stock as they would have been screened in theaters before 1950. The theater also features a custom-made organ that provides live music accompaniment for silent movies. During the year the theater offered public screenings of more than 200 titles held by the library. More than 17,000 people attended these screenings.

Films

It is estimated that half of the films produced before 1950 and 80 percent to 90 percent made before 1920 have disappeared forever. The Library of Congress is working with many organizations to prevent such losses and to preserve motion pictures through the National Film Registry.

Under the terms of the National Film Preservation Act of 1992, the Librarian of Congress—with advice from the National Film Preservation Board—began selecting 25 films a year to be preserved for all time. The films are chosen based on whether they are "culturally, historically, or aesthetically significant." The library works to ensure that registry films are preserved by its staff or through collaboration with other archives, motion picture studios, and independent filmmakers.

In December 2010 the librarian named the following 25 films to the registry, bringing the total to 550:

Airplane! (1980)
All the President's Men (1976)
The Bargain (1914)

Cry of Jazz (1959)
Electronic Labyrinth: THX 1138 4EB (1967)
The Empire Strikes Back (1980)
The Exorcist (1973)
The Front Page (1931)
Grey Gardens (1976)
I Am Joaquin (1969)
It's a Gift (1934)
Let There Be Light (1946)
Lonesome (1928)
Make Way for Tomorrow (1937)
Malcolm X (1992)
McCabe and Mrs. Miller (1971)
Newark Athlete (1891)
Our Lady of the Sphere (1969)
The Pink Panther (1964)
Preservation of the Sign Language (1913)
Saturday Night Fever (1977)
Study of a River (1996)
Tarantella (1940)
A Tree Grows in Brooklyn (1945)
A Trip Down Market Street (1906)

Sound Recordings

In September 2010 the Library of Congress National Recording Preservation Board released a study titled *The State of Recorded Sound Preservation in the United States: A National Legacy at Risk in the Digital Age.* Mandated by Congress under the National Recording Preservation Act of 2000 (P.L. 106-174), it is the first comprehensive U.S. study that examines the state of sound-recording preservation on a national level and outlines the issues that threaten the long-term survival of the nation's sound-recording history. It also identifies public and private policy issues that bear on whether culturally and historically important sound recordings will be preserved for future generations. The report is available for purchase and as a free download at http://www.clir.org/pubs/abstract/pub148abst.html.

The National Recording Preservation Act of 2000 also tasks the Librarian of Congress with annually choosing recordings that are "culturally, historically or aesthetically significant." In June 2010 the librarian announced the addition of 25 sound recordings to the National Recording Registry, bringing the total to 300:

"Fon der Choope" (From the Wedding), Abe Elenkrig's Yidishe Orchestra (1913)
"Canal Street Blues," King Oliver's Creole Jazz Band (1923)

"Tristan und Isolde," Metropolitan Opera, featuring Kirsten Flagstad and Lauritz Melchior, NBC Broadcast of March 9, 1935

"When You Wish Upon a Star," Cliff Edwards (recorded 1938, released 1940)

"America's Town Meeting of the Air: Should Our Ships Convoy Materials to England?" (May 8, 1941)

The Library of Congress Marine Corps Combat Field Recording Collection, Second Battle of Guam (July 20–August 11, 1944)

"Evangeline Special" and "Love Bridge Waltz," Iry LeJeune (1948)

"The Little Engine That Could," narrated by Paul Wing (1949)

Leon Metcalf Collection of recordings of the First People of Western Washington State (1950–1954)

"Tutti Frutti," Little Richard (1955)

"Smokestack Lightning," Howlin' Wolf (1956)

Gypsy, original cast recording (1959)

The Complete Village Vanguard Recordings, Bill Evans Trio (1961)

"Daisy Bell" ("Bicycle Built for Two"), Max Mathews (1961)

I Started Out As a Child, Bill Cosby (1964)

Azucar Pa Ti, Eddie Palmieri (1965)

"Today!" Mississippi John Hurt (1966)

"Silver Apples of the Moon," Morton Subotnick (1967)

Soul Folk in Action, The Staple Singers (1968)

The Band, The Band (1969)

"Coal Miner's Daughter," Loretta Lynn (1970)

Red Headed Stranger, Willie Nelson (1975)

"Horses," Patti Smith (1975)

"Radio Free Europe," R.E.M. (1981)

"Dear Mama," Tupac Shakur (1995)

Oral History

The American Folklife Center continued its mandate to "preserve and present American folklife" through a number of outreach and oral-history programs such as the Veterans History Project and StoryCorps.

Established by Congress in 2000, the Veterans History Project (VHP) is a major program of the folklife center. For the past decade, the program has preserved the memories of both those in the nation's armed services and those at home.

During 2010 the project collected more than 6,400 personal recollections, bringing the total to 73,700. More than 8,000 collections are accessible on the VHP Web site at http://www.loc.gov/vets. Special presentations added to the site during the year honored American Indians, Korean War veterans, and women pilots of World War II. In honor of its tenth anniversary, the project developed a Web presentation, "VHP: The First Ten Years," which highlights the stories of

20 veterans whose accounts represent a cross section of the more than 73,000 collections donated to the project during its first decade of existence.

StoryCorps, launched in 2003 by David Isay and his award-winning documentary company Sound Portraits Productions, was inspired by the Works Progress Administration's Federal Writers' Project of the Depression years, which recorded oral history interviews with everyday Americans across the country. In FY 2010 more than 8,800 audio files of interviews were added to the StoryCorps collection, bringing the total to more than 33,000 housed in the American Folklife Center. In addition to weekly broadcasts on National Public Radio's "Morning Edition," selected StoryCorps stories are available as downloadable podcasts. During 2010 StoryCorps launched its "Historias" mobile booth to gather contemporary personal narrative recordings of Latinos and Latinas in 20 cities in the United States and Puerto Rico. These will be the folklife center's first major collection of recorded oral narratives and life stories from Latino Americans.

The Civil Rights History Project Act of 2009 (P.L. 111-19) was signed into law on May 12, 2009. The law requires the Library of Congress and the Smithsonian Institution's National Museum of African American History and Culture to establish a joint five-year oral history project to collect and make publicly accessible documentation relevant to the personal histories of participants in the Civil Rights movement. A total of $500,000 was designated through the Library of Congress and Smithsonian Institution budgets to support the program in FY 2010. A cooperative agreement between the library and the Smithsonian specified that the library's American Folklife Center would take the lead in undertaking a survey of libraries, archives, museums, and other institutions to determine the extent of existing documentary recordings of the Civil Rights movement. The Smithsonian will take the lead in collecting future interviews.

Digital Preservation and Management

The library continues development of its National Digital Information Infrastructure and Preservation Program (NDIIPP), a unique strategic initiative mandated by Congress in 2000 to collect and preserve at-risk digital content of cultural and historical importance. Under the auspices of the library's Office of Strategic Initiatives, NDIIPP has grown to a decentralized network of 170 partners with expertise in handling digital content. These partners are seeking to preserve a wide range of born-digital records, including public and commercial content, and are working collaboratively to establish standards for digital preservation. The project also includes Web capture to address the problem of the limited lifespan of the average online site as well as plans to manage the influx of born-digital collections.

To formalize the partnerships that have been forged through NDIIPP, the National Digital Stewardship Alliance was launched at the partners meeting in July 2010. By October 1 a total of 53 organizations had joined the alliance. Alliance members will work together to build a national digital collection, develop and adopt digital preservation standards, share tools and services, support innovation of practice and research, and promote national outreach for digital preservation.

Work accomplished in 2010 includes the following:

State Records

Most states lack the resources to ensure the preservation of the information they produce in digital form only, such as legislative records, court case files, and executive agency records. As a result, much state government digital information, including content useful to policymakers, is at risk. In 2010 the four projects making up the NDIIPP Preserving State Government Information initiative worked with institutions in 35 states, adding valuable digital information to the network.

Commercial Partners

NDIIPP continued to support private sector partners engaged in preserving creative works in digital formats. These works include photographs, cartoons, motion pictures, sound recordings, and video games. In 2010 work focused on developing and improving standards and practices that will ultimately benefit public archives as well as commercial communities. Participating partners including the Society of American Archivists and the Stock Artists Alliance continued their mission to promote the use of standard metadata to support long-term archiving and content exchange.

Web Archiving

In FY 2010 the library's Web Archiving team provided project management and technical support for a growing number of library collections. The team managed 13 Web archive collections, which included almost 4,000 nominated Web sites. The team built and managed Web archives for the 2010 U.S. elections, the Brazilian presidential election, Sri Lankan presidential and general elections, the Burma/Myanmar general elections, and an Afghanistan Web archive. The team also continued to develop tools and strengthen the infrastructure at the library for the long-term storage and preservation of Web archive content.

Standards

The Federal Agency Digitization Guidelines Working Group under NDIIPP is a collaborative effort by 15 federal agencies to define common guidelines, methods, and practices to digitize historical content in a standard manner. Two working groups were formed to address two distinct formats: still images and audiovisual material. In 2010 the Still Image Working Group published a comprehensive guidelines document, *Technical Guidelines for Digitizing Cultural Heritage Materials*. The document includes a detailed treatment of objective, quantifiable measures for scanning performance. Several federal agencies are now using these guidelines. The Audiovisual Working Group began the process of drafting an application specification relating to the Material Exchange Format (MXF) standard, suitable for the creation and management of files for video and other moving-image content.

U.S. Copyright Office

The U.S. Copyright Office in the Library of Congress administers the U.S. copyright law, under which authors of creative works register claims to protect their intellectual property. Congress enacted the first copyright law in May 1790, and in 1870 it centralized the national copyright function in the Library of Congress. The library's collections have been created largely through the copyright deposit system.

During 2010 the Copyright Office registered 636,527 copyright claims. Significant progress was made in reducing a large backlog of claims. This was accomplished with assistance from 51 library staff members detailed to the Copyright Office and the successful implementation of a new version of the IT system for electronic copyright registration (eCO). The eCO system accommodates traditional formats as well as items that are born digital. As of October 1, 2010, electronic submissions accounted for more than 80 percent of all incoming claims.

Since 2006 the Copyright Royalty Judges have administered the provisions of Chapter 8 of Title 17 of the Copyright Act, which is related to setting royalty rates and terms as well as determining the distribution of royalties for certain copyright statutory licenses. In their fifth year of operation, the judges set rates and terms for various statutory licenses and distributed royalty fees collected by the Copyright Office. In 2010 the judges facilitated the collection of $274 million in royalties and directed distribution of nearly $249 million to copyright owners.

National Library Service for the Blind and Physically Handicapped

Established in 1931 when President Herbert Hoover signed the Pratt-Smoot Act into law, the National Library Service for the Blind and Physically Handicapped (NLS) currently circulates more than 25 million copies of braille and recorded books and magazines to some 800,000 readers through a network of 131 cooperating libraries. NLS also provides a free service known as the 102 Talking-Book Club to more than 3,700 patrons who are 100 years of age or older.

Since April 2009 the permanent version of the online Braille and Audio Reading Download (BARD) service has made audiobooks available as downloadable files over the Internet. In March 2010 the system reached its 1 millionth download. As of October, 25,000 patrons were registered to use BARD, which delivers an average of 100,000 copies of audiobooks and magazines over the Internet monthly.

In its first full year of operation, the new Digital Talking-Book Program produced and shipped approximately 20,000 digital players and more than 100,000 copies of digital talking books to its network of cooperating libraries. In compliance with Public Law 89-522, the network libraries reported that nearly all veterans registered to receive materials from NLS had received a player and their first digital talking books.

John W. Kluge Center

The John W. Kluge Center was established in 2000 with a gift of $60 million from John W. Kluge, founding chairman of the James Madison Council (the library's private sector advisory group). Kluge, who built a communications empire, Metromedia, died on September 7, 2010, at his home in Charlottesville, Virginia, at the age of 95.

Located within the library's Office of Scholarly Programs, the Kluge Center's goal is to bring the world's best thinkers to the Library of Congress, where they can use the institution's resources and can interact with policymakers in Washington.

During the year, the Kluge Center continued to attract outstanding senior scholars and postdoctoral fellows. Working with the American Folklife Center, the Kluge Center supported the first competition for a postdoctoral fellowship for advanced research based on the Alan Lomax Collection, beginning in 2012. Donated to the library in 2004, the Lomax Collection comprises the ethnographic documentation collected by the folklorist over a period of 60 years.

In conjunction with the donation to the library of the Jack Kemp papers, plans were made to establish the Jack Kemp Chair in Political Economy in the Kluge Center. For more information about the center, visit http://www.loc.gov/kluge.

Publications

Each year the library publishes books, calendars, and other printed products featuring its vast content, often in cooperation with trade publishers.

Among the titles published in 2010 were works featuring the library's photographic collections (*Framing the West: The Survey Photographs of Timothy H. O'Sullivan* and three new titles in the Fields of Vision series featuring photographs by Esther Bubley, Jack Delano, and John Vachon). Three new titles feature maps of California, Texas, and Virginia. In addition, the *Poets Laureate Anthology* features works by each of the 43 U.S. poets laureate. This work charts the course of American poetry over the past 75 years.

Exhibitions

From pre-Colombian artifacts to rare 15th-century Bibles, from the nation's founding documents to Thomas Jefferson's personal library, continuing exhibitions that compose the Library of Congress Experience offer something for everyone. In January 2010 the Matteo Ricci World Map (1602)—the first in Chinese to show the Americas—made its North American debut at the library and remained on view for three months.

The exhibition "Voices from Afghanistan" (February–May 2010) was made possible by a recent gift to the library from Radio Free Europe/Radio Liberty (RFE/RL) of a collection of 15,000 letters from listeners of Radio Azadi, RFE/RL's Afghan Service.

Nearly a century after its creation, *The Red Book* by Swiss psychiatrist Carl Jung (1875–1961) was the centerpiece of a library exhibition, "The Red Book of Carl G. Jung: Its Origins and Influence." This seminal work, along with items from the library's Sigmund Freud collection, was on display June 17–September 25, 2010.

The Bob Hope Gallery in the Thomas Jefferson Building reopened in June 2010 with the exhibition "Hope for America: Performers, Politics and Pop Culture." The new exhibition examines the interplay of politics and entertainment in

American public life, drawing from the Bob Hope Collection, which was donated to the library by the comedian's family starting in 1998.

In late September the library launched a new traveling exhibition, "Gateway to Knowledge." Mounted on a truck and accompanied by two docents, the exhibition will bring facsimiles of many of the library's top treasures to the public. More information about the touring exhibition can be found at http://www.loc.gov/gateway.

The library's exhibitions can be viewed online at http://www.loc.gov/exhibits/ and http://myLOC.gov.

Special Events

During the year the library presented hundreds of public events such as poetry and literary programs, concerts, lectures, and symposia, many of which were broadcast live or archived on the library's Web site at http://www.loc.gov/webcasts. For a list of upcoming events, visit http://www.loc.gov/loc/events.

Literary Events

Setting a new attendance record, the tenth annual National Book Festival drew an estimated 150,000 book-lovers to the National Mall on September 25. The 2010 festival marked "A Decade of Words and Wonder." In May David M. Rubenstein, cofounder and managing director of the Carlyle Group, announced his intention to donate $5 million over the next five years to support the annual event. The festival has drawn nearly 1 million people since its inception in 2001.

With President Barack Obama and First Lady Michelle Obama serving as the 2010 festival's honorary chairpersons, the event featured more than 70 authors, poets, and illustrators, among them former First Lady Laura Bush, Hunger Games trilogy author Suzanne Collins, best-selling author Ken Follett, National Book Award-winner Jonathan Franzen, and "Top Chef" contestant Spike Mendelssohn. Making her first appearance at the festival, Chilean American author Isabel Allende was presented the National Book Festival Creative Achievement Award.

During the year the library's Poetry and Literature Center sponsored a number of programs featuring new and renowned poets reading from their works. Kay Ryan served a second term as the library's Poet Laureate Consultant in Poetry for the 2009–2010 literary season. Ryan, who has spent most of her career teaching at the College of Marin in California, focused her second year as laureate on community college students. During the year she launched "Poetry for the Mind's Joy," which included a poetry-writing contest, a video conference with students at community colleges, and the designation of April 1 as Community College Poetry Day.

On October 6, Ryan was joined by six former U.S. Poets Laureate Consultants in Poetry for "A Celebration of American Poets Laureate." The event featured readings by Ryan, Billy Collins, Rita Dove, Daniel Hoffman, Maxine Kumin, Charles Simic, and Mark Strand. On October 25 W. S. Merwin began his tenure as the library's 17th Poet Laureate Consultant in Poetry for 2010–2011.

The library also sponsored numerous book talks during the year, many offered as part of the Center for the Book's Books and Beyond lecture series.

Concerts

Since 1925 the library's Coolidge Auditorium has been the venue for world-class performers and world premieres of commissioned works. Sponsored by the library's Music Division, the annual concert series reflects the diversity of American music and features many genres: classical, jazz, musical theater, dance, pop, and rock.

The art of the string quartet was the centerpiece of the library's 84th concert season (2009–2010), which offered 32 concerts, three film series, and 25 lectures by notable scholars, scientists, and other experts. On April 30 the Jack Quartet premiered a new work for strings by California composer Caleb Burhans, which was commissioned by the library with support from the Boris and Sonya Kroyt Fund. Two concerts capped the 16-event series marking the bicentennial of the birth of Felix Mendelssohn. Concerts also marked the bicentennials of the birth of Robert Schumann and the death of Joseph Haydn.

The noontime folklife concert series known as "Homegrown: The Music of America" features diverse musical traditions. Presented by the American Folklife Center and the Music Division in cooperation with the Kennedy Center Millennium Stage, the series featured traditional Passamaquoddy music from Maine, cowboy music from Montana, Texas rhythm and blues, and Norwegian American dance music from Virginia.

Symposia and Lectures

During the year various library divisions sponsored hundreds of programs and lectures on a wide range of topics. These programs provided an opportunity to share ideas, celebrate diversity, and showcase the library's collections.

The library celebrated diversity with public programs marking the contributions to the nation of women, African Americans, Asians, Hispanics, veterans, persons with disabilities, and members of the gay and lesbian community.

The library's Manuscript Division held a symposium, "The NAACP: Reflections on the First 100 Years," in February 2010 to mark the centennial of the organization, whose records are housed in the Library of Congress.

In April historian Jonathan D. Spence, a noted expert on modern China, delivered the fourth Jay I. Kislak lecture, "Mapping the Way: The Chinese Quests of Matteo Ricci." In conjunction with the display of the 1602 Ricci map, Spence discussed the place that Ricci, an Italian Jesuit, made for himself in China and how he encouraged the Chinese to think about knowledge.

The library's Japanese collections, comprising 1.17 million items, were the subject of a display and symposium in September. In December the American Folklife Center sponsored a two-day public symposium on the documentation of work, workers, and the culture of work in contemporary America.

Honors and Awards

Gershwin Prize for Popular Song

The library's Gershwin Prize for Popular Song, which President Obama presented to former Beatle Paul McCartney, who performed at a special concert in the East Room of the White House on June 2, commemorates composer and lyricist George and Ira Gershwin. The Gershwins' extensive manuscript collection resides in the library. The prize is awarded to musicians whose lifetime contributions in the field of popular song exemplify the standard of excellence associated with the Gershwins. The first Gershwin Prize was awarded in May 2007 to Paul Simon, and the second to Stevie Wonder in February 2009.

In conjunction with the award, the library hosted a press conference with McCartney on June 1. That evening in the library's Coolidge Auditorium, the Loma Mar Quartet performed a selection of McCartney's songs on stringed instruments from the library's Cremonese collection, and Chinese pianist Lang Lang performed on George Gershwin's piano. They were joined on stage by McCartney, who performed two of his works.

Living Legend Award

Baritone Thomas Hampson received the library's Living Legend medal during a concert on October 28 in the Coolidge Auditorium. Hampson, with pianist Wolfram Rieger, performed pieces to mark the birth anniversaries of composers Samuel Barber and Gustav Mahler, and also offered a selection of American favorites. The Living Legend award recognizes individuals who have made significant contributions to the nation's diverse cultural, scientific, and social heritage.

Additional Sources of Information

Library of Congress telephone numbers for public information:

Main switchboard (with menu)	202-707-5000
Reading room hours and locations	202-707-6400
General reference	202-707-3399
	TTY 202-707-4210
Visitor information	202-707-8000
	TTY 202-707-6200
Exhibition hours	202-707-4604
Reference assistance	202-707-6500
Copyright information	202-707-3000
Copyright hotline (to order forms)	202-707-9100
Sales shop (credit card orders)	888-682-3557

Center for the Book

Library of Congress, Washington, DC 20540
World Wide Web http://www.loc.gov/cfbook

John Y. Cole
Director

Congress established the Center for the Book in the Library of Congress by statute (Public Law 95-129) in 1977. The center's purpose is to use the resources and prestige of the Library of Congress to stimulate public interest in books and reading. Through the years, the center's mission has expanded to include literacy and library promotion and encouragement of the historical study of books, reading, libraries, and the printed word.

The center's audience, which is international as well as national, has always included readers and potential readers of all ages. The Center for the Book is a successful public-private partnership, relying on outside funding for all of its activities; the Library of Congress supports its five staff positions.

Highlights of 2010

During 2010 the Center for the Book

- Completed its first full year of administering the new Young Readers Center in the library's Jefferson Building, the first space in the library's history devoted to the reading interests of people under the age of 16
- Hosted "Reading in the White House," a symposium celebrating the publication of *The First White House Library: A History and Annotated Catalogue* by Pennsylvania State University Press (cosponsors were the Bibliographical Society of America and the National First Ladies' Library)
- Played a major role in the organization and administration of the National Book Festival, which attracted approximately 150,000 people to the National Mall on September 25
- Became a sponsor of the annual awards ceremony for the National Collegiate Book Collecting Contest and hosted the ceremony at the Library of Congress on October 15 (cosponsors were the Antiquarian Booksellers Association of America and the Fellowship of American Bibliographic Societies)
- Coordinated more than 30 public events at the library, many of them booktalks and signings in the center's Books & Beyond series, which features new books based on the library's collections

Young Readers Center

Opened in October 2009, the Young Readers Center is a showcase for Center for the Book and Library of Congress projects that encourage reading and literacy among young people. Young readers of all ages are welcome to browse and use its collection of award-winning books and classics; they need only to be accompanied by an adult.

The Young Readers Center's immediate focus is on providing personal and family "read-aloud" experiences, which can be supplemented by demonstrations of the library's online educational projects and films of author presentations aimed at younger audiences at previous National Book Festivals. In 2010 the Young Readers Center averaged more than 1,000 visitors a month. It inaugurated scheduled story hours and a series of public events featuring writers and guest speakers from other parts of the library, including the Rare Book and Special Collections Division, the Preservation Office, and the Educational Outreach Office. In October and November 2010, in cooperation with the Spanish Embassy and the Kids Euro Festival, it hosted five public programs highlighting toy theaters from Spain.

National Ambassador

Award-winning children's author Katherine Paterson completed her first year as National Ambassador for Young People's Literature, a program developed with the Children's Book Council to promote the importance of young people's literature nationwide. Like her predecessor, Jon Scieszka, she was a featured author at the National Book Festival, appearing in three different sessions including the "Exquisite Corpse Adventure" session (see below) in the Children's pavilion. A few days prior to the festival, she spoke to a crowd of more than 200 young people at the center's inaugural Jonah S. Eskin Memorial Lecture.

Letters About Literature

The six national winners of the 2009–2010 Letters About Literature reading and writing contest were announced in April 2010. To enter, a young reader (grades 4 through 12) writes a personal letter to an author, living or dead, from any genre—fiction or nonfiction, contemporary or classic—explaining how that author's work changed the student's way of thinking about the world or himself or herself. A record of more than 70,000 letters were submitted. The contest is jointly sponsored by the Center for the Book, its state centers, and the Target store chain, which donates $10,000 to a library designated by each of the six national winners and $1,000 to a library designated by each of the 12 honorable mention winners.

The Center for the Book organized a special Letters About Literature program in the Teens and Children pavilion at the National Book Festival in which two participating authors, Katherine Paterson and Michael Buckley, talked with students who had written prize-winning letters to them.

River of Words

The center has cosponsored the River of Words, an annual environmental poetry and art competition for students ages 5–19, for the past 15 years. On June 30, 2010, an awards and recognition ceremony was held in the Jefferson Building.

The master of ceremonies was River of Words cofounder Robert Hass, who was U.S. poet laureate from 1995 to 1997. Young people and their families traveled to the event from across the country.

Online Resources

A new multimedia Web site overseen by the Center for the Book, http://www.read.gov, was launched in September 2009. The center's Web site, http://www.loc.gov/cfbooks, is part of it. Read.gov comprises four sub-sites tailored to children, teens, adults, and educators and parents. A National Ambassador for Young People's Literature sub-site was added in 2010 to focus on the new ambassador, Katherine Paterson. Read.gov is one of the few places on the Library of Congress Web site that focuses on current events and literature. All of the center's Books & Beyond author programs are filmed for webcasting, which increases their reach, and an accompanying Books & Beyond on Facebook encourages further discussion of these authors' current works.

An exclusive highlight of Read.gov is the original sequential story "The Exquisite Corpse Adventure," whose first episode debuted and was read by its author, Jon Scieszka, during the opening session in the Children's pavilion at the 2009 National Book Festival. Twenty-seven episodes later, it concluded when ambassador Katherine Paterson read the final episode, which she wrote, at the opening session in the same pavilion at the 2010 National Book Festival. Several of the more than 20 writers and illustrators who contributed biweekly episodes and art to this unpredictable story joined Paterson in "acting out" the episode. They included M. T. Anderson, Timothy Basil Ering, Linda Sue Park, and James Ransome.

The Exquisite Corpse Adventure was a project of the Center for the Book and one of its reading promotion partners, the National Children's Book and Literacy Alliance. Another partner, PBS's Reading Rockets, ran two very successful contests in association with Exquisite Corpse to encourage young people to write their own stories or create their own videos.

The Center for the Book Web site includes links to organizations including national reading promotion partners and affiliated state centers that share the center's interest in promoting books and reading and in encouraging the study of books, libraries, and print culture.

National Book Festival

For the tenth year, the Center for the Book took the lead in organizing the program for the National Book Festival. Held September 25 and covering more than four blocks on the National Mall, the 2010 festival featured 71 nationally known and award-winning authors, illustrators, and poets. Approximately 150,000 members of the public attended—a new record. President Barack Obama and First Lady Michelle Obama were honorary chairpersons.

In addition to the writers and illustrators of books for young people mentioned above, the festival highlighted outstanding writers and notable personalities including two Nobel Prize winners (Orhan Pamuk and Harold Varmus), Isabel Allende (who received the Library of Congress National Book Festival Creative Achievement Award), 2010 Newbery Medal winner Rebecca Stead, 2009 National Book Award winner Phillip Hoose, 2010 Pulitzer Prize-winning poet Rae Armantrout, 1993 Pulitzer Prize-winning historian Gordon S. Wood, international best-selling authors Ken Follett and Mem Fox, popular favorite Diana Gabaldon, legal thriller best-selling writer Scott Turow, *New Yorker* editor David Remnick, and literary sensations Jonathan Franzen, Jane Smiley, and Gail Godwin.

The Center for the Book also organized the Pavilion of the States for festival-goers to learn about the center and its reading and literacy programs and about the literary traditions of the 50 states, the District of Columbia, and the U.S. territories. Representatives of state centers for the book provided information and answered questions about their states' writers, libraries, book festivals, book awards, and reading promotion activities. In addition, several festival authors and illustrators made scheduled visits to their state's table to greet fans and sign autographs.

An especially popular Pavilion of the States feature among young readers and their families was "Discover Great Places Through Reading," a free map of the United States that visitors could present at each table for an appropriate state sticker or stamp. The map included "52 Great Reads About Great Places," a reading list of books for young people compiled through recommendations of books from each state.

Reading Promotion Networks

The center's partnership program, which includes more than 80 national nonprofit and governmental organizations, strengthens and supports its reading and literacy projects nationwide. The annual partners' idea exchange meeting was held at the Library of Congress in March 2010.

The Center for the Book has 52 official affiliates that renew their partnerships with the national center every three years: the 50 states, the District of Columbia, and the Virgin Islands. The purpose of the network is to link reading promotion resources and ideas from the Library of Congress with related projects and interests at the local level. The annual idea exchange meeting is an opportunity for representatives from the state centers to come together to learn how their peers around the country promote reading, literacy, and libraries.

At the 2010 state center idea exchange, coordinators from 40 state affiliates discussed current and potential projects as well as topics such as fund raising and board development. Brief presentations were made by two new reading promotion partners who described their organizations and organizational goals: Charles Trueheart, director of the American Library in Paris, and Malcolm O'Hagan, president of the American Writers Museum Foundation.

The national center cohosted poetry readings with the California and Massachusetts state centers during 2010, both featuring readings by young home-state poets to whom Poet Laureate Kay Ryan had awarded Library of Congress Witter Bynner Fellowships. On May 11, Atsuro Riley gave a reading at the Stanford

Humanities Center; Jill McDonough's program was on November 9 at the Boston Athenaeum.

Publications

In late 2009, in cooperation with Oak Knoll Press, the Center for the Book published an important two-volume work by collector Carol Fitzgerald: *Series Americana: Post Depression Era Regional Literature, 1938–1980, A Descriptive Bibliography.* This collection of 163 titles, issued as part of 13 series including American Folkways, Regions of America, and the American Lakes Series, was featured in Fitzgerald's October 15, 2010 presentation at the awards ceremony for the National Collegiate Book Collecting Contest. Her presentation and the awards ceremony itself were filmed by C-SPAN. In November she and her husband presented the Series Americana books and archive as a gift to the Rare Book and Special Collections Division of the Library of Congress.

"The Library of Congress and the Center for the Book: Essays in Honor of John Y. Cole" was published as the first 2010 issue of the University of Texas Press quarterly *Libraries and the Cultural Record: Exploring the History of Collections of Recorded Knowledge.* This festschrift will be published in an expanded and illustrated clothbound edition in 2011.

National Agricultural Library

U.S. Department of Agriculture, Abraham Lincoln Bldg.,
10301 Baltimore Ave., Beltsville, MD 20705-2351
E-mail agref@nal.usda.gov
World Wide Web http://www.nal.usda.gov

Mary Ann Leonard
Special Assistant to the Director

The U.S. Department of Agriculture's National Agricultural Library (NAL) is one of the world's largest and most accessible agricultural research libraries, offering service directly to the public and via its Web site, http://www.nal.usda.gov. The library was instituted in 1862 at the same time as the U.S. Department of Agriculture (USDA). It became a national library in 1962 when Congress established it as the primary agricultural information resource of the United States (7 USCS § 3125a).

Congress assigned to the library the responsibilities to:

- Acquire, preserve, and manage information resources relating to agriculture and allied sciences
- Organize agricultural information products and services and provide them within the United States and internationally
- Plan, coordinate, and evaluate information and library needs relating to agricultural research and education
- Cooperate with and coordinate efforts toward development of a comprehensive agricultural library and information network
- Coordinate the development of specialized subject information services among the agricultural and library information communities

NAL is the only library in the United States with the mandate to carry out these national and international responsibilities for the agricultural community. With that mandate in mind, the library has established its vision as "advancing access to global information for agriculture."

NAL is located in Beltsville, Maryland, near Washington, D.C., on the grounds of USDA's Henry A. Wallace Beltsville Agricultural Research Center. Its 15-story Abraham Lincoln Building is named in honor of the president who created the Department of Agriculture and signed several of the major U.S. laws affecting agriculture.

The library employs about 155 librarians, information specialists, computer specialists, administrators, and clerical personnel, supplemented by about 55 volunteers, contract staff, and cooperators from NAL partnering organizations.

NAL's reputation as one of the world's foremost agricultural libraries is supported and burnished by its expert staff, ongoing leadership in delivering information services, expanding collaborations with other U.S. and international agricultural research and information organizations, and its extensive collection of agricultural information, searchable through the renowned AGRICOLA (AGRICultural On-Line Access) bibliographic database.

The Collection

The NAL collection dates to the congressionally approved 1839 purchase of books for the Agricultural Division of the Patent Office, predating the 1862 establishment of USDA itself. Today NAL provides access to billions of pages of agricultural information—an immense collection of scientific books, journals, audiovisuals, reports, theses, artifacts, and images—and to a widening array of digital media, as well as databases and other information resources germane to the broad reach of agriculture-related sciences.

The library's collection contains nearly 3.6 million items, dating from the 16th century to the present, including the most complete repository of USDA publications and the world's most extensive set of materials on the history of U.S. agriculture. The collection covers all aspects of agriculture and related sciences and is a comprehensive resource for agricultural scientists, policymakers, regulators, and scholars.

Networks of Cooperation

The NAL collection and information resources are supplemented by networks of cooperation with other institutions, including arrangements with agricultural libraries at U.S. land-grant universities, other U.S. national libraries, agricultural libraries in other countries, and libraries of the United Nations and other international organizations.

AgNIC

The library serves as secretariat for the Agriculture Network Information Center (AgNIC) Alliance (http://www.agnic.org), a voluntary, collaborative partnership that hosts a distributed network of discipline-specific agricultural information Web sites. AgNIC provides access to high-quality agricultural information selected by its partner members. These 62 partners include land-grant universities, NAL, and other institutions globally. Together they offer 68 subject-specific sites and reference services. Additional sites and resources are being developed.

During 2010 AgNIC partners continued to build full-text content through a variety of projects. One such project, metadata harvesting, uses the Open Archives Initiative (OAI) protocols to harvest metadata for full-text resources from targeted institutional repositories and collections. Once the metadata is harvested, AgNIC delivers it through a single point of access. AgNIC then links the bibliographic citations to another service so that users can find items in nearby libraries. Over the past year, AgNIC expanded the content available by harvesting the NAL AGRICOLA database and the National Library of Medicine's (NLM's) PubMed database. The AgNIC system now links to more than 5 million full-text and bibliographic items.

AgNIC has also extended its reach through the launch of an Animal Health Portal. Developed in conjunction with veterinary librarians at Oklahoma State and Washington State universities, the portal contains more than 2 million full-text and bibliographic citations drawn from the AGRICOLA database and the NLM's PubMed database. The Animal Health Portal also includes topical pages, news, and events relating to animal health. AgNIC also has added social networking capabilities to its services.

AGLINET

Through the Agricultural Libraries Network (AGLINET), NAL serves as the U.S. node of an international agricultural information system that brings together agricultural libraries with strong regional or country coverage and other specialized collections. NAL functions as a gateway to U.S. agricultural libraries and resources, fulfilling requests for information via reciprocal agreements with several other libraries, information centers, and consortia. As an AGLINET member, NAL agrees to provide low-cost interlibrary loan and photocopy service to other AGLINET libraries. Most materials requested through AGLINET are delivered digitally, although reproductions via fiche or photocopy are used when appropriate. AGLINET is administered by the Food and Agriculture Organization of the United Nations.

Animal Science Image Gallery

NAL and the American Society of Animal Science are collaborators on the Animal Science Image Gallery, a Web site of animal science images at http://anscigallery.nal.usda.gov. The images, animations, and videos, which also have accompanying text, are intended for classroom and educational outreach. The gallery was originally funded through a USDA Higher Education Challenge Grant; NAL now hosts it in perpetuity. Gallery editors, reviewers, and submitters come from the membership of the American Society of Animal Science, the American Dairy Science Association, the Poultry Science Association, the Equine Science Society, the American Society for Nutrition, the Society for the Study of Reproduction, and the American College of Theriogenologists.

Building the NAL Collection

NAL annually acquires approximately 16,700 serial titles, including nearly 9,000 digital journals. More than 3,000 of those digital journals in agriculture and related sciences are purchased with permanent data storage rights. NAL has primary responsibility for collecting and retaining publications of USDA and its agencies, and is the only U.S. national library with a legislated mandate to collect in the following disciplines: plant and animal health, welfare, and production; agricultural economics, products, and education; aquaculture; forestry; rural sociology and rural life; family and consumer science; and food science, safety, and nutrition. In addition to collecting as comprehensively as possible in these core subject areas, NAL collects extensively in many related subject areas, such as biology, bioinformatics, biochemistry, chemistry, entomology, environmental science, genetics, invasive species, meteorology, natural resources, physics, soil science, sustainability, water quality, and zoology.

Since the mid-1800s NAL has carried out a strong global program to acquire international publications. In the past, direct purchasing was paired with the exchange of USDA publications with foreign partners. Over the past decade the changes in publishing practice from paper to digital have essentially eliminated the opportunities for exchange.

In general, NAL's acquisition program and collection development policy are based upon its responsibility to provide service to the staff of the Department of Agriculture, U.S. land-grant universities, and the general public in all subjects pertaining to agriculture. The NAL Collection Development Policy (http://www.nal.usda.gov/about/policy/coll_dev_toc.shtml) outlines the scope of subjects collected and the degree of coverage for each subject. This policy is regularly revised to include emerging subject areas and to incorporate guidelines for collecting new formats, especially digital formats. NAL collection policies reflect and differentiate the collecting responsibilities of National Library of Medicine and the Library of Congress. These three national libraries have developed cooperative collection development policy statements for the following subject areas: biotechnology, human nutrition and food, and veterinary sciences.

Rare and Special Collections

The NAL special collections program emphasizes access to and preservation of rare and unique materials documenting the history of agriculture and related sciences. Items in the library's special collections include rare books, manuscripts, nursery and seed trade catalogs, posters, objects, photographs, and other rare materials documenting agricultural subjects. Materials date from the 1500s to the late 1900s and include many international sources. Detailed information about NAL special collections is available on the NAL Web site at http://www.nal.usda.gov/speccoll.

NAL special collections of note include the following:

- The U.S. Department of Agriculture History Collection (http://www.nal.usda.gov/speccoll/collect/history.html), assembled over 80 years by USDA historians, includes letters, memoranda, reports, and papers of USDA officials, as well as photographs, oral histories, and clippings covering the activities of the department from its founding through the early 1990s. A guide to this collection is viewable via the NAL Web site.
- The U.S. Department of Agriculture Pomological Watercolor Collection (http://www.nal.usda.gov/speccoll/collectionsguide/mssindex/pomology) includes more than 7,000 detailed, botanically accurate watercolor illustrations of fruits and nuts representing newly introduced varieties, healthy and diseased fruits, and depictions of various stages of development. Created between 1880 and the 1940s, the watercolor illustrations served as official documentation of the work of the Office of the Pomologist and were used for creation of chromolithographs in publications distributed widely by the department. Although created for scientific accuracy, the works in this collection are artistic treasures in their own right. The library received a grant to preserve and digitize the entire collection and put it on the Web. This project will be completed in 2011.
- The Henry G. Gilbert Nursery and Seed Trade Catalog Collection (http://www.nal.usda.gov/speccoll/collectionsguide/nurserycatalogs.shtml) is a

rich collection of historic catalogs of the nursery and seed trade. Started in 1904 by USDA economic botanist Percy L. Ricker, the collection is used by researchers to document the introduction of plants to the United States, study economic trends, and illustrate early developments in American landscape design. The earliest catalogs document the trade beginning in the mid-1700s. NAL continues to collect nursery and seed catalogs.

- The Rare Book Collection (http://www.nal.usda.gov/speccoll/collectionsguide/rarebooks.shtml) highlights agriculture's printed historical record and covers a wide variety of subjects. International in scope, the collection documents early agricultural practices in Britain and Europe as well as the Americas. In 2010 records of 480 items in the NAL Rare Book and Manuscript collections were added to AGRICOLA. NAL holdings of Carl Linnaeus, the "father of taxonomy," include more than 300 books by or about Linnaeus, among them a rare first edition of his 1735 work *Systema Naturae*.
- NAL offers access to more than 400 manuscript collections documenting the story of American agriculture and its influence on the world; see http://www.nal.usda.gov/speccoll/collectionsguide/mssindex1.shtml.

In recent years, special collections staff have enhanced access to the program's unique materials by putting digitized images on its Web site. NAL provides in-house research and reference services for its special collections and offers fee-based duplication services. Detailed indexes to the content of many manuscript collections are available in print as well as on the Web. AGRICOLA—NAL's catalog and index to its collections—includes bibliographic entries for special collection items, manuscripts, and rare books.

Preservation

NAL is committed to the preservation of its print and non-print collections. It continues to monitor and improve the environmental quality of its stacks to extend the longevity of all materials in the collection. The library has instituted a long-term strategy to ensure the growing body of agricultural information is systematically identified, preserved, and archived.

NAL's digital conversion program has resulted in a growing digital collection of USDA publications, including *Agriculture Handbook; Agriculture Information Bulletin; Agricultural Economic Report; Century of Service: The First 100 Years of the United States Department of Agriculture; Home and Garden Bulletin; Journal of Agricultural Research; Report of the Commissioner of Agriculture (1862 to 1888),* continued by the *Report of the Secretary of Agriculture (1889 to 1893); Yearbook of the United States Department of Agriculture;* the Plant Inventory series and its complement, the Plant Immigrants series; and several series of Fruit and Vegetable Market News Reports of the Agricultural Marketing Service.

The library provides online access to these and other full-text publications, including many non-USDA historical materials not restricted by copyright, via the NAL digital repository.

Digital Collections

The library has undertaken several projects to digitize, store, and provide online access to nearly 1 million pages of historic print documents, primarily from USDA. These various projects within NAL are at different stages of development and implementation, but work is under way to unify them. The library is developing procedures and policies to collect, store, and make publicly available federally funded research outcomes published by USDA scientists and researchers. Long-range plans include collecting, maintaining, and providing access to a broad range of agricultural information in a wide variety of digital formats. The end result will be a perpetual, reliable, publicly accessible collection of digital documents, datasets, images, and other items relating to agriculture.

AGRICOLA

AGRICOLA catalogs and indexes NAL collections and delivers worldwide access to agricultural information through its searchable Web interface (http://agricola.nal.usda.gov). Alternatively, users can access AGRICOLA on a fee basis through several commercial vendors, or they can subscribe to the complete AGRICOLA file, also on a fee basis, from the National Technical Information Service within the U.S. Department of Commerce.

The AGRICOLA database covers materials in all formats, including printed works from the 16th century onward. The records describe publications and resources encompassing all aspects of agriculture and allied disciplines. Tens of thousands of AGRICOLA records contain links to networked Web resources. The AGRICOLA database is updated with records for newly cataloged and indexed materials that are searchable separately or together via the following two components:

- NAL Public Access Catalog, containing more than 1 million citations to books, audiovisual materials, serial titles, and other materials in the NAL collection (the catalog also contains some bibliographic records for items cataloged by other libraries but not held in the NAL collection)
- NAL Article Citation Database, consisting of 3.8 million citations to serial articles, book chapters, reports, and reprints

Information Management and Information Technology

Over the past quarter century, NAL has applied increasingly sophisticated information technology to support the ever more complex and demanding information needs of researchers, practitioners, policymakers, and the general public. Technological developments spearheaded by the library date back to the 1940s and 1950s, when NAL Director Ralph Shaw invented "electronic machines" such as the photo charger, rapid selector, and photo clerk. Over the years NAL has made numerous technological improvements, from automating collections information to delivering full-text and image collections digitally on the Internet.

NAL has fully implemented the Voyager integrated library management system from Ex Libris, Ltd. The system supports ordering, receiving, and invoice processing for purchases; creating and maintaining indexing and cataloging records for AGRICOLA; circulating print holdings; and providing a Web-based online catalog for public searching and browsing of the collection. In addition, the system is fully integrated with an automated interlibrary loan and document delivery system by Relais International that streamlines services and provides desktop delivery of needed materials.

English-Spanish Agricultural Thesaurus and Glossary

NAL is known for its expertise in developing and using a thesaurus, or controlled vocabulary, a critical component of effective digital information systems. The NAL Agricultural Thesaurus (NALT) (http://agclass.nal.usda.gov/agt.shtml) is a hierarchical vocabulary of agricultural and biological terms. Updated annually, NALT broadly defines the subject scope of agriculture, organized according to 17 subject categories and with 2,970 definitions. The thesaurus comprises primarily biological nomenclature, although it also includes terminology supporting the physical and social sciences.

Originally prepared to meet the needs of Agricultural Research Service scientists, NALT is now extensively used to aid retrieval in agricultural information systems within USDA and elsewhere. For example, NALT is the indexing vocabulary for NAL's Article Citation Database in AGRICOLA.

In January 2011 NAL released the tenth edition of NALT, which has grown to approximately 82,000 terms. This edition now includes terminology associated with nanotechnology, life cycle assessment, and sustainable agriculture. In addition, collaboration with the Joint Institute for Food Safety and Applied Nutrition at the University of Maryland resulted in the significant addition of food safety risk assessment terminology. Important Latin American plant species also were added to this edition and verified in the Germplasm Resource Information Network.

The associated NAL Glossary provides definitions of agricultural terms. The 2010 edition contains 2,970 definitions ranging across agriculture and its many ancillary subjects, an increase of 321 new definitions (in both Spanish and English) over last year. Most definitions are composed by NALT staff. Suggestions for new terms or definitions can be sent by e-mail to NAL.thesaurus@ars.usda.gov.

NAL publishes Spanish-language versions of NALT and the glossary, which carry the names *Tesauro Agrícola* and *Glosario*, respectively. The Spanish-language versions of NALT and the glossary support increased Spanish-language access to agricultural information.

During 2010 the Inter-American Institute for Cooperation on Agriculture (IICA) (http://www.iica.int) and NAL expanded their collaboration to include the involvement of other Latin American experts, including the Mexican Network of Agricultural Libraries (REMBA). With the aid of Latin American experts, IICA and NAL cooperatively develop and maintain these terminology tools to support the advancement of agricultural information in the Americas.

The Spanish-language version of NALT is updated concurrently with the annual release of the English-language version of NALT. The 2011 edition contains more than 77,000 terms. The thesaurus Web site is available in both English and Spanish.

Although these compilations are primarily intended for indexers, computer programmers working with Web search engines, and others who gather and organize information, the glossary and thesaurus are also suitable for students from fifth grade up as well as for teachers, writers, translators, and people who work in agriculture. Users can download all four publications in a variety of formats (pdf, XML, Word, MARC 21, and RDF-SKOS) at http://agclass.nal.usda.gov/download.shtml.

Library Services

NAL serves the agricultural information needs of customers through a combination of Web-based and traditional library services, including reference, document delivery, and information center services. The NAL Web site offers access to a wide variety of full-text resources as well as online access to reference and document delivery services. In 2010 the library delivered more than 90 million direct customer service transactions throughout the world via its Web site and other Internet-based services.

The main reading room in the library's Beltsville facility features a walk-up service desk, access to an array of digital information resources (including full-text scientific journals), a current periodicals collection, and an on-site request service for materials from NAL's print collection. NAL also operates a walk-in reference and digital services center at USDA headquarters in downtown Washington, D.C. Services at both facilities are available 8:30 to 4:30 Monday through Friday, except federal holidays. NAL's reference services are accessible online using "contact us" links on the NAL Web pages; by use of e-mail addressed to agref@ars.usda.gov; by telephone at 301-504-5755; or by mail to Reference Research Services, National Agricultural Library ARS/USDA, 10301 Baltimore Avenue, Beltsville, MD 20705. The Reference Research Services staff cover all areas and aspects of agriculture, but particularly answer questions and provide research guidance for subjects and topic areas not addressed by the various subject-focused information centers of the library.

NAL's information centers are reliable sources of comprehensive, science-based information on key aspects of U.S. agriculture, providing timely, accurate, and in-depth coverage of their specialized subject areas. Their expert staff offer extensive Web-based information resources and advanced reference services. Each NAL information center has its own Web site and is a partner in AgNIC.

Presently, NAL has seven information centers:

- The Alternative Farming Systems Information Center (AFSIC) (http://afsic.nal.usda.gov) specializes in identifying and accessing information relating to farming methods that maintain the health and productivity of the entire farming enterprise, including the world's natural resources. This focus includes sustainable and alternative agricultural systems, crops, and livestock.

- The Animal Welfare Information Center (AWIC) (http://awic.nal.usda.gov) provides scientific information and referrals to help ensure the proper care and treatment of animals used in biomedical research, testing, teaching, and exhibitions, and by animal dealers. Among its varied outreach activities, the center conducts workshops for researchers on meeting the information requirements of the Animal Welfare Act.
- The Food and Nutrition Information Center (FNIC) (http://fnic.nal.usda.gov), a leader in food and human nutrition information dissemination since 1973, provides credible, accurate, and practical resources for nutrition and health professionals, educators, government personnel, and consumers. FNIC maintains a staff of registered dietitians, specialists with training in food science and human nutrition, who can answer questions on food and human nutrition.
- The Food Safety Information Center (FSIC) (http://fsrio.nal.usda.gov) collects, organizes, and disseminates reliable and timely food safety resources for researchers, educators, and consumers. The center's main focus is the Food Safety Research Information Office (FSRIO), which was mandated by Congress to provide to the research community and the general public information on publicly funded—and, to the extent possible, privately funded—food safety research initiatives. FSRIO fulfills this mandate through its Web site, which provides a gateway to food safety research information, and through its Research Projects Database. With more than 5,400 projects cited, the database provides ready access to the largest searchable collection of food safety research being conducted within U.S. and international governmental agencies.
- The National Invasive Species Information Center (NISIC) (http://www.invasivespeciesinfo.gov) is a gateway to invasive species information, covering federal, state, local, and international sources. The Web site provides accessible, accurate, referenced, up-to-date, and comprehensive information on invasive species.
- The Rural Information Center (http://ric.nal.usda.gov) provides services for local officials, organizations, businesses, and rural residents working to maintain the vitality of rural areas. It collects and disseminates information on such diverse topics as community economic development, small business development, health care, finance, housing, environment, quality of life, community leadership, and education.
- The Water Quality Information Center (WQIC) (http://wqic.nal.usda.gov) collects, organizes, and communicates scientific findings, educational methodologies, and public policy issues relating to water resources and agriculture. The center provides access to numerous bibliographies and a database of online documents relating to water and agriculture.

In addition to these information centers, NAL manages the popular Nutrition.gov Web site (http://www.nutrition.gov) in collaboration with other USDA agencies and the Department of Health and Human Services. This site provides vetted, science-based nutrition information for the general consumer and highlights the latest in nutrition news and tools from across federal government agencies. A team of registered dietitians at NAL's Food and Nutrition Information Center maintains Nutrition.gov and answers questions on food and nutrition issues.

The site is an important tool for developing food- and exercise-based strategies for weight management and for disseminating the work of multiple federal agencies in a national obesity prevention effort. Nutrition.gov includes databases, recipes, interactive tools, and specialized information for infants and children, adult men and women, and seniors. It provides a comprehensive source of information on nutrition and dietary guidance from multiple federal agencies.

Web-Based Products and Services

In 2010 the NAL Web sites collectively received an average of 8 million hits a month from people seeking agricultural information. As NAL continues to improve its Web site functionality, search capability, and content, it anticipates that usage will continue to increase.

NAL was an early adopter of social media/Web 2.0 technologies and has a strong and growing presence on Twitter.

DigiTop

DigiTop, USDA's Digital Desktop Library, delivers the full text of thousands of journals and hundreds of newspapers worldwide, provides 18 agriculturally significant citation databases, supplies a range of digital reference resources, and offers focused, personalized services. DigiTop is available to the entire USDA work force worldwide—more than 100,000 people—around the clock. NAL staff provides help desk and reference services, continuous user education, and training for DigiTop users. During fiscal year 2010 more than 1,350,000 articles were downloaded from DigiTop.

Document Delivery Services

NAL's document delivery operation responds to thousands of requests each year for agricultural information materials from USDA employees and from libraries and organizations around the world. For USDA employees, NAL also acquires needed materials that are not otherwise available from NAL collections.

NAL uses the Relais Enterprise document request and delivery system that is integrated with the Voyager library system, with DigiTop, and with other OpenURL and ISO ILL compliant systems to support document delivery. With the system fully integrated and online, NAL customers can request materials or check on the status of their requests via the Web, and materials are easily delivered electronically. Library requests can also come via OCLC (NAL's symbol is AGL) and DOCLINE (NAL's libid is MDUNAL). Visit http://www.nal.usda.gov/services/request.shtml for details.

National Library of Medicine

8600 Rockville Pike, Bethesda, MD 20894
301-496-6308, 888-346-3656, fax 301-496-4450
E-mail publicinfo@nlm.nih.gov
World Wide Web http://www.nlm.nih.gov

Kathleen Cravedi
Director, Office of Communications and Public Liaison

Melanie Modlin
Deputy Director, Office of Communications and Public Liaison

Founded in 1836—celebrating its 175th anniversary in 2011—the National Library of Medicine (NLM) is the world's largest biomedical library and the producer of electronic information services used by millions of people the world over. Scientists, health professionals, and the public search the library's resources more than 2 billion times a year; trillions of bytes of data are disseminated every day. Located in Bethesda, Maryland, NLM is part of the National Institutes of Health (NIH), U.S. Department of Health and Human Services (DHHS).

What started as a modest shelf of books in the library of the U.S. Army Surgeon General has grown to a collection of more than 17 million books, journals, artworks, audiovisuals, and other materials in more than 150 languages. The library's scope has expanded too, to include such things as DNA sequences, clinical trials data, toxicology and environmental health data, and consumer health information. NLM also conducts and supports informatics research and development in electronic health records, clinical decision making, information retrieval, advanced imaging, computational biology, telecommunications, and disaster response.

In its mission to enable biomedical research, support health care and public health, and promote healthy behavior, NLM

- Acquires, organizes, and works to preserve the world's scholarly biomedical literature, including addressing the challenges of making digital information permanent
- Provides access to biomedical and health information in partnership with the 5,800-member National Network of Libraries of Medicine
- Receives high-throughput screening output and serves as a leading international resource for building, curating, and providing sophisticated access to molecular biology and genomic databases via its National Center for Biotechnology Information
- Creates and maintains information services on toxicology, environmental health, health services research, public health, and disaster management
- Develops information systems and resources to ensure uninterrupted access to critical health information during national and international disasters

- Supports and conducts advanced biomedical informatics and health information technology research and development
- Develops and supports standards for electronic health records to enable efficient health information exchange and support health care reform
- Works to reinvigorate the research community through outreach programs to interest young people in scientific and health careers and by being the primary supporter of research training in biomedical informatics at 18 U.S. universities

Working with libraries and other partners, NLM develops and tests new methods to expand awareness and use of its information and services. Twitter and other social media outlets, programs for mobile devices, interactive tutorials, a free consumer magazine, and online games are some of the tools that help to generate widespread access to NIH's high-quality health information.

NLM also remains focused on the goals of its 2006–2016 long-range plan, including key activities in such areas as interoperable electronic health records, more-effective disaster and emergency response, and development of a robust knowledge base for personalized health care.

Scientific Information Services

MEDLINE/Pub Med is NLM's premier publicly available database of references and abstracts for medical journal articles. It is the world's most frequently consulted online scientific medical resource. It covers the period 1947 to the present and added its 20 millionth citation on July 27, 2010.

Coincidentally, on the same day PubMed Central—the library's digital archive of free, unrestricted full-text biomedical literature—added its 2 millionth article from some 700 journals. It also celebrated its tenth anniversary in 2010.

GenBank, which is maintained by NLM's National Center for Biotechnology Information (NCBI), is NIH's annotated collection of all publicly available DNA sequences. This open access resource contains more than 250 billion base pairs and continues to grow exponentially, doubling in size every 18 months. Integrated retrieval tools allow seamless searching of GenBank data and more than 40 integrated biomedical databases, including related literature and curated reference gene and genome databases developed by NCBI to support rapid advances in research.

New sequencing, microarray, and small molecule screening technologies are exponentially increasing NCBI's genomic data. For example, 10 trillion base pairs of high-throughput sequences were absorbed into the new Sequence Read Archive (SRA) last year. With more than one terabyte of sequence data being added each month, SRA is one of the fastest-growing biological databases ever.

Access to these data and associated NCBI databases provide the foundation for the translation of basic science into new diagnoses and treatments. Examples are dbGaP, which promises to spur discovery of genetic variations associated with common diseases and to which clinical phenotype and genomic data from 20 new Genome Wide Association Studies was recently added; PubChem, which provides bioactivity results from more than 50 million tests of small molecules, the new Peptidome database of mass spectrometry peptide and protein data; and numerous DNA, protein, and gene databases, all linked to the scientific literature.

The Lister Hill Center for Biomedical Communications, established in 1968 to research biomedical informatics in support of NLM, conducts and supports research in such areas as the development and dissemination of health information technology standards; the dissemination, processing, and use of high-quality imagery; medical language processing; high-speed access to biomedical information; next generation electronic health records (EHRs); and advanced technology for emergency and disaster management.

As the central coordinating body for clinical terminology standards within DHHS, NLM works closely with the Office of the National Coordinator for Health Information Technology to enable meaningful use of EHRs. NLM support allows them to be regularly updated to include new drugs and tests, and changes in biomedical knowledge and health practice, and also permits them to be used free of charge in U.S. systems that support health care, public health, and biomedical research.

NLM is committed to improving the nation's ability to ensure uninterrupted access to critical health information resources during disasters. As part of the Bethesda Hospital Emergency Preparedness Partnership, NLM's Disaster Information Management Research Center (DIMRC), within the Division of Specialized Information Services (SIS), is developing backup communications systems for patient tracking, information sharing, and responder training to serve as a model for hospitals across the nation. The center also produces information systems for first responders and others engaged in disaster management.

For example, after the January 2010 earthquake in Haiti, DIMRC quickly put together a Web page filled with links tailored to the people responding to the disaster, including information in Haitian Creole. The Lister Hill Center created a "people locator," a Web site to help reunite families, with an iPhone application to submit information. Additional resources were added to aid in the aftermath of the earthquake in Chile and the Gulf oil spill, and SIS activated the Emergency Access Initiative to provide free reference materials to Haiti and Pakistan.

Information Services for the Public

NLM creates and maintains numerous outreach programs to alert biomedical researchers, health professionals, librarians, patients, their families, and the public to its information and numerous services.

MedlinePlus is the library's main portal for consumer health information. Available in English and Spanish, with selected materials in almost 50 other languages, it includes information from NIH and other trusted sources on more than 850 diseases and conditions, and is updated daily. There are directories, a medical encyclopedia and medical dictionary, easy-to-understand tutorials on common conditions, medical tests and treatments, extensive information on prescription and over-the-counter drugs, health information from the media, and links to thousands of clinical trials.

During 2010 MedlinePlus was redesigned to make it more user-friendly, and more than 155 million unique visitors entered the site. The "medlineplus4you"

Twitter feed, a companion to the MedlinePlus.gov Web site, is one of several successful social media initiatives and now has thousands of followers. Another new free service, MedlinePlus Connect, was also begun, to allow EHR systems to easily link users to MedlinePlus and its deep bank of health and wellness information.

Along with its heavily used Web-based information services, *NIH MedlinePlus* magazine and its popular Spanish-language counterpart *NIH MedlinePlus Salud* continued to transmit the latest useful research findings, in plain language, to the public. Produced in cooperation with the Friends of the National Library of Medicine, *NIH MedlinePlus* is distributed free of charge each quarter to hundreds of thousands of doctors' offices, hospital waiting rooms, clinics, medical libraries, and individual subscribers, reaching more than 5 million readers.

Another widely used public resource is NIHSeniorHealth.gov, a collaboration of NLM and the National Institute on Aging, as well as other NIH institutes and centers. Designed with seniors' special cognitive needs in mind, it offers larger font sizes and a "talking" function, permitting users to listen to text as it is read.

ClinicalTrial.gov is a unique resource for scientific and clinical information that can assist in giving patients, healthcare providers, and researchers comprehensive information about ongoing and completed research. Containing information on more than 97,000 public and private research studies in 174 countries, the site celebrated a decade of service in 2010. It is the most comprehensive source of information about clinical trials for researchers, health professionals, and the public. NLM also has enhanced ClinicalTrials.gov to accommodate summary results and mandatory adverse events data, in response to the Food and Drug Administration Amendments Act of 2007.

NLM works with libraries and community organizations to increase public awareness and use of its many valuable resources. Among those with which it partners are members of the National Network of Libraries of Medicine, Partners in Information Access for the Public Health Workforce, the Environmental Health Information Outreach Program involving Historically Black Colleges and Universities, tribal colleges, and other minority-serving institutions.

NLM also fosters informal partnerships, such as the Information ℞ program to promote MedlinePlus usage by encouraging physicians to write "information prescriptions" for their patients. Recognizing the critical importance of reducing health disparities, NLM uses exhibitions, the media, and new technologies in its efforts to reach underserved populations.

As part of its outreach efforts, NLM continually solicits feedback from users on how existing resources can be improved. Dozens of community-based projects were funded to enhance awareness and generate access to health information, using a combination of high tech and "high touch" approaches. In 2010 social media activity in particular was developed at the library. To reach its diverse audiences all over the world, NLM now hosts more Twitter feeds and Facebook accounts than any other NIH institute or center.

During 2010 NLM expanded its successful traveling exhibitions program as another means of highlighting the library's collections and services and promoting interest in careers in science and medicine in public libraries and other venues. The exhibitions are free, but recipients pay the cost of shipping. The popular "Harry Potter's World: Renaissance Science, Magic, and Medicine" is fully booked through 2012.

Administration

The director of NLM, Donald A. B. Lindberg, M.D., is guided in matters of policy by a Board of Regents consisting of 10 appointed and 11 ex officio members.

Table 1 / Selected NLM Statistics*

Library Operations	Volume
Collection (book and non-book)	17,941,368
Items cataloged	18,820
Serial titles received	20,465
Articles indexed for MEDLINE	699,420
Circulation requests processed	401,699
For interlibrary loan	256,459
For on-site users	145,240
Computerized searches (MEDLINE/ PubMed)	1,578,714,477
Budget authority	$340,386,000
Staff	800

*For the year ending September 30, 2010.

United States Government Printing Office

732 North Capitol St. N.W., Washington, DC 20401
World Wide Web http://www.gpo.gov

Gary Somerset
Media and Public Relations Manager
202-512-1957, e-mail gsomerset@gpo.gov

The U.S. Government Printing Office (GPO) is the federal government's primary centralized resource for gathering, cataloging, producing, disseminating, and preserving published information in all forms. Since GPO opened its doors on March 4, 1861, the agency has offered Congress, the courts, and government agencies a set of centralized services, enabling them to produce tangible and electronic documents easily and cost effectively according to a uniform set of federal government specifications. In addition, GPO has offered these publications for sale to the public and made them widely available at no cost through the Federal Depository Library Program (FDLP).

Today GPO is at the epicenter of technological change as it fulfills its historic mission while embracing the technological challenges of today's digital world. GPO has transformed itself into a 21st century printing, digital media, and secure credentialing facility.

GPO is part of the legislative branch of the federal government and operates under the authority of the public printing and documents chapters of Title 44 of the U.S. Code. All three branches of the federal government rely on GPO's services. Congressional documents, Supreme Court decisions, federal regulations and reports, IRS tax forms, and U.S. passports all are produced by or through GPO.

GPO's headquarters, which includes a bookstore, is located in Washington, D.C. Nationwide, GPO maintains 15 field locations and two major distribution facilities, in Pueblo, Colorado, and Laurel, Maryland.

GPO's information dissemination activities include FDLP, which disseminates information products from all three branches of government to more than 1,200 libraries nationwide; GPO's Federal Digital System (FDsys), the successor to GPO Access, provides online access to titles on GPO servers as well as links to titles on other federal Web sites; and a Publication and Information Sales program that sells government publications to the public.

GPO also administers the Cataloging and Indexing (C&I) Program, the By-Law Program, and the distribution component of the International Exchange Program for the Library of Congress. To achieve its mission to provide timely, permanent, no-fee public access to federal government publications, GPO coordinates a network of libraries that assist the public in using U.S. government information resources; provides access to tools such as the Catalog of Government Publications to identify, describe, locate, and obtain publications; and maintains a permanent collection of government publications.

Together, these activities disseminate one of the world's largest volumes of published information.

Federal Digital System

GPO's Federal Digital System (FDsys) is a one-stop site for authentic, published government information. This system automates the collection and dissemination of electronic information from all three branches of the federal government.

Information is submitted directly into FDsys, permanently available in electronic format, authenticated and versioned, and publicly accessible for searching and downloading. FDsys is a content management system; it securely controls digital content throughout its lifecycle to ensure content integrity and authenticity. It is a preservation repository that follows archival system standards to ensure long-term preservation and access of digital content. And it is an advanced search engine, combining extensive metadata creation with modern search technology to ensure the highest-quality search experience.

Fiscal year (FY) 2010 saw considerable progress toward the completion of FDsys. The foundational system has been put into place, along with the content management system, preservation repository, and search component.

All 40 GPO Access content collections have been migrated to the system.

FDsys was expected to fully replace GPO Access in FY 2011; at that time, it will become the electronic system of record, and GPO Access will be shut down.

Authentication

To help meet the challenge of the digital age, GPO has been implementing digital signatures to electronic documents on GPO Access and FDsys that not only establish GPO as a trusted information disseminator but also provide assurance that an electronic document has not been altered since GPO disseminated it.

A digital signature, viewed through the GPO Seal of Authenticity, verifies document integrity and authenticity on GPO online federal documents at no cost to the customer.

FDsys is continuing with the essential work of authenticating U.S. government online publications that began with GPO Access.

A workshop was hosted at GPO in June 2010 pertaining to document authentication. GPO stakeholders from the library community, academia, and federal government agencies were invited to attend. The objective of the workshop was to facilitate input from stakeholders relating to

- User community requirements for different levels of authentication assurance on the same content (some parties willing to use less robust means and others requiring the current digital signature approach)
- Standards and techniques that should be used for native XML authentication
- Standards and techniques that should be used for "Chain of Custody" (if content originators support it)
- User community requirements for "granular authentication"

GPO next hosted an Industry Day in October 2010 to gather information on technology options for XML digital signatures that would be of use to GPO and its end-user community and stakeholders.

GPO continues to be a leader within the federal government for document authentication. The transcripts and summary documentation from these events are available at http://www.gpoaccess.gov/authentication.

Online Learning

Online Programming for All Libraries (OPAL)

GPO, as well as depository staff and representatives of federal agencies, has presented several programs on topics relating to FDLP through Online Programming for All Libraries (OPAL), a Web conferencing service (see http://www.opal-online.org). All past presentations are available for viewing in the GPO OPAL archive at http://www.opal-online.org/archivegpo.htm.

In the past year GPO started a new program titled "Chat with GPO." During these interactive sessions, GPO staff present information on timely and relevant topics, and depository staff have the opportunity to engage in Q&A with the presenters. "Chat with GPO" sessions held in FY 2010 included

- An Overview of the Microfiche Program of the Federal Depository Library Program
- A Brief Overview of Microfiche, Shipping Lists, and SuDoc Classification in the Federal Depository Library System
- Cataloging Records Distribution Pilot Project
- Discards, Needs, and Offers—Oh My! What's One to Do?
- Helping GPO Identify Fugitive Publications
- The GPO Historic Shelflist Project
- GPO's Federal Digital System
- Needs Assessment and 2009 Biennial Survey: What Did We Learn?
- Going Mostly Electronic: Part I—The Basics

Other OPAL presentations for FY 2010 included

- Searching for Free Government Full Text Docs Online: Where to Begin?
- Department of Energy Office of Science and Technology Information (OSTI): A Very Brief Overview of OSTI Offerings
- Trademarks: What Every Librarian Should Know

Also, for the first time, OPAL and GPO hosted the Six-State Virtual Government Information Conference, which included 15 separate presentations.

Visit FDLP Desktop at http://www.fdlp.gov/outreach/onlinelearning/68-opal to view the OPAL archive or submit a proposal for a program.

Education Modules

During the fiscal year GPO enhanced online learning opportunities through the availability of educational training modules. As of late 2010 it had made WEBTech Notes available, and FDLP Desktop and other modules are planned for future releases.

To view the first module, visit http://www.fdlp.gov/webtechnotes.

Federal Depository Library Program

FDLP continues to provide public access to U.S. government publications in tangible documents maintained by designated federal depository libraries (FDLs) and with direct online access through FDsys at http://www.fdsys.gov.

Cataloging and Indexing

GPO is charged with cataloging and indexing all publications issued by the federal government that are not confidential in character. This task serves libraries and the public nationwide and enables people to locate desired government publications in all formats. The main public interface for the access of cataloging records is the *Catalog of U.S. Government Publications* (*CGP*) (http://catalog.gpo.gov/F).

GPO's goal is to expand *CGP* to a more comprehensive online index of public documents, both historic and current, to increase the visibility and use of government information products. Electronic information dissemination and access have greatly expanded the number of publications that require cataloging and indexing.

Beginning in January 2010, metadata transcription of the complete set of more than 1 million three-by-five cards from the GPO's historic shelflist began. By the end of FY 2010, more than 25,000 bibliographic records from the shelflist were made available in *CGP*. The Web-based catalog currently provides access to approximately 700,000 records dating from the late 1880s to the present.

Integrated Library System

FY 2010 saw significant progress regarding the Integrated Library System (ILS).

MetaLib was released with an initial collection of 53 resources. A direct link to a pre-populated category in askGPO "Suggest a Resource" on the MetaLib banner leverages expert knowledge of federal government documents in depository libraries and in the user base at large by facilitating recommendations to GPO for additional resources to add to MetaLib.

The FDLP login page was also released during the fiscal year. The page gives depository libraries access to authenticated services in *CGP*. These include the setup of selective dissemination of information (SDI) searches whose results can be returned via RSS or e-mail. In addition, the page provides the ability to add desired records to the Bookshelf, to create folders to organize and store them, and save them across sessions. Moreover, there is the option to save to the authenticated user's local computer and the option to set and save such user preferences as number of results per page and result format.

GPO's authority control initiative has led to the validation of Library of Congress name and subject headings in monthly files of bibliographic records. The ILS Aleph software has also been configured so that new or updated Library of Congress name and subject authority records now automatically update bibliographic records in *CGP*. Aleph software has been upgraded from version 18 to the latest version 20 and is now in production.

New hardware was brought into production and the software has been upgraded for the ILS Citrix implementation. This enhancement gives GPO staff users secure, thin client access to the Aleph staff client.

Another layer of systems support has been added to the Federal Depository Library Directory that includes monitoring and data capture.

Additionally, GPO's Library Services and Content Management (LSCM) staff conducted a stress test with depository library volunteers on the z39.50 server. The test results demonstrated that the existing hardware could handle an increased load, and the z39.50 per-session record limit therefore was raised from 1,000 records to 10,000 records.

A new format was added to the New Electronic Titles Monthly Archive Reports. As of June 2010 the reports are available in both HTML and CSV (comma-separated values) formats. The CSV format allows depository libraries greater flexibility in manipulating the report data.

Registry of U.S. Government Publication Digitization Projects

The Registry of U.S. Government Publication Digitization Projects contains records for projects that include digitized copies of publications originating with the U.S. government. It serves as a locator tool for publicly accessible collections of digitized U.S. government publications; increases awareness of U.S. government publication digitization projects that are planned, in progress, or completed; fosters collaboration for digitization projects; and provides models for future digitization projects.

GPO, in collaboration with the Depository Library Council, identified the opportunity for several enhancements to the registry. During FY 2010 a plan was developed to address the full scope of the possible modifications, including both long-term and short-term possibilities. Several modifications were implemented, and it was determined that some modifications would require more-complex solutions and systems for both LSCM as a provider and the registry contributing members. As a next step, content requirements were established, and work began. A revamp to the registry page was in process late in 2010, and links to other relevant sites were being added.

Some minor changes had already been made to the existing registry page, such as a link to the grants summary document. Additionally, work has been done on the FDLP Desktop to make the link to the registry more visible there.

For more about the Registry of U.S. Government Publication Digitization Projects, visit http://registry.fdlp.gov.

Preservation

During FY 2010 David Walls, formerly of Yale University, joined GPO's team as its first preservation librarian. He is working on numerous preservation-related issues, including development of preservation policies and procedures in LSCM and liaison activities with FDsys.

GPO Partnerships

During FY 2010 GPO developed a new partnership with the Cornell University Law Library for a pilot project to evaluate a conversion process of the Code of

Federal Regulations (CFR) into XML (extensible markup language) format. The Cornell Legal Information Institute is converting various titles into XML and making them accessible on the university's Web site for research. GPO and Cornell will use the lessons learned from the pilot project to find ways of providing public access to government documents.

Partnerships with Southern Methodist University for the Historic Publications from World War II Digital Library and with the Library of Michigan for regional depository library information were renewed. The renewal of the agreement with the Library of Michigan also brought a change to the location of regional information that was moved off the library's Web site and onto the FDLP Community site.

A partnership with the Association of Schools of Public Health (ASPH) to provide electronic access to public health reports was announced in September 2009 and was fully implemented in January 2010. Nearly 700 depositories now have electronic access to this ASPH material.

Several institutions marked anniversaries as GPO partners in FY 2010. They included the University of Illinois at Chicago and DOSFAN (13 years); Louisiana State University and the List of Federal Agency Internet Sites (8 years); Oklahoma State University and Browse Topics (7 years); and the Federal Reserve Bank of St. Louis and FRASER (5 years).

GPO entered a new service partnership with St. Mary's University for its Government Information on the Web Subject Index, which provides a starting point for browsing subject areas, bringing both broad and detailed subject listings from many libraries together in one index.

GPO also released Cooperative Cataloging Guidelines in August 2010, establishing guidelines under which GPO will undertake partnerships with a cataloging component. The Cooperative Cataloging Guidelines are available at http://www.fdlp.gov/outreach/partnerships/757-catalogingpartnershipguide.

Also in the past year, GPO joined the Lots of Copies Keep Stuff Safe (LOCKSS) Alliance.

Public Access Assessments

Conducting Public Access Assessments is the primary way that LSCM fulfills the legal requirement "to make firsthand investigation of conditions for which need is indicated" (44 USC §1909). Public Access Assessments (PAAs) are a review and consulting opportunity that LSCM outreach librarians conduct of a library's federal depository operations and services. The PAA focuses on how they provide access to federal government information products and serve the community's needs. The review identifies strengths of the depository and also any areas needing improvement. Individual depository libraries have the flexibility to determine locally how to apply the requirements. PAA reviews also provide LSCM and library staff with opportunities to share depository management best practices, with the goal of enhancing depository services to the public and promoting greater efficiency and effectiveness within FDLP. Any library can request an assessment at any time.

During FY 2010 PAAs were conducted in Arizona, Connecticut, Georgia, Massachusetts, Mississippi, Nebraska, Oklahoma, New Mexico, and Texas. For more information about the program, visit http://www.fdlp.gov/outreach/paa.

During the fiscal year four additional outreach librarians were hired, tripling the staff who consult on depository management issues, provide training, and perform PAAs.

FDLP Marketing Plan and Customer Relations Program

The services provided by federal depository libraries and administered by GPO are unique and essential to the public. Many critical calls for help with marketing the services and benefits of FDLs and FDLP have been made by the Depository Library Council and depository librarians throughout the country. In response to these calls, GPO is proposing a variety of marketing strategies and activities.

The FDLP Marketing Plan is designed to give FDLs the tools they need to market their valuable services to all audiences in the most effective way possible. The FDLP Marketing Plan, Phases 1 and 2, is available at http://www.fdlp.gov/outreach/promotionalresources/98-fdlpmarketingplan.

The performance framework of government is increasingly "customer-centric," yet is still outpaced by the rising expectations of customers. The necessity to understand those whom government serves, and their needs, is therefore of the utmost importance. While GPO has long had channels to obtain feedback and suggestions from the depository library community, these methods have not been cyclical or embedded into the planning and business processes.

During FY 2009 LSCM was asked specifically to develop and implement a formal customer relations program for FDLs that would delineate them by type of library. Establishing such a plan allows LSCM to better serve depository library needs. It also allows LSCM to monitor and document business operations to ensure provision of appropriate customer care, response to mission requirements, and solicitation of feedback from depository libraries on performance.

The Customer Relations Program: Plan for FDL Partners identifies two goals: (1) develop a customer relations program that will identify needed improvements in services to and communication with FDLs, address identified needs, and use quantitative metrics for success measures; and (2) develop a customer relations program that will identify and report on needed improvements in business processes that support services provided to FDLs.

The segmentation survey of depository libraries conducted in spring 2009 was a first step in doing research to understand the varied needs of FDLP's diverse libraries and depository users. A formal customer relations plan is now in place, and work has begun to implement action items from the program.

Community Outreach

Public Access Assessments are just one of the outreach activities conducted by LSCM. Related outreach activities pertaining to library visits, training, and other outreach activities by LSCM staff are detailed at http://www.fdlp.gov/outreach/events/450-fdlp-on-the-go. The page also provides for submission of requests for GPO staff to participate in state and local meetings and speaking engagements, and to hold training sessions.

The Outreach section of the FDLP Desktop was updated to include information about LSCM's interaction, communication, and consultation with FDLP libraries about depository management activities. This includes information about GPO's consultation services relating to depository management and spotlight articles about depository libraries.

Daily consultation with individual library staff in person, on the phone, or by e-mail is of importance to GPO staff. LSCM also continues to develop educational articles, tools, and conference programs to assist library personnel as they strive to make the most of their depository operations.

LSCM staff have been regularly involved in working groups and conferences that focus on major issues in FDLP. Among these, GPO staff—particularly LSCM's Archival Manager, James Mauldin—have been heavily involved in the recent release of "Technical Guidelines for Digitizing Cultural Heritage Materials: Creation of Raster Image Master Files." The guidelines represent shared best practices followed by agencies participating in the Federal Agencies Digitization Guidelines Initiative (FADGI) Still Image Working Group for digitizing cultural heritage materials. This group is involved in a cooperative effort to develop common digitization guidelines for still image materials (such as textual content, maps, and photographic prints and negatives) found in cultural heritage institutions.

The guidelines were prepared by members of the working group during the winter of 2009–2010. This document draws substantially on the National Archives and Records Administration's (NARA's) "Technical Guidelines for Digitizing Archival Records for Electronic Access: Creation of Production Master Files—Raster Images" (June 2004), but has been revised and updated in several areas to reflect the current recommendations of the working group and to reflect changes that have occurred in the digitization field during the last five years.

The document is available at http://webcache.googleusercontent.com/search?q=cache:http://www.digitizationguidelines.gov/stillimages/documents/FADGI_Still_Image-Tech_Guidelines_2010-08.pdf.

A Look at Metrics

The following statistics reflect notable LSCM metrics for FY 2010 (through July 2010).

- New titles acquired (online and tangible): 15,281
- Searches of the Catalog of U.S. Government Publications: 15,800,348
- Total titles cataloged: 13,830
- Total PURLs (persistent uniform resource locators) created: 9,019
- Total titles distributed: 6,952
- Total copies distributed: 1,607,369
- Number of federal depository libraries: more than 1,220

By-Law Program

LSCM administers the dissemination of certain tangible publications as specified by public law. Under Title 44 of the United States Code, GPO is required to provide copies of publications to certain federal agencies and others at the direction of Congress. Two or more copies of every publication printed are provided to the Library of Congress, regardless of whether the publication is distributed to federal depository libraries. NARA is entitled to receive three copies of every publication printed. Additionally, on behalf of the Department of State, LSCM distributes copies of publications to foreign legions. LSCM also maintains mailing lists for by-law distribution of specific publications.

A database created to track by-law publications more efficiently continues to provide excellent results. Protocols were recently established between various GPO business units that further ensure that all by-law publications are identified as such by the Superintendent of Documents.

International Exchange Service

Under the direction of the Library of Congress, GPO distributes tangible government publications to foreign governments that agree to send to the United States similar publications of their governments for the library's collections. The following statistics reflect International Exchange Service (IES) activity for FY 2010 (through July 2010).

Distributed IES Publications

Full sets:	88,546
Congressional Record:	8,862
Federal Register:	6,243
Serial set (paper):	900
Serial set (microfiche):	8,228
Total boxes shipped:	2,561

Ben's Guide to U.S. Government

Ben's Guide to U.S. Government (http://bensguide.gpo.gov) strives to introduce and explain the workings of the three branches of the federal government. Through the use of primary source materials, grade-appropriate explanations, and a stimulating site design, Ben's Guide not only increases the public's access to and knowledge of the government, but makes learning fun.

The site is broken down into four grade levels (K–2, 3–5, 6–8, and 9–12) and also provides an area for parents and educators. The material in each of these sections is tailored specifically for its intended audience. Ben's Guide includes historical documents and information on legislative processes, elections, and citizenship. The site also features learning activities and a list of federal Web sites designed for students, parents, and educators.

FDLP Desktop and the FDLP Community

FDLP Desktop

The FDLP Desktop (http://www.fdlp.gov) serves as a centralized resource for FDLP. Through FDLP Desktop, users can stay up to date with the latest innovations and progress of the program, and federal depository libraries can utilize various tools in order to enhance public services.

All of the content on this comprehensive resource for depository librarians is created and maintained by GPO staff and serves as the main informational hub for FDLP. An easy-to-use navigation system, including RSS feeds and links to social bookmarks, provides multiple ways to stay in touch with the latest developments in FDLP.

FDLP Community

The FDLP Community Web site (http://community.fdlp.gov) is designed to give members of the federal library community an opportunity to connect, collaborate, and learn from each other in a secure environment. All members of the federal depository library community can create an account, then share knowledge, experiences, and resources through such means as writing blogs, posting to a forum, collaborating in groups, uploading documents, or submitting Web links.

While GPO maintains informational pages and at times will generate forum topics, most of the content on FDLP Community is generated by its members. As participation increases, the resources become more helpful and relevant to the members.

Biennial Survey and Needs Assessments Survey

In FY 2009 LSCM developed and implemented a formal Customer Relations Program (CRP) for federal depository libraries. The CRP allows LSCM to better serve depository library needs based upon unique characteristics (such as library segment) and data analysis. It also allows LSCM to monitor and document business operations to ensure provision of appropriate customer care, response to mission requirements, and solicitation of feedback from depository libraries on performance.

GPO contracted with Outsell, Inc. to develop and administer data gathering activities. As a first step, in 2009, a segmentation survey was conducted to develop an understanding of the number and characteristics of various types of libraries that make up FDLP and to map these libraries to specified library types.

As a follow-up to the segmentation survey, in FY 2010 a needs assessment was conducted and incorporated into an abbreviated 2009 biennial survey. The needs assessment was conducted to determine how well GPO was providing services to depositories and how to better support depository needs. The survey is required of all FDLP libraries as it provides the tool for them to fulfill their legal requirement to report conditions to the Superintendent of Documents every two years.

Some highlights of the survey:

- 92 percent of respondents planned to remain in FDLP
- 7 percent were reconsidering their designation
- Nine regional depositories were considering changing their designation to selective depository
- More than 80 percent of respondents reported having piece-level records for online books and serials
- 37 percent of libraries reported an interest in receiving digital files on deposit

The full report with aggregate overview, segmentation analysis, and individual responses is available at http://www.fdlp.gov/home/about/723-crp-segmentation-needsassessment.

In July 2010 an OPAL session was conducted: "Needs Assessment and 2009 Biennial Survey: What Did We Learn?" This archived session is available at http://www.fdlp.gov/outreach/onlinelearning/68-opal.

Promotional Initiatives

In continuing its efforts to spread awareness of FDLP, LSCM undertook several promotional initiatives in FY 2010.

GPO has been disseminating public service announcements to radio stations across the country. GPO staff has created two separate radio spots, one directed at stations on college campuses with a depository and the other for public stations and for college campuses without a depository. Nearly 150 radio stations are airing the announcements.

GPO also contracted with North American Precis Syndicate (NAPS) to help disseminate informational articles about FDLP to 10,000 print and online publications nationwide, as well as a radio spot to about 400 radio stations. A new FDLP screensaver was also created for public access workstations at depository libraries.

In addition, an FDsys promotional plan was created and is being executed. FDsys promotional initiatives currently in process include a revamp of all promotional brochures offered for free ordering via FDLP Desktop, a new FDsys Web page on the FDLP Desktop with FDsys training materials, a new NAPS campaign focused on FDsys, and new FDsys mouse pads for free ordering on the FDLP Desktop.

Selling Government Publications

GPO's sales program currently offers approximately 2,500 individual government titles on a broad array of subjects. These are sold principally via the Internet, e-mail, telephone, fax, and mail. The program operates on a cost-recovery basis. Publications for sale include books, forms, posters, pamphlets, and CD-ROMs. Subscription services for both dated periodicals and basic-and-supplement services (involving an initial volume and supplemental issues) also are offered.

GPO's U.S. Government Online Bookstore (http://bookstore.gpo.gov) is the prime source of information on its sales inventory. The online bookstore includes a searchable database of all in-print publications as well as an extensive archive of recently out-of-print titles. It also includes a broad spectrum of special publication collections featuring new and popular titles and key product lines. GPO uses Pay.gov, a secure financial management transaction portal available around the clock, to provide processing of online orders. The online bookstore also gives customers the options of expedited shipping, new and improved shopping cart and order-confirmation e-mails, and expanded ordering options for international transactions.

Express service, which includes priority handling and expedited delivery, is available for orders placed by telephone for domestic delivery. Orders placed before noon Eastern time for in-stock publications and single-copy subscriptions are delivered within two working days. Call the GPO Contact Center using the toll-free number 866-512-1800 (or 202-512-1800 within the Washington, D.C., area) for more information. The GPO Contact Center is open from 8 A.M. to 5:30 P.M. Eastern time.

GPO also offers publications for sale through the main bookstore at 710 North Capitol St., N.W., Washington, D.C. The bookstore has recently undergone a major renovation. In addition to offering a browse-and-purchase experience, the bookstore also has an exhibit space that outlines the history of printing and GPO's role in printing for the federal government. Hours of operation are 8 A.M. to 4 P.M. The telephone number is 202-512-0132 and e-mail mainbks@gpo.gov.

Consumer-oriented publications also are either sold or distributed at no charge through the Federal Citizen Information Center in Pueblo, Colorado, which GPO operates on behalf of the General Services Administration.

Members of the public can register free of charge to receive e-mail updates when new publications become available for sale through GPO's New Titles by Topic e-mail alert service, which can be accessed at http://bookstore.gpo.gov/alertservice.jsp.

Standing order service is available to ensure automatic receipt of many of GPO's most popular recurring and series publications. Standing order customers receive each new edition automatically as soon as it is published. This service can be set up using a Visa, MasterCard, American Express, or Discover credit card, or through a Superintendent of Documents deposit account. For more information on how to set up a standing order for recurring or series publications, e-mail contactcenter@gpo.gov or call 866-512-1800 (toll free) or 202-512-1800 within the Washington, D.C., area.

The GPO sales program has begun using print-on-demand technology with a print-on-demand vendor to increase the long-term availability of publications. Sales also has brought its bibliographic practices more in line with those of the commercial publishing sector by utilizing ONIX (Online Information Exchange), the publishing industry's standard electronic format for sharing product data with wholesale and retail booksellers, other publishers, library buyers, and anyone else involved in the sale of books. ONIX enables GPO to have government publications listed, promoted, and sold by commercial book dealers worldwide. GPO sales titles are listed on Amazon.com, Barnesandnoble.com, and other online commercial bookselling sites. In 2010 GPO began Government Book Talk (http://govbooktalk.gpo.gov), a blog that reviews government publications past and present. In its first six months, the blog received more than 70,000 page views and added more than 800 subscribers.

National Technical Information Service

U.S. Department of Commerce, Alexandria, VA 22312
800-553-NTIS (6847) or 703-605-6000
World Wide Web http://www.ntis.gov

Wayne Strickland
Manager, Office of Product and Program Management

The National Technical Information Service (NTIS) is the nation's largest and most comprehensive source of government-funded scientific, technical, engineering, and business information produced or sponsored by U.S. and international government sources. NTIS is a federal agency within the U.S. Department of Commerce.

Since 1945 the NTIS mission has been to operate a central U.S. government access point for scientific and technical information useful to American industry and government. NTIS maintains a permanent archive of this declassified information for researchers, businesses, and the public to access quickly and easily. Release of the information is intended to promote U.S. economic growth and development and to increase U.S. competitiveness in the world market.

The NTIS collection of more than 2 million titles contains products available in various formats. Such information includes reports describing research conducted or sponsored by federal agencies and their contractors; statistical and business information; U.S. military publications; multimedia training programs; databases developed by federal agencies; and technical reports prepared by research organizations worldwide. NTIS maintains a permanent repository of its information products.

More than 200 U.S. government agencies contribute to the NTIS collection, including the National Aeronautics and Space Administration; the Environmental Protection Agency; the departments of Agriculture, Commerce, Defense, Energy, Health and Human Services, Homeland Security, Interior, Labor, Treasury, Veterans Affairs, Housing and Urban Development, Education, and Transportation; and numerous other agencies. International contributors include Canada, Japan, Britain, and several European countries.

NTIS on the Web

NTIS offers Web-based access to information on government scientific and technical research products. Visitors to http://www.ntis.gov can search the entire collection dating back to 1964 free of charge. NTIS provides many of the technical reports for purchase on CD, paper copies, or downloaded pdf files. RSS feeds of recently catalogued materials are available in 39 major subject categories at http://www.ntis.gov/rss/RSSNTISCategoryList.aspx.

NTIS Database

The NTIS Database offers unparalleled bibliographic coverage of U.S. government and worldwide government-sponsored research information products acquired by NTIS since 1964. Its contents represent hundreds of billions of research dollars and cover a range of important topics including agriculture, biotechnology, business, communication, energy, engineering, the environment, health and safety, medicine, research and development, science, space, technology, and transportation.

The NTIS Database can be leased directly from NTIS and can also be accessed through several commercial services. For an updated list of organizations offering NTIS Database products, see http://www.ntis.gov/products/commercial.aspx.

To lease the NTIS Database directly from NTIS, contact the NTIS Office of Product Management at 703-605-6515. For more information, see http://www.ntis.gov/products/ntisdb.aspx.

NTIS National Technical Reports Library

The National Technical Reports Library (NTRL) enhances accessibility to the NTIS technical reports collection. Subscription rates are based on institutional FTE levels. NTRL operates on a system interface that allows users to do queries on the large NTIS bibliographic database. The intent is to broadly expand and improve access to more than 2.5 million bibliographic records (pre-1960 to the present) and 500,000 full-text documents in pdf format that are directly linked to that bibliographic database. For more information, visit http://www.ntis.gov/products/ntrl.aspx.

Other Databases Available from NTIS

NTIS offers several valuable research-oriented database products. To find out more about accessing the databases, visit http://www.ntis.gov/products/data.aspx.

AGRICOLA

As one of the most comprehensive sources of U.S. agricultural and life sciences information, the AGRICOLA (Agricultural Online Access) Database contains bibliographic records for documents acquired by the U.S. Department of Agriculture's National Agricultural Library. To access an updated list of organizations offering AGRICOLA Database products, see http://www.ntis.gov/products/agricola.aspx.

AGRIS

The International Information System for the Agricultural Science and Technology (AGRIS) Database is a cooperative system for collecting and disseminating information on the world's agricultural literature. More than 100 national and multinational centers take part in the system. References to citations for U.S. publications given coverage in the AGRICOLA Database are not included in AGRIS. To access an updated list of organizations offering AGRIS Database products, see http://www.ntis.gov/products/agris.aspx.

Energy Science and Technology

The Energy Science and Technology Database (EDB) is a multidisciplinary file containing worldwide references to basic and applied scientific and technical research literature. The information is collected for use by government managers, researchers at the national laboratories, and other research efforts sponsored by the U.S. Department of Energy, and the results of this research are transferred to the public. To access an updated list of organizations offering EDB products, see http://www.ntis.gov/products/engsci.aspx.

FEDRIP

The Federal Research in Progress Database (FEDRIP) provides access to more than 150,000 current government-sponsored research projects in such fields as the physical sciences, engineering, and life sciences. To access an updated list of organizations offering FEDRIP Database products, see http://www.ntis.gov/products/fedrip.aspx.

Online Subscriptions

NTIS offers quick, convenient online access, on a subscription basis, to the following resources:

World News Connection

World News Connection (WNC) is an NTIS online news service accessible only via the World Wide Web. WNC makes available English-language translations of time-sensitive news and information from thousands of non-U.S. media. Particularly effective in its coverage of local media, WNC provides the power to identify what is happening in a specific country or region. The information is obtained from speeches, television and radio broadcasts, newspaper articles, periodicals, and books. The subject matter focuses on socioeconomic, political, scientific, technical, and environmental issues and events.

The information in WNC is provided to NTIS by the Open Source Center (OSC), a U.S. government agency. For more than 60 years, analysts from OSC's domestic and overseas bureaus have monitored timely and pertinent open source material, including gray literature. Uniquely, WNC allows subscribers to take advantage of the intelligence-gathering experience of OSC. WNC is updated every government business day. New information is added hourly.

Access to WNC is available through Dialog Corporation. To use the service, complete the WNC form at http://www.dialog.com/contacts/forms/wnc.shtml.

U.S. Export Administration Regulations

U.S. Export Administration Regulations (EAR) provides the latest rules controlling the export of U.S. dual-use commodities, technology, and software. Step by step, EAR explains when an export license is necessary and when it is not, how to obtain an export license, policy changes as they are issued, new restrictions on exports to certain countries and of certain types of items, and where to obtain further help.

This information is available through NTIS in looseleaf form, on CD-ROM, and online. An e-mail update notification service is also available. For more information, see http://www.ntis.gov/products/export-regs.aspx.

Special Subscription Services

NTIS Alerts

More than 1,000 new titles are added to the NTIS collection every week. NTIS prepares a list of search criteria that is run against all new studies and research and development reports in 16 subject areas. An NTIS Alert provides a twice-monthly information briefing service covering a wide range of technology topics.

For more information, call the NTIS Subscriptions Department at 703-605-6060 or see http://www.ntis.gov/products/alerts.aspx.

NTIS Selected Research Service

NTIS Selected Research Service (SRS) is a tailored information service that delivers complete electronic copies of government publications based on your needs, automatically, within a few weeks of announcement by NTIS. SRS includes the full bibliographic information in XML format. Customers choose between Standard SRS (selecting one or more of the 320 existing subject areas) or Custom SRS, which creates a new subject area to meet their particular needs. Custom SRS requires a one-time fee to cover the cost of strategy development and computer programming to set up a profile. Except for this fee, the cost of Custom SRS is the same as the Standard SRS. Through this ongoing subscription service, customers download copies of new reports pertaining to their field(s) of interest, as NTIS obtains the reports.

For more information, see http://www.ntis.gov/products/srs.aspx. To place an order, call 800-363-2068 or 703-605-6060.

This service is also available in microfiche form as Selected Research in Microfiche (SRIM), which delivers full-text microfiche copies of technical reports based on a customer's needs, and in CD-ROM format as Science and Technology on CD, which delivers the documents digitized and stored in pdf format.

For more information on SRIM, see http://www.ntis.gov/products/srim.aspx. To place an order, call 800-363-2068 or 703-605-6060. For more information on Science and Technology on CD, see http://www.ntis.gov/products/STonCD.aspx.

NTIS Customer Service

NTIS's automated systems keep it at the forefront when it comes to customer service. Shopping online at NTIS is safe and secure; its secure socket layer (SSL) software is among the best available.

Electronic document storage is fully integrated with NTIS's order-taking process, allowing it to provide rapid reproduction for the most recent additions to the NTIS document collection. Most orders for shipment are filled and delivered anywhere in the United States in five to seven business days. Rush service is available for an additional fee.

Key NTIS Contacts for Ordering

Order by Phone

Sales Desk 8:30 A.M.–5:00 P.M. Eastern time, Monday–Friday	800-553-6847 or 703-605-6000
Subscriptions 8:30 A.M.–5:00 P.M. Eastern time, Monday–Friday	800-363-2068 or 703-605-6060
TDD (hearing impaired only) 8:30 A.M.–5:00 P.M. Eastern time, Monday–Friday	703-487-4639

Order by Fax

24 hours a day, seven days a week To verify receipt of fax, call 703-605-6090, 7:00 A.M.–5:00 P.M. Eastern time, Monday–Friday	703-605-6900

Order by Mail

National Technical Information Service
5301Shawnee Rd.
Alexandria, VA 22312

RUSH Service (available for an additional fee) Note: If requesting RUSH Service, please do not mail your order	800-553-6847 or 703-605-6000

Order Online

Direct and secure online ordering	http://www.ntis.gov

National Archives and Records Administration

8601 Adelphi Rd., College Park, MD 20740
301-837-2000
World Wide Web http://www.archives.gov

The National Archives and Records Administration (NARA), an independent federal agency, is the nation's record keeper. NARA safeguards and preserves the records of the federal government so that the people can discover, use, and learn from this documentary heritage. NARA ensures continuing access to the essential documentation of the rights of American citizens and the actions of their government.

NARA is singular among the world's archives as a unified federal institution that accessions and preserves materials from all three branches of government. It carries out its mission through a national network of archives and records services facilities including presidential libraries documenting administrations back to that of Herbert Hoover. NARA assists federal agencies in documenting their activities, administering records management programs, scheduling records, and retiring non-current records to federal records centers. It also assists administers the National Historical Publications and Records Commission in its grant program for state and local records and edited publications of the papers of prominent Americans; it archives the papers of key figures in American history, and state and local government records; publishes the laws, regulations, presidential documents, and other official notices of the federal government through the *Federal Register*. In cooperation with other federal agencies, NARA administers the new National Declassification Center, providing a systematic, collaborative approach to the referral process, essential to the proper declassification and release of information. It also administers the Information Security Oversight Office, which oversees the government's security classification program, and the Office of Government Information Services, which is responsible for the review of agencies' Freedom of Information Act (FOIA) administration practices and compliance with FOIA.

NARA constituents include the federal government, educators and their students at all levels, the public, family historians, the media, the archival community, and a broad spectrum of professional associations and researchers in such fields as history, political science, law, library and information services, and genealogy.

The size and breadth of NARA's holdings are staggering. Together, NARA's facilities hold approximately 4 million cubic feet (equivalent to more than 10 billion pieces of paper) of original textual and non-textual materials from the executive, legislative, and judicial branches of the federal government. Its multimedia collections include more than 120,000 motion picture films; more than 8 million maps, charts, and architectural drawings; about 250,000 sound and video recordings; more than 27 million aerial photographs; more than 14 million still pictures and posters; and about 110 terabytes of electronic records.

Strategic Directions

NARA's strategic priorities are laid out in *Preserving the Past to Protect the Future: The Strategic Plan of the National Archives and Records Administration 2006–2016,* which was revised in 2009. Success for the agency as envisioned in the plan centers on six strategic goals:

- As the nation's record keeper, NARA will ensure the continuity and effective operation of federal programs by expanding its leadership and services in managing the government's records.
- NARA will preserve and process records to ensure access by the public as soon as legally possible.
- NARA will address the challenges of electronic records in government to ensure success in fulfilling NARA's mission in the digital era.
- NARA will provide prompt, easy, and secure access to its holdings anywhere, anytime.
- NARA will increase access to its records in ways that further civic literacy through its museum, public outreach, education, and grants programs.
- NARA will equip itself to meet the changing needs of its customers.

The plan lays out strategies for reaching these goals, sets milestone targets for accomplishments through 2016, and identifies measurements for gauging progress. The targets and measurements are further delineated in NARA's annual performance plans.

NARA's strategic plan and annual performance plans, together with performance and accountability reports, are available on the NARA Web site at http://www.archives.gov/about/plans-reports or by calling 301-837-1850.

NARA employs approximately 3,500 people, of whom nearly 2,600 are full-time permanent staff members.

Records and Access

Electronic Records Archives

The Electronic Records Archives (ERA) system captures electronic records and information, regardless of format, saves them permanently, and provides access to them. In 2010 NARA achieved a major milestone with the deployment of the Congressional Records Instance, providing for management and access to congressional assets. It met another major milestone in late 2011 with the release of a prototype of Online Public Access (OPA), the portal for public access to and information about NARA's holdings. NARA also drafted a Preservation Framework, defining the principles for long-term preservation and access to permanent electronic records in ERA.

NARA works to continue moving data from its legacy systems into ERA, as well as ingesting new electronic records from federal agencies. Electronic records from the presidential libraries brings the total volume in ERA to more than 97 terabytes, an information content equivalent to more than 25 billion textual pages of records. In summer 2010 the White House announced that ERA was one of the Office of Management and Budget's high-priority information technology investments. In early 2011 the system was being made ready for use by Chief Information Officers Council agencies beginning in March 2011, and for federal agencies and their components by mid-summer. ERA development is scheduled to be complete by the end of fiscal year (FY) 2011, and ERA will move to an operations and maintenance phase at the beginning of FY 2012. The focus will shift to advancing user adoption in anticipation of ERA becoming mandatory by the end of 2012 for federal agency use in scheduling and transferring permanent electronic records to NARA. In addition, NARA's current goal of transferring 10 terabytes per quarter from agencies will be quickly dwarfed in late 2011 when it plans to accept 488 terabytes of 2010 Census records into a secured part of the system. For more information about ERA, visit http://www.archives.gov/era.

NCAST

NARA established the National Archives Center for Advanced Systems and Technologies (NCAST) to serve as its premier center for advanced and applied research capabilities in the fields of computer science, engineering, and archival science. NCAST conducts research on new technologies, both to be aware of new types of electronic records NARA will need to preserve and to evaluate new technologies that might be incorporated into the ERA system or other systems. The center will also help NARA managers and employees acquire the new knowledge and skills they need to function effectively in e-government. For more information about NCAST, visit http://www.archives.gov/ncast.

National Declassification Center

In an executive order signed in December 2009, President Barack Obama directed an overhaul of the way documents created by the federal government are classified and declassified. This initiative is aimed at promoting transparency and accountability of government. The president also directed the creation of the National Declassification Center (NDC), now located within NARA.

NDC is leading the streamlining of the declassification process throughout the federal government. In particular, it is accelerating the processing of historically valuable classified records in which more than one federal agency has an interest. It oversees the development of common declassification processes among agencies and is prioritizing declassification based on public interest and the likelihood of declassification. For more information about NDC, visit http://www.archives.gov/declassification.

Online Research Catalog

Today anyone connected to the Internet can search descriptions of more than 70 percent of NARA's nationwide holdings and view digital copies of some of its most popular documents through its newly available Online Public Access portal prototype. Because of the volume of NARA holdings, it will take several more years to fully populate the catalog. At present, the catalog contains nearly 5.3

million descriptions of archival holdings. Included in the catalog are more than 157,000 digital copies of high-interest documents, representing many of the holdings highlighted in the Public Vaults, NARA's permanent interactive exhibition. The catalog is available at http://www.archives.gov/research.

Office of Government Information

Congress refers to NARA's Office of Government Information Services (OGIS) as "the Federal FOIA ombudsman." In short, this means OGIS serves as a bridge between requesters and agencies, particularly in situations where clear, direct communication has been lacking.

OGIS was created within NARA when the OPEN Government Act of 2007 amended FOIA (5 U.S.C. 552). Its key responsibilities include the following:

- *Review compliance and policy.* OGIS reviews policies and procedures of administrative agencies under FOIA, reviews compliance with FOIA by agencies, and recommends policy changes to Congress and the president to improve the administration of FOIA.
- *Mediate disputes.* OGIS offers mediation services to resolve disputes between persons making FOIA requests and agencies (as a nonexclusive alternative to litigation). It may issue advisory opinions if mediation has not resolved the dispute.
- *Serve as ombudsman.* OGIS solicits and receives comments and questions from federal agencies and the public regarding the administration of FOIA to improve FOIA processes and facilitate communication between agencies and FOIA requesters.

In addition to these responsibilities, OGIS also provides dispute resolution training for FOIA staff of federal agencies, and works closely with key FOIA stakeholders including the requester community and open government advocates. For more information, visit http://www.archives.gov/ogis.

Internet

NARA's Web site, http://www.archives.gov, redesigned in late 2010, provides the most widely available means of electronic access to information about and services from NARA. Feedback from visitors, as well as visitors to the National Archives Building in Washington, D.C., led to portals designed to support the particular needs of researchers, veterans and their families, educators and students, and the general public, as well as easily found information for records managers, journalists, information security specialists, members of Congress, and federal employees.

The site includes directions on how to contact NARA and do research at its facilities; descriptions of holdings in an online catalog at http//:www.archives.gov/research/search; direct access to certain archival electronic records at http//:www.archives.gov/aad; digital copies of selected archival documents; a Web form at www.archives.gov/contact/inquire-form.html for customer questions, reference requests, comments, and complaints; electronic versions of

Federal Register publications; online exhibits; classroom resources for students and teachers; and online tools including the Web-based, interactive inquiry program at http//:www.archives.gov/veterans/evetrecs, which allows veterans and the next-of-kin of deceased veterans to complete and print, for mail-in submission, requests for their service records. At http//:www.archives.gov/presidential-libraries, visitors can link to individual presidential library Web sites.

Copies of military pension records from the American Revolution through World War I, census pages, land files, court records, and microfilm publications can be ordered online, as can books, apparel, and accessories, at http//:www.archives.gov/order. Researchers can also submit reference questions about various research topics online.

Visitors to the Web site can interact with NARA staff through a wide variety of social media including Facebook, Twitter, blogs, Flickr, and YouTube, as well as obtaining Really Simple Syndication (RSS) feeds for the "Document for Today" feature, NARA news, and press releases.

In cooperation with several federal agencies, NARA also has established a Web portal, http//:www.regulations.gov, providing access to federal rules and instructions for submitting comments on federal regulatory actions.

Digitization Projects

NARA is working to digitize its traditional holdings to benefit their preservation and to provide greater access to the public. Although the online NARA catalog gives users the ability to identify many archival holdings (except for the relatively small amount of material digitized and made available via catalog), it does not provide online access to the holdings themselves. Most of NARA's holdings currently are available only from the archival facility in which they are stored. Through a series of digitization projects, NARA is working to vastly increase online public access. In 2008 it created a strategy to deal with digitization efforts, which includes working with partners in the private sector. Currently, more than 1,300 catalog descriptions link to millions of digital copies on partners' Web sites, and many thousands more will be made available in the future; for example, the 1940 census will be available online April 1, 2012. More information about the digitization partnerships is available at http://www.archives.gov/digitization/index.html.

Social Media

The worldwide use of social media continues to grow, as does its use at the National Archives. NARA has embraced social media as an important tool for open government. Its main goals in the social media sphere are to increase awareness about archival holdings and programs and to enrich NARA's relationship with the public through conversations about its services and holdings. Social media projects are also a way for NARA to learn more about its researchers and the general public and what they would like from the National Archives.

NARA shares historical videos from its holdings and videos of recent public events through YouTube, and photographs and documents from its collections through Flickr Commons. NARA can also be found on Facebook, and NARA regularly tweets about news and events around the country.

The AOTUS (Archivist of the United States) and NARAtions blogs have sparked many engaging conversations about ideas NARA is exploring. It also plans to use a blog to share information and collect feedback from the public on updating NARA's Open Government plan and activities in the coming year. NARA uses IdeaScale, an idea-generation and social-voting tool, as a way to get input from the general public, stakeholders, and staff.

More information about NARA's Web 2.0 projects is available online at http://www.archives.gov/social-media.

National Archives Experience

The National Archives Experience, a set of interconnected resources made possible by a public-private partnership between NARA and the Foundation for the National Archives, provides a variety of ways to explore the power and importance of America's records.

The Rotunda for the Charters of Freedom at the National Archives Building in Washington, D.C., is the cornerstone of the National Archives Experience. On display are the Declaration of Independence, the Constitution, and the Bill of Rights, known collectively as the Charters of Freedom. The Public Vaults is a 9,000-square-foot permanent exhibition that conveys the feeling of going beyond the walls of the rotunda and into the stacks and vaults of the working archives. Dozens of individual exhibits, many of them interactive, reveal the breadth and variety of NARA's holdings. Complementing the Public Vaults, the O'Brien Gallery hosts a changing array of topical exhibits based on National Archives records. The 290-seat McGowan Theater is a state-of-the-art showplace for NARA's extensive audiovisual holdings and serves as a forum for lectures and discussion. It also is home to the Charles Guggenheim Center for the Documentary Film at the National Archives. Inside the Boeing Learning Center, the ReSource Room is an access point for teachers and parents to explore documents found in the exhibits and to use our records as teaching tools. The center's "Constitution-in-Action" learning lab is designed to provide an intense field-trip adventure for middle and high school students.

The newly launched DocsTeach is an education Web site designed to provide instruction to teachers in the best practices of teaching with primary sources. Using documents in the National Archives as teachable resources, DocsTeach strongly supports NARA's goal to promote civic literacy. This tool gives teachers access to primary sources, instruction in best practices, and opportunities to interact with their counterparts across the nation. In developing the site, NARA established an online community that served as a virtual meeting place for its education team and colleagues from schools, institutions, and organizations to collaborate and share innovative ideas and best practices. For more information, visit http//:www.docsteach.org.

A set of Web pages now makes the entire National Archives Experience available to people who may not be able to travel to Washington. An illustrated history of the Charters of Freedom can be found there, as well as information on educational programs, special events, and exhibits currently at the National Archives. Those traveling to Washington can make online reservations at http://

www.recreation.gov. For more information, visit http//:www.archives.gov/national-archives-experience.

Research Center

At the Robert M. Warner Research Center, researchers can consult with staff experts on records in the National Archives building and submit requests to examine original documents. The research center houses approximately 275,000 rolls of microfilmed records, documenting military service prior to World War I, immigration into the United States, the federal census, Congress, federal courts in the District of Columbia, the Bureau of Indian Affairs, and the Freedmen's Bureau. The center also contains an extensive and expanding system of reference reports, helping researchers conduct research in federal documents.

Archives Library Information Center

The Archives Library Information Center (ALIC) provides access to information on American history and government, archival administration, information management, and government documents. ALIC is physically located in the National Archives at College Park, Maryland, but is also on the Internet at http//:www.archives.gov/research/alic. The Web site includes "Reference at Your Desk" Internet links, staff-compiled bibliographies and publications, an online library catalog, and other features. ALIC can be reached by phone at 301-837-3415.

Government Documents

U.S. government publications are generally available to researchers at many of the 1,250 congressionally designated federal depository libraries throughout the United States. A record set of these publications also is part of NARA's archival holdings. Publications of the U.S. Government (Record Group 287) is a collection of selected publications of government agencies, arranged by the SuDoc classification system devised by the Office of the Superintendent of Documents, Government Printing Office (GPO). The core of the collection is a library established in 1895 by GPO's Public Documents Division. By 1972, when NARA acquired the library, it included official publications dating from the early years of the federal government and selected publications produced for and by federal government agencies. Since 1972 the 25,000-cubic-foot collection has been augmented periodically with accessions of government publications selected by the Office of the Superintendent of Documents as a byproduct of its cataloging activity. As with the federal depository library collections, the holdings in NARA's Record Group 287 comprise only a portion of all official publications published by the U.S. government.

NARA Publications

NARA publishes guides and indexes to various portions of its archival holdings; catalogs of microfilmed records; informational leaflets and brochures; general interest books about NARA and its holdings that will appeal to anyone with an interest in U.S. history; more-specialized publications that will be useful to scholars, archivists, records managers, historians, researchers, and educators; facsimiles of certain documents; and *Prologue,* a scholarly journal published quarterly. Some publications are also available on NARA's Web site at http//:www.archives.gov/publications/online.html. Many are available from NARA's Customer Service Center in College Park by phoning 800-234-8861 or 866-272-6272 or faxing 301-837-0483. (In the Washington, D.C., area, call 301-837-2000.) The NARA Web site's publications home page, http//:www.archives.gov/publications, provides more-detailed information about available publications and ordering.

Federal Register

The *Federal Register* is the daily gazette of the U.S. government, containing presidential documents, proposed and final federal regulations, and public notices of federal agencies. The *Federal Register* is published by the Office of the Federal Register and printed and distributed by GPO. The two agencies collaborate in the same way to produce the annual revisions of the *Code of Federal Regulations* (*CFR*). Free access to the full text of the electronic version of the *Federal Register* and *CFR,* and to an unofficial, daily-updated electronic *CFR* (the *e-CFR*), is available at http//:www.federalregister.gov. Federal Register documents scheduled for future publication are available for public inspection at the Office of the Federal Register (800 North Capitol St. N.W., Washington, D.C.) or online at the electronic Public Inspection Desk (http//:www.federalregister.gov). Access to rules published in the *Federal Register* and open for public comment, as well as a portal for submitting comments, are provided through the multiagency Web site http//:www.regulations.gov.

Access to the full texts of other Federal Register publications, including the *Compilation of Presidential Documents, Public Papers of the President,* slip laws, *U.S. Statutes at Large,* and the *United States Government Manual* is available via http//:www.federalregister.gov. Printed editions of these publications also are maintained at all federal depository libraries. The Public Law Electronic Notification Service (PENS) is a free subscription e-mail service available for notification of recently enacted public laws. The *Federal Register* Table of Contents Service is a free e-mail service available for delivery of the daily table of contents of the *Federal Register* with direct links to documents.

The Office of the Federal Register also publishes information about its ministerial responsibilities associated with the operation of the Electoral College and ratification of constitutional amendments, and provides access to related records. The office also provides publication information concerning laws, regulations, and presidential documents and services (telephone 202-741-6000). Additional finding aids for Federal Register publications, the Electoral College, and constitutional amendments are also available via http//:www.archives.gov/federal-register.

Publications can be ordered by contacting GPO at http//:bookstore.gpo.gov, and by toll-free telephone at 866-512-1800. To submit orders by fax or by mail, see http://bookstore.gpo.gov/help/index.jsp.

Customer Service

Few records repositories serve as many customers as NARA. In FY 2010 there were nearly 140,000 researcher visits to NARA facilities nationwide, including archives, presidential libraries, and federal records centers. At the same time, more than 1.5 million customers requested information in writing. NARA also served the executive agencies of the federal government, the courts, and Congress by providing records storage, reference service, training, advice, and guidance on many issues relating to records management. Federal records centers replied to more than 8.2 million requests for information and records, including more than 1.4 million requests for information regarding military and civilian service records provided by the National Personnel Records Center in St. Louis. NARA also provided informative public programs at its various facilities for nearly 15,000 people. More than a million visited the National Archives Experience, and exhibits in the presidential library museums were visited by more than 2.4 million people.

NARA knows it must understand its customers to ensure that people can discover, use, and learn from their documentary heritage in the National Archives. Customers are surveyed regularly to help NARA align its standards of performance with their expectations. By repeating surveys at frequent, systematic intervals, changes in NARA's performance are measured and appropriate management actions are taken to ensure that service levels reflect an appropriate balance between customer needs and NARA resources. NARA also maintains an Internet Web form (http://www.archives.gov/contact/inquire-form.html) to facilitate continuous feedback from customers about what is most important to them and what NARA might do better to meet their needs.

Grants

The National Historical Publications and Records Commission (NHPRC) is the grant-making affiliate of NARA's national grants program. The Archivist of the United States chairs the commission and makes grants on its recommendation. The commission's 14 other members represent the President of the United States (two appointees), the U.S. Supreme Court, the Senate and House of Representatives, the U.S. Departments of State and Defense, the Librarian of Congress, the American Association for State and Local History, the American Historical Association, the Association for Documentary Editing, the National Association of Government Archives and Records Administrators, the Organization of American Historians, and the Society of American Archivists.

The commission carries out a statutory mission to ensure understanding of the nation's past by promoting the preservation and use of essential historical documents. The commission supports the creation and publication of documentary editions and research in the management and preservation of authentic electronic records, and it works in partnership with a national network of state archives and state historical records advisory boards to develop a national archival infrastructure. NHPRC grants help state and local governments, and archives, universities, historical societies, professional organizations, and other nonprofit organizations establish or strengthen archival programs, improve training and techniques, preserve and process records collections, and provide access to them through finding aids, digitization of collections, and documentary editions of the papers of significant historical figures and movements in American history. For more information about the commission, visit http://www.archives.gov/nhprc.

Information Security Oversight Office

The Information Security Oversight Office (ISOO) is responsible for policy and oversight of the government-wide security classification system and the National Industrial Security Program. ISOO is a component of NARA and receives policy and program guidance from the National Security Council. ISOO oversees the security classification programs (classification, safeguarding, and declassification) in both government and industry. It is also responsible for carrying out NARA's authorities and responsibilities as the executive agent for "controlled unclassified" information. ISOO contributes materially to the effective implementation of the government-wide security classification program and has a direct impact on the performance of thousands of government employees and contract personnel who work with classified national security information.

For more information on ISOO, visit http://www.archives.gov/isoo.

Federal Library and Information Center Committee

101 Independence Ave. S.E., Washington, DC 20540-4935
202-707-4800, fax 202-707-4818, e-mail flicc@loc.gov

Blane K. Dessy
Executive Director

Highlights of the Year

FLICC welcomed its new permanent executive director, Blane K. Dessy, in June 2010, following the retirement of Charles Stanhope, who had served as acting executive director for the first half of the fiscal year. Dessy previously was director of the U.S. Department of Justice Library staff.

The FLICC working groups completed an ambitious agenda in fiscal year (FY) 2010. The Human Resources Working Group launched its formal mentoring and coaching program initiative and held its third annual networking fair for those interested in positions as federal librarians. The Education Working Group presented a variety of seminars, workshops, and institutes on such topics as gray literature, content management, and writing for the Web.

In conjunction with the working groups, FLICC offered a total of 32 seminars, workshops, and lunchtime discussions to nearly 1,500 members of the federal library and information center community.

FLICC's cooperative network, FEDLINK, continued to enhance its fiscal operations while providing its members with $87.3 million in transfer-pay services, $6.7 million in direct-pay services, and an estimated $34.9 million in Direct Express services, saving federal agencies more than $17.6 million in vendor volume discounts and approximately $17.7 million more in cost avoidance. On average, this saved federal agencies 20 percent on their information purchases and 80 percent on their purchasing time requirements.

FLICC's budgeting efforts projected both costs and revenue for FY 2011, looking at both private sector and historic costs based on vendor and Government Accountability Office (GAO) predictions. After examining FEDLINK program growth and realized savings through program management and program reserves, FLICC/FEDLINK's governing bodies recommended that fees remain the same in FY 2011.

FEDLINK gave federal agencies cost-effective access to automated information retrieval services for online research, cataloging, and resource sharing. FEDLINK members procured print serials, electronic journals, books and other publications, document delivery, and digitization and preservation services via Library of Congress/FEDLINK contracts with more than 120 major vendors. The program obtained further discounts through consortia and enterprise-wide licenses for journals, aggregated information retrieval services, and electronic books. New this year are foreign language software vendors, expanded book and electronic database vendors, and an integrated library system for the National Defense University.

Quarterly Membership Meetings

FLICC membership focused its quarterly meetings on a variety of broad federal information topics including "Collection Development Issues at the Library of Congress: Building Resources for Federal Agencies"; a panel presentation on "Major Initiatives and Issues in Federal Libraries" with a legislative update from Wendy Ginsburg of the Congressional Research Service; a report on the OCLC Record Use Policy Task Force and the Unified Search Project by Chris Cole of the National Agricultural Library; and overviews on Environmental Protection Agency (EPA) libraries, the American Library Association (ALA) Midwinter Meeting, and the Special Libraries Association (SLA) Military Libraries Division.

FLICC Executive Board

The FLICC Executive Board focused its efforts on a number of initiatives relating to the FLICC/FEDLINK Business Plan and planned 2011 environmental scan, the EPA Advisory Board's recommendations for EPA libraries, gray literature issues, Library of Congress collection development, and federal library surveys. The board agreed to review its bylaws and established FEDGrey, its new working group on federal agencies and gray literature.

FLICC Working Groups

Awards

To honor the many ways in which federal libraries, librarians, and library technicians fulfill the information demands of government, business, research, scholarly communities, and the public, the Awards Working Group administered a series of national awards for federal librarianship.

Winners of the FY 2009 Awards, awarded in FY 2010, were:

- Federal Library/Information Center of the Year (large library/information center, with a staff of 11 or more federal and/or contract employees). National Institutes of Health (NIH) Library, Bethesda, Maryland; (small library/information center) Gorgas Memorial Library, Walter Reed Army Institute of Research
- Federal Librarian of the Year. Eleanor S. Uhlinger, university librarian, Dudley Knox Library, Naval Postgraduate School, Monterey, California
- Federal Library Technician of the Year. Gary B. Baker, Army Counterintelligence Center, Fort Meade, Maryland

Budget and Finance

The FLICC Budget and Finance Working Group developed the FY 2011 FEDLINK budget and fee structure in the spring quarter. The group produced an online budget questionnaire for FEDLINK members and used the results to verify assumptions for the FY 2011 budget. The final budget for FY 2011 held membership fees steady for transfer-pay customers to 6 percent on amounts exceeding $100,000; fees remain 6.75 percent below $100,000 and 4 percent on amounts exceeding $1,000,000. Direct-pay fees remained at FY 2009 levels, as did Direct Express fees of 0.75 percent for all participating commercial online information services vendors. Library of Congress officials approved the budget in September 2010.

Consortia and Interagency Cooperative Activities

Consortia activities concentrated on establishing support of CENDI, an interagency working group of senior scientific and technical information (STI) managers from 14 U.S. federal agencies representing 97 percent of the federal research and development budget.

Education

During FY 2010 the Education Working Group, in concert with other FLICC working groups, sponsored 32 seminars, workshops, brokered conferences, and lunchtime discussions for members of the federal library and information center community. These programs covered such topics as "second life," marketing for libraries, writing for the Web, federal appropriations law, and gray literature. The week-long Institute for Federal Library Technicians focused on developing competencies for federal library technicians.

The working group sponsored a series of orientations to help federal librarians become acquainted with a variety of institutions and collections in the Washington, D.C., area. They included the National Transportation Library, Census Bureau Library, National Geographic Society Library, Law Library of Congress, and Executive Office of the President Library.

The group continued to promote federal librarianship to new library school graduates and other job seekers by cosponsoring a fourth annual Careers in Federal Libraries preconference event at the ALA 2010 Annual Conference in Washington. A total of 75 registrants (students, new librarians, mid-career librarians) took part in the preconference, which covered basic advice about federal applications, interviews, and the selection process. More than 80 registered when the group cosponsored this program for the first time during the ALA Midwinter Meeting in Boston.

Human Resources

The Human Resources Working Group spent the year designing the FLICC Mentoring and Coaching Program and the FLICC Job Fair. The group created guidelines for the Mentoring and Coaching Program and drafted Web application forms and began database development.

In August the working group's Careers in Federal Libraries program attracted 350 registrants and vendors from nearly 25 agencies. The program also featured a series of well-attended sessions on résumé writing, federal applications, interviews, and the selection process.

Integrated Library System

The information gathered by the ad hoc Integrated Library System (ILS) working group was used in a pilot project to procure a new ILS for the National Defense University.

Libraries and Emerging Technologies

The Libraries and Emerging Technologies working group focused its discussions on a variety of topics that ranged from cybersecurity problems to ways to make content available to teleworkers or those working at remote locations. The group also reviewed federal efforts to ensure continuity of operations (e.g., proxy servers, electronic licensing issues), e-books, Web scale discovery solutions, electronic records management, cooperative systems, integrated systems, federated search technologies, and the impact of emerging technologies on the changing physical shape of libraries.

Nominating

The FLICC Nominating Working Group oversaw the 2010 election process for FLICC rotating members, FLICC Executive Board members, the FEDLINK Advisory Council (FAC), and a FEDLINK delegate to the OCLC Members Council. Librarians representing a variety of federal agencies agreed to place their names in nomination for these positions.

Preservation and Digitization

By the end of the fiscal year, the Preservation Working Group and the Disaster Preparedness Working Group combined to encompass all areas concerned with preservation of federal cultural and intellectual resources, including traditional library preservation and reformatting, digitization, and disaster preparedness. The working group sponsored two workshops for the Library of Congress, "Materials Science for Conservators" and "Library Binding: A Review of Principles and Practices." The digitization survey committee continued work on its survey of digitization in federal libraries. The chair of the committee presented preliminary findings in several venues, most recently for the new workshop series "Issues and Answers in Digitization." The Disaster Preparedness Working Group continued to oversee the Safety Net, the Washington, D.C., regional federal network for disaster response and also sponsored two educational programs—"FLICC Disaster Preparedness Update," which informed members about recent activities of three local organizations concerned with emergency preparedness, and "Can We Relax Yet? Assessing the Risks to Library Collections and Operations." Members also updated the FLICC online finding aid for information resources on disaster preparedness.

Executive Director's Office

In addition to strategic planning, budgeting, and administrative efforts, the executive director's office hosted visitors from the Netherlands, Denmark, Germany, South

Korea, and Japan, all of whom were interested in emulating FLICC/FEDLINK concepts. The executive director also served on the search committee for a new National Agricultural Library director and on the OCLC Review Board.

Additional outreach efforts included serving as a program moderator for the ALA Careers Workshop, supporting the American Association of Law Libraries' Federal Law Librarians' caucus, and attending the sessions on e-Content and the World Future Society to prepare for FLICC's environmental scan.

Publications and Education Office

In FY 2010 FLICC continued its publication program as a digital communication provider and used the FEDLIB listserv to communicate critical advocacy and program information to more than 3,000 electronic subscribers.

FLICC revised mission-critical materials and developed targeted resources to support the FEDLINK program, including the FLICC authorization, meetings on revising the FEDLINK member handbook, and five FEDLINK information alerts. FLICC also produced the minutes of the four FY 2010 FLICC Quarterly Meetings and six FLICC Executive Board meetings, and all FLICC education program promotional and support materials. Publications and Education also produced 25 FLICC meeting announcements to promote FLICC education programs, FEDLINK membership and OCLC users' meetings, brown-bag discussions, and education institutes, along with badges, programs, certificates of completion, and other supporting materials.

FLICC staff members continued to convert all publications, announcements, alerts, member materials, meeting minutes, and working group resources into HTML and pdf formats. Staff members maintained the Web links throughout the FLICC/FEDLINK Web site, worked on quality assurance efforts with Library Services and the Office of Strategic Initiatives, and enhanced and expanded the site via an inter-unit Web team of content, design, editorial, and technical personnel. Staff also participated in the Federal Consortium on Second Life as part of ongoing efforts to influence federal agency use of Web 2.0 emerging technologies.

Distance-learning offerings were heightened through the use of Web conferencing software for a number of events, and electronic versions of PowerPoint and other presentation materials were incorporated to enhance access to the resources available at educational programs. To make the discussions and presentations at the FLICC quarterly membership meetings available for members at remote locations, staff members used Web conferencing services to offer live and interactive attendance to these and other meetings to remote participants.

In collaboration with FEDLINK Network Operations staff members, publications staff continued to offer dynamic resources for the FEDLINK Membership Meetings, pricing data, and many other new documents, including an updated FEDLINK serials handbook, promotional program fact sheets, and a variety of training resources. Staff members also worked with Library of Congress Contracts and Grants staff to make electronic versions of FEDLINK's requests for proposals (RFPs) available online for prospective vendors.

During FY 2010 publications staff continued to support the Member Services Unit and its Online Registration/Online Interagency Agreement (IAG) system. Staff redesigned and updated online registration Web resources, revised the online registration booklet, and began efforts to update the FEDLINK member handbook to enable members to achieve seamless fiscal year transitions and manage their accounts effectively.

FLICC demonstrated its ongoing commitment to library technicians' continuing education by hosting its Institute for Federal Library Technicians and its annual teleconference series "Soaring to . . . Excellence," produced by the College of DuPage. Federal and academic librarians also joined FLICC professionals to discuss various areas of librarianship, including virtual reference, preservation and disaster preparedness, Web writing and content management, and federal appropriations law. The ongoing FLICC "Great Escapes" series returned in FY 2010 with tours of the Executive Office of the President, the National Transportation Library, the Census Bureau Library, the Naval Observatory Library, and the Law Library of Congress.

FLICC also provided organizational, promotional, and logistical support for FEDLINK meetings and events including the FEDLINK Fall and Spring Membership Meetings, one FEDLINK OCLC Users Group meeting, and 82 vendor presentations with 411 customers attending.

Staff members also continued to support a variety of initiatives and projects of all FLICC governing bodies, including meetings, listservs, projects, graphic design initiatives, surveys, and the development of multimedia resource materials.

FEDLINK

During FY 2010 the Federal Library and Information Network (FEDLINK) continued to give federal agencies cost-effective access to an array of automated information-retrieval services for online research, cataloging, information management and resource sharing. FEDLINK members also procured print and electronic journals, print and electronic books, sound recordings, audiovisual materials, document delivery, technical processing services, digitization, and preservation and conservation services via Library of Congress/FEDLINK contracts with more than 120 major vendors. The program obtained further discounts for customers through consortia and enterprise-wide licenses for journals, aggregated information retrieval services, and books. Staff welcomed a consortia coordinator on detail for a year to assist in investigating more opportunities for group discounts and expanded access to content and services.

FEDLINK issued RFPs for both serials subscription services and monograph acquisitions, awarding agreements with five subscription agents and 30 book jobbers. FEDLINK developed a new service category, online language learning systems, issuing an RFP and awarding agreements with four companies and an integrated library system for one agency. FEDLINK also worked with CENDI, an interagency working group of senior scientific and technical information (STI) managers from 14 U.S. federal agencies representing 97 percent of the federal research and development budget.

FEDLINK awarded nine new contracts for electronic retrieval services and assisted seven agencies in their use of preservation contracts to digitize and conserve special collections, and create related metadata. It assisted one agency in the procurement of a software application for managing digital collections locally. Staff also assisted five agencies as they began to work with Internet Archive to create digital archives, and supported ongoing projects for five more agencies. They assisted two more agencies in procuring contract cataloging services.

The FEDLINK Advisory Council met six times during the fiscal year. In addition to its general oversight activities, the council provided valuable insight into trends in the information industry and supported adoption of the proposed FY 2011 budget.

The annual fall FEDLINK Membership Meeting featured an overview of virtual reference options and best practices. The spring FEDLINK Membership Meeting featured MaryBeth Dowdell of the Naval Research Laboratory, chair of the FLICC Budget and Finance Working Group, who presented the proposed budget for FY 2011 and an overview of the U.S. test of Resource Description and Access (RDA). FAC members reported on key projects at their libraries.

In the area of outreach, FLICC/FEDLINK staff continued to support Web conferencing via the Elluminate application and produced a monthly electronic newsletter to communicate training opportunities and items of interest relating to contracts and program activities.

Staff highlighted services at national conferences including those of ALA, the Military Librarians Workshop, and SLA, as well as regional events such as the Government Accountability Office Expo. FEDLINK staff also assisted the ALA Federal and Armed Forces Librarians Round Table (FAFLRT) in tracking legislative initiatives affecting federal libraries. During ALA's Annual Conference in Washington, D.C., FLICC cosponsored with FAFLRT a very successful session on careers in federal libraries.

Staff members participated in additional national conferences, workshops, and meetings, including CENDI, the American Society for Information Science and Technology (ASIS&T), the National Federation of Abstracting and Indexing Services (NFAIS), the Military Librarians Workshop, Computers in Libraries, Internet Librarian, and the DTIC 2009 Conference. They also represented federal libraries' needs at national discussions focused on disaster recovery and preservation best practices, including presenting a paper at the digital curation curriculum symposium DigCCurr 2009: Digital Curation Practice, Promise, and Prospects.

FEDLINK negotiated discounted rates for several national conferences with Information Today, Inc: 253 attendees registered through FEDLINK to attend Computers in Libraries 2010, saving the government nearly $70,000; a total of 29 members attended WebSearch University, saving the government $5,000; a total of 17 members registered for the Internet Librarian conference, for a savings of $4,000, and 6 FEDLINK members registered for the KMWorld conference, for a savings of $1,200.

FEDLINK Fiscal Operations

FEDLINK continued to enhance its fiscal operations while providing its members with $87.3 million in transfer-pay services, $6.7 million in direct-pay services, and an estimated $34.9 million in Direct Express services, saving federal agencies more than $17.6 million in vendor volume discounts and approximately $17.7 million more in cost avoidance. On average, this saved federal agencies 20 percent on their information purchases and 80 percent on their purchasing time requirements.

Staff members supported business plan goals for improving processes and expanding the market for products and services through streamlining invoicing and payment process, meeting with selected vendors and members on requirements and acquisition of company data for electronic invoicing, and reviewing and analyzing the development documentation for the new FEDLINK Customer Account Management System (FCAMS) and the system upgrade development for the FEDLINK Subsidiary Financial System (SYMIN II).

FEDLINK Vendor Services

Total FEDLINK vendor service dollars for FY 2010 were made up of $87.3 million for transfer-pay customers, $6.7 million for direct-pay customers, and $34.9 million of estimated vendor billings to Direct Express customers. Database retrieval services, available only through the transfer-pay and Direct Express options, represented $81.8 million. Publication acquisition services, available through the transfer-pay and direct-pay options, represented $38.6 million. Within this service category, serials subscription services comprised the largest procurement for transfer-pay and direct-pay customers, representing $19.8 million and $6.5 million, respectively. Library support and other miscellaneous services, available only through the transfer-pay option, represented $8.3 million. Within this service category, bibliographic utilities constituted the largest procurement area, representing $5.1 million.

Accounts Receivable and Member Services

FEDLINK processed FY 2010 registrations from federal libraries, information centers, and other federal offices for a total of 401 signed interagency agreements (IAGs). In addition, FEDLINK processed 1,755 IAG amendments (909 for current-year and 846 for prior-year adjustments) for agencies that added, adjusted, or ended service funding. These IAGs and IAG amendments represented 6,476 individual service requests to begin, move, convert, or cancel service from FEDLINK vendors. FEDLINK executed service requests by generating 6,030 delivery orders that Library of Congress Contracts and Grants issued to vendors.

For FY 2010 alone, FEDLINK processed $87.3 million in service dollars for 2,005 transfer-pay accounts and $6.7 million in service dollars for 11 direct-pay accounts. Included in the above member service transactions were 3,647 member requests to move prior-year (no-year and multiyear) funds across fiscal year boundaries. These no-year and multiyear service request transactions represented an additional contracting volume of $28 million.

Transfer-Pay Accounts Payable Services

For transfer-pay users, FEDLINK processed 57,010 invoices for payment during FY 2010 for both current and prior-year orders. Staff members efficiently processed vendor invoices and earned $24,607 in discounts in excess of interest payment penalties levied for the late payment of invoices to FEDLINK vendors.

Direct Express Services

The FEDLINK Direct Express program now includes 61 vendors offering database retrieval services. The program is set up to provide customers procurement and payment options similar to the General Services Administration (GSA); vendors pay a quarterly service fee to FEDLINK based on customer billings for usage. Direct Express eliminates the process steps required of customers and vendors to set up an IAG for the direct purchase of online services. During FY 2010, the Direct Express program generated 64 percent of the fee revenue initially anticipated in the budget and the forecast for the fiscal year.

Financial Management, Reporting, and Control

FEDLINK successfully passed the Library of Congress Financial Audit of FY 2009 transactions and completed vulnerability assessments of program financial risks for Library Services. It continued to provide central accounting for customer agency account balances to meet U.S. Treasury Department reporting requirements. FEDLINK also completed all aspects of its revolving fund status reporting, including preparation, review, and forecasts of revenue and expenses for the accounting period.

National Center for Education Statistics Library Statistics Program

U.S. Department of Education, Institute of Education Sciences
Elementary/Secondary and Libraries Studies Division
1990 K St. N.W., Washington, DC 20006

Tai A. Phan
Program Director

In an effort to collect and disseminate more-complete statistical information about libraries, the National Center for Education Statistics (NCES) initiated a formal library statistics program in 1989 that included surveys on academic libraries, school library media centers, public libraries, and state libraries.* At the end of December 2007, the Public Libraries Survey and the State Library Agencies Survey were transferred to the Office of Library Programs of the Institute of Museum and Library Services (IMLS). The Academic Libraries Survey (ALS) and the School Library Media Centers Survey (SLMCS) continue to be administered and funded by NCES, under the leadership of Tai A. Phan, program director, Library Statistics Program. [For detailed information on the surveys now being handled by IMLS, see "Institute of Museum and Library Services Library Programs" in Part 2 and "Highlights of IMLS and NCES Surveys" in Part 4—*Ed.*]

The library surveys conducted by NCES are designed to provide comprehensive nationwide data on the status of libraries. Federal, state, and local officials, professional associations, and local practitioners use these surveys for planning, evaluating, and making policy. These data are also available to researchers and educators.

The NCES Library Statistics Program's Web site, http://nces.ed.gov/surveys/libraries, provides links to data search tools, data files, survey definitions, and survey designs for each survey. The two library surveys conducted by NCES—ALS and SLMCS—are described below.

Academic Libraries

The Academic Libraries Survey (ALS) provides descriptive statistics from approximately 3,800 academic libraries in the 50 states, the District of Columbia, and the outlying areas of the United States. NCES surveyed academic libraries on a three-year cycle between 1966 and 1988. From 1988 to 1998, the ALS was a component of the Integrated Postsecondary Education Data System (IPEDS), and was on a two-year cycle. Beginning with fiscal year 2000, the survey is no longer a component of IPEDS, but remains on a two-year cycle. IPEDS and ALS data can still be linked by the identification codes of the postsecondary education institutions. In aggregate, these data provide an overview of the status of academic libraries nationally and by state. The ALS collects data on libraries in the

*The authorization for the National Center for Education Statistics (NCES) to collect library statistics is included in the Education Sciences Reform Act of 2002 (PL 107-279), under Title I, Part C.

entire universe of degree-granting postsecondary institutions, using a Web-based data collection system.

The ALS has an established working group composed of representatives of the academic library community. Its mission is to improve data quality and the timeliness of data collection, processing, and release. NCES also works cooperatively in the collection of ALS data with the American Library Association and its Association of College and Research Libraries, the Association of Research Libraries, and academic libraries.

The ALS collects data on the number of academic libraries, operating expenditures, full-time-equivalent library staff, number of service outlets, collection size, circulation, interlibrary loans, number of public service hours, library visits, reference transactions, consortia services, number of presentations, attendance at presentations, electronic services, and information literacy. Academic libraries are also asked whether they provide reference services by e-mail or the Internet, have technology for patrons with disabilities, and whether documents are digitized by library staff.

An NCES First Look report, *Academic Libraries, 2008* (NCES 2010-348), was released on the NCES Web site in December 2009. The final data file and documentation for the 2008 ALS public use data file (NCES 2010-310) were released on the Web site at the same time. NCES has developed a Web-based peer analysis tool for the ALS called "Compare Academic Libraries," which currently uses the ALS 2008 data.

Additional information on academic library statistics is available from Tai A. Phan, National Center for Education Statistics, telephone 202-502-7431, e-mail tai.phan@ed.gov.

School Library Media Centers

National surveys of school library media centers in elementary and secondary schools in the United States were conducted in 1958, 1962, 1974, 1978, and 1986, 1993–1994, 1999–2000, 2003–2004, and 2007–2008. The 2007–2008 data was available in the summer of 2009.

NCES, with the assistance of the U.S. Bureau of the Census, conducts the School Library Media Centers Survey as part of the Schools and Staffing Survey (SASS). SASS is the nation's largest sample survey of teachers, schools and principals in U.S. K–12 public and private schools. Data from the school library media center questionnaire provide a national picture of public school library staffing, collections, expenditures, technology, and services. Results from the 2007–2008 survey can be found in *Public and Bureau of Indian Education Elementary and Secondary School Library Media Centers in the United States: 2007–08 Schools and Staffing Survey* (NCES 2009-322).

NCES also published a historical report about school libraries titled *Fifty Years of Supporting Children's Learning: A History of Public School Libraries and Federal Legislation from 1953–2000.* Drawn from more than 50 sources, this report presents descriptive data about public school libraries since 1953. Along with key characteristics of school libraries, the report also presents national and regional standards, and federal legislation affecting school library media centers.

Data from sample surveys are presented at the national, regional, and school levels, and by state.

NCES has included some library-oriented questions relevant to the library usage and skills of the parent and the teacher instruments of its Early Childhood Longitudinal Study (ECLS). For additional information, visit http://nces.ed.gov/ecls. Library items also appear in National Household Education Survey (NHES) instruments. For more information about that survey, visit http://nces.ed.gov/nhes.

NCES also included a questionnaire about high school library media centers in the Education Longitudinal Study of 2002 (ELS: 2002). This survey collected data from tenth graders about their schools, their school library media centers, their communities, and their home life. The report *School Library Media Centers: Selected Results from the Education Longitudinal Study of 2002 (ELS: 2002)* (NCES 2005-302) is available on the NCES Web site. For more information about this survey, visit http://nces.ed.gov/surveys/els2002.

Additional information on school library media center statistics is available from Tai A. Phan, National Center for Education Statistics, telephone 202-502-7431, e-mail tai.phan@ed.gov.

How to Obtain Printed and Electronic Products

Reports are currently published in the First Look format. First Look reports consist of a short collection of tables presenting state and national totals, a survey description, and data highlights. NCES also publishes separate more in-depth studies analyzing these data.

Internet Access

Many NCES publications (including out-of-print publications) and edited raw data files from the library surveys are available for viewing or downloading free of charge through the Electronic Catalog on the NCES Web site at http://nces.ed.gov/pubsearch.

Ordering Printed Products

Many NCES publications are also available in printed format. To order one free copy of recent NCES reports, contact the Education Publications Center (ED Pubs) at http://www.edpubs.org, by e-mail at edpubs@edpubs.ed.gov, by toll-free telephone at 877-4-ED-PUBS (877-433-7827) (TTY/TDD 877-576-7734), by fax at 703-605-6794, or by mail at ED Pubs, P.O. Box 22207, Alexandria, VA 22304.

Many publications are available through the Educational Resources Information Clearinghouse (ERIC) system. For more information on services and products, visit the EDRS Web site at http://www.eric.ed.gov.

Out-of-print publications and data files may be available through the NCES Electronic Catalog on the NCES Web site at http://nces.ed.gov/pubsearch or through one of the 1,250 Federal Depository Libraries throughout the United States. Use the NCES publication number included in the citations for publications and data files to quickly locate items in the NCES Electronic Catalog; use the GPO number to locate items in a Federal depository library.

Defense Technical Information Center

Fort Belvoir, VA 22060
World Wide Web http://www.dtic.mil

Sandy Schwalb
Public Affairs Officer

The Defense Technical Information Center (DTIC) marked its 65th anniversary in 2010. Formed in 1945 to collect and catalog scientific and technical documents from World War II, DTIC traces its beginnings to the Air Documents Division of the Air Technical Service (U.S. Army Air Corps). In the 21st century it continues to serve as a vital link in the transfer of information within the defense community.

DTIC offers access to more than 2 million publications for engineers, researchers, scientists, information professionals, and those in laboratories, universities, and the acquisition field. The center consists of six directorates and the Information Analysis Center (IAC) Program Management Office. Headquartered at Fort Belvoir, Virginia, DTIC has four regional offices, in Dayton, Albuquerque, Boston, and Los Angeles, and a satellite office in San Diego.

DTIC's mission is "to provide essential, technical, research, development, testing and evaluation information rapidly, accurately and reliably to support our DoD customers' needs." A Department of Defense (DoD) field activity, the center is in the office of the undersecretary of defense for acquisition, technology, and logistics, and reports to the assistant secretary of defense, research and engineering.

Reaching Customers

DTIC offers its suite of services to a diverse population of the defense community, but DTIC's customers can also be found in academia, the intelligence community, and foreign governments (through negotiated agreements with countries including Australia, Canada, France, Germany, the Netherlands, South Korea, and Britain), as well as military school students and faculty and the general public. Because of the nature of the information DTIC handles, users must qualify for its services.

DTIC's registered users include acquisition instructors, active duty military, congressional staff, DoD contractors, historians, librarians and other information professionals, logistics management specialists, business owners, security managers, and software engineers and developers.

Registered users can order documents directly from DTIC. Individuals who are not eligible to register with DTIC can order documents in the "unclassified, unlimited" category by contacting the National Technical Information Service (NTIS) at 800-553-NTIS (553-6847) or via http://www.ntis.gov.

Simplified Access

Late in 2010 DTIC successfully unveiled a seamless registration process. This enables DoD personnel and contractors with DoD-issued "common access cards" (CACs) immediate access to DoDTechipedia, DoD's science and technology wiki; Aristotle, DoD's professional networking tool; and "unclassified, limited" information in DTIC's collections through DTIC Online Access Controlled.

New users will automatically be registered for DTIC's products and services when they access a DTIC Web site for the first time with their CAC. Federal employees and contractors, potential defense contractors, and some academic institutions also qualify for registration with DTIC. Those without a CAC now have a simplified application process to complete. Once their application is verified, they will be able to get additional "unclassified, limited" information and to apply to upgrade their account to classified and export-controlled information. DTIC is the first component/organization within DoD to implement a seamless CAC registration.

Suite of Services

To ensure that the user has easier access to its material, DTIC has consolidated its resources into two Web sites: DTIC Online (available to the public at http://www.dtic.mil) and DTIC Online Access Controlled, a registration-only site. In addition, the organization has continued to expand its use of Web 2.0 technologies.

DoDTechipedia

Designed for use by the defense community, DoDTechipedia is a wiki application launched in 2008. It is a secure online system facilitating the sharing of knowledge and collaboration throughout the U.S. defense community. DoDTechipedia ensures greater transparency and communication among DoD scientists, engineers, program managers, and military service personnel. This tool helps members of the DoD community collaborate, identify solutions for technology challenges, and ensure that taxpayer dollars are spent efficiently. Among its numerous features are a live forum, a "sandbox" for users to practice posting and editing content, acronyms and definitions, technology areas where discussions about scientific and technical investment areas or enabling technology take place, interest area pages for DoD personnel and DoD contractors to work together on challenges and solutions, and capabilities to post blogs. DoDTechipedia use requires registration.

Aristotle

Aristotle, launched in August 2010, is the newest addition to DTIC's suite of services. It is a secure, Web-based professional networking tool designed for federal government and DoD employees and contractors in the science and technology community. Aristotle connects federal and DoD customers, users, and collaborators and provides for searching not only people but projects and topics. It offers an evolving snapshot of what is going on across the scientific and technical community. Use of Aristotle requires registration.

DTIC Online Access Controlled

This protected site is a gateway to DoD "unclassified, controlled" science and technology and research and engineering information. It contains resources from DTIC's former Research and Engineering portal and DoDTechipedia. Users of DTIC Online Access Controlled can get congressional budget information, DoD scientific and technical planning documents, the Biomedical Research Database, the Militarily Critical Technologies List, more than 2 million technical reports, research summaries, and numerous other resources, all free of charge.

Web Hosting Expertise

DTIC hosts more than 100 Web sites sponsored by components of the Office of the Secretary of Defense, military service headquarters organizations, and several defense agencies, among them the Federal Voting Assistance Program, Joint Chiefs of Staff, and Defense Prisoner of War/Mission Personnel Office. As a leader in information storage and retrieval, DTIC has been able to advise DoD components concerning policy, law, best practices, and security strategies that relate to the transmission and use of all types of information. This is an effective support program for senior-level planners and other users of information resources. The shared infrastructure allows many organizations to obtain technologies and resources that a single organization might not be able to afford on its own.

Iraqi Virtual Science Library

In June 2010 the Iraqi Virtual Science Library (IVSL) was formally transferred to Iraqi ownership and support. DTIC was an integral part of IVSL since its inception; its role was to oversee the design of the site and then to build, test, and host it from 2006. IVSL offers Iraqi scientists, engineers, and university students free-of-charge access to more than 17,000 full-text journal articles on developments in science and technology, online training and educational materials, and information about funding opportunities. The goal of the project is to ensure that Iraqi scientists and engineers can access information to help rebuild Iraq's infrastructure, since many scientific information sources were lost before and during the war. This was a successful public-private partnership that included several U.S. government agencies, 13 publishers of scientific journals, and technology companies.

Security of Information

A DTIC priority in handling information is to safeguard national security, export control, and intellectual property rights. While there is much publicly accessible material in the DTIC collection, some information is restricted by security classifications. DoD's scientific and technical information is always categorized (or "marked," the term used in the defense community) by the office that originates the document. This marking ("unclassified, controlled," "unclassified, unlimited," and so forth) determines how, and to whom, the information can be disseminated.

Resources

DTIC's holdings include technical reports on completed research; research summaries of planned, ongoing, and completed work; independent research and development summaries; defense technology transfer agreements; DoD planning documents; DoD directives and instructions; conference proceedings; security classification guides; command histories; and special collections that date back to World War II. DoD-funded researchers are required to search DTIC's collections to ensure that they do not "reinvent the wheel" and undertake unnecessary or redundant research.

Primary Collections

The DTIC Technical Reports database contains more than 2 million reports in print, nonprint (CDs, DVDs, software, data files, databases, and video recordings), and electronic formats conveying the results of defense-sponsored research, development, and test and evaluation efforts. It includes journal articles, DoD-sponsored patent applications, studies, analyses, open source literature from other countries, conference proceedings, and theses. During 2010 nearly 20 percent more technical reports were processed than in 2009, and the processing time was cut in half.

The Research Summaries database contains descriptions of DoD research that provide information on technical content, responsible individuals and organizations, principal investigators, and funding sources at the work unit level. Available only to certain registered users, this collection is controlled by individual access restrictions. It consists of more than 315,000 active and inactive summaries from 1965 to the present.

The Independent Research and Development (IR&D) database contains more than 175,000 descriptions of research and development projects initiated by DoD contractors but not performed under contract and independent of DoD control. The database includes basic and applied research, technology development efforts, and systems and concept formulation studies. Defense contractors and potential contractors are encouraged to submit project descriptions to the IR&D database. The proprietary IR&D database is restricted to registered users and is used to identify contractors with expertise in areas of interest to DoD and to avoid DoD duplication of industry research and development efforts.

Information Sources

DTIC information is derived from many sources, including DoD organizations (civilian and military) and DoD contractors; U.S. government organizations and their contractors; nonprofit organizations working on DoD scientific, research, and engineering activities; academia; and foreign governments. DTIC accepts information in print, nonprint (CDs and DVDs), and electronically over the World Wide Web. DTIC obtains information from the defense community, for the defense community, about defense and beyond. Having a full range of science and technology and research and development information within the DTIC collection ensures that technological innovations are linked to defense development and acquisition efforts. New research projects can begin with the highest level of information available. This avoids duplication of effort, maximizing the use of DoD project dollars.

Information Analysis Centers

The Information Analysis Centers (IACs) are research and analysis organizations established by DoD and managed by DTIC to help researchers, engineers, scientists, and program managers use existing scientific and technical information. IACs identify, analyze, and use scientific and technical information in specific technology areas and develop information and analysis products for the defense science and engineering communities. Staffed by experienced technical area scientists, engineers, and information specialists, they help users locate and analyze scientific and technical information in specific subject areas.

Products and services produced by IACs include announcements of reports relevant to the particular IAC's field of interest, authoritative bibliographic search reports, latest scientific and engineering information on specific technical subjects, consultation with or referral to recognized technical experts, and status of current technologies. Many of the products and services are offered free of charge. See http://iac.dtic.mil.

The DTIC-managed IACs (12/10) are AMMTIAC: Advanced Materials, Manufacturing and Testing; CBRNIAC: Chemical, Biological, Radiological, Nuclear Defense; CPIAC: Chemical Propulsion; DACS: Data and Analysis Center for Software; IATAC: Information Assurance Technology Analysis Center; MSIAC: Modeling and Simulation; RIAC: Reliability; SENSIAC: Sensors; SURVIAC: Survivability; and WSTIAC: Weapons Systems Technology.

Annual Conference

DTIC held its 36th annual conference March 22–24, 2010, in Alexandria, Virginia. A record-setting event, it attracted more than 400 attendees, many of them first-timers. The sessions focused on DTIC's support to the combatant commands, social networking, Web 2.0 tools, virtual worlds, and developments in information security management.

DTIC's 2011 annual conference was a virtual event, taking place April 4–5 at DTIC headquarters and viewable over a secure DoD network, although a limited number of people were able to participate in person. The theme was "DTIC: Your Authoritative Source of Defense Information for the Front Line and Homeland."

Boot Camps and Webinars

During 2010 DTIC revamped its training program to provide targeted sessions for DoD laboratories and related organizations. "DTIC Boot Camp: S&T Resources for Labs" offers hands-on training, including sessions on DTIC Online Access Controlled, DoDTechipedia, and Aristotle, as well as instruction on submitting documents and leveraging the use of the DTIC IACs. Demand for training increased during 2010. DTIC users have requested additional training sessions at Fort Belvoir and at their own locations. Another facet of DTIC's free training was the introduction of the "DoDTechipedia 101" Webinars. DTIC has also produced online tutorials to help individuals learn how to use the wiki's key features.

Traditional classroom training is also available to customers at DTIC headquarters and at the regional offices in Dayton, Boston, Albuquerque, and Los

Angeles. Additionally, customized and on-site courses can be provided, with travel expenses paid by the hosting organization. The training curriculum includes searching DTIC databases, and DoD Scientific and Technical Information (STINFO) management.

DTIC Review

The *DTIC Review* (http://www.dtic.mil/dtic/stresources/dticreview/index.html) provides the full text of selected technical reports and a bibliography of other references of interest in a single publication. Each volume features a sampling of documents from the DTIC collection on a specific topic of current interest. Topics highlighted in 2010 included "Maritime Domain Awareness," "Airships," and "WMD: The Terrorist Threat."

DTIC Regional Offices

DTIC's four regional offices provide a range of products and services including reference, registration, and assistance in accessing the center's numerous offerings. There is also a satellite office in San Diego that focuses on human systems and biomedical research and development and provides information support to small businesses.

Midwestern Regional Office
Wright-Patterson Air Force Base, Ohio
Tel. 937-255-7905, fax 937-986-7002
E-mail dayton@dtic.mil

Northeastern Regional Office
Hanscom Air Force Base, Massachusetts
Tel. 781-377-2413, fax 781-377-5627
E-mail boston@dtic.mil

Southwestern Regional Office
Kirtland Air Force Base, New Mexico
Tel. 505-846-6797, fax 505-846-6799
E-mail albuq@dtic.mil

Western Regional Office
El Segundo, California
Tel. 310-653-2483, fax 310-363-2159
E-mail losangel@dtic.mil

DTIC-A, San Diego
NAS North Island
Box 357011
San Diego, CA 92135-7011
Tel. 619-545-7384
E-mail dticasd@dticam.dtic.mil

Note: DTIC is a registered service mark of the Defense Technical Information Center.

National Library of Education

Knowledge Utilization Division
National Center for Education Evaluation and Regional Assistance
Institute of Education Sciences, U.S. Department of Education
400 Maryland Ave. S.W., Washington, DC 20202
World Wide Web http://ies.ed.gov/ncee/projects/nat_ed_library.asp

Christina Dunn

Director, National Library of Education
202-219-1012, e-mail christina.dunn@ed.gov

The U.S. Department of Education's National Library of Education (NLE), which marked 16 years of service in 2010, is the primary resource center for education information in the federal government, serving the research needs of the education community through the Education Resources Information Center, better known as ERIC, and the Education Department Research Library/Reference Center (RL/RC). These programs are the center for the collection, preservation, discovery, and retrieval of education information, especially information produced by and for the U.S. Department of Education. The program resides in the department's Institute of Education Sciences and reports to the Commissioner for Education Evaluation and Regional Assistance through the Knowledge Utilization Division.

Created by Public Law 103-227, the Educational Research, Development, Dissemination, and Improvement Act of 1994, and reauthorized under Public Law 107-279, the Education Sciences Reform Act of 2002, NLE is directed to perform four primary functions:

- Collect and archive information, including products and publications developed through, or supported by, the Institute of Education Sciences; and other relevant and useful education-related research, statistics, and evaluation materials and other information, projects, and publications that are consistent with scientifically valid research or the priorities and mission of the institute, and developed by the department, other federal agencies, or entities
- Provide a central location within the federal government for information about education
- Provide comprehensive reference services on matters relating to education to employees of the Department of Education and its contractors and grantees, other federal employees, and members of the public
- Promote greater cooperation and resource sharing among providers and repositories of education information in the United States

NLE's programs—ERIC and RL/RC—share these functions by complementing and supporting one another and by eliminating duplication of effort. ERIC collects and archives information and provides a central location within the federal government for information about education, while RL/RC offers comprehensive reference services. Both address promoting cooperation and resource sharing, although in different ways. To carry out these responsibilities, the NLE director, who is required by the legislation to be qualified in library science, is assisted by six federal staff, including the ERIC director, as well as ERIC and NLE contractors.

ERIC, established in 1966, pre-existed NLE, but became part of the library upon its creation in 1994. ERIC is responsible for providing a comprehensive, easy-to-use, searchable, Internet-based bibliographic and full-text database of education research and information for educators, researchers, and the general public. Its digital library is centered around a collection of more than 1.3 million bibliographic records of education resources, including journal articles, books, research syntheses, conference papers, technical reports, policy papers, and other education-related materials, and more than 330,000 full-text documents. In 2010 ERIC users conducted more than 125 million searches through the ERIC Web site (http://www.eric.ed.gov); and commercial and noncommercial sites. Because ERIC serves as the major public program and outreach arm of NLE, it is covered separately. [See the following article, "Education Resources Information Center"—*Ed.*] This article, providing only a brief overview of NLE, is devoted to the activities of RL/RC.

Research Library/Reference Center

RL/RC has as its prime responsibility providing information services to agency staff and contractors, the general public, other government agencies, and other libraries. Located in the agency's headquarters building in Washington, D.C., it houses current and historical collections and archives of information on education issues, research, statistics, and policy; there is a special emphasis on agency publications and contractor reports, as well as current and historical federal education legislation. RL/RC makes a special effort to support Institute of Education Sciences programs by collecting journals indexed in the ERIC database, and through research supporting the What Works Clearinghouse and the Regional Educational Laboratories. Because of space considerations and increasing customer demand, RL/RC is moving toward a predominately electronic collection; to date, about 98 percent of current journal subscriptions are received in electronic format, and about two-thirds of all monographs added to the collection in 2010 were electronic—about 2,100 new electronic titles as opposed to 320 paper titles.

In addition to providing more electronic books and journals, RL/RC provides agency staff with desktop access to a comprehensive collection of digital information resources covering the subjects of education, psychology, sociology, public policy, and law. To promote its information services, manage customer requests, and grow its own internal information bank, RL/RC employs virtual reference technology to provide reference services to department staff and contractors and to support the activities of the IES Regional Educational Laboratories Virtual Reference Desk Program. In 2010 RL/RC continued to deliver about 95 percent of its products and services in digital formats, with usage increasing about 2 percent over 2009. Promoting and improving services remains a primary consideration in achieving RL/RC initiatives.

With a staff of 14—five full-time federal staff and nine contract librarians—RL/RC has two units: Collection Management (formerly Technical Services and

Serials Management) and Public Services (formerly Reference and Document Delivery). Staffing and organizational structure are kept flexible to support changing needs and to allow for fast, competent response to customer requests, institutional initiatives, and advances in technology. The RL/RC primary customer base includes about 5,000 department staff nationwide; department contractors performing research; education organizations and media; and academic, special, and government libraries. All services are supported by NLE's budget for RL/RC, which in fiscal year 2010 was $2 million.

Use of the Library

During 2010 RL/RC use was similar to that of the previous three years, with about 18,500 requests received. Document delivery and interlibrary loan continue to show the greatest growth, with requests for reference assistance remaining constant. While most information requests continue to come from the general public, most staff time (about 72 percent) is devoted to responding to the information needs of department staff and contractors as their requests tend to be complex, often requiring services that extend over several weeks or months. This group generated around 6,800 requests or about 37 percent of all requests received in 2010. It also accessed more electronic journal articles and conducted more database searches than in 2009, showing an increase in usage of 6.1 percent. With most access taking place on the RL/RC portal, usage of the "Ask a Librarian" feature nearly doubled over the previous year.

The general public generated almost 7,000 requests—about 38 percent of the total number of requests—down slightly from 2009; most were for reference assistance. Of these, around 12 percent were referrals generated by the department's EDPubs service, the 800-USA-LEARN service, Regional Education Laboratories Virtual Reference Desk, and ERIC Help Desk. The characteristics of public users remain almost the same as in previous years. Over 71.5 percent of the general public contacting RL/RC in 2010 were K–12 educators, students in institutions of higher education, or researchers; 26 percent were parents; and about 2.5 percent were unknown. As in 2009 the majority of these customers continued to access RL/RC by telephone (55 percent) and e-mail (43.2 percent); less than 1.8 percent visited the facility.

Academic, government, and special libraries make up RL/RC's third-largest user group; together they generated slightly more than 4,700 requests (25 percent of total requests), which was somewhat higher than in 2009. Most requests continued to be for interlibrary loan services. While in the past the most frequently requested items were historical documents of all types (such as policy, research, and contractor reports, including those on ERIC microfiche) and other publications released prior to 1985, in 2010 more than 50 percent of all requests were for more recently published documents (since 1990), with libraries in institutions of higher education initiating the largest number of requests. About 79 percent of RL/RC's library customers are institutions of higher education, followed by special libraries, including law libraries (15 percent) and government libraries (5 percent). Public and school libraries represent less than 1 percent. Outreach to academic libraries includes interlibrary loan and a gift books program that has become increasingly popular in recent years with more than 200 libraries participating in 2010.

Collections

RL/RC's collection focus has remained the same since its creation: education issues, with an emphasis on research and policy; and related topics, including law, public policy, economics, urban affairs, sociology, history, philosophy, psychology, cognitive development, and library and information science. In 2010 RL/RC added about 2,100 new electronic titles and 320 paper titles to its monograph collection. This represents a significant change in collection development, as in 2009 the RL/RC added about 2,650 print monographs and 404 electronic publications, excluding agency publications. The number of paid journal subscriptions increased to 418, up from 322 in 2009. With 98 percent of current subscriptions being desktop-accessible, staff demand for journals has increased, which explains why RL/RC added 96 new titles during the year.

RL/RC has maintained special collections of historical documents associated with its parent agency, having a complete collection of ERIC microfiche; research reports supporting the work of the What Works Clearinghouse and special panels; and publications of or relating to the department's predecessor agencies, including the National Institute of Education and the U.S. Office of Education in the Department of Health, Education, and Welfare. These collections include reports, studies, manuals, statistical publications, speeches, and policy papers. With the digitization of the ERIC microfiche collection of about 340,000 documents, RL/RC now has electronic access to the full text of all ERIC microfiche indexed between 1966 and 1992. In contrast, the ERIC Web site at http://www.ed.eric.gov provides public access only to those documents for which copyright clearance was obtained—the full text of nearly 192,000 documents or almost 55 percent of the collection. All digitized documents from the ERIC microfiche collection are available through interlibrary loan upon request. RL/RC also serves as a federal depository library under the Government Printing Office program.

Services

RL/RC provides reference and other information services, including legislative reference and statistical information services, to department staff and contractors, to the education community at large, and to the general public, as well as providing document delivery services to department staff and contractors and interlibrary loan services to other libraries and government agencies. Services to agency staff and contractors continue to grow, resulting in additional resources continuing to be focused on serving this community. Through its involvement in the Regional Education Laboratories Virtual Reference Desk, the library provides resources and reference services to researchers and end users alike.

On another front, RL/RC has seen an increased interest in news feeds by various offices and individuals within the agency, especially by those with responsibility for communications; during 2010 there were five new requests, bringing the total number of daily/weekly news feeds to nine. In addition, RL/RC tracks research on specific topics for agency and contractor staff and publishes, at least weekly, an electronic newsletter on education research of general interest to agency staff.

Of the nearly 7,000 inquiries from the general public received in 2010, most pertained to the same issues that were of interest in the previous year: agency programs, student achievement and assessment, charter schools, teacher quality and preparation, early childhood education, and national statistics. Requests for information on No Child Left Behind dropped from the previous year; however, new to this list is the reauthorization of the Elementary and Secondary Education Act (ESEA). Other topics of public interest in 2010 included agency policy and budget; federal funding to states and local school districts; current education issues in the news, such as Common Core State Standards, local school funding, technology in the schools, community colleges, after-school and summer programming, school choice, and failing schools; teacher certification requirements; school safety; and bullying and cyberbullying.

Agency staff conducted more than 31,000 searches of RL/RC's databases. Results of these searches coupled with department staff and contractor requests for specific titles generated requests for almost 7,100 journal articles and other documents. Although more full-text journal articles are available to agency staff online, the number of requests for journal articles and other documents continues to grow steadily, up from the 6,800 requests in 2009 and the 6,000 requests in 2008. The library filled about 65 percent of requests from its own collections, with the remaining 35 percent filled from other sources—about 8 percent were borrowed from other libraries, 19 percent came from document delivery services, and 8 percent were purchased from vendors and sponsoring organizations. Increasingly, RL/RC has been able to fill more staff and contractor requests from its own collections; this was especially true during 2010 because of the addition of 96 new journal titles. Also, with the increased acquisition of e-books, RL/RC is able to provide access to new publications more quickly than in previous years.

The U.S. Department of Education Research Library/Reference Center can be contacted by e-mail at library@ed.gov. The library's reference desk is available by telephone at 800-424-1616 (toll free), 202-205-5015, 202-205-5019, or 202-205-7561 (TTY); and by fax at 202-401-0547. Located in the department's headquarters building at 400 Maryland Ave. S.W, it is open from 9 A.M. to 5 P.M. weekdays, except federal holidays.

Education Resources Information Center

National Library of Education
National Center for Education Evaluation and Regional Assistance
Institute of Education Sciences, U.S. Department of Education
400 Maryland Ave. S.W., Washington, DC 20202
World Wide Web http://www.eric.ed.gov

Luna Levinson
Director, ERIC Program

202-208-2321, e-mail Luna.Levinson@ed.gov

The Education Resources Information Center (ERIC) is the world's largest education library, featuring an electronic collection of more than 1.3 million bibliographic records from 1966 to the present along with about 332,000 full-text documents. The U.S. Department of Education's Institute of Education Sciences (IES) administers ERIC as part of the National Library of Education.

Background

For decades ERIC has served the information needs of schools, institutions of higher education, educators, parents, administrators, policymakers, researchers, and public and private entities through a variety of library services and formats, first in paper copy, then in microfiche, and today exclusively in electronic format. ERIC provides service directly to the public via its Web site, http://www.eric.ed.gov.

With a 44-year history of public service, ERIC is one of the oldest programs in the U.S. Department of Education. As the world's largest education resource, it is distinguished by two hallmarks: free dissemination of bibliographic records, and the collection of gray literature such as research conference papers and government contractor reports.

The authorizing legislation for ERIC is part of the Education Sciences Reform Act of 2002, Public Law 107-279. This legislation envisioned ERIC subject areas or topics (previously covered by the ERIC Clearinghouses) as part of the totality of enhanced information dissemination to be conducted by the Institute of Education Sciences. In addition, information dissemination includes material on closing the achievement gap and educational practices that improve academic achievement and promote learning. The Department of Education awarded a single contract for the operation of ERIC to Computer Sciences Corporation (CSC) in 2009.

ERIC Mission

The ERIC mission is to provide a comprehensive, easy-to-use, searchable, Internet-based bibliographic and full-text database of education research and information for educators, researchers, and the general public. Terms defining the ERIC mission are explained as follows:

- *Comprehensive,* consisting of journal articles and non-journal materials, including materials not published by commercial publishers, that are directly related to education
- *Easy-to-use and searchable,* allowing database users to find the information they need quickly and efficiently
- *Electronic,* making ERIC operations accessible to the maximum extent feasible and linking to publishers and commercial sources of journal articles
- *Bibliographic and full-text,* with bibliographic records conveying the information that users need in a simple and straightforward manner, and whenever possible including full-text journal articles and non-journal materials free of charge

Following this mission, the overarching goal of ERIC is to increase the availability and quality of research and information for ERIC users.

Activities that fulfill the ERIC mission are broadly categorized as collection development, content authorizations and agreements, acquisitions and processing, database and Web site operations, and communications. These five functions continue to evolve and improve as suggestions and guidance are received from a variety of sources including public comments and the ERIC Steering Committee, Content Experts, and Library Committee.

Selection Standards

The broad selection standard provides that all materials added to the ERIC database are directly related to the field of education. The majority of the journals indexed in ERIC are peer-reviewed, and the peer-reviewed status is indicated for all journals indexed from 2004 forward, when this data began to be documented by the ERIC system. The collection scope includes early childhood education through higher education, vocational education, and special education; it includes teacher education, education administration, assessment and evaluation, counseling, information technology, and the academic areas of reading, mathematics, science, environmental education, languages, and social studies. In addition, the collection also includes resources addressing one of the three objectives identified in Section 172 of the Education Sciences Reform Act: closing the achievement gap, encouraging educational practices that improve academic achievement, and conducting education research.

Within that standard, there are three sets of specific criteria providing guidance for document selection. The quality criteria consist of five basic factors: completeness, integrity, objectivity, substantive merit, and utility/importance. Selection is further determined by sponsorship criteria, and preference for inclusion in ERIC is given to those resources with identified sponsorship (for example, professional societies and government agencies). Detailed editorial criteria also provide factors for consideration, especially with regard to journals considered for comprehensive indexing.

All submissions considered for selection must be in digital format and accompanied by author permission for dissemination. For individual document submissions, authors (copyright holders) register through the ERIC Web site feature "My ERIC"; follow the steps to enter bibliographic information, abstract, and document file; and submit the electronic document release form authorizing ERIC to disseminate the materials. Journal publishers, associations, and other entities with multiple documents also submit electronic content following guidance and instructions consistent with provider agreements from ERIC. Once publishers have signed an ERIC agreement, files can be submitted by e-mail or disk or by upload to ERIC's FTP site.

ERIC Collection

In addition to being the largest education library, ERIC is one of the few collections to index non-journal materials as well as journal literature. The largest share of the collection consists of citations to journal articles (874,100 records), and a smaller portion consists of non-journal materials (499,500 records). The non-journal materials are frequently called gray literature, materials that are not easy to find and are not produced by commercial publishers. In ERIC, the gray literature consists of research syntheses, dissertations, conference proceedings, and such selected papers as keynote speeches, technical reports, policy papers, literature reviews, bibliographies, congressional hearings and reports, reports on federal and state standards, testing and regulations, U.S. Department of Education contractor reports (e.g., What Works Clearinghouse and the National Center for Education Statistics), and working papers for established research and policy organizations.

To support consistency and reliability in content coverage, most education journals are indexed comprehensively so that all articles in each issue are included. ERIC currently indexes a total of 1,143 journals; 1,046 journals comprehensively and 97 selectively. Articles from selectively covered journals are acquired by ERIC subject specialists who identify individual documents for the ERIC database according to the ERIC selection policy.

The complete list of journals indexed in ERIC, including the years of coverage and the number of articles indexed, is a tool on the ERIC Web site enabling users to identify more easily specific journal literature. There is also a non-journal source list of more than 800 organizations producing education-related materials providing content to ERIC. Another convenience for users that is designed to streamline the process of obtaining full text is the "Find in a Library" feature, which leverages the Open URL Gateway and WorldCat to provide a link from ERIC records to electronic and print resources available in libraries. For all journals currently indexed in ERIC, there are links to publishers' Web sites if users choose to purchase full-text articles.

To facilitate electronic access to more archived materials, ERIC launched a microfiche digitization project in 2006; this project was concluded in 2009. The project scope was to digitize and archive microfiche full-text documents containing an estimated 43 million pages and to provide copyright due diligence by seeking permission from the copyright holders to make the electronic version available to users.

Approximately 340,000 full-text documents, indexed 1966–1992, were converted from microfiche to digital image files, and more than 65 percent of these documents were added to the ERIC digital library. The ERIC Web site provides various lists for librarians to manage microfiche collections in their institutions based on what is now available in PDF format on the ERIC Web site.

In 2010 ERIC established a partnership with ProQuest to begin indexing education-related doctoral dissertations from 700 academic institutions worldwide. More than 1,700 recent records from the ProQuest Dissertations and Thesis Database have been added to the ERIC collection. As the project expands, records will reach back to 1997, the year digital copies of dissertations were first acquired.

ERIC Web Site

Recent enhancements to ERIC focus on increased access for special audiences and new search features. For example, the home page provides links with information for publishers and authors, librarians, and licensors of the ERIC database. Searchers can mark records for placement in a temporary workspace called "My Clipboard." This feature permits users to print, e-mail, or export records, or save them to a "My ERIC" account. Additional Web site improvements include search-term highlighting so that users see where and how frequently their search terms occur in the results set; a metadata field indicating peer-reviewed articles for records acquired 2004 to the present; and quicker loading of search results. Search facets are a new feature, allowing users to narrow searches by author, descriptor, date, audience, source, education level, and publication type, with each category offering the most frequently occurring names or terms in the results set.

Refinements to ERIC's technical architecture continue to improve system functionality and user satisfaction. Usability tests with participant groups including librarians, researchers, and students provide input on issues such as online submission, the "Help" section, and an extensive range of search operations. With all database enhancements, the development process contributes to increasing accessibility, efficiency, and quality.

Automated systems for acquisition and processing help to reduce the total time required to produce a database record, and most records are processed in less than 30 days. New content is added to the ERIC database every day, and ERIC publishes approximately 4,000 new records to the ERIC digital library each month. Commercial vendors receive updates to the database monthly.

RSS feeds enable users to keep up to date with new content from several sources. For example, users can receive regular updates from specific U.S. Department of Education programs: the Regional Educational Laboratories, the What Works Clearinghouse, and the National Assessment of Educational Progress (NAEP). Moreover, any ERIC search can become an RSS feed, or users can click to one of several education topics including community colleges, financial aid for college, and teacher effectiveness.

Tutorials provide added support for users searching the ERIC collection, helping searchers take advantage of Web site features. Tutorials include author search using full name, citation management, field code search, refining a search, and many more titles found under the ERIC "Help" section.

While the ERIC database has traditionally used narrative abstracts to describe full-text documents, database contributors now have the option of writing structured abstracts for their research papers and conference presentations. Structured abstracts present important details about research studies and their outcomes under predefined headings or elements such as research design types and study sample.

The Web site also provides links to find ERIC on Facebook and Twitter. This feature provides frequent news updates, links, and downloadable materials, with the goal of broadening ERIC outreach.

ERIC Access

There were more than 125 million searches of the ERIC digital library in 2010. In addition to the government-sponsored Web site at http://www.eric.ed.gov, ERIC is carried by search engines, including Goggle and Google Scholar, MSN, and Yahoo!, and by commercial database providers, including EBSCO, OCLC, OVID, ProQuest, SilverPlatter, and Dialog. ERIC is also available through statewide networks in Ohio, Texas, Kentucky, and North Carolina.

The ERIC digital library can be reached by toll-free telephone in the United States, Canada, and Puerto Rico at 800-LET-ERIC (800-538-3742), Monday through Friday, 8:00 A.M. to 8:00 P.M. eastern time. Questions can also be transmitted via the message box on the "Contact Us" page on the ERIC Web site.

National Association and Organization Reports

American Library Association

50 E. Huron St., Chicago, IL 60611
800-545-2433
World Wide Web http://www.ala.org

Roberta A. Stevens
President

The American Library Association (ALA) was founded in 1876 in Philadelphia and later chartered in the Commonwealth of Massachusetts; it is the oldest, largest, and most influential library association in the world. ALA has more than 61,000 members, including librarians, library trustees, and other interested people from every state and many nations. The association serves public, state, school, and academic libraries, as well as special libraries for people working in government, commerce and industry, the arts, and the armed services or in hospitals, prisons, and other institutions.

ALA's mission is "to provide leadership for the development, promotion, and improvement of library and information services and the profession of librarianship in order to enhance learning and ensure access to information for all."

ALA is governed by an elected council, its policy making body, and an executive board, which acts for the council in the administration of established policies and programs. Within this context, the executive board is the body that manages the affairs of the association, delegating management of the day-to-day operation to the association's executive director. ALA also has 37 standing committees, designated as committees of the association or of the council. ALA operations are implemented by staff through a structure of programmatic offices and support units.

ALA is home to 11 membership divisions, each focused on a type of library or library function. They are the American Association of School Librarians (AASL), the Association for Library Collections and Technical Services (ALCTS), the Association for Library Service to Children (ALSC), the Association of College and Research Libraries (ACRL), the Association of Library Trustees, Advocates, Friends, and Foundations (ALTAFF), the Association of Specialized and Cooperative Library Agencies (ASCLA), the Library and Information Technology Association (LITA), the Library Leadership and Management Association (LLAMA), the Public Library Association (PLA), the Reference and

User Services Association (RUSA), and the Young Adult Library Services Association (YALSA).

The association also hosts 18 roundtables for members who share interests that do not fall within the scope of any of the divisions. A network of affiliates, chapters, and other organizations enables ALA to reach a broad audience.

Key action areas include diversity, equitable access to information and library services, education and lifelong learning, intellectual freedom, advocacy for libraries and the profession, literacy, and organizational excellence.

ALA offices are units of the association that address the broad interests and issues of concern to ALA members; they track issues and provide information, services, and products for members and the general public. Current ALA offices are the Chapter Relations Office, the Development Office, the Governance Office, the International Relations Office, the Office for Accreditation, the Office for Diversity, the Office of Government Relations, the Office for Human Resource Development and Recruitment, the Office for Information Technology Policy, the Office for Intellectual Freedom, the Office for Library Advocacy, the Office for Literacy and Outreach Services, the Office for Research and Statistics, the Public Information Office, the Public Programs Office, and the Washington Office.

ALA's headquarters is in Chicago; the Office of Government Relations and the Office for Information Technology Policy are housed at ALA's Washington Office. The association also has an editorial office for *Choice,* a review journal for academic libraries, in Middletown, Connecticut.

ALA is a 501(c)(3) charitable and educational organization.

Focus on Author Advocates and Fund Raising

In her presidential year, 2010–2011 ALA President Roberta Stevens implemented key initiatives that addressed advocacy and fund raising.

Stevens's Our Authors, Our Advocates presidential initiative aimed to establish a cadre of nationally known writers who were ready and willing to speak out on behalf of libraries. "This initiative will focus on using these well-known, articulate, and impassioned spokespeople to highlight the key role libraries and library staff play in the economic, social, and educational fabric of our nation," Stevens said in announcing the effort, which highlighted authors in support of libraries through interviews, posters, podcasts, publications, and other media support. Much like the ALA's READ posters, the initiative was designed to build a broad base of support for libraries over time. Additionally, it can be used as a model for creating advocates for libraries at the community level through the ALA toolkit "Cultivating Your Local Notables," which provides guidance on identifying and enlisting local celebrities, such as writers, as library advocates.

Stevens's Frontline Fund Raising initiative, responding to reduced resources at libraries throughout the nation, offers tools that can be used by everyone, regardless of the size or type of library, who needs to supplement their institutional budget with additional funding. The initiative helps libraries develop and utilize the tools and skills needed at the local level, with a primary focus on the development of an online toolkit and webinars that can be broadly accessed by ALA members.

Highlights of the Year

ALA Helps Libraries Weather 'Perfect Storm'

Faced with a "perfect storm" of growing demand for library services but shrinking resources to meet that demand, libraries worked in 2010 to provide critically needed materials and services, amplify advocacy efforts, and ask their users and supporters to speak out on their behalf.

In June more than 2,000 people turned out for Library Advocacy Day in Washington, D.C. The event, nearly five times larger than any previous National Library Legislative Day, included a rally on Capitol Hill, meetings with elected officials, and a virtual component that drew another 1,053 participants to advocate for libraries by e-mailing members of Congress.

ALA continued to provide Capwiz advocacy software to ALA chapters, which used the online tool to send nearly 200,000 messages on the value of libraries to their legislators and governors. These online campaigns helped reinstate $20 million in state aid for libraries in Florida and millions in New Jersey and Pennsylvania.

Writers Marilyn Johnson, Paula Poundstone, Barbara Kingsolver, Lisa Scottoline, and Roy Blount, Jr. were the first to join "Authors for Libraries," an effort by ALTAFF to encourage authors to advocate for libraries on local, state, and national levels. The program shares quotes from participating authors about the importance of libraries on the ALTAFF Web site and through promotional materials; it also keeps authors informed of opportunities to advocate for libraries.

ACRL embarked on a multiyear Value of Academic Libraries initiative to increase recognition of the value of libraries and librarians by leaders in higher education, information technology, funding agencies, and campus decision making. Megan Oakleaf, an assistant professor in the School of Information Studies (iSchool) at Syracuse University, led a review of the literature, methodologies, and best practices already in place to demonstrate the value of academic libraries. The findings were released in September 2010 in *The Value of Academic Libraries: A Comprehensive Research Review and Report.*

Responding to Disasters in Haiti and Chile

ALA set up efforts to rebuild libraries in Haiti and Chile after devastating earthquakes in early 2010. The association raised an initial $25,000 to rebuild three libraries in Haiti: the Petit-Goave Public Library, the Centre Culturel Pyepoudre Community Library, and the Bibliothèque Haïtienne des Pères du Saint-Esprit, which was founded in 1873 and holds resources documenting the history of Haiti, French colonization, slavery, and emancipation. In Chile, in addition to seeking funding, ALA worked to have U.S. libraries "adopt" libraries in the southern region of the country that were destroyed or damaged during the February 27 earthquake and aftershocks.

New Online Learning Site Debuts

As ALA divisions and offices continued to expand their online education offerings, the association launched a new Online Learning Web site (http://www.ala.org/ala/onlinelearning), a collaboration of all units providing e-learning through a variety of methods, including podcasts, webinars, and e-courses. The easy-to-search site is organized into five general areas: Collection Management, Issues and Advocacy, Management Issues for Library Leaders, School Libraries, and Service Delivery in Libraries.

Library Copyright Alliance Speaks Out

The Library Copyright Alliance (LCA)—which includes ALA, ACRL, and the Association of Research Libraries (ARL)—continued to work to present a unified voice for the library community concerning national and international copyright law and policy for the digital environment. During 2010 LCA filed comments on a World Intellectual Property Organization (WIPO) draft proposal to facilitate access to copyrighted works for people with visual impairments and other reading disabilities, issued a series of briefs relating to international copyright and libraries, and called for openness in the discussion of a proposed anti-counterfeiting trade agreement. The group also filed friend-of-the-court briefs in cases dealing with consumers' rights and the right of Internet service providers to not be held liable for copyright infringement by third-party users.

Google Book Search Agreement Guide

ALA, ARL, and ACRL continued to play an active role in the ongoing response to the Google Book Search Settlement, releasing "A Guide for the Perplexed Part III: The Amended Settlement Agreement," which described the major changes in the amended settlement agreement submitted by Google, the Authors Guild, and the Association of American Publishers, with an emphasis on those changes relevant to libraries. In addition, the three groups submitted a letter to the U.S. Department of Justice Antitrust Division, recommending that the court presiding over the settlement closely supervise its implementation, particularly the pricing of institutional subscriptions and the selection of the Book Rights Registry board.

Priorities for 2015 Strategic Plan

In preparation for the drafting of ALA's 2015 strategic plan, association members were invited to share their thoughts on ALA priorities and performance. Nearly 9,000 members participated in the survey, which evaluated the importance and the performance of 37 statements of ALA activities. The top ten in terms of importance were legislative advocacy, accreditation, continuing education, intellectual freedom, public awareness, standards for library services, the ALA Web site, networking opportunities, ALA divisions, and media relations.

'Choose Privacy Week' Highlights Digital Age Rights

The ALA Office for Intellectual Freedom's two-year National Conversation on Privacy initiative, which invited library users to take part in a national conversation about privacy rights in a digital age, culminated in Choose Privacy Week during the first week of May. Events took place in Florida, Indiana, Massachusetts, Maine, Missouri, New Hampshire, Ohio, Pennsylvania, Rhode Island, Vermont, and Virginia. In addition, more than 160 people attended an online

Choose Privacy Week event sponsored by ACRL, and 44 librarians participated in an online workshop on learning how to host community forums on privacy.

'Turning the Page' Comes to Close

After benefiting more than 3,500 librarians and library supporters in 32 states, the groundbreaking program "Turning the Page: Building Your Library Community" ended May 31, 2010. Begun in 2007 with a grant from the Bill and Melinda Gates Foundation, the program provided advocacy training for public libraries participating in the Gates Foundation Opportunity Online hardware grants program. PLA has since released the program as a free Web-based training guide that leads participants through the creation of an advocacy work plan. Library staff and supporters can learn how to create and tell their library's story, deliver effective presentations, develop a compelling case for support, and build and sustain partnerships along the way.

Banned Books Week Urges Independent Thinking

The 29th celebration of Banned Books Week, the Office for Intellectual Freedom (OIF) campaign about challenges to library materials, promoted the slogan "Think for Yourself and Let Others Do the Same," featuring an illustration of a robot who has unplugged from the Internet and is reading a book. To start the week, OIF, the Newberry Library, and the McCormick Foundation Civics Program hosted a Banned Books Week Read-Out! on September 25. The event was emceed by acclaimed young adult writer Chris Crutcher and featured the authors of the top-ten most frequently challenged books of 2009, including Lauren Myracle, author of the TTYL series of young adult books. The week also saw the first awards from the Freedom to Read Foundation's Judith F. Krug Fund, which gave grants to seven libraries and organizations.

Teen Read Week

Observed October 17–23, Teen Read Week 2010 used the theme "Books with Beat @ your library," encouraging teens to read poetry, audiobooks, books about music, and more. Since 1998 Teen Read Week has encouraged teens and their parents to follow the main theme and a sub-theme that changes each year, serving as a basis for developing programs in schools, public libraries, and bookstores. More than 8,000 teens voted in the 2010 Teens' Top Ten, with *Catching Fire* by Suzanne Collins topping the list as the most popular book from the previous year; teens also chose the 2011 theme, "Picture It @ your library."

AASL Adopts Title of 'School Librarian'

In January 2010 the AASL board of directors officially adopted for the profession the title "school librarian" after an AASL survey indicated confusion, misperceptions, and inconsistencies about various job titles in the school librarian profession. The board voted to adopt the title to reflect the roles of the 21st century school library professional as a leader, instructional partner, information specialist, teacher, and program administrator.

Public Access Study Draws Record Response

Continuing the largest and longest-running national study of Internet connectivity and services in public libraries, the 2009–2010 survey—conducted by the ALA Office for Research and Statistics and the Center for Library and Information Innovation at the University of Maryland—received a record 82.4 percent response from public libraries in every state. Preliminary findings were detailed in the report *A Perfect Storm Brewing: Budget Cuts Threaten Public Library Services at Time of Increased Demand.*

Ethnic Affiliates Develop Family Literacy Programs

Through ALA 2009–2010 President Camila Alire's Family Literacy Focus, ALA's five ethnic affiliates received funding to develop innovative, culturally focused family literacy programs emphasizing oral and written traditions and exploring new literacies. The American Indian Library Association and Asian/Pacific American Librarians Association combined resources to create "Talk Story: Sharing Stories, Sharing Culture"; the Black Caucus of ALA held an author-centered intergenerational literacy program, "Reading Is Grand," for "Grand Families @ your library"; the Chinese American Librarians Association brought generations together through literacy and cultural activities with "Bridging Generations, a Bag at a Time"; and REFORMA, the National Association to Promote Library and Information Services to Latinos and the Spanish-Speaking, created "Noche de Cuentos" to preserve cultures and support storytelling and oral traditions. By June 16 public libraries in diverse communities had held 21 family literacy events attended by 1,117 children, adults, and elders.

First National Bookmobile Day

The first-ever celebration of National Bookmobile Day—a collaborative effort of the ALA Office for Literacy and Outreach Services, the Association of Bookmobile and Outreach Services, and the Association for Rural and Small Libraries—was held April 14, 2010. The event received notable media coverage, including almost 100 placements in national and local newspapers and magazines.

Quran Read-Out

To protest a Florida Christian clergyman's threat to burn the Quran on the anniversary of the September 11, 2001, terrorist attacks, the ALA Office for Intellectual Freedom and ALA's *American Libraries* magazine joined with representatives of local Chicago Islamic organizations on September 11, 2010, to read from the Quran. More than 50 people attended the reading outside ALA headquarters, where OIF Director Barbara Jones and *American Libraries* Editor Leonard Kniffel joined Gerald Hankerson of the Council on American-Islamic Relations and Kiran Ansari of the Council of Islamic Organizations of Greater Chicago to read verses from the Quran. The event received local, national, and international coverage from print, newswire, television, and radio organizations.

Campaign for the World's Libraries

In 2010 the Library and Information Association of Jamaica became the newest member of the Campaign for the World's Libraries, which was developed by ALA and the International Federation of Library Associations and Institutions (IFLA) to showcase the unique and vital roles played by public, school, academic, and special libraries worldwide. To date, 36 countries have joined the campaign, and the "@ your library" brand has been translated into 29 languages.

Programs and Partners

Campaign Partnerships

Campaign partner Dollar General Literacy Foundation provided funding for 75 public libraries in 24 states to receive "The American Dream Starts @ your library" grants to add or expand literacy services for adult English-language learners. Especially notable about the 2010 round was the awarding of grants to support mobile outreach to immigrant communities, particularly bookmobile service.

The "Step Up to the Plate @ your library" program, developed by ALA and the National Baseball Hall of Fame and Museum in Cooperstown, New York, concluded its fourth season with a grand prize drawing at the Hall of Fame. Program spokesperson and Hall of Famer Ozzie Smith chose 11-year-old Elizabeth Ann Bishop of Chambersburg, Pennsylvania, as the winner. "Step Up to the Plate" encouraged fans of all ages to use the print and electronic resources at their library to answer a series of trivia questions focused on multiculturalism in baseball and baseball around the world. Season five of the program launched in April 2010; library staff at the Hall of Fame developed trivia questions reflecting the Hall of Fame's role in preserving the history of baseball, with questions about exhibits at the museum.

For the second year, Univision Radio, the nation's largest Spanish-language radio broadcaster, aired Spanish-language public service announcements about the value of libraries and librarians for the "en tu biblioteca" campaign, which encourages members of the Latino community to use their local libraries. A Spanish-language Web site for the public supports the messages of the radio public service announcements and offers tools and materials to help librarians reach out to their Spanish-speaking audience.

Continuing a nine-year partnership with the Campaign for America's Libraries, *Woman's Day* magazine featured the four winners of its latest library initiative, which asked readers how they used the resources at their libraries to save money and cope with tough economic times. Winners included a woman who uses the resources and programs at her library to help home-school her son, one who used interlibrary loan to check out college textbooks, another who used the library's free resources to find her place in a new community, and another who used books from the library to learn how to renovate her 1880s home. Also in the March 2010 issue, *Woman's Day* announced its next initiative, asking women to submit stories of why the library is important to their community. Four submissions were to be featured in March 2011.

Smart investing @ your library

With sections for lessons learned and downloadable tools, the redesigned Web site for "Smart investing @ your library" encourages grantees, grant applicants, or anyone interested in starting a financial literacy program to borrow and share resources and strategies. Through 2009 the program from the FINRA Investor Education Foundation and RUSA had awarded three rounds of grants totaling $3,256,122. More than 90 percent of first-round programs have been incorporated into regular operations budgets and are continuing beyond the grant cycle.

Traveling Exhibitions

The ALA Public Programs Office (PPO) toured nine ongoing traveling exhibits to 110 libraries, reaching an audience of 773,000 library patrons: "Benjamin Franklin: In Search of a Better World," "Changing the Face of Medicine: Celebrating America's Women Physicians," "Forever Free: Abraham Lincoln's Journey to Emancipation," "Harry Potter's World: Renaissance Science, Magic, and Medicine," "John Adams Unbound," "Lewis and Clark and the Indian Country," "Lincoln: The Constitution and the Civil War," "Pride and Passion: The African American Baseball Experience," and "Visions of the Universe: Four Centuries of Discovery."

We the People Bookshelf

The National Endowment for the Humanities (NEH) collaborated with PPO for the seventh year to present the We the People Bookshelf, which aims to encourage young people to read and understand great literature while exploring themes in American history through library programming. The 2010 program provided sets of 17 books for young readers on the theme "A More Perfect Union," along with bonus materials for audiences of all ages, to 4,000 school and public libraries. Since 2003 NEH and ALA have distributed 17,000 book sets to school and public libraries.

Pilot Program Engages Chicago Teens

In the summer of 2010 more than 500 teens met in nine Chicago Public Library branches to discuss American art, current issues, and ways to get involved in the community through a series of pilot programs titled "Engage! Teens, Art, and Civic Engagement." Following the discussions, participants brainstormed action plans for improving their environment and undertook a variety of projects, including painting murals, planting community gardens, and installing sculpture in public spaces. Funding for the PPO pilot initiative was provided by grants from the Searle Funds at the Chicago Community Trust and the Terra Foundation for American Art.

Teen Tech Week

The fourth annual Teen Tech Week in March 2010 drew more than 1,700 library registrants with the theme "Learn Create Share @ your library." YALSA's week-long initiative encourages teens to explore the nonprint resources available at their libraries—including DVDs, databases, audiobooks, and electronic games. Promotional partners were ALA Graphics, Evanced Solutions, Galaxy Press, Rosen Publishing, and Tutor.com.

Support Teen Literature Day

YALSA worked with Readergirlz, Guys' Lit Wire, and If I Can Read, I Can Do Anything to distribute 10,000 young adult books to libraries on native reservations and tribal lands on Support Teen Literature Day in April 2010. The books, donated by publishers of young adult works, were worth roughly $175,000. In its third year, Operation Teen Book Drop is part of a massive effort by librarians, young adult authors, and avid readers to spur reading on a nationwide scale. Participating publishers included Abrams Books, Bloomsbury/Walker Books/ Candlewick Press, Chronicle Books, Hachette Book Group, Boyds Mills Press, Houghton Mifflin Harcourt, Milkweed, Mirrorstone Books, Orca Book Publishers, Scholastic, Simon & Schuster Children's Publishing, Tor/Forge/Starscape/ Tor Teen/Roaring Brook Press, and Better World Books.

Conferences and Workshops

2010 Annual Conference

Nearly 20,000 librarians participated in more than 2,400 sessions, meetings, and events at the 2010 Annual Conference, held June 24–29 in Washington, D.C. The issue of advocacy dominated the conference, which culminated in a closing-day rally on Capitol Hill that drew 1,600 librarians and an additional 400 library supporters. Speakers included author Lauren Myracle, Rep. Vern Ehlers (R-Mich.), Sen. Jack Reed (D-R.I.), ALA President Alire, and ALA Executive Director Keith Michael Fiels.

At a meeting with the AASL board and elected leaders from state school library organizations, U.S. Department of Education Secretary Arne Duncan urged school librarians to lobby Congress for passage of the jobs bill.

Alire's President's Program featured Eppo van Nispen, who spoke of his vision for the future of media and libraries. In addition, Alire, Past President Jim Rettig, and President-Elect Stevens launched the Spectrum Presidential Fundraising Initiative with the goal of raising $1 million to support the Spectrum Scholarship Program.

More than 600 attended the annual Coretta Scott King Book Awards Breakfast to celebrate winners of the 2010 awards and the inaugural Coretta Scott King/Virginia Hamilton Award for Lifetime Achievement. [For a complete list of the award winners, see "Literary Prizes" in Part 5—*Ed.*]

More than 800 turned out to hear Francine Berman, vice president of research at Rensselaer Polytechnic Institute, at the ALCTS President's Program, "Got Data? New Roles for Libraries in Shaping 21st-Century Research." Berman described the emerging role for libraries as stewards of valued digital research collections.

Authors, and the relationship between authors and libraries, as usual played a strong role at the conference. "I suspect that every single author that speaks to librarians can tell you about his or her intimate, steady, and vital relationships to libraries," said Pulitzer Prize winner Toni Morrison at the opening general session. President-elect Stevens's Inaugural Program included authors Maria Arana, Brad Meltzer, Sharon Draper, and Carmen Agra Deedy, who spoke of their experiences with and support for libraries.

The Auditorium Series of speakers featured novelist John Grisham, who is the honorary chairman of National Library Week 2011. Other speakers included Dave Isay of StoryCorps, puzzle expert Will Shortz, and authors Salman Rushdie, Dennis Lehane, Nancy Pearl, Mary McDonough, Sue Monk Kidd, and Ann Kidd Taylor.

PPO presented the LIVE! @ your library Reading Stage on the exhibits floor with a special focus on poetry, offering readings from award-winning, popular, and up-and-coming poets. Featured poets and authors on the stage included Laurie Halse Anderson, Roy Blount, Jr., Henri Cole, Heid E. Erdrich, Marilyn Johnson, and Adriana Trigiani.

Two groups marked 40th anniversaries. The Gay, Lesbian, Bisexual, and Transgendered Round Table's milestone was officially recognized with a resolution of congratulations from the U.S. House of Representatives; and the Leroy C. Merritt Humanitarian Fund, founded in 1970 to help librarians who have been denied employment rights because of their defense of intellectual freedom or because of discrimination, marked its anniversary at a celebratory dinner at the Folger Shakespeare Library.

The Jean E. Coleman Library Outreach Lecture was presented by Kathleen de la Peña McCook, professor at the University of South Florida School of Library and Information Science. McCook discussed "Librarians and Human Rights," a historical and cultural analysis of the librarian's role in human rights, highlighting the convergence of the goals of library workers and the human rights movement.

A strong exhibits program concluded with a performance by songwriter and performer Natalie Merchant, with a set of songs adapted from the works of various classic and contemporary poets.

Closing out the program, Battledecks, which made its first ALA appearance in the "Networking Uncommons" at the 2010 Midwinter Meeting, returned with an enlarged field of contestants. LITA's Jason Griffey prevailed over eight other participants to win first prize.

Official figures for the conference were 19,513 attendees and 6,688 exhibitors, for a total of 26,201.

2011 Midwinter Meeting

A total of 7,549 attendees and 2,561 exhibitors took part in the 2011 Midwinter Meeting January 7–11 in San Diego.

Among topics explored was the future of libraries in an increasingly digital world. At the session "Turning the Page on E-Books," panelist Brewster Kahle, founder of the Internet Archive, suggested that e-books fit well with the core of library services. "What libraries do is we buy stuff and we lend it," Kahle noted. "Let's do our jobs, digitize what we have to, buy what we can, but make sure we've got great collections for our patrons."

The meeting was also an opportunity to unveil key initiatives. ALA President Stevens introduced her Our Authors, Our Advocates initiative and also launched a video contest, "Why I Need My Library," which encourages teens 13 to 18 to create original videos on why they think libraries are needed now more than ever. The winning videos will be showcased on ALA Web sites and at the 2011 ALA Annual Conference.

Actor, environmental activist, and author Ted Danson delivered the keynote speech at the President's Program.

At the annual Youth Media Awards, held every year to celebrate the best in children's and young adult literature, *Moon over Manifest* by Clare Vanderpool earned the John Newbery Medal for the most outstanding contribution to children's literature, and *A Sick Day for Amos McGee,* illustrated by Erin E. Stead and written by Philip C. Stead, won the Randolph Caldecott Medal for the most distinguished American picture book. *Ship Breaker* by Paolo Bacigalupi took the Michael L. Printz Award for excellence in literature written for young adults; *One Crazy Summer* by Rita Williams-Garcia won the Coretta Scott King Author Book Award; and *Dave the Potter: Artist, Poet, Slave,* illustrated by Bryan Collier and written by Laban Carrick Hill, won the 2011 Coretta Scott King Illustrator Book Award.

Author events included librarian Nancy Pearl, author of *Book Lust* and the inspiration for the Librarian Action Figure, and 2009 Newbery Medal winner Neil Gaiman discussing Gaiman's *The Graveyard Book.* The ALA/Exhibits Round Table/*Booklist* Author forum featured glimpses into the minds of prominent authors including David Levithan, Stewart O'Nan, Armistead Maupin, and Susan Vreeland. Journalist and historian Richard Rhodes delivered the Arthur Curley Memorial Lecture.

Other meeting highlights included the launch of the Buy India a Library project, aimed at raising enough money to build a library in an impoverished neighborhood in India; the annual Martin Luther King, Jr. Sunrise Celebration, which featured keynote speaker Michael K. Honey, professor of labor and ethnic studies and American history at the University of Washington, and the Sunrise Speaker Series, which included forensic anthropologist Kathy Reichs and Andre Dubus III, author of *Townie, The Garden of Last Days,* and *House of Sand and Fog.*

Also during the meeting, the ALA Council passed a measure encouraging clarification within job listings as to the presence or absence of domestic partner benefits.

PLA National Conference Draws 7,500

More than 7,500 attendees gathered for the Public Library Association's 13th National Conference March 23–27, 2010, in Portland, Oregon. With programming focused on such key issues as advocacy, technology, literacy, and serving adults and youth, the conference provided a national platform for sharing ideas on ways to weather the "perfect storm" of increased library use and reduced budgets. Special events included presentations by author Sarah Vowell and columnist Nicholas Kristof and author luncheons with Scott Turow, Patrick Somerville, Kadir Nelson, and Alberto Urrea.

LITA Annual Forum

The 13th Annual LITA National Forum, with the theme "Crowd and the Cloud," was held in Atlanta September 30–October 3, 2010. Speakers included Ross Singer of Talis Information, Roy Tennant of the Online Computer Library Center (OCLC), and Amy Bruckman of the Georgia Institute of Technology. Two preconference workshops were offered: "Redesigning a Web Site Using Information Architecture Principles" by Jenny Emanuel of the University of Illinois and "Virtualize IT: Laying the Foundation for the Library of the Future," by Maurice York of North Carolina State University.

Publishing

ALA Editions

In addition to launching more new print books (37) in one year than ever before, the range of online publishing offered by ALA Editions was stepped up with the incorporation of ALA TechSource and its staff into the unit. Additionally, eEditions allows customers to buy ALA Editions books and ALA TechSource's *Library Technology Reports* in electronic format directly from the ALA Store, with file formats readable using a variety of software and devices, including the digital book readers Amazon Kindle, Sony Reader, iPhone's Stanza, Adobe Digital Editions, and the MobiPocket. The reports can also be read on desktop and laptop computers using free software. A new bundle option was introduced so that customers can download ALA Editions books and begin reading immediately while the print version is being shipped.

ALA TechSource

ALA TechSource published eight print issues of *Library Technology Reports,* which can now be purchased through the ALA Editions catalog and the ALA Store. Content (including an archive of issues) is also available on an ongoing basis via e-journal host MetaPress, along with the monthly *Smart Libraries* newsletter. Among the year's issues were two by Karen Coyle addressing metadata and RDA (Resource Description and Access). More than 600 attendees signed up for Coyle's related webinar, Directions in Metadata.

ALA Graphics

Celebrity and character posters came thick and fast in 2009–2010 with sought-after stars of movies, TV shows, and books helping ALA Graphics to promote libraries, literacy, and reading. As in the past, ALA Graphics partnered with several ALA divisions and units to develop and distribute posters and other items promoting library-related events such as National Library Week, Banned Books Week, and Teen Read and Teen Tech Weeks. New partnerships were formed, notably with the Office of Intellectual Freedom for Choose Privacy Week, with ALTAFF for National Friends of Libraries Week, and with ALCTS for Preservation Week.

Movie stars were the source of several widely appreciated new READ campaign posters. Building on the success of the "Twilight" poster of 2009 were Taylor Lautner holding *New Moon* and Dakota Fanning holding *Eclipse.* Robert Downey, Jr. and Jude Law were featured in a fast-selling poster that tied in to release of the movie *Sherlock Holmes.* Other celebrities included Taraji P. Henson holding *Green Eggs and Ham,* Nathan Fillion holding *The Softwire: Awakening on Orbis 4,* Rachel Maddow with *All the King's Men,* and Seth Meyers holding *Catch-22.* The READ campaign received a regal touch with Queen Rania al Abdullah of Jordan holding *The Prophet* on the first-ever English/Arabic READ poster.

ALA JobLIST

ALA JobLIST, the association's one-stop library jobs site for both job seekers and employers, continued to add and improve features in response to user feedback. Thanks to the increased ways to find JobLIST content—including through the site, RSS, Twitter, Facebook, LinkedIn, Indeed.com, SimplyHired.com, search engine optimization, and e-newsletters—exposure to the site continued to grow. Despite the reduced number of jobs available during the ongoing economic crisis, this joint project of ACRL, *American Libraries,* and the ALA Office for Human Resource Development and Recruitment (HRDR) listed more than 1,200 open positions in 2009–2010 and showed a slight increase in online advertising revenue.

Building on JobLIST's home page redesign the previous year, an updated appearance and navigation structure was carried through to other areas of the site, nearly doubling the number of pages viewed per visit since the updated site was launched. In addition, advertising employers have more options to control how candidates respond to ads and contact them.

JobLIST also added new formatting options for ad content, more specific and advanced treatment of salary ranges in ads and searches, and improved banner advertising opportunities.

The ALA Placement Center run by HRDR at both Midwinter Meeting and the Annual Conference was renamed the ALA JobLIST Placement Center to emphasize the centrality of JobLIST to ALA's support of job seekers and employers. The center provided one-on-one career counseling sessions with a professional counselor for job seekers at both Midwinter and Annual Conference, a résumé review service, and career-guidance workshops.

American Libraries

Representing a fundamental shift in how news and information are published, a new *American Libraries* Web site was launched in January 2010, with content open to all. Columns, features, and news are posted regularly, with links appearing weekly in the e-newsletter *American Libraries Direct.* Other benefits include expanded news content, Web-only spotlights, HTML versions of most of the print magazine's content, comment-enabled articles, an archive of every issue of *American Libraries Direct,* and RSS feeds for new issues. The site was developed in the open source software Drupal, making it easier to keep the site dynamic. Since March, each new issue of *American Libraries* is accompanied by a digital edition, and readers can choose to receive print plus digital, or digital-only.

A new professional-development column was introduced in the double January-February 2010 issue. "Next Steps" by Brian Mathews, assistant university librarian at the University of California, Santa Barbara, spotlights professional leadership strategies for creating and sustaining inspirational libraries. In addition, content in the print issues offered the usual eclectic range of library-related features and information, including online library degree programs and related opportunities, an evaluation of e-readers, notions of childhood that shape children's programs and services, and drawing Spanish-speaking families into the library. Newsmakers in 2009–2010 included Mohammad Abbas, head of the Library Department of the Iraqi Council of Representatives in Baghdad; David Weinberger, one of the authors of the influential *Cluetrain Manifesto*; and Els van der Plas, director of the Prince Klaus Fund, a "platform for intercultural exchange."

AL Focus published new photo and video reports throughout the year, from Library Advocacy Day to ALA conference coverage, from interviews with librarians to general library events.

Booklist Publications

Booklist Publications had another year marked by innovation in digital media—expansion of existing blogs, e-newsletters, and social media, an iPhone app, and a new sponsored webinar program that helped the imprint overcome the challenging current magazine advertising environment—all while maintaining the quality and depth of its print publications. The whole suite of publications offered numerous features, posts, articles, top-ten lists, read-alikes, and listen-alikes, in addition to the growing number of 8,500-plus titles reviewed and recommended in adult, youth, media, and reference.

The new sponsored webinar series drew more than 26,000 registrants. Each webinar includes a lineup of expert panelists from the library and publishing worlds as well as *Booklist* editors. The series began with "The Scoop on Series Nonfiction" and has since included "Sweet Talk: Romance Fiction in the Library"; "Twenty-first Century Reference Collections"; "Now Hear This: Audiobooks A to Z"; "Youth Spring Announcements"; "Series Nonfiction for Youth"; "Let's Get Graphic: Kids' Comics in Classrooms and Libraries"; "Crime Fiction Past and Present"; and "Trends in Teen Lit: The Independent View."

Book Links magazine made a smooth transition in the fall to publication as a quarterly print supplement to *Booklist* rather than as a stand-alone magazine. The editorial focus and original content continue to fulfill the mission of connecting children with books and related media, and the supplement is offered at no additional cost.

RDA: Resource Description and Access

The new cataloging standard RDA: Resource Description and Access went into beta testing, and in June 2010 the RDA Toolkit was launched by ALA, the

Canadian Library Association, and Facet Publishing (the publishing arm of Britain's CILIP: The Chartered Institute of Library and Information Professionals) with a complimentary open access period through August 31. More than 5,500 people (both institutions and solo users) signed up during this period and took advantage of a webinar on how to make the most of the toolkit. Highlights of the RDA Toolkit include searchable and browsable RDA instructions; AACR2 Rule Number Search of RDA instructions; workflows, mappings, and examples as tools to customize the RDA instruction set to support organizational training and processes; and the full text of AACR2 with links to RDA.

Testing of RDA is under way; the process was expected to be completed in June 2011, when the three U.S. national libraries will develop recommendations about the adoption of RDA based on their analysis of its testing. In collaboration with ALA Digital Reference, ALA Editions is set to publish the full-text print version of RDA that offers a snapshot serving as an offline access point for the single and partial cataloger institutions to evaluate RDA, as well as to support training and classroom use.

Leadership

Roberta Stevens, outreach projects and partnerships officer at the Library of Congress and project manager of the National Book Festival, was inaugurated as ALA president at the 2010 Annual Conference in Washington, D.C.

Stevens's 36-year career in libraries includes positions as a school library/media specialist, chairperson of media services for the National Technical Institute for the Deaf at the Rochester Institute of Technology in Rochester, New York, and director of technical operations for the Fairfax County (Virginia) Public Library. Other positions at the Library of Congress included managing product development, marketing, customer support, and accounting operations for its Cataloging Distribution Service; high-profile positions working with members of Congress and their staff, individuals at the highest levels of government, and top donors to the library; and managing the library's three-year bicentennial program, which included exhibitions, publications, symposia, concerts, a nationwide Local Legacies Project, and the Gifts to the Nation program that raised $80 million for the library's collections, projects, and a scholarly center.

Molly Raphael, retired director of the Multnomah County Library in Portland, Oregon, was chosen as president-elect in the 2010 election. Raphael, who will be inaugurated as ALA president at the 2011 Annual Conference in New Orleans, said she looks forward to working with everyone in the ALA to ensure that the critical roles of libraries in our society are sustained.

Two new ALA Executive Board members were elected by the ALA Council in a vote taken at the 2010 ALA Midwinter Meeting. They are Kevin Reynolds, assistant university librarian for learning and access services at the Jessie Ball duPont Library at the University of the South in Sewanee, Tennessee, and J. Linda Williams, coordinator of library media services for Anne Arundel County Public Schools in Annapolis, Maryland. Each is serving a three-year term that runs from July 2010 to June 2013.

Grants and Contributions

Office for Diversity Receives IMLS Grant for Recruitment

In June 2010 the ALA Office for Diversity Spectrum Scholarship Program was awarded a $432,495 grant under the Institute of Museum and Library Services' Laura Bush 21st-Century Librarian Program to fund a three-year project to recruit ethnically diverse high school and college students to careers in libraries. "Discovering Librarianship: The Future Is Overdue" will enlist a cohort of 35 early-career librarians from previously successful diversity initiatives, including the Spectrum Scholarship Program, to develop recruitment materials and serve as in-the-field recruiters to a new generation of professionals. Field recruiters will be provided with funding to participate in 70 national, regional, and local career recruitment and education events. ALA will host an institute for up to 50 college undergraduates interested in careers in librarianship, with information on preparing for graduate school admissions, selecting a library and information science program, finding funding for graduate school, and making the most of graduate education in library and information science.

Beyond Words Grants

Beyond Words issued grants totaling more than $90,000 to school libraries nationwide that have sustained materials losses because of a major disaster. The Beyond Words grants, sponsored by national discount retailer Dollar General and administered by AASL in collaboration with the National Education Association, provide funds that can be used for buying books, media, and/or library equipment that support learning in a school library environment.

Louisa May Alcott Library Outreach Program

In May 2010 the Public Programs Office announced that 30 libraries would receive grants of $2,500 to support five reading, viewing, and discussion programs featuring the documentary *Louisa May Alcott: The Woman Behind 'Little Women'* and the companion biography of the same name. The library outreach program is operated in collaboration with NEH and Nancy Porter and Harriet Reisen for Filmmakers Collaborative.

Picturing America Program Grants

In June 2010 PPO selected 30 libraries to receive $3,000 programming grants from NEH to support public programs featuring the Picturing America collection. The selected programs represented a diverse group of program formats, including discussions of local history, musical performances, a photography contest, storytelling events, author visits, hands-on art workshops, a celebration of Native American heritage, scholarly lectures, and "Let's Talk About It" reading and discussion programs.

Major Awards and Honors

Joseph W. Lippincott Award

Thomas C. Phelps, director of public programs at NEH, received the Joseph W. Lippincott Award for 2010. The award, founded in 1938, is given annually to an individual for distinguished service to the profession of librarianship. As assistant director and then director of public programs at NEH, Phelps essentially invented the idea of awarding grants to libraries across the country, in collaboration with ALA, to engage in humanities programming for the general public. The initiative began in 1984 with the highly popular "Let's Talk About It" reading and discussion program in all 50 states. A member of ALA for more than 40 years, Phelps was at the Salt Lake City Public Library from 1968 to 1980, rising to the position of director of the system's central library; he joined NEH in 1980.

James Madison Award

Joint winners of the 2010 James Madison Award were Meredith Fuchs, general counsel to the National Security Archive, and the group Citizens for Responsibility and Ethics in Washington (CREW). Named in honor of President James Madison, the award was established by ALA in 1986 to honor individuals or groups who have championed, protected, and promoted public access to government information and the public's "right to know" on the national level.

Association of American Publishers

71 Fifth Ave., New York, NY 10010
212-255-0200, fax 212-255-7007

455 Massachusetts Ave. N.W., Washington, DC 20001
202-347-3375, fax 202-347-3690

World Wide Web http://www.publishers.org

Judith Platt
Director, Communications/Public Affairs

The Association of American Publishers (AAP) is the national trade association of the U.S. book publishing industry. The association was created in 1970 through the merger of the American Book Publishers Council, a trade publishing group, and the American Educational Publishers Institute, an organization of textbook publishers. AAP's more than 300 corporate members include most of the major commercial book publishers in the United States as well as smaller and medium-sized houses, not-for-profit publishers, university presses, and scholarly societies.

AAP members publish hardcover and paperback books in every field including general fiction and nonfiction; poetry; children's books; textbooks; Bibles and other religious works; reference works; scientific, medical, technical, professional, and scholarly books and journals; computer software; and a range of digital products and services.

AAP policy is set by a board of directors, elected by the membership for four-year terms, under a chair who serves for two years. There is an executive committee composed of the chair, vice chair, secretary, and treasurer and a minimum of two at-large members. Management of the association, within the guidelines set by the board, is the responsibility of AAP's president and CEO.

Highlights of 2010

- Will Ethridge (Pearson Education) served the second year of a two-year term as AAP chairman.
- The Professional and Scholarly Publishing Division's R. R. Hawkins Award went to University of Chicago Press for *Plato's Philosophers: The Coherence of the Dialogues* and to John Wiley & Sons for *Wiley Interdisciplinary Reviews (WIREs).*
- Book sales for 2009 were an estimated $23.9 billion, a drop of 1.8 percent from the previous year.
- Hong Kong publishing house New Century Press received the Jeri Laber International Freedom to Publish Award.
- AAP continued to press for an exemption for children's books from the lead-content testing and certification provisions of the Consumer Product Safety Improvement Act (CPSIA).
- AAP achieved a major legislative victory with passage of the SPEECH Act, a new law to protect Americans against "libel tourism."

- AAP and Britain's Publishers Association continued joint efforts to combat infringement of higher education textbooks and trade book piracy in China.
- AAP's Young to Publishing Group hosted its first "House Party," giving young publishing professionals live webstream access to the National Book Awards.
- AAP and the Book Industry Study Group (BISG) embarked on an ambitious initiative to develop a new joint industry statistics model.
- The AAP School Division launched a series of initiatives to help school publishers make the transition to Common Core State Standards in reading/language arts and math.

Copyright

The AAP Copyright Committee coordinates efforts to protect and strengthen intellectual property rights and to enhance public awareness of the importance of copyright as an incentive to creativity. The committee monitors intellectual property legislation in the United States and abroad and serves as an advisory body to the AAP Board of Directors in formulating policy on legislation and compliance activities, including litigation. The committee coordinates AAP's efforts to promote understanding and compliance with U.S. copyright law on America's college and university campuses. Ken Carson (Cengage Learning) chaired the committee in 2010.

Google Settlement

In 2010 the committee continued to monitor copyright issues relating to the Google Book Search Program, including the lawsuit filed in federal court in the fall of 2005 by five major AAP members (McGraw-Hill, Pearson Education, Penguin Group USA, Simon & Schuster, and John Wiley & Sons) asserting that the Google Library Project's mass digitization of in-copyright books was not protected by the "fair use" provision of copyright law.

The case was settled in October 2008 with the announcement of a groundbreaking agreement that would expand online access to millions of in-copyright books and other written materials in the United States from the collections of a number of major U.S. libraries participating in Google Book Search. The agreement, reached after two years of negotiation, resolved the class-action lawsuit brought by book authors and the Authors Guild, as well as the separate publishers' lawsuit. Heavy opposition to approval of the settlement agreement resulted in the postponement of the court hearing and the filing of a revised settlement agreement in November 2009 addressing major concerns of the U.S. Department of Justice and foreign publishers, among others.

AAP believes the agreement has the potential to benefit readers and researchers and to enhance the ability of authors and publishers to distribute their content in digital form, by significantly expanding online access to works through Google Book Search, an ambitious effort to make millions of books searchable via the Internet. [The court ruled in mid-March in favor of the publishers and authors—*Ed.*]

The committee also monitored a number of important court decisions in cases filed against Google, along with domestic and foreign news media coverage of Google's views and business transactions.

E-Reserves: Georgia State Suit

Litigation filed by three AAP member publishers (Oxford University Press, Cambridge University Press, and Sage Publications) in 2008 citing "systematic, widespread and unauthorized copying and distribution of a vast amount of copyrighted works" at Georgia State University (GSU) continued through 2010. GSU is one of three state universities that refused to engage in discussions with AAP regarding their e-reserves policies and practices, and the lawsuit charged that GSU officials were violating the law by systematically enabling professors to give students digital copies of copyrighted course readings published by the plaintiffs and numerous other publishers without their authorization. The lawsuit seeks injunctive relief to bring an end to such practices, but does not seek monetary damages.

The parties filed cross motions for summary judgment in February 2010. GSU argued that none of the defendants were liable for copyright infringement because none of them engaged in volitional acts of copying or materially contributed to such copying; rather, it claimed the defendants actively sought to prevent infringement, citing the issuance of new policies by the regents and GSU during the litigation. This argument placed responsibility for any infringing activity squarely on the faculty. The judge rejected the publishers' motion for summary judgment in September, ruling that defendants were not liable for direct infringement nor for vicarious liability. However, the court ruled that the publishers could still proceed with their claim of "contributory infringement" if they could show that the current GSU policy had resulted in "ongoing and continuous misuse" of the fair use defense. The case was still pending at the time this report was prepared.

Amicus Briefs

The committee also filed several friend-of-the-court (amicus) briefs in important copyright cases in 2010.

Costco Wholesale Corp. v. *Omega, SA*

AAP filed an amicus brief in September asking the U.S. Supreme Court to uphold a ruling by the Ninth Circuit holding that the "first sale doctrine" does not apply to the unauthorized importation into the United States of copyrighted works that are manufactured overseas and acquired abroad. Although the case involved the importation of wristwatches rather than books, it was seen as critically important to U.S. publishers because the Supreme Court ruling would determine whether the "first sale doctrine" (which allows the owner of a copy of a work protected by U.S. copyright to sell or otherwise dispose of that particular copy without having to get the permission of the copyright holder) would operate to legalize the importation of books that were manufactured abroad for distribution in foreign markets and never intended for sale in the United States. AAP's brief noted that it was book publishers who had persuaded Congress that a copyright owner's exclusive right to distribute copies of a copyrighted work would be meaningless if the copyright owner did not also have the right to ban the unauthorized importation into the United States of copies of the work that were created under foreign law solely for use abroad.

On December 13, in a 4-4 split decision (Justice Elena Kagan recused herself because the government had filed an amicus brief on the other side when she was solicitor general), the Supreme Court left the lower court ruling intact. While the ruling is a victory for publishing interests, it is more limited than it might have been as the split decision means that the ruling is binding only on judges in the Ninth Circuit.

Viacom v. *YouTube*

In May 2010 AAP joined in filing an amicus brief supporting Viacom in its copyright infringement suit against YouTube and its parent company, Google. The suit, filed in February 2007, accuses the popular video-sharing Web site of massive intentional copyright infringement and seeks more than $1 billion in damages. The amicus brief, filed in federal district court in New York, argues that YouTube should not be able to claim immunity from copyright infringement liability under the "safe harbor" provisions of the Digital Millennium Copyright Act (DMCA) for infringing material posted by its users. Those provisions, the brief argues, were enacted by Congress to encourage technological innovation by protecting telephone companies, cable television services, and other Internet service providers (ISPs) from liability for the occasional, isolated acts of infringement on their networks by their subscribers, as well as for the incidental, automatically generated electronic "copies" made in the course of simply transmitting information over the Internet. Congress never meant the safe harbors to indemnify "companies that knowingly make infringing content available online and benefit from the infringement . . .," the brief states, noting that "Businesses built on the backs of others' content cannot be said to be 'innovation' in any constructive sense of the word. . ."

On June 23, the district court ruled in favor of YouTube, holding that the video-sharing Web site is entitled to claim immunity from copyright infringement liability under the "safe harbor" provisions of DMCA for infringing materials posted by its users. In granting summary judgment, U.S. District Court Judge Louis Stanton held that it was not the intent of Congress to "impose responsibility on service providers to discover which of their users' postings infringe a copyright," but only to take down infringing material when duly notified of specific infringements.

Particularly troubling to AAP members was the court's rejection of the argument that DMCA's safe harbor provisions should not be available to a service provider when there is a widespread and general awareness that there are infringements on the service provider's system. The case is on appeal to the Second Circuit.

Penguin USA v. *American Buddha*

An issue pending before the New York Court of Appeals (the state's highest appellate court) has enormous significance for the future ability of publishers to fight Internet piracy. The question concerns the location (*situs*) of the injury suffered by a New York copyright holder when the copyright infringement takes place outside New York. Penguin USA filed suit in federal district court in New York against American Buddha, a free online library, for uploading Penguin titles without permission and making them available online to their patrons. Dismissing the case on a very narrow reading of New York's "long-arm" statute (which allows the state to exercise jurisdiction over out-of-state defendants under certain circumstances), the district court held that since the infringing activity and injury took place outside New York (American Buddha's servers are located in Arizona and Oregon), the court lacked personal jurisdiction over the defendant. The case has gone up on appeal to the Second Circuit, which has asked the New York Court of Appeals to decide the question of the *situs* of the injury in copyright infringement cases for purposes of New York's long-arm statute. AAP filed an amicus brief with the New York Court of Appeals in December focusing on the growth of global e-book piracy and stressing the absolute imperative of allowing a U.S. copyright owner to sue a "foreign" infringer in the federal court that is local to the owner and the infringed work. ". . . it is critical that New York, the home of the publishing industry, interpret [the statute] to provide long-arm jurisdiction to a New York copyright holder seeking injunctive relief against a defendant distributing its pirated materials on the Internet," the brief states.

Public Access to Federally Funded Research

In 2010 the committee continued to support the Fair Copyright in Research Works Act (H.R. 801), introduced in February 2009 to repeal the mandatory National Institutes of Health (NIH) public access policy that requires government-funded researchers to submit their final peer-reviewed electronic manuscripts of journal articles to NIH within 12 months of publication, making the article freely available to the public on NIH's PubMed Central Web site. At the same time, publishers actively lobbied against the Federal Research Public Access Act (S. 1373), which would have extended the NIH mandated public access policy to 11 federal agencies with an even narrower (six-month) window.

Publishers were disheartened by a report growing out of roundtable discussions sponsored by the House Science and Research Subcommittee and the White House Office of Science and Technology Policy in summer 2010 regarding public access to federally funded research. Although the report did not recommend "mandatory" public access policies such as the one in place at NIH, and urged government agencies to "consult and cooperate" with the publishing community in formulating and implementing such policies, it failed to acknowledge the publishing community's central contention—that articles published in peer-reviewed science journals, even at the "final peer-reviewed manuscript accepted for publication stage," are simply not funded by government research grants.

Limitations and Exceptions, Visually Impaired Persons

Accessibility of copyrighted works for people with print disabilities was an issue of international as well as domestic concern in 2010, with continuing discussions of a possible treaty at the World Intellectual Property Organization (WIPO). A treaty drafted by the World Blind Union in 2009 that would allow cross-border use of copyrighted works reproduced and distributed in specialized formats without permission from rightsholders for the benefit of users with print disabilities was tabled by Brazil, Paraguay, and Ecuador. WIPO established a Stakeholders' Platform to move forward on a parallel track with its own "trusted intermediary" pilot project as an alternative to facilitate cross-border distribution of accessible versions of works consistent with national copyright laws. The pilot project would last three years, during which trusted intermediaries appointed in ten countries would conduct a pragmatic test of the planned cross-border transfer program. AAP is following the progress of this initiative through the International Publishers Association, which is one of the planning parties.

Combating Online Infringement and Counterfeits Act

In September 2010 Senate Judiciary Committee Chairman Patrick Leahy (D-Vt.) and other committee members introduced S. 3804, the Combating Online Infringement and Counterfeits Act (COICA). The legislation targets "rogue" Web sites—the worst of the worst Internet pirate sites—and provides law enforcement with important resources to stop Web sites dedicated to online piracy and the sale of counterfeit goods. Since its introduction, the bill has been the target of anticipated criticism, mostly from copyleft groups ("copyleft" is defined as using copyright law to offer the right to distribute copies and modified versions of a work). The bill authorizes the U.S. attorney general to bring actions against such sites to secure court orders that would help to eliminate the legitimate support that such sites receive from ISPs, financial payment services, and other third-party intermediaries. Despite rapid approval by the Senate Judiciary Committee in November, the 111th Congress ran out of time. The bill was expected to be introduced and hearings held early in the 112th Congress. AAP supported COICA and is continuing to work in support of the legislation in the new Congress.

Rights and Permissions Advisory Committee

AAP's Rights and Permissions Advisory Committee (RPAC), which operates under the aegis of the Copyright Committee, sponsors educational programs for rights and permissions professionals. Chaired by Bonnie Beacher (McGraw-Hill), RPAC hosted its annual conference in New York City in May 2010, drawing more than 80 professionals to its day-long program. The conference featured sessions on copyright basics, fighting online piracy, accessibility issues, multimedia licensing, and pertinent legislation. RPAC also held a 90-minute webinar on copyright basics in November, which drew more than 70 rights and permissions professionals. RPAC members are in the process of revising and updating the *Copyright Primer,* and the revision is expected to be released during 2011.

Digital Issues

AAP's Digital Issues Working Group, a forum for publishers to share information and learn about business opportunities and strategies in the digital world, holds luncheon meetings throughout the year featuring guest speakers on a range of subjects. Peter Balis (John Wiley & Sons) and Leslie Hulse (HarperCollins) are the working group's co-chairs.

Meeting topics in 2010 included technical standards and protocols relating to international distribution of digital products, enhanced e-book products, the .EPUB standard for production and rendering of e-books, and cloud-based e-book distribution platforms and associated technical security.

Diversity/Recruit and Retain

AAP's Diversity/Recruit and Retain Committee (DRRC) continued its work to attract a talented and diverse work force to book publishing with its Bookjobs Web site and "Book Yourself a Career" campaign. The committee, composed of senior human-resource professionals from trade and academic houses, is chaired by Ann Wienerman (Random House).

The focus for 2010 included outreach to area colleges with diverse student populations where AAP hosted summer and autumn presentations on careers in book publishing. In 2010 AAP partnered with the Eastern Association of Colleges and Employers on two events to educate career counselors from colleges and universities along the eastern seaboard about the various functions within a publishing house. Speakers represented both trade and academic publishing with representatives of some 40 colleges in attendance. The committee hosted a similar event for colleges and universities based in New York, along with a targeted session for college students. AAP's Young to Publishing members, as recent college graduates, are being trained to present programs at their alma maters.

AAP hosted its annual Young to Publishing conference in December 2010 with an unprecedented 250 young professionals in attendance at the event, "Driving Careers by Driving Content."

Young to Publishing Group

The Young to Publishing Group (YPG), a subcommittee of DRRC, boasts a membership of more than 1,500 young professionals who have been in the industry from one to five years. YPG hosts monthly brown-bag lunches with guest speakers from every area of publishing.

In an effort to enhance access to industry events for junior professionals, YPG, in concert with the National Book Foundation, hosted an inaugural "House Party" that provided live webstream access to the National Book Awards. The event was sponsored by the Huffington Post and proceeds of the evening's auction benefited Literacy Partners.

The group continues to maintain an active Web site for junior publishing professionals and has expanded its outreach with community service programs throughout the New York metro area. The committee is exploring the possibility of creating branch chapters in Boston and San Francisco.

Freedom to Read

The mandate of the AAP Freedom to Read Committee is to protect the free marketplace of ideas for American publishers. The committee serves as the publishing industry's early warning system on issues such as libel, privacy, school and library censorship, journalists' privilege, Internet censorship, government regulation of protected speech, and third-party liability for protected speech. The committee coordinates AAP participation in First Amendment (freedom of expression) court cases, sponsors educational programs, plays an active role in Media Coalition (a trade association of business-oriented groups concerned with censorship issues), and works with groups within and beyond the book community to advance common interests in the area of intellectual freedom. Terry Adams (Little, Brown/Hachette Book Group) chaired the committee in 2010.

U.S. v. *Stevens*

In July 2009 AAP filed an amicus brief asking the U.S. Supreme Court to strike down a federal statute prohibiting the creation, sale, or possession of "a depiction of animal cruelty" and to reject arguments by the government that a whole category of speech can be denied First Amendment protection when Congress finds the "value" of the speech to be outweighed by the government's interest in suppressing it.

On April 20, 2010, the court, strongly affirming First Amendment principles and refusing to create a new category of unprotected speech, struck down the statute.

Oregon Harmful to Minors Law Challenge

In early 2008 AAP joined other Media Coalition plaintiffs in challenging two Oregon statutes that criminalized the dissemination of sexually explicit material to anyone under the age of 13 or the dissemination of such material to anyone under 18 with the intent to sexually arouse the recipient or the provider. The statutory language contained no provision for judging the material as a whole, nor for considering its value as the Supreme Court has mandated. The federal district court, relying on legislative history rather than statutory language, refused to strike them down and the case went up on appeal to the U.S. Court of Appeals for the Ninth Circuit.

On September 20, 2010, in a strong First Amendment ruling, the Ninth Circuit overturned the lower court, saying that the legislative goal did not match the statutory language. In its ruling the court specifically mentioned books by noted children's and young adult author Judy Blume as the kind of material that would be swept up by the statutes.

Campaign for Reader Privacy

With several USAPatriot Act provisions, including the controversial Section 215, due to expire at the end of 2009, AAP joined its fellow organizations in the Campaign for Reader Privacy in launching another phase of the five-year campaign to restore reader privacy safeguards that were stripped away by the act. Intensive lobbying efforts produced a bill approved by the Senate Judiciary Committee that provided important safeguards for library records. Without voting on the bill, however, in February 2010 Congress approved a one-year extension of the provisions with no changes. The campaign welcomed an announcement in June by the Justice Department's inspector general of plans to begin a new investigation into how the government is using USAPatriot Act domestic surveillance powers.

Libel Tourism and the SPEECH Act

After an intensive, multiyear lobbying effort, AAP secured a major legislative victory when President Barack Obama signed the SPEECH Act on August 10. The new law gives American authors and publishers important new legal protections against "libel tourists" and others who would use foreign courts to stifle free expression in the United States.

The new law prohibits federal courts from recognizing or enforcing foreign libel judgments that do not pass First Amendment muster and allows American authors and publishers to go into court and seek a declaration that such a foreign judgment is "repugnant" to constitutional values and not enforceable in the United States. American authors and publishers do not have to wait for the foreign litigant to move to enforce the judgment before seeking declaratory relief from a U.S. court.

AAP was one of the earliest supporters of U.S. author Rachel Ehrenfeld's efforts to have an English libel judgment against her thrown out by a U.S. court. It was the Ehrenfeld case, involving her book *Funding Evil: How Terrorism Is Financed and How to Stop It,* that called public attention to the problem of libel tourism, generating calls for Congress to act.

Royall v. *Main*

AAP filed an amicus brief in a defamation suit in Texas that raises serious First Amendment questions for book authors and publishers. The suit, *Royall* v. *Main,* was brought by a developer against author Carla Main over her book *Bulldozed,* which deals with an eminent domain situation in Freeport, Texas. Following the trial court's refusal to dismiss the case, Main and her publisher filed an appeal under a state statute that allows media defendants to file such an "interlocutory" appeal to protect their First Amendment interests. The plaintiff has opposed their right to appeal, arguing that book authors and publishers are not "media" as defined by the statute. AAP's brief deals with two key issues, arguing that books are "print media" subject to First Amendment protection under Texas law, and that because of the circumstances surrounding the public controversy, the plaintiff is a limited-purpose public figure and must prove the author and publisher acted with "actual malice."

Funeral Protest Case

AAP joined with other media and free speech groups in filing an amicus brief in *Phelps* v. *Snyder,* which the Supreme Court heard October 6. The court is considering a multi-million-dollar judgment for intentional infliction of emotional distress awarded to the father of a Marine killed in Iraq stemming from protests staged by a church group at his son's funeral in Maryland. The award of damages by a federal district court was overturned on appeal by the Fourth Circuit. The brief addresses the question of whether speech on a matter of public concern may be too offensive to merit First Amendment protection, and, while noting that "This case tests the mettle of even the most ardent free speech advocates because the underlying speech is so repugnant," the amicus brief argues that what is at stake is the central tenet of the First Amendment: "that the government must remain neutral in the marketplace of idcas."

California Video Game Statute

In September AAP joined in filing an amicus brief urging the Supreme Court to uphold a Ninth Circuit ruling that struck down a California statute prohibiting the sale of "violent" video games to anyone under the age of 18. Similar state laws have been overturned by the Seventh and Eighth Circuits. In arguing for a new exception to First Amendment protection for "offensively violent material," California asserts the right of the state to regulate anything it deems likely to harm the "ethical or moral development" of a minor. The amicus brief urges the court to reject the attempt to create a whole new category of speech that lies out side the protection of the First Amendment.

Harmful to Minors Statutes

In October a federal district court issued a preliminary injunction barring enforcement of a Massachusetts statute that extends the state's harmful to minors law to the Internet. The ruling came in a lawsuit filed in July by AAP and other members of Media Coalition, several Massachusetts booksellers, and the Massachusetts ACLU. The law, which was signed in April, could make a Web site operator or anyone who communicates via a listserv criminally liable for constitutionally protected material containing nudity or sexual content that could be considered harmful to minors, in effect reducing all Internet communication to a level suitable for children.

Earlier, in August, AAP and other Media Coalition members filed a lawsuit in federal court in Anchorage to overturn a new Alaska statute that would criminalize the distribution—via the Internet, or through retail establishments or libraries—of constitutionally protected material that might be considered harmful to minors. On October 20 the judge issued a preliminary injunction barring enforcement of the statute.

Personal Privacy Rights for Corporations

AAP filed an amicus brief asking the Supreme Court to rule that a corporation does not have personal privacy rights under the Freedom of Information Act (FOIA). In 2008 the Federal Communications Commission (FCC) ruled that an exemption to FOIA designed to prevent public disclosure of law enforcement records that could constitute "an unwarranted invasion of personal privacy" did not apply to corporations. AT&T sued to prevent FCC from releasing records pursuant to a FOIA request pertaining to an investigation into whether the company had overcharged the government for contract work. In 2009 the Third Circuit overruled FCC, holding that, for purposes of the FOIA exemption, corporations qualify for personal privacy rights. FCC successfully petitioned for Supreme Court review. The question has significant implications for access to information on government investigations into corporate conduct, such as the BP Gulf of Mexico oil spill and the financial crisis.

Book Banning

Continuing to voice support for the right of young people to read a wide variety of books of their own choosing, AAP joined with like-minded groups in opposing attempts to remove books with "objectionable" content from school and public libraries and classroom reading lists across the country.

- AAP co-signed a letter opposing the removal of Judy Blume's book *Forever* from a school library in Florida. The Book Reconsideration Committee mandated by school district policy voted to retain the book without restrictions on open library shelves.
- AAP joined in urging a New Jersey school board not to remove three books in the high school library that were targeted because they appear on a list of gay-themed books created by the Gay Lesbian Straight Education Network.
- AAP participated in a successful fight against the removal of Toni Morrison's *Song of Solomon* from 11th grade AP English classes in Indianapolis.
- AAP was part of a coalition of education and free speech organizations supporting citizens in Stockton, Missouri, in an unsuccessful fight to retain Sherman Alexie's award-winning novel *The Absolutely True Diary of a Part-Time Indian* in the high school curriculum and library.
- AAP again weighed in on a challenge to the Alexie book, this time in Helena, Montana, where it was being used in high school English classes as part of an Indian education curriculum. The Montana challenge was defeated.

AAP members again actively participated in 2010 Banned Books Week. This annual celebration was created in 1982 by the American Library Association (ALA), the American Booksellers Association, and AAP in response to the growing number of attempts to remove or restrict access to books in public and school libraries, classrooms, and bookstores.

Educational Programs

The Freedom to Read Committee joined with the ALA Intellectual Freedom Committee to sponsor a program at the ALA Annual Conference in Washington, D.C., in June 2010. The program—titled "Blasphemy!"—explored the occasional clash of religious values with intellectual freedom. It featured feminist author and journalist Irshad Manji and Paul Sturges, a leader in the fight for free expression in the international library community.

The committee and the American Booksellers Foundation for Free Expression cosponsored a program at the annual book trade fair BookExpo America on the free speech implications of the Supreme Court's ruling in the Citizens United case, in which the court held that corporate funding of independent political broadcasts in candidate elections could not be limited under the First Amendment. AAP President and CEO Tom Allen moderated the discussion.

Government Affairs

AAP's Washington office is the industry's front line on matters of federal legislation and government policy. Washington keeps AAP members informed about developments on Capitol Hill and in the executive branch, to enable the membership to develop consensus positions on national policy issues. AAP's government affairs professionals serve as the industry's voice in advocating the views and concerns of American publishers on questions of national policy.

CPSIA

A major concern for AAP grew out of passage of the Consumer Product Safety Improvement Act (CPSIA) in August 2008. Enacted in response to a series of highly publicized recalls because of lead contamination of toys manufactured primarily in China, CPSIA requires that all products intended for children under the age of 12 be certified not to contain lead over prescribed statutory levels. AAP has been pressing to have ordinary paper-based books and other paper-based print materials excluded from the testing and certification requirements since they have never posed a threat of lead exposure to children.

In early December 2010 the Senate Committee on Commerce, Science, and Transportation's Subcommittee on Consumer Protection, Product Safety, and Insurance held an oversight hearing, with testimony from the Consumer Products Safety Commission chair and one of the commissioners. Seeing the hearing as an opportunity to focus on issues raised by CPSIA, AAP staff visited Capitol Hill in advance of the hearing to press the case for extending the stay on enforcement of the lead testing and certification requirements that would otherwise expire on February 10, 2011. In visits with key Senate staff, AAP stressed that the stay was both necessary and appropriate in light of the still-unissued testing rules and the inadequate time that industries would have to comply with them if they were issued in the coming weeks and the stay allowed to expire.

Higher Education

AAP's Higher Education group serves the needs and interests of AAP members who publish for the postsecondary education market. John Isley (Pearson Education) chaired the Higher Education Executive Committee in 2010.

A significant portion of AAP's efforts focused on informing policymakers of significant strides in the development of course materials that best meet the needs of students and their instructors. These efforts often require responding to legislative initiatives.

The group continued two major initiatives in 2010.

The AccessText Network (ATN) is a membership exchange network that facilitates and supports nationwide delivery of alternative files for students with diagnosed print-related disabilities. More than 500 colleges and universities in 49 states are enrolled in the system, with more than 360,000 textbook titles available. In 2010 three statewide agreements were made with ATN: in California, Georgia, and Ohio.

ATN makes it quicker and easier for students with disabilities such as blindness, dyslexia, and physical impairments that prevent the use of traditional hardcopy textbooks to get the alternative electronic textbooks they need for college.

The Alternative Media Access Center (AMAC) at the Georgia Institute of Technology is now working with CourseSmart.com to convert the most popular electronic textbooks on the site to make them accessible to all students. Hundreds of titles made available during the fall 2010 semester and CourseSmart.com and AMAC announced in October that they had been awarded a Student E-Rental Pilot Program (STEPP) grant of $1.1 million from the U.S. Department of Education to produce 1,000 more rentable accessible textbooks over a two-year period.

Funding for the development of ATN was provided by eight AAP member publishers: Cengage Learning, CQ Press, John Wiley & Sons, Macmillan, McGraw-Hill, Pearson, Reed Elsevier, and W. W. Norton. Operating from Atlanta, ATN is administered through the Board of Regents of the University System of Georgia, the Georgia Institute of Technology Enterprise Innovation Institute, and the Alternative Media Access Center.

The second initiative, Cost-Effective Solutions for Student Success, an effort to expand publisher outreach to educators and policymakers, enabled publishers to provide information about new technologies and options that will improve student success, increasing retention and pass rates while reducing student costs for course materials and reducing per-pupil instruction costs for colleges and universities.

Since the initiative's inception, publishers have crisscrossed the nation, sharing information, exploring new business models and cost-saving options to offset funding cutbacks, and analyzing ways in which they can help meet the challenges facing states, university systems, and individual schools and faculty.

Higher Ed Critical Issues Task Force

The Higher Education Group's Critical Issues Task Force (CITF) works exclusively on issues involving the provision of accessible instructional materials to postsecondary students with print-related disabilities.

CITF members helped to fund and develop ATN, which launched in beta in August 2009. ATN's membership grew in 2010 to more than 500 individual postsecondary institutions nationwide, plus four system-wide alternative media centers. By December, ATN had already facilitated publishers' fulfillment of more than 32,000 e-text and permissions requests from college Disability Services to Students (DSS) offices.

AAP also participated in the Advisory Commission on Accessible Instructional Materials in Postsecondary Education for Students with Disabilities, which is tasked with making recommendations to Congress after "conducting a comprehensive study to assess the barriers and systemic issues that may affect, and technical solutions available that may improve, the timely delivery and quality of accessible instructional materials for postsecondary students with print disabilities." The commission convened in September and remains active in 2011.

International Copyright Protection

AAP's International Copyright Protection Committee works to combat international copyright piracy, to increase fair access to foreign markets, and to strengthen intellectual property laws. Maria Danzilo (John Wiley & Sons) chaired the committee in 2010.

AAP's enforcement and advocacy efforts extend to a number of key Asian markets including China, Hong Kong, Malaysia, the Philippines, South Korea, Taiwan, and Thailand. In several of these, AAP works with local industry representatives to shape policy and strengthen enforcement through engagement with relevant government agencies. AAP and its member publishers have also been engaged in efforts in Brazil, Egypt, India, Japan, and Vietnam.

China was again a focus of AAP's ongoing enforcement and advocacy efforts in 2010. Key priorities include the following:

- Addressing a pervasive piracy problem affecting both the hard goods and online markets. The U.S.-Chinese government dialogue under the auspices of the Joint Commission on Commerce and Trade (JCCT) continues to be a key forum through which the problem of online piracy of STM (scientific, technical, and medical) journals is addressed. AAP participated in a JCCT-IPR (Intellectual Property Rights) Working Group meeting during which it had an opportunity to directly address the Chinese government on this issue. Online journal piracy and the implementation of the 2009 JCCT Chinese government commitment to strengthen copyright protection at libraries were again high on the U.S. government bilateral agenda with China.
- Legal reform issues, including clarification of Internet intermediary liability under Chinese law.
- World Trade Organization (WTO) Market Access Case compliance. Following the WTO Appellate Body's decision on the market-access case in favor of the United States in December 2009, the U.S. and Chinese governments agreed in July 2010 that the reasonable period of time for China to implement the recommendations and rulings of the Dispute Settlement Body would be 14 months from the date of adoption of the Appellate Body report, or March 19, 2011. The Chinese government had expressed its intent to implement the rulings, noting that the relevant Chinese government agencies had begun to actively study how implementation could be accomplished, but there were no significant developments in 2010.

AAP and its member publishers hope for full and meaningful compliance by China.

Collaborative efforts continued between AAP and Britain's Publishers Association to combat infringement of higher education textbooks at institutions of higher learning as well as trade book piracy throughout China. In the coming year both organizations will intensify engagement with the Chinese government on Internet piracy, particularly online piracy of medical and scientific journals.

Copyright law reform remains a key component of AAP's advocacy efforts. Working through local industry representatives and coalitions, AAP has provided input for a number of government consultations. With online piracy a rapidly expanding threat, legislative reform to facilitate cooperation between rights holders (particularly publishers) and Internet service providers to combat infringing activity continues to be among the highest priorities for AAP and its International Copyright Protection Committee.

AAP is a founding member of the International Intellectual Property Alliance (IIPA). Through IIPA, in February 2010 AAP again provided information and submitted specific recommendations regarding the adequacy of intellectual property protection in a number of countries to the U.S. Trade Representative (USTR) as part of USTR's annual Special 301 review of intellectual property and market-access problems worldwide.

International Freedom to Publish

AAP's International Freedom to Publish (IFTP) Committee defends and promotes freedom of written communication worldwide. The committee monitors human rights issues and provides moral support and practical assistance to publishers and authors outside the United States who are denied basic freedoms. The committee carries on its work in close cooperation with other human rights groups, including the International Publishers Association's Freedom to Publish Committee, Human Rights Watch, and PEN American Center. Hal Fessenden (Viking Penguin) served as committee chairman in 2010.

Jeri Laber, who directed the work of IFTP for more than three decades and who was one of its founding members, retired in spring 2010. Acknowledging her role in the forefront of the international human rights movement as a founder and executive director of Helsinki Watch and as senior advisor to Human Rights Watch, and noting that her accomplishments had "brought honor to the Association of American Publishers," the AAP Board of Directors adopted a resolution at its June meeting expressing the gratitude of the association and its members.

In 2003 IFTP established the Jeri Laber International Freedom to Publish Award, to be given annually to a book publisher outside the United States who has demonstrated courage in the face of political persecution. The award, which carries a cash prize, has been given to publishers in Iran, Turkey, Indonesia, Egypt, Cambodia, and Tibet.

The 2010 Laber award went to Hong Kong-based New Century Press. Established in 2005, the press is committed to making available in Chinese books of historic and political interest that have been banned on the Chinese mainland, a virtually unprecedented initiative in the Chinese-language publishing world.

IFTP members undertake missions to meet with writers, publishers, human rights activists, and others in areas where freedom of expression is seriously threatened. Several years ago committee members Fessenden and Wendy Wolf, together with Larry Siems of PEN and others, traveled to Cambodia to assess the state of publishing in that country. During that trip Cambodian writer and human rights activist Kho Tararith came to the attention of the committee as the founding director of the Nou Hach Literary Project. Tararith and the Nou Hach Literary Project were awarded the 2008 Jeri Laber Award for their work in attempting to revitalize Cambodia's literary life and to revitalize the development of modern Cambodian literature. After receiving the prize, Tararith's activities and outspokenness on human rights issues continued to draw the attention and wrath of government authorities and it became increasingly evident that he would need to leave the country. As a result of the committee's advocacy efforts, working in concert with groups including PEN and Scholars at Risk, Tararith and his family obtained visas to come to the United States, and he is now a visiting scholar at the Watson Institute for International Studies at Brown University. In December 2010 Tararith attended an IFTP meeting in New York and spoke about his ongoing work in support of free expression.

The committee, together with the AAP president, sends letters of protest to officials of foreign governments (and often to U.S. officials as well) regarding violations of free expression in their respective countries. In separate letters sent in August to the president of China and to Secretary of State Hillary Rodham Clinton, the committee issued an urgent call for the release of Tibetan author and editor Tragyal, who was arrested following the publication of his book *The Line Between Sky and Earth,* an indictment of China's policies in Tibet. The arrest appears to be part of a wider crackdown on Tibetan writers and intellectuals. The committee also wrote to Turkish officials protesting the arrest of writer and human rights activist Dogan Akhanli, a German citizen who was arrested at the Istanbul Airport as he attempted to enter Turkey to visit his ailing father.

In October IFTP and AAP joined with publishing colleagues around the world in cheering the announcement that the 2010 Nobel Peace Prize had been awarded to imprisoned Chinese writer Liu Xiabo. Liu, a former president of the Independent Chinese PEN Center, is serving an 11-year jail sentence. The committee had previously protested Liu's arrest.

Professional and Scholarly Publishing

The association's Professional and Scholarly Publishing Division (PSP) serves AAP member organizations that publish books, journals, serials, and electronic products. These span a wide variety of disciplines including technology, science, medicine, business, law, humanities, the social and behavioral sciences, and scholarly reference. Commercial organizations, professional societies, and university presses are the mainstay of the PSP membership. The rapid introduction of e-products throughout this sector of the industry has meant that PSP is increasingly oriented toward digital issues, and there has been increased attention to electronic publishing in all facets of the division's activities. Glen Campbell (Elsevier) chaired the PSP Executive Council in 2010 and Susan King (American Chemical Society) was vice chair. They will continue their two-year term in these roles through 2011.

The PSP Annual Conference is among the division's major membership activities. The 2010 conference, themed "The New Reality: Disruption, Innovation, Relevance," was held in Washington, D.C., in February and saw a rebound in attendance (to 229) after a disappointing turnout the previous year. The 2010 preconference, "The Culture of Free," attracted 97 registrants, also a rebound from the previous year's modest attendance.

The PROSE Awards luncheon is a highlight of the conference. For the second year, the number of competing titles reached new highs, with a 2010 total of 441 submissions in 47 categories. The most prestigious award, the 34th annual R. R. Hawkins Award, was presented to two publishers, University of Chicago Press for *Plato's Philosophers: The Coherence of the Dialogues* and John Wiley & Sons for *Wiley Interdisciplinary Reviews (WIREs).* A new video, "PROSE 2009: Publishers . . . on Publishing," premiered at the luncheon and was posted to the PROSE Web site and YouTube.

In response to members' demand for current information on several fronts—technology development, industry knowledge, and legislative developments—PSP maintained an active and diverse program of communications and industry outreach.

Launched in 2008, *PSP . . . Links* published 23 issues in 2010 to keep PSP member organizations up to date on information posted to the AAP and PSP Web sites as well as the association's professional development programs and industry job postings. The alerting service also provides links to articles and Web sites that contain information relevant to the needs and concerns of PSP members. The *PSP Bulletin* continued its quarterly publication schedule. In 2010 it expanded the number of pages published annually and focused on recruiting articles of interest from external writers.

Two long-planned information initiatives became a reality in 2010. A section on frequently asked questions about public access was developed by the PSP Public Relations Committee and posted to the PSP Web site in May. In addition, a training program titled "What Is Journals Publishing?" was completed at the end of the year and was launched at the February 2011 Annual Conference. Plans call for the development of several additional presentations dealing with specific topics, such as a book-publishing overview, a focus on the importance of peer review, and issues in public access.

PSP Executive Director John Tagler serves as a member of the Chicago Collaborative, an organization that brings together librarians, academics, and publishers to share experiences, educate each other about their respective communities, and develop recommendations that represent their shared views. One of the first programs to be launched is an educational module, Biomedical Publishing 101, designed to educate librarians about biomedical publishing.

In trying to meet the continuing need for information about scholarly journals publishing, the division worked closely with the AAP Statistics Program to get feedback from PSP members for the journals section of the AAP Annual Professional and Scholarly Journals and Books Surveys for 2009.

Education remains a critical component of PSP's service to members. In 2010 the Books Boot Camp was held twice—in the spring in New York and in the fall in Washington, D.C. Collaboration with the Copyright Clearance Center enabled PSP to offer two well-attended webinars on copyright, one on copyright for marketing professionals and a second on international copyright. Other seminars included e-products usage statistics, coverage of semantic publishing, online advertising, and a particularly popular program on social networking that may be repeated in 2011.

PSP committees continued to offer guest speakers at meetings throughout the year. The Electronic Information Committee continued with a second year of its seminars on electronic publishing, offering separate spring and fall series onsite at AAP's New York office and via webinar.

AAP continues to play an active role in legislative matters, submitting comments on three federal legislative and regulatory issues during the first half of 2010, including a joint letter from AAP and the DC Principles Coalition to the White House Office of Science and Technology Policy regarding public access policies for science and technology funding agencies across the federal government, and a letter expressing PSP members' position on the House Science and Technology Committee's Scholarly Publishing Roundtable report. A joint letter from AAP and the DC Principles Coalition was submitted in response to the Federal Research Public Access Act introduced in the House in spring 2010. An important congressional development was reapproval of the America COMPETES Act, which calls for federal grant-funding agencies to work with all constituencies in developing policies for public access to federally funded research projects. Late in the year the National Institutes of Health (NIH) announced an online database, "Images," which offers public access to images contained in articles posted to PubMed Central. The publishing community responded with a letter from AAP and letters from individual publishers expressing concern that a database of images represents a derivative product beyond the boundaries of a manuscript, and that the NIH policy infringes copyright.

PSP continued its support of public service programs to provide medical information where it is needed throughout the world. PSP maintained its active roles in Research4Life, a United Nations-coordinated global initiative for developing countries, and patientINFORM, which collaborates with a growing number of health organizations in the United States to provide patients and caregivers with free access to research articles to help patients better understand disease treatment in such areas as cancer, diabetes, cardiology, lupus, and arthritis. The most tangible outreach program in 2010 was the Emergency Access Initiative (EAI), developed by PSP's American Medical Publishers Committee and the National Library of Medicine. The program gives healthcare professionals and libraries free access to full-text articles from a list of more than 200 biomedical serial titles and select reference books. The January 2010 earthquake in Haiti, which was followed weeks later by a cholera outbreak, was the first crucial test of EAI's viability. Later in the year EAI enabled caregivers in Pakistan to access emergency medical information following devastating floods there.

PSP continues to collaborate with international publishing associations to protect copyright on the global level and address some of the issues that affect U.S. publishers both domestically and abroad. AAP's Online Piracy Working Group gives PSP members an opportunity to understand this escalating challenge and participate in programs that may lead to better control of online copyright infringement.

Resources for the Book Publishing Industry

Book Data Joint Venture

AAP and the Book Industry Study Group (BISG) are embarking on an ambitious initiative to develop a new joint industry statistics model to better track the dramatic changes in the ways book content is produced and sold in the digital age.

In 2010 AAP and BISG interviewed more than 40 industry players, including large and independent publishers, distributors, wholesalers, retailers, allied data providers, associations, and press, and conducted a comprehensive review of survey responses from more than 400 industry participants, in an effort to pressure-test a proposed new industry statistics product.

The new data product, to be released annually in its initial phase, will provide a comprehensive view of book publishing sales aggregated by revenue, units, categories, formats, and distribution channels. A review of the first cut of the data model can be found at http://www.publishers.org/main/IndustryStats/indStats_01.htm.

Response to the joint venture has been overwhelmingly positive, and publisher participation is expected to increase substantially, with data provided by all vertical markets (trade, academic, professional).

A new algorithm is being developed to estimate the size of the industry, to complement actual reports from participants. This new methodology will incorporate data from non-publishing partners including other industry data collection services, associations, retailers, distributors, and wholesalers.

Bowker has been retained as the data collection provider for the new joint venture, with support from AAP's longstanding statistics provider, Management Practice, Inc. The project is being directed by the Statistics Steering Committee, with representation from Hachette Book Group, Sourcebooks, Barnes & Noble, BISG, and AAP.

AAP-Bowker Webinars on Consumer Book Buying

Bowker's PubTrack and AAP joined forces to cohost two educational events in 2011 aimed at helping publishing professionals make the most of consumer information. Each event is intended to provide an overview on the publishing companies' use of consumer data as a business tool, followed by a focused presentation on how editorial, marketing, and sales professionals can use consumer data to acquire, market, and sell their titles more effectively.

Compensation Reports

AAP continues to provide valuable aggregate data reports, including the annual Survey on Compensation and Personnel Practices in the Book Publishing Industry, widely regarded as the most comprehensive and reliable source of data in this area. AAP's Compensation Committee, composed of senior compensation and human resources professionals, met throughout 2010 to create job descriptions and manage the survey process. Purchase of the report is contingent upon participation in the survey.

Total Compensation Solutions, which produces the report for AAP, presented highlights of the 2010 report at AAP's annual human resources seminar, "Compensation and Human Resources Practices in the Book Publishing Industry," in November.

The association also tracks holiday benefits for the publishing community and shares data with a compensation committee composed of publishing industry professionals who independently oversee holiday and vacation compensation for their respective houses.

Annual Statistics

AAP publishes industry statistics for all segments of book publishing, on a monthly and annual basis. Committees for consumer, trade, higher education, and professional publishing met throughout 2010 to revise the program and develop a strategy and implementation process for disseminating consumer and K–12 monthly reports. More than 80 publishers participate in AAP's monthly statistical reports, which aggregate revenue and compile raw data on market size on a month-to-month basis and provide year-to-date growth based on a cross section of the industry. Additional data points were produced for the el-hi market for the third quarter of the year. Outreach to journals publishers resulted in substantially increased representation.

Smaller and Independent Publishers

AAP's Smaller and Independent Publishing Committee was created in 1998. In 2010 the committee continued to work with partners to create educational programming for the independent publishing community. A session on maximizing special market sales was planned for 2011, and the committee will focus on a revitalized membership drive.

School Division

The School Division is concerned with publishing for the elementary and secondary school (K–12) market. The division works to enhance the role of instructional materials in the education process, to maintain categorical funding for instructional materials and increase the funds available for the purchase of these materials, to simplify and rationalize the process of state adoptions for instructional materials, and to generally improve the climate in which educational publishers do business. Paul McFall (Pearson Education) chaired the School Division Executive Committee in 2010.

In 2010 the division continued to play a key role in supporting the el-hi publishing industry through a range of public policy initiatives.

The year saw slightly improving economic conditions in the states and school districts, which led to an increase of 3.2 percent in elementary and secondary annual net sales. Sales in the adoption states were strongest, with an increase of 15.4 percent; sales in the non-adoption states fell 7.6 percent for the year.

Major Initiatives and Meetings

During 2010 the School Division launched a series of initiatives to assist school publishers as they, along with states and school districts across the nation, make the transition to Common Core State Standards in reading/language arts and math. This transition will require publishers to develop instructional materials and assessments that align with the new Common Core standards rather than existing state standards. To support publishers in this transition, the School Division convened a series of meetings and presentations on Common Core implementation. In addition, the division's Fall Summit on K–12 publishing was devoted to a series of topics relating to implementation of the Common Core State Standards.

At the state level, the division was active in more than a dozen states on issues ranging from instructional materials funding to legislation relating to accessibility issues concerning textbooks for blind and print-disabled students. At the federal level, AAP and its members were active on Capitol Hill in early March when they met with more than three dozen members of Congress to discuss the division's priorities for reauthorization of the Elementary and Secondary Education Act.

The division was also active on international issues in 2010. Jay Diskey, the division's executive director, participated in International Publishers Association (IPA) meetings on school publishing issues including digital piracy and open educational resources. A working group of educational publishers and IPA members convened in London, Barcelona, and Frankfurt to develop policy papers and public relations strategies relating to the two issues.

Trade Publishing

AAP's Trade Publishing Group includes publishers of fiction, general nonfiction, poetry, children's literature, religious books, and reference publications, in hardcover, paperback, and electronic formats, and represents the most senior committee within the association's trade publishing core. Susan Peterson Kennedy (Penguin Group USA) became chair of the Trade Executive Committee in 2010.

In 2010 the executive committee focused its efforts on communicating the value of trade publishing, including the ability to discover and nurture talent. The committee has articulated the role of the trade publisher in its mission statement: "Bringing writers to readers is what we do. The role of the publisher is to invest in good writers and good books, connecting authors to readers. Publishers curate and invest in many ideas, looking for the best, the most meaningful and the most original. Publishers focus the cultural conversation and develop market innovations which help bring eyes to writers' works."

In cooperation with the National Book Foundation, the Trade Publishing Group played an active role in lobbying the White House for heightened national recognition of National Book Award winners. The goal is to raise the public profile of existing programs, create new ones, and cultivate press coverage in order to build general public awareness of the contribution contemporary writers make to American culture, to enhance the place of writers and writing among the arts, and to emphasize the essential role of writers and books in the public dialogue that is central to democratic society.

Get Caught Reading

As inheritors of the existing Get Caught Reading campaign, a subcommittee under the direction of the Trade Executive Committee plans to create a new reading-promotion campaign in the digital arena. The target demographic for the new campaign is 18- to 35-year-olds, built on the existence of a new generation of readers—"the Harry Potter Generation"—as reflected in the rise in reading rates reported by the National Endowment for the Arts. The subcommittee is considering a new tagline ("What Are You Reading?") and is exploring partnerships with various social media/digital platforms, advertising agencies, and retail partners. The current Get Caught Reading Web site will be refreshed with new content, including videos of authors discussing the importance of libraries.

Trade Libraries Committee

AAP's Trade Libraries Committee, chaired by Talia Ross (Macmillan), is made up of representatives of major book publishing houses in partnership with such organizations as ALA. The committee continued to focus its efforts in 2010 on promoting titles, hosting educational sessions for librarians at various trade conventions including BookExpo America (BEA), the ALA Midwinter Meeting, and the Texas Library Association meeting. The committee hosted several successful author events at BEA 2010 in New York with speakers including Cory Doctorow, Rachel Vincent, Jane Green, Ann Brashares, Susan Isaacs, Jonathan Adler, Joshilyn Jackson, Caroline Leavitt, Deborah Coonts, and Adriana Trigiani.

At BEA the committee also hosted educational sessions on leveraging the popularity of romance novels and a first "Librarians Shout and Share," in which librarians shared their top book picks.

In fall 2010 the committee hosted a spring catalog preview exclusively for adult collection development librarians in the greater New York area. In collaboration with *Library Journal,* the committee provides its own ongoing book reviews in the magazine's online newsletter "BookSmack."

American Booksellers Association

200 White Plains Rd., Tarrytown, NY 10591
914-591-2665
World Wide Web http://www.BookWeb.org

The American Booksellers Association (ABA) and its approximately 1,500 bookstore members had a busy year of accomplishment in 2010. Despite ongoing challenges posed by the economy, independent booksellers reported improved sales and strong and growing community support. ABA's year included an important merger with the Association of Booksellers for Children (ABC); policy and administration changes to better serve members; increased advocacy efforts on the national, state, and local levels; significant new initiatives in technology; growth in its IndieBound marketing program; and a continued emphasis on member education.

Staff Reorganization

In early 2010 the association announced that it had begun a process of staff reorganization. Several new senior staff positions were announced:

- Meg Smith was named membership and marketing officer.
- Dan Cullen was named content officer to head a newly created content department.
- Mark Nichols was named industry relations officer.
- Jill Perlstein was named meetings and planning officer, a newly created officer-level position in which she will oversee all meeting and event logistics, including such high-profile events as the ABA Winter Institute and the association's participation in BookExpo America.

Len Vlahos continues as ABA's chief operating officer, and Eleanor Chang continues in her role as chief financial officer.

Said ABA Chief Executive Officer Oren Teicher, "I was charged by the association's board of directors to make ABA both more efficient and better prepared to meet the new and myriad challenges facing independent booksellers. This reorganization, which is the result of many months of analysis and investigation, is the first step in that process."

New Dues Structure

In an August 2010 letter to the membership, ABA President Michael Tucker announced the launch of a new dues structure to go into effect as of February 1, 2011. Under the changes, the association reduced the annual dues of smaller stores and established a separate category for new stores. In addition, the entire dues renewal process, which had gone unchanged for a decade, was made less complex, and used bookstores were made eligible for ABA membership.

"ABA is making these changes because we believe in the opportunities inherent for community-based, indie booksellers in this time of substantial change, and the importance of making sure that bookstores have the resources and support necessary to take root and grow," Tucker said.

Member Relations

In March 2010 ABA launched a Member Relations Department to ensure that booksellers have a convenient way to get information about the opportunities available to them as part of their membership. Under the new structure, two member relations managers serve as the main contacts for all bookstore and provisional members. At the launch of the new department, Smith explained that "We heard from members that they weren't sure which ABA staff members they should speak to about different issues, and while booksellers are welcome to contact any staff members, this new member-relations structure gives them an easy way to get an answer to any question."

Elections

In May ABA announced the results of balloting by bookstore members to elect three board directors and to ratify the board's selection for president and vice president. Elected to serve three-year terms as directors beginning June 2010 were Sarah Bagby of Watermark Books in Wichita, Kansas; Steve Bercu of BookPeople in Austin, Texas; and Tom Campbell of the Regulator Bookshop in Durham, North Carolina. Bercu and Campbell are now in their second three-year terms on the board. ABA membership also ratified the board's choice of Tucker, of Books Inc. in San Francisco, to serve a second one-year term as president, and Becky Anderson, of Anderson's Bookshops in Naperville, Illinois, as vice president/secretary. Ending her second term as a board director was Cathy Langer of Tattered Cover Book Store in Denver.

Merger with ABC

In the culmination of a process that took almost two years, voting members of the Association of Booksellers for Children (ABC) cast ballots in October in favor of a merger with ABA. ABC members approved the merger by a margin of better than 4 to 1. A total of 127 ballots were returned, with 105 stores voting in favor of the merger (nearly 83 percent), and 23 opposed (18 percent). This represented a 67 percent majority of ABC's eligible stores.

"I'm very proud of the stores of the ABC," said ABC Executive Director Kristen McLean. "This vote was much larger than the issue of who will administer ABC's programming. We are in a time of unprecedented industry evolution, and I believe the independent booksellers of the ABC are sending a message that they can also evolve to meet the demands of the changing industry positively. I'm very excited that many more stores will have access to the expertise of ABC, and that children's issues will continue to be an important part of the ongoing dialogue that ABA is cultivating at the national level."

The merger comes at a time when children's books are playing an increasingly important role in the bottom line of many bookstores as they try to hedge against uncertainty in the marketplace. "Children's bookselling continues to be one of the vital bright spots in a struggling industry, and we are delighted to share our collective knowledge and expertise with all of our colleagues at the ABA," said ABC President Elizabeth Bluemle, of the Flying Pig Bookstore in Shelburne, Vermont. "After such a long process, it will be wonderful to see new programming and resources evolve and, we hope, reach a broader membership."

The merger also reflects the trend toward consolidation at all levels of the book industry as the traditional model streamlines in the face of changes in consumer behavior, technology, and distribution. "The merger of ABC and ABA comes at a time when all independent booksellers need to unite their resources, passion, and expertise to build for our future," said ABA Vice President Anderson, a past president of ABC. "Children's issues are a huge part of this future for all stores. Together we can take independent children's bookselling to new heights and continued growth."

ABA CEO Teicher commented that "Recognizing the rich history and many accomplishments of the Association of Booksellers for Children, coupled with all the enormous changes taking place in retail bookselling, we at ABA see this [merger] as an opportunity to be able to accomplish more to serve the present and future needs of children's booksellers.

In addition, the ABA board amended the association's Ends Policies to include the following language: "Members will have access to programs specifically aimed at growing and expanding the reach of children's books to a wide audience of both consumers and booksellers and would include such things as communication vehicles, appropriate awards, and educational programs."

Survey Partnership

In an important enhancement of a key association initiative, ABA announced that it would produce the 2010 ABACUS Survey through a new partnership with the National Association of College Stores (NACS). ABACUS is a yearly financial survey for ABA member bookstores that provides a tool for evaluating and improving a bookstore's financial performance, and for helping in key strategic business decisions.

Signs of Growth

Against a backdrop of measured economic recovery, there were many positive markers of innovation and growth among independent booksellers. Twenty-six ABA member bookstores opened in 2010, with several filling voids left by the closing of major chain stores. The openings, and neighborhood response, suggest continued and growing support for locally owned businesses and bricks-and-mortar stores. Some of the new stores are branches of existing businesses, while others offer interesting twists on traditional business models. All of the stores have been welcomed by their communities. Key elements of their business strategy are strong community ties; a distinctive, curated inventory; and intriguing nonbook offerings.

Despite the numerous challenges faced by independent retailers throughout 2010, many booksellers reported to ABA that they had a strong holiday season, with both an overall increase from last year's sales and a significant improvement from 2009. Independent booksellers continued to distinguish themselves by showcasing local authors and artists and boosted sales by creating attractive pairings of books and sidelines. Many booksellers noted an overall positive shift in consumer confidence and in shoppers' spending behavior during the 2010 holiday season.

Numerous member bookstores reported that they again used ABA's innovative marketing materials from the IndieBound holiday design initiative. The materials, which can be adapted and personalized, all emphasized community and the value of books as gifts.

The resilience of independent businesses was borne out by a post-holiday national survey. For the fourth consecutive year, the survey revealed that those in communities with active "buy local" campaigns had experienced markedly stronger revenue growth compared with those located in areas without such initiatives.

The survey, conducted in January, gathered data from 2,768 independent businesses, including retailers (among them hundreds of ABA member booksellers), service providers, restaurants, and others. The survey found that those in communities with a "buy local" initiative reported revenue growth of 5.6 percent on average in 2010, compared with 2.1 percent for those in areas without such a campaign. Among independent retailers, which accounted for nearly half the respondents, there was a similar gap in holiday sales performance, with those in "buy local" communities seeing a 5.2 percent increase in holiday sales while those elsewhere reported an average gain of 0.8 percent. "Buy local" campaigns run by American Independent Business Alliance organizations and Local First groups are now under way in about 140 U.S. cities.

Nearly two-thirds of respondents said that public awareness of the benefits of supporting locally owned businesses had increased in the past year, while 24 percent said awareness had stayed the same, and only 3 percent said it had decreased. Business owners in cities with active "buy local" campaigns reported a wide range of positive impacts on their businesses. Almost half reported that the campaign had brought new customers to their business, and 55 percent said it had made existing customers more loyal. More than two-thirds said local media coverage of independent businesses had increased, and 51 percent said that local government officials were now more aware and supportive of the needs of independent businesses.

Throughout the year, there was ongoing media coverage highlighting the opportunities for independent booksellers in a society of hyper-connectivity and technological saturation. In August *New York* magazine reported that "against all odds, a small army of neighborhood bookshops has arrived" in the city and noted that, despite the closing of some of New York's bookselling institutions, the city was "suddenly, unexpectedly in the midst of an indie-bookstore renaissance."

The same month, Portfolio.com surveyed industry trends and news updates—falling sales at chain book superstores, the growing market share of big-box discounters like Walmart, Amazon.com's competitive advantage gained from its refusal to collect state sales tax—and asked, "Do these stories leave an opening for small businesses?" The piece also cited the growing importance of localism to consumers and, importantly, the inherent abilities of smaller entrepreneurs to respond quickly and effectively to business conditions and trends. As Jessica Stockton Bagnulo, co-owner of Greenlight Bookstore in Brooklyn, New York, said in a Reuters story headlined "U.S. Neighborhood Bookstores Thrive in Digital Age," "People are rediscovering the value of an independent store that's connected to their neighborhood and understands them and their tastes."

In what has become an annual tradition, several ABA senior staff members volunteered at member stores during the 2010 holiday season. Their goal was to help out wherever needed and to gather information about bookselling on the frontlines. In 2010 ABA's CEO and COO and its industry relations officer, Mark Nichols, hand-sold and gift-wrapped at Russo's Books in Bakersfield, California; R. J. Julia Booksellers in Madison, Connecticut; and Posman Books in New York, respectively.

IndieCommerce Links with Google eBooks

ABA continued its ongoing upgrades and enhancements to IndieCommerce, its e-commerce business solution for member stores. In December it was announced that member stores with IndieCommerce Web sites could now sell Google eBooks.

"This partnership with Google is an important chapter in the renaissance we've been seeing in independent bookselling," said ABA President Tucker. "It allows our membership to better compete with corporate retailers on selection, price, and convenience. It levels the playing field."

A Google eBook is a new form of cloud-based digital book that allows readers to access their personal libraries on almost any device from a single repository, regardless of where the e-book was purchased. Google offers hundreds of thousands of titles for sale, ranging from new releases and bestsellers in every category to classics in the public domain.

In conjunction with the launch, ABA announced IndieCommerce.com, a new Web site that offers a wealth of resources to help IndieCommerce stores answer consumer questions about e-books and e-readers. The site also provides information for bookstores interested in learning more about the IndieCommerce program.

During the year the ABA board approved the use of resources to substantially upgrade the IndieCommerce platform. The first phase of the upgrade consists of improvements to the search and checkout processes on IndieCommerce Web sites, which were the improvements most frequently requested by IndieCommerce users.

IndieBound

ABA's IndieBound program saw continued development in 2010, including debuts in Britain and Australia. The Booksellers Association of the United Kingdom and Ireland licensed IndieBound marketing materials, and independent booksellers there began receiving those materials in May. In July the Australian Booksellers Association launched an Australia-based IndieBound. The Australian association will license for its members' use certain IndieBound designs, and marketing and collateral materials.

In a major initiative, in September bestselling thriller-writer James Patterson launched a new program to support college-bound high school students. "Book Dollars for Scholars" is a contest open to high school seniors who will have an opportunity to win one of 56 gift certificates, ranging from $250 to $5,000, for use at any IndieBound-affiliated independent bookstore. High school students can enter to win the certificates by participating in an essay contest via JamesPatterson.com (http://www.JamesPatterson.com). The essay question asks, "How has your favorite book inspired you toward what you'd like to do in life?" Essays will be read by Patterson and select members from his ReadKiddoRead.com board.

April 17, 2010, marked the first celebration of e-Free Day, created by IndieBound as a way for booksellers to encourage customers to put down their electronic gadgets and pick up a book instead. The ready-made marketing campaign featured downloadable e-Free posters, bag stuffers, and a list of activity ideas that stores could use to create in-store events.

Indies Choice Book Awards

ABA again sponsored the Indies Choice Book Awards, reflecting the spirit of independent bookstores nationwide and the IndieBound movement.

The 2010 winners were chosen by the owners and staff at ABA member stores nationwide in more than four weeks of voting. Winners were all titles appearing on the 2009 Indie Next lists. [For a listing of the Indies Choice winners and other major book awards, see "Literary Prizes, 2010" in Part 5—*Ed.*]

ABA members also inducted three of their all-time favorites into the Indies Choice Book Awards Picture Book Hall of Fame: *Alexander and the Terrible, Horrible, No Good Very Bad Day* by Judith Viorst and Ray Cruz (Atheneum); *Madeline* by Ludwig Bemelmans (Viking), and *The Story of Ferdinand* by Munro Leaf and Robert Lawson (Viking).

Winter Institute

ABA's 2010 ABA Winter Institute (Wi5), a three-day education program, gave booksellers, both new and experienced, practical ideas and guidance on how to respond to the rapidly changing digital environment. Sessions on everything from e-books and technology issues to handselling and alternative business models were interspersed with opportunities for networking, opportunities for booksellers to hear about upcoming spring titles, and keynote speeches featuring industry leaders including Ingram's Andrew Weinstein, Google Books' Daniel Clancy, Verso's Jack McKeown, and Daniel Pink, author of *Drive: The Surprising Truth That Motivates Us* (Riverhead).

The results of a consumer survey presented by McKeown showed that independent booksellers' "mind share" (book buyers' preferred shopping location as opposed to their actual shopping location) was equal to the major bookstore chains' and more than online sellers'.

BookExpo America

Several hundred ABA member bookstores were represented at BookExpo America 2010 (BEA) in May. Packed educational sessions at the New York trade show reflected booksellers' interest in staying abreast of changes in the industry.

ABA again provided a full day of education at BEA, which began with "Opening Plenary: A CEO Panel on the Value of the Book." The panel, cosponsored by ABA and BEA, featured Bob Miller, group publisher, Workman; Esther Newberg, executive vice president, International Creative Management (ICM); Skip Prichard, chief executive officer, Ingram; David Shanks, chief executive officer, Penguin Group (USA); ABA CEO Oren Teicher; and Scott Turow, author and incoming president of the Authors Guild. Other sessions included roundtable discussions and seminars on a range of issues, including techniques and tactics for Web site promotion.

ABA again worked closely with BookExpo America on a number of initiatives, including limited free BEA attendance for ABA members. In addition, ABA and BEA provided "crossover" attendance to the organizations' concurrent retailer education tracks.

Advocacy

As part of its reorganization in 2010, ABA increased its advocacy efforts on behalf of member bookstores. An important step was the establishment of an online E-Fairness Action Kit (E-FACT) that provides booksellers with crucial, state-specific tools to help them in their E-Fairness outreach efforts. The E-Fairness campaign urges state lawmakers to enact regulations to require online-only booksellers to collect sales taxes as bricks-and-mortar businesses must do. E-FACT, located on the ABA Web site BookWeb.org, gives booksellers state-specific template letters to their state legislators and governor, as well as suggested op-ed pieces, lists of FAQs, and relevant articles to help advocate on behalf of e-fairness.

Throughout the year, ABA worked with booksellers to help them make their views known to elected officials regarding the importance of e-fairness and sales tax equity, assisting them in meeting with legislators and state officials, offering important background information and support materials, and working with a growing number of allied trade associations and organizations. Among the meetings ABA helped facilitate were bookseller meetings with the attorneys general of Connecticut and Texas.

ABA continued its efforts to represent the needs of small businesses in Washington, D.C. In April 2010 ABA President Tucker and CEO Teicher met with Karen Gordon Mills, head of the Small Business Administration (SBA), to discuss issues of importance to independent booksellers. Joining them at the meeting was SBA Chief of Staff Ana M. Ma. Two key topics of the discussion were access to capital and small business tax credits in the new health insurance reform law.

Recognizing the importance of communication and institutional cooperation, leaders of trade associations and other organizations representing independent businesses joined together in January in Washington, D.C., for the Advocates for Independent Retail (AIR) Summit, organized by ABA.

American Booksellers Foundation for Free Expression

The American Booksellers Foundation for Free Expression (ABFFE) is the bookseller's voice in the fight against censorship.

In November 2010 the U.S. Supreme Court debated the constitutionality of a California law that bans minors from purchasing violent video games. ABFFE filed a friend-of-the-court brief arguing that upholding the law would open the door to the regulation of violent content in books and other media. A few months earlier, the Supreme Court handed down a decision in another important case, overturning a law that banned the depiction of animal cruelty; ABFFE had filed a brief opposing the law on the grounds that it created a new category of "low-value" speech that could be expanded to include almost anything that someone finds offensive.

On the state level, ABFFE won three major court victories in a five-week period in fall 2010. The Ninth Circuit Court of Appeals struck down an unconstitutional Oregon law that blocked minors' access to material containing images or narrative accounts of sexual conduct. ABFFE became a plaintiff in the case because the law was so broad that it could have criminalized the sale to minors of sex education books and many young adult titles. ABFFE was also a plaintiff in challenges to laws in Alaska and Massachusetts that restricted the sale of First Amendment-protected material considered "harmful to minors." Both laws were struck down a month after the decision in the Oregon case.

Meanwhile, ABFFE continued to engage in the daily struggle against book-banning in schools and libraries. The American Library Association (ALA) reported more than 400 such challenges in 2009. With ALA, ABFFE cosponsored Banned Books Week to make Americans aware of widespread challenges to free speech. With the National Coalition Against Censorship (NCAC), ABFFE cosponsored the Kids' Right to Read Project, which communicates with school officials when books are challenged. ABFFE also joined with ALA, NCAC, and others in protesting efforts by Common Sense Media (CSM) to create a book-rating system that could have a chilling effect on the sale of books that CSM reviewers consider controversial.

ABFFE was founded by ABA in 1990. Its address is 19 Fulton St., New York, NY 10038 (telephone 212-587-4025, fax 212-587-2436, World Wide Web http://www.abffe.com). Its president is Chris Finan.

Association of Research Libraries

21 Dupont Circle N.W., Washington, DC 20036
202-296-2296, e-mail arlhq@arl.org
World Wide Web http://www.arl.org

Lee Anne George
Publications Program Officer

The Association of Research Libraries (ARL) is a nonprofit organization of 126 research libraries in the United States and Canada. Its mission is to influence the changing environment of scholarly communication and the public policies that affect research libraries and the diverse communities they serve. ARL pursues this mission by advancing the goals of its member research libraries, providing leadership in public and information policy to the scholarly and higher education communities, fostering the exchange of ideas and expertise, facilitating the emergence of new roles for research libraries, and shaping a future environment that leverages ARL's interests with those of allied organizations.

Following a year-long review involving several rounds of member input, in November 2009 the ARL board adopted the ARL Strategic Plan for 2010–2012. A special issue of *Research Library Issues* focuses on the new plan. In an introductory essay, ARL Executive Director Charles B. Lowry highlights some of the challenges that ARL will address during the next three years "where ARL can play a role in finding a solution that can be achieved principally through collective action and with modest resources." Lowry provides examples of the association's efforts that tie directly to the outcomes and strategies targeted by the strategic plan. *Research Library Issues* 268 (February 2010), containing the article, is posted at http://publications.arl.org/rli/r26s2.

Influencing Public Policies

A primary goal of ARL's Public Policies program is to influence legislative action that is favorable to the research library and higher education communities. To achieve this goal, the program helps ARL members keep abreast of the legislative landscape, as well as rapidly changing issues, players, regulations, and community priorities. Program staff track the activities of state and federal legislatures as well as regulatory and government agencies in the United States and Canada and abroad. The program analyzes, responds to, and seeks to influence public initiatives on information, intellectual property, and telecommunications policies, among others. In addition, the program promotes funding for numerous agencies and national institutions and advances ARL members' interests on these issues. The Public Policies program monitors Canadian information policies, such as copyright and intellectual property and access to government information, through the Canadian Association of Research Libraries. Additional information about this ARL strategic direction is available at http://www.arl.org/pp.

Copyright and Intellectual Property

Court Cases and Related Activities

During 2010 ARL filed and/or participated in nine amicus (friend of the court) legal briefs. Although the majority of the cases focused on copyright issues (e.g., safe harbor under the Digital Millennium Copyright Act in *Viacom* v. *YouTube* and *UMG* v. *Veoh*), several others concerned free speech, affirmative action, and freedom of information. For example, in July ARL joined the American Council on Education and others in the higher education community in an amicus brief supporting the Hastings College of Law. In this case, the U.S. Supreme Court ruled in favor of public institutions' First Amendment right to academic freedom. The brief is available at http://www.acenet.edu/AM/Template.cfm?Section=Legal_Issues_and_Policy_Briefs2&TEMPLATE=/CM/ContentDisplay.cfm&CONTENTID=35884.

In November ARL joined Citizens for Responsibility and Ethics in Washington, the Electronic Frontier Foundation (EFF), and four other organizations in filing an amicus brief before the U.S. Supreme Court concerning whether privacy protections under the Freedom of Information Act (FOIA) are applicable to corporations. The ruling in the case, *Federal Communications Commission* v. *AT&T*, will have a significant impact on government transparency and accountability. The brief is available at http://www.arl.org/bm~doc/fccvs_att_amicus.pdf.

Several cases concerned the first sale doctrine. As the case *Timothy S. Vernor* v. *Autodesk, Inc.* (which concerns software licensing and the first sale doctrine) moved through the courts in 2010, ARL joined EFF and others in the public interest sector in filing amicus briefs about the importance of the first sale doctrine. In its ruling, determining that software is licensed, not owned, the U.S. Federal Court of Appeals for the Ninth Circuit acknowledged policy concerns raised by its decision, including the possibility that sellers of books and music could use licenses to significantly impair the ability of libraries to obtain and circulate materials. The brief is available at http://www.librarycopyrightalliance.org/bm~doc/lca_vernor12oct10.pdf.

The Library Copyright Alliance (LCA) filed an amicus brief before the U.S. Supreme Court in another case concerning first sale, *Costco* v. *Omega*. The U.S. Court of Appeals for the Ninth Circuit ruled that the first sale doctrine applied only to copies manufactured in the United States. If a book does not specify that it was printed in the United States, a library would not know whether it could lend it without being exposed to a copyright lawsuit. The Supreme Court let the Ninth Circuit ruling stand. For more information, see http://www.arl.org/news/pr/lcaamicus-8july10.shtml.

ARL joined in several cases relating to fair use. In September ARL—along with the American Library Association (ALA), the Association of College and Research Libraries (ACRL), the International Documentary Association, and the WGBH Educational Foundation—joined an amicus brief asking for the full U.S. Court of Appeals for the Fourth Circuit to rehear the case of *Bouchat* v. *Ravens* and reconsider a ruling concerning fair use. The court has yet to rule. The brief is available at http://www.arl.org/bm~doc/amicus_bouchatvravens092010.pdf.

In September a preliminary decision was issued in a closely watched case concerning alleged copyright infringement. A trio of academic publishers, two of which are university presses, brought a copyright infringement suit in 2008 against administrators and trustees of Georgia State University. Following the preliminary ruling, the ARL executive director sent a letter to the president of the Copyright Clearance Center (CCC) expressing ARL's concerns with CCC's decision to underwrite 50 percent of the legal fees of the three publishers in the litigation against Georgia State. The letter states:

> As the CCC notes on its website, the not-for-profit organization was founded 'by a collaboration of content creators, content publishers, and content users.' The CCC also notes that it 'serves the interests of those who supply content as well as those who use it.' Balancing the interests of these communities can be a challenging task, and many efforts have been made over the years to that end with the understanding that collaboration is a far more successful strategy. Unfortunately, this action by the CCC signals to the content user community that the CCC no longer seeks to serve the interests of all of the partners in the scholarly communications enterprise.

The letter asks that CCC seriously reconsider its role and participation in litigation against members of the academic community. The letter is available at http://www.arl.org/bm~doc/ltccc-final.pdf. For additional information, see http://policynotes.arl.org/post/1242815160/federal-court-narrows-georgia-state-e-reserves-case.

International Copyright Activities

The main focus of ARL's and LCA's international activities was twofold: to respond to draft treaties on traditional cultural expression, on the blind, the visually impaired, and the print disabled; on an upcoming 2011 World Intellectual Property Organization (WIPO) meeting to consider limitations and exceptions for libraries and archives; and to formulate positions on the Anti-Counterfeiting Trade Agreement negotiations. For example, with regard to traditional cultural expression, in a letter to WIPO, LCA noted that such a treaty would have a negative impact on the public domain, intellectual freedom, access to information held in library collections, and a library's ability to meet the educational and research needs of the community it serves. The letter is available at http://www.librarycopyrightalliance.org/bm~doc/lca_wipo_comments_072210.pdf.

Fair Use and Related Initiatives

ARL received a grant from the Andrew W. Mellon Foundation to develop a code of best practices in fair use for academic and research libraries. ARL is undertaking the three-year project with the Center for Social Media at American University and the Program on Information Justice and Intellectual Property in American University's Washington College of Law. The project will be conducted in three phases: a research phase, in which the project team will conduct interviews with members of the library and legal communities; a development phase, in which the project team, with members of the academic and research library community, will draft and publish the code of best practices; and an outreach phase, in which the project team will distribute and publicize the code of best practices. In December ARL released the results of Phase 1: "Fair Use Challenges in Academic and Research Libraries," a report that summarizes research into the current application of fair use and other copyright exemptions to meet the missions of U.S. academic and research libraries. The report is available at http://www.arl.org/bm~doc/arl_csm_fairusereport.pdf. For additional information, see http://www.arl.org/pp/ppcopyright/codefairuse/index.shtml.

In February 2010 LCA released an issue brief that reviews the legal status of streaming entire films to students located outside of the traditional classroom. The discussion was prompted, in part, by the disagreement between University of California, Los Angeles (UCLA) and a media equipment trade association, Association for Information Media and Equipment (AIME), over the streaming of films to students as part of an online courseware system. In December AIME and Ambrose Video Publishing filed suit against the regents and chancellor of UCLA in federal court, claiming that UCLA's video streaming program violates copyright and contract law. UCLA has said its practices are permissible under the copyright limitations and exceptions, and licensing terms and conditions. For more information, see http://www.librarycopyrightalliance.org/bm~doc/ibstreamingfilms_021810.pdf.

In December LCA filed comments in regard to a notice of inquiry from the Department of Commerce. The comments focused on a broad range of topics relating to the impact of restrictions on the free flow of information on the Internet on innovation, global economic growth, trade, and investment. The comments are available at http://www.arl.org/bm~doc/lcadocnoi.pdf.

Every three years the Librarian of Congress is allowed to adopt exemptions to Section 1201(a)(1) of the Digital Millennium Copyright Act (DMCA), the anticircumvention provisions that place technological protections on copyrighted works. In the latest round of exemptions, the librarian ruled in accordance with requests made by LCA members. LCA applauded the decision by the librarian to expand the exemption for the creation of film-clip compilations for classroom and educational use to all college and university faculty, regardless of academic discipline. For more information, see http://www.arl.org/news/pr/1201exempt-27july10.shtml.

Public Access Policies

Open and Public Access Policies

There was a great deal of momentum around adoption of open and public access policies in 2010. For example, the Federal Research Public Access Act was introduced in the House of Representatives and the Senate. Congress reauthorized the America COMPETES Act, a law intended to promote U.S. competitiveness through a renewed focus on improvements in math and science education and a strong commitment to research, which included language on public access policies to federally funded research and data. In addition, the National Science Board's Task Force on Data Policy began to examine the management and sharing of data and decided to include public access to peer-reviewed journal literature in their deliberations. See http://www.nsf.gov/nsb/committees/tskforce_dp_charge.jsp.

The White House Office of Science and Technology requested public comment on extending public access to federally funded research to all science and technology agencies. These federal initiatives follow a growing number of academic institutions adopting institutional policies concerning the work of their faculty, students, and researchers. ARL comments are available at http://www.arl.org/bm%7Edoc/ostp-15jan2010.pdf.

Open Government

Throughout the year ARL joined OpenTheGovernment.org and other groups focused on transparency issues to write letters to Congress and federal agencies. These included issues concerning FOIA agency practices, destruction of agency e-mails, Wikileaks, the Gulf of Mexico oil spill, and other topics. For example, ARL and 32 other organizations joined OpenTheGovernment.org in a letter to the Senate supporting the Faster FOIA Act, which would result in recommendations on how to reduce delays in processing FOIA requests. In addition, ARL joined OpenTheGovernment.org and seven other nonprofit organizations in hosting a discussion on open government at the Center for American Progress in Washington, D.C., on March 19. Leading experts on transparency issues from inside and outside government discussed if and how the Obama administration's Open Government Directive and related initiatives have made the federal government more open, and what remains to be done. For a report on this event, see http://www.americanprogress.org/events/2010/03/sunshine.html.

Federal Depository Library Program

Following on the ARL/COSLA study by Ithaka, "Documents for a Digital Democracy: A Model for the Federal Depository Library Program in the 21st Century," the ARL Board of Directors endorsed a set of principles on October 14 that recognizes that federal documents collections are valuable assets of the individual libraries, the states and regions where the collections are located, and for the nation as a whole. The statement also notes that the best means of providing broad public access to these collections is through online access to digital and digitized copies. Therefore, the management of these tangible collections should include efforts to support or participate in initiatives to create a comprehensive digital collection in the public domain. The principles are available at http://www.arl.org/bm~doc/fdlpprinciples14oct10.pdf. The Ithaka report is available at http://www.arl.org/bm~doc/documents-for-a-digital-democracy.pdf.

Privacy and Civil Liberties Issues

ARL, as a member of Digital Due Process—a coalition of technology, communications, and other organizations focused on privacy issues in the Internet age—filed comments in June 2010 with the National Telecommunications and Information Administration, U.S. Department of Commerce, regarding how best to update the Electronic Communications Privacy Act. The comments are available at http://www.digitaldueprocess.org/index.cfm?objectid=7A1286F6-78C1-11DF-8BFB000C296BA163.

In December ARL and ALA endorsed comments filed by the Center for Democracy and Technology (CDT) in response to a Department of Commerce notice of inquiry regarding the free flow of information on the Internet. CDT, ARL, and ALA also provided recommendations on how the Department of Commerce could implement policies that promote the free flow of information. The comments are available at http://www.arl.org/bm~doc/commentscdt-arl-ala_noi.pdf.

Net Neutrality

Ensuring the availability of low-cost, high-speed, nondiscriminatory Internet services is essential for research libraries and academic institutions to achieve their missions in the 21st century. As a consequence, ARL actively participated in debates concerning network neutrality or ensuring that every network operator that provides Internet access to the public must allow every user to access and use all desired content, applications, and services on the Internet without interference or discrimination. Activities included meeting with staff and commissioners of the Federal Communications Commission (FCC), congressional visits, joint statements, and numerous filings before FCC. For example, in January, ARL, EDUCAUSE, Internet2, ACUTA, and NYSERNet filed comments with FCC in support of preserving "network neutrality"—keeping the Internet open—which is a priority of the Obama administration. ARL, as a member of the Open Internet Coalition (OIC), also joined in OIC's comments to FCC and to Congress. More information is available at http://publications.arl.org/rli273 and http://www.arl.org/pp/telecom.

Federal Agency Funding

During 2010 ARL wrote to Congress in support of appropriations for the National Science Foundation, the U.S. Government Printing Office, and the National Endowment for the Humanities. For more information, see http://www.arl.org/pp/fedfund.

Policy Notes Blog

ARL also launched a blog, "ARL Policy Notes" (http://policynotes.arl.org). The blog reports on public policy issues and their impact on the research library community, from copyright and intellectual property (such as the Google Book Search Settlement, fair use issues, and net neutrality), access to federally funded research, and to the Federal Depository Library Program.

Reshaping Scholarly Communication

ARL's Reshaping Scholarly Communication program works to develop effective, extensible, sustainable, and economically viable models of scholarly communication that provide barrier-free access to high-quality information in support of the mission of research institutions. The program articulates the dynamic system of scholarly communication, encourages the creation and implementation of new models for scholarly exchange that build on the widespread adoption of digital technologies, advocates for improved terms and conditions under which content is made available, and establishes alliances and develops relationships that promote open collaboration among stakeholders in the scholarly communication system. More information about this ARL strategic direction is available at http://www.arl.org/sc.

Institute on Scholarly Communication Webinar Series

The ARL-ACRL Institute on Scholarly Communication (ISC) offered an eight-part webinar series in 2010 to help libraries continue developing their scholarly communication programs. Targeted to individuals from institutions that have sent representatives to previous ISC events or were in the midst of creating their own institutional scholarly communication program, the series provided an opportunity for participants to develop and build on a network of colleagues. The series identified how local successes and activities can grow into a comprehensive program plan and strengthen local planning. Featured speakers provided perspectives on emerging areas in scholarly communication.

The first "Building on Success" webinar program provided a brief overview of the changes in scholarly communication. Speakers presented implementations of comprehensive scholarly communication programs. Participants discussed and assessed their current programs and identified opportunities for building on current successes.

Two programs assisted participants in understanding how libraries that are involved in advocating for and supporting open access mandates and policies are managing these roles. Panelists explored the type of work that goes into getting buy-in for policy changes and transforming behaviors after a mandate or policy change. One session focused on specific campus issues, the other on federal policy issues.

The third set of programs helped libraries that are increasingly involved in providing journal hosting and support services to explore transitional models for economic support from subscriptions to open access. The first focused on library as publisher, the second on library experiments in economic support for open access.

Two programs focused on organizing and training librarians and library staff to achieve library scholarly communications roles. Speakers addressed shifting roles of libraries and the infrastructure needed to sustain programs, allocating/reallocating staff resources, and building internal education programs to support outreach efforts.

Participants in the final webinar joined library leaders to envision the long-term future for libraries, librarians, and scholarship. Discussion and independent post-work were designed to help libraries complete long-term program planning scenarios at their own institutions. For more information, see http://www.arl.org/sc/institute/iscwebseries.

Strategies for Opening Up Content

Issue 269 of *Research Library Issues,* a special issue guest-edited by ARL's Julia Blixrud, focused on approaches now being deployed to increase the amount of content that is open and available to the research library community and, by extension, the larger world. Included are articles on the University of Kansas open access policy, open access publishing funds, model license language for author rights, and HathiTrust. *RLI* 269 is available on the Web at http://publications.arl.org/s68n7.

Partnering to Publish

ARL cosponsored a seminar with the Society for Scholarly Publishing in November in Washington, D.C., to give research libraries, small society publishers, and federal agency librarians and research staff an opportunity to learn about current partnerships and explore new opportunities for cost-effective and innovative joint ventures. The seminar was organized into four panel sessions. The first provided an overview of the new landscape of collaboration, and other panels discussed the changing roles for editing, production, and marketing. An overview of the seminar is available at http://www.arl.org/sc/models/lib-publishing/partnering2publish. The proceedings, with links to slides and videos of each session, can be found at http://www.arl.org/sc/models/lib-publishing/partnering2publish/p2p-proceedings.shtml. The videos were filmed and edited courtesy of Columbia University's Center for Digital Research and Scholarship.

Scholarly Communication Visiting Program Officer

Nancy Eaton, dean emerita, Pennsylvania State University Libraries, has begun serving as an ARL Visiting Program Officer on behalf of the Steering Committee on Reshaping Scholarly Communication. In this role, she will be investigating and developing a white paper characterizing economic models both in use and in development that are serving to sustain scholarly communication activities in research libraries. The study will provide a useful overview for ARL and for individual libraries.

Access to ARL Titles

ARL has made nearly 400 of its titles 100 percent viewable in Google Book Search and more than 400 titles in HathiTrust. This has largely been possible because many ARL titles have been scanned through the Google Library Partners Program and, because ARL is a Google Books Partner, bibliographic data for ARL content has been exposed in Google Book Search. ARL will continue to open more of its titles in the future.

ARL-AAUP Joint Working Group

A joint meeting between ARL library directors and university press directors resulted in the establishment of a joint working group by ARL and the American Association of University Presses (AAUP). Several areas of shared interest and activity were identified during the meeting. The working group will be responsible for maintaining a constructive dialogue between the communities represented by the associations and finding effective initiatives to advance their common interests and values.

Transforming Research Libraries

The transformation of research libraries mirrors, to a large degree, the ongoing evolution of research institutions and the practices of research and scholarship. An ARL strategic direction focuses on articulating, promoting, and facilitating new and expanding roles for ARL libraries that support, enable, and enrich the transformations affecting research and research-intensive education. Additional information about this ARL strategic direction is available at http://www.arl.org/rtl.

2030 Scenarios Project

In spring 2010 ARL launched a scenario-based visioning project to look decades into the future at potential interactions among key social, technological, economic, political/regulatory, and environmental forces that will shape research organizations and their libraries. Particularly in turbulent times, scenario development offers opportunities to move beyond environmental scanning, extrapolations of past trends, or individual forecasting. It challenges ingrained assumptions and focuses on a small set of drivers, exploring the implications and interactions of drivers to uncover previously unthinkable outcomes.

In collaboration with an experienced consultant with expertise working with leaders in diverse industries and sectors, the project created four high-level descriptions of potential future states that research libraries can use to inform their own planning and decision making. The set of scenarios captures broad environmental drivers affecting research libraries—describing the situation of research libraries in the future.

At ARL's 2010 April Membership Meeting in Seattle, the Transforming Research Libraries Steering Committee presented a briefing session on "Envisioning Research Library Futures: ARL's Scenario Thinking Project," providing an overview of plans for the visioning project.

In July ARL sponsored a webcast, "Envisioning the Future of Research Libraries: ARL's Scenario Development Project." During it, the project consultant, Susan Stickley of Stratus, Inc., introduced the concept of scenario planning and highlighted how it compares with other prediction-oriented tools for planning, such as forecasting or trend analysis. Stickley also presented an update on the ARL project. The webcast can be seen at http://www.youtube.com/arladmin#p/f/0/D2iCPqs3R2I.

ARL released *The ARL 2030 Scenarios: A User's Guide for Research Libraries* in October. This publication includes the "ARL 2030 Scenario Set" and an accompanying user's guide. The ARL 2030 Scenario Set is a rich description of four possible futures. As a set, the four scenarios are designed to tell widely divergent stories that collectively explore a broad range of possible developments over time. The user's guide builds on the scenarios by identifying several strategic implications for research libraries and provides extensive how-to resources for library leaders, planners, and facilitators who want to use the scenarios for visioning and planning. To download a free interactive pdf of *The ARL 2030 Scenarios: A User's Guide for Research Libraries* or purchase a bound copy from ARL, see http://www.arl.org/news/pr/scenariosguide19oct10.shtml.

In November ARL sponsored the webcast "An Introduction to Using the ARL 2030 Scenarios for Research Library Planning." The 90-minute session introduced the user's guide and highlighted the ways in which the scenarios can be used to enhance leaders' own thinking about the dynamics that shape the future of research libraries and how to integrate scenario-planning techniques into their libraries' planning activities. View the webcast on ARL's YouTube channel at http://www.youtube.com/watch?v=WSUynutYC3g.

Special Collections

The Transforming Special Collections in the Digital Age Working Group is charged with monitoring and advising on the role of special collections in research libraries. It identifies the issues distinctive to research libraries that are most critical for special collections in the digital age, and recommends any policies or actions that ARL is in a unique position to adopt. The renaming of the former Working Group on Special Collections corresponded to a revision of the group's charge. The choice of new directions for the group was informed by ARL's adoption of its new strategic plan as well as the 2009 report "Special Collections in ARL Libraries: A Discussion Report from the ARL Working Group" and the forum "An Age of Discovery: Distinctive Collections in the Digital Age." To view the new charge and related documents, visit the working group's Web site http://www.arl.org/rtl/speccoll/spcollwg2010.

The ARL board unanimously voted on July 26 to endorse nine principles, recommended by the working group, to guide vendor/publisher relations in large-scale digitization projects of special collections materials. The board's vote strongly encourages ARL member libraries to refrain from signing future agreements with publishers or vendors that do not adhere to the principles. The principles address issues including implications of the distinctive character of special collections, the need for libraries to retain their own copies of the products of digitization projects, the importance of promoting broad access to digitized collections, and concerns regarding the collection of data about users of digitized collections. For more information and a link to the principles, see http://www.arl.org/news/pr/principles-4august10.shtml.

ARL, in partnership with Ithaka S+R, was awarded a $464,286 grant under the Institute of Museum and Library Services' National Leadership Grants program to fund a two-year study of how libraries, archives, and museums are creating sustainable digitized special collections. This study will provide actionable recommendations, best practices, and planning tools to help project leaders plan for sustaining their own special collections digitization projects. Building on past work by Ithaka S+R examining sustainability of digital resources done, activities under this cooperative agreement will include a survey of digitized special collections and focused interviews with leaders and project staff in selected cultural heritage organizations managing digitized special collections. The study's final report of lessons learned, recommendations, and case studies will be freely shared through the partners' Web sites and other mechanisms. For more information about the project, see http://www.arl.org/rtl/speccoll/sustaindigsc.

E-Science

In August ARL published *E-Science and Data Support Services: A Study of ARL Member Institutions* by Catherine Soehner, Catherine Steeves, and Jennifer Ward. The study was sponsored by the ARL E-Science Working Group to build an understanding of how libraries can contribute to e-science activities in their institutions and identify organizations that have similar interests in e-science to leverage research library interests. The report presents the findings of a 2009 survey of ARL member libraries, includes six case studies compiled by the authors to elaborate library e-science activities and collaborations, and includes a bibliography of related articles, reports, and Web sites, along with the survey instrument and a selection of recent research library position descriptions with significant e-science support components. The report is available at http://www.arl.org/bm~doc/escience_report2010.pdf.

In December ARL released a Web-based resource that unpacks the recently announced National Science Foundation (NSF) Data Sharing Policy and offers links to resources developed by librarians to support researchers in meeting the policy's data management requirements. The NSF policy, which went into effect in January 2011, requires researchers to submit data management plans as part of their grant proposals. The *Guide for Research Libraries: The NSF Data Sharing Policy* by Patricia Hswe and Ann Holt reviews the policy, explains its implications for research libraries, and provides resources for communicating with researchers about data management and funder policies and educating researchers in the basics of developing data management plans. The site is a dynamic resource collection that will be updated as libraries continue to develop resources to support this activity. See http://www.arl.org/rtl/eresearch/escien/nsf. To promote information sharing among librarians advancing data management activities, ARL also launched a Google group for library-based data management professionals.

Diversity, Professional Workforce, Leadership

ARL works closely with member libraries, graduate library and information programs, and other libraries and library associations to promote awareness of career opportunities in research libraries and support the success of library professionals from racial and ethnic groups currently under-represented in the profession. ARL's diversity programs support member libraries as they strive to reflect society's diversity in their staffing, collections, leadership, and programs. Central to the diversity agenda are programs that facilitate the recruitment, preparation, and advancement of librarians into leadership positions in research libraries. The themes and curricula of these programs introduce participants to major trends affecting research libraries and the communities they serve: the changing nature of scholarly communication, the influence of information and other public policies, and new and expanding library roles in support of research and scholarship.

Leadership Institute

More than 70 MLIS students attended the sixth annual ARL Leadership Symposium in Boston January 14–17, 2010. Program participants included 17 ARL

Career Enhancement Program fellows, 19 ARL diversity scholars, and other MLIS students from the Boston area and throughout the Northeast. The symposium curriculum included presentations by ARL staff on the major strategic areas of the association, as well as on developing job-search skills, and on the evolving professional roles of library and information professionals in ARL libraries. More information about the annual leadership symposium and diversity program participants can be found at http://www.arl.org/diversity.

Initiative to Recruit a Diverse Workforce

During 2010 ARL celebrated ten years of its Initiative to Recruit a Diverse Workforce (IRDW), one of the most successful minority-recruitment programs in the library and information science profession. IRDW provides support for graduate school in library and information science and other professional development opportunities to students from traditionally under-represented racial and ethnic minority groups over three years. Participants in IRDW, known as ARL diversity scholars, receive a generous compensation package worth, potentially, more than $13,000 over the course of the program. In addition, diversity scholars participate in a formal mentoring program, research library visits, and numerous other program components. Since 2000 IRDW has supported the library and information science education of more than 125 students.

In April 2010 Purdue University Libraries hosted the 2009–2011 ARL diversity scholars for a research libraries visit. The annual visit, which Purdue has hosted for six years, gives the scholars an in-depth view of the daily workings of a major research library and life in a midwestern college community. Diversity scholars attended presentations on such topics as embedded librarianship, the promotion and tenure process on campus, and library liaisons. The agenda included formal presentations, library tours, and social events attended by Purdue library and campus administrators and Purdue library staff. For more information on the diversity scholars and ARL's IRDW, visit http://www.arl.org/diversity/init.

In June 2010 more than 140 people—including numerous ARL directors, current and former IRDW diversity scholars, current and former mentors of the program, ARL staff, and many other supporters—attended a luncheon in Washington, D.C., celebrating the tenth anniversary of IRDW. The program included an address by National Public Radio correspondent Claudio Sanchez as well as presentations by 2004–2006 diversity scholar LaVerne Gray and current diversity scholar Jeffrey Cruz. Jim Williams, dean of libraries at the University of Colorado at Boulder, moderated the program.

Also in June ARL was awarded a $543,014 grant under the IMLS Laura Bush 21st-Century Librarian Program to fund the next iteration of IRDW. This is the third grant awarded by IMLS in support of ARL's diversity recruitment programs since 2003. The grant will provide support for graduate school in library and information science and other professional development opportunities to 30 students over the next three years. Recruitment for the program will focus on students with academic training in science, technology, engineering, and mathematics disciplines. In October the ARL Committee on Diversity and Leadership selected 15 MLIS students to participate in the 2010–2012 IRDW as ARL diversity scholars. For a full roster of the 2010–2012 diversity scholars and more information on the program, see the press release at http://www.arl.org/news/pr/Diversity-Scholars-28oct10.shtml.

Leadership and Career Development

Since 2007 ARL has offered its Leadership and Career Development Program (LCDP) to help prepare mid-career librarians from under-represented racial and ethnic groups to take on increasingly demanding leadership roles in research libraries. The 2009–2010 "vanguard class" is the sixth class to complete the program.

The LCDP fellows were guests of the Kent State University Libraries during the February Institute on Scholarly Communication and Public Policy. The program included presentations by Barbara Schloman, associate dean of public services, and Tom Sanville, executive director of the consortium OhioLINK.

In May 2010 the program hosted a webcast on "Digital Access and Scholarly Publishing: Re-envisioning the Research Library Future." Presenting for the LCDP fellows were three University of Michigan Library administrators, Paul Courant, Maria Bonn, and John Wilkin. An archive of the webcast is online at http://sas-origin.onstreammedia.com/origin/infiniteconferencing/DatedRecordings/052710/ARL/052710ARL.html.

The closing ceremonies for the vanguard class were held June 26 in Washington, D.C. The event featured a poster session highlighting the research projects completed by the LCDP fellows during their 18-month fellowship. Photos from the closing ceremonies are on ARL's Flickr stream at http://www.flickr.com/photos/arl-pix/sets/72157624311171159. View abstracts of the projects along with pdfs of the posters at http://www.arl.org/diversity/lcdp/projects. For more information about the LCDP, visit http://www.arl.org/diversity/lcdp.

Career Enhancement Program

In November the ARL Career Enhancement Program (CEP) Coordinating Committee selected 19 fellows to participate in the third and final year of this competitive fellowship program. CEP, funded by IMLS and ARL member libraries, gives MLIS students from under-represented groups assistance in starting their careers in research libraries by providing a fellowship experience that includes an internship in an ARL member library. This program reflects the commitment of ARL members to create a diverse research library community that will better meet the challenges of changing demographics in higher education and the emphasis on global perspectives in the academy. For more information about CEP, visit http://www.arl.org/diversity/cep.

Research Library Leadership Fellows

The Research Library Leadership Fellows Program is ARL's executive leadership program for future senior-level leaders in research libraries. Seven ARL libraries sponsored the 2009–2010 class of fellows: Brigham Young, Florida, Georgia Tech, Houston, Michigan, Utah, and Western Ontario.

Boston College Libraries hosted a "mini site visit" in January 2010 for the 2009–2010 fellows that included discussions with University Librarian Thomas Wall and a visit by Provost Cutberto Garza. University of Florida Libraries hosted an institute in February that included presentations by Dean of University Libraries Judith Russell and university administrators on the topics of fund development and donor relations. The last major program experience for this class of fellows was the Strategic Issues Institute hosted by the University of Houston in late September. The 2009–2010 class came to a close at the 157th ARL Membership Meeting in October at which the 21 graduating fellows were recognized. An overview of the program, as well as a complete list of the fellows, is available at http://www.arl.org/leadership/rllf.

Synergy: News from ARL Diversity Programs

In the June 2010 issue of *Synergy,* an open access publication featuring news about ARL diversity and leadership programs and their participants, three 2009 Diversity Program participants wrote about their experiences in programmatic activities and shared insights about information learned, skills developed, and relationships forged as part of the process. A pdf of the issue is available at http://www.arl.org/bm~doc/synergy0610.pdf.

Statistics and Assessment

The ARL Statistics and Assessment program focuses on describing and measuring the performance of research libraries and their contributions to research, scholarship, and community service. ARL serves a leadership role in the development, testing, and application of academic library performance measures, statistics, and management tools. Grounded in the tradition of the U.S. and Canadian research library environment, the program provides analysis and reports of quantitative and qualitative indicators of library collections, personnel, and services by using a variety of evidence-gathering mechanisms and tools. The program hosts the StatsQUAL (Statistics and Service Quality) suite of services that focus on developing new approaches for describing and evaluating library service effectiveness, value and return on investment, digital library services, the impact of networked electronic services, diversity, leadership, and organizational climate, among others. StatsQUAL tools include LibQUAL+, ClimateQUAL, MINES for Libraries, DigiQUAL, and ARL Statistics. More information is available at http://www.arl.org/stats and http://www.statsqual.org.

LibQUAL+

In January 2010 in Boston and in May in Glasgow, Scotland, well-attended LibQUAL+ training events covered research, application, and best practices. The training covered features of the new LibQUAL+ Web site, including improved capability for managing survey languages and implementing the survey in as many languages as an institution wishes to offer; a streamlined customization process that allows libraries to implement a shorter version of the survey known as LibQUAL+ Lite; and the availability of all of the LibQUAL+ notebook analyses to all participants for all implementation years, upon subscription.

Three libraries were selected to receive in-kind grants to facilitate their participation in the 2010 LibQUAL+ survey. The selection of grantees was based on financial need, contribution to the growth of LibQUAL+, and potential for surfacing best practices in the area of library service improvements. The 2010 LibQUAL+ grant recipients were G. R. Little Library, Elizabeth City State University, North Carolina; Castleton State College Library, Vermont; and Capital Community College Library, Hartford, Connecticut. For details, see the press release http://www.arl.org/news/pr/LibQUAL-Grants-15feb10.shtml.

During 2010 the LibQUAL+ survey was completed by more than 217,000 faculty members, graduate and undergraduate students, and staff at 195 institutions in 16 countries. The countries with the largest cohorts of participating libraries were the United States, with 99 libraries, and Canada, with 53. The 2010 LibQUAL+ Canada effort was the second countrywide implementation in Canada; the first LibQUAL+ Canada effort took place in 2007. View highlights from 2010 at http://libqual.org/documents/LibQual/publications/LibQUAL Highlights2010_Full.pdf.

The Bibliothèque Nationale et Universitaire de Strasbourg engaged in a creative marketing campaign that resulted in more than 7,000 users responding to their 2010 LibQUAL+ survey, a record number among all institutions implementing the survey over the past ten years. More about this marketing success is found in the Spring 2010 LibQUAL+ Update (http://libqual.org/documents/LibQual/publications/LQUpdate_Spring_2010.pdf).

LibQUAL+ Lite

The new LibQUAL+ Lite protocol, which presents a short version of the survey to each respondent by asking all of the questions but having each respondent answer only a few randomly selected questions, proved to be a popular choice among LibQUAL+ participants in 2010. A total of 195 institutions collected more than 217,000 complete surveys from undergraduate and graduate students, faculty, university staff, and library staff. About 65 percent of all surveys presented to users have been of the LibQUAL+ Lite version. In addition to decreasing the response time, LibQUAL+ Lite increases the response rate: 44 percent of long surveys generate complete responses, compared with 53 percent of Lite surveys.

ClimateQUAL

The ClimateQUAL learning community—which is composed of those libraries that have implemented or are interested in implementing an internal staffing survey on organizational culture, climate, and diversity issues—convened in January 2010 in Boston and again in June in Washington, D.C. The group reviewed plans regarding upcoming participation in ClimateQUAL and research questions to be explored in 2010. A rich exchange of ideas took place, spurred by presentations from the participating libraries bringing a variety of perspectives regarding organizational improvement strategies. The discussion continues on the ClimateQUAL blog.

Library Assessment Forum

The 2010 Library Assessment Forum featured a discussion relating to the recent IMLS grant to study the value of academic libraries awarded to the University of Tennessee, University of Illinois at Urbana-Champaign, and ARL. Carol Tenopir, co-principal investigator, led a discussion of the research that has taken place to date and engaged the participants to shape the return on investment methodology with their input. Her presentation is available at http://www.arl.org/bm~doc/libvaluemidwinter2010.ppt. The forum also included a presentation by Linda Plunket of Boston University regarding the university's efforts to create a culture of assessment. See http://www.arl.org/bm~doc/plunket2010.ppt.

At the June forum, attendees focused on how libraries are using data to support budget reallocation and justifications, how data are driving our understanding of trends in funding higher education and libraries, and how libraries are surviving the tough economic climate. The meeting featured two presentations. Rachel Besara and Kirsten Kinsley of Florida State University spoke about using assessment data to pursue alternative funding sources. Jim Self of the University of Virginia delivered an overview of his library's budget. Presentations are available at http://libraryassessment.info/?p=536.

Library Assessment Conference

The 2010 Library Assessment Conference, held October 25–7 in Baltimore, drew nearly 500 participants. As one of the themes of the conference was "Library As Place," the Peabody Library provided an ideal backdrop for the conference reception. The opening poster reception showcased 80 posters, including 12 that received the Judges' Choice Award. David Shulenburger of the Association of Public and Land-grant Universities spoke on "The Relationship Between University Assessment and Library Assessment." Keynote papers by Fred Heath, Danuta Nitecki, Megan Oakleaf, Stephen Town, and Joe Matthews were published in the January 2011 issue of *Library Quarterly*; the papers are available at http://libraryassessment.org/bm~doc/2010_lac_plenaries.pdf.

Lib-Value

In collaboration with the University of Tennessee, the University of Illinois at Urbana-Champaign, and George Washington University, ARL organized a Lib-Value workshop about the current state of the art regarding value and return on investment methods in academic libraries. The workshop reviewed methodologies developed and applied to date, and engaged the audience in expanding their understanding of how to measure, describe, and articulate the value of libraries in today's competitive environment. Lib-Value is a three-year study, funded by an IMLS grant, with the goal of understanding how to measure value and return on investment in all aspects of academic libraries. For more information on the workshop, including videos of the presentations, see http://www.arl.org/stats/statsevents/return-on-investment-roi-lib-value-workshop.shtml.

Special Issue on Assessing Performance

ARL published a special issue of *Research Library Issues* (*RLI*) on demonstrating library value by assessing organizational performance. The issue focuses on ways in which ARL assessment tools help libraries improve their services and programs and prove their value to stakeholders. The articles cover several different applications of LibQUAL+, the qualitative ARL library profiles, the ARL library scorecard pilot project, the Lib-Value project to measure the value and return on investment of academic libraries, and Measuring the Impact of Networked Electronic Services (MINES for Libraries). See http://publications.arl.org/rli271.

ARL Balanced Scorecard Pilot Activities

A variety of presentations at the ARL/CNI Forum and the Library Assessment Conference in Baltimore featured the ARL Balanced Scorecard Pilot Activities, capturing the rich learning and engaging work that has taken place. Four ARL libraries participated in the ARL Library Scorecard Pilot (Johns Hopkins University, McMaster University, University of Virginia, and University of Washington), based on the Balanced Scorecard framework created by Harvard business professors Robert S. Kaplan and David P. Norton. McMaster recently unveiled a new strategic plan based on the Balanced Scorecard model. The scorecard allows users to examine current and future performance based on four balanced perspectives: the user, staff learning and growth, internal processes, and financial health. Slides from the presentation "Building Scorecards in Academic Research Libraries: Organizational Issues and Measuring Performance," are available for download at http://libraryassessment.org/bm~doc/lewis_vivian.pdf.

ARL is working with Ascendant Strategy Management and the four pilot libraries in designing the next phase of the ARL Balanced Scorecard activities. A call of participation for a new cohort of libraries for a collaborative learning, development, and implementation process is forthcoming.

ARL Statistics Analytics Interface

All ARL institutions have access to the ARL Statistics Analytics as soon as the data are submitted through the StatsQUAL password-protected gateway at http://www.arlstatistics.org. ARL offers a subscription service to the ARL Statistics Analytics for organizations that are interested in accessing the final verified data through an interactive interface; the subscription fee is $750 for for-profit organizations and $500 for nonprofit organizations. For more information, e-mail stats@arl.org.

Publications

Annual electronic and print publications produced by the publications program describe salary compensation and collection, staffing, expenditures, and service trends for research libraries. The series includes the *ARL Annual Salary Survey, ARL Statistics, ARL Academic Law Library Statistics, ARL Academic Health Sciences Library Statistics,* and *ARL Supplementary Statistics. ARL Preservation Statistics* is being discontinued with future work in this area focusing on the development of a vision for 21st century research library collections that will address strategic directions for preservation activities.

Every year ARL calculates for its member libraries the proportion of the university budget devoted to libraries; this ratio continues to decline. For the 40 ARL libraries tracked since 1982, library expenditures as a percentage of university expenditures was 2.09 percent in 2007–2008 (the most recent data set available), a slight decrease from 2.21 percent in the previous year. Possible explanations of this trend may include the need for universities to invest more in technology and other infrastructure; the increased collaboration that is occurring in libraries through consortia and centralized purchasing; and the embedding of library functions within the teaching, learning, and research processes. These data are compiled using the ARL Statistics for library expenditures and the Integrated Postsecondary Education Data System (IPEDS) finance form for university expenditures. Updated graphs and machine-readable data files can be downloaded from http://www.arl.org/stats/annualsurveys/eg.

The SPEC survey program gathers information on current research library operating practices and policies on topics relevant to ARL's strategic directions; it publishes the SPEC Kit series as guides for libraries as they face ever-changing management issues. Six SPEC Kits were published in 2010: *SPEC Kit 316 Evaluating E-resources, SPEC Kit 317 Special Collections Engagement, SPEC Kit 318 Impact Measures in Research Libraries, SPEC Kit 319 Diversity Plans and Programs, SPEC Kit 320 Core Benefits,* and *SPEC Kit 321 Services for Users with Disabilities.* Links to the tables of contents and executive summaries of SPEC Kits are available at http://www.arl.org/resources/pubs/spec/complete.shtml, and pdfs of complete SPEC Kits from 1977 through 2005 are available through Google Books (http://books.google.com) and HathiTrust (http://www.hathitrust.org).

Workshops and Other Events

The program also offers various workshops on topics such as METS, Google Analytics, and an introduction to XML. Presentations at various research conferences on topics relating to analytics and library assessment also took place throughout the year. For more information, see http://www.arl.org/stats/statsevents/index.shtml.

Communications and Alliances

The Communications and Alliances enabling capability is engaged in many activities that support ARL's strategic directions. These include acquainting ARL members with current, important developments of interest to research libraries; influencing policy and decision-makers within the higher education, research, and scholarly communities; educating academic communities about issues relating to scholarly communication and research libraries; and providing the library community with information about activities in which research libraries are engaged. Using print and electronic media as well as direct outreach, the communications capability disseminates information about ARL to the higher education and scholarly communities, as well as to ARL member institutions, and publishes a full range of timely, accurate, and informative resources to assist library and higher education communities in their efforts to improve the delivery of scholarly communication.

News about ARL activities and publications is available through several e-mail lists that are distributed widely to the library and higher education communities. To subscribe, visit http://www.arl.org/resources/emaillists. The following channels can also be used to keep up with the latest from ARL: Twitter, Facebook, YouTube, Flickr, and blogs. To learn about public policy issues that affect the research library community, see the Policy Notes Blog at http://policynotes.arl.org; for discussions of library service assessment, evaluation, and improvement, see the Library Assessment Blog at http://libraryassessment.info. To learn more about managing these and other news feeds from ARL, visit http://www.arl.org/news/feeds.

ARL makes many of its publications available electronically via the ARL Web site; some are available in excerpted form for preview before purchase and others are available in their entirety. See http://www.arl.org/resources/pubs/ for more information.

Governance and Membership Meetings

In March 2010, M. Sue Baughman joined ARL as associate deputy executive director. Baughman was formerly assistant dean for organizational development at the University of Maryland, College Park. The primary role of ARL's associate deputy executive director is to promote and facilitate the strategic development of ARL policies and programs. For details, see the press release http://www.arl.org/news/pr/Baughman-27jan10.shtml.

A total of 107 ARL member library representatives participated in the 156th ARL Membership Meeting April 28–30, 2010, in Seattle. The program theme "Globalization of Higher Education and Research Libraries" was developed by ARL President Brinley Franklin to examine globalization, business models for interdependent collections, and shared infrastructure for university press e-books. Meeting participants discussed such issues as intellectual property, partnerships and services in other countries, scholarly communication trends in China, new business models for interdependent collections, university presses and e-books, and approaches to global collections. Most of the speakers' remarks and slides are available on the ARL Web site. See http://www.arl.org/resources/pubs/mmproceedings/156mm-proceedings.shtml.

At the business meeting, ARL membership voted to invite the University of Ottawa Library to join as the 125th member. The university is a bilingual institution and a member of the Canadian research-intensive "G-13" institutions based on sponsored research and number of Ph.D.'s. The library brings together people, expertise, and knowledge resources in physical and virtual environments that foster research, teaching, and learning in English and French. University Librarian Leslie Weir accepted the invitation.

The 157th ARL Membership Meeting was held October 13–14 in Washington, D.C. The program theme was "Imperatives for Change." More than 100 ARL member library representatives participated in sessions examining copyright and fair use best practices; scenario planning; mobile technologies; measuring library value; and models for leadership development. David E. Shulenburger, vice president, academic affairs, of the Association of Public and Land-grant Universities, presented the keynote address, "The Future of Research Libraries." Speakers' remarks and slides are available at http://www.arl.org/resources/pubs/mmproceedings/157mm-proceedings.shtml.

At the business meeting, member library representatives ratified the ARL Board of Directors' election of Winston Tabb as ARL vice president/president-elect and elected three new board members: Deborah Carver, Ernie Ingles, and Anne Kenney. Members also voted to invite the National Archives and Records Administration to join as the 126th member. Archivist of the United States David S. Ferriero accepted the invitation. At the conclusion of the business meeting, Franklin presented the gavel to Carol Mandel, who began her term as ARL president.

Immediately following the October meeting, ARL and the Coalition for Networked Information co-hosted a forum on "Achieving Strategic Change in Research Libraries." This forum explored the strategic questions that leaders must ask in order to ensure that research libraries are meeting the mission of their institution and the research, teaching, and learning needs of faculty and students. To listen to audio and view slides from the forum presentations, see http://www.arl.org/resources/pubs/fallforumproceedings/forum10.shtml.

SPARC—The Scholarly Publishing and Academic Resources Coalition

Executive Director, Heather Joseph
21 Dupont Circle, Suite 800, Washington, DC 20036
202-296-2296, fax 202-872-0884, e-mail sparc@arl.org
World Wide Web http://www.arl.org/sparc

Background and Mission

SPARC (the Scholarly Publishing and Academic Resources Coalition) promotes expanded sharing of scholarship in the networked digital environment. It believes that faster and wider sharing of outputs of the research process increases the impact of research, fuels the advancement of knowledge, and increases the return on research investments.

Established in 1997, SPARC was launched by the Association of Research Libraries to act on library concern that the promise of the Internet to improve scholarly communication was inhibited by pricing and access barriers in the journals marketplace. SPARC has been an innovative leader in the rapidly expanding international movement to make scholarly communication more responsive to the needs of researchers, students, the academic enterprise, funders, and the public.

SPARC is a catalyst for action. Its pragmatic agenda focuses on collaborating with other stakeholders to stimulate the emergence of new scholarly communication norms, practices, and policies that leverage the networked digital environment to support research, expand the dissemination of research findings, and reduce financial pressures on libraries.

As support for and conversations about open access have emerged at ever-higher levels, SPARC has had increasing opportunities to participate and contribute to policy making in multiple arenas. SPARC's expertise is being sought by the White House, the National Science Foundation, and other advisory groups as new policies are being crafted. During 2010 SPARC was invited to provide the keynote address for Freedom of Information Day at the New York Public Library and to participate in the Higher Education Big Ideas Fest. The growth of SPARC's influence parallels that of the open access movement, which is expanding in scale and becoming more global. Open access is also showing its strength as it becomes a factor on Wall Street in the valuation of multinational companies in the publishing arena.

SPARC is supported by a membership of more than 220 academic and research libraries, and works in cooperation with affiliates in Europe and Japan. Together, SPARC North America, SPARC Europe, and SPARC Japan represent more than 800 libraries worldwide.

Strategy

SPARC's strategy focuses on reducing barriers to the access, sharing, and use of scholarship. SPARC's highest priority is advancing the understanding and implementation of policies and practices that ensure open access to scholarly research outputs. While much of SPARC's focus to date has been on journal literature, its evolving strategy reflects an increasing focus on open access to research outputs and digital data of all kinds, in all subject areas. SPARC's role in stimulating change centers on three key program areas:

- Educating stakeholders about the problems facing scholarly communication and the opportunities for them to play a role in achieving positive change
- Advocating policy changes that advance scholarly communication and that explicitly recognize that dissemination of scholarship is an essential, inseparable component of the research process
- Incubating demonstrations of new publishing and sustainability models that benefit scholarship and academe

Priorities

SPARC actions during 2010 were designed to advance acceptance and long-term sustainability of a more open system of scholarship, with a primary focus on advancing open access models for both publishing and archiving the results of scholarly research. In particular, as interest in public access to the results of federally funded research continues to accelerate, SPARC has worked to deploy a focused and disciplined advocacy strategy.

SPARC's program activity recognizes that cultural, economic, and technical differences exist in various disciplines and that, in some areas, the interests of scholarship may best be served in the near term by equitable fee-based publishing solutions. Its programs aim at building a broader understanding of opportunities for change in all fields, and place an emphasis on identifying areas of common advantage to all stakeholders in the scholarly communications community—particularly scholarly and scientific researchers, universities and colleges, and university presses and society publishers.

Key areas of focus in 2010 included expanding adoption of public access policies throughout the U.S. federal government, expanding SPARC's role in supporting the open data and open educational resources movements, and establishing a framework for international expansion of SPARC.

Key Program Activities and Outcomes

Advocacy and Policy Front

During 2010 SPARC continued policy advocacy with the Open Access Working Group, an alliance of leading organizations that support open access, and served as the organizational focal point for the Alliance for Taxpayer Access.

As legislative and policy proposals affecting open access were explored in Washington, D.C., SPARC played an active role in championing the expansion of the successful National Institutes of Health (NIH) public access policy. During the year the Federal Research Public Access Act was introduced in the Senate (having been introduced in the House in 2009). It would make the results of federally funded research supported by most government agencies available to the public within six months after publication in scholarly journals. It would cover agencies with research budgets of more than $100 million, including the Department of Defense, the National Science Foundation, the Centers for Disease Control and Prevention, and the U.S. Department of Agriculture.

In July 2010 the Information Policy, Census, and National Archives Subcommittee of the House Committee on Government Oversight and Reform held the first-ever hearing on the issue of public access to federally funded research. The subcommittee invited ten witnesses, representing a broad cross-section of the stakeholder communities affected by this issue, to testify on the implications of opening access to the results of publicly funded research. The hearing signals persistent and growing interest in public access policies among U.S. legislators and mirrors activity at the executive branch level.

SPARC responded to a request for information (RFI) from the White House Office of Science and Technology Policy on potential executive action regarding public access policies. SPARC members and allies advocated for the expansion of the successful NIH policy across federal science and technology agencies. News of executive action following the RFI was expected at the time this report was prepared.

Research supported by SPARC revealed the substantial return on investment on access to publicly funded research outputs. The study, "The Economic and Social Returns on Investment in Open Archiving Publicly Funded Research Outputs," focused on research in the United States and was written by John Houghton, with Bruce Rasmussen and Peter Sheehan at the Centre for Strategic Economic Studies at Victoria University in Melbourne, Australia. It measured the potential return on investment from government spending on research and development that was disseminated freely among scholars and the public. Preliminary modeling suggested that over 30 years from implementation, the potential incremental benefits of a mandate for all federally funded research and development might be worth about three times the estimated cost, using the higher end lifecycle costing; six times the cost, using the NIH costing; and 17 times the cost, using Cornell University's arXiv costing. The study suggests that in the United States, national benefits might be 2 to 11 times the cost of the investment.

SPARC continued to support campus-based policy action in conjunction with the panel of experts first convened in 2009 to help develop a set of resources that support data-driven, community-engaging, and successful open access policy development. A total of 84 institutions had taken advantage of the project to initiate policy discussions as of early 2011.

In response to media requests for information on public access issues, SPARC provided materials to reporters and expert sources for interviews. SPARC sources have been quoted in *Inside Higher Ed,* the *Scientist, Library Journal,* and the *Chronicle of Higher Education.* Its staff has also prepared articles for various publications. For examples of SPARC in the press, see http://www.arl.org/sparc/media/inthenews/index.html.

Because change in scholarly communication is needed on a global scale, SPARC continued to amplify its impact by working in collaboration with global allies such as SPARC Japan, SPARC Europe, the Canadian Association of Research Libraries (CARL), EIFL in Europe, and various national and regional library associations.

Also within the scope of SPARC's advocacy program in 2010:

- SPARC actively promoted broad library participation in the SCOAP3 (Sponsoring Consortium for Open Access Publishing in Particle Physics) initiative to educate the U.S. community on potential benefits of the proposed project and encourage library participation.
- SPARC and allies actively secured a commitment to bring Berlin 9 Open Access Conference to the U.S. in 2011.
- SPARC monitored efforts to create open access digitization projects, such as the Open Knowledge Commons and the Open Content Alliance.
- SPARC participated in a new Open Educational Resources (OER) advocacy coalition to leverage messaging and membership in support of open access and OER policies.
- Work continued with the Committee for Economic Development, a Washington, D.C.-based think tank whose board of trustees includes several dozen university and college presidents as well as leaders in private industry.
- SPARC continued to consult in support of open access policies with nonprofit and health groups.

International Expansion

During the year SPARC played a pivotal role in international developments in scholarly communications and open access by convening regular conversations among key SPARC international leaders in partnership with SPARC Japan and SPARC Europe. It issued a statement in support of the Confederation of Open Access Repositories (COAR), which is committed to implementing digital repositories, promoting open access policies, collaborating on the development of international interoperability guidelines for repositories, and supporting regional and national repository initiatives. SPARC also was a driver in getting large-scale international collaborative support for SPARC Japan.

Campus Education

In 2010 SPARC developed a new set of Web resources designed to assist institutions interested in setting up funds in support of open access publishing. These new resources survey the current North American landscape of open access funds and explore key emerging questions on how such funds are considered and developed on college and university campuses. SPARC also worked with the Harvard University Office of Scholarly Communication to explore support for the Compact for Open Access Publishing Equity (http://www.oacompact.org). SPARC officially endorsed the compact, which encourages universities and colleges to establish funds to underwrite the cost for authors to publish in fee-based open access journals and has been signed by seven major North American campuses and the Memorial Sloan-Kettering Cancer Center.

SPARC sponsored International Open Access Week in October 2010, in partnership with a several organizations in the United States and internationally, to highlight the research community's commitment to open access. Building on the growing awareness of the issue and strengthening network, the event became a wider global phenomenon. Participation expanded greatly in 2010 with thousands of students and scholars observing the week on campuses in more than 90 countries. As a testament to the maturity of the open access movement, the concept has become more of the norm on college campuses than an alternative. The 2011 Open Access Week is scheduled for October 24–30.

On college and university campuses, SPARC continued to encourage and aid libraries' grassroots advocacy efforts to support open access with presentations, consulting, and new or enhanced resources. During 2010 SPARC provided more than three dozen presentations and webcasts to library, publishing, and higher education institutions in the United States and abroad. Its staff met directly with faculty members, department heads, deans, and campus administrators on SPARC member campuses to provide one-on-one information and advice on campus open access advocacy and other scholarly communication issues.

Author rights management continues to be a core element in SPARC's effort to engage faculty and advance more open practices for sharing research.

The short animated video "Open Access 101," illustrating the basic concept and benefits of open access, was translated into Spanish and French. A new suite of video resources was also made available online, featuring testimonials from student leaders on the value of free access to scholarly research.

During the year SPARC supported Peter Suber's monthly *SPARC Open Access Newsletter* and the "Open Access News" blog. SPARC continued and expanded members-only communication channels to connect directors with thought leaders in scholarly communication. Directors' briefings featured a number of speakers. Among them:

- Claudio Aspesi, senior market analyst with the Bernstein Group, who coauthored a report on Elsevier: "Professional Publishers: Academics with Pitchforks—Academic Libraries Start to Revolt Against Price Increases"
- Nick Shockey, director of the SPARC-sponsored, student-led Right to Research Coalition, discussing the important contributions students have been making to create change in scholarly publishing
- Stuart Shieber, director of the Harvard University Office of Scholarly Communication and architect of the Compact for Open-Access Publishing Equity (http://www.oacompact.org).

The popular SPARC Innovator Series continued in 2010, highlighting the efforts of key individuals and institutions in successfully promoting positive change in scholarly communications. Profiled in 2010 were the Optical Society of America and the authors of the *Panton Principles: Principles for Open Data in Science,* Cameron Neylon, Rufus Pollock, Peter Murray-Rust, and John Wilbanks.

SPARC-ACRL Forum

A major component of SPARC's community outreach occurs at the Annual Conference and Midwinter Meeting of the American Library Association (ALA), when SPARC works with ALA's Association of College and Research Libraries and its scholarly communication committee to bring current issues to the attention of the community. The 2010 SPARC-ACRL forum at the Midwinter Meeting in Boston covered ambitious initiatives to deliver free online access to scholarly monographs. The June Annual Conference in Washington hosted a discussion of the state of key developments in the move to expand access to scholarly research, including federal policy action and major campus-based moves to push for change and exert collective power.

Digital Repositories Meeting

The SPARC meeting on digital repositories in November highlighted the power of repositories as the engine for the open access movement. The 2010 international gathering focused on four key trends: repository-based publishing strategies, global repository networks, open data, and making the case for financial sustainability. In addition to the panel discussions and keynote speeches, an innovation fair featured new technologies and participants shared creative practices on campuses.

Student Campaign

SPARC continued to expand its partnership with student groups and to educate the next generation of academics on issues relating to scholarly communication. It increased the scope and number of organizations in the student Right to Research Coalition and, to solidify and publicize the "Right to Research" brand, SPARC created a new logo and Web presence at http://www.righttoresearch.org. The coalition is now an established body representing organizations with more than 5.5 million students.

During 2010 the coalition gave invited presentations at several national meetings of coalition member organizations, including Apple AcademiX and the European Medical Student Association.

SPARC has helped fuel this movement by engaging and supporting networks of students through the Right to Research Coalition and provided a unified home for exchanging best practices and organizing. With the help of a new grant secured by SPARC, the coalition is working aggressively to expand internationally.

SPARC hosted the second annual "Student Leadership Summit" in Washington, D.C., which brought together active leaders from campuses. Students talked about strategies and ways to deepen engagement in the coalition. The summit was coupled with an advocacy day and Capitol Hill visit.

To help students articulate the characteristics they value about the open Web and electronic communication using new media and technology, SPARC hosted the fourth annual SPARKY Awards contest, in which students are asked to create short videos promoting open access. It was cosponsored by Campus MovieFest, Open Video Alliance, New Media Consortium, Center for Social Media, Students for Free Culture, Association of Research Libraries, Association of College and

Research Libraries, Penn Libraries at the University of Pennsylvania, and the Student PIRGs (Public Interest Research Groups) organization.

Publisher Partnership Programs

SPARC supports and promotes useful examples of open access or other innovative publishing initiatives and participates in programs that highlight areas of common concern to libraries and not-for-profit publisher communities and where collaborative action can be beneficial.

SPARC continued to assist arXiv, BioOne, and Project Euclid in evolving sound, sustainable business practices needed to become leading platforms for digital dissemination of independent journals.

In 2010 SPARC expanded webcast conversations with the university press community, some in partnership with the American Association of University Presses. The events were well attended.

Business Consulting Services

SPARC provides ongoing consulting support to the library and publishing communities. Subsidized advisory services were made available to more than a dozen organizations and alternative publishing ventures during the year.

Council on Library and Information Resources

1752 N St. N.W., Suite 800, Washington, DC 20036
202-939-4754, fax 202-939-4765
World Wide Web http://www.clir.org

Kathlin Smith
Director of Communications

The Council on Library and Information Resources (CLIR) is an independent, nonprofit organization that works at the intersection of libraries, scholarship, and technology. CLIR helps organize, structure, and sustain the collaborative effort needed to realize a new digital environment for research, teaching, and learning. Its staff of ten is led by Charles Henry, CLIR president.

CLIR is supported by fees from sponsoring institutions, grants from public and private foundations, contracts with federal agencies, and donations from individuals. CLIR's board of directors establishes policy, oversees the investment of funds, sets goals, and approves strategies for their achievement. In 2010 the board appointed new members W. Joseph King, executive director of the National Institute for Technology in Liberal Education (NITLE); David Rumsey, founder of the David Rumsey Map Collection and president of Cartography Associates; and John C. Vaughn, executive vice president of the Association of American Universities. A full listing of CLIR board members can be found at http://www.clir.org/about/board.html.

G. Sayeed Choudhury and Elliott Shore continued their affiliations with CLIR as senior presidential fellows in 2010. Choudhury is associate dean for library digital programs and Hodson director of the Digital Research and Curation Center at the Sheridan Libraries, Johns Hopkins University. Shore is chief information officer and Constance A. Jones director of libraries and professor of history at Bryn Mawr College.

In May 2010 CLIR appointed Rachel Frick program director of the Digital Library Federation (DLF) and established a DLF Advisory Committee. DLF was created as a CLIR program in 1995 and became independent in 2006; it then merged back into CLIR in July 2009. As a program within CLIR, DLF is building upon its original mission to pioneer the use of electronic technology to extend collections and services, while refocusing on challenges specific to the second decade of the 21st century. The 2010 DLF Fall Forum was held in Palo Alto, California, November 1–3.

Activities

While continuing its work in leadership, preservation, and scholarly communication, CLIR is increasingly focused on identifying models of collaboration that could redefine the concept of the research library and produce more cost-effective services and programs to improve support of research and teaching. Such collaboration might include building campus cyberinfrastructures, developing connections between institutional repositories, collectively negotiating with commercial and external entities in large-scale digitization, cooperative cataloging, participating in academic and research computing roles on campus, and creating print repository and "insurance" models, among other activities.

Toward a Cloud Library

With support from the Andrew W. Mellon Foundation, CLIR initiated a research project titled "Toward a Cloud Library." This project evaluated combining large-scale virtual and print repositories as surrogates for library collections, using the New York University libraries as a case study. The goal was to identify the policies, procedures, logistics, and infrastructure that print and digital repositories need to make their services more widely available to university libraries, and to enable libraries to make more effective use of these repositories in managing their own collections. In this research project, CLIR also worked with the Columbia University Libraries and their off-site book-depository program (ReCAP), the HathiTrust, and OCLC. A report on the project will be available in 2011.

Global Digital Libraries Collaborative

The Global Digital Libraries Collaborative was established in November 2009 as a means to identify opportunities for international collaboration in digital library research and development. Sixty-one library administrators and senior technologists, representing 13 countries and 24 institutions, met at Stanford University for three days to discuss the challenges and opportunities afforded by the prospect of developing truly integrated global digital libraries.

Participants were enthusiastic about extending their collections and services through unprecedented integration of their digital collections with those of others, and identified a list of promising initiatives that are worthy of support by the international library community. This list is available on CLIR's Web site and is included in a report of the meeting issued in January 2010. The British Library hosted a second meeting of the group in May 2010, devoted to the topic of linked data. That meeting's discussions resulted in the identification of key areas for development relating to the implementation of linked data in libraries. Reports from the January and May meetings are available at http://www.clir.org/globaldigitallibraries/index.html.

Infrastructure for Humanities Scholarship

In October 2009 CLIR and Tufts University began a collaborative planning process to identify what is needed to advance an infrastructure to support humanities scholarship, with particular focus on the classics. The project, funded by the Institute of Museum and Library Services (IMLS), engaged scholars and academic librarians in examining the services and digital objects classicists have developed, the future needs of the discipline, and the roles of libraries and other curatorial institutions in fostering the infrastructure on which the core intellectual activities of classics and many other disciplines depend. On the basis of consultation with librarians, archivists, and humanities scholars, project staff sought to identify and describe a set of shared services layered over a distributed storage architecture that is seamless to end users, allows multiple contributors, and leverages institutional resources and facilities. Much of this architecture exists at the individual project and institutional levels; the challenge is to identify the suite of shared services to be developed.

A steering committee composed of librarians, subject bibliographers, archivists, research scholars, and library-based computer scientists was organized, and principal investigators Gregory Crane and Amy Friedlander consulted with scholars and other stakeholders. Meanwhile, Alison Jones of Tufts University undertook a review of digital projects in the classics to identify existing services, resources, and needs. The report was discussed at a meeting in October 2010 and then posted for public comment. A final version of the review and a plan for next steps will be released in 2011.

Assessment of 'DID Challenge'

In January 2010 CLIR entered a cooperative agreement with the National Endowment for the Humanities (NEH) Office of Digital Humanities to provide a strategic assessment of the Digging into Data (DID) Challenge, a grant competition jointly sponsored by NEH, Britain's Joint Information Systems Committee (JISC), the U.S. National Science Foundation (NSF), and Canada's Social Sciences and Humanities Research Council (SSHRC). The goals of the DID Challenge are to encourage multidisciplinary collaborations that explore the application of computational techniques to large corpora and to begin to understand the kinds of research that become possible when advanced search algorithms are applied to these corpora. The program's sponsors announced the first eight awards in December 2009.

The CLIR-NEH cooperative assessment will address how well the DID Challenge met its objectives and will identify the next steps agencies and researchers might take to best support continued development in this area. The project team is organizing focus group meetings, interviews, and site visits with grantees, program officers, and experts to inform the assessment.

Following the conclusion of the DID Challenge funding cycle in June 2011, CLIR will issue two final reports. The first will be a technical summary that addresses the assessment's goals, administrative history, methodology, summary of findings, next steps, and recommendations. The second report will discuss implications of the findings for the future of computationally intensive scholarship in the humanities, and for the roles of public and private funding agencies in fostering this research.

Task Force on Sustainable Digital Preservation and Access

In February 2010 the Blue Ribbon Task Force on Economically Sustainable Digital Preservation and Access issued its final report, *Sustainable Economics for a Digital Planet: Ensuring Long-Term Access to Digital Information.* CLIR had been an institutional participant in the task force since its formation in 2007. Funded by the National Science Foundation and the Andrew W. Mellon Foundation, the task force was created to identify sustainable economic models for providing access to the ever-growing amount of digital information in the public interest.

Preserving Recorded Sound Heritage

Since 2004 CLIR has conducted work under contract with the Library of Congress and the National Recording Preservation Board in support of a congressionally mandated study of the state of recorded-sound preservation and restoration. The study comprises a series of reports examining issues relevant to the long-term survival of the nation's recorded sound heritage. In the first half of 2010 CLIR staff worked in an editorial partnership with Rob Bamberger and Sam Brylawski, authors of *The State of Recorded Sound Preservation in the United States: A National Legacy at Risk in the Digital Age*. The report, copublished by CLIR and the Library of Congress in August 2010, is the culmination of nearly ten years of investigation and commissioned research on technical, legal, and educational dimensions of the challenges facing recorded sound preservation. The report lays the groundwork for a National Recording Preservation Plan, which the Library of Congress is to present to Congress in 2011.

Workshops

In 2010 CLIR continued to offer faculty research behavior workshops, which teach library and IT professionals ethnographic techniques that enable them to understand faculty members' work practices and how library and information services can address real faculty needs. Teams of librarians and instructional technologists from more than 60 colleges and universities have attended the workshops. Sites have included Wesleyan University; Kenyon College; Cornell University; the University of California, Berkeley; George Washington University; the University of Rochester; New York University; the University of Miami; the University of New Mexico; and the University of Washington. The workshops are led by Nancy Fried Foster, director of anthropological research at the River Campus Libraries, University of Rochester.

Building on the success of the faculty workshops, in late 2009 CLIR initiated a series of undergraduate work practices workshops, also led by Foster. At these sessions, teams from CLIR's sponsoring institutions learn techniques for understanding how undergraduates do their work, especially how they use library resources, staff, and facilities in writing research papers and completing research-based assignments. Following the workshops, participants share ideas, current research and publications, and suggestions through a listserv.

Leadership Through New Communities of Knowledge

Leadership Through New Communities of Knowledge, a partnership between CLIR and the Council of Independent Colleges (CIC), offers professional development opportunities for library staff at small-to-midsize private colleges and universities. Launched in July 2009, the project is supported with funds from IMLS.

In May 2010 CLIR sent 12 participants from CIC schools to the University of North Carolina at Chapel Hill's 2010 DigCCurr Professional Institute on "Curation Practices for the Digital Object Lifecycle." Participants benefited from sessions on such issues as digital preservation and managing in response to technological change; they also engaged in hands-on sessions with software such as

DRAMBORA. In July 2010 Maureen Sullivan of Maureen Sullivan Associates conducted a workshop titled "Work Restructuring in the Library." This was followed in October 2010 by the workshop "Archives for Non-Archivists," led by Holly Mengel and Courtney Smerz, project manager and project archivist, respectively, for the PACSCL Hidden Collections Processing Project. In November Nancy Fried Foster of the University of Rochester led a workshop on "Undergraduate Research Behavior."

Frye Leadership Institute

During 2010 the Frye Leadership Institute took a one-year hiatus to develop and articulate a new program that addresses higher education's leadership needs in an era of unprecedented change. The next institute, to be jointly sponsored by CLIR, EDUCAUSE, and Emory University, was scheduled for Atlanta June 5–10, 2011.

In its new iteration, Frye will engage those who are already leaders in their profession and further develop their skills, particularly in the area of advocacy. The institute will address challenges in higher education through a variety of topics, empowering librarians and information technologists to start conversations and take action on issues that are important not only to their own institutions but also to the entire higher education community. The Frye Leadership Institute seeks to foster leaders, particularly in the information sector, who can inspire, advocate, and implement fundamental collaborative change.

CLIR Chief Information Officers Group

CLIR's Chief Information Officers Group is composed of 35 directors of organizations that have merged their library and technology units on liberal arts college campuses. The group met in May and October 2010 to discuss organizational and policy issues that are unique to their environments. They explored such topics as open access; how the recession has affected organizational structure, technology, business strategies, and attitudes; cloud computing; portals versus Web 2.0; measuring the use and effectiveness of services; and ideas for prioritizing services. Throughout the year, members exchange ideas and solutions through a listserv.

Affiliation with Taiga Forum

In August CLIR announced that DLF had established an affiliation with the Taiga Forum, a community of assistant/associate university librarians and deans who meet to share ideas and strategies for developing organizational structures for research and academic libraries that are more flexible, agile, and effective.

By partnering with Taiga, DLF strengthens its ability to facilitate conversations between administrators and developers/project managers. The partnership creates opportunities to develop a shared understanding around changing technology, user expectations, and the idea that the "digital library" is not a separate function of the library but is integrated with all aspects of library service. The Taiga Steering Committee is eager to work with CLIR/DLF to explore potential new strategic directions for Taiga and the synergies that might be attained by working together. Both entities are concerned with exploring the impact and potential of the new digital information environment, and how challenges can be faced.

In November the Taiga Forum was held independently in conjunction with the DLF Fall Forum, an arrangement that will continue for at least one more year.

Scholarly Communication Institute

CLIR continues to serve on the planning committee for the Scholarly Communication Institute (SCI), which in 2010 focused on new-model scholarly communication. SCI began in 2003 with the goal of providing an opportunity for scholars and leaders in scholarly disciplines and societies, academic libraries, information technology, and higher education administration to design, test, and implement strategies that advance the humanities through the use of innovative technologies. Since 2006, the University of Virginia has hosted SCI, which is now under the direction of Abby Smith-Rumsey. Information about SCI is available at http://www.uvasci.org.

Awards

Cataloging Hidden Special Collections and Archives

Launched in 2008 with the support of the Andrew W. Mellon Foundation, CLIR's Cataloging Hidden Special Collections and Archives Program supports heritage organizations engaged in describing valuable cultural materials that are unknown or underutilized. In 2010 CLIR issued the program's third call for proposals. A review panel selected 17 projects, to which a total of $4 million was awarded.

The projects funded to date represent a wide range of institutions from across the United States and involve collections of books, other printed matter, manuscripts, personal papers, photography, audio and video recordings, specimens, artworks, artifacts, maps, posters, ephemera, architectural materials, and other items.

To gain a better understanding of the concerns of the librarians and archivists tasked with describing hidden collections, CLIR began work with a team of researchers to develop an outreach program framed as a study titled "Observations on Scholarly Engagement with Hidden Special Collections and Archives." The team includes eight former participants in CLIR's Postdoctoral Fellowship in Academic Libraries Program. The aim of the study is to describe successful strategies for engaging expert users with collections. The team has collected data from 2008 and 2009 grant recipients through an anonymous survey and a series of on-site interviews with project staff. In spring 2010 the team summarized findings in an interim report that is available at http://www.clir.org/hiddencollections/engagement/engagement.html.

In March 2010 CLIR sponsored a symposium for grant recipients in Washington, D.C. Seventy-two participants attended the two-day meeting. The agenda, presentation slides, and digital copies of posters contributed by participants are available at http://www.clir.org/hiddencollections/symposium20100329.html.

Postdoctoral Fellowship in Academic Libraries

The Postdoctoral Fellowship in Academic Libraries Program, now in its seventh year, gives recent Ph.D. recipients an opportunity to develop expertise in new forms of scholarly research and the information resources that support them, both traditional and digital. CLIR postdoctoral fellows work on projects that forge, renovate, and strengthen connections between academic library collections and their users. Fellows have consulted on integrating library materials and resources into the classroom, designed and implemented metadata standards, curated exhibitions in libraries and museums, organized conferences and colloquia, taught courses, written successful grant proposals for host institutions, managed archives, and created Web portals. Participating libraries benefit from the expertise of accomplished humanists, social scientists, and scientists who invigorate approaches to collection use and teaching, contribute field-specific knowledge, and provide insight into the future of scholarship. As of early 2011, a total of 45 fellows had participated in the program.

Mellon Dissertation Fellowships

Fourteen graduate students were selected to receive Mellon Dissertation Fellowships in 2010. The fellowship program, now entering its tenth year, is intended to help graduate students in the humanities and related social science fields pursue doctoral research using original sources and gain skill and creativity in using primary source materials in libraries, archives, museums, and related repositories. Each fellowship carries a maximum stipend of $25,000 and supports dissertation research for up to 12 months. By early 2011 the program had supported 111 graduate students who carried out their dissertation research in public and private libraries and archives worldwide.

A. R. Zipf Fellowship in Information Management

Named in honor of A. R. Zipf, a pioneer in information management systems, the $10,000 Zipf fellowship is awarded annually to a student who is enrolled in graduate school in the early stages of study and shows exceptional promise for leadership and technical achievement in information management. Lynn Yarmey, a master's degree student in the Graduate School of Library and Information Science at the University of Illinois at Urbana-Champaign, was selected to receive the fellowship for 2010. Her research focuses on the role of controlled vocabularies in translating knowledge into machine-readable form and increasing local retrieval through improved information capture and discovery.

Rovelstad Scholarship in International Librarianship

Instituted in 2002, the Rovelstad Scholarship encourages library students who have an interest in international library work by enabling them to attend the World Library and Information Congress, the annual meeting of the International Federation of Library Associations and Institutions (IFLA). Amy Neeser, who is pursuing her MLIS degree at the University of Wisconsin–Milwaukee's School of Information Studies, received the award in 2010. She has a bachelor's degree in German studies from the University of Minnesota, and for the past three years has been working as the language services, publicity, and technology coordinator at the nonprofit Germanic-American Institute in St. Paul, Minnesota.

Publications

The Idea of Order: Transforming Research Collections for 21st-Century Scholarship. June 2010. Available at http://www.clir.org/pubs/abstract/pub147abst.html.

This three-report volume explores the transition from an analog to a digital environment for knowledge access, preservation, and reconstitution, and the implications of this transition for managing research collections. The first report, "Can a New Research Library Be All-Digital?" by Lisa Spiro and Geneva Henry, explores the degree to which a new research library can eschew print. The second, "On the Cost of Keeping a Book" by Paul Courant and Matthew "Buzzy" Nielsen, argues that from the perspective of long-term storage, digital surrogates offer a considerable cost savings over print-based libraries. The final report, "Ghostlier Demarcations," examines how well large text databases being created by Google Books and other mass-digitization efforts meet the needs of scholars, and the larger implications of these projects for research, teaching, and publishing.

A Distant Symmetry. Final Report: U.S. Intelligence Community Tools, by Amelia Acker and Katie Shilton. August 2010. Available in electronic format only at http://www.clir.org/pubs/archives/AckerShilton2010.pdf.

This study investigates the relevance of declassified tools developed by the intelligence community to humanistic scholarship for such tasks as processing vast corpora of texts and translating and working in multiple languages. The authors' research focused on identifying what tools exist in the intelligence communities and whether these tools are accessible to humanities scholars; in cases where a scholar can find a link to a tool, they looked at whether there is sufficient information for the investigator to understand its requirements as well as the relevance of the tool to the proposed research.

The State of Recorded Sound Preservation in the United States: A National Legacy at Risk in the Digital Age, by Rob Bamberger and Sam Brylawski. Commissioned for and sponsored by the National Recording Preservation Board, Library of Congress. August 2010. Available at http://www.clir.org/pubs/abstract/pub148abst.html.

This is the first comprehensive, national-level study of the state of sound recording preservation ever conducted in the United States. The authors have produced a study outlining the web of interlocking issues that now threaten the long-term survival of the nation's sound-recording history. This study tells us that major areas of America's recorded sound heritage have already been destroyed or remain inaccessible to the public. It suggests that the lack of conformity between federal and state laws may adversely affect the long-term survival of pre-1972-era sound recordings in particular. Finally, it warns that the continued lack of national coordination among interested parties in the public and private sectors, in addressing the challenges in preservation, professional education and public access, makes it difficult to arrest permanent loss of irreplaceable sound recordings in all genres.

Digital Forensics and Born-Digital Content in Cultural Heritage Collections, by Matthew G. Kirschenbaum, Richard Ovenden, and Gabriela Redwine with research assistance from Rachel Donahue. December 2010. Available at http://www.clir.org/pubs/abstract/pub149abst.html.

This report introduces the field of digital forensics in the cultural heritage sector and explores some points of convergence between the interests of those charged with collecting and maintaining born-digital cultural heritage materials and those charged with collecting and maintaining legal evidence.

Most records today are born digital, and libraries and other collecting institutions increasingly receive computer storage media as part of their acquisition of "papers" from writers, scholars, scientists, musicians, and public figures. This poses new challenges to librarians, archivists, and curators—challenges related to accessing and preserving legacy formats, recovering data, ensuring authenticity, and maintaining trust. The methods and tools developed by forensics experts represent a novel approach to these demands.

Association for Library and Information Science Education

ALISE Headquarters, 65 E. Wacker Place, Suite 1900, Chicago, IL 60601-7246
312-795-0996, fax 312-419-8950, e-mail contact@alise.org
World Wide Web http://www.alise.org

Lorna Peterson
President 2010–2011

The Association for Library and Information Science Education (ALISE) is an independent, nonprofit professional association. Its mission is to promote excellence in research, teaching, and service for library and information science (LIS) education through leadership, collaboration, advocacy, and dissemination of research. ALISE was founded in 1915 as the Association of American Library Schools (AALS). In 1983 it changed its name to its present form to reflect more accurately the mission, goals, and membership.

Membership

Membership categories are personal and institutional. Personal members can include anyone who has an interest in the objectives of the association. Personal membership categories are full-time (faculty member, administrator, librarian, researcher, or other interested individual); part-time/adjunct (retired or part-time faculty member); and doctoral student. Institutional members are schools with programs accredited by the American Library Association (ALA) and other U.S. and Canadian schools that offer a graduate degree in library and information science (LIS) or a cognate field. International affiliate institutional membership is open to any school outside the United States or Canada that offers a program to educate persons for the practice of librarianship or other information work at the professional level as defined or accepted by the country in which the school is located.

Structure and Governance

Operational groups within ALISE include its board of directors; committees; council of deans, directors, and program chairs; school representatives; and special interest groups. Since 2006 the Medical Library Association has managed ALISE. Kathleen Combs is ALISE executive director.

The board of directors includes seven elected officers serving three-year terms. Officers for 2010–2011 were Lorna Peterson (University at Buffalo, State University of New York), president; Lynne Howarth (University of Toronto), vice president/president-elect; Linda C. Smith (University of Illinois at Urbana-Champaign), past president; Jean Preer (Indiana University), secretary/treasurer; Ann Carlson Weeks (University of Maryland), director for membership services;

Susan Roman (Dominican University), director for external relations; and Andrew Wertheimer (University of Hawaii at Manoa), director for special interest groups. In January 2011 Linda Smith and Susan Roman concluded their board terms and newly elected officers Melissa Gross (Florida State University), vice president/president-elect, and Louise Spiteri (Dalhousie University), director for external relations, joined the board.

The ALISE board establishes policy, sets goals and strategic directions, and provides oversight for the management of the association. Face-to-face meetings are held in January and April. For the remainder of the year, business is conducted through teleconferences and e-mail.

Committees have important roles in carrying out the work of the association. An open call for volunteers to serve on committees has been used since 2008 to ensure broader participation in committee service, with members for the coming year appointed by the vice president/president-elect. Principal areas of activity include awards, budget and finance, conference program planning, governance, membership, nominations, publications, research competitions, and tellers (see http://www.alise.org/mc/page.do?sitePageId=86452 for a full list). Each committee is given an ongoing term of reference to guide its work as well as the specific charges for the year. Task forces can be charged to carry out tasks outside the scope of the existing standing committees. For example, a Code of Ethics for Library and Information Science Educators task force was established in 2007 and chaired by Toni Carbo (Drexel University). The task force presented a draft of "Ethical Guidelines for Library and Information Science Educators" at the 2010 ALISE Annual Conference with the expectation of finalizing the document during the year in response to feedback from ALISE members. The document was completed, and in November 2010 the code was approved by 87 percent of the voting membership.

The ALISE council of deans, directors, and program chairs consists of the chief executive officers of each of the association's institutional member schools. The group convenes at the Annual Conference and can discuss issues via electronic mail in the interim. Stephen Bajjaly (Wayne State University), Edwin Cortez (University of Tennessee), and Hope Olson (University of Wisconsin–Milwaukee) co-chaired the council for 2010–2011.

Within each institutional member school, a school representative is named to serve as a direct link between the membership and the ALISE board of directors. These individuals communicate to the faculty of their school about ALISE and the organization's events and initiatives and provide input on membership issues to the ALISE board.

Special interest groups (SIGs) enable members with shared interests to communicate and collaborate, with a particular emphasis on programs at the Annual Conference. New SIGs are established as new areas of interest emerge among ALISE members. There are currently 19 SIGs, grouped by broad theme. Notable activities for the SIGs at the 2011 conference were the 20th anniversary of the Multicultural, Ethnic, and Humanistic Concerns SIG and a special luncheon hosted by San José State University for the Part-time and Adjunct Faculty SIG.

Publications

The ALISE publications program has four components.

The *Journal of Education for Library and Information Science* (*JELIS*) is a peer-reviewed quarterly journal edited by Kathleen Burnett and Michelle Kazmer of Florida State University. Under their leadership, *JELIS* has published a number of research articles, brief communications and discussions of research in progress, and the ALISE 2010 Best Conference Papers. The journal will continue to showcase outstanding contributed papers presented at each Annual Conference. The editors maintain a companion Web site for *JELIS* at http://jelis.org. The goal is to raise the visibility of the journal and to develop an interactive Web site that engages the ALISE membership and others interested in scholarly conversation. Examples in advancing that goal are announcements such as the posting of the 2010 ALISE Best Conference Paper Award winners. Articles developed from these papers appeared in Volume 51, no. 4, published in October 2010.

The *ALISE Directory of LIS Programs and Faculty in the United States and Canada* is published annually. It is now made available only in electronic form, to members, through the ALISE Web site. Listings of faculty for each school include indications of teaching and research areas, using codes from the LIS Research Areas Classification Scheme that ALISE maintains.

The *ALISE Library and Information Science Education Statistical Report* publishes data collected in cooperation with the ALA Committee on Accreditation. It is an annual compilation of statistical data on curriculum, faculty, students, income and expenditures, and continuing professional education. Since his appointment as ALISE statistical data manager in 2008, Danny Wallace (University of Alabama) has worked to bring publication of the annual volumes up to date. Currently, members can access the 2005, 2006, and 2009 reports on the members-only site. Wallace is also planning ahead for enhancements to move from static annual reports to ongoing maintenance of a database that could support customized reporting. He recently resubmitted a grant proposal to the Institute of Museum and Library Services (IMLS) seeking support for the design, development, and implementation of a sophisticated database system for managing all aspects of the annual statistical data gathering process and retrospective inclusion of data for all years since 1980.

The ALISE Web site is the association's official communication mechanism. It keeps members informed of association activities and publishes issues of *ALISE News* three times a year. Information compiled from each Annual Conference, and made available on the Web site, includes abstracts of papers and posters presented and the president's report. ALISE supports the leadership efforts of SIG conveners to use social networking tools in fostering constituent communication. Two such recent examples are the leadership by Lesley Farmer (California State University, Long Beach) of the ALISE Gender SIG and Susan Maret (San José), of the ALISE Part-time and Adjunct Faculty SIG. The Gender SIG wiki created by Farmer offers ALISE members opportunities to share ideas about gender as they apply to the profession. Goals for the communication vehicles established by Maret include fostering opportunities for increased discussion among LIS part-time and adjunct faculty through both a discussion list on Yahoo User Groups (ALISEadjunct@yahoogroups.com) and a Facebook page.

Annual Conference

The ALISE Annual Conference is held each year immediately before the ALA Midwinter Meeting. The 2011 conference drew 470 attendees to San Diego January 4–7 to explore the theme "Competitiveness and Innovation." The program co-chairs, Mary Stansbury (University of Denver) and Dan O'Connor (Rutgers University), put together an array of program sessions, including keynote speaker Jorge Reina Schement, dean of Rutgers University's School of Communication and Information whose presentation was titled "'Big, Complex, Demanding, and Competitive': The Road to Library and Information Science Education in the 21st Century."

Two poster sessions, Work-in-Progress and Doctoral Student Research, offered opportunities to discuss a wide range of research. A "birds-of-a-feather" brown-bag lunch fostered discussion of teaching various content areas. Scheduled sessions included presentation of papers, panel discussions, a presidential program on diversity, and SIG-sponsored programs. The first day of the conference was devoted to continuing professional development, with a workshop on online pedagogy sponsored by the Web-based Information Science Education consortium (WISE), and the ALISE Academy sponsored by the H. W. Wilson Foundation.

The ALISE Academy initiative, in its third year, is a continuing-education opportunity designed to provide support and inspiration to members at all stages of their careers. For the 2011 conference, the concentration was on educators in archives, preservation, rare books and special collections, and museum studies. Anne Gilliand (University of California, Los Angeles) and Cecilia Salvatore (Dominican University) worked with their committee to plan three workshops: "Early Career Planning for Doctoral Students and Junior Faculty" (Anne Gilliland, UCLA and Sidney Berger, Simmons College); "From the Outside In: Bringing Cultural Heritage Institutions Into the Classroom" (Michèle Cloonan and Martha Mahard, Simmons); and "Developing Research and Collaborative Programs for Cultural Heritage: Connecting the Dots" (Tula Giannini, Pratt, and Kevin Cherry, IMLS). Planners also sought to stimulate post-conference research and teaching collaborations through the networking opportunities afforded by the conference. "Unconference" activities, where research conversations could continue, were made available through scheduled hospitality suite programs.

The Annual Conference has an active placement service, facilitating support for job candidates through vita and portfolio reviews and scheduled interviews. Despite the economic downturn, representatives from several institutional member schools conducted interviews for open positions.

A memorial resolution at the business meeting was presented to Annie Horrocks Baert, honoring her father, Norman Horrocks, ALISE past president and parliamentarian, who died October 14, 2010.

Grants and Awards

ALISE seeks to stimulate research and recognize accomplishments through its grants and awards programs. Research competitions include the ALISE Research

Grant Competition, the ALISE/Bohdan S. Wynar Research Paper Competition, the ALISE/Dialog Methodology Paper Competition, the ALISE/Eugene Garfield Doctoral Dissertation Competition, the ALISE/Linworth Youth Services Paper Award, and the OCLC/ALISE Library and Information Science Research Grant Competition. Support for conference participation is provided by the University of Washington Information School Youth Services Graduate Student Travel Award and the Doctoral Student to ALISE Award. Awards recognizing outstanding accomplishments include the ALISE/Norman Horrocks Leadership Award (for early career leadership), the ALISE/Pratt-Severn Faculty Innovation Award, the ALISE Service Award, the ALISE Award for Teaching Excellence, and the ALISE Award for Professional Contribution. Winners are recognized at an awards reception at the Annual Conference.

Collaboration

ALISE seeks to collaborate with other organizations on activities of mutual interest. ALISE is represented on the ALA Committee on Education (COE) by Susan Roman, director for external relations. ALISE jointly sponsored a forum with COE at the 2011 ALA Midwinter Meeting on "LIS Faculty and Practitioners Surviving and Thriving Together."

ALISE Past President Linda Smith serves on the LSTA (Library Services and Technology Act) Reauthorization Subcommittee of the ALA Committee on Legislation. This provides an opportunity to advocate for continuing funding of the IMLS Laura Bush 21st Century Librarian Grant program, which has benefited many ALISE institutional members since the first awards were made in 2003.

Several ALISE institutional members collaborate on staffing an ALISE booth anchoring the LIS Education Pavilion area of the exhibit hall at the ALA Annual Conference each summer.

ALISE members joined the ALA rally for support of libraries, librarians and library workers, research programs, scholarships, and other funding needs on Library Advocacy Day, June 29, on Capitol Hill. With 1,600 ALA members and advocates of all ages present, ALISE was part of the largest federal advocacy event in library history. In collaboration with the Federal Library Information Center Committee (FLICC), ALISE invited its members to a special session held at the Justice Department regarding intelligence analysis as an alternative career path for librarians. The program, "Intelligence Analysis: A Discussion of Convergent Skills and the Future," held during the 2010 ALA Annual Conference, attracted more than 60 attendees.

ALISE is seeking to build more international connections. ALISE organized a dinner for ALISE members attending the IFLA World Library and Information Congress in Gothenburg, Sweden, in August, as it had done at two previous IFLA conferences. ALISE continues to seek opportunities to partner with the IFLA Sections on Education and Training and Library Theory and Research. ALISE collaborated in the planning and management of an IFLA-ALISE-EUCLID satellite meeting, "Cooperation and Collaboration in Teaching and Research: Trends in Library and Information Studies Education" held August 8–9 at the Swedish School of Library and Information Science in Borås prior to the conference in Gothenburg. ALISE will be represented at the IFLA Conference in Puerto Rico in August.

Past President Linda Smith participated as an interviewee in the research project "Re-conceptualising and Re-positioning Australian Library and Information Science Education for the 21st Century." This project is funded by the Australian Learning and Teaching Council and is part of an effort to develop a framework for the education of information professionals in Australia. More information is available at http://www.altc.edu.au/project-reconceptualising-repositioning-library-education-qut-2009.

ALISE was a cosponsor of the Third International Symposium on Library and Information Science Education in the Digital Age at Wuhan University in China, celebrating the 90th anniversary of the university's School of Information Management. ALISE Secretary/Treasurer Jean Preer represented the association. She presented to Dean Chuanfu Chen a complimentary ALISE membership and a proclamation commemorating the accomplishments of the school, and delivered a paper, "Looking Back to the Future: The Origins of the Information Age in the 1920s."

ALISE board members have served on the Advisory Committee for the IMLS-funded WILIS (Workforce Issues in Library and Information Science) project for which Joanne Gard Marshall (University of North Carolina–Chapel Hill) is principal investigator. ALISE is also contributing to the next phase of the study, which is gathering data for several more programs beyond the six North Carolina programs that participated in the initial study. For more information, see http://www.wilis.unc.edu.

Conclusion

ALISE will mark its centennial in 2015, and the association's board is working with ALISE headquarters staff and the University of Illinois Archives, where the ALISE archives are housed, to ensure that records documenting the work of the association continue to be maintained. Michèle Cloonan (Simmons) is providing early leadership planning for the centennial celebration. The 2012 conference theme "Extending Our Reach: Expanding Horizons, Creating Opportunities" continues the association's forward-looking viewpoint.

International Reports

International Federation of Library Associations and Institutions

P.O. Box 95312, 2509 CH The Hague, Netherlands
Tel. 31-70-314-0884, fax 31-70-383-4827, e-mail ifla@ifla.org
World Wide Web http://www.ifla.org

Beacher Wiggins
Director for Acquisitions and Bibliographic Access, Library of Congress

American Library Association Representative to the IFLA Standing Committee on Government Libraries, 2011–2015

The International Federation of Library Associations and Institutions (IFLA) is the preeminent international organization representing librarians, other information professionals, and library users. Like many other nonprofit and international organizations, in 2010 IFLA was challenged by worldwide economic constraints. Nevertheless, IFLA promoted high standards of provision and delivery of library and information services; encouraged widespread understanding of the value of good library and information services; and represented the interests of its members throughout the world. Throughout the year IFLA promoted an understanding of libraries as cultural heritage resources that are the patrimony of every nation.

World Library and Information Congress

The World Library and Information Congress (WLIC) and 76th IFLA General Conference and Council attracted approximately 3,236 registered participants from approximately 120 countries to Gothenburg (Göteborg), Sweden, August 10–15, 2010. The conference was relocated from Brisbane, Australia, to Gothenburg in response to the global recession of 2008–2009. Swedish national sponsor Axiell Library Group and other corporate sponsors were generous with support. The number of registered participants, nevertheless, was 9.3 percent lower than the 3,568 who registered at the previous year's conference in Milan. Many prominent libraries reported budget reductions, often in the neighborhood of 20 percent to 25 percent, and formal and informal discussions of how to cope with budgetary constraints dominated the conference.

The conference theme, "Open Access to Knowledge: Promoting Sustainable Progress," showed the resilience and ingenuity of libraries throughout the world while acknowledging current economic realities.

Thirteen satellite meetings permitted intensive focus on special topics. Within Sweden, satellite meetings addressed "Building Strong Communities: Unleashing the Potential of Public Libraries to Build Community Capacity, Engagement and Identity"; "New Techniques for Old Documents: Scientific Examination Methods in the Service of Preservation and Book History"; "Cooperation and Collaboration in Teaching and Research Trends in Library and Information Studies Education"; "Open Access and the Changing Role of Libraries"; "The Global Librarian"; "Open Access to Parliamentary Information"; "Information Literacy: Context, Community, Culture"; "Marketing Libraries in a Web 2.0 World"; "Measuring Usage and Understanding Users! E-resources Statistics and What They Teach Us"; and "The Future of School Libraries in a National and International Perspective." In Denmark, participants discussed "Libraries in a Multicultural Society" while Norway was the setting for "With the Right to Read," sponsored by the IFLA Sections on Library Services to People with Special Needs, Libraries Serving People with Print Disabilities, and Literacy and Reading, with the International DAISY Consortium and International Network for Easy to Read. The most distant satellite meeting took place in Crete: "Open Access to Science, Medical and Technical Information: Trends, Models, and Strategies for Libraries."

The next World Library and Information Congresses will take place in San Juan, Puerto Rico (2011) and Helsinki, Finland (2012). Under IFLA's current WLIC planning guidelines, the 2013 conference will take place in Asia or Oceania.

The IFLA Governing Board is committed to continuously improving both the conference experience for participants and the financial security of the organization. The conference budget is usually about 2 million euros, approximately equal to the rest of IFLA's overall annual budget, and will probably have to increase to meet participants' expectations for on-site free wifi and other services. About half the conference budget comes from registration fees, about 25 percent from local subsidies by the host city or library association, and about 25 percent from exhibitor fees. Although the exhibitor fees and registration are higher than for most conferences in the library community, WLIC does not make money for IFLA, and the custom of convening all registered participants in opening and closing ceremonies limits the number of cities that can host the conference to those with halls seating at least 3,000 people. Furthermore, member organizations have reported that the scheduling requirements make it difficult to send representatives to both the general conference and the numerous specialized satellite meetings. To address these concerns, the governing board charged a conference review committee under Patrice Landry, chair of the IFLA Professional Committee, to review the format and planning model for future conferences. The committee contracted with Pleiade Management and Consultancy, headquartered in Amsterdam, for a consultation process, from January through March 2010, among four major stakeholder groups: delegates and members who were represented at the conferences in 2008 and 2009; IFLA section standing committees, special interest groups, and core activities; former national conference committee members; and conference sponsors and exhibitors.

All stakeholder groups reacted favorably to proposals that IFLA adopt a seven-year planning cycle for its annual general conference and organize each conference around three to five themes or tracks. Stakeholders also generally favored the idea of a three-pronged governance model for each conference. In this model, IFLA, through its governing board, would retain overall ownership of each conference, and the governing board, IFLA headquarters, and the conference national committee (the local organizing committee) would be responsible for each conference overall. Program content would be guided by the IFLA Professional Committee. Actual conference planning and services would be contracted to a "provider of conference organization," or event management company. Stakeholders had mixed reactions to the ideas of changing the conference format in order to permit IFLA to meet in a wider range of cities and of holding the IFLA conference jointly with other national or regional conferences. The stakeholders' divided opinions revealed the value that IFLA members place on the sense of community that distinguishes WLIC from most professional conferences.

Conference of Directors of National Libraries

The Conference of Directors of National Libraries (CDNL) is an independent association that meets in conjunction with IFLA's WLIC to promote cooperation on matters of common interest to national libraries around the world. At the 2010 meeting, CDNL continued to promote its long-term vision of a global, distributed digital library and discussed electronic legal deposit, copyright, and the role of literacy and reading programs in national libraries. Through 2010 the chair of CDNL was Penny Carnaby of the National Library of New Zealand, which hosted the CDNL Secretariat. In 2011 the secretariat moves to the National Library of South Africa, with John Tsebe, South Africa's national librarian, as incoming chair.

Response to War and Natural Disaster

IFLA was a founding member of the International Committee of the Blue Shield (ICBS), which since 1996 has aimed to protect cultural property in the event of natural and human disasters. IFLA's current partners in ICBS are the International Council on Archives, the International Council on Monuments and Sites, the International Council of Museums, and the Coordinating Council of Audiovisual Archives Associations. In 2010 ICBS continued its concern for the preservation of cultural heritage in the ongoing aftermath of war and of natural disasters such as the massive earthquake in Bam, Iran, in 2003, the Asian tsunami of December 2004, Hurricane Katrina in August 2005, and the earthquake that devastated Haiti on January 12, 2010. The IFLA North American regional center for preservation and conservation, hosted at the Library of Congress, continued to develop a network of colleague institutions to provide a safety net for library collections during emergencies. In summer 2010 the president and president-elect of IFLA visited Haiti and on behalf of ICBS co-signed an agreement with the Haitian government to support restoration of ruined libraries, temporary library initiatives, and improvement of professional library skills in the country. In particular, IFLA cooperated with the Haitian Ministry of Culture to open the "Ark" center to rescue damaged documents. The Haiti earthquake was the topic of a special update session at the Gothenburg conference. At the close of 2010 IFLA announced two major projects: the financing of a mobile library program to restore library services and a one-week training seminar in restoration of damaged documents.

Bibliographic Control

IFLA has worked steadily over the decades to improve bibliographic control through practical workshops, support of the International Standard Bibliographic Description, and research that seeks to establish basic principles of bibliographic control and to identify areas where cataloging practices in different cultures can be harmonized to make library catalogs less expensive to produce and easier for patrons to use.

In 2009 IFLA reshaped its core activity ICABS, the IFLA-CDNL Alliance for Bibliographic Standards, into ICADS, the IFLA-CDNL Alliance for Digital Strategies, with a broader mission that also encompasses issues relating to long-term archiving, digital preservation, and rights metadata. The founding members of ICADS are the British Library, the Biblioteca Nacional de Portugal, the Deutsche Nationalbibliothek, the Library of Congress, the National Library of Australia, the National Library of New Zealand, the Koninklijke Bibliotheek (Netherlands), and the Conference of Directors of National Libraries (CDNL).

Closely related to ICADS is the separate IFLA UNIMARC Core Activity (UCA), which maintains, develops, documents, and promotes the four UNIMARC formats for bibliographic, authority, classification, and holdings data. Since 2003, when it succeeded IFLA's former Universal Bibliographic Control and International MARC program, UCA has been hosted by the National Library of Portugal. Under UCA, the Permanent UNIMARC Committee maintains the formats and also advises ICADS on matters relating to UNIMARC. The Permanent UNIMARC Committee is currently chaired by Alan Hopkinson of Middlesex University in the United Kingdom.

Copyright Issues

The IFLA Committee on Copyright and Other Legal Matters (CLM) works to ensure a proper balance between the claims of intellectual property rights holders and the needs of library users worldwide. In 2009 CLM developed a list of 12 basic "Core Exceptions to Copyright" law that are deemed essential if libraries throughout the world are to fulfill their mission of providing open access to information and knowledge for all people. In 2010 CLM encouraged the World Intellectual Property Organization (WIPO) to recognize the core exceptions, striving for a global copyright strategy based on libraries' real-life needs. In November the WIPO Standing Committee on Copyright and Related Rights adopted a work plan for 2011–2012 that placed the core exceptions and their possible adoption in treaty form on the agenda for formal discussion by WIPO member states in 2011.

With WIPO, the National Diet Library of Japan, the International Federation of Reproduction Rights Organizations, and the International Publishers Association, IFLA sponsored a major conference on "Enhancing the Culture of Reading and Books in the Digital Age: Copyright as a Means to Foster Creativity and Access," held at the National Diet Library, Japan, December 1–2.

FAIFE

One of IFLA's core activities is Freedom of Access to Information and Freedom of Expression, or FAIFE, which is defined in Article 19 of the United Nations Universal Declaration of Human Rights as a basic human right.

FAIFE has been a leader within IFLA in adopting social media such as Facebook and YouTube and began publishing a new online newsletter in 2010. FAIFE has a presence at the annual Internet Governance Forum, which in 2010 took place in Vilnius, Lithuania, in September. FAIFE also held numerous workshops, particularly in Latin America, on health information, use of the Internet, and the IFLA/UNESCO Internet Manifesto that was prepared by FAIFE in 2002 to safeguard the right to freedom of information in the Internet age.

Grants and Awards

IFLA continues to collaborate with corporate partners and national libraries to maintain programs and opportunities that would otherwise not be possible, especially for librarians and libraries in developing countries.

The Jay Jordan IFLA/OCLC Early Career Development Fellowships bring library and information science professionals from countries with developing economies who are in the early stages of their careers to the OCLC headquarters in Dublin, Ohio, for four weeks of intensive experience in librarianship, followed by a week at OCLC's offices in Leiden, the Netherlands. The fellows for 2010 were from Azerbaijan, China, Egypt, Jamaica, Kenya, and Pakistan. As announced at the Gothenburg conference, the fellows for 2011 will be from Botswana, China, Malawi, Nepal, the Philippines, and Serbia. The American Theological Library Association is the third sponsor of the program, and one of the fellows must be a theological librarian. Since its inception in 2001, the program has supported 56 librarians from 31 developing countries.

The Frederick Thorpe Awards, established in 2003, are administered by the IFLA Libraries Serving Persons with Print Disabilities Section and the Ulverscroft Foundation of Leicester, England, which Thorpe founded to support the visually impaired. The Ulverscroft Foundation renewed the program as the Ulverscroft/IFLA Best Practice Awards (Frederick Thorpe Awards) in 2006, 2007, and 2008, with no award in 2009. In 2010 the Ulverscroft/IFLA Best Practice Awards were presented to Shanghai Pudong New Area Library, China, to expand its free information and communications technology (ICT) training program for visually impaired people; to three British individuals: Mark Freeman, manager of the South Tyneside Library Service and chair of Share the Vision, United Kingdom; Kathy Teague and Wendy Taylor, librarians at the Royal National Institute of Blind People; and Yasmine Youssef of the Taha Hussein Library for the Blind and Print Disabled at the Bibliotheca Alexandrina, Egypt. In an example of convergence of IFLA's work on cataloging standards and on special-needs libraries, Teague and Taylor used their award to study an implementation of the *Functional Requirements for Bibliographic Records,* produced by an IFLA working group, in a catalog for print-disabled library users.

The Bill and Melinda Gates Foundation Access to Learning Award in 2010 was presented to the Veria Central Public Library, Greece, during the Gothenburg conference. This annual award presents up to $1 million to libraries, library agencies, or comparable organizations outside the United States that have been innovative in providing free public access to information.

Numerous awards and grants encourage travel to the annual IFLA conferences. For the 2010 conference in Gothenburg, De Gruyter Saur Publishers provided grants for travelers from the Pacific Region; the Swedish Library Association and the Stichting IFLA Foundation made 60,000 euros available to support participation from developing countries; and Axiell Library Group provided 16,000 euros for travel grants. The IFLA Academic and Research Libraries Section instituted an essay contest, awarding conference registration for three contestants from Africa, Latin America, and the Asia/Pacific region. The IFLA International Marketing Award includes a stipend and travel to the conference. In 2002, 2003, and 2004, IFLA and 3M Library Systems cosponsored the marketing awards. After a hiatus in 2005, IFLA cosponsored the awards with SirsiDynix in 2006 and 2007. The Emerald Group has sponsored the award since 2008. The Dr. Shawky Salem Conference Grant supports conference attendance from an Arab country. While many national library professional associations subsidize travel to the IFLA conference, the *Comité Français IFLA* supports travelers from any francophone country.

The Guust van Wesemael Literacy Prize of 3,000 euros is awarded biennially to a school or public library in a country with a developing economy; the most recent award took place in 2009. The Harry Campbell Conference Attendance Grant, supporting travel to the IFLA Conference from a developing country that has not had conference participants in recent years, was not awarded in 2010.

The IFLA Honorary Fellowships, the IFLA Medal, and the IFLA Scroll of Appreciation recognize service to IFLA by individuals.

Membership and Finances

IFLA has more than 1,700 members in 150 countries around the world. Established at a conference in Edinburgh, Scotland, in 1927, it has been registered in the Netherlands since 1971 and has headquarters facilities at the Koninklijke Bibliotheek (Royal Library) in The Hague. Although IFLA did not hold a General Conference outside Europe and North America until 1980, there has been steadily increasing participation from Asia, Africa, South America, and Australia. The federation now maintains regional offices for Africa (in Pretoria, South Africa); Asia and Oceania (in Singapore); and Latin America and the Caribbean (in Rio de Janeiro). The organization has seven official working languages—Arabic, Chinese, English, French, German, Russian, and Spanish—and offers a range of membership categories: international library associations, national library associations, other associations (generally regional or special library associations), institutions, institutional sub-units, one-person libraries, school libraries, personal affiliates, and student affiliates. Association and institution members have voting rights in the IFLA General Council and IFLA elections and may nominate candidates for IFLA offices. Institutional sub-units, one-person libraries, school libraries, and personal affiliates do not have voting rights but may submit nominations for any IFLA office; personal affiliates may run for office. Except for personal and student affiliates, membership fees are keyed to the UNESCO Scale of Assessment and the United Nations List of Least Developed Countries to encourage participation regardless of economic circumstances. The IFLA Core Activity Fund is supported by national libraries worldwide.

UNESCO has given IFLA formal associate relations status, the highest level of relationship it accords to non-governmental organizations. In addition, IFLA has observer status with the United Nations, WIPO, the International Organization for Standardization, and the World Trade Organization, and associate status with the International Council of Scientific Unions. The federation continues several follow-up activities with the World Summit on the Information Society, most recently convened in Tunis, Tunisia, in 2005, to ensure that libraries have a role in providing information and knowledge to all people.

More than two dozen corporations in the information industry have formed working relationships with IFLA as corporate partners, providing financial and in-kind support. Gold Corporate Partners that contributed more than 3,500 euros to IFLA in 2010 were Australian Science; OCLC, Inc.; SirsiDynix; and publishers De Gruyter Saur, Elsevier, Emerald, nbd/biblion, Sabinet, and Sage.

The IFLA Foundation (Stichting IFLA) was established in 2007. The foundation accepts private donations and also is funded by all other IFLA income. It gives funding priority to proposals and projects that promise to have a long-term impact in developing and strengthening IFLA, are clearly related to at least one of the federation's three pillars, and are not likely to be funded by other bodies.

IFLA's Three Pillars: Society, Members, and Profession

The operational model for IFLA is based on the three pillars of society, membership, and professional matters. All of the federation's core functions relate to three strategic factors: the societal contexts in which libraries and information services operate; the membership of the federation; and the library profession.

Although the three pillars and the infrastructure of IFLA are interdependent, they can be roughly analyzed as follows: The Society Pillar focuses on the role and impact of libraries and information services in society. Activities supported by the Society Pillar include FAIFE, CLM, Blue Shield, IFLA's presence at the World Summit on the Information Society, and the advocacy office at IFLA headquarters—all activities that preserve memory, feed development, enable education and research, and support international understanding and community wellbeing. The Profession Pillar focuses on IFLA's role as the global voice for libraries and information services. The Members Pillar includes IFLA's member services, conferences, and publications.

The federation's operational infrastructure, consisting of IFLA Headquarters, the IFLA.org Web site, and the IFLA governance structure, support and receive strategic direction from the three pillars. The three pillars enable IFLA to promote its four core values: freedom of access to information and expression, as stated in Article 19 of the Universal Declaration of Human Rights; the belief that such access must be universal and equitable access to support human wellbeing; delivery of high-quality library and information services in support of that access; and the commitment to enabling all members of IFLA to participate without regard to citizenship, disability, ethnic origin, gender, geographical location, political philosophy, race, or religion.

In 2010 the IFLA Governing Board adopted a new strategic plan for the years 2010–2105. The plan, grounded in the four core values, sets forth four strategic directions: empowering libraries to enable their user communities to have equitable access to information; building the strategic capacity of IFLA and that of its members; transforming the profile and standing of the library profession; and representing the interests of IFLA's members and their users throughout the world. The plan also delineates priority activities for 2010–2011, including support for FAIFE, CLM, ICADS, Action for Development through Libraries (ALP), advocacy, and IFLA's Preservation and Conservation core activity (PAC). The governing board will determine priority activities every two years under the strategic plan.

Personnel, Structure, and Governance

The secretary general of IFLA is Jennefer Nicholson, former executive director of the Australian Library and Information Association. Nicholson succeeded Peter Johan Lor, who retired in 2008. Sjoerd M. J. Koopman is coordinator of professional activities, an IFLA headquarters position. The editor of the quarterly *IFLA Journal* is J. Stephen Parker. In 2008 IFLA hired Stuart Hamilton as its first senior policy advisor for advocacy, also a headquarters position. The IFLA conference officer is Josche Ouwerkerk.

The current president of IFLA is Ellen R. Tise, senior director for library and information services, University of Stellenbosch, South Africa. "Libraries Driving Access to Knowledge" was her presidential theme when she began her two-year term as president in August 2009 at the close of the 75th World Library and Information Congress in Milan. In addition to the WLIC programs, Tise chairs the annual IFLA Presidential Meeting. In 2010 her presidential meeting, "Knowing Is Not Enough: Engaging in the Knowledge Economy," took place in conjunction with the University of Stellenbosch Library's annual symposium in February. Tise continued to call for libraries and librarians to become more user-oriented and active in advocacy. Librarians, she stressed, must create partnerships with other societal stakeholders, other cultural heritage communities, and commercial and private enterprises, and must promote awareness of the library as space and place—a "Wow!" environment and experience.

The current president-elect of IFLA is Ingrid Parent, who had a long career at Library and Archives Canada before becoming University Librarian at the University of British Columbia in Vancouver. She has adopted the theme "Convergence: Ensuring Access and Diversity for a Shared Future."

The current treasurer of IFLA is Barbara Schleihagen, executive director, Deutsche Bibliotheksverband.

Under the revised 2008 IFLA Statutes, the 19 members of the federation's governing board (plus the secretary general, ex officio) are responsible for IFLA's general policies, management, and finance. Additionally, the board represents the federation in legal and other formal proceedings. The board is composed of the president, president-elect, treasurer, ten directly elected members, the chair of the IFLA Professional Committee, the chairs of each IFLA division, and the chair of the standing committee of the Management of Library Associations Section, currently Janice Lachance, chief executive officer, Special Libraries Association. Current members, in addition to Tise, Parent, Schleihagen, Nicholson, and Lachance, are Helena Asamoah-Hassan (Ghana), Danielle Mincio (Switzerland), Tone Eli Moseid (Norway), Pascal Sanz (France), Donna Scheeder (USA), Paul Whitney (Canada), and Qiang Zhu (China), plus the chair and eight members of the professional committee. In addition, Jesus Lau, Universidad Veracruzana, Mexico, and Sinikka Sipilä, Finnish Library Association, have been co-opted to the governing board since 2009 to provide special expertise.

The governing board delegates responsibility for overseeing the direction of IFLA between board meetings to the IFLA Executive Committee, which includes the president, president-elect, treasurer, chair of the professional committee, two members of the governing board (elected every two years by members of the board from among its elected members), and IFLA's secretary general, ex officio. The current elected governing board members of the executive committee are Lau and Sanz.

The IFLA Professional Committee monitors the planning and programming of professional activities carried out by IFLA's two types of bodies: professional groups—five divisions, 48 sections, and discussion groups—and core activities (formerly called core programs). The IFLA Professional Committee is composed of one elected officer from each division, plus a chair elected by the outgoing committee; the president, the president-elect, and the coordinator of professional activities, who serves as secretary; the chairs of the CLM and FAIFE committees, and two elected members of the governing board, currently Asamoah-Hassan and Moseid. Patrice Landry, chief of classification and indexing, Swiss National Library, chairs the professional committee.

The five divisions of IFLA and their representatives on the professional committee are I: Library Types (Steve W. Witt, USA); II: Library Collections (Ann Okerson, USA); III: Library Services (Judith J. Field, USA); IV: Support of the Profession (Michael Heaney, Britain); and V: Regions (Buhle Mbambo-Thata, South Africa). The chair of the IFLA Copyright and Legal Matters Committee is Winston Tabb (USA). The chair of the IFLA Freedom of Access to Information and Freedom of Expression Committee is Kai Ekholm (Finland). A total of 44 sections focus on topical interests, such as statistics and evaluation, library theory and research, and management and marketing, or on particular types of libraries or parts of the world.

The six IFLA core activities are Action for Development through Libraries (ALP, formerly Advancement of Librarianship); Preservation and Conservation (PAC); IFLA-CDNL Alliance for Digital Strategies (ICADS); IFLA UNIMARC Core Activity, which maintains and develops the Universal MARC Format, UNIMARC; Free Access to Information and Freedom of Expression (FAIFE); and

Copyright and Other Legal Matters (CLM). Two other longstanding IFLA projects are the IFLA World Wide Web site IFLANET and the IFLA Voucher Scheme, which replaced the IFLA Office for International Lending. The voucher scheme enables libraries to pay for international interlibrary loan requests using vouchers purchased from IFLA rather than actual currency or credit accounts. By eliminating bank charges and invoices for each transaction, the voucher scheme reduces the administrative costs of international library loans and allows libraries to plan budgets with less regard to short-term fluctuations in the value of different national currencies. The voucher scheme has also encouraged participating libraries to voluntarily standardize their charges for loans at the rate of one voucher for up to fifteen pages.

To ensure an arena within IFLA for discussion of new social, professional, or cultural issues, the professional committee approves the formation of special interest groups for a limited time period. There currently are discussion groups for Access to Information Network/Africa (ATINA); Agricultural Libraries; E-Learning; E-Metrics; Environmental Sustainability and Libraries; Indigenous Matters; Library and Information Science Education in Developing Countries; Library History; National Organizations and International Relations; New Professionals; and Women, Information, and Libraries.

Canadian Libraries in 2010: Funding Pinches, Copyright Legislation, Studies, Collaborations

Karen Adams
Director of Libraries, University of Manitoba

Introduction

The minority government led by Conservative Prime Minister Stephen Harper remained in power throughout 2010. The emphasis of the government continued to be on economic recovery, with the 2010–2011 budget reducing the deficit from C$53.8 billion to C$49.2 billion, and the announcement of continued stimulus spending.[1] National gross domestic product grew 3.2 percent during the 12 months from December 2009 to December 2010. The largest growth was in mining, oil, and gas; industrial production; and durable manufacturing industries. The only decrease was in utilities, at 0.1 percent. Information and cultural industries grew 2.2 percent over the period.[2] The Canadian dollar remained strong, ending the year valued at US$1.002.

Libraries benefited from federal stimulus/infrastructure funding, with many renovation and construction projects being announced across the country. Among the largest of these was an award of C$18.3 million for the new C$55 million central library in Halifax.[3] Some provinces also had programs of their own, including the Quebec government, which provided C$3 million to expand Boisbriand Public Library.[4] Newfoundland and Labrador allocated C$250,000 for renovations to libraries.

Operating grants for publicly funded libraries were mixed across the country. In Alberta, they remained stable with an overall adjustment to allow for increased populations in some municipalities.[5] Prince Edward Island added C$400,000 for an integrated library system for its school libraries, but nothing for public libraries.[6] Public libraries in British Columbia had a long lead time to prepare for a 22 percent cut in provincial funding in 2010, with the actual event resulting in such measures as cutting hours, book budgets, and programs.[7] In addition, public libraries lost the ability to participate in AskAway, the province-wide reference service, as well as provincially funded database licenses, which remained available only to the postsecondary sector, whose funding came from a different provincial department. British Columbia also saw a decline in funding for school library programs.[8] In Manitoba, grants to public libraries remained stable, but the public library agency's budget was reduced by C$143,000.[9] In New Brunswick, the government increased the cap on its matching grant to the New Brunswick Libraries' Foundation to $200,000 to encourage corporate and individual donations to the foundation, as well as allocating nearly C$750,000 for special projects in public libraries.[10]

There were funding challenges at the municipal level as well. The city of Edmonton sought a tax increase, and awarded additional funds to Edmonton Public Library to avoid Christmas closures in 2010.[11] After a public campaign to avoid planned budget cuts, Winnipeg Public Library received a C$80,000 increase to its materials budget.[12] Planning its 2011 budget, the Toronto Public Library Board sought a 3.3 percent increase of C$5.5 million in the face of the city's request for a 10 percent cut.[13]

Copyright

On June 2, 2010, Bill C-32, "An Act to amend the Copyright Act," was introduced in the House of Commons by Industry Minister Tony Clement.[14] Observers of the copyright scene noted that in 2005 and 2008 the introduction of a copyright bill signaled that an election would be called before the bill would be approved. Library associations generally responded positively to the bill, which expanded fair dealing to include educational purposes, but unfortunately also introduced technological protection measures (see, for example, the submission of the Canadian Association of Research Libraries[15] and the Canadian Urban Libraries Council[16]). Creators groups, such as the Writers' Union of Canada, were "outraged" at the inclusion of education in fair dealing.[17] Canada's English-language licensing collective, Access Copyright, was concerned that the inclusion of education signaled the government's support for ceasing to pay creators.[18] The bill received second reading in November, and was referred to a specially created committee prior to third reading.[19] Committee meetings and hearings continued into 2011.

The bigger news around copyright was a surprise move by Access Copyright (AC) in March 2010, wherein the collective applied to the Copyright Board of Canada for a tariff for the postsecondary sector with a levy rate of $45 per student. The new regime proposed to cover, scanning, uploading, and e-mailing, rather than just photocopying.[20] Universities and colleges responded negatively, given that the rates under the existing agreement, which expired August 31, 2010, were C$3.38 per student, and $C0.10 per page for course packs—resulting in a national aggregate average cost per student of some C$20. The negative response was also caused by the fact that most of the electronic copying rights being offered were rights that are largely already covered and paid for through licenses with publishers for electronic books and journals, not to mention a decline in the use of course packs in an environment that included course-management software becoming more common.[21]

By the end of summer, 101 objections to the proposed postsecondary educational institutions tariff had been filed with the copyright board, necessitating a decision by the board identifying those who would be able to participate fully in the process of establishing the tariff. The Association of Universities and Colleges Canada and the Association of Canadian Community Colleges were both accepted as full participants. Over the summer months, Access Copyright proposed a license extension agreement, which would enable institutions that signed to continue current practices at current rates until December 31, 2011. Access Copyright also proposed an interim tariff pending the copyright board ruling, potentially no sooner that 2013. The interim tariff essentially continued the conditions of the expired agreement, with signatories agreeing to make payments as they had in past, with a retroactive adjustment once the final tariff is established. The copyright board approved this interim tariff on December 23, 2010, and at the time this report was prepared each university and college was deciding whether to operate under the interim tariff.

The K–12 educational system also had issues with Access Copyright. Following on the copyright board education tariff of 2009 with its rate of C$5.16 per student, the Council of Ministers of Education, Canada (CMEC) had sought relief from the Supreme Court of Canada with respect to the definition of fair dealing used in the tariff and other matters. The high court upheld the tariff, and CMEC launched an appeal of that decision in September.[22] Access Copyright applied in June for a new tariff of C$15.00 per student for the 2011–2012 term, with expanded coverage to include sheet music, scanned copies, and reproducibles.[23]

The first Canadian to be jailed for pirating movies—both distributing them and filming them—was sentenced in March 2010 to two-and-a-half months after pleading guilty.[24]

Access to Information

The federal government's earliest funding program in support of free Internet access to all Canadians, the Community Access Program (CAP), was reaffirmed for 2010–2011 after having been reduced to C$2 million in the previous fiscal year. While the budget available was not announced, Industry Canada indicated that previously funded organizations would not be cut off, in spite of letters stating that sites within 25 kilometers of a public library would no longer be eligible.[25] However, the focus of the umbrella program—Broadband Canada: Connecting Rural Canadians—had clearly shifted to connecting individual homes rather than communities.[26]

The Canadian Radio-Television and Telecommunications Commission (CRTC) reminded Canadians that television stations in major urban areas switch from analog to digital broadcasting by the end of August 2011.[27] This prompted concerns about a new digital divide for those without access to cable or satellite services.[28]

In spring 2010 the federal government's interim access commissioner issued a report on access to federal information, including a department-by-department "A to F" letter grade. There were more F's than A's.[29] The privacy commissioner initiated consultations into privacy and cloud computing, an increasing issue because of personal data stored in the United States and thus subject to the USAPatriot Act.[30]

In May 2010 the government launched bill C-28, the Fighting Internet and Wireless Spam Act, and bill C-29, the Safeguarding Canadians' Personal Information Act. C-28 was well received, and had been passed by both houses of Parliament by year's end, but had not received royal assent; C-29 had not reached second reading.

Studies

The *Globe and Mail* published comparative data on Internet access over 15 years, finding that in 1995 just 6 percent of Canadians had Internet access at home compared with 82 percent in 2010. In 1995, 5 percent of Canadian Internet users had high-speed access, compared with 95 percent in 2010.[31]

Primary Research Group discovered that Canadian librarians spent 60-plus percent more than U.S. librarians on travel, meals, and lodging to attend library conferences.[32]

The federal government launched a review of the revised foreign investment policy in book publishing and distribution in July, receiving 44 submissions on the review Web site. The existing policy was introduced in 1985 and revised in 2002. The goals of the review were to determine if the policy still provided healthy competition in the Canadian book publishing, distribution, and retail industries, and still contributed to ensuring that Canadian content was accessible nationally and internationally.[33]

The Audit Bureau of Circulations analyzed 56 major Canadian consumer magazines, and found that, in spite of modest growth by some titles, overall circulation of these magazines declined almost 5.4 percent, with the decline occurring solely in subscriptions. Single-copy sales increased by 0.52 percent.[34]

A survey of newspaper readership by NADbank found that 78 percent of Canadians read a print or online edition of a newspaper once a week, with the print edition still being most popular among adults; 47 percent read a print daily newspaper on a weekday; 4 percent of adults read newspapers only online.[35]

The Conference Board of Canada released its report on intellectual property policy in Canada, after having withdrawn three "plagiarized" reports in 2009. The report recommended greater adoption of open access strategies, and recommended a shift in the debate over balance, from balance in intellectual property regimes between creators and users, to balance between the incentive to create and the incentive to diffuse.[36]

Events

In January the *Globe and Mail* reported on the renaissance in Canadian public libraries, noting a 5 percent increase in the number of items borrowed from and an 8.5 percent increase in visits to Toronto Public Library in 2009. The article also noted a 23 percent increase in circulation and a 19 percent increase at Edmonton Public Library, highlighting that library's new children's center with built-in aquarium.[37]

Calgary Public Library launched a unique advertising campaign with ads for the library in produce and deli departments at ten food stores—also a first for Canadian grocery stores.[38]

Ottawa Public Library claimed the first library vending machines in Canada in July, with two kiosks stocked with books and DVDs.[39] In September Edmonton Public Library announced its first vending machine at a light rail transit station, and upped the service ante by including a return drop-off box.[40]

An Edmonton man was jailed for two years after pleading guilty to arson in a fire that caused C$3 million in damage to the library at Victoria School of Performing and Visual Arts. He was arrested while carrying a fire extinguisher.[41]

A new 5,500-square-foot library opened in Cap-Pelé, New Brunswick, with the village and its 2,300 citizens contributing C$1.55 million, and C$600,000 coming from the provincial and regional governments.[42]

Woodlawn Public Library (Dartmouth, Nova Scotia) opened a 16,000-square-foot library in a former movie theater.[43]

Initiatives

In December 2010 Library and Archives Canada (LAC) announced its seven-year plan for a suite of digital services, including replacing paper copies sent to clients with electronic copies, doubling its online content, and becoming a trusted digital repository for Canada's digital heritage. LAC will also preserve all federal government digital records and make them accessible.[44]

The first Canadian Virtual Health Library was announced in June, with funding support of C$800,000 over three years from the Canadian Institutes of Health Research (CIHR). The goal of the library will be to provide all Canadian health professionals with easy access to authoritative information online.[45]

The Canadian National Institute for the Blind (CNIB) launched its "Right to Read" campaign in support of its quest for funding from federal and provincial governments. As part of the funding campaign, CNIB announced that it would not continue its partner programs with public libraries in jurisdictions that did not contribute money to CNIB. Five provincial/territorial jurisdictions responded during 2010, with the Province of New Brunswick committing C$130,459 to CNIB.[46, 47] The Northwest Territories, Ontario, and Alberta also contributed.[48] The government of Newfoundland and Labrador made a one-time contribution of C$200,000.[49] Early in 2011 the government of Canada announced a one-time contribution over two years of C$7million.[50]

The University of British Columbia (UBC) Library and the Korean National Assembly Library (NAL) announced a collaboration that will see users of the UBC Library being able to access some 119 million full-text pages from NAL, one of South Korea's two national depositories.[51]

Manitoba's University College of the North secured C$15 million in funding for renovations to the existing campus, and a new 13,500-square-foot library at its campus in The Pas.[52]

BC Books Online was launched in May 2010, following three years of work preparing for the digital delivery of a collection of books published in British Columbia. The initiative was the first-ever collaboration between publishers and libraries with the goal of delivering e-content to an entire province.[53]

CANARIE, Canada's Advanced Research and Innovation Network, announced the addition of 250,000 books to the Internet Archive from the University of Toronto Libraries. The goal was to complete digitization of half a million items.[54]

AIDS P.E.I. launched Prince Edward Island's first lesbian, gay, bisexual, and transgender library in Charlottetown in May.[55]

Notes

1. http://www.budget.gc.ca/2010/glance-apercu/brief-bref-eng.html.
2. http://www.statcan.gc.ca/daily-quotidien/110228/dq110228a-eng.htm.
3. http://www.halifaxcentrallibrary.ca/funding.
4. http://communiques.gouv.qc.ca/gouvqc/communiques/GPQF/Aout2010/09/c9286.html?slang=en.
5. http://www.calgarycvo.org/our-work/policy-issues/provincial-government/provincial-budget-2010.
6. http://www.gov.pe.ca/budget/2010/address.php.
7. http://www.martlet.ca/martlet/article/Library-books-suffer-budget-cuts.
8. http://www.cla.ca/AM/Template.cfm?Section=Home&TEMPLATE=/CM/ContentDisplay.cfm&CONTENTID=9353.
9. http://www.winnipegfreepress.com/local/wage-freeze—100-m-savings-officials-89098062.html.
10. http://www.gnb.ca/cnb/news/pet/2010e0685pe.htm.
11. http://www.cbc.ca/canada/edmonton/story/2009/12/08/edmonton-city-budget-passed.html.
12. http://www.mla.mb.ca, February 2, 2010.
13. http://www.thestar.com/news/article/917751—library-board-defies-ford-to-seek-increase.
14. http://www2.parl.gc.ca/HousePublications/Publication.aspx?DocId=4580265&Language=e&Mode=1.
15. http://www.carl-abrc.ca/projects/copyright/copyright-e.html.
16. http://www.culc.ca/news/post/CULCCBUC-commends-government-for-Bill-C-32-%28Copyright%293b-still-some-changes-requested.aspx.
17. http://www.writersunion.ca/av_pr060810.asp.
18. http://www.marketwire.com/press-release/Access-Copyright-Is-Deeply-Concerned-Governments-Lack-Support-Remuneration-Creators-1270887.htm.
19. http://www.marketwire.com/press-release/Bill-C-32-Receives-Support-at-Second-Reading-Now-to-Committee-for-Review-1349081.htm.
20. http://www.accesscopyright.ca/default.aspx?id=310.
21. http://www.edmontonjournal.com/business/copyright+will+students+more+learning+materials/2904884/story.html.
22. http://www.cmec.ca/Press/2010/Pages/2010-09-29.aspx.
23. http://www.cb-cda.gc.ca/home-accueil-e.html.
24. http://www.cbc.ca/arts/story/2010/03/17/bc-copyright-movie-pirate-conviction.html?ref=rss.
25. http://www.cbc.ca/news/canada/story/2010/03/16/cap-internet-funding.html?ref=rss.
26. http://www.ic.gc.ca/eic/site/719.nsf/eng/home.
27. http://www.crtc.gc.ca/eng/info_sht/bdt14.htm.
28. http://www.cbc.ca/news/canada/story/2009/06/01/f-digital-tv-transition.html.
29. http://www.oic-ci.gc.ca/eng/med-roo-sal-med_nr-cp_2010_5.aspx.
30. http://www.priv.gc.ca/media/nr-c/2010/nr-c_100211_e.cfm.
31. Report on Business (Toronto: *Globe and Mail*, July/August 2011) pp. 30–31.
32. http://www.primaryresearch.com/read_more.php?press_release_id=33.
33. http://www.pch.gc.ca/eng/1278438951595/1278425798049.
34. http://www.theglobeandmail.com/news/arts/majority-of-canadian-magazine-see-circulation-decline/article1667075/?cmpid=rss1&utm_source=feedburner&utm_medium=feed&utm_

campaign=Feed%3A+TheGlobeAndMail-Entertainment+%28The+Globe+and+Mail+-+Arts+News%29&utm_content=Bloglines.

35. http://www.mediapost.com/publications/?fa=Articles.showArticle&art_aid=124681.
36. http://www.conferenceboard.ca/documents.aspx?did=3452.
37. http://www.theglobeandmail.com/news.national/toronto/the-new-library-not-just-about-books-anymore.
38. http://www.cbc.ca/news/canada/calgary/story/2010/01/27/calgary-library-superstore-ads.html.
39. http://www.yourottawaregion.com/news/article/961556—library-kiosk-popular-after-a-year-in-hunt-club.
40. http://www.epl.ca/releases/2010Sep21%20%20Library%20Opens%20Lending%20Machine%20at%20LRT%20Station.
41. http://www.edmontonjournal.com/news/Edmonton+jailed+years+Victoria+School+library+arson/3300517/story.html.
42. http://www.gnb.ca/cnb/news/pet/2010e0024pe.htm.
43. http://www.halifaxpubliclibraries.ca/about/news/woodlawn-library-expansion.html.
44. http://www.collectionscanada.gc.ca/whats-new/013-503-e.html.
45. http://www.cihr-irsc.gc.ca/e/40995.html.
46. http://righttoread.cnib.ca/default.aspx.
47. http://www.gnb.ca/cnb/news/pet/2010e0154pe.htm.
48. http://www.cbc.ca/news/health/story/2010/01/19/cnib-library-funding.html.
49. http://www.releases.gov.nl.ca/releases/2010/health/0415n06.htm.
50. http://news.gc.ca/web/article-eng.do?m=/index&nid=590979.
51. http://blogs.ubc.ca/librarynews/2010/11/03/ubc-library-korea%E2%80%99s-nal-to-collaborate.
52. http://news.gov.mb.ca/news/index.html?archive=2010-6-01&item=8766.
53. http://www.quillandquire.com/google/article.cfm?article_id=11303.
54. http://www.canarie.ca/templates/news/releases/19_04_10_E.pdf.
55. http://www.cbc.ca/news/canada/prince-edward-island/story/2010/05/13/pei-gay-library-584.html.

Canadian Library Association

1150 Morrison Drive, Suite 400, Ottawa, ON K2H 8S9
613-232-9625, fax 613-563-9895, e-mail info@cla.ca
World Wide Web http://www.cla.ca

Kelly Moore
Executive Director

The Canadian Library Association/Association Canadienne des Bibliothèques (CLA) is Canada's major national professional association for the library and information community. It is predominantly English-language, with selected activities also in French. Its mission reads: "CLA is my advocate and public voice, educator and network. We build the Canadian library and information community and advance its information professionals."

Founded in 1946, CLA is a federally incorporated not-for-profit organization. It is governed by a 12-person Executive Council, which is advised by appointed standing committees and as-needed task forces.

Membership is composed both of individuals (librarians and other information professionals and library board trustees) and of institutions (mainly libraries, but also suppliers to the library and information community).

Much of CLA's work is done through its five divisions:

- Canadian Association of College and University Libraries (CACUL), which includes the Community and Technical College Libraries (CTCL) section
- Canadian Association of Public Libraries (CAPL), which includes the Canadian Association of Children's Librarians (CACL) section
- Canadian Library Trustees Association (CLTA)
- Canadian Association for School Libraries (CASL)
- Canadian Association of Special Libraries and Information Services (CASLIS)

There are CLA Student Chapters at six English-language library and information science postgraduate programs in Canada, and there is a student chapter at one library technician program.

To facilitate sharing of information in specific areas of interest, CLA has 19 interest groups focusing on topics as diverse as access to government information, action for literacy, library and information needs of native people, and new librarians and information professionals.

Governance

In June 2010 the role of CLA president was assumed by Keith Walker, director of library services, Medicine Hat College Library. He succeeded John Teskey, director of libraries at the University of New Brunswick, who had served as president since May 2009.

Serving as officers for 2010–2011 in addition to Walker are Vice President Karen Adams, Treasurer Ingrid Langhammer, and Executive Director Kelly Moore.

Major Activities

In early 2010 CLA's Executive Council started a major strategic planning exercise. A draft CLA Future Plan was distributed to members and the wider professional community for consultation in October. Changes to both the governance and organizational structure were proposed. Based on responses to the plan, amendments to the CLA Constitution and Bylaws will be presented as resolutions at the 2011 annual general meeting.

CLA continues to lead a variety of national advocacy initiatives and to offer professional development opportunities. Major activities have focused on these two elements, with additional efforts directed at a number of other important issues.

Advocacy and Public Awareness

Canada Post decided to maintain the Library Book Rate for 2011 with no increase in costs since 2005. CLA continues to support Member of Parliament Merv Tweed (Brandon-Souris) on his private member's bill (C-509) to create legislation supporting the rate. The bill has the support of the government and all opposition parties.

During 2010 CLA met with members of parliament and officials and staff in federal government ministries to raise awareness of key issues, including copyright and infrastructure resources for libraries. CLA continues to lead a cooperative effort on the development of the Initiative for Equitable Library Access.

CLA has been monitoring national and international developments in the area of copyright and related rights. It produced an analysis of the federal government's latest proposed copyright legislation titled "Protecting the Public Interest in the Digital World: The Views of the Canadian Library Association/ Association Canadienne des Bibliothèques on Bill C-32, An Act to Amend the Copyright Act." With other library organizations, CLA has been present at meetings of the World Intellectual Property Organization's (WIPO's) Standing Committee on Copyright and Related Rights, and has engaged in efforts to ensure that WIPO would consider limitations and exceptions for libraries and archives in its 2011–2012 work plan.

The association continued to spearhead Canadian Library Month/Le Mois Canadien des Bibliothèques, partnering with provincial, regional, and territorial library associations and governments. Under the theme "Your Library Your World" with the 2010 tagline "Opening Doors to the Future," this bilingual collection of events helped raise awareness of all types of libraries—public, academic, school, and special—and their roles for Canadians of all ages.

Professional Development

CLA's major contribution to continuing professional development continues to be its National Conference. The 2010 National Conference and Trade Show was held in Edmonton, Alberta, June 2–5.

International Activities

CLA has maintained strong contact with the international library community, mainly through its involvement with the International Federation of Library Associations and Institutions (IFLA). CLA President Walker and Executive Director Moore attended the 2010 IFLA Congress in Gothenburg, Sweden, along with a large Canadian delegation. The Canadian library community is organizing its support for Ingrid Parent as Canada's first president-elect of IFLA; she is scheduled to assume presidency of the federation in August.

Communications

Canadian librarians depend on timely and attractive publications and resources from CLA, and those outside the library community look to their professional association as a significant source of information.

CLA's bimonthly publication *Feliciter,* published since 1956, continues to explore core themes in the library community: international activities by Canadian librarians, service to patrons with print disabilities, information policy, and emerging technologies in libraries. The *CLA Digest* is a biweekly e-newsletter for members, with links to more in-depth news.

Awards and Honors

CLA recognized individuals from the library and information community with awards and honors in 2010.

The association's most significant award is for Outstanding Service to Librarianship, which is presented only when there is a candidate considered worthy of the honor. In 2010 CLA presented the award to Lynn Copeland, university librarian and dean of library services at Simon Fraser University.

The 2010 CLA Award for the Advancement of Intellectual Freedom was presented to Kent Weaver, manager of systems operations, information technology services, at the University of Toronto Library. Since 1988 the award has recognized outstanding contributions to intellectual freedom of individuals and groups, both in and outside the library community.

The CLA/Ken Haycock Award—established in honor of educator, administrator, advocate, and former CLA President Ken Haycock—honors an individual for demonstrating exceptional success in enhancing public recognition and appreciation of librarianship. The 2010 recipient was Wendy Newman, senior fellow at the Faculty of Information Studies, University of Toronto.

The CLA/Information Today Award for Innovative Technology went to Knowledge Ontario (KO). The award was given in recognition of both the breadth and depth and equity of access KO initiatives have brought to the province of Ontario.

The CLA/3M Canada Award for Achievement in Technical Services was presented to the Ottawa Public Library for the project "New Cataloguing Strategy for World Languages Material."

The CLA 27th annual Student Article contest was won by Jessica Rovito for "The LibQUAL Culture of Assessment: Institutionalizing the Need to Study People More Than Books."

[For a complete listing of 2010 awards, see "Library Scholarship and Award Recipients, 2010" in Part 3—*Ed.*]

Conclusion

CLA celebrated a number of successes in 2010 in the areas of advocacy and professional development, which members identified as priorities. CLA achieved tangible success with government on some key issues, including the Library Book Rate and library infrastructure investment, and efforts continued to advance other concerns, including copyright and equitable library access. Through continued progress in increasing public awareness of the role and importance of libraries and literacy, and taking public positions on critical issues in the library and information community, CLA fulfilled its mission during the year.

Special Libraries Association

331 South Patrick St., Alexandria, VA 22314
703-647-4900, fax 703-647-4901
E-mail sla@sla.org
World Wide Web http://www.sla.org

Janice R. Lachance
Chief Executive Officer

Founded in 1909 and headquartered in Alexandria, Virginia, the Special Libraries Association (SLA) is a global organization for information professionals and their strategic partners. SLA represents thousands of information experts and knowledge managers in more than 80 countries who collect, analyze, evaluate, package, and disseminate information to facilitate strategic decision making.

SLA members are known for finding innovative ways to contribute to the overall goals of their organizations, regardless of industry.

SLA's nearly 10,000 members work in various settings including Fortune 500 companies, not-for-profit organizations, consulting firms, government agencies, technical and academic institutions, museums, law firms, and medical facilities. SLA promotes and strengthens its members through learning, advocacy, and networking initiatives.

History

SLA was founded in 1909 by John Cotton Dana and a group of librarians who believed that libraries serving business, government, social agencies, and the academic community were very different from other libraries. Dana recognized a need for unity within the special librarian profession, and his initial goal was to provide numerous and continuous opportunities to achieve that unity. The association still identifies with this initial goal. The founders believed that these libraries operated using a different philosophy and more-diverse resources than the typical public or school library.

These "special"—or more aptly, "specialized"—libraries at first were distinguished by being subject collections with a specialized clientele, but gradually it was recognized that their chief characteristic was that they existed to serve the organization of which they were a part. Their purpose was not education per se, but the delivery of practical, focused, and decision-ready information to the executives and other clients within their organizations. Specialist librarians, commonly referred to today as "information professionals," are unique in their relationship with their users and customers, and are proactive partners in information and knowledge management.

Over the past century, SLA members have been working on the technological cutting edge, moving into knowledge services, and adapting to new roles to keep up with the times. They are entrepreneurial, innovative, and perpetually open to new technology tools, embracing change and using their knowledge and vision to further the goals of their organizations. Corporate information professionals synthesize strategic information to help executives make the decisions necessary for business to thrive. Government information professionals organize and deliver information for congressional, parliamentary, judicial, and executive leaders to make policy decisions. Academic special librarians organize, digitize, and deliver research information so that instructors can effectively relay knowledge to students, and students can follow the right methods of gathering information for research projects and other assignments.

With the increasingly rapid growth of technology, a common discussion topic among SLA members regards effectively digitizing, archiving, and preserving copyright requirements of the varied resources they are responsible for organizing and delivering.

SLA's strengths in serving its membership have always been focused on three areas: learning, networking, and advocacy. These are the underpinnings that prompted the founders to form a cooperative association, and they are still the fundamental benefits SLA provides the information specialists of the 21st century.

Core Values

The association's core values are

- Leadership—Strengthening members' roles as information leaders in their organizations and communities, including shaping information policy, and ethical use and gathering of information
- Service—Responding to clients' needs, adding qualitative and quantitative value to information services and products
- Innovation and continuous learning—Embracing innovative solutions for the enhancement of services and intellectual advancement within the profession
- Results and accountability—Delivering measurable results in the information economy and members' organizations; the association and its members are expected to operate with the highest level of ethics and honesty
- Collaboration and partnering—Providing opportunities to meet, communicate, collaborate, and partner within the information industry and the business community

Chapters, Divisions, and Caucuses

SLA chapter membership provides a network of information professionals in geographic community or region, while SLA division membership links members to information professionals within topical areas of expertise. SLA membership includes membership in one chapter and one division. For a small fee, members can join additional chapters, divisions, and caucuses.

SLA has 58 regional chapters in the United States, Canada, Europe, Asia, and the Middle East; 27 divisions representing a variety of industries; and 10 special-interest caucuses.

SLA's regional chapters elect officers, issue bulletins or meeting announcements, hold three to nine program meetings during a year, and initiate special projects. Members may affiliate with the chapter nearest to their preferred mailing address (either business or residence).

A caucus is an informal network of members gathered to discuss a specific topic or discipline not necessarily related to their individual day-to-day work. Examples include SLA's Futurist Caucus (using science fiction films and stories to find parallels to where the profession is headed in the digital age); User-Experience Caucus (examining how the user experience can be improved upon as it relates to the user interaction with various forms of media and staff within libraries); and Baseball Caucus (discussing everything from current events in the baseball community to methods of organizing and recalling baseball statistics).

SLA divisions represent subject interests, fields, or types of information-handling techniques. Each division elects officers and publishes a bulletin or newsletter. Most conduct professional programs during the association's annual conferences. The association added an Academic Division in 2008 and a Taxonomy Division in 2009.

Governance

SLA is governed by a board of directors elected by the membership. The board and the association both operate on a calendar year, with newly elected officers, as well as chapter and division leaders, taking office in January. SLA's president for 2011 is Cindy Romaine of Romainiacs Intelligent Research, and its president-elect is Brent Mai of Concordia University. Janice R. Lachance is the association's chief executive officer. [Additional officers are listed in SLA's directory entry in Part 6 of this volume—*Ed.*].

Alignment Project

In 2009 SLA completed the research phase of the SLA Alignment Project, a two-year extensive look at how employers and decision-makers value knowledge managers, information professionals, and special librarians and the services they provide. The research was conducted using a variety of methods, including surveys of large groups of managers and executives, dial-testing, and word association. A multidisciplinary team unveiled research that will not only help refine the current positioning of the profession in the information marketplace but will also provide a framework for discussing the inherent value in the profession and SLA in a concise and cohesive voice.

In late 2010 feedback was solicited from all members of SLA regarding its core mission, vision, and value statements via an online "share portal" that was accessed through the association's Web site. The 2011 SLA Board of Directors reviewed the feedback and decided to put any changes in the statements on hold for the 2011 fiscal year.

Programs and Services

Click University

SLA's Click University (Click U), launched in 2005, is an online learning community focusing on continuing professional education for information professionals. Click U is primarily designed to give SLA members state-of-the-art learning opportunities in partnership with today's information industry experts. Courses on software, new technology, management, communications, copyright laws, and leadership are designed to enhance the skills acquired through traditional library and information science education. Click U and its programs are available to SLA members and nonmembers. The majority of the webinars offered through Click U are offered free of charge, included as part of membership benefits, and are available to members only. Those offerings that carry an additional fee are noted as "Click U Premium," including Click U at Annual Conference and Click U Certificate Programs.

Click U is constantly adding programs and courses on topics ranging from public speaking to copyright law.

Click U Certificate Programs (Premium)

Click U provides certificate programs for information professionals looking to take the next step into a new career and utilize their traditional information skills in fields such as competitive intelligence, knowledge management, and copyright management. Eight Certificate in Copyright Management courses were scheduled to take place online throughout 2011 and at SLA Annual Conference and INFO-EXPO 2011 June 12–15.

Click U @ Annual Conference (Premium)

SLA offers in-person training and continuing education at the SLA Annual Conference. SLA "workshops" (half day) and "learning forums" (full day) are designed to educate and inspire participants to make an impact in their organizations. These premium courses give professionals tools that they can use to make improvements in their organizations or bolster their résumés.

Innovation Laboratory

The SLA Innovation Laboratory is a resource for members to discover popular and new technologies. The laboratory offers a wide variety of Web 2.0 software learning tools (including guides on how to use wikis, blogs, and social networking sites like Twitter, Facebook, and LinkedIn) to help information professionals become more business-savvy and technologically adept.

Advocacy

SLA serves the profession by advocating publicly on the value of the information profession. Its activities range from communicating with executives and hiring professionals on the important role information professionals play in the workplace to sharing the membership's views and opinions with government officials worldwide.

Public Policy Program

Government bodies and related international organizations play a critical role in establishing the legal and social framework within which SLA members conduct information services. Because of the importance of governments and international organizations to its membership, SLA maintains an active public policy program. SLA staff and the association's Public Policy Advisory Council monitor and proactively work to shape legislation and regulatory proposals that affect the association's membership.

SLA supports government policies that

- Strike a fair and equitable balance among the rights and interests of all parties in the creation, distribution, and use of information and other intellectual property
- Strengthen the library and information management operations of government agencies
- Promote access to government public information through the application of modern technologies and sound information management practices
- Encourage the development and application of new information and communications technologies to improve library services, information services, and information management
- Protect individual intellectual freedom and the confidentiality of library records, safeguard freedom of expression, and oppose government censorship
- Foster international exchange of information

With regard to the actions of government bodies and related international organizations in the policy areas listed above, the association will

- Monitor executive, legislative, and judicial actions and initiatives at the national and international level, and to the extent practical at various local levels
- Educate key decision-makers on the concerns of SLA's members, and highlight the importance of these concerns
- Provide timely updates to the membership on critical issues and actions
- Encourage and empower members to influence public action and legislature by expressing their opinions
- Develop cooperative relationships with other like-minded organizations to expand SLA's visibility and impact

SLA plans to support in 2011 such initiatives as the British-based Voices for the Library campaign, BadInfo.org (a Dow Jones study), the Open Book Alliance, and OpenTheGovernment.org.

Employment and Career Services

The online SLA Career Center includes a variety of services to meet the career needs of members, including career coaching, articles and resources such as podcasts, and career disruption assistance mentoring. It includes a job board that gives employers an opportunity to publicize their current information and library position opportunities to a highly targeted audience of professionals with MLIS degrees. SLA members and nonmembers have access to the listings on the job board, but only members are able to utilize such resources as career coaching articles.

SLA partners with a number of information industry professionals and job coaches to ensure that its members keep their résumés current and their skill sets relevant in today's ever-changing economy.

SLA Career Connection combines digital tools with the benefit of meeting in person. By participating online in SLA Career Connection, job seekers and employers are able to connect online and then meet face-to-face at the next SLA Annual Conference to take part in mock-interviews, career coaching seminars, and one-on-one sessions with certified career-resource associates. Meeting in person gives SLA members the opportunity to receive individualized tips and resources. A variety of three to five topic-based sessions are scheduled to be held at SLA Annual Conference and INFO-EXPO 2011.

Information Center

The SLA Information Center provides referral services and resources to members to assist them in their day-to-day tasks and management decisions, and in their roles as SLA leaders.

Professional and Student Networks

SLA's student groups, located throughout the world, are affiliated with accredited graduate schools of library and information science. Through membership in SLA, students gain professional experience and make industry contacts well in advance of officially starting their careers as information professionals.

Publications, Blogs, and Newsletters

SLA's monthly magazine, *Information Outlook,* provides news, features, and evaluation of trends in information management. SLA also gives members a weekly e-newsletter, *SLA Connections,* which covers breaking information industry news as well as association news and updates on upcoming Click University courses and important deadlines. In addition, SLA has a number of association blogs designed to keep members informed about SLA and professional news. Blogs are divided by category; "Leadership Connections," for example, supplies SLA's volunteer-leadership community with vital information and initiatives they can implement to improve their chapters and divisions.

Unit-Blogs, Industry-Outreach Blogs, Division Newsletters

Aside from blogs on the association level, many chapters and divisions of SLA actively write their own blogs to keep their members and the rest of the association community informed of their recent activities. Many divisions (such as the Science and Technology Division) publish a monthly bulletin or newsletter featuring industry information as it relates to new technologies. SLA President Cindy Romaine launched an industry outreach blog to be hosted by SLA titled "Future Ready 365." The blog is an ongoing collaborative effort among SLA members, staff, industry vendors, and celebrity/guest bloggers such as Silicon Valley venture capitalist Guy Kawasaki. The blog consists of a post-per-day, with each post sharing a new idea on how SLA's community of information professionals will become prepared for the future within their organization and their profession.

SLA's Social Media Community

SLA has presence in various social media networking sites, among them Twitter, LinkedIn, and Facebook. Each of these sites gives members the opportunity to build community among themselves virtually when physical meetings aren't possible. They also provide members with an easy way to share SLA information among their friends and networks, along with an easy outlet for customer service inquiries directed to SLA staff.

SLA Awards and Honors

The SLA awards and honors program was created in 1948 to honor exceptional individuals, achievements, and contributions to the association and the information profession. The program's purpose is to bring attention to the important work of special librarians and information professionals within the corporate and academic setting.

The association offers nine different awards and recognitions annually. SLA's highest honor is named after its founder, John Cotton Dana, and is granted to professionals to recognize a lifetime of professional achievement and contribution to the association. The recipient for 2010 was Jim Tchobanoff. [For a full list of SLA award recipients, visit the "Awards and Honors" page at http://www.sla.org/content/SLA/awardsrecognition/index.cfm, or see "Library Scholarship and Award Recipients, 2010" in Part 3—*Ed.*].

Research

SLA funds surveys and projects, endowment fund grants, and research studies relating to all aspects of information management.

Grants

SLA offers grants for research projects for the advancement of library sciences, the support of programs developed by SLA chapters, divisions, or committees, and the support of the association's expanding international agenda. Additionally, grants, scholarships, and stipends are offered by many of SLA's chapters and divisions. A recent grant-funded study was conducted by Betsy Rolland and Emily Glenn, Ph.D. candidates and SLA members. It found that information professionals are being relied on to play a greater role in biomedical research projects. For full information on the study, see http://www.sla.org/content/SLA/pressroom/pressrelease/10pr/pr1024.cfm.

Events and Conferences

SLA's Annual Conference and INFO-EXPO brings together thousands of information professionals and provides a forum for discussion of issues shaping the information industry. The conference offers more than 400 events, programs, panel discussions, and seminars, and includes an exhibit hall with more than 300 participating companies.

SLA's Annual Conference and INFO-EXPO 2011 is set for June 12–15 in Philadelphia. The theme of the conference will be "Future Ready: Building Community," which entails an effort to establish a support structure for SLA members to be ready for whatever the future may bring their way—in their organizations, transitioning between jobs or careers, and within the information profession itself.

Part 2
Legislation, Funding, and Grants

Legislation

Legislation and Regulations Affecting Libraries in 2010

Emily Sheketoff
Executive Director, Washington Office, American Library Association

Jenni Terry
Press Officer, Washington Office, American Library Association

The second session of the 111th Congress proved to be a waiting game for those engaged in library-related federal legislation. Some key bills were finally passed in the December lame-duck session, but while patience and diligence paid off regarding some issues, library proponents must renew their resolve to continue fighting familiar battles in the 112th Congress.

At the start of 2010 the American Library Association (ALA) and library grassroots supporters anxiously anticipated movement on two major issues in particular: education reform to address school library issues under a new Elementary and Secondary Education Act (ESEA), and the reauthorization of the Library Services and Technology Act (LSTA). However, when Congress wrapped up on December 22, 2010, only one of those critical items—LSTA—had been checked off the list.

Congress passed the Museum and Library Service Act (MLSA), which includes the Library Services and Technology Act (LSTA) and reauthorizes all of the programs under the Institute of Museum and Library Services (IMLS). President Obama signed MLSA into law on December 22. This down-to-the-wire congressional accomplishment was a major legislative victory, and it was accomplished through the diligence of ALA's grassroots network and collaboration among ALA staff and congressional leaders, primarily library champion U.S. Sen. Jack Reed (D-R.I.) who authored the Senate bill.

ESEA, however, was postponed until the 112th Congress, along with several other library-related issues.

As 2010 ended, the other unfinished issues included privacy, surveillance and reauthorization of key sections of the USAPatriot Act, net neutrality, access to government information, and copyright. The waiting game therefore continues, as do ALA's lobbying and grassroots efforts.

Appropriations

While the reauthorization of MLSA and LSTA was a clear victory for the library community, Congress failed to take the next steps in the federal funding process by the end of December 2010—passing the fiscal year (FY) 2011 budget bills, including funding for LSTA and the Improving Literacy Through School Libraries program.

In fact, it failed to pass any of the 12 FY 2011 budget bills by the end of the 111th Congress. Faced with the government running out of money and shutting down, it passed a continuing resolution (CR) until February 2011. Under the CR, all federal programs including LSTA and Improving Literacy Through School Libraries were to be funded at FY 2010 levels, leaving the duty of passing the FY 2011 budget to the 112th Congress.

While LSTA can fund all types of libraries, it is the only annual source of funding in the federal budget at this time for academic and public libraries. LSTA includes several titles supporting unique library programs, the largest of which is a state program providing funds to every state library agency (including the District of Columbia and the U.S. territories), administered and distributed by IMLS on a population-based formula. Each state librarian determines how to distribute the LSTA funds based upon his or her state's needs. When President Obama sent his FY 2011 budget request to Congress in February 2010, he asked that LSTA be funded at the FY 2010 level of $213.5 million. ALA continues its efforts to push Congress to appropriate $300 million to LSTA in FY 2011 and FY 2012. During the 111th Congress, 35 senators and 22 representatives asked both the House and Senate appropriations committees to fund LSTA at ALA's requested amount in a "Dear Colleague" letter.

Improving Literacy Through School Libraries is administered by the U.S. Department of Education and is intended to help low-income areas update their school libraries. Authorized since 2002 at $250 million, the program has never been funded above $20 million. In President Obama's FY 2011 budget request, the program was consolidated with five other Department of Education literacy programs, meaning that Improving Literacy Through School Libraries would be competing for funding every year with those other programs. ALA asked Congress to give Improving Literacy its own appropriation, at $100 million, and that the program be a population-based grant distributed through the school librarians, similar to LSTA. A "Dear Colleague" letter from 21 House members and 35 senators was sent to the Appropriations Committee during the 111th Congress asking for the Improving Literacy Through School Libraries to be funded at $100 million.

School Libraries

Elementary and Secondary Education Act (ESEA)

Under the Obama administration, the Department of Education changed the name of the No Child Left Behind (NCLB) Act back to the previously used name for comprehensive education legislation, the Elementary and Secondary Education Act (ESEA).

ESEA/NCLB was scheduled to be reauthorized in 2009, but the legislation was not completed during the 111th Congress despite the efforts of U.S. Sen. Tom Harkin (D-Iowa), chairman of the Senate Health, Education, Labor, and Pensions Committee, and U.S. Rep. George Miller (D-Calif.), chairman of the House Education and Labor Committee. The 112th Congress was to resume work on this critical legislation, which has been described as a priority by both Harkin and the new House Republican majority.

In the meantime, programs were to operate the same in 2011 and beyond until Congress passes reauthorization. ALA continues to lobby both the House and Senate for inclusion of language that will ensure all public schools have effective school library programs staffed by full-time, state-certified school librarians.

SKILLs Act

The Strengthening Kids' Interest in Learning and Libraries (SKILLs) Act was reintroduced in the 111th Congress as H.R. 3928 on October 26, 2009. Originally introduced in the 110th Congress by Sens. Reed and Thad Cochran (R-Miss.) and Reps. Raul Grijalva (D-Ariz.) and Vernon Ehlers (R-Mich.), the act would require school districts, to the extent feasible, to ensure that every school employ at least one state-certified school librarian in each library. The Senate did not introduce a companion bill.

As the SKILLs Act didn't advance during the 111th Congress, it is ALA's goal to secure the bill's provisions in the reauthorization of ESEA during the 112th.

Privacy and Surveillance

Confidentiality of library records is a core value of librarianship. Privacy is essential to the exercise of free speech, free thought, and free association. These privacy policies guide ALA's work to protect personal privacy in other areas, including debate on federal laws such as the USAPatriot Act, the Electronic Communications Privacy Act (EPCA), and the Computer Assistance for Law Enforcement Act (CALEA).

USAPatriot Act and Section 215 Reauthorization

During 2010 ALA continued to focus on reform of Section 215, the business records section (often called the "library provision") of the USAPatriot Act. Section 215 and two other sections of the act—the "lone wolf" and "roving wire-tap" provisions—were scheduled to sunset on February 28, 2010. The 111th Congress made additional extensions, which, at the time this report was prepared, scheduled these three sections to expire on February 28, 2011. This extended deadline was agreed to in February 2010 when Congress ran out of time, in part because of the continuing health care reform debate.

The actual reauthorization bills under consideration in the 111th Congress were H.R. 3845 and S. 1692. Both bills attempted modest changes to the USAPatriot Act, including some improvements to Section 215 relating to judicial review and oversight. The approach in H.R. 3845 was preferred over the Senate version, in part because it included improvements to the national security letter (NSL) standards. It is unclear whether the 112th Congress would start with the above proposals or begin whole new approaches to reauthorize the three expiring sections.

Electronic Communications Privacy Act

ALA joined the Digital Due Process (DDP) coalition and worked on efforts to reauthorize the Electronic Communications Privacy Act (ECPA) throughout 2010. The overarching goal of the coalition's work was to balance the law enforcement interests of the government, the privacy interests of users, and the interests of communications service providers in certainty, efficiency, and public confidence. The coalition took a cautious and considered approach to this reauthorization, which was also one of the issues expected to be addressed with new legislative proposals in the 112th Congress.

ECPA sets specific standards for law enforcement access to electronic communications and associated data, affording important privacy protections to subscribers of emerging wireless and Internet technologies. The statute has not undergone a significant revision since it was enacted in 1986, and ALA believes the statute therefore can no longer be applied in a clear and consistent way. Since enactment of ECPA, there have been fundamental changes in communications technology and the way people use it, including e-mail, mobile communications, cloud computing, and social networking.

DDP developed a set of principles articulated in a stated mission: "To simplify, clarify, and unify the ECPA standards, providing stronger privacy protections for communications and associated data in response to changes in technology and new services and usage patterns, while preserving the legal tools necessary for government agencies to enforce the laws, respond to emergency circumstances, and protect the public." DDP worked over the past year with privacy advocates, legal scholars, and major Internet and communications service providers to explore how ECPA would apply to new services and technologies. Significant consensus evolved about providing clearer privacy protections for users, taking into account changes in technology and usage patterns while preserving the legal tools necessary for government agencies to enforce the laws and protect the public. ALA hopes that the advance homework done by the DDP coalition during 2010 will lead Congress to improve ECPA this year.

Accessibility and Open Access

21st Century Communications and Video Accessibility Act of 2010

On October 8, 2010, President Obama signed into law the 21st Century Communications and Video Accessibility Act of 2010 (Public Law 111-260). This legislative action was a big win for libraries and their patrons, including the disabled. ALA strongly supported the legislation and adopted, during the ALA 2010 Annual Conference, the Resolution on Equal Access to 21st Century Communications (ALA CD 20.10).

The bill required Internet providers to make Internet and telecommunications services accessible to persons with disabilities,

- Requiring that equipment and services for advanced communications be usable by individuals with disabilities
- Requiring that the equipment or service be compatible with existing commonly used peripheral devices or specialized customer equipment
- Establishing an accessible and publicly available products and services clearinghouse

Federal Research Public Access Act of 2009

The Federal Research Public Access Act (FRPAA) of 2009 (S. 1373) was introduced in June 2009, and the House version, H.R. 5037, in April 2010. According to the bills' identical language, their purpose was "to provide for federal agencies to develop public access policies relating to research conducted by employees of that agency or from funds administered by that agency."

Specifically, the bills would have required federal agencies and departments with annual extramural research budgets of more than $100 million to make available, via the Internet, the final manuscript of articles resulting from research funded by taxpayers. The manuscripts would be maintained and preserved in a digital archive, ensuring that the research was available to the public.

Essentially, the bills would have advanced and expanded the National Institutes of Health (NIH) Public Access Policy that became mandatory via the Consolidated Appropriations Act of 2008, and would have required public access to taxpayer-funded research to an additional 11 agencies. The ability to search and access the archives of non-classified research of these agencies and departments—the departments of Agriculture, Commerce, Defense, Education, Energy, Health and Human Services, Homeland Security, and Transportation, the Environmental Protection Agency, the National Aeronautics and Space Administration, and the National Science Foundation—would have provided open online access to research. Undoubtedly, such an archive would allow librarians the ability to better assist library patrons with their information and research needs as well as allow direct access by the public.

Both bills died at the conclusion of the 111th Congress. While it was unclear whether similar bills would be reintroduced in the 112th, ALA strongly supports legislation that improves or expands public access to taxpayer-funded research.

Open the Congressional Research Service

Librarians, academics, journalists, open government advocates, and concerned citizens have for several years urged Congress to provide free, public access through the Internet to the unclassified, taxpayer-funded reports produced by the Congressional Research Service (CRS), a division of the Library of Congress. Taxpayers spend more than $100 million a year to fund CRS, which generates detailed reports for lawmakers.

CRS reports play a critical role in the political process, but have never been made available in a consistent manner to the public. Although lawmakers may provide copies of the reports to their constituents upon request, this is a slow, unreliable process, and there is no way for taxpayers to know what reports have been published.

Senate Resolution 118 was sponsored by Sen. Joseph Lieberman (I-Conn.) in April 2009 to provide Internet access to certain CRS publications. The resolution was referred to the Committee on Rules and Administration, but no further action occurred.

Congressional Research Service Electronic Accessibility Act of 2009

Rep. Frank Kratovil (D-Md.) introduced the Congressional Research Service Electronic Accessibility Act of 2009, H.R. 3762, in October 2009. The bill would have provided public Internet access to certain CRS publications, including briefs, reports, and authorization of appropriations products, but excluded information determined confidential or originating from a confidential research request. The bipartisan legislation would have made published CRS reports available to the public in an effort to increase government transparency.

Fair Copyright in Research Works Act

Rep. John Conyers, Jr. (D-Mich.), chairman of the U.S. House of Representatives Committee on the Judiciary during the 111th Congress, introduced the Fair Copyright in Research Works Act (H.R. 801) on February 3, 2009. This bill sought to amend copyright code and create a new category of copyrighted work, and was very similar to its predecessor in the 110th Congress (H.R. 6845). Just as in the 110th Congress (and the 109th), H.R. 801 would have negated or reversed the National Institutes of Health (NIH) Public Access Policy currently in place, rolling back progress on public access to taxpayer-funded NIH research on the Internet. Library advocates expressed to their members of Congress their strong opposition to the bill. It was unclear at the time this report was prepared whether a similar bill would be reintroduced in the 112th Congress.

Broadband and Telecommunications

Network Neutrality

During 2010 network (net) neutrality emerged as a leading issue in the broadband and telecommunications arena, setting the stage for congressional and Federal Communications Commission (FCC) activity in the 112th Congress.

Over the course of the year ALA worked with the Association of Research Libraries (ARL) and EDUCAUSE to lobby FCC commissioners and key members of Congress to inform and improve FCC Chairman Julius Genachowski's latest legal strategy to attempt to codify net neutrality principles. Specifically, the organizations asked FCC to address the following concerns prior to the scheduled vote on the net neutrality order:

- The definition of Broadband Internet Access Service should not be limited to "consumer" retail services. If the word "consumer" is defined as a "residential" consumer, then libraries and higher education would not be protected by the proposed net neutrality rules and policies.

- ALA, ARL, and EDUCAUSE believe "paid prioritization" should be banned altogether. Higher education and libraries already pay subscriber fees to obtain access to the Internet. The concern is that such prioritization puts not-for-profit educational institutions at a disadvantage compared with entertainment and for-profit educational entities.
- Net neutrality protections should be limited to "lawful traffic." Broadband operators should not be given absolute discretion to block traffic based on their own private determination that it is unlawful. It is inconsistent with core First Amendment values to allow broadband operators to impose prior restraints on Internet speakers without the benefit of a prior judicial determination or other adequate due process.
- Wireless services should be treated the same as wireline services. All Internet subscribers, whether using wireline or wireless technologies, should have the same right to a neutral, non-prioritized Internet.

In a long-awaited action on December 21, FCC passed (by a 3–2 vote) a net neutrality order. From ALA's perspective, the order did not go far enough to ensure that libraries and other community anchor institutions' content and services could be equally accessed by the public. While FCC addressed the broadband Internet access service definition issue raised in a letter by U.S. Reps. Doris Matsui (D-Calif.), Edward Markey (D-Mass.), and Anna Eshoo (D-Calif.) on behalf of ALA, the association believes the additional provisions it sought (outlined above) were not sufficiently met.

The order did not hold wireless to the same nondiscriminatory standards as wireline access, despite the growing number of libraries, higher education institutions, and users that utilize wireless technology to access content, information, and other applications. Additionally, ALA sought that the practice of paid prioritization be banned in order to protect libraries and educational interests from being charged more to provide the public with the same quality of access to educational and nonprofit content.

ALA immediately began the process to encourage FCC to address these additional concerns and to provide long-term oversight and enforcement of the rule. In addition, ALA began preparations for significant congressional activity on net neutrality as individual members of Congress signaled their intent to address the issue in the 112th Congress.

E-Rate

In the 111th Congress, Rep. Markey introduced the E-rate 2.0 Act of 2010 (H.R. 4619). The bill would have amended the Communications Act of 1934 to create a pilot program to bridge the "digital divide" by providing vouchers for broadband service to eligible students, to increase access to advanced telecommunications and information services for community colleges and Head Start programs, to establish a pilot program for discounted electronic books, and for other purposes. The E-rate provides lower "electronic" telecommunications rates for K–12 schools and public libraries. ALA worked with members of Congress to ensure that the discounts provided to public libraries for access to advanced telecommunications and information services were not endangered or eroded in any way (i.e., extending E-rate eligibility to cover additional purposes without increasing the cap).

The bill died at the end of the 111th Congress, but ALA began to actively monitor any E-rate and Universal Service Reform legislation to be ready for any proposals that might be introduced in the 112th Congress. The Universal Service Fund was created under the Telecommunications Act of 1996, which provides, in part, that all schools, classrooms, health care providers, and libraries should have access to advanced telecommunications services.

Universal Service Fund Exemption from Antideficiency Act Rules

The E-rate discount program was frozen for several months in 2004 following a major shift in requirements that made FCC comply with government accounting rules under the Antideficiency Act (ADA). This sudden application of ADA cash-flow rules forced FCC to freeze E-rate funds and temporarily halt pending commitments to E-rate participants for the subsequent year. There was major disruption for participants in the program because funds were withheld from vendors as well as libraries and schools, making it impossible for them to plan and budget for pending E-rate related services. The freeze was lifted when Congress passed a one-year exemption, which has had to be done again each year since, including again during December 2010.

ALA and others continued to seek a permanent exemption in order to provide stability and certainty to the E-rate program for participants and for service providers. ALA argued that after several years of one-year exemptions, the program demonstrated reasonable cash-flow procedures at FCC and at the Universal Service Administrative Company (USAC), and that these organizations continued to work effectively on the E-rate and should not be subject to ADA requirements.

ALA urged passage of S. 348, a bill introduced by Sens. John D. Rockefeller (D-W. Va.) and Olympia Snowe (R-Maine), two of the original sponsors of the E-rate program in the Telecommunications Act of 1996. ALA also urged passage of a companion bill, H.R. 2135, introduced by U.S. Rep. Denny Rehberg (R-Mont.), to provide a permanent exemption. Both S. 348 and H.R. 2135 would have amended Section 254 of the Communications Act of 1934 (which includes the Telecommunications Act of 1996). Unfortunately, the legislation died at the end of the 111th Congress.

As a matter of equity, at the end of 2010 the E-rate discount program under the Universal Service program at FCC remained an important way to ensure that public libraries and public and private schools could afford the ongoing monthly costs of telecommunications services in order to serve students and library users of all ages. ALA, as a member of the Education and Libraries Networks Coalition (EdLiNC), argued that every state benefited, with the deepest discounts going to the poorest communities. By the end of 2010, and over the 13 years of the program, public libraries received telecommunications discounts of more than $600 million. School libraries also continued to benefit. ALA will advocate reintroduction of an ADA Exemption bill during the 112th Congress.

Government Information

Freedom of Information Act (FOIA)

On May 5, 2010, the Senate Judiciary Committee passed S. 3111, the Faster FOIA Act. U.S. Rep. Brad Sherman (D-Calif.) introduced a similar bill, H.R. 5087, in the House, and it was referred to the House Committee on Oversight and Government Reform. Both bills would have created a commission that was required to make recommendations to Congress and the president for reducing impediments to the processing of FOIA requests. By undertaking a thorough study of the root causes of FOIA processing delays and developing concrete recommendations, a commission would help agencies successfully implement President Obama's directive to reduce significant backlogs of outstanding FOIA requests. This bill died at the conclusion of the 111th Congress.

Presidential Records Act

Rep. Edolphus Towns (D-N.Y.) introduced the Presidential Records Act Amendments of 2009 (H.R. 35) in the 111th Congress. The bill would have revoked an executive order of President George W. Bush (E.O. 13233) and other restrictions on access to presidential records. However, a U.S. District Court judge ruled in 2007 that presidents do not have authority to control executive records after they leave office. This ruling invalidates a part of E.O. 13233 that allows former presidents and vice presidents to review executive records before they are released under FOIA. Presidential records have been an important resource for historians, and ALA holds that it continues to be vital to the public interest that these papers are publicly available. H.R. 35 passed in January 2010 (by a vote of 359–58) and was sent to the Senate. The majority leader placed it on the Senate's legislative calendar, but it never came to a vote. ALA continued to work on this issue throughout 2010 and is prepared to seek passage of similar bills during the 112th Congress.

Preserve America's Historical Records Act

During the 111th Congress ALA supported H.R. 2256 and S. 3227, the Preserving the American Historical Record Act. These bills—sponsored by U.S. Reps. Maurice Hinchey (D-N.Y.) and John McHugh (R-N.Y.) and Sens. Orrin Hatch (R-Utah) and Carl Levin (D-Mich.)—demonstrated a bipartisan effort to ensure the proper preservation of historical records and allow for a wide variety of access tools to records. Congress did not take action on either bill before the end of the 111th Congress.

Whistleblower Protection Legislation

ALA worked again during 2010 to support whistleblower legislation to ensure the American public's "right to know," the cornerstone of government accountability and informed public participation. In the 111th Congress, Sen. Daniel Akaka (D-Alaska) introduced S. 372, the Whistleblower Protection Enhancement Act of 2009. The bill passed the Senate by unanimous consent on December 10, 2010. When the bill was sent to the House it passed without objection on December 22, after discussion raised by the WikiLeaks release of classified government documents led to a bipartisan agreement that it would only provide coverage to non-intelligence employees for unclassified whistleblower disclosures. Although this bill initially passed both houses of Congress, when it returned to the Senate for approval of the changes made in the House an anonymous hold was placed on it that stopped it from continuing on in the process toward becoming law.

During the 111th Congress a number of bills were introduced in the House and Senate that would overturn a U.S. Supreme Court decision from 2006, in *Garcetti* v. *Ceballos,* in which the high court ruled that the more than 21 million public employees could not claim freedom of speech rights under the First Amendment when they voice concerns to their supervisors.

Another bill, S. 1745, introduced by Sen. Claire McCaskill (D-Mo.) on October 1, 2009, would have protected government contractors if they were to bring forward any evidence of the misuse of federal funds. The bill was referred to the Committee on Homeland Security and Governmental Affairs and died at the end of the 111th Congress.

Over-Classification of Government Information and WikiLeaks

Despite slow and quiet activity throughout 2010 on legislative issues relating to whistleblowers and public access to government information, public debate exploded on December 7, 2010, when the Web site WikiLeaks posted a large number of classified documents, including classified material from U.S. Department of State cables. Vigorous debate about whether WikiLeaks founder Julian Assange was a saint for providing public access to the internal workings of government or a criminal for releasing classified documents spread across both official and grassroots venues. Internal ALA discussions began immediately about how libraries should handle this type of material and provide public access consistent with library principles of open access. As the debate within ALA moved forward on blogs and e-lists, some ALA members prepared draft resolutions relating to WikiLeaks and over-classification of government information for debate at ALA's Midwinter Conference in San Diego in January 2011.

By December 22, 2010, ALA had created a site on its Web pages to collect a full range of information, discussion, and varying perspectives about the multitude of issues raised by the release of the classified materials. The WikiLeaks activities raised many important policy issues for the library community. These policy issues include access to government information, censorship and the blocking of Web sites, government secrecy and the over-classification of government information, treatment of whistleblowers, government transparency, and the legalities surrounding classified information—all issues addressed by ALA policies and of concern to the library community.

Also on December 22, ALA joined a number of other open government and public access/First Amendment organizations in "An Open Letter to U.S. Government Officials Regarding Free Expression in the Wake of the WikiLeaks Controversy." The group, including the American Civil Liberties Union, the Association of Research Libraries, the Electronic Frontier Foundation, OpenTheGovernment.org, and others, emphasized the importance of the constitutional rights of the public and of publishers. The letter concluded: "It will be especially critical for members of Congress to keep these rights in mind as they consider any future legislation that may impact freedom of expression. . . . As the robust public debate about WikiLeaks continues, please make sure that it includes the rights of all involved."

With only days left in the 111th lame-duck session, two bills were introduced. One was S. 4004, the SHIELD (Securing Human Intelligence and Enforcing Lawful Dissemination) Act, which sought to "amend section 798 of title 18, United States Code, to provide penalties for disclosure of classified information relating to certain intelligence activities of the United States and for other purposes . . ." In the House, the same bill was introduced as H.R. 6506. Time ran out and the 111th Congress ended, but the bills were expected to be reintroduced in the new Congress.

James Madison Award

The 2010 James Madison Award was presented to Meredith Fuchs, general counsel to the National Security Archive, and Citizens for Responsibility and Ethics in Washington (CREW) for their work in resolving the missing White House e-mail lawsuit filed first by the National Security Archive in September 2007.

This award is given each year to honor individuals or groups who have championed, protected, and promoted public access to government information and the public's "right to know" on the national level.

Funding Programs and Grant-Making Agencies

National Endowment for the Humanities

1100 Pennsylvania Ave. N.W., Washington, DC 20506
202-606-8400, 1-800-634-1121
TDD (hearing impaired) 202-606-8282 or 866-372-2930 (toll free)
E-mail Info@neh.gov, World Wide Web http://www.neh.gov

The National Endowment for the Humanities (NEH) is an independent federal agency created in 1965. It is the largest funder of humanities programs in the United States.

Because democracy demands wisdom, NEH promotes excellence in the humanities and conveys the lessons of history to all Americans, seeking to develop educated and thoughtful citizens. It accomplishes this mission by providing grants for high-quality humanities projects in six funding areas: education, preservation and access, public programs, research, challenge grants, and digital humanities.

Grants from NEH enrich classroom learning, create and preserve knowledge, and bring ideas to life through public television, radio, new technologies, museum exhibitions, and programs in libraries and other community places. Recipients typically are cultural institutions, such as museums, archives, libraries, colleges and universities, and public television and radio stations, as well as individual scholars. The grants

- Strengthen teaching and learning in the humanities in schools and colleges
- Preserve and provide access to cultural and educational resources
- Provide opportunities for lifelong learning
- Facilitate research and original scholarship
- Strengthen the institutional base of the humanities

Over the past 45 years, NEH has reached millions of Americans with projects and programs that preserve and study the nation's culture and history while providing a foundation for the future.

The endowment's mission is to enrich cultural life by promoting the study of the humanities. According to the National Foundation on the Arts and the Humanities Act, "The term 'humanities' includes, but is not limited to, the study of the following: language, both modern and classical; linguistics; literature; history; jurisprudence; philosophy; archaeology; comparative religion; ethics; the history, criticism, and theory of the arts; those aspects of social sciences which have humanistic content and employ humanistic methods; and the study and application of the humanities to the human environment with particular attention to reflecting our diverse heritage, traditions, and history and to the relevance of the humanities to the current conditions of national life."

The act, adopted by Congress in 1965, provided for the establishment of the National Foundation on the Arts and the Humanities in order to promote progress and scholarship in the humanities and the arts in the United States. The act included the following findings:

- The arts and the humanities belong to all the people of the United States.
- The encouragement and support of national progress and scholarship in the humanities and the arts, while primarily matters for private and local initiative, are also appropriate matters of concern to the federal government.
- An advanced civilization must not limit its efforts to science and technology alone, but must give full value and support to the other great branches of scholarly and cultural activity in order to achieve a better understanding of the past, a better analysis of the present, and a better view of the future.
- Democracy demands wisdom and vision in its citizens. It must therefore foster and support a form of education, and access to the arts and the humanities, designed to make people of all backgrounds and locations masters of technology and not its unthinking servants.
- It is necessary and appropriate for the federal government to complement, assist, and add to programs for the advancement of the humanities and the arts by local, state, regional, and private agencies and their organizations. In doing so, the government must be sensitive to the nature of public sponsorship. Public funding of the arts and humanities is subject to the conditions that traditionally govern the use of public money. Such funding should contribute to public support and confidence in the use of taxpayer funds. Public funds provided by the federal government ultimately must serve public purposes the Congress defines.
- The arts and the humanities reflect the high place accorded by the American people to the nation's rich culture and history and to the fostering of mutual respect for the diverse beliefs and values of all persons and groups.

What NEH Grants Accomplish

Since its founding, NEH has awarded more than 67,700 competitive grants.

Interpretive Exhibitions

Interpretive exhibitions provide opportunities for lifelong learning in the humanities for millions of Americans. Since 1967 NEH has awarded more than $268 million in grants for interpretive exhibitions, catalogs, and public programs, which are among the most highly visible activities supported by the endowment.

During 2011 NEH support is financing 30 exhibitions; reading, viewing, and discussion programs; Web-based programs; and other public education programs at venues across the country.

Renewing Teaching

Over NEH's history, more than 95,578 high school and college teachers have deepened their knowledge of the humanities through intensive summer study supported by the endowment; tens of thousands of students benefit from these better-educated teachers every year.

Reading and Discussion Programs

Since 1982 NEH has supported reading and discussion programs in the nation's libraries, bringing people together to discuss works of literature and history. Scholars in the humanities provide thematic direction for the discussion programs. Using selected texts and themes such as "Work," "Family," "Diversity," and "Not for Children Only," these programs have attracted more than 2 million Americans to read and talk about what they've read.

Chronicling America

NEH's National Digital Newspaper Program is supporting projects to convert microfilm of historically important U.S. newspapers into fully searchable digital files. Developed in partnership with the Library of Congress, this long-term project ultimately will make more than 30 million pages of newspapers accessible online. For more on this project, visit http://chroniclingamerica.loc.gov.

Stimulating Private Support

More than $1.685 billion in humanities support has been generated by NEH's Challenge Grants program, which requires most grant recipients to raise $3 in nonfederal funds for every dollar they receive.

Presidential Papers

Ten presidential papers projects, from Washington to Eisenhower, have received support from NEH. Matching grants for the ten projects have leveraged $7.65 million in nonfederal contributions.

New Scholarship

NEH grants enable scholars to do in-depth study. Jack Rakove explored the making of the Constitution in his *Original Meanings* and James McPherson chronicled the Civil War in his *Battle Cry of Freedom.* Projects supported by NEH grants have earned 18 Pulitzer Prizes and 20 Bancroft Prizes.

History on Screen

Since 1967 NEH has awarded more than $291 million to support the production of films for broad public distribution, including the Emmy Award-winning series *The Civil War,* the Oscar-nominated films *Brooklyn Bridge, The Restless Con-*

science, and *Freedom on My Mind,* and film biographies of John and Abigail Adams, Eugene O'Neill, and Ernest Hemingway. Twenty million Americans have watched Ken Burns's critically acclaimed *The War* (2007), which chronicles the United States in World War II. More than 8 million people saw the April 2010 debut of *The Buddha,* a documentary made for PBS by filmmaker David Grubin, and it has been streamed into 548 classrooms across the country.

American Voices

NEH support for scholarly editions makes the writings of prominent and influential Americans accessible. Ten presidents are included, along with such key figures as Martin Luther King, Jr., George C. Marshall, and Eleanor Roosevelt. Papers of prominent writers—among them Emily Dickinson, Walt Whitman, Mark Twain, and Robert Frost—are also available.

Library of America

Millions of books have been sold as part of the Library of America series, a collection of the riches of the nation's literature. Begun with NEH seed money, the more than 170 published volumes include the work of such figures as Henry Adams, Edith Wharton, William James, Eudora Welty, and W. E. B. DuBois.

The Library of America also received a $150,000 grant for the publication of *American Poetry: The Seventeenth and Eighteenth Centuries* (two volumes) and an expanded volume of selected works by Captain John Smith—a key figure in the establishment of the first permanent English settlement in North America, at Jamestown, Virginia—and other early exploration narratives.

Technical Innovation

NEH support for the digital humanities is fueling innovation and new tools for research in the humanities. Modern 3D technology allows students to walk the sands of ancient Egypt alongside Ramses II in Digital Karnak (http://dlib.etc.ucla.edu/projects/Karnak) or visit the 1964–1965 New York World's Fair (http://mcl.ucf.edu/nywf). Spectral imaging is being used to create an online critical edition of explorer David Livingstone's previously unreadable field diary.

Science and the Humanities

The scientific past is being preserved with NEH-supported editions of the letters of Charles Darwin, the works of Albert Einstein, and the 14-volume papers of Thomas Edison. Additionally, NEH and the National Science Foundation have joined forces in Documenting Endangered Languages (DEL), a multiyear effort to preserve records of key languages that are in danger of becoming extinct.

EDSITEment

EDSITEment (http://www.edsitement.neh.gov) assembles the best humanities resources on the Web, drawing more than 400,000 visitors each month. Incorporating these Internet resources, particularly primary documents, from more than 200 peer-reviewed Web sites, EDSITEment features more than 400 online lesson plans in all areas of the humanities. Teachers use EDSITEment's resources to enhance lessons and to engage students through interactive technology tools that hone critical-thinking skills.

Federal-State Partnership

The Office of Federal-State Partnership links NEH with the nationwide network of 56 humanities councils, which are located in each state, the District of Columbia, Puerto Rico, the U.S. Virgin Islands, the Northern Mariana Islands, American Samoa, and Guam. Each humanities council funds humanities programs in its own jurisdiction.

Directory of State Humanities Councils

Alabama

Alabama Humanities Foundation
1100 Ireland Way, Suite 101
Birmingham, AL 35205-7001
205-558-3980, fax 205-558-3981
http://www.ahf.net

Alaska

Alaska Humanities Forum
161 E. First Ave., Door 15
Anchorage, AK 99501
907-272-5341, fax 907-272-3979
http://www.akhf.org

Arizona

Arizona Humanities Council
Ellis-Shackelford House
1242 N. Central Ave.
Phoenix, AZ 85004-1887
602-257-0335, fax 602-257-0392
http://www.azhumanities.org

Arkansas

Arkansas Humanities Council
407 President Clinton Ave., Suite 201
Little Rock, AR 72201
501-320-5761, fax 501-537-4550
http://www.arkhums.org

California

California Council for the Humanities
312 Sutter St., Suite 601
San Francisco, CA 94108
415-391-1474, fax 415-391-1312
http://www.calhum.org

Colorado

Colorado Humanities
1490 Lafayette St., Suite 101
Denver, CO 80218
303-894-7951, fax 303-864-9361
http://www.coloradohumanities.org

Connecticut

Connecticut Humanities Council
37 Broad St.
Middletown, CT 06457
860-685-2260, fax 860-685-7597
http://www.ctculture.org

Delaware

Delaware Humanities Forum
100 W. Tenth St., Suite 1009
Wilmington, DE 19801
302-657-0650, fax 302-657-0655
http://www.dhf.org

District of Columbia

Humanities Council of Washington, D.C.
925 U St. N.W.
Washington, DC 20001
202-387-8391, fax 202-387-8149
http://wdchumanities.org

Florida

Florida Humanities Council
599 Second St. South
St. Petersburg, FL 33701-5005
727-873-2000, fax 727-873-2014
http://www.flahum.org

Georgia

Georgia Humanities Council
50 Hurt Plaza S.E., Suite 595
Atlanta, GA 30303-2915
404-523-6220, fax 404-523-5702
http://www.georgiahumanities.org

Hawaii

Hawai'i Council for the Humanities
First Hawaiian Bank Bldg.
3599 Waialae Ave., Room 25
Honolulu, HI 96816
808-732-5402, fax 808-732-5432
http://www.hihumanities.org

Idaho

Idaho Humanities Council
217 W. State St.
Boise, ID 83702
208-345-5346, fax 208-345-5347
http://www.idahohumanities.org

Illinois

Illinois Humanities Council
17 N. State St., No. 1400
Chicago, IL 60602-3296
312-422-5580, fax 312-422-5588
http://www.prairie.org

Indiana

Indiana Humanities Council
1500 N. Delaware St.
Indianapolis, IN 46202
317-638-1500, fax 317-634-9503
http://www.indianahumanities.org

Iowa

Humanities Iowa
100 LIB RM 4039
Iowa City, IA 52242-5000
319-335-4153, fax 319-335-4154
http://www.humanitiesiowa.org

Kansas

Kansas Humanities Council
112 S.W. Sixth Ave., Suite 210
Topeka, KS 66603
785-357-0359, fax 785-357-1723
http://www.kansashumanities.org

Kentucky

Kentucky Humanities Council
206 E. Maxwell St.
Lexington, KY 40508
859-257-5932, fax 859-257-5933
http://www.kyhumanities.org

Louisiana

Louisiana Endowment for the Humanities
938 Lafayette St., Suite 300
New Orleans, LA 70113-1782
504-523-4352, fax 504-529-2358
http://www.leh.org

Maine

Maine Humanities Council
674 Brighton Ave.
Portland, ME 04102-1012
207-773-5051, fax 207-773-2416
http://www.mainehumanities.org

Maryland

Maryland Humanities Council
108 W. Centre St.
Baltimore, MD 21201-4565
410-685-0095, fax 410-685-0795
http://www.mdhc.org

Massachusetts

Mass Humanities
66 Bridge St.
Northampton, MA 01060
413-584-8440, fax 413-584-8454
http://www.masshumanities.org

Michigan

Michigan Humanities Council

119 Pere Marquette Drive, Suite 3B
Lansing, MI 48912-1270
517-372-7770, fax 517-372-0027
http://michiganhumanities.org

Minnesota

Minnesota Humanities Center
987 E. Ivy Ave.
St. Paul, MN 55106-2046
651-774-0105, fax 651-774-0205
http://www.minnesotahumanities.org

Mississippi

Mississippi Humanities Council
3825 Ridgewood Rd., Room 311
Jackson, MS 39211
601-432-6752, fax 601-432-6750
http://www.mshumanities.org

Missouri

Missouri Humanities Council
543 Hanley Industrial Court, Suite 201
St. Louis, MO 63144-1905
314-781-9660, fax 314-781-9681
http://www.mohumanities.org

Montana

Humanities Montana
311 Brantly
Missoula, MT 59812-7848
406-243-6022, fax 406-243-4836
http://www.humanitiesmontana.org

Nebraska

Nebraska Humanities Council
215 Centennial Mall South, Suite 330
Lincoln, NE 68508
402-474-2131, fax 402-474-4852
http://www.nebraskahumanties.org

Nevada

Nevada Humanities
P.O. Box 8029
Reno, NV 89507
775-784-6587, fax 775-784-6527
http://www.nevadahumanities.org

New Hampshire

New Hampshire Humanities Council
19 Pillsbury St.
Concord, NH 03301
603-224-4071, fax 603-224-4072
http://www.nhhc.org

New Jersey

New Jersey Council for the Humanities
28 W. State St., 6th floor
Trenton, NJ 08608
609-695-4838, fax 609-695-4929
http://www.njch.org

New Mexico

New Mexico Humanities Council
MSC06 3570
1 University of New Mexico
Albuquerque, NM 87131-0001
505-277-3705, fax 505-277-6056
http://www.nmhum.org

New York

New York Council for the Humanities
150 Broadway, Suite 1700
New York, NY 10038
212-233-1131, fax 212-233-4607
http://www.nyhumanities.org

North Carolina

North Carolina Humanities Council
122 North Elm St.
Greensboro, NC 27401
336-334-5325, fax 336-334-5052
http://www.nchumanities.org

North Dakota

North Dakota Humanities Council
418 E. Broadway, Suite 8
Bismarck, ND 58501
701-255-3360, fax 701-223-8724
http://www.nd-humanities.org

Ohio

Ohio Humanities Council
471 E. Broad St., Suite 1620
Columbus, OH 43215-3857

614-461-7802, fax 614-461-4651
http://www.ohiohumanities.org

Oklahoma

Oklahoma Humanities Council
Festival Plaza
428 W. California, Suite 270
Oklahoma City, OK 73102
405-235-0280, fax 405-235-0289
http://www.okhumanitiescouncil.org

Oregon

Oregon Council for the Humanities
813 S.W. Alder St., Suite 702
Portland, OR 97205
503-241-0543, fax 503-241-0024
http://www.oregonhum.org

Pennsylvania

Pennsylvania Humanities Council
325 Chestnut St., Suite 715
Philadelphia, PA 19106-2607
215-925-1005, fax 215-925-3054
http://www.pahumanities.org

Rhode Island

Rhode Island Council for the Humanities
131 Washington St., Suite 201
Providence, RI 02903
401-273-2250, fax 401-454-4872
http://www.rihumanities.org

South Carolina

Humanities Council of South Carolina
P.O. Box 5287
Columbia, SC 29250
803-771-2477, fax 803-771-2487
http://www.schumanities.org

South Dakota

South Dakota Humanities Council
1215 Trail Ridge Rd., Suite A
Brookings, SD 57006
605-688-6113, fax 605-688-4531
http://sdhumanities.org

Tennessee

Humanities Tennessee
306 Gay St., Suite 306
Nashville, TN 37201
615-770-0006, fax 615-770-0007
http://www.humanitiestennessee.org

Texas

Humanities Texas
1410 Rio Grande St.
Austin, TX 78701
512-440-1991, fax 512-440-0115
http://www.humanitiestexas.org

Utah

Utah Humanities Council
202 W. 300 North
Salt Lake City, UT 84103
801-359-9670, fax 801-531-7869
http://www.utahhumanities.org

Vermont

Vermont Humanities Council
11 Loomis St.
Montpelier, VT 05602
802-262-2626, fax 802-262-2620
http://www.vermonthumanities.org

Virginia

Virginia Foundation for the Humanities and Public Policy
145 Ednam Drive
Charlottesville, VA 22903-4629
434-924-3296, fax 434-296-4714
http://www.virginiafoundation.org

Washington

Humanities Washington
1204 Minor Ave.
Seattle, WA 98101-2825
206-682-1770, fax 206-682-4158
http://www.humanities.org

West Virginia

West Virginia Humanities Council
1310 Kanawha Blvd. East

Charleston, WV 25301
304-346-8500, fax 304-346-8504
http://www.wvhumanities.org

Wisconsin

Wisconsin Humanities Council
222 S. Bedford St., Suite F
Madison, WI 53703-3688
608-262-0706, fax 608-263-7970
http://www.wisconsinhumanities.org

Wyoming

Wyoming Humanities Council
1315 E. Lewis St.
Laramie, WY 82072-3459
307-721-9243, fax 307-742-4914
http://www.uwyo.edu/humanities

American Samoa

Amerika Samoa Humanities Council
P.O. Box 5800
Pago Pago, AS 96799
684-633-4870, fax 684-633-4873
http://amerikasamoahumanitiescouncil.org

Guam

Guam Humanities Council
222 Chalan Santo Papa
Reflection Center, Suite 106
Hagatna, Guam 96910
671-472-4460, fax 671-472-4465
http://www.guamhumanitiescouncil.org

Northern Mariana Islands

Northern Mariana Islands Council for the Humanities
P.O. Box 506437
Saipan, MP 96950
670-235-4785, fax 670-235-4786
http://www.nmihumanities.org

Puerto Rico

Fundación Puertorriqueña de las Humanidades
Box 9023920
San Juan, PR 00902-3920
787-721-2087, fax 787-721-2684
http://www.fphpr.org

Virgin Islands

Virgin Islands Humanities Council
1829 Kongens Gade
St. Thomas, VI 00802-6746
340-776-4044, fax 340-774-3972
http://www.vihumanities.org

NEH Overview

Division of Education Programs

Through grants to educational institutions and professional development programs for scholars and teachers, this division is designed to support study of the humanities at all levels of education.

Grants support the development of curriculum and materials, faculty study programs among educational institutions, and conferences and networks of institutions.

Eligible applicants: Public and private elementary and secondary schools, school systems, colleges and universities, nonprofit academic associations, and cultural institutions such as libraries and museums

Application deadlines: Humanitics Initiatives at Historically Black Colleges and Universities, Humanities Initiatives at Institutions with High Hispanic Enrollment, and

	Humanities Initiatives at Tribal Colleges and Universities, April 14, 2011
Contact:	202-606-8500, e-mail education@neh.gov

Seminars and Institutes

Grants support summer seminars and institutes in the humanities for college and school teachers. These faculty development activities are conducted at colleges and universities in the United States and abroad. Those wishing to participate in seminars should submit their seminar applications to the seminar director.

Eligible applicants:	Individuals and institutions of higher learning, as well as cultural institutions
Application deadlines:	Participants, March 1, 2011, for summer seminars and institutes in 2011; Directors, March 1, 2011, for summer seminars and institutes in 2012

Landmarks of American History and Culture

Grants for Landmarks workshops provide support to school teachers and community college faculty. These professional development workshops are conducted at or near sites important to American history and culture (e.g., presidential residences or libraries, colonial era settlements, major battlefields, historic districts, and sites associated with major writers or artists) to address central themes and issues in American history, government, literature, art history, and other related subjects in the humanities.

Eligibility:	Individuals, institutions of higher learning, cultural institutions
Application deadlines:	School teacher and community college faculty participants, March 1, 2011, for summer workshops in 2011; directors, March 1, 2011, for summer workshops in 2012
Contact:	202-606-8463, e-mail sem-inst@neh.gov

Division of Preservation and Access

Grants are made for projects that will create, preserve, and increase the availability of resources important for research, education, and public programming in the humanities.

Projects may encompass books, journals, newspapers, manuscript and archival materials, maps, still and moving images, sound recordings, and objects of material culture held by libraries, archives, museums, historical organizations, and other repositories.

Preservation and Access Projects

Support may be sought to preserve the intellectual content and aid bibliographic control of collections; to compile bibliographies, descriptive catalogs, and guides to cultural holdings; and to create dictionaries, encyclopedias, databases, and electronic archives. Applications also may be submitted for education and training projects dealing with issues of preservation or access; for research and development leading to improved preservation and access standards, practices, and tools; and for projects to digitize historic American newspapers and to document endangered languages. Grants are also made to help smaller cultural repositories preserve and care for their humanities collections.

Proposals may combine preservation and access activities within a single project.

Eligible applicants:	Nonprofit institutions, cultural organizations, state agencies, and institutional consortia
Application deadlines:	May, June, July, September, and December 2011
Contact:	202-606-8570, e-mail preservation@neh.gov

Division of Public Programs

Public humanities programs promote lifelong learning in American and world history, literature, comparative religion, philosophy, and other fields of the humanities. They offer new insights into familiar subjects and invite conversation about important humanities ideas and questions.

The Division of Public Programs supports a wide range of public humanities programs that reach large and diverse public audiences through a variety of program formats, including interpretive exhibitions, radio and television broadcasts, lectures, symposia, interpretive multimedia projects, printed materials, and reading and discussion programs.

Grants support the development and production of television, radio and digital media programs; the planning and implementation of museum exhibitions, the interpretation of historic sites, the production of related publications, multimedia components, and educational programs; the planning and implementation of reading and discussion programs, lectures, symposia, and interpretive exhibitions of books, manuscripts, and other library resources.

Eligible applicants:	Nonprofit institutions and organizations including public television and radio stations and state humanities councils
Application deadlines:	Planning, implementation, development, production: January, June, and August 2011
Contact:	202-606-8269, e-mail publicpgms@neh.gov

Division of Research Programs

Through fellowships to individual scholars and grants to support complex, frequently collaborative research, the Division of Research Programs contributes to the creation of knowledge in the humanities.

Fellowships and Stipends

Grants provide support for scholars to undertake full-time independent research and writing in the humanities. Grants are available for a maximum of one year and a minimum of two months of summer study.

Eligible applicants:	Individuals
Application deadlines:	Fellowships, May 2011; awards for faculty at Historically Black Colleges and Universities, Institutions with High Hispanic Enrollment, and Tribal Colleges and Universities, April 2011. Summer stipends, September 2011
Contact:	202-606-8200, e-mail (fellowships) fellowships@neh.gov, (summer stipends) stipends@neh.gov

Research

Grants provide up to three years of support for collaborative research in the preparation of publication of editions, translations, and other important works in the humanities, and in the conduct of large or complex interpretive studies including archaeology projects and humanities studies of science and technology. Grants also support research opportunities offered through independent research centers and international research organizations.

Eligible applicants:	Individuals, institutions of higher education, nonprofit professional associations, scholarly societies, and other nonprofit organizations
Application deadlines:	Collaborative research and scholarly editions, October 2011; Fellowship programs at independent research institutions, August 2011
Contact:	202-606-8200, e-mail research@neh.gov

Office of Challenge Grants

Nonprofit institutions interested in developing new sources of long-term support for educational, scholarly, preservation, and public programs in the humanities may be assisted in these efforts by an NEH Challenge Grant. Grantees are required to raise $3 in nonfederal donations for every federal dollar offered. Both federal and nonfederal funds may be used to establish or increase institutional endowments and therefore guarantee long-term support for a variety of humanities needs. Funds also may be used for limited direct capital expenditures where such needs are compelling and clearly related to improvements in the humanities.

Eligible applicants:	Nonprofit postsecondary, educational, research, or cultural institutions and organizations working within the humanities
Application deadlines:	Challenge grants, May 2011
Contact:	202-606-8309, e-mail challenge@neh.gov

Office of Digital Humanities

The Office of Digital Humanities encourages and supports projects that utilize or study the impact of digital technology on research, education, preservation, and public programming in the humanities. First launched as an initiative in 2006, the Digital Humanities initiative was made permanent as an office within NEH in spring 2008.

NEH is interested in fostering the growth of digital humanities and lending support to a wide variety of projects, including those that deploy digital technologies and methods to enhance understanding of a topic or issue; those that study the impact of digital technology on the humanities; and those that digitize important materials, thereby increasing the public's ability to search and access humanities information.

The office coordinates the endowment's efforts in the area of digital scholarship. Currently, NEH has numerous programs throughout the agency that are actively funding digital scholarship, including Humanities Collections and Resources, Institutes for Advanced Topics in the Digital Humanities, Digital Humanities Challenge Grants, Digital Humanities Start-Up Grants, and many others. NEH is also actively working with other funding partners, both in the United States and abroad, in order to better coordinate spending on digital infrastructure for the humanities.

Eligible applicants:	Nonprofit postsecondary, educational, research, or cultural institutions and organizations working within the humanities
Application deadlines:	Digital Humanities Start-Up Grants, February 2011; Institutes for Advanced Topics in the Digital Humanities, February 2011
Contact:	202-606-8401, e-mail odh@neh.gov

A full list of NEH grants programs and deadlines is available on the endowment's Web site, http://www.neh.gov.

Institute of Museum and Library Services Office of Library Services

1800 M St. N.W., Ninth Floor, Washington, DC 20036-5802
202-653-4657, fax 202-653-4625
World Wide Web http://www.imls.gov

Susan Hildreth
Director

Mary L. Chute
Deputy Director for Libraries

Mission

The Institute of Museum and Library Services (IMLS) is the primary source of federal support for the nation's 123,000 libraries and 17,500 museums. The institute's mission is to create strong libraries and museums that connect people to information and ideas. IMLS works at the national level and in coordination with state and local organizations to sustain heritage, culture, and knowledge; enhance learning and innovation; and support professional development.

Leadership

Susan Hildreth was appointed in 2010 to a four-year term as IMLS director by President Barack Obama. Her nomination was confirmed by unanimous consent by the U.S. Senate on December 22, and her term of office began on January 23.

Hildreth previously served for two years as city librarian in Seattle and five years as state librarian of California. She succeeds IMLS Deputy Director for Museums Marsha Semmel, who served as acting director of IMLS following the departure of Anne-Imelda Radice in March 2010 at the conclusion of her four-year term.

Overview

Libraries and museums help create vibrant, energized learning communities. Our achievement as individuals and our success as a democratic society depend on learning continually, adapting to change readily, and evaluating information critically.

Museums and Libraries—as stewards of cultural heritage, information, and ideas—traditionally have played a vital role in helping people experience, explore, discover, and make sense of the world. Through building technological infrastructure and strengthening community relationships, libraries and museums can offer the public unprecedented access and expertise in transforming information overload into knowledge.

The role of IMLS is to provide leadership and funding for libraries and museums, resources these institutions need to fulfill their mission of becoming centers of learning for life crucial to achieving personal fulfillment, a productive work force, and an engaged citizenry.

Specifically, the Museum and Library Services Act authorizes the Institute to support the following activities:

Library Services and Technology Act (LSTA)

- To promote improvements in library services in all types of libraries to better serve the people of the United States
- To facilitate access to resources and in all types of libraries for the purpose of cultivating an educated and informed citizenry
- To encourage resource sharing among all types of libraries for the purpose of achieving economical and efficient delivery of library services to the public

Museum Services Act

- To encourage and support museums in carrying out their public service role of connecting the whole society to cultural, artistic, historic, natural, and scientific understandings that constitute its heritage
- To encourage and support museums in carrying out their educational role as core providers of learning and in conjunction with schools, families, and communities
- To encourage leadership, innovation, and application of the most current technologies and practices to enhance museum services
- To assist, encourage, and support museums in carrying out their stewardship responsibilities to achieve the highest standards in conservation and care of the cultural, historic, natural, and scientific heritage of the United States to benefit future generations
- To assist, encourage, and support museums in achieving the highest standards of management and service to the public, and to ease the financial burden borne by museums as a result of their increasing use by the public
- To support resource sharing and partnerships among museums, libraries, schools, and other community organizations

Impact of Museum and Library Services

A general provision of the Museum and Library Services Act states that "the Director shall carry out and publish analyses of the impact of museum and library services. Such analyses

- Shall be conducted in ongoing consultation with state library administrative agencies; state, regional, and national library and museum organizations; and other relevant agencies and organizations

- Shall identify national needs for, and trends of, museum and library services provided with funds made available under subchapters II and III of this chapter
- Shall report on the impact and effectiveness of programs conducted with funds made available by the Institute in addressing such needs
- Shall identify, and disseminate information on, the best practices of such programs to the agencies and entities described."

Fiscal Year 2010

In fiscal year (FY) 2010 Congress appropriated $228,042,560 for the programs and administrative support authorized by LSTA. The Office of Library Services within IMLS, under the policy direction of the IMLS director and deputy director, administers LSTA programs. The office comprises the Division of State Programs, which administers the Grants to States program, and the Division of Discretionary Programs, which administers the National Leadership Grants for Libraries program, the Laura Bush 21st Century Librarian program, the Native American Library Services program, and the Native Hawaiian Library Services program. IMLS also presents annual awards to libraries through the National Medal for Museum and Library Service program. Additionally, IMLS is one of the sponsoring organizations supporting the National Arts and Humanities Youth Program Awards (formerly the Coming Up Taller awards) in conjunction with the President's Committee on the Arts and the Humanities, the National Endowment for the Arts, and the National Endowment for the Humanities); the Big Read program (in partnership with the National Endowment for the Arts); and Save America's Treasures (in partnership with the National Park Service, the National Trust for Historic Preservation, Heritage Preservation, the National Endowment for the Arts, and the National Park Foundation).

Library Statistics

President Obama's budget request for FY 2009 included funds for IMLS to continue administering the Public Libraries Survey and the State Library Agencies Survey, effective October 1, 2008. FY 2009 marked the first year that IMLS administered the Public Libraries Survey and the State Library Agencies Survey over a full collection cycle, from survey planning to collection and dissemination. Responding to concerns from the professional community, IMLS has reduced by six months the time it takes to release survey results. In addition to producing annual reports on the survey data, IMLS introduced new, shorter research products to highlight report findings. These new reports leverage the survey data to address a wide range of public policy priorities, including education, employment, community and economic development, and telecommunications policy.

In the Library Statistics section of the IMLS Web site (http://www.imls.gov/statistics), visitors can link to data search tools, the latest available data for each survey, other publications, data files, and survey definitions.

Public Libraries Survey

Descriptive statistics for more than 9,000 public libraries are collected and disseminated annually through a voluntary census, the Public Libraries Survey. The survey is conducted through the Public Library Statistics Cooperative (PLSC, formerly the Federal-State Cooperative System [FSCS]). In FY 2011 IMLS will complete the 14th collection of this data.

The Public Libraries Survey collects identifying information about public libraries and each of their service outlets, including street address, mailing address, Web address, and telephone number. The survey collects data about public libraries, including data on staffing, type of legal basis, type of geographic boundary, type of administrative structure, type of interlibrary relationship, type and number of public service outlets, operating revenue and expenditures, capital revenue and expenditures, size of collection (including number of electronic books and databases), current serial subscriptions (including electronic), and service measures, such as number of reference transactions, interlibrary loans, circulation, public service hours, library visits, circulation of children's materials, number of children's programs, children's program attendance, total number of library programs, total attendance at library programs, number of Internet terminals used by the general public, and number of users of electronic resources per year.

This survey also collects several data items about outlets, including the location of an outlet relative to a metropolitan area, number of books-by-mail-only outlets, number of bookmobiles by bookmobile outlet, and square footage of the outlet.

The 50 states and the District of Columbia have participated in data collection from the survey's inception in 1989. In 1993 Guam, the Commonwealth of the Northern Mariana Islands, Puerto Rico, and the U.S. Virgin Islands joined in the survey. The first release of Public Libraries Survey data occurred with the release of the updated Compare Public Libraries Tool on the Library Statistics section of the IMLS Web site (http://www.imls.gov/statistics). The data used in this Web tool are final, but do not include imputations for missing data (imputation is a statistical means for providing an estimate for each missing data item).

Final imputed data files that contain FY 2008 data on more than 9,000 responding libraries and identifying information about their outlets were made available in November 2008 in the Library Statistics section of the IMLS Web site. The FY 2007 data were aggregated to state and national levels in a report, *Public Libraries in the United States: Fiscal Year 2008,* and released in June 2010 on the IMLS Web site. The Compare Public Libraries Tool and the Find Public Libraries Tool were updated with FY 2008 data. FY 2009 data are expected to be available on these tools in spring 2011.

An important feature recently added to the public library data tools is the availability of locale codes for all administrative entities and outlets. These codes allow users to quickly identify which library outlets and administrative entities are located in cities, suburbs, towns, or rural areas. The new locale codes are based on an address's proximity to an urbanized area (a densely settled core with densely settled surrounding areas). The locale code system classifies territory into four major types: city, suburban, town, and rural. Each type has three subcategories. For city and suburb, these gradations are based on population size—

large, midsize, and small. Towns and rural areas are further distinguished by their distance from an urbanized area; they can be characterized as fringe, distant, or remote. The coding methodology was developed by the U.S. Census Bureau as a way to identify the location of public schools in the National Center for Education Statistics' (NCES's) Common Core of Data. As of FY 2008 each library outlet and administrative entity survey has one of the 12 locale codes assigned to it.

Locale codes provide a new way to analyze library services. By incorporating objective measures of rurality and urbanicity into the data files, researchers and practitioners can benchmark services in a fundamentally different way by basing comparisons on community attributes as well as the attributes of the libraries themselves. In other words, library services in rural remote areas can now be compared with library services in other rural remote areas of the state or country using a standardized urbanicity/rurality metric that is applied consistently to each library. Once communities of interest have been selected, comparisons can be made to any data that is available in the Public Library Survey, whether it be financial, operational, or service output related.

State Library Agencies Survey

The State Library Agencies Survey collects and disseminates information about the state library agencies in the 50 states and the District of Columbia. A state library agency (StLA) is the official unit of state government charged with statewide library development and the administration of federal funds under LSTA. StLAs' administrative and developmental responsibilities affect the operation of thousands of public, academic, school, and special libraries. StLAs provide important reference and information services to state government and sometimes also provide service to the general public. StLAs often administer state library and special operations such as state archives and libraries for the blind and physically handicapped and the state Center for the Book.

The State Library Agencies Survey began in 1994 and was administered by NCES until 2007. The FY 2009 State Library Agencies Survey collected data on the following areas: direct library services; adult literacy and family literacy; library development services; resources assigned to allied operations such as archive and records management; organizational and governance structure within which the agency operates; electronic networking; staffing; collections; and expenditures. The FY 2009 survey was the 15th in the StLA series. These data are edited electronically, and before FY 1999 missing data were not imputed. Beginning with FY 1999 data, however, national totals included imputations for missing data. Another change is that beginning with FY 1999 data, the StLA became a Web-based data collection system. The most recent data available are for FY 2009. The survey database and report were released in December 2010.

National Medal for Museum and Library Service

The National Medal for Museum and Library Service honors outstanding institutions that make significant and exceptional contributions to their communities. The winning institutions demonstrate extraordinary and innovative approaches to public service, exceeding the expected levels of community outreach and core programs generally associated with their services. The honor includes a prize of $10,000 to each recipient and an awards ceremony held in Washington, D.C. The 2010 ceremony was held at the White House on December 17; First Lady Michelle Obama presented the awards.

The winners of the 2010 National Medal for Museum and Library Service were (libraries) Nashville Public Library; Patchogue-Medford Library, Patchogue, New York; Peter White Public Library, Marquette, Michigan; Rangeview Library District and Anythink Libraries, Adams County, Colorado; West Bloomfield Township (Michigan) Public Library; (museums) New York Botanical Garden; Conner Prairie Interactive History Park, Fishers, Indiana; Explora, Albuquerque; Japanese American National Museum, Los Angeles; and Mississippi Museum of Art, Jackson.

State-Administered Programs

In FY 2010 approximately 65 percent of the annual federal appropriation under LSTA was distributed through the Grants to States program to the State Library Administrative Agencies (SLAAs) according to a population-based formula. The formula consists of a minimum amount set by law plus a supplemental amount based on population. Population data were based on the information available from the U.S. Census Bureau Web site on October 1, 2009. The 2003 reauthorization requires that base allotments of $680,000 go to the states and $60,000 go to the Pacific Territories.

For FY 2010 the Grants to States program total appropriation was $172,561,000 (see Table 1). State agencies may use the appropriation for statewide initiatives and services. They may also distribute the funds through competitive subgrants or cooperative agreements to public, academic, research, school, or special libraries. For-profit and federal libraries are not eligible applicants. LSTA state grant funds have been used to meet the special needs of children, parents, teenagers, the unemployed, senior citizens, and the business community, as well as adult learners. Many libraries have partnered with community organizations to provide a variety of services and programs, including access to electronic databases, computer instruction, homework centers, summer reading programs, digitization of special collections, access to e-books and adaptive technology, bookmobile service, and development of outreach programs to the underserved. The act limits the amount of funds available for administration at the state level to 4 percent and requires a 34 percent match from nonfederal state or local funds.

Grants to the Pacific Territories and the Freely Associated States (FAS) are funded under a Special Rule, 20 USCA 9131(b)(3), which authorizes a small competitive grants program in the Pacific region and the U.S. Virgin Islands. There are seven eligible entities: Guam, American Samoa, the Commonwealth of Northern Mariana Islands, the Federated States of Micronesia, the Republic of the Marshall Islands, the Republic of Palau, and the U.S. Virgin Islands. The funds for this grant program are taken from the allotment amounts for the FAS (Federated States of Micronesia, Marshall Islands, and Palau). The territories (Guam, Samoa, the Marianas, and the Virgin Islands) receive allotments through

Table 1 / Library Services and Technology Act, State Allotments, FY 2010 (P.L. 111-117)
Total Distributed to States: $172,561,000[1]

State	Federal Funds from IMLS (66%)[2]	State Matching Funds (34%)	Total Federal and State Funds
Alabama	$2,746,218	$1,414,718	$4,160,936
Alaska	984,174	506,999	1,491,173
Arizona	3,560,969	1,834,439	5,395,408
Arkansas	1,945,548	1,002,252	2,947,800
California	16,971,056	8,742,665	25,713,721
Colorado	2,869,234	1,478,090	4,347,324
Connecticut	2,231,803	1,149,717	3,381,520
Delaware	1,066,966	549,649	1,616,615
Florida	8,803,371	4,535,070	13,338,441
Georgia	4,972,854	2,561,773	7,534,627
Hawaii	1,250,947	644,427	1,895,374
Idaho	1,355,376	698,224	2,053,600
Illinois	6,398,149	3,296,016	9,694,165
Indiana	3,506,281	1,806,266	5,312,547
Iowa	2,010,773	1,035,853	3,046,626
Kansas	1,921,944	990,092	2,912,036
Kentucky	2,572,188	1,325,067	3,897,255
Louisiana	2,634,925	1,357,386	3,992,311
Maine	1,263,471	650,879	1,914,350
Maryland	3,176,887	1,636,578	4,813,465
Massachusetts	3,559,988	1,833,933	5,393,921
Michigan	5,113,653	2,634,306	7,747,959
Minnesota	2,993,749	1,542,234	4,535,983
Mississippi	1,982,436	1,021,255	3,003,691
Missouri	3,300,104	1,700,054	5,000,158
Montana	1,108,783	571,191	1,679,974
Nebraska	1,470,441	757,500	2,227,941
Nevada	1,832,430	943,979	2,776,409
New Hampshire	1,263,185	650,732	1,913,917
New Jersey	4,528,274	2,332,747	6,861,021
New Mexico	1,559,494	803,376	2,362,870
New York	9,318,366	4,800,370	14,118,736
North Carolina	4,767,500	2,455,985	7,223,485
North Dakota	964,313	496,767	1,461,080
Ohio	5,770,712	2,972,791	8,743,503
Oklahoma	2,294,344	1,181,935	3,476,279
Oregon	2,359,806	1,215,658	3,575,464
Pennsylvania	6,197,247	3,192,521	9,389,768
Rhode Island	1,145,724	590,221	1,735,945
South Carolina	2,665,509	1,373,141	4,038,650
South Dakota	1,036,430	533,918	1,570,348
Tennessee	3,434,523	1,769,300	5,203,823
Texas	11,462,047	5,904,691	17,366,738
Utah	1,892,820	975,089	2,867,909
Vermont	955,355	492,153	1,447,508
Virginia	4,123,366	2,124,158	6,247,524

Washington	3,582,706	1,845,636	5,428,342
West Virginia	1,484,197	764,586	2,248,783
Wisconsin	3,174,392	1,635,293	4,809,685
Wyoming	916,086	471,923	1,388,009
District of Columbia	942,308	485,431	1,427,739
Puerto Rico	2,432,483	1,253,097	3,685,580
American Samoa	89,087	45,893	134,980
Northern Marianas	82,818	42,664	125,482
Guam	139,083	71,649	210,732
Virgin Islands	108,676	55,985	164,661
Pacific Territories[3]	265,431	136,737	402,168
Total[4]	$172,561,000	$88,895,061	$261,456,061

Plus: Supplemental Carryover	$2,917,995
Total Allotted to States	$175,478,995

1 The amount available to states is based on the estimated appropriation for FY 2010.

2 Calculation is based on minimum set in the law (P.L. 108-81).

Population data is from the Bureau of Census (BOC) estimates. Data used in the state allotment table are the most current published population estimates available the first day of the fiscal year. Therefore, the population data used in the 2009 table is what was available on the BOC Web site http://www.census.gov/popest/states/index.html on October 1, 2009.

Population data for American Samoa, Northern Marianas, Guam, Virgin Islands, Marshall Islands, Federated States of Micronesia, and Palau may be accessed at http://www.census.gov/cgi-bin/ipc/idbrank.pl This table reflects what was available on October 1, 2009.

3 Aggregate allotments (including administrative costs) for Palau, Marshall Islands, and Federated States of Micronesia are awarded on a competitive basis to eligible applicants, and are administered by Pacific Resources for Education and Learning (PREL).

4 Because of rounding to whole dollar amounts in the state allotments, some totals may be slightly adjusted to reflect actual total amounts.

the Grants to States program and, in addition, may apply for funds under the competitive program. In FY 2010 a total of $265,431 was available for the seven entities. This amount included a set-aside of 5 percent for Pacific Resources for Education and Learning (PREL), based in Hawaii, to facilitate the grants review process. Therefore, the total amount awarded in FY 2010 was $252,159.

The LSTA-funded programs and services delivered by each SLAA support the purposes and priorities set forth in legislation. The individual SLAAs set goals and objectives for their state regarding the expenditure of Grants to States funds within the statutorily required five-year plan on file with IMLS. These goals and objectives are determined through a planning process that includes statewide needs assessments.

On a rotating basis, IMLS Grants to State program staff members conduct site visits to SLAAs to provide technical support and to monitor the states' success in administering the LSTA program. This year, program officers visited ten SLAAs, in Alabama, Colorado, Delaware, Florida, Idaho, Maine, Mississippi, Montana, New Jersey, and Vermont. Each site visit includes the critical review of the administration of the LSTA program at the SLAA as well as trips into the field to visit libraries that are recipients of subgrants or beneficiaries of statewide LSTA projects.

Discretionary Grants Programs

IMLS began administering the discretionary grants programs of LSTA in 1998. In FY 2010 a total of $40,962,000 was allocated for discretionary programs, distributed as follows: National Leadership Grants, $12,437,000; Laura Bush 21st Century Librarian Program, $24,525,000; Native American Library Services, $3,430,000; Native Hawaiian Library Services, $570,000.

National Leadership Grants for Libraries

The National Leadership Grants for Libraries program provides funding for research and innovative model programs to enhance the quality of library services nationwide. National Leadership Grants are competitive and intended to produce results useful for the broader library community.

In 2010 IMLS awarded 35 National Leadership Grants totaling $11,538,376. The program received a total of 145 applications, requesting more than $56,000,000. Projects were funded in four categories: Advancing Digital Resources, Demonstration, Research, and Library-Museum Collaboration (see Table 2). In addition, IMLS offered Collaborative Planning Grants in all categories of the National Leadership Grants program. Collaborative Planning Grants were offered at two levels: Level 1 planning grants of up to $50,000 enable project teams from libraries, museums, or other partner organizations to work together on the planning of a single collaborative project in any of the National Leadership Grants categories; and Level 2 planning grants of up to $100,000 support workshops, symposia, or other convenings of experts to discuss issues of national importance to libraries, archives, and/or museums, with the goal of producing a white paper that encourages multiple National Leadership Grant proposals addressing issues raised in the report. Partnerships with museums are not required for any projects except those in the Library-Museum Collaboration category.

Advancing Digital Resources (Maximum award $1 million)

Advancing Digital Resources grants support the creation, use, preservation, and presentation of significant digital resources as well as the development of tools to manage digital assets, incorporating new technologies or new technology practice. IMLS supported projects that

- Developed and disseminated new tools to facilitate management, preservation, sharing, and use of digital resources
- Increased community access to institutional resources through innovative use of existing technology-based tools
- Increased community access to institutional resources by improving practice in use, dissemination, and support of existing technology-based tools
- Developed or advanced participation in museum and/or library communities using social technologies in new ways
- Developed new approaches or tools for digital curation

Demonstration (maximum award $1 million)

Demonstration projects use available knowledge to address key needs and challenges facing libraries and museums, and transform that knowledge into formal practice. Funded projects

- Demonstrated and/or tested new practices in library and/or museum operations
- Demonstrated how libraries and/or museums serve their communities by fostering public value and implementing systemic changes in the field
- Established and/or tested standards and tools for innovative learning
- Demonstrated and/or tested an expansion of preservation or conservation practices

Research (maximum award $1 million)

Research grants support projects that have the potential to improve library and museum practice, resource use, programs, and services. Both basic and applied research projects are encouraged. Funded projects

- Evaluated the impact of library or museum services
- Investigated how learning takes place in libraries and museums, and how use of library and/or museum resources enhance learning
- Investigated how to improve the quality, effectiveness, or efficiency of library or museum management programs or services
- Investigated ways to enhance the archiving, preservation, management, discovery, and use of digital assets and resources
- Investigated or conducted research to add new knowledge or make improvements in the conservation and preservation of collections

Library-Museum Collaboration (maximum award $1 million)

This award category helps to create new opportunities for libraries and museums to engage with each other, and with other organizations as appropriate, to support the educational, economic, and social needs of their communities. A partnership of at least one eligible library entity and one eligible museum entity is required. Additional partners are encouraged where appropriate. Both research and implementation projects are eligible. Grant funds supported innovative collaborative projects, whether they were new partnerships or were building on an existing collaboration. Funded projects

- Addressed community civic and educational needs
- Increased the organizations' capacity to serve as effective venues and resources for learning, or
- Used technology in innovative ways to serve audiences more effectively

Table 2 / National Leadership Grants for Libraries, FY 2010

Advancing Digital Resources

California Academy of Sciences, San Francisco $428,753

The California Academy of Sciences will partner with the Academy of Natural Sciences, Harvard University's Herbaria and Botany Libraries and its Museum of Comparative Zoology, the Missouri Botanical Garden, the New York Botanical Garden, and the Smithsonian Institution's U.S. National Herbarium to develop a system for integrating biological researchers' field and specimen notes with museum specimens and related electronically published literature.

Center for Research Libraries, Chicago $335,905

The center will partner with the American Antiquarian Society to jointly assemble a comprehensive directory of newspapers published in the United States and abroad from the 17th to the 21st centuries, supplemented with details on where titles are held in print, microfilm, and digital format.

Clemson University $773,444

Clemson will partner with Purdue University, the National Parks Service—Southeast Region, South Carolina State Parks, Georgia State Parks, and North Carolina State Parks to build an online research repository of park-related publications, including the National Parks Service directors' papers.

George Mason University $249,761

Building on the success of its open source Omeka Web publishing software, the university's Center for History and New Media will pilot test a new Omeka Commons. This centralized repository service will be designed to meet the needs of smaller cultural heritage and scholarship organizations that often have difficulty creating, delivering, and sustaining online digital collections.

Trustees of Columbia University $974,998

Architectural works and the built environment are the focus of this project, in which the Avery Architectural and Fine Arts Library at Columbia will partner with ARTstor, Inc., and other collaborators to develop a Built Works Registry, a freely available data resource for scholars, catalogers, and other users across all types of academic and cultural heritage organizations.

Research

Association of Research Libraries $464,286

The association, in partnership with Ithaka S+R, will study how libraries, archives, and museums are sustaining digital collections. This study will provide actionable recommendations, best practices, and planning tools to help project leaders in higher education, public libraries, museums, historical societies, and other organizations plan for sustaining their own digital projects.

National Academy of Sciences $50,000

The academy will form a committee to identify and prioritize a research agenda on the impact of copyright policies on innovation. Project activities will include conversations with relevant experts on key topics, commissioning a small number of background papers, convening a multi-disciplinary workshop, and soliciting ideas and feedback via a project Web site.

Regents of the University of Michigan $589,728

The university's School of Information—with the Inter-university Consortium for Social and Political Research, the University of Michigan Museum of Zoology, and the nonprofit Alexandria Archive Institute—will study how contextual information about data sets can best be created and preserved along with the data to promote greater potential for reuse and repurposing of the data.

Table 2 / National Leadership Grants for Libraries, FY 2010 *(cont.)*

Regents of the University of Michigan $674,722

The university's School of Information and its university libraries, in collaboration with the HathiTrust and the University of Minnesota Libraries, will investigate possible methods for detecting and measuring errors and other quality issues within mass-digitized literature and analyze the potential impact of found errors on educational and scholarly use of these digital collections.

San José State University Research Foundation $335,156

The university's School of Library and Information Science and the Center on Juvenile and Criminal Justice will examine current library practices regarding the creation and uses of space for young adults. The three-year study will document, analyze, and share project findings on current practices in a selected sample of representative libraries.

University of Illinois Board of Trustees $785,898

The university will collaborate with the University of Maryland, the Rochester Institute of Technology, and Stanford University to study effective strategies for preserving educational computer games and other complex interactive materials.

University of North Texas $271,344

The university will partner with Wuhan University in China and the Autonomous University of the State of Mexico to facilitate multilingual information access to digital collections. This project will evaluate the extent to which current machine translation technologies generate adequate translation for metadata records and identify the most effective metadata records translation strategies for digital collections.

Vanderbilt University Medical Center $421,737

The Eskind Biomedical Library at the medical center and partner University Community Health Services will test patients' ability to understand health information and their best way to learn, whether through seeing, reading, listening, or doing. The results will be used to build an Internet-based tool that will to give patients more-understandable information about their illness.

Demonstration

American Library Association $581,609

The association will partner with the University of Illinois, the University of Maryland, and Florida State University to develop a Web-based resource to help libraries and governments provide better e-government-related services in such areas as filing taxes, applying for citizenship, enrolling children in schools, and applying for social services.

Center for Research Libraries $590,766

To mitigate the high costs of acquiring, storing, and maintaining extensive physical collections in research libraries, the Chicago-based center will partner with the Law Library Microfilm Consortium and the U.S. Agricultural Information Network to build a sustainable and scalable plan for cooperative management of legacy print materials at the local, regional, state, and national levels.

Hartford (Connecticut) Public Library $637,896

The library will partner with Catholic Charities Migration and Refugee Resettlement Services, the City of Hartford's Office of Human Relations, Everyday Democracy, and the University of Connecticut's School of Social Work to promote immigrant civic engagement. Focusing on legal permanent residents within Hartford's immigrant community, the partners will train a core group of volunteer immigrants who will help other newly arrived immigrants in such tasks such as accessing community services.

Table 2 / National Leadership Grants for Libraries, FY 2010 *(cont.)*

North Carolina State University $313,655

The university's libraries and its distance education and learning technology applications will partner with strategic consultant DEGW to design, share, and promote an updated model for college and university libraries to support emerging new learning environments. This project will build on the libraries' previous leadership in building and promoting a first-generation learning commons, a model that has been widely adopted in academic libraries.

Trustees of the University of Pennsylvania $200,002

The University of Pennsylvania Libraries will develop an open source decision support system called MetriDoc to support evidence-based strategic planning in libraries. Building on a decade of work in this area by project staff, the project will create a scalable software platform to collect, store, and analyze a wide array of service data flowing from user activities and interactions with the library.

University of Maine $821,065

The university will partner with Bates College, Bowdoin College, Colby College, Maine InfoNet, Maine State Library, Portland Public Library, Bangor Public Library, and the University of Southern Maine in a statewide Maine Shared Collections Strategy project. The project will define a strategy for shared management of legacy print collections and explore new ways of delivering content to library users by designing and testing a print-on-demand and e-book-on-demand service for available digital collections from the Open Content Alliance and Google Books.

University of North Carolina at Chapel Hill $262,115

The university's Odum Institute for Research in Social Science Data Archive will collaborate with partners from the National Network of State Polls to demonstrate the feasibility of a streamlined and timely workflow for getting research data into data archives.

Library-Museum Collaboration

Athens-Clarke County (Georgia) Library $343,100

The library will partner with the Lyndon House Arts Center to develop new services and programs for the aging Baby Boom population, born between 1946 and 1964. The goals and objectives are to provide lifelong learning opportunities for and by older, active adults, expanding museum and library services beyond existing walls.

Denver Public Library $461,257

The library will collaborate with several partners—Colorado Historical Society, Historic Denver, Rocky Mountain Jewish Historical Society and Beck Archives, Aurora History Museum, Four Mile Historic Park, Lakewood Heritage Center, Colorado Genealogy Society, Auraria Library and Center for Colorado and the West, Douglas County Libraries, and the Inscribe/Zion Baptist Church—to create an online community archive and preservation education project for the public.

Maine Historical Society $745,313

In partnership with the Maine State Library, the society will build on previous efforts to implement a statewide outreach and training program. This project is designed to foster collaboration and resource sharing among libraries, historical organizations, and schools through the exploration of local history and use of technology.

Pennsylvania Heritage Society $806,183

The society and three partners—the State Library of Pennsylvania, the Pennsylvania Humanities Council, and the Pennsylvania Historical and Museum Commission—will produce innovative programming through a Pennsylvania Civil War Road Show. This project will use the sesquicentennial of the Civil War as a catalyst to engage new and underserved public audiences and to involve local communities in dialogue that links the historical context for issues of race, equality, and freedom with these issues today.

Table 2 / National Leadership Grants for Libraries, FY 2010 *(cont.)*

Rhodes College $257,767

Rhodes College, the Memphis Public Library, the National Civil Rights Museum, and other community partners in Memphis will create the Memphis Coalition for Cultural Heritage (MCCH) and the Memphis Preservation Corps. MCCH will constitute an organizational framework that will address the need to build capacity for preservation and access to significant primary resources about the history of the community.

Collaborative Planning Grants, Level 1

Ann Arbor Hands-On Museum $49,257

The museum, the Mideastern Michigan Library Cooperative, and Michigan State University Extension 4-H Youth Development will engage with other regional and national partners to develop plans for a regional program promoting scientific and environmental literacy and interest among school-age children and other populations in the Great Lakes region.

Dance Heritage Coalition $48,435

The Dance Heritage Coalition will partner with the Theatre Library Association, the National Dance Education Organization, and the New York City office of Dance/USA to identify long-range plans for making digital dance resources available. In facilitated meetings and a strategic planning session, the partners will bring together content creators such as dance artists and choreographers, content users such as scholars and teachers, and content providers such as librarians and archivists.

Drexel University $47,621

Drexel and its partners, the University at Buffalo and Getty Research Institute, will bring together library, archives, and museum practitioners, researchers, and domain experts to discuss current practices and problems with knowledge organization systems with the goal of planning and researching more meaningful, useful, and interoperable systems.

LYRASIS $49,984

With its partners—the Center for Research Libraries, the California Digital Library, and the Committee on Institutional Cooperation—the library consortium LYRASIS will define the characteristics of a national, collaborative model for managing print monographs and identify issues that need testing or research.

Trident Technical College $46,047

Trident Technical College Library and the Avery Research Center for African American History and Culture will establish the Low Country Foodways Project to document the African, Caribbean, English, French, and Native American roots of the food-related traditions of the Low Country region between Wilmington, North Carolina, and Jacksonville, Florida.

Trustees of Indiana University $49,504

Indiana University Libraries and its partner Northwestern University will work with New York University, the University of Miami, Ohio State University, the nonprofit organization DuraSpace, and other participants to define the scope, requirements, and technical architecture to extend Indiana University's open source Variations digital music library system.

University of Massachusetts Medical School $49,894

The libraries of the medical school and Worcester Polytechnic Institute will develop and test an instructional framework and delivery system for openly accessible, online instructional modules on preserving, managing, and sharing digital data.

Collaborative Planning Grants, Level 2

Heart of Brooklyn Cultural Institutions $100,000

The Brooklyn, New York, organization Heart of Brooklyn will partner with the Institute for Learning Innovation and the Center for the Study of Brooklyn to examine factors that encourage or inhibit meaningful collaborations among cultural institutions.

Table 2 / National Leadership Grants for Libraries, FY 2010 *(cont.)*

Michigan State University	$98,173
Centering on the Quilt Index, this project will identify key challenges for globally constructed and shared online resources, and develop a model plan that responds to those challenges. Partners are the Michigan State University Museum; the MATRIX Center for Humane Arts, Letters, and Social Sciences Online; the Alliance for American Quilts; and the International Quilt Study Center.	
Purdue University	$100,000
Purdue University Libraries and partner libraries at the Georgia Institute of Technology and the University of Utah will investigate existing organizational and service models for library-based publishing, identify best practices for such operations, and identify areas of critical or high need for capacity development, including opportunities for collaboration with university and other publishers.	

Laura Bush 21st Century Librarian Program

This program was established in 2003 as the Librarians for the 21st Century program; the name was changed in 2006 in accordance with the provisions of IMLS's congressional appropriation. The program provides competitive funding (up to $1 million) to support projects to recruit and educate the next generation of librarians and library leaders, build institutional capacity in graduate schools of library and information science and develop faculty who will help in this endeavor, conduct needed research on the demographics and needs of the profession, and support programs of continuing education and training in library and information science for librarians and library staff.

In FY 2010 IMLS awarded 39 grants totaling $23,423,477 under the program (see Table 3). A total of 110 applications requesting $68,242,619 were received.

The 2010 priorities for Laura Bush 21st Century Librarian Program funding were

Doctoral Programs

- To develop faculty to educate the next generation of library professionals; in particular, to increase the number of students enrolled in doctoral programs that will prepare faculty to teach master's degree students who will work in school, public, and academic libraries
- To develop the next generation of library leaders; in particular, to increase the number of students enrolled in doctoral programs that will prepare them to assume positions as library managers and administrators

Master's Programs

- To educate the next generation of librarians; in particular, to increase the number of students enrolled in nationally accredited graduate library programs preparing for careers of service in libraries

Research

- *Early Career Development Program*—To support the early career development of new faculty members who are likely to become leaders in library and information science by supporting innovative research by untenured, tenure-track faculty
- *Research*—To provide the library community with information needed to support successful recruitment and education of the next generation of librarians; in particular, through funded research, to establish baseline data on professional demographics and job availability, and to evaluate current programs in library education for their capacity to meet the identified needs; and to conduct research and establish ongoing research capacity in the field of library and information science, particularly the evaluation of library and information services, assessment of the value and use of public libraries and their services by the public, and assessment of the public value and use of the Internet

Preprofessional Programs

- To recruit future librarians; in particular, to attract promising junior high school, high school, or college students to consider careers in librarianship through statewide or regional pilot projects employing recruitment strategies that are cost-effective and measurable; and to introduce high school or college students to potential careers in library and information science

Programs to Build Institutional Capacity

- To develop or enhance curricula within graduate schools of library and information science; in particular, to develop or enhance courses or programs of study for library and archives professionals in the creation, management, preservation, presentation, and use of digital assets; to broaden curricula by incorporating perspectives from other disciplines and fields of scholarship; to develop or enhance programs of study that address knowledge, skills, abilities, and issues of common interest to libraries, museums, archives, and data repositories; and to develop projects or programs in data curation as training programs for graduate students in library and information science

Continuing Education

- To increase professional development and library and archive staff knowledge, skills, and abilities through programs of continuing formal education, informal education, and training

Table 3 / Laura Bush 21st Century Librarian Program, FY 2010

Doctoral Programs

Board of Regents of the University of Wisconsin $815,340

The School of Information Studies (SOIS) at the University of Wisconsin–Milwaukee will recruit six Ph.D. students to add to the knowledge base of library and information science through their research on overcoming barriers to information access.

Board of Trustees of the University of Illinois at Urbana-Champaign $988,543

The university's Graduate School of Library and Information Science, the University of Tennessee School of Information Sciences, and the National Center for Atmospheric Research have established Data Curation Education in Research Centers, which will develop a model for educating LIS master's and doctoral students in data curation.

University of South Carolina Research Foundation $857,489

The USC School of Library and Information Science will support seven doctoral fellowships participating in an experimental course based on the Responsive Ph.D. model recently developed by the Woodrow Wilson Fellowship Foundation.

Master's Programs

Association of Research Libraries $543,015

The association's Initiative to Recruit a Diverse Workforce will provide financial support, mentoring, leadership development, and career placement services for 30 MLIS students from traditionally underrepresented racial and ethnic minority groups.

Drexel University $622,963

Drexel will partner with the School District of Philadelphia to recruit and educate current professional and paraprofessional employees to receive a master's degree and become eligible for Pennsylvania's "Library Science, K–12" certification.

Mansfield University of Pennsylvania $999,940

The university's online School of Library and Information Technologies program will partner with Chicago Public Schools and the New York City Department of Education to recruit and graduate 48 newly certified school librarians in a project that will address the school librarian shortage while building greater skills and leadership abilities among graduates.

Pratt Institute $971,407

Project CHART (Cultural Heritage, Access, Research, and Technology) is a three-year partnership among Pratt Institute, the Brooklyn (New York) Public Library, Brooklyn Museum, and Brooklyn Historical Society designed to prepare 18 master's degree students for leadership roles as digital managers and curators in libraries, museums, and archives.

Regents of the University of California, Riverside $974,259

This project will recruit 25 non-degreed library staff interested in pursuing an MLIS degree and give them scholarships, internships, mentoring, and professional development. The project involves the university and several partners—San Bernardino County Library System, San Bernardino County Law Library, San Bernardino Public Library, Rancho Cucamonga Public Library, San Bernardino Valley Community College, Riverside Community College, Moreno Valley Campus, Riverside County Law Library, and the University of Redlands.

San José State University Research Foundation $842,532

The university's School of Library and Information Science and the American Indian Library Association will launch the Circle of Learning project, the only scholarship program designed exclusively for Native American students who want to earn a fully online ALA-accredited MLIS degree.

Table 3 / Laura Bush 21st Century Librarian Program, FY 2010 *(cont.)*

University of Alabama $882,416

Library schools at the University of Alabama and the University of South Florida will partner to recruit and prepare 30 students to provide universal information access. Particularly benefiting from this master's degree program initiative are users who have physical impairments but do not meet the legal definition of "disabled," a population referred to as "extra-legally ably challenged" (ELAC).

University of Memphis, Office of Research Support Services $552,168

The university's School Librarian SOS (Support for Online Study) project will increase by 30 the number of fully qualified school librarians working in three high-need school districts. This project will recruit teachers and non-degreed librarians into an online MLIS program and provide them with scholarships and computers in exchange for a minimum three-year commitment to work in a sponsoring library.

University of North Carolina, Greensboro $889,401

The university libraries and the Department of Library and Information Studies will lead the second cohort of the Academic and Cultural Enrichment Scholars Program, recruiting and preparing 15 students from underserved communities with diverse backgrounds for professional positions in academic libraries.

University of North Texas $999,363

The university's College of Information, Library Science, and Technologies and the university libraries will collaborate with Pacific Resources for Education and Learning (PREL) to increase the number and diversity of degreed library professionals for the geographically dispersed and economically depressed area of the U.S.-affiliated Pacific islands.

University of Maryland, College Park $799,493

To better meet the needs of the nation's rapidly diversifying library-user base, the university will provide scholarships to 20 students who will enroll in the Information and Diverse Populations Concentration of the school's master of library science degree program.

Research

University of North Carolina at Chapel Hill, Office of Sponsored Research $298,385

The School of Information and Library Science, the Institute on Aging, and the Howard Odum Institute for Research in Social Science at the university will collaborate to document the process of data archiving and sharing. The major aims of the WILIS 3 project are to create publicly accessible de-identified datasets; to develop an interactive program-specific data system to enable library and information science programs to explore their own data and benchmark with other programs; and to produce a data archiving toolkit for use by other researchers.

Research: Early Career Development

Regents of the University of Michigan $601,837

This grant will provide support for Tiffany Veinot, an assistant professor, to study the information activities and networks of chronically ill people and their family members and the roles they play in chronic-illness-related coping, care, and support within families.

Research Foundation of the State University of New York $325,780

Xiaojun Yuan, an assistant professor at the University at Albany, will use this grant to support research about problems of enhanced query length and enhanced user interaction with digital libraries and other information systems. A result of the project will be a new model for user interaction with digital libraries.

Table 3 / Laura Bush 21st Century Librarian Program, FY 2010 *(cont.)*

San José State University Research Foundation $122,683

Lili Luo, an assistant professor in the university's School of Library and Information Science, will conduct research regarding text messaging as a platform for providing virtual reference services.

Syracuse University $280,550

Assistant Professor Megan Oakleaf of the university's School of Information Studies will conduct research on assessing student learning and will develop a standards-based rubric that will measure the information literacy skills of college students.

Preprofessional Programs

American Library Association $432,495

The association will launch a three-year national initiative to recruit 50 ethnically diverse high school and college students to careers in libraries by developing a stronger professional presence at local career, education, and cultural events. New professionals from ALA's Spectrum Scholarship Program and other national diversity recruitment programs will serve as field recruiters at such events.

Kent State University $552,908

Kent State University School of Library and Information Science, Case Western Reserve University Libraries, and the Cleveland Art Museum are partnering with 19 academic and special libraries to recruit undergraduate college students. Project goals are to attract minorities to the library profession and to direct good candidates to particular subject areas (e.g., art, health sciences, music) with shortages of qualified people.

Miami Dade College $559,973

Project PIPELINE is a preprofessional project to identify, educate, and support library support staff at the college, Florida International University, Miami Dade Public Library System, and Miami Dade County Public Schools, with the goal of improving the staff's language and computer skills in order to better serve diverse clients.

Nebraska Library Commission $721,033

The commission and Central Community College will foster recruitment, education, and 21st century skills development for at least 165 preprofessional and professional students through scholarships, internships, and stipends.

Palau Community College $216,405

The college will develop a distance education library and information services program accredited through the Accrediting Commission for Community and Junior Colleges of the Western Association of Schools and Colleges with the goal of providing a formal training opportunity for approximately 30 library staff.

Rose State College $86,421

Rose State and the Oklahoma Library Association will continue the Information Matrix Camp, a week-long summer program for middle school students. The goals of the camp are to promote librarianship and to encourage the participants to consider library careers.

Santa Ana (California) Public Library $626,767

The library and the Orange County Chapter of REFORMA will provide opportunities for 1,257 at-risk bilingual teens and college-age young adults from foreign-born families to learn about libraries and the library profession and to pursue successful careers as librarians.

Programs to Build Institutional Capacity

Northeastern State University. $972,337

Project I'm Ready is an innovative program designed by the university and Maryetta Public

Table 3 / Laura Bush 21st Century Librarian Program, FY 2010 *(cont.)*

School to educate 20 school librarians to serve in high-poverty rural areas of Oklahoma, and to provide annual conferences in northeast Oklahoma to discuss Native American educational improvement.

University of North Carolina at Chapel Hill, Office of Sponsored Research $891,451

The university's School of Information and Library Science, in partnership with its Carolina Center for the Study of the Middle East and Muslim Civilization, will launch a program to promote graduate-level education in library and information science at the American University in Cairo, Egypt, and Al Akhawayn University in Morocco.

Continuing Education

Alaska Department of Education and Early Development $185,427

The state's Division of Libraries, Archives, and Museums will support paraprofessional and professional continuing education and training, organizing a summit of 83 library, archive, and museum staff who are Alaska Native or serve significant Alaska Native populations.

American Library Association $590,110

This project focuses on disseminating information on the availability, accessibility, and value of the Library Support Staff Certification (LSSC) program. Among activities will be additional approved courses and competency sets for specializations; collaborating with state libraries and library technical assistant programs to develop reciprocity agreements and promote the LSSC program; and measuring the impact of the program on an estimated 900 participants and the services they provide in their libraries.

Carroll County (Kentucky) Public Schools $578,818

Project Catalyst—developed by the school system, the Ohio Valley Educational Cooperative, six other school districts, and six county public libraries—will train 35 librarians to collaborate more effectively in addressing the needs of students with limited proficiency in reading and information literacy.

College Library Directors' Mentor Program $137,854

IMLS funding will directly support the program's transition to new leadership. Headquartered in Kearney, Nebraska, the program has served 271 participants representing 244 small colleges from 43 states. This project will assess the strengths and areas of needed improvement of the program, improve guidance to mentors, identify and integrate new leaders, and facilitate wider participation.

HistoryMakers Resources Center $731,699

Chicago-based HistoryMakers will recruit, train, and place 12 library school graduates in a one-year fellowship program for those interested in African American archival collections. The program will begin with an intensive three-month training institute at HistoryMakers, followed by a nine-month residency at a host institution.

Online Computer Library Center/WebJunction Seattle $940,750

WebJunction and the State Library of North Carolina will conduct needs assessments to outline unemployment impacts in all U.S. regions and will create a corresponding curriculum that can be tailored to meet local needs. WebJunction will conduct a train-the-trainer workshop and up to 75 local workshops for an estimated 1,875 public library staff working in the highest unemployment areas.

Pacific Resources for Education and Learning $323,792

Pacific Resources for Education and Learning (PREL) of Honolulu will continue, expand, and enhance informal continuing education opportunities for 20 preprofessional school library staff in the U.S.-affiliated Pacific islands.

Table 3 / Laura Bush 21st Century Librarian Program, FY 2010 *(cont.)*

Peabody Essex Museum	$164,031
The Phillips Library of the Peabody Essex Museum in Salem, Massachusetts, will host two symposia for approximately 75 professional librarians working in museums, their museum counterpart practitioners, and preprofessional students to explore the special issues of libraries in museums.	
Purdue University	$187,242
Purdue will create a series of workshops to expand the expertise of academic librarians about data curation issues, particularly the effects of technology on research and its dissemination.	
Syracuse University	$482,130
The university's School of Information Studies, the Center for Digital Literacy, and the Burton Blatt Institute will create a comprehensive continuing education program for teacher-librarians to better serve pre-K–12 students with disabilities. Forty-five teams of New York State school librarians and educators will be involved.	
Texas State Library and Archives Commission	$674,270
The commission will lead a team of partners representing statewide collaborative projects (the American Association for State and Local History, Clemson University, Florida Association of Museums, Maine State Museum, Newark [New Jersey] Museum, Washington State Library, Oklahoma Department of Libraries, South Dakota State Historical Society, and the Board of Library Commissioners for the Commonwealth of Massachusetts) that will work with IMLS to develop the Connecting to Collections Continuing Conversation Exchange, a series of meetings planned, managed, and hosted by recipients of Connecting to Collections Statewide Planning Grants.	

Native American Library Services

The Native American Library Services program provides opportunities for improved library services to an important part of the nation's community of library users. The program offers three types of support to serve the range of needs of Indian tribes and Alaska Native villages and corporations.

In FY 2010 IMLS distributed $3,546,562 in grants under the program (including some funds recovered from previous budget years and reallocated to the 2010 awards).

The program offers three types of support:

- Basic library services grants in the amount of $6,000, which support core library operations on a noncompetitive basis for all eligible Indian tribes and Alaska Native villages and corporations that apply for such support. IMLS awarded basic grants to 31 tribes in 2010.
- Basic library services grants with a supplemental education/assessment option of $1,000, totaling $7,000. IMLS awarded basic grants with the education/assessment option to 190 tribes. The purpose of the education/assessment option is to provide funding for library staff to attend continuing education courses and/or training workshops onsite or offsite, for library staff to attend or give presentations at conferences relating to library services, and/or to hire a consultant for an onsite professional library assessment.

- Enhancement grants, which support new levels of library service for activities specifically identified under LSTA. Of the 46 applications received, IMLS awarded 17 enhancement grants for a total of $2,030,562 (see Table 4).

Native Hawaiian Library Services

The Native Hawaiian Library Services program provides opportunities for improved library services through grants to nonprofit organizations that primarily serve and represent Native Hawaiians, as the term "Native Hawaiian" is defined in section 7207 of the Native Hawaiian Education Act (20 U.S.C. 7517). In FY 2010 two Native Hawaiian Library Services grants were awarded: to Alu Like, Inc.'s Native Hawaiian Library for $420,000, and to Hawaii Maoli for $150,000.

Table 4 / Native American Library Services Enhancement Grants, FY 2010

Traditional Knowledge and Language Project, Bay Mills Indian Community $147,968

The Bay Mills Indian Community of Brimley, Michigan, will focus on two high-priority needs: documenting traditional knowledge and language for future generations, and establishing a branch library at the Brimley Area Public School.

Virtual Library of Cherokee Knowledge $150,000

The Cherokee Nation, based in Tahlequah, Oklahoma, will establish a virtual library intended to give Cherokee citizens and the general public access to a comprehensive digital repository of authentic knowledge relating to the Cherokee Nation's history, language, traditions, culture, and leaders.

Kuwan.omp'tap Sikisve (Computer Technology on Wheels) $150,000

The Hopi Tribe of Arizona will add Computer Technology on Wheels to its successful Hopi Tutuqayki Sikisve (Library on Wheels), which was funded by an earlier Enhancement Grant. The mobile computer lab will operate in tandem with the current bookmobile's schedule to bring public computer and Internet access to the remote villages throughout the Hopi service area.

Igiugig Tribal Library Digitization Project $118,220

Igiugig Village, on the shore of Lake Iliamna in southwestern Alaska, maintains an active joint school-public library that will use this grant to gather local knowledge, oral history, and elder recollections of the community. Material collected will be the basis for a digitization project of historic photos, other images, and stories relating to the early history of the village.

Starting Points Literacy, Educational, and Employment Resource Office $87,365

The Iowa Tribe of Oklahoma will develop the program, which will establish a Literacy, Educational, and Employment Resource Office within the tribal library to assist community members in need of literacy and employment training.

Promoting Karuk Life: Capturing Our Culture $145,165

This Karuk Tribe of California project will improve and expand on existing library operations in Happy Camp and Orleans, California. With the assistance of a consultant, library staff will organize and catalog their collections and make them Web-accessible. Local storytellers will entertain Karuk Head Start children and introduce them to the library environment. Trainings and workshops on how to use the library's resources will be held for adults at the Karuk Tribe Community Computer Centers.

Kaw Nation Library Enhancement Program $74,494

The Kaw Nation in Oklahoma, which recently opened its new Kaw Nation Library and Learning Center, will hire a library coordinator who will establish policies and a long-range plan in

Table 4 / Native American Library Services Enhancement Grants, FY 2010 *(cont.)*

cooperation with an advisory board. Library staff will purchase materials to enhance the current collection and will implement a library automation system to organize it and make it accessible.

Aabiji-miinidiiwin (Endless Gift) Project $133,779

This project, planned by Michigan's Keweenaw Bay Indian Community, is a cooperative effort of the Keweenaw Bay Tribal Education Department, Ojibwa Community Library, the Head Start/Early Head Start Program, and the Pre-Primary Education Center. It will focus on expanding and enhancing existing library services to children up to the age of 5 and their caregivers.

Lummi Nation Library Enhancement Grant Program $148,580

On behalf of the Lummi Tribe, the Lummi Library at Northwest Indian College in Bellingham, Washington, will implement an early literacy project, "The Lummi Road to Reading." This will leverage proven methods for improving early childhood literacy through its alignment with the Raising A Reader program, the college's Early Childhood Education program, Lummi Head Start, and Lummi Daycare.

Makahs: In Pursuit of Knowledge $48,377

The Makah Culture and Research Center, on behalf of the Makah Indian Tribe of Neah Bay, Washington, will offer a program titled "Makahs: In Pursuit of Knowledge" (MIPOK), which will build on an earlier IMLS enhancement grant project, "We Are All Family."

Digitizing Special Menominee Collections $74,520

The Menominee Tribe of Wisconsin is working in partnership with the College of Menominee Nation Library Special Collections Department and Wisconsin Heritage Online to house, preserve, catalog, and digitize a large collection of rare and historically significant archival materials, many relating directly to the personal, legal, and national story of the Menominee Tribe's struggle for sovereignty during the Termination and Restoration period from 1954 to 1973.

Library Services Opportunity and Renovation $149,936

On behalf of the Leech Lake Band of the Minnesota Chippewa Tribe, the Bug-O-Nay-Ge-Shig School in Bena, Minnesota, will implement the Library Services Opportunity and Renovation Project to better serve students and surrounding communities. While adding extensive collection materials for all ages, the school library also will be made available to community members after school and during special events. A new library assistant will help with processing new materials and assisting community members learn how to use the library's resources, and patron computer availability will be increased.

Newborn to Pre-School Literacy Program: Enhancing P'oe Tsawa's Literacy Education Programs $83,930

Ohkay Owingeh of New Mexico will enhance its existing P'oe Tsawa Community Library services and activities for library patrons of all ages, particularly preschoolers, students, parents, caregivers, and educators, through strengthening their current literacy programs by adding storytelling events and initiating a "Newborn to Pre-School Literacy Program" based on Every Child Ready to Read @ your library.

Oneida Community Library Enhancement $102,824

Oneida Community Public Libraries, on behalf of the Oneida Nation of Wisconsin, are planning a library makeover with new furnishings to provide a comfortable, safe, and inviting environment for the community. The project will include new computers, a Nintendo Wii for fitness and educational gaming, and video equipment.

Table 4 / Native American Library Services Enhancement Grants, FY 2010 *(cont.)*

Chukchansi Family Library Services Program	$148,655
The Picayune Rancheria of Chukchansi Indians in Coarsegold, California, will implement the Chukchansi Family Library Services Program, focusing on cultural discovery, cultural literacy, and computer knowledge.	
Preserving our Language and Culture through Technology and Beyond	$150,000
The Jemez Pueblo Community Library in Jemez, New Mexico, will undertake a project focusing on the preservation of the Towa language and Jemez Pueblo culture, traditions, and knowledge. The new Towa Cultural Resource Center in the library will serve as a centralized place to collect, house, and make resources available to tribal members.	
Spirit Lake Tribe Library Enhancement Grant	$116,749
On behalf of Spirit Lake Tribe, the Valerie Merrick Memorial Library at the Cankdeska Cikana Community College in Fort Totten, North Dakota, will build a community literacy program focusing on improving reading skills through an outreach campaign that will emphasize family literacy activities.	

Partnerships

The Big Read

The Big Read, a program of the National Endowment for the Arts (NEA) offered in partnership with IMLS and in cooperation with Arts Midwest, is designed to restore reading to the center of culture. The program offers grants to organizations in local communities to engage citizens in the reading of literature by exploring and discussing a single book within their communities. Organizations selected to participate receive a grant, financial support to attend a national orientation meeting, educational and promotional materials for broad distribution, an organizer's guide for developing and managing Big Read activities, and additional resources. IMLS's contribution was made through the Laura Bush 21st Century Librarian Program. FY 2010 was the IMLS's final year of support for this program.

NEA inaugurated the Big Read as a pilot project in 2006 with ten communities featuring four books. The Big Read expanded to include more U.S. communities, programming in four countries abroad, and 31 book selections. By the end of 2010 more than 850 U.S. communities will have hosted a Big Read since the program's 2007 national launch.

In 2009 and 2010 IMLS supported several opportunities for the State Library Administrative Agencies (SLAAs) to access, free of charge, Big Read program materials. The SLAAs and their communities were the beneficiaries of 361,000 reader's guides, 98,000 teacher's guides, and 305,000 audio guides. For more information, see http://www.neabigread.org.

Picturing America

Picturing America, an initiative of the National Endowment for the Humanities (NEH), promotes the teaching, study, and understanding of American art, history, and culture. IMLS has been a key partner in this initiative. The project has distributed large, high-quality, laminated color reproductions of 40 iconic works of American art, along with a comprehensive teacher's resource guide, to libraries and schools. More than 76,000 sets of Picturing America color reproductions were distributed to schools and public libraries across the country. IMLS continues to work with NEH and its partner, the American Library Association (ALA), on ways to leverage these materials for robust cultural programming and partnership opportunities, and to build the capacity of public librarians to use the materials in meaningful and effective ways.

IMLS funds supported the distribution of Picturing America to public libraries nationwide, as well as the online portal Programming Librarian (http://www.programminglibrarian.org) that hosts resources to assist public librarians in using the Picturing America materials. ALA hosted five online training programs to help public librarians maximize the impact of the materials. All of these online programs are available in an archived format on the Web portal. ALA continues to add content to the site, including resources for adult programs, reading lists and support materials on Picturing America-related themes, poetry programming resources developed in cooperation with the Academy of American Poets, and film viewing and discussion lists developed by ALA's Video Round Table.

In 2009 and 2010 IMLS partnered with WNET (Thirteen, New York Public Media) to cosponsor a preconference day at the Celebration of Teaching and Learning conference. The annual national convening is a K–12 professional development event that attracts more than 8,000 teachers, librarians, media experts, and policymakers for a two-day conference devoted to best practices, education philosophy, and in-the-classroom experiences. IMLS supported the attendance of school and public librarians, including a preconference day that focused exclusively on Picturing America materials.

National Arts and Humanities Youth Program Awards

The National Arts and Humanities Youth Program (NAHYP) Awards are given for out-of-school, after-school, and summer arts and humanities programs that celebrate the creativity of America's youth, particularly those from underserved communities. Each year the NAHYP Awards recognize and support excellence in programs that open new pathways to learning, self-discovery, and achievement, in addition to presenting high-quality arts and humanities learning opportunities. Award recipients receive $10,000 each, a plaque, and an opportunity to attend the annual awardees conference in Washington, D.C., where they receive capacity-building and communications support designed to strengthen their organizations.

Launched in 1998 as the Coming Up Taller awards, this program is a signature initiative of the President's Committee on the Arts and the Humanities, in partnership with IMLS, NEA, and NEH. Libraries and museums are encouraged to apply. For more information, see http://www.nahyp.org.

21st Century Skills, Competitive Work Force, Engaged Citizens

President Obama has called for the development of 21st century skills, including problem solving, critical thinking, entrepreneurship, and creativity. Combining traditional strengths in creating powerful learning experiences with strategic investment in modern communications infrastructures, libraries and museums are trusted institutions positioned to build the skills needed to succeed in the 21st century.

As part of its effort to engage libraries and museums, community stakeholders, and policymakers at the national, state, and local levels to meet the educational, economic, civic, and cultural needs of communities, IMLS worked with more than 100 museum and library experts as well as representatives of the private and education sectors to produce *Museums, Libraries, and 21st Century Skills.* The publication and companion Web site (http://www.imls.gov/about/21stCSkills.shtm) provide a framework for museums and libraries to align their programs and services to deliver 21st century skills and outline possibilities for broader community partnerships and engagement.

Since its release in August 2009, the publication has been received with enthusiasm; more than 10,000 copies have been distributed. Success stories range from individual institutions to statewide initiatives that use the framework as a strategic planning tool.

IMLS is continuing a robust dissemination, training, and communications effort to raise awareness and encourage action. This involves grantmaking with a 21st century skills focus as well as outreach to federal, state, and local policymakers.

In addition, IMLS has launched "Making the Learning Connection," an eight-city tour to spotlight success stories and identify barriers to success. The tour began in FY 2010 and will continue in FY 2011 and 2012. Webinars, a blog, and a contest will follow. Making the Learning Connection workshops bring together museum and library leaders with representatives of local community foundations, the United Way, AARP, the K–12 education system, and representatives of universities and colleges to foster collaboration and coordination of communitywide efforts. As of the end of December 2010, workshops had been held in Baltimore, San Francisco, Miami, and Columbia, South Carolina. Future workshops were slated for Chicago and Albuquerque, with two other cities still to be determined.

These workshops build on IMLS's long history of supporting collaborative activity among libraries, museums, and other community partners with significant results.

IMLS and STEM

The 21st century skills initiative includes a focus on STEM (science, technology, engineering, and mathematics). In his speech to the National Academies of Science, President Obama challenged Americans to join the cause of elevating STEM education as a national priority. He announced a series called "Educate to Innovate" to highlight public/private partnerships to advance this goal. In accordance with Office of Management and Budget (OMB) guidance on cross-agency goals, IMLS is working with the White House Office of Science and Technology Policy to highlight ongoing IMLS support for library and museum STEM programming and to leverage private support.

Working with the John D. and Catherine T. MacArthur Foundation, IMLS will build the capacity of library and museum professionals to develop effective

STEM programs by disseminating research, design, and programming principles and seeding demonstration projects, including a national competition to create 30 new learning labs in libraries and museums across the country. Recognizing that a real change in science education requires the participation of many national and community partners, the John S. and James L. Knight Foundation, the Pearson Foundation, the New York Community Trust, the Chicago Community Trust, the Mozilla Foundation, and the Grable Foundation will provide additional resources to support the design and construction of the new learning labs. In addition, organizations such as the Boys and Girls Clubs, National 4-H, Maker Faire, FabLab, Boy Scouts, and Girl Scouts will be eligible as local partners to the libraries and museums as they prepare plans for new, dynamic learning centers that will redefine the purpose of libraries and museums and make them hubs for youth engagement, creativity, and learning. The competition application process will be announced in 2011.

IMLS support also encourages such innovations as the development of new finding tools, including a project that was recently highlighted at a White House meeting on ideation, and widgets and apps to bring homework help to students' social networks. National Leadership Grants are creating open source solutions for use in library and museum systems with the potential of increasing efficiency and information sharing and saving communities millions of dollars. IMLS also participated in the planning for the National Research Council's benchmark study *Learning Science in Informal Environments: People, Places and Pursuits* (2009), which describes how people learn in informal environments, synthesizes the state of knowledge about learning in informal environments, and articulates a common framework for new research. IMLS also invested in the study's companion volume, *Surrounded by Science: Learning Science in Informal Environments* (2010), which offers examples and questions for practitioners.

Learning Labs at Libraries and Museums

In September 2010 IMLS and the John D. and Catherine T. MacArthur Foundation announced plans to create 30 new youth learning labs in public libraries and museums across the country. Inspired by an innovative teen space at the Chicago Public Library called YOUmedia and innovations in science and technology centers, these labs will help young people become makers and creators of content rather than just consumers of it. The labs will be based on new research about how young people learn. Information on the competition application process will be announced in 2011. IMLS funds will be contributed from the National Leadership Grants program.

IMLS and the Department of Labor

Through communications, grantmaking, and federal partnerships, IMLS is working to support libraries in their roles as "first responders" in the economic downturn. As the nation experiences its first recession in the online age, job seekers are turning to libraries in record numbers. People are seeking library services to get assistance in looking for and applying for work, using e-government services, and developing new businesses. IMLS issued a series of podcast interviews with state library chief officers in five states who described how libraries were stepping up to meet new needs. Many libraries are working in cooperation with state work force organizations.

Recognizing that throngs of job seekers were using the library for support, on June 29, 2010 IMLS and the Employment and Training Administration (ETA) at the U.S. Department of Labor announced a partnership to encourage collaborations between the work force investment system and public libraries aimed at improving the quality of employment and training services to job seekers and the unemployed. Assistant Secretary of Labor Jane Oates released a training and education notice to the entire public work force system encouraging work with public libraries.

IMLS and ETA have hosted webinars with the National Governors Association and other private partners to help public libraries and the work force system share data, best practices, and tools. In addition, IMLS has awarded grants to the online learning community WebJunction and to the State Library of North Carolina for Project Compass, which seeks to assess the needs of libraries and provide nationwide work force development training for librarians. In the past year, Project Compass has supported training and assessment opportunities for every state library, and in the coming year it will offer local training opportunities in high-need areas for nearly 2,000 librarians.

IMLS plans additional work with other federal agencies particularly in the area of developing better e-government-related services, such as filing taxes, applying for citizenship, enrolling children in schools, and applying for social services—activities that increasingly take place at the public library.

International Collaboration

Salzburg Global Seminar

IMLS and the Salzburg Global Seminar partnered to host "Connecting to the World's Collections: Making the Case for Conservation and Preservation of Our Cultural Heritage" in Salzburg, Austria, October 28–November 1, 2009 (http://www.imls.gov/collections/tour/sgs.htm). This seminar built on the findings of the institute's multiyear initiative on collections care, "Connecting to Collections: A Call to Action," by putting them into a global perspective. At the convening, 59 cultural heritage leaders from 32 countries unanimously passed the Salzburg Declaration on the Conservation and Preservation of Cultural Heritage.

Film Forward

Film Forward: Advancing Cultural Dialogue (formerly AFI: 20/20) is an international filmmaker and film exchange program supported by IMLS since 2006, in partnership with the President's Committee on the Arts and the Humanities, NEA, and NEH, in cooperation with the Sundance Institute. The goal of the program is to foster intercultural dialogue and engage domestic and global audiences around films. Through this program, U.S. and international filmmakers are paired and sent to U.S. embassies around the world and to various U.S. domestic film venues, including libraries, museums, arts organizations, and theaters. These venues screen the films and convene educational programs. The 2011 film program launched in December 2010.

'Digging into Data' Grant Competition

Digging into Data is a grant competition sponsored by eight leading funding agencies from the United States, Canada, the Netherlands, and Britain. The purposes of the competition are to

- *Explore how scale affects research in the humanities and social sciences*—Now that vast amounts of text and other information resources are available in digital form, data-mining techniques can allow scholars to search digital resources automatically, which may change the kinds of questions that can be asked.
- *Promote international cooperation*—Each team must have members from at least two of the sponsoring countries. The participating organizations are the Social Sciences and Humanities Research Council (Canada); the Netherlands Organisation for Scientific Research; the Joint Information Systems Committee, the Arts and Humanities Research Council, and the Economic and Social Research Council (Britain); and NEH, the National Science Foundation, and IMLS. The awards will next be announced in fall 2012. For more information see http://www.diggingintodata.org.

Partnership for Cultural Exchange

Building on a June 2007 cultural accord, IMLS in November 2008 entered into the Partnership for Cultural Exchange with the Ministry of Culture of the People's Republic of China in an effort to strengthen cultural cooperation between the two countries. The agreement calls for sharing best practices in library and museum services, including enhancement of public service and access to information in libraries, promotion of youth engagement, education in museums, and applications of new technologies in libraries and museums to engage audiences and increase the availability of information online.

One major component of this partnership is Think Globally, Act Globally, a library professional exchange program. With IMLS funding through the Laura Bush 21st Century Librarian Program, the University of Illinois at Urbana-Champaign (UIUC) Libraries—in partnership with UIUC's Mortenson Center for International Library Programs, the Library Society of China, and the Chinese American Library Association—will develop a three-year partnership between librarians in the United States and China. The project is providing workshops in both countries for Chinese librarians and library educators on U.S. practices in library public services, and for teaching U.S. librarians about Chinese resources that can be made available online to meet a growing demand for Chinese-language information about China. The project has a Web-based portal at http://www.library.illinois.edu/China.

Closing the Digital Curation Gap

Scientists, researchers, and scholars across the world generate vast amounts of digital data, but the scientific record and the documentary heritage created in digital form are at risk—from technology obsolescence, the fragility of digital media, and the lack of baseline practices for managing and preserving digital data. The University of North Carolina Chapel Hill School of Information and Library Science is collaborating with IMLS and the Joint Information Systems Committee (JISC), which supports innovation in digital technologies in British colleges and universities, and its funded entities, the Strategic Content Alliance and the Digital Curation Centre, on the Closing the Digital Curation Gap project. The goal of the project is to establish baseline practices for the storage, maintenance, and preservation of digital data to help ensure their enhancement and continuing long-term use.

Bloomsbury Conference on E-Publishing and E-Publications

IMLS partnered with the University College London's Department of Information Studies to cohost the fourth annual Bloomsbury Conference on E-Publishing and E Publications in London June 24–25, 2010. The conference theme was "Valued Resources: Roles and Responsibilities of Digital Curators and Publishers." A June 26 invitational workshop following the conference brought together experts from Britain, Germany, the Netherlands, and the United States to discuss the role of library and information science in digital curation and opportunities for collaboration among digital curators and publishers in research and practice. See http://www.imls.gov/pdf/Bloomsbury.pdf.

Evaluation of IMLS Programs

In addition to outcome-based evaluation support for grantees, IMLS has instituted a new series of in-depth evaluations of its own programs on a rolling basis. In FY 2010 IMLS contracted two research firms to conduct independent evaluations for two IMLS grant programs, Museums for America and the Laura Bush 21st Century Librarian Program. The evaluations, which span approximately 18 months, employ mix method techniques for determining the impact of federal grant receipts on individual program participants and the institutions that receive support. Data used for these studies include application data, financial and narrative reports, post-award follow-up surveys, and qualitative case studies.

Research Sponsored and Conducted by IMLS

In July 2010 IMLS published *Opportunity for All.* This study provides the first large-scale investigation of the ways library patrons use public computers and Internet access in public libraries, why they use it, and how it affects their lives. A national telephone survey, nearly 45,000 online surveys at public libraries, and hundreds of interviews reveal the central role modern libraries play in a digital society. The study, which was released in March 2010, was funded in partnership with the Bill and Melinda Gates Foundation and conducted by the University of Washington Information School.

Future research from the IMLS Office of Policy, Planning, Research, and Communication (OPPRC) will examine library services in a variety of contexts, from small towns and remote rural areas to central cities and suburbs. OPPRC also will look at the intersection of library service with other public policy priorities, including education, employment, immigration, and public health.

IMLS Conferences and Activities

Grants to States Conference

The tenth Grants to States Conference was held in Washington, D.C., in mid-February 2010. One hundred participants representing the State Library Administrative Agencies in 49 states, the District of Columbia, and Puerto Rico took part. The conference included a two-day grants management course on the audit process, which is a primary area of federal grants administration. The third day of the conference featured table talks covering IMLS programs and initiatives, a plenary session on the program's match and maintenance of effort requirements, and a presentation and participatory session on the topic of 21st century skills.

WebWise

The 11th annual WebWise conference on Libraries and Museums in the Digital World was held in March 2010 in Denver. The theme was "Imagining the Digital Future." Cosponsors were the University of Denver, the Denver Art Museum, the Bibliographical Center for Research, the MacArthur Foundation, and the Morgridge Family Foundation. More than 400 participants attended the event.

Pacific Grantees Workshop

IMLS hosted a Pacific Grantees Workshop in Honolulu in May 2010. Grantees attended from the three Pacific Territories and the three Freely Associated States. The agenda included presentations from each of the six grantees on their library grants and Connecting to Collections planning grants, and sessions on 21st century skills, grants administration, disaster preparedness, and the 2009 American Samoa tsunami. Additionally, individual technical assistance meetings were held with each grantee.

Library Statistics State Data Coordinators Conference

The third IMLS-sponsored Library Statistics State Data Coordinators Conference was held in Washington, D.C., November 30–December 2, 2010. There were 55 participants representing the 50 states, the District of Columbia, Puerto Rico, and Palau. The conference included training on data collection and input, review of existing data elements included in the Public Libraries Survey, workshops on data presentation and analysis, and discussion and balloting of new data elements for the FY 2010 survey and beyond.

IMLS Web Site and Publications

The Grants to States program provides SLAA LSTA program administrators with around-the-clock access to a Web site that facilitates communication about program requirements and guidance.

IMLS's Web site (http://www.imls.gov) provides information on the various grant programs, the National Medal for Museum and Library Service, funded projects, application forms, and staff contacts. The Web site also highlights model projects developed by libraries and museums throughout the country and provides information about IMLS-sponsored conferences, publications, and studies. Through an electronic newsletter, *Primary Source,* IMLS provides information on grant deadlines and opportunities. Information on subscribing to the IMLS newsletter is located on the Web site.

The following recent publications are available at the IMLS Web site: the 2011 *Grant and Award Opportunities* booklet; *Opportunity for All: How the American Public Benefits from Internet Access at U.S. Libraries*; *Advancing Research and Practice in Digital Curation and Publishing,* a white paper stemming from the 2010 Bloomsbury Conference; *Connecting to Collections: A Report to the Nation;* the *2010 National Medal for Museum and Library Service* brochure; and guidelines for each of the grant programs.

Part 3
Library/Information Science Education, Placement, and Salaries

Library Employment Sources on the Internet

Catherine Barr
Contributing Editor

The continuing economic crisis hit libraries hard in 2010, with reductions in budgets and staffing; for graphic representations of the impact of these cuts on public libraries, visit http://www.losinglibraries.org, where there is also a link to the site called A Nation Without School Librarians, which monitors schools and school districts where librarians have been eliminated.

New library school graduates reported various obstacles to finding jobs, including the fact that expected retirements were not taking place (see *Library Journal*'s editorial "Sold on a Graying Profession" at http://www.libraryjournal.com/lj/careerscareernews/887165-300/editorial_sold_on_a_graying.html.csp). *Library Journal*'s annual "Placements and Salaries" report for 2010 reported that 7.8 percent of 2009 library school graduates were unemployed, 10.6 percent in temporary jobs, 19.4 percent in nonprofessional employment, and 22.8 percent in part-time positions. [See the following article for the full report.—*Ed.*]

This is not a comprehensive list of the hundreds of job-related sites on the Internet of interest to librarians and information professionals. These are, however, the best starting places for a general job search in this area. Many offer additional information that will be helpful to those considering a career in librarianship, including advice on conducting a successful search, writing résumés, preparing for interviews, and negotiating salaries.

Before spending a lot of time on any Web site, users should check that the site has been updated recently and that out-of-date job listings no longer appear. Many sites do not reflect the current difficulties that jobseekers are encountering.

The Directory of Organizations in Part 6 of this volume may also prove useful.

Background Information

The Bureau of Labor Statistics of the Department of Labor provides a thorough overview of the work of a librarian, necessary qualifications, and the job and salary outlook at http://www.bls.gov/oco/ocos068.htm. Similar pages are available for archivists, curators, and museum technicians (http://www.bls.gov/oco/ocos065.htm) and for library technicians and library assistants http://www.bls.gov/oco/ocos316.htm). Salary information can also be found at http://www.salary.com/salary/index.asp, which offers a page of library options at http://www1.salary.com/Library-Services-Salaries.html.

The American Library Association (ALA) provides a user-friendly overview of librarianship at all levels—from page and library assistant to managers and directors—at LibraryCareers.org (http://www.ala.org/ala/educationcareers/

careers/librarycareerssite/home.cfm), and Info*Nation: Choose a Career in Libraries (http://www.cla.ca/infonation/welcome.htm) is an excellent Canadian site that describes the work of librarians, combining brief information on a variety of career options with statements by individual librarians about why they love their jobs. These two sites will be particularly useful for young people considering a possible career in librarianship.

The October 2010 issue of *Knowledge Quest* has a feature story titled "Public Librarian" in which three public librarians describe their jobs and the aspects that they particularly enjoy. And the April 2010 issue of *College and Research Library News* includes an article—"Making the Best of the Worst of Times: Global Turmoil and Landing Your First Library Job"—that looks at job listings and how to prepare for an interview.

Also of interest to aspiring librarians is Rachel Singer Gordon's article in the September 15, 2009, *Library Journal* (http://www.libraryjournal.com/article/CA605244.html), "How to Become a Librarian—Updated." In this, she covers all the basics and recommends paths to the profession.

In response to the difficulties facing both new and mid-career librarians, ALA in 2009 created a site called Get a Job! (http://www.getajob.ala.org). Subtitled "ALA's Toolkit for Getting a Job in a Tough Economy," this provides helpful information under such headings as "Especially in a Tough Job Market." Podcasts and stories offer real-life experiences and users can ask questions and contribute comments.

Finally, How to Apply for a Library Job (http://www.liswiki.com/wiki/HOWTO:Apply_for_a_library_job) offers thoughtful advice and practical interview tips.

General Sites/Portals

American Library Association:
Education and Careers http://www.ala.org/ala/educationcareers/index.cfm

Maintained by ALA. A useful source of information on library careers, education and professional development, scholarships, and salaries.

ALA JobLIST http://joblist.ala.org

Sponsored by ALA and the Association of College and Research Libraries. This site incorporates the former job sites of *American Libraries* magazine and *C&RL News.* Registration is free for jobseekers, who can post their résumés and search jobs by library type, date, state, institution name, salary range, and other parameters. Employers can choose from a menu of print and electronic posting combinations.

Canadian Library Association:
Library Careers http://www.cla.ca/AM/Template.cfm?Section=Library_Careers

The Canadian Library Association lists Canadian job openings here (select Job Search) and provides guidance on recognition of foreign credentials.

Employment Resources: Organizations
and Associations http://slisweb.sjsu.edu/resources/employment.htm

Maintained by San José State University's School of Library and Information Science. Gives links to organizations that will be of interest to students at the university, including a number of California sites. A related page, Professional Associations in the Information Sciences (http://slisweb.sjsu.edu/resources/orgs.htm), is a comprehensive listing of associations in the United States and abroad. And excellent information on conducting job searches and professional development in general can be found at http://slisgroups.sjsu.edu/alumni/jobseekers/index.html.

LibGig http://www.libgig.com

This professional networking site offers jobs, "who's hiring" job alerts, résumé consultation, career profiles, news, blogs, and a Job Market full of current advice (http://libgig.com/jobmarket).

Library Job Postings on the Internet http://www.libraryjobpostings.org

Compiled by Sarah (Nesbeitt) Johnson of Booth Library, Eastern Illinois University, coauthor of *The Information Professional's Guide to Career Development Online* (Information Today, Inc., 2002); there is a link to the book's companion Web site on this site. Provides links to library employment sites in the United States and abroad, with easy access by location and by category of job.

LIScareer.com: Career Strategies for Librarians http://www.liscareer.com

Relaunched in 2009, this helpful site is maintained by Priscilla Shontz and offers "practical career development advice for new librarians and information professionals, MLS students, and those considering a library-related career." There are no job listings but the site offers interesting articles in the areas of career exploration, education, job searching, experience, networking, mentoring, interpersonal skills, leadership, publishing and presenting, and work/life balance. This is an excellent place to begin research on library jobs. Shontz also offers career consulting services via this site. Shontz and Richard Murray are coeditors of *A Day in the Life: Career Options in Library and Information Science* (Libraries Unlimited, 2007). Shontz is also the author of *The Librarian's Career Guidebook* (Scarecrow, 2004) and *Jump Start Your Career in Library and Information Science* (Scarecrow, 2002).

Lisjobs.com—Jobs for Librarians and Information Professionals http://www.lisjobs.com

Maintained by Rachel Singer Gordon, author of books including *What's the Alternative? Career Options for Librarians and Info Pros* (Information Today, Inc., 2008), *Information Tomorrow: Reflections on Technology and the Future of Public and Academic Libraries* (Information Today, Inc., 2007), *The NextGen Librarian's Survival Guide* (Information Today, Inc., 2006), and *The Accidental Library Manager* (Information Today, Inc., 2005).

This newly updated site includes a searchable database of job listings (RSS feed available), links to job banks, and useful job hunting and career development resources. Job seekers can post résumés for a small fee. The site also features information on scholarships and funding for continuing education, and a section called "Career Q&A with the Library Career People," which provides detailed answers to users' questions.

The Riley Guide: Employment Opportunities and Job Resources on the Internet http://www.rileyguide.com

Compiled by Margaret F. Dikel, a private consultant and coauthor with Frances Roehm of *The Guide to Internet Job Searching* (McGraw-Hill, 2006). A general site rich in advice for the job seeker, from résumé writing and how to target a new employer to tips on networking and interviewing. Links to job sites are organized by type of opportunity; Information Delivery, Design, and Management is found under Humanities, Social Sciences, and Personal Services.

Sites by Sector

Public Libraries

Public library openings can be found at all the general sites/portals listed above.

Careers in Public Librarianship http://www.ala.org/ala/mgrps/divs/pla/placareers/index.cfm

The Public Library Association offers information on public librarianship, with a section on the experiences of PLA members.

Competencies for Librarians Serving Children in Public Libraries http://www.ala.org/ala/mgrps/divs/alsc/edcareeers/alsccorecomps

A detailed listing of skills and knowledge required to be a children's librarian in a public library.

School Libraries

School library openings can be found at many of the sites listed above. Sites with interesting material for aspiring school librarians include those listed below.

AASL: Recruitment to School Librarianship http://www.ala.org/ala/mgrps/divs/aasl/aasleducation/recruitmentlib/aaslrecruitment.cfm

The American Association of School Librarians hosts this site, which describes the role of school librarians, salary and job outlooks, and mentoring programs; provides testimonials from working library media specialists; and offers state-by-state information on licensure, scholarships, library education, job hunting, mentoring, and recruitment efforts.

General education sites usually include school library openings. Among sites with nationwide coverage is:

Education America http://www.educationamerica.net

Library openings can be searched by geographic location.

Special and Academic Libraries

AALL Career Center http://www.aallnet.org/careers

Maintained by the American Association of Law Librarians, this site, with an online job board, also links to the excellent Careers in Law Librarianship site (http://www.lawlibrarycareers.org), which answers the question "Is a career as a law librarian right for you?"

Association of College and Research Libraries
See ALA JobLIST above.

ALISE: Job Placement http://www.alise.org

The Association for Library and Information Science Education posts jobs (under the heading Job Placement) for deans, directors, and faculty, organized by position and alphabetically by school.

ASIS&T: Careers http://www.asist.org/careers.html

The Careers page maintained by the American Society for Information Science and Technology offers access to a Jobline, Placement Center, and Continuing Education information.

Association of Research Libraries: Career Resources http://www.arl.org/resources/careers/index.shtml

In addition to listings of openings at ARL member institutions and at other organizations, there is information on ARL's diversity programs plus a database of research library residency and internship programs.

Chronicle of Higher Education http://chronicle.com/jobs

Listings can be browsed, with geographical options, under the category "Library/information sciences" (found under "Professional fields") or searched by simple keyword such as "library." Articles and advice on job searching are also available.

EDUCAUSE Job Posting Service http://www.educause.edu/jobpost

EDUCAUSE member organizations post positions "in the broad field of information technology in higher education."

HigherEdJobs.com http://www.higheredjobs.com

The category "Libraries" is found under Administrative Positions.

Major Orchestra Librarians' Association http://www.mola-inc.org

A nice site for a field that might be overlooked. The Resources section includes an introduction to the work of an orchestra librarian.

Medical Library Association: Career Development http://www.mlanet.org/career/index.html

The Medical Library Association offers much more than job listings here, with brochures on medical librarianship, a video, career tips, and a mentor program.

Music Library Association Job Openings http://www.musiclibraryassoc.org/employmentanded/joblist/openings.shtml

Along with job postings and a résumé review service, this site features an article titled "Music Librarianship—Is It for You?" and a listing of resources for both beginning and mid-career music librarians.

SLA: Career Center http://www.sla.org/content/jobs/index.cfm

In addition to salary information and searchable job listings that are available to all users, the Special Libraries Association provides many services for association members.

Government

Library of Congress http://www.loc.gov/hr/employment

Current job openings, internships, fellowships, and volunteering.

National Archives and Records Administration http://www.archives.gov/careers

In addition to information on employment opportunities, internships, and volunteering, NARA provides profiles of employees and interns, describing the kinds of work they do.

Serials

NASIG Jobs http://jobs.nasig.org

Managed by the North American Serials Interest Group. Accepts serials-related job postings.

Library Periodicals

American Libraries

See ALA JobList above.

Library Journal http://www.libraryjournal.com

Job listings are found under the Careers tab.

School Library Journal http://www.schoollibraryjournal.com

Click on the Jobs tab for access to a general list of job openings (jointly maintained with *Library Journal*; you must filter by Children's/Young Adult to access school positions.

Employment Agencies/Commercial Services

A number of employment agencies and commercial services in the United States and abroad specialize in library-related jobs. Among those that keep up-to-date listings on their Web sites are:

Advanced Information Management http://www.aimusa.com

Specializes in librarians and support staff in a variety of types of libraries across the country.

Library Associates http://www.libraryassociates.com

An easy-to-use list of openings that can be sorted by function, department, and location.

TPFL: The Information People: Recruitment and Executive Search http://www.tfpl.com/permanent_recruitment/candidates/pjobs.cfm

Specializes in jobs in the fields of knowledge management, library and information management, records management, and Web and content management. Jobs around the world are listed, with the majority in the United Kingdom.

Listservs

Many listservs allow members to post job openings on a casual basis.

jESSE http://web.utk.edu/~gwhitney/jesse.html

This worldwide discussion group focuses on library and information science education; LIS faculty position announcements frequently appear here.

LIBJOBS http://www.ifla.org/en/mailing-lists

LIBJOBS is a mailing list for librarians and information professionals seeking employment. It is managed by the International Federation of Library Associations and Institutions (IFLA). Subscribers to this list receive posted job opportunities by e-mail.

PUBLIB http://lists.webjunction.org/publib

Public library job openings often appear on this list.

Blogs

The Blogging Libraries Wiki (http://www.blogwithoutalibrary.net/links/index.php?title=Welcome_to_the_Blogging_Libraries_Wiki) provides lists of library blogs in the following fields: Academic Libraries, Public Libraries, School Libraries, Special Libraries, Internal Library Communication, Library Associations, and Library Director.

Beyond the Job http://www.beyondthejob.org

Compiled by Sarah Johnson and Rachel Singer Gordon, this blog focuses on job-hunting advice and professional development.

Career Q&A with the Library Career People http://www.lisjobs.com/careerqa_blog

This attractive and user-friendly blog is maintained by librarians Tiffany Allen and Susanne Markgren and is intended to "create an enlightening discussion forum of professional guidance and advice for librarians, library staff, and those thinking of entering the profession." Categories include job satisfaction, job seeking, and professional development.

Placements and Salaries 2010: The Recession's Toll

Stephanie L. Maatta

"Jobs . . . What jobs?" asked many of the 2009 library and information science (LIS) graduating class following another year of stagnating salaries and rising unemployment. Participants in this annual study relayed many tales of triumph and travail, illustrating another struggling job market with a few glimmers of hope and achievement. There was strong participation in the survey—the 1,996 respondents represented 38.7 percent of the year's approximately 5,160 LIS graduates.

The job search for the graduates followed the laws of physics: for every positive gain there was an equally negative reversal. While the average starting salary recovered the ground lost in 2008, improving 1.5 percent to $42,215 (up from $41,579), reports of unemployment continued to rise to a rate of 7.8 percent among the respondents. The length of the search to find a position of any kind inched up to more than five months. Those who graduated in the first half of 2009 had a slightly easier time—a four-and-a-half-month job search compared with those in the second half, who averaged well over five and half months.

Much like the graduates themselves, the LIS programs have their own stories to tell. In 2009 there appeared to be an overall decrease in the number of students graduating, with an average reduction of approximately 7 percent reported. This suggests that students may be taking longer to complete their studies given the current economic environment; there may be a decrease in overall enrollment in the LIS programs; or students might not be completing programs because of a lack of available financial assistance through employer tuition reimbursement or student loans.

The trends hinted at by the 2008 graduating class came to fruition in 2009. Too many applicants for too few jobs, continued hiring freezes, and mandated furloughs without pay continued to affect job placement, forcing graduates to seek positions outside the library and information science professions or to take on part-time and nonprofessional work. "I'm working in a job that requires the educational equivalent of a GED," said one graduate, while others reported that they stayed on as pages or shelvers or took on jobs in bookstores as cashiers and children's specialists.

In Search of Stability

Unlike the previous two years, when approximately 87 percent of graduates reported employment, in 2009 the employment status slid backward to 83.3 percent, compounded by an overall 7.8 percent unemployment rate. The fact that full-time placements improved slightly to 72.9 percent from a low of 69.8 percent in 2008—though not reaching the levels of 2007 (89.2 percent)—remains

Stephanie L. Maatta has been on faculty at the University of South Florida School of Library and Information Science, Tampa.

Adapted from *Library Journal,* October 15, 2010.

Table 1 / Status of 2009 Graduates*

	Number of Schools Reporting	Number of Graduates Responding	Permanent Professional	Temporary Professional	Non-professional	Total	Graduates Outside of Profession	Unemployed or Status Unreported
Northeast	14	769	344	60	135	539	72	159
Southeast	10	271	149	23	31	203	34	34
Midwest	10	536	313	57	65	435	44	57
Southwest	5	147	93	8	15	116	15	16
West	4	198	74	23	21	118	21	46
Total	43	1,996	1,017	174	284	1,475	189	333

* Table based on survey responses from schools and individual graduates. Figures will not necessarily be fully consistent with some of the other data reported. Tables do not always add up, individually or collectively, since both schools and individuals omitted data in some cases.

Table 2 / Placements and Full-Time Salaries of 2009 Graduates/Summary by Region*

					Low Salary $		High Salary $		Average Salary $			Median Salary $		
Region	Total	Women	Men	Total	Women	Men	Women	Men	Women	Men	All	Women	Men	All
Northeast	299	220	36	252	15,600	18,000	104,000	70,000	42,101	37,695	42,346	42,000	40,000	42,000
Southeast	250	168	51	218	13,104	15,000	75,000	72,500	39,622	38,068	39,525	40,000	36,000	39,000
Midwest	321	205	65	270	12,000	18,720	82,000	112,500	38,965	44,999	40,418	37,500	42,500	38,200
Southwest	121	94	18	113	15,000	25,000	85,000	88,000	41,921	46,980	42,780	40,648	44,000	41,000
West	154	87	32	119	20,000	30,500	95,000	98,000	48,170	56,251	50,343	46,000	53,500	46,000
International	24	8	3	11	22,000	32,000	80,000	61,400	45,716	47,133	46,103	43,871	48,000	48,000
Combined	1,220	793	206	998	12,000	15,000	104,000	112,500	41,514	4 4,945	42,215	40,000	42,000	40,000

*All International salaries converted to American dollars based on conversion rates for August 26, 2010. This table represents only salaries and placements reported as full-time. Some data were reported as aggregate without break-down by gender or region. Comparison with other tables will show different numbers of placements.

Table 3 / 2009 Total Graduates and Placements by School*

Schools	Graduates			Employed		
	Women	Men	Total	Women	Men	Total
Alabama	72	25	97	8	5	13
Albany	64	26	90	16	4	20
Arizona***	64	8	72	—	—	—
Buffalo**	31	7	38	28	6	34
Catholic	60	18	78	17	4	21
Clarion	222	45	267	27	2	29
Denver	35	11	46	8	1	9
Dominican**	—	1	1	—	—	—
Drexel	209	91	300	48	19	68
Florida State**	63	15	78	54	13	67
Hawaii	39	8	47	14	3	17
Illinois**	56	7	63	51	5	56
Indiana	187	64	251	50	16	66
Iowa	27	6	33	25	3	28
Kent State	201	59	260	67	21	88
Kentucky	70	18	88	25	10	35
Long Island	108	34	142	27	5	32
Louisiana State**	1	—	1	1	—	1
Michigan***	67	62	162	67	62	129
Missouri–Columbia	75	9	84	23	3	26
N.C. Chapel Hill	62	49	111	11	2	13
North Texas	400	65	465	24	5	29
Oklahoma	47	12	59	12	4	16
Pittsburgh**	52	8	60	44	7	51

bittersweet because permanent professional placements continued to decline, from 75.8 percent of the number in 2007 to 61 percent in 2009, while temporary placements increased once again (from 7.8 percent in 2008 to 10.6 percent in 2009), as did nonprofessional jobs (from 13.5 percent of placements in 2008 to 19.4 percent in 2009).

Similar trends appear in the number of jobs reported in many types of library and information agencies, with academic librarians seeing a staggering drop in placements, from 31 percent of all jobs in 2008 to 20 percent in 2009. Agencies outside of libraries, on the other hand, experienced an increase in reported placements from just over 15 percent in the previous year to more than 27 percent this year, though salaries in these same agencies did not follow suit, remaining flat with less than 1 percent growth. Not surprisingly, public libraries, which were hit again by severely restricted public funding, hired fewer new librarians, dropping 8.4 percent, though the average public librarian salary held steady at $37,308 (within 1 percent of a year earlier). Government libraries, while overall numbers continue to be low, displayed more positive growth in placements (increasing another 13 percent from 2008) and in salaries (edging up 4.4 percent to $43,904 to recover losses experienced between 2007 and 2008).

Many graduates indicated a reluctance to relinquish their current jobs when they received their master's degrees, even when it meant remaining in a nonpro-

Pratt	110	29	139	42	4	47
Queens**	1	—	1	1	—	1
Rhode Island	66	14	80	31	4	35
Rutgers	136	26	162	61	10	71
San José	319	120	439	91	22	113
Simmons***	192	35	227	134	22	156
So. Connecticut	121	17	138	35	4	39
So. Mississippi	47	8	55	4	—	4
South Carolina	15	2	17	13	2	15
South Florida	21	4	25	17	2	19
St. John's**	10	—	10	9	—	9
Syracuse	84	8	92	18	2	20
Tennessee	42	9	51	37	6	43
Texas (Austin)	88	15	103	38	7	45
Texas Women's	220	6	226	30	1	32
UCLA	56	23	79	5	—	5
Washington	106	29	135	18	2	20
Wayne State**	36	3	39	30	3	33
Wisconsin (Madison)**	52	16	68	37	14	51
Wisconsin (Milwaukee)	164	49	213	45	15	60
Total	4,098	1,061	5,192	1,343	320	1,666

* Tables do not always add up, individually or collectively, since both schools and individuals omitted data in some cases.

** For schools that did not fill out the institutional survey, data were taken from graduate surveys, thus there is not full representation of their graduating classes.

*** Some schools completed the institutional survey, but responses were not received from graduates; or schools conducted their own survey and provided reports. This table represents placements of any kind. Comparison with other tables will show different numbers of placements.

Other categories: Students: 22 women, 6 men, with a total of 34. Unemployed: 119 women, 37 men, with a total of 156. Unknown: 2,636 women; 704 men, with a total of 3,400.

fessional position as a library assistant or clerk. Several graduates said they could not afford to give up their current income in order to risk finding a professional position elsewhere, particularly in light of a national recession and high national unemployment. More respondents remained with their current employer after graduation (44.6 percent compared with 42.3 percent in 2008 and 43.8 percent in 2007), and of these graduates, a full 25 percent (a significant increase from 20.1 percent in 2008 and 16.7 percent in 2007) accepted or stayed in nonprofessional positions rather than entering the ranks of the jobless. For some, this meant lower wages, fewer professional responsibilities, and minimal benefits (health insurance, paid vacation/sick days, and so on).

Compromise for Many

The graduating class of 2009 made numerous compromises to find jobs. Approximately 41 percent accepted placement in an agency other than that for which they had originally trained. For example, graduates accepted positions in government agencies and corporations although they had prepared for positions in archives or academic libraries. Their reaction was mixed; some noted disappointment and frustration in not being able to find the right environment, while others said such things as "It's not what I planned, but I love what I'm doing now."

(text continues on page 338)

Table 4 / Placements by Average Full-Time Salary of Reporting 2009 Graduates*

	Average Salary			Median Salary		Low Salary		High Salary		Salaries		
	Women	Men	All	Women	Men	Women	Men	Women	Men	Women	Men	Total Placements
Long Island	$59,971	$41,000	$57,261	$57,000	$41,000	$41,000	$32,000	$104,000	$50,000	12	2	20
Michigan	49,789	62,736	55,716	45,000	62,500	30,000	33,250	95,000	112,500	45	38	118
UCLA	49,250	—	49,250	48,500	—	45,000	—	55,000	—	4	—	4
San José	47,451	46,295	47,220	42,500	45,000	20,000	38,500	89,000	60,000	48	12	79
Catholic University	47,412	38,000	46,688	49,872	38,000	24,000	38,000	62,000	38,000	12	1	17
North Texas	44,750	57,333	46,638	45,000	52,000	26,000	50,000	58,000	70,000	17	3	26
Rutgers	45,595	45,766	45,625	47,000	45,500	20,000	35,000	92,000	60,000	37	8	56
Pratt	44,535	52,367	44,783	43,000	50,000	29,000	37,100	65,000	70,000	32	3	37
Washington	44,538	42,500	44,267	43,500	42,500	27,000	42,000	65,000	43,000	13	2	17
Denver	43,859	—	43,859	36,000	—	28,000	—	83,000	—	5	—	6
South Carolina	42,481	47,500	43,318	43,000	47,500	27,500	4,000	58,000	55,000	10	2	13
Iowa	44,270	36,167	43,054	42,000	42,500	18,000	21,000	82,000	45,000	17	3	22
Drexel	42,676	43,924	42,959	41,750	38,520	25,000	32,000	74,000	70,000	34	10	56
Southern Mississippi	42,667	—	42,667	36,000	—	30,000	—	62,000	—	3	—	3
Texas (Austin)	41,413	47,691	42,570	42,000	40,000	24,000	27,840	64,000	88,000	31	7	39
Illinois	42,584	41,000	42,395	42,500	38,000	19,000	34,000	72,000	55,000	37	5	48
NC Chapel Hill	42,401	40,750	42,126	43,442	40,750	22,000	31,500	55,000	50,000	10	2	12
Texas Women's	42,521	25,000	41,948	42,000	25,000	15,000	25,000	85,000	25,000	19	1	24
Hawaii	42,384	37,000	41,487	45,500	37,000	21,000	36,000	55,344	38,000	10	2	14
Southern Connecticut	41,173	42,333	41,307	40,000	37,000	27,000	33,000	62,225	57,000	23	3	31
Wisconsin–Milwaukee	40,459	42,497	41,086	42,000	39,000	20,000	32,500	72,000	57,360	27	12	48

Simmons	41,087	40,138	40,924	40,000	38,000	13,000	24,000	76,000	69,000	64	13	91
Tennessee	38,832	46,300	40,037	39,500	48,000	13,104	23,000	56,000	72,500	26	5	34
Indiana	38,306	45,686	39,930	38,890	43,000	20,800	30,500	68,000	71,000	39	11	53
Wisconsin–Madison	40,688	36,995	39,391	37,750	36,000	28,000	20,800	63,000	51,630	24	13	41
Clarion	39,449	33,000	38,933	37,500	33,000	28,000	32,000	70,000	34,000	23	2	26
Rhode Island	38,544	37,250	38,415	37,750	37,250	20,000	33,500	52,000	41,000	18	2	25
Wayne State	37,036	60,000	38,387	40,000	60,000	16,000	60,000	52,741	60,000	16	1	19
Buffalo	38,148	39,322	38,368	40,000	36,566	29,000	20,000	48,000	61,400	13	3	16
Syracuse	38,150	35,500	37,742	35,000	35,500	21,450	18,000	50,500	53,000	11	2	17
Kent State University	36,414	39,966	37,389	36,000	42,000	12,000	18,720	59,000	65,000	37	14	59
Albany	38,177	32,500	37,231	40,319	32 500	22,000	21,000	46,770	44,000	10	2	14
Florida State	37,740	32,250	36,704	40,000	31,000	19,000	23,000	56,990	42,000	44	10	63
St John's	36,683	—	36,683	38,000	—	15,600	—	51,500	—	6	—	6
Oklahoma	35,666	39,267	36,497	38,150	36,000	19,000	31,000	60,000	50,800	10	3	13
Kentucky	37,737	32,777	36,026	36,000	34,000	18,500	15,000	75,000	43,767	19	10	30
Pittsburgh	35,369	39,400	35,979	34,812	36,000	16,354	25,000	68,000	58,000	28	5	37
Missouri–Columbia	34,870	38,833	35,496	35,750	38,000	28,000	35,000	42,000	43,500	16	3	20
Alabama	31,110	31,827	31,379	26,500	30,480	22,048	29,000	41,500	36,000	5	3	11
South Florida	29,799	35,000	30,272	34,296	35,000	14,400	35,000	40,000	35,000	10	1	13

* This table represents only placements and salaries reported as full-time. Some individuals or schools omitted some information, rendering information unusable. Comparisons with other tables will show different numbers of placement and salary.

(continued from page 335)

Part-time employment has become a way of life for many LIS graduates, and it has steadily risen from 16.3 percent in 2007 to 22.8 percent in 2009. For some graduates, this is a deliberate choice, but more than 34 percent of the part-timers in 2009 accepted multiple jobs (two or more) to create a semblance of a full-time salary, often without benefits. Common combinations were academic librarian by day/public librarian by night, part-time retail or office work meshed with jobs at local libraries, and children's programming at a public library mixed with work as a school media assistant or substitute teacher. The Northeast and the Midwest had the highest rates of part-time employment in 2009 (37.5 percent and 26.5 percent, respectively). As anticipated, public libraries offered the highest level of part-time employment at 32.7 percent, but surprisingly jobs considered "other"—falling outside of library and information agencies—experienced higher-than-average rates as well, with these being 23.3 percent of the part-time jobs.

Where Are the Jobs?

Regional economic instability appeared to have limited impact on average starting salaries for new graduates; however, the same economic uncertainty is reflected in the levels of regional unemployment among these same graduates. The two regions that felt salary compression were the Northeast ($42,346, or 3.7 percent below 2008) and the Southeast ($39,525, or 1.1 percent below 2008). The Northeast and Southeast also experienced moderately high levels of unemployment in 2009 at 7 percent and 8.5 percent, respectively. By comparison, the other regions had notable salary increases over 2008, ranging from a positive 3.4 percent in the Midwest ($40,418, up $1,371 from 2008 levels) to 6.5 percent in the Southwest ($42,780, up $2,780 from 2008 levels). Regionality continued to affect salaries, with the West having the highest starting salaries at $50,343 (16 percent higher than the national average of $42,268), and the Southeast hovering at $39,525 (6.9 percent lower than the overall national average).

The real bright spot in the LIS job market during 2009 was the Southwest. Across-the-board starting salaries there enjoyed healthy growth of 6.6 percent between 2008 and 2009, rising from an average of $40,000 in 2008 to $42,780. In the same vein, part-time employment among LIS graduates in the Southwest declined for a second year, to 4.3 percent of the reported placements (down considerably from 6.9 percent in 2008 and 8.2 percent in 2007). Women experienced the best salary growth in the Southwest, increasing a healthy 7.5 percent from $38,997 in 2008 to $41,921 in 2009, surpassing the salary levels of 2007 ($40,795). Southwestern public libraries saw a similar improvement, jumping 7.5 percent to an average of $38,904 and topping the national starting salary for all public libraries ($37,308).

Comparing region to region, the Midwest experienced the highest placement rates, with 26.7 percent of the overall reported jobs (full-time and part-time combined). The region also experienced small but positive salary improvement, up 3.5 percent to an average of $40,418 from $39,047 in 2008, helped along by improved salaries for graduates entering government libraries and vendors in the Midwest. The Midwest had the highest placements in college and university

Table 5 / Average Salary Index Starting Library Positions, 1999–2009

Year	Library Schools	Average Starting Salary	Dollar Increase in Average Salary	Salary Index	BLS-CPI*
1999	37	$33,976	$2,061	192.03	168.7
2000	37	34,871	895	197.26	175.1
2001	40	36,818	1,947	208.09	177.1
2002	30	37,456	638	211.70	179.9
2003	43	37,975	519	214.63	184.0
2004	46	39,079	1,104	220.87	188.9
2005	37	40,115	1,036	226.73	195.3
2006	45	41,014	899	231.81	201.6
2007	43	42,361	1,347	239.42	207.3
2008	40	41,579	-782	235.00	215.3
2009	42	42,215	636	238.60	214.5

* U.S. Department of Labor, Bureau of Labor Statistics, Consumer Price index, All Urban Consumers (CPI-U), U.S. city average, all items, 1982–1984=100. The average beginning professional salary for that period was $17,693.

libraries, compared with the other types of libraries and information agencies—these jobs accounted for approximately 40 percent of new academic librarians' placements. Meanwhile, placements in public libraries fell sharply from 39.5 percent in 2008 to 27.8 percent in 2009, while salaries in Midwestern public libraries held steady at $34,966 (still among the lowest in the nation). This reversed a placement trend set in 2008 when public libraries in the Midwest had the best overall growth rate. Graduates in the Midwest, however, saw the best job growth (27 percent between 2008 and 2009) in other types of agencies, especially in private industry where placements doubled between 2008 and 2009—although it was only 13.3 percent of total placements.

Graduates in the Southeast were not quite so lucky. Overall placement in all types of libraries and other agencies dropped almost 20 percent compared with the previous year; salaries in many types of libraries were among the lowest in the nation, especially for public librarians; unemployment among graduates was 8.5 percent. However, the region also experienced pockets of good news. The Southeast was the only region in which minority graduates reported salary growth, improving 2.8 percent to $43,259 (an increase of $1,175 from 2008), nearly 10 percent higher than all graduates in the Southeast (with an average starting salary of $39,440). Graduates negotiated higher salaries in government libraries than their peers in other regions, with an average starting salary of $45,858 (approximately 11.5 percent higher on average). This improvement is due in part to graduates accepting work in the Washington, D.C., area, which traditionally offers better-than-average salaries.

The class of 2009 saw a decline in available positions, averaging 11.5 percent below the previous year's reports. However, this does not begin to tell the whole story. Several roles, including archives and records management and research specialists (i.e., independent research and research analysts), experienced modest growth. Graduates also found a number of new and interesting job titles in the areas of intellectual property, copyright, and scholarly communica-

Table 6 / Salaries of Reporting Professionals by Area of Job Assignment*

Assignment	No.	Percent of Total	Low Salary	High Salary	Average Salary	Median Salary
Access Services	17	1.00	$19,000	$84,000	$42,182	$40,000
Acquisitions	23	1.00	20,000	48,000	33,717	33,150
Administration	93	5.80	18,000	83,000	45,266	41,000
Adult Services	41	2.56	22,000	46,280	34,912	34,000
Archives	90	5.61	13,000	55,000	37,631	38,000
Automation/Systems	12	0.75	31,000	70,000	49,488	48,000
Cataloging and Classification	66	4.11	17,000	68,640	37,558	35,750
Children's Services	67	4.18	13,104	55,000	39,704	40,398
Circulation	92	5.74	18,000	52,000	30,515	30,000
Collection Development	13	0.81	27,000	55,000	36,113	35,180
Database Management	7	0.44	37,000	65,000	53,000	55,000
Electronic or Digital Services	46	2.87	27,500	70,000	43,229	42,113
Government Documents	7	0.44	19,000	51,500	35,667	37,750
Information Architecture	6	0.37	48,000	70,000	60,100	60,000
Info Technology	56	3.49	23,000	112,500	52,337	49,000
Instruction	40	2.49	16,000	60,000	42,663	43,500
Interlibrary Loans/ Document Delivery	15	0.94	30,000	60,000	39,145	37,500
Knowledge Management	24	1.50	24,000	87,000	48,329	47,960
Metadata	12	0.75	27,040	92,000	45,640	43,500
Other	212	13.22	14,400	104,000	45,312	42,000
Preservation/ Conservation	10	0.62	18,500	46,396	36,066	38,000
Public Services	46	2.87	19,000	72,000	39,135	41,500
Reference/Info Services	247	15.40	18,720	84,000	41,795	41,000
Research Services	21	1.31	38,000	60,000	44,250	42,000
School Library Media Specialist	165	10.29	20,000	89,000	46,299	45,000
Solo Librarian	49	3.05	15,000	58,000	37,449	38,000
Technical Services	34	2.12	24,000	51,000	35,301	34,000
Usability/User Experiences	22	1.37	47,500	95,000	66,346	65,000
Youth Services	71	4.43	20,800	61,400	37,525	38,000
Total	1,604		13,000	112,500	42,177	40,000

* This table represents placements of any type reported by job assignment, but only salaries reported as full-time. Some individuals omitted placement information, rendering some information unusable. Comparison with other tables will show different numbers of placements.

tions. Salaries resembled a roller coaster ride with an equal number of dips and rises.

Reference service continued to be a popular choice among LIS graduates, with positions spread among academic, public, and special libraries. Following a pattern that emerged over the last couple of years, however, reference jobs declined again, making up 15.4 percent of the overall number of jobs (compared wirh 20.6 percent in 2008 and 21.6 percent in 2007). It also comprised 23.7 percent of the reported part-time positions in 2009. In the plus column, new reference librarians saw improved salaries, up 3.4 percent after declining in 2008 ($41,795 compared with $40,368 in 2008 and $41,172 in 2007). When discussing their jobs at the reference desk, graduates frequently described multitasking as a strong element of their daily routine, combining reference with collection development, outreach, and/or instruction. In public libraries, they switched between adult reference services and children's or teen services, or floated among multiple units, covering the circulation desk, technical services, and the reference desk. While the overall numbers are low, graduates acknowledged accepting positions in academic reference and user services in newly established learning commons and as digital librarians along with standard reference desk activities.

Jobs in administration provided another small area of genuine improvement. While administrative placements held steady, hovering right around 6 percent of the jobs in 2008 and again in 2009, salaries jumped 8.3 percent to a starting average of $45,266 after dropping the previous year ($43,849 in 2007; $41,809 for 2008). Administrative jobs were seen across all library types and outside of library and information agencies. Job titles included department head, library director, project manager, higher education administration, and manager. Interestingly, high-level administrative positions were offered almost equally between new graduates with prior professional experience (33 percent reporting) and those seeking their first professional jobs (31 percent reporting), suggesting that the combination of personal skills plus an interest in administration is as important to the job as is prior experience.

Circulation and technical services continue to be areas where graduates struggle to find better-than-average salaries. After rebounding in 2008, salaries for jobs in circulation plummeted more than 10 percent to $30,515 (a huge drop of 38.5 percent below the national average of $42,268 for starting salaries in 2009). In addition, circulation jobs made up nearly 25 percent of nonprofessional positions in 2009, equaling low pay and few benefits. Technical services also experienced a similar decline in salary levels, losing 9.5 percent between 2008 and 2009 ($38,652 and $35,301, respectively). This may be due in part to an increase in the level of nonprofessional positions filled by LIS graduates in 2009. Catalogers, on the other hand, while still trying to recover the losses between 2007 ($39,607) and 2008 ($36,812), mustered a modest salary improvement of $746 ($37,558, up 2 percent).

New archivists saw increased demand for their skills. Over the previous two years, there had been small but steady growth in the number of reported archival jobs, rising from 4.4 percent in 2007 to 5.7 percent in 2009. Unfortunately, salaries for new archivists did not keep pace, falling 7.4 percent to $37,631 (compared with $40,397 in 2008). They found themselves employed in a range of agencies, including museums, nonprofits, and regional and national archival organizations, many of which were affected by a struggling economy; others landed jobs in large corporations that maintain their own records-management facilities. In a related area, a small number of graduates identified jobs in preservation and conservation, including digitization and digital preservation. Salaries here, while slightly less than archival salaries ($36,066 compared with $37,631), enjoyed a modest 4.2 percent growth from 2008 (averaging $34,620).

(text continues on page 344)

Table 7 / Comparison of Salaries by Type of Organization*

	Total Placements	Salaries		Low Salary		High Salary		Average Salary			Median Salary		
		Women	Men	Women	Men	Women	Men	Women	Men	All	Women	Men	All
Public Libraries													
Northeast	99	73	7	$16,354	$21,000	$52,000	$48,000	$38,006	$37,962	$37,628	$40,000	$41,500	$39,697
Southeast	50	33	10	13,104	27,000	48,500	44,920	34,158	33,790	34,073	35,000	32,000	34,625
Midwest	80	61	10	18,720	20,800	60,000	65,000	34,643	36,759	34,966	34,320	36,500	34,750
Southwest	27	22	2	15,000	50,000	72,000	50,800	37,859	50,400	38,904	38,150	50,400	38,900
West	23	15	1	27,000	40,000	84,000	40,000	47,963	40,000	47,465	48,000	40,000	46,000
Canada/Intl.	6	2	1	52,741	61,400	80,000	61,400	66,371	61,400	64,714	66,371	61,400	61,400
All Public	289	214	30	13,104	20,800	84,000	65,000	37,207	37,717	37,319	36,700	36,000	36,500
School Libraries													
Northeast	71	57	4	19,000	24,000	75,454	57,000	45,628	39,642	45,235	44,232	38,873	44,000
Southeast	30	25	2	18,500	40,000	58,000	50,000	41,642	45,000	41,891	40,000	45,000	40,000
Midwest	30	22	1	29,000	57,360	72,000	57,360	46,800	57,360	47,259	44,500	57,360	45,000
Southwest	28	26	1	28,000	48,000	60,000	48,000	46,143	48,000	46,212	45,425	48,000	45,850
West	14	9	2	24,650	34,000	89,000	58,000	54,642	46,000	53,071	49,126	46,000	49,126
Canada/Intl.	3	2	1	29,000	32,000	56,990	32,000	42,995	32,000	39,330	42,995	32,000	32,000
All School	178	141	11	18,500	24,000	89,000	58,000	45,737	43,448	45,571	45,000	41,000	45,000
College/University Libraries													
Northeast	81	51	12	18,500	25,000	64,000	62,000	39,796	41,067	40,038	40,000	42,000	40,500
Southeast	87	56	24	17,500	18,000	58,000	72,500	38,762	37,740	38,455	40,000	36,000	40,000
Midwest	99	67	21	22,000	28,000	62,000	55,000	38,463	41,014	39,072	38,000	42,000	38,990
Southwest	32	26	6	19,000	25,000	83,000	46,000	39,575	34,500	38,623	38,678	35,500	38,678
West	44	25	11	20,000	35,000	78,000	68,000	43,943	47,773	45,113	42,500	45,000	44,250
Canada/Intl.	8	3	—	22,000	—	60,000	—	39,000	—	39,000	35,000	—	35,000
All Academic	247	230	74	17,500	18,000	83,000	72,500	39,551	40,437	40,065	40,000	40,500	40,000
Special Libraries													
Northeast	31	23	3	20,000	20,000	87,000	39,040	49,108	31,680	47,097	47,000	36,000	45,500
Southeast	18	15	3	30,000	29,000	56,000	33,280	40,073	31,843	38,701	38,000	33,250	36,250
Midwest	17	12	5	19,000	28,000	55,000	60,000	36,745	44,100	38,909	38,750	42,500	40,000
Southwest	6	4	—	38,000	—	56,000	—	48,000	—	48,000	49,000	—	49,000

West	10	9	—	28,000	—	58,000	—	43,056	—	43,056	42,000	—	42,000
All Special	85	65	13	19,000	28,000	87,000	60,000	43,798	39,256	43,090	42,000	37,520	41,870
Government Libraries													
Northeast	8	8	—	13,000	—	70,000	—	44,125	—	44,125	45,250	—	45,250
Southeast	27	20	6	31,000	36,000	64,000	51,630	46,303	45,377	45,858	45,350	47,500	45,850
Midwest	5	3	2	30,000	37,500	39,000	51,300	35,367	44,400	39,160	38,000	44,400	38,000
Southwest	5	5	—	31,000	—	50,150	—	37,830	—	37,830	35,000	—	35,000
West	5	3	2	21,000	40,040	60,000	43,000	46,000	41,520	44,208	57,000	41,520	43,000
All Government	50	39	10	13,000	36,000	70,000	51,630	43,774	44,410	43,904	42,000	44,000	43,000
Library Cooperatives/Networks													
Midwest	2	—	2	—	32,000	—	48,000	—	40,000	40,000	—	40,000	40,000
Southwest	1	—	1	—	41,000	—	41,000	—	41,000	41,000	—	41,000	41,000
All Co-op./Networks	3	—	3	—	32,000	—	48,000	—	40,333	40,333	—	41,000	41,000
Vendors													
Northeast	7	5	1	33,000	50,000	92,000	50,000	49,457	50,000	49,547	37,000	50,000	43,500
Southeast	2	1	—	43,000	—	43,000	—	43,000	—	43,000	43,000	—	43,000
Midwest	4	3	1	35,000	35,000	55,000	35,000	48,333	35,000	45,000	55,000	35,000	45,000
Southwest	1	1	—	24,000	—	24,000	—	24,000	—	24,000	24,000	—	24,000
West	2	2	—	32,000	—	45,000	—	38,500	—	38,500	38,500	—	38,500
All Vendors	16	14	2	24,000	35,000	92,000	50,000	43,753	42,500	44,377	36,000	42,500	40,000
Other Organizations													
Northeast	88	47	14	15,600	18,000	104,000	70,000	43,131	48,443	43,264	42,000	47,050	44,500
Southeast	40	20	6	14,400	15,000	75,000	65,000	45,349	40,000	44,114	42,000	35,500	41,250
Midwest	83	37	22	12,000	18,720	82,000	112,500	42,568	53,528	46,655	40,000	55,250	42,000
Southwest	22	12	8	24,960	27,840	85,000	88,000	44,942	56,105	49,407	48,250	55,000	49,500
West	99	26	16	27,000	30,500	95,000	98,000	52,365	66,219	57,643	45,500	67,500	55,000
Canada/Intl.	8	1	1	30,000	48,000	30,000	48,000	30,000	48,000	39,000	30,000	48,000	39,000
All Other	324	148	70	12,000	15,000	104,000	112,500	45,204	53,796	47,790	42,250	54,000	45,000

This table represents only full-time salaries and placements reported by type. Some individuals omitted placement information, rendering some information unusable.

* Comparison with other tables will show different numbers of total placements due to completeness of the data reported by individuals and schools.

(continued from page 341)

Graduates reported new job titles related to digital repositories and scholarly communications along with ones related to intellectual property management and copyright. The majority of these placements were in conjunction with academic and special libraries (law and business in particular). Not surprisingly, these jobs were snapped up by graduates of heavily information science (IS) programs where they used more of their technology, metadata, and database management skills. In addition, jobs in the areas of usability, user experience design, and interactive design were increasingly identified as roles by the IS graduates, replete with fat starting salaries (averaging $66,346 in 2009).

The Attractive 'Other'

Once again, jobs in the "other" category—falling outside of library and information agencies—provided an unusual look at the LIS professions. The number of graduates describing positions in other agencies outstripped the levels set in 2008 (15.5 percent) and 2007 (16.3 percent) by making up more than 27 percent of the reported placements in 2009. This growth was helped in part by the number of graduates from University of Michigan who landed jobs in private industry (56 percent in 2009) and from Drexel, which placed more than 67 percent of its responding graduates in other agencies. Placements ran the gamut from jobs in large corporations and hospitals to historical societies and state government agencies. Along the way, graduates took up positions in consulting, bookstores, publishing, and entrepreneurial endeavors (self-employed). More than one graduate explained that while the jobs fell outside of libraries and information science, they used their LIS skills daily in dealing with complex information questions and information-management activities. Their educational experiences were expanded to applications well beyond the library environment.

The type of other agency that hires LIS graduates plays a role in salary levels. Private industry continues to maintain strong earning potential, with an annual average of $55,301, but it was not immune to the economic recession of 2009—salary levels didn't quite reach the high of $58,194 in 2008. Private industry was once again dominated by jobs focusing on information technology, social media, and high-level business operations and analysis. By comparison, salaries for nonprofit agencies ($42,522) and other types of organizations ($43,427) were much closer to each other and in line with overall national starting salaries for new LIS graduates (an average of 1.6 percent higher). The gap between private industry and nonprofits—$55,301 and $42,522, respectively—narrowed to 30 percent compared with the previous year's divergence of a solid 40 percent.

Gender Equity Gap Grows

Each year's survey provides an opportunity to examine the health of the profession through multiple lenses, focusing on the experiences of individual subsets of graduates. Across the profession, women continue to dominate (representing 80 percent of the graduating class), and with that comes an inherent salary gap and glass ceiling. At the high end of starting salaries, women have yet to achieve salaries consistently as high as or higher than men's. Men still command higher average starting salaries than women ($44,945 compared with $41,514). The gender gap widened this year with the national average for women's starting salaries falling 8.3 percent below their male peers', increasing from the 7.4 percent differential of 2008. Part of this may be accounted for by the large percentage of men who landed jobs in private industry (40 percent in 2009) at salary levels that were 24 percent above those of female colleagues. The gap is further compounded by the larger percentages of women who enter the field at lower-paying jobs, such as circulation, children's services, and youth or teen services, and take on nonprofessional positions.

While growth in salaries year to year was slow, women and men found starting salaries that were slightly better in 2009. Women, while still below the national average starting salary ($41,537 compared with $42,215), improved their lot by 1.5 percent, and men by 1.7 percent ($44,945, up $773 from 2008). However, women claiming minority status felt a stark departure in starting salaries, erasing gains made in the previous years, with a 2009 average of $39,566 (9.2 percent below 2008). This situation for minority women can be partially attributed to high placement in libraries and jobs with notoriously lower salary levels, such as public libraries, and in roles that are more often given nonprofessional status, such as those in circulation and technical services.

Women achieved better starting salaries than their male counterparts in both special libraries ($43,858 over $41,006) and in school library media centers ($45,894 compared with $44,136). In fact, women seeking jobs in special libraries saw a significant salary increase over the previous year's levels (up nearly 15 percent), while the men were hit with a small decline in earnings (down by almost 3 percent). The increase was most noticeable in the Northeast, where women in special libraries made a solid leap of 29.7 percent from $37,850 in 2008 to an above-average $49,108 in 2009.

Both men and women experienced a reversal of fortunes in academic libraries, narrowing the gender gap to 2 percent. Men lost approximately 5.1 percent in earnings (dropping from $42,523 in 2008 to $40,347 in 2009), while women dipped just under 3 percent ($39,551 in 2009 compared with $40,749 in 2008). For women, this altered the trend between 2007 and 2008, when they gained 1.5 percent on their starting salaries in academic libraries, but for the men, the downward trend accelerated from a loss of 1.5 percent to 5.4 percent within the same time period. This downward trend speaks to the overall economic environment in which academic libraries found themselves in 2009, replete with hiring freezes and staff reductions. The 2009 graduates also spoke of applicant pools of 200 to 300 for one or two available positions and of academic libraries seeking individuals with highly specialized skills including atypical foreign language abilities (such as speaking and reading Middle Eastern and little-known Asian languages) along with Web design and knowledge of instructional technologies.

While they continued to lag behind their male colleagues, women experienced positive growth both in starting salaries and in placement in other types of agencies. In the Northeast and in the West, the number of women reporting jobs outside library and information agencies more than doubled from 2008 levels. The starting salaries in each of these regions also showed improvement, moving upward 6.4 percent ($43,199 compared with $40,586) and 2.7 percent ($52,365 compared with $51,000), respectively. In comparing nonprofit organizations to private industry and the ubiquitous "other," women experienced strong salary improvement in the "other" category, gaining 6.7 percent to $42,665 (up from $39,977 in 2008) and, surprisingly, in nonprofits, with a 2 percent increase to $41,547 (up from $40,732 in 2008). However, in the category of "other," minority graduates salaries took a serious hit, dropping more than 19 percent to $40,993 (down from $50,776 in 2008), despite an increased level of placement in these same agencies (climbing from 12.8 percent of minority placements in 2008 to just over 20 percent in 2009).

Minorities Lose Ground

Graduates identifying themselves as minorities struggled in 2009 to achieve the same levels of earnings their counterparts had achieved in previous years. In 2009 approximately 10 percent of the graduates claimed minority status, remaining in the same range as previously (between 9 percent and 13 percent annually). Unlike the gains of previous years, when, compared with all of the LIS graduates, the minority grads fell below the national starting averages ($40,475, or 4.2 percent below $42,268). A strong gender gap between men and women was readily apparent in an $8,500 difference in starting salaries between the two groups (women's starting average at $39,566, men's $48,151).

Minority graduates felt the best growth and highest level of salaries in school library media centers, with an average starting salary of $52,745. This was more than 17.8 percent higher than equivalent positions the previous year (when they started at $44,790), and 13.2 percent higher salary than received by all graduates entering school libraries in 2009. The only region in which the minority graduates experience positive improvements in salary and placements was in the Southeast. While salaries in general in the Southeast dropped slightly (declining 1.1 percent to $39,525), minority graduates moved upward 2.8 percent to $43,259 (compared with $42,084 in 2008), reversing the downward trend experienced between 2007 and 2008.

Minority placements in academic libraries grew from 25 percent of all minority jobs reported in 2008 to 31 percent in 2009. However, salaries in academic libraries did not keep pace and followed the overall pattern of decline, losing 15 percent from the high of 2008 ($37,539 compared with $44,182). A portion of this reduction can be attributed to 36 percent of the jobs accepted in academic libraries by minority candidates being nonprofessional positions with lower salaries (circulation, tech services, and interlibrary loan, for example).

On a bright note, these same graduates were able to negotiate higher starting salaries than all of their peers in both the Northeast and the Southeast (both regions that experienced salary compression in 2009). In the Northeast, minority graduates started 10 percent higher ($45,901 compared with $41,727), while in the Southeast they started out 9.7 percent higher ($43,259 compared with $39,440). In both instances, these graduates obtained salaries that were higher than the overall national average for new LIS graduates in 2009 (a combined average of 5.4 percent higher than $42,268). However, in the Northeast starting salaries were significantly below those negotiated in 2008.

As the Grads See It

Disappointment and disillusionment were words that the 2009 graduates used frequently when describing their postgraduate experiences. Some even expressed the wish that they had selected different areas for their graduate studies, such as health care administration or nursing. Still others felt great satisfaction with their new jobs, but tempered it with comments that they considered themselves "very, very lucky" to have found a full-time, permanent position with an adequate salary in a struggling economy.

As in the past, LIS graduates continue to be career changers, with 48 percent of the 2009 graduating class describing first and second professional careers before entering library and information science. Former professions continued to range from education, publishing, and human services to computer science, life sciences, and engineering. However, having a prior profession did not make the job search much easier. Those reporting job experience and other professional backgrounds averaged a job search of four and half months before finding a placement (full-time and part-time combined). Many of these career changers explained that if they did not have any library experience, either through internships and fieldwork or through nonprofessional jobs prior to graduating with an MLIS degree, the job search was difficult at best. Many employers were looking for two or three years of library experience. Interestingly, career changers had a much higher rate of unemployment compared with their peers seeking a first profession (7.3 percent unemployed compared with 4.5 percent). This suggests that not only was lack of library experience a detriment, but career changers encountered difficulty in parlaying previous experience into equivalent library experience.

Reports of layoffs occurred more frequently among the 2009 graduating class than in previous years. While the actual numbers appear to be small, for some the "last hired, first fired" principle held true. All types of libraries and information agencies were subjected to staff reductions. After a job search that lasted several months, hopes were dashed when budget cuts and reduced hours meant being laid off and back in the applicant pool. The frustration and disappointment was further compounded by the necessity of taking civil service exams that are offered infrequently, thus causing potential candidates an additional burden of being ineligible for public service jobs after being laid off from other types of agencies.

Members of the graduating class of 2009 did offer words of encouragement to their future colleagues, however. They repeatedly said "Be flexible," acknowledging that while the job search was difficult, for those willing to compromise something would come along. They also advised that future graduates must be willing to start small in order to move up and that graduates need to think about their information skills as valuable to other agencies beyond a traditional environment.

Graduates who found employment observed several key factors. First, job search is a process that will take time and effort and that the process must be managed carefully. Many felt that their application letters were incredibly important, and those letters required a high degree of customization to show how closely the applicant matched the available position. Some graduates explained that once they began focusing their job search and writing strong letters, the search eased—not necessarily becoming shorter, but at least generating interviews rather than outright rejections.

Fieldwork and internship opportunities have been highly cited in previous surveys as important to securing employment, and the 2009 graduates reemphasized that these activities were crucial to job success. Fieldwork and internships aided in putting classroom learning into practice and exposed graduates to potential employers. More than one graduate suggested completing an internship or volunteering in the place where the candidate wants a job. In addition, graduates who interned or volunteered said they gained valuable on-the-job experience required by employers as well as making connections within the professional community. They also gathered insider information about potential openings.

Early indications from the 2010 graduating class suggest that it will be another challenging year for finding jobs. They are sending out 50 to 60 résumés without landing an initial interview or even acknowledgements that a résumé has been received. Applicant pools continue to be huge, with employers having a wide range of experience levels and skills from which to select. LIS grads will need to continue to make compromises and be flexible in managing their education and job searches.

As a group, the 2009 graduates offer the suggestion that job candidates need to keep "all options open," "be diverse in their coursework," and take time to prepare through internships, volunteering, and networking.

Accredited Master's Programs in Library and Information Studies

This list of graduate programs accredited by the American Library Association is issued by the ALA Office for Accreditation. Regular updates and additional details appear on the Office for Accreditation's Web site at http://www.ala.org/Template.cfm?Section=lisdirb&Template=/cfapps/lisdir/index.cfm. More than 150 institutions offering both accredited and nonaccredited programs in librarianship are included in the 64th edition (2011–2012) of *American Library Directory* (Information Today, Inc.)

Northeast: Conn., D.C., Md., Mass., N.J., N.Y., Pa., R.I.

Catholic University of America, School of Lib. and Info. Science, 620 Michigan Ave. N.E., Washington, DC 20064. Ingrid Hsieh-Yee, Interim dean. Tel. 202-319-5085, fax 202-219-5574, e-mail cua-slis@cua.edu, World Wide Web http://slis.cua.edu. Admissions contact: Louise Gray. Tel. 202-319-5085, e-mail grayl@cua.edu.

Clarion University of Pennsylvania, College of Educ. and Human Services, Dept. of Lib. Science, 210 Carlson Lib. Bldg., 840 Wood St., Clarion, PA 16214. Janice M. Krueger, chair. Tel. 866-272-5612, fax 814-393-2150, World Wide Web http://www.clarion.edu/libsci. Admissions contact: Lois Dulavitch. Tel. 866-272-5612, e-mail ldulavitch@clarion.edu.

Drexel University, College of Info. Science and Technology, 3141 Chestnut St., Philadelphia, PA 19104-2875. David E. Fenske, dean. Tel. 215-895-2474, fax 215-895-2494, e-mail istinfo@drexel.edu, World Wide Web http://www.ischool.drexel.edu. Admissions contact: Matthew Lechtenburg. Tel. 215-895-1951, e-mail ml333@ischool.drexel.edu.

Long Island University, Palmer School of Lib. and Info. Science, C. W. Post Campus, 720 Northern Blvd., Brookville, NY 11548-1300. Linda M. Ryan, director. Tel. 516-299-2866, fax 516-299-4168, e-mail palmer@cwpost.liu.edu, World Wide Web http://www.liu.edu/palmer. Admissions contact: Geraldine Kopczynski. Tel. 516-299-2857, e-mail gkopski@liu.edu.

Pratt Institute, School of Info. and Lib. Science, 144 W. 14 St., New York, NY 10011. Tula Giannini, dean. Tel. 212-647-7682, fax 202-367-2492, e-mail infosils@pratt.edu, World Wide Web http://www.pratt.edu/academics/information_and_library_sciences. Admissions contact: Quinn Lai. E-mail infosils@pratt.edu.

Queens College, City Univ. of New York, Grad. School of Lib. and Info. Studies, Rm. 254, Rosenthal Lib., 65-30 Kissena Blvd., Flushing, NY 11367-1597. Thomas T. Surprenant, dir. Tel. 718-997-3790, fax 718-997-3797, e-mail gc_gslis@qc.cuny.edu, World Wide Web http://www.qc.edu/gslis. Admissions contact: Roberta Brody. E-mail roberta_brody@qc.edu.

Rutgers University, School of Communication and Info., Dept. of Lib. and Info. Science, New Brunswick, NJ 08901-1071. Claire R. McInerney, chair. Tel. 732-932-7500 ext. 8218, fax 732-932-6916, e-mail scilsmls@comminfo.rutgers.edu, World Wide Web http://www.comminfo.rutgers.edu. Admissions contact: Kay Cassell. Tel. 732-932-7500 ext. 8264.

Saint John's University, College of Liberal Arts and Sciences, Div. of Lib. and Info. Science, 8000 Utopia Pkwy., Queens, NY 11439. Jeffery E. Olson, dir. Tel. 718-990-6200, fax 718-990-2071, e-mail dlis@stjohns.edu, World Wide Web http://www.stjohns.edu/libraryscience. Admissions contact: Deborah Martinez. Tel. 718-990-6209.

Simmons College, Grad. School of Lib. and Info. Science, 300 The Fenway, Boston, MA 02115. Michele Cloonan, dean. Tel.

617-521-2800, fax 617-521-3192, e-mail gslis@simmons.edu, World Wide Web http://www.simmons.edu/gslis.

Southern Connecticut State University, School of Educ., Communication, Dept. of Info., and Lib. Science, 501 Crescent St., New Haven, CT 06515. Chang Suk Kim, chair. Tel. 203-392-5781, fax 203-392-5780, e-mail ils@southernct.edu, World Wide Web http://www.southernct.edu/ils. Admissions contact: Kathy Muldowney.

Syracuse University, School of Info. Studies, 343 Hinds Hall, Syracuse, NY 13244. Elizabeth D. Liddy, dean. Tel. 315-443-2911, fax 315-443-6886, e-mail ischool@syr.edu, World Wide Web http://www.ischool.syr.edu. Admissions contact: R. David Lankes. Tel. 315-443-2911, e-mail mslis@syr.edu.

University at Albany, State Univ. of New York, College of Computing and Info., Dept. of Info. Studies, Draper 113, 135 Western Ave., Albany, NY 12222. Terrence A. Maxwell, chair. Tel. 518-442-5110, fax 518-442-5367, e-mail infostudies@albany.edu, World Wide Web http://www.albany.edu/cci/informationstudies/index.shtml. Admissions contact: Frances Reynolds. E-mail reynolds@albany.edu.

University at Buffalo, State Univ. of New York, Graduate School of Educ., Lib. and Info. Studies, 534 Baldy Hall, Box 1020, Buffalo, NY 14260. Dagobert Soergel, chair. Tel. 716-645-2412, fax 716-645-3775, e-mail ub-lis@buffalo.edu, World Wide Web http://www.gse.buffalo.edu/lis. Admissions contact: Radhika Suresh. Tel. 716-645-2110, e-mail gse-info@buffalo.edu.

University of Maryland, College of Info. Studies, 4105 Hornbake Bldg., College Park, MD 20742. Jennifer Preece, dean. Tel. 301-405-2033, fax 301-314-9145, e-mail ischooladmission@umd.edu, World Wide Web http://ischool.umd.edu. Admissions contact: Cassandra B. Jones. Tel. 301-405-2038, e-mail ischooladmission@umd.edu.

University of Pittsburgh, School of Info. Sciences, 135 N. Bellefield Ave., Pittsburgh, PA 15260. Mary K. Biagini, chair. Tel. 412-624-9420, fax 412-648-7001, e-mail lisinq@mail.sis.pitt.edu, World Wide Web http://www.sis.pitt.edu. Admissions contact: Debbie Day. Tel. 412-624-9420, e-mail dday@sis.pitt.edu.

University of Rhode Island, Grad. School of Lib. and Info. Studies, Rodman Hall, 94 W. Alumni Ave., Kingston, RI 02881. Gale Eaton, dir. Tel. 401-874-2878, fax 401-874-4964, e-mail gslis@etal.uri.edu, World Wide Web http://www.uri.edu/artsci/lsc.

Southeast: Ala., Fla., Ga., Ky., La., Miss., N.C., S.C., Tenn., P.R.

Florida State University, College of Communication and Info., School of Lib. and Info. Studies, 142 Collegiate Loop, P.O. Box 3062100, Tallahassee, FL 32306-2100. Corinne Jorgensen, dir. Tel. 850-644-5775, fax 850-644-9763, World Wide Web http://slis.fsu.edu. Admissions contact: Delores Bryant. Tel. 850-645-3280, e-mail delores.bryant@cci.fsu.edu.

Louisiana State University, School of Lib. and Info. Science, 267 Coates Hall, Baton Rouge, LA 70803. Beth Paskoff, dean. Tel. 225-578-3158, fax 225-578-4581, e-mail slis@lsu.edu, World Wide Web http://slis.lsu.edu. Admissions contact: LaToya Coleman Joseph. E-mail lcjoseph@lsu.edu.

North Carolina Central University, School of Lib. and Info. Sciences, P.O. Box 19586, Durham, NC 27707. Irene Owens, dean. Tel. 919-530-6485, fax 919-530-6402, World Wide Web http://www.nccuslis.org. Admissions contact: Tysha Jacobs. Tel. 919-530-7320, e-mail tjacobs@nccu.edu.

University of Alabama, College of Communication and Info. Sciences, School of Lib. and Info. Studies, 515 Gorgas Lib., Capstone Drive, Box 870252, Tuscaloosa, AL 35487-0252. Elizabeth Aversa, dean. Tel. 205-348-4610, fax 205-348-3746, e-mail info@slis.ua.edu, World Wide Web http://www.slis.ua.edu. Admissions contact: Beth Riggs. Tel. 205-348-1527, e-mail briggs@slis.ua.edu.

University of Kentucky, School of Lib. and Info. Science, 320 Little Lib., Lexington, KY 40506-0224. Jeffrey T. Huber, dir. Tel. 859-257-8876, fax 859-257-4205, e-mail ukslis@uky.edu, World Wide Web http://www.uky.edu/CIS/SLIS. Admissions contact: Will Buntin. Tel. 859-257-3317, e-mail wjbunt0@uky.edu.

University of North Carolina at Chapel Hill, School of Info. and Lib. Science, CB 3360, 100 Manning Hall, Chapel Hill, NC 27599-3360. Gary Marchionini, dean. Tel. 919-962-8366, fax 919-962-8071, e-mail info@ils.unc.edu, World Wide Web http://www.sils.unc.edu. Admissions contact: Lara Bailey.

University of North Carolina at Greensboro, School of Educ., Dept. of Lib. and Info. Studies, 349 Curry Bldg., Greensboro, NC 27402-6170. Clara M. Chu, chair. Tel. 336-334-3477, fax 336-334-5060, World Wide Web http://lis.uncg.edu. Admissions contact: Cindy Felts. E-mail cpfelts@uncg.edu.

University of Puerto Rico, Info. Sciences and Technologies, P.O. Box 21906, San Juan, PR 00931-1906. Luisa Vigo-Cepeda, acting dir. Tel. 787-763-6199, fax 787-764-2311, e-mail egcti@uprrp.edu, World Wide Web http://egcti.upr.edu. Admissions contact: Migdalia Dávila-Perez. Tel. 787-764-0000 ext. 3530, e-mail migdalia.davila@upr.edu.

University of South Carolina, College of Mass Communications and Info. Studies, School of Lib. and Info. Science, 1501 Greene St., Columbia, SC 29208. Samantha K. Hastings, dir. Tel. 803-777-3858, fax 803-777-7938, e-mail hastings@sc.edu, World Wide Web http://www.libsci.sc.edu. Admissions contact: Tilda Reeder. Tel. 800-304-3153, e-mail tildareeder@sc.edu.

University of South Florida, College of Arts and Sciences, School of Lib. and Info. Science, 4202 E. Fowler Ave., CIS 1040, Tampa, FL 33620. James Andrews, interim dir. Tel. 813-974-3520, fax 813-974-6840, e-mail lisinfo@cas.usf.edu, World Wide Web http://slis.usf.edu. Admissions contact: Daniel Kahl. Tel. 813-974-8022, e-mail djkahl@usf.edu.

University of Southern Mississippi, College of Educ. and Psychology, School of Lib. and Info. Science, 118 College Drive, No. 5146, Hattiesburg, MS 39406-0001. M. J. Norton, dir. Tel. 601-266-4228, fax 601-266-5774, e-mail slis@usm.edu, World Wide Web http://www.usm.edu/slis. Admissions tel. 601-266-5137, e-mail graduatestudies@usm.edu.

University of Tennessee, College of Communication and Info., School of Info. Sciences, 451 Communication Bldg., Knoxville, TN 37996. Edwin M. Cortez, dir. Tel. 865-974-2148, fax 865-974-4967, World Wide Web http://www.sis.utk.edu. Admissions contact: Tanya Arnold. Tel. 865-974-2858, e-mail tnarnold@utk.edu.

Valdosta State Univ., Dept. of Info. Studies, 1500 N. Patterson St., Valdosta, GA 31698-0133. Wallace Koehler, dir. Tel. 229-333-5966, fax 229-259-5055, e-mail mlis@valdosta.edu, World Wide Web http://www.valdosta.edu/mlis. Admissions contact: Sheila Peacock.

Midwest: Ill., Ind., Iowa, Kan., Mich., Mo., Ohio, Wis.

Dominican University, Grad. School of Lib. and Info. Science, 7900 W. Division St., River Forest, IL 60305. Susan Roman, dean. Tel. 708-524-6845, fax 708-524-6657, e-mail gslis@dom.edu, World Wide Web http://www.gslis.dom.edu. Admissions contact: Bruce Zimmerman. Tel. 708-524-6848, e-mail bzimmerman@dom.edu.

Emporia State University, School of Lib. and Info. Management, 1200 Commercial, Campus Box 4025, Emporia, KS 66801. Gwen Alexander, dean. Tel. 620-341-5203, fax 620-341-5233, e-mail sliminfo@emporia.edu, World Wide Web http://slim.emporia.edu. Admissions contact: Candace Boardman. Tel. 620-341-6159, e-mail sliminfo@emporia.edu.

Indiana University, School of Lib. and Info. Science, 1320 E. 10 St., LI011, Bloomington, IN 47405-3907. Blaise Cronin, dean. Tel. 812-855-2018, fax 812-855-6166, e-mail slis@indiana.edu, World Wide Web http://www.slis.indiana.edu. Admissions contact: Rhonda Spencer.

Kent State University, School of Lib. and Info. Science, P.O. Box 5190, Kent, OH 44242-0001. Don A. Wicks, interim dir. Tel. 330-672-2782, fax 330-672-7965, e-mail inform@slis.kent.edu, World Wide Web http://www.slis.kent.edu. Admissions contact: Cheryl Tennant.

University of Illinois at Urbana-Champaign, Grad. School of Lib. and Info. Science, 501 E. Daniel St., Champaign, IL 61820-6211. John Unsworth, dean. Tel. 217-333-3280, fax 217-244-3302, e-mail gslis@Illinois.edu, World Wide Web http://www.lis.uiuc.edu. Admissions contact: Penny Ames. Tel. 217-333-7197, e-mail pames@illinois.edu.

University of Iowa, Graduate College, School of Lib. and Info. Science, 3087 Main Lib., Iowa City, IA 52242-1420. James K. Elmborg, dir. Tel. 319-335-5707, fax 319-335-5374, e-mail slis@uiowa.edu, World Wide Web http://slis.uiowa.edu/~slisweb. Admissions contact: Kit Austin. E-mail caroline-austin@uiowa.edu.

University of Michigan, School of Info., 4322 North Quad, 105 W. St., Ann Arbor, MI 48109-1285. Jeffrey MaKie-Mason, dean. Tel. 734-763-2285, fax 734-764-2475, e-mail si.admissions@umich.edu, World Wide Web http://www.si.umich.edu. Admissions contact: Laura Elgas. E-mail si.admissions@umich.edu.

University of Missouri, College of Educ., School of Info. Science and Learning Technologies, 303 Townsend Hall, Columbia, MO 65211. John Wedman, dir. Tel. 877-747-5868, fax 573-884-0122, e-mail sislt@missouri.edu, World Wide Web http://sislt.missouri.edu. Admissions tel. 573-882-4546.

University of Wisconsin–Madison, College of Letters and Sciences, School of Lib. and Info. Studies, Rm. 4217, H. C. White Hall, 600 N. Park St., Madison, WI 53706. Christine Pawley, dir. Tel. 608-263-2900, fax 608-263-4849, e-mail uw-slis@slis.wisc.edu, World Wide Web http://www.slis.wisc.edu. Admissions contact: Andrea Poehling. Tel. 608-263-2909, e-mail student-services@slis.wisc.edu.

University of Wisconsin–Milwaukee, School of Info. Studies, P.O. Box 413, Milwaukee, WI 53211. Hope Olson, acting dean. Tel. 414-229-4707, fax 414-229-6699, e-mail soisinfo@uwm.edu, World Wide Web http://www4.uwm.edu/sois. Admissions tel. 414-229-4707.

Wayne State University, School of Lib. and Info. Science, 106 Kresge Lib., Detroit, MI 48202. Stephen T. Bajjaly, dir. Tel. 313-577-1825, fax 313-577-7563, e-mail asklis@wayne.edu, World Wide Web http://www.slis.wayne.edu. Admissions contact: Matthew Fredericks. Tel. 313-577-2446, e-mail mfredericks@wayne.edu.

Southwest: Ariz., Okla., Texas

Texas Woman's University, School of Lib. and Info. Studies, P.O. Box 425438, Denton, TX 76204-5438. Ling Hwey Jeng, dir. Tel. 940-898-2602, fax 940-898-2611, e-mail slis@twu.edu, World Wide Web http://www.twu.edu/library-studies. Admissions contact: Brenda Mallory. E-mail bmallory@mail.two.edu.

University of Arizona, College of Social and Behavioral Sciences, School of Info. Resources and Lib. Science, 1515 E. 1 St., Tucson, AZ 85719. P. Bryan Heidorn, dir. Tel. 520-621-3565, fax 520-621-3279, e-mail sirls@email.arizona.edu, World Wide Web http://www.sirls.arizona.edu. Admissions contact: Geraldine Fragoso. Tel. 520-621-5230, e-mail gfragoso@u.arizona.edu.

University of North Texas, College of Info., Dept. of Lib. and Info. Sciences, 1155 Union Circle, No. 311068, Denton, TX 76203-5017. Herman L. Totten, dean. Tel. 940-565-2445, fax 940-565-3101, e-mail ci-dean@unt.edu, World Wide Web http://www.ci.unt.edu/main. Admissions contact: John Pipes. Tel. 940-565-3562, e-mail john.pipes@unt.edu.

University of Oklahoma, School of Lib. and Info. Studies, College of Arts and Sciences, Rm. 120, 401 W. Brooks, Norman, OK 73019-6032. Cecelia Brown, dir. Tel. 405-325-3921, fax 405-325-7648, e-mail slisinfo@ou.edu, World Wide Web http://www.ou.edu/cas/slis. Admissions contact: Maggie Ryan.

University of Texas at Austin, School of Info., Suite 5.202, 1616 Guadalupe St., Austin, TX 78701-1213. Andrew Dillon, dean. Tel. 512-471-3821, fax 512-471-3971, e-mail info@ischool.utexas.edu, World Wide Web http://www.ischool.utexas.edu. Admissions contact: Carla Criner. Tel. 512-471-5654, e-mail criner@ischool.utexas.edu.

West: Calif., Colo., Hawaii, Wash.

San José State University, School of Lib. and Info. Science, 1 Washington Sq., San José, CA 95192-0029. Sandy Hirsh, dir. Tel. 408-924-2490, fax 408-924-2476, e-mail sanjoseslis@gmail.com, World Wide Web http://slisweb.sjsu.edu. Admissions contact: Linda Main. Tel. 408-924-2494, e-mail Linda.main@ sjsu.edu.

University of California, Los Angeles, Graduate School of Educ. and Info. Studies, Dept. of Info. Studies, Box 951520, Los Angeles, CA 90095-1520. Gregory Leazer, interim chair. Tel. 310-825-8799, fax 310-206-3076, e-mail info@gseis.ucla.edu, World Wide Web http://is.gseis.ucla.edu. Admissions contact: Susan Abler. Tel. 310-825-5269, e-mail abler@gseis.ucla.edu.

University of Denver, Morgridge College of Educ., Lib. and Info. Science Program, 1999 E. Evans Ave., Denver, CO 80208-1700. Mary Stansbury, chair. Tel. 303-871-2747, fax 303-871-2709, World Wide Web http://www.du.edu/lis. Admissions contact: Nick Heckart. E-mail nheckart@du.edu.

University of Hawaii, College of Natural Sciences, Lib. and Info. Science Program, 2550 McCarthy Mall, Honolulu, HI 96822. Peter Jacso, chair. Tel. 808-956-7321, fax 808-956-3548, e-mail slis@hawaii.edu, World Wide Web http://www.hawaii.edu/slis.

University of Washington, The Info. School, 370 Mary Gates Hall, Seattle, WA 98195-2840. Harry Bruce, dean. Tel. 206-685-9937, fax 206-616-3152, e-mail ischool@uw.edu, World Wide Web http://ischool.uw.edu. Admissions contact: Admissions coordinator. Tel. 206-543-1794, e-mail mlis@ischool.uw.edu.

Canada

Dalhousie University, School of Info. Management, Kenneth C. Rowe Management Bldg., Halifax, NS B3H 3J5. Louise Spiteri, dir. Tel. 902-494-3656, fax 902-494-2451, e-mail sim@dal.ca, World Wide Web http://www.sim.management.dal.ca. Admissions contact: JoAnn Watson. E-mail mlis@dal.ca.

McGill University, School of Info. Studies, 3661 Peel St., Montreal, QC H3A 1X1. France Bouthillier, dir. Tel. 514-398-4204, fax 514-398-7193, e-mail sis@mcgill.ca, World Wide Web http://www.mcgill.ca/sis. Admissions contact: Kathryn Hubbard, Tel. 514-398-4204 ext. 0742.

Université de Montréal, École de Bibliothéconomie et des Sciences de l'Information, C.P. 6128, Succursale Centre-Ville, Montreal, QC H3C 3J7. Clément Arsenault, dir. Tel. 514-343-6044, fax 514-343-5753, e-mail ebsiinfo@ebsi.umontreal.ca, World Wide Web http://www.ebsi.umontreal.ca. Admissions contact: Alain Tremblay. Tel. 514-343-6044, e-mail alain.tremblay.1@umontreal.ca.

University of Alberta, School of Lib. and Info. Studies, 3-20 Rutherford S., Edmonton, AB T6G 2J4. Ernie Ingles, dir. Tel. 780-492-4578, fax 780-492-2430, e-mail slis@ualberta.ca, World Wide Web http://www.slis.ualberta.ca. Admissions contact: Aman Powar-Grewal. Tel. 780-492-4140, e-mail slisadmissions@ualberta.ca.

University of British Columbia, School of Lib., Archival, and Info. Studies, Irving K.

Barber Learning Centre, Vancouver, BC V6T 1Z1. Caroline Haythornthwaite, dir. Tel. 604-822-2404, fax 604-822-6006, e-mail slais@interchange.ubc.ca, World Wide Web http://www.slais.ubc.ca. Admissions contact: Michelle Mallette. E-mail slaisad@interchange.ubc.ca.

University of Toronto, Faculty of Info., Rm. 211, 140 George St., Toronto, ON M5S 3G6. Seamus Ross, dean. Tel. 416-978-3202, fax 416-978-5762, e-mail inquire@ischool.utoronto.ca, World Wide Web http://www.ischool.utoronto.ca. Admissions contact: Judy Dunn. Tel. 416-978-3934, e-mail judy.dunn@utoronto.ca.

University of Western Ontario, Grad. Programs in Lib. and Info. Science, Faculty of Info. and Media Studies, Room 240, North Campus Bldg., London, ON N6A 5B7. Thomas Carmichael, dean. Tel. 519-661-4017, fax 519-661-3506, e-mail mlisinfo@uwo.ca, World Wide Web http://fims.uwo.ca. Admissions contact: Shelley Long.

Library Scholarship Sources

For a more complete list of scholarships, fellowships, and assistantships offered for library study, see *Financial Assistance for Library and Information Studies,* published annually by the American Library Association (ALA). The document is also available on the ALA Web site at http://www.ala.org/ala/educationcareers/education/financialassistance/index.cfm.

American Association of Law Libraries. (1) A varying number of scholarships of a minimum of $1,000 for graduates of an accredited law school who are degree candidates in an ALA-accredited library school; (2) a varying number of scholarships of varying amounts for library school graduates working on a law degree and non-law graduates enrolled in an ALA-accredited library school; (3) the George A. Strait Minority Stipend of $3,500 for varying numbers of minority librarians working toward a library or law degree; and (4) a varying number of $500 scholarships for law librarians taking courses relating to law librarianship. For information, write to: Scholarship Committee, AALL, 53 W. Jackson Blvd., Suite 940, Chicago, IL 60604, or see http://www.aallnet.org/services/scholarships.asp.

American Library Association. (1) The Marshall Cavendish Scholarship of $3,000 for a varying number of students who have been admitted to an ALA-accredited library school; (2) the David H. Clift Scholarship of $3,000 for a varying number of students who have been admitted to an ALA-accredited library school; (3) the Tom and Roberta Drewes Scholarship of $3,000 for a varying number of library support staff; (4) the Mary V. Gaver Scholarship of $3,000 for a varying number of individuals specializing in youth services; (5) the Miriam L. Hornback Scholarship of $3,000 for a varying number of ALA or library support staff; (6) the Christopher J. Hoy/ERT Scholarship of $5,000 for a varying number of students who have been admitted to an ALA-accredited library school; (7) the Tony B. Leisner Scholarship of $3,000 for a varying number of library support staff; (8) the Peter Lyman Memorial/SAGE Scholarship in New Media of $2,500 for a student admitted to an ALA accredited library school and specializing in new media; (9) the Cicely Phippen Marks Scholarship of $1,500 for a student admitted to an ALA-accredited program and specializing in federal librarianship; (10) Spectrum Initiative Scholarships of $6,500 for a varying number of minority students admitted to an ALA-accredited library school. For information, write to: ALA Scholarship Clearinghouse, 50 E. Huron St., Chicago, IL 60611, or see http://www.ala.org/scholarships.

ALA/Association for Library Service to Children. (1) The Bound to Stay Bound Books Scholarship of $7,000 each for four students who are U.S. or Canadian citizens, who have been admitted to an ALA-accredited master's or doctoral program, and who will work with children in a library for one year after graduation; (2) the Frederic G. Melcher Scholarship of $6,000 each for two U.S. or Canadian citizens admitted to an ALA-accredited library school who will work with children in school or public libraries for one year after graduation. For information, write to: ALA Scholarship Clearinghouse, 50 E. Huron St., Chicago, IL 60611, or see http://www.ala.org/scholarships.

ALA/Association of College and Research Libraries and Thomson Reuters. (1) The ACRL Doctoral Dissertation Fellowship of $1,500 for a student who has completed all coursework, and submitted a dissertation proposal that has been accepted, in the area of academic librarianship; (2) the Samuel Lazerow Fellowship of $1,000 for a research, travel, or writing project in acquisitions or technical services in an academic or research library; (3) the ACRL and Coutts Nijhoff International

West European Specialist Study Grant of $3,000 to pay travel expenses, room, and board for a ten-day trip to Europe for an ALA member (selection is based on proposal outlining purpose of trip). For information, write to: Megan Griffin, ALA/ACRL, 50 E. Huron St., Chicago, IL 60611.

ALA/Association of Specialized and Cooperative Library Agencies. Century Scholarship of up to $2,500 for a varying number of disabled U.S. or Canadian citizens admitted to an ALA-accredited library school. For information, write to: ALA Scholarship Clearinghouse, 50 E. Huron St., Chicago, IL 60611, or see http://www.ala.org/scholarships.

ALA/International Relations Committee. The Bogle Pratt International Library Travel Fund grant of $1,000 for a varying number of ALA members to attend a first international conference. For information, write to: Michael Dowling, ALA/IRC, 50 E. Huron St., Chicago, IL 60611.

ALA/Library and Information Technology Association. (1) The LITA/Christian Larew Memorial Scholarship of $3,000 for a disabled U.S. or Canadian citizen admitted to an ALA-accredited library school; (2) the LITA/OCLC Minority Scholarship in Library and Information Technology of $3,000 and (3) the LITA/LSSI Minority Scholarship of $2,500, each for a minority student admitted to an ALA-accredited program. For information, write to: ALA Scholarship Clearinghouse, 50 E. Huron St., Chicago, IL 60611, or see http://www.ala.org/scholarships.

ALA/Public Library Association. The Demco New Leaders Travel Grant Study Award of up to $1,500 for a varying number of PLA members with MLS degrees and five years or less experience. For information, write to: PLA Awards Program, ALA/PLA, 50 E. Huron St., Chicago, IL 60611.

American-Scandinavian Foundation. Fellowships and grants for 25 to 30 students, in amounts from $5,000 to $23,000, for advanced study in Denmark, Finland, Iceland, Norway, or Sweden. For information, write to: Fellowships and Grants, American-Scandinavian Foundation, 58 Park Ave., New York, NY 10026, or see http://www.amscan.org/fellowships_grants.html.

Association for Library and Information Science Education (ALISE). A varying number of research grants of up to $2,500 each for members of ALISE. For information, write to: Association for Library and Information Science Education, 65 E. Wacker Place, Suite 1900, Chicago, IL 60601.

Association of Jewish Libraries. The AJL Scholarship Fund offers up to two scholarships of $500 each for MLS students who plan to work as Judaica librarians. For information, write to: Lynn Feinman, 92nd St. Y Library, 1395 Lexington Ave., New York, NY 10128 (e-mail lfeinman@92Y.org).

Association of Seventh-Day Adventist Librarians. The D. Glenn Hilts Scholarship of $1,200 for a member of the Seventh-Day Adventist Church in a graduate library program. For information, write to: Lee Wisel, Association of Seventh-Day Adventist Librarians, Columbia Union College, 7600 Flower Ave., Takoma Park, MD 20912.

Beta Phi Mu. (1) The Sarah Rebecca Reed Scholarship of $2,000 for a person accepted in an ALA-accredited library program; (2) the Frank B. Sessa Scholarship of $1,500 for a Beta Phi Mu member for continuing education; (3) the Harold Lancour Scholarship of $1,750 for study in a foreign country relating to the applicant's work or schooling; (4) the Blanche E. Woolls Scholarship for School Library Media Service of $2,250 for a person accepted in an ALA-accredited library program; (5) the Eugene Garfield Doctoral Dissertation Scholarship of $3,000 for a person who has approval of a dissertation topic. For information, write to: Christie Koontz, Executive Director, Beta Phi Mu, College of Information, Florida State University, 101H Louis Shores Building, 142 Collegiate Loop, Tallahassee, FL 32306-2100.

Canadian Association of Law Libraries. The Diana M. Priestly Scholarship of $2,500 for a student with previous law library experience or for entry to an approved

Canadian law school or accredited Canadian library school. For information, write to: Janet Mass, Chair, CALL/ACBD Scholarship and Awards Committee, Gerard V. La Forest Law Library, University of New Brunswick, Bag Service 44999, Fredericton, NB E38 6C9.

Canadian Federation of University Women. (1) The Alice E. Wilson Award of $6,000 for five mature students returning to graduate studies in any field, with special consideration given to those returning to study after at least three years; (2) the Margaret McWilliams Pre-Doctoral Fellowship of $13,000 for a female student who has completed at least one full year as a full-time student in doctoral-level studies; (3) the Marion Elder Grant Fellowship of $11,000 for a full time student at any level of a doctoral program; (4) the CFUW Memorial Fellowship of $10,000 for a student who is currently enrolled in a master's program in science, mathematics, or engineering in Canada or abroad; (5) the Beverly Jackson Fellowship of $2,000 for a student over the age of 35 at the time of application who is enrolled in graduate studies at an Ontario university; (6) the 1989 Ecole Polytechnique Commemorative Award of $7,000 for graduate studies in any field; (7) the Bourse Georgette LeMoyne award of $7,000 for graduate study in any field at a Canadian university (the candidate must be studying in French); (8) the Margaret Dale Philp Biennial Award of $3,000 for studies in the humanities or social sciences; (9) the Canadian Home Economics Association Fellowship of $6,000 for a student enrolled in a postgraduate program in Canada. For information, write to: Fellowships Program Manager, Canadian Federation of University Women, 305-251 Bank St., Suite 305, Ottawa, ON K2P 1X3, Canada, or see http://www.cfuw.org.

Canadian Library Association. (1) The CLA Dafoe Scholarship of $5,000; and (2) the H. W. Wilson Scholarship of $2,000, each given to a Canadian citizen or landed immigrant to attend an accredited Canadian library school; (3) the Library Research and Development Grant of $1,000 for a member of the Canadian Library Association, in support of theoretical and applied research in library and information science. For information, write to: CLA Membership Services Department, Scholarship Committee, 1150 Morrison Drive, Suite 400, Ottawa, ON K2H 8S9, Canada.

Catholic Library Association. (1) The World Book, Inc., Grant of $1,500 divided among no more than three CLA members for continuing education in children's or school librarianship; (2) the Rev. Andrew L. Bouwhuis Memorial Scholarship of $1,500 for a student accepted into a graduate program in library science. For information, write to: Jean R. Bostley, SSJ, Scholarship Chair, Catholic Library Association, 100 North St., Suite 224, Pittsfield, MA 01201-5109.

Chinese American Librarians Association. (1) The Sheila Suen Lai Scholarship and (2) the C. C. Seetoo/CALA Conference Travel Scholarship each offer $500 to a Chinese descendant who has been accepted in an ALA-accredited program. For information, write to: MengXiong Liu, Clark Library, San José State University, 1 Washington Sq., San Jose, CA 95192-0028.

Church and Synagogue Library Association. The Muriel Fuller Memorial Scholarship of $200 (including texts) for a correspondence course offered by the association. For information, write to: CSLA, 2920 S.W. Dolph Court, Suite 3A, Portland, OR 97280-0357.

Council on Library and Information Resources. (1) The Rovelstad Scholarship in International Librarianship, to enable a student enrolled in an accredited LIS program to attend the IFLA Annual Conference; (2) the A. R. Zipf Fellowship in Information Management of $10,000, awarded annually to a U.S. citizen enrolled in graduate school who shows exceptional promise for leadership and technical achievement. For more information, write to: A. R. Zipf Fellowship, Council on Library and Information Resources, 1752 N St. N.W., Suite 800, Washington, DC 20036.

Massachusetts Black Librarians' Network. Two scholarships of at least $500 and $1,000 for minority students entering an ALA-accredited master's program in library science with no more 12 semester hours completed toward a degree. For information, write to: Pearl Mosley, Chair, Massachusetts Black Librarians' Network, 17 Beech Glen St., Roxbury, MA 02119.

Medical Library Association. (1) The Cunningham Memorial International Fellowship of $3,500 for each of two health sciences librarians from countries other than the United States and Canada; (2) a scholarship of $5,000 for a person entering an ALA-accredited library program, with no more than one-half of the program yet to be completed; (3) a scholarship of $5,000 for a minority student for graduate study; (4) a varying number of Research, Development, and Demonstration Project Grants of $100 to $1,000 for U.S. or Canadian citizens who are MLA members; (5) the MLA Doctoral Fellowship of $2,000 for doctoral work in medical librarianship or information science; (6) the Rittenhouse Award of $500 for a student enrolled in an ALA-accredited library program or a recent graduate working as a trainee in a library internship program. For information, write to: Professional Development Department, Medical Library Association, 65 E. Wacker Place, Suite 1900, Chicago, IL 60601-7298.

Society of American Archivists. (1) The Colonial Dames Awards, two grants of $1,200 each for specific types of repositories and collections. For information, write to: Debra Noland, Society of American Archivists, 521 S. Wells St., 5th fl., Chicago, IL 60607.

Southern Regional Education Board. A varying number of grants of varying amounts to cover in-state tuition for graduate or postgraduate study in an ALA-accredited library school for residents of various southern U.S. states (qualifying states vary year by year). For information, write to: Academic Common Market, c/o Southern Regional Education Board, 592 Tenth St. N.W., Atlanta, GA 30318-5790.

Special Libraries Association. (1) Three $6,000 scholarships for students interested in special-library work; (2) the Plenum Scholarship of $1,000 and (3) the ISI Scholarship of $1,000, each also for students interested in special-library work; (4) the Affirmative Action Scholarship of $6,000 for a minority student interested in special-library work; and (5) the Pharmaceutical Division Stipend Award of $1,200 for a student with an undergraduate degree in chemistry, life sciences, or pharmacy entering or enrolled in an ALA-accredited program. For information on the first four scholarships, write to: Scholarship Committee, Special Libraries Association, 331 S. Patrick St., Alexandria, VA 22314-3501. For information on the Pharmaceutical Stipend, write to: Susan E. Katz, Awards Chair, Knoll Pharmaceuticals Science Information Center, 30 N. Jefferson St., Whippany, NJ 07981.

Library Scholarship and Award Recipients, 2010

Compiled by the Staff of the Library and Book Trade Almanac

Scholarships and awards are listed by organization.

American Association of Law Libraries (AALL)

AALL Public Access to Government Information Award. *Winner:* Legal Information Institute, Cornell Law School.

AALL Scholarships. *Winners:* (library degree for law school graduates) Scott Akehurst-Moore, Benita Ghura, Ellen Richardson, Grace Rosales; (library school for non-law school graduates) Joanne Gialelis, Jeffrey Nelson; (law school for those seeking a dual law degree/MLIS) Jennifer Ekblaw.

AALL Spectrum Article of the Year Award. *Winner:* James M. Donovan for "Back Away from the Survey Monkey! Optimize Research Results with an Honest Assessment of Methodology" (*AALL Spectrum,* November 2009).

AALL and Thomson West/George A. Strait Minority Scholarship. *Winners:* Andrew Christensen, Donyele Darrough, Benita Ghura, Jeffrey Nelson, Grace Rosales.

Joseph L. Andrews Bibliographic Award. *Winner:* Kent C. Olson for *Principles of Legal Research* (West).

Marian Gould Gallagher Distinguished Service Award. To recognize extended and sustained service to law librarianship. *Winner:* Marie E. Whited.

Law Library Journal Article of the Year. *Winner:* Stephanie L. Plotin for "Legal Scholarship, Electronic Publishing, and Open Access: Transformation or Steadfast Stagnation." *Law Library Journal* vol. 101, no. 31 (2009).

Law Library Publications Award (nonprint division). *Winner:* Rutgers University Law School Library for "Same-Sex Marriage: A Selective Bibliography of the Legal Literature."

LexisNexis/John R. Johnson Memorial Scholarships. *Winners:* (library degree for law school graduates) Ronald Fuller; (law degree for library school graduates) Robert Malesko; (dual library degree and law degree) Jennifer Ekblaw.

Minority Leadership Development Award. *Winner:* Sean H. Crane.

Robert L. Oakley Member Advocacy Award. *Winner:* Ohio Regional Association of Law Libraries County Law Library Special Interest Group.

American Library Association (ALA)

ALA/Information Today Library of the Future Award ($1,500). For a library, consortium, group of librarians, or support organization for innovative planning for, applications of, or development of patron training programs about information technology in a library setting. *Donor:* Information Today, Inc. *Winner:* University of Michigan, Ann Arbor, for its "Enriching Scholarship" program.

ALA Presidential Citations for Innovative International Library Projects. To libraries outside the United States for significant contributions to the people they serve. *Winners:* Fondation Connaissance et Liberté / Fondasyon Konesans Ak Libète (FOKAL) Community Libraries Initiative; International Children's Digital Library, Afghanistan Centre at Kabul University Box Library Extension (ABLE); Library Society of China National Library Volunteering Project, World Digital Library.

Leo Albert Spectrum Scholarship. To a designated Spectrum Scholarship recipient. *Donor:* Leo Albert. *Winner:* Lisa West.

Hugh C. Atkinson Memorial Award. For outstanding achievement (including risk taking) by academic librarians that has contributed significantly to improvements in library automation, management, and/or development or research. *Offered by:*

ACRL, ALCTS, LLAMA, and LITA divisions. *Winner:* Paula T. Kaufman.

Carroll Preston Baber Research Grant (up to $3,000). For innovative research that could lead to an improvement in library services to any specified group(s) of people. *Donor:* Eric R. Baber. *Winner:* Betsy Simpson for "Shifting Patterns: Examining the Impact of Hiring Non-MLS Librarians."

Beta Phi Mu Award ($1,000). For distinguished service in library education. *Donor:* Beta Phi Mu International Library Science Honorary Society. *Winner:* Ken Haycock.

Bogle-Pratt International Library Travel Fund Award ($1,000). To ALA member(s) to attend their first international conference. *Donors:* Bogle Memorial Fund and Pratt Institute School of Information and Library Science. *Winner:* Susan Matveyeva.

W. Y. Boyd Literary Novel Award. *Winner:* See "Literary Prizes, 2010" in Part 5.

David H. Clift Scholarship ($3,000). To worthy U.S. or Canadian citizens enrolled in an ALA-accredited program toward an MLS degree. *Winner:* Laura Sue Manley.

Eileen Cooke State and Local James Madison Award. To recognize individuals or groups who have championed public access to government information. *Winner*: Not awarded in 2010.

Melvil Dewey Medal ($2,000). To an individual or group for recent creative professional achievement in library management, training, cataloging and classification, and the tools and techniques of librarianship. *Donor:* OCLC/Forest Press. *Winner:* Brian E. C. Schottlaender.

Tom and Roberta Drewes Scholarship ($3,000). To a library support staff member pursuing a master's degree. *Donor:* Quality Books. *Winner:* Brenda Sevigny-Killen.

EBSCO/ALA Conference Sponsorship Award ($1,000). To enable librarians to attend the ALA Annual Conference. *Donor:* EBSCO. *Winners:* Sonnet Erin Brown, Min Chou, Jaime Corris Hammond, Hyun-Duck Chung, Judith A. Downie, Jenny Emanuel, Valeria Gallo Stampino.

Equality Award ($1,000). To an individual or group for an outstanding contribution that promotes equality in the library profession. *Donor:* Scarecrow Press. *Winner:* Patricia Tarin.

Elizabeth Futas Catalyst for Change Award ($1,000). A biennial award to recognize a librarian who invests time and talent to make positive change in the profession of librarianship. *Donor:* Elizabeth Futas Memorial Fund. *Winner:* Loida García-Febo.

Loleta D. Fyan Public Library Research Grant (up to $10,000). For projects in public library development. *Donor:* Fyan Estate. *Winner:* Pamela MacKellar for "Online Management Course for New Library Directors in New Mexico."

Gale Cengage Learning Financial Development Award ($2,500). To a library organization for a financial development project to secure new funding resources for a public or academic library. *Donor:* Gale Cengage Learning. *Winner:* Friends of the Princeton (New Jersey) Public Library.

Mary V. Gaver Scholarship ($3,000). To a student pursuing an MLS degree and specializing in youth services. *Winner:* Bridget Ward.

Louise Giles Spectrum Scholarship. To a designated Spectrum Scholarship recipient. *Donor:* Louise Giles. *Winner:* Mosi Kamau.

William R. Gordon Spectrum Scholarship. To a designated Spectrum Scholarship recipient. *Donor:* William R. Gordon and friends. *Winner:* Christian Minter.

Greenwood Publishing Group Award for Best Book in Library Literature ($5,000). To recognize authors of U.S. or Canadian works whose books improve library management principles and practice. *Donor:* Greenwood Publishing Group. *Winners:* Robert E. Dugan, Peter Hernon, and Danuta A. Nitecki for *Viewing Library Metrics from Different Perspectives: Inputs, Outputs, and Outcomes* (Libraries Unlimited).

Ken Haycock Award for Promoting Librarianship ($1,000). For significant contribution to public recognition and appreciation of librarianship through professional performance, teaching, or writing. *Winner:* Michael Gorman.

Honorary ALA Membership. To recognize outstanding contributions of lasting importance to libraries and librarianship. *Honoree:* Not awarded in 2010.

Miriam L. Hornback Scholarship ($3,000). To an ALA or library support staff person pursuing a master's degree in library science. *Winner:* Diana J. Lennon.

Paul Howard Award for Courage ($1,000). Awarded biennially to a librarian, library board, library group, or an individual for exhibiting unusual courage for the benefit of library programs or services. *Donor:* Paul Howard Memorial Fund. *Winners (2009):* Judith Flint, Amy Grasmick, Christine Lesinski.

John Ames Humphry/OCLC/Forest Press Award ($1,000). To one or more individuals for significant contributions to international librarianship. *Donor:* OCLC/Forest Press. *Winners:* H. Lea Wells and Jordan Scepanski.

Tony B. Leisner Scholarship ($3,000). To a library support staff member pursuing a master's degree program. *Donor:* Tony B. Leisner. *Winner:* Madeline Bentley.

Joseph W. Lippincott Award ($1,000). For distinguished service to the library profession. *Donor:* Joseph W. Lippincott, III. *Winner:* Thomas C. Phelps, director, Division of Public Programs, National Endowment for the Humanities.

Peter Lyman Memorial/Sage Scholarship in New Media ($2,500). *Donor:* Sage Publications. *Winner:* Cynthia Lovett.

James Madison Award. To recognize efforts to promote government openness. *Winners:* Meredith Fuchs, General Counsel to the National Security Archive, and the Citizens for Responsibility and Ethics in Washington (CREW).

Marshall Cavendish Excellence in Library Programming Award ($2,000). To recognize either a school library or public library that demonstrates excellence in library programming by providing programs that have community impact and respond to community need. *Donor:* Marshall Cavendish. *Winner:* Queens (New York) Library for HealthLink, which brings cancer information and treatment referrals to Queens Borough's medically underserved communities.

Marshall Cavendish Scholarship ($3,000). To a worthy U.S. or Canadian citizen to begin an MLS degree in an ALA-accredited program. *Winner:* Mackenzie Brooks.

Grolier Foundation Award. See Scholastic Library Publishing Award.

Medical Library Association/National Library of Medicine Spectrum Scholarship. To a designated Spectrum Scholarship recipient or recipients. *Donors:* Medical Library Association, National Library of Medicine. *Winners:* Holly Beeman, Mariaelena de la Rosa.

Schneider Family Book Awards. *Winners:* See "Literary Prizes, 2010" in Part 5.

Scholastic Library Publishing Award (formerly the Grolier Foundation Award) ($1,000). For stimulation and guidance of reading by children and young people. *Donor:* Scholastic Library Publishing. *Winner:* Joni Richards Bodart.

Spectrum Doctoral Fellowships. To provide full tuition support and stipends to minority U.S. and Canadian LIS doctoral students. *Donor:* Institute of Museum and Library Services. *Winners:* Not awarded in 2010.

Spectrum Initiative Scholarships ($5,000). Presented to minority students admitted to ALA-accredited library schools. *Donors:* ALA and Institute of Museum and Library Services. *Winners:* Ameerah Al-Mateen, Ana-Elisa Arredondo, Sheena Barbour, JaTara Barnes, Julianna Barrera-Gomez, Sofia Becerra-Licha, Holly Beeman, Joseph Bellanca, Felipe Alberto Castillo, Vivian Choy, Grace Chung, Carla-Mae Crookendale, Sherry Elaine Cuadrado, Mariaelena de la Rosa, LaNesha "Gail" DeBardelaben, Wendy Dere, Hoan-Vu Do, Janis Elmore, Emmanuel L. Faulkner, Concepcion Flores, Yrenes Fornes, Sylvia Franco, Nancy Gallegos, Yvonne Garcia, Katrina Gardner, Jennifer Irene Garrett, Benita Ghura, Mary E. Gibson, Peter Grassman, Aron B. Gutierrez, Darla Rose Gutierrez, Jennifer Hamada, Dorothy Hargett, Brandon Hodge, Julie Hong, Amiya P. Hutson, Latanya Ingraham, Angelica Johnson, Andrea G. Johnson, Mosi Kamau, Emily

Kornak, Christopher Kyauk, Jacqueline Macias, Katy Mahraj, Sylvia Martinez, Leni Matthews, Ramona Melody, Claudia M. Melton, Christian Minter, Jeri C. Morton, Julie Motooka, Karla Anne Merino Nielsen, Jefferson Perales, Vanessa Pozan, Erin Prentiss, Daniel Ramirez, Anna Lisa Raya Rivera, Yesenia Rosado, Sarah Hashemi Scott, Sandy Shitanishi, Mishalla Spearing, Rachel Keiko Stark, Sean Sullivan, Julie Tanaka, Adoracion Thomas, Jade Torres-Morrison, Susan Trujillo, Kia Vang, James W. Wallace, Jr., Amanda Webb-Trujillo, Kui Wedemeyer, Lisa West, LaMonica Wiggins, Stacie Williams, Haruko Yamauchi.

Sullivan Award for Public Library Administrators Supporting Services to Children. To a library supervisor/administrator who has shown exceptional understanding and support of public library services to children. *Donor:* Peggy Sullivan. *Winner:* Neel Parikh, Pierce County (Washington) Library System.

Howard M. and Gladys B. Teeple Spectrum Scholarship. To a designated Spectrum Scholarship recipient. *Donor:* Religion and Ethics Institute. *Winner:* Janis Elmore.

Dr. Betty J. Turock Spectrum Scholarship. To a designated Spectrum Scholarship recipient. *Winner:* Anna Lisa Raya Rivera.

H. W. Wilson Library Staff Development Grant ($3,500). To a library organization for a program to further its staff development goals and objectives. *Donor:* H. W. Wilson Company. *Winner:* Kelvin Smith Library, Case Western Reserve University, for "Traveling and Training with Technology (T3): A Tool Kit for Staff Development."

Women's National Book Association Award. To a living American woman who derives part or all of her income from books and allied arts and who has done meritorious work in the world of books. *Winner:* Masha Hamilton.

Women's National Book Association (WNBA)/Ann Heidbreder Eastman Grant ($500). To support library association professional development in a state in which WNBA has a chapter. *Winner:* North Carolina School Library Media Association.

World Book/ALA Information Literacy Goal Awards ($5,000). To promote exemplary information literacy programs in public and school libraries. *Donor:* World Book. *Winners:* Not awarded in 2010.

ALA/Allied Professional Association

SirsiDynix Award for Outstanding Achievement in Promoting Salaries and Status for Library Workers. *Donor:* SirsiDynix. *Winners:* Award discontinued.

American Association of School Librarians (AASL)

AASL/ABC-CLIO Leadership Grant (up to $1,750). For planning and implementing leadership programs at state, regional, or local levels to be given to school library associations that are affiliates of AASL. *Donor:* ABC-CLIO. *Winner:* Alabama Instructional Media Association (AIMA).

AASL/Baker & Taylor Distinguished Service Award ($3,000). For outstanding contributions to librarianship and school library development. *Donor:* Baker & Taylor Books. *Winner:* Marcia A. Mardis.

AASL Collaborative School Library Media Award ($2,500). For expanding the role of the library in elementary and/or secondary school education. *Donor:* Highsmith, Inc. *Winners:* librarian Marilyn Rothberg and her teacher collaborator, Barbara Masters, General Wayne Elementary, Malvern, Pennsylvania, for "Listen My Children and You Shall Hear . . . The 18th Century Project: Inquiry, Collaboration, and a Social Studies Year."

AASL Crystal Apple Award. To an individual, individuals, or group for a significant impact on school libraries and students. *Winner:* Ohio Governor Ted Strickland.

AASL Distinguished School Administrators Award ($2,000). For expanding the role of the library in elementary and/or secondary school education. *Donor:* ProQuest. *Winner:* Vince Barnes, principal, North Elementary School, Noblesville, Indiana.

AASL/Frances Henne Award ($1,250). To a school library media specialist with five or fewer years in the profession to attend an AASL regional conference or ALA Annual Conference for the first time. *Donor:* Greenwood Publishing Group. *Winner:* Melanie Gibson.

AASL Innovative Reading Grant ($2,500). To support the planning and implementation of an innovative program for children that motivates and encourages reading, especially with struggling readers. *Sponsor:* Capstone Publishers. *Winner:* Myra Oleynik, Bower Hill Elementary School, Venetia, Pennsylvania.

Information Technology Pathfinder Award ($1,000 to the specialist and $500 to the library). To library media specialists for innovative approaches to microcomputer applications in the school library media center. *Donor:* Follett Software Company. *Winners:* Not awarded in 2010.

Intellectual Freedom Award ($2,000 plus $1,000 to the media center of the recipient's choice). To a school library media specialist and AASL member who has upheld the principles of intellectual freedom. *Donor:* ProQuest. *Winner:* Karyn Storts-Brinks, school librarian, Knox County (Tennessee) School District.

National School Library Media Program of the Year Award ($10,000). To school districts and two single schools for excellence and innovation in outstanding library media programs. *Donor:* Follett Library Resources. *Winners:* (district) Not awarded in 2010; (single school) Perry Meridian Middle School, Indianapolis, Indiana; New Canaan (Connecticut) High School.

Association for Library Collections and Technical Services (ALCTS)

ALCTS/LBI George Cunha and Susan Swartzburg Preservation Award ($1,250). To recognize cooperative preservation projects and/or individuals or groups that foster collaboration for preservation goals. *Donor:* LBI. *Winners:* Jeffrey Field and Robert Harriman, U.S. Newspaper Project.

ALCTS Presidential Citations for Outstanding Service. *Winners:* Pamela Bluh, Jeanne Drewes, Dina Giambi, Kate Harcourt, Keisha Manning, Karen Motylewski.

Hugh C. Atkinson Memorial Award. *See under* American Library Association.

Ross Atkinson Lifetime Achievement Award. To recognize the contribution of an ALCTS member and library leader who has demonstrated exceptional service to ALCTS and its areas of interest. *Donor:* EBSCO. *Winner:* Peggy Johnson.

Paul Banks and Carolyn Harris Preservation Award ($1,500). To recognize the contribution of a professional preservation specialist who has been active in the field of preservation and/or conservation for library and/or archival materials. *Donor:* Preservation Technologies. *Winner:* Michèle V. Cloonan.

Best of *LRTS* Award ($250). To the author(s) of the year's best paper published in the division's official journal. *Winner:* Patricia Dragon for "Name Authority Control in Local Digitization Projects and the Eastern North Carolina Postcard Collection."

Blackwell's Scholarship Award. See Outstanding Publication Award.

Coutts Award for Innovation in Electronic Resources Management ($2,000) To recognize significant and innovative contributions to electronic collections management and development practice. *Donor:* Coutts Information Services. *Winners:* Galadriel Chilton and William Doering.

First Step Award (Wiley Professional Development Grant) ($1,500). For librarians new to the serials field to attend the ALA Annual Conference. *Donor:* John Wiley & Sons. *Winner:* Rebecca Kemp.

Leadership in Library Acquisitions Award ($1,500). For significant contributions by an outstanding leader in the field of library acquisitions. *Donor:* Harrassowitz. *Winner:* Not awarded in 2010.

Margaret Mann Citation (includes $2,000 award to the U.S. or Canadian library school of the winner's choice). To a cataloger or classifier for achievement in the areas of cataloging or classification. *Donor:* Online Computer Library Center. *Winner:* Olivia M. A. Madison.

Outstanding Collaboration Citation. For outstanding collaborative problem-solving efforts in the areas of acquisition, access, management, preservation, or archiving of library materials. *Winners:* Biodiversity

Heritage Library and the Rakow Research Library of the Corning Museum of Glass.

Outstanding Publication Award (formerly the Blackwell's Scholarship Award). To honor the author(s) of the year's outstanding monograph, article, or original paper in the field of acquisitions, collection development, and related areas of resource development in libraries. *Winners:* Kristin Blake and Jacquie Samples for "Creating Organization Name Authority Within an Electronic Resources Management System" in *Library Resources and Technical Services,* vol. 53, no. 2.

Esther J. Piercy Award ($1,500). To a librarian with no more than ten years' experience for contributions and leadership in the field of library collections and technical services. *Donor:* YBP Library Services. *Winner:* Kelly McGrath.

Ulrich's Serials Librarianship Award ($1,500). For distinguished contributions to serials librarianship. *Sponsor:* Ulrich's. *Winner:* Steven C. Shadle.

Association for Library Service to Children (ALSC)

ALSC/Book Wholesalers, Inc. BWI Summer Reading Program Grant ($3,000). To an ALSC member for implementation of an outstanding public library summer reading program for children. *Donor:* Book Wholesalers, Inc. *Winner:* Gail Borden Public Library, Elgin, Illinois.

ALSC/Booklist/YALSA Odyssey Award. To the producer of the best audiobook for children and/or young adults available in English in the United States. *Sponsor: Booklist. Winner:* Live Oak Media for *Louise, the Adventures of a Chicken,* written by Kate DiCamillo, narrated by Barbara Rosenblat.

ALSC/Candlewick Press "Light the Way: Library Outreach to the Underserved" Grant ($3,000). To a library conducting exemplary outreach to underserved populations. *Donor:* Candlewick Press. *Winner:* Fayetteville (Arkansas) Public Library.

May Hill Arbuthnot Honor Lectureship. To an author, critic, librarian, historian, or teacher of children's literature who prepares a paper considered to be a significant contribution to the field of children's literature. *Winner:* author Lois Lowry.

Mildred L. Batchelder Award. *Winner:* See "Literary Prizes, 2010" in Part 5.

Louise Seaman Bechtel Fellowship ($4,000). For librarians with 12 or more years of professional-level work in children's library collections, to read and study at Baldwin Library, University of Florida. *Donor:* Bechtel Fund. *Winner:* Christina H. Dorr.

Pura Belpré Award. *Winners:* See "Literary Prizes, 2010" in Part 5.

Bookapalooza Program Awards. To provide three libraries with a collection of materials that will help transform their collection. *Winners:* Foundation Schools (Maryland), Monterey County (California) Free Libraries, Richmond (California) Public Library.

Bound to Stay Bound Books Scholarships ($7,000 each). For men and women who intend to pursue an MLS or advanced degree and who plan to work in the area of library service to children. *Donor:* Bound to Stay Bound Books. *Winners:* Leah Biado, Marsha Burrola, Susan Dominguez, Alejandro Picazo.

Randolph Caldecott Medal. *Winner:* See "Literary Prizes, 2010" in Part 5.

Andrew Carnegie Medal. To the U.S. producers of the most distinguished video for children in the previous year. *Sponsor:* Carnegie Corporation of New York. *Winners:* Paul R. Gagne and Mo Willems of Weston Woods Studios for "Don't Let the Pigeon Drive the Bus!"

Carnegie-Whitney Awards (up to $5,000). For the preparation of print or electronic reading lists, indexes, or other guides to library resources that promote reading or the use of library resources at any type of library. *Donors:* James Lyman Whitney and Andrew Carnegie Funds. *Winners:* Christine Bombaro for *Finding History*; Kimberley Bugg for *The Study of Black Popular Culture: An Annotated Electronic Index*; Susan Irwin for *A Companion Guide to the Sacks Collection of the American West*; Peggy Johnson for *Facilitating the Writing of Literature Reviews*; Stephanie Kueen for *Teen Read Week and Teen*

Tech Week: The Best of YALS; Teresa Welsh for *A Selected Bibliography of Resources Related to Disaster Preparedness*; Camilla Yamada for *Children of the Storm: An Educational Database for Children in Disasters.*

Distinguished Service Award ($1,000). To recognize significant contributions to, and an impact on, library services to children and/or ALSC. *Winner:* Margaret Bush.

Theodor Seuss Geisel Award. *Winner:* See "Literary Prizes, 2010" in Part 5.

Maureen Hayes Author/Illustrator Visit Award (up to $4,000). For an honorarium and travel expenses to enable a library talk to children by a nationally known author/illustrator. *Sponsor:* Simon & Schuster Children's Publishing. *Winner:* Abbeville (South Carolina) County Library System.

Frederic G. Melcher Scholarships ($6,000). To two students entering the field of library service to children for graduate work in an ALA-accredited program. *Winners:* Sarah Avant, Whitney Chamberlin.

John Newbery Medal. *Winner:* See "Literary Prizes, 2010" in Part 5.

Penguin Young Readers Group Awards ($600). To children's librarians in school or public libraries with ten or fewer years of experience to attend the ALA Annual Conference. *Donor:* Penguin Young Readers Group. *Winners:* Elizabeth Dalton, Marisa Glaviano, Kathleen Houlihan, Susan Ridgeway.

Robert F. Sibert Medal. *Winner:* See "Literary Prizes, 2010" in Part 5.

Laura Ingalls Wilder Medal. *Winner:* See "Literary Prizes, 2010" in Part 5.

Association of College and Research Libraries (ACRL)

ACRL Academic or Research Librarian of the Year Award ($5,000). For outstanding contribution to academic and research librarianship and library development. *Donor:* YBP Library Services. *Winner:* Maureen Sullivan.

ACRL Distinguished Education and Behavioral Sciences Librarian Award ($2,500). To an academic librarian who has made an outstanding contribution as an education and/or behavioral sciences librarian through accomplishments and service to the profession. *Donor:* John Wiley & Sons. *Winner:* Penny Minton Beile.

ACRL/DLS Haworth Press Distance Learning Librarian Conference Sponsorship Award ($1,200). To an ACRL member working in distance-learning librarianship in higher education. *Winner:* Thomas E. Abbott.

ACRL Doctoral Dissertation Fellowship ($1,500). To a doctoral student in the field of academic librarianship whose research has potential significance in the field. *Donor:* Thomson Reuters. *Winner:* Christine Madsen, Oxford Internet Institute, University of Oxford, for her proposal "Library Futures: Building a New Knowledge Architecture in Academic Libraries."

ACRL Special Presidential Recognition Award. To recognize an individual's special career contributions to ACRL and the library profession. *Winners:* Not awarded in 2010.

ACRL/WSS Award for Career Achievement in Women's Studies Librarianship ($1,000). *Donor:* Greenwood Publishing Group. *Winner:* Cindy Ingold.

ACRL/WSS Award for Significant Achievement in Women's Studies Librarianship ($1,000). *Donor:* Greenwood Publishing Group. *Winner:* Award discontinued.

Hugh C. Atkinson Memorial Award. *See under* American Library Association.

Community College Learning Resources Leadership/Library Achievement Awards ($500). To recognize outstanding achievement in library programs or leadership. *Sponsor:* EBSCO Information Services. *Winner:* Northwest Vista College Library, San Antonio.

Coutts Nijhoff International West European Specialist Study Grant ($3,000). Supports research pertaining to West European studies, librarianship, or the book trade. *Sponsor*: Coutts Information Services. *Winner:* Timothy Robert Shipe, University of Iowa, for his proposal "The Franco-Romanian Literary Avant-garde in Bucharest Libraries."

Miriam Dudley Instruction Librarian Award ($1,000). For a contribution to the advancement of bibliographic instruction in a college or research institution. *Sponsor:* LOEX. *Winner:* Beth S. Woodward.

Excellence in Academic Libraries Awards ($3,000). To recognize outstanding community college, college, and university libraries. *Donor:* Blackwell's Book Services. *Winners:* (university) Indiana University Bloomington; (college) Elmhurst College, Elmhurst, Illinois; (community college) Bucks County (Pennsylvania) Community College.

Instruction Section Innovation Award ($3,000). To librarians or project teams in recognition of a project that demonstrates creative, innovative, or unique approaches to information literacy instruction or programming. *Donor:* LexisNexis. *Winners:* Nancy Goebel and Dylan Anderson, University of Alberta, for developing WASSAIL, an information literacy assessment project.

Marta Lange/CQ Press Award ($1,000). To recognize an academic or law librarian for contributions to bibliography and information service in law or political science. *Donor:* CQ Press. *Winner:* Bruce Pencek.

Samuel Lazerow Fellowship for Research in Acquisitions or Technical Services ($1,000). To foster advances in acquisitions or technical services by providing librarians a fellowship for travel or writing in those fields. *Sponsor:* Thomson Reuters. *Winner:* Award discontinued.

Katharine Kyes Leab and Daniel J. Leab Exhibition Catalog Awards (citations). For the best catalogs published by American or Canadian institutions in conjunction with exhibitions of books and/or manuscripts. *Winners:* (category I–expensive) Rare Books and Special Collections Department, Firestone Library, Princeton University, for *Liberty and the American Revolution: Selections from the Collection of Sid Lapidus, Class of 1959*; (category II–moderately expensive) Rare Books and Special Collections Department, Firestone Library, Princeton University, for *Beauty and Bravado in Japanese Woodblock Prints: Highlights from the Gilbert G. Griffin Collection*; (category III–inexpensive) Special Collections Department, University of Victoria Libraries, for *The Lion and the Fox: Art and Literary Works by Wyndham Lewis from the C. J. Fox Collection*; (category IV–brochures) Harry Ransom Center at the University of Texas at Austin for *The Mystique of the Archive*; (category V–electronic exhibition) University of Maryland Libraries' Special Collections Department for "Nancy Drew and Friends: Girls' Series Books Rediscovered" (online at http://www.lib.umd.edu/RARE/SpecialCollection/nancy/index.html).

Oberly Award for Bibliography in the Agricultural or Natural Sciences. Awarded biennially for the best English-language bibliography in the field of agriculture or a related science in the preceding two-year period. *Donor:* Eunice Rockwood Oberly Memorial Fund. *Winner:* To be awarded next in 2011.

Ilene F. Rockman Instruction Publication of the Year Award ($3,000). To recognize an outstanding publication relating to instruction in a library environment in the past two years. *Sponsor:* Emerald Group. *Winner:* Heidi L. M. Jacobs for "Information Literacy and Reflective Pedagogical Praxis," published in the May 2008 issue of *The Journal of Academic Librarianship.*

Association of Library Trustees, Advocates, Friends and Foundations (ALTAFF)

ALTAFF/Baker & Taylor Awards. To recognize library friends groups for outstanding efforts to support their libraries. *Winners:* (public library group with assistance from paid staff) Friends of the Johnson County (Kansas) Library, Friends of the Seattle (Washington) Public Library; (public library group without assistance from paid staff) Friends of the Nederland (Colorado) Public Library, Friends of the Castro Valley (California) Library, Friends of the Fitchburg (Wisconsin) Public Library.

ALTAFF/Gale Outstanding Trustee Conference Grant Award ($850). *Donor:* Gale Cengage Learning. *Winner:* Gail F. Graske.

ALTAFF Major Benefactors Citation. To individuals, families, or corporate bodies that have made major benefactions to public libraries. *Winner:* Ouida Bedingfield.

ALTAFF Public Service Award. To a legislator who has been especially supportive of libraries. *Winner:* To be awarded next in 2011.

Trustee Citations. To recognize public library trustees for individual service to library development on the local, state, regional, or national level. *Winners:* Robert O. Bonam, Margaret J. Danhof.

Association of Specialized and Cooperative Library Agencies (ASCLA)

ASCLA Cathleen Bourdon Service Award. To recognize an ASCLA personal member for outstanding service and leadership to the division. *Winner:* Jerry Krois.

ASCLA Century Scholarship ($2,500). For a library school student or students with disabilities admitted to an ALA-accredited library school. *Winner:* Not awarded in 2010.

ASCLA Exceptional Service Award. To recognize exceptional service to patients, the homebound, inmates, and to medical, nursing, and other professional staff in hospitals. *Winner:* Barbara T. Mates.

ASCLA Leadership and Professional Achievement Award. To recognize leadership and achievement in the areas of consulting, multitype library cooperation, statewide service and programs, and state library development. *Winner:* Not awarded in 2010.

Francis Joseph Campbell Award. For a contribution of recognized importance to library service for the blind and physically handicapped. *Winner:* Daniel W. Boyd, former director of the South Dakota Braille and Talking Book Library.

KLAS/National Organization on Disability Award for Library Service to People with Disabilities ($1,000). To a library organization to recognize an innovative project to benefit people with disabilities. *Donor:* Keystone Systems. *Winner:* Resource Library of the Wyoming Institute for Disabilities (WIND) for its project "Disability Etiquette Infusion Units: Changing Attitudinal Barriers at University of Wyoming."

Black Caucus of the American Library Association (BCALA)

Distinguished Service to BCALA Award. *Winner:* Cassandra Allen.

BCALA Distinguished Service to the Library Profession Award. *Winner:* Rose Timmons Dawson.

BCALA Library Advocacy Award. *Winner:* Rudolph Clay.

BCALA Professional Achievement Award. *Winner:* Joyce Jelks.

BCALA Trailblazer's Award. Presented once every five years in recognition of outstanding and unique contributions to librarianship. *Winner:* Robert Wedgeworth.

DEMCO/BCALA Excellence in Librarianship Award ($500). To a librarian who has made significant contributions to promoting the status of African Americans in the library profession. *Winner:* Irene Owens.

E. J. Josey Scholarship Awards ($2,000). To two African American students enrolled in or accepted by ALA accredited MLIS programs. *Winners:* Alice Etim, Ashanti White.

Ethnic and Multicultural Information and Exchange Round Table (EMIERT)

David Cohen/EMIERT Multicultural Award ($300). To recognize articles of significant research and publication that increase understanding and promote multiculturalism in North American libraries. *Donor:* Routledge. *Winner:* Not awarded in 2010.

Gale/EMIERT Multicultural Award ($1,000). For outstanding achievement and leadership in serving the multicultural/multiethnic community. *Donor:* Gale Research. *Winner:* Not awarded in 2010.

Exhibits Round Table (ERT)

Christopher J. Hoy/ERT Scholarship ($5,000). To an individual or individuals who will work toward an MLS degree in an ALA-accredited program. *Donor:* Family of Christopher Hoy. *Winner:* Holly Michelle Byers.

Federal and Armed Forces Librarians Round Table (FAFLRT)

FAFLRT Achievement Award. For achievement in the promotion of library and information service and the information profession in the federal government community. *Winner:* Shirley Loo, Congressional Research Service, Library of Congress.

Adelaide del Frate Conference Sponsorship Award ($1,000). To encourage library school students to become familiar with federal librarianship and ultimately seek work in federal libraries; for attendance at ALA Annual Conference and activities of the Federal and Armed Forces Librarians Round Table. *Winner:* Julie K. Williams.

Distinguished Service Award (citation). To honor a FAFLRT member for outstanding and sustained contributions to the association and to federal librarianship. *Winner:* Nancy G. Faget, U.S. Government Printing Office.

Cicely Phippen Marks Scholarship ($1,500). To a library school student with an interest in working in a federal library. *Winner:* Megan Myers.

Gay, Lesbian, Bisexual, and Transgendered Round Table (GLBT)

Stonewall Book Awards. *Winners:* See "Literary Prizes, 2010" in Part 5.

Government Documents Round Table (GODORT)

James Bennett Childs Award. To a librarian or other individual for distinguished lifetime contributions to documents librarianship. *Winner:* Sandee McAninch.

Bernadine Abbott Hoduski Founders Award. To recognize documents librarians who may not be known at the national level but who have made significant contributions to the field of local, state, federal, or international documents. *Winner:* Liza Duncan.

LexisNexis Documents to the People Award ($3,000). To an individual, library, organization, or noncommercial group that most effectively encourages or enhances the use of government documents in library services. *Winner:* Maliaca Oxnam.

NewsBank/Readex Catharine J. Reynolds Award ($2,000). To documents librarians for travel and/or study in the field of documents librarianship or area of study benefiting performance as documents librarians. *Donor:* NewsBank and Readex Corporation. *Winner:* Not awarded in 2010.

W. David Rozkuszka Scholarship ($3,000). To provide financial assistance to an individual who is currently working with government documents in a library while completing a master's program in library science. *Winner:* Lindsay Braddy.

Intellectual Freedom Round Table (IFRT)

John Phillip Immroth Memorial Award for Intellectual Freedom ($500). For notable contribution to intellectual freedom fueled by personal courage. *Winner:* Ron Critchfield.

Eli M. Oboler Memorial Award. See "Literary Prizes, 2010" in Part 5.

ProQuest/SIRS State and Regional Achievement Award ($1,000). To an innovative and effective intellectual freedom project covering a state or region during the calendar year. *Donor:* ProQuest Social Issues Resource Series (SIRS). *Winner:* Not awarded in 2010.

Library and Information Technology Association (LITA)

Hugh C. Atkinson Memorial Award. *See under* American Library Association.

Ex Libris Student Writing Award ($1,000 and publication in *Information Technology and Libraries*). For the best unpublished manuscript on a topic in the area of libraries and information technology written by a student or students enrolled in an ALA-accredited library and information studies graduate program. *Donor:* Ex Libris. *Winner:* Andromeda Yelton.

LITA/Brett Butler Entrepreneurship Award ($5,000). To recognize a librarian or library for demonstrating exemplary entrepreneurship by providing innovative products or services through the application of information technology. *Winner:* Award discontinued in 2009.

LITA/Christian Larew Memorial Scholarship ($3,000). To encourage the entry of qualified persons into the library and information technology field. *Sponsor*: Informata.com. *Winner:* Katy Rebecca Mahraj.

LITA/Library Hi Tech Award ($1,000). To an individual or institution for a work that shows outstanding communication for continuing education in library and information technology. *Donor:* Emerald Group Publishing. *Winner:* Marshall Breeding.

LITA/LSSI Minority Scholarship in Library and Information Science ($2,500). To encourage a qualified member of a principal minority group to work toward an MLS degree in an ALA-accredited program with emphasis on library automation. *Donor:* Library Systems and Services. *Winner:* Julianna Barrera-Gomez.

LITA/OCLC Frederick G. Kilgour Award for Research in Library and Information Technology ($2,000 and expense-paid attendance at the ALA Annual Conference). To bring attention to research relevant to the development of information technologies. *Donor:* OCLC. *Winner:* John Willinsky.

LITA/OCLC Minority Scholarship in Library and Information Technology ($3,000). To encourage a qualified member of a principal minority group to work toward an MLS degree in an ALA-accredited program with emphasis on library automation. *Donor:* OCLC. *Winner:* Sophia Beccerra-Licha.

Library History Round Table (LHRT)

Phyllis Dain Library History Dissertation Award ($500). Awarded biennially to the author of a dissertation treating the history of books, libraries, librarianship, or information science. *Winner:* To be awarded next in 2011.

Donald G. Davis Article Award (certificate). For the best article written in English in the field of U.S. and Canadian library history. *Winner:* Kate McDowell for "Surveying the Field: The Research Model of Women in Librarianship," in *Library Quarterly* vol. 79, no. 3.

Eliza Atkins Gleason Book Award. Presented every third year to the author of the best book in English in the field of library history. *Winner:* David Allan, University of St. Andrews, for *A Nation of Readers: The Lending Library in Georgian England* (British Library).

Justin Winsor Prize Essay ($500). To an author of an outstanding essay embodying original historical research on a significant subject of library history. *Winner:* Pamela Bleisch for "Spoilsmen and Daughters of the Republic: Political Interference in the Texas State Library during the Tenure of Elizabeth Howard West, 1911–1925."

Library Leadership and Management Association (LLAMA)

Hugh C. Atkinson Memorial Award. *See under* American Library Association.

Diana V. Braddom Fundraising and Financial Development Section Scholarship ($1,000). To enable attendance at the ALA Annual Conference. *Donor:* Diana V. Braddom. *Winner:* Award discontinued in 2009.

John Cotton Dana Library Public Relations Awards ($5,000). To libraries or library organizations of all types for public relations programs or special projects ended during the preceding year. *Donors:* H. W. Wilson Company and H. W. Wilson Foundation. *Winners:* Hackney Library at Barton College, Wilson, North Carolina; King County Library System, Issaquah, Washington; New Jersey State Library, Trenton; Pasco County Library System, Hudson, Florida; San Francisco (California) Public Library; Westbank Community Library District, Austin, Texas.

LLAMA Group Achievement Award. *Winner:* Award discontinued.

LLAMA Leadership Award. *Winner:* Award discontinued.

LLAMA President's Award. *Winner:* Award discontinued.

Library Research Round Table (LRRT)

Ingenta Research Award (up to $6,000). To sponsor research projects about acquisition, use, and preservation of digital information; the award includes $1,000 to support travel to a conference to present the results of that research. *Sponsor:* Ingenta. *Winner:* Not awarded in 2010.

Jesse H. Shera Award for Distinguished Published Research ($500). For a research article on library and information studies published in English during the calendar year. *Winner:* Jane Greenberg, for "Theoretical Considerations of Lifecycle Modeling: An Analysis of the Dryad Repository Demonstrating Automatic Metadata Propagation, Inheritance, and Value System Adoption," published in *Cataloging & Classification Quarterly* 47 (3–4).

Jesse H. Shera Award for Support of Dissertation Research ($500). To recognize and support dissertation research employing exemplary research design and methods. *Winner:* Hea Lim Rhee for "The Relationship Between Archival Appraisal Practice and the User Study in U.S. State Archives and Records Management Programs: An Exploratory Study."

Map and Geography Round Table

MAGERT Honors Award. *Winner:* Pete Reehling.

New Members Round Table (NMRT)

NMRT/Marshall Cavendish Award (tickets to the Newbery/Caldecott/Wilder Banquet at the ALA Annual Conference). *Winners:* Megan Hodge, Charlene Gross, Miranda Johnson.

Shirley Olofson Memorial Award ($1,000). To an individual to help defray costs of attending the ALA Annual Conference. *Winner:* Rachel Slough.

Student Chapter of the Year Award. To an ALA student chapter for outstanding contributions to ALA. *Winner:* ALA student chapter at San Jose State University.

3M Professional Development Grant. To new NMRT members to encourage professional development and participation in national ALA and NMRT activities. *Donor:* 3M. *Winners:* Erin Dorney, Cesar Garza, Cheryl Lee.

Office for Diversity

Achievement in Diversity Research Honor. To an ALA member who has made significant contributions to diversity research in the profession. *Winner:* Stanton Biddle.

Diversity Research Grants ($2,500). To the authors of research proposals that address critical gaps in the knowledge of diversity issues within library and information science. *Winners:* Elizabeth Friese for "Selecting Racially Diverse Literature for Elementary School Libraries"; Sandra Hughes-Hassell and Casey Rawson for "Promoting Equity in Literacy Instruction for Adolescent African American Males through the Use of Enabling Texts"; Jennifer K. Sweeney for "Helping Teens Help Themselves: A National Survey of Library Services to Juveniles in Detention."

Office for Information Technology Policy

L. Ray Patterson Copyright Award. To recognize an individual who supports the constitutional purpose of U.S. copyright law, fair use, and the public domain. *Sponsor:* Freedom to Read Foundation. *Winner:* Fred von Lohmann.

Office for Intellectual Freedom

Freedom to Read Foundation Roll of Honor (citation): To recognize individuals who have contributed substantially to the foundation. *Winner:* Robert M. O'Neil, director, Thomas Jefferson Center for the Protection of Free Expression, University of Virginia.

Freedom to Read Foundation Gordon M. Conable Conference Scholarship. To enable a library school student or new professional to attend the ALA Annual Conference. *Winner:* Aubrey Madler.

Office for Literacy and Outreach Services (OLOS)

Jean E. Coleman Library Outreach Lecture. *Sponsor:* OLOS Advisory Committee. *Winner:* Kathleen de la Peña McCook.

Diversity Fair Awards. To outreach librarians for their institutions' diversity-in-action initiatives. *Winners:* (first place) Ellen Halliday, Brooklyn (New York) Public Library, for "Reading is Fundamental"; (second place) Christina Wray, Center for Disability Information and Referral, for "It's 2 a.m. and I Finally Have Time for the Library! Providing Disability Information to Patrons When it's Best for Them"; (third place) Ben Gulyas, Cleveland Heights (Ohio) Library, Coventry Branch, for "Services and Programming for the Deaf and Hard of Hearing."

Estela and Raúl Mora Award ($1,000 and plaque). For exemplary programs celebrating Día de Los Niños/Día de Los Libros. *Winners:* Arthur F. Turner Community Library, West Sacramento, California; Pima County Public Library, Tucson, Arizona; Santa Barbara (California) Public Library System.

Public Awareness Committee

Scholastic Library Publishing National Library Week Grant ($3,000). To libraries or library associations of all types for a public awareness campaign in connection with National Library Week in the year the grant is awarded. *Sponsor:* Scholastic Library Publishing. *Winner:* Poudre River Public Library District, Fort Collins, Colorado.

Public Library Association (PLA)

Advancement of Literacy Award (plaque). To a publisher, bookseller, hardware and/or software dealer, foundation, or similar group that has made a significant contribution to the advancement of adult literacy. *Winner:* Award discontinued in 2009.

Baker & Taylor Entertainment Audio Music/Video Product Grant ($2,500 worth of audio music or video products). To help a public library to build or expand a collection of either or both formats. *Donor:* Baker & Taylor. *Winner:* Bailey Cove Branch Library, Huntsville, Alabama.

Gordon M. Conable Award ($1,500). To a public library staff member, library trustee, or public library for demonstrating a commitment to intellectual freedom and the Library Bill of Rights. *Sponsor:* LSSI. *Winner:* Oak Park (Illinois) Public Library.

Demco New Leaders Travel Grants (up to $1,500). To PLA members who have not attended a major PLA continuing-education event in the past five years. *Winners:* Emma Mejia, Kathy Smith.

EBSCO Excellence in Small and/or Rural Public Service Award ($1,000). Honors a library serving a population of 10,000 or less that demonstrates excellence of service to its community as exemplified by an overall service program or a special program of significant accomplishment. *Donor:* EBSCO Information Services. *Winner:* Gilpin County Public Library, Blackhawk, Colorado.

Highsmith Library Innovation Award ($2,000). To recognize a public library's innovative achievement in planning and implementing a creative community service program. *Donor:* Highsmith. *Winner:* Calcasieu Parish (Louisiana) Public Library.

Allie Beth Martin Award ($3,000). To honor a public librarian who has demonstrated extraordinary range and depth of knowledge about books or other library materials and has distinguished ability to share that knowledge. *Donor:* Baker & Taylor. *Winner:* Rebecca Vnuk.

Polaris Innovation in Technology John Iliff Award ($1,000). To a library worker, librarian, or library for the use of technology and innovative thinking as a tool to improve services to public library users. *Sponsor:* Polaris. *Winner:* Ellen Schmid, Geneva (Illinois) Public Library District.

Charlie Robinson Award. To honor a public library director who, over a period of seven years, has been a risk taker, an innovator, and/or a change agent in a public library. *Donor:* Baker & Taylor. *Winner:* Patrick Losinski, Columbus (Ohio) Metropolitan Library.

Romance Writers of America Library Grant ($4,500). To a library to build or expand a fiction collection and/or host romance fiction programming. *Donor:* Romance Writers of America. *Winner:* Huntsville-Madison County (Alabama) Public Library.

Public Programs Office

Sara Jaffarian School Library Program Award ($4,000). To honor a K–8 school library that has conducted an exemplary program or program series in the humanities. *Donors:* Sara Jaffarian and ALA Cultural Communities Fund. *Winner:* Jefferson Elementary School, Elmhurst, Illinois, for "Elmhurst History Project."

Reference and User Services Association (RUSA)

ABC-CLIO Online History Award ($3,000). A biennial award to recognize professional achievement in historical reference and librarianship. *Donor:* ABC-CLIO. *Winner:* To be awarded next in 2011.

ALA/RUSA Zora Neale Hurston Award. To recognize the efforts of RUSA members in promoting African American literature. *Sponsored by:* Harper Perennial Publishing. *Winner:* Anthony Loum, Brooklyn Public Library.

Virginia Boucher-OCLC Distinguished ILL Librarian Award ($2,000). To a librarian for outstanding professional achievement, leadership, and contributions to interlibrary loan and document delivery. *Winner:* Cherié Weible, University of Illinois at Urbana-Champaign.

BRASS Emerald Research Grant Awards ($5,000). To ALA members seeking support to conduct research in business librarianship. *Donor:* Emerald Group Publishing. *Winners:* Tao Jin, Kevin Harwell.

BRASS Gale Cengage Learning Student Travel Award ($1,000). To enable a student enrolled in an ALA-accredited master's program to attend the ALA Annual Conference. *Donor:* Gale Cengage Learning. *Winner:* Nancy Origer Poole.

BRASS Public Librarian Support Award ($1,000). To support attendance at the ALA Annual Conference of a public librarian who has performed outstanding business reference service. *Donor:* Morningstar. *Winner:* Ed Rossman.

BRASS Standard and Poor's Award for Outstanding Service to Minority Business Communities ($2,000). To a librarian or library to recognize creation of an innovative service to a minority business community or achievement of recognition from that community for providing outstanding service. *Winner:* Not awarded in 2010.

Sophie Brody Medal. *Winner:* See "Literary Prizes, 2010" in Part 5.

Gale Cengage Award for Excellence in Business Librarianship ($3,000). For distinguished activities in the field of business librarianship *Donor:* Gale Cengage Learning. *Winner:* Jennifer Boettcher.

Gale Cengage Award for Excellence in Reference and Adult Library Services ($3,000). To recognize a library or library system for developing an imaginative and unique library resource to meet patrons' reference needs. *Donor:* Gale Cengage Learning. *Winner:* J. Y. Joyner Library Digital Collections, East Carolina University, for "Seeds of Change: The Daily Reflector Image Collection."

Genealogical Publishing Company/History Section Award ($1,500). To encourage and commend professional achievement in historical reference and research librarianship. *Donor:* Genealogical Publishing Company. *Winner:* Thomas Jay Kemp.

Margaret E. Monroe Library Adult Services Award (citation). To a librarian for his or her impact on library service to adults. *Winner:* Nancy Pearl.

Isadore Gilbert Mudge–Gale Cengage Award ($5,000). For distinguished contributions to reference librarianship. *Donor:* Gale Cengage Learning. *Winner:* Marie L. Radford, Rutgers University.

Reference Service Press Award ($2,500). To the author or authors of the most outstanding article published in *RUSQ* during the preceding two volume years. *Donor:* Reference Service Press. *Winners:* Luke Vilelle and Christopher C. Peters for "Don't Shelve the Questions: Defining Good Customer Service for Shelvers," *RUSQ* 48:1 (Fall 2008).

John Sessions Memorial Award (plaque). To a library or library system in recognition of work with the labor community. *Donor:*

Department of Professional Employees, AFL/CIO. *Winner:* Murray-Green Library at Roosevelt University, Chicago.

Louis Shores–Greenwood Publishing Group Award ($3,000). To an individual, team, or organization to recognize excellence in reviewing of books and other materials for libraries. *Donor:* Greenwood Publishing Group. *Winner:* Heather McCormack, *Library Journal.*

STARS-Atlas Systems Mentoring Award ($1,000). To a library practitioner new to the field of interlibrary loan, resource sharing, or electronic reserves, to attend the ALA Annual Conference. *Donor:* Atlas Systems. *Winner:* Naomi I. Chow.

Social Responsibilities Round Table (SRRT)

Coretta Scott King Awards. *Winners:* See "Literary Prizes, 2010" in Part 5.

Jackie Eubanks Memorial Award ($500). To honor outstanding achievement in promoting the acquisition and use of alternative media in libraries. *Donor:* SRRT Alternatives in Publication Task Force. *Winner:* Not awarded in 2010.

Young Adult Library Services Association (YALSA)

Alex Awards. *Winners:* See "Literary Prizes, 2010" in Part 5.

Baker & Taylor/YALSA Scholarship Grants ($1,000). To young adult librarians in public or school libraries to attend the ALA Annual Conference for the first time. *Donor:* Baker & Taylor. *Winners:* Barbara Kinast, Carol Anne Geary.

BWI/YALSA Collection Development Grants ($1,000). To YALSA members who represent a public library and work directly with young adults, for collection development materials for young adults. *Donor:* Book Wholesalers, Inc. *Winners:* Amy Young, Jessica Neiweem.

Margaret A. Edwards Award. *Winner:* See "Literary Prizes, 2010" in Part 5.

Great Books Giveaway (books, videos, CDs, and audiocassettes valued at a total of $25,000). *Winners:* Benjamin Banneker High School, Atlanta; Conley-Caraballo High School, New Haven Unified School District, Hayward, California; Farmington (New Mexico) High School Library.

Frances Henne/YALSA/VOYA Research Grant ($1,000). To provide seed money to an individual, institution, or group for a project to encourage research on library service to young adults. *Donors: Voice of Youth Advocates* and Scarecrow Press. *Winners:* Janet Newsum and Marcia Mardis.

Michael L. Printz Award. *Winner:* See "Literary Prizes, 2010" in Part 5.

YALSA/Greenwood Publishing Group Service to Young Adults Achievement Award ($2,000). Awarded biennially to a YALSA member who has demonstrated unique and sustained devotion to young adult services. *Donor:* Greenwood. *Winner:* Patty Campbell.

YALSA/MAE Award ($500 for the recipient plus $500 for his or her library). For an exemplary young adult reading or literature program. *Sponsor:* Margaret A. Edwards Trust. *Winner:* Susan Bohn.

YALSA William C. Morris YA Debut Award. *Winner:* See "Literary Prizes, 2010" in Part 5.

YALSA/Sagebrush Award. See YALSA/MAE Award.

YALSA Spectrum Scholarship. To a designated Spectrum Scholarship recipient. *Winner:* Hoan-Vu Do.

American Society for Information Science and Technology (ASIS&T)

ASIS&T Award of Merit. For an outstanding contribution to the field of information science. *Winner:* Linda C. Smith.

ASIS&T Best Information Science Book. *Winner:* Adrian Johns for *Piracy: The Intellectual Property Wars from Gutenberg to Gates* (University of Chicago).

ASIS&T Best Research Paper Award ($500). *Winner:* Sarah Buchanan for "Name's the Same? The Los Angeles Chapter of ASIS&T upon its Semicentennial."

ASIS&T History Fund Grant Award Winner ($1,000). *Winner:* Andrew Russell for "An

Open World: Ideological Origins of Network Standards."

ASIS&T New Leaders Award. To recruit, engage, and retain new ASIS&T members and to identify potential for new leadership in the society. *Winners:* Andrea Baer, Laura Christopherson, Alex Garnett, Margaret Gross, Thomas Heverin, Tina Jayroe, Sara Mooney, Denise Pasquinelli.

ASIS&T ProQuest Doctoral Dissertation Award ($1,000 plus expense-paid attendance at ASIS&T Annual Meeting). *Winner:* Alberto Pepe for "Structure and Evolution of Scientific Collaboration Networks in a Modern Research Collaboratory."

ASIS&T Research in Information Science Award. For a systematic program of research in a single area at a level beyond the single study, recognizing contributions in the field of information science. *Winner:* Susan Leigh Star.

ASIS&T Special Award. To recognize long-term contributions to the advancement of information science and technology and enhancement of public access to information and discovery of mechanisms for improved transfer and utilization of knowledge. *Winner:* Not awarded in 2010.

James M. Cretsos Leadership Award. *Winner:* Crystal Fulton.

Watson Davis Award. For outstanding continuous contributions and dedicated service to the society. *Winner:* Barbara Wildemuth.

Thomson ISI Doctoral Dissertation Proposal Scholarship. *Winner:* Jaime Snyder for "Image-Enabled Discourse: An Investigation of the Creation of Visual Information as Communicative Practice."

John Wiley Best *JASIST* Paper Award. *Winners:* Max L. Wilson, M. C. Schraefel, and Ryen W. White for "Evaluating advanced search interfaces using established information-seeking models."

Art Libraries Society of North America (ARLIS/NA)

ARLIS/NA Conference Attendance Award. *Winner:* Sonja Staum.

ARLIS/NA Internship Award. To provide financial support for students preparing for a career in art librarianship or visual resource librarianship. *Winner:* Bailey Diers.

ARLIS/NA Student Conference Attendance Award. *Winner:* Marie Botkin.

ARLIS/NA Worldwide Books Award for Electronic Resources. *Winner:* Kitty Chibnik, Avery Library, Columbia University, for digitization of its New York Real Estate Brochure Collection.

ARLIS/NA Worldwide Books Award for Publications. *Winner:* Jeff Gunderson for his essay "A Combination of Accidents: The San Francisco Art Scene in the 1940s."

AskART Conference Attendance Award. *Winner:* Lee Viverette.

Melva J. Dwyer Award. To the creators of exceptional reference or research tools relating to Canadian art and architecture. *Winner:* Oliver Botar for *Andor Weininger: A Bauhausler in Canada* (Robert McLaughlin Gallery).

Judith A. Hoffberg Award for Student Attendance. *Winner:* Rachel Isaac-Menard.

Howard and Beverly Joy Karno Award. *Winner:* Gilda Santana.

Samuel H. Kress Foundation Award for European Travel. *Winner:* Holly Hatheway.

Gerd Muehsam Award. To one or more graduate students in library science programs to recognize excellence in a graduate paper or project. *Winner:* Diane Bockrath for the Walters Islamic Manuscript digital project.

Merrill Wadsworth Smith Travel Award in Architecture Librarianship. *Winner:* Elizabeth Schaub.

Student Diversity Award for Conference Attendance. *Winner:* April Fernandez.

H.W. Wilson Foundation Research Grant. *Winner:* Tom McNulty.

George Wittenborn Memorial Book Awards. See "Literary Prizes, 2010" in Part 5.

Asian/Pacific Americans Libraries Association (APALA)

APALA Scholarship ($1,000). For a student of Asian or Pacific background who is enrolled, or has been accepted into, a master's or doctoral degree program in library and/or information science at an ALA-accredited school. *Winner:* Harrison W. Inefuku.

APALA Travel Award ($500). To a library professional possessing a master's-level degree in library and/or information science to attend the ALA Annual Conference. *Winner:* Lessa Kanani'opua Pelayo-Lozado.

Association for Library and Information Science Education (ALISE)

ALISE Award for Teaching Excellence in the Field of Library and Information Science Education. *Winner:* Denise Agosto, iSchool at Drexel.

ALISE/Dialog Methodology Paper Competition ($500). To stimulate communication on research methodologies at ALISE annual conferences. *Sponsor:* Dialog. *Winners:* Heather Archibald and Lisa Given, University of Alberta, for "Visual Traffic Sweeps (VTS): A Research Method for Mapping User Activities in the Library Space."

ALISE/Eugene Garfield Doctoral Dissertation Award ($500). *Winner:* Charles Kamau Maina, University of Western Ontario, for "The Traditional Knowledge Protection Debate: Identifying and Listening to the Voices of Traditional Knowledge Holders."

ALISE Professional Contribution to Library and Information Science Education Award. *Winner:* Ken Haycock.

ALISE Research Grant Awards (one or more grants totaling $5,000): *Winners:* Kyung-won Koh, Sung Jae Park, and Kathleen Burnett, Florida State University, for "Online Collaborative Learning in the Web 2.0 Era."

ALISE/University of Washington Information School Youth Services Graduate Student Travel Award ($750). To support the costs associated with travel to and participation in the ALISE Annual Conference. *Winner:* Minjie Chen.

Doctoral Students to ALISE Grant ($500). To support the attendance of one or more promising LIS doctoral students at the ALISE Annual Conference. *Winner:* Sarah Sutton, Texas Woman's University.

OCLC/ALISE Library and Information Science Research Grant Program. To promote independent research that helps librarians integrate new technologies into areas of traditional competence and contributes to a better understanding of the library environment. *Winners:* Louise Spiteri and Laurel Tarulli, Hsin-liang Chen and Barbara Albee, Besiki Stvilia and Corinne Jorgensen.

Service to ALISE Award. *Winner:* Connie Van Fleet.

Association of Jewish Libraries (AJL)

AJL Scholarships ($1,000). For students enrolled in accredited library schools who plan to work as Judaica librarians. *Winners:* Haim Gottschalk, Rachel Isaac-Menard.

Association of Research Libraries

ARL Diversity Scholarships (stipend of up to $10,000). To a varying number of MLS students from under-represented groups who are interested in careers in research libraries. *Sponsors:* ARL member libraries and the Institute of Museum and Library Services. *Winners (2010–2012):* JaTara Barnes, Bertha Chang, Steven Chong, Manuel de la Cruz-Gutierrez, LaNesha DeBardelaben, Mariaelena De la Rosa, Hoan-Vu Do, Angel Durr, Mayu Ishida, Abraham de Jesus, Soyeong Jeon, Ashley Rayner, Yasmeen Shorish, Marina Torres-Aiello, Qinqin Zhang.

Association of Seventh-Day Adventist Librarians

D. Glenn Hilts Scholarship ($1,500) for a member of the Seventh-Day Adventist Church in a graduate library program. *Winner:* Melissa Faifer.

Beta Phi Mu

Beta Phi Mu Award. *See under* American Library Association.

Eugene Garfield Doctoral Dissertation Fellowships ($3,000). *Winners:* Kim Anderson for "Appraisal Learning Networks: How University Archivists Learn to Appraise Through Social Interaction"; Jeanette de Richemond for "What Is Enough Information?"; Carolyn Hank for "Scholars and their Blogs: Characteristics, Preferences, and Perceptions Impacting Digital Preservation"; Kyungwon Koh for "Proposing a Theoretical Framework for Digital Age Youth Information Behavior Building upon Radical Change Theory"; Ellen Pozzi for "The Public Library in an Immigrant Neighborhood: A Case Study of Italian Immigrants' Literacies in Newark (New Jersey), 1889–1919"; Ellen Rubenstein for "Ethnography of an Online Breast Cancer Support Group."

Harold Lancour Scholarship for Foreign Study ($1,500). For graduate study in a foreign country related to the applicant's work or schooling. *Winner:* Dorian Lange.

Sarah Rebecca Reed Scholarship ($2,000). For study at an ALA-accredited library school. *Winner:* Aaron G. Prosser.

Frank B. Sessa Scholarship for Continuing Professional Education ($1,250). For continuing education for a Beta Phi Mu member. *Winner:* Samantha Schmehl Hines.

Blanche E. Woolls Scholarship ($1,500). For a beginning student in school library media services. *Winner:* Katharine St. Laurent.

Bibliographical Society of America (BSA)

BSA Fellowships ($1,500–$6,000). For scholars involved in bibliographical inquiry and research in the history of the book trades and in publishing history. *Winners:* (Katharine F. Pantzer Senior Fellowship in Bibliography and the British Book Trades, $6,000) Kathryn Gucer; (BSA-Mercantile Library Fellowship in North American Bibliography, $2,000) John K. Young; (McCorison Fellowship for the History and Bibliography of Printing in Canada and the United States, ($2,000) Everett Wilkie; (Reese Fellowship for American Bibliography and the History of the Book in the Americas, $2,000) Sarah Wadsworth; (Katharine Pantzer Fellowship in the British Book Trades, $2,000) Jacob Heil; (one-month fellowships, $2,000) Meaghan Brown, Stephen Lubell, Thomas McSweeny, Willa Silverman; (Fredson Bowers Award, $1,500) Troy Bassett.

William L. Mitchell Prize for Research on Early British Serials ($1,000). Awarded triennially for the best single work published in the previous three years. *Winners:* To be awarded next in 2012.

St. Louis Mercantile Library Prize in American Bibliography ($2,000). Awarded triennially to encourage scholarship in the bibliography of American history and literature. *Sponsor:* St. Louis Mercantile Library, University of Missouri, St. Louis. *Winner:* To be awarded next in 2011.

Justin G. Schiller Prize for Bibliographical Work on Pre-20th-Century Children's Books ($2,000). A triennial award to encourage scholarship in the bibliography of historical children's books. *Winner:* Jill Shefrin for *The Dartons: Publishers of Educational Aids, Pastimes and Juvenile Ephemera, 1787–1876. A Bibliographic Checklist* (Cotsen Occasional Press).

Canadian Library Association (CLA)

Olga B. Bishop Award ($C200). To a library school student for the best paper on government information or publications. *Winner:* Not awarded in 2010.

Chancellor Group Conference Grant ($C500). To support attendance of newly qualified teacher-librarians at the next conference of the Canadian Association for School Libraries (CASL). *Winners:* Vivianne Fogarty, Shirley McGowan.

CLA Award for the Advancement of Intellectual Freedom in Canada. *Winner:* Kent Weaver.

CLA Elizabeth Dafoe Scholarship ($C5,000). *Winner:* Wayne Pender.

CLA/Ken Haycock Award for Promoting Librarianship ($C1,000). For significant contributions to the public recognition and appreciation of librarianship. *Winner:* Wendy Newman.

CLA/Information Today Award for Innovative Technology. *Donor:* Information Today, Inc. *Winner:* Knowledge Ontario (KO).

CLA Outstanding Service to Librarianship Award. *Donor:* R. R. Bowker. *Winner:* Lynn Copeland.

CLA Research and Development Grant ($C1,000). *Winner:* Allan Wilson and John Shepherd for "Performance Metrics: A Board Level View of Library Performance."

CLA Student Article Award. *Winner:* Jessica Rovito for "The LibQUAL Culture of Assessment: Institutionalizing 'the need to study people more than books.'"

CLA/3M Canada Award for Achievement in Technical Services ($C1,000). *Winner:* Ottawa Public Library.

CLA/YBP Award for Outstanding Contribution to Collection Development and Management ($C1,000). To recognize a CLA member who has made an outstanding local, national, or international contribution in the field of library collection development or management. *Sponsor:* YBP Library Services. *Winner:* Tony Horava.

W. Kaye Lamb Award for Service to Seniors. *Sponsored by:* Ex Libris Association and CLA. *Winner:* Not awarded in 2010.

H. W. Wilson Scholarship ($2,000). *Winner:* Emily Thompson.

World Book Graduate Scholarship in Library Science ($2,500). *Winner:* Award discontinued in 2009.

Canadian Association for School Libraries (CASL)

CASL Follett International Teacher Librarian of the Year Award. *Winner:* Pat Parungao.

CASL Margaret B. Scott Award of Merit. For the development of school libraries in Canada. *Winner:* Diana Gauthier.

CASL Angela Thacker Memorial Award. To honor teacher-librarians who have made contributions to the profession through publications, productions, or professional development activities. *Winner:* CASL Publications Editorial Board (Derrick Grose, Victoria Pennell, Linsey Hammond, Richard Beaudry, John Tooth, Judith Sykes).

Canadian Association of College and University Libraries (CACUL)

CACUL/Robert H. Blackburn Distinguished Paper Award ($200). To acknowledge notable research published by CACUL members. *Winners:* Guoying "Grace" Liu and Danielle Winn, University of Windsor, for "Chinese Graduate Students and the Canadian Academic Library: A User Study at the University of Windsor," published in the *Journal of Academic Librarianship.*

CACUL/Miles Blackwell Award for Outstanding Academic Librarian. *Sponsor:* Baker & Taylor/YBP Library Services. *Winner:* Michael Ridley.

CACUL Innovation Achievement Award ($1,000). *Sponsor:* OCLC. *Winners:* University of Prince Edward Island for the Islandora Project, Council of Prairie and Pacific University Libraries (COPPUL) for its Private LOCKSS Network.

CTCL Award for Outstanding College Librarian. *Winner:* Carole Compton-Smith, director of learning resources at Douglas College in New Westminster, British Columbia.

CTCL Innovation Achievement Award. *Sponsor:* OCLC. *Winners:* British Columbia Institute of Technology Library for its "ehPod," Mohawk College of Applied Arts and Technology Library for its Evergreen ILS project.

Canadian Association of Public Libraries (CAPL)

CAPL/Brodart Outstanding Public Library Service Award. *Winner:* Beth Hovius.

Canadian Association of Special Libraries and Information Services (CASLIS)

CASLIS Award for Special Librarianship in Canada. *Winner:* Kirsten Wurmann.

Canadian Library Trustees Association (CLTA)

CLTA/Stan Heath Achievement in Literacy Award. For an innovative literacy program by a public library board. *Donor:* ABC Canada. *Winners (tie):* Regina Public Library Board, Lethbridge Public Library Board.

CLTA Merit Award for Distinguished Service as a Public Library Trustee. *Winner:* Judith Umbach.

Catholic Library Association

Regina Medal. For continued, distinguished contribution to the field of children's literature. *Offered by:* Catholic Library Association. *Winner:* Ashley Bryan.

Chinese-American Librarians Association (CALA)

CALA Distinguished Service Award. To a librarian who has been a mentor, role model, and leader in the fields of library and information science. *Winner:* Ling Hwey Jeng.

CALA President's Recognition Award. *Winners:* Not awarded in 2010.

CALA Scholarship of Library and Information Science ($500). *Winner:* Qinqin Zhang.

Sheila Suen Lai Scholarship ($500). *Winner:* Teresa Nesbitt.

C. C. Seetoo/CALA Conference Travel Scholarship ($500). For a student to attend the ALA Annual Conference and CALA program. *Winner:* Yang Yang.

Sally T. Tseng Professional Development Grant ($1,000). *Winner:* Ying Xu for "Beyond Words and Into Action: Library Services for the Language Minorities."

Huang Tso-ping and Wu Yao-yu Scholarship Memorial Research Grant ($200): *Winner:* Laura Fu.

Church and Synagogue Library Association (CSLA)

CSLA Award for Outstanding Congregational Librarian. For distinguished service to the congregation and/or community through devotion to the congregational library. *Winner:* Not awarded in 2010.

CSLA Award for Outstanding Congregational Library. For responding in creative and innovative ways to the library's mission of reaching and serving the congregation and/or the wider community. *Winner:* Preston Hollow Presbyterian Church, Dallas, Texas.

CSLA Award for Outstanding Contribution to Congregational Libraries. For providing inspiration, guidance, leadership, or resources to enrich the field of church or synagogue librarianship. *Winner:* Not awarded in 2010.

Helen Keating Ott Award for Outstanding Contribution to Children's Literature. *Winner:* Not awarded in 2010.

Pat Tabler Memorial Scholarship Award. *Winner:* Not awarded in 2010.

Coalition for Networked Information

Paul Evan Peters Award. Awarded biennially to recognize notable and lasting international achievements relating to high-performance networks and the creation and use of information resources and services that advance scholarship and intellectual productivity. *Sponsors:* Association of Research Libraries, Coalition for Networked Information, EDUCAUSE. *Winner:* Christine L. Borgman, professor and presidential chair in information studies, University of California, Los Angeles.

Paul Evan Peters Fellowship ($5,000 a year for two years). Awarded biennially to a student pursuing a graduate degree in librarianship or the information sciences. *Sponsors:* Association of Research Libraries, Coalition for Networked Information, EDUCAUSE. *Winner:* Jessica A. Koepfler.

Council on Library and Information Resources (CLIR)

CLIR Postdoctoral Fellowships in Scholarly Information Resources. *Current fellows:* Andrew Asher, Tamar Boyadjian, Brian

Croxall, John Maclachlan, Julia Osman, Yi Shen, Mike Snowdon.

Mellon Fellowship Program for Dissertation Research in the Humanities in Original Sources (stipends of up to $20,000 to support dissertation research). *Current fellows:* Faiz Ahmed, Norah Andrews, Megan Barber, Juandrea Bates, Jacob Baum, Roland Clark, Christine DeLucia, Amy Dunagin, Rohit Goel, Benjamin Graham, Philipp Lehmann, Pablo Palomino, Kelly Summers, Samuel Thrope.

Rovelstad Scholarship in International Librarianship. To enable a student enrolled in an accredited LIS program to attend the IFLA World Library and Information Congress. *Winner:* Amy Neeser.

A. R. Zipf Fellowship in Information Management ($10,000). To a student enrolled in graduate school who shows exceptional promise for leadership and technical achievement. *Winner:* Lynn Yarmey.

Friends of the National Library of Medicine

Michael E. DeBakey Library Services Outreach Award. To recognize outstanding service and contributions to rural and underserved communities by a practicing health sciences librarian. *Winner:* Rita Smith, Medical Library and Peyton T. Anderson Learning Resources Center, Mercer University School of Medicine.

Bill and Melinda Gates Foundation

Access to Learning Award ($1 million). To public libraries or similar organizations outside the United States for innovative programs that provide the public free access to information technology. *Administered by:* Gates Foundation Global Libraries initiative. *Winner:* Veria Central Public Library, Veria, Greece.

Institute of Museum and Library Services

National Medal for Museum and Library Service. For extraordinary civic, educational, economic, environmental, and social contributions ($10,000). *Winners:* (libraries) Nashville (Tennessee) Public Library; Patchogue-Medford (New York) Library; Peter White Public Library, Marquette, Michigan; Rangeview Library District and Anythink Libraries, Adams County, Colorado; West Bloomfield Township (Michigan) Public Library.

International Association of School Librarians (IASL)

Ken Haycock and Jean Lowrie Leadership Development Grants ($1,000). To enable applicants in developing nations to attend their first IASL Annual Conference. *Winners:* (Haycock award) Keith Kuda Munyuengeterwa, Zimbabwe; (Lowrie award) Rachmawati (Indonesia).

International Federation of Library Associations and Institutions (IFLA)

De Gruyter Saur/IFLA Research Paper Award (€1,000). For the best unpublished research paper on a topic of importance to publishing and access to information by an author or authors with no more than eight years of professional experience in library and information services. *Sponsors:* IFLA and De Gruyter Saur. *Winner:* Pauline Nicholas, Main Library, University of the West Indies, Mona, Jamaica.

Gates Foundation Access to Learning Award. See under Bill and Melinda Gates Foundation.

Dr. Shawky Salem Conference Grant (up to $1,900). To enable an expert in library and information science who is a national of an Arab country to attend the IFLA Conference for the first time. *Winner:* Elham Abdallah, Université Saint Esprit Kaslik, Jounieh, Lebanon.

Frederick Thorpe Individual Awards (up to £5,000 total). To librarians working in libraries for the blind. *Donor:* Ulverscroft Foundation. *Winners:* Not awarded in 2010.

Frederick Thorpe Organizational Award (up to £15,000). To a library organization for development of service delivery to the visually impaired. *Winners:* Not awarded in 2010.

Ulverscroft Foundation/IFLA Libraries Serving Persons with Print Disabilities Section (£20,000 total). To assist the development of library services for print-disabled people and foster cooperation between library services serving these persons. *Winners:* (organization award) Shanghai Pudong New Area Library, China; (individual awards) Mark Freeman, South Tyneside Library Service and Share the Vision; Kathy Teague and Wendy Taylor, RNIB National Library Service; Yasmine Youssef, Taha Hussein Library for the Blind and Print Disabled, Bibliotheca Alexandrina, Egypt.

Library Journal

Library Journal Teaching Award ($5,000). To recognize excellence in LIS education. *Offered by: Library Journal. Sponsored by:* ProQuest. *Winner:* Steven L. McCall, University of Alabama, Tuscaloosa.

Medical Library Association (MLA)

Virginia L. and William K. Beatty MLA Volunteer Service Award. To recognize a medical librarian who has demonstrated outstanding, sustained service to the Medical Library Association and the health sciences library profession. *Winner:* Ann C. Weller.

Estelle Brodman Award for the Academic Medical Librarian of the Year. To honor significant achievement, potential for leadership, and continuing excellence at midcareer in the area of academic health sciences librarianship. *Winner:* Stephanie Fulton.

Lois Ann Colaianni Award for Excellence and Achievement in Hospital Librarianship. To a member of MLA who has made significant contributions to the profession in the area of overall distinction or leadership in hospital librarianship. *Winner:* Michele A. Spatz.

Cunningham Memorial International Fellowships. Provides grants and travel expenses in the United States and Canada for one or more librarians from other countries. Includes attendance at the MLA Annual Meeting and observation and supervised work in one of more medical libraries. *Winners:* Petros Demilew Miskir, Ethiopia; Marie-Therese Mitri, Lebanon.

Louise Darling Medal. For distinguished achievement in collection development in the health sciences. *Winner:* C. Trenton Boyd.

Janet Doe Lectureship. *Winner:* T. Scott Plutchak.

EBSCO/MLA Annual Meeting Grants (up to $1,000). To enable four health sciences librarians to attend the MLA Annual Meeting. *Winners:* Rienne Johnson, Elizabeth Kiscaden, Susan Warthman, Andrea Wright.

Ida and George Eliot Prize. To recognize a work published in the preceding calendar year that has been judged most effective in furthering medical librarianship. *Winners:* Ana Cleveland and Donald Cleveland.

Carla J. Funk Governmental Relations Award ($500). To recognize a medical librarian who has demonstrated outstanding leadership in the area of governmental relations at the federal, state, or local level, and who has furthered the goal of providing quality information for improved health. *Winner:* Logan Ludwig.

Murray Gottlieb Prize. For the best unpublished essay on the history of medicine and allied sciences written by a health sciences librarian. *Donors:* Ralph and Jo Grimes. *Winner:* Lindsay E. Blake for "The Tuskegee Syphilis Study: Medical Research versus Human Rights."

T. Mark Hodges International Service Award. To honor outstanding achievement in promoting, enabling, or delivering improved health information internationally. *Winner:* Lenny Rhine.

Hospital Libraries Section/MLA Professional Development Grants. *Winners:* Not awarded in 2010.

David A. Kronick Traveling Fellowship ($2,000). *Sponsor:* Bowden-Massey Foundation. *Winner:* Keith Cogdill.

Joseph Leiter NLM/MLA Lectureship. *Winner:* John D. Halamka.

Donald A. B. Lindberg Research Fellowship ($10,000). To fund research aimed at expanding the research knowledgebase, linking the information services provided by librarians to improved health care and advances in biomedical research. *Winner:* Joanne Gard Marshall for "The Value of Library and Information Services for Patient Care."

Lucretia W. McClure Excellence in Education Award. To an outstanding educator in the field of health sciences librarianship and informatics. *Winner:* Lauren Maggio.

Majors/MLA Chapter Project of the Year Award. *Sponsor:* J. A. Majors Co. *Winner:* Southern Chapter of MLA for its oral history project.

John P. McGovern Award Lectureship. *Winner:* Daniel H. Pink.

Medical Informatics Section Career Development Grant ($1,500). To support a career development activity that will contribute to advancement in the field of medical informatics. *Winners:* Not awarded in 2010.

MLA Continuing Education Awards. *Winners:* Marie K. Saimbert, Lin Wu.

MLA Fellowships. For sustained and outstanding contributions to health sciences librarianship and to the advancement of the purposes of MLA. *Honorees:* Margaret Allen, Shelley A. Bader, Margaret Bandy, Mark E. Funk, Connie Schardt.

MLA/NLM Spectrum Scholarships. To support minority students in their goals to become health sciences information professionals. *Winners:* Holly Beeman, Mariaelena de la Rosa.

MLA Research, Development, and Demonstration Project Grants ($100 to $1,000). To provide support for research, development, or demonstration projects that will help to promote excellence in the field of health sciences librarianship and information sciences. *Winner:* Catherine Mary Boss for "A Research Study: Does Exemplary Library Services to Patients and Their Family Members, Friends, and Caregivers Influence Patient Satisfaction Scores?"

MLA Scholarship (up to $5,000). For graduate study at an ALA-accredited library school. *Winner:* Kathryn Elliott.

MLA Scholarship for Minority Students (up to $5,000). For graduate study at an ALA-accredited library school. *Winner:* Maria Tan.

Marcia C. Noyes Award. For an outstanding contribution to medical librarianship. *Winner:* Sherrilynne Fuller.

President's Award. To an MLA member for a notable or important contribution made during the past association year. *Winner:* Not awarded in 2010.

Rittenhouse Award. For the best unpublished paper on medical librarianship submitted by a student enrolled in, or having been enrolled in, a course for credit in an ALA-accredited library school or a trainee in an internship program in medical librarianship. *Donor:* Rittenhouse Medical Bookstore. *Winner:* Melody Ramsey.

Thomson Reuters/Frank Bradway Rogers Information Advancement Award. To recognize outstanding contributions for the application of technology to the delivery of health science information, to the science of information, or to the facilitation of the delivery of health science information. *Sponsor:* Thomson Reuters. *Winner:* Not awarded in 2010.

Thomson Reuters/MLA Doctoral Fellowship ($2,000). To encourage superior students to conduct doctoral work in an area of health sciences librarianship or information sciences and to provide support to individuals who have been admitted to candidacy. *Sponsor:* Thomson Reuters. *Winner:* Shelagh Genuis.

Music Library Association

Carol June Bradley Award. To support studies that involve the history of music libraries or special collections. *Winner:* Not awarded in 2010.

Vincent H. Duckles Award. For the best book-length bibliography or other research tool in music. *Winner:* Laurie J. Sampsel for *Music Research: A Handbook* (Oxford University Press).

Dena Epstein Award for Archival and Library Research in American Music. To support research in archives or libraries internationally on any aspect of American music. *Winner:* Ursula Crosslin.

Kevin Freeman Travel Grants. To colleagues who are new to the profession to enable them to attend the association's annual meeting. *Winners:* Dyann S. Bishop, Matthew Ertz, Bracken Klar, Yi Hong Sim, Jennifer Ward.

Walter Gerboth Award. To members of the association who are in the first five years of their professional library careers, to assist research-in-progress in music or music librarianship. *Winner:* Mac Nelson.

Richard S. Hill Award. For the best article on music librarianship or article of a music-bibliographic nature. *Winner:* Rupert Ridgewell for "Artaria Plate Numbers and the Publication Process, 1778–87" in *Music and the Book Trade: From the Sixteenth to the Twentieth Century* (Oak Knoll).

MLA Citation. Awarded in recognition of contributions to the profession over a career. *Winner:* Not awarded in 2010.

Eva Judd O'Meara Award. For the best review published in *Notes*. *Winner:* Daniel F. Boomhower for reviews of Bach B-minor Mass editions, *Notes* 65:2 (December 2008).

National Library Service for the Blind and Physically Handicapped, Library of Congress

Library of the Year Awards ($1,000). *Winners:* (network library of the year) Washington Talking Book and Braille Library, Seattle; (network subregional library of the year) Special Services Library for the Blind and Physically Handicapped, Virginia Beach.

REFORMA (National Association to Promote Library and Information Services to Latinos and the Spanish-Speaking)

REFORMA scholarships ($1,500). To students who qualify for graduate study in library science and who are citizens or permanent residents of the United States. *Winners:* Concepción Flores, Candelaria Mendoza, Jefferson Perales, Mirna Turcios, Yesenia Villar-Villalobos.

Arnulfo D. Trejo Librarian of the Year Award. To recognize a librarian who has promoted and advocated services to the Spanish-speaking and Latino communities and made outstanding contributions to REFORMA. *Winners:* Oralia Garza de Cortés, Susana Hinojosa.

K. G. Saur Verlag (Munich, Germany)

Award for Best *Libri* Student Paper (500 euros). To recognize the most outstanding article published in *Libri* during the preceding year. *Donor:* K. G. Saur Verlag. *Winner:* Niamh Corbett, Curtin University, Perth, Western Australia, for "Parliamentary Petitions: An Information Studies Perspective," published December 2010.

Society of American Archivists (SAA)

C. F. W. Coker Award for Description. To recognize creators of tools that enable archivists to produce more effective finding aids. *Winner:* North Carolina State University Libraries Special Collections Research Center.

Colonial Dames of America Scholarship (up to $1,200). To enable new archivists to attend the Modern Archives Institute of the National Archives and Records Administration. *Winner:* Not awarded in 2010.

Distinguished Service Award. To recognize an archival institution, education program, nonprofit organization, or governmental organization that has given outstanding service to its public and has made an exemplary contribution to the archives profession. *Winner:* American Heritage Center (AHC), University of Wyoming.

Fellows' Ernst Posner Award. For an outstanding essay dealing with a facet of archival administration, history, theory, or methodology, published in *American Archivist. Winner:* Scott Cline for "To the Limit of Our Integrity: Reflections on Archival Being," *American Archivist* 72:2.

F. Gerald Ham Scholarship ($7,500). To recognize an individual's past performance in a graduate archival studies program and his or her potential in the field. *Winner:* Venus E. Van Ness.

Philip M. Hamer and Elizabeth Hamer Kegan Award. For individuals and/or institutions that have increased public awareness of a specific body of documents. *Winner:* Giza Archives at the Museum of Fine Arts, Boston, for promoting its holdings of early 20th century archaeological expedition records.

Oliver Wendell Holmes Travel Award. To enable overseas archivists already in the United States or Canada for training to attend the SAA annual meeting. *Winner:* Elaine Goh.

J. Franklin Jameson Award. For individuals and/or organizations that promote greater public awareness of archival activities and programs. *Winner:* Gladys Krieble Delmas Foundation.

Sister M. Claude Lane, O.P., Memorial Award. For a significant contribution to the field of religious archives. *Winner:* Sister Jane Aucoin.

Waldo Gifford Leland Prize. For writing of superior excellence and usefulness in the field of archival history, theory, or practice. *Winners:* Karen D. Paul, Glenn R. Gray, and L. Rebecca Johnson Melvin for *An American Political Archives Reader* (Scarecrow).

Theodore Calvin Pease Award. For the best student paper. *Winner:* Emily Monks-Leeson, for "Archives on the Internet: Representing Contexts and Provenance from Repository to Website."

Donald Peterson Student Scholarship Award (up to $1,000). To enable a student or recent graduate to attend the SAA Annual Meeting. *Winner:* Keara Duggan.

Harold T. Pinkett Minority Student Award. To encourage minority students to consider careers in the archival profession, and to promote minority participation in SAA. *Winners:* Miranda N. Rivers, Vivian Wong.

Preservation Publication Award. To recognize an outstanding work published in North America that advances the theory or the practice of preservation in archival institutions. *Winner:* Michele F. Pacifico and Thomas P. Wilsted, editors, for *Archival and Special Collections Facilities: Guidelines for Archivists, Librarians, Architects, and Engineers* (SAA).

SAA Fellows. To a limited number of members for their outstanding contribution to the archival profession. *Honored*: Daria D'Arienzo, David Haury, Diane Kaplan, Leon Miller, Christopher J. Prom, Scott Schwartz, Becky Haglund Tousey.

SAA Mosaic Scholarship ($5,000). To minority students pursuing graduate education in archival science. *Winners:* LaNesha DeBardelaben, Susan Gehr.

SAA Spotlight Award. To recognize the contributions of individuals who work for the good of the profession and of archival collections, and whose work would not typically receive public recognition. *Winners:* Ann Russell.

Special Libraries Association (SLA)

Dialog Member Achievement Award ($1,000). To an SLA member for raising visibility, awareness, and appreciation of the profession, SLA unit, or the association. *Winners:* Richard P. Hulser, Dianna Wiggins.

Diversity Leadership Development Award ($1,000 stipend). *Sponsor:* EBSCO. *Winner:* Nancy Snell.

Dow Jones Leadership Award ($2,000). For excellence in special librarianship. *Winner:* Stacey Greenwell.

SLA John Cotton Dana Award. For exceptional support and encouragement of special librarianship. *Winner:* Jim Tchobanoff.

SLA Fellows. *Honored:* Rebecca Jones, Dee Magnoni, James E. Manasco, Jill Strand, Libby Trudell.

SLA Hall of Fame Award. For outstanding performance and distinguished service to SLA. *Winners:* Judy Field, John V. Ganly, Guy St. Clair.

SLA/J. J. Keller Innovations in Technology Award ($1,000). *Winner:* Not awarded in 2010.

SLA Research Grant (incorporating the Steven I. Goldspiel Memorial Research Grant Fund) (up to $25,000). To support outstanding research. *Winner:* Not awarded in 2010.

Rose L. Vormelker Award. *Winner:* Jan Chindlund.

Other Awards of Distinction

Robert B. Downs Intellectual Freedom Award. To recognize individuals or groups who have furthered the cause of intellectual freedom, particularly as it impacts libraries and information centers and the dissemination of ideas. *Offered by:* Graduate School of Library and Information Science, University of Illinois at Urbana-Champaign. *Winner:* Comic Book Legal Defense Fund.

I Love My Librarian Awards ($5,000, a plaque, and a $500 travel stipend to attend the awards ceremony). To recognize librarians for service to their communities, schools, and campuses. Winners are nominated by library patrons. *Sponsors:* Carnegie Corporation of New York and the *New York Times*. *Winners:* (public librarians) Paul Clark, Ellen M. Dolan, Melissa McCollum, Christina Wagner; (school librarians) Kelley I. McDaniel, Patricia J. Updike, Doug Valentine; (college, community college, and university librarians) Laura Farwell Blake, Jeff Dowdy, Stefanie Wittenbach.

RWA Librarian of the Year. To a librarian who demonstrates outstanding support of romance authors and the romance genre. *Offered by:* Romance Writers of America. *Winner:* Jennifer Lohmann, Durham County (North Carolina) Library.

Part 4
Research and Statistics

Research and Statistics on Libraries and Librarianship in 2010

Denise M. Davis

This article focuses on e-books, both because of the enormous increase in this media format in consumer and library markets and because of the digital rights management issues that hinder its use in libraries. For this review I draw upon research employing quantitative and observational (qualitative) methods in the library, education, and business disciplines.

The article also highlights library statistics for the year, including the Public Library Funding and Technology Access Study, the Association of College and Research Libraries (ACRL) value studies, the latest "Public Libraries in the United States" report generated by the Institute of Museum and Library Services (IMLS), and the recent American Association of School Librarians (AASL) study "School Libraries Count!"

Winners of research awards and grants conferred by the American Library Association and its divisions, the American Society for Information Science and Technology, the Association for Library and Information Science Education, and the Medical Library Association also are highlighted.

E-Books

One of the more demanding issues facing libraries is the integration of e-books. Academic libraries have struggled with book format issues for a longer period than public or school libraries, addressing challenges of scholarly publishing of books, monographic series, and "born digital" content. Public libraries have been challenged with mass-market content to a greater extent than academic and school libraries. However, the consumer-model sales paradigm embraced by publishers affects the access and license agreements for all types of libraries, most notably agreements with public libraries.

The chasm between library need and content distributor behavior is at a tipping point, and an unpleasant one for such major distributors as Overdrive. Based on expenditure data reported by IMLS (2008 public libraries) and the National Center for Education Statistics (NCES) (2008 academic libraries and 2006–2007

Denise M. Davis was director of the American Library Association's Office for Research and Statistics through late 2010. She is now deputy director of the Sacramento (California) Public Library.

school libraries), public, academic, and school libraries spend an estimated combined $6.08 billion for collections each year. Regarding e-books, public libraries reported owning nearly 14 million items (IMLS FY 2008, Table 14) and spending about $155.6 million on electronic materials (IMLS FY 2008, Table 22, which includes e-books and databases)[1]; academic libraries owned about 102.5 million e-books and added more than 20 million in 2008 (NCES, Tables 5 and 6)[2].

A 2010 study, "COSLA: eBook Feasibility Study for Public Libraries," conducted for the Chief Officers of State Library Agencies (COSLA) by consultants at PinPointLogic, raised serious questions about file format limitations, device dependency, user demographics and consumer behavior.[3] One statistic mentioned in the COSLA study came from the 2009 North American Technographics Media and Marketing survey conducted by Forrester Research: ". . . nearly 70% of adults say they won't buy an eBook reader that is more than $100, which may indicate people place low value on single-purpose devices" (COSLA, p. 9). However, a 2009 study conducted by Citi Investment Research found that Kindle units sold in 2008 totaled an estimated 500,000 and that sales rose to about 3.5 million in 2010, an increase of nearly 86 percent. The Kindle unit price dropped from about $350 in 2008 to $253 in 2010, but also accounted for an estimated 4.4 percent of Amazon's total sales in 2010 ($27.5 million).[4] Consider if the price were to drop to $100—the barrier point reported in 2009. What might the Kindle price point be in 2011, having already dropped nearly 28 percent in two years?

A September 2010 Harris Poll found that only 8 percent of Americans used digital book readers.[5] But those with e-readers reported reading more than those reading only print. "Overall, 2 in 5 Americans (40%) read 11 or more books a year with 1 in 5 reading 21 or more books in a year (19%). But among those who have an e-reader, over one-third read 11–20 books a year (36%) and over one-quarter read 21 or more books in an average year (26%)." The Harris Poll also found that about 1 in 10 Americans would purchase a digital book reader in the next six months.

In a small 2008 study of fifth graders' acclimation to e-readers, Lotta C. Larson (Kansas State University) found that the utilities in the reader software appealed most to the students, drawing them into the text in ways not possible in print.[6] Another study, conducted by Vanessa Ratten (Duquesne University) of 18- to 29-year-old university students in the Brisbane, Australia, metropolitan area, tested the research question "What influences a person's intention to adopt an e-book device?"[7] Of five hypotheses developed and tested in the study, only two were determined to be statistically significant: "The more exposure a person has to e-book devices, the greater their intention to use an e-book," and "The greater a person's entrepreneurial orientation, the greater their intention to use an e-book device." (Ratten, pp. 8–9) The other three hypotheses tested were found to be statistically insignificant—modeling of others, outcome expectancy, and learning orientation (Ratten, p. 12).

Based on the adoption rates reported by Citi Investment Research and Harris Poll, will Americans continue to adapt to digital book readers at the reported rate? Will e-reader owners purchase titles, or will there be a rising expectation to borrow them from their local library? And what does this mean for libraries and their migration away from print collections to more digital content?

Access barriers for libraries caused by licensing agreements were presented in the COSLA study: "Despite the rising demand for eBooks, all agreed that getting eBooks from libraries is not convenient or easy to do. We heard just as many concerns about this as assurances that eBooks will bring patrons to libraries. 'One copy, one user' e-book licensing is hard to explain: the title is listed, digital, but not 'checked out.' Plus, users must navigate through multiple layers and interfaces to find e-books on a library site. To get one, they must load proprietary software on a personal computer, download the title there, then transfer it onto a reading device. Improving the e-book browsing and downloading experience for library patrons is critical for competing more effectively with commercial alternatives. When someone values convenience, as you might expect from e-book lovers, ease of use matters greatly." (COSLA 2010, p. 9)

Evidence shows that not only are e-book devices growing in popularity; an individual's age is insignificant in determining adoption. The Harris Poll (2010) study found no significant difference in adoption rates based on age. In fact, the poll found greater adoption at ages 34–45 (Gen X, 15 percent) and ages 46–64 (Baby Boomers, 14 percent), followed by ages 18–33 (Echo Boomers, 11 percent). Public library use in these age ranges is quite strong. A 2010 study by Harris Interactive for the American Library Association found that 80 percent of those ages 18–24, 70 percent of those 25–34, and 73 percent of those 35–44 had used their library in the past year.[8] Good news for libraries only if the format and use challenges are mitigated.

[For more on e-books, see the Special Report "E-books Pose Major Challenge for Publishers, Libraries" in Part 1—*Ed.*]

Facts and Figures About Libraries

Public Libraries

IMLS includes ten-year trend graphics and narrative in its annual "Public Libraries in the United States" reports. The most recent—covering fiscal year (FY) 2008—did have some reporting problems and, although the data file has been reissued, the full report had not been revised at the time this article was prepared. Notably, public libraries saw a 4.7 percent increase in in-person visits in FY 2008, at 1.50 billion from 1.43 billion in fiscal year 2007.[9] Also up were circulations, 2.28 billion in FY 2008 from 2.17 billion the previous year, an increase of about 5 percent (IMLS, p. 5). For the ten-year period 1999–2008, public libraries saw a per capita increase in circulation of about 19.7 percent. Declining print materials acquisition, which became visible in fiscal year 2003 reported data, has been coupled by a steady rise in other formats, such as audio and video materials (IMLS, Figures 6 and 7). IMLS reported that for the ten-year period FY 1999–2008 video materials increased from 73.5 video materials per 1,000 people to 166.7, a rise of about 126.8 percent (Figure 7). Audio materials also increased during this period, rising from 112.4 materials per 1,000 people in FY 1999 to 168.2 in FY 2008, about 49.6 percent.

The American Library Association's *Libraries Connect Communities: Public Library Funding and Technology Access Study 2009–2010* determined that despite the increased use of libraries, funding cuts were more prevalent and services were being reduced. About 15 percent of libraries reported decreased operating hours in 2009–2010, up 4.5 percent from 2008–2009. State libraries in 13 states reported awareness of public library closures due to budget problems as compared with the previous 12 months.[10] Further, 56.4 percent of public libraries reported flat or decreased FY 2010 operating budgets (an increase of about 16 percent in one year), and about 27 percent of libraries anticipated further reductions in the current (FY 2010) operating year. More than half (54.6 percent) of urban libraries anticipated reductions compared with 41.6 percent of suburban and 26.5 percent of rural public libraries (ALA, p. 11). An issues brief from the 2009–2010 study *A Perfect Storm Brewing: Budget Cuts Threaten Public Library Services at Time of Increased Demand* highlights the significance of the budget reductions.[11]

Academic Libraries

ACRL produced two reports in 2010—*Value of Academic Libraries: A Comprehensive Research Review and Report,*[12] developed by Megan Oakleaf of the iSchool at Syracuse University, and *Futures Thinking for Academic Librarians: Higher Education in 2025,* prepared by David J. Staley, director of the Harvey Goldberg Center for Excellence in Teaching at Ohio State University, and Kara J. Malenfant, ACRL scholarly communications and government relations specialist.[13]

The Oakleaf study presents a comprehensive literature review including methodologies and current best practices in academic libraries regarding "library value." The significance of this review is that it identifies the research currently in place as well as the gaps in research in order to position those practices and measures reasonably correlated to academic library performance.

The Staley and Malenfant study presents 26 long-term scenarios (through 2025) resulting from an "implications assessment of current trends." The scenarios are presented through a visualization tool and include assessments from ACRL members regarding probability of each scenario occurring. The study also includes a "suggested activity" document, customizable to individual library conditions, and a discussion (audio clip) with the authors about the value of the scenarios.

School Libraries

"School Libraries Count!"—an annual longitudinal study from AASL—is in its fourth year and now includes customizable results reports.[14] The AASL research is a voluntary survey of public and private K–12 schools; the national estimates published annually are compiled from a stratified random sample of all responding libraries. The 2010 report presents data from 5,191 responses and summarizes findings, as well as presenting responses as percentiles. This study included supplemental questions regarding digital content and related resources.

The average number of hours worked by school library staffs declined about 2.4 hours from 2009 to 2010, but the number of hours worked by "librarians" (which excludes other library staff) increased from 2009 by 0.8 hours, as did time spent providing instruction, by about 0.5 hours. The decline in hours worked by other staff was most evident in the Northeast and Midwest.

Variation in collections is evident in the 2010 study. Books declined about 2.6 percent, periodicals about 11 percent, and video materials about 5 percent (ALA-AASL, p. 80). Expenditures on information resources also declined, to an average of $12,260 in 2010 compared with $13,525 in 2009 (a decline of about 9.35 percent overall). Greater declines were noted in high-poverty areas where average expenditures dropped by $3,557 (more than 25 percent) to $10,378 in 2010 from $13,935 last year (ALA-AASL, p. 12).

The supplemental questions were related to digital content. School libraries reported slow movement in print-to-digital replacement, with about 72 percent indicating increases of less than 5 percent and only about 4 percent reporting 25 percent or greater increases to digital from print.[15] The largest schools (enrollment above 2,000) were least likely to report the smaller percentage shifts from print to digital—45 percent of the largest schools compared with 79 percent of the smallest (enrollment under 300). Nearly half (49 percent) of all schools reported having more than five database subscriptions for their students in addition to retaining print collections. Adding digital content directly impacts the quality of the technology infrastructure; about 61 percent of schools reported there was an important impact, although about 15 percent reported digital content had no impact on access needs.

Awards and Grants that Support Excellent Research

The professional library associations offer many awards and grants to recognize and encourage research. The 2010 awards and grants here are listed under the name of the sponsoring association, and in the case of ALA by the awarding division, in alphabetical order. More-detailed information about the prizes and prizewinners can be found at the association Web sites. [For additional library awards, see "Library Scholarship and Award Recipients, 2010" in Part 3—*Ed.*]

American Library Association

Carroll Preston Baber Research Grant
Winner: Betsy Simpson, University of Florida, for "Shifting Patterns: Examining the Impact of Hiring Non-MLS Librarians."

Jesse H. Shera Award for Excellence in Published Research
Winner: Jane Greenberg for "Theoretical Considerations of Lifecycle Modeling: An Analysis of the Dryad Repository Demonstrating Automatic Metadata Propagation, Inheritance, and Value System Adoption," published in *Cataloging and Classification Quarterly* 47 (3-4): 380–402.

Jesse H. Shera Award for Support of Dissertation Research
Winner: Hea Lim Rhee, University of Pittsburgh School of Information Sciences, for "The Relationship Between Archival Appraisal Practice and the User Study in U.S. State Archives and Records Management Programs: An Exploratory Study."

Association of College and Research Libraries (ACRL)

Coutts Nijhoff International West European Specialist Study Grant
Winner: Timothy Robert Shipe, University of Iowa, for "The Franco-Romanian Literary Avant-garde in Bucharest Libraries."

Doctoral Dissertation Fellowship
Winner: Christine Madsen for "Library Futures: Building a New Knowledge Architecture in Academic Libraries."

Ilene F. Rockman Instruction Publication of the Year Award
Winner: Heidi L. M. Jacobs, University of Windsor, for "Information Literacy and Reflective Pedagogical Praxis."

Library and Information Technology Association

Frederick G. Kilgour Award for Research in Library and Information Technology
Winner: John Willinsky, Khosla Family Professor of Education at Stanford University and founder of the Public Knowledge Project (PKP).

American Society for Information Science and Technology

ASIS&T Best Information Science Book
Winner: Adrian Johns for *Piracy: The Intellectual Property Wars from Gutenberg to Gates* (University of Chicago).

John Wiley Best *JASIST* Paper Award
Winners: Max L. Wilson, M. C. Schraefel, and Ryen W. White for "Evaluating Advanced Search Interfaces Using Established Information-Seeking Models."

ProQuest Doctoral Dissertation Award
Winner: Alberto Pepe for "Structure and Evolution of Scientific Collaboration Networks in a Modern Research Collaboratory."

Research in Information Science Award
Winner: Susan Leigh Star, whose contributions to research in information science over a 15-year period are exemplified in two key monographs and a number of other highly cited publications. The monographs are "Sorting Things Out: Classification and Its Consequences" (1999) and "Standards and Their Stories: How Quantifying, Classifying, and Formalizing Practices Shape Everyday Life" (2009).

Thomson ISI Doctoral Dissertation Proposal Scholarship
Winner: Jaime Snyder for "Image-Enabled Discourse: An Investigation of the Creation of Visual Information as Communicative Practice."

Association for Library and Information Science Education

ALISE/Eugene Garfield Doctoral Dissertation Competition
Winner: Charles Kamau Maina for "The Traditional Knowledge Protection Debate: Identifying and Listening to the Voices of Traditional Knowledge Holders."

ALISE Research Grant Competition

Winner: Kyungwon Koh, Sung Jae Park, and Kathleen Burnett for "Online Collaborative Learning in the Web 2.0 Era."

Medical Library Association

Janet Doe Lectureship

Winner: T. Scott Plutchak.

Ida and George Eliot Prize

Winners: Ana D. Cleveland and Donald Cleveland for "Health Informatics for Medical Librarians."

Donald A. B. Lindberg Research Fellowship

Winner: Joanne Gard Marshall for "The Value of Library and Information Services for Patient Care."

Notes

1. IMLS. "Public Libraries Survey Fiscal Year 2008." Calculation for e-books estimated by taking the percentage of collection expenditures for electronic materials reported in Table 23 (11.8 percent, or $155,646,650).
2. National Center for Education Statistics. "Academic Libraries: 2008." NCES 2010 348. Accessed December 5, 2010. http://nces.ed.gov/pubs2010/2010348.pdf.
3. Chief Officers of State Library Agencies. "COSLA: eBook Feasibility Study for Public Libraries—Final Report." 2010. Accessed December 5, 2010. http://www.cosla.org/documents/COSLA2270_Report_Final1.pdf.
4. Schonfeld, Eric. "Is the Kindle Outpacing Early iPod Sales?" *Tech Crunch,* February 3, 2009. Accessed December 8, 2010. http://techcrunch.com/2009/02/03/is-the-kindle-outpacing-early-ipod-sales.
5. Harris Poll. Regina Corso, director. Harris Poll No. 108 (September 22, 2010). Survey question: "Do you use an electronic reader device, such as a Kindle, an iPad or a Nook, to read books?" Accessed December 8, 2010. http://www.harrisinteractive.com/NewsRoom/HarrisPolls/tabid/447/ctl/ReadCustom%20Default/mid/1508/ArticleId/568/Default.aspx.
6. Larson, Lotta C. "Digital Literacies. e-Reading and e-Responding: New Tools for the Next Generation of Readers." *Journal of Adolescent and Adult Literacy* 53(3): 255–258 (November 2008).
7. Ratten, Vanessa. "Social Cognitive Theory and the Adoption of E-book Devices." *International Journal of e-Business Management* 4(2): 3–16 (2010).
8. Harris Interactive. January 2010 Harris Poll Quorum. P.1. Accessed December 8, 2010. http://www.ala.org/ala/research/librarystats/2010HarrisPoll.pdf.
9. Institute of Museum and Library Services. "Public Libraries in the United States, Fiscal Year 2008." *Figure 1: Per Capita Visitation in U.S. Public Libraries, FY1999.* Accessed December 5, 2010. http://harvester.census.gov/imls/pubs/pls/pub_detail.asp?id=130#.
10. American Library Association. "Libraries Connect Communities: Public Library Funding and Technology Access Study 2009–2010." Executive Summary, p. 9. Accessed December 5, 2010. http://www.ala.org/ala/research/initiatives/plftas/2009_2010/index.cfm.
11. American Library Association. *A Perfect Storm Brewing: Budget Cuts Threaten Public Library Services at Time of Increased Demand.* Published January 14, 2010; revised March

4, 2010. Accessed December 5, 2010 http://www.ala.org/ala/research/initiatives/plftas/issuesbriefs/issuebrief_perfectstorm.pdf.

12. American Library Association, Association of College and Research Libraries. *Value of Academic Libraries: A Comprehensive Research Review and Report.* Prepared by Megan Oakleaf. 2010. Accessed December 5, 2010. http://www.acrl.ala.org/value.
13. Staley, David J., and Kara J. Malenfant. "Futures Thinking for Academic Librarians: Higher Education in 2025." Accessed December 5, 2010. http://www.ala.org/ala/mgrps/divs/acrl/issues/value/futures2025.pdf.
14. ALA. American Association of School Librarians. "School Libraries Count!" Accessed December 5, 2010. http://www.ala.org/ala/mgrps/divs/aasl/researchandstatistics/slcsurvey/2010/slc2010.pdf.
15. ALA. American Association of School Librarians. "School Libraries Count!". Supplemental Report on Digital Content and Resources. Accessed December 5, 2010. http://www.ala.org/ala/mgrps/divs/aasl/researchandstatistics/slcsurvey/2010/slc2010extra.cfm.

The Consortial Effect: Is a Consortium Greater Than the Sum of Its Parts?

Robert E. Molyneux

In the library world, the term "consortium" is a flag of convenience. Libraries band together for different and often overlapping purposes, and it seems that no two are alike. This article deals with one type of consortium—those made up of public libraries wishing to share resources—and it attempts to analyze the effect on library use of an independent library after joining such a consortium.

What spurred this analysis is two cases in which the author noted a striking increase in use of formerly independent public libraries that had joined such a resource-sharing consortium. Consider Figure 1, which shows the experience of the libraries, Florence County Library System (FCLS) (http://florencelibrary.org/wordpress) in Florence, South Carolina, and the York County Library (YCLS) (http://www.yclibrary.org) in Rock Hill, South Carolina. York County joined the SC LENDS consortium in October 2009 and Florence County joined in early December of that year. SC LENDS is a new resource-sharing consortium of South Carolina public libraries and the South Carolina State Library.

What Figure 1 shows is the sum of ILL (interlibrary loan) transactions—items lent to other libraries plus the items borrowed from others—up to the go-live date of each library's participation in the new consortium; after that the series is spliced with SC LENDS data reporting intra-consortial borrowing and lending. Upon entering a resource-sharing consortium, the libraries' holdings are joined with those of the other members, and users of the libraries can then see these consortial resources; that is, items available locally and at other libraries in the consortium.

For York, the sum of lent and borrowed items went from 264 in September 2009 to 665 in the month it joined, then to 2,571 in November, and on from there. FCLS went from ten ILL transactions in November to more than 1,500 holds in January of 2010, an increase of 1,500 percent. That is an impressive change in the use of the libraries and one that bespeaks library users taking advantage of the newly available consortial resources.

December is typically the low month for public library circulations and other types of library use, and Memorial Day usually marks the uptick that results from summer being a reading season and the fact that public libraries commonly have such activities as summer reading programs. We see this pattern for both libraries in Figure 1.

The second case of an increase in library use from independent libraries joining such a consortium comes from the many anecdotes surrounding the founding of the PINES consortium (http://pines.georgialibraries.org) in Georgia. This consortium got its electronic start as a result of the "Y2K" problem as January 1, 2000, approached. Many Georgia public libraries had software that

Robert E. Molyneux has worked on compiling, documenting, and analyzing library data for more than 25 years and has taught a variety of library school classes dealing with the integration of computers and networking technology in libraries. He is vice president for business development at Equinox Software, Inc. Sue Easun of the publishing consultancy Second Hand Knowledge assisted in the preparation of this report.

Figure 1 / Pre and Post Evergreen Go-Live, Items Loaned to and Borrowed from Other Libraries (time of go-live circled)

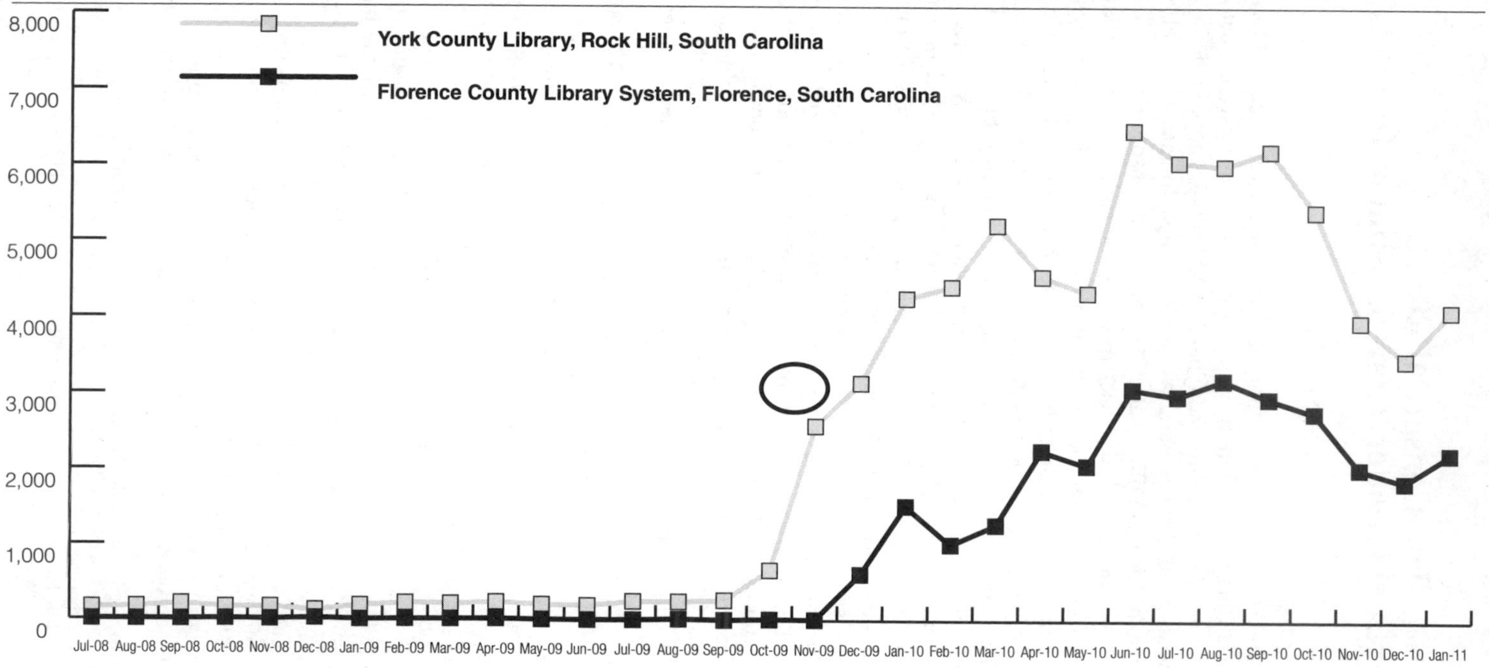

could not handle the date change, and it was decided to migrate those that had inadequate software to a resource-sharing consortium running Unicorn, from SirsiDynix. Twenty-six public library systems migrated in December 1999 and 16 more in 2001.

A story that is relevant here results from the Georgia universal-borrower card. A Georgia resident has no access to PINES through his or her local library if it is not a member of the PINES consortium. However, that resident can get a system card at any PINES library and then borrow items through PINES. One often-repeated anecdote is that the users of libraries not in PINES started going to nearby PINES libraries to have access to the resources of the larger PINES union catalog. Of course, the staff of non-PINES libraries noticed this behavior, and there was therefore an incentive to join the system.

PINES currently has 51 system members with around 280 separate outlets (central libraries, branches, and bookmobiles) and 10 million items. In 2010 the total circulations figure was 19 million.

Is this kind of experience borne out by other such consortia? We can posit that users who find their local library has extended its resources by sharing with others like the resulting access to the larger tail of information. There is ample experience that indicates information-seekers generally do not like information silos—management systems that cannot operate reciprocally with other related systems. Resource-sharing consortia, then, may be a response of the library community to break down these silos.

How can we test whether there is an increase in use of libraries joining resource-sharing consortia? Do data back up the anecdotes and confirm the experience of the two South Carolina libraries? The data gathered for this study provide evidence that there is a consortial effect, and it can be speculated that it results from library users being able to gain ready access to a much greater wealth of materials through the resources of the other libraries sharing through the consortium—such as the 10 million items held by PINES members.

The public library data series used in this analysis comprises longitudinal data from each of the U.S. public library systems (http://drdata.lrs.org/pldf3). This series is based on the data compilations issued first by the National Center for Educational Statistics and now by the Institute for Museum and Library Services (http://harvester.census.gov/imls/publib.asp). The data begin in fiscal year (FY) 1987 for some states and are currently available through FY 2008. The data are reported on a fiscal year basis because of varying local reporting requirements in the several states.

We will examine these variables, which seem relevant:

- Population served
- Total annual circulations
- Items lent to other libraries
- Items borrowed from other libraries

("Population served" is probably the most commonly used number in the public library world to describe a library. It is different from "registered borrowers." Registered borrowers has been reported only since FY 2006, and this variable is not used here.)

A problem with reported total circulations affects the analysis. When these library systems use one integrated library system (ILS), circulations increase steadily. In the three cases used here, when these systems migrate to another, the circulations drop for the next year or two. In the case of PINES, the consortium experienced a steady increase in total circulations, but PINES members had two declines: when the separate libraries joined the consortium in the first place, and when the PINES consortium moved from Unicorn to Evergreen (http://www.open-ils.org).

In the first year of PINES, one library had a decline in circulations of close to 1 million and the total for the Phase 1 libraries declined by about 400,000. A similar result occurred during the transition from Unicorn to Evergreen, where the decline for the Phase 1 and Phase 2 libraries was about 600,000*. Why? This result seems to reflect different definitions used by different systems and affects the results here. For one who has analyzed circulation statistics on many occasions, this discovery is not a complete surprise but still chastening.

We cannot be confident of circulation data that cross a migration from one library system to another. This experience is not as noticeable with items lent to and borrowed from other libraries. Although both sets of numbers are not independently audited, the circulation figures are much larger and more noticed. It can also be speculated that the definition of what a circulation is becomes more consistent between libraries after they form a consortium.

The third case is discussed below. The Bergen County Cooperative Library System (BCCLS) in New Jersey had a similar decline after migrating to a new system.

What we have done here is to use data from the estimated year after the consortium is formed or expanded to examine a set of consortia in three tables. The consortia are introduced near the tables with more information on them in the Appendix.

Table 1 / PINES, Phase 1 and Phase 2 Libraries

Consortium	Variables	Estimated Initial year FY 2002	FY 2006	% Change
PINES				
40 systems, 217 outlets	Total Circulation	15,724,171	16,846,059	7.1
	Items lent to others	11,746	218,071	1,757
	Items borrowed from others	10,638	195,317	1,736
	Population served (sum)	3,651,783	3,999,765	10
	% lent to + borrowed from ==> as a % of total circulations	0.1	2.5	

* The Georgia library fiscal year is July–June. The 2006 data, then, are for a complete year under Unicorn.

The first consortium we will consider is PINES. Table 1 has the summary data we will use here and on the other consortia. There are four variables and a few calculations using these data.

PINES was initially formed in the two phases mentioned above. Published reports mentioned 26 public library systems in Phase 1 (in 1999) and 16 in Phase 2 (in 2001), a total of 42 public library systems. One of those is the Georgia Public Library Service, the state library of Georgia, which has a small collection and is not included in this analysis. An analysis of the records has not helped us discover the last library. We have 40 for this analysis with 217 outlets. The estimated first year of the consortium, then, is 2002 and the data are from that year. In addition, note that the last year of data used here is FY 2006. The reader will recall that in early September 2006, PINES moved from Unicorn to Evergreen.

As we see in Table 1, total annual circulations for these libraries went from 15.7 million to 16.8 million from FY 2002 through FY 2006. The last column shows the percentage change between those the figures from those two years. Total circulations of these founding members of the PINES consortium went up more than 7 percent during these years.

The items lent to other libraries went up a substantially greater percent: 1,757 percent—almost 18 times. Items borrowed from other libraries increased about 17 times. The two numbers at the bottom of the two columns (for FY 2002 and for FY 2006) are a percentage of the total circulations from the total items lent to and borrowed from others. For FY 2006, then, the sum of the 11,746 items loaned to others plus the 10,638 items borrowed from others equal 0.1 percent of the 15.7 million total circulations for FY 2002. Between that year and FY 2006, both of these categories grew dramatically as noted, and this calculated percentage of the total from items loaned to and borrowed from others increased as well. Meanwhile, population served increased by 10 percent. Of course, even though these data are for these Phase 1 and Phase 2 libraries, as the consortium has grown these libraries are borrowing from and lending to a larger set of libraries. The influence of the larger set of libraries is reflected in the data in this table.

With the case of PINES, then, circulations do rise, but not nearly as much as the items coming into each of the systems from others and going out, nor as much as the population served. However, the items moving around the system have become a more important part of the circulation patterns of the consortium's members. Their users were requesting items not available locally and doing it more frequently. For comparison, the sum of these to variables in FY 2008 is 860,000, so the number more than doubles in the next two years.

Table 2 has two more consortia, eiNetwork, a large consortium in western Pennsylvania, and Portage Library Consortium, a smaller consortium in northeastern Ohio. The estimated initial year is different for the two—1997 for eiNetwork and 1996 for Portage—but the final year for these consortia and those in Table 3 is for the last year of available data: FY 2008.

In the case of eiNetwork, the growth in everything but population served has gone up substantially. Total circulations for the consortium are up 48 percent from the estimated initial year, and the percentage of those circulations that are due to items lent plus those borrowed has also gone up in absolute terms as well as in their contribution to all circulations at this consortium (1.1 percent to 29.4 percent). These numbers are greater than those for PINES, albeit for more years.

Table 2 / eiNetwork and Portage Library Consortium

Consortium	Variables	Estimated Initial year FY 1997	FY 2008	% Change
eiNetwork				
44 public library systems, 69 outlets	Total Circulation	6,971,228	10,328,707	48
	Items lent to others	38,737	1,523,451	3,833
	Items borrowed from others	34,923	1,515,502	4,240
	Population served (sum)	1,295,814	1,259,567	-3
	% lent to + borrowed from ==> as a % of total circulations	1.1	29.4	
Portage		**FY 1996**		
3 systems, 8 outlets				
	Total Circulation	1,313,064	1,704,534	30
	Items lent to others	2,777	46,217	1,564
	Items borrowed from others	1,254	37,181	2,865
	Population served (sum)	149,571	155,870	4
	% lent to + borrowed from ==> as a % of total circulations	0.3	4.9	

Portage Library Consortium has increased its total circulations by 30 percent, and the percentage of total circulations resulting from the sum of loans to other libraries and those borrowed has also gone up, but not nearly at the level we find with eiNetwork.

In these two, there is an increase in the materials moving around within their systems, as we saw with PINES, but both have increases in circulations that are larger than the changes in population served, which was not the case with PINES.

Table 3 presents summary data for several sets of libraries in New Jersey and is complicated but also telling.

The Bergen County Cooperative Library System (BCCLS) is a resource-sharing consortium in northeast New Jersey. According to its Web site (http://www.bccls.org/buckles/history.shtml), it was formed in 1979—before our data begin—-but "Thirteen libraries from Essex, Hudson, and Passaic counties have joined BCCLS since 1991." This group of libraries is analyzed separately in the second group, but also is included in the system data. The consortium migrated from a library system created by Data Research Associates (DRA) to Unicorn in 2004, according to lib-web-cats (http://www.librarytechnology.org/libwebcats), Marshall Breeding's invaluable site. DRA had been absorbed by Sirsi some years before. The circulations did drop with this migration, as we found with PINES, but for the purposes of Table 3, this fact was ignored—by 2008, BCCLS circulations had recovered handily. BCCLS has just moved to the Polaris ILS (http://www.polarislibrary.com). The data used here are from the DRA and Unicorn systems.

The PALS Plus Consortium (http://www.palsplus.org) has offered "Interlocal Cooperation since 1992," or about the same time as libraries in Passaic and Essex counties. This consortium includes two academic libraries, but we will only consider the public libraries in this analysis.

Table 3 / Three New Jersey Public Library Systems

Consortium	Variables	Estimated Initial year FY 1992	FY 2008	% Change
Bergen County Cooperative Library System (BCCLS)				
75 systems, 78 outlets	Total Circulation	8,589,224	11,198,501	30
	Items lent to others	64,433	833,940	1,194
	Items borrowed from others	102,054	809,271	693
	Population served (sum)	1,040,548	1,100,064	6
	% lent to + borrowed from ==> as a % of total circulations	1.9	14.7	
Essex, Hudson, and Passaic Libraries in BCCLS				
13 systems, 15 outlets	Total Circulation	1,860,061	2,236,656	20
	Items lent to others	6,303	111,131	1,663
	Items borrowed from others	15,661	204,066	1,203
	Population served (sum)	289,679	304,015	5
	% lent to + borrowed from ==> as a % of total circulations	1.2	14.1	
PALS Plus				
18 public library systems, 24 outlets	Total Circulation	1,786,472	1,862,224	4
	Items lent to others	3,647	66,751	1,730
	Items borrowed from others	7,934	66,440	737
	Population served (sum)	448,604	484,565	8
	% lent to + borrowed from ==> as a % of total circulations	0.6	7.2	
Essex, Hudson, and Passaic Libraries Not in BCCLS or Pals Plus				
18 systems, 25 outlets	Total Circulation	4,306,822	3,984,565	-7
	Items lent to others	24,212	82,479	241
	Items borrowed from others	16,026	76,404	377
	Population served (sum)	1,330,098	1,416,083	6
	% lent to + borrowed from ==> as a % of total circulations	0.9	4.0	

The fourth group in the table are those public libraries in these three counties that are not members of either BCCLS or PALS Plus. We will use the FY 1992 data for the initial year for the four groups in Table 3 and follow them to the end of the published data in FY 2008.

In Table 3 we see that the libraries in BCCLS have a 30 percent increase in circulations and that their percentage of total circulations that are a result of loans to and from these individual systems is nearing 15 percent over the period. The libraries in the three counties that joined "since 1991" have a somewhat lower increase in circulations as a percentage; otherwise, their experience is similar to the other libraries in BCCLS, and it would appear that joining BCCLS was a successful move. Looking at their figures, they are borrowing a bit more than 90,000 items more than they are lending.

PALS Plus libraries show increases in all measures, also. But these increases were not as great as we observed in the libraries in BCCLS nor their newer members. Note, though, that the FY 1992 data for this group shows them borrowing about twice what they lend, but in FY 2008 these two numbers are almost in balance. Contrast this result with the 13 new library systems that joined BCCLS after 1991 that have been net borrowers since joining BCCLS.

The 18 systems that are in neither BCCLS nor PALS Plus have an absolute decline in total circulations and do not show the kind of strong growth seen in loans to and items borrowed from all other libraries that we see at those two consortia. For the libraries represented in this table, at least, resource sharing has proved a success.

Conclusion

From these opportunistic samples, it appears that there is a consortial effect that is clearest in considering inter-consortial lending, but in most of the cases here is apparent in total circulations as well. The group of libraries not in a consortium did not fare as well as those that were.

These facts may be a result of a consortial effect, but of course local conditions may be a more important aspect of the story. National-level data such as are used here allow an analysis based on a few data items but remove the context that may well be useful in understanding what is being observed. That said, these results do confirm the wealth of anecdotal evidence from across the nation.

Generally, the economics of integrated library system software favor larger libraries or consortia on a per-unit basis; there are scale economies, and libraries joining large consortia will save money on software. However, much of the money saved may go to paying for a courier service to move the items requested by the expanded users of the consortium. The net result is happier users at a lower cost than found in independent systems.

Appendix

Details on the Consortia

Bergen County Cooperative Library System (BCCLS). BCCLS is a resource-sharing consortium centered in Bergen County, New Jersey (with member libraries from some nearby counties). It reported 75 systems and 78 outlets in 2008. Our analysis begins with data from 1992. Its history page says the system was founded in 1979, but that 13 libraries from three nearby counties have joined BCCLS "since 1991" (http://www.bccls.org/buckles/history.shtml).

BCCLS was formed before the beginning of the longitudinal data series used here to analyze these consortia, and for that reason we have no base year for comparison. However, we can examine the 13 libraries that joined from that date by treating them separately. To compare the four groups of libraries, Table 3 treats the estimated first year for all four of these groups of libraries used in this table as 1992. Although our focus is on the 13 libraries that joined "since 1991," Table 3 also includes the BCCLS data for comparison.

Those libraries not in either group are also included in Table 3. There are 18 library systems and 25 outlets. They use a variety of integrated library systems.

eiNetwork (http://www.einetwork.net). This consortium is located in western Pennsylvania. It was founded in 1996 (http://en.wikipedia.org/wiki/Allegheny_County_Library_Association) and from the beginning has used software from Innovative Interfaces (http://www.iii.com) for its integrated library system. It has 44 public library systems, one special library, and 70 outlets. Data from the special library are not included.

PINES. This is the geographically dispersed Georgia resource-sharing consortium discussed above. We start our analysis after the 41 Phase 2 libraries joined in 2001. PINES used Unicorn until 2006 when it became the first system to run the open source Evergreen consortial library system (http://www.open-ils.org). This analysis uses data from Unicorn alone.

Portage. This is a three-public-library system in Ohio with eight outlets. The Kent Free Library and Reed Memorial Library each have a central library and no branches; the Portage County District Library has six outlets. The estimated first year is 2006. This date was chosen from the "Brief History of the Portage County Library District (http://www.portagecounty.lib.oh.us/page.cfm?ID=334), which says the library joined with the others in the mid-1990s. Portage also uses the Millenium system from Innovative Interfaces.

SC LENDS. This system began in May of 2009 with the first migrations to the Evergreen (http://www.open-ils.org) open source library system.

Number of Libraries in the United States and Canada

Statistics are from *American Library Directory* (*ALD*) *2010–2011* (Information Today, Inc., 2010). Data are exclusive of elementary and secondary school libraries.

Libraries in the United States

Public Libraries	16,992*
Public libraries, excluding branches	9,744†
Main public libraries that have branches	1,420
Public library branches	7,248
Academic Libraries	3,745*
Community college	1,160
Departmental	208
Law	1
Medical	11
Religious	11
University and college	2,585
Departmental	1,371
Law	182
Medical	245
Religious	237
Armed Forces Libraries	284*
Air Force	84
Medical	5
Army	132
Medical	27
Marine Corps	12
Navy	56
Law	1
Medical	12
Government Libraries	1,113*
Law	399
Medical	150
Special Libraries (excluding public, academic, armed forces, and government)	7,195*
Law	853
Medical	1,427
Religious	523
Total Special Libraries (including public, academic, armed forces, and government)	8,476
Total law	1,436
Total medical	1,877
Total religious	1,022
Total Libraries Counted(*)	29,329

Libraries in Regions Administered by the United States

Public Libraries	29*
Public libraries, excluding branches	11†
Main public libraries that have branches	3
Public library branches	18
Academic Libraries	37*
Community college	4
Departmental	3
Medical	0
University and college	33
Departmental	21
Law	3
Medical	2
Religious	1
Armed Forces Libraries	2*
Air Force	1
Army	1
Navy	0
Government Libraries	6*
Law	1
Medical	2
Special Libraries (excluding public, academic, armed forces, and government)	7*
Law	3
Medical	1
Religious	1
Total Special Libraries (including public, academic, armed forces, and government)	16
Total law	7
Total medical	5
Total religious	2
Total Libraries Counted(*)	81

Libraries in Canada

Public Libraries	2,057*
Public libraries, excluding branches	819†
Main public libraries that have branches	136
Public library branches	1,238
Academic Libraries	350*
Community college	85
Departmental	13
Medical	0
Religious	4

University and college	265
Departmental	177
Law	16
Medical	21
Religious	34
Government Libraries	288*
Law	36
Medical	7
Special Libraries (excluding public, academic, armed forces, and government)	929*
Law	104
Medical	178
Religious	26
Total Special Libraries (including public, academic, armed forces, and government)	1,047
Total law	156
Total medical	206
Total religious	91
Total Libraries Counted(*)	3,624

Summary

Total U.S. Libraries	29,329
Total Libraries Administered by the United States	81
Total Canadian Libraries	3,624
Grand Total of Libraries Listed	33,034

Note: Numbers followed by an asterisk are added to find "Total libraries counted" for each of the three geographic areas (United States, U.S.-administered regions, and Canada). The sum of the three totals is the "Grand total of libraries listed" in *ALD*. [For details on the count of libraries, see the preface to the 63rd edition of *ALD—Ed.*]

†Federal, state, and other statistical sources use this figure (libraries *excluding* branches) as the total for public libraries.

Highlights of IMLS and NCES Surveys

The Institute of Museum and Library Services (IMLS) and the National Center for Education Statistics (NCES) collect and disseminate statistical information about libraries in the United States and its outlying areas. Two major surveys are conducted by NCES, the Academic Libraries Survey and the School Library Media Centers Survey; two others, the Public Libraries Survey and the State Library Agencies Survey, were formerly conducted by NCES, but are now handled by IMLS.

Both IMLS and NCES also conduct surveys on related topics. This article presents highlights from two of the most recently conducted surveys.

For more information, see "National Center for Education Statistics Library Statistics Program" in Part 1 and "Institute of Museum and Library Services Library Programs" in Part 2 of this volume.

Public Libraries

The following are highlights from the publication *Public Libraries Survey: Fiscal Year 2008,* released in June 2010 by IMLS.

Number of Libraries

- There were 9,221 public libraries (administrative entities) in the 50 states and the District of Columbia in fiscal year (FY) 2008, slightly up from 9,214 in FY 2007.
- Public libraries are widely distributed across the United States; 98.4 percent of counties have at least one administrative entity or library outlet. Public library service areas encompassed 97.47 percent of the total population of the states and the District of Columbia in FY 2008, either in legally established geographic service areas or in areas under contract.
- Slightly less than 12 percent of the U.S. public libraries served 72.8 percent of the population of legally served areas during FY 2008; each of these public libraries had a legal service area population of 50,000 or more.

Visits

- Library visitation per capita has steadily increased over the past ten years. In FY 2008 the average individual in a library service area visited the library just over 5 times (5.1), compared with 4.3 visits per person in 1999, an increase of 19.7 percent. Overall, there were 1.50 billion public library visits in FY 2008, up from 1.43 billion total visits the previous year.

Circulation

- Circulation per capita has generally increased during the past ten years, rising by 19.7 percent since FY 1999 when per person circulation stood at 6.5. The nation's libraries recorded 7.7 circulations per capita in FY 2008, up from 7.4 the previous year.

- Overall, the nation's public libraries circulated 2.28 billion materials during FY 2008, up from 2.17 billion in FY 2007 and 1.69 billion in FY 1999. Overall circulation has increased by 34.5 percent since FY 1999.
- The circulations per 1,000 visits metric provides a rough measure of the likelihood that library visitors will check out materials and shows how patterns of library use are evolving. Circulation per 1,000 visits was virtually the same in FY 2008 (1,513) as it was in FY 1999 (1,512). Fluctuation between these two points in time was rather modest; the difference between the low point (1,495 circulations per 1,000 visits in FY 2000) and the high point (1,530 circulations per 1,000 visits in FY 2003) was only 2.3 percent. Even though circulations per visit remained relatively flat during the ten-year study period, it is worth noting that in FY 1997 there were 1,598 circulations per visit, so circulations per visit have declined 5.3 percent since then.

Computer Use and Availability

- The availability of Internet terminals in public libraries has nearly doubled over the past ten years in response to patron demand; Internet PCs per 5,000 people rose from 1.9 in FY 1999 to 3.7 in FY 2008. (The number of uses of Internet PCs per person is a relatively new data element that was introduced in the FY 2006 Public Libraries Survey, so it cannot be traced back as far as most of the other metrics.)
- Internet PC uses per capita has remained at the same basic level since FY 2006. There were 1.16 Internet uses per person in FY 2006, 1.22 Internet uses per person in FY 2007, and 1.21 Internet uses per person in FY 2008.

Collections

- The composition of library collections has changed somewhat over the past ten years. The number of print materials per 1,000 people has fluctuated over the time period, but on balance it has declined, from 2,846 print materials per 1,000 people in FY 1999 to 2,767 print materials per 1,000 people in FY 2008, a decrease of 2.8 percent. The high point during the study period was FY 2003, when libraries reported 2,860 print materials per 1,000 people.
- At the same time that print materials per person have decreased slightly, the amount of video and audio materials per person has increased considerably. Video materials per capita more than doubled during the study period, increasing from 73.5 video materials per 1,000 people in FY 1999 to 166.7 video materials per 1,000 people in FY 2008, an increase of 126.6 percent. The availability of audio materials also increased markedly, going from 112.4 materials per 1,000 people in FY 1999 to 168.1 materials per 1,000 people in FY 2008, an increase of nearly 50 percent (49.6 percent).

Reference Transactions

- Unlike circulation per capita and per capita visitation, per capita reference transactions have generally declined over the past ten years, going from

1.12 reference transactions per capita in FY 1999 to 1.02 in FY 2008, a decline of 9.0 percent.

- Not only have reference transactions declined relative to population; they have also declined relative to visitation. In FY 1999 there were 263.1 reference transactions per 1,000 visits. By FY 2008 the figure had declined to 200.0 reference transactions per 1,000 visits, a decrease of 24.0 percent. This decline in reference transactions is likely due to the rise of the Internet as an alternate source for information; patrons may be using the Internet to answer more straightforward questions and enlisting the help of library staff to answer questions that require more time, expertise, and research experience.

Program Attendance

- Children's program attendance at public libraries gradually rose during the study period, incrementally increasing from 181.7 children's program attendances per 1,000 people in FY 1999 to 206.8 program attendances per 1,000 people in FY 2008, an increase of 13.9 percent.
- Information on overall program attendance (children's program attendance plus other program attendance) has been collected at the national level only since FY 2004; since then, overall program attendance has increased from 237.6 attendances per 1,000 people to 279.4 attendances per 1,000 people in FY 2008, an increase of 17.6 percent. Program attendance per 1,000 visits increased by 7.5 percent (from 50.9 to 54.8) from FY 2004 to FY 2008.
- The majority of people who attend programs at libraries are attending children's programs, although children's program attendance as a share of all program attendance has decreased during the past few years. Children's programs accounted for 81.1 percent of all library program attendance in FY 2004; since then, it has declined every year until reaching its FY 2008 level of 74.0 percent of overall program attendance.

Staffing

- The number of public librarians per 25,000 people has remained more or less the same over the past decade, hovering around 4.0. There were 4.0 librarians per 25,000 people in FY 1999 and 4.1 in FY 2008. Libraries reported having fewer than four librarians per 25,000 people during only two of the last ten years, FY 2004 and FY 2005.
- The number of paid staff per 25,000 people has similarly remained flat over the past ten years. There were 12.3 paid staffers per 25,000 people in FY 2008, up from 12.2 in FY 1999. The year with the highest relative number of staff persons was FY 2007, when there were 12.4 paid staffers per 25,000 people; the lowest was in FY 2004, when there were 12.0 paid staffers per 25,000 people.
- The percentage of librarians with American Library Association-accredited master's degrees in library science (ALA-MLS degrees) fell slightly during the study period. In FY 1999 a total of 69.0 percent of public librarians had ALA-MLS degrees; this percentage fell from then until FY

2003, when it reached its low during the study period of 67.6 percent. From there, the percentage increased each year until it reached 68.3 percent in FY 2006.

- In FY 2008 the percentage of librarians with ALA-MLS degrees stood at 67.9 percent. In contrast, the number of library systems with at least one ALA-MLS-degreed librarian increased somewhat during the study period, rising from 44.1 percent in FY 1999 to 48.4 percent in FY 2008. This means that on average, public library systems were 9.9 percent more likely to have ALA-MLS-degreed librarians in FY 2008 than they were in FY 1999.

Expenditures

- Total operating expenditures in public libraries steadily rose during the study period, going from $8.29 billion in FY 1999 to $10.72 billion in FY 2008 (figures are in constant 2008 dollars), an absolute increase of $2.43 billion and a percentage increase of 29.4 percent. Per capita operating expenditures increased during the period as well. Per capita operating expenditures rose from $31.56 in FY 1999 to $36.36 in FY 2008, an absolute increase of $4.80 per person and a percentage increase of 15.2 percent.
- In the past ten years, local governments have borne a growing share of the responsibility for funding libraries. In FY 2000 local governments supplied 77.1 percent of public library operating revenue. This percentage has gradually risen since then, reaching a high of 82.7 percent in FY 2008.
- This trend of increasing local contributions to operating revenue has been paralleled by a decrease in the share of operating revenue that is supplied by state governments. During FY 1999–2001, state government funds provided 12.7 to 12.8 percent of public library operating revenue. After that, the state share of operating revenue steadily declined, reaching its low of 8.7 percent in FY 2008.
- Revenue from federal (0.6 percent in FY 1999, 0.4 percent in FY 2008) and "other" sources (9.0 percent in FY 1999, 8.2 percent in FY 2008) remained relatively flat over the same time period.

Service Outlets, Legal Basis, Interlibrary Relationships

- The majority of public libraries (85.2 percent) are public agencies connected to some form of local government. In FY 2008 a total of 52.9 percent of public libraries were part of a municipal government, 14.6 percent were separate government units known as library districts, 9.8 percent were part of a county or parish, 3.4 percent had multijurisdictional legal basis under an intergovernmental agreement, 2.0 percent were part of a school district, 1.0 percent were part of a city or county, and 1.5 percent reported their legal basis as "other."
- Just under 15 percent (14.9) of public libraries were operated by nonprofit associations/agencies; this means that they were privately controlled but met the legal definition of a public library in the states in which they were located.
- Although the majority of public libraries report single jurisdictions, many belong to broader service networks. More than three-quarters (75.6) percent of public libraries were members of a federation or cooperative service,

while 23.2 percent were not. And 1.2 percent served as the headquarters of a federation or cooperative service.

Summary

- The survey data suggest that demand for library services is continuing to increase over time. Per person visitation and per person circulation both increased by nearly 20 percent from FY 1999 to FY 2008, and library program attendance per person increased 17.6 percent from FY 2004 to FY 2008.
- The availability of information technology resources in libraries has increased rapidly in response to patron demand; the number of Internet PCs per person nearly doubled from FY 2000 to FY 2008.
- There is evidence that library use patterns have changed somewhat. Library visitors are making fewer reference inquiries per visit and checking out fewer materials per visit—reference transactions per visit declined by nearly 25 percent from FY 1999 to FY 2008 and circulations per visit declined by 5.3 percent from FY 1997 to FY 2008. At the same time, visitors are becoming more likely to attend library programs such as youth reading events, book clubs, and literacy classes; library program attendance per visit increased by 7.5 percent from FY 2004 to FY 2008.
- The survey data also show that libraries have become more expensive to run and more dependent on local funding sources. Per person operating expenditures increased by 15.2 percent from FY 1999 to FY 2008 and total operating expenditures increased by nearly 30 percent during the same period. The share of operating revenues from local sources increased from 77.7 percent to 82.7 percent from FY 1999 to FY 2008 while the share of operating revenue from state sources decreased from 12.7 percent to 8.7 percent during the same period.

Academic Libraries

The following are highlights from the First Look publication *Academic Libraries, 2008,* released in December 2009 by NCES.

Services

- During FY 2008, there were about 138.1 million circulation transactions from academic libraries' general collections.
- Academic libraries loaned some 11.1 million documents to other libraries in FY 2008. Academic libraries also borrowed approximately 10.7 million documents from other libraries and commercial services. Documents from commercial services accounted for about 936,000 of the documents borrowed.
- The majority of academic libraries, 2,530, were open between 60 and 99 hours during a typical week in FY 2008. Another 683 academic libraries were open between 40 and 59 hours per typical week, and 532 were open more than 100 hours per typical week.
- During a typical week in the fall of 2008, approximately 1.1 million academic library reference transactions were conducted, including computer searches.

Collections

- At the end of FY 2008, there were 226 academic libraries that held 1 million or more books, serial backfiles, and other paper materials including government documents.
- Academic libraries held approximately 102.5 million e-books and about 3.6 million electronic reference sources and aggregation services at the end of FY 2008.
- In FY 2008 academic libraries added approximately 24.0 million books, serial backfiles, and other paper materials including government documents.

Staff

- Academic libraries reported 93,438 full-time-equivalent (FTE) staff working in academic libraries during the fall of 2008.
- Academic libraries reported 27,030 FTE librarians during the fall of 2008. Librarians accounted for about 29 percent of the total number of FTE staff in academic libraries during the fall of 2008.

Expenditures

- Academic libraries' expenditures totaled approximately $6.8 billion during FY 2008.
- During FY 2008 academic libraries spent about $3.3 billion on salaries and wages, representing approximately 49 percent of total library expenditures.
- Academic libraries spent about $2.7 billion on information resources during FY 2008.
- Academic libraries spent approximately $133.6 million for electronic books, serial backfiles, and other materials in FY 2008.
- Expenditures for electronic current serial subscriptions were about $1.0 billion.
- During FY 2008 academic libraries spent approximately $113.4 million for bibliographic utilities, networks, and consortia.

Electronic Services

- In fall 2008 some 72 percent of academic libraries provided library reference service by e-mail or the Web.
- Nearly half (49 percent) reported providing technology to assist patrons with disabilities in fall 2008.

Information Literacy

- During FY 2008 some 46 percent of academic libraries reported that their postsecondary institution defined information literacy or the information-literate student.
- During FY 2008 about 33 percent of academic libraries reported that their postsecondary institution had incorporated information literacy into its mission.

Library Acquisition Expenditures, 2009–2010: U.S. Public, Academic, Special, and Government Libraries

The information in these tables is taken from *American Library Directory* (*ALD*) *2010–2011* (Information Today, Inc., 2010). The tables report acquisition expenditures by public, academic, special, and government libraries.

The total number of libraries in the United States and in regions administered by the United States listed in this 63rd edition of *ALD* is 29,410, including 17,021 public libraries, 3,782 academic libraries, 7,202 special libraries, and 1,119 government libraries.

Understanding the Tables

Number of libraries includes only those U.S. libraries in *ALD* that reported annual acquisition expenditures (1,798 public libraries, 768 academic libraries, 136 special libraries, and 44 government libraries). Libraries that reported annual income but not expenditures are not included in the count. Academic libraries include university, college, and junior college libraries. Special academic libraries, such as law and medical libraries, that reported acquisition expenditures separately from the institution's main library are counted as independent libraries.

The amount in the *total acquisition expenditures* column for a given state is generally greater than the sum of the categories of expenditures. This is because the total acquisition expenditures amount also includes the expenditures of libraries that did not itemize by category.

Figures in *categories of expenditure* columns represent only those libraries that itemized expenditures. Libraries that reported a total acquisition expenditure amount but did not itemize are only represented in the total acquisition expenditures column.

Table 1 / Public Library Acquisition Expenditures

State	Number of Libraries	Total Acquisition Expenditures	Categories of Expenditures (in U.S. dollars)								
			Books	Other Print Materials	Periodicals/ Serials	Manuscripts & Archives	AV Equipment	AV Materials	Microforms	Electronic Reference	Preservation
Alabama	25	18,117,287	1,319,215	15,641	46,388	2,000	297	218,506	1,963	20,519	400
Alaska	13	879,646	161,601	5,123	21,886	0	0	29,800	500	15,818	0
Arizona	21	13,859,286	3,521,476	4,727,824	180,271	0	0	2,394,456	50,656	2,085,324	8,876
Arkansas	17	4,163,551	2,568,285	22,064	172,135	0	23,105	454,518	1,640	314,435	8,270
California	69	86,947,336	32,295,338	1,831,597	3,779,542	4,500	0	9,636,389	188,083	5,886,329	10,019,775
Colorado	36	16,174,123	6,073,544	16,500	509,134	0	17,200	2,913,634	1,000	1,185,087	450
Connecticut	65	9,859,638	4,895,197	665,498	857,712	600	10,600	917,648	118,040	1,317,042	25,444
Delaware	5	632,708	130,294	0	0	0	0	26,263	0	1,500	0
District of Columbia	0	0	0	0	0	0	0	0	0	0	0
Florida	34	35,752,311	13,239,609	535,373	1,139,270	1,500	129,966	5,442,785	208,013	2,661,415	2,000
Georgia	14	9,111,629	2,534,175	1,068	151,211	0	2,026	606,483	740	425,695	583
Hawaii	1	2,930,469	0	0	170,259	0	0	0	67,819	1,487,608	0
Idaho	11	487,307	166,844	500	19,638	0	0	21,774	900	3,824	1,500
Illinois	91	25,537,406	8,269,824	82,257	652,399	10,000	73,980	2,586,701	333,410	2,422,192	20,042
Indiana	62	24,108,549	11,553,824	57,538	1,276,026	0	167,935	4,165,684	197,190	854,940	87,209
Iowa	58	6,965,316	1,959,289	90,161	220,437	0	13,768	548,144	1,709	183,747	0
Kansas	38	13,011,037	2,585,741	129,822	844,230	15	23,600	864,894	2,950	658,465	400
Kentucky	18	6,352,765	1,820,935	2,486	79,634	0	15,329	705,687	13,685	325,269	0
Louisiana	7	6,307,976	2,437,122	5,000	299,118	3,000	77,168	797,547	54,882	544,823	0
Maine	46	1,736,746	835,244	1,350	118,433	2,000	5,350	123,669	1,200	202,861	1,000
Maryland	3	10,351,925	1,832,335	0	115,097	0	0	908,338	0	201,766	0
Massachusetts	87	18,584,283	3,724,911	66,372	467,929	0	8,257	1,116,172	36,530	328,233	4,500
Michigan	80	24,524,401	8,080,962	18,763	614,408	0	34,000	1,932,688	26,440	1,080,787	13,275
Minnesota	37	17,062,002	4,672,515	6,589	154,837	0	4,500	1,261,693	6,039	543,490	668
Mississippi	9	3,891,855	470,525	0	36,506	0	0	153,005	6,414	1,421,336	2,162

Missouri	29	18,784,211	2,299,161	0	199,807	0	21,197	667,013	2,154	829,635	0
Montana	17	823,572	496,346	6,491	97,821	200	10,316	136,362	2,873	51,288	1,710
Nebraska	27	2,145,397	1,168,540	399,866	45,094	278	47	58,894	540	253,668	2,346
Nevada	5	1,157,270	128,500	1,193	10,558	0	0	19,634	200	20,000	0
New Hampshire	66	2,677,363	1,193,170	3,000	153,801	0	7,428	283,609	23,891	111,031	7,050
New Jersey	90	29,966,294	14,442,821	79,641	1,484,290	500	31,000	3,361,264	125,915	2,085,624	4,850
New Mexico	11	2,386,311	1,198,446	427	58,122	0	9,225	246,055	11,799	73,268	0
New York	130	38,189,253	18,177,491	431,350	1,839,913	5,000	145,713	3,779,367	142,618	2,245,974	28,628
North Carolina	28	12,227,238	7,552,253	1,344,458	261,286	0	26,040	963,356	15,540	522,032	0
North Dakota	16	1,713,832	741,349	4,085	86,568	0	35,000	135,462	3,500	121,887	1,000
Ohio	62	50,369,394	22,607,247	481,804	3,614,569	1,031	108,708	10,732,229	374,113	6,546,785	322,565
Oklahoma	10	12,919,852	5,299,024	11,498	860,566	0	0	1,579,149	2,910	917,153	0
Oregon	38	6,982,100	2,688,267	22,827	308,361	0	1,500	578,229	21,968	173,772	1,872,003
Pennsylvania	71	19,743,519	6,531,186	1,099,981	1,738,460	156,260	39,208	2,804,371	678,405	1,890,106	225,723
Rhode Island	9	9,932,476	768,963	54,994	102,744	0	1,846	121,734	70	72,440	3,500
South Carolina	17	11,246,743	6,763,833	22,222	423,116	5,000	90,907	1,724,307	23,809	1,339,716	12,235
South Dakota	19	1,909,249	962,881	1,000	97,075	0	395	298,134	50	116,006	0
Tennessee	24	6,135,120	1,769,129	0	252,973	0	11,177	331,529	1,200	463,767	1,315
Texas	85	27,250,208	12,088,741	528,768	1,192,494	0	274,345	2,275,405	55,041	1,639,410	9,224
Utah	11	4,478,938	1,448,387	1,203	108,063	245,000	0	517,610	30,367	108,754	72,000
Vermont	44	1,272,948	531,719	221	21,079	0	0	83,847	276	21,205	500
Virginia	27	8,908,160	3,890,329	9,551	415,633	6,278	0	976,374	19,578	658,370	4,800
Washington	25	24,165,990	2,855,283	490,238	139,990	0	54,230	705,893	4,100	544,011	900
West Virginia	16	4,036,148	1,580,939	1,086	109,543	9,000	24,000	227,112	10,310	776,375	6,000
Wisconsin	61	7,574,596	3,737,265	90,842	226,841	0	6,475	1,102,635	9,920	575,925	2,700
Wyoming	13	1,503,731	401,929	4,694	35,337	0	6,000	71,095	55	32,251	0
Puerto Rico	0	0	0	0	0	0	0	0	0	0	0
Total	1,798	665,849,465	236,472,004	13,372,966	25,810,604	452,162	1,511,838	71,607,147	2,881,005	46,362,958	12,775,603
Estimated % of Acquisition Expenditures			35.51	2.01	3.8	0.07	0.23	10.75	0.43	6.96	1.92

Table 2 / Academic Library Acquisition Expenditures

State	Number of Libraries	Total Acquisition Expenditures	Categories of Expenditures (in U.S. dollars)								
			Books	Other Print Materials	Periodicals/ Serials	Manuscripts & Archives	AV Equipment	AV Materials	Microforms	Electronic Reference	Preservation
Alabama	14	14,244,892	1,921,832	9,017	4,622,376	0	20,000	157,877	58,490	1,562,907	132,642
Alaska	5	6,695,613	532,433	10,000	2,446,408	0	300	74,887	17,307	888,392	18,827
Arizona	9	3,150,530	717,122	67,581	650,462	17,979	6,675	110,561	39,301	1,354,392	14,153
Arkansas	6	11,607,143	1,657,615	0	6,624,194	0	0	94,323	180,909	2,955,144	94,958
California	59	86,919,147	9,722,326	486,555	17,365,684	2,000	65,419	464,426	614,036	11,276,273	518,388
Colorado	12	25,100,426	3,347,653	898,159	9,785,900	0	0	114,063	70	7,815,956	68,945
Connecticut	11	8,206,135	1,808,862	340	3,846,592	0	20,478	162,881	155,138	1,416,991	86,588
Delaware	3	8,346,310	40,000	0	8,419	0	0	0	0	0	0
District of Columbia	3	11,667,126	1,973,224	0	6,269,488	0	0	8,100	99,300	1,012,392	94,154
Florida	30	26,443,500	4,726,391	722,211	10,100,935	0	26,000	577,046	203,213	8,136,955	291,468
Georgia	18	13,687,486	1,009,367	2,000	1,441,247	0	4,075	124,973	51,714	1,913,632	56,037
Hawaii	2	659,932	128,000	0	176,200	0	3,000	16,047	14,000	77,438	18,700
Idaho	4	9,452,279	832,363	0	3,584,197	2,470	0	28,897	0	879,501	56,780
Illinois	29	71,271,924	8,863,187	9,966	16,674,705	0	33,598	321,340	49,996	12,253,365	158,618
Indiana	17	22,994,511	3,746,709	24,211	12,984,721	0	44,452	175,948	33,331	2,040,908	94,563
Iowa	19	27,293,945	3,333,203	264,492	13,397,441	0	31,139	110,515	44,924	3,331,771	144,563
Kansas	17	9,135,940	1,612,694	24,000	6,230,318	0	8,718	50,198	23,753	729,016	62,577
Kentucky	13	21,235,399	2,337,491	11,300	9,423,855	32,109	2,747	117,978	192,266	4,910,261	203,176
Louisiana	8	5,302,035	535,867	35,173	3,400,999	3,427	3,720	6,387	68,382	1,091,779	46,632
Maine	3	7,905,379	1,509,525	0	5,842,437	0	0	44,812	62,500	251,231	74,374
Maryland	11	11,526,653	1,114,063	6,209	5,223,280	14,926	0	63,154	10,986	875,687	69,981
Massachusetts	27	180,071,469	4,091,367	49,981	9,105,271	0	107,000	206,800	46,938	9,067,518	163,675
Michigan	29	22,320,208	3,220,975	159,640	7,603,896	26,000	48,588	148,793	212,882	6,697,929	132,012
Minnesota	17	12,951,972	2,238,180	4,500	4,699,991	0	25,705	227,040	102,007	2,231,915	95,701
Mississippi	6	3,489,772	341,867	0	1,365,001	0	1,000	36,853	116,000	1,309,437	45,818

Missouri	16	10,665,931	790,641	0	2,441,071	2,765	8,326	115,875	134,171	668,640	55,764
Montana	5	374,497	164,301	0	154,767	0	10,000	9,069	3,000	20,000	0
Nebraska	9	10,445,456	569,759	123,250	2,230,224	15,000	34,909	134,477	49,043	604,778	18,220
Nevada	2	415,295	136,754	0	11,877	0	0	15,908	217	49,926	613
New Hampshire	5	8,349,884	1,195,724	0	4,180,222	0	0	700	21,116	1,351,794	76,271
New Jersey	12	7,902,037	1,311,323	71,023	1,638,820	0	0	47,205	83,376	1,457,888	27,530
New Mexico	6	5,944,302	44,000	0	8,800	0	0	11,000	4,300	24,400	2,200
New York	51	78,151,538	10,289,237	361,102	22,376,457	28,433	153,648	522,429	232,753	20,368,147	423,237
North Carolina	30	50,979,216	9,828,749	15,003	28,015,137	2,000	16,933	547,124	358,343	3,119,310	195,371
North Dakota	3	4,699,658	368,210	10,000	2,095,007	0	1,080	28,734	684	1,027,799	22,732
Ohio	31	28,909,653	5,742,476	78,695	8,959,421	2,461	27,829	266,771	143,789	6,485,451	281,732
Oklahoma	9	4,602,790	684,493	56,186	2,379,851	2,000	0	150,125	18,127	475,497	12,646
Oregon	16	29,464,004	1,438,337	4,488	3,509,981	0	43,675	116,010	0	1,734,265	102,981
Pennsylvania	30	19,943,642	4,045,500	9,500	9,431,537	35,314	71,203	275,502	265,735	2,915,219	201,039
Rhode Island	5	4,138,699	549,357	2,100	1,071,593	9,500	36,338	44,958	21,021	613,363	23,538
South Carolina	17	10,531,133	2,189,098	103,196	2,687,601	20,000	10,000	125,933	90,085	2,327,455	94,116
South Dakota	4	3,381,770	280,605	0	641,458	0	3,592	12,688	12,480	626,286	18,339
Tennessee	15	18,755,820	957,884	0	1,539,729	0	0	55,750	68,400	2,643,068	11,101
Texas	36	59,613,807	10,170,492	18,140	24,620,357	6,050	235,748	344,779	364,918	4,323,366	374,621
Utah	4	4,846,673	1,008,900	0	2,964,773	0	16,000	71,500	3,500	782,000	0
Vermont	6	1,845,478	488,155	0	796,812	3,000	5,000	39,620	2,580	379,240	10,500
Virginia	26	34,209,722	6,751,645	625,166	13,014,893	2,000	25,938	336,952	128,643	6,150,505	109,133
Washington	17	14,033,124	2,641,226	11,644	7,596,794	34,449	57,793	183,261	41,238	1,634,236	60,109
West Virginia	13	5,811,573	351,666	638,661	861,787	12,696	19,000	47,453	35,295	840,980	9,005
Wisconsin	18	21,734,783	2,675,120	10,256	6,119,951	0	23,109	140,423	113,439	949,447	69,402
Wyoming	3	7,480,309	3,458,937	0	2,201,321	0	0	13,200	0	863,481	0
Puerto Rico	7	6,235,838	804,121	1,000	4,649,922	5,000	34,527	49,638	0	674,235	10,000
Total	768	1,075,146,358	130,299,026	4,924,745	319,074,180	279,579	1,287,262	7,150,983	4,593,696	147,191,566	4,953,530
Estimated % of Acquisition Expenditures			12.12	0.46	29.68	0.03	0.12	0.67	0.43	13.69	0.46

Table 3 / Special Library Acquisition Expenditures

State	Number of Libraries	Total Acquisition Expenditures	Categories of Expenditures (in U.S. dollars)								
			Books	Other Print Materials	Periodicals/ Serials	Manuscripts & Archives	AV Equipment	AV Materials	Microforms	Electronic Reference	Preservation
Alabama	1	1,375	250	0	525	0	0	0	0	500	100
Alaska	0	0	0	0	0	0	0	0	0	0	0
Arizona	4	20,324	0	0	0	0	0	0	0	0	0
Arkansas	0	0	0	0	0	0	0	0	0	0	0
California	13	392,098	52,198	2,000	167,059	0	2,500	1,100	0	69,741	7,500
Colorado	1	10,000	7,000	0	1,000	0	0	2,000	0	0	0
Connecticut	0	0	0	0	0	0	0	0	0	0	0
Delaware	0	0	0	0	0	0	0	0	0	0	0
District of Columbia	3	877,714	124,027	0	57,110	0	0	261	25,000	13,000	504,877
Florida	5	105,900	46,350	1,000	35,300	0	0	0	0	7,500	11,800
Georgia	0	0	0	0	0	0	0	0	0	0	0
Hawaii	0	0	0	0	0	0	0	0	0	0	0
Idaho	0	0	0	0	0	0	0	0	0	0	0
Illinois	10	2,745,600	93,300	500	146,500	200	1,900	4,000	1,500	72,000	4,700
Indiana	2	43,625	37,725	0	120	500	0	0	3,780	0	1,500
Iowa	2	203,058	35,362	0	12,408	0	0	0	155,288	0	0
Kansas	2	12,581	4,400	4,000	4,081	0	0	0	0	0	100
Kentucky	0	0	0	0	0	0	0	0	0	0	0
Louisiana	0	0	0	0	0	0	0	0	0	0	0
Maine	1	200	0	0	0	0	0	0	0	0	0
Maryland	3	166,950	23,150	0	130,450	50	0	0	0	12,000	100
Massachusetts	3	81,891	0	0	0	0	0	0	0	0	0
Michigan	1	12,000	3,000	500	3,600	0	0	400	0	0	0
Minnesota	2	54,850	21,350	5,000	11,500	0	0	1,000	0	16,000	0
Mississippi	0	0	0	0	0	0	0	0	0	0	0

Missouri	2	68,745	24,000	0	30,145	0	0	0	600	14,000	0
Montana	1	17,348	15,848	0	0	0	0	0	0	1,500	0
Nebraska	2	2,600	950	0	1,500	0	0	0	0	0	0
Nevada	1	1,000	0	0	0	0	0	0	0	0	0
New Hampshire	2	69,000	16,000	2,000	4,000	15,000	0	0	0	22,000	9,000
New Jersey	4	37,000	15,000	0	10,900	0	0	6,000	0	1,900	3,200
New Mexico	1	2,600	0	300	500	0	500	0	0	0	1,300
New York	22	690,956	164,545	50	191,450	20,000	3,452	11,662	1,000	36,775	26,820
North Carolina	0	0	0	0	0	0	0	0	0	0	0
North Dakota	2	11,598	2,660	0	5,475	2,000	0	0	0	0	1,463
Ohio	12	1,585,713	119,527	550	670,162	1,200	150	1,549	500	775,615	11,260
Oklahoma	3	101,050	15,000	1,250	36,800	12,000	20,000	1,000	3,000	12,000	0
Oregon	1	600	200	0	0	0	0	0	0	400	0
Pennsylvania	6	459,057	41,108	58,812	85,859	18,351	0	9,671	10,000	204,322	25,034
Rhode Island	1	75,313	44,726	0	5,000	15,387	0	0	0	0	10,200
South Carolina	1	29,600	14,000	0	5,000	0	0	6,000	3,000	0	0
South Dakota	0	0	0	0	0	0	0	0	0	0	0
Tennessee	2	26,000	12,500	0	6,000	0	500	3,000	0	4,000	0
Texas	10	1,167,759	46,237	45,992	19,759	500	1,474	1,587	0	96,000	500
Utah	1	75,000	5,000	5,000	10,000	0	5,000	0	0	50,000	0
Vermont	0	0	0	0	0	0	0	0	0	0	0
Virginia	5	383,110	102,159	12,600	51,030	40,373	48,265	5,380	4,200	27,975	91,128
Washington	1	1,500	0	0	0	0	0	0	0	0	0
West Virginia	1	11,000	4,000	0	5,000	0	0	500	0	1,500	0
Wisconsin	2	128,500	11,300	0	74,000	0	0	0	0	43,000	0
Wyoming	0	0	0	0	0	0	0	0	0	0	0
Puerto Rico	0	0	0	0	0	0	0	0	0	0	0
Total	136	9,673,215	1,102,872	139,554	1,782,233	125,561	83,741	55,110	207,868	1,481,728	710,582
Estimated % of Acquisition Expenditures			11.40	1.44	18.42	1.30	0.87	0.57	2.15	15.32	7.35

Table 4 / Government Library Acquisition Expenditures

State	Number of Libraries	Total Acquisition Expenditures	Categories of Expenditures (in U.S. dollars)								
			Books	Other Print Materials	Periodicals/ Serials	Manuscripts & Archives	AV Equipment	AV Materials	Microforms	Electronic Reference	Preservation
Alabama	2	626,295	243,777	0	575	0	0	0	0	381,472	471
Alaska	0	0	0	0	0	0	0	0	0	0	0
Arizona	0	0	0	0	0	0	0	0	0	0	0
Arkansas	0	0	0	0	0	0	0	0	0	0	0
California	10	2,553,176	781,727	174,358	537,590	0	7,472	6,245	17,804	399,163	4,432
Colorado	0	0	0	0	0	0	0	0	0	0	0
Connecticut	0	0	0	0	0	0	0	0	0	0	0
Delaware	1	50,000	7,000	1,000	9,000	0	0	0	0	33,000	0
District of Columbia	0	0	0	0	0	0	0	0	0	0	0
Florida	1	19,545	3,750	0	14,170	0	0	1,625	0	0	0
Georgia	0	0	0	0	0	0	0	0	0	0	0
Hawaii	0	0	0	0	0	0	0	0	0	0	0
Idaho	0	0	0	0	0	0	0	0	0	0	0
Illinois	0	0	0	0	0	0	0	0	0	0	0
Indiana	0	0	0	0	0	0	0	0	0	0	0
Iowa	0	0	0	0	0	0	0	0	0	0	0
Kansas	2	801,526	303,156	0	407,919	0	0	0	0	83,534	6,917
Kentucky	0	0	0	0	0	0	0	0	0	0	0
Louisiana	2	1,042,318	28,500	0	123,000	0	500	1,000	0	15,000	0
Maine	1	257,079	0	0	0	0	0	0	0	0	0
Maryland	3	589,000	358,000	11,800	196,000	0	0	7,700	0	0	3,500
Massachusetts	3	348,868	195,036	0	0	0	0	0	0	68,332	7,500
Michigan	1	35,000	0	0	0	0	0	0	0	0	0
Minnesota	2	134,500	18,000	0	61,500	0	0	0	0	55,000	0
Mississippi	1	2,500	0	0	0	0	0	0	0	0	0

Missouri	0	0	0	0	0	0	0	0	0	0	0
Montana	1	425,961	328,391	0	0	0	0	0	0	97,570	0
Nebraska	0	0	0	0	0	0	0	0	0	0	0
Nevada	1	768,769	562,656	0	10,803	0	0	0	3,151	186,357	5,802
New Hampshire	1	70,000	0	0	0	0	0	0	0	0	0
New Jersey	0	0	0	0	0	0	0	0	0	0	0
New Mexico	0	0	0	0	0	0	0	0	0	0	0
New York	3	1,367,180	0	0	0	0	0	0	0	0	5,300
North Carolina	0	0	0	0	0	0	0	0	0	0	0
North Dakota	1	40,000	5,000	0	30,000	0	0	0	0	5,000	0
Ohio	0	0	0	0	0	0	0	0	0	0	0
Oklahoma	0	0	0	0	0	0	0	0	0	0	0
Oregon	0	0	0	0	0	0	0	0	0	0	0
Pennsylvania	4	575,000	71,500	0	500	0	0	0	0	10,000	0
Rhode Island	1	43,425	9,961	0	31,764	0	0	814	0	886	0
South Carolina	0	0	0	0	0	0	0	0	0	0	0
South Dakota	0	0	0	0	0	0	0	0	0	0	0
Tennessee	1	125,000	0	0	0	0	0	0	0	0	0
Texas	0	0	0	0	0	0	0	0	0	0	0
Utah	0	0	0	0	0	0	0	0	0	0	0
Vermont	0	0	0	0	0	0	0	0	0	0	0
Virginia	1	63,090	13,355	0	42,453	0	0	6,271	0	1,011	0
Washington	0	0	0	0	0	0	0	0	0	0	0
West Virginia	1	650,000	50,000	0	400,000	0	0	0	0	200,000	0
Wisconsin	0	0	0	0	0	0	0	0	0	0	0
Wyoming	0	0	0	0	0	0	0	0	0	0	0
Puerto Rico	0	0	0	0	0	0	0	0	0	0	0
Total	44	10,588,232	2,979,809	187,158	1,865,274	0	7,972	23,655	20,955	1,536,325	33,922
Estimated % of Acquisition Expenditures			28.14	1.77	17.62	0.00	0.08	0.22	0.20	14.51	0.32

Public Library State Rankings, 2008

State	Library Visits per Capita[1]	Reference Transactions per Capita	Circulation Transactions per Capita	Interlibrary Loans Received per 1,000 Population	Public-use Computers per Stationary Outlet
Alabama	46	34	46	32	13
Alaska	29	46	36	29	48
Arizona	40	38	27	25	3
Arkansas	45	41	43	43	40
California	34	25	40	22	12
Colorado	13	8	6	20	9
Connecticut	5	6	16	15	18
Delaware	25	48	11	13	19
District of Columbia[2]	32	5	50	50	29
Florida	36	3	37	39	1
Georgia	43	18	45	28	6
Hawaii[3]	33	40	41	51	35
Idaho	12	29	15	26	38
Illinois	8	9	19	6	23
Indiana	2	19	3	36	7
Iowa	14	45	13	17	45
Kansas	16	12	7	12	41
Kentucky	37	27	32	41	5
Louisiana	50	10	49	35	25
Maine	19	47	25	10	49
Maryland	21	15	12	31	2
Massachusetts	10	26	22	4	32
Michigan	26	21	24	8	15
Minnesota	27	32	9	14	28
Mississippi	51	49	51	48	39
Missouri	24	14	14	27	26
Montana	35	51	34	16	42
Nebraska	3	24	10	34	44
Nevada	42	43	33	37	27
New Hampshire	23	44	20	18	51
New Jersey	20	16	28	11	16
New Mexico	31	28	35	44	30
New York	17	4	23	7	20
North Carolina	39	7	39	49	11
North Dakota	38	35	29	21	47
Ohio	1	1	1	5	10
Oklahoma	30	36	31	42	33
Oregon	7	33	2	2	34
Pennsylvania	41	39	38	9	31
Rhode Island	18	30	30	3	17
South Carolina	44	13	42	46	8
South Dakota	22	23	21	24	46
Tennessee	47	42	48	45	21
Texas	48	37	44	40	4
Utah	6	2	4	47	24

State	Library Visits per Capita[1]	Reference Transactions per Capita	Circulation Transactions per Capita	Interlibrary Loans Received per 1,000 Population	Public-use Computers per Stationary Outlet
Vermont	11	31	26	23	50
Virginia	28	20	17	38	14
Washington	9	17	5	33	22
West Virginia	49	50	47	30	43
Wisconsin	15	22	8	1	36
Wyoming	4	11	18	19	37

State	Public-use Internet Computers per 5,000 Population	Print Materials per Capita	Audio Materials per 1,000 Population	Video Materials per 1,000 Population	Current Print Serial Subscriptions per 1,000 Population
Alabama	9	40	41	42	49
Alaska	23	17	23	5	9
Arizona	47	51	44	44	48
Arkansas	32	39	47	46	43
California	49	44	45	41	45
Colorado	24	37	16	19	31
Connecticut	13	9	11	6	15
Delaware	46	34	34	26	19
District of Columbia[2]	48	20	29	40	32
Florida	31	49	36	30	41
Georgia	36	50	51	49	51
Hawaii[3]	50	29	39	47	39
Idaho	16	23	25	27	33
Illinois	18	16	9	15	11
Indiana	6	7	5	2	7
Iowa	7	13	14	11	3
Kansas	5	10	13	4	12
Kentucky	28	42	37	38	36
Louisiana	11	30	46	33	30
Maine	8	1	22	12	10
Maryland	37	31	20	32	23
Massachusetts	27	3	8	9	14
Michigan	12	22	15	23	24
Minnesota	22	28	28	28	25
Mississippi	33	46	50	48	46
Missouri	19	19	27	29	16
Montana	15	24	35	31	29
Nebraska	2	2	10	13	5
Nevada	51	43	30	25	44
New Hampshire	20	5	17	10	2
New Jersey	26	18	26	22	26
New Mexico	17	25	32	37	21
New York	29	15	6	17	6
North Carolina	39	48	49	51	42
North Dakota	21	11	24	24	18

State	Public-use Internet Computers per 5,000 Population	Print Materials per Capita	Audio Materials per 1,000 Population	Video Materials per 1,000 Population	Current Print Serial Subscriptions per 1,000 Population
Ohio	10	14	3	1	1
Oklahoma	30	38	40	45	38
Oregon	40	27	7	16	27
Pennsylvania	44	36	19	34	34
Rhode Island	14	12	33	20	22
South Carolina	35	41	42	39	35
South Dakota	4	8	21	14	17
Tennessee	43	45	48	50	50
Texas	42	47	43	43	47
Utah	45	35	4	18	28
Vermont	1	4	12	8	4
Virginia	38	33	31	36	37
Washington	34	32	18	21	20
West Virginia	41	26	38	35	40
Wisconsin	25	21	1	3	13
Wyoming	3	6	2	7	8

State	Total Paid FTE Staff per 25,000 Population	Paid FTE Librarians per 25,000 Population	Paid FTE Librarians with ALA-MLS per 25,000 Population	Other Paid FTE Staff per 25,000 Population	Total Operating Revenue per Capita
Alabama	39	32	43	43	47
Alaska	30	30	26	26	13
Arizona	46	46	33	40	37
Arkansas	40	43	50	35	43
California	48	47	27	42	28
Colorado	14	27	15	10	7
Connecticut	8	6	1	12	9
Delaware	38	31	36	39	31
District of Columbia[2]	5	17	2	3	1
Florida	41	44	23	34	27
Georgia	49	51	39	37	46
Hawaii[3]	33	37	11	29	40
Idaho	23	36	47	15	34
Illinois	6	13	9	5	3
Indiana	3	10	8	2	11
Iowa	19	5	32	41	30
Kansas	4	1	19	14	14
Kentucky	28	12	40	38	26
Louisiana	24	25	31	20	17
Maine	17	7	13	25	32
Maryland	10	14	16	11	12
Massachusetts	15	9	6	21	19
Michigan	25	24	12	22	16
Minnesota	31	33	21	28	21
Mississippi	36	23	51	46	51

State	Total Paid FTE Staff per 25,000 Population	Paid FTE Librarians per 25,000 Population	Paid FTE Librarians with ALA-MLS per 25,000 Population	Other Paid FTE Staff per 25,000 Population	Total Operating Revenue per Capita
Missouri	13	34	35	6	18
Montana	43	19	46	50	42
Nebraska	11	8	28	18	24
Nevada	44	49	44	32	23
New Hampshire	9	2	10	27	20
New Jersey	12	29	7	8	5
New Mexico	29	26	24	33	38
New York	7	15	4	7	4
North Carolina	45	50	34	36	44
North Dakota	42	22	45	49	45
Ohio	1	11	5	1	2
Oklahoma	34	18	37	45	36
Oregon	27	35	17	17	10
Pennsylvania	37	41	25	31	39
Rhode Island	16	16	3	16	15
South Carolina	35	40	22	30	41
South Dakota	26	20	42	24	35
Tennessee	51	48	49	48	50
Texas	50	45	38	44	48
Utah	32	42	41	23	33
Vermont	21	4	30	47	29
Virginia	22	38	18	13	25
Washington	18	39	14	9	8
West Virginia	47	28	48	51	49
Wisconsin	20	21	20	19	22
Wyoming	2	3	29	4	6

State	State Operating Revenue per Capita	Local Operating Revenue per Capita	Other Operating Revenue per Capita	Total Operating Expenditures per Capita
Alabama	27	44	30	47
Alaska	24	11	31	13
Arizona	46	30	35	39
Arkansas	18	40	46	46
California	32	24	29	25
Colorado	48	7	10	11
Connecticut	36	10	6	8
Delaware	7	34	34	32
District of Columbia[2]	51	1	51	1
Florida	20	23	44	31
Georgia	8	46	49	45
Hawaii[3]	2	51	32	40
Idaho	33	31	20	37
Illinois	12	3	9	4
Indiana	10	9	16	9
Iowa	31	28	21	24
Kansas	19	13	13	14

State	State Operating Revenue per Capita	Local Operating Revenue per Capita	Other Operating Revenue per Capita	Total Operating Expenditures per Capita
Kentucky	17	25	23	38
Louisiana	15	16	24	28
Maine	40	37	3	26
Maryland	5	19	4	10
Massachusetts	23	17	14	16
Michigan	28	12	18	18
Minnesota	22	21	17	19
Mississippi	9	50	37	51
Missouri	34	14	15	20
Montana	38	39	26	42
Nebraska	37	20	25	23
Nevada	25	35	2	30
New Hampshire	49	15	22	17
New Jersey	29	2	27	5
New Mexico	21	33	45	34
New York	11	5	5	3
North Carolina	16	41	43	44
North Dakota	26	43	28	43
Ohio	1	45	7	2
Oklahoma	30	32	38	36
Oregon	42	8	19	12
Pennsylvania	4	47	12	35
Rhode Island	3	26	8	15
South Carolina	14	38	48	41
South Dakota	50	29	42	33
Tennessee	47	48	47	49
Texas	41	42	50	48
Utah	39	27	41	29
Vermont	45	36	1	27
Virginia	13	22	40	22
Washington	44	4	36	7
West Virginia	6	49	39	50
Wisconsin	35	18	33	21
Wyoming	43	6	11	6

State	Total Collection Expenditures per Capita	Total Staff Expenditures per Capita	Salaries and Wages Expenditures per Capita	Number of Registered Borrowers per Capita
Alabama	48	45	44	39
Alaska	23	13	17	24
Arizona	30	39	39	20
Arkansas	43	48	48	26
California	42	24	28	31
Colorado	9	14	13	30
Connecticut	15	6	3	16
Delaware	28	31	32	37
District of Columbia[2]	2	1	1	41
Florida	34	35	35	28

State	Total Collection Expenditures per Capita	Total Staff Expenditures per Capita	Salaries and Wages Expenditures per Capita	Number of Registered Borrowers per Capita
Georgia	44	44	45	51
Hawaii[3]	35	38	25	8
Idaho	39	32	33	33
Illinois	4	7	5	48
Indiana	3	10	10	7
Iowa	19	26	26	10
Kansas	11	16	14	2
Kentucky	36	41	40	32
Louisiana	40	33	34	27
Maine	41	25	22	14
Maryland	6	9	11	21
Massachusetts	14	15	9	25
Michigan	20	20	21	40
Minnesota	26	19	18	3
Mississippi	51	51	51	45
Missouri	7	23	23	17
Montana	45	43	43	42
Nebraska	17	22	24	1
Nevada	13	30	30	50
New Hampshire	21	17	15	36
New Jersey	10	4	6	34
New Mexico	29	34	38	4
New York	8	3	4	18
North Carolina	46	42	42	29
North Dakota	38	46	46	46
Ohio	1	2	2	6
Oklahoma	33	37	36	5
Oregon	18	11	16	22
Pennsylvania	31	36	37	47
Rhode Island	22	12	12	44
South Carolina	32	40	41	38
South Dakota	25	29	29	23
Tennessee	50	49	49	43
Texas	47	47	47	35
Utah	16	28	31	12
Vermont	37	27	27	15
Virginia	27	21	19	19
Washington	5	8	8	9
West Virginia	49	50	50	49
Wisconsin	24	18	20	13
Wyoming	12	5	7	11

FTE=full-time equivalent.

1 Per capita is based on the total unduplicated population of legal service areas.

2 The District of Columbia, while not a state, is included in the state rankings. Special care should be used in comparing its data to state data.

3 Caution should be used in making comparisons with the state of Hawaii, as Hawaii reports only one public library for the entire state.

Source: Compiled by Carol Collier from *Survey of Public Libraries in the United States, Fiscal Year 2008,* Institute of Museum and Library Services, 2010.

Library Buildings 2010: Comfort and Joy

Bette-Lee Fox
Managing Editor, *Library Journal*

Today's library is more than the mere sum of its parts. As evidenced by 125 public library and 12 academic library projects completed between July 1, 2009, and June 30, 2010, the thinking these days is for the library to harmonize with and extend both into and beyond its community, to become a warm and welcoming place for its constituents, and to present a safe harbor for everyone who enters.

These libraries embrace brilliant artwork, panoramic views through glass walls, extensive collections of varied materials, high-tech elements of every imaginable kind, and more energy-efficient features than you can shake a bioswale at. That's beyond comfort—that's a complete joy.

Nothing shouts comfort like a fireplace. The Dan A. Williams Branch in Lincoln, Nebraska, part of an elementary school complex, has the first in its system. Novi Library in Michigan, meanwhile, gives folks the option of warming up in its fireplace lounge or cooling off on its outdoor patio. (The library also notably houses the Novi Special, a 1941 racing car designed by a local engineer.)

Inside Out, Outside In

Patios and other outdoor spaces also figure prominently at the Tustin (California) Library, which boasts three age-appropriate indoor/outdoor patios; at Maple Grove Branch of Hennepin County (Minnesota) Library, which has a summer reading porch and a reading lounge that looks out onto the new urban park; and at the Reynolds Corners Branch of Toledo-Lucas County (Ohio) Public Library, which features a fountain reading court.

When it comes to kids-only amenities, the Donald W. Reynolds Library in Mountain Home, Arkansas, has a gazebo in its children's space; the Ingleside Branch of San Francisco Public Library incorporates a bench seat window in its children's room; and the Eastern Avenue Branch of the Davenport (Iowa) Public Library features a children's garden for presentations and storytelling.

Indeed, the demarcation between the inside and outside world in libraries is increasingly blurred. The Orange Cove Branch of Fresno County (California) Public Library incorporates community interest in herbs and *cuarandero*—a healer's garden—with its landscape of plants historically used as food and medicine. Rural life in Fergus Falls, Minnesota, figures into the design of the Viking Library System headquarters, which includes a grain wagon and elements from an antique grain elevator. And the Sayville (New York) Library features sand and seashell tables in its "beach" area.

The Carnegie Library of Pittsburgh-Allegheny, bedecked with large storefront windows, has in its reading room a table crafted from a tree from the lawn of the Allegheny Observatory. The Sammamish (Washington) Library features skylights, a gas fireplace, and a view of a nature preserve. And the Sachem Pub-

Adapted from *Library Journal,* December 2010

lic Library in Holbrook, New York, has a new Inside/Out outdoor extension as a summer performance space.

Preserving Local Interests

Like Novi Library's 1941 Novi Special race car, locally designed artistic elements further help to create a community feel within libraries. The Hamilton Mill Branch of Gwinnett County Public Library, Lawrenceville, Georgia, illuminates its massive glass walls with an installation by artist Maria Artemis called "Poiesis," consisting of 67 glass paintings throughout the building. Lauderdale Lakes Library/Education and Cultural Center in Florida displays interactive work by artist George Gadson. And the South Regional Library, Durham, North Carolina, features the library system's only outdoor work of public art, an 18-foot structure by Thomas Sayre.

Also creating a community feel is the preservation of nostalgic historic elements. The recent renovation to the Bernal Heights Branch maintains San Francisco Public Library's 1940s heritage with its hand-painted ceiling stencils and original hanging fixtures. The staff room of the Prairie Trails Public Library District, Burbank, Illinois, harks back to old-time diners. And the giant addition/renovation of the Cambridge (Massachusetts) Public Library enhanced the original 1889 structure fourfold as it restored WPA-era murals in the iconic reading room.

South San Francisco Main Library staff worked with their architect to create a "marketplace" connecting the building's two entrances, while the Portland (Maine) Public Library remodeling offers an art gallery, a conference center, and cafe-style atrium seating to engage with the city's commercial and social locus in Monument Square. The Martha Washington Library in Alexandria, Virginia, includes a serpentine metal wall that leads patrons from the front porch to the circulation desk. The Albert Wisner Public Library in Warwick, New York, uses reading niches to lure readers; the Lochwood Branch of the Dallas Public Library has a black-box theater; and Baltimore Public Library's Storyville @ Woodlawn features a 3,150-square-foot "village" as an early literacy and learning center.

Multiple joint-use projects take the library to that next step, combining with elementary schools, like the Rice Branch of Cleveland Public Library; civic buildings, like the Kendall Neighborhood Library and Community Center in Houston; and even with a transitional housing project for the former homeless and low-income seniors, like the Hispanic Branch of Miami-Dade Public Library.

The academic library projects spotlighted in this article include a huge renovation at the University of Utah, a new Partnership Center between Seminole State College of Florida and the University of Central Florida, and a renovation and addition at the University of Wyoming.

Increased Accessibility

Accessibility is another way libraries are extending a warm welcome. The new ground floor of Walnut Creek (California) Library operates independently of the main library, enabling extended hours for the lending of new and AV materials, the use of public computers, and pick up of holds. The new Anacostia Neighborhood Library in Washington, D.C., features a tower that lights up at night to draw in passers-by. And the Plainsboro (New Jersey) Public Library has a private room called the Health Education Center, where patrons can access health information. An inlaid chessboard on the third floor, too, has become a hit with the teen crowd.

Today's libraries are probably as comfortable as most people's homes, with plush seating areas; fireplaces, patios, gardens, and gazebos; and accent works by local artists. They are also a model for flexible and sustainable building practices that many homeowners can emulate. One exemplar is the Leadership in Energy and Environmental Design (LEED) Platinum-certified Silver Lake Branch of Los Angeles Public Library.

The best of all possible worlds. Restful places, green spaces, touching all the bases. That's joy; that's the library.

Table 1 / New Academic Library Buildings, 2010

Institution	Project Cost	Gross Square Feet	Square Foot Cost	Construction Cost	Furniture/ Equip. Cost	Book Capacity	Architect
McCarthy Library, Napa Valley College, CA	$27,000,000	62,000	$387.10	$24,000,000	$3,000,000	80,000	TLCD Architecture
SSC-UCF Partnership Center, Seminole State College of Florida, Sanford	25,749,665	109,675	233.59	25,618,665	131,000	120,000	Harvard Jolly

Table 2 / Academic Library Buildings, Additions and Renovations, 2010

Institution	Status	Project Cost	Gross Square Feet	Square Foot Cost	Construction Cost	Furniture/ Equip. Cost	Book Capacity	Architect
William Robertson Coe Library, University of Wyoming, Laramie	Total	$47,930,000	268,614	$138.35	$37,162,280	$5,837,937	2,311,900	GSG Architecture
	New	27,547,655	89,365	238.99	21,357,341	3,737,937	111,900	
	Renovated	20,382,345	179,249	88.17	15,804,939	2,100,000	2,200,000	
Rio Hondo College Library, Whittier, CA	Total	34,700,000	94,000	326.6	30,700,000	4,000,000	85,000	AC Martin
	New	n.a.	n.a.	n.a.	n.a.	n.a.	n.a.	
	Renovated	n.a.	n.a.	n.a.	n.a.	n.a.	n.a.	
Ryan Library, Iona College, New Rochelle, NY	Total	9,250,000	26,000	307.69	8,000,000	600,000	n.a.	Anthony Pucillo
	New	n.a.	15,800	n.a.	n.a.	n.a.	n.a.	
	Renovated	n.a.	10,200	n.a.	n.a.	n.a.	n.a.	

n.a. = not available.

Table 3 / Academic Library Buildings, Renovations Only, 2010

Institution	Project Cost	Gross Square Feet	Square Foot Cost	Construction Cost	Furniture/ Equip. Cost	Book Capacity	Architect
J. Willard Marriott Library, University of Utah, Salt Lake City	$79,322,771	300,000	$202.56	$60,767,034	$7,034,491	4,500,000	MJSA Architecture & Interior Design
Kresge Law Library, University of Notre Dame	17,163,000	107,000	106.93	11,442,000	2,561,500	500,000	S/L/A/M Collaborative
Robert W. Woodruff Library, Atlanta University Center	16,200,000	100,000	114	11,400,000	2,000,000	1,600,000	Shepley Bulfinch
Maps Library, Penn State University, University Park	2,300,000	8,000	207.5	1,660,000	100,000	437,000 *	Hayes Large Architects & Engineers
William Madison Randall Library, University of North Carolina, Wilmington	502,219	10,884	25.23	274,581	223,338	n.a.	UNCW Project Management
College-Conservatory of Music Library, University of Cincinnati	488,026	15,343	24.49	375,800	112,226	117,500	University of Cincinnati Planning +Design+ Construction
Franklin D. Schurz Library, Indiana University South Bend	198,920	3,978	33.79	134,420	64,500	11,812	Indiana University Architect's Office

* The library holds 400,000 maps and 37,000 monographs.

n.a. = not available.

Table 4 / New Public Library Buildings, 2010

Community	Pop. ('000)	Code	Project Cost	Construction Cost	Gross Sq. Ft.	Sq. Ft. Cost	Equipment Cost	Site Cost	Other Costs	Volumes	Federal Funds	State Funds	Local Funds	Gift Funds	Architect
Arizona															
Prescott Valley	39	M	$21,158,000	$17,650,000	55,000	$320.91	$1,976,000	Owned	$1,532,000	8,136	$85,000	0	$20,100,000	$973,000	richärd+bauer
Scottsdale	235	B	10,469,000	7,265,000	21,000	345.95	1,384,000	Owned	1,820,000	60,000	0	0	10,403,000	66,000	DWL Archs.; Douglas Sydnor
Sun City	30	B	161,845	0	4,365	0	161,845	Leased	0	8,000	0	0	11,845	150,000	not reported
Arkansas															
Mountain Home	42	M	10,497,885	7,593,847	35,500	213.91	1,414,925	$450,000	1,039,113	11,015	0	0	450,000	10,296,885	Sapp Design Assocs.
California															
Castro Valley	61	B	17,129,236	12,463,380	34,537	360.87	1,460,973	Owned	3,204,883	160,000	0	$12,519,001	4,610,235	0	Noll & Tam
La Crescenta	18	B	14,800,000	8,800,000	15,010	586.27	1,000,000	1,800,000	3,200,000	1,175	1,437,000	0	13,363,000	0	Carde-Ten Architects
Lafayette	24	O	47,500,000	30,100,000	70,000	430	1,970,000	2,075,000	13,355,000	117,000	0	11,900,000	24,100,000	11,500,000	Killefer Flammang
Los Angeles	33	B	16,770,000	12,600,000	13,760	915.7	385,000	2,907,000	378,000	50,000	0	0	16,770,000	0	M2A
Orange Cove	11	B	4,878,612	3,292,758	10,072	326.92	312,021	51,000	1,222,833	32,200	0	2,807,698	2,070,914	19,920	Taylor Teter Partnership
Riverside	37	MS	15,407,000	12,493,000	39,133	319.24	180,000	2,000,000	734,000	70,000	2,000,000	0	13,407,000	0	Kroh Architects
Sacramento	46	B	13,391,030	10,867,475	20,500	530.12	701,627	502,500	1,319,428	82,000	0	0	13,391,030	0	Noll & Tam
Sacramento	37	B	13,732,131	7,794,305	22,400	347.96	2,582,900	1,500,000	1,354,926	117,000	0	7,924,893	5,807,238	0	Nacht & Lewis
San Diego	29	B	11,247,007	9,083,000	25,000	363.32	574,000	900,000	690,007	106,648	3,383,000	5,359,724	3,950,000	1,899,373	Martinez + Cutri
San Francisco	13	B	7,534,000	1,451,707	6,075	238.96	500,000	1,839,205	3,743,088	2,198	0	3,751,943	3,282,057	500,000	Fougeron Arch./Group 4
San José	57	B	12,342,231	9,399,486	22,000	427.25	455,856	Owned	2,486,889	123,663	0	0	12,342,231	0	Studios Architecture
Tustin	75	B	24,900,000	15,100,000	32,000	471.88	0	Leased	0	209,000	0	218,000	24,682,000	0	Field Paoli
Walnut Creek	66	B	39,900,000	28,300,000	93,000	304.3	2,300,000	Owned	9,300,000	120,000	0	0	34,400,000	5,500,000	Group 4 Architecture
Colorado															
Brighton	31	M	6,700,000	5,180,000	20,000	259	620,000	Owned	900,000	3,926	0	0	6,430,000	270,000	Humphries Poli
Thornton	159	M	9,420,000	6,650,000	25,000	266	775,000	735,000	1,260,000	5,221	0	0	9,420,000	0	Humphries Poli
District of Columbia															
Washington	12	B	14,741,204	10,116,427	22,728	445.11	464,333	Owned	4,160,439	80,000	0	0	14,741,204	0	Freelon Group
Washington	11	B	15,707,441	9,951,328	22,980	433.04	566,973	Owned	5,189,140	80,000	274,570	0	15,432,871	0	Davis Brody Bond Aedas
Washington*	25	O	n.a.	n.a.	4,500	n.a.	n.a.	Owned	n.a.	25,000	n.a.	n.a.	2,500,000	n.a.	Hord Coplan Macht
Washington	15	O	981,672	807,322	4,909	164.46	63,000	Leased	111,350	27,000	126,818	0	854,854	0	Moody Nolan

Symbol Code: B=Branch Library; BS=Branch and System Headquarters; M=Main Library; MS=Main and System Headquarters; S=System Headquarters; O=combined use space; n.a. = not available.

Table 4 / New Public Library Buildings, 2010 *(cont.)*

Community	Pop. ('000)	Code	Project Cost	Construction Cost	Gross Sq. Ft.	Sq. Ft. Cost	Equipment Cost	Site Cost	Other Costs	Volumes	Federal Funds	State Funds	Local Funds	Gift Funds	Architect
Florida															
Cape Coral	53	B	$14,123,823	$6,809,977	41,142	$165.52	$1,080,746	Owned	$6,233,100	145,000	0	$500,000	$13,623,823	0	BSSW Architects
Clermont	50	O	14,035,637	12,078,152	64,971	185.9	894,848	Owned	1,062,637	14,529	0	6,108,331	7,250,000	$677,306	Harvard Jolly
Lauderdale Lakes	32	B	3,632,199	2,900,000	10,000	290	379,699	Leased	352,500	50,000	0	500,000	3,132,199	0	Pierce Goodwin Alexander
Miami	36	B	3,448,287	2,950,852	12,000	245.9	497,435	Owned	0	40,000	0	0	3,448,287	0	Eddy Frances & Assocs.
Pensacola	50	B	3,003,978	2,363,724	12,100	195.34	339,788	Owned	300,466	3,200	0	500,000	2,503,978	0	Strobel and Hunter
Tampa	69	B	5,691,451	3,513,316	24,000	146.39	1,003,465	$199,315	975,355	150,000	0	0	5,691,451	0	FleischmanGarcia
Georgia															
Augusta	250	MS	24,635,000	16,692,519	90,000	185.47	2,780,789	2,032,482	3,129,210	38,370	0	2,000,000	22,635,000	0	Craig Gaulden Davis/Studio 3
Dacula	45	O	5,792,260	4,615,890	20,805	221.86	601,530	175,000	399,840	75,000	0	2,000,000	3,792,260	0	Precision Planning
Iowa															
Davenport	30	B	6,636,628	5,232,946	26,000	201.27	721,418	Owned	682,264	6,294	$112,000	1,439,841	3,981,977	1,102,810	Engberg Anderson
Kentucky															
Louisville	20	B	2,279,113	1,696,604	8,300	204.41	112,999	Owned	469,510	30,000	0	0	1,949,855	329,258	MS&R Ltd.
Louisiana															
Gretna	53	B	2,575,545	1,406,687	5,615	250.52	149,250	296,200	723,408	12,900	504,025	0	2,057,020	14,500	Burgdahl & Graves
Lafitte	5	O	1,946,357	1,609,229	4,545	354.06	196,990	Owned	140,138	12,400	1,581	0	2,618,153	10,000	Meyer Engineers
Maine															
Orono	10	M	1,952,685	1,485,140	6,000	247.52	186,287	150,000	131,258	55,000	0	45,000	1,080,423	863,931	WBRC Architects
Massachusetts															
Mashpee	14	M	8,330,190	4,395,945	22,000	199.82	2,775,645	Owned	1,158,600	63,400	0	2,934,541	5,320,649	75,000	Johnson Roberts Assocs.
Townsend**	10	O	n.a.	n.a.	17,000	n.a.	n.a.	n.a.	n.a.	44,153	0	0	0	n.a.	Johnson Roberts Assocs.
Michigan															
Novi	52	M	16,000,000	n.a.	66,000	n.a.	n.a.	Owned	n.a.	207,000	n.a.	n.a.	14,700,000	1,300,000	BEI Assocs; Diamond & Schmitt

Symbol Code: B=Branch Library; BS=Branch and System Headquarters; M=Main Library; MS=Main and System Headquarters; S=System Headquarters; O=combined use space; n.a. = not available.

Minnesota															
Fergus Falls	124	S	1,230,000	997,243	8,156	122.27	61,000	65,000	106,757	18,000	0	1,100,000	130,000	0	Design Intent Archs.
Maple Grove	63	B	25,855,000	15,340,000	40,000	383.5	1,940,000	1,096,000	7,479,000	114,000	0	0	24,759,000	1,096,000	MS&R Ltd.
Plymouth	73	B	16,600,000	10,400,000	30,000	346.67	1,932,000	Owned	4,268,000	30,000	0	0	16,600,000	0	Bentz/Thompson/Rietow
Missouri															
Republic	14	B	299,235	0	10,000	0	170,421	Leased	128,814	38 750	0	0	215,735	83,500	B. Cinalli Designs
Smithville	6	B	6,125,013	4,690,000	15,300	306.55	118,000	1,001,513	315,500	65 000	0	0	6,125,013	0	Tognascioli & Assocs.
Willard	6	B	165,703	0	5,000	0	137,652	Leased	28,051	23 000	0	0	74,879	90,824	Grooms Office Environments
Nebraska															
Lincoln	5	O	444,117	337,856	2,000	168.93	106,261	Leased	0	6,600	0	0	416,292	27,825	DLR Group
Nevada															
Henderson	62	B	5,180,277	2,880,188	19,919	144.6	53,220	2,005,963	240,906	6,582	0	0	4,888 583	291,694	RSJ Architecture
New Jersey															
Plainsboro	20	M	16,655,552	12,310,216	46,501	264.73	1,211,129	1,000,000	2,134,207	102,282	0	120,000	15,300,000	1,863,000	BKSK Architects
New York															
Albany	93	B	5,831,000	4,957,000	12,000	413.08	204,000	Owned	670,000	75,000	0	0	5,831,000	0	H+G Architects
Albany	93	B	3,755,000	3,046,000	8,500	358.35	195,000	Owned	514,000	30,000	0	0	3,755,000	0	H+G Architects
Mount Kisco	10	M	9,656,306	7,967,476	18,000	442.64	0	Owned	1,688,830	78,000	0	457,409	9,656,306	150,250	Lothrop Assocs.
Sayville	18	O	14,703,368	12,175,245	42,823	284.32	744,703	Owned	1,783,420	14,288	0	662,879	14,961,291	39,056	h2m architects + engineers
Warwick	22	M	9,100,000	6,700,000	20.000	335	660,000	200,000	1,540,000	120,000	0	143,454	8,500,000	451,546	Butler Rowland Mays
Westhampton Beach	6	M	7,137,773	4,228,014	14,250	296.7	670,173	Owned	2,289,586	5,512	0	287,365	6,900,408	0	Ward Associates
North Carolina															
Charlotte	42	B	4,635,000	3,200,000	16,000	200	170,000	635,000	630,000	100,000	0	0	4,635,000	0	Wagner-Murray
Durham	38	B	9,628,544	5,935,500	27,300	217.41	2,005,144	1,000,000	687,900	100,700	0	0	9,628,544	0	Freelon Group
Raleigh	112	B	3,976,040	2,444,721	8,560	285.6	266,029	Owned	1,265,290	3,860	0	0	4,103,923	0	Cherry Huffman
Ohio															
Cleveland***	26	B	5,011,667	4,121,531	14,000	294.4	320,653	0	569,483	3,167	0	0	5,011,667	0	Bostwick Design
West Chester	95	B	14,988,260	10,011,918	48,350	207.07	866,579	2,141,450	1,978,313	26,556	0	0	14,988,260	0	glaserworks
Pennsylvania															
Pittsburgh	30	B	5,522,000	4,300,000	15,000	286.67	545,000	Owned	677,000	29,327	0	2,200,000	31,500	3,970,000	Loysen & Kreuthmeier

Symbol Code: B=Branch Library; BS=Branch and System Headquarters; M=Main Library; MS=Main and System Headquarters; S=System Headquarters; O=combined use space; n.a. = not available.

Table 4 / New Public Library Buildings, 2010 *(cont.)*

Community	Pop. ('000)	Code	Project Cost	Construction Cost	Gross Sq. Ft.	Sq. Ft. Cost	Equipment Cost	Site Cost	Other Costs	Volumes	Federal Funds	State Funds	Local Funds	Gift Funds	Architect
South Carolina															
Johnsonville	3	B	$1,570,102	$1,175,886	6,500	$180.91	$211,014	$150,000	$33,202	10,000	$48,000	$550,000	$972,102	0	Craig Gaulden Davis
Olanta	1	B	1,468,011	1,022,904	6,500	157.37	203,242	100,000	141,865	10,000	26,739	250,000	191,272	$1,000,000	Craig Gaulden Davis
Timmonsville	3	B	1,597,195	1,079,415	6,500	166.06	227,239	150,000	140,541	10,000	39,385	0	407,810	1,150,000	Craig Gaulden Davis
Texas															
Dallas	60	B	6,655,011	3,914,277	20,200	193.78	500,000	750,000	1,490,734	70,000	0	0	6,655,011	0	MS&R Ltd.
Houston	72	B	6,388,988	4,828,667	11,979	403.09	1,030,000	Owned	530,321	3,672	0	0	6,388,988	0	mArchitects
Houston	45	O	9,234,332	6,618,116	19,000	348.33	1,964,901	Owned	651,315	6,009	0	0	9,234,332	0	English + Associates
Houston	38	O	7,702,985	5,776,590	19,864	290.81	1,476,043	Owned	450,352	5,031	0	0	7,702,985	0	AutoArch Architects
Washington															
Sammamish	48	B	13,688,603	9,738,751	19,500	499.42	891,428	904,803	2,153,621	103,425	0	0	13,688,603	0	Perkins + Will
Vancouver	57	B	10,262,455	7,879,254	24,175	325.93	571,882	Leased	1,811,319	90,000	0	0	10,200,000	96,000	Opsis Architecture
Wyoming															
Alta	3	B	1,022,400	731,160	2,500	292.46	41,000	169,000	81,240	8,500	0	812,400	169,000	41,000	Humphries Poli

* Mixed used development (with K–8 school and recreation center); overall project cost $33 million
** Building a gift of one firm and includes a meeting hall and a senior center; costs not disclosed
*** Land swap

Symbol Code: B=Branch Library; BS=Branch and System Headquarters; M=Main Library; MS=Main and System Headquarters; S=System Headquarters; O=combined use space; n.a. = not available.

Table 5 / Public Library Buildings, Additions and Renovations, 2010

Community	Pop. ('000)	Code	Project Cost	Constr. Cost	Gross Sq. Ft.	Sq. Ft. Cost	Equipment Cost	Site Cost	Other Costs	Volumes	Federal Funds	State Funds	Local Funds	Gift Funds	Architect
Arizona															
Sun City	57	B	$387,628	$168,628	13,545	$12.45	$203,077	Leased	$15,923	18 750	0	0	$387,628	0	MRT Design
California															
Anaheim	98	MS	2,014,316	1,487,844	20,000	74.39	212,000	Owned	314,472	70,000	$412,000	$750,000	792,316	$60,000	CWA
Foster City	32	B	1,073,823	184,588	23,708	7.79	688,594	Owned	200,641	140,000	0	0	868,823	205,000	Anderson Brulé
Menifee	30	B	3,915,000	3,220,000	10,500	306.67	180,000	$500,000	15,000	36,000	2,000,000	0	2,200,000	0	JCJ Architecture
Sacramento	35	B	67,460	52,000	5,425	9.58	15,460	Owned	0	25,000	0	0	67,460	0	not reported
Sacramento	61	B	513,000	222,000	11,000	20.18	196,000	Owned	95,000	32,000	0	0	243,000	270,000	not reported
San Francisco	25	B	6,243,000	4,035,836	8,777	459.82	500,000	Owned	1,707,164	2,585	0	0	5,743,000	500,000	Dept. of Public Works
San Francisco	26	B	4,922,000	2,628,152	6,465	406.52	500,000	Owned	1,793,848	2,679	0	0	4,422,000	500,000	Dept. of Public Works
San Francisco	11	B	5,926,847	3,829,735	5,428	705.55	500,000	Owned	1,597,112	1,705	0	0	5,426,347	500,000	Dept. of Public Works
San José	30	B	10,052,247	7,274,557	10,200	713.19	284,136	Owned	2,493,554	40,797	0	0	10,052,247	0	GouldEvans
South San Francisco	45	M	765,752	294,964	14,500	20.34	422,562	Owned	48,226	90,000	46,183	0	469,569	250,000	Group 4 Architecture
Sunnyvale	140	M	1,051,680	50,000	20,000	2.5	887,480	Owned	114,200	300,000	0	0	978,723	72,957	none
Torrance	24	B	189,000	169,000	3,973	42.54	15,000	Owned	5,000	42,000	0	0	192,000	15,000	none
Torrance	24	B	272,000	217,000	4,000	54.25	50,000	Owned	5,000	45,000	0	0	192,000	95,000	none
Torrance	24	B	189,000	169,000	3,973	42.54	15,000	Owned	5,000	36,000	0	0	192,000	15,000	none
Visalia	121	MS	5,890,170	5,247,100	43,600	120.35	595,634	Owned	47,436	250,000	0	3,730,539	1,489,138	670,493	Charles Rhoads
Florida															
Fort Lauderdale	180	MS	653,155	168,321	7,000	24.05	450,081	Owned	34,753	0	0	0	653,155	0	Saltz Michelson Arch.
Tampa	9	O	970,277	685,365	3,500	195.82	199,725	Owned	35,187	10,000	0	0	970,277	0	FleischmanGarcia
Georgia															
Conyers	89	M	7,102,801	5,979,861	46,500	128.6	502,678	Owned	620,262	16,500	0	2,000,000	5,102,801	0	Craig Gaulden Davis/Studio 3
Illinois															
Burbank	29	M	319,134	277,134	4,694	59.04	0	Owned	42,000	96,000	0	26,000	293,134	0	Frega Associates
Indiana															
Bloomington	129	M	1,086,000	938,000	54,185	17.31	70,000	Owned	78,000	450,000	28,000	0	1,058,000	0	Woollen, Molzan & Partners

Symbol Code: B=Branch Library; BS=Branch and System Headquarters; M=Main Library; MS=Main and System Headquarters; S=System Headquarters; O=combined use space; n.a. = not available.

Table 5 / Public Library Buildings, Additions and Renovations, 2010 *(cont.)*

Community	Pop. ('000)	Code	Project Cost	Constr. Cost	Gross Sq. Ft.	Sq. Ft. Cost	Equipment Cost	Site Cost	Other Costs	Volumes	Federal Funds	State Funds	Local Funds	Gift Funds	Architect
Kentucky															
Danville	28	M	$9,254,431	$7,097,065	43,910	$161.63	$1,037,675	$572,458	$547,233	13,347	$191,000	$300,000	$6,522,205	$2,241,226	Pearson & Peters
Union	20	B	1,006,120	682,700	35,000	19.5	235,252	Owned	88,168	130,000	0	0	1,006,120	0	Robert Ehmet Hayes
Maine															
Portland	70	BS	7,340,000	5,738,911	47,077	121.9	371,978	Owned	1,229,111	196,951	200,000	200,000	4,000,000	2,940,000	Scott Simons Architects
Maryland															
Westminster	61	B	1,821,472	1,160,676	22,921	50.64	604,298	Owned	56,498	127,161	0	683,000	1,018,472	120,000	Ruebling & Associates
Whiteford	7	B	4,678,400	3,150,000	13,280	237.2	1,138,400	Owned	390,000	70,000	0	373,000	4,238,400	67,000	Edmeades & Stromdahl
Woodlawn	339	B	1,268,228	1,005,078	3,150	319.07	38,150	Owned	225,000	50	0	225,000	1,043,228	0	Sanders Design
Massachusetts															
Bolton	5	M	7,087,067	5,743,657	16,945	338.96	335,000	Owned	914,410	44,370	0	2,539,117	3,500,000	1,047,950	Lerner Ladds + Bartels
Cambridge*	101	M	n.a.	69,000,000	141,600	529.66	n.a.	Owned	n.a.	315,000	0	10,700,000	58,300,000	0	Wm. Rawn.a.nn Beha
North Easton	23	M	2,499,324	2,254,688	13,476	167.31	45,126	Owned	199,510	80,000	0	0	0	2,499,324	James Thomas
Architects															
Minnesota															
Roseville	131	BS	16,583,000	13,032,118	74,175	175.69	2,683,000	Owned	867,882	209,000	400,000	0	17,534,988	346,000	MS&R, Ltd.
New York															
Albany	93	B	3,584,000	2,966,000	9,500	312.21	268,000	Owned	350,000	35,000	0	0	3,584,000	0	CS Arch
Albany	93	B	5,323,000	4,623,000	12,000	385.25	225,000	Owned	475,000	30,000	0	0	5,323,000	0	CS Arch
Albany	93	B	5,020,000	4,169,000	19,000	219.42	410,000	Owned	441,000	50,000	0	0	5,020,000	0	CS Arch
Holbrook	82	M	998,200	476,200	38,000	12.53	11,800	370,000	140,200	n.a.	0	56,171	906,629	35,400	Beatty, Harvey, Coco
New City	47	M	212,300	137,950	2,000	68.97	65,350	Owned	9,000	153	0	8,082	204,218	0	Robert Hoene Assocs.
Plainview	28	O	89,040	15,560	3,850	4.04	73,480	Owned	0	n.a.	0	40,330	46,910	1,800	Library Interiors, Inc.
Poughkeepsie	74	M	15,500,000	11,930,000	40,000	298.25	1,300,000	Owned	2,270,000	140,000	0	615,000	14,345,000	540,000	Clark Patterson Lee
Spencerport	18	M	420,452	240,662	8,500	28.31	130,051	Owned	49,739	66,000	0	100,000	332,255	0	Bergmann Associates
Syracuse	21	M	3,139,700	2,515,467	18,600	135.24	328,557	Owned	295,676	4,222	0	3,000,000	104,700	35,000	Schopfer Architects

Symbol Code: B=Branch Library; BS=Branch and System Headquarters; M=Main Library; MS=Main and System Headquarters; S=System Headquarters; O=combined use space; n.a. = not available.

North Carolina															
Durham	50	B	6,390,394	4,070,162	25,000	162.8	1,320,982	600,000	399,250	100,700	0	0	6,390,394	0	Cherry Huffman
North Dakota															
Bismarck	77	M	679,000	503,000	7,429	67.71	114,000	Owned	62,000	42,000	0	5,000	50,000	624,000	Architectural Concepts
Ohio															
Toledo	34	B	2,218,263	1,702,450	17,758	95.87	365,585	Owned	150,228	130,000	0	0	2,195,513	22,750	Buehrer Group
Vermilion	11	M	5,389,375	4,161,734	35,410	117.53	368,358	Owned	859,283	7,263	0	2,000,000	3,389,365	10,000	CBLH Design Inc.
South Dakota															
Sioux Falls	192	MS	11,437,542	9,315,569	61,832	150.66	1,162,789	Owned	959,184	150,000	0	0	11,437,542	0	FEH Associates
Texas															
Denton	38	B	2,570,696	1,934,434	20,700	93.45	303,244	Owned	333,018	65,000	0	0	2,570,696	0	Booziotis & Co.
Houston	2229	B	12,875,096	10,559,685	26,007	406.03	1,058,208	Owned	1,257,203	2,436	6,830,648	0	6,044,448	0	Smith & Co.
Keller	40	M	4,108,575	3,338,803	22,500	148.39	363,582	Owned	406,190	98,661	0	22,025	4,000,000	86,550	PSA-Dewberry
Virginia															
Alexandria	24	B	6,375,191	4,966,000	16,663	298.03	468,191	Owned	941,000	62,000	0	0	6,375,191	0	Ritter Architects
Arlington	210	O	23,062,300	16,000,000	62,000	258.06	62,300	Owned	7,000,000	43,300	0	0	23,062,300	0	Cox Graae + Spack
Falls Church	33	B	7,696,308	5,843,000	17,000	343.71	479,308	Owned	1,374,000	73,000	0	0	7,696,308	0	Hughes Group
Springfield	56	B	7,267,758	5,550,000	17,753	312.62	447,758	Owned	1,270,000	71,500	0	0	7,267,758	0	BeeryRio Architects
Washington															
Colfax	16	M	1,035,000	944,000	12,000	78.66	10,400	Owned	30,600	65,000	550,000	113,563	232,133	139,304	Castellaw • Kom
Wisconsin															
Town of Merton	9	M	2,500,000	1,916,583	15,000	127.77	216,646	175,441	131,330	80,000	0	0	1,250,000	1,250,000	MSI General
Milwaukee	605	M	1,451,221	1,303,118	30,700	42.45	12,500	Owned	135,603	n.a.	0	0	1,011,000	440,221	HGA

* Massive project includes an addition, a renovation, and underground parking. Funding from two state grants and the city

Symbol Code: B=Branch Library; BS=Branch and System Headquarters; M=Main Library; MS=Main and System Headquarters; S=System Headquarters; O=combined use space; n.a. = not available.

Table 6 / Public Library Buildings, Six-Year Cost Summary

	Fiscal 2005	Fiscal 2006	Fiscal 2007	Fiscal 2008	Fiscal 2009	Fiscal 2010
Number of new buildings	91	81	82	95	80	70
Number of ARRs*	94	79	86	88	90	55
Sq. ft. new buildings	2,349,670	2,050,087	2,245,929	2,235,853	1,772,434	1,608,324
Sq. ft. ARRs	1,530,382	1,505,326	2,300,619	1,782,204	1,942,810	1,271,709
New Buildings						
Construction cost	$420,241,028	$421,856,723	$491,240,609	$539,109,943	$486,722,590	$453,517,944
Equipment cost	57,152,920	51,541,695	60,666,368	73,468,236	54,212,351	49,087,060
Site cost	43,892,631	43,897,019	37,089,067	36,331,029	37,658,061	28,981,431
Other cost	75,384,007	90,240,356	105,271,399	86,508,406	75,202,090	110,238,949
Total—Project cost	596,670,586	611,502,793	705,543,661	736,767,614	656,020,880	669,591,384
ARRs—Project cost	235,915,173	293,982,768	426,681,990	334,871,847	482,214,848	234,485,743
New and ARR Project Cost	$832,585,759	$905,485,561	$1,132,225,651	$1,071,639,461	$1,138,235,728	$904,077,127
Fund Sources						
Federal, new buildings	$3,657,196	$9,733,136	$9,701,152	$6,797,857	$17,049,910	$8,038,118
Federal, ARRs	3,692,293	4,150,883	2,971,210	7,733,967	7,873,278	10,657,831
Federal, total	$7,349,489	$13,884,019	$12,672,362	$14,531,824	$24,923,188	$18,695,949
State, new buildings	$28,458,752	$26,218,139	$65,941,808	$47,484,015	$63,038,118	$67,097,479
State, ARRs	12,816,996	28,803,122	23,951,016	25,725,016	40,827,176	27,486,827
State, total	$41,275,748	$55,021,261	$89,892,824	$73,209,031	$103,865,294	$94,584,306
Local, new buildings	$537,391,416	$534,202,531	$560,754,782	$620,037,382	$518,738,443	$558,427,058
Local, ARRs	193,115,934	236,808,805	369,691,281	258,453,050	392,376,170	251,796,891
Local, total	730,507,350	771,011,336	930,446,063	878,490,432	911,114,613	810,223,949
Gift, new buildings	$27,464,751	$43,422,990	$71,784,153	$62,835,806	$58,532,660	$45,898,678
Gift, ARRs	26,579,726	24,780,729	31,906,464	43,718,655	42,456,942	15,599,975
Gift, total	$54,044,477	$68,203,719	$103,690,617	$106,554,461	$100,989,602	$61,498,653
Total Funds Used	$833,177,064	$908,120,335	$1,136,701,866	$1,072,785,748	$1,140,892,697	$985,002,857

*ARR: Additions, Renovations and Remodels

Expenditures for Resources in School Library Media Centers, 2009–2010

Lesley Farmer

Thank goodness we're a resourceful bunch. How else could media specialists have survived this protracted recession, where our colleagues continue to get pink slips, budgets keep getting slashed, and we constantly have to defend what we do?

How have things changed since we published our last spending survey in April 2009? Our latest *School Library Journal* (*SLJ*) survey of school expenditures and collections, for 2009–2010, shows that librarians have used a variety of coping techniques to weather this economic storm, whether it's serving more than one school, using additional volunteers, taking on more tasks, or seeking outside funding ("Nearly all resource purchases are done via donation or grant writing," wrote one of the resourceful 833 library staffers who responded to the survey).

No doubt knowing how others are holding up helps us better gauge where we stand—and provides more ammunition when it comes to asking for what we need. What the survey found is that huge inequities remain. Overall, elementary school libraries continued to be short-staffed, and they had shorter operating hours than other school levels. Middle schools had the least technology. And high schools were the hardest hit budget-wise. But it was media specialists in western states like California and Arizona who had it the hardest, having suffered the brunt of the financial fallout. While the economy continued to chip away at library budgets nationwide, western states—although they have the largest schools—had less library staff and smaller budgets than their counterparts in other regions.

Disappearing Dollars, Beleaguered Budgets

Although some states, such as North Carolina and Texas, saw new K–12 schools sprout up and receive sizeable financial support, for the most part states were scrambling for money. In general, the western states fared worst. For that reason, both the mean and median figures are reported in Table 1. Generally, federal funding failed to relieve strained budgets, which suggests a greater reliance on local discretionary allocations and fund raising as the recession thins donors' pockets.

Fortunately, some materials and services, such as periodicals and technology, were funded from other budgets at the local, district, and state levels. In addition, almost all states provided school libraries with statewide database subscriptions.

Some differences in budgets by grade level and region are shown in Table 2. Middle school libraries fared worse than other grade levels, and in the Northeast the amount of money spent per student was more than double the amount spent

Lesley Farmer coordinates the librarianship program at California State University, Long Beach.
Adapted from *School Library Journal*, March 2011.

Table 1 / Comparison of Mean and Median Expenditures for All Resources and Funding Sources
2009–2010

	Number of Respondents	Mean	Median
Total local funds	637	$14,969	$5,438
Total federal funds	269	5,407	0
Total fund-raising/gifts	422	4,415	0
Total all funds	817	11,384	7,350
Books	637	10,390	4,500
e-Books	348	790	0
Periodicals	554	834	500
AV resources/equipment	459	1,857	200
Computer resources/equipment	319	7,402	0
Telecommunications	261	141	0
Web-based resources	382	3,153	238
Technical processing	358	624	0

Table 2 / Student Enrollment, Median Library Books, Acquisitions, and Budgets
2009–2010

	Average Student Enrollment	Books Added (median)	Books Added per Student	Total Budget (median)	Expenditure per Student
Elementary school, K–8	540	400	0.74	$5,177	$9.59
Middle school	748	414	0.55	6,023	8.05
High school, K–12	1,269	421	0.33	12,485	9.84
Northeast	600	400	0.66	10,000	16.67
South	650	435	0.67	7,000	10.77
North Central	644	450	0.70	7,000	10.87
West	609	383	0.63	4,500	7.39

Table 3 / Number of Nonprint Items in Library Collection
2009–2010

	e-books (average/median)	Videos	DVDs Added	DVDs	Audios Added	Audios	Software
Elementary school, K–8 (N=356)	172/0	217/200	72/40	12/5	80/38	22/0	9/0
Middle school (N=163)	89/0	265/150	87/50	13/5	80/45	10/2	9/5
High school, 7–12 (N=231)	135/6	428/200	192/100	27/11	78/30	8/2	14/4
Other (N=74)	688/0	213/100	72/37	15/5	55/40	9/0	15/5

by school libraries in the West. It should be noted that in our last survey, for the 2008–2009 school year, it was anticipated that the mean high school library budget for 2009–2010 would be $17,818. In actuality, it was $18,165, but the median was less than $13,000; and the range was $0 to $300,000. The top tenth of school libraries were very well funded (especially new ones with strong opening collections), were successful at fund raising, or had strong administrative support. But the majority of school libraries didn't experience robust financial health.

Throughout the nation, about a third of libraries had their budgets slashed, while half had no change and only an eighth saw an increase. High school libraries seemed to be hardest hit, probably because their collections tend to be bigger than those in middle and elementary schools so that it appears they're not in much need of funds. Even though high school libraries are increasingly using digital resources, only a tenth of them had increased budgets, and almost 40 percent had decreased budgets. For those libraries whose budgets increased, the national median was 20 percent for elementary school libraries, 13 percent for middle school libraries, and 10 percent for high school libraries. On the other hand, the median decrease was 28 percent for elementary school libraries and 20 percent for both middle school and high school libraries. As for changes in budgets, more variation existed within regions than among them.

Elementary school and middle school libraries were twice as likely to get outside funding (about 40 percent) than high school libraries (20 percent). They were also more likely to host book fairs and receive community donations. Interestingly, about half of K–12 school libraries received outside funding. As the economy continues to struggle and government funding diminishes, the message seems to be that schools in general, and school libraries in particular, need to supplement their income in order to maintain quality collections and services. No one funding group (such as book fair vendors) was listed by more than 10 percent of the respondents. Local funders such as businesses, nonprofits, and parents were the main sources of funding and were five times more likely than nonlocal funders to provide financial help. At every grade level, outside funding was used for many purposes, but mainly for resource sharing (11 percent), books (10 percent), supplies (10 percent), and telecommunications (7 percent).

Staffing, Pay, Hours

Geography plays a huge role in library staffing. Schools in the West were less likely to have a professional librarian than those in other parts of the country, which tended to have at least one full-time librarian. The South seemed to be better staffed than most regions, with an average of 1.3 librarians per school, but it also tended to have less paraprofessional help. Around half the time, libraries in the Northeast and the South had full-time paraprofessionals, and two-thirds of schools in the North Central states had one. Once again, the West was in the worst shape, with only about a third of its libraries having full-time paraprofessionals. The West was also most likely to have a half-time school librarian. Not surprisingly, then, the West was more likely to have adult volunteers (an average of 3.5, with a median of at least one) and student volunteers (a median of three) as opposed to one for sites in the Northeast and two for the South and North

Central areas. One might speculate that the differences in staff are due to budget, school size, and state or regional accreditation mandates.

Not that the western school librarians earned more. That privilege went to those in the Northeast, with a median annual salary of $62,000 in comparison with $50,000 for the rest of the nation. It should also be noted that high school librarians nationwide had a median salary of $57,800, as opposed to school librarians at other levels (elementary median salary was $50,000, middle school average salary was $56,000, and other school levels' average salaries were about $48,000).

The average number of work experience for head library staff was between nine and ten years, regardless of site level or region; the South and West had more veteran K–12 staff, averaging about 18 years. High school librarians averaged 17 years of work experience in education, in comparison with elementary and middle school librarians who averaged 15 years.

The West also has the largest student enrollments, most sharply at the high school level; the median enrollment was 1,450, compared to 1,225 in the South, 980 in the Northeast, and 820 in the North Central states. The South and West had about 800 average enrollment in middle schools (compared with 660 in the Northeast and 600 in the North Central states), and 500 in elementary schools (compared with 450 in the Northeast and North Central states).

It should be noted that there was no significant difference in library hours relative to region. On the other hand, about a third of elementary school libraries were open less than 34 hours a week, as opposed to one-sixth of middle school libraries and 9 percent of high school libraries.

Collections

In collections, there were slight net gains across the board. There was no regional difference in the size of collections at any grade level. Nationwide, the median number of books at the elementary and middle school levels was 12,000, and the median number at the high school level was 14,000. Around the nation, the median number of books weeded in elementary libraries was 200, in middle school libraries 300, and in high school libraries 250.

Most librarians, regardless of school level or geography, said that between 11 and 30 percent of their collections were out of date (respondents self-defined the term). Elementary collections were more likely to be current (about a quarter of respondents thought that 90 percent or more of their collections were current), and high school collections were most likely to be largely out of date (almost a tenth of respondents).

A little less than half of southern and western school libraries included non-English materials, and about 55 percent of school libraries in the Northeast and 36 percent of those in the North Central states. Looking at the languages that respondents mentioned, it appears that the two main reasons for collecting non-English materials are curriculum and student population ethnicity. Nationwide, a small majority of high school libraries collected non-English materials; 43 percent of middle school and 39 percent of elementary libraries did. Spanish materials were overwhelming the top choice, at 95 percent. Second in popularity (about one-sixth) were materials in French, and a distant third (about 5 percent) were Chinese or German materials.

Digital Resources

Across grade levels, two-thirds of school libraries had access to statewide digital resources. A third of school libraries (a quarter at the elementary and middle school levels, and a slight majority of high school libraries) chose digital resources beyond those provided by the district or state. More than 70 digital products, such as reference titles, database aggregators, and e-books (which were usually identified by company name) were identified by respondents as part of their collections or subscribed to by them. Not counting video-streaming products (noted below), the products most often acquired were from Gale, identified by one-sixth of the schools. EBSCO's products were named by a tenth, and ProQuest, Wilson, eLibrary, SIRS, Infotrac, JSTOR, Project Muse, and NetTrekker were also mentioned. World Book was the most popular online encyclopedia, cited by 13 percent of the respondents. Britannica was noted by 5 percent and Grolier by 4 percent.

Other digital products mentioned by 1 to 3 percent of school libraries included:

- Reference: Facts on File, Marshall Cavendish, Oxford University Press (especially its dictionary), Salem Press, Sharpe, ABC-CLIO, Scholastic
- Health: Teen Health and Wellness
- Geopolitical: Culture Grams, Country Watch, Country Reports, World & I, Congressional Quarterly, Current Biography, and several map collections
- Other subject-specific sources: Art Museum Gallery, Mango (language)
- Newspapers: Newsbank, America's Historical Newspapers
- Reading: Renaissance Learning (Accelerated Reader), PebbleGo, TumbleBooks
- General learning sites: Enchanted Learning, Study Island, Teaching.net
- Bibliographics: Novelist, LibGuides
- Intellectual property tools: Noodle Tools, EasyBib, Turn It In

The variety of topic and titles was impressive, and all levels of libraries subscribed to these products. While the standard general database aggregator companies such as Gale, EBSCO, and ProQuest, are well-represented, the specific digital resources chosen show that school libraries are focused on subscribing to digital resources that are tailored to their curricular needs.

About three-quarters of elementary and middle school libraries and almost two-thirds of high school libraries subscribe to streaming video services. Discovery Education streaming is the favorite at all levels; Safari is a distant second.

At the time of the survey, a little more than 50 percent of elementary school libraries and almost 60 percent of middle school libraries and about 43 percent of high school libraries had no access to e-books. About 20 percent of elementary and middle school libraries had access to more than 100 e-books, and about a third of high school libraries had such access. However, a little over 10 percent of high school libraries had access to more than 1,000 e-books.

As for other nonprint materials and multimedia products, growth was consistently small: about 20 percent across media, for relatively small collections, although some school libraries had significant nonprint collections. Audio collections grew about 50 percent across levels since 2007–2008, while videos and DVDs remained fairly flat in the same time period.

Table 4 / Sources for Collection Development

	Online Vendor	Direct from Publisher	Local Bookstore
Elementary school	24%	11%	36%
Middle school	46%	13%	41%
High school	51%	23%	47%

Vendor Choices

About 90 percent of school libraries at all levels handle book selection at the local level, enabling them to address community-specific needs. Only about 1 percent, scattered by level and region, had centralized selection only. Roughly a tenth used a combination of site and centralized selection.

While about two-thirds of school librarians across all levels used Follett as their main vendor for book purchasing, most used another vendor as well. The second most popular vendor among elementary school librarians (10 percent) was Bound to Stay Bound, and among middle school libraries it was Permabound and Mackin, tied at 6 percent. High school librarians, however, had little consensus in their choice of vendors, with Amazon being the second most popular at 4 percent. Junior Library Guild and Barnes & Noble were frequently used at all levels. Middle school and high school librarians turned to Baker & Taylor, while elementary and middle school librarians favored Scholastic. Gumdrop was also popular among elementary school librarians. The use of other types of vendors increased with grade level.

Follett was most cited as the library's integrated library management system at all levels, about a third of the time. At a distant second (less than 5 percent of the time) was Alexandria. Surprisingly, in-house solutions came in third. Sirsi was fourth most popular, and TLC was fifth. No significant difference existed between school levels.

Computers and Cataloging

The days of a remote computer lab maintained by the school librarian seem to be over. On the other hand, the equivalent of one has moved into the library, with about seven out of eight media centers now housing a bank of computers. The median number of computers in the school library at the elementary and K–8 level was nine; at the high school level it was 25, and other levels had a median of 16 computers. Across the board, school librarians tended to buy a couple of computers and said they didn't plan to buy another during the present school year.

Cataloging was a function that often involved in-house, district, and vendor cataloging. About three out of four libraries at all levels cataloged in-house. A central system, usually at the district level, was used by 22 percent of elementary school libraries, 14 percent of middle school libraries, and 18 percent of high school libraries. Vendors were also used in cataloging: 43 percent of elementary schools, 46 percent of middle schools, and 53 percent of high school libraries.

Online computer catalogs seemed to go hand-in-hand with library computers; if the library had computers, it had an OPAC, which was accessible from all student stations—and between 85 and 90 percent (lowest at middle schools and highest at high schools) had classroom remote access; either all the classes or none had access to the library OPAC. These same libraries also had Web home pages.

The school librarian maintained the Web page at about 88 percent of elementary and middle school libraries and at 83 percent of high school libraries. In elementary and middle school settings, a school technology specialist maintained the home page 6 percent of the time, compared with about 10 percent of high schools. District staff handled that job 2 percent of the time across levels.

Collaboration

Regardless of level, most school librarians plan with 20 percent or fewer of classroom teachers. Almost 10 percent of elementary school librarians did no planning with classroom teachers (in comparison to 5 percent of middle school and 3 percent of high school librarians). On the other hand, about 5 percent of elementary school librarians plan with more than 80 percent of classroom teachers in comparison with 6 percent of middle school and 1 percent of high school librarians.

A little more than half (52 percent) of elementary school libraries had fixed schedules, as opposed to less than 6 percent of middle school and 4 percent of high school libraries. About two-thirds of middle school and seven-eighths of high school libraries had flexible schedules. About a third of elementary and middle school libraries had a mix of flexible and fixed schedules.

About 40 percent of elementary school librarians did not talk with public librarians, perhaps because many of those sites are managed by paraprofessionals, while almost all middle and high school librarians talked yearly with public librarians, and about a third of them talked a couple of times a term. In all cases, about a tenth talked more frequently than monthly with public librarians.

Technology

School librarians routinely incorporated technology into teaching and learning. The new American Association of School Librarians learning standards that encourage student production can be seen to be reflected in the technology uses in Table 5. In general, technology use increased in the higher grades, and reading programs such as Accelerated Reader and Reading Rockets continued to be used mainly in lower grades (but were used less than was reported in previous sur-

Table 5 / How Library Computers Are Used for Teaching and Learning
2009–2010

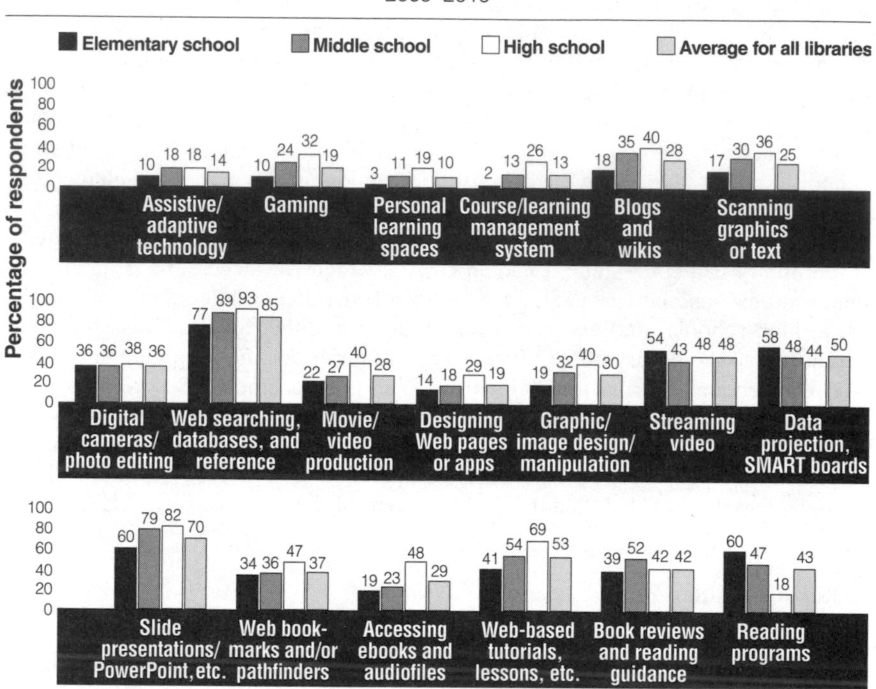

veys). Most technology uses listed in Table 5 stabilized since our 2009 survey, which covered the 2007–2008 school year. However, access to e-books and audio files has also jumped significantly: to almost half of high school libraries. The survey measured the following applications for the first time: gaming, movie production, course management systems, and personal learning spaces. The first two items seemed to have taken off to the greatest extent; about a third of high school libraries incorporated gaming, and almost 40 percent produced movies.

Using the data

About a third of the survey respondents made use of *SLJ*'s previous spending surveys or data, mainly when asking for a budget increase or as a resource for general library advocacy. The surveys helped people inform decision-makers, particularly in terms of comparing resource support. Other respondents used the surveys as a site assessment tool, again to make comparisons nationally and to provide a benchmark for improving in resource allocation. Respondents have used the information to help in budget planning, technology acquisitions, and collection development and replacement. Library educators use it for school librarian preservice instruction and research.

Think Globally, Act Locally

As Thomas Jefferson said, an informed citizenry is the only true repository of the public will. Now, more than ever, school librarians need to know how their colleagues are faring, if for no other reason than for equitable educational experiences for students around the country. That's one of the main reasons we're committed to doing these surveys.

With the growing use of technology, we were interested to see how school libraries were taking advantage of it. We discovered that technology is an integral part of most school libraries in terms of collection development and retrieval, teaching and instruction, and program administration. Increasingly, collection development didn't seem to quibble between access and ownership. Nor is the book format sacred: rather, the ideas are what are central, and the format accommodates learners. Technology acquisition decisions seemed to be site-based and student-centered. Both sites and districts shared in resources and administrative functions relative to technology. Multiple teaching strategies incorporated technology, and facilitated student generation of knowledge products. One respondent noted: "I feel like my job is changing, and I am struggling to keep up with the changes in technology." Another said: "The numbers may be small, but I do not think that is a good measure of a successful library in today's world of technology." Furthermore, school libraries are having to address school-wide technology efforts such as one-to-one laptop programs and open textbook initiatives, which can affect access to information.

Schools continue to be local entities, and school libraries derive much support from them in terms of resources, money, and time. Respondents' comments indicated that local support—or the lack of it—can make or break a library's effectiveness. So the final message for school librarians is this: Make connections with your school and local community; plan informally and formally with teachers, administrators, and public librarians; share your stories and your successes; build resources and services in response to local interests and needs; express library needs in terms of how they are essential to student learning; and let student voices speak on behalf of the library to their families. We need to involve our communities in supporting and advancing what we do.

About the Study

In December 2010 the survey was e-mailed to *SLJ*'s nearly 26,000 newsletter subscribers; a total of 833 returned the completed survey within the month. Almost 98 percent of those who responded work in public school libraries, while the remainder work in charter school libraries and just a few work in private schools. Of those numbers, 45 percent work in elementary (K–8), schools, about 20 percent in middle schools, almost 30 percent in high school or grades 7–12 libraries, and 0.5 percent in K–12 settings. Based on information from the National Center for Education Statistics, librarians from the Northeast and West were a bit higher represented proportionally, and those from the South were a bit under-represented (although that region had the highest proportion of elementary schools represented).

Book Trade Research and Statistics

2010: Digital Publishing's Impact Felt Across Industry

Jim Milliot
Co-Editorial Director, *Publishers Weekly*

In a year-end letter to employees, Simon & Schuster CEO Carolyn Reidy said 2010 was the year that publishing was irrecoverably changed—a viewpoint shared by many, if not all, in the industry.

The year was dominated by digital developments. Sales of e-books skyrocketed, as did sales of digital readers, following the launch of Apple's iPad, Barnes & Noble's Nookcolor and the third edition of Amazon's Kindle. Meanwhile, publishers and booksellers implemented new business practices to deal with the ramifications of the strong digital growth. Through the first 11 months of 2010, e-book sales at 14 major trade houses were up 166 percent, but accompanying that boom was a decline in sales of print books.

The year also saw the industry slowly recovering from the recession that gripped the country for much of 2009, with pay raises and other benefits being restored as 2010 moved forward.

Digital news seemed to be made nearly every day, and that situation seemed destined to continue. One announcement eagerly awaited throughout 2010 didn't come until mid-March 2011—a decision in the Google Book Search settlement. Judge Denny Chin of the U.S. Court of Appeals for the Second Circuit, who had heard final arguments in the case February 18, 2010, ruled in mid-March against Google and in favor of the publishers and authors who had brought the suit. Google's plans for pursuing the case were unknown at the time of this writing.

Another source of frustration for publishers, authors, and booksellers—Amazon's decision to sell e-books for $9.99—came to a head in early 2010 when five of the six largest trade houses adopted the so-called agency pricing model. Under this model, publishers establish the price for e-books (usually between $12.99 and $14.99) and booksellers receive a 30 percent commission. Under the traditional wholesale model used to sell print books and carried over by Amazon for e-books, publishers sold books at a discount off list price and booksellers could charge whatever they wanted. When Macmillan became the first publisher to implement the agency model, Amazon removed the "buy" buttons from Macmillan titles on its Web site in protest. After a ten-day standoff, Amazon relented, restored the "buy" buttons, and agreed to adopt the agency model from certain publishers. Amazon used a similar tactic against Penguin when it moved to the agency model, preventing Penguin's frontlist titles from being sold for the

Kindle. The dispute lasted for about a month. (Of the major houses, the only publisher not using the agency model to sell e-books was Random House.)

The adoption of the agency model cooled debate about what price e-books should be, although price experimentation continued throughout the year. The move to the agency model also brought a quick end to the debate about when e-books should be released, with most publishers choosing to release e-books and print books simultaneously. Some publishers had favored a "window" approach in which the e-book would be released about three months after publication of the hardcover version.

The biggest business battle in the year was over control of Barnes & Noble, the country's largest bookstore chain. Ron Burkle, its largest outside shareholder, launched a proxy contest during the summer, contending that B&N's stock price was undervalued because of ineffective leadership on the part of founder and chairman Len Riggio. Burkle maintained that the B&N board was too closely aligned with Riggio and other insiders and failed to exercise proper oversight of Riggio's decisions. The action that most upset Burkle was the acquisition of Barnes & Noble College Booksellers, a company owned by Riggio that Burkle argued B&N had paid too much to acquire. In response, B&N announced it was conducting a strategic review of the entire company, a process that included its possible sale. The review was expected to be completed in the first quarter of 2011. The company also nominated two new directors to run with Riggio for three board slots; in a vote in early September, the Riggio slate defeated the Burkle candidates in a close vote.

The country's second-largest bookstore chain, Borders, was at the center of another major business story in 2010. The retailer took on new leadership early in the year when Mike Edwards was appointed CEO, succeeding Ron Marshall who resigned to join the supermarket chain A&P. Later in the year, investor Bennett LeBow bought a substantial stake in Borders, making him the largest shareholder, and he was named chairman. Throughout the year Borders engaged in an aggressive effort to close unprofitable stores, especially in its mall operations, while also laying off 100 people in its warehouse and cutting its corporate work force. The fireworks over Borders, however, didn't really start until December when the chain reported another dismal quarter and revealed it could face a potential cash crunch early in 2011 unless it was able to obtain new financing. On December 30, Borders further acknowledged that it had delayed payments to the major publishers and in the first week of 2011 began discussions with the major houses to turn those missed payments into interest-bearing notes as part of a refinancing effort. Publishers reacted coolly to the offer, and early in 2011 Borders filed for bankruptcy and announced a major restructuring.

Borders' problems reflected the steady drop in the purchase of print books in favor of e-books. To make up for this decline, bookstores began adding more non-book items, such as educational toys and games. Bookstores also scrambled to find ways to compete with Amazon and Barnes & Noble in the e-book market. Borders opened its own e-bookstore in the summer, as did the nation's third-largest chain, Books-A-Million; BAM also starting selling the Nook family of digital devices in the fall. To accompany the launch of the iPad, Apple opened the iBookstore in the spring and a Canadian iBookstore in the summer. After months of delays, Google finally launched Google Editions late in the fall and renamed it Google eBooks. The enterprise is Google's entry into the e-book market, and it teamed with the American Booksellers Association (ABA) to sell Google e-books.

The industry's book show, BookExpo America (BEA), moved to a midweek schedule in 2010, and while the switch from a Friday–Sunday show met with a good reception the decision to reduce the number of days the exhibit floor was open from three to two did not, and BookExpo officials announced that the 2011 show will once again be three days. BEA executives also held discussions in the year with the American Library Association regarding the possibility of holding BEA and the ALA annual meeting in the same city on the same dates in what was described as a "co-location" deal. Although it appeared an agreement was likely, ALA decided to continue to hold its annual meeting on its own.

The Wylie Agency started a new front in the battle over control of digital rights when it launched Odyssey Editions in the summer. Wylie took the position that it owned the digital rights to a number of backlist books by well-established authors, and rather than accept the standard 25 percent royalty it signed a deal with Amazon to sell digital editions exclusively through the Kindle store for a substantially higher royalty. Random reacted by saying it would not do business with Wylie until the question of who owned the rights was resolved. After some back-and-forth, the parties reached a deal under which Random took control of backlist rights in exchange for a higher, sliding-scale royalty that went up to 40 percent. At the end of 2010 Wylie was still operating Odyssey Editions, although it hadn't signed any new authors (and wasn't selling Random authors).

Finances

The impact of the recession, though less evident than in 2009, still influenced events in 2010, particularly in the first part of the year. Educational Media & Publishing Group (EM&PG), parent company of Houghton Mifflin Harcourt, restructured its financing in a move that saw EM&PG Chairman Barry O'Callaghan lose day-to-day control over the company. Educational and audiobook publisher Haights Cross Communications filed for prepackaged bankruptcy in January as part of a plan to reduce its debt. The company emerged from Chapter 11 in the spring. Another company that exited bankruptcy in 2010 was Reader's Digest, after successfully restructuring its debt. As part of its effort to reduce expenses, the company moved out of its longtime headquarters in Pleasantville, New York (which it had previously sold) to offices in White Plains and New York City.

F+W Media restructured its debt, with ABRY Partners moving from its position as F+W's largest shareholder to a minority position. F+W CEO David Nussbaum was named the head of a new board of directors.

Library e-content vendor OverDrive received new funding from Insight Venture Partners, and the e-book distributor LibreDigital received $8.1 million in additional venture capital funding to expand its e-book distribution services. Scholastic repurchased 5.2 million shares in a $157 million Dutch auction.

Although the number of independent booksellers held fairly steady in 2010, Joseph-Beth Booksellers, which operated eight bookstores in Tennessee, Kentucky, and Ohio, filed for Chapter 11 in November and closed four stores.

Texas issued an assessment against Amazon, claiming the company owed the state $269 million in uncollected sales tax for the 2005–2009 period. Amazon has long held that it does not need to collect sales tax in states where it has no physical presence, and said it would vigorously fight the ruling.

BookLocker and Amazon reached an out-of-court settlement in BookLocker's antitrust lawsuit against Amazon, which claimed that Amazon was forcing print-on-demand companies to use its CreateSpace division. As part of the agreement, Amazon agreed to pay BookLocker's court costs.

Mergers and Acquisitions

The weak economy and uncertain direction of the book market because of the rapid changes being brought about by digital developments combined to limit mergers and acquisitions in 2010. Three industry publications, however, changed hands in the year. *Publishers Weekly* was sold to its one-time publisher George Slowik, Jr. by Reed Business Information, which also sold *Library Journal* and *School Library Journal* to Media Source.

Kirkus Reviews, temporarily closed by Nielsen Company at the end of 2009, was acquired by Herb Simon, a billionaire shopping center developer and owner of the Indiana Pacers (and a *Kirkus* subscriber).

In one of the bigger acquisitions of the year, an investor group led by Zelnick Media acquired Alloy, Inc. in a deal valued at $126 million. Alloy, whose businesses include developing book series for the young adult market, has annual sales of about $205 million. Religious book publisher Thomas Nelson got a new owner during 2010 when Kohlberg & Company acquired a majority stake as part of a financial restructuring of the publisher's debt. InterMedia Partners, which took Nelson private in 2006, held on to a minority stake. Nelson CEO Michael Hyatt was named chairman.

The majority of acquisitions during the year involved small deals aimed at filling holes in a company's portfolio. Skyhorse Publishing closed three deals in 2010. The New York City independent was the winner in the bankruptcy auction for Arcade Publishing, paying $548,000 to acquire approximately 500 titles. Later in the year, Skyhorse bought Allworth Press, and just before the end of 2010 bought the assets of Sports Publishing. Allworth has a backlist of more than 300 titles focused on business and self-help books for artists, photographers, graphic designers, and authors. Publisher Tad Crawford will continue to oversee Allworth's operations. The purchase of the assets of Sports Publishing, which went bankrupt in 2008, added 700 titles, and Skyhorse will relaunch Sports Publishing as a standalone imprint releasing 40 revised and updated titles annually.

Turner Publishing was another independent that made multiple deals in the year. Early in 2010 it acquired about 100 publishing contracts of Ancestry Publishing from parent company Ancestry.com. Turner followed that deal with the purchase of the publishing assets or Fieldstone Alliance, publisher of about 50 business management titles for nonprofit agencies. Guideposts acquired Ellie

Claire Gift & Paper Expressions in a deal that also included Ellie Claire's Christian book imprint Summerside Press. Summerside has a backlist of 84 titles in fiction and nonfiction, while Ellie Claire produces a range of items for the gift market. Square One Publishers acquired the book assets of diet, health, and nutrition publisher Safe Goods Publishing.

Children's book publisher Charlesbridge acquired year-old Imagine Publishing. Imagine founders Jeremy and Charles Nurnberg moved to Charlesbridge with Charles remaining Imagine publisher and Jeremy becoming vice president of sales.

Amazon added to its publishing holdings in the year, acquiring the rights to 120 titles from Toby Press that the company said it would republish under its AmazonEncore and AmazonCrossing imprints. Toby owner Matthew Miller refocused his operations on his Koren and Maggid imprints and moved from Connecticut to Israel. David Lamb acquired Vantage Press and began to overhaul the company, one of the original self-publishing companies (back when self-publishing was called vanity publishing). As part of the reorganization, Lamb created Vantage Point, an imprint in which, rather than authors paying a publishing fee, Vantage will publish the books in exchange for a split of the royalties.

Bowker bought BML, a leading provider of research on the British book market. Peter Goodman, founder of the Berkeley, California, publisher Stone Bridge Press, reacquired that company from the Japanese book distributor Yohan. Alibris, online marketplace for books, acquired smaller rival Monsoon, Inc. in February. Alibris would later change its name to Monsoon. Harlequin bought out the 50 percent stake in its German publishing operation, Cora Verlag, held by its partner Axel Springer.

In retail, struggling Borders sold its stationery group, Paperchase, to the British private equity firm Private Capital Limited for $31 million. The spoken word audio segment saw AudioGo Limited, a British media company, acquire an 85 percent stake in BBC Audiobooks, a deal that included the U.S. division, BBC Audiobooks America. The company's name was changed to AudioGo.

The biggest deal in the industry was on the manufacturing side where Wisconsin-based Quad/Graphics bought World Color Press in a move that created North America's second-largest printer with annual sales of approximately $4.8 billion.

Launched and Closed

Langenscheidt Publishing Group, the U.S. arm of the German travel and reference publisher, closed late in 2010 after attempts to restructure the company failed. In March Langenscheidt had named John Muchnicki, a turnaround expert, as president, replacing Marc Jennings, but Muchnicki was unable to reverse the company's fortunes. Langenscheidt reached an agreement with Ingram Publishers Services for IPS to distribute the company's titles in the United States.

HarperCollins closed its HarperStudio imprint following the departure of founder Bob Miller to Workman. HarperStudio sought to redefine the traditional publishing model by offering lower advances to authors in exchange for a higher portion of revenue, and to sell books on a non-returnable basis. HarperStudio's list was divided among various HarperCollins imprints, and Associate Publisher Debbie Stier left the company late in 2010. DC Comics closed Zuda.com, a Web site started to solicit original Web comics.

After losing his job as head of Simon & Schuster's flagship imprint in spring 2010, David Rosenthal was named president and publisher of a new, general imprint at Penguin. Rosenthal hoped to release his first titles in fall 2011 and publish 24–36 titles annually. Another major new adult imprint was announced by Little, Brown, which said it planned to launch Mulholland Books, a suspense fiction imprint, in spring 2011. With John Schoenfelder as editor, Mulholland plans to release one hardcover and one paperback per month. Sterling Publishing teamed with British publisher Quercus to form the Silver Oak imprint. Silver Oak will publish fiction titles in the United States that have appeared on Quercus's British list. Sterling also announced plans to start a new teen fiction imprint, Splinter.

Sterling was not the only company to announce initiatives in the children's market. Margaret Ferguson, publisher and editorial director of FSG Books for Young Readers, was given her own imprint, Margaret Ferguson Books, with plans for a 2011 launch. Skyhorse Publishing announced that it was creating a new children's imprint, Sky Pony Press, set for fall 2011. The line, which will start with 15 to 20 new titles, is being launched with the help of children's book publishing veteran Jean Reynolds, who is working as a consultant on the project. Candlewick Press partnered with *New Yorker* art director Françoise Mouly's comics line, Toon Books, to launch the Toon Books imprint.

Rick Richter, former head of Simon & Schuster Children's Publishing, formed Ruckus Media, a family entertainment company that will specialize in creating animation apps for the children's market.

With the growth in self-publishing, Barnes & Noble launched PubIt!, a service that allows independent publishers and self-publishers to distribute digital editions of their works through B&N.com and the Barnes & Noble e-bookstore. In some other nontraditional areas, Harvard Common Press and a group of investors launched Yummly, a Web site aimed at putting recipes, including those from cookbook publishers, online and charging for access. Adams Media announced an agreement to develop a new line of print and e-books with the children's music brand Kidz Bop. North Atlantic Books launched Evolver Editions with Evolver LLC, an online magazine focused on psychic evolution. Midwestern library and educational publisher Abdo formed Abdo Digital to offer online access to e-book versions of Abdo print titles.

With print review sources in decline, Ted Sturtz launched the *New York Journal of Books,* an online book review site. Yale University launched a new weeklong publishing program in July, looking to fill the void left by the closure of the Stanford Professional Publishing Course.

Reorganizations

Reflecting the growing importance of digital publishing, Random House, the nation's largest trade publisher, promoted a number of executives to head new teams that will support all of the company's digital programs. Amanda Close was named vice president, digital sales and business development; Nina von Moltke was appointed vice president, digital publishing development; and Peter McCarthy was named vice president, online and digital marketing. As part of the restructuring, von Moltke was put in charge of Random House Audio and the Fodor's Travel Group, while the Princeton Review, Sylvan Learning, and Prima Games imprints were put under Chip Gibson, president of Random House Children's Books.

Random didn't limit its restructuring to the digital arena in 2010. In a long-awaited move, the company merged its Bantam Dell imprint with that of Ballantine to form Ballantine Bantam Dell. The move united all of Random's mass-market imprints under the direction of Libby McGuire, with Nita Taublib (executive vice president, publisher, and editor-in-chief of Bantam Dell) leaving the company. The Crown Publishing Group also continued to tweak its operations, eliminating some positions in its illustrated-book unit and cutting five jobs in its WaterBrook Multnomah religious book imprint. Random's children's division discontinued the frontlist publishing program of Tricycle Press, laying off publisher Nicole Geiger and her four-person editorial team. Random will continue to sell the Tricycle backlist.

HarperCollins formed two new units in response to the growing influence of digital publishing. HarperCollins Digital is a digital marketing unit, while the Digital Technology Services group will support all of the company's digital initiatives. Barron's broke out its test prep imprint into a separate division and named Bob O'Sullivan publisher; the unit publishes 50 titles a year.

Simon & Schuster fired David Rosenthal, president and publisher of its flagship S&S imprint, and replaced him with Twelve publisher Jonathan Karp, who immediately began revamping the imprint around smaller editorial and marketing teams. Among the editors brought to S&S by Karp were Ben Loehnen and Jofie Ferrari-Adler, who were appointed senior editors. Loehnen had been at HarperCollins and Ferrari-Adler at Grove/Atlantic. As a result of the reorganization, longtime publicity director Victoria Meyer was among those who left S&S.

The combination of a weak economy and shrinking shelf space for mass-market paperbacks led to the overhaul of mass-market house Dorchester Publishing. After laying off several staffers, Dorchester CEO John Prebich left the company and was succeeded by Robert Anthony, and the company said it was ending its mass-market program in favor of doing original titles in both e-book and trade paperback formats. Print titles will be released under the Dorchester Trade Publishing name, rather than its existing Love Spell and Leisure Arts imprints. As sales of mass-market paperbacks plunged, Dorchester was criticized for late and missed payments to authors, resulting in some authors leaving the house. The new management team promised to address all outstanding issues with authors. The Hard Case Crime series, which had been published by Dorchester, found a new partner with Titan Publishing, and planned to release its first title in the partnership in September 2011.

Here Media, Inc., owner of one of the country's oldest gay publishers, Alyson Books, closed the house's print operations and said it would turn it into an e-book-only publisher. Publisher Don Weise left the company and later announced he was forming Magnus Books, which plans to publish about 15 titles annually for the gay and lesbian market.

After a two-year process, the Association of Booksellers for Children merged with the American Booksellers Association. Zondervan cut 30 positions from its sales, marketing, and creative teams in order to free resources to devote to expansion in digital publishing. Ingram continued to move away from its role as a traditional distributor of print books by adding more digital capabilities. The company also reached a deal with Macmillan to manage Macmillan's traditional print inventory and long-tail titles. DC Entertainment moved its digital and multimedia operations from New York to Burbank while keeping DC Comics in New York. The shift resulted in about 100 layoffs.

John Wiley took over the publishing program of Bloomberg Press, which was being shut down by its parent company Bloomberg L.P. The transition was not without controversy, however; the Authors Guild protested a letter sent by Wiley to Bloomberg authors about changing terms of the contracts they had with Bloomberg. The dispute ended when Wiley said it would not hold authors to any contract it signed.

Keen Communications closed the Berkeley, California, office of its Wilderness Press imprint and split its operations among its Menasha Ridge and Clerisy Press imprints, with editorial and production functions shifted to Menasha Ridge and marketing and publicity conducted by Clerisy. Counterpoint Press closed its New York offices, laying off two editors, and consolidated all operations in its Berkeley offices.

Penguin realigned its international sales team, putting more emphasis on Spanish-language territories, and named Barbara O'Shea president of international non-trade sales and special markets. Key Porter Books, one of Canada's most prestigious houses, closed its Toronto office and laid off 11 people while trimming its list. Its operations were moved to parent company H. B. Fenn's Bolton, Ontario, offices.

People

David Davidar, Penguin Canada publisher and a leader in the Canadian publishing industry, resigned after sexual harassment charges were filed against him. A settlement was reached in the dispute, and Mike Bryan, head of Penguin India, was named president of Penguin Canada, which also formed a new advisory board and appointed Rob Prichard as company chairman. Stephen Smith, chief operating officer at John Wiley & Sons, was named to succeed CEO Will Pesce when Pesce retires from the company in April 2011. Deborah Wiley, longtime head of corporation communications, retired and was succeeded by Susan Spilka. Bob Miller left HarperCollins where he was head of HarperStudio to become president of Workman Publishing.

Susan Kamil was appointed publisher of the Random House Publishing Group, taking over that role from Gina Centrello, who remained president. Kamil continued as editor-in-chief of Little Random and Dial Press. Other promotions within the group included that of Tom Perry to deputy publisher and that of Theresa Zoro, who was named senior vice president and director of publicity. Also in the Random family, Molly Stern joined Crown as senior vice president and publisher of Crown and Broadway Books. Stern had been editor-in-chief at

Viking. Former *Gourmet* Editor-in-Chief Ruth Reichl joined Random as editor-at-large, while former *Newsweek* Editor Jon Meacham was named executive vice president and executive editor of Random House Publishing Group. Random also hired away Cyrus Kheradi from Simon & Schuster, where he was head of S&S's international sales operation, to become senior vice president and director of international sales at Random House.

Evan Schnittman left Oxford University Press to become managing director of group sales and marketing, print and digital, for Bloomsbury. Tim Barton, president of Oxford University Press, was named to a new position that combined OUP USA with the press's British academic and journals divisions. Artist Jim Lee and Dan Didio, senior vice president of DC Comics, were named co-publishers of the company. Jim King resigned as head of Nielsen BookScan, where he was later replaced by Jonathan Stolper. Farrar, Straus & Giroux editor Lorin Stein was named editor of the *Paris Review,* succeeding Philip Gourevitch. Jon Thurber was named book review editor of the *Los Angeles Times,* taking over from David Ulin who stayed at the paper as book critic. Motoko Rich, who covered the publishing industry for the *New York Times,* left the beat, replaced by Julia Bosman.

Three regional bookselling associations gained new leaders in the fall. Deborah Leonard replaced Jim Dana as executive director of Great Lakes Independent Booksellers Association. Leonard, a sales manager at Cengage Learning, began her career in the book industry as a bookseller at Zibart's in Nashville. Dana joined the Peace Corps. Mountains and Plains Independent Booksellers Association replaced longtime Director Lisa D. Knudsen with Laura P. Ayrey, while Carrie Obry, an acquisitions editor at Llewellyn Worldwide, was named the new executive director of the Midwest Booksellers Association. Obry replaced Susan Walker, who moved back to her native North Carolina to care for her aging parents after serving as MBA head for 23 years.

Ralph Munsen, formerly vice president of technology at Clear Channel Communications, was named chief information officer at Hachette Book Group. Laurie Brown was named senior vice president, sales and marketing, at Houghton Mifflin Harcourt's trade and reference group. As part of the restructuring, Bridget Marmion, senior vice president for marketing, left the company. Susan Van Metre was named publisher of Abrams Books for Young Readers and Amulet Books, succeeding Howard Reeves, who moved to an editor-at-large position. Lottchen Shivers, longtime publicity and marketing executive at Holt who had also run her own firm, joined Abrams in the new post of executive director of adult marketing and publicity. Nicole Dewey moved from Henry Holt to Little, Brown where she was appointed executive director of publicity. Pat Eisemann was named to succeed Dewey at Holt.

Jane Friedman's Open Road Integrated Media startup added children's publishing veteran Barbara Marcus and Pablo Defendini to its roster. Marcus, onetime head of Scholastic's trade publishing and distribution group, was appointed to head Open Road's children's division. Defendini had been a producer at Tor.com. Haights Cross Communications named Ron Schlosser chairman and CEO. Karen Lotz, president and publisher of Candlewick Press, was named joint group managing director of parent company Walker Group and was slated to become sole managing director in July 2011. Lotz will continue to oversee

Candlewick. Lori Benton, former vice president and publisher of Harcourt Children's Books, was named vice president and publisher of the Scholastic Trade Publishing division, succeeding Suzanne Murphy, who was named vice president and publisher of books at Disney Publishing Worldwide. Murphy took over from Jonathan Yaged, who resigned in February to become COO of the marketing company House Party. Yaged returned to publishing just before the end of the year as head of the Macmillan Children's Publishing Group, succeeding Dan Farley.

In a major appointment in the agent world, Nick Harris was named co-head of ICM's book-to-film department. Former Collins publisher Steve Ross joined the Abrams Artists Agency, working both as an agent and heading up the company's newly formed Abrams Author Services.

Bestsellers

Stieg Larsson's Millennium trilogy—*The Girl with the Dragon Tattoo, The Girl Who Played with Fire,* and *The Girl Who Kicked the Hornet's Nest*—made the late Swedish author the biggest selling writer in the United States in 2010 with all three titles hitting, and dominating, the *Publishers Weekly* bestsellers lists (not to mention selling more than 1 million e-books at Amazon). *Hornet's Nest* was a fixture on the hardcover bestsellers list following its release in July, while *Tattoo* spent all of 2010 on the trade paperback list and 38 weeks on the mass-market list. *Fire* was a trade paperback bestseller for 38 weeks and also spent the same amount of time on the mass-market list. Another title that showed remarkable staying power was Kathryn Stockett's *The Help,* a hardcover mainstay in 2010, while *Outliers* by Malcolm Gladwell and *Women, Food and God* by Geneen Roth spent 28 weeks on the nonfiction list.

Larsson's strong paperback showing helped publisher Random House grab the largest share of the paperback market away from Penguin. Although Penguin had more titles hit the paperback list than Random by a count of 83 to 50, Larsson's durability resulted in Random putting books on the paperback list for a total of 370 weeks compared with 321 weeks for Penguin. Overall, Random commanded 24.2 percent of the paperback market in 2010, up from 21.0 percent in 2009, while Penguin's share fell to 20.2 percent from 22.0 percent. Hachette Book Group USA edged Simon & Schuster as the third-most-successful paperback publisher; its market share rose from 11.0 percent in 2009 to 12.7 percent in 2010, and although S&S's share also rose, its 0.6 percent increase put its total market share at 12.0 percent. Hachette and S&S both had 30 titles hit the paperback bestsellers lists in 2010. HarperCollins was in fifth position among paperback publishers with an 8.8 percent market share.

Larsson had less impact on the hardcover list, but Random still managed to hang onto the most book real estate in 2010. The nation's largest trade book publisher had a 20.8 percent share of the *Publishers Weekly* hardcover bestsellers list, down from 25.4 percent in 2009, placing 93 books on the list for 318 weeks. Penguin was close on Random's heels, increasing its market share to 20.2 percent from 18.2 percent with 83 hardcover bestsellers in the year for 309 weeks. Hachette once again managed to put a fewer number of bestsellers (46) and the hardcover list for a longer period of time than S&S, which had 54 bestsellers. Hachette's bestsellers spent 280 weeks on the list compared with 220 for S&S, giving Hachette an 18.3 percent share of the hardcover market compared with the 14.4 percent claimed by S&S. Similar to the paperback rankings, HarperCollins was in fifth place among hardcover publishers with a 10.3 percent market share.

Prices of U.S. and Foreign Published Materials

Narda Tafuri
Editor, ALA ALCTS Library Materials Price Index Editorial Board

The Library Materials Price Index (LMPI) Editorial Board of the American Library Association's Association for Library Collections and Technical Services' Publications Committee continues to monitor prices for a range of library materials from sources within North America and from other key publishing centers around the world.

The U.S. Consumer Price Index (CPI) dropped to 1.5 percent in 2010, a substantial decrease from the 2.7 percent registered for 2009. Continuing high unemployment and lower oil prices during that time period may have acted to restrain inflation. During 2010 the prices of hardcover books, legal serials services, and the average price of serials saw the greatest overall increases for library materials, outperforming the CPI. The price of college books, audiobooks, and British academic books declined; however, the average price of trade paperbacks dropped drastically in comparison. CPI data are obtained from the Bureau of Labor Statistics Web site at http://www.bls.gov.

The U.S. Periodicals Price Index (USPPI) (Table 1) has not been updated this year and is being repeated from last year's article. The index is unavailable this year due to a change in data provider. Beginning next year, data will be provided by EBSCO. Percent changes in average prices from previous years are noted in the chart below under the category "Periodicals."

A new index, a re-established index, and a new table make their debut in this year's article. The new table, Average Price of Serials, established by compiler Stephen Bosch, is based on titles in select serials indexes and shows average price trends from 2007 through 2011. This table is based on titles indexed in ISI Arts and Humanities Citation Index, ISI Science Citation Index, ISI Social Sciences Citation Index, EBSCO Academic Search Complete, and EBSCO Masterfile Premier. It differs from the data that appears in the USPPI by its inclusion of foreign serials prices, as well as using approximately three times the number of serials in its compilation. This appears as Table 8. Changes in average prices from previous years are noted in the chart below under the category "Serials."

Also new this year is the Legal Serials Services Index (LSSI). This index was previously included in the more general Serials Services Index. Due to the shift of a majority of serials services away from print to online-only access, the LMPI Editorial Board decided to focus on legal serials, which continue to produce a large number of publications in print. The base year established for this new index is 2009. This index appears as Table 2.

The British Academic Book index has been reestablished by compiler Judy Jeng, using data provided by Baker & Taylor. The base year for this index is 2009. The re-established index appears as Table 9.

Of special note to readers is a change in data source for the North American Academic Books Index. Beginning with the data for 2009, this table is being indexed using combined data from Coutts Information Services and YBP Library Services. Prior years' data may not be applicable if compared with those presented in this year's table.

Table 1 / U.S Periodicals: Average Prices and Price Indexes, 2008–2010
Index Base: 1984 = 100

Subject Area	1984	2008		2009		2010	
	Average Price	Average Price	Index	Average Price	Index	Average Price	Index
U.S. periodicals excluding Russian translations	$54.97	$436.90	794.8	$467.82	851.1	$497.63	905.3
U.S. periodicals including Russian translations	72.47	559.96	772.7	603.85	833.3	642.62	886.8
Agriculture	24.06	169.99	706.5	181.40	754.0	201.60	837.9
Business and economics	38.87	245.27	631.0	263.64	678.3	287.64	740.0
Chemistry and physics	228.90	2,333.37	1,019.4	2,482.16	1,084.4	2,622.14	1,145.5
Children's periodicals	12.21	29.98	245.5	33.43	273.8	35.87	293.8
Education	34.01	240.80	708.0	258.73	760.8	276.33	812.5
Engineering	78.70	688.98	875.5	734.14	932.8	786.72	999.6
Fine and applied arts	26.90	84.94	315.8	89.40	332.4	94.10	349.8
General interest periodicals	27.90	60.11	215.5	63.91	229.1	66.70	239.1
History	23.68	106.55	450.0	113.94	481.2	123.57	521.8
Home economics	37.15	225.51	549.5	246.26	600.1	260.64	635.1
Industrial arts	30.40	170.51	560.9	172.22	566.5	188.27	619.3
Journalism and communications	39.25	182.41	464.8	192.89	491.4	210.49	536.3
Labor and industrial relations	29.87	201.12	673.3	220.96	739.8	234.50	785.1
Law	31.31	141.02	450.4	149.04	476.0	157.88	504.2
Library and information sciences	38.85	161.15	414.8	172.63	444.4	179.80	462.8
Literature and language	23.02	96.35	418.5	102.92	447.1	109.32	474.9
Mathematics, botany, geology, general science	106.56	925.61	868.6	991.88	930.8	1,024.13	961.1
Medicine	125.57	1,224.41	975.1	1,317.81	1,049.5	1,427.56	1,136.9
Philosophy and religion	21.94	99.33	452.8	107.44	489.7	117.24	534.3
Physical education and recreation	20.54	81.79	398.2	87.73	427.1	91.48	445.4
Political science	32.43	241.37	744.3	261.05	805.0	273.80	844.3
Psychology	69.74	631.79	905.9	686.52	984.4	726.87	1,042.3
Russian translations	381.86	3,080.51	806.7	3,390.04	887.8	3,580.13	937.6
Sociology and anthropology	43.87	367.59	837.9	400.08	912.0	432.76	986.5
Zoology	78.35	911.89	1 163.9	980.66	1,251.6	1,047.35	1,336.8
Total number of periodicals							
Excluding Russian translations	3,731	3.728		3,728		3,728	
Including Russian translations	3,942	3,910		3,910		3,912	

Compiled by Brenda Dingley, University of Missouri, Kansas City, based on subscription information supplied by Swets Information Services.

	Percent Change				
Index	2006	2007	2008	2009	2010
CPI	2.50	4.10	0.10	2.70	1.50
Periodicals	7.30	7.20	8.00	6.40	n.a.
Legal serials services	n.a.	n.a.	n.a.	n.a.	3.50
*Hardcover books	5.90	-39.00	2.81	0.34	2.72
†Academic books	2.90	1.10	3.90	-1.20	n.a.
†E-Books	n.a.	n.a.	13.10	-18.40	n.a.
†Textbooks	n.a.	n.a.	2.80	1.70	n.a.
College books	3.00	0.47	3.30	4.10	-2.30
*Mass market paperbacks	0.47	0.47	1.56	3.08	1.79
*Trade paperbacks	1.06	27.29	-9.75	-0.41	-10.48
*Audiobooks	-9.61	8.44	11.39	9.88	-0.74
Serials	n.a.	n.a.	7.70	8.30	3.80
British academic books	n.a.	n.a.	n.a.	n.a.	-1.80

n.a. = not available
* = figures revised based on BISAC categories
† = Beginning with 2009, new data source

U.S. Published Materials

Tables 1 through 7A indicate average prices and price indexes for library materials published primarily in the United States. These indexes are U.S. Periodicals (Table 1), Legal Serials Services (Table 2), U.S. Hardcover Books (Table 3), North American Academic Books (Table 4), North American Academic E-Books (Table 4A), North American Academic Textbooks (Table 4B), U.S. College Books (Table 5), U.S. Mass Market Paperback Books (Table 6), U.S. Paperbacks (Excluding Mass Market) (Table 7), and U.S. Audiobooks (Table 7A).

Periodicals and Serials Prices

The LMPI Committee and Swets Information Services jointly produced the U.S. Periodicals Price Index (Table 1). The subscription prices shown are publishers' list prices, excluding publisher discount or vendor service charges. This report includes 2008, 2009, and 2010 data indexed to the base year of 1984. Table 1 was compiled by Brenda Dingley and is being repeated from last year. A new table is being re-indexed using data provided by EBSCO and should appear in next year's *Library and Book Trade Almanac*.

More extensive reports from the periodicals price index were published annually through 1992 in the April 15 issue of *Library Journal,* in the May issue of *American Libraries* from 1993 to 2002, and in the October 2003 issue of *Library Resources and Technical Services.*

The Legal Serials Services Index (Table 2) was compiled by Ajaye Bloomstone using data collected from a number of different legal serials vendors. The base year for this new index is 2009. This index presents price data covering the years 2009, 2010, and 2011. Vendors were asked to provide cost data on particular titles with the assumption that the title/set has been held by a large academic research law library, and the cost recorded in the index is that for upkeep of the title in question, *not* the cost incurred in purchasing a new set.

Table 2 / Legal Serials Services: Average Prices and Price Indexes, 2009–2011
Index Base: 2009 = 100

Year	Number of Titles	Average Price	Percent Change	Index
2009	217	$1,658.20	n.a.	100.0
2010	217	1,716.30	3.5	103.5
2011	217	1,905.20	11.0	114.9

n.a. = not available.

Finding serials publications available in print is challenging now and will undoubtedly become more challenging in the future as more of these publications migrate to an electronic-only status. Because the type of serial publication that is being tracked for this index is most commonly found in library collections—and not in private collections—vendors may be more likely to discontinue the print versions in favor of electronic versions. As the pool of available print titles becomes even smaller than it is now, there is concern that meaningful comparisons will become more difficult to make. The use of a new base year (2009) for this index shows smaller dollar amounts for the average costs than the previous base year used, in part because some of the more expensive materials may have already migrated to an electronic-only format. This lower dollar amount also reflects a smaller sample available.

As in the past, legal serials services titles were selected on the basis of their format: print, with the same continuing titles being tracked over time. In many cases, especially for U.S. state statutes and codes, there may be little or no consistency in the number of new volumes/revised volumes/updates and so forth. that are published for any one title from any given year to the next, so the cost of those items may well bear no resemblance to the cost of the previous year(s).

Book Prices

Tables 3 (hardcover books), 6 (mass market paperbacks), 7 (other, essentially trade, paperbacks), and 7A (audiobooks), prepared by Catherine Barr, are derived from data provided by book wholesaler Baker & Taylor. Figures for 2009 are revised to reflect late updates to the Baker & Taylor database (publishers were still adding 2009 titles in early 2010); the 2010 figures given here may be similarly revised in next year's tables and should be considered preliminary. These four tables use the Book Industry Study Group's BISAC categories; for more information on the BISAC categories, visit http://www.bisg.org.

Average book prices were mixed in 2010. List prices for hardcovers (Table 3) rose 2.72 percent, and those for hardcovers under $81 (Table 3) rose 2.61 percent. Mass market paperback prices (Table 6) also continued their slow but steady increase, rising another 1.79 percent; trade paperback prices (Table 7), on the other hand, continued to fall, declining 10.48 percent. And after steady increases over the last few years, audiobook prices (Table 7A) saw a drop of 0.74 percent in 2010.

(text continues on page 481)

Table 3 / U.S. Hardcover Books:Average Prices and Price Indexes, 2007–2010
Index Base: 2005 = 100

	2005	2007 Final			2008 Final			2009 Final			2010 Preliminary		
BISAC Category	Average Prices	Volumes	Average Prices	Index	Volumes	Average Prices	Index	Volumes	Average Prices	Index	Volumes	Average Prices	Index
Antiques and collectibles	$71.07	200	$65.02	91.5	195	$80.84	113.7	159	$46.98	66.1	178	$51.25	72.1
Architecture	66.99	788	71.47	106.7	853	77.54	115.7	842	84.46	126.1	772	83.16	124.1
Art	62.33	1,651	82.55	132.4	1,681	84.79	136.0	1,688	75.13	120.5	1,667	71.54	114.8
Bibles	48.05	176	41.20	85.7	191	49.19	102.4	165	46.32	96.4	198	38.55	80.2
Biography and autobiography	46.20	1,825	52.75	114.2	1,714	57.55	124.6	1,652	50.08	108.4	1,606	53.40	115.6
Body, mind and spirit	26.76	208	31.50	117.7	233	26.12	97.6	194	27.60	103.1	167	35.67	133.3
Business and economics	120.56	3,452	126.71	105.1	3,581	134.29	111.4	3,913	123.46	102.4	3,983	130.92	108.6
Children	23.14	14,959	24.07	104.0	13,235	27.35	118.2	12,396	25.01	108.1	11,501	24.29	105.0
Comics and graphic novels	32.75	324	33.46	102.2	462	32.65	99.7	732	32.07	97.9	692	31.23	95.4
Computers	113.07	769	116.67	103.2	731	146.42	129.5	786	155.86	137.8	826	133.93	118.4
Cooking	28.68	878	27.65	96.4	1,015	29.99	104.6	814	29.54	103.0	955	27.73	96.7
Crafts and hobbies	28.82	338	26.78	92.9	267	27.57	95.7	237	29.94	103.9	214	33.72	117.0
Design	59.41	385	87.10	146.6	358	62.22	104.7	331	66.52	112.0	448	76.36	128.5
Drama	60.81	84	66.77	109.8	192	53.65	88.2	81	83.00	136.5	55	77.88	128.1
Education	95.10	1,245	111.28	117.0	1,330	111.90	117.7	1,392	105.56	111.0	1,347	111.89	117.7
Family and relationships	25.37	324	26.68	105.2	301	29.37	115.8	296	33.57	132.3	257	31.73	125.1
Fiction	28.37	4,627	33.61	118.5	4,976	29.03	102.3	4,556	28.78	101.4	4,355	32.27	113.7
Foreign language study	116.89	211	113.35	97.0	146	110.68	94.7	120	132.01	112.9	115	121.37	103.8
Games	32.07	154	29.50	92.0	145	39.16	122.1	167	37.48	116.9	172	43.30	135.0
Gardening	38.20	189	37.56	98.3	149	42.41	111.0	140	36.98	96.8	118	35.87	93.9
Health and fitness	54.05	405	54.06	100.0	449	61.08	113.0	356	50.78	94.0	305	46.52	86.1
History	88.17	4,766	85.18	96.6	4,795	87.46	99.2	4,687	84.41	95.7	5,022	80.92	91.8
House and home	31.51	152	36.80	116.8	117	40.85	129.6	113	40.44	128.3	93	44.24	140.4
Humor	19.00	227	20.71	109.0	241	20.42	107.5	229	20.24	106.5	214	22.44	118.1

Language arts and disciplines	120.71	1,404	130.09	107.8	1,300	133.45	110.6	1,485	131.36	108.8	1,614	113.28	93.8
Law	155.28	1,409	167.87	108.1	1,516	163.59	105.4	1,515	166.60	107.3	1,687	170.87	110.0
Literary collections	74.92	472	139.70	186.5	383	89.75	119.8	373	90.08	120.2	318	84.72	113.1
Literary criticism	123.84	1,823	102.68	82.9	1,707	106.08	85.7	1,903	108.05	87.2	2,026	112.38	90.7
Mathematics	144.88	1,029	122.66	84.7	916	127.81	88.2	895	117.08	80.8	959	124.37	85.8
Medical	156.54	3,118	153.14	97.8	3,076	154.91	99.0	2,924	165.92	106.0	3,188	166.41	106.3
Music	77.63	486	76.07	98.0	485	69.34	89.3	520	77.34	99.6	519	86.16	111.0
Nature	67.75	447	63.67	94.0	435	62.58	92.4	411	65.83	97.2	370	69.46	102.5
Performing arts	71.74	577	80.10	111.7	618	81.63	113.8	540	80.97	112.9	574	74.73	104.2
Pets	25.45	225	24.12	94.8	181	29.39	115.5	176	25.04	98.4	139	24.50	96.3
Philosophy	127.22	1,007	94.62	74.4	973	98.56	77.5	990	93.78	73.7	1,065	106.96	84.1
Photography	56.77	895	66.57	117.3	882	82.64	145.6	805	81.82	144.1	824	109.65	193.1
Poetry	36.58	351	42.30	115.6	339	42.50	116.2	293	45.48	124.3	273	40.88	111.8
Political science	103.39	2,315	99.59	96.3	2,492	97.13	93.9	2,698	108.10	104.6	2,768	108.71	105.1
Psychology	93.85	1,112	103.14	109.9	1,063	101.94	108.6	1,031	104.29	111.1	1,099	103.71	110.5
Reference	202.23	644	266.10	131.6	613	290.72	143.8	558	274.83	135.9	560	306.31	151.5
Religion	62.29	2,510	65.68	105.4	2,449	68.04	109.2	2,353	72.64	116.6	2,534	80.85	129.8
Science	203.44	3,214	213.59	105.0	3,171	204.74	100.6	3,161	190.41	93.6	3,465	171.33	84.2
Self-help	22.43	326	24.14	107.6	322	25.67	114.4	311	21.51	95.9	238	25.60	114.1
Social science	96.17	2,932	108.85	113.2	2,948	97.93	101.8	3,019	102.73	106.8	3,201	99.03	103.0
Sports and recreation	38.77	670	39.62	102.2	746	41.47	107.0	619	38.66	99.7	636	40.81	105.3
Study aids	105.28	21	87.52	83.1	17	78.49	74.6	24	114.64	108.9	18	98.79	93.8
Technology and engineering	187.80	1,947	156.46	83.3	2,145	158.80	84.6	2,439	160.83	85.6	2,519	159.27	84.8
Transportation	68.68	287	57.40	83.6	312	64.24	93.5	245	75.98	110.6	287	85.26	124.1
Travel	37.11	754	53.63	144.5	457	34.80	93.8	384	41.22	111.1	362	41.73	112.4
True crime	29.28	97	28.44	97.1	94	26.32	89.9	93	29.36	100.3	65	34.81	118.9
Young adult	50.17	2,749	50.68	101.0	2,256	49.41	98.5	2,466	37.38	74.5	2,670	35.96	71.7
Totals	$80.36	71,158	$82.24	102.3	69,253	$84.55	105.2	68,277	$84.84	105.6	69,238	$87.15	108.4

Compiled by Catherine Barr from data supplied by Baker & Taylor.

Table 4 / North American Academic Books: Average Prices and Price Indexes 2007–2009
(Index Base: 1989 = 100)

		1989		2007		2008		2009			
Subject Area	LC Class	No. of Titles	Average Price	No. of Titles	Average Price	No. of Titles	Average Price	No. of Titles	Average Price	% Change 2008–2009	Index
Agriculture	S	897	$45.13	1,183	$77.64	1,295	$96.70	1,253	$98.24	1.6%	217.7
Anthropology	GN	406	32.81	486	70.79	515	77.29	488	73.55	-4.8	224.2
Botany	QK	251	69.02	245	109.21	272	172.18	286	118.52	-31.2	171.7
Business and economics	H	5979	41.67	8,134	75.77	9,852	92.69	10,070	89.33	-3.6	214.4
Chemistry	QD	577	110.61	602	182.61	621	222.95	562	225.48	1.1	203.8
Education	L	1685	29.61	3,728	62.01	4,314	70.83	4,295	75.75	6.9	255.8
Engineering and technology	T	4569	64.94	6,391	101.60	7,363	121.74	7,137	124.72	2.4	192.1
Fine and applied arts	M-N	3040	40.72	6,573	49.95	6,767	54.17	6,647	54.07	-0.2	132.8
General works	A	333	134.65	115	70.05	133	72.42	116	57.09	-21.2	42.4
Geography	G	396	47.34	884	83.48	1,108	100.87	1,124	102.13	1.2	215.7
Geology	QE	303	63.49	249	112.06	318	123.68	278	125.35	1.3	197.4
History	C-D-E-F	5549	31.34	8,531	54.46	10,380	59.10	10,415	55.98	-5.3	178.6
Home economics	TX	535	27.10	750	44.40	1,153	41.74	961	42.85	2.6	158.1
Industrial arts	TT	175	23.89	279	37.56	246	40.89	281	38.05	-6.9	159.3
Law	K	1252	51.10	3,237	99.49	4,119	103.47	4,522	113.24	9.4	221.6
Library and information science	Z	857	44.51	640	66.32	705	77.00	738	86.67	12.6	194.7

Literature and language	P	10812	24.99	17,351	41.93	18,368	45.69	19,707	48.32	5.7	193.4
Mathematics and computer science	QA	2707	44.68	3,641	82.90	4,204	101.69	3,902	103.90	2.2	232.5
Medicine	R	5028	58.38	7,266	89.13	9,089	109.35	8,603	101.97	-6.8	174.7
Military and naval science	U-V	715	33.57	811	67.18	872	63.21	849	62.51	-1.1	186.2
Philosophy and religion	B	3518	29.06	6,628	59.18	7,522	65.79	7,574	67.91	3.2	233.7
Physical education and recreation	GV	814	20.38	1,414	42.76	1,728	49.51	1,807	49.75	0.5	244.1
Physics and astronomy	QB	1219	64.59	1,409	109.43	1,522	134.91	1,551	138.92	3.0	215.1
Political science	J	1650	36.76	2,706	71.17	3,167	88.21	3,196	85.12	-3.5	231.6
Psychology	BF	890	31.97	1,270	64.48	1,499	71.82	1,626	63.97	-10.9	200.1
Science (general)	Q	433	56.10	421	96.12	515	106.31	552	122.02	14.8	217.5
Sociology	HM	2742	29.36	5,580	65.31	6,199	76.44	6,240	73.58	-3.7	250.6
Zoology	QH,L,P,R	1967	71.28	2,568	112.52	2,964	138.00	2,973	126.24	-8.5	177.1
Average for all subjects		59,299	$41.69	93,092	$68.51	106,310	$80.25	107,753	$79.32	-1.2%	190.2

Compiled by Stephen Bosch, University of Arizona, from electronic data provided by Coutts Information Services and YBP Library Services. The data represent all titles (includes hard-cover, trade, and paperback books, as well as annuals) treated for all approval plan customers serviced by the vendors. This table covers titles published or distributed in the United States and Canada during the calendar years listed.

This index does include paperback editions. The inclusion of these items does impact pricing in the index.

Table 4A / North American Academic E-Books: Average Prices and Price Indexes 2007–2009
(Index Base: 2007 = 100)

		2007		2008		2009			
Subject Area	**LC Class**	**No. of Titles**	**Average Price**	**No. of Titles**	**Average Price**	**No. of Titles**	**Average Price**	**% Change 2008–2009**	**Index**
Agriculture	S	894	$128.59	600	$158.42	1,416	$141.69	-10.6%	110.2
Anthropology	GN	382	105.28	197	117.18	521	87.65	-25.2	83.3
Botany	QK	287	168.18	191	244.5	347	167.31	-31.6	99.5
Business and economics	H	9,807	97.25	5,892	105.84	12,542	87.02	-17.8	89.5
Chemistry	QD	934	213.76	537	262.82	1,559	244.65	-6.9	114.5
Education	L	2,565	107.62	1,425	118.84	3,650	84.24	-29.1	78.3
Engineering and technology	T	7,176	133.60	4,032	159.82	9,128	142.86	-10.6	106.9
Fine and applied arts	M-N	1,141	84.30	924	86.89	2,174	70.91	-18.4	84.1
General works	A	60	107.85	28	140.81	83	81.79	-41.9	75.8
Geography	G	888	132.67	542	138.69	1,308	109.83	-20.8	82.8
Geology	QE	201	136.49	187	172.39	358	135.90	-21.2	99.6
History	C-D-E-F	4,452	93.55	3,220	90.04	8,519	73.99	-17.8	79.1
Home economics	TX	255	104.31	149	113.72	468	80.49	-29.2	77.2
Industrial arts	TT	20	52.73	19	55.08	72	36.91	-33.0	70.0
Law	K	1,743	99.61	1,415	120.39	3,711	113.49	-5.7	113.9
Library and information science	Z	308	74.70	192	125.90	561	84.44	-32.9	113.0
Literature and language	P	5,517	90.59	4,676	104.93	11,470	84.08	-19.9	92.8
Mathematics and computer science	QA	4,285	102.93	2,559	129.34	4,387	109.20	-15.6	106.1
Medicine	R	7,420	123.59	4,897	142.04	10,680	118.45	-16.6	95.8
Military and naval science	U-V	684	82.89	399	92.37	736	86.28	-6.6	104.1
Philosophy and religion	B	3,612	93.77	3,531	111.98	6,843	87.18	-22.1	93.0
Physical education and recreation	GV	610	96.00	409	79.67	1,255	61.11	-23.3	63.7
Physics and astronomy	QB	1,965	142.11	1,237	163.76	2,197	143.77	-12.2	101.2
Political science	J	2,447	102.72	1,583	118.11	4,053	88.44	-25.1	86.1
Psychology	BF	1,113	83.51	747	96.46	1,729	77.42	-19.7	92.7
Science (general)	Q	468	117.19	340	135.07	640	107.75	-20.2	91.9
Sociology	HM	4,139	98.02	2,953	105.59	7,141	82.60	-21.8	84.3
Zoology	QH,L,P,R	3,394	154.01	2,124	189.08	4,066	145.77	-22.9	94.6
Average for all subjects		66,767	$110.82	45,005	$125.33	101,614	$102.21	-18.4%	92.2

Compiled by Stephen Bosch, University of Arizona, from electronic data provided by Coutts Information Services and YBP Library Services. The data represent all e-book titles treated for all approval plan customers serviced by the vendors. This table covers titles published or distributed in the United States and Canada during the calendar years listed. It is important to note that e-books that were released in a given year may have been published in print much earlier.

Table 4B / North American Academic Textbooks: Average Prices and Price Indexes 2007–2009

(Index Base: 2007 = 100)

		2007		2008		2009			
Subject Area	LC Class	No. of Titles	Average Price	No. of Titles	Average Price	No. of Titles	Average Price	% Change 2008–2009	Index
Agriculture	S	68	$134.75	67	$103.67	50	$102.37	-1.3%	76.0
Anthropology	GN	40	89.15	31	90.75	27	82.21	-9.4	92.2
Botany	QK	4	98.00	12	124.29	21	126.81	2.0	129.4
Business and economics	H	666	110.18	740	115.69	674	115.47	-0.2	104.8
Chemistry	QD	80	138.70	95	123.83	76	131.24	6.0	94.6
Education	L	235	79.58	269	84.55	220	84.49	-0.1	106.2
Engineering and technology	T	668	106.13	835	110.98	790	113.64	2.4	107.1
Fine and applied arts	M-N	82	73.69	75	79.99	72	86.44	8.1	117.3
General works	A	1	48.00	2	53.48	1	90.00	68.3	187.5
Geography	G	59	100.42	72	105.24	82	104.79	-0.4	104.4
Geology	QE	26	118.28	26	114.15	20	124.78	9.3	105.5
History	C-D-E-F	72	78.41	102	73.85	72	87.34	18.3	111.4
Home economics	TX	54	68.23	40	108.45	32	92.59	-14.6	135.7
Industrial arts	TT	13	73.90	16	86.76	13	91.87	5.9	124.3
Law	K	163	87.67	271	90.51	241	100.38	10.9	114.5
Library and information science	Z	24	65.54	31	70.46	21	71.61	1.6	109.3
Literature and language	P	269	71.35	263	73.50	284	73.56	0.1	103.1
Mathematics and computer science	QA	732	91.42	821	88.93	679	89.50	0.6	97.9
Medicine	R	1,210	126.37	1,375	133.27	1,375	131.12	-1.6	103.8
Military and naval science	U-V	10	104.58	10	109.19	8	138.90	27.2	132.8
Philosophy and religion	B	85	55.51	107	56.83	98	57.11	0.5	102.9
Physical education and recreation	GV	47	72.14	59	74.89	45	84.99	13.5	117.8
Physics and astronomy	QB	237	107.05	197	112.42	200	109.28	-2.8	102.1
Political science	J	104	74.21	116	80.58	100	86.36	7.2	116.4
Psychology	BF	120	100.17	126	107.08	102	101.51	-5.2	101.3
Science (general)	Q	24	111.30	25	84.82	24	86.36	1.8	77.6
Sociology	HM	330	84.88	339	84.50	261	84.05	-0.5	99.0
Zoology	QH,L,P,R	250	116.73	249	110.45	231	114.93	4.1	98.5
Average for all subjects		5,673	$102.52	6,371	$105.34	5,819	$107.17	1.7%	104.5

Compiled by Stephen Bosch, University of Arizona, from electronic data provided by YBP Library Services. The data represent all textbook titles treated for all approval plan customers serviced by the vendor. This table covers titles published or distributed in the United States and Canada during the calendar years listed. This index does include paperback editions. The inclusion of these items does impact pricing in the index.

Table 5 / US College Books: Average Prices and Price Indexes 1989, 2008–2010
(Index Base : 1989 = 100)

	1989		2008				2009				2010				
Subject	No. of Titles	Avg. Price per Title	No. of Titles	Avg. Price per Title	Indexed to 1989	Indexed to 2007	No. of Titles	Avg. Price per Title	Indexed to 1989	Indexed to 2008	No. of Titles	Avg. Price per Title	Indexed to 1989	Indexed to 2009	Percent Change 2009–2010
General*	19	$40.19	n.a.	n.a.	n.a.	n.a.	n.a.	n.a.	n.a.	n.a.	n.a.	n.a.	n.a.	n.a.	n.a.
Humanities	21	$32.33	73	$56.95	176.15	103.55	80	$55.38	171.30	97.24	91	$58.99	182.46	106.52	6.52
Art and Architecture	276	55.56	150	57.84	104.10	100.50	161	58.30	104.93	100.80	149	61.69	111.03	105.81	5.81
*Fine Arts***	n.a.	n.a.	116	68.77	n.a.	112.70	88	64.79	n.a.	94.21	92	67.13	n.a.	103.61	3.61
*Architecture***	n.a.	n.a.	50	77.12	n.a.	135.30	55	62.38	n.a.	80.89	48	61.53	n.a.	98.64	-1.36
Photography	24	44.11	18	46.64	105.74	90.11	30	54.44	123.42	116.72	28	53.02	120.20	97.39	-2.61
Communication	42	32.70	98	54.17	165.66	92.08	90	61.00	186.54	112.61	112	59.97	183.39	98.31	-1.69
Language and Literature	110	35.17	70	64.77	184.16	118.02	73	60.76	172.76	93.81	94	68.66	195.22	113.00	13.00
*Africa and Middle East***	n.a.	n.a.	26	49.03	n.a.	98.89	30	48.68	n.a.	99.29	24	62.28	n.a.	127.94	27.94
*Asia and Oceania***	n.a.	n.a.	25	62.27	n.a.	115.17	23	55.94	n.a.	89.83	24	71.99	n.a.	128.69	28.69
Classical	75	43.07	29	81.64	189.55	105.71	29	74.51	173.00	91.27	24	78.76	182.87	105.70	5.70
English and American	547	30.27	420	58.83	194.35	101.96	382	62.74	207.27	106.65	394	61.96	204.69	98.76	-1.24
Germanic	38	32.18	29	66.89	207.86	108.48	25	65.85	204.63	98.45	22	70.36	218.65	106.85	6.85
Romance	97	30.30	70	53.94	178.02	105.19	70	63.77	210.46	118.22	70	59.00	194.72	92.52	-7.48
Slavic	41	27.92	20	44.41	159.06	66.27	16	55.17	197.60	124.23	32	35.95	128.76	65.16	-34.84
Other	63	25.09	n.a.	n.a.	n.a.	n.a.	n.a.	n.a.	n.a.	n.a.	n.a.	n.a.	n.a.	n.a.	n.a.
Performing Arts	20	29.41	29	54.42	185.04	107.66	34	55.77	189.63	102.48	30	61.97	210.71	111.12	11.12
Film	82	33.00	159	58.12	176.12	110.83	163	66.89	202.70	115.09	130	64.13	194.33	95.87	-4.13
Music	156	35.34	157	56.97	161.21	106.29	116	54.62	154.56	95.88	123	61.01	172.64	111.70	11.70
Theater and Dance	58	34.18	41	64.11	187.57	125.21	48	62.44	182.68	97.40	45	62.38	182.50	99.90	-0.10
Philosophy	185	37.25	183	58.00	155.70	98.91	198	70.02	187.97	120.72	198	63.45	170.34	90.62	-9.38
Religion	174	33.49	250	48.32	144.28	95.25	213	50.23	149.99	103.95	272	57.18	170.74	113.84	13.84
Total Humanities	2,009	$36.09	2,013	$58.37	161.73	104.06	1,924	$60.85	168.61	104.25	2,002	$61.60	170.68	101.23	1.23

Science and Technology	99	46.90	109	53.68	114.46	115.54	89	64.47	137.46	120.10	110	58.09	123.86	90.10	-9.90
History of Science and Technology	74	40.56	96	46.72	115.19	97.88	90	61.47	151.55	131.57	78	54.10	133.38	88.01	-11.99
Astronautics and Astronomy	22	50.56	68	50.64	100.16	100.54	82	54.41	107.61	107.44	63	55.58	109.93	102.15	2.15
Biology	97	51.01	145	71.31	139.80	122.57	140	72.10	141.34	101.11	151	72.74	142.60	100.89	0.89
Botany	29	63.91	85	77.65	121.50	139.61	82	86.09	134.71	110.87	85	85.09	133.14	98.84	-1.16
Zoology	53	49.21	94	67.63	137.43	88.57	107	64.28	130.62	95.05	121	64.33	130.73	100.08	0.08
Chemistry	21	70.76	70	109.05	154.11	93.47	50	103.32	146.01	94.75	42	115.42	163.11	111.71	11.71
Earth Science	34	79.44	95	73.74	92.82	92.60	111	77.25	97.24	104.76	102	63.33	79.72	81.98	-18.02
Engineering	87	66.74	90	95.23	142.69	105.45	101	102.62	153.76	107.76	103	88.38	132.42	86.12	-13.88
Health Sciences	94	34.91	156	56.29	161.24	106.71	191	52.90	151.53	93.98	146	56.14	160.81	106.12	6.12
Information and Computer Science	70	40.35	90	75.86	188.00	119.37	82	93.54	231.82	123.31	83	73.50	182.16	78.58	-21.42
Mathematics	60	48.53	98	68.98	142.14	105.51	117	67.75	139.60	98.22	108	61.97	127.69	91.47	-8.53
Physics	22	43.94	65	63.43	144.36	80.16	47	64.30	146.34	101.37	50	54.74	124.58	85.13	-14.87
Sports and Physical Education	18	27.46	65	38.72	141.01	103.20	56	51.82	188.71	133.83	67	54.06	196.87	104.32	4.32
Total Science	780	$49.54	1,326	$67.34	135.93	101.80	1,345	$71.00	143.32	105.44	1,309	$67.13	135.51	94.55	-5.45
Social and Behavioral Sciences	92	$37.09	108	$60.31	162.60	99.44	95	$64.92	175.03	107.64	129	$66.32	178.81	102.16	2.16
Anthropology	96	39.94	142	56.41	141.24	83.51	125	68.14	170.61	120.79	139	63.60	159.24	93.34	-6.66
Business Management and Labor	145	35.72	151	53.01	148.40	104.39	150	54.88	153.64	103.53	150	58.00	162.37	105.69	5.69
Economics	332	40.75	263	62.36	153.03	98.41	292	63.56	155.98	101.92	270	61.16	150.09	96.22	-3.78
Education	71	34.50	163	52.71	152.78	101.86	170	58.33	169.07	110.66	158	62.56	181.33	107.25	7.25
History, Geography and Area Studies	59	42.10	111	51.33	121.92	104.05	102	53.59	127.29	104.40	154	58.16	138.15	108.53	8.53
Africa	44	34.85	29	62.02	177.96	112.89	24	63.61	182.53	102.56	38	69.05	198.13	108.55	8.55
*Ancient History***	n.a.	n.a.	48	80.66	n.a.	112.81	44	63.06	n.a.	78.18	49	57.90	n.a.	91.82	-8.18
Asia and Oceania	76	34.75	86	54.73	157.50	97.66	82	71.83	206.71	131.24	72	60.88	175.19	84.76	-15.24
*Central and Eastern Europe***	n.a.	n.a.	60	57.24	n.a.	102.58	60	68.85	n.a.	120.28	56	66.53	n.a.	96.63	-3.37
Latin America and Caribbean	42	37.23	71	53.15	142.76	102.09	60	55.14	148.11	103.74	54	59.31	159.31	107.56	7.56

Table 5 / US College Books: Average Prices and Price Indexes 1989, 2008–2010 *(cont.)*
(Index Base : 1989 = 100)

	1989		2008				2009				2010				
Subject	No. of Titles	Avg. Price per Title	No. of Titles	Avg. Price per Title	Indexed to 1989	Indexed to 2007	No. of Titles	Avg. Price per Title	Indexed to 1989	Indexed to 2008	No. of Titles	Avg. Price per Title	Indexed to 1989	Indexed to 2009	Percent Change 2009–2010
Middle East and North Africa	30	$36.32	45	$50.17	138.13	77.40	44	$68.44	188.44	136.42	43	$65.57	180.53	95.81	-4.19
North America	349	30.56	382	45.07	147.48	105.97	396	49.30	161.32	109.39	444	45.50	148.89	92.29	-7.71
*United Kingdom***	n.a.	n.a.	91	58.62	n.a.	103.06	62	64.55	n.a.	110.12	80	69.56	n.a.	107.76	7.76
Western Europe	287	42.08	134	65.03	154.54	133.04	144	69.55	165.28	106.95	138	59.14	140.54	85.03	-14.97
Political Science	28	33.56	6	54.30	161.80	89.19	3	103.00	306.91	189.69	4	84.36	251.37	81.90	-18.10
Comparative Politics	236	37.82	207	60.16	159.07	103.42	185	70.93	187.55	117.90	183	66.34	175.41	93.53	-6.47
International Relations	207	35.74	166	59.46	166.37	112.15	171	66.19	185.20	111.32	213	65.64	183.66	99.17	-0.83
Political Theory	59	37.76	81	62.43	165.33	103.34	89	61.13	161.89	97.92	73	56.74	150.26	92.82	-7.18
U.S. Politics	212	29.37	218	49.15	167.35	104.84	218	50.30	171.26	102.34	253	53.03	180.56	105.43	5.43
Psychology	179	36.36	125	61.59	169.39	104.05	122	65.45	180.01	106.27	126	60.55	166.53	92.51	-7.49
Sociology	178	36.36	237	61.09	168.01	106.91	258	59.86	164.63	97.99	226	60.71	166.97	101.42	1.42
Social and Behavioral Sciences	2,722	$36.43	2,924	$56.40	154.82	103.56	2,896	$60.65	166.48	107.54	3,052	$59.09	162.20	97.43	-2.57
Total General, Humanities	5,511	$38.16	6,263	$59.35	155.53	103.85	6,165	$62.97	165.02	106.10	6,363	$61.53	161.24	97.71	-2.29
Science, and Social Science Reference	636	$61.02	20	$72.36	n.a.	53.10	39	$93.36	153.00	129.02	29	$61.17	65.52	65.52	-34.48
Humanities**	n.a.	n.a.	144	102.95	n.a.	89.90	115	112.72	n.a.	109.49	128	117.12	n.a.	103.90	3.90
Science and Technology**	n.a.	n.a.	89	145.94	n.a.	150.83	85	117.06	n.a.	80.21	76	133.19	n.a.	113.78	13.78
Social and Behavioral Sciences**	n.a.	n.a.	198	162.60	n.a.	113.48	185	150.72	n.a.	92.69	216	152.91	n.a.	101.45	1.45
Total Reference	636	$61.02	451	$136.26	223.30	106.01	424	$128.60	210.75	94.38	449	$133.44	218.68	103.76	3.76
Grand Total	6,147	$40.52	6,714	$64.52	159.23	103.33	6,589	$67.18	165.79	104.12	6,812	$66.27	163.55	98.65	-1.35

Compiled by Frederick Lynden, Brown University. *General category no longer appears after 1999. ** Began appearing as separate sections after 1989. n.a. = not available.

Table 6 / U.S. Mass Market Paperback Books: Average Prices and Price Indexes, 2007–2010

Index Base: 2005 = 100

	2005	2007 Final			2008 Final			2009 Final			2010 Preliminary		
BISAC Category	Average Prices	Volumes	Average Prices	Index	Volumes	Average Prices	Index	Volumes	Average Prices	Index	Volumes	Average Prices	Index
Antiques and collectibles	$7.69	9	$7.99	103.9	10	$8.59	111.7	9	$8.66	112.6	9	$8.77	114.0
Architecture	n.a.	n.a.	n.a.	n.a.	n.a.	n.a.	n.a.	0	n.a.	n.a.	0	n.a.	n.a.
Art	n.a.	n.a.	n.a.	n.a.	n.a.	n.a.	n.a.	0	n.a.	n.a.	0	n.a.	n.a.
Bibles	n.a.	n.a.	n.a.	n.a.	n.a.	n.a.	n.a.	0	n.a.	n.a.	0	n.a.	n.a.
Biography and autobiography	7.83	9	7.87	100.5	8	7.87	100.5	13	7.48	95.5	13	7.51	95.9
Body, mind and spirit	7.11	22	7.62	107.2	14	7.13	100.3	13	7.99	112.4	15	7.99	112.4
Business and economics	12.47	n.a.	n.a.	n.a.	1	7.99	64.1	1	9.99	80.1	3	9.32	74.7
Children	5.29	284	5.61	106.0	239	5.94	112.3	238	6.12	115.7	263	6.21	117.4
Comics and graphic novels	8.47	n.a.	n.a.	n.a.	n.a.	n.a.	n.a.	0	n.a.	n.a.	0	n.a.	n.a.
Computers	n.a.	n.a.	n.a.	n.a.	n.a.	n.a.	n.a.	0	n.a.	n.a.	0	n.a.	n.a.
Cooking	7.50	n.a.	n.a.	n.a.	n.a.	n.a.	n.a.	0	n.a.	n.a.	0	n.a.	n.a.
Crafts and hobbies	n.a.	n.a.	n.a.	n.a.	n.a.	n.a.	n.a.	0	n.a.	n.a.	0	n.a.	n.a.
Design	n.a.	n.a.	n.a.	n.a.	n.a.	n.a.	n.a.	0	n.a.	n.a.	0	n.a.	n.a.
Drama	6.32	4	6.47	102.4	2	5.99	94.8	3	5.98	94.6	3	6.30	99.7
Education	n.a.	n.a.	n.a.	n.a.	n.a.	n.a.	n.a.	0	n.a.	n.a.	0	n.a.	n.a.
Family and relationships	6.98	3	8.32	119.2	n.a.	n.a.	n.a.	1	4.99	71.5	1	7.99	114.5
Fiction	6.34	4,227	6.40	100.9	4,162	6.48	102.2	4,013	6.68	105.4	3,995	6.80	107.3
Foreign language study	n.a.	4	6.74	n.a.	5	6.19	n.a.	4	6.99	n.a.	6	7.08	n.a.
Games	7.14	19	5.54	77.6	13	5.45	76.3	5	4.99	69.9	0	n.a.	n.a.
Gardening	n.a.	n.a.	n.a.	n.a.	n.a.	n.a.	n.a.	0	n.a.	n.a.	0	n.a.	n.a.
Health and fitness	7.43	18	7.49	100.8	18	7.66	103.1	15	7.79	104.8	14	7.92	106.6
History	7.90	13	7.76	98.2	3	5.83	73.8	5	7.89	99.9	1	9.95	125.9
House and home	5.99	n.a.	n.a.	n.a.	n.a.	n.a.	n.a.	0	n.a.	n.a.	0	n.a.	n.a.
Humor	6.99	4	7.49	107.2	3	6.32	90.4	0	n.a.	n.a.	1	3.50	50.1
Language arts and disciplines	6.99	n.a.	n.a.	n.a.	n.a.	n.a.	n.a.	0	n.a.	n.a.	2	13.25	189.6
Law	n.a.	n.a.	n.a.	n.a.	n.a.	n.a.	n.a.	0	n.a.	n.a.	0	n.a.	n.a.
Literary collections	n.a.	n.a.	n.a.	n.a.	1	4.99	n.a.	1	7.95	n.a.	1	5.95	n.a.

Table 6 / U.S. Mass Market Paperback Books: Average Prices and Price Indexes, 2007–2010 *(cont.)*
Index Base: 2005 = 100

	2005	2007 Final			2008 Final			2009 Final			2010 Preliminary		
BISAC Category	Average Prices	Volumes	Average Prices	Index	Volumes	Average Prices	Index	Volumes	Average Prices	Index	Volumes	Average Prices	Index
Literary criticism	7.95	n.a.	n.a.	n.a.	1	7.95	100	1	7.99	100.5	1	7.99	100.5
Mathematics	n.a.	n.a.	n.a.	n.a.	n.a.	n.a.	n.a.	0	n.a.	n.a.	0	n.a.	n.a.
Medical	$7.83	4	$6.87	87.7	1	$7.50	95.8	0	n.a.	n.a.	1	$8.99	114.8
Music	7.95	n.a.	n.a.	n.a.	n.a.	n.a.	n.a.	0	n.a.	n.a.	0	n.a.	n.a.
Nature	n.a.	n.a.	n.a.	n.a.	n.a.	n.a.	n.a.	0	n.a.	n.a.	0	n.a.	n.a.
Performing arts	8.23	3	8.64	105.0	1	9.99	121.4	1	$9.99	121.4	1	9.99	121.4
Pets	n.a.	n.a.	n.a.	n.a.	1	7.99	n.a.	0	n.a.	n.a.	1	7.99	n.a.
Philosophy	7.49	5	7.78	103.9	2	5.95	79.4	0	n.a.	n.a.	2	6.47	86.4
Photography	n.a.	n.a.	n.a.	n.a.	n.a.	n.a.	n.a.	0	n.a.	n.a.	0	n.a.	n.a.
Poetry	5.75	1	5.95	103.5	2	4.95	86.1	5	6.95	120.9	1	7.95	138.3
Political science	n.a.	1	6.99	n.a.	2	7.99	n.a.	1	5.95	n.a.	2	7.97	n.a.
Psychology	7.97	2	7.97	100.0	n.a.	n.a.	n.a.	0	n.a.	n.a.	0	n.a.	n.a.
Reference	6.85	3	6.49	94.7	3	7.16	104.5	3	7.66	111.8	1	7.99	116.6
Religion	9.96	2	6.99	70.2	4	7.74	77.7	3	6.98	70.1	2	7.99	80.2
Science	n.a.	n.a.	n.a.	n.a.	1	6.95	n.a.	0	n.a.	n.a.	0	n.a.	n.a.
Self-help	12.45	6	7.80	62.7	3	9.64	77.4	2	7.99	64.2	1	7.99	64.2
Social science	7.08	1	7.99	112.9	n.a.	n.a.	n.a.	0	n.a.	n.a.	0	n.a.	n.a.
Sports and recreation	7.62	2	7.49	98.3	3	7.99	104.9	3	6.99	91.7	1	7.99	104.9
Study aids	n.a.	n.a.	n.a.	n.a.	n.a.	n.a.	n.a.	0	n.a.	n.a.	0	n.a.	n.a.
Technology and engineering	n.a.	n.a.	n.a.	n.a.	n.a.	n.a.	n.a.	0	n.a.	n.a.	0	n.a.	n.a.
Transportation	12.95	n.a.	n.a.	n.a.	n.a.	n.a.	n.a.	1	14.00	108.1	0	n.a.	n.a.
Travel	n.a.	n.a.	n.a.	n.a.	1	6.95	n.a.	1	4.95	n.a.	0	n.a.	n.a.
True crime	7.19	51	7.42	103.2	53	7.35	102.2	52	7.47	103.9	54	7.64	106.3
Young adult	6.46	159	6.79	105.1	142	7.10	109.9	96	7.63	118.1	90	8.12	125.7
Totals	$6.34	4,856	$6.40	100.9	4,699	$6.50	102.5	4,490	$6.70	105.7	4,485	$6.82	107.6

Compiled by Catherine Barr from data supplied by Baker & Taylor.
n.a. = not available.

Table 7 / U.S. Paperback Books (Excluding Mass Market): Average Prices and Price Indexes, 2007–2010

Index Base: 2005 = 100

	2005	2007 Final			2008 Final			2009 Final			2010 Preliminary		
BISAC Category	Average Prices	Volumes	Average Prices	Index	Volumes	Average Prices	Index	Volumes	Average Prices	Index	Volumes	Average Prices	Index
Antiques and collectibles	$24.80	275	$121.12	488.4	239	$27.08	109.2	191	$27.25	109.9	178	$24.99	100.8
Architecture	38.90	717	40.17	103.3	694	41.89	107.7	692	44.89	115.4	711	45.65	117.4
Art	31.28	1,692	34.43	110.1	1,581	37.55	120.0	1,491	37.63	120.3	1,433	37.39	119.5
Bibles	36.87	291	40.08	108.7	363	49.29	133.7	307	40.67	110.3	424	39.00	105.8
Biography and autobiography	19.19	2,278	20.92	109.0	2,211	20.31	105.8	2,347	20.54	107.0	2,250	19.67	102.5
Body, mind and spirit	17.48	1,045	17.67	101.1	1,072	18.47	105.7	1,009	18.16	103.9	946	18.00	103.0
Business and economics	71.12	11,053	106.82	150.2	5,937	73.97	104.0	5,930	62.07	87.3	5,077	64.38	90.5
Children	11.11	9,136	10.43	93.9	9,099	10.79	97.1	9,716	10.91	98.2	8,296	10.28	92.5
Comics and graphic novels	12.75	2,167	15.18	119.1	2,407	14.15	111.0	2,173	15.42	120.9	1,996	15.82	124.1
Computers	57.01	3,809	79.96	140.3	3,279	87.12	152.8	3,795	97.47	171.0	3,141	64.26	112.7
Cooking	18.30	1,068	17.98	98.3	1,271	18.84	103.0	1,006	19.59	107.0	1,053	19.59	107.0
Crafts and hobbies	18.49	906	20.31	109.8	943	19.98	108.1	1,002	19.29	104.3	1,049	19.43	105.1
Design	32.87	415	35.91	109.2	381	34.18	104.0	397	37.00	112.6	425	65.52	199.3
Drama	16.40	578	18.16	110.7	521	18.66	113.8	581	21.70	132.3	475	17.07	104.1
Education	35.10	4,166	36.98	105.4	3,929	37.21	106.0	3,262	41.43	118.0	3,133	39.97	113.9
Family and relationships	17.10	983	18.23	106.6	951	17.78	104.0	884	19.63	114.8	741	18.52	108.3
Fiction	15.74	9,517	17.74	112.7	9,480	16.30	103.6	9,694	17.32	110.0	8,638	16.66	105.8
Foreign language study	41.90	1,209	34.78	83.0	1,405	30.19	72.1	977	32.31	77.1	998	32.92	78.6
Games	16.53	847	16.90	102.2	800	17.08	103.3	787	17.59	106.4	782	16.48	99.7
Gardening	20.59	241	19.86	96.5	368	18.93	91.9	256	20.96	101.8	238	23.03	111.9
Health and fitness	22.81	1,539	22.39	98.2	1,373	24.19	106.0	1,333	23.67	103.8	1,227	26.17	114.7
History	33.53	6,743	35.19	105.0	5,856	31.85	95.0	6,436	31.80	94.8	6,549	34.37	102.5
House and home	19.33	327	20.72	107.2	295	20.23	104.7	226	21.96	113.6	198	20.98	108.5
Humor	12.96	477	13.29	102.5	463	13.49	104.1	486	13.79	106.4	417	14.18	109.4
Language arts and disciplines	49.14	2,022	51.59	105.0	1,654	53.38	108.6	2,088	65.35	134.0	2,147	61.86	125.9
Law	$60.92	2,857	$80.75	132.6	3,781	$115.14	189.0	2,711	$75.41	123.8	2,945	$69.38	113.9
Literary collections	28.07	559	43.66	155.5	540	35.23	125.5	581	35.01	124.7	640	35.76	127.4

Table 7 / U.S. Paperback Books (Excluding Mass Market): Average Prices and Price Indexes, 2007–2010 *(cont.)*
Index Base: 2005 = 100

	2005	2007 Final			2008 Final			2009 Final			2010 Preliminary		
BISAC Category	**Average Prices**	**Volumes**	**Average Prices**	**Index**	**Volumes**	**Average Prices**	**Index**	**Volumes**	**Average Prices**	**Index**	**Volumes**	**Average Prices**	**Index**
Literary criticism	31.99	1,577	36.60	114.4	1,446	36.57	114.3	1,770	38.66	120.9	1,621	34.58	108.1
Mathematics	75.77	989	74.91	98.9	961	61.82	81.6	885	68.93	91.0	786	65.59	86.6
Medical	64.27	4,153	69.32	107.9	3,986	74.82	116.4	3,937	76.34	118.8	4,050	66.92	104.1
Music	22.66	2,659	26.95	118.9	2,921	21.67	95.6	2,975	23.22	102.5	2,865	22.86	100.9
Nature	26.90	698	25.98	96.6	604	25.42	94.5	613	27.02	100.4	505	27.79	103.3
Performing arts	27.85	1,100	30.43	109.3	991	31.01	111.3	934	33.65	120.8	1,003	33.98	122.0
Pets	18.86	321	17.53	92.9	292	18.70	99.2	299	19.01	100.8	250	17.50	92.8
Philosophy	31.40	1,619	32.69	104.1	1,271	30.93	98.5	1,465	34.33	109.3	1,196	34.70	110.5
Photography	27.74	480	31.94	115.1	535	32.87	118.5	539	31.13	112.2	524	30.47	109.8
Poetry	16.09	1,863	17.19	106.8	1,784	16.50	102.5	1,720	16.88	104.9	1,569	16.76	104.2
Political science	45.65	3,663	59.46	130.3	3,142	37.58	82.3	3,220	37.91	83.0	3,553	40.53	88.8
Psychology	45.74	1,575	45.22	98.9	1,377	41.37	90.4	1,256	43.08	94.2	1,464	42.53	93.0
Reference	52.54	1,276	65.70	125.0	1,353	68.97	131.3	1,307	90.69	172.6	1,079	79.71	151.7
Religion	20.54	5,549	20.51	99.9	5,796	20.12	98.0	6,052	21.31	103.7	6,108	21.82	106.2
Science	71.05	2,346	74.30	104.6	2,099	70.80	99.6	2,462	78.19	110.0	2,233	62.16	87.5
Self-help	16.36	1,216	16.92	103.4	1,148	17.17	105.0	1,047	17.84	109.0	1,048	17.91	109.5
Social science	36.83	4,061	38.53	104.6	4,037	40.16	109.0	3,998	42.51	115.4	3,886	39.70	107.8
Sports and recreation	21.82	1,381	22.74	104.2	1,331	23.77	108.9	1,259	23.39	107.2	1,179	22.61	103.6
Study aids	30.90	682	32.02	103.6	880	32.14	104.0	669	30.82	99.7	1,502	40.35	130.6
Technology and engineering	85.80	2,689	139.50	162.6	2,583	154.07	179.6	2,681	153.11	178.4	1,613	80.92	94.3
Transportation	40.19	414	35.30	87.8	430	39.28	97.7	459	36.61	91.1	458	34.16	85.0
Travel	19.18	3,449	21.03	109.6	3,077	20.33	106.0	2,852	20.51	106.9	2,478	20.45	106.6
True crime	17.71	154	18.65	105.3	144	18.17	102.6	156	19.00	107.3	179	20.86	117.8
Young adult	14.06	3,108	13.85	98.5	2,555	13.76	97.9	2,462	16.79	119.4	2,176	14.54	103.4
Totals	$33.90	113,939	$43.61	128.6	105,636	$39.36	116.1	105,375	$39.20	115.6	99,432	$35.09	103.5

Compiled by Catherine Barr from data supplied by Baker & Taylor.

Table 7A / U.S. Audiobooks: Average Prices and Price Indexes, 2007–2010
Index Base: 2005 = 100

BISAC Category	2005 Average Prices	2007 Final Volumes	2007 Final Average Prices	2007 Final Index	2008 Final Volumes	2008 Final Average Prices	2008 Final Index	2009 Final Volumes	2009 Final Average Prices	2009 Final Index	2010 Preliminary Volumes	2010 Preliminary Average Prices	2010 Preliminary Index
Antiques and collectibles	n.a.	1	$11.95	n.a.	n.a.	n.a.	n.a.	1	$74.95	n.a.	3	$36.66	n.a.
Architecture	$68.95	n.a.	n.a.	n.a.	2	$37.47	54.3	0	n.a.	n.a.	3	39.99	58.0
Art	57.51	5	40.18	69.9	5	40.99	71.3	7	59.41	103.3	9	58.21	101.2
Bibles	47.08	34	51.45	109.3	20	41.83	88.8	9	75.53	160.4	6	47.16	100.2
Biography and autobiography	37.68	453	44.53	118.2	641	47.05	124.9	685	50.75	134.7	697	51.15	135.7
Body, mind and spirit	26.74	81	33.52	125.4	83	38.28	143.2	87	37.95	141.9	68	33.65	125.8
Business and economics	42.11	295	34.17	81.1	426	39.54	93.9	436	46.15	109.6	322	49.99	118.7
Children	26.57	876	28.80	108.4	733	31.09	117.0	832	36.22	136.3	767	37.78	142.2
Comics and graphic novels	n.a.	n.a.	n.a.	n.a.	n.a.	n.a.	n.a.	0	n.a.	n.a.	0	n.a.	n.a.
Computers	41.39	n.a.	n.a.	n.a.	4	31.23	75.5	5	46.99	113.5	2	45.00	108.7
Cooking	14.45	7	35.40	245.0	4	14.71	101.8	14	44.70	309.3	2	44.97	311.2
Crafts and hobbies	n.a.	10	26.96	n.a.	9	42.20	n.a.	4	38.72	n.a.	1	24.98	n.a.
Design	n.a.	n.a.	n.a.	n.a.	n.a.	n.a.	n.a.	0	n.a.	n.a.	0	n.a.	n.a.
Drama	23.45	27	29.74	126.8	48	36.67	156.4	151	34.54	147.3	89	34.27	146.1
Education	27.46	27	40.39	147.1	17	29.78	108.4	22	45.34	165.1	18	41.05	149.5
Family and relationships	24.58	47	31.52	128.2	73	36.73	149.4	54	39.41	160.3	69	41.07	167.1
Fiction	41.47	3,644	44.08	106.3	4,379	48.43	116.8	6,278	52.62	126.9	7,360	50.42	121.6
Foreign language study	70.04	314	41.17	58.8	394	37.63	53.7	260	40.74	58.2	156	48.88	69.8
Games	32.68	n.a.	n.a.	n.a.	1	14.95	45.7	6	14.12	43.2	0	n.a.	n.a.
Gardening	n.a.	3	30.62	n.a.	2	39.97	n.a.	0	n.a.	n.a.	6	47.82	n.a.
Health and fitness	26.61	60	31.89	119.8	83	33.32	125.2	82	46.09	173.2	83	42.07	158.1
History	41.61	480	48.35	116.2	577	54.71	131.5	450	57.69	138.6	533	58.28	140.1
House and home	25.00	1	29.95	119.8	n.a.	n.a	n.a.	0	n.a.	n.a.	0	n.a.	n.a.
Humor	29.60	59	30.31	102.4	65	36.20	122.3	79	42.37	143.1	91	36.93	124.8
Language arts and disciplines	60.84	31	55.43	91.1	14	36.96	60.7	18	46.65	76.7	11	33.42	54.9
Law	55.32	24	59.46	107.5	18	54.21	98.0	9	49.75	89.9	11	59.44	107.4
Literary collections	24.71	16	28.73	116.3	16	38.91	157.5	20	32.34	130.9	13	49.82	201.6

Table 7A / U.S. Audiobooks: Average Prices and Price Indexes, 2007–2010 *(cont.)*
Index Base: 2005 = 100

	2005	2007 Final			2008 Final			2009 Final			2010 Preliminary		
BISAC Category	**Average Prices**	**Volumes**	**Average Prices**	**Index**	**Volumes**	**Average Prices**	**Index**	**Volumes**	**Average Prices**	**Index**	**Volumes**	**Average Prices**	**Index**
Literary criticism	$26.41	18	$35.63	134.9	35	$49.61	187.8	20	$42.43	160.7	17	$42.68	161.6
Mathematics	n.a.	1	89.99	n.a.	n.a.	n.a.	n.a.	0	n.a.	n.a.	0	n.a.	n.a.
Medical	153.72	20	68.55	44.6	25	96.61	62.8	13	60.66	39.5	21	36.65	23.8
Music	29.83	121	27.58	92.5	144	29.46	98.8	108	38.41	128.8	68	35.76	119.9
Nature	28.92	21	33.07	114.3	27	39.18	135.5	37	47.09	162.8	55	41.33	142.9
Performing arts	25.78	18	25.38	98.4	39	38.32	148.6	21	46.23	179.3	16	40.60	157.5
Pets	33.05	10	29.28	88.6	20	34.05	103.0	23	43.51	131.6	49	38.23	115.7
Philosophy	35.30	24	40.01	113.3	37	41.33	117.1	36	51.39	145.6	37	54.27	153.7
Photography	n.a.	n.a.	n.a.	n.a.	n.a.	n.a.	n.a.	0	n.a.	n.a.	0	n.a.	n.a.
Poetry	22.87	54	24.30	106.3	45	25.88	113.2	50	35.88	156.9	27	33.24	145.3
Political science	42.66	151	40.97	96.0	174	44.16	103.5	177	49.69	116.5	219	48.54	113.8
Psychology	35.70	30	36.19	101.4	31	37.38	104.7	54	52.13	146.0	40	46.91	131.4
Reference	21.20	7	34.10	160.8	15	32.78	154.6	7	40.55	191.3	1	69.99	330.1
Religion	26.52	377	27.07	102.1	313	30.20	113.9	418	33.50	126.3	360	33.10	124.8
Science	39.86	30	39.73	99.7	61	48.59	121.9	64	47.75	119.8	64	51.48	129.2
Self-help	23.58	297	27.61	117.1	207	29.98	127.1	289	38.30	162.4	187	39.48	167.4
Social science	35.73	63	35.52	99.4	55	40.17	112.4	79	50.36	140.9	89	47.59	133.2
Sports and recreation	28.46	45	38.44	135.1	57	39.75	139.7	41	45.78	160.9	57	48.03	168.8
Study aids	41.85	9	43.36	103.6	18	67.10	160.3	21	33.92	81.1	7	19.41	46.4
Technology and engineering	61.47	12	33.88	55.1	10	52.09	84.7	7	48.56	79.0	23	53.33	86.8
Transportation	28.00	n.a.	n.a.	n.a.	n.a.	n.a.	n.a.	3	36.66	130.9	7	46.28	165.3
Travel	41.91	45	46.24	110.3	39	44.73	106.7	15	51.57	123.0	44	49.89	119.0
True crime	35.97	30	41.90	116.5	59	51.41	142.9	45	50.69	140.9	36	52.79	146.8
Young adult	35.68	273	39.87	111.7	269	45.52	127.6	527	44.85	125.7	830	44.90	125.8
Totals	$40.49	8,151	$39.69	98.0	9,294	$44.21	109.2	11,564	$48.58	120.0	12,574	$48.22	119.1

Compiled by Catherine Barr from data supplied by Baker & Taylor.
n.a. = not available.

(continued from page 465)

The North American Academic Books Price Indexes (Tables 4, 4A, and 4B) are prepared by Stephen Bosch. The most significant change in the North American Academic Books Price Index (NAABPI) for 2009 is that the vendors supplying the data have changed, and this has resulted in modifications. (In 2010 Blackwell Book Services was purchased by YBP Library Services. Blackwell and YBP had been the data sources for the index. Starting with 2009 the data sources are now Coutts Information Services and YBP. The index was reconstructed back to 2007 using data from Coutts Information Services and YBP.) Both the number of titles and the average prices have increased in comparison with the previous NAABPI. The total number of titles in the index increased 49 percent (rising from 72,159 to 107,753), and the overall average price increased 12 percent (from $70.64 to $79.32). These changes indicate significant variations, and the prior years' versions index should not be compared with the version for 2009 and beyond. The year-to-year comparisons are now based on this new data model and the changes in price and number of titles are not as dramatic when looking at comparable data.

Two indexes were added in 2008, one for e books (Table 4A) and another for textbooks (Table 4B). With the change in vendors, the index for e-books continues to use data blended from both vendors. For the time being, the textbook index will only use data from YBP.

Both of these areas are of high interest to users, and the indexes will continue to use the base index year of 2007. In the academic market, it has always been assumed that e-books are more expensive than their print counterparts because the $9.95 versions of e-books available to consumers through channels such as Amazon are not available to libraries. The new index clearly points out the difference in price—the average price of an e-book in 2009 was $102.21 and the average price for a print book was $79.32. Responding to customer demands, vendors offer multiple platforms and pricing models for e-books; consequently there may be multiple prices for the same title. Only the first instance of a unique ISBN is included in the data, so if the same book was treated by a vendor from one e-book aggregator and then treated again from another aggregator, only the first instance of the e-book is in the index. Because electronic access is where the market is going, it is appropriate to have e-books as a separate index. It is also important to note that the e-book market is rapidly changing. This is reflected in the large swing in numbers of titles between 2007, 2008, and 2009. Vendors report large jumps in numbers because they are adding "catch up" titles to their database or adding titles from new suppliers.

Rising cost of textbooks has been a hot topic on many campuses. The index for textbooks will try to document price changes in this area. Indications are that textbook prices tend to be higher, with an average price of $107.17 in 2009, but the rate of inflation has not seen a huge increase.

The average price of North American Academic Books in 2009 (Table 4) decreased slightly (1.2 percent) from 2008. This is mainly due to a larger increase in the number of titles treated in the lower part of the price bands ($0–$30). Nearly all price bands showed fewer titles between 2008 and 2009 except for the lower price band, which showed a 5 percent increase. This led to a slight decrease in the average price for all books. See Figure 1.

Figure 1 / Comparison of Titles in Sample Grouped by Price

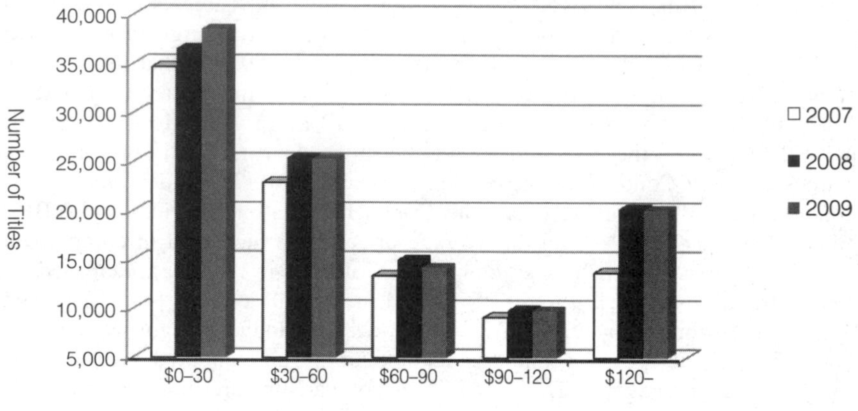

Number of Titles
40,000
35,000
30,000
25,000
20,000
15,000
10,000
5,000
$0–30
$30–60
$60–90
$90–120
$120–
2007
2008
2009

One thing that really stands out when looking at the data by price band is that the highest end ($120.00 and up) has seen huge growth in the past two years, nearly doubling in overall costs represented by the band ($2.6 million to $4.5 million). The impact on pricing from the titles in the $120 and up price band is confirmed if you look at the actual dollar values in groups (sum of all prices for titles in the group). It is clear that the increase in the top end of the index was the main component in the overall increase in the index for 2008 as well as for 2009. Although the $0–$30 price area has the largest number of titles, dollar-wise it is the smallest portion as far as total cost (sum of all prices) goes in the index. The increase in the prices in the upper end of the index was what added to the overall level of increase.

Although the average price decreased from 2008 to 2009, if you compare the 2009 average price to 2007 the average increased 16 percent and this is due to growth in the high end of the data. See Figure 2.

Figure 2

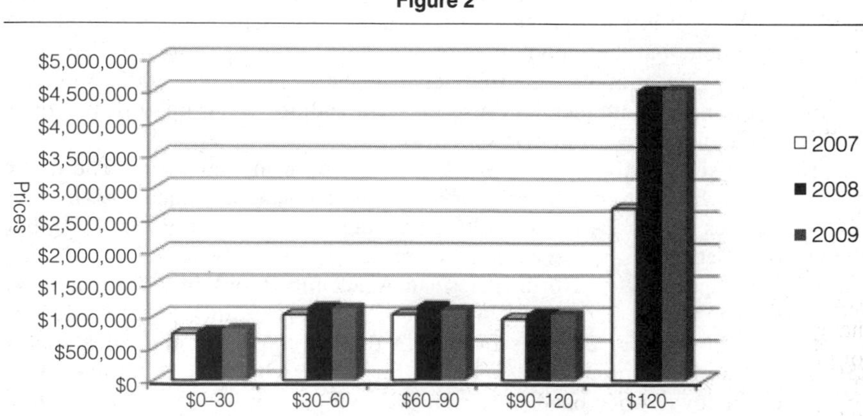

The data used for this index is derived from all titles treated by Coutts Information Services and YBP Library Services in their approval plans during the calendar years listed. The index does include paperback editions as supplied by these vendors and this inclusion of paperbacks as distributed as part of the approval plans has clearly influenced the prices reflected in the index figures.

E-books are now being treated in a separate index (Table 4A), so the impact of separating out e-books on the index will have to be monitored. Currently the vast majority of titles are published in both print and "e" versions, so the number of titles in the print index should not be affected until the industry moves toward more e-publishing with print as an added component to the electronic version. It is safe to say that in the future the number of titles in the print-only index could decline. At the same time the number of e-books should rise, especially as we see more publishers move to publishing primarily "e" versions of their books. Many e-book pricing models add extra charges of as much as 50 percent to the retail price, and this pricing model is reflected in the higher prices for e-books. The overall price for e-books did show a decline from 2007 to 2009, but because the number of titles treated had a huge variation it is not really possible to draw sound conclusions about pricing trends in e-books at this time. The index does clearly show that for the library market, e-books are more expensive than print. Many publishers and e-book aggregators are still adding "e" versions of print books from backlists and these are showing up in the index; this is also the basis of the wide swings in numbers of titles in the index from year to year.

The first year of the price index for textbooks (Table 4B) shows a 2.8 percent increase for overall prices between 2008 and 2009. This increase is higher than the increase seen for the broader print index, and the overall prices are also higher. These are indicators that the angst experienced by students as they purchase their texts may well be justified—prices appear to be increasing at a faster clip, and the overall cost is 35 percent higher than the average academic book. It will take a little more time and data before any real trends can be identified.

Price changes vary, as always, among subject areas. There were several double-digit increases in subject areas and even more areas saw double-digit price decreases. If you look at the top areas for price increases, in 2009 there were relatively few areas showing large increases, with science, library and information science, and law leading the way. Library and information science was also one area that had double-digit increases the previous year. Apart from science, most of the higher increases were seen in social science and humanities. It is interesting to note that some areas that showed high increases last year (for example, botany) are now at the other end of the spectrum of price decreases.

It is good to remember that price indexes become less accurate at describing price changes the smaller the sample becomes. Botany, general works, and library and information science areas are small samplings and showed very large price changes, but to then conclude that all books in the area increased or decreased at like amounts is not correct. These areas have a small sample size (fewer than 500 titles) and the inclusion of just a few large, expensive items can have a major impact on prices for the category. In these areas there will be a lot of encyclopedias and other large reference works, so price volatility is expected. The inclusion of a few expensive items can really affect the overall average price when the number of titles in an area is small. Also, with the change in data sources, it will take a few more years for the historical data to build; the resulting broader set of data will help us better understand price changes.

The U.S. College Books Price Index (Table 5), prepared by Frederick C. Lynden, contains price and indexing information for the years 2008 through 2010 (index base year of 1989), and also the percentage change between 2009 and 2010. Data for the index were compiled from 6,849 reviews of books published in *Choice* during 2010; expensive titles ($500 or more) were omitted from the analysis, so the total number of titles reported is smaller than the number published. As with the North American Academic Books data (Table 4), this index includes some paperback prices; as a result, the average price of books is less than if only hardcover books were included.

The average price for humanities titles in 2010 increased by 1.23 percent over the previous year. The average price for science and technology titles decreased by 5.45 percent, and the average price for social and behavioral sciences titles decreased by 2.57 percent. Calculated separately, reference books for 2010 showed a 3.76 percent increase over the previous year. For all titles, there has been a 63.56 percent average price increase since 1989.

For 2010 the overall average price for books in the humanities, sciences, and social and behavioral sciences (including reference books) was $66.27, a small price decrease of 1.35 percent from the average 2009 book price of $67.18. Reference books calculated separately had an average price increase of 3.76 percent over the previous year, with a 2010 average of $133.44 compared with 2009's average price of $128.60. Excluding reference books, the 2010 average price was $61.53, a 2.29 percent decrease compared with the average 2009 price of $62.97.

Questions regarding this index should be addressed to the author: Frederick Lynden, Retired Director, Scholarly Communication and Library Research, Brown University Library, Providence, RI 02912 (e-mail flynden@stanford alumni.org).

Prices of Other Media

The LMPI Editorial Board is continuing to work on developing a price index for electronic journals. It is hoped that a pricing model and index will be available in the near future.

Foreign Prices

The dollar has posted a modest gain against the euro and the British pound sterling since 2009. While the dollar showed a modest decline against the Canadian dollar, it showed a steep decline against the Japanese yen. World economies remain in flux.

Serials Prices

Table 8 (Average Price of Serials) provides the average prices and percent increases for serials based on titles in select serials indexes. The serials included

(text continues on page 488)

Table 8 / Average Price of Serials, Based on Titles in Select Serials Indexes: 2007–2011

Subject	LC Class	2007		2008			2009			2010			2011		
		No. of Titles	Avg. Price	No. of Titles	Avg. Price	% of Price Increase	No. of Titles	Avg. Price	% of Price Increase	No. of Titles	Avg. Price	% of Price Increase	No. of Titles	Avg. Price	% of Price Increase
Agriculture	S	285	$703	287	$760	8.1%	286	$819	7.8%	288	$869	6.1%	289	$958	10.2%
Anthropology	GN	80	271	84	286	5.5	80	316	10.5	81	335	6.0	84	367	9.6
Arts and architecture	N	161	245	168	272	11.0	165	294	8.1	169	324	10.2	171	343	5.9
Astronomy	QB	44	1,608	46	1,722	7.1	47	1,852	7.5	47	1,968	6.3	50	2,067	5.0
Biology	QH	363	1,570	370	1,693	7.8	369	1,836	8.4	371	1,937	5.5	369	2,091	8.0
Botany	QK	89	1,317	91	1,416	7.5	92	1,537	8.5	92	1,631	6.1	94	1,725	5.8
Business and economics	HA-HJ	675	547	684	584	6.8	683	628	7.5	693	668	6.4	694	716	7.2
Chemistry	QD	305	3,121	308	3,334	6.8	313	3,548	6.4	315	3,702	4.3	320	3,969	7.2
Education	L	437	313	437	343	9.6	437	369	7.6	437	387	4.9	440	468	20.9
Engineering	T	532	1,388	536	1,488	7.2	539	1,604	7.8	540	1,690	5.4	543	1,796	6.3
Food science	TX	57	568	59	588	3.5	59	635	8.0	60	674	6.1	60	727	7.9
General science	Q	135	866	137	934	7.9	137	1,005	7.6	137	1,064	5.9	141	1,146	7.7
General works	A	238	124	238	132	6.5	235	135	2.3	233	142	5.2	236	149	4.9
Geography	G-GF	147	702	147	773	10.1	153	818	5.8	153	886	8.3	151	949	7.1
Geology	QE	125	1,265	129	1,191	-5.8	131	1,438	20.7	132	1,511	5.1	126	1,621	7.3
Health sciences	R	2,410	1,047	2,435	1,137	8.6	2,440	1,241	9.1	2,444	1,233	-0.6	2,474	1,382	12.1

Table 8 / Average Price of Serials, Based on Titles in Select Serials Indexes: 2007–2011 *(cont.)*

		2007		2008			2009			2010			2011		
Subject	LC Class	No. of Titles	Avg. Price	No. of Titles	Avg. Price	% of Price Increase	No. of Titles	Avg. Price	% of Price Increase	No. of Titles	Avg. Price	% of Price Increase	No. of Titles	Avg. Price	% of Price Increase
History	C,D,E,F	581	$202	591	$226	11.9	599	$245	8.4	522	$267	9.0	630	$284	6.4%
Language and literature	P	593	202	600	223	10.4	598	216	-3.1	626	260	20.4	660	271	4.2
Law	K	183	280	187	310	10.7	178	339	9.4	193	412	21.5	198	431	4.6
Library science	Z	137	327	139	352	7.6	138	372	5.7	139	385	3.5	142	399	3.6
Math and computer science	QA	362	1,230	371	1,317	7.1	371	1,411	7.1	372	1,466	3.9	384	1,550	5.7
Military and naval science	U,V	50	264	51	295	11.7	51	333	12.9	45	406	21.9	45	414	2.0
Music	M	94	151	94	198	31.1	93	210	6.1	95	220	4.8	96	238	8.2
Philosophy and religion	B-BD, BH-BX	342	240	343	262	9.2	341	289	10.3	386	322	11.4	396	344	6.8
Physics	QC	348	2,922	353	3,077	5.3	356	3,256	5.8	360	3,386	4.0	360	3,531	4.3
Political science	J	153	429	158	463	7.9	158	508	9.7	163	527	3.7	166	577	9.5
Psychology	BF	175	533	176	581	9.0	177	638	9.8	181	679	6.4	182	722	6.3
Recreation	QV	73	173	72	193	11.6	70	212	9.8	71	218	2.8	73	230	5.5
Social sciences	H	101	418	101	456	9.1	100	501	9.9	101	525	4.8	103	547	4.2
Sociology	HM-HX	340	435	343	484	11.3	348	518	7.0	350	552	6.6	353	590	6.9
Technology	TA-TT	97	784	99	853	8.8	98	979	14.8	98	1,038	6.0	99	1,098	5.8
Zoology	QL	168	1,160	171	1,278	10.2	171	1,394	9.1	176	1,452	4.2	179	1,512	4.1
Totals		9,880	$882	10,005	$950	7.7%	10,013	$1,029	8.3%	10,075	$1,068	3.8%	10,308	$1,144	7.1%

Compiled by Stephen Bosch, University of Arizona, from data on serials pricing supplied by EBSCO based on titles indexed in ISI Arts and Humanities Citation Index, ISI Science Citation Index, ISI Social Sciences Citation Index, EBSCO Academic Search Complete, and EBSCO Masterfile Premier.

Table 9 / British Academic Books : Average Prices and Price Indexes 2009–2010

(Index Base: 2009 = 100)

Subject	LC Class	2009		2010			
		No. of Titles	Average Price (£)	No. of Titles	Average Price (£)	% Change 2009–2010	Index
Agriculture	S	140	£53.96	154	£63.97	18.6%	118.6
Anthropology	GN	109	53.60	154	50.85	-5.1	94.9
Botany	QK	22	145.94	45	66.08	-54.7	45.3
Business and economics	H	2,439	59.12	2,874	61.09	3.3	103.3
Chemistry	QD	88	101.14	96	105.68	4.5	104.5
Education	L	386	49.70	558	52.21	5.1	105.1
Engineering and technology	T	716	65.60	655	65.73	0.2	100.2
Fine and applied arts	M, N	762	39.71	1,037	37.00	-6.8	93.2
General works	A	15	76.73	30	60.03	-21.8	78.2
Geography	G	233	50.98	660	64.95	27.4	127.4
Geology	QE	41	53.80	33	52.28	-2.8	97.2
History	C,D,E,F	1,572	41.0[illegible]	1,822	48.13	17.4	117.4
Home economics	TX	59	39.02	46	30.48	-21.9	78.1
Industrial arts	TT	21	24.32	41	28.47	17.1	117.1
Law	K	1,117	76.13	1,153	83.10	9.2	109.2
Library and information science	Z	98	60.32	100	53.58	-11.2	88.8
Literature and language	P	2,928	34.77	3,987	31.58	-9.2	90.8
Mathematics and computer science	QA	216	49.30	207	48.29	-2.0	98.0
Medicine	R	1,110	48.50	1,182	55.12	13.6	113.6
Military and naval sciences	U, V	112	83.99	184	38.00	-54.8	45.2
Philosophy and religion	B	1,091	46.45	1,336	45.24	-2.6	97.4
Physics and astronomy	QB, QC	196	54.54	214	59.69	9.4	109.4
Political Science	J	621	59.74	737	71.88	20.3	120.3
Psychology	BF	195	44.46	265	39.69	-10.7	89.3
Science (general)	Q	55	42.12	69	36.32	-13.8	86.2
Sociology	HM	153	74.17	208	70.13	-5.4	94.6
Sports and recreation	GV	181	30.90	192	36.76	19.0	119.0
Zoology	QH, QL, QP, QR	326	66.20	373	72.30	9.2	109.2
Total, All Books		15,432	£52.91	18,490	£51.97	-1.8%	98.2

Compiled by Judy Jeng, University of Illinois at Urbana-Champaign, based on information provided by Baker & Taylor.

(continued from page 484)

Dates	12/31/06	12/30/07	12/31/08	12/31/09	12/31/10
Canada	1.1720	0.9990	1.1910	1.0510	1.0200
Euro	0.7590	0.6800	0.7310	0.6950	0.7700
U.K.	0.5120	0.4860	0.6570	0.6160	0.6400
Japan	119.5300	110.8800	92.6500	92.3900	83.8300

Source: Data from Financial Management Services. U.S. Treasury Department (http://fms.treas.gov/intn.html).

here are published in the United States as well as overseas and are indexed in ISI Arts and Humanities Citation Index, ISI Science Citation Index, ISI Social Sciences Citation Index, EBSCO Academic Search Complete, and EBSCO Masterfile Premier.

This table covers prices for periodicals and serials for a five-year period, 2007 through 2011. The 2011 pricing is the renewal pricing for 2011. Table 8 is a departure from the U.S. Periodicals Price Index: Average Prices and Price Indexes (USPPI) that appears as Table 1 in this report. Table 8 is derived from pricing data supplied by EBSCO Subscription Services and reflects broad pricing changes aggregated from titles that are indexed in the five major products mentioned above. The USPPI table is based on price changes seen in a static set of approximately 3,700 serial titles. This new table is based on a much broader set of titles, approximately 10,000, that are not static; therefore this pricing study does not rise to the level of a price index. This study is still useful in showing price changes for periodicals. The indexes selected for this price survey were deemed to be fairly representative of serials that are frequently purchased in academic and public libraries. There are some foreign titles, so the scope is broader and this may give a better picture of the overall price pressures experienced in libraries. This new table is not a replacement for the USPPI, which is being reconfigured. The Average Price of Serials Index (Table 8) will serve as a complement to the USPPI data.

The most important trend seen in this data is that after a modest increase in prices for 2010 (3.8 percent), the overall price increase has risen to 7.1 percent in 2011. The respite in price increases seen in 2010 appears to be ending. Libraries were very vocal about not being able to sustain high rates of inflation, and in 2010 price increases moderated significantly. That moderation now seems to be over. The price increase in 2011 is lower than those for 2008 (7.7 percent) and 2009 (8.3 percent), but it is still closer to those figures than to the 3.8 percent seen in 2010.

Another interesting trend is that the science and technology subject areas do not show the largest price increases. Instead, subjects in the social sciences and life sciences (political science, anthropology, agriculture, health sciences, and education) reflected the highest price increases, with agriculture, health sciences, and education all showing double-digit increases. In the past, price increases in science and technology areas were seen as drivers in serials inflation, but that is no longer that case.

In this price study, as in similar surveys, the data become less accurate at describing price changes as the sample becomes smaller. For that reason, conclusions about price changes in subject areas with a limited number of titles will be less accurate than for large areas or the broader price survey. Price changes are far more volatile where smaller data sets are used. For example, language and literature (about 600 titles) showed price changes of 10.4 percent, -3.1 percent, 20.4 percent, and 4.2 between 2007 and 2011. Librarians are encouraged to look at an average price change over the time period or the overall price change to calculate inflation rates. Year-to-year price changes are too unstable to be used for this purpose.

Book Prices

The British Academic Books Price Index (Table 9), compiled by Judy Jeng, indicates the average prices and price indexes for 2009 through 2010. This index has been re-established using data compiled from Baker & Taylor. The previous index, compiled by Curt Holleman, was based on data supplied by Blackwell's Book Services, and may not be comparable.

The average price of a British academic book fell 1.8 percent over the period covered, declining from £52.91 in 2009 to £51.97 in 2010. This index uses prices for cloth editions except when these are not available, and does not separate out more expensive reference titles. The index does not include e-book prices.

The index shows that British academic book production has risen significantly, from 15,432 titles in 2009 to 18,490 titles in 2010, an increase of 19.82 percent.

Using the Price Indexes

Librarians are encouraged to monitor trends in the publishing industry and changes in economic conditions when preparing budget forecasts and projections. The ALA ALCTS Library Materials Price Index Editorial Board endeavors to make information on publishing trends readily available by sponsoring the annual compilation and publication of price data contained in Tables 1 to 9. The indexes cover newly published library materials and document prices and rates of percent changes at the national and international level. They are useful benchmarks against which local costs can be compared, but because they reflect retail prices in the aggregate, they are not a substitute for cost data that reflect the collecting patterns of individual libraries, and they are not a substitute for specific cost studies.

Differences between local prices and those found in national indexes arise partially because these indexes exclude discounts, service charges, shipping and handling fees, and other costs that the library might incur. Discrepancies may also relate to a library's subject coverage; mix of titles purchased, including both current and backfiles; and the proportion of the library's budget expended on domestic or foreign materials. These variables can affect the average price paid by an individual library, although the individual library's rate of increase may not differ greatly from the national indexes.

The LMPI board is interested in pursuing studies that would correlate a particular library's costs with the national prices. The group welcomes interested parties to its meetings at the ALA Annual Conference and Midwinter Meeting.

The Library Materials Price Index Editorial Board consists of compilers Catherine Barr, Ajaye Bloomstone, Stephen Bosch, Brenda Dingley, Judy Jeng, Frederick C. Lynden, and editor Narda Tafuri.

Book Title Output and Average Prices: 2007–2010

Catherine Barr
Contributing Editor

Constance Harbison
Baker & Taylor

The economic downturn continues to depress the print publishing industry even as the surge in popularity of e-books has focused attention on that sector. From a high of 190,502 titles in 2007, there has been a steady decrease in American book title output, with preliminary figures for 2010, at 174,066, falling below the 2005 level. The number of titles published dropped by 5.5 percent in 2008, 0.66 percent in 2009, and preliminary figures for 2010 showed a further decline of 2.7 percent (publishers were still submitting late 2010 titles in early 2011).

The figures for this edition of the *Library and Book Trade Almanac* were provided by book wholesaler Baker & Taylor and are based on the Book Industry Study Group's BISAC categories. The BISAC juvenile category (fiction and non-fiction) has been divided into children's and young adult. Figures for 2009 have been restated, reflecting late updates to the Baker & Taylor database.

For more information on the BISAC categories, visit http://www.bisg.org.

Output by Format and by Category

Hardcovers and audiobooks were the only formats to show growth in 2010, with hardcover titles and editions rising by 961 (1.41 percent) following a decline of the same percent in 2009. Audiobook output continued to increase but at a slower pace, up only 8.73 percent in 2010 after posting gains of 14.02 percent in 2008 and 24.42 percent in 2009. This growth is caused in part by the introduction of new formats. Hardcovers priced at less than $81—whose share of the hardcover market has been declining but still exceeds 60 percent—fell by 1,270 titles (2.64 percent) in 2008, 2,121 (4.53 percent) in 2009, and 1,103 titles (2.47 percent) in 2010. After registering declines of 3.23 percent (157 titles) and 4.45 percent (209 titles) in 2008 and 2009, respectively, mass market paperback output dropped only 0.11 percent (5 titles) in 2010. Trade paperbacks did not fare so well, following decreases of 7.29 percent (8,303 titles) in 2008 and 0.25 percent (261 titles) in 2009 with a fall of 5.64 percent (5,943 titles) in 2010.

Fiction, a key category, broke through the 18,000-title mark in 2007 and showed resilience in 2008 and 2009, posting output of 18,638 titles and 18,272 titles respectively; however, 2010 saw a 6.99 percent drop to 16,995 titles. Hardcover fiction (less than $81) rose 10.50 percent in 2008, but fell 8.20 percent in 2009, and a further 4.83 percent in 2010. In the paperback sector, mass market fiction dropped 3.58 percent in 2009 and 0.45 percent in 2010 while trade fiction rose 2.25 percent in 2009 only to fall 10.89 percent in 2010. Audiobook fiction, which had jumped 20.17 percent in 2008 and an impressive 43.36 percent in 2009, registered a more modest increase of 17.23 percent in 2010.

Table 1 / American Book Production, 2006–2010

BISAC Category	2006	2007	2008	2009	2010
Antiques and collectibles	503	485	445	359	365
Architecture	1,366	1,504	1,548	1,534	1,484
Art	3,083	3,347	3,261	3,181	3,108
Bibles	684	467	554	474	622
Biography and autobiography	3,916	4,116	3,935	4,012	3,869
Body, mind and spirit	1,258	1,276	1,319	1,216	1,128
Business and economics	9,689	14,593	9,593	10,006	9,232
Children	22,115	24,440	22,603	22,395	20,100
Comics and graphic novels	2,277	2,491	2,869	2,906	2,688
Computers	4,020	4,590	4,014	4,589	3,985
Cooking	1,842	1,957	2,294	1,835	2,022
Crafts and hobbies	1,322	1,247	1,212	1,240	1,266
Design	640	800	739	728	874
Drama	505	666	714	665	533
Education	5,322	5,428	5,277	4,673	4,506
Family and relationships	1,389	1,317	1,256	1,185	1,002
Fiction	17,059	18,471	18,638	18,272	16,995
Foreign language study	1,568	1,431	1,550	1,114	1,152
Games	1,181	1,022	958	959	954
Gardening	414	431	517	397	356
Health and fitness	2,056	1,962	1,847	1,710	1,553
History	10,503	11,526	10,658	11,157	11,622
House and home	475	481	412	340	291
Humor	699	710	708	715	632
Language arts and disciplines	3,132	3,436	2,967	3,590	3,793
Law	4,547	4,318	5,363	4,266	4,662
Literary collections	640	1,031	922	955	959
Literary criticism	3,039	3,401	3,158	3,679	3,660
Mathematics	2,063	2,025	1,888	1,829	1,829
Medical	7,141	7,331	7,092	6,891	7,276
Music	3,241	3,149	3,408	3,497	3,399
Nature	1,133	1,145	1,039	1,025	877
Performing arts	1,489	1,681	1,610	1,481	1,580
Pets	536	546	474	475	390
Philosophy	2,044	2,631	2,246	2,456	2,267
Photography	1,363	1,375	1,417	1,344	1,348
Poetry	2,042	2,215	2,126	2,018	1,843
Political science	5,126	5,988	5,655	5,927	6,387
Psychology	2,564	2,698	2,456	2,339	2,652
Reference	2,203	1,933	1,975	1,872	1,640
Religion	8,128	8,065	8,276	8,415	8,646
Science	5,611	5,596	5,324	5,740	5,805
Self-help	1,381	1,548	1,474	1,360	1,287
Social science	6,662	6,997	6,998	7,037	7,118
Sports and recreation	2,185	2,054	2,081	1,882	1,816
Study aids	1,186	704	898	694	1,524

Technology and engineering	3,957	4,642	4,739	5,134	4,143
Transportation	994	701	742	706	746
Travel	3,313	4,206	3,542	3,238	2,843
True crime	230	303	291	301	298
Young adult	5,120	6,025	4,950	5,028	4,939
Totals	174,956	190,502	180,032	178,841	174,066

The important juveniles category is broken down into children's (Pre-K–6) and young adult (YA; grades 7–12) titles. Both these sectors have showed mixed results in the last few years. For children's books, hardcover titles priced at less than $81 fell steadily from 2007's high, posting declines of 12.33 percent in 2008, 5.65 percent in 2009, and 7.69 percent in 2010; mass market paperbacks moved up and down over the four-year period, with 2010's output 7.39 percent lower than that of 2007; and trade paperbacks rose 6.78 percent in 2009 but lost this ground in 2010, falling by 14.6 percent. YA titles showed a similar mix, with output of hardcovers less than $81 falling in 2008 but rising again in 2009 and 2010 (by 11.47 percent and 9.56 percent respectively), and of mass market paperbacks (down 32.39 percent in 2009 and a further 6.25 percent in 2010) and trade paperbacks (down 3.64 percent in 2009 and a further 11.62 percent in 2010) falling steadily across the four-year period. And the audiobook sector showed differing trends in the children's and YA markets, with children's output falling in 2008 and 2010 and the YA market showing strong growth in 2009 and 2010 (95.9 and 57.5 percent, respectively).

Comics and graphic novels—a category that can include both fiction and nonfiction—rose 63.6 percent in hardcovers under $81 in 2009 before slipping 5.21 percent in 2010; and lost ground in the trade paperback sector, dropping 9.72 percent in 2009 and 8.15 percent in 2010.

A review of overall output in nonfiction categories (Table 1) shows the usual variations. As expected, many categories lost ground in 2010. A few registered double-digit increases in title output in 2010—among them, Bibles (up 31.22 percent), cooking (up 10.19 percent), design (up 20.05 percent), psychology (up 13.38 percent), and study aids (up an impressive 119.60 percent). Categories posting double-digit losses were children's (down 10.25 percent), computers (down 13.16 percent), drama (down 19.85 percent), family and relationships (down 15.44 percent), gardening (down 10.33 percent), house and home (down 14.41 percent), humor (down 11.61 percent), nature (down 14.44 percent), pets (down 17.89 percent), reference (down 12.39 percent), technology and engineering (down 19.30 percent), and travel (down 12.20 percent).

Average Book Prices

Average book prices were mixed in 2010. List prices for hardcovers (Table 2) rose 2.72 percent, and those for hardcovers under $81 (Table 3) rose 2.61 percent.

Mass market paperback prices (Table 4) also continued their slow but steady increase, rising another 1.79 percent; trade paperback prices (Table 5), on the

(text continues on page 504)

Table 2 / Hardcover Average Per-Volume Prices, 2007–2010

	2007			2008			2009			2010		
BISAC Category	Vols.	$ Total	Prices	Vols.	$ Total	Prices	Vols.	$ Total	Prices	Vols.	$ Total	Prices
Antiques and collectibles	200	$13,003.84	$65.02	195	$15,763.28	$80.84	159	$7,469.68	$46.98	178	$9,121.95	$51.25
Architecture	788	56,321.04	71.47	853	66,141.71	77.54	842	71,115.56	84.46	772	64,196.37	83.16
Art	1,651	136,283.82	82.55	1,681	142,524.38	84.79	1,688	126,824.23	75.13	1,667	119,257.02	71.54
Bibles	176	7,251.88	41.20	191	9,396.02	49.19	165	7,643.10	46.32	198	7,631.99	38.55
Biography and autobiography	1,825	96,276.98	52.75	1,714	98,643.35	57.55	1,652	82,734.86	50.08	1,606	85,765.92	53.40
Body, mind and spirit	208	6,551.93	31.50	233	6,085.82	26.12	194	5,355.04	27.60	167	5,957.08	35.67
Business and economics	3,452	437,415.74	126.71	3,581	480,896.85	134.29	3,913	483,112.81	123.46	3,983	521,448.95	130.92
Children	14,959	360,012.83	24.07	13,235	362,043.14	27.35	12,396	310,031.58	25.01	11,501	279,400.07	24.29
Comics and graphic novels	324	10,840.21	33.46	462	15,084.50	32.65	732	23,474.46	32.07	692	21,614.31	31.23
Computers	769	89,715.87	116.67	731	107,032.74	146.42	786	122,508.69	155.86	826	110,628.27	133.93
Cooking	878	24,276.18	27.65	1,015	30,443.41	29.99	814	24,041.89	29.54	955	26,484.30	27.73
Crafts and hobbies	338	9,050.47	26.78	267	7,361.24	27.57	237	7,094.80	29.94	214	7,215.09	33.72
Design	385	33,532.68	87.10	358	22,273.82	62.22	331	22,019.63	66.52	448	34,208.40	76.36
Drama	84	5,608.74	66.77	192	10,300.98	53.65	81	6,723.29	83.00	55	4,283.33	77.88
Education	1,245	138,539.83	111.28	1,330	148,820.74	111.90	1,392	146,944.34	105.56	1,347	150,713.56	111.89
Family and relationships	324	8,644.62	26.68	301	8,839.56	29.37	296	9,936.85	33.57	257	8,153.76	31.73
Fiction	4,627	155,507.10	33.61	4,976	144,477.84	29.03	4,556	131,127.58	28.78	4,355	140,521.90	32.27
Foreign language study	211	23,915.86	113.35	146	16,159.40	110.68	120	15,840.79	132.01	115	13,957.93	121.37
Games	154	4,543.19	29.50	145	5,678.75	39.16	167	6,258.91	37.48	172	7,448.39	43.30
Gardening	189	7,099.09	37.56	149	6,318.83	42.41	140	5,177.87	36.98	118	4,232.16	35.87
Health and fitness	405	21,893.76	54.06	449	27,425.63	61.08	356	18,078.72	50.78	305	14,187.77	46.52
History	4,766	405,946.42	85.18	4,795	419,378.14	87.46	4,687	395,609.19	84.41	5,022	406,380.57	80.92
House and home	152	5,593.30	36.80	117	4,779.14	40.85	113	4,569.88	40.44	93	4,114.35	44.24
Humor	227	4,701.10	20.71	241	4,921.32	20.42	229	4,635.89	20.24	214	4,801.87	22.44

Language arts and disciplines	1,404	182,644.90	130.09	1,300	173,479.85	133.45	1,435	195,067.50	131.36	1,614	182,840.73	113.28
Law	1,409	236,529.80	167.87	1,516	247,998.43	163.59	1,515	252,397.29	166.60	1,687	288,258.12	170.87
Literary collections	472	65,940.69	139.70	383	34,373.11	89.75	373	33,600.00	90.08	318	26,939.83	84.72
Literary criticism	1,823	187,184.88	102.68	1,707	181,073.91	106.08	1,903	205,616.68	108.05	2,026	227,688.80	112.38
Mathematics	1,029	126,215.07	122.66	916	117,073.40	127.81	895	104,786.72	117.08	959	119,267.41	124.37
Medical	3,118	477,496.29	153.14	3,076	476,516.50	154.91	2,924	485,153.60	165.92	3,188	530,505.20	166.41
Music	486	36,967.71	76.07	485	33,628.05	69.34	520	40,214.72	77.34	519	44,714.63	86.16
Nature	447	28,459.99	63.67	435	27,221.52	62.58	411	27,055.02	65.83	370	25,701.54	69.46
Performing arts	577	46,217.96	80.10	618	50,450.12	81.63	540	43,721.93	80.97	574	42,894.35	74.73
Pets	225	5,427.23	24.12	181	5,318.82	29.39	176	4,407.15	25.04	139	3,405.33	24.50
Philosophy	1,007	95,281.98	94.62	973	95,896.54	98.56	990	92,845.84	93.78	1,065	113,914.25	106.96
Photography	895	59,582.47	66.57	882	72,886.61	82.64	805	65,864.70	81.82	824	90,353.60	109.65
Poetry	351	14,845.72	42.30	339	14,406.45	42.50	293	13,324.37	45.48	273	11,161.51	40.88
Political science	2,315	230,550.20	99.59	2,492	242,055.07	97.13	2,698	291,658.10	108.10	2,768	300,914.98	108.71
Psychology	1,112	114,696.17	103.14	1,063	108,360.07	101.94	1,031	107,518.67	104.29	1,099	113,974.17	103.71
Reference	644	171,371.20	266.10	613	178,211.72	290.72	558	153,354.85	274.83	560	171,531.95	306.31
Religion	2,510	164,865.97	65.68	2,449	186,622.19	68.04	2,353	170,926.23	72.64	2,534	204,869.50	80.85
Science	3,214	686,473.09	213.59	3,171	649,242.37	204.74	3,161	601,882.90	190.41	3,465	593,642.96	171.33
Self-help	326	7,871.19	24.14	322	8,265.48	25.67	311	6,690.61	21.51	238	6,093.92	25.60
Social science	2,932	319,137.90	108.85	2,948	288,701.80	97.93	3,019	310,154.24	102.73	3,201	316,986.39	99.03
Sports and recreation	670	26,546.21	39.62	746	30,938.26	41.47	619	23,927.64	38.66	636	25,958.26	40.81
Study aids	21	1,838.00	87.52	17	1,334.40	78.49	24	2,751.35	114.64	18	1,778.19	98.79
Technology and engineering	1,947	304,618.30	156.46	2,145	340,632.86	158.80	2,439	392,271.18	160.83	2,519	401,196.89	159.27
Transportation	287	16,474.77	57.40	312	20,043.82	64.24	245	18,614.53	75.98	287	24,468.89	85.26
Travel	754	40,433.70	53.63	457	15,904.23	34.80	384	15,827.41	41.22	362	15,104.64	41.73
True crime	97	2,758.97	28.44	94	2,474.48	26.32	93	2,730.42	29.36	65	2,262.58	34.81
Young adult	2,749	139,330.93	50.68	2,256	111,464.02	49.41	2,466	92,170.46	37.38	2,670	96,019.84	35.96
Totals	71,158	$5,852,287.77	$82.24	69,253	$5,855,364.67	$84.55	68,277	$5,792,863.75	$84.84	69,238	$6,034,173.77	$87.15

Table 3 / Hardcover Average Per-Volume Prices, Less Than $81, 2007–2010

	2007			2008			2009			2010		
BISAC Category	Vols.	$ Total	Prices	Vols.	$ Total	Prices	Vols.	$ Total	Prices	Vols.	$ Total	Prices
Antiques and collectibles	164	$6,880.05	$41.95	158	$6,091.85	$38.56	140	$5,250.25	$37.50	145	$4,590.13	$31.66
Architecture	579	28,797.91	49.74	613	31,148.56	50.81	564	29,288.70	51.93	526	27,488.38	52.26
Art	1,319	60,267.17	45.69	1,333	62,046.12	46.55	1,364	63,705.85	46.71	1,318	61,954.19	47.01
Bibles	171	6,591.96	38.55	177	6,708.32	37.90	158	6,370.23	40.32	188	6,423.07	34.17
Biography and autobiography	1,623	50,892.84	31.36	1,510	47,377.50	31.38	1,482	45,428.56	30.65	1,415	44,730.65	31.61
Body, mind and spirit	195	4,763.98	24.43	222	4,861.07	21.90	183	4,031.74	22.03	157	4,101.18	26.12
Business and economics	1,503	59,611.00	39.66	1,615	66,649.41	41.27	1,814	72,002.39	39.69	1,647	66,555.00	40.41
Children	14,595	279,188.12	19.13	12,796	250,571.44	19.58	12,073	236,547.64	19.59	11,144	216,834.04	19.46
Comics and graphic novels	310	9,328.87	30.09	434	12,220.74	28.16	710	20,811.69	29.31	673	19,209.36	28.54
Computers	247	14,769.55	59.80	240	14,827.83	61.78	181	10,900.85	60.23	207	12,516.80	60.47
Cooking	864	22,518.11	26.06	987	26,659.53	27.01	805	23,192.54	28.81	936	23,928.17	25.56
Crafts and hobbies	335	8,795.47	26.26	266	7,276.24	27.35	232	6,590.35	28.41	207	6,060.14	29.28
Design	324	15,389.93	47.50	307	14,911.87	48.57	277	13,520.48	48.81	347	16,015.65	46.15
Drama	58	2,316.24	39.94	168	6,923.43	41.21	37	1,680.29	45.41	32	1,686.43	52.70
Education	648	35,228.48	54.36	625	35,825.96	57.32	649	36,057.56	55.56	485	26,231.04	54.08
Family and relationships	308	6,540.27	21.23	279	6,119.71	21.93	271	6,413.10	23.66	234	5,545.31	23.70
Fiction	4,466	122,128.45	27.35	4,935	136,931.49	27.75	4,530	127,152.18	28.07	4,311	121,577.75	28.20
Foreign language study	79	3,803.36	48.14	71	3,764.05	53.01	46	2,152.49	46.79	36	1,733.15	48.14
Games	151	4,221.25	27.96	139	4,415.85	31.77	161	5,377.91	33.40	167	4,613.39	27.63
Gardening	182	6,286.39	34.54	141	5,084.13	36.06	134	4,558.07	34.02	115	3,872.16	33.67
Health and fitness	350	10,054.34	28.73	342	10,366.78	30.31	303	10,085.59	33.29	261	8,560.17	32.80
History	3,013	130,476.75	43.30	3,210	139,908.95	43.59	3,066	136,103.66	44.39	3,224	150,069.42	46.55
House and home	145	4,883.90	33.68	110	3,874.20	35.22	107	3,928.93	36.72	89	3,253.78	36.56
Humor	224	4,092.22	18.27	238	4,483.44	18.84	226	4,301.94	19.04	210	4,318.92	20.57

Language arts and disciplines	565	31,625.58	55.97	517	28,871.62	55.84	551	32,192.66	58.43	715	41,656.97	58.26
Law	309	16,280.97	52.69	331	17,692.70	53.45	278	15,704.82	56.49	342	18,973.13	55.48
Literary collections	215	8,925.14	41.51	265	12,426.71	46.89	237	10,737.27	45.30	211	10,300.58	48.82
Literary criticism	902	49,423.99	54.79	841	47,022.07	55.91	872	47,594.62	54.58	927	55,135.55	59.48
Mathematics	234	13,701.65	58.55	255	16,019.92	62.82	264	16,163.72	61.23	268	17,049.29	63.62
Medical	591	32,684.76	55.30	572	32,413.01	56.67	450	25,644.77	56.99	481	27,253.18	56.66
Music	315	12,872.91	40.87	351	15,137.90	43.13	352	15,543.74	44.16	334	14,832.32	44.41
Nature	338	12,825.60	37.95	342	12,455.23	36.42	294	10,642.04	36.20	254	9,548.14	37.59
Performing arts	351	17,790.33	50.68	378	18,878.72	49.94	314	14,787.15	47.09	366	18,476.63	50.48
Pets	221	4,954.33	22.42	179	4,356.83	24.34	173	4,112.20	23.77	138	3,255.33	23.59
Philosophy	433	23,065.71	53.27	489	26,490.89	54.17	441	23,240.50	52.70	451	25,407.07	56.33
Photography	833	35,558.62	42.69	793	34,612.03	43.65	706	31,564.61	44.71	724	35,108.91	48.49
Poetry	311	9,355.67	30.08	303	9,594.30	31.66	255	7,652.03	30.01	246	7,589.25	30.85
Political science	1,128	55,757.29	49.43	1,258	61,728.66	49.07	1,175	57,443.46	48.89	1,117	54,911.74	49.16
Psychology	487	24,857.24	51.04	460	23,722.51	51.57	477	24,580.38	51.53	471	24,819.02	52.69
Reference	297	11,236.10	37.83	270	9,210.17	34.11	238	8,588.83	36.09	221	7,595.13	34.37
Religion	1,762	53,473.09	30.35	1,762	55,636.12	31.58	1,614	53,692.99	33.27	1,612	54,930.44	34.08
Science	631	30,823.80	48.85	645	32,356.74	50.17	683	33,617.88	49.22	696	36,268.39	52.11
Self-help	318	7,035.21	22.12	311	6,884.98	22.14	309	6,458.71	20.90	232	5,436.27	23.43
Social science	1,496	76,093.02	50.86	1,657	86,305.63	52.09	1,622	85,039.38	52.43	1,600	85,408.13	53.38
Sports and recreation	630	19,560.31	31.05	690	22,765.11	32.99	579	18,414.49	31.80	583	18,802.56	32.25
Study aids	14	586.65	41.90	12	558.50	46.54	15	661.50	44.10	13	574.59	44.20
Technology and engineering	226	12,396.32	54.85	305	16,902.02	55.42	269	15,258.54	56.72	311	17,616.05	56.64
Transportation	245	9,542.87	38.95	259	10,541.22	40.70	196	8,252.63	42.11	232	9,261.86	39.92
Travel	733	28,686.75	39.14	439	12,882.88	29.35	365	11,560.17	31.67	326	9,604.24	29.46
True crime	95	2,511.47	26.44	94	2,474.48	26.32	91	2,550.42	28.03	62	1,809.59	29.19
Young adult	2,524	68,724.52	27.23	2,093	56,380.12	26.94	2,333	67,217.00	28.81	2,556	72,063.52	28.19
Totals	48,057	$1,568,176.51	$32.63	46,787	$1,583,369.54	$33.84	44,666	$1,524,369.50	$34.13	43,563	$1,525,556.16	$35.02

Table 4 / Mass Market Paperbacks Average Per-Volume Prices, 2007–2010

	2007			2008			2009			2010		
BISAC Category	Vols.	$ Total	Prices	Vols.	$ Total	Prices	Vols.	$ Total	Prices	Vols.	$ Total	Prices
Antiques and collectibles	9	$71.91	$7.99	10	$85.90	$8.59	9	$77.91	$8.66	9	$78.91	$8.77
Architecture	n.a.	n.a.	n.a.	n.a.	n.a.	n.a.	0	0.00	n.a.	0	0.00	n.a.
Art	n.a.	n.a.	n.a.	n.a.	n.a.	n.a.	0	0.00	n.a.	0	0.00	n.a.
Bibles	n.a.	n.a.	n.a.	n.a.	n.a.	n.a.	0	0.00	n.a.	0	0.00	n.a.
Biography and autobiography	9	70.87	7.87	8	62.92	7.87	13	97.30	7.48	13	97.67	7.51
Body, mind and spirit	22	167.74	7.62	14	99.86	7.13	13	103.87	7.99	15	119.85	7.99
Business and economics	n.a.	n.a.	n.a.	1	7.99	7.99	1	9.99	9.99	3	27.97	9.32
Children	284	1,593.33	5.61	239	1,420.29	5.94	238	1,456.16	6.12	263	1,633.39	6.21
Comics and graphic novels	n.a.	n.a.	n.a.	n.a.	n.a.	n.a.	0	0.00	n.a.	0	0.00	n.a.
Computers	n.a.	n.a.	n.a.	n.a.	n.a.	n.a.	0	0.00	n.a.	0	0.00	n.a.
Cooking	n.a.	n.a.	n.a.	n.a.	n.a.	n.a.	0	0.00	n.a.	0	0.00	n.a.
Crafts and hobbies	n.a.	n.a.	n.a.	n.a.	n.a.	n.a.	0	0.00	n.a.	0	0.00	n.a.
Design	n.a.	n.a.	n.a.	n.a.	n.a.	n.a.	0	0.00	n.a.	0	0.00	n.a.
Drama	4	25.88	6.47	2	11.98	5.99	3	17.93	5.98	3	18.89	6.30
Education	n.a.	n.a.	n.a.	n.a.	n.a.	n.a.	0	0.00	n.a.	0	0.00	n.a.
Family and relationships	3	24.97	8.32	n.a.	n.a.	n.a.	1	4.99	4.99	1	7.99	7.99
Fiction	4,227	27,051.87	6.40	4,162	26,965.85	6.48	4,013	26,824.43	6.68	3,995	27,151.28	6.80
Foreign language study	4	26.96	6.74	5	30.95	6.19	4	27.96	6.99	6	42.45	7.08
Games	19	105.28	5.54	13	70.87	5.45	5	24.95	4.99	0	0.00	n.a.
Gardening	n.a.	n.a.	n.a.	n.a.	n.a.	n.a.	0	0.00	n.a.	0	0.00	n.a.
Health and fitness	18	134.84	7.49	18	137.82	7.66	15	116.85	7.79	14	110.86	7.92
History	13	100.87	7.76	3	17.48	5.83	5	39.46	7.89	1	9.95	9.95
House and home	n.a.	n.a.	n.a.	n.a.	n.a.	n.a.	0	0.00	n.a.	0	0.00	n.a.
Humor	4	29.96	7.49	3	18.97	6.32	0	0.00	n.a.	1	3.50	3.50

Language arts and disciplines	n.a.	n.a.	n.a.	n.a.	n.a.	n.a.	0	0.00	n.a.	2	26.49	13.25
Law	n.a.	n.a.	n.a.	n.a.	n.a.	n.a.	0	0.00	n.a.	0	0.00	n.a.
Literary collections	n.a.	n.a.	n.a.	1	4.99	4.99	1	7.95	7.95	1	5.95	5.95
Literary criticism	n.a.	n.a.	n.a.	1	7.95	7.95	1	7.99	7.99	1	7.99	7.99
Mathematics	n.a.	n.a.	n.a.	n.a.	n.a.	n.a.	0	0.00	n.a.	0	0.00	n.a.
Medical	4	27.47	6.87	1	7.50	7.50	0	0.00	n.a.	1	8.99	8.99
Music	n.a.	n.a.	n.a.	n.a.	n.a.	n.a.	0	0.00	n.a.	0	0.00	n.a.
Nature	n.a.	n.a.	n.a.	n.a.	n.a.	n.a.	0	0.00	n.a.	0	0.00	n.a.
Performing arts	3	25.93	8.64	1	9.99	9.99	1	9.99	9.99	1	9.99	9.99
Pets	n.a.	n.a.	n.a.	1	7.99	7.99	0	0.00	n.a.	1	7.99	7.99
Philosophy	5	38.91	7.78	2	11.90	5.95	0	0.00	n.a.	2	12.94	6.47
Photography	n.a.	n.a.	n.a.	n.a.	n.a.	n.a.	0	0.00	n.a.	0	0.00	n.a.
Poetry	1	5.95	5.95	2	9.90	4.95	5	34.75	6.95	1	7.95	7.95
Political science	1	6.99	6.99	2	15.98	7.99	1	5.95	5.95	2	15.94	7.97
Psychology	2	15.94	7.97	n.a.	n.a.	n.a.	0	0.00	n.a.	0	0.00	n.a.
Reference	3	19.48	6.49	3	21.48	7.16	3	22.97	7.66	1	7.99	7.99
Religion	2	13.98	6.99	4	30.96	7.74	3	20.93	6.98	2	15.98	7.99
Science	n.a.	n.a.	n.a.	1	6.95	6.95	0	0.00	n.a.	0	0.00	n.a.
Self-help	6	46.82	7.80	3	28.93	9.64	2	15.98	7.99	1	7.99	7.99
Social science	1	7.99	7.99	n.a.	n.a.	n.a.	0	0.00	n.a.	0	0.00	n.a.
Sports and recreation	2	14.98	7.49	3	23.97	7.99	3	20.97	6.99	1	7.99	7.99
Study aids	n.a.	n.a.	n.a.	n.a.	n.a.	n.a.	0	0.00	n.a.	0	0.00	n.a.
Technology and engineering	n.a.	n.a.	n.a.	n.a.	n.a.	n.a.	0	0.00	n.a.	0	0.00	n.a.
Transportation	n.a.	n.a.	n.a.	n.a.	n.a.	n.a.	1	14.00	14.00	0	0.00	n.a.
Travel	n.a.	n.a.	n.a.	1	6.95	6.95	1	4.95	4.95	0	0.00	n.a.
True crime	51	378.49	7.42	53	389.47	7.35	52	388.48	7.47	54	412.46	7.64
Young adult	159	1,080.06	6.79	142	1,007.71	7.10	96	732.61	7.63	90	730.61	8.12
Totals	4,856	$31,087.47	$6.40	4,699	$30,523.50	$6.50	4,490	$30,089.32	$6.70	4,485	$30,589.96	$6.8

n.a. = not available.

Table 5 / Trade Paperbacks Average Per-Volume Prices, 2007–2010

	2007			2008			2009			2010		
BISAC Category	Vols.	$ Total	Prices	Vols.	$ Total	Prices	Vols.	$ Total	Prices	Vols.	$ Total	Prices
Antiques and collectibles	275	$33,306.69	$121.12	239	$6,471.72	$27.08	191	$5,204.12	$27.25	178	$4,447.37	$24.99
Architecture	717	28,801.97	40.17	694	29,074.36	41.89	692	31,060.73	44.89	711	32,459.31	45.65
Art	1,692	58,262.19	34.43	1,581	59,368.38	37.55	1,491	56,100.80	37.63	1,433	53,583.60	37.39
Bibles	291	11,662.34	40.08	363	17,891.83	49.29	307	12,484.70	40.67	424	16,537.05	39.00
Biography and autobiography	2,278	47,660.75	20.92	2,211	44,895.41	20.31	2,347	48,201.37	20.54	2,250	44,246.49	19.67
Body, mind and spirit	1,045	18,462.36	17.67	1,072	19,799.35	18.47	1,009	18,319.98	18.16	946	17,024.02	18.00
Business and economics	11,053	1,180,679.39	106.82	5,937	439,177.68	73.97	5,930	368,094.31	62.07	5,077	326,844.17	64.38
Children	9,136	95,293.74	10.43	9,099	98,172.30	10.79	9,716	105,976.59	10.91	8,296	85,288.18	10.28
Comics and graphic novels	2,167	32,904.80	15.18	2,407	34,048.57	14.15	2,173	33,503.48	15.42	1,996	31,576.96	15.82
Computers	3,809	304,573.90	79.96	3,279	285,682.16	87.12	3,795	369,895.63	97.47	3,141	201,829.19	64.26
Cooking	1,068	19,200.62	17.98	1,271	23,940.09	18.84	1,006	19,711.24	19.59	1,053	20,627.89	19.59
Crafts and hobbies	906	18,399.77	20.31	943	18,840.65	19.98	1,002	19,331.96	19.29	1,049	20,379.93	19.43
Design	415	14,902.92	35.91	381	13,021.49	34.18	397	14,690.39	37.00	425	27,847.76	65.52
Drama	578	10,493.96	18.16	521	9,719.82	18.66	581	12,607.20	21.70	475	8,108.47	17.07
Education	4,166	154,046.24	36.98	3,929	146,190.54	37.21	3,262	135,148.69	41.43	3,133	125,231.39	39.97
Family and relationships	983	17,918.59	18.23	951	16,908.59	17.78	884	17,351.78	19.63	741	13,721.52	18.52
Fiction	9,517	168,794.52	17.74	9,480	154,544.25	16.30	9,694	167,906.96	17.32	8,638	143,867.70	16.66
Foreign language study	1,209	42,048.22	34.78	1,405	42,411.50	30.19	977	31,564.73	32.31	998	32,853.74	32.92
Games	847	14,314.60	16.90	800	13,664.44	17.08	787	13,844.60	17.59	782	12,889.58	16.48
Gardening	241	4,787.39	19.86	368	6,967.28	18.93	256	5,364.93	20.96	238	5,481.21	23.03
Health and fitness	1,539	34,458.41	22.39	1,373	33,213.71	24.19	1,333	31,558.58	23.67	1,227	32,105.12	26.17
History	6,743	237,306.47	35.19	5,856	186,490.43	31.85	6,436	204,677.72	31.80	6,549	225,110.72	34.37
House and home	327	6,774.33	20.72	295	5,966.45	20.23	226	4,963.14	21.96	198	4,153.36	20.98
Humor	477	6,337.84	13.29	463	6,245.21	13.49	486	6,700.28	13.79	417	5,914.77	14.18

Language arts and disciplines	2,022	104,307.32	51.59	1,654	88,284.87	53.38	2,088	137,490.40	65.85	2,147	132,808.27	61.86
Law	2,857	230,700.59	80.75	3,781	435,331.41	115.14	2,711	204,427.95	75.41	2,945	204,318.48	69.38
Literary collections	559	24,407.35	43.66	540	19,026.29	35.23	581	20,338.04	35.01	640	22,888.49	35.76
Literary criticism	1,577	57,723.82	36.60	1,446	52,882.23	36.57	1,770	68,422.50	38.66	1,621	56,057.87	34.58
Mathematics	989	74,089.98	74.91	961	59,407.06	61.82	385	61,007.20	68.93	786	51,549.94	65.59
Medical	4,153	287,874.33	69.32	3,986	298,247.53	74.82	3,337	300,540.69	76.34	4,050	271,044.35	66.92
Music	2,659	71,667.90	26.95	2,921	63,289.38	21.67	2,375	69,079.36	23.22	2,865	65,494.64	22.86
Nature	698	18,134.27	25.98	604	15,354.00	25.42	513	16,565.41	27.02	505	14,035.13	27.79
Performing arts	1,100	33,474.19	30.43	991	30,729.49	31.01	334	31,428.80	33.65	1,003	34,080.72	33.98
Pets	321	5,627.67	17.53	292	5,460.59	18.70	299	5,683.91	19.01	250	4,374.55	17.50
Philosophy	1,619	52,920.03	32.69	1,271	39,313.80	30.93	1,465	50,292.43	34.33	1,196	41,505.73	34.70
Photography	480	15,330.39	31.94	535	17,583.24	32.87	539	16,778.30	31.13	524	15,965.44	30.47
Poetry	1,863	32,019.27	17.19	1,784	29,429.78	16.50	1,720	29,025.11	16.88	1,569	26,301.42	16.76
Political science	3,663	217,800.56	59.46	3,142	118,071.58	37.58	3,220	122,070.40	37.91	3,553	143,994.38	40.53
Psychology	1,575	71,221.17	45.22	1,377	56,963.01	41.37	1,256	54,111.63	43.08	1,464	62,267.59	42.53
Reference	1,276	83,832.08	65.70	1,353	93,313.31	68.97	1,307	118,538.30	90.69	1,079	86,003.94	79.71
Religion	5,549	113,803.78	20.51	5,796	116,639.69	20.12	6,052	128,974.55	21.31	6,108	133,297.42	21.82
Science	2,346	174,316.32	74.30	2,099	148,609.73	70.80	2,462	192,498.92	78.19	2,233	138,800.61	62.16
Self-help	1,216	20,571.68	16.92	1,148	19,714.93	17.17	1,047	18,675.96	17.84	1,048	18,770.49	17.91
Social science	4,061	156,469.26	38.53	4,037	162,110.83	40.16	3,998	169,968.27	42.51	3,886	154,261.42	39.70
Sports and recreation	1,381	31,400.10	22.74	1,331	31,637.86	23.77	1,259	29,445.35	23.39	1,179	26,652.13	22.61
Study aids	682	21,836.71	32.02	880	28,279.44	32.14	669	20,617.83	30.82	1,502	60,611.38	40.35
Technology and engineering	2,689	375,124.65	139.50	2,583	397,972.78	154.07	2 681	410,478.85	153.11	1,613	130,517.48	80.92
Transportation	414	14,615.31	35.30	430	16,891.62	39.28	459	16,804.27	36.61	458	15,645.10	34.16
Travel	3,449	72,525.62	21.03	3,077	62,556.02	20.33	2 852	58,486.95	20.51	2,478	50,664.99	20.45
True crime	154	2,872.86	18.65	144	2,616.49	18.17	156	2,964.75	19.00	179	3,734.43	20.86
Young adult	3,108	43,036.58	13.85	2,555	35,166.01	13.76	2 462	41,325.07	16.79	2,176	31,640.71	14.54
Totals	113,939	$4,969,095.80	$43.61	105,636	$4,157,589.68	$39.36	105 375	$4,130,305.11	$39.20	99,432	$3,489,416.60	$35.09

Table 6 / Audiobook Average Per-Volume Prices, 2007–2010

	2007			2008			2009			2010		
BISAC Category	**Vols.**	**$ Total**	**Prices**	**Vols.**	**$ Total**	**Prices**	**Vols.**	**$ Total**	**Prices**	**Vols.**	**$ Total**	**Prices**
Antiques and collectibles	1	$11.95	$11.95	n.a.	n.a.	n.a.	1	$74.95	$74.95	3	$109.97	$36.66
Architecture	n.a.	n.a.	n.a.	2	74.94	37.47	0	0.00	n.a.	3	119.97	39.99
Art	5	200.89	40.18	5	204.96	40.99	7	415.86	59.41	9	523.90	58.21
Bibles	34	1,749.17	51.45	20	836.66	41.83	9	679.75	75.53	6	282.94	47.16
Biography and autobiography	453	20,173.61	44.53	641	30,161.85	47.05	685	34,762.98	50.75	697	35,648.73	51.15
Body, mind and spirit	81	2,715.33	33.52	83	3,177.53	38.28	87	3,302.01	37.95	68	2,288.41	33.65
Business and economics	295	10,079.10	34.17	426	16,843.14	39.54	436	20,121.06	46.15	322	16,097.43	49.99
Children	876	25,229.59	28.80	733	22,787.18	31.09	832	30,132.89	36.22	767	28,975.60	37.78
Comics and graphic novels	n.a.	n.a.	n.a.	n.a.	n.a.	n.a.	0	0.00	n.a.	0	0.00	n.a.
Computers	n.a.	n.a.	n.a.	4	124.91	31.23	5	234.95	46.99	2	89.99	45.00
Cooking	7	247.78	35.40	4	58.83	14.71	14	625.78	44.70	2	89.94	44.97
Crafts and hobbies	10	269.58	26.96	9	379.79	42.20	4	154.88	38.72	1	24.98	24.98
Design	n.a.	n.a.	n.a.	n.a.	n.a.	n.a.	0	0.00	n.a.	0	0.00	n.a.
Drama	27	803.01	29.74	48	1,760.14	36.67	151	5,214.79	34.54	89	3,049.78	34.27
Education	27	1,090.65	40.39	17	506.32	29.78	22	997.47	45.34	18	738.98	41.05
Family and relationships	47	1,481.66	31.52	73	2,681.09	36.73	54	2,128.07	39.41	69	2,833.82	41.07
Fiction	3,644	160,624.65	44.08	4,379	212,093.98	48.43	6,278	330,348.73	52.62	7,360	371,119.37	50.42
Foreign language study	314	12,928.46	41.17	394	14,826.58	37.63	260	10,592.04	40.74	156	7,625.55	48.88
Games	n.a.	n.a.	n.a.	1	14.95	14.95	6	84.74	14.12	0	0.00	n.a.
Gardening	3	91.85	30.62	2	79.94	39.97	0	0.00	n.a.	6	286.89	47.82
Health and fitness	60	1,913.20	31.89	83	2,765.84	33.32	82	3,779.22	46.09	83	3,491.53	42.07
History	480	23,208.18	48.35	577	31,569.53	54.71	450	25,959.35	57.69	533	31,063.46	58.28
House and home	1	29.95	29.95	n.a.	n.a.	n.a.	0	0.00	n.a.	0	0.00	n.a.
Humor	59	1,788.54	30.31	65	2,353.30	36.20	79	3,347.29	42.37	91	3,360.45	36.93

Language arts and disciplines	31	1,718.18	55.43	14	517.38	36.96	18	839.65	46.65	11	367.64	33.42
Law	24	1,426.92	59.46	18	975.80	54.21	9	447.79	49.75	11	653.89	59.44
Literary collections	16	459.60	28.73	16	622.55	38.91	20	646.71	32.34	13	647.69	49.82
Literary criticism	18	641.35	35.63	35	1,736.31	49.61	20	848.60	42.43	17	725.61	42.68
Mathematics	1	89.99	89.99	n.a.	n.a.	n.a.	0	0.00	n.a.	0	0.00	n.a.
Medical	20	1,371.08	68.55	25	2,415.28	96.61	13	788.59	60.66	21	769.57	36.65
Music	121	3,337.78	27.58	144	4,241.96	29.46	108	4,148.22	38.41	68	2,431.92	35.76
Nature	21	694.44	33.07	27	1,057.98	39.18	37	1,742.43	47.09	55	2,273.20	41.33
Performing arts	18	456.75	25.38	39	1,494.32	38.32	21	970.78	46.23	16	649.63	40.60
Pets	10	292.79	29.28	20	681.06	34.05	23	1,000.67	43.51	49	1,873.21	38.23
Philosophy	24	960.23	40.01	37	1,529.12	41.33	36	1,850.21	51.39	37	2,008.03	54.27
Photography	n.a.	n.a.	n.a.	n.a.	n.a.	n.a.	0	0.00	n.a.	0	0.00	n.a.
Poetry	54	1,312.04	24.30	45	1,164.63	25.88	50	1,794.08	35.88	27	897.47	33.24
Political science	151	6,186.44	40.97	174	7,684.54	44.16	177	8,795.18	49.69	219	10,629.27	48.54
Psychology	30	1,085.65	36.19	31	1,158.63	37.38	54	2,815.00	52.13	40	1,876.25	46.91
Reference	7	238.70	34.10	15	491.73	32.78	7	283.85	40.55	1	69.99	69.99
Religion	377	10,205.68	27.07	313	9,452.23	30.20	418	14,002.55	33.50	360	11,915.78	33.10
Science	30	1,191.99	39.73	61	2,964.04	48.59	64	3,055.70	47.75	64	3,295.01	51.48
Self-help	297	8,200.73	27.61	207	6,205.85	29.98	289	11,067.31	38.30	187	7,382.32	39.48
Social science	63	2,237.70	35.52	55	2,209.62	40.17	79	3,978.46	50.36	89	4,235.55	47.59
Sports and recreation	45	1,729.93	38.44	57	2,265.59	39.75	41	1,877.15	45.78	57	2,737.67	48.03
Study aids	9	390.20	43.36	18	1,207.83	67.10	21	712.23	33.92	7	135.88	19.41
Technology and engineering	12	406.58	33.88	10	520.92	52.09	7	339.94	48.56	23	1,226.54	53.33
Transportation	n.a.	n.a.	n.a.	n.a.	n.a.	n.a.	3	109.97	36.66	7	323.93	46.28
Travel	45	2,080.75	46.24	39	1,744.45	44.73	15	773.58	51.57	44	2,195.09	49.89
True crime	30	1,256.85	41.90	59	3,033.48	51.41	45	2,281.13	50.69	36	1,900.35	52.79
Young adult	273	10,884.11	39.87	269	12,244.65	45.52	527	23,638.46	44.85	830	37,265.15	44.90
Totals	8,151	$323,493.61	$39.69	9,294	$410,921.41	$44.21	11,564	$561,765.05	$48.58	12,574	$606,308.33	$48.22

n.a. = not available.

(continued from page 493)

other hand, continued to fall, declining 10.48 percent. And after steady increases over the last few years, audiobook prices (Table 6) saw a drop of 0.74 percent in 2010.

Average book prices for fiction were also mixed in 2010. Hardcover fiction titles priced at less than $81 edged up 13 cents (0.46 percent) and mass market fiction increased 12 cents (1.80 percent), but trade fiction slipped 3.81 percent to $16.66. Audiobook fiction also fell, losing 4.18 percent.

Average prices for hardcovers under $81 in the important children's category fell 0.66 percent in 2010. Children's mass market paperbacks, however, rose 1.47 percent while the more important sector of trade paperbacks saw a decline of 5.77 percent. Children's audiobook prices continued to rise (up 4.31 percent) even as output declined.

Young adult prices declined in 2010. Prices in the hardcovers under $81 sector fell by 2.15 percent while trade paperbacks plunged 13.4 percent and YA audiobooks slipped 0.11 percent.

Hardcover categories (Table 2) showing substantial price increases in 2010 were body, mind, and spirit (up 29.23 percent), crafts and hobbies (12.63 percent), design (14.78 percent), games (15.55 percent), humor (10.84 percent), music (11.40 percent), philosophy (14.05 percent), photography (34.02 percent), reference (11.45 percent), religion (11.30 percent), self-help (19.02 percent), transportation (12.21 percent), and true crime (18.56 percent). Double-digit declines were seen in books on computers (down 14.07), language arts and disciplines (down 13.76 percent), poetry (down 10.10 percent), science (down 10.02 percent), and study aids (down 13.83 percent).

In the trade paperback sector, there were some substantial swings in prices—down more than 34 percent for computer books and more than 47 percent in the area of technology and engineering, while design books (a small universe) rose just over 77 percent and study aids were up 30.9 percent.

The rise in audiobook prices generally stalled or declined in 2010, with the most popular categories of biography and autobiography rising only 0.78 percent and history by 1.03 percent. (Fiction, children's, and YA sectors are discussed above.)

'Black Swan' Confronts Book Exports and Imports in 2010

Albert N. Greco
Professor of Marketing, Gabelli School of Business, Fordham University
E-mail agreco@fordham.edu

In 2007 Nassim Nicholas Taleb published his groundbreaking study *The Black Swan: The Impact of the Highly Improbable.* The book was viewed as an intellectual assault on the use of sophisticated mathematical models employed by hedge funds, private equity firms, and investment banks in the United States and in major financial centers around the world.

Taleb warned of possible global financial crises—events that unfortunately materialized within a few months of the book's publication. Two hedge funds managed by Lehman Brothers imploded in June 2007. By August the phrase "subprime mortgages" was appearing in newspapers, magazines, and television news reports on a daily basis. And the financial literature covered these events in great detail, including the works of Bhide (2010), Frydman and Goldberg (2011), and Borio and Disyatat (2010).

Clearly Taleb's book was, and remains, an important contribution to the financial literature. However, what do Taleb's theses have to do with U.S. book exports and imports?

In 2010 the U.S. book industry confronted its own "Black Swan," triggering a series of events that will change permanently the domestic and global structure of this industry.

At first glance, the book export and import data sets released in March 2011 by the International Trade Administration (ITA) revealed some deeply unsettling trends. Revenue data on U.S. domestic exports of books in 2010 showed a modest increase, although totals were still down from the high point reached in 2008 (Figure 1).

Figure 2 indicates another modest increase in total export units, although export units had been dropping precipitously since 2003. Unfortunately, similar patterns were evident in import revenues (Figure 3), also down sharply from 2007, and units (Figure 4), down from the 2006 high.

The statistical tables provide a clear understanding of the state of U.S. book exports and imports. While exports increased between 2004 and 2008, the results for 2009 and again for 2010 were, at best, disappointing, slipping 8.06 percent between 2008 and 2010. Imports in 2008 also posted the best results since 1970, yet the decline between 2008 and 2010 was 20.15 percent. Table 1 outlines in detail exports and imports since 1970.

Table 2 lists total U.S. book industry shipments (i.e., revenues) between 1970 and 2010. The year 2007 represents the high point of revenues, reaching $29.296 billion. The impact of the recession and general economic uncertainty depressed total sales for several years; they declined 1.16 percent between 2007 and 2010. During those same years, exports declined 5.83 percent; and exports as a percentage of sales stood at 6.9 percent in 2010, down from a high of 9.4 percent in 1990 and 7.3 percent in 2007. Table 2 lists these totals.

Figure 1 / U.S. Domestic Exports—Annual Data—Revenues

Figure 2 / U.S. Domestic Exports—Annual Data—Units

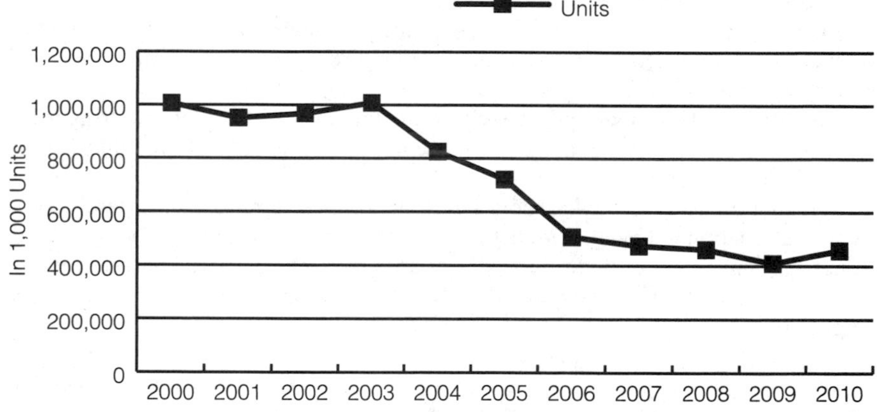

A review of the top ten export destinations in 2010 revealed no significant shift in market share. Canada, as usual, remained the United States' preeminent trading partner, accounting for more than $960.3 million. The United Kingdom was a distant second at $281.46 million, but declined 1.7 percent from 2009 ($286.3 million). Impressive totals were posted by Mexico (up 7.6 percent), India (up 24.2 percent), and, surprisingly, China (up 30.7 percent between 2009 and 2010 and up 124.4 percent between 2000 and 2010).

Japan also experienced a positive result in 2010 (up 12.3 percent). However, the devastating March 2011 earthquake and tsunami in Japan are certain to adversely affect its international trade in 2011 and beyond.

Table 3 provides an overview of these results.

Table 4 is a more-focused list of book exports to the top 25 nations between 2006 and 2010. What is striking about this cluster of markets was the steep

Figure 3 / U.S. Imports for Consumption—Annual Data—Revenues

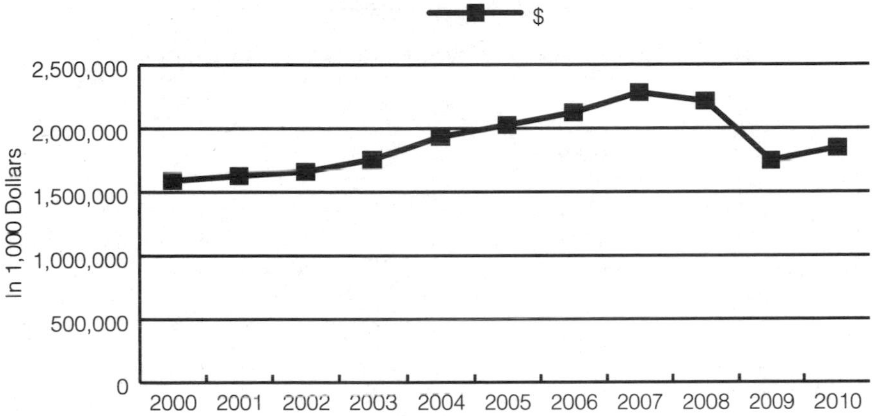

Figure 4 / U.S. Imports—Annual Data—Units

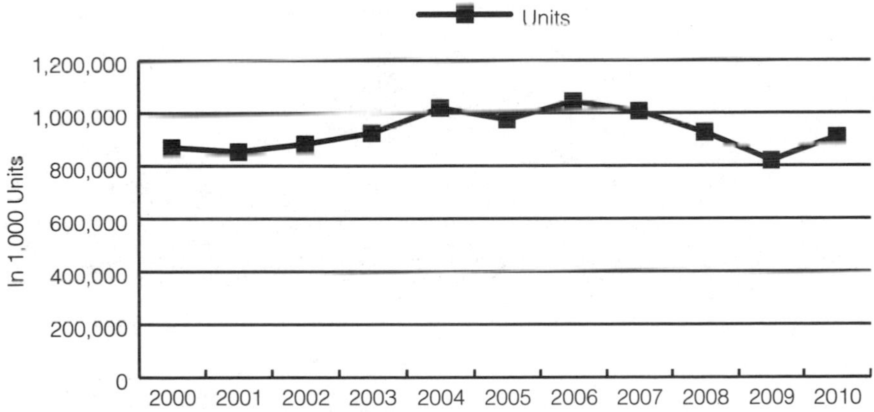

decline in exports between 2009 and 2010 to many of the United States' traditional trading partners in Europe (Germany was down 13.8 percent, the Netherlands 12.1 percent) and in the important Asian and the Pacific Rim areas (Australia was down 3.2 percent, Singapore 7.6 percent, Hong Kong 9.1 percent, Taiwan 30.1 percent). Impressive increases were generated by Brazil (up 23.1 percent), South Africa (33.9 percent), and Thailand (56.9 percent).

Overall, the top 25 nations were up 2.2 percent; all of the other nations tracked by ITA posted an 11.4 percent decline. The final 2010 tally stood at a slim increase of 1.2 percent. Table 4 outlines these patterns.

The top ten sources of book imports revealed a slight shift in market shares. China again emerged as the largest source of printed books (although it is unlikely that very many books imported from that nation are printed and published in China). Canada's share slipped in 2010, falling 14.3 percent; the United King-

Table 1 / U.S. Trade in Books, 1970–2010
($ million)

Year	U.S. Book Exports	U.S. Book Imports	Ratio: U.S. Book Exports/Imports
1970	$174.9	$92.0	1.90
1975	269.3	147.6	1.82
1980	518.9	306.5	1.69
1985	591.2	564.2	1.05
1990	1,415.1	855.1	1.65
1995	1,779.5	1,184.5	1.50
1996	1,775.6	1,240.1	1.43
1997	1,896.6	1,297.5	1.46
1998	1,841.8	1,383.7	1.33
1999	1,871.1	1,441.4	1.30
2000	1,877.0	1,590.5	1.18
2001	1,712.3	1,627.8	1.05
2002	1,681.2	1,661.2	1.01
2003	1,693.6	1,755.9	0.96
2004	1,740.5	1,934.4	0.90
2005	1,894.3	2,026.3	0.93
2006	1,948.1	2,124.3	0.92
2007	2,135.2	2,281.3	0.94
2008	2,187.0	2,313.8	0.95
2009	1,987.3	1,746.1	1.13
2010	2,010.8	1,847.5	1.09

Source: U.S. Department of Commerce, International Trade Administration. All totals are rounded off to one decimal point. Data for individual categories may not add to totals due to statistical rounding. Due to changes in the classification of "U.S. traded products" and what constitutes products classified as "books," data prior to 1990 are not strictly comparable to data beginning in 1990. All totals are rounded off to one decimal point. Commerce often updates previously released data incorporating changes in collection methodologies.

dom inched ahead of Canada, with an increase of 8.7 percent. Italy (up 21.4 percent) and Mexico (up 32.7 percent, in all probability more printed than printed-and-published books) also had positive results in 2010. Table 5 lists the figures. Also see Guerrero, Clouse, Platt, Iskyan, and Chaze (2011); and Kattel (2010).

As for the top 25 sources of books imported into the United States, China's commanding presence ($3.87 billion between 2006 and 2010) represented the largest share of the revenue market, easily outpacing Canada ($1.35 billion between 2006 and 2010). In 2010 China generated an impressive 13.5 percent increase ($807.1 million) over its 2009 results ($711.4 million). Other countries with strong increases in 2010 included Japan (11.4 percent) and South Korea (18.0 percent).

Other results were impressive, with Italy up 21.4 percent, Denmark up a remarkable 274.2 percent, and Sweden up 45.3 percent . The top 25 countries together climbed 6 percent between 2009 and 2010, as nations outside of the top

Table 2 / U.S. Book Industry Shipments Compared with U.S. Book Exports: 1970–2010
($ million)

Year	Total Shipments	U.S. Book Exports	Exports as a Percent of Total Shipments
1970	$2,434.2	$174.9	7.2
1975	3,536.5	269.3	7.6
1980	6,114.4	518.9	8.5
1985	10,165.7	591.2	5.8
1990	14,982.6	1,415.1	9.4
1995	19,471.0	1,779.5	9.1
1996	20,285.7	1,775.6	8.8
1997	21,131.9	1,896.6	9.0
1998	22,480.0	1,841.8	8.2
1999	24,129.9	1,871.1	7.8
2000	25,235.0	1,877.0	7.4
2001	26,096.0	1,712.3	6.6
2002	27,203.0	1,681.2	6.2
2003	26,326.0	1,693.6	6.4
2004	27,903.0	1,740.5	6.2
2005	27,905.0	1,894.3	6.8
2006	28,236.0	1,948.1	6.9
2007	29,296.0	2,135.2	7.3
2008	28,266.0	2,187.0	7.7
2009	28,314.0	1,987.3	7.0
2010	28,957.0	2,010.8	6.9

Source: U.S. Department of Commerce, International Trade Administration; and calculations by the author. Due to changes in the classification of U.S. traded products and what constitutes products classified as "books," data prior to 1990 are not strictly comparable to data beginning in 1990. All totals are rounded off to one decimal point. Data for individual categories may not add to totals due to statistical rounding. Commerce often updates previously released data incorporating changes in collection methodologies. Data for 2008, 2009, and 2010 revised based on new datasets from the U.S. Department of Commerce.

25 fell by 4.5 percent. Table 6 lists these results as well as the overall growth rate of 5.8 percent of all countries monitored by ITA.

Between 2000 and 2004 China sent the United States slightly more than 1 million books (representing 23.4 percent of all shipments), with Singapore a distant second at 215,000 (a 4.7 percent market share). Overall, the Asian and Pacific Rim nations shipped more than 2.1 million books to the United States, accounting for slightly more than 48 percent of all imports. Table 7 details these trends.

The detailed 2005–2010 statistical data in Table 8 reveal the continuing importance of China in the U.S. book import market. In 2010 its book tallies were up 18.1 percent, accounting for more than 2.36 million units between 2005 and 2010 and a commanding market share of 41.5 percent during those years. See Table 8 for the other Asian and Pacific Rim countries (2005–2010) and Table 9 for the years 2000–2010.

(text continues on page 515)

Table 3 / Top Ten Export Destinations for U.S. Books, 1999–2010
($'000)

Country	2000	2001	2002	2003	2004	2005	2006	2007	2008	2009	2010	Percent Change 2009–2010
Canada	756,667	727,698	742,619	776,441	812,833	866,173	918,250	962,509	999,309	934,517	960,308	2.8
United Kingdom	264,230	250,031	270,622	274,596	289,196	284,993	291,376	300,150	340,864	286,309	281,463	-1.7
Australia	116,302	66,010	70,806	76,067	78,549	100,769	107,754	110,922	110,922	93,885	90,905	-3.2
Mexico	73,886	63,804	64,938	68,132	66,087	102,658	71,316	79,685	78,578	74,430	80,080	7.6
Japan	123,100	129,316	100,804	95,835	98,436	93,394	78,219	78,301	76,594	66,238	74,372	12.3
Singapore	60,669	48,985	49,570	48,358	57,974	53,395	49,734	52,689	58,541	55,703	51,472	-7.6
Germany	34,341	34,007	29,081	34,128	27,174	35,789	38,298	76,176	44,837	42,457	36,594	-13.8
South Korea	36,793	35,499	29,131	24,698	26,670	38,557	33,432	44,400	42,922	40,234	38,909	-3.3
India	14,430	15,992	19,513	16,807	18,967	22,497	21,757	40,022	32,537	25,340	31,477	24.2
China	12,019	10,711	11,739	15,491	18,110	16,532	25,777	29,715	28,058	20,640	26,972	30.7

Source: U.S. Department of Commerce, International Trade Administration.

Note: Individual shipments are excluded from the foreign trade data if valued under $2,500. All totals are rounded off to one decimal point. Data for individual categories may not add to totals due to statistical rounding. Commerce often updates previously released data incorporating changes in collection methodologies.

Table 4 / U.S. Book Exports to 25 Principal Countries: 2006–2010
($'000)

	Value					Percent Change
Country	**2006**	**2007**	**2008**	**2009**	**2010**	**2009–2010**
Canada	$918,250	$962,509	$999,309	$934,517	$960,308	2.8%
United Kingdom	291,376	300,150	340,864	286,309	281,463	-1.7
Australia	107,754	110,922	105,822	93,885	90,905	-3.2
Mexico	71,316	79,685	78,578	74,430	80,080	7.6
Japan	78,219	78,301	76,594	66,238	74,372	12.3
Singapore	49,734	52,689	58,541	55,703	51,472	-7.6
Germany	38,298	76,176	44,837	42,457	36,594	-13.8
South Korea	33,432	44,400	42,922	40,234	38,909	-3.3
India	21,757	40,022	32,537	25,340	31,477	24.2
Hong Kong	17,844	19,722	18,879	24,677	22,430	-9.1
Philippines	19,131	18,883	19,997	21,281	17,763	-16.5
China	25,777	29,715	28,058	20,640	26,972	30.7
United Arab Emirates	5,483	9,999	17,349	19,111	19,975	4.5
Brazil	13,758	21,676	21,829	18,997	23,390	23.1
South Africa	21,172	18,627	22,772	18,100	24,232	33.9
Taiwan	16,144	18,663	15,065	17,182	12,011	-30.1
Saudi Arabia	9,804	10,109	12,770	15,707	15,345	-2.3
Netherlands	11,879	12,260	11,759	13,723	12,065	-12.1
Malaysia	9,801	9,913	9,946	9,799	9,345	-4.6
Nigeria	7,970	11,635	14,044	9,407	10,236	8.8
Thailand	6,799	7,922	10,102	7,961	12,488	56.9
New Zealand	11,731	14,385	12,000	7,905	9,478	19.9
Ireland	4,946	5,511	6,580	6,725	6,575	-2.2
Jordan	3,827	5,436	4,265	4,999	6,895	39.7
Argentina	5,084	13,461	7,028	6,140	6,708	9.2
Total, Top 25 Countries	$1,807,575	$1,970,011	$2,016,978	$1,848,463	$1,881	2.2
All Others	$140.53	$165.18	$170.07	$138.82	$129.19	-11.4
Grand Total	$1,948,103	$2,135,195	$2,187,049	$1,987,282	$2,010.80	1.2%

Source: U.S. Department of Commerce, International Trade Administration. Note: Individual shipments are excluded from the foreign trade data if valued under $2,500. All totals are rounded off to one decimal point. Data for individual categories may not add to totals due to statistical rounding. Commerce often updates previously released data incorporating changes in collection methodologies.

Table 5 / Top Ten Import Sources of Books: 2000–2010
($'000)

Country	2000	2001	2002	2003	2004	2005	2006	2007	2008	2009	2010	Percent Change 2009–2010
China	220,895	267,582	338,489	413,065	5,335,241	605,229	724,742	815,677	806,695	711,438	807,134	13.5
United Kingdom	317,660	303,897	267,853	287,972	304,619	307,517	286,624	332,579	289,280	195,495	212,502	8.7
Canada	229,045	243,689	251,085	275,053	289,423	281,120	292,273	298,633	308,340	247,509	212,040	-14.3
Singapore	86,630	96,325	100,610	103,383	113,900	115,314	115,609	120,867	115,740	93,988	82,894	-11.8
Hong Kong	224,834	229,719	223,452	189,783	185,963	176,079	136,617	125,138	107,406	76,092	74,031	-2.7
Germany	57,345	53,092	55,993	52,055	57,353	68,211	76,657	82,088	88,075	56,780	51,717	-8.9
Japan	59,268	49,956	47,198	45,277	48,726	50,765	63,822	88,062	96,681	52,285	58,238	11.4
South Korea	29,430	35,559	40,459	39,083	46,265	54,303	54,398	54,252	55,545	47,290	55,800	18.0
Italy	94,983	87,779	83,360	84,167	78,567	69,463	69,571	69,393	62,430	40,800	49,531	21.4
Mexico	24,656	19,272	18,627	21,828	22,627	40,956	47,089	32,380	30,667	29,559	38,240	32.7

Source: U.S. Department of Commerce, International Trade Administration.

All totals are rounded off to one decimal point. Data for individual categories may not add to totals due to statistical rounding. Commerce often updates previously released data incorporating changes in collection methodologies.

Table 6 / U.S. Book Imports from 25 Principal Countries: 2006–2010
($'000)

Country	Value					Percent Change
	2006	2007	2008	2009	2010	2009–2010
China	$724,742	$815,677	$806,695	$711,438	$807,134	13.5
Canada	292,273	298,633	308,340	247,509	201,040	-14.3
United Kingdom	286,624	332,579	289,280	195,495	212,502	8.7
Singapore	115,609	120,867	115,740	93,988	82,894	-11.8
Hong Kong	136,617	125,138	107,406	76,092	74,031	-2.7
Germany	76,657	82,088	88,075	56,780	51,717	-8.9
Japan	63,822	88,062	96,681	52,285	58,238	11.4
South Korea	54,398	54,252	55,545	47,290	55,800	18.0
Italy	69,571	69,393	62,430	40,800	49,531	21.4
Mexico	47,089	32,380	30,667	29,559	39,240	32.7
Colombia	22,102	36,274	31,159	27,479	27,829	1.3
Spain	36,901	32,646	32,679	26,274	22,593	-14.0
India	14,222	16,439	16,161	19,180	22,405	16.8
France	31,006	25,562	22,503	17,222	17,253	0.2
Malaysia	14,011	13,816	15,063	12,666	12,777	0.9
Israel	12,874	14,309	13,686	11,122	11,895	6.9
Thailand	19,476	18,747	15,454	9,345	14,683	57.1
Netherlands	8,570	8,084	21,557	7,901	6,436	-18.5
Taiwan	8,860	9,866	10,303	7,820	7,803	-0.2
Australia	6,828	6,811	6,564	7,673	7,171	-6.5
Denmark	1,095	2,086	3,165	1,751	6,553	274.2
United Arab Emirates	6,748	6,075	6,578	6,095	5,447	-10.6
Indonesia	3,431	3,254	6,145	3,249	3,630	11.7
Brazil	5,994	5,882	2,380	3,163	4,222	33.5
Sweden	5,527	5,526	3,974	2,568	3,731	45.3
Total: Top 25 Countries	$2,083,079	$2,235,137	$2,174,609	$1,719,275	$1,817	6.0
All Others	$41,227	$46,138	$39,203	$26,801	$30	-4.5
Grand Total	$2,124,306	$2,281,275	$2,113,812	$1,746,076	$1,847	5.8

Source: U.S. Department of Commerce, International Trade Administration. All totals are rounded off to one decimal point. Data for individual categories may not add to totals due to statistical rounding. Individual shipments are excluded from the foreign trade data if valued under $2,500. Commerce often updates previously released data incorporating changes in collection methodologies.

Table 7 / Book Units Imported from 11 Asian and Pacific Rim Nations: 2000–2004
('000 Units)

Country	2000	2001	2002	2003	2004	Total 2000–2004
China	151,594	183,228	213,236	232,049	284,844	1,064,951
Singapore	34,945	40,582	44,076	45,085	50,762	215,450
South Korea	12,324	17,586	22,082	20,443	36,910	109,345
Hong Kong	130,582	121,142	117,091	102,881	107,997	579,693
India	1,436	3,782	2,777	4,015	9,993	22,003
Malaysia	5,739	5,245	8,111	9,330	6,142	34,567
Taiwan	8,637	6,648	6,827	6,966	6,562	35,640
Thailand	6,906	7,665	8,293	7,891	4,765	35,520
Japan	18,741	12,668	12,293	12,724	11,311	67,737
Indonesia	2,583	1,273	2,864	1,948	3,765	12,433
Australia	2,573	4,292	2,645	2,171	2,874	14,555
Total	376,060	404,111	440,295	445,503	525,925	2,191,894
Total All Imported Books	869,114	858,310	882,606	924,184	1,019,474	4,553,688
11 Nations Percentage of All Imported Books	43.3	47.1	49.9	48.2	51.6	48.1

Source: U.S. Department of Commerce, International Trade Administration. All totals are rounded off to one decimal point. Data for individual categories may not add to totals due to statistical rounding. Commerce often updates previously released data incorporating changes in collection methodologies.

Table 8 / Book Units Imported from 11 Asian and the Pacific Rim Nations: 2005–2010
('000 Units)

Country	2005	2006	2007	2008	2009	2010	Percent Change 2009–2010	Total 2005–2010
China	318,269	394,795	432,716	420,852	362,395	427,841	18.1	2,356,868
Singapore	47,467	47,948	52,607	53,522	41,237	36,223	-12.2	279,004
South Korea	34,671	33,465	34,823	38,783	37,280	49,695	33.3	228,717
Hong Kong	96,742	65,752	60,140	47,097	33,692	29,700	-11.8	333,123
India	7,628	6,723	7,392	5,713	7,143	6,643	-7.0	41,242
Malaysia	6,796	5,950	6,836	7,287	6,096	7,264	19.2	40,229
Taiwan	6,626	6,762	6,732	6,411	5,776	6,224	7.8	38,531
Thailand	5,777	8,869	7,537	6,153	5,290	5,747	8.6	39,373
Japan	9,611	8,781	10,064	9,574	5,194	4,493	-13.5	47,717
Indonesia	4,495	2,152	2,649	4,220	2,662	2,484	-6.7	18,662
Australia	2,643	1,215	1,070	778	1,221	n.a.	n.a.	6,927
Total	540,725	582,412	622,566	600,390	507,986	576,314	—	3,430,393
Total All	975,459	1,044,165	1,007,257	926,324	819,433	909,426	5,682,064	
11 Nations Percentage of All Imported Books	55.4	55.8	61.8	64.8	62.0	63.4	60.4	

Source: U.S. Department of Commerce, International Trade Administration. All totals are rounded off to one decimal point. Data for individual categories may not add to totals due to statistical rounding. Commerce often updates previously released data incorporating changes in collection methodologies. Totals for 2001 were updated by Commerce.

n.a. = not available.

Table 9 / Book Units Imported From 11 Asian and Pacific Rim Nations: 2000–2010
('000 Units)

	2000–2010	Percent of Total Imports
China	3,421,819	33.43
Singapore	494,454	4.83
South Korea	338,062	3.30
Hong Kong	912,816	8.92
India	63,245	0.62
Malaysia	74,796	0.73
Taiwan	74,171	0.72
Thailand	74,893	0.73
Japan	115,454	1.13
Indonesia	31,095	0.30
Australia	21,482	0.21
Total	5,622,287	—
Total All Imported Books	10,235,752	—
11 Nations Percentage of All Imported Books	54.93	

Source: U.S. Department of Commerce, International Trade Administration. All totals are rounded off to one decimal point. Data for individual categories may not add to totals due to statistical rounding. Commerce often updates previously released data incorporating changes in collection methodologies.

(continued from page 509)

Looking to the Future

What other events in 2010 influenced exports and imports and will have a significantly larger impact on the years 2011–2015?

Michael Porter, preeminent scholar of competitive strategy and analysis, insisted correctly that, when evaluating a nation's competitiveness, everything counts (Porter 1985; 1998a and 1998b). Following Porter's advice, a number of data sets were evaluated.

Books are imported into the United States to be sold to consumers or institutions (e.g., public libraries, academic libraries, governmental libraries, special libraries at corporations and laboratories) (Greco 2005). An analysis of U.S. Department of Commerce, Bureau of the Census bookstore sales data (covering national and regional chains and independent bookstores) revealed important trends. First, bookstore sales increased sharply between 1992 ($8.34 billion) and 2000 ($14.9 billion), up an impressive 78.6 percent. (To be counted as a bookstore by the Department of Commerce, a retail store had to have at least 51 percent of its revenues from books; consequently, mass merchants, price clubs, terminals, supermarkets, convenience stores, and so forth whose book sales fall below the 51 percent threshold are excluded from the department's monthly and annual tallies.) Table 10 provides monthly and annual revenues.

Table 10 / Bookstore Monthly Sales: 1992–2000
($ million)

	1992	1993	1994	1995	1996	1997	1998	1999	2000
January	790	999	1,055	1,309	1,375	1,559	1,467	1,514	1,506
February	540	568	636	720	758	825	923	990	1,091
March	536	602	635	696	743	813	883	976	1,031
April	524	583	610	689	751	806	854	934	975
May	553	613	684	786	855	893	920	977	1,105
June	589	619	726	808	839	876	939	1,032	1,123
July	593	608	679	783	787	830	882	1,024	1,049
August	895	985	1,156	1,248	1,361	1,301	1,385	1,388	1,595
September	863	905	1,023	1,103	1,042	1,159	1,247	1,242	1,407
October	647	669	733	747	899	926	954	1,020	1,015
November	642	693	772	851	908	996	991	1,090	1,100
December	1,166	1,275	1,410	1,468	1,600	1,771	1,849	1,998	1,895
Annual Total	8,338	9,119	10,119	11,208	11,918	12,755	13,294	14,185	14,892
Percent Change	—	9.37	10.97	10.76	6.33	7.02	4.23	6.70	4.98

Source: U.S. Department of Commerce, Bureau of the Census. Monthly Retail Trade Survey.

However, the figures for 2001–2010 reveal disturbing patterns. Overall, sales at the nation's bookstores increased by 9.2 percent during that period. A detailed analysis of the data released by the Department of Commerce revealed a sharp increase between 2001 ($15.1 billion) and 2007 ($17.2 billion), but a dramatic 4.1 percent decline between 2007 and 2010 ($16.5 billion). The prognosis for 2011 (and in all likelihood through 2015) is not optimistic.

In February 2011 Borders, the nation's second-largest book chain, went into Chapter 11 bankruptcy, announcing the closing of more than 200 stores and possibly as many as 275. In March Borders's CEO also announced that the chain would reconfigure its stores, with 60 percent of the space allocated to books and the remaining 40 percent to be stocked with toys, games, and other non-book merchandise. The average Borders superstore stocks approximately 100,000 books. A 40 percent reduction means that about 40,000 books will be removed from a superstore, and some of these are books imported into the United States (imports include higher education textbooks; large, illustrated, four-color books; juvenile titles; dictionaries; and more).

Barnes & Noble, the only larger U.S. bookstore chain, reported uneven financial results for 2010, announcing that it also would reconfigure many of its stores with more non-book products (including the Nook, its e-book reader; toys and games, and so forth). Books-A-Million (the number three chain) also reported lower sales in 2010. Clearly, the amount of shelf space allocated for books will be reduced at the two largest chains, and it is likely that Books-A-Million will follow this trend. Fewer bookshelves mean fewer books for sale in stores, although all three chains expressed hope that their online book sales would increase. Table 11 has the monthly and annual data for 2001–2010.

The economic outlook for the United States remains subdued. The Congressional Budget Office (CBO) in January 2011 released its projections for 2011–2013 for annual changes in the major economic indicators. These include

Table 11 / Bookstore Monthly Sales: 2001–2010
($ million)

	2001	2002	2003	2004	2005	2006	2007	2008	2009	2010
January	1,586	1,973	2,056	2,149	2,077	2,227	2,228	2,295	2,254	2,294
February	1,070	1,001	992	1,109	1,088	1,103	1,044	1,153	1,019	1,013
March	1,063	1,009	927	1,074	1,102	1,094	1,032	1,022	997	1,013
April	935	968	977	1,024	999	989	934	1,001	966	918
May	1,071	1,118	1,109	1,113	1,121	1,178	1,139	1,156	1,116	1,087
June	1,078	1,046	1,183	1,207	1,155	1,241	1,165	1,075	1,105	1,095
July	1,006	1,038	1,131	1,173	1,216	1,138	1,224	1,123	1,105	1,080
August	1,821	1,799	2,141	2,121	2,222	2,147	2,334	2,433	2,447	2,300
September	1,407	1,491	1,575	1,562	1,556	1,559	1,580	1,489	1,625	1,525
October	1,016	998	1,047	1,070	1,065	1,058	1,128	1,043	1,026	1,000
November	1,099	1,060	1,038	1,089	1,152	1,146	1,225	1,059	1,031	1,084
December	1,958	1,949	2,067	2,201	2,260	2,140	2,175	2,058	2,041	2,088
Annual Total	15,110	15,450	16,243	16,892	17,013	17,020	17,208	16,907	16,732	16,497
Percent Change	1.46	2.25	5.13	4.00	0.72	0.04	1.10	-1.75	-1.04	-1.40

Source: U.S. Department of Commerce, Bureau of the Census. Monthly Retail Trade Survey. Book gift cards and book gift certificates: "Upon the purchase of a gift card or a gift certificate, a liability is established for the cash value of the gift card or gift certificate. Revenue from a gift card or gift certificate is recognized at the time of redemption. The liability remains on the books until the earlier of redemption, escheatment, or 60 months. After 60 months, the remaining portion of the liability is relieved and recognized as 'other Income.' It is our historical experience that the likelihood of redemption after 60 months is remote. The liability for gift cards and gift certificates is recorded in accounts payable on the Consolidated Balance Sheets."

Table 12 / Congressional Budget Office Economic Assumptions, 2010–2013

	2010	2011	2012	2013
Real GDP Percent Change	2.8	2.7	3.1	4.4
PCE Price Index Percent Change	1.8	1.3	1.2	1.7
CPI Percent Change	1.6	1.6	1.3	1.9
Three-Month T-Bill Rate (Percent)	0.1	0.3	1.1	3.6
Ten Year T-Note Rate (Percent)	3.2	3.4	3.8	4.7
Unemployment Rate (Percent)	9.6	9.4	8.4	6.4

Source: Congressional Budget Office; revised as of January 2011.
GDP: Gross Domestic Product; PCE: Personal Consumption Expenditures; CPI: Consumer Price Index; T-Bill: U.S. Treasury bills; T-Note: U.S. Treasury notes.

real gross domestic product (GDP) (which was up 2.8 percent for 2010 and is forecast to increase 4.4 percent in 2013), personal consumptions expenditures (PCE), the consumer price index (CPI), various U.S. Treasury bills and notes, and the unemployment rate. Table 12 shows these CBO projections.

The satellite and cable television business news channel CNBC reported in March 2011 that housing prices and sales "will be a real challenge . . . New home sales reached a record 47-year low this past year with an annual decrease of 14 percent." Nationally, about 23 percent of all home mortgages were "under water" in 2010—that is, the value of the property was lower than the amount owed on the mortgage. Library budgets were curtailed again in 2010, with the result that book purchases were trimmed at public, academic, special, and government libraries. All of these events affected the sale of books in the United States as well as book imports and exports. But while these trends were significant, one event in 2010 changed the course of history in the book publishing, book retailing, and the book distribution sectors.

Enter the Black Swan

E-readers have been sold in the United States for a number of years, among them the Sony Reader and the Rocket e-book. However, the first signs of an e-reader "black swan" appeared in 2007 with the introduction of an exceptionally popular device (the various Kindles released by Amazon.com), although the Kindle screen only had 16 shades of gray. Barnes & Noble also entered the market with its Nook; the first model had a screen with 16 shades of gray, but eventually a color Nook appeared.

By December 2010 it was estimated that the various Kindles and Nooks had total sales somewhere in the 3 million to 5 million range; neither Amazon.com nor Barnes & Noble has released precise sales figures. The 3 million to 5 million total does not include other devices capable of reading book content (such as smart phones and computers).

However, April 3, 2010, was the "turning point" in the history of e-readers. That was the day Apple released its iPAD (which is an "entertainment" electronic device, not just an e-reader, although it is estimated that about 70 percent of iPAD owners use their iPAD to read books). That was also the day that the black swan began to affect U.S. physical book sales, physical book exports, and physical book imports.

Between April 3 and December 31, 2010, Apple announced it sold 15 million iPADS. As many as 30 million iPADS are expected to be sold in 2011; in fact the launch in March 2011 of the iPAD 2 was overwhelming, with more than 500,000 units sold within a few days (waiting lists for the iPAD 2 were expected to last four to six weeks, or—because of the earthquake and tsunami in Japan—even longer).

Despite a sluggish economy, high unemployment rates, and problems with mortgages and retail sales, consumers in the United States bought and used their Nooks, Kindles, and iPADS to buy and download books. This trend was also evident in the library sector.

Among the results of this metamorphosis in the book industry:

- The *Wall Street Journal* reported on November 9, 2010, that John Grisham's publisher had cut the print run of his newest novel from 2.8 million printed copies to 1.5 million. In October 2010 Grisham's novel sold 160,000 print copies and 70,000 e-book downloads.
- *Crain's New York Business* reported on November 24, 2010, that former President George W. Bush's autobiography had sold 1.1 million printed books and 135,000 e-books (e-books represented about 12 percent of the total sales).
- *Publishers Weekly* reported on November 1, 2010, that numerous authors had had significant e-book sales in 2010, among them several whose e-

book sales were a third of the books' total sales. These included Stieg Larsson's *The Girl Who Kicked the Hornet's Nest,* Vince Flynn's *American Assassin,*Rick Riordan's *The Lost Hero,* and Michael Connelly's *The Reversal.*

The bottom line is clear. Printed books are in a zero-sum game with e-books. Every e-book purchased and downloaded by a consumer is a printed book that is not printed and sold, and, in many instances, a book that is not imported into the United States.

According to preliminary estimates from the Association of American Publishers, as reported by *Publishers Weekly,* e-book sales from 16 reporting companies jumped 115.8 percent in January to \$69.9 million, while no other trade segment posted a sales increase for the month.

Why did consumers buy e-readers and e-books? A review of U.S. demographic data released by the Department of Commerce revealed some reasons.

Basic consumer marketing trends have illustrated the acceptance of new technologies by certain demographic groups known as the "innovators" and the "early adopters." One such segment is the juvenile market, specifically teenagers who spend approximately \$170 billion annually on such products as music, iPODS, films, clothing, young adult books (such as the Harry Potter series and the Twilight series). They are not paying for such things as mortgages, rent, life insurance policies, and so forth.

Table 13 provides an overview of the total number of juveniles in the United States in 2010 in the ages 10–14 cohort (19.77 million) and the number likely by 2015 (20.98 million), an increase of more than 6 percent.

Table 14 outlines in more detail annual increases in the under 5 and 5–9 age groups and the 10–14.

Table 15 lists detailed information about the growing 15–19, 20–24, 25–29, 30–34, 35–39, and 40–44 cohorts in 2010 (126.66 million) and in 2015 (129.26 million). While the growth will be only 2.05 percent, individuals in these age

Table 13 / Demographic Data, Juveniles: 1980–2015
('000)

	1980	1990	2000	2006	2010	2015
Under 5 Years						
Total	16,348	18,765	19,176	20,418	21,426	22,358
Male	8,362	9,603	9,811	10,442	10,947	11,423
Female	7,986	9,162	9,365	9,976	10,479	10,935
Ages 5–9						
Total	16,700	18,042	20,550	19,710	20,726	21,623
Male	8,539	9,236	10,523	10,077	10,575	11,044
Female	8,161	8,806	10,026	9,633	10,131	10,579
Ages 10–14						
Total	18,242	17,067	20,528	20,627	19,767	20,984
Male	9,316	8,742	10,520	10,563	10,109	10,718
Female	8,926	8,325	10,008	10,065	9,658	10,265

Source: U.S. Department of Commerce, Bureau of the Census.

Table 14 / Demographic Data, Juveniles, Totals for Ages: 2000–2015
('000)

	Under 5 Years	5–9 Years	10–14 Years
2000	19,176	20,550	20,528
2001	19,354	20,241	20,898
2002	19,544	19,990	21,121
2003	19,783	19,774	21,212
2004	20,070	19,624	21,143
2005	20,315	19,558	20,879
2006	20,418	19,710	20,627
2007	20,724	19,849	20,314
2008	n.a.	n.a.	n.a.
2009	n.a.	n.a.	n.a.
2010	21,426	20,706	19,767
2015	22,358	21,623	20,984

Source: U.S. Department of Commerce, Bureau of the Census.
n.a. = not available.

Table 15 / Demographic Data, Adults 15–44: 2000–2025
('000)

Year	15–19	20–24	25–29	30–34	35–39	40–44
2000	20,219	18,963	19,382	20,511	22,707	22,442
2001	20,317	19,823	18,957	20,745	22,289	22,850
2002	20,384	20,350	18,937	20,831	21,849	22,954
2003	20,497	20,709	19,113	20,717	21,403	22,985
2004	20,737	20,957	19,539	20,467	21,047	23,050
2005	21,063	21,053	20,054	20,090	21,006	22,860
2006	21,275	20,994	20,575	19,607	21,119	22,436
2007	21,474	21,032	21,058	19,533	21,176	21,985
2010	21,770	21,779	21,418	20,400	20,287	21,010
2015	21,209	22,342	22,400	22,099	20,841	20,460
2020	22,554	21,799	22,949	23,112	22,586	21,078
2025	23,545	23,168	22,417	23,699	23,645	22,651

Source: U.S. Department of Commerce, Bureau of the Census.

clusters tend to be innovators and early adopters of new products, including technology. This group accounted for a large percentage of iPAD sales in 2010, and it is likely they will purchase a significant percentage of the 30 million iPADS in 2011.

The 15–44 age cohorts are very important to manufacturers of consumer products (durables and consumables), technology, e-readers, and e-books. However, the remaining demographic groups cannot be discounted, especially as they account for the largest percentage of net assets and disposable incomes in the United States and they traditionally have been heavy users of media products, including books. Consumer marketing data shows that the average buyer and reader of a book in the United States in 2010 was a 45-year-old female.

Table 16 / Demographic Data, Adults 45–83: 2000–2015
('000)

Year	45–49	50–54	55–59	60–64	65–74	75–84
2000	20,093	17,586	13,469	10,806	18,391	12,361
2001	20,713	18,665	13,935	11,106	18,324	12,591
2002	21,281	18,701	15,086	11,504	18,286	12,761
2003	21,766	19,043	15,725	12,113	18,355	12,887
2004	22,121	19,498	16,487	12,589	18,480	12,981
2005	22,486	20,001	17,353	13,002	18,650	13,060
2006	22,798	20,481	18,224	13,362	18,917	13,047
2007	22,861	21,013	18,236	14,476	19,352	13,024
2010	22,596	22,109	19,517	16,758	21,463	13,015
2015	21,001	22,367	21,682	18,861	26,967	n.a.
2020	20,502	20,852	21,994	21,009	32,313	n.a.
2025	21,154	20,404	20,575	21,377	36,356	n.a.

Source: U.S. Department of Commerce, Bureau of the Census.
n.a. = not available.

Between 2010 and 2015, the number of people in the 45–49, 50–54, 55–59, 60–64, and the 65–74 age clusters is forecast to increase 8.23 percent, from 102.44 million to 110.88 million.

How much did consumers spend in 2010 to buy and download consumer books? How much was spent in the other e-book categories? In order to answer these questions, a large data set of highly reliable statistics was reviewed, including studies, reports, working research papers, and books released by the U.S. Department of Commerce Bureau of the Census, Bureau of Economic Analysis, and International Trade Administration; the U.S. Department of Education; the U.S. Department of Labor, Bureau of Labor Statistics; the U.S. Department of the Treasury; the Federal Reserve Bank; the Congressional Budget Office; the Chicago Board of Options Exchange; The National Bureau of Economic Research; quarterly and annual financial reports, presentations, and press releases from major U.S. book-publishing firms; the *Wall Street Journal*; and the *Financial Times.*

Data back to 1947 were reviewed in order to develop reliable printed book and e-book revenues and ARIMA models for the years 2011–2015. ARIMA models are considered to be among the most accurate among the class of forecasting models know as "time series" models, and have been used by most major corporations, the Congressional Budget Office, and many federal government departments.

A series of major economic, demographic, and book industry data sets were evaluated in order to determine the inputs used in the ARIMA models to create projections for the years 2011 through 2015.

The models created print and e-book revenues in five distinct book categories: consumer books (adult; juvenile/YA; religion); K–12 textbooks; higher education textbooks; university press books; and professional and scholarly books (STM—science, technology, and medical; LTR—legal, tax, and regulatory; and HSS—humanities and the social sciences, including business).

Each of these book categories has its own market drivers, and they are moving toward a digital e-book world at different speeds.

Consumer e-books get the most attention, but they posted rather conservative results. In 2008 they accounted for only $78 million, though the figure grew to $166 million in 2009. The emergence of the iPAD, the color Nook, and newer Kindle models triggered an impressive growth rate in 2010, topping $600 million. The ARIMA model, which was subjected to a myriad of validation tests, indicated that this e-book sector should reach $3.5 billion in 2015.

K–12 digital e-books (e-textbooks) are purchased by more than 14,000 U.S. school districts, and these school districts rely on funding, generated by taxes, from the federal government, the state, and local jurisdictions. State and local taxes dropped in 2008 and 2009, with a slight rebound in 2010. This e-book sector declined slowly in 2008 ($151 million), in 2009 ($143 million), and in 2010 ($136 million). A more impressive growth rate is forecast to take place between 2011 and 2015 (when state and local taxes are expected to increase), reaching $600 million the final year.

Higher education e-textbooks saw solid gains in 2008 ($200 million) and 2009 ($400 million) because more than 98 percent of U.S. college students have a laptop, netbook, desktop computer, or iPAD. In addition, the creation and expansion of CourseSmart, an online provider of e-textbooks and other "e-resources," contributed to this sector's growth. By 2010 e-textbooks reached $750 million, with $6.5 billion projected for 2015. By that year, this book category is expected to be more than 95 percent digital.

University presses made slow progress in the transformation from a print to a digital e-book market, growing from $8 million in 2008 to about $95 million in 2015.

The largest e-book category has been the professional and scholarly book sector. Clearly, the STM component grew rapidly between 2008 and 2010, with larger gains possible by 2015. The LTR segment sustained some setbacks because of the recession, but it should also post impressive results by 2015. The HSS portion is the smallest and slowest-growing part of professional and scholarly publishing. Overall, professional and scholarly books should top $3.77 billion by 2015.

Table 17 lists the results of the analysis of historical data and the ARIMA forecasts.

Table 17 / E-Book Projections: 2008–2015
($ million)

Category	2008	2009	2010	2015
Consumer Books	78	166	600	3,500
K–12 Textbooks	151	143	136	600
Higher Education Textbooks	200	400	750	6,530
University Press Books	8	10	12	95
Professional and Scholarly Books	1,142	1,337	1,552	3,770

Source: Albert N. Greco.

In 2008 e-book revenues stood at $1.58 billion; by 2015 the figure should reach $14.5 billion, an increase of 818 percent. Consumers have purchased millions of e-readers and e-books. The end result will be a movement toward e-books and a decrease in the number of printed books sold in the United States, especially in the following categories: mass market paperbacks, textbooks, professional and scholarly books (especially in the STM and LTR subcategories), and university press books. Some book categories will move slowly toward a digital e-book marketplace, including juvenile books, some YA books, and large, illustrated four-color books.

This shift toward a digital e-book world will have a direct impact on the number of books printed and sold in the United States, print runs, the number of U.S. printed books exported to other countries, and the number of printed books imported into the United States.

In this reconfiguration of the U.S. book publishing industry, there will be winners and losers. The winners will include consumers, who will have access to more books at lower prices; libraries, which will have e-books that never get lost or damaged; and college students, who may save about 49 percent on the cost of textbooks. In addition, publishers will have lower book returns, smaller investments in distribution centers, and higher margins in a digital e-book market and will be able to move from a print-oriented import and export business to a foreign rights business (Karier 2010). And authors will be able to get books into wider channels of distribution.

The losers will include

- Publishers and authors adversely affected by e-book piracy (see Taylor, Ishida, and Wallace 2009; Wilson 2010; "U.S. Book Anti-Piracy Research Findings;" and "Special 301")
- Retail bricks-and-mortar bookstores (Lewis and Dart 2010)
- Owners and operators of shopping malls (which will have fewer bricks-and-mortar bookstores)
- Trucking companies (which will handle fewer books to and from bookstores)
- Foreign publishers and printers—particularly in Asia, the Pacific Rim, and Latin America—that have profited from the book export and import trade

If these trends continue—if Americans continue to buy e-readers and e-books, if publishers move aggressively toward a rights-oriented business model—then a sharp decline in printed book exports and imports will be evident each year between 2011 and 2015.

As baseball great Yogi Berra once said, "The future ain't what it used to be."

References

Auld, Graeme, Benjamin Cashore, Christina Balboa, Laura Bozzi, and Stefan Renckens. "Can Technological Innovations Improve Private Regulation in the Global Economy?" *Business & Politics* 12, 3 (2010): 1–39.

Bhide, Amar. *A Call for Judgment: Sensible Finance for a Dynamic Economy* (Oxford University Press, 2010).

Borio, Claudio, and Piti Disyatat. "Global Imbalances and Financial Crisis: Reassessing the Role of International Finance." *Asian Economic Policy Review* 5, 2(December 2010): 198–216.

"For Housing Rebound, Once Again It's Wait Until Next Year." CNBC, March 14, 2011 (http://www.cnbc.com).

Frydman, Roman, and Michael D. Goldberg. *Beyond Mechanical Markets: Asset Price Swings, Risk, and the Role of the State* (Princeton University Press, 2011).

Greco, Albert N. *The Book Publishing Industry,* 2nd ed. (Erlbaum, 2005).

Guerrero, Antomio, Thomas Clouse, Gordon Platt, Kim Iskyan, and Aaron Chaze. "Emerging Markets Roundup." *Global Finance* 25, 2 (February 2011): 10–14.

Karier, Thomas. *Intellectual Capital: Forty Years of the Nobel Prize in Economics* (Cambridge University Press, 2010).

Kattel, Rainer. "Financial and Economic Crisis in Eastern Europe." *Journal of Post Keynesian Economics* 33, 1(Fall 2010): 41–60.

Lewis, Robin, and Michael Dart. *The New Rules of Retail: Competing in the World's Toughest Marketplace* (Palgrave Macmillan, 2010).

Porter, Michael E. *Competitive Advantage: Creating and Sustaining Superior Performance* (Free Press, 1985).

Porter, Michael E. *Competitive Strategy: Techniques for Analyzing Industries and Competitors* (Free Press, 1998a).

Porter, Michael E. *On Competition* (Harvard Business School Press, 1998b).

"Special 301." International Intellectual Property Alliance (http://www.iipa.com).

Taleb, Nassim Nicholas. *The Black Swan: the Impact of the Highly Improbable* (Random, 2007).

Taylor, Steven A., Chiharu Ishida, and David W. Wallace. "Intention to Engage in Digital Piracy: A Conceptual Model and Empirical Test." *Journal of Service Research* 11, 3(February 2009): 246–262.

"U.S. Book Anti-Piracy Research Findings." Attributor, January 14, 2010 (http://www.attributor.com).

Wilson, Arlene. "Digital Rights Management—An Overview." *Business Law Review* 31, 1(January 2010): 2–7.

Number of Book Outlets in the United States and Canada

The *American Book Trade Directory* (Information Today, Inc.) has been published since 1915. Revised annually, it features lists of booksellers, wholesalers, periodicals, reference tools, and other information about the U.S. and Canadian book markets. The data shown in Table 1, the most current available, are from the 2010–2011 edition of the directory.

Table 1 / Bookstores in the United States and Canada, 2010

Category	United States	Canada
Antiquarian General	742	68
Antiquarian Mail Order	279	11
Antiquarian Specialized	135	5
Art Supply Store	69	2
College General	3,102	161
College Specialized	115	6
Comics	214	26
Computer Software	2	0
Cooking	278	10
Department Store	1,574	7
Educational*	180	35
Federal Sites†	223	1
Foreign Language*	17	2
General	3,534	594
Gift Shop	139	7
Juvenile*	106	19
Mail Order General	88	9
Mail Order Specialized	345	20
Metaphysics, New Age, and Occult	154	19
Museum Store and Art Gallery	490	30
Nature and Natural History	40	6
Newsdealer	29	2
Office Supply	14	2
Other††	2,499	450
Paperback§	96	4
Religious*	1,883	162
Self Help/Development	20	7
Stationer	5	3
Toy Store	45	18
Used*	545	83
Totals	16,968	1,769

* Includes Mail Order Shops for this topic, which are not counted elsewhere in this survey.

† National Historic Sites, National Monuments, and National Parks.

††Stores specializing in subjects or services other than those covered in this survey.

§ Includes Mail Order. Excludes used paperback bookstores, stationers, drugstores, or wholesalers handling paperbacks.

The 18,737 stores of various types shown are located throughout the United States, Canada, and regions administered by the United States. "General" bookstores stock trade books and children's books in a general variety of subjects. "College" stores carry college-level textbooks. "Educational" outlets handle school textbooks up to and including the high school level. "Mail order" outlets sell general trade books by mail and are not book clubs; all others operating by mail are classified according to the kinds of books carried. "Antiquarian" dealers sell old and rare books. Stores handling secondhand books are classified as "used." "Paperback" stores have more than 80 percent of their stock in paperbound books. Stores with paperback departments are listed under the appropriate major classification ("general," "department store," "stationer," and so forth.). Bookstores with at least 50 percent of their stock on a particular subject are classified by subject.

Review Media Statistics

Compiled by the staff of the *Library and Book Trade Almanac*

Number of Books and Other Media Reviewed by Major Reviewing Publications 2009–2010

	Adult		Juvenile		Young Adult		Total	
	2009	**2010**	**2009**	**2010**	**2009**	**2010**	**2009**	**2010**
Booklist[1]	4,737	4,876	3,542	3,581	—	—	8,279	8,457
Bookmarks	692	702	—	—	—	10	692	712
BookPage[2]	758	653	109	116	34	59	901	828
Bulletin of the Center for Children's Books[3]	—	—	790	726	—	—	790	726
Chicago Sun Times	n.a.	n.a.	n.a.	n.a.	—	—	n.a.	n.a.
Chicago Tribune Sunday Book Section[4]	350	250	200	250	50	—	600	500
Choice[5]	6,632	6,851	—	—	—	—	6,632	6,851
Horn Book Guide	—	—	3,272	3,046	1,101	921	4,373	3,967
Horn Book Magazine[6]	3	1	335	301	116	126	454	428
Kirkus Reviews[4]	2,311	2,279	2,155	2,245	—	—	4,466	4,524
Library Journal[7]	5,741	6,099	—	—	—	—	5,741	6,099
Los Angeles Times	n.a.	n.a.	—	—	—	—	n.a.	n.a.
Multicultural Review[8]	331	226	127	121	63	31	521	378
New York Journal of Books[9]	n.a.	975	n.a.	150	n.a.	100	n.a.	1,225
New York Review of Books[10]	n.a.	394	—	—	—	—	n.a.	394
New York Times Sunday Book Review	n.a.	n.a.	n.a.	n.a.	—	—	n.a.	n.a.
Publishers Weekly[11]	6,352	6,119	1,243	1,765	—	—	7,595	7,884
School Library Journal[4]	172	19	5,528	5,755	—	—	5,700	5,774
Washington Post Book World[4]	860	839	50	45	—	—	910	884

n.a. = not available.

1 All figures are for a 12-month period from September 1, 2009, to August 31, 2010 (vol. 106). YA books are included in the juvenile total. *Booklist* also reviewed 499 other media.

2 Of the total count, 118 were Web-only reviews. BookPage also published 37 audio reviews.

3 All figures are for a 12-month period beginning September and ending July/August. YA books are included in the juvenile total.

4 YA books are included in the juvenile total.

5 All materials reviewed in *Choice* are scholarly publications intended for undergraduate libraries. *Choice* also reviewed 438 Internet sites and 1 CD-ROM.

6 *Horn Book Magazine* also reviewed 18 audiobooks.

7 In addition, *Library Journal* reviewed 422 audiobooks, 447 DVDs/videos, 88 magazines and zines, 260 books in Collection Development, and 120 online databases, and previewed 1,447 books in "Prepub Alert."

8 *MultiCultural Review* also published 7 audio or video reviews. The magazine published three issues in 2010 rather than the usual four.

9 *New York Journal of Books,* which began publication in 2010, is online only.

10 *New York Review of Books* published 280 articles dealing directly with books or other media. These articles treated a cumulative 435 individual items, of which 10 were films, 2 operas, 2 television series, 3 plays, and 24 art exhibitions. The remainder (394) were adult books.

11 Of the total of 7,884 reviews, 989 were online only. *Publishers Weekly* also reviewed 362 audiobooks.

Part 5
Reference Information

Bibliographies

The Librarian's Bookshelf

Mary Ellen Quinn
Editor, *Booklist/Reference Books Bulletin,* American Library Association

Most of the books on this selective bibliography have been published since 2008; a few earlier titles are retained because of their continuing importance.

General Works

American Library Directory, 2011–2012. 2v. Information Today, Inc., 2011. $329. Also available online.

Annual Review of Information Science and Technology (ARIST). Ed. by Blaise Cronin. Information Today, Inc., 2011. $124.95.

Charleston Conference Proceedings, 2008. Ed. by Beth R. Bernhardt and others. Libraries Unlimited, 2009. Paper $40.

Library and Book Trade Almanac, 2011. Information Today, Inc., 2011. $229.

Encyclopedia of Library and Information Science. 3rd ed. Ed. by Miriam A. Drake. CRC, 2009. $3,000. Also available online.

Library Literature and Information Science Full Text. H. W. Wilson (http://www.hwwilson.com).

Library Literature and Information Science Index. H. W. Wilson, 1921–. Also available online, 1984–.

Library Literature and Information Science Retrospective: 1905–1983. H. W. Wilson (http://www.hwwilson.com).

The Oxford Guide to Library Research. 3rd ed. By Thomas Mann. Oxford University Press, 2005. Paper $19.99.

The Whole Library Handbook 4. Ed. by George Eberhart. American Library Association, 2006. Paper $48.

Academic Libraries

ARL Statistics. Association of Research Libraries. Annual. 1962– (http://www.arl.org/stats/annualsurveys/arlstats).

Academic Librarianship. By Camila A. Alire and G. Edward Evans. Neal-Schuman, 2010. Paper $65.

The Academic Library Building in the Digital Age: A Study of Construction, Planning, and Design of New Library Space. By Christopher Stewart. Association of College and Research Libraries, 2010. Paper $44.

Academic Library Outreach: Beyond the Campus Walls. By Nancy Courtney. Libraries Unlimited, 2008. Paper $45.

Academic Library Trends and Statistics, 2009. Association of College and Research Libraries/American Library Association, 2010. 3 vols. $550.

Advocacy, Outreach and the Nation's Academic Libraries: A Call for Action. Ed. by William C. Welburn, Janice Welburn, and Beth McNeil. Association of College and Research Libraries, 2010. Paper $40.

Building Bridges: Connecting Faculty, Students, and the College Library. By Monty L. McAdoo. American Library Association, 2010. Paper $55.

Convergence and Collaboration of Campus Information Services. Ed. by Peter Hernon and Ronald R. Powell. Libraries Unlimited, 2008. Paper $50.

Creating the Customer-Driven Academic Library. By Jeannette Woodward. American Library Association, 2008. Paper $58.

Envisioning Future Academic Library Services: Initiatives, Ideas and Challenges. Ed. by Sue Knight. Facet Publishing, 2010. Paper $125.

The Expert Library: Staffing, Sustaining, and Advancing the Academic Library in the 21st Century. By Scott Walter and Karen Williams. Association of College and Research Libraries, 2010. Paper $48.

A Field Guide to the Information Commons. By Charles Forrest and Martin Halbert. Scarecrow, 2009. Paper $65.

Managing the Small College Library. By Rachel Applegate. Libraries Unlimited, 2010. Paper $55.

Mistakes in Academic Library Management: Grievous Errors and How to Avoid Them. Ed. by Jack E. Fritts, Jr. Scarecrow, 2009. Paper $50.

Starting, Strengthening, and Managing Institutional Repositories: A How-to-Do-It Manual. By Jonathan A. Nabe. Neal-Schuman, 2010. Paper $85.

Transforming Library Service Through Information Commons: Case Studies for the Digital Age. By D. Russell Bailey and Barbara Gunter Tierney. American Library Association, 2008. Paper $60.

Administration and Personnel

Assessing Information Needs: Managing Transformative Library Services. By Robert J. Grover, Roger C. Greer, and John Agada. Libraries Unlimited, 2010. Paper $60.

The Complete Library Trustee Handbook. By Sally Gardner Reed and Jillian Kolonick. Neal-Schuman, 2010. Paper $55.

Developing a Compensation Plan for Your Library. 2nd ed. By Paula M. Singer and Laura L. Francisco. American Library Association, 2009. Paper $55.

Even More Ideas for Libraries and Friends. By Sally Gardner Reed and Beth Nawalinski. Neal-Schuman, 2008. Paper $69.95.

Hiring, Training, and Supervising Library Shelvers. By Patricia Tunstall. American Library Association, 2010. Paper $50.

Implementing for Results: Your Strategic Plan in Action. By Sandra Nelson. American Library Association, 2009. Paper $65.

Inside, Outside, and Online: Building Your Library Community. By Chrystie Hill. American Library Association, 2009. Paper $48.

Library Data: Empowering Practice and Persuasion. Ed. by Darby Orcutt. Libraries Unlimited, 2010. Paper $50.

The Library Security and Safety Guide to Prevention, Planning, and Response. By Miriam B. Kahn. American Library Association, 2008. Paper $52.

Moving Materials: Physical Delivery in Libraries. Ed. by Valerie Horton and Bruce Smith. American Library Association, 2010. Paper $70.

Our New Public, A Changing Clientele: Bewildering Issues or New Challenges for Managing Libraries? Ed. by Janes R. Kennedy, Lisa Vardaman, and Gerard B. McCabe. Libraries Unlimited, 2008. $45.

Privacy and Confidentiality Issues: A Guide for Libraries and Their Lawyers. By Theresa Chmara. American Library Association, 2009. Paper $47.

The Quality Library: Guide to Staff-Driven Improvement, Better Efficiency, and Happier Customers. By Sara Laughlin and Ray W. Wilson. American Library Association, 2008. Paper $55.

Staff Development Strategies That Work: Stories and Strategies from New Librarians. Ed. by Georgie L. Donovan and Miguel A. Figueroa. Neal-Schuman, 2008. Paper $75.

Strategic Planning for Results. By Sandra Nelson. American Library Association, 2008. Paper $72.

Streamlining Library Services: What We Do, How Much Time It Takes, What It Costs, and How We Can Do It Better. By Richard M. Dougherty. Scarecrow, 2008. Paper $49.50.

The Successful Library Trustee Handbook. 2nd ed. By Mary Y. Moore. American Library Association, 2009. Paper $45.

Succession Planning in the Library: Developing Leaders, Managing Change. By Paula

M. Singer with Gail Griffith. American Library Association, 2010. Paper $55.

Archives

Archives: Principles and Practices. By Laura A. Millar. Neal-Schuman, 2010. Paper $75.

Leading and Managing Archives and Records Programs: Strategies for Success. Ed. by Bruce W. Dearstyne. Neal-Schuman, 2008. Paper $75.

Special Collections 2.0: New Technologies for Rare Books, Manuscripts, and Archival Collections. By Beth M. Whittaker and Lynne M. Thomas. Libraries Unlimited, 2009. Paper $45.

Buildings and Space Planning

Building Science 101: A Primer for Librarians. By Lynn M. Piotrowicz and Scott Osgood. American Library Association, 2010. Paper $40.

Countdown to a New Library: Managing the Building Project. 2nd ed. By Jeannette Woodward. American Library Association, 2010. Paper $75.

Libraries Designed for Kids By Nolan Lushington. Neal-Schuman, 2008. Paper $85.

Moving Your Library: Getting the Collection from Here to There. By Steven Carl Fortriede. American Library Association, 2010. Paper $70.

Cataloging and Bibliographic Control

Beginning Cataloging. By Jean Weihs and Sheila S. Intner. Libraries Unlimited, 2009. Paper $40.

Cataloging Correctly for Kids: An Introduction to the Tools. 5th ed. By Sheila S. Intner and Joanna F. Fountain. American Library Association, 2010. Paper $55.

Collection-Level Cataloging: Bound-with Books. By Jain Fletcher. Libraries Unlimited, 2010. Paper $45.

Describing Electronic, Digital, and Other Media Using AACR2 and RDA. By Mary Beth Weber and Fay Austin. Neal-Schuman, 2010. Paper $75.

FRBR: A Guide for the Perplexed. By Robert L. Maxwell. American Library Association, 2008. Paper $60.

Introducing RDA: A Guide to the Basics. By Chris Oliver. American Library Association, 2010. Paper $45.

Metadata. By Marcia Lei Zeng and Jian Qin. Neal-Schuman, 2008. Paper $65.

Next-Gen Library Catalogs. By Marshall Breeding. Neal-Schuman, 2010. Paper $55.

Radical Cataloging: Essays at the Front. Ed. by K. R. Roberto. McFarland, 2008. Paper $45.

The RDA Primer: A Guide for the Occasional Cataloger. By Amy Hart. Linworth, 2010. Paper $40.

Children's and Young Adult Services and Materials

Children's Literature in Action: A Librarian's Guide. By Sylvia Vardell. Libraries Unlimited, 2008. $65.

Children's Services: Partnerships for Success. Ed. by Betsy Diamant-Cohen. American Library Association, 2010. Paper $50.

Connecting Young Adults and Libraries. 4th ed. By Michele Gorman and Tricia Suellentrop. Neal-Schuman, 2009. Paper $85.

Core Collection for Children and Young Adults. By Rachel E. Schwedt and Janice DeLong. Scarecrow, 2008. $55.

Crash Course in Library Services to Preschool Children. By Betsy Diamant-Cohen. Libraries Unlimited, 2010. Paper $30.

Managing Children's Services in the Public Library. 3rd ed. By Adele M. Fasick and Leslie E. Holt. Libraries Unlimited, 2007. Paper $45.

More Than MySpace: Teens, Librarians, and Social Networking. Ed. by Robyn M. Lupa. Libraries Unlimited, 2009. Paper $40.

Multicultural Programs for Teens and Tweens. Ed. by Linda B. Alexander and Nahyun Kwan. American Library Association, 2010. Paper $50.

The Newbery and Caldecott Awards 2010: A Guide to the Medal and Honor Books. Association for Library Service to Children/American Library Association, 2010. Paper $25.

Risky Business: Taking and Managing Risks in Library Services for Teens. By Linda W. Braun, Hillias J. Martin, and Connie Urquhart. American Library Association, 2010. Paper $55.

Serving Urban Teens. By Paula Brehm-Heeger. Libraries Unlimited, 2008. Paper $40.

Start to Finish YA Programs: Hip-Hop Symposiums, Summer Reading Programs, Virtual Tours, Poetry Slams, Teen Advisory Boards, Term Paper Clinics, and More! By Ella W. Jones. Neal-Schuman, 2009. Paper $75.

Teen-Centered Library Service: Putting Youth Participation into Practice. By Diane P. Tuccillo. Libraries Unlimited, 2009. Paper $45.

Teen Spaces: The Step-by-Step Library Makeover. 2nd ed. By Kimberly Bolan. American Library Association, 2009. Paper $47.

Young Adults Deserve the Best: YALSA's Competencies in Action. By Sarah Flowers. American Library Association, 2010. Paper $48.

Collection Development

Developing an Outstanding Core Collection. By Carol Alabaster. American Library Association, 2010. Paper $60.

Fundamentals of Collection Development and Management. 2nd ed. By Peggy Johnson. American Library Association, 2009. Paper $70.

The Kovacs Guide to Electronic Library Collection Development. By Diane K. Kovacs. Neal-Schuman, 2009. Paper $150.

Copyright

Smart Copyright Compliance for Schools: A How-To-Do-It Manual. By Rebecca P. Butler. Neal-Schuman, 2009. Paper $75.

Digital Libraries

Building Digital Libraries. By Terry Reese, Jr. and Kyle Banerjee. Neal-Schuman, 2008. Paper $75.

Digitization in the Real World: Lessons Learned from Small and Medium-Sized Digitization Projects. Ed. by Kwong Bor Ng and Jason Kucsma. Metropolitan New York Library Council, 2010. Paper $60.

Licensing Digital Content: A Practical Guide for Librarians. 2nd ed. By Lesley Ellen Harris. American Library Association, 2009. Paper $57.

What Every Librarian Should Know About Electronic Privacy. By Jeanette Woodward. Libraries Unlimited, 2008. Paper $40.

History

The First White House Library: A History and Annotated Catalogue. Ed. by Catherine M. Parisian. Pennsylvania University Press, 2010. $55.

The History of Public Library Access for African Americans in the South, or, Leaving Behind the Plow. By David M. Battles. Scarecrow, 2008. Paper $44.

Librarianship in Gilded Age America: An Anthology of Writings, 1868–1901. Ed. by Leonard Schlup and Stephen H. Paschen. McFarland, 2009. Paper $55.

Reading Places: Literacy, Democracy, and the Public Library in the Cold War. By Christine Pawley. University of Massachusetts Press, 2010. Paper $28.95.

Information Literacy

Best Practices for Credit-Bearing Information Literacy Courses. By Christopher Hollister. Association of College and Research Libraries, 2010. Paper $48.

Information Literacy Instruction: Theory and Practice. 2nd ed. By Esther S. Grassian and Joan R. Kaplowitz. Neal-Schuman, 2009. Paper $75.

Information Science

Foundations of Library and Information Science. 3rd. ed. By Richard E. Rubin. Neal-Schuman, 2010. Paper $75.

Structures for Organizing Knowledge: Exploring Taxonomies, Ontologies, and Other Schema. By June Abbas. Neal-Schuman, 2010. Paper $85.

Intellectual Freedom

Banned Books Resource Guide. American Library Association/Office of Intellectual Freedom, 2010. Paper $48.

Intellectual Freedom Manual. 8th ed. American Library Association/Office of Intellectual Freedom, 2010. Paper $65.

Protecting Intellectual Freedom in Your Academic Library. By Barbara M. Jones. American Library Association, 2009. Paper $50.

Protecting Intellectual Freedom in Your Public Library. By June Pinnell-Stephens. American Library Association, 2009. Paper $50.

Protecting Intellectual Freedom in Your School Library. By Pat R. Scales. American Library Association, 2009. Paper $55.

Internet/Web

Going Beyond Google: The Invisible Web in Learning and Teaching. By Jane Devine and Francine Egger-Sider. Neal-Schuman, 2008. Paper $65.

I Found It on the Internet: Coming of Age Online. 2nd ed. By Frances Jacobson Harris. American Library Association, 2010. Paper $45.

Making Library Web Sites Usable: A LITA Guide. Ed. by Tom Lehman and Terry Nikkel. Neal-Schuman, 2008. Paper $65.

Knowledge Management

Perspectives on Knowledge Management. Ed. by I. V. Malhan and Shivarama Rao K. Scarecrow, 2008. Paper. $71.50.

Leadership

Developing Library Leaders: A How-To-Do-It Manual for Coaching, Team Building, and Mentoring Library Staff. By Robert D. Stueart with Maureen Sullivan. Neal-Schuman, 2010. Paper $75.

Interpersonal Skills, Theory, and Practice: The Librarian's Guide to Becoming a Leader. By Brooke E. Sheldon. Libraries Unlimited, 2010. Paper $48.

"Leading from the Middle," and Other Contrarian Essays on Library Leadership. By John Lubans, Jr. Libraries Unlimited, 2010. Paper $50.

Shaping the Future: Advancing the Understanding of Leadership. Ed. by Peter Hernon. Libraries Unlimited, 2010. Paper $50.

Librarians and Librarianship

The ALA-APA Salary Survey 2010: Librarian—Public and Academic. ALA-Allied Professional Association and the ALA Office for Research and Statistics. American Library Association, 2010. Paper $90. Also available online.

ARL Annual Salary Survey, 2009–2010. Association of Research Libraries, 2009. http://www.arl.org/bm~doc/ss09.pdf.

How to Pay for Your Degree in Library and Information Studies 2010–2012. By Gail Ann Schlachter and R. David Webber. Reference Service Press, 2010. Paper $30.

Information Technology in Librarianship: New Critical Approaches. Ed. by Gloria J. Leckie and John E. Buschman. Libraries Unlimited, 2009. Paper $50.

Libraries in the Information Age: An Introduction and Career Exploration. By Denise K. Fourie and David R. Dowell. Libraries Unlimited, 2009. Paper $45.

Library Ethics. By Jean Preer. Libraries Unlimited, 2008. Paper $45.

Library World Records. 2nd ed. By Godfrey Oswald. 2nd ed. McFarland, 2009. Paper $39.95.

The MLS Project: An Assessment After Sixty Years. By Boyd Keith Swigger. Scarecrow, 2010. Paper $50.

The Portable MLIS: Insights from the Experts. Ed. by Ken Haycock and Brooke E. Sheldon. Libraries Unlimited, 2008. Paper $50.

Self-Examination: The Present and Future of Librarianship. By John M. Budd. Libraries Unlimited, 2008. Paper $60.

Service Learning: Linking Library Education and Practice. By Loriene Roy, Kelly Jensen, and Alex Hershey Meyers. American Library Association, 2009. Paper $65.

Public Libraries

Crash Course in Public Library Administration. By Wayne Disher. Libraries Unlimited, 2010. Paper $30.

The Customer-Focused Library: Re-Inventing the Public Library from the Outside-In. By Joseph R. Matthews. Libraries Unlimited, 2009. Paper $50.

Defining Relevancy: Managing the New Public Library. Ed. by Janet McNeil Hurlbert. Libraries Unlimited, 2008. Paper $45.

DIY Programming and Book Displays: How to Stretch Your Programming Without Stretching Your Budget and Staff. By Amanda Moss Struckmeyer and Svetha Hetzler. Libraries Unlimited, 2010. Paper $36.

Everyone Plays at the Library: Creating Great Gaming Experiences for All Ages. By Scott Nicholson. Information Today, Inc., 2010. Paper $39.50.

Introduction to Library Public Services. By G. Edward Evans and Thomas L. Carter. Libraries Unlimited, 2008. $65.

The PLA Reader for Public Library Directors and Managers. Ed. by Kathleen M. Hughes. Neal-Schuman, 2009. Paper $65.

Pop Goes the Library: Using Pop Culture to Connect with Your Whole Community. By Sophie Brookover and Elizabeth Burns. Information Today, 2008. Paper $39.50.

Public Libraries and Internet Service Roles: Measuring and Maximizing Internet Services. By Charles R. McClure and Paul T. Jaeger. American Library Association, 2008. Paper $45.

Public Libraries and the Internet: Roles, Perspectives, and Implications. By John Carlo Bertot and Paul T. Jaeger. Libraries Unlimited, 2010. Paper $45.

Public Libraries Going Green. By Kathryn Miller. American Library Association, 2010. Paper $45.

Public Libraries in the 21st Century. By Ann E. Prentice. Libraries Unlimited, 2010. Paper $65.

Public Library Data Service Statistical Report 2010. Public Library Association/American Library Association, 2010. Paper $120.

The Public Library Policy Writer: A Guidebook with Model Policies on CD-ROM. By Jeanette C. Larson and Herman L.Totten. Neal-Schuman, 2008. Paper and CD-ROM $75.

The Small Public Library Survival Guide: Thriving on Less. By Herbert B. Landau. American Library Association, 2008. Paper $47.

Public Relations/Marketing

Bite-Sized Marketing: Realistic Solutions for the Overworked Librarian. By Nancy Dowd, Mary Evangelista, and Jonathan Silberman. American Library Association, 2010. Paper $48.

Building a Buzz: Libraries and Word-of-Mouth Marketing. By Peggy Barber and Linda Wallace. American Library Association, 2010. Paper $45.

Creating Your Library Brand: Communicating Your Relevance and Value to Your Patrons. By Elizabeth Doucett. American Library Association, 2008. Paper $50.

The Library PR Handbook: High-Impact Communications. Ed. by Mark R. Gould. American Library Association, 2009. Paper $55.

Look, It's Books! Marketing Your Library with Displays and Promotions. By Gayle Skaggs. McFarland, 2008. Paper $49.95.

Merchandising Made Simple: Using Standards and Dynamite Displays to Boost Circulation. By Jenny LaPierre and Trish Christiansen. Libraries Unlimited, 2008. Paper $36.

Readers' Advisory

A Few Good Books: Using Contemporary Reader's Advisory Strategies to Connect Readers with Books. By Stephanie L. Maatta. Neal-Schuman, 2009. Paper $69.95.

Integrated Advisory Service: Breaking Through the Book Boundary to Better Serve Library Users. Ed. by Jessica E. Moyer. Libraries Unlimited, 2010. $58.

The Readers' Advisory Guide to Genre Fiction. 2nd ed. By Joyce G. Saricks. American Library Association, 2009. Paper $65.

Readers' Advisory Service for Children and 'Tweens. By Penny Peck. Libraries Unlimited, 2010. Paper $36.

The Reader's Advisory Handbook. Ed. by Jessica E. Moyer and Kaite Mediatore Stover. American Library Association, 2010. Paper $55.

Research-Based Readers' Advisory. By Jessica E. Moyer. American Library Association, 2008. Paper $55.

Serving Boys Through Readers' Advisory. By Michael Sullivan. American Library Association, 2010. Paper $48.

Reference Services

Conducting the Reference Interview. 2nd ed. By Catherine Sheldrick Ross, Kristi Nilsen, and Marie L. Radford. Neal-Schuman, 2009. Paper $75.

Crash Course in Reference. By Charlotte Ford. Libraries Unlimited, 2008. Paper $30.

Guide to Reference. American Library Association. Online database. http://guidetoreference.org.

Reference and Information Services in the 21st Century: An Introduction. By Kay Ann Cassell and Uma Hiremath. Neal-Schuman, 2009. Paper $69.95.

Reference Renaissance: Current and Future Trends. Ed. by Marie L. Radford and R. David Lankes. Neal-Schuman, 2010. Paper $75.

Training Paraprofessionals for Reference Service. By Pamela J. Morgan. Neal-Schuman, 2008. Paper $65.

Virtual Reference Best Practices: Tailoring Services to Your Library. By M. Kathleen Kern. American Library Association, 2008. Paper $50.

School Libraries/Media Centers

Administering the School Library Media Center. 5th ed. By Betty J. Morris. Libraries Unlimited, 2010. Paper $45.

Enhancing Teaching and Learning: A Leadership Guide for School Library Media Specialists. 2nd ed. By Jean Donham. Neal-Schuman, 2008. Paper $65.

Ensuring Intellectual Freedom and Access to Information in the School Library Media Program. By Helen R. Adams. Libraries Unlimited, 2008. Paper $40.

Essential Documents for School Libraries. 2nd ed. By Colleen MacDonell. Linworth, 2010. Paper and CD $50.

Essential Reference Services for Today's School Media Specialist. 2nd ed. Ed. by Scott Lanning and John Bryner. Libraries Unlimited, 2009. Paper $45.

Fundamentals of School Library Media Management. By Barbara Stein Martin and Marco Zannier. Neal-Schuman, 2009. Paper $59.95.

Guide for Developing and Evaluating School Library Programs. 7th ed. By Nebraska Educational Media Association. Libraries Unlimited, 2010. Paper $45.

Independent School Libraries: Perspectives on Excellence. Ed. by Dorcas Hand. Libraries Unlimited, 2010. Paper $45.

Leadership for Excellence: Insights of National School Library Media Program of the Year Award Winners. Ed. by Joanne Carr. American Library Association, 2008. Paper $45.

The Neal-Schuman Technology Management Handbook for School Library Media Centers. By Lesley S. J. Farmer and Marc E. McPhee. Neal-Schuman, 2010. Paper $59.95.

Personal Learning Networks: Professional Development for the Isolated School Librarian. By Mary Ann Harlan. Libraries Unlimited, 2009. Paper $30.

The Resilient School Library. By Carol A. Doll and Beth Doll. Libraries Unlimited, 2010. Paper $40.

The School Library Media Manager. 4th ed. By Blanche Woolls. Libraries Unlimited, 2008. Paper $45.

The School Library Media Specialist's Policy and Procedure Writer. By Elizabeth Downs. Neal-Schuman, 2010. Paper and CD-ROM $75.

Simply Indispensable: An Action Guide for School Librarians. By Janice Gilmore-See. Libraries Unlimited, 2010. Paper $35.

Teaching Generation M: A Handbook for Librarians and Educators. Ed. by Vibiana Bowman Cvetkovic and Robert J. Lackie. Neal-Schuman, 2009. Paper $85.

The Tech-Savvy Booktalker: A Guide for 21st-Century Educators. By Terence Cavanaugh and Nancy Keane. Libraries Unlimited, 2009. Paper $35.

Technology and the School Library: A Comprehensive Guide for Media Specialists and Other Educators. By Odin Jurkowski. Scarecrow, 2010. Paper $45.

Technology for the School Librarian: Theory and Practice. By William O. Scheeren. Libraries Unlimited, 2010. Paper $50.

21st Century Learning in School Libraries: Putting the AASL Standards to Work. Ed. by Kristin Fontichiaro. Libraries Unlimited, 2009. Paper $40.

Your School Library: Check It Out!. By Lesley S. J. Farmer. Libraries Unlimited, 2009. Paper $35.

Services for Special Groups

Crash Course in Serving Spanish-Speakers. By Salvador Avila. Libraries Unlimited, 2008. Paper $30.

Easy Information Sources for ESL, Adult Learners, and New Readers. By Rosemarie Riechel. Neal-Schuman, 2008. Paper $64.

¡Hola, Amigos! A Plan for Latino Outreach. By Susana G. Baumann. Libraries Unlimited, 2010. Paper $40.

Librarians Serving Diverse Populations: Challenges and Opportunities. By Lori Mestre. Association of College and Research Libraries, 2010. Paper $54.

Public Library Services to the Poor: Doing All We Can. By Leslie Edmonds Holt and Glen E. Holt. American Library Association, 2010. Paper $48.

Social Media

Blogging and RSS: A Librarian's Guide. 2nd ed. By Michael P. Sauers. Information Today, 2010. Paper $35.

Effective Blogging for Libraries. By Connie Crosby. Neal-Schuman, 2010. Paper $55.

Game On! Gaming at the Library. By Beth Gallaway. Neal-Schuman, 2009. Paper $55.

Gaming in Libraries. By Kelly Czarnecki. Neal-Schuman, 2010. Paper $55.

Microblogging and Lifestreaming in Libraries. By Robin Hastings. Neal-Schuman, 2010. Paper $55.

A Social Networking Primer for Librarians. By Cliff Landis. Neal-Schuman, 2010. Paper $55.

Wikis for Libraries. By Lauren Pressley. Neal-Schuman, 2010. Paper $55.

Technical Services

Acquisitions in the New Information Universe: Core Competencies and Ethical Practices, By Jesse Holden. Neal-Schuman, 2010. Paper $75.

Fundamentals of Technical Services Management. By Sheila S. Intner, with Peggy Johnson. American Library Association, 2008. Paper $50.

Introduction to Technical Services. 8th ed. By C. Edward Evans, Sheila S. Intner, and Jean Weihs. Libraries Unlimited, 2010. Paper $60.

More Innovative Redesign and Reorganization of Library Technical Services. By Bradford Lee Eden. Libraries Unlimited, 2008. Paper $50.

Technology

Core Technology Competencies for Librarians and Library Staff: A LITA Guide Ed. by Susan M. Thompson. Neal-Schuman, 2009. Paper $65.

Library Camps and Unconferences. By Steve Lawson. Neal-Schuman, 2010. Paper $55.

Library Mashups: Exploring New Ways to Deliver Library Data. Ed. by Nicole C. Engard. Information Today, Inc., 2009. Paper $39.50.

Library Programs Online: Possibilities and Practicalities of Web Conferencing. By Thomas A. Peters. Libraries Unlimited, 2009. Paper $40.

Library Videos and Webcasts. By Sean Robinson. Neal-Schuman, 2010. Paper $55.

Mobile Technology and Libraries. By Jason Griffey. Neal-Schuman, 2010. Paper $55.

More Technology for the Rest of Us: A Second Primer on Computing for the Non-IT Librarian. Ed. By Nancy Courtney. Libraries Unlimited, 2010. Paper $50.

Neal-Schuman Library Technology Companion: A Basic Guide for Library Staff. 3rd ed. By John J. Burke. Neal-Schuman, 2009. Paper $65.

Searching 2.0. By Michael Sauers. Neal-Schuman, 2009. Paper $65.

Technology Training in Libraries. By Sarah Houghton-Jan. Neal-Schuman, 2010. Paper $55.

Web 2.0 for Librarians and Information Professionals. By Ellyssa Kroski. Neal-Schuman, 2008. Paper $75.

Periodicals

Advanced Technology Libraries
Against the Grain
American Archivist
American Libraries
ARL
Behavioral and Social Sciences Librarian
Booklist
Booklist Online
The Bottom Line: Managing Library Finances
Cataloging and Classification Quarterly
Catholic Library World
Children and Libraries: The Journal of the Association for Library Services to Children
CHOICE
CHOICE Reviews Online
Collection Management
College and Research Libraries
College and Undergraduate Libraries
Community and Junior College Libraries
Computers in Libraries
Congregational Libraries Today
IFLA Journal
Information Outlook
Information Technology and Libraries
Internet Reference Services Quarterly
Journal of Academic Librarianship
Journal of Education for Library and Information Science
Journal of Electronic Resources Librarianship
Journal of Information Ethics
Journal of Interlibrary Loan, Document Delivery and Information Supply
Journal of Library Administration
Journal of the American Society for Information Science and Technology
Journal of the Medical Library Association
Knowledge Quest
Law Library Journal
Legal Reference Services Quarterly
Libraries and the Cultural Record
Library Administration and Management
Library and Archival Security
Library and Information Science Research (LIBRES)
Library Hi-Tech News
Library Issues: Briefings for Faculty and Academic Administrators
Library Journal
Library Media Connection
The Library Quarterly
Library Resources and Technical Services
Library Technology Reports
Library Trends
Librarysparks
Marketing Library Services
Medical Reference Services Quarterly
MultiMedia and Internet @ Schools
Music Library Association Notes
Music Reference Services Quarterly
New Review of Children's Literature and Librarianship
Portal: Libraries and the Academy
Public Libraries
Public Library Quarterly
Reference and User Services Quarterly
Reference Librarian
Resource Sharing & Information Networks
RSR: Reference Services Review
School Library Journal

School Library Media Research
Searcher: The Magazine for Database Professionals
Serials Librarian
Serials Review
Technical Services Quarterly
Technicalities
Video Librarian
Voice of Youth Advocates (*VOYA*)
World Libraries
Young Adult Library Services

Blogs

025.431: The Dewey Blog. By Joan Mitchell (http://ddc.typepad.com).

AASL Blog (http://www.aasl.ala.org/aaslblog).

ACRLog (http://acrlog.org).

ALA TechSource (http://www.alatechsource.org/blog).

ALSL Blog (http://www.alsc.ala.org/blog).

Annoyed Librarian (http://www.libraryjournal.com/annoyedlibrarian).

Audiobooker. By Mary Burkey (http://audiobooker.booklistonline.com).

Awful Library Books. By Holly Hibner and Mary Kelly (http://awfullibrarybooks.net).

Beyond the Job. By Sarah Johnson and Rachel Singer Gordon (http://www.beyondthejob.org).

Blue Skunk. By Doug Johnson (http://doug-johnson.squarespace.com).

Book Group Buzz (http://bookgroupbuzz.booklistonline.com).

Catalogablog. By David Bigwood (http://catalogablog.blogspot.com).

A Chair, a Fireplace, and a Tea Cozy. By Liz Burns (http://blog.schoollibraryjournal.com/teacozy).

Copyfight. By Ernest Miller, Elizabeth Rader, JasonSchultz, Wendy Seltzer, Aaron Schwartz, and Adam Wexelblat (http://copyfight.corante.com).

David Lee King. By David Lee King (http://www.davidleeking.com).

Digitization 101. By Jill Hurst-Wahl (http://hurstassociates.blogspot.com).

Early Word. By Nora Rawlinson (http://www.earlyword.com).

Free Range Librarian. By Karen G. Schneider (http://freerangelibrarian.com).

Hey Jude. By Judy O'Connell (http://heyjude.wordpress.com).

Information Wants to Be Free. By Meredith Farkas (http://meredith.wolfwater.com/wordpress).

Librarian.net. By Jessamyn West (http://www.librarian.net).

LibrarianInBlack. By Sarah Houghton-Jan (http://librarianinblack.net).

Library Juice. By Rory Litwin (http://libraryjuicepress.com/blog).

LibraryLaw Blog. By Mary Minow (http://blog.librarylaw.com).

Library Web Chic. By Karen A. Coombs (http://www.librarywebchic.net).

A Library Writer's Blog. By Corey Seeman (http://librarywriting.blogspot.com).

Likely Stories. By Keir Graff (http://blog.booklistonline.com).

LIS News. By Blake Carver (http://lisnews.org).

LITA Blog (http://litablog.org).

The 'M' Word—Marketing in Libraries. By Kathy Dempsey (http://themwordblog.blogspot.com).

NeverEndingSearch. By Joyce Valenza (http://blog.schoollibraryjournal.com/neverendingsearch).

No Shelf Required. By Sue Polanka (http://www.libraries.wright.edu/noshelfrequired).

Pattern Recognition. By Jason Griffey (http://www.jasongriffey.net/wp).

Phil Bradley's Weblog. By Phil Bradley (http://www.philbradley.typepad.com).

PLA Blog (http://plablog.org).

Points of Reference (http://pointsofreference.booklistonline.com).

ResourceShelf. By Gary Price (http://www.resourceshelf.com).

RUSA Blog (http://rusa.ala.org/blog).

See Also . . . By Steve Lawson (http://stevelawson.name/seealso).

ShelfRenewal. By Karen Kleckner and Rebecca Vnuk (http://blog.libraryjournal.com/shelfrenewal).

The Shifted Librarian. By Jenny Levine (http://www.theshiftedlibrarian.com).

Stephen's Lighthouse. By Stephen Abram (http://stephenslighthouse.syrsidynix.com).

Swiss Army Librarian. By Brian Herzog (http://www.swissarmylibrarian.net).

Tame the Web: Libraries and Technology. By Michael Stephens (http://tametheweb.com).

The Travelin' Librarian. By Michael Sauers (http://www.travelinlibrarian.info).

Walking Paper. By Aaron Schmidt (http://www.walkingpaper.org/blog).

Walt at Random. By Walt Crawford (http://walt.lishost.org).

What I Learned Today. By Nicole C. Engard (http://www.web2learning.net).

YALSA Blog (http://yalsa.ala.org/blog).

Ready Reference

How to Obtain an ISBN

Beat Barblan and Louise Timko
United States ISBN/SAN Agency

The International Standard Book Numbering (ISBN) system was introduced into the United Kingdom by J. Whitaker & Sons Ltd. in 1967 and into the United States in 1968 by R. R. Bowker. The Technical Committee on Documentation of the International Organization for Standardization (ISO TC 46) is responsible for the international standard.

The purpose of this standard is to "establish the specifications for the International Standard Book Number (ISBN) as a unique international identification system for each product form or edition of a monographic publication published or produced by a specific publisher." The standard specifies the construction of an ISBN, the rules for assignment and use of an ISBN, and all metadata associated with the allocation of an ISBN.

Types of monographic publications to which an ISBN may be assigned include printed books and pamphlets (in various product formats); electronic publications (either on the Internet or on physical carriers such as CD-ROMs or diskettes); educational/instructional films, videos, and transparencies; educational/instructional software; audiobooks on cassette or CD or DVD; braille publications; and microform publications.

Serial publications, printed music, and musical sound recordings are excluded from the ISBN standard as they are covered by other identification systems.

The ISBN is used by publishers, distributors, wholesalers, bookstores, and libraries, among others, in 217 countries and territories as an ordering and inventory system. It expedites the collection of data on new and forthcoming editions of monographic publications for print and electronic directories used by the book trade. Its use also facilitates rights management and the monitoring of sales data for the publishing industry.

The "new" ISBN consists of 13 digits. As of January 1, 2007, a revision to the ISBN standard was implemented in an effort to substantially increase the numbering capacity. The 10-digit ISBN identifier (ISBN-10) is now replaced by the ISBN 13-digit identifier (ISBN-13). All facets of book publishing are now expected to use the ISBN-13, and the ISBN agencies throughout the world are now issuing only ISBN-13s to publishers. Publishers with existing ISBN-10s need to convert their ISBNs to ISBN-13s by the addition of the EAN prefix 978 and recalculation of the new check digit:

ISBN-10: 0-8352-8235-X
ISBN-13: 978-0-8352-8235-2

When the inventory of the ISBN-10s has been exhausted, the ISBN agencies will start assigning ISBN-13s with the "979" prefix instead of the "978." There is no 10-digit equivalent for 979 ISBNs.

Construction of an ISBN

An ISBN currently consists of 13 digits separated into the following parts:

1 A prefix of "978" for an ISBN-10 converted to an ISBN-13
2 Group or country identifier, which identifies a national or geographic grouping of publishers
3 Publisher identifier, which identifies a particular publisher within a group
4 Title identifier, which identifies a particular title or edition of a title
5 Check digit, the single digit at the end of the ISBN that validates the ISBN-13

For more information regarding ISBN-13 conversion services provided by the U.S. ISBN Agency at R. R. Bowker, LLC, visit the ISBN Agency Web site at http://www.isbn.org, or contact the U.S. ISBN Agency at isbn-san@bowker.com.

Publishers requiring their ISBNs to be converted from the ISBN-10 to ISBN-13 format can use the U.S. ISBN Agency's free ISBN-13 online converter at http://isbn.org/converterpub.asp. Large list conversions can be requested by e-mailing isbnconversion@bowker.com. Publishers can also subscribe to view their ISBN online log book by accessing their personal account at http://www.bowkerlink.com.

Displaying the ISBN on a Product or Publication

When an ISBN is written or printed, it should be preceded by the letters ISBN, and each part should be separated by a space or hyphen. In the United States, the hyphen is used for separation, as in the following example: ISBN 978-0-8352-8235-2. In this example, 978 is the prefix that precedes the ISBN-13, 0 is the group identifier, 8352 is the publisher identifier, 8235 is the title identifier, and 2 is the check digit. The group of English-speaking countries, which includes the United States, Australia, Canada, New Zealand, and the United Kingdom, uses the group identifiers 0 and 1.

The ISBN Organization

The administration of the ISBN system is carried out at three levels—through the International ISBN Agency in the United Kingdom, through the national agencies, and through the publishing houses themselves. The International ISBN

Agency, which is responsible for assigning country prefixes and for coordinating the worldwide implementation of the system, has an advisory panel that represents the International Organization for Standardization (ISO), publishers, and libraries. The International ISBN Agency publishes the *Publishers International ISBN Directory,* which is a listing of all national agencies' publishers with their assigned ISBN publisher prefixes. R. R. Bowker, as the publisher of *Books In Print* with its extensive and varied database of publishers' addresses, was the obvious place to initiate the ISBN system and to provide the service to the U.S. publishing industry. To date, the U.S. ISBN Agency has entered more than 180,000 publishers into the system.

ISBN Assignment Procedure

Assignment of ISBNs is a shared endeavor between the U.S. ISBN Agency and the publisher. Publishers can make online application through the ISBN Agency's Web site, or by phone or fax. After an application is received and processed by the agency, an ISBN Publisher Prefix is assigned, along with a computer-generated block of ISBNs that is mailed or e-mailed to the publisher. The publisher then has the responsibility to assign an ISBN to each title, keep an accurate record of each number assigned, and register each title in the *Books In Print* database at http://www.bowkerlink.com. It is the responsibility of the ISBN Agency to validate assigned ISBNs and keep a record of all ISBN publisher prefixes in circulation.

ISBN implementation is very much market-driven. Major distributors, wholesalers, retailers, and so forth recognize the necessity of the ISBN system and request that publishers register with the ISBN Agency. Also, the ISBN is a mandatory bibliographic element in the International Standard Bibliographical Description (ISBD). The Library of Congress Cataloging in Publication (CIP) Division directs publishers to the agency to obtain their ISBN prefixes.

Location and Display of the ISBN

On books, pamphlets, and other printed material, the ISBN shall be printed on the verso of the title leaf or, if this is not possible, at the foot of the title leaf itself. It should also appear on the outside back cover or on the back of the jacket if the book has one (the lower right-hand corner is recommended). The ISBN shall also appear on any accompanying promotional materials following the provisions for location according to the format of the material.

On other monographic publications, the ISBN shall appear on the title or credit frames and any labels permanently affixed to the publication. If the publication is issued in a container that is an integral part of the publication, the ISBN shall be displayed on the label. If it is not possible to place the ISBN on the item or its label, then the number should be displayed on the bottom or the back of the container, box, sleeve, or frame. It should also appear on any accompanying material, including each component of a multi-type publication.

Printing of ISBN in Machine-Readable Coding

All books should carry ISBNs in the EAN-13 bar code machine-readable format. All ISBN EAN-13 bar codes start with the EAN prefix 978 for books. As of January 1, 2007, all EAN bar codes should have the ISBN-13 appearing immediately above the bar code in eye-readable format, preceded by the acronym "ISBN." The recommended location of the EAN-13 bar code for books is in the lower right-hand corner of the back cover (see Figure 1).

Figure 1 / Printing the ISBN in Bookland/EAN Symbology

Five-Digit Add-On Code

In the United States, a five-digit add-on code is used for additional information. In the publishing industry, this code is used for price information. The lead digit of the five-digit add-on has been designated a currency identifier, when the add-on is used for price. Number 5 is the code for the U.S. dollar, 6 denotes the Canadian dollar, 1 the British pound, 3 the Australian dollar, and 4 the New Zealand dollar. Publishers that do not want to indicate price in the add-on should print the code 90000 (see Figure 2).

Figure 2 / Printing the ISBN Bookland/EAN Number in Bar Code with the Five-Digit Add-On Code

978 = ISBN Bookland/EAN prefix
5 = Code for U.S. $
2499 = $24.99

90000 means no information in the add-on code

Reporting the Title and the ISBN

After the publisher reports a title to the ISBN Agency, the number is validated and the title is listed in the many R. R. Bowker hard-copy and electronic publications, including *Books in Print; Forthcoming Books; Paperbound Books in Print; Books in Print Supplement; Books Out of Print; Books in Print Online; Books in Print Plus-CD ROM; Children's Books in Print; Subject Guide to Children's Books in Print; Books Out Loud: Bowker's Guide to AudioBooks; Bowker's Complete Video Directory; Software Encyclopedia; Software for Schools;* and other specialized publications.

For an ISBN application and information, visit the ISBN Agency Web site at http://www.isbn.org, call the toll-free number 888-269-5372, fax 908-219-0188, or write to the United States ISBN Agency, 630 Central Ave., New Providence, NJ 07974.

The ISSN, and How to Obtain One

U.S. ISSN Center
Library of Congress

In the early 1970s the rapid increase in the production and dissemination of information and an intensified desire to exchange information about serials in computerized form among different systems and organizations made it increasingly clear that a means to identify serial publications at an international level was needed. The International Standard Serial Number (ISSN) was developed and became the internationally accepted code for identifying serial publications.

The ISSN is an international standard, ISO 3297: 2007, as well as a U.S. standard, ANSI/NISO Z39.9. The 2007 edition of ISO 3297 expands the scope of the ISSN to cover continuing resources (serials, as well as updating databases, looseleafs, and some Web sites).

The number itself has no significance other than as a brief, unique, and unambiguous identifier. The ISSN consists of eight digits in Arabic numerals 0 to 9, except for the last—or check—digit, which can be an X. The numbers appear as two groups of four digits separated by a hyphen and preceded by the letters ISSN—for example, ISSN 1234-5679.

The ISSN is not self-assigned by publishers. Administration of the ISSN is coordinated through the ISSN Network, an intergovernmental organization within the UNESCO/UNISIST program. The ISSN Network consists of national ISSN centers, coordinated by the ISSN International Centre, located in Paris. National ISSN Centers are responsible for registering serials published in their respective countries. Responsibility for the assignment of ISSN to titles from multinational publishers is allocated among the ISSN Centers in which the publisher has offices. A list of these publishers and the corresponding ISSN centers is located on International Centre's web site, http://www.issn.org.

The ISSN International Centre handles ISSN assignments for international organizations and for countries that do not have a national center. It also maintains and distributes the ISSN Register and makes it available in a variety of products, most commonly via the ISSN Portal, an online subscription database. The ISSN Register is also available via Z39.50 access, and as a data file. Selected ISSN data can also be obtained in customized files or database extracts that can be used, for example, to check the accuracy or completeness of a requestor's list of titles and ISSN. The ISSN Register contains bibliographic records corresponding to each ISSN assignment as reported by national ISSN centers. The database contains records for well over 1.5 million ISSNs.

The ISSN is used all over the world by serials publishers to identify their serials and to distinguish their titles from others that are the same or similar. It is used by subscription services and libraries to manage files for orders, claims, and back issues. It is used in automated check-in systems by libraries that wish to process receipts more quickly. Copyright centers use the ISSN as a means to collect and disseminate royalties. It is also used as an identification code by postal services and legal deposit services. The ISSN is included as a verification element in interlibrary lending activities and for union catalogs as a collocating device. In recent years, the ISSN has been incorporated into bar codes for optical recognition of serial publications and into the standards for the identification of issues and articles in serial publications. Other growing uses for the ISSN are in online systems where it can serve to connect catalog records or citations in abstracting and indexing databases with full-text journal content via OpenURL resolvers or reference linking services, and as an identifier and link in archives of electronic and print serials.

Because serials are generally known and cited by title, assignment of the ISSN is inseparably linked to the key title, a standardized form of the title derived from information in the serial issue. Only one ISSN can be assigned to a title in a particular medium. For titles issued in multiple media—e.g., print, online, CD-ROM—a separate ISSN is assigned to each medium version. If a major title change occurs or the medium changes, a new ISSN must be assigned. Centers responsible for assigning ISSNs also construct the key title and create an associated bibliographic record.

A significant new feature of the 2007 ISSN standard is the Linking ISSN (ISSN-L), a mechanism that enables collocation or linking among different media versions of a continuing resource. The Linking ISSN allows a unique designation (one of the existing ISSNs) to be applied to all media versions of a continuing resource while retaining the separate ISSN that pertains to each version. When an ISSN is functioning as a Linking ISSN, the eight digits of the base ISSN are prefixed with the designation "ISSN-L." The Linking ISSN facilitates search, retrieval, and delivery across all medium versions of a serial or other continuing resource for improved ISSN functionality in OpenURL linking, search engines, library catalogs, and knowledge bases. The 2007 standard also supports interoperability by specifying the use of ISSN and ISSN-L with other systems such as DOI, OpenURL, URN, and EAN bar codes. ISSN-L was implemented in the ISSN Register in 2008. To help ISSN users implement the ISSN-L in their databases, two free tables are available from the ISSN International Centre's home page: one lists each ISSN and its corresponding ISSN-L; the other lists each ISSN-L and its corresponding ISSNs.

In the United States, the U.S. ISSN Center at the Library of Congress is responsible for assigning and maintaining the ISSNs for all U.S. serial titles. Publishers wishing to have an ISSN assigned should download an application from the Center's Web site, and mail, e-mail, or fax the form to the U.S. ISSN Center. Assignment of the ISSN is free, and there is no charge for use of the ISSN.

To obtain an ISSN for a U.S. publication, or for further information about ISSN in the United States, libraries, publishers, and other ISSN users should visit the U.S. ISSN Center's Web site, http://www.loc.gov/issn, or contact the U.S. ISSN Center, U.S. and Publisher Liaison Division, Library of Congress, 101 Independence Ave. S.E., Washington, DC 20540-4284 (telephone 202-707-6452, fax 202-707-6333, e-mail issn@loc.gov).

For information about ISSN products and services, and for application procedures that non-U.S. parties should use to apply for an ISSN, visit the ISSN International Centre's Web site at http://www.issn.org or contact the International Centre at 45 rue de Turbigo, 75003 Paris, France (telephone 33-1-44-88-22-20, fax 33-1-40-26-32-43, e-mail issnic@issn.org).

How to Obtain an SAN

Beat Barblan and Louise Timko
United States ISBN/SAN Agency

SAN stands for Standard Address Number. The SAN system, an American National Standards Institute (ANSI) standard, assigns a unique identification number that is used to positively identify specific addresses of organizations in order to facilitate buying and selling transactions within the industry. It is recognized as the identification code for electronic communication within the industry.

For purposes of this standard, the book industry includes book publishers, book wholesalers, book distributors, book retailers, college bookstores, libraries, library binders, and serial vendors. Schools, school systems, technical institutes, and colleges and universities are not members of this industry, but are served by it and therefore included in the SAN system.

The purpose of the SAN is to ease communications among these organizations, of which there are several hundreds of thousands that engage in a large volume of separate transactions with one another. These transactions include purchases of books by book dealers, wholesalers, schools, colleges, and libraries from publishers and wholesalers; payments for all such purchases; and other communications between participants. The objective of this standard is to establish an identification code system by assigning each address within the industry a unique code to be used for positive identification for all book and serial buying and selling transactions.

Many organizations have similar names and multiple addresses, making identification of the correct contact point difficult and subject to error. In many cases, the physical movement of materials takes place between addresses that differ from the addresses to be used for the financial transactions. In such instances, there is ample opportunity for confusion and errors. Without identification by SAN, a complex record-keeping system would have to be instituted to avoid introducing errors. In addition, problems with the current numbering system—such as errors in billing, shipping, payments, and returns—are significantly reduced by using the SAN system. The SAN also eliminates one step in the order fulfillment process: the "look-up procedure" used to assign account numbers. Previously a store or library dealing with 50 different publishers was assigned a different account number by each of the suppliers. The SAN solved this problem. If a publisher prints its SAN on its stationery and ordering documents, vendors to whom it sends transactions do not have to look up the account number, but can proceed immediately to process orders by SAN.

Libraries are involved in many of the same transactions as book dealers, such as ordering and paying for books and charging and paying for various services to other libraries. Keeping records of transactions—whether these involve buying, selling, lending, or donations—entails operations suited to SAN use. SAN stationery speeds up order fulfillment and eliminate errors in shipping, billing, and crediting; this, in turn, means savings in both time and money.

History

Development of the Standard Address Number began in 1968 when Russell Reynolds, general manager of the National Association of College Stores (NACS), approached R. R. Bowker and suggested that a "Standard Account Number" system be implemented in the book industry. The first draft of a standard was prepared by an American National Standards Institute (ANSI) Committee Z39 subcommittee, which was co-chaired by Russell Reynolds and Emery Koltay of Bowker. After Z39 members proposed changes, the current version of the standard was approved by NACS on December 17, 1979.

Format

The SAN consists of six digits plus a seventh *Modulus 11* check digit; a hyphen follows the third digit (XXX-XXXX) to facilitate transcription. The hyphen is to be used in print form, but need not be entered or retained in computer systems. Printed on documents, the Standard Address Number should be preceded by the identifier "SAN" to avoid confusion with other numerical codes (SAN XXXXXXX).

Check Digit Calculation

The check digit is based on *Modulus 11*, and can be derived as follows:

1.	Write the digits of the basic number.	2 3 4 5 6 7
2.	Write the constant weighting factors associated with each position by the basic number.	7 6 5 4 3 2
3.	Multiply each digit by its associated weighting factor.	14 18 20 20 18 14
4.	Add the products of the multiplications.	14 + 18 + 20 + 20 + 18 + 14 = 104
5.	Divide the sum by *Modulus 11* to find the remainder.	104 ÷ 11 = 9 plus a remainder of 5
6.	Subtract the remainder from the *Modulus 11* to generate the required check digit. If there is no remainder, generate a check digit of zero. If the check digit is 10, generate a check digit of X to represent 10, since the use of 10 would require an extra digit.	11 - 5 = 6
7.	Append the check digit to create the standard seven-digit Standard Address Number.	SAN 234-5676

SAN Assignment

R. R. Bowker accepted responsibility for being the central administrative agency for SAN, and in that capacity assigns SANs to identify uniquely the addresses of organizations. No SANs can be reassigned; in the event that an organization should cease to exist, for example, its SAN would cease to be in circulation entirely. If an organization using an SAN should move or change its name with no change in ownership, its SAN would remain the same, and only the name or address would be updated to reflect the change.

The SAN should be used in all transactions; it is recommended that the SAN be imprinted on stationery, letterheads, order and invoice forms, checks, and all other documents used in executing various book transactions. The SAN should always be printed on a separate line above the name and address of the organization, preferably in the upper left-hand corner of the stationery to avoid confusion with other numerical codes pertaining to the organization, such as telephone number, zip code, and the like.

SAN Functions

The SAN is strictly a Standard Address Number, becoming functional only in applications determined by the user; these may include activities such as purchasing, billing, shipping, receiving, paying, crediting, and refunding. It is the method used by Pubnet and PubEasy systems and is required in all electronic data interchange communications using the Book Industry Systems Advisory Committee (BISAC) EDI formats. Every department that has an independent function within an organization could have a SAN for its own identification.

For additional information or to make suggestions, write to ISBN/SAN Agency, R. R. Bowker, LLC, 630 Central Ave., New Providence, NJ 07974, call 888-269-5372, or fax 908-219-0188. The e-mail address is san@bowker.com. The SAN Web site for online applications is at http://www.isbn.org.

Distinguished Books

Notable Books of 2010

The Notable Books Council of the Reference and User Services Association, a division of the American Library Association, selected these titles for their significant contribution to the expansion of knowledge or for the pleasure they can provide to adult readers.

Fiction

Bass, Rick. *Nashville Chrome* (Houghton Mifflin Harcourt).

Donoghue, Emma. *Room* (Little, Brown).

Egan, Jennifer. *A Visit from the Goon Squad* (Knopf).

Franklin, Tom. *Crooked Letter, Crooked Letter* (Morrow).

Franze, Jonathan. *Freedom* (Farrar, Straus & Giroux).

Hynes, James. *Next* (Reagan Arthur).

Lee, Chang Rae. *The Surrendered* (Riverhead).

Marlantes, Karl. *Matterhorn: A Novel of the Vietnam War* (Atlantic Monthly).

Mitchell, David. *The Thousand Autumns of Jacob de Zoet.* (Random).

Murray, Paul. *Skippy Dies* (Faber).

Soli, Tatjana. *The Lotus Eaters* (St. Martin's).

Udall, Brady. *The Lonely Polygamist* (Norton).

Nonfiction

Chernow, Ron. *Washington: A Life* (Penguin).

de Waal, Edmund. *The Hare with Amber Eyes: A Family's Century of Art and Loss* (Farrar, Straus & Giroux)

Demick, Barbara. *Nothing to Envy: Ordinary Lives in North Korea* (Spiegel & Grau).

Frazier, Ian. *Travels in Siberia* (Farrar, Straus & Giroux).

Harman, Oren. *The Price of Altruism: George Price and the Search for the Origins of Kindness* (Norton).

Okrent, Daniel. *Last Call: The Rise and Fall of Prohibition* (Scribner).

Olson, Lynne. *Citizens of London: The Americans Who Stood with Britain in Its Darkest, Finest Hour* (Random).

Philbrick, Nathaniel. *The Last Stand: Custer, Sitting Bull, and the Battle of the Little Bighorn* (Viking).

Skloot, Rebecca. *The Immortal Life of Henrietta Lacks* (Crown).

Smith, Patti. *Just Kids* (Ecco).

Vaillant, John. *The Tiger: A True Story of Vengeance and Survival* (Knopf).

Wilkerson, Isabel. *The Warmth of Other Suns: The Epic Story of America's Great Migration* (Random).

Poetry

Hoagland, Tony. *Unincorporated Persons in the Late Honda Dynasty* (Graywolf).

Williams, C. K. *Wait* (Farrar, Straus & Giroux).

Best Fiction for Young Adults

Each year a committee of the Young Adult Library Services Association YALSA, a division of the American Library Association, compiles a list of the best fiction appropriate for young adults ages 12 to 18. Selected on the basis of each book's proven or potential appeal and value to young adults, the titles span a variety of subjects as well as a broad range of reading levels.

Alonzo, Sandra. *Riding Invisible,* illustrated by Nathan Huang (Disney-Hyperion).

Anderson, Laurie Halse. *Forge* (Simon & Schuster).

Avasthi, Swati. *Split* (Random).

Ayarbe, Heidi. *Compromised* (HarperCollins).

Bacigalupi, Paolo. *Ship Breaker* (Little, Brown).

Black, Holly. *White Cat* (Simon & Schuster).

Bow, Erin. *Plain Kate* (Scholastic).

Boyce, Frank. *Cosmic* (Walden Pond).

Boyd, Maria. *Will* (Random).

Brande, Robin. *Fat Cat* (Random).

Bunce, Elizabeth C. *Star Crossed* (Scholastic).

Calame, Don. *Beat the Band* (Candlewick).

Carbone, Elisa. *Jump* (Penguin).

Chima, Cinda Williams. *The Demon King: A Seven Realms Novel* (Disney-Hyperion).

Christopher, Lucy. *Stolen* (Scholastic).

Cohn, Rachel and David Levithan. *Dash and Lily's Book of Dares* (Random).

Combres, Elisabeth. *Broken Memory: A Novel of Rwanda,* translated by Shelley Tanaka (Groundwood).

Condie, Ally. *Matched* (Dutton).

Crowley, Cath. *A Little Wanting Song* (Random).

Dashner, James. *The Maze Runner* (Random).

David, Keren. *When I Was Joe* (Frances Lincoln).

De Goldi, Kate. *The 10 P.M. Question* (Candlewick).

De Vigan, Delphine. *No and Me* (Bloomsbury).

DeGramont, Nina. *Every Little Thing in the World* (Simon & Schuster).

Derting, Kimberly. *The Body Finder* (HarperCollins).

Diamand, Emily. *Raiders' Ransom* (Scholastic).

Donnelly, Jennifer. *Revolution* (Random).

Edwardson, Debby Dahl. *Blessing's Bead* (Farrar, Straus & Giroux).

Erskine, Kathryn. *Mockingbird* (Penguin).

Fisher, Catherine. *Incarceron* (Penguin).

Flood, Nancy Bo. *Warriors in the Crossfire* (Boyds Mills).

Funke, Cornelia. *Reckless* (Little, Brown).

George, Jessica Day. *Princess of Glass* (Bloomsbury).

Gleitzman, Morris. *Once* (Macmillan).

Gonzalez, Christina Diaz. *The Red Umbrella* (Random).

Goto, Hiromi. *Half World,* illustrated by Jillian Tamaki (Penguin).

Gray, Keith. *Ostrich Boys* (Random).

Green, John, and David Levithan. *Will Grayson, Will Grayson* (Penguin).

Healey, Karen. *Guardian of the Dead* (Little, Brown).

Henry, April. *Girl, Stolen* (Macmillan).

Hoffman, Alice. *Green Witch* (Scholastic).

Holt, Kimberly Willis. *The Water Seeker* (Macmillan).

Kelly, Tara. *Harmonic Feedback* (Macmillan).

Kephart, Beth. *The Heart Is Not a Size* (HarperCollins).

King, A. S. *Please Ignore Vera Dietz* (Random).

Koertge, Ron. *Shakespeare Makes the Playoffs* (Candlewick).

Lockhart, E. *Real Live Boyfriends* (Random).

Lynch, Chris. *Hothouse* (HarperCollins).

Maberry, Jonathan. *Rot and Ruin* (Simon & Schuster).

Marchetta, Melina. *Finnikin of the Rock* (Candlewick).

Matson, Morgan. *Amy and Roger's Epic Detour* (Simon & Schuster).

McBride, Lish. *Hold Me Closer, Necromancer* (Macmillan).

McCaughrean, Geraldine. *The Death-Defying Pepper Roux* (HarperCollins).

McMullan, Margaret. *Sources of Light* (Houghton Mifflin Harcourt).

Milford, Kate. *The Boneshaker* (Clarion).

Millard, Glenda. *A Small Free Kiss in the Dark* (Holiday House).

Mulligan, Andy. *Trash* (David Fickling).

Myers, Walter Dean. *Lockdown* (HarperCollins).

Nelson, Jandy. *The Sky is Everywhere* (Penguin).

Nolan, Han. *Crazy* (Houghton Mifflin Harcourt).

O'Brien, Caragh M. *Birthmarked* (Roaring Brook).

Oliver, Lauren. *Before I Fall* (HarperCollins).

Oppel, Kenneth. *Half Brother* (Scholastic).

Paulsen, Gary. *Woods Runner* (Random).

Perkins, Lynne Rae. *As Easy As Falling Off the Face of the Earth* (HarperCollins).

Perkins, Mitali. *Bamboo People* (Charlesbridge).

Quick, Matthew. *Sorta Like a Rock Star* (Little, Brown).

Reeve, Philip. *Fever Crumb* (Scholastic).

Reinhardt, Dana. *The Things a Brother Knows* (Random)

Richards, Jame. *Three Rivers Rising: A Novel of the Johnstown Flood* (Random).

Roy, Jennifer. *Mindblind* (Marshall Cavendish).

Ruiz Zafón, Carlos. *The Prince of Mist* (Little, Brown).

Sachar, Louis. *The Cardturner* (Random).

Saenz, Benjamin. *Last Night I Sang to the Monster* (Cinco Puntos).

Sedgwick, Marcus. *Revolver* (Roaring Brook).

Shimko, Bonnie. *The Private Thoughts of Amelia E. Rye* (Macmillan).

Shinn, Sharon. *Gateway* (Penguin).

Shulman, Mark. *Scrawl* (Roaring Brook).

Shulman, Polly. *The Grimm Legacy* (Penguin).

Slade, Arthur. *The Hunchback Assignments* (Random).

Smith, Andrew. *The Marbury Lens* (Macmillan).

Sonnenblick, Jordan. *After Ever After* (Scholastic).

Standiford, Natalie. *Confessions of the Sullivan Sisters* (Scholastic).

Stork, Francisco X. *The Last Summer of the Death Warriors* (Scholastic).

Stratton, Allan. *Borderline* (HarperCollins).

Stuber, Barbara. *Crossing the Tracks* (Simon & Schuster).

Summers, Courtney. *Some Girls Are* (St. Martin's).

Supplee, Suzanne. *Somebody Everybody Listens To* (Penguin).

Teller, Janne. *Nothing*, translated by Martin Aitken (Simon & Schuster).

Tomlinson, Heather. *Toads and Diamonds* (Macmillan).

Turner, Megan Whalen. *A Conspiracy of Kings* (HarperCollins).

Vivian, Siobhan. *Not That Kind of Girl* (Scholastic).

Ward, Rachel. *Numbers* (Scholastic).

Wesselhoeft, Conrad. *Adios, Nirvana* (Houghton Mifflin).

Whitney, Daisy. *The Mockingbirds* (Little, Brown).

Williams, Carol Lynch. *Glimpse* (Simon & Schuster).

Williams, Gabrielle. *Beatle Meets Destiny* (Marshall Cavendish).

Yancey, Rick. *The Curse of the Wendigo* (Simon & Schuster).

Yovanoff, Brenna. *Replacement* (Penguin).

Quick Picks for Reluctant Young Adult Readers

The Young Adult Library Services Association, a division of the American Library Association, annually chooses a list of outstanding titles that will stimulate the interest of reluctant teen readers. This list is intended to attract teens who, for whatever reason, choose not to read.

The list includes fiction and nonfiction titles published from late 2009 through early 2011.

Fiction

Barnes, Erica. *Immortal* (Urban).

Benoit, Charles. *You.* (HarperCollins).

Bodeen, S. A. *The Gardener* (Macmillan).

Borris, Albert. *Crash Into Me* (Simon & Schuster).

Carman, Patrick. *Thirteen Days to Midnight* (Little, Brown).

Condie, Allie. *Matched* (Penguin).

Dashner, James. *The Maze Runner* (Random).

De la Pena, Matt. *I Will Save You* (Random).

Devlin, Ivy. *Low Red Moon* (Bloomsbury).

Divine, L. *Drama High: Culture Clash* (Drama High Series) (Kensington).

Elkeles, Simone. *Return to Paradise* (Llewellyn).

Elkeles, Simone. *Rules of Attraction* (Bloomsbury).

Fehlbaum, Beth. *Hope in Patience* (Westside).

Giles, Gail. *Dark Song* (Little, Brown).

Greene, Michele Dominguez. *Keep Sweet* (Simon & Schuster).

Hautman, Pete. *Blank Confession* (Simon & Schuster).

Henry, April. *Girl Stolen* (Macmillan).

Hubbard, Jennifer. *The Secret Year* (Penguin).

Jacobson, Jennifer Richard. *The Complete History of Why I Hate Her* (Simon & Schuster).

Keplinger, Kody. *The D.U.F.F. (Designated Ugly Fat Friend)* (Little, Brown).

Kimani Tru Imprint (Kimani Publishing): Byrd, A. J. *Losing Romeo* (BFF novel); Cross, Cecil. *Next Semester*; McKayhan, Monica. *Step Up* (Indigo novel); Sewell, Earl. *Myself and I* (Keysha novel).

Maldonado, Torrey. *Secret Saturdays* (Penguin).

Myers, Walter Dean. *Lockdown* (HarperCollins).

Night Fall Series (Lerner): Duke, Shirley. *Unthinkable*; Jasper, Rick. *Skin*; Jasper, Rick. *Thaw*; Watson, Stephanie. *The Club.*

Omololu, C. J. *Dirty Little Secrets* (Bloomsbury).

Peirce, Lincoln. *Big Nate: In a Class By Himself* (Big Nate series) (HarperCollins).

Peters, Julie Anne. *By the Time You Read This, I'll Be Dead* (Disney-Hyperion).

Price, Charlie. *The Interrogation of Gabriel James.* (Farrar, Straus & Giroux).

Rainfield, Cheryl. *Scars* (Westside).

Reed, Amy. *Beautiful* (Simon & Schuster).

Schraff, Anne (Urban Underground series, Saddleback Educational). *Outrunning the Darkness*; *Shadows of Guilt*; *A Boy Called Twister*; *If You Really Loved Me*; *Like a Broken Doll*; *To Be A Man.*

Schutz, Samantha. *You Are Not Here* (Scholastic).

Scott, Elizabeth. *The Unwritten Rule* (Simon & Schuster).

Shan, Darren. *Birth of a Killer* (Little, Brown).

Shulman, Mark. *Scrawl* (Roaring Brook).

Simone, Ni-Ni. *Teenage Love Affair* (Kensington).

Smith, Alexander Gordon. *Solitary: Escape from Furnace* (Farrar, Straus & Giroux).

Stine, R. L. *Fear: 13 Stories of Suspense* (Speak).

Strasser, Todd. *Blood on My Hands* (Egmont USA).

Strasser, Todd. *Wish You Were Dead* (Egmont USA).

Summers, Courtney. *Some Girls Are* (St. Martin's).

Teller, Janne. *Nothing* (Simon & Schuster).

Templar Company Ltd. *Vampireology: The True History of the Fallen* (Candlewick).

Van Tol, Alex. *Knifepoint* (Orca Soundings).

Volponi, Paul. *Rikers High* (Penguin).

Wells, Dan. *Mr. Monster* (Tor).

Williams, Carol Lynch. *Glimpse* (Simon & Schuster).

Nonfiction

Amason, Jessica, and Richard Blakeley. *This is Why You're Fat: Where Dreams Become Heart Attacks* (HarperCollins).

Believe it or Not! Ripley's. *Ripley's Believe it or Not! Enter If You Dare* (Ripley).

Balestier, Courtney. *Would You Rather. . .? BFF!! Over 300 Fiercely Fascinating Questions to Ask your Friends.* (Seven Footer).

Bellows, Melina Gerosa. *NatGeo Amazing! 100 People, Places, and Things That Will Wow You* (National Geographic).

Berger, Melvin and Gilda. *101 Freaky Animals* (Scholastic).

Bos, Samone, et al. *Ask Me Everything: Facts, Stats, Lists, Records and More* (Penguin).

Brereton, Catherine, Philip Steele, and Hannah Wilson. *Warriors Versus Warriors: Ten Fighters, Five Battles, One Winner* (Macmillan).

Buller, Laura. *Danger! Open with Extreme Caution* (Penguin).

Cassidy, John, and Brendan Boyle. *The Klutz Book of Inventions* (Scholastic).

Choron, Harry and Sandra. *Look! It's Jesus! Amazing Holy Visions in Everyday Life* (Chronicle).

Claybourne, Anna. *100 Most Disgusting Things on the Planet* (Scholastic).

Conley, Erin. *Kiss: a Girl's Guide to Puckering Up* (Zest/Orange Avenue).

Eaton, Jim. *Ghosts Caught on Film 2: Photographs of the Unexplained* (F+W Media).

Felisbret, Eric. *Graffiti New York* (Abrams).

Goldblatt, David, and Johnny Acton. *The Soccer Book* (Penguin).

Hasler, Nikol. *Sex: A Book for Teens: An Uncensored Guide to Your Body, Sex and Safety* (Zest/Orange Avenue).

Henry, Nathan. *Good Behavior: A Memoir* (Bloomsbury).

Hines-Stephens, Sarah. *Show Off: How to Do Absolutely Everything One Step at a Time* (Candlewick).

Jackson, Julie, and Jill Johnson. *Glamourpuss: The Enchanting World of Kitty Wigs* (Chronicle).

Kamikaze Factory Studio. *Kodomo Manga: Super Cute!* (HarperCollins).

Leto, Lauren, and Ben Bator. *Texts From Last Night: All the Texts No One Remembers Sending* (Penguin).

Lipkowitz, Daniel. *The Lego Book* (Penguin).

Mockus, Steve. *How to Speak Zombie: A Guide for the Living* (Chronicle).

Mora, Pat. *Dizzy in Your Eyes: Poems About Love* (Random).

Munro, Nicky, and Sharon Spencer. *Life in the Wild* (Penguin).

National Geographic. *Weird but True! 300 Outrageous Facts* (National Geographic).

Neri, G., and Randy DuBurke. *Yummy: The Last Days of a Southside Shorty* (Lee & Low).

Pluto, Terry, and Brian Windhorst. *Lebron James: The Making of an MVP* (Gray & Company).

Sansweet, Stephen J., and Anne Neumann. *Star Wars: 1,000 Collectibles: Memorabilia and Stories from a Galaxy Far, Far Away* (Abrams).

Sartore, Joel. *Rare: Portraits of America's Endangered Species* (National Geographic).

Scholastic. *Ripley's Believe It or Not: Special Edition* (Scholastic).

Setchfield, Neil. *Yuck! The Things People Eat* (Merrell).

Seventeen Magazine. *Seventeen Presents . . . 500 Beauty Tips: Look Your Best for School, Weekend, Parties and More* (Hearst).

Tack, Karen, and Alan Richardson. *What's New Cupcake: Ingeniously Simple Designs for Every Occasion*. (Houghton Mifflin Harcourt).

Talmadge, Eve, and Justin Taylor. *The Word Made Flesh: Literary Tattoos from Bookworms Worldwide* (HarperCollins).

Teen Vogue. *The Teen Vogue Handbook* (Penguin).

Thompson, Alicia. *The Secret Language of Birthdays: Teen Edition* (Penguin).

Valentino, Serena. *How To Be A Zombie: The Essential Guide for Anyone Who Craves Brains* (Candlewick).

Veasey, Nick. *X-treme X-ray: See the World Inside Out!* (Scholastic).

Von D, Kat, with Sandra Bark. *The Tattoo Chronicles* (HarperCollins).

Yates, Jen. *Cake Wrecks: When Professional Cakes Go Hilariously Wrong* (Andrews McMeel).

Audiobooks for Young Adults

Each year a committee of the Young Adult Library Services Association, a division of the American Library Association, compiles a list of the best audiobooks for young adults ages 12 to 18. The titles are selected for their teen appeal and recording quality, and because they enhance the audience's appreciation of any written work on which the recordings may be based. While the list as a whole addresses the interests and needs of young adults, individual titles need not appeal to this entire age range but rather to parts of it.

Nonfiction

A Savage Thunder: Antietam and the Bloody Road to Freedom by Jim Murphy, read by Kevin Orton. Recorded Books, 3 hours, 3 discs (978-1-4407-1409-2).

Fiction

Alchemy and Meggy Swann by Karen Cushman, read by Katherine Kellgren. Listening Library, 4 hours and 23 minutes, 4 discs (978-0-3077-1024-6).

Beat the Band by Don Calame, read by Nick Podehl. Brilliance Audio, 8 hours and 17 minutes, 7 discs (978-1-4418-1493-7).

The Best Bad Luck I Ever Had by Kristin Levine, read by Kirby Heyborne. Listening Library, 7 hours and 9 minutes, 6 discs (978-0-3077-1058-1).

The Boy Book: A Study of Habits and Behaviors, Plus Techniques for Taming Them by E. Lockhart, read by Kirsten Potter. Listening Library, 5 hours and 5 minutes, 4 discs (978-0-7393-8107-6).

Dreamdark Silksinger by Lani Taylor, read by Cassandra Campbell. Brilliance Audio, 13 hours and 18 minutes, 11 discs (978-1-4418-0231-6).

Enola Holmes: The Case of the Peculiar Pink Fan by Nancy Springer, read by Katherine Kellgren. Recorded Books, 3 hours and 54 minutes, 4 discs (978-1-4361-6162-6).

Finnikin of the Rock by Melina Marchetta, read by Jeffrey Cummings. Brilliance Audio, 12 hours and 29 minutes, 11 discs (978-1-4418-8871-6).

Heist Society by Ally Carter, read by Angela Dawe. Brilliance Audio, 6 hours and 10 minutes, 5 discs (978-1-4418-2674-9).

Impulse by Ellen Hopkins, read by Laura Flanagan, Jeremy Guskin, and Steve Coombs. HighBridge, 6 hours and 45 minutes, 6 discs (978-1-598-87-7564).

Incarceron by Catherine Fisher, read by Kim Mai Guest. Listening Library, 11 hours and 37 minutes, 10 discs (978-0-3077-0707-9).

It's Not Summer Without You by Jenny Han, read by Jessica Almasy. Recorded Books,

6 hours and 45 minutes, 6 discs (978-1-4498-2017-6).

Jerk, California by Jonathan Friesen, read by Andy Paris. Recorded Books, 9 hours and 30 minutes, 8 discs (978-1-4498-0647-7).

The Knife of Never Letting Go by Patrick Ness, read by Nick Podehl. Brilliance Audio, 12 hours, 10 discs (978-1-4418-5267-0).

Leviathan by Scott Westerfeld, read by Alan Cumming. Simon & Schuster, 8 hours and 20 minutes, 7 discs (978-0-7435-8388-6).

Muchacho by Louanne Johnson, read by Ozzie Rodriguez. Listening Library, 4 hours and 48 minutes, 4 discs (978-0-7393-8599-9).

One Crazy Summer by Rita Garcia Williams, read by Sisi Aisha Johnson. Recorded Books, 5 hours and 15 minutes, 5 discs (978-1-4498-2196-8).

Ostrich Boys by Keith Gray, read by Bruce Mann. Listening Library, 6 hours and 10 minutes, 5 discs (0-7393-7914-3).

Precious by Sapphire, read by Bahni Turpin. Random House, 5 hours and 5 minutes, 4 discs (0-3075-7811-9).

Rapture of the Deep by L. A. Meyer, read by Katherine Kellgren. Listen and Live Audio, 12 hours, 10 discs (978-1-59316-483-6).

Revolution by Jennifer Donnelly, read by Emily Janice Card and Emma Bering. Listening Library, 15 hours and 4 minutes, 12 discs (978-0-3077-4629-0).

The Rock and the River by Kekla Magoon, read by Dion Graham. Brilliance Audio, 6 hours and 47 minutes, 6 discs (978-1-4418-5865-8).

Seth Baumgartner's Love Manifesto by Eric Luper, read by Nick Podehl. Brilliance Audio, 6 hours and 33 minutes, 6 discs (978-1-4418-5964-8).

Split by Swati Avasthi, read by Joshua Swanson. Listening Library, 8 hours and 17 minutes, 7 discs (978-0-3075-7996-6).

Stop in the Name of Pants! by Louise Rennison, read by Stina Nielsen. Recorded Books, 6 hours and 30 minutes, 6 discs (978-1-4407-7774-5).

Swim the Fly by Don Calame, read by Nick Podehl. Brilliance Audio, 7 hours and 36 minutes, 7 discs (978-1-4418-1488-3).

This Full House by Virginia Euwer Wolff, read by Heather Alicia Simms. Listening Library, 7 hours and 41 minutes, 6 discs (978-0-7393-8000-0).

This World We Live In by Susan Beth Pfeffer, read by Emily Bauer. Listening Library, 6 discs (978-0-3075-8227-0).

The True Meaning of Smekday by Adam Rex, read by Bahni Turpin. Listening Library, 10 hours and 38 minutes, 9 discs (978-0-3077-1112-0).

What I Saw and How I Lied by Judy Blundell, read by Caitlin Greer. Scholastic Audiobooks, 6 hours and 20 minutes, 5 discs (978-0-545-16091-9).

White Cat by Holly Black, read by Jesse Eisenberg. Listening Library, 6 hours and 41 minutes, 6 discs (978-0-3077-1183-0).

Will Grayson, Will Grayson by John Green and David Levithan, read by MacLeod Andrews and Nick Podehl. Brilliance Audio, 7 hours and 57 minutes, 7 discs (978-1-4418-4260-2).

The Reading List

Established in 2007 by the Reference and User Services Association (RUSA), a division of the American Library Association, this list highlights outstanding genre fiction that merits special attention by general adult readers and the librarians who work with them.

RUSA's Reading List Council, which consists of 12 librarians who are experts in readers' advisory and collection development, selects books in eight categories: Adrenaline (suspense, thrillers, and action adventure), Fantasy, Historical Fiction, Horror, Mystery, Romance, Science Fiction, and Women's Fiction.

Adrenaline

The Nearest Exit by Olen Steinhauer (Minotaur).

Fantasy

Under Heaven by Guy Gavriel Kay (Roc).

Historical Fiction

The Invisible Bridge by Julie Orringer (Knopf).

Horror

The Dead Path by Stephen M. Irwin (Doubleday).

Mystery

Bury Your Dead by Louise Penny (Minotaur).

Romance

A Matter of Class by Mary Balogh (Vanguard).

Science Fiction

The Dervish House by Ian McDonald (Pyr).

Women's Fiction

Solomon's Oak by Jo-Ann Mapson (Bloomsbury).

Notable Recordings for Children

This list of notable CD recordings for children was selected by the Association for Library Service to Children, a division of the American Library Association. Recommended titles are chosen by children's librarians and educators on the basis of their originality, creativity, and suitability.

Alchemy and Meggy Swann. Listening Library, 4 hours and 23 minutes. Ages 9–14. Katherine Kellgren tells the story, set in medieval London, of a girl who has to make herself useful to her alchemist father.

Boom! Listening Library, 3 hours and 46 minutes. Ages 10–14. When Jimbo and Charlie overhear their teachers speaking a strange language, they embark on an adventure that involves them in foiling space alien plans. Julian Rhind-Tutt tells the humorous story.

The Call of the Wild. Listening Library, 3 hours and 10 minutes. Ages 10 up. Jeff Daniels tells the classic story of Buck, a dog who is stolen from his family home and becomes part of a dog sled team in Alaska.

Cantilena: Night Songs from Around the World. Yellow Tail Records, 56 minutes. Ages 0–5 years. Soothing lullabies, with multilingual vocals by Patrice O'Neill, demonstrate that people calm babies with similar music around the world.

Chicken Little. Weston Woods, 7 minutes. Ages 3–7. Walter Mayes narrates the tale of the chicken who thought the sky was falling.

Clementine: Friend of the Week. Recorded Books, two hours. Ages 7–10. Jessica Almasy's warm-hearted storytelling brings young Clementine to life.

Crocodile Tears (Alex Rider series). Recorded Books, 9 hours and 45 minutes. Ages 10–14. Alex is again involved in fantastic spy escapades and nearly is fed to a crocodile. Simon Prebble narrates.

The Curious Garden. Weston Woods, 8 minutes. Ages 5–8. David Mansfield's music and Katherine Kellgren's narration dramatize the story of a boy whose special garden spills over into the dreary city outside.

The Dinosaurs of Waterhouse Hawkins. Weston Woods, 20 minutes. Ages 8–10. Jonathan Pryce's reading and Ernest Troost's music enliven a reading of this 2002 Caldecott honor book.

Epossumondas Plays Possum. Recorded Books, 15 minutes. Ages 4–8. Cynthia Darlow tells this funny, slightly scary story of an adventurous baby opossum.

Forge. Brilliance Audio, 7 hours and 51 minutes. Laurie Halse Anderson's sequel to *Chains,* read by Tim Cain, brings to life what it took for runaway slaves to forge their own paths in the midst of the American Revolution.

Here in Harlem: Poems in Many Voices. Live Oak Media, 1 hour and 30 minutes. Ages 12–up. Walter Dean Myers's poems give voice to the New York City community where he grew up.

If You Were a Penguin. Live Oak Media, 9 minutes. Ages 3–7. Antonia Bath reads this introduction, with music, to members of the penguin family.

Jungle Gym. Carpet Square Records, 40 minutes. Ages 4–9. Twelve children's songs about everyday events, including fire drills, trick or treating, snow days, and sleepovers.

The King and the Thrush: Tales of Goodness and Greed. Eastern Coyote Recordings, 49 minutes. Ages 6–up. Earrings made of frogs, a jackal who thinks he's a god, and a bird wearing a tiny suit show up in these traditional folk tales told by Tim Jennings and Leanne Ponder.

The Magician's Elephant. Brilliance Audio, 2 hours and 55 minutes. Ages 9–12. Juliet Stevenson creates multiple voices for this story of an elephant and an orphan in the imaginary city of Baltese.

Mockingbird. Recorded Books, 4 hours and 30 minutes. Ages 10–14. Listeners learn how Caitlin copes with Asperger's syndrome, the loss of her brother, and learning to interact with others. Angela Jayne Rogers is the storyteller.

The New Explorers Club. Flannery Brothers, 45 minutes. Ages 5–8. Original music features lyrics about bugs, boots, pirates, and parrots.

One Crazy Summer. Recorded Books, 5 hours and 15 minutes. Ages 10–14. Delphine and her two sisters travel to California in the summer of 1968 to visit their estranged mother, but instead spend most of their time in a nearby Black Panthers summer camp.

Ranky Tanky. Mayhem Music, 50 minutes. Ages 4–8. Seventeen new and classic songs are performed by Rani Arbo and Daisy Mayhem.

Splat the Cat. Weston Woods, 7 minutes. Ages 4–7. Rob Scotton's humorous story about the first day of school is voiced by John Keating and scored by Scotty Huff and Robert Reynolds.

They Called Themselves the K.K.K. Brilliance Audio, 4 hours. Ages 12–up. Dion Graham narrates the story of the rise and evolution of the Ku Klux Klan.

The True Meaning of Smekday. Listening Library, 10 hours and 38 minutes. Ages 9–14. Adam Rex's popular novel is read by Bahni Turpin.

The Water Seeker. Listening Library, 7 hours and 3 minutes. Ages 12–14. Will Patton tells the story of young Amos Kincaid's westward journey to the Oregon territory in the early 19th century.

What to Do about Alice? Weston Woods, 15 minutes. Ages 7–10. The story of the life and times of Alice Roosevelt, daughter of President Theodore Roosevelt, is told by Katherine Kellgren.

Great Interactive Software for Kids

This list is chosen by a committee of the Association for Library Service to Children, a division of the American Library Association. Titles are selected on the basis of their originality, creativity, and suitability for children.

Kerpoof Studios. Disney Online (http://www.kerpoof.com). Ages 2–12. Children can create cards, drawings, and movies, tell a story, and more. New activities are added on a regular basis. Online.

Generation Cures: Caduceus. FableVision (http://www.fablevisionstudios.com/project.php?id=1). Ages 10–13. Caduceus takes children on a quest to master alchemy and save the land of Alterica. The game was developed in partnership with the Children's Hospital Trust to encourage civic consciousness in preteens. Online.

Zoodles 3.4.4. Inquisitive Minds (http://www.zoodles.com). Ages 3–10. Zoodles offers a wide range of games for children, from math and reading games to adventure games and computer games. A free version includes advertising. Download.

Notable Children's Books

A list of notable children's books is selected each year by the Notable Children's Books Committee of the Association for Library Service to Children, a division of the American Library Association. Recommended titles are selected by children's librarians and educators based on originality, creativity, and suitability for children. [See "Literary Prizes, 2010" later in Part 5 for Caldecott, Newbery, and other award winners—*Ed.*]

Books for Younger Readers

Baker, Keith. *LMNO Peas* (Beach Lane).

DiCamillo, Kate, and Alison McGhee. *Bink and Gollie,* illustrated by Tony Fucile (Candlewick).

Elliott, David. *In the Wild,* illustrated by Holly Meade (Candlewick).

Elya, Susan Middleton. *Rubia and the Three Osos,* illustrated by Melissa Sweet (Hyperion).

French, Vivian. *Yucky Worms,* illustrated by Jessica Ahlberg (Candlewick).

Graham, Bob. *April and Esme, Tooth Fairies* (Candlewick).

Hacohen, Dean. *Tuck Me In!* illustrated by Sherry Scharschmidt (Candlewick).

Khan, Rukhsana. *Big Red Lollipop,* illustrated by Sophie Blackall (Viking).

Lin, Grade. *Ling and Ting: Not Exactly the Same!* (Little, Brown).

Markle, Sandra. *Hip-Pocket Papa,* illustrated by Alan Marks (Charlesbridge).

Mavor, Salley. *Pocketful of Posies: A Treasury of Nursery Rhymes* (Houghton Mifflin Harcourt).

Reynolds, Aaron. *Back of the Bus,* illustrated by Floyd Cooper (Philomel).

Stead, Philip C. *A Sick Day for Amos McGee,* illustrated by Erin E. Stead (Roaring Brook).

Stein, David Ezra. *Interrupting Chicken* (Candlewick).

Tafolla, Carmen. *Fiesta Babies,* illustrated by Amy Córdova. (Tricycle).

Thompson, Bill. *Chalk* (Marshall Cavendish).

Tonatiuh, Duncan. *Dear Primo: A Letter to My Cousin* (Abrams).

Willems, Mo. *City Dog, Country Frog,* illustrated by Jon J Muth (Hyperion).

Willems, Mo. *We Are in a Book!* (Disney-Hyperion).

Woodson, Jacqueline. *Pecan Pie Baby,* illustrated by Sophie Blackall (Putnam).

Underwood, Deborah. *The Quiet Book,* illustrated by Renata Liwska (Houghton Mifflin Harcourt).

Velasquez, Eric. *Grandma's Gift* (Walker).

Middle Readers

Ancona, George. *¡Ole! Flamenco* (Lee & Low).

Angleberger, Tom. *The Strange Case of Origami Yoda* (Amulet).

Bishop, Nic. *Nic Bishop Lizards* (Scholastic).

Burns, Loree Griffin. *The Hive Detectives: Chronicle of a Honey Bee Catastrophe,* illustrated by Ellen Harasimowicz (Houghton Mifflin Harcourt).

Campbell, Sarah C. *Growing Patterns: Fibonacci Numbers in Nature* (Boyds Mills).

Carson, Mary Kay. *The Bat Scientists,* illustrated by Tom Uhlman (Houghton Mifflin Harcourt).

Dembicki, Matt, editor. *Trickster: Native American Tales—A Graphic Collection* (Fulcrum).

Gidwitz, Adam. *A Tale Dark and Grimm* (Dutton).

Greenberg, Jan, and Sandra Jordan. *Ballet for Martha: Making Appalachian Spring,* illustrated by Brian Floca (Roaring Brook).

Hill, Laban Carrick. *Dave the Potter: Artist, Poet, Slave,* illustrated by Bryan Collier (Little, Brown).

Holm, Jennifer L. *Turtle in Paradise* (Random).

Jenkins, Steve, and Robin Page. *How to Clean a Hippopotamus: A Look at Unusu-*

al Animal Partnerships (Houghton Mifflin Harcourt).

Montgomery, Sy. *Kakapo Rescue: Saving the World's Strangest Parrot,* illustrated by Nic Bishop (Houghton Mifflin Harcourt).

Novesky, Amy. *Me, Frida,* illustrated by David Diaz (Abrams).

O'Connor, Barbara. *The Fantastic Secret of Owen Jester* (Farrar, Straus & Giroux).

Raczka, Bob. *Guyku: A Year of Haiku for Boys,* illustrated by Peter H. Reynolds (Houghton Mifflin Harcourt).

Ramsey, Calvin Alexander, and Gwen Strauss. *Ruth and the Green Book,* illustrated by Floyd Cooper (Carolrhoda).

Rhodes, Jewell Parker. *Ninth Ward* (Little, Brown).

Schlitz, Laura Amy. *The Night Fairy,* illustrated by Angela Barrett (Candlewick).

Stamaty, Mark Alan. *Shake, Rattle and Turn That Noise Down! How Elvis Shook Up Music, Me and Mom* (Knopf).

Telgemeier, Raina. *Smile,* illustrated by the author and Stephanie Yue (Scholastic).

Tingle, Tim. *Saltypie: A Choctaw Journey from Darkness into Light,* illustrated by Karen Clarkson (Cinco Puntos).

Williams-Garcia, Rita. *One Crazy Summer* (Harper).

Older Readers

Bacigalupi, Paolo. *Ship Breaker* (Little, Brown).

Bartoletti, Susan Campbell. *They Called Themselves the K.K.K.: The Birth of an American Terrorist Group* (Houghton Mifflin Harcourt).

Bondoux, Anne-Laure. *Time of Miracles,* translated by Y. Maudet (Random).

Engle, Margarita. *The Firefly Letters: A Suffragette's Journey to Cuba* (Holt).

Erskine, Kathryn. *Mockingbird* (Philomel).

Flores-Galbis, Enrique. *90 Miles to Havana* (Roaring Brook).

Freedman, Russell. *Lafayette and the American Revolution* (Holiday House).

Matti, Truus. *Departure Time,* translated by Nancy Forest-Flier (Namelos).

Nelson, S. D. *Black Elk's Vision: A Lakota Story* (Abrams).

Neri, G. *Yummy: The Last Days of a Southside Shorty,* illustrated by Randy DuBurke (Lee & Low).

Preus, Margi. *Heart of a Samurai* (Abrams).

Reeve, Philip. *Fever Crumb* (Scholastic).

Ryan, Pam Muñoz. *The Dreamer,* illustrated by Peter Sís (Scholastic).

Sidman, Joyce. *Ubiquitous: Celebrating Nature's Survivors,* illustrated by Beckie Prange (Houghton Mifflin Harcourt).

Stotts, Stuart. *We Shall Overcome: A Song that Changed the World,* illustrated by Terrance Cummings (Houghton Mifflin Harcourt).

Teller, Janne. *Nothing,* translated by Martin Aitken (Simon & Schuster).

Vanderpool, Clare. *Moon Over Manifest* (Random).

Wiles, Deborah. *Countdown* (Scholastic).

All Ages

Cooper, Elisha. *Farm* (Scholastic).

Jenkins, Steve. *Bones: Skeletons and How They Work* (Scholastic).

Lee, Suzy. *Shadow* (Chronicle).

Shiga, Jason. *Meanwhile* (Abrams).

Sidman, Joyce. *Dark Emperor and Other Poems of the Night,* illustrated by Rick Allen (Houghton Mifflin Harcourt).

Singer, Marilyn. *Mirror, Mirror: A Book of Reversible Verse,* illustrated by Josée Masse (Dutton).

Notable Children's Videos

These DVD titles are selected by a committee of the Association for Library Service to Children, a division of the American Library Association. Recommendations are based on originality, creativity, and suitability for children.

The American Presidents, 1754–1861: Revolution and the New Nation, Expansion and Reform. Disney, 45 minutes. Ages 9–13.

Anatomy of a Puff. Human Relations Media, 15 minutes. Ages 12–up.

Chicken Little. Weston Woods, 9 minutes. Ages 2–6.

Cliques: Where Do You Fit In? Human Relations Media, 15 minutes. Ages 10–14.

Crow Call. Weston Woods, 16 minutes. Ages 2–6.

The Curious Garden. Weston Woods, 8 minutes. Ages 5–8.

The Dinosaurs of Waterhouse Hawkins. Weston Woods, 20 minutes. Ages 6–9.

Getting to Know Edgar Degas. Getting to Know, Inc., 22 minutes. Ages 7–10.

Katie Loves the Kittens. Weston Woods, 9 minutes. Ages 2–7.

Louise, The Adventures of a Chicken. Nutmeg Media, 15 minutes. Ages 3–7.

May I Pet Your Dog? Nutmeg Media, 13 minutes. Ages 4–8.

Naked Mole Rat Gets Dressed. Weston Woods, 9 minutes. Ages 2–7.

The Pigeon Finds a Hot Dog! Weston Woods, 7 minutes. Ages 2–7.

The Pluto Files. PBS, 60 minutes. Ages 10–14.

Songs of Freedom. Blue Sky Project, 27 minutes. Ages 7–10.

Splat the Cat. Weston Woods, 9 minutes. Ages 5–8.

Spoon. Weston Woods, 8 minutes. Ages 5–8.

That Book Woman. Weston Woods, 12 minutes. Ages 6–9.

Two Bobbies. Nutmeg Media, 12 minutes. Ages 6–9.

Bestsellers of 2010

E-books Rock

Daisy Maryles
Contributing Editor, *Publishers Weekly*

Back in March 2000, the big publishing news was Stephen King's novella *Riding the Bullet* being published exclusively in e-book format. King was the first major bestselling author to publish in an electronic format. At the time, Simon & Schuster spokesperson Adam Rothberg was widely quoted as saying: "This could change the model of publishing."

This year, for the first time in *Publishers Weekly*'s (*PW*'s) more than 100 years of annual features on bestsellers, the magazine collected statistics on e-book sales. We asked publishers (and only publishers that had print bestsellers with sales of more than 100,000 in 2010) to submit e-books with sales of more than 10,000 in 2010. The response from the houses was mixed. Many declined to share this information, others only submitted selected titles. Still, *PW* collected statistics on about 275 books—enough to underscore that the publishing model has indeed changed and that what is available in e-book format is ubiquitous.

The list shows familiar authors in familiar spots. Many top-selling authors on the 2010 hardcover chart are among the e-book top-sellers, including Stieg Larsson for *The Girl Who Kicked the Hornet's Nest,* which had electronic sales of 775,000 compared to 1.9 million in print. John Grisham, James Patterson (at least 12 e-book hits), Nicholas Sparks, Stephen King, and more are high and plentiful on both charts. There is also plenty of backlist, as classics like *Gone with the Wind, The Great Gatsby,* and *How to Win Friends and Influence People* reap solid e-book sales.

A recent blog by Mike Shatzkin, who specializes in digital change in the book publishing industry, was headlined "E-books are making me recall the history of mass market publishing." He also wrote: "The anti-paperback snobbery was widespread, and the separation between trade and mass market publishing persisted for a long time. For at least a couple of decades, paperback houses didn't do hardcovers." That's history now. But Shatzkin's last sentence resonates in today's fast-changing book marketplace. "Much less expensive editions, combined with access to audiences for authors that couldn't get past the gatekeepers in the established houses, can create millions of new readers." Anything that creates more readers is a boon for all kinds of publishers.

"The times they are a-changin'," sang Bob Dylan back in 1964. It is the first part of that sentence that publishers are all singing: "You better start swimmin' or you'll sink like a stone."

(Note: titles with an asterisk were submitted in confidence, for use in placing titles on the lists. Those numbers are rounded down to indicate their relationship to figures for other titles; in several cases the sales figures were omitted entirely, at the publishers' request.)

Adapted from *Publishers Weekly,* March 21, 2011.

Top 10 Hardcover Print/e-book Combined Sales as Reported (2010)

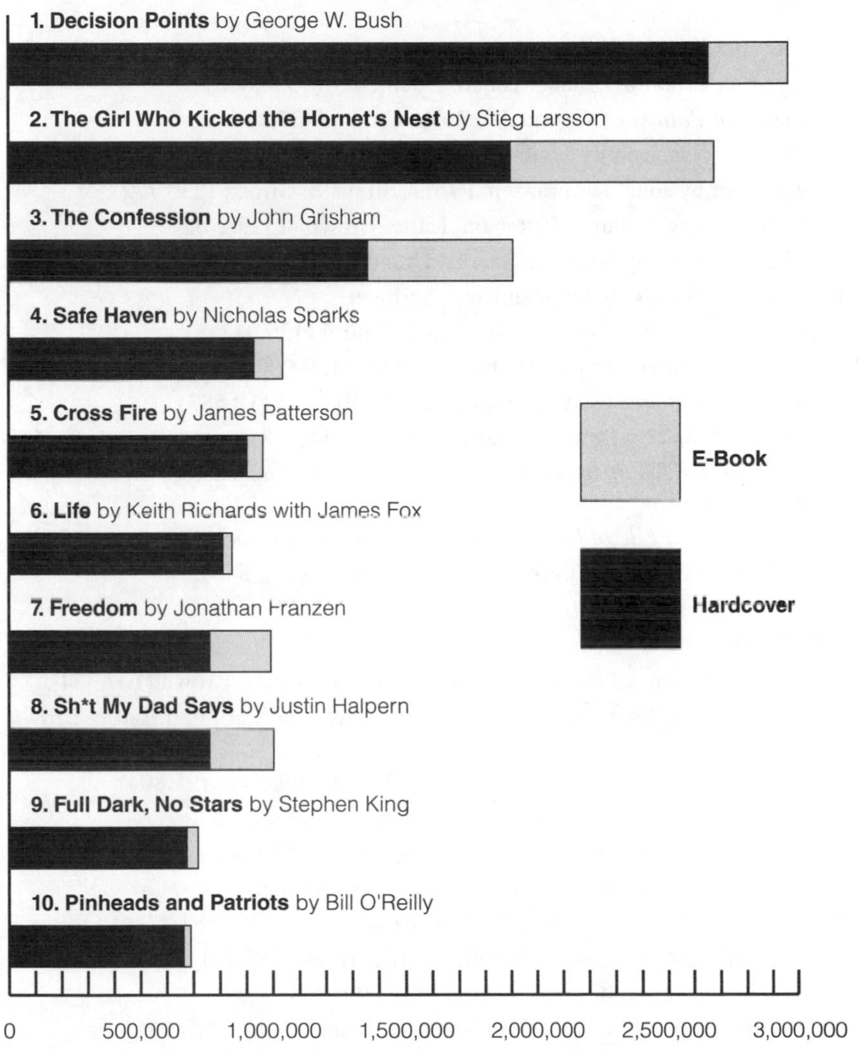

E-book Sales, 2010

100,000+

1. *The Girl Who Kicked the Hornet's Nest* by Stieg Larsson. Knopf (775,000).
2. *The Confession* by John Grisham. Doubleday (*550,000).
3. *Decision Points.* by George W. Bush. Crown (307,216).
4. *Sh*t My Dad Says* by Justin Halpern. HarperCollins/It Books (242,000).
5. *Freedom* by Jonathan Franzen. Farrar, Straus & Giroux (230,772).
6. *I, Alex Cross* by James Patterson. Little, Brown (152,626).
7. *The Last Song* by Nicholas Sparks. Grand Central (134,934).
8. *Under the Dome* by Stephen King. Scribner.
9. *Dear John* by Nicholas Sparks. Grand Central (130,042).
10. *American Assassin* by Vince Flynn. Atria (*120,000).
11. *The Lovely Bones* by Alice Sebold. Little, Brown (118,583).
12. *Shutter Island* by Dennis Lehane. Morrow (115,528).
13. *The 9th Judgment* by James Patterson and Maxine Paetro. Little, Brown (114,998).
14. *The Immortal Life of Henrietta Lacks* by Rebecca Skloot. Crown (110,273).
15. *Safe Haven* by Nicholas Sparks. Grand Central (108,849).

E-book Runners-Up

16. *Private* by James Patterson and Maxine Paetro. Little, Brown (107,334).
17. *The Postcard Killers* by James Patterson and Liza Marklund. Little, Brown (100,490).
18. *The 4-Hour Body* by Timothy Ferriss. Crown Archetype (91,804).
19. *Dead Witch Walking* by Kim Harrison. Eos (90,922).
20. *Little Bee* by Chris Cleave. Simon & Schuster (*90,000).
21. *The Lion* by Nelson DeMille. Grand Central (85,819).
22. *Fly Away Home* by Jennifer Weiner. Atria.
23. *The Reversal* by Michael Connelly. Little, Brown (85,121).
24. *House Rules* by Jodi Picoult. Atria (*80,000).
25. *Deliver Us from Evil* by David Baldacci. Grand Central (78,951).
26. *Rage of Angels* by Sidney Sheldon. Morrow (77,264).
27. *Innocent* by Scott Turow. Grand Central (73,215).
28. *Don't Blink* by James Patterson and Howard Roughan. Little, Brown (72,776).
29. *Room* by Emma Donoghue. Little, Brown (71,919).
30. *Half Broke Horses* by Jeannette Walls. Scribner (*66,000).

50,000+

Heat Wave by Richard Castle. Hyperion (65,785).

Outliers by Malcolm Gladwell. Little, Brown (65,705).

Star Island by Carl Hiaasen. Knopf (65,624).

Hell's Corner by David Baldacci. Grand Central (64,094).

Naked Heat by Richard Castle. Hyperion (62,803).

The Shack by William P. Young. Windblown Media (61,907).

Worst Case by James Patterson and James Ledwidge. Little, Brown (61,249).

Beautiful Lies by Lisa Ungar. Broadway (61,191).

Cross Fire by James Patterson. Little, Brown (59,907).

Chelsea Chelsea Bang Bang by Chelsea Handler. Grand Central (56,372).

Foreign Influence by Brad Thor. Atria (*55,000).

A Dog's Purpose by Bruce Cameron. Forge (51,767).

The Glass Castle by Jeannette Walls. Scribner.

Tough Customer by Sandra Brown. Simon & Schuster (*50,000).

20,000+

Are You There, Vodka? It's Me, Chelsea by Chelsea Handler. Gallery.

Pursuit of Honor by Vince Flynn. Atria (*48,000).

At Home by Bill Bryson. Doubleday (*47,000).

Ender's Game by Orson Scott Card. Tor (46,003).

My Horizontal Life by Chelsea Handler. Bloomsbury (45,781).

Think of a Number by John Verdun. Crown (45,475).

Born to Run by Christopher McDougall. Vintage (45,000).

War by Sebastian Junger. Grand Central (44,917).

The Overton Window by Glenn Beck. Threshold Editions.

The 8th Confession by James Patterson and Maxine Paetro. Little, Brown (42,791).

Spoken from the Heart by Laura Bush. Scribner.

Full Dark, No Stars by Stephen King. Scribner.

True Blue by David Baldacci. Grand Central (41,208).

The Shadow of Your Smile by Mary Higgins Clark. Simon & Schuster.

I'd Know You Anywhere by Laura Lippman. Morrow (40,372).

The 4-Hour Workweek, Expanded and Updated by Timothy Ferriss. Crown Archetype (39,798).

Obama's Wars by Bob Woodward. Simon & Schuster (38,625).

Forgotten Garden by Kate Morton. Atria (38,473).

The Red Queen by Philippa Gregory. Touchstone (37,922).

Moonlight Mile by Dennis Lehane. Morrow (37,918).

The Particular Sadness of Lemon Cake by Aimee Bender. Doubleday.

The Host by Stephenie Meyer. Little, Brown (37,232).

Spider Bones by Kathy Reichs. Scribner.

The Glass Rainbow by James Lee Burke. Simon & Schuster (*36,000).

The Burning Wire by Jeffrey Deaver. Simon & Schuster (*35,000).

SuperFreakonomics by Steven D. Levitt and Stephen J. Dubner. Morrow (34,800).

Life by Keith Richards with James Fox. Little, Brown (34,467).

Wolf Hall by Hilary Mantel. Henry Holt (34,336).

The Ritual Bath by Faye Kellerman. Morrow (33,940).

Transfer of Power by Vince Flynn. Atria.

I, Sniper by Stephen Hunter. Simon & Schuster.

Leslie Sansone's Eat Smart, Walk Strong by Leslie Sansone. Hachette/Center Street (33,634).

I Remember Nothing and Other Reflections by Nora Ephron. Knopf (32,556).

What the Dog Saw by Malcolm Gladwell. Little, Brown (33,364).

Abraham Lincoln: Vampire Hunter by Seth Grahame-Smith. Grand Central (33,325).

World War Z: An Oral History of the Zombie War by Max Brooks. Three Rivers (32,188).

Fever Dream by Lincoln Child. Grand Central (31,418).

Not My Daughter by Barbara Delinsky. Doubleday.

Freakonomics, revised edition by Steven D. Levitt and Stephen J. Dubner. Morrow (30,934).

Switch: How to Change Things When Change Is Hard by Chip Heath and Dan Heath. Crown Business (30,912).

The Hobbit by J. R. R. Tolkien. Morrow (30,907).

Oprah: A Biography by Kitty Kelley. Crown Archetype (29,654).

The Island by Elin Hildebrand. Little, Brown (29,623).

Nine Dragons by Michael Connelly. Little, Brown (29,072).

Best Friends Forever by Jennifer Weiner. Atria (*28,000).

The Tipping Point by Malcolm Gladwell. Little, Brown (27,756).

The White Queen by Philippa Gregory. Touchstone (27,294).

Altar of Eden by James Rollins. Morrow (26,902).

Pinheads and Patriots by Bill O'Reilly. Morrow (26,290).

One for the Money by Janet Evanovich. Scribner.

Third Option by Vince Flynn. Atria. (26,075).

Black Magic Sanction by Kim Harrison. Eos (25,730).

Roses by Leila Meacham. Grand Central (25,493).

Last Night at Chateau Marmont by Lauren Weisberger. Atria.

Lone Survivor by Marcus Luttrell. Little, Brown (25,368).

Hangman by Faye Kellerman. Morrow (25,452).

Noah's Compass by Anne Tyler. Knopf (25,000).

Blink by Malcolm Gladwell. Little, Brown (24,680).

This Time Together by Carol Burnett. Crown Archetype (24,662).

Squirrel Seeks Chipmunk by David Sedaris. Little, Brown (24,499).

Fragile by Lisa Ungar. Crown (24,423).

Rework by Jason Fried and David Heinemeier Hansson. Crown Business (24,332).

The Finkler Question by Howard Jacobson. Bloomsbury (24,026).

The Double Comfort Safari Club by Alexander McCall Smith. Pantheon (24,000).

Change Your Brain, Change Your Body by Dr. Daniel G. Amen. Crown Archetype (23,924).

In Fifty Years We'll All Be Chicks by Adam Carolla. Crown Archetype (23,607).

Alex Cross's Trial by James Patterson and Richard DiLallo. Little, Brown (23,411).

Empire of the Summer Moon by S. C. Gynne. Scribner.

Pleasure of a Dark Prince by Kresley Cole. Pocket.

Crooked Letter, Crooked Letter by Tom Franklin. Morrow (22,262).

Barefoot by Elin Hildebrand. Little, Brown (22,659).

Way of Kings by Brandon Sanderson. Tor (22,195).

Rainwater by Sandra Brown. Simon & Schuster (22,048).

The Man from Beijing by Henning Mankell. Knopf (22,000).

Term Limits by Vince Flynn. Atria.

First Family by David Baldacci. Grand Central (21,834).

The Lucky One by Nicholas Sparks. Grand Central (21,834).

Still Alice by Lisa Genova. Pocket.

Separation of Power by Vince Flynn. Atria.

Broke: The Plan to Restore Our Trust, Truth and Treasure by Glenn Beck. Threshold Editions.

90 Minutes in Heaven by Don Piper. Revell (21,197).

Mennonite in a Little Black Dress by Rhoda Janzen. Henry Holt (20,915).

Unbearable Lightness by Portia De Rossi. Atria.

The Burnt House by Faye Kellerman. Morrow (20,567).
The Strain by Guillermo Del Toro. Morrow (20,478).
Demon from the Dark by Kresley Cole. Pocket.
A Hunger Like No Other by Kresley Cole. Pocket.
Angels and Demons by Dan Brown. Atria.

10,000+

Warlord by Ted Bell. Morrow (19,994).
Cleopatra by Stacy Schiff. Little, Brown (19,807).
Radical: Taking Back Your Faith from the American Dream by David Platt. Multnomah (19,770).
Assholes Finish First by Tucker Max. Gallery.
First Drop of Crimson by Jeaniene Frost. Avon (19,700).
Operation Mincemeat by Ben Macintyre. Crown (19,679).
Edge by Jeffery Deaver. Simon & Schuster.
I Am Nujood, Age 10 and Divorced by Nujood Ali with Delphine Minoui. Broadway (19,364).
Two for the Dough by Janet Evanovich. Scribner.
A Short History of Nearly Everything by Bill Bryson. Broadway (19,318).
Sliding into Home by Kendra Wilkinson. Gallery.
The Good, the Bad, and the Undead by Kim Harrison. Eos (19,159).
Memorial Day by Vince Flynn. Atria.
The Choice by Nicholas Sparks. Grand Central (18,894).
Nanny Returns by Emma McLaughlin and Nicola Straus. Atria.
Handle with Care by Jodi Picoult. Atria (18,741).
Robert Ludlum's The Bourne Objective by Eric Van Lustbader. Grand Central (18,723).
True Compass by Edward Kennedy. Grand Central (18,574).
The Checklist Manifesto by Atul Gawande. Metropolitan (18,516).
The Watchman by Robert Crais. Simon & Schuster.
Her Fearful Symmetry by Audrey Niffenegger. Scribner.
Consent to Kill by Vince Flynn. Atria.
The Zombie Survival Guide by Max Brooks. Crown Archetype (17,875).
Secrets of Eden by Chris Bohjalian. Crown (17,812).
Extreme Measures by Vince Flynn. Atria (17,734).
1st to Die by James Patterson. Little, Brown (17,723).
Kitchen House by Kathleen Grissom. Touchstone (17,705).
The Last Lecture by Randy Pausch. Hyperion (17,461).
The Secret by Rhonda Byrne. Atria (17,392).
Gone with the Wind by Margaret Mitchell. Scribner.
Ten Things I Love About You by Julia Quinn. Avon (17,239).
Eternal Kiss of Darkness by Jeaniene Frost. Avon (17,202).
Shadow of Power by Steve Martini. Morrow (17,178).
Wicked by Gregory Maguire. Morrow (17,169).
Lions of Lucerne by Brad Thor. Atria.
Executive Power by Vince Flynn. Atria (*16,000).
206 Bones by Kathy Reichs. Scribner.
Déjà Dead by Kathy Reichs. Scribner.
The Fall by Guillermo Del Toro. Morrow (16,641).
Redeeming Love by Francine Rivers. Multnomah (16,553).
7th Heaven by James Patterson and Maxine Paetro. Little, Brown (16,523).
The Obama Diaries by Laura Ingraham. Threshold Editions.
Her Mother's Hope by Francine Prose. Tyndale (16,291).
The Walk by Richard Paul Evans. Simon & Schuster.
Dark Descent by Christine Feehan. Avon (16,243).
The Great Gatsby by F. Scott Fitzgerald. Scribner.
The Athena Project by Brad Thor. Atria.
Run for Your Life by James Patterson and Michael Ledwidge. Little, Brown (16,079).
Protect and Defend by Vince Flynn. Atria.

Three to Get Deadly by Janet Evanovich. Scribner.

Nine Rules to Break When Romancing a Rake by Sarah MacLean. Avon (15,699).

Swimsuit by James Patterson and Maxine Paetro. Little, Brown (15,683).

My Sister's Keeper by Jodi Picoult. Pocket.

The Wave by Susan Casey. Doubleday (15,660).

The Rule of Nine by Steve Martini. Morrow (15,410).

This Is Why You're Fat (And How to Get Thin Forever) by Jackie Warner. Grand Central (15,337).

Resilience: Reflections on the Burdens and Gifts of Facing Life's Adversities by Elizabeth Edwards. Broadway (15,185).

Act of Treason by Vince Flynn. Atria.

Deception Point by Dan Brown. Atria.

Every Which Way But Dead by Kim Harrison. Eos (15,038).

Apostle by Brad Thor. Atria.

The Lion's Game by Nelson DeMille. Grand Central (14,931).

Master Your Metabolism by Jillian Michaels. Crown Archetype (14,861).

The Harry Bosch Novels by Michael Connelly. Little, Brown (14,679).

Nineteen Minutes by Jodi Picoult. Atria.

On the Brink by Henry M. Paulson, Jr. Grand Central (14,579).

Decision Points Deluxe E-book Edition by George W. Bush. Crown (14,529).

The Notebook by Nicholas Sparks. Grand Central (14,436).

Delivering Happiness by Tony Hsieh. Grand Central (14,431).

Is It Just Me? Or Is It Nuts Out There? by Whoopi Goldberg. Hyperion (14,214).

Three Stations by Martin Cruz Smith. Simon & Schuster.

Afraid by Jack Kilborn. Grand Central (13,844).

No Rest for the Wicked by Kresley Cole. Pocket.

Hero at Large by Janet Evanovich. Harper (13,823).

Promise Me by Richard Paul Evans. Simon & Schuster.

A Bold Fresh Piece of Humanity: A Memoir by Bill O'Reilly. Broadway (13,573).

Path of the Assassin by Brad Thor. Atria.

Smash Cut by Sandra Brown. Simon & Schuster.

Arguing with Idiots: How to Stop Small Minds and Big Government by Glenn Beck. Threshold Editions.

Second Chance by James Patterson. Little, Brown (13,401).

Wicked Deeds on a Winter's Night by Kresley Cole. Pocket.

The Quants by Scott Patterson. Crown Business (13,299).

Dark Dream by Christine Feehan. Avon (13,231).

The Vampire and the Virgin by Kerrelyn Sparks. Avon (13,167).

The Lost Symbol: Special Illustrated Edition by Dan Brown. Doubleday.

New Day, New You by Joyce Meyer. FaithWords (13,135).

Aftershock by Robert B. Reich. Knopf (13,000).

Riding the Bullet by Stephen King. Scribner.

In the Name of Honor by Richard North Patterson. Henry Holt (12,746).

Born to Bite by Lynsay Sands. Avon (12,727).

Takedown by Brad Thor. Atria.

House at Riverton by Kate Morton. Atria (12,800).

Cross Country by James Patterson. Little, Brown (12,646).

Devil's Punchbowl by Greg Iles. Scribner.

I Am Ozzy by Ozzy Osbourne. Grand Central (12,479).

A Walk to Remember by Nicholas Sparks. Grand Central (12,475).

The Swan Thieves by Elizabeth Kostova. Little, Brown (12,453).

How to Win Friends and Influence People by Dale Carnegie. Simon & Schuster.

The Apothecary's Daughter by Julie Klassen. Bethany House (12,226).

Happiness by Matthieu Ricard and Daniel Goleman. Little, Brown (12,163).

The Perfect Someone by Johanna Lindsey. Pocket.

The Boy Who Came Back from Heaven by Kevin Malarkey. Tyndale (12,141).

Days of Gold by Jude Deveraux. Atria.

New Atkins for a New You by Dr. Eric C. Westman. Touchstone (12,073).

A Is for Alibi by Sue Grafton. Henry Holt (12,029).
The Truth about Lord Stoneville by Sabrina Jeffries. Pocket.
Seven Year Switch by Claire Cook. Hyperion (11,957).
The Bride Collector by Ted Dekker. Hachette/Center Street (11,950).
Hungry for You by Lynsay Sands. Avon (11,948).
Nothing but Trouble by Rachel Gibson. Avon (11,815).
Dark Needs at Night's Edge by Kresley Cole. Pocket.
Dark Desires after Dusk by Kresley Cole. Pocket.
State of the Union by Brad Thor. Atria.
Last Call: The Rise and Fall of Prohibition by Daniel Okrent. Scribner.
The Scarecrow by Michael Connelly. Little, Brown (11,578).
The Wedding by Nicholas Sparks. Grand Central (11,517).
Lavender Morning by Jude Deveraux. Atria.
Kiss of a Demon King by Kresley Cole. Pocket.
A Hellion in Her Bed by Sabrina Jeffries. Pocket.
Her Daughter's Dream by Francine Prose. Tyndale (11,383).
Scarlet Nights by Jude Deveraux. Atria.
Blowback by Brad Thor. Atria (11,340).
Eat Prey Love by Kerrelyn Sparks. Avon (11,335).
3rd Degree by James Patterson and Andrew Gross. Little, Brown (11,330).
The Good Mood Diet by Susan Kleiner. Grand Central (11,325).
Stone Cold by David Baldacci. Grand Central (11,281).
Just Take My Heart by Mary Higgins Clark. Simon & Schuster (11,028).
Hitch-22 by Christopher Hitchens. Grand Central (10,931).
The Reckless Bride by Stephanie Laurens. Avon (10,776).
The Greatest Trade Ever by Gregory Zuckerman. Crown Business (10,763).
Pleasure Unbound by Larissa Ione. Grand Central (10,760).
Tuesdays with Morrie by Mitch Albom. Broadway (10,694).
Along Came a Spider by James Patterson. Little, Brown (10,618).
How to Raise the Perfect Dog by Cesar Millan with Melissa Jo Peltier. Crown Archetype (10,616).
Courage and Consequence: My Life as a Conservative in the Fight by Karl Rove. Threshold Editions.
Double Cross by James Patterson. Little, Brown (10,513).
Brooklyn by Colm Tóibín. Scribner.
Rich Dad Poor Dad by Robert T. Kiyosaki. Grand Central (10,466).
4th of July by James Patterson and Maxine Paetro. Little, Brown (10,433).
Team of Rivals by Doris Kearns Goodwin. Simon & Schuster (10,321).
The 6th Target by James Patterson and Maxine Paetro. Little, Brown (10,285).
Last Words: A Memoir by George Carlin. Free Press.
First Commandment by Brad Thor. Atria.
The Rook by Steve James. Revell (10,162).
12-Day Body-Shaping Miracle by Michael Thurmond. Grand Central (10,145).
The Elusive Bride by Stephanie Laurens. Avon (10,117).
The Brass Verdict by Michael Connelly. Little, Brown (10,051).
Deep Kiss of Winter by Kresley Cole and Gena Showalter. Pocket.
Gunn's Golden Rules: Life's Little Lessons for Making It Work by Tim Gunn. Gallery.
The Brazen Bride by Stephanie Laurens. Avon (10,015).
A Kiss at Midnight by Eloisa James. Avon (10,012).
The Historian by Elizabeth Kostova. Little, Brown (10,004).

Hardcover: The Usual Suspects, and More

Daisy Maryles

What's new in the hardcover fiction bestsellers of 2010? Very little. Almost every author in the fiction top 30 has been on these charts in previous years—most several times. The sole exception is the No. 1 fiction bestseller, *The Girl Who Kicked the Hornet's Nest,* with sales of 1.9 million. Stieg Larsson enjoyed a quadruple play, heading fiction, mass market, trade paper, and the e-book list of bestsellers.

Still, a number of veteran bestselling novelists dominate. Chief among them is James Patterson. With his stable of coauthors, he managed to rack up six of the top 25 fiction bestsellers, with combined sales of 3,332,263. Clive Cussler had four bestsellers in 2010, with combined sales of 1,006,132; Nora Roberts had three, with combined sales of 900,000 copies. And the bestselling female author last year was Janet Evanovich; she had two of the top 15 bestsellers, with sales of more than 1.5 million.

The only novel to make a second appearance in the top 15 is Kathryn Stockett's *The Help.* A debut fiction hitting the 1 million-plus sales mark for the second year in a row, it is also the only hardcover that did not miss a single showing on the 2010 weekly charts.

First novels that score are always an inspiration, and four others achieved sales of more than 100,000 last year—*Matterhorn: A Novel of the Vietnam War*; *The Imperfectionists*; *Major Pettigrew's Last Stand*; and *The Postmistress.* Each enjoyed rave reviews, proving that there is still room for quality in this competitive game.

What has changed dramatically for bestsellers, including books by list veterans, is that fewer books have double-digit tenure on the weekly charts, revealing the greater difficulty in getting the higher annual sales figures of years past. In 2010 three hardcover fiction titles sold more than 1 million copies, and five sold more than 750,000 copies. The year before, six books went over the 1 million mark and six more sold 750,000+ copies. In fact, each year during the past decade, there were at least six (and often eight) books with 1 million-plus sales.

There were 126 works of fiction that claimed sales of more than 100,000, only slightly fewer than the 130 in 2009, but 19 percent fewer than the 156 in 2008. Nonfiction titles with sales of more than 100,000 in 2010 were up, with 108 titles—more than the 91 in 2009 but fewer than the 132 in 2008.

Almost all of the nonfiction books are by familiar names from outside of the book-publishing arena, many by authors who have landed on *Publishers Weekly*'s annual charts in previous years. Media personalities abound—Glenn Beck, Jon Stewart, Bill O'Reilly, and Chelsea Handler, to name just a few. Politicians and books about them were plentiful on the bestseller charts, but the biggest victory can be claimed by George W. Bush. His *Decision Points* garnered good reviews and record-breaking sales; it is the only 2010 nonfiction title to sell more than 1 million copies—2,653,565, to be exact. Crown claimed sales of 775,000 in the title's first week and noted that it was the biggest opening of any Random House title since 2004. Former First Lady Laura Bush also landed in the top 15, with sales of more than 600,000 copies for *Spoken from the Heart.*

Other politicians made the top 15 list. It was Sarah Palin's second visit—in 2010 she made it to No. 5, with sales of 797,955 for *America by Heart*; a year earlier she topped the charts with sales of more than 2,670,000 for *Going Rogue.* There were no books by President Obama this year, but if you peruse the nonfiction list, you will find many about him.

Political memoirs by Karl Rove and Mitt Romney made the charts, as did ones written by rock star Keith Richards and hip-hop star Jay-Z. Food Network star Ina Garten landed among the top 15, and many of her cooking colleagues were on the 2010 charts.

Then there was that bestseller *Autobiography of Mark Twain,* whose author gave explicit instructions not to publish his book until 100 years after his death. Patience to all authors who are waiting for publication—your time may come.

The Usual Disclaimer

As in previous years, all calculations in the lists are based on shipped-and-billed figures supplied by publishers for new books with sales of more than 100,000; all reflect only 2010 domestic retail sales for print books (one title, marked with a #, was published in 2009). We asked publishers to take into account returns through February 15, 2011; it would be safe to assume that not all did. Sales figures on these pages should not be considered final. For many books, especially those published in the final third of the year, returns were not yet calculated.

The figures for all books listed marked with an asterisk—hardcover, paperback, and e-books—were submitted to *Publishers Weekly* in confidence, for use in placing titles on the lists. Those numbers are rounded down to indicate their relationship to figures for other titles; in several cases the sales figures were omitted entirely.

Hardcover Fiction

1. *The Girl Who Kicked the Hornet's Nest* by Stieg Larsson. Knopf (1,900,000).
2. *The Confession* by John Grisham. Doubleday (*1,360,000).
3. #*The Help* by Kathryn Stockett. Putnam/Amy Einhorn (1,317,397).
4. *Safe Haven* by Nicholas Sparks. Grand Central (929,397).
5. *Dead or Alive* by Tom Clancy. Putnam (921,358).
6. *Sizzling Sixteen* by Janet Evanovich. St. Martin's (903,000).
7. *Cross Fire* by James Patterson. Little, Brown (902,906).
8. *Freedom* by Jonathan Franzen. Farrar, Straus & Giroux (761,701).
9. *Port Mortuary* by Patricia Cornwell. Putnam (700,000).
10. *Full Dark, No Stars* by Stephen King. Scribner (*675,000).
11. *Dead in the Family* by Charlaine Harris. Ace (625,000).
12. *Fall of Giants* by Ken Follett. Dutton (621,562).
13. *Wicked Appetite* by Janet Evanovich. St. Martin's (598,763).
14. *American Assassin* by Vince Flynn. Atria (*522,000).

15. *Hell's Corner* by David Baldacci. Grand Central (520,423).
16. *The 9th Judgment* by James Patterson and Maxine Paetro. Little, Brown (516,780).
17. *Worst Case* by James Patterson and Michael Ledwidge. Little, Brown (475,321).
18. *The Postcard Killers* by James Patterson and Liza Marklund. Little, Brown (468,311).
19. *Private* by James Patterson and Maxine Paetro. Little, Brown (465,292).
20. *The Search* by Nora Roberts. Putnam (450,000).
21. *Heart of the Matter* by Emily Giffin. St. Martin's (444,261).
22. *Don't Blink* by James Patterson and Howard Roughan. Little, Brown (443,653).
23. *House Rules* by Jodi Picoult. Atria.
24. *Squirrel Seeks Chipmunk: A Modest Bestiary* by David Sedaris. Little, Brown (420,473).
25. *Crescent Dawn: A Dirk Pitt Novel* by Clive Cussler and Dirk Cussler. Putnam (427,082).
26. *In the Company of Others: A Father Tim Novel* by Jan Karon. Viking (412,891).
27. *Towers of Midnight: Book 13 of the Wheel of Time* by Robert Jordan and Brandon Sanderson. Tor (406,346).
28. *Deliver Us from Evil* by David Baldacci. Grand Central (340,042).
29. *The Reversal* by Michael Connelly. Little, Brown (317,168).
30. *Worth Dying For* by Lee Child. Delacorte (317,000).

300,000+

The Lion by Nelson DeMille. Grand Central (311,484).

The Passage by Justin Cronin. Ballantine (309,000).

Caught by Harlan Coban. Dutton (303,456).

200,000+

The Shadow of Your Smile by Mary Higgins Clark. Simon & Schuster (*290,000).

61 Hours by Lee Child. Delacorte (284,000).

Innocent by Scott Turow. Grand Central (270,636).

Winter Garden by Kristin Hannah. St. Martin's (257,893).

Indulgence in Death by J. D. Robb. Putnam (250,000).

Getting to Happy by Terry McMillan. Viking (240,350).

Storm Prey by John Sandford. Putnam (237,152).

Abraham Lincoln: Vampire Hunter by Seth Grahame-Smith. Grand Central. (232,708).

Moonlight Mile by Dennis Lehane. Morrow (217,917).

Promise Me by Richard Paul Evans. Simon & Schuster.

The Spy: An Isaac Bell Adventure by Clive Cussler and Justin Scott. Putnam (210,182).

Fly Away Home by Jennifer Weiner. Atria.

Fantasy in Death by J. D. Robb. Putnam (200,000).

150,000+

Altar of Eden by James Rollins. Morrow (199,775).

No Mercy by Sherrilyn Kenyon. St. Martin's (198,565).

The Silent Sea: A Novel of the Oregon Files by Clive Cussler. Putnam (197,705).

Think Twice by Lisa Scottoline. St. Martin's (196,465).

Room by Emma Donoghue. Little, Brown (194,171).

Tough Customer by Sandra Brown. Simon & Schuster.

Mini Shopaholic by Sophie Kinsella. Dial (192,000).

World War Z: An Oral History of the Zombie War by Max Brooks. Three Rivers (187,052).

Bad Blood: A Virgil Flowers Novel by John Sandford. Putnam (185,158).

The Rembrandt Affair by Daniel Silva. Putnam (184,645).

I Still Dream About You by Fannie Flagg. Random House (184,000).

Deception by Jonathan Kellerman. Ballantine (180,000).

An Object of Beauty by Steve Martin. Grand Central (179,331).

Whiplash by Catherine Coulter. Putnam (176,905).

Big Girl by Danielle Steel. Delacorte (175,000).

Family Ties by Danielle Steel. Delacorte (175,000).

Legacy by Danielle Steel. Delacorte (175,000).

Lost Empire: A Fargo Adventure by Clive Cussler. Putnam (171,163).

The Athena Project by Brad Thor. Atria.

What the Night Knows by Dean Koontz. Bantam (170,000).

The Outlaws: A Presidential Agent Novel by W. E. B. Griffin. Putnam (168,854).

Eight Days to Live by Iris Johansen. St. Martin's (167,530).

The Christmas Journey by Donna VanLiere. St. Martin's (165,359).

Matterhorn: A Novel of the Vietnam War by Karl Marlantes. Atlantic Monthly (164,907).

Chasing the Night by Iris Johansen. St. Martin's (164,743).

Poor Little Bitch Girl by Jackie Collins. St. Martin's (163,440).

Her Mother's Hope by Francine Rivers. Tyndale (157,407).

Secrets to the Grave by Tami Hoag. Dutton (153,926).

Hannah's List by Debbie Macomber. Mira (152,117).

Ice Cold by Tess Gerritsen. Ballantine (150,000).

Lover Mine by J. R. Ward. NAL (150,000).

125,000+

Call Me Mrs. Miracle by Debbie Macomber. Mira (148,332).

Star Island by Carl Hiaasen. Knopf (147,804).

Changes by Jim Butcher. Roc (145,000).

Robert Ludlum's The Bourne Objective by Eric Van Lustbader. Grand Central (143,969).

The Red Queen by Philippa Gregory. Touchstone (141,588).

Bite Me by Christopher Moore. Morrow (137,578).

Foreign Influence by Brad Thor. Atria.

Horns by Joe Hill. Morrow (134,447).

Every Last One by Anna Quindlen. Random House (134,000).

A Dog's Purpose by Bruce Cameron. Forge (133,710).

Edge by Jeffery Deaver. Simon & Schuster.

Blockade Billy by Stephen King. Scribner (133,240).

Naked Heat by Richard Castle. Hyperion (130,039).

100,000+

Her Daughter's Dream by Francine Rivers. Tyndale (124,954).

Rescue by Anita Shreve. Little, Brown (123,436).

The Emperor's Tomb by Steve Berry. Ballantine (122,000).

The Imperfectionists by Tom Rachman. Dial (122,000).

Fever Dream by Douglas Preston and Lincoln Child. Grand Central (121,288).

A Secret Kept Tatiana De Rosnay. St. Martin's (120,932).

This Body of Death by Elizabeth George. HarperCollins (120,921).

The Rule of Nine by Steve Martini. Morrow (120,294).

Split Image: A Jesse Stone Novel by Robert B. Parker. Putnam (120,128).

Spider Bones by Kathy Reichs. Scribner.

Flirt by Laurell K. Hamilton. Berkley (120,000).

The Double Comfort Safari Club by Alexander McCall Smith. Pantheon (120,000).

The Swan Thieves by Elizabeth Kostova. Little, Brown (118,218).
Bullet by Laurell K. Hamilton. Berkley (115,000).
Redeeming Love by Francine Rivers. Multnomah (114,542).
The Walk by Richard Paul Evans. Simon & Schuster.
Shadow Zone by Iris Johansen. St. Martin's (112,583).
Our Kind of Traitor by John le Carré. Viking (112,325).
Christmas Eve at Friday Harbor by Lisa Kleypas. St. Martin's (111,237).
Lucid Intervals: A Stone Barrington Novel by Stuart Woods. Putnam (110,440).
Dark Peril by Christine Feehan. Berkley (110,000).
The Thousand Autumns of Jacob De Zoet by David Mitchell. Random House (105,000).
Warlord by Ted Bell. Morrow (104,888).
Major Pettigrew's Last Stand by Helen Simonson. Random House (104,000).
Painted Ladies: A Spenser Novel by Robert B. Parker. Putnam (103,623).
The Last Surgeon by Michael Palmer. St. Martin's (103,576).
The Valcourt Heiress by Catherine Coulter. Putnam (103,469).
Heat Wave by Richard Castle. Hyperion (101,907).
Valley Forge by Newt Gingrich and William R. Forstchen. St. Martin's (101,477).
The Fall by Guillermo Del Toro and Chuck Hogan. Morrow (101,136).
The Postmistress by Sarah Blake. Putnam (100,320).
Silver Borne by Patricia Briggs. Ace (100,000).
Side Jobs by Jim Butcher. Roc (100,000).

Hardcover Nonfiction

1. *Decision Points* by George W. Bush. Crown (2,653,565).
2. *Broke: The Plan to Restore Our Trust, Truth, and Treasure* by Glenn Beck. Threshold Editions (*860,002).
3. *Women Food and God: An Unexpected Path to Almost Everything* by Geneen Roth. Scribner (*850,000).
4. *Life* by Keith Richards with James Fox. Little, Brown (811,596).
5. *America by Heart: Reflections on Family, Faith, and Flag* by Sarah Palin. HarperCollins (797,955).
6. *The Daily Show with Jon Stewart Presents Earth (The Book): A Visitor's Guide to the Human Race* by Jon Stewart. Grand Central (782,871).
7. *Sh*t My Dad Says* by Justin Halpern. HarperCollins/It Books (761,000).
8. *Barefoot Contessa How Easy Is That?* by Ina Garten. Clarkson Potter (722,608).
9. *Pinheads and Patriots: Where You Stand in the Age of Obama* by Bill O'Reilly. Morrow (662,950).
10. *Chelsea Chelsea Bang Bang* by Chelsea Handler. Grand Central 653,321).
11. *Straight Talk, No Chaser: How to Find, Keep and Understand a Man* by Steve Harvey. Amistad (626,732).
12. *Spoken from the Heart* by Laura Bush. Scribner (*605,000).
13. *The Big Short: Inside the Doomsday Machine* by Michael Lewis. Norton (*600,000).
14. *The Power* by Rhonda Byrne. Atria (*525,000).

15. *Unbroken: A World War II Story of Survival, Resilience, and Redemption* by Laura Hillenbrand. Random House (518,000).
16. *Game Change: Obama and the Clintons, McCain and Palin, and the Race of a Lifetime* by John Heileman and Mark Halperin. HarperCollins (490,298).
17. *Obama's Wars* by Bob Woodward. Simon & Schuster (*430,000).
18. *The Immortal Life of Henrietta Lacks* by Rebecca Skloot. Crown (393,064).
19. *The Pacific* by Hugh Ambrose. NAL Caliber (330,000).
20. *So Long, Insecurity (You've Been a Bad Friend to Us)* by Beth Moore. Tyndale (327,180).
21. *Autobiography of Mark Twain,* edited by Harriet Elinor Smith. University of California.
22. *Double Delicious* by Jessica Seinfeld. Morrow (300,434).
23. *The 4-Hour Body: An Uncommon Guide to Rapid Fat-Loss, Incredible Sex, and Becoming Superhuman* by Timothy Ferriss. Crown Archetype (299,176).
24. *The Pioneer Woman Cooks* by Ree Drummond. Morrow (291,860).
25. *The Grand Design* by Stephen Hawking and Leonard Mlodinow. Bantam (286,000).
26. *Decoded* by Jay-Z. Random/Spiegel & Grau (283,000).
27. *Have a Little Faith: A True Story* by Mitch Albom. Hyperion (275,234).
28. *Cleopatra* by Stacy Schiff. Little, Brown (271,327).
29. *Power Thoughts: 12 Strategies to Win the Battle of the Mind* by Joyce Meyer. FaithWords (266,958).
30. *Delivering Happiness: A Path to Profits, Passion, and Purpose* by Tony Hsieh. Grand Central (263,028).

200,000+

The Politician by Andrew Young. St. Martin's (242,811).

The Last Boy: Mickey Mantle and the End of America's Childhood by Jane Leavy. HarperCollins (242,211).

Switch: How to Change Things When Change Is Hard by Chip Heath and Dan Heath. Crown Business (236,879).

No Apology by Mitt Romney. St. Martin's (224,684).

Dewey's Nine Lives: The Legacy of a Small-Town Library Cat Who Inspired Millions by Vicki Myron. Dutton (222,301).

Trickle Up Poverty by Michael Savage. Morrow (220,517).

Sexy Forever: How to Fight Fat After Forty by Suzanne Somers. Crown Archetype (218,340).

Oprah: A Biography by Kitty Kelley. Crown Archetype (217,818).

Coming Back Stronger by Drew Brees with Chris Fabry. Tyndale (215,982).

I Remember Nothing and Other Reflections by Nora Ephron. Knopf (210,817).

Bringing Up Girls by James Dobson. Tyndale (210,555).

The Secret by Rhonda Byrne. Atria (*210,000).

Change Your Brain, Change Your Body: Use Your Brain to Get and Keep the Body You Have Always Wanted by Dr. Daniel G. Amen. Crown Archetype (203,944).

Giada at Home: Family Recipes from Italy and California by Giada De Laurentiis. Clarkson Potter (203,932).

Outliers: The Story of Success by Malcolm Gladwell. Little, Brown (202,191).

Born to Run: A Hidden Tribe, Superathletes, and the Greatest Race the World Has Never Seen by Christopher McDougall. Knopf (200,000).

150,000+

Medium Raw: A Bloody Valentine to the World of Food and the People Who Cook by Anthony Bourdain. Ecco (197,858).

Oogy: The Dog Only a Family Could Love by Larry Levin. Grand Central (190,222).

At Home: A Short History of Private Life by Bill Bryson. Doubleday (*186,000).

The Christmas Spirit: Memories of Family, Friends and Faith by Joel Osteen. Free Press (*185,000).

War by Sebastian Junger. Grand Central (181,057).

Unbearable Lightness: A Story of Loss and Gain by Portia De Rossi. Atria.

Choosing to See: A Journey of Struggle and Hope by Mary Beth Chapman and Ellen Vaughn. Revell (178,015).

Kardashian Konfidental by Kim Kardashian, Kourtney Kardashian, and Khloe Kardashian. St. Martin's (177,674).

Colonel Roosevelt by Edmund Morris. Random House (177,000).

The Coming Economic Armageddon: What Bible Prophecy Warns about the New Global Economy by David Jeremiah. FaithWords (173,651).

The Happiness Project: Or Why I Spent a Year Trying to Sing in the Morning, Clean My Closets, Fight Right, Read Aristotle, and Generally Have More Fun by Gretchen Rubin. HarperCollins (173,202).

This Time Together: Laughter and Reflection by Carol Burnett. Crown Archetype (167,168).

Act Like a Lady, Think Like a Man: What Men Really Think About Love, Relationships, Intimacy, and Commitment by Steve Harvey. Amistad (162,759).

The Life You Want: Get Motivated, Lose Weight, and Be Happy by Bob Greene, Ann Kearney-Cooke, and Janis Jibrin. Simon & Schuster.

The Kind Diet: A Simple Guide to Feeling Great, Losing Weight, and Saving the Planet by Alicia Silverstone. Rodale (158,211).

Simple Times: Crafts for Poor People by Amy Sedaris. Grand Central (154,458).

The Checklist Manifesto: How to Get Things Right by Atul Gawande. Metropolitan (154,000).

Angelina: An Unauthorized Biography by Andrew Morton. St. Martin's (151,258).

125,000+

My Passion for Design by Barbra Streisand. Viking.

I Am Ozzy by Ozzy Osbourne with Chris Ayres. Grand Central (145,364).

The Master Your Metabolism Cookbook by Jillian Michaels. Crown Archetype (144,996).

The Last Stand: Custer, Sitting Bull, and the Battle of the Little Bighorn by Nathaniel Philbrick. Viking (143,900).

Bobby Flay's Throwdown! by Bobby Flay. Clarkson Potter (136,783).

Me by Ricky Martin. Celebra (135,000).

Drive: The Surprising Truth About What Motivates Us by Daniel H. Pink. Riverhead (134,693).

Bloody Crimes by James Swanson. Morrow (132,266).

Empire of the Summer Moon by S. C. Gwynne. Scribner.

Not Without Hope by Nick Schuyler. Morrow (131,298).

The 4-Hour Work Week, Expanded and Updated by Timothy Ferriss. Crown Archetype (125,935).

Washington: A Life by Rob Chernow. Penguin (*125,000).

This Is Why You're Fat (And How to Get Thin Forever): Eat More, Cheat More, Lose More—And Keep the Weight Off by Jackie Warner. Grand Central (124,227).

100,000+

Divine Transformation by Zhi Gang Sha. Atria (*119,000).

Extraordinary, Ordinary People: A Memoir of Family by Condoleezza Rice. Crown Archetype (116,643).

Cake Boss: Stories and Recipes from Mia Famiglia by Buddy Valastro. Free Press.

Love, Lust and Faking It: The Naked Truth About Sex, Lies, and True Romance by Jenny McCarthy. HarperCollins (115,176).

Eat the Cake . . . Buy the Shoes: Giving Yourself Permission to Lighten Up by Joyce Meyer. FaithWords (113,355).

My Reading Life by Pat Conroy. Doubleday.

The Boy Who Came Back from Heaven by Kevin Malarkey. Tyndale (112,386).

The Warmth of Other Suns by Isabel Wilkerson. Random House (110,000).

The Emperor of All Maladies: A Biography of Cancer by Siddhartha Mukherjee. Scribner.

Take Back America: A Battle Plan by Dick Morris. HarperCollins (109,186).

Is It Just Me? Or Is It Nuts Out There? by Whoopi Goldberg. Hyperion (108,866).

The Wave: In Pursuit of the Rogues, Freaks, and Giants of the Ocean by Susan Casey. Doubleday.

Home Cooking with Trisha Yearwood by Trisha Yearwood. Clarkson Potter (105,296).

They Call Me Baba Booey by Gary Dell'Abate. Random/Spiegel & Grau (105,000).

Master Your Metabolism: The Three Diet Secrets to Naturally Balancing Your Hormones for a Hot and Healthy Body by Jillian Michaels. Crown Archetype (103,968).

The Prodigal God: Recovering the Heart of the Christian Faith by Timothy Keller. Dutton (103,458).

Rework by Jason Fried and David Heinemeier Hansson. Crown Business (101,516).

Paperbacks: Big Names on Top—Larsson, Brown, Sparks, Gilbert

Daisy Maryles

It's the Stieg Larsson show in 2010 paperback bestsellers. The first two books of his enormously successful trilogy racked up sales of more than 10,942,000 in their mass market and paperback editions. That's more than the combined sales of two other stellar sellers—James Patterson and Nora Roberts. Their combined sales total for 15 titles in mass and trade amounted to a bit more than 7,734,200.

As noted every year, the mass market bestsellers are by veterans of these annual charts, with almost no surprises. Nicholas Sparks had three mass market titles, with a combined sale of 2,770,816; Debbie Macomber had four with sales of 2,513,394; Danielle Steel's big three in 2010 had a 2,313,583 sales combination. Janet Evanovich was the only woman in 2010 with a single title that enjoyed sales of more than 1 million; her two 2010 titles sold 1,855,946 combined. In 2009 she was one of five women with single-title sales of more than 1 million.

The only two names that were not the usual on the mass market annual list were Harper Lee and J. D. Salinger. Lee's *To Kill a Mockingbird* was celebrated in a 50th anniversary edition and had sales of 804,752; sales for Salinger's *The Catcher in the Rye* amounted to 578,141 (Salinger died in January 2010).

Waning Mass Market Sales

In mass market, we asked publishers to report 2010 sales for titles that sold 500,000 copies or more during the 12-month period. This is the same criteria we have used since 2002. In that year there were 107 books with sales of 500,000 copies or more (compare that to 1990, when 123 mass markets enjoyed sales of 1 million or more). The number of titles peaked in 2005, when 131 titles went over the 500,000 mark. In 2010 only 58 titles reported sales of at least 500,000. And in 2010 only 13 books exceeded sales of 750,000 copies or more; by contrast, in 2005, 39 titles broke the 1-million-copy mark.

The high rollers also saw their unit sales melt away. In 2005 Nora Roberts had nine titles with sales of more than 1 million, and two of them were over 2 million; her highest sale in 2010 was 785,000. Patterson had two over the 1 million mark in 2005, but his highest in 2010 was 927,681; Dean Koontz had three titles over 1 million in 2005, but only one got as high as 948,000 copies in 2010. Nonfiction was never a major factor in mass market, but these days it is a total no-show. The 2005 list had seven nonfiction titles.

Trade Paper Faltering

Again, back in 2002 we asked publishers to submit trade paperback sales for 100,000 or more copies. Previously, the number was 50,000 unit sales, and *Publishers Weekly* raised the number because sales picked up in the 100,000-plus category. That year we counted 166 titles with sales of 100,000-plus, twice as many as the 1995 figure of 83 books. In 2005 the 100,000-plus figure soared to 226; in 2010 it dropped to 134. As for the big sellers, there were 12 titles with sales of 500,000 or more in 2010; a year earlier, the number was almost double, at 22.

The trade paperback list, as always, is much more eclectic than its mass market counterpart. And while popular commercial fiction is always strong, this is the list where literary fiction, including prize winners, get to shine. *Little Bee, Cutting for Stone, The Finkler Question,* and *The Old Cape Magic* all had strong sales. And Oprah's most recent (perhaps last?) book club pick—*A Tale of Two Cities and Great Expectations: Two Novels*—racked up sales of more than 480,000.

Food and diet were the most popular categories, with 18 top sellers on the 2010 charts. Movie tie-ins helped, and two figured in the 1-million-plus category: *Eat, Pray, Love* and *The Last Song.* While the reviews for both were generally harsh, that did not seem to have an impact on book sales.

And that is the good news despite a falloff in bestseller sales. This listing is only a drop in the bucket of books published in 2010. Just keep reading.

Paperback Fiction

2,000,000+

The Girl with the Dragon Tattoo by Stieg Larsson. Vintage (2,429,055).

The Lost Symbol by Dan Brown. Vintage (2,367,052).

The Girl Who Played with Fire by Stieg Larsson. Vintage (2,177,705).

1,000,000+

The Last Song (movie tie-in) by Nicholas Sparks. Grand Central (1,397,441).

Ford County: Stories by John Grisham. Dell (1,050,000).

Finger Lickin' Fifteen by Janet Evanovich. St. Martin's (1,045,363).

750,000+

Pirate Latitudes by Michael Crichton. Harper (986,990).

Breathless by Dean Koontz. Bantam (948,000).

I, Alex Cross by James Patterson. Grand Central (927,681).

One Night by Debbie Macomber. Avon (901,618).

Alex Cross's Trial by James Patterson and Richard DiLallo. Rep. Grand Central (889,151).

Live to Tell by Lisa Gardner. Bantam (872,000).

61 Hours by Lee Child. Dell (857,000).

Southern Lights by Danielle Steel. Dell (869,000).

Hero at Large by Janet Evanovich. Harper (809,583).

To Kill a Mockingbird by Harper Lee (50th anniversary edition). Grand Central (804,752).

Black Hills by Nora Roberts. Jove (785,000).

Blood Games by Iris Johansen. St. Martin's (781,190).

500,000+

One Day at a Time by Danielle Steel. Dell (769,000).

The Doomsday Key by James Rollins. Harper (741,774).

Just Take My Heart by Mary Higgins Clark. Pocket (*715,000).

Dear John by Nicholas Sparks (movie tie-in). Grand Central (711,995).

First Family by David Baldacci. Grand Central (713,384).

Run for Your Life by James Patterson and Michael Ledwidge. Grand Central (672,849).

True Blue by David Baldacci. Grand Central (663,960).

The Lucky One by Nicholas Sparks. Grand Central (661,380).

Matters of the Heart by Danielle Steel. Dell (635,000).

The Neighbor by Lisa Gardner. Bantam (631,000).

Rainwater by Sandra Brown. Pocket (*625,000).

Eight Days to Live by Iris Johansen. St. Martin's (617,205).

Smash Cut by Sandra Brown. Pocket (*610,000).

Guardian of Lies by Steve Martini. Harper (606,591).

Gone Tomorrow by Lee Child. Dell (600,000).

The Elusive Bride by Stephanie Laurens. Avon (598,543).

The Catcher in the Rye by J. D. Salinger. Little, Brown (578,141).

The Reckless Bride by Stephanie Laurens. Avon (577,493).

1012 Evergreen Place by Debbie Macomber. Mira (575,091).

Fugitive by Phillip Margolin. Harper (563,735).

The Christmas Sweater by Glenn Beck. Pocket.

The Brazen Bride by Stephanie Laurens. Avon (560,571).

The Scarpetta Factor by Patricia Cornwell. Berkley (550,000).

Relentless by Dean Koontz. Bantam (536,000).

U Is for Undertow by Sue Grafton. Berkley (535,000).

Heart and Soul by Maeve Binchy. Vintage (527,940).

Ten Things I Love About You by Julia Quinn. Avon (527,316).

Orchard Valley Grooms by Debbie Macomber. Mira (526,133).

Storm Cycle by Iris Johansen. St. Martin's (516,998).

Summer on Blossom Street by Debbie Macomber. Mira (510,552).

Hot Rocks by Nora Roberts. Jove (510,000).

Fire and Ice by J. A. Jance. Harper (509,788).

McKettricks of Texas: Tate by Linda Lael Miller. HQN (508,507).

Wallflower Christmas by Lisa Kleypas. St. Martin's (505,963).

The 8th Confession by James Patterson and Maxine Paetro. Grand Central (504,691).

Love in the Afternoon by Lisa Kleypas. St. Martin's (503,254).

Evidence by Jonathan Kellerman. Ballantine (503,000).

Not My Daughter by Barbara Delinsky. Vintage (501,296).

Play Dead by Harlan Coben. Signet (500,000).

Deeper than the Dead by Tami Hoag. Signet (500,000).

Trade Paperbacks

1,000,000+

The Girl with the Dragon Tattoo by Stieg Larsson. Vintage (3,685,909).

The Girl Who Played with Fire by Stieg Larsson. Vintage (2,650,033).

Eat, Pray, Love by Elizabeth Gilbert. Penguin (2,153,835, including movie tie-in edition).

The Last Song by Nicholas Sparks. Grand Central (1,386,834).

Little Bee by Chris Cleave. Simon & Schuster (*1,045,000).

500,000+

Happy Ever After by Nora Roberts. Berkley (900,000).

Cutting for Stone by Abraham Verghese. Vintage (825,029).

Savor the Moment by Nora Roberts. Berkley (775,000).

Dear John by Nicholas Sparks. Grand Central (703,226).

A Reliable Wife by Robert Goolrick. Algonquin (658,000).

Radical: Taking Back Your Faith from the American Dream by David Platt. Multnomah (526,174).

Hunted by P. C. Cast and Kristin Cast. St. Martin's Griffin (511,306).

250,000+

The Host by Stephenie Meyer. Little, Brown/Back Bay (492,615).

A Tale of Two Cities and Great Expectations: Two Novels by Charles Dickens (Oprah Book Club pick). Penguin (481,002).

House Rules by Jodi Picoult. Washington Square (472,086).

Best Friends Forever by Jennifer Weiner. Washington Square (467,490).

Three Cups of Tea: One's Man Mission to Promote Peace by Greg Mortenson and David Oliver Relin. Penguin (450,447).

Look Again by Lisa Scottoline. St. Martin's Griffin (444,769).

Are You There, Vodka? It's Me, Chelsea by Chelsea Handler. Gallery (436,967).

The Blind Side: Evolution of a Game by Michael Lewis (movie tie-in). Norton (408,323).

The 8th Confession by James Patterson and Maxine Paetro. Grand Central (384,767).

My Horizontal Life: A Collection of One-Night Stands by Chelsea Handler. Bloomsbury (383,829).

Under the Dome by Stephen King. Gallery (*380,000).

Hungry Girl 1-2-3 by Lisa Lillien. St. Martin's Griffin (368,064).

Conservative Victory by Sean Hannity. Harper (357,000).

The Lost City of Z by David Grann. Vintage (350,583).

One Day by David Nicholls. Vintage (345,505).

Half Broke Horses by Jeannette Walls. Scribner (*340,000).

The Forgotten Garden by Kate Morton. Washington Square (335, 920).

Rachael Ray's Look + Cook by Rachael Ray. Clarkson Potter (332,433).

The Last Child by John Hart. St. Martin's Minotaur (327,527).

The Lovely Bones by Alice Sebold (movie tie-in). Little, Brown/Back Bay (326,807).

Swimsuit by James Patterson and Maxine Paetro. Grand Central (322,691).

The Glass Castle by Jeannette Walls. Scribner (320,000).

Mennonite in a Little Black Dress by Rhoda Janzen. Henry Holt (315,076).

Water for Elephants by Sara Gruen. Algonquin (310,000).

Eat This, Not That 2011 by David Zinczenko with Matt Goulding. Rodale (309,071).

Food Rules: An Eater's Manual by Michael Pollan. Penguin (307,541).

Winter Garden by Kristin Hannah. St. Martin's Griffin (305,670).

Worst Case by James Patterson and Michael Ledwidge. Grand Central (273,136).

Alex Cross's Trial by James Patterson and Richard Dilallo. Grand Central (271,885).

Where Men Win Glory by Jon Krakauer. Anchor.

What the Dog Saw: And Other Adventures by Malcolm Gladwell. Little, Brown/Back Bay (267,050).

Cook This, Not That: Easy and Awesome 350 Calorie Meals by David Zinczenko with Matt Goulding. Rodale (263,184).

True Colors by Kristin Hannah. St. Martin's Griffin (257,840).

Fledgling Handbook 101 by P. C. Cast. St. Martin's Griffin (252,283).

Never Let Me Go by Kazuo Ishiguro. Vintage (250,159).

125,000+

The Zombie Survival Guide: Complete Protection from the Living Dead by Max Brooks. Three Rivers (247,122).

Inside of a Dog; What the Dogs See, Smell and Hear by Alexandra Horowitz. Scribner.

America's Most Wanted Recipes by Ron Douglas. Atria (243,405).

South of Broad by Pat Conroy. Dial (240,000).

Blink: The Power of Positive Thinking Without Thinking by Malcolm Gladwell. Little, Brown/Back Bay (237,884).

The Accidental Billionaires by Ben Mezrich (movie tie-in). Anchor.

The Lucky One by Nicholas Sparks. Grand Central (234,776).

The Guernsey Literary and Potato Peel Pie Society by Mary Ann Shaffer and Annie Barrows. Dial (234,000).

The Kite Runner by Khaled Hosseini. Riverhead (225,000).

The Castaways by Elin Hilderbrand. Little, Brown/Back Bay (218,614).

Stones into Schools: Promoting Peace with Education in Afghanistan and Pakistan by Greg Mortenson. Penguin (217,922).

More of America's Most Wanted Recipes by Ron Douglas. Atria (217,151).

New Atkins for a New You by Dr. Eric C. Westman. Fireside (213,627).

The White Queen by Philippa Gregory. Touchstone (213,456).

Open by Andre Agassi. Vintage (211,945).

Shanghai Girls by Lisa See. Random House (208,000).

The Curious Incident of the Dog in the Night-Time by Mark Haddon (movie tie-in). Vintage (204,169).

Her Fearful Symmetry by Audrey Niffenegger. Scribner (*197,000).

Zeitoun by Dave Eggers. Vintage (195,974).

Olive Kitteridge by Elizabeth Strout. Random House (191,000).

Push (also known as *Precious*) by Sapphire. Vintage (187,595).

World War Z: An Oral History of the Zombie War by Max Brooks. Three Rivers (187,052).

Hungry Girl Happy Hour by Lisa Lillien. St. Martin's Griffin (186,377).

That Old Cape Magic by Richard Russo. Vintage (178,158).

Choosing to See: A Journey of Struggle and Hope by Mary Beth Chapman and Ellen Vaughn. Revell (178,015).

Half the Sky by Nicholas D. Kristof. Vintage (175,139).

The Master Your Metabolism Calorie Counter by Jillian Michaels. Three Rivers (172,622).

The Lacuna by Barbara Kingsolver. Harper Perennial (171,000).

Now Eat This! by Rocco Dispirito. Ballantine (169,000).

Cook This, Not That! Kitchen Survival Guide by David Zinczenko and Matt Goulding. Rodale (162,813).

Duets by Nora Roberts. Silhouette (157,167).

The Finkler Question by Howard Jacobson. Bloomsbury (155,581).

Lit: A Memoir by Mary Karr. Harper Perennial (154,000).

Dewey: The Small-Town Library Cat Who Touched the World by Vicki Myron with Bret Witter. Grand Central (153,434).

Tea Time for the Traditionally Built by Alexander McCall Smith. Anchor (*150,000).

Vision in White by Nora Roberts. Berkley (145,000).

Awkward Family Photos by Mike Bender and Doug Chernack. Three Rivers (143,923).

The Angel's Game by Carlos Ruiz Zafón. Anchor.

Brooklyn by Colm Tóibín. Scribner.

Fix-It and Forget-It: 700 Great Slow Cooker Recipes by Phyllis Pellman Good. Good Books (139,041).

Arguing with Idiots: How to Stop Small Minds and Big Government by Glenn Beck. Threshold Editions.

Soft Place to Land by Susan Rebecca White. Touchstone (136,473).

Fix-It and Forget-It Christmas Cookbook: 600 Slow Cooker Holiday Recipes by Phyllis Pellman Good. Good Books (134,399).

Tuesdays with Morrie by Mitch Albom. Broadway (133,100).

Helmet for My Pillow by Robert Leckie. Bantam (133,000).

Everyday Food: Fresh Flavor Fast by Martha Stewart Living Magazine. Clarkson Potter (131,938).

Secretariat by William Nack. Hyperion (131,580).

The Next 100 Years by George Friedman. Anchor.

The Sweetness at the Bottom of the Pie by Alan Bradley. Bantam (128,000).

The Black Swan by Nissim Nichol Taleb. Random House (127,000).

Midnight Sons, Vol. 3 by Debbie Macomber. Mira (125,215).

My Booky Wook by Russell Brand. HarperCollins/It Books (125,000).

100,000+

Commencement by J. Courtney Sullivan. Vintage (124,816).

Ford County: Stories by John Grisham. Bantam (124,000).

Twenties Girl by Sophie Kinsella. Dial (123,000).

Green Zone by Raji Chandrasekaran. Vintage (122,574).

Drink This, Not That! by David Zinczenko and Matt Goulding. Rodale (121,984).

Roses by Leila Meacham. Grand Central (122,570).

A Bold Fresh Piece of Humanity by Bill O'Reilly. Broadway (121,319).

Let Me In by John Ajvide Lindqvist. St. Martin's Griffin (120,024).

I Am Nujood, Age 10 and Divorced by Nujood Ali. Broadway (119,265).

A Gate at the Stairs by Lorrie Moore. Vintage (119,184).

No Angel: My Harrowing Undercover Journey to the Inner Circle of Hell's Angels by Jay Dobyns and Nils Johnson-Shelton. Broadway (115,147).

Redeeming Love by Francine Rivers. Multnomah (114,542).

Major Pettigrew's Last Stand by Helen Simonson. Bantam (114,000).

The Murder of King Tut by James Patterson and Martin Dugard. Grand Central (113,503).

The Girl from Ames: A Story of Women and a Forty-Year Friendship by Jeffrey Zaslow. Gotham (113,078).

Saving CeeCee Honeycutt by Beth Hoffman. Penguin (112,629).

Liar's Poker: Rising Through the Wreckage on Wall Street by Michael Lewis. Norton.

An Echo in the Bone by Diana Gabaldon. Bantam (111,000).

Biggest Loser Dessert Cookbook by Devin Alexander et al. Rodale (109,199).

Bart Simpson Class Clown by Matt Groening. Harper (109,000).

Secrets and Sunsets by Nora Roberts. Silhouette (108,488).

A Change in Altitude by Anita Shreve. Little, Brown/Back Bay (108,214).

Skinny Italian: Eat It and Enjoy It—Live La Bella Vita and Look Great, Too! by Teresa Giudice. Hyperion (107,612).

Knit the Season by Kate Jacobs. Berkley (105,000).

Thursday at Eight by Debbie Macomber. Mira (104,824).

Pygmy by Chuck Palahniuk. Anchor.

Charlie St. Cloud by Ben Sherwood. Bantam (104,000).

What Color Is Your Parachute? 2011 by Richard N. Bolles. Ten Speed (102,374).

The Tourist by Olen Steinhauer. St. Martin's Minotaur (102,109).

The Wedding Girl by Madeleine Wickham. St. Martin's Griffin (101,195).

Summer Dreams by Nora Roberts. Silhouette (101,096).

It's Your Time: Activate Your Faith, Achieve Your Dreams, and Increase in God's Favor by Joel Osteen. Free Press.

Holidays on Ice by David Sedaris. Little, Brown/Back Bay (100,570).

Hope in a Jar by Beth Harbison. St. Martin's Griffin (100,175).

Home Made Simple by the Experts at Home Made Simple. St. Martin's (100,048).

Children's Bestsellers: Series Dominate with Huge Numbers, E-Book Needle Jumps

Diane Roback

Senior Editor, Children's Books, *Publishers Weekly*

If you want to sell in the mega-numbers, write or publish a series. That's the clear message from our compilation of 2010's bestselling titles. Eighteen books for children and teens sold more than a million copies last year, and all of them were from authors of big franchises: Jeff Kinney, Stephenie Meyer, Rick Riordan, Suzanne Collins, P. C. and Kristin Cast. The Wimpy Kid had a not-very-wimpy total: 11.5 million copies sold, of seven titles. Sales of Twilight books, while still significant, cooled somewhat—just over 8.5 million books sold in 2010 vs. 26.5 million in 2009 and 27.5 million in 2008. Riordan's various series added up to more than 10 million copies sold; nearly 4 million Hunger Games books were sold; and James Patterson's assorted series sold just over 2.5 million copies.

Want more? Four-and-a-half million Fancy Nancy books, 3.2 million House of Night books, 2.4 million Pretty Little Liars books, 1.5 million in the Immortals series, 1.8 million copies of The 39 Clues.

Some newer, up-and-coming series made strong showings in 2010, including Dork Diaries, Fallen, the Adventures of Ook and Gluk, Big Nate, the Carrie Diaries, and the first volume in John Grisham's Theodore Boone series for middle-graders.

And there's still room on the lists for some one-offs: *Justin Bieber: First Step 2 Forever*; President Barack Obama's picture book *Of Thee I Sing*; Lauren Oliver's debut young adult novel, *Before I Fall*; and the middle-grade hit *The Strange Case of Origami Yoda.*

This was the first year *Publishers Weekly* collected e-book sales figures, and as one might expect, the big series raked in the biggest numbers. Stephenie Meyer and Rick Riordan each sold around half a million e-books. With Meyer's enormous crossover audience, it's fair to assume that many of those buyers were adults, but Riordan's numbers indicate that the e-needle has begun to move significantly for younger readers as well. Elsewhere around the e-list, the Hunger Games series sold a combined 350,000 e-books, House of Night sold 187,000, Pretty Little Liars sold 167,000, and James Patterson sold 135,000. Other strong e-book sellers, all with crossover in readership: *The Book Thief* by Markus Zusak; *Fallen* and *Torment* by Lauren Kate; *Clockwork Angel* by Cassandra Clare; and *The Carrie Diaries* by Candace Bushnell.

Please note that the figures that follow were provided by the publishers. They reflect sales in calendar year 2010 (minus returns). An asterisk denotes a title for which sales figures were provided in confidence, to be used for ranking purposes only.

Children's Hardcover Frontlist

1,000,000+

1. *The Ugly Truth* (Diary of a Wimpy Kid No. 5) by Jeff Kinney. Abrams/Amulet (3,316,509).
2. *The Short Second Life of Bree Tanner: An Eclipse Novella* by Stephenie Meyer. Little, Brown/Tingley (2,284,066).
3. *The Wimpy Kid Movie Diary* by Jeff Kinney. Abrams/Amulet (1,656,631).
4. *Mockingjay* (Hunger Games No. 3) by Suzanne Collins. Scholastic (1,493,654).
5. *The Lost Hero* (Heroes of Olympus No. 1) by Rick Riordan. Disney-Hyperion (1,315,637).
6. *The Red Pyramid* (Kane Chronicles No. 1) by Rick Riordan. Disney-Hyperion (1,075,749).
7. *Burned* (House of Night No. 7) by P. C. and Kristin Cast. St. Martin's Griffin (1,020,279).

300,000+

8. *The Gift* (Witch and Wizard No. 2) by James Patterson and Ned Rust. Little, Brown (579,001).
9. *Justin Bieber: First Step 2 Forever* by Justin Bieber. HarperCollins (503,447).
10. *Last Sacrifice* (Vampire Academy No. 6) by Richelle Mead. Penguin/Razorbill (484,849).
11. *Fang* (Maximum Ride No. 6) by James Patterson. Little, Brown (463,562).
12. *Disney/Pixar Toy Story 3* by Annie Auerbach, illustrated by Adrian Molina. Golden/Disney. (423,181).
13. *Spirit Bound* (Vampire Academy No. 5) by Richelle Mead. Penguin/Razorbill (420,485).
14. *Of Thee I Sing* by Barack Obama, illustrated by Loren Long. Knopf (420,455).
15. *Theodore Boone: Kid Lawyer* by John Grisham. Dutton (415,800).
16. *Dark Flame* (Immortals No. 4) by Alyson Noël. St. Martin's Griffin (362,572).
17. **Dork Diaries 2: Tales from a Not-So-Popular Party Girl* by Rachel Renée Russell. Simon & Shuster/Aladdin.
18. **Dork Diaries: Tales from a Not-So-Fabulous Life Girl* by Rachel Renée Russell. Simon & Shuster/Aladdin.
19. *Torment* (Fallen No. 2) by Lauren Kate. Delacorte (338,881).
20. **Clockwork Angel* by Cassandra Clare. Simon & Shuster/McElderry.
21. *Sweet Little Lies* by Lauren Conrad. HarperTeen (328,450).
22. *The Adventures of Ook and Gluk: Kung Fu Cave Men from the Future* by Dav Pilkey. Scholastic/Blue Sky (327,662).

23. *The Vampire Diaries: The Return—Shadow Souls* by L. J. Smith. HarperTeen (326,621).
24. *Big Nate* by Lincoln Peirce. HarperCollins (325,362).
25. *The Carrie Diaries* by Candace Bushnell. HarperCollins/Balzer & Bray (321,911).
26. *Star Wars Scanimation* by Rufus Butler Seder. Workman (316,000).
27. *Percy Jackson and the Olympians (The Ultimate Guide)* by Rick Riordan. Disney-Hyperion (306,313).
28. *Night Star* (Immortals No. 5) by Alyson Noël. St. Martin's Griffin (303,938).

200,000+

29. *Fancy Nancy: Ooh La La! It's Beauty Day* by Jane O'Connor, illustrated by Robin Preiss Glasser. HarperCollins (283,566).
30. *Into the Gauntlet* (39 Clues No. 10) by Margaret Peterson Haddix. Scholastic (272,404).
31. *Artemis Fowl: The Atlantis Complex* by Eoin Colfer. Disney-Hyperion (261,806).
32. *Storm Warning* (39 Clues No. 9) by Linda Sue Park. Scholastic (261,709).
33. *The Viper's Nest* (39 Clues No. 7) by Peter Lerangis. Scholastic (250,249).
34. *The Emperor's Code* (39 Clues No. 8) by Gordon Korman. Scholastic (247,683)
35. *Big Nate Strikes Again* by Lincoln Peirce. HarperCollins (244,877).
36. *Demons and Druids* (Daniel X) by James Patterson and Adam Sadler. Little, Brown (243,677).
37. *Fancy Nancy: Poet Extraordinaire!* by Jane O'Connor, illustrated by Robin Preiss Glasser. HarperCollins (241,010).
38. *Sugar and Spice* by Lauren Conrad. HarperTeen (233,667).
39. *Reckless* by Cornelia Funke. Little, Brown (231,350).
40. *Leprechaun in Late Winter* (Magic Tree House No. 43) by Mary Pope Osborne, illustrated by Sal Murdocca. Random House (222,506).
41. *Linger* by Maggie Stiefvater. Scholastic (221,721).
42. *Toy Story Storybook Collection*. Disney (220,601).
43. *Llama Llama Holiday Drama* by Anna Dewdney. Viking (214,103).
44. *Infinity* by Sherrilyn Kenyon. St. Martin's Griffin (208,795).
45. *The Black Book of Buried Secrets* (39 Clues). Scholastic (205,061).
46. *Wanted* (Pretty Little Liars No. 8) by Sara Shepard. HarperTeen (203,350).
47. *The Necromancer* (Secrets of the Immortal Nicholas Flamel No. 4) by Michael Scott. Delacorte (202,614).
48. *Fancy Nancy and the Fabulous Fashion Boutique* by Jane O'Connor, illustrated by Robin Preiss Glasser. HarperCollins (202,350).
49. *LEGO Brickmaster: Star Wars*. DK (200,074).

100,000+

50. *Misguided Angel* (Blue Bloods) by Melissa de la Cruz. Hyperion (194,393).
51. **Crescendo* by Becca Fitzpatrick. Simon & Schuster.
52. *A Ghost Tale for Christmas Time* (MTH No. 44). Mary Pope Osborne, illustrated by Sal Murdocca. Random House (175,049).
53. *Lauren Conrad Style* by Lauren Conrad. HarperTeen (173,764).
54. *Walt Disney's Alice in Wonderland.* Golden/Disney (171,947).
55. *The Cat in the Hat Knows a Lot About That! The Thinga-ma-jigger Is Coming Today!* by Tish Rabe, illustrated by Christopher Moroney. Random House/Golden (169,973).
56. *Fallout* by Ellen Hopkins. Simon & Schuster/McElderry.
57. *Tangled* by Ben Smiley, illustrated by Victoria Ying. Random House/Golden (168,664).
58. *On the Night You Were Born* (board book) by Nancy Tillman. Feiwel and Friends (167,327).
59. *My Mommy Hung the Moon* by Jamie Lee Curtis, illustrated by Laura Cornell. HarperCollins/Balzer & Bray (161,333).
60. *Monster High* by Lisi Harrison. Little, Brown/Poppy (156,322).
61. *Before I Fall* by Lauren Oliver. HarperCollins (154,346).
62. *Marley and the Kittens* by John Grogan, illustrated by Richard Cowdrey. HarperCollins (153,959).
63. *Only the Good Spy Young* by Ally Carter. Disney-Hyperion (151,765).
64. *Knuffle Bunny Free* by Mo Willems. HarperCollins/Balzer & Bray (151,613).
65. *Fading Echoes* (Warriors: Omen of the Stars No. 2) by Erin Hunter. HarperCollins (150,524).
66. *Beautiful Darkness* (Caster Chronicles No. 2) by Kami Garcia and Margaret Stohl. Little, Brown (150,019).
67. *Halt's Peril* (Ranger's Apprentice No. 9) by John Flanagan. Philomel (148,553).
68. *Star Wars: Millennium Falcon: A 3-D Owner's Guide* by Ryder Windham. Scholastic (147,467).
69. *Disney/Pixar Toy Story 3: Read-Aloud Storybook* by Christine Peymani, illustrated by Caroline Egan. Random House (147,382).
70. *The Reckoning* by Kelley Armstrong. HarperCollins (143,884).
71. **Disney/Pixar Toy Story 3: Magnet Book.* Random House.
72. *Barbie in a Mermaid Tale* by Mary Man-Kong. Random House/Golden (138,866).
73. *Twelfth Grade Kills* (Chronicles of Vladimir Tod) by Heather Brewer. Dutton (136,651).
74. *Meet the Gang! A Moving Pictures Book* by Annie Auerbach. Disney Press (134,242).
75. *The Kings of Clonmel* (Ranger's Apprentice No. 8) by John Flanagan. Philomel (133,888).

76. *Wherever You Are My Love Will Find You* by Nancy Tillman. Feiwel and Friends (133,388).
77. *Scaredy-Cat, Splat!* by Rob Scotton. HarperCollins (132,294).
78. *The Lying Game* by Sara Shepard. HarperTeen (129,965).
79. *Matched* by Ally Condie. Dutton (126,803).
80. *The Strange Case of Origami Yoda* by Tom Angelberger. Abrams/Amulet (125,000).
81. *I Am Number Four* by Pittacus Lore. HarperCollins (123,771).
82. *Night Whispers* (Warriors: Omen of the Stars No. 3) by Erin Hunter. HarperCollins (123,058).
83. *Disney Tangled: Read-Aloud Storybook* by Christine Peymani, illustrated by Jean-Paul Orpinas. Random House (121,682).
84. **Olivia Goes to Venice* by Ian Falconer. Simon & Schuster/Atheneum.
85. *Dora's Birthday Surprise!* by Molly Reisner, illustrated by David Aikins. Random House/Golden (118,893).
86. **Heads* by Matthew Van Fleet. Simon & Schuster/Wiseman.
87. *The Big Red Book of Beginner Books* by P. D. Eastman. Random House. (113,742).
88. *Bloody Valentine* (Blue Bloods) by Melissa de la Cruz. Hyperion (105,731).
89. *DC Super Heroes: The Ultimate Pop-Up Book* by DC Comics and Matthew Reinhart. Little, Brown (105,200).
90. *The Scorch Trials* (Maze Runner No. 2) by James Dashner. Delacorte (102,574).
91. *Dinosaur Train: Triceratops for Lunch* by Golden Books, illustrated by Caleb Meurer. Random House/Golden (101,297).
92. *I'm a T. Rex!* by Dennis Shealy, illustrated by Brian Biggs. Random House/Golden (100,590).
93. *SkyClan's Destiny* (Warriors Super Edition) by Erin Hunter. HarperCollins (101,590).
94. *It's a Book* by Lane Smith. Roaring Brook (101,531).
95. *Hourglass* by Claudia Gray. HarperTeen (100,755).
96. *Revolution* by Jennifer Donnelly. Delacorte (100,578).
97. *The Easter Egg* by Jan Brett. Putnam (100,085).

Hardcover Backlist

1,000,000+

1. *Diary of a Wimpy Kid* by Jeff Kinney. Abrams/Amulet, 2007 (1,512,578).
2. *Diary of a Wimpy Kid Do-It-Yourself Book* by Jeff Kinney. Abrams/ Amulet, 2008 (1,455,253).
3. *Rodrick Rules* (Diary of a Wimpy Kid No. 2) by Jeff Kinney. Abrams/ Amulet, 2008 (1,304,968).

4. *The Last Straw* (Diary of a Wimpy Kid No. 3) by Jeff Kinney. Abrams/ Amulet, 2009 (1,294,019).

300,000+

5. *Dog Days* (Diary of a Wimpy Kid No. 4) by Jeff Kinney. Abrams/Amulet, 2009 (954,180).
6. *The Last Olympian* (Percy Jackson and the Olympians No. 5) by Rick Riordan. Disney-Hyperion, 2009 (945,056).
7. *Catching Fire* (Hunger Games No. 2) by Suzanne Collins. Scholastic, 2009 (918,821).
8. *Breaking Dawn* (Twilight Saga No. 4) by Stephenie Meyer. Little, Brown/ Tingley, 2008 (720,032).
9. *Goodnight Moon* (board book) by Margaret Wise Brown, illustrated by Clement Hurd. HarperFestival, 1991 (599,353).
10. *Green Eggs and Ham* by Dr. Seuss. Random House, 1960 (581,787).
11. *Are You My Mother?* (board book) by Dr. Seuss. Random House, 1998 (517,035).
12. *Oh, the Places You'll Go!* by Dr. Seuss. Random House, 1990 (479,683).
13. *One Fish Two Fish Red Fish Blue Fish* by Dr. Seuss. Random House, 1960 (472,551).
14. *The Hunger Games* by Suzanne Collins. Scholastic, 2008 (471,027).
15. *LEGO Star Wars: The Visual Dictionary.* DK, 2009 (470,514).
16. *The Cat in the Hat* by Dr. Seuss. Random House, 1957 (467,977).
17. *Brown Bear, Brown Bear, What Do You See?* 25th anniversary edition (board book) by Bill Martin, Jr., illustrated by Eric Carle. Priddy Books, 1996 (424,096).
18. *Guess How Much I Love You* (board book) by Sam McBratney, illustrated by Anita Jeram. Candlewick, 1995 (376,399).
19. *The Very Hungry Caterpillar* (board book) by Eric Carle. Philomel, 2004 (405,311).
20. *Dr. Seuss's ABC* (board book) by Dr. Seuss. Random House, 1996 (356,143).
21. *The Maze of Bones* (39 Clues No. 1) by Rick Riordan. Scholastic, 2008 (333,549).
22. *The Poky Little Puppy* by Janette Sebring Lowery, illustrated by Gustaf Tenggren. Golden, 2001 (301,559).

200,000+

23. *Fancy Nancy: Splendiferous Christmas* by Jane O'Connor, illustrated by Robin Preiss Glasser. HarperCollins, 2009 (296,307).
24. *Big Board First 100 Words* (board book) by Roger Priddy. Priddy Books, 2005 (265,066).

25. *I Love You Through and Through* (board book) by Bernadette Rossetti Shustak, illustrated by Caroline Jayne Church. Scholastic/Cartwheel, 2005 (263,588).
26. *Disney Bedtime Favorites*. Disney, 2007 (260,899).
27. *Mr. Brown Can Moo! Can You?* (board book) by Dr. Seuss. Random House, 1996 (256,376).
28. *Hop on Pop* by Dr. Seuss. Random House, 1963 (255,794).
29. **Going-to-Bed Book* (board book) by Sandra Boynton. Little Simon, 1982.
30. *Are You My Mother?* by Dr. Seuss. Random House, 1960 (241,713).
31. **Moo, Baa, La La La!* (board book) by Sandra Boynton. Little Simon, 1982.
32. *Disney/Pixar Toy Story: Toy Story*. Random House/Disney, 2009 (219,753).
33. *How the Grinch Stole Christmas!* by Dr. Seuss. Random House, 1957 (219,489).
34. *Dr. Seuss's ABC* by Dr. Seuss. Random House, 1960 (215,247).
35. *Baby Einstein: First Words*. Disney, 2008 (214,265).
36. *Waddle!* by Rufus Butler Seder. Workman, 2009 (213,000).
37. *The Giving Tree* by Shel Silverstein. HarperCollins, 2003 (211,624).
38. *My First Read and Learn Bible* by American Bible Society. Scholastic/Little Shepherd, 2006 (200,988).

100,000+

39. *A Treasury of Curious George* by H. A. Rey. Houghton Mifflin, 2004 (189,215).
40. *Go, Dog Go!* by Dr. Seuss. Random House, 1961 (186,973).
41. *Tempted* (House of Night No. 6) by P. C. and Kristin Cast. St. Martin's Griffin, 2009 (181,528).
42. *Fox in Socks* by Dr. Seuss. Random House, 1965 (176,970).
43. *SpongeBob SquarePants: Mr. FancyPants!* by Geof Smith, illustrated by Caleb Meurer. Random/Golden, 2009 (175,180).
44. *The Big Green Book of Beginner Books* by Dr. Seuss, illustrated by James Stevenson. Random House, 2009 (174,754).
45. *The Polar Express* by Chris Van Allsburg. Houghton Mifflin, 1985 (174,000).
46. **Where Is Baby's Belly Button?* (board book) by Karen Katz. Little Simon, 2000.
47. *Baby Einstein: Mirror Me!* by Julie Aigner-Clark. Disney, 2002 (168,254).
48. *The Big Blue Book of Beginner Books* by P. D. Eastman. Random House, 2008 (161,984).
49. *Pat the Bunny* by Dorothy Kunhardt. Golden, 2001 (161,755).
50. **Toes, Ears and Nose* (board book) by Marion Dane Bauer. Little Simon, 2003.

51. *On the Night You Were Born* by Nancy Tillman. Feiwel and Friends, 2006 (159,610).
52. *There's No Place Like Space* by Tish Rabe, illustrated by Aristides Ruiz. Random House, 1999 (158,672).
53. *Barnyard Dance* by Sandra Boynton. Workman, 1993 (158,000).
54. *Eclipse* (Twilight Saga No. 3) by Stephenie Meyer. Little, Brown/Tingley, 2007 (155,451).
55. *5 Little Monkeys Jumping on the Bed* (board book) by Eileen Christelow. Clarion, 1989 (154,242).
56. *Go, Dog. Go!* (board book) by Dr. Seuss. Random House, 1997 (154,142).
57. *Pinkalicious* by Victoria and Elizabeth Kann. HarperCollins, 2006 (151,260).
58. *One False Note* (39 Clues No. 2) by Gordon Korman. Scholastic, 2008 (150,023).
59. *How Do I Love You?* by Marion Dane Bauer, illustrated by Caroline Jayne Church. Scholastic/Cartwheel, 2008 (147,307).
60. *Hand, Hand, Fingers, Thumb* (board book) by Al Perkins, illustrated by Eric Gurney. Random House, 1998 (146,214).
61. *Disney Princess Collection.* Disney, 2009 (145,973).
62. *Goodnight Gorilla* (board book) by Peggy Rathmann. Putnam, 1996 (144,356).
63. *The Foot Book* (board book) by Dr. Seuss. Random House, 1996 (143,575).
64. *When You Reach Me* by Rebecca Stead. Random/Lamb, 2009 (142,791).
65. *Oh, Say Can You Say Di-no-saur?* by Bonnie Worth. Random House, 1999 (142,746).
66. *The Runaway Bunny* (board book) by Margaret Wise Brown, illustrated by Clement Hurd. HarperFestival, 1991 (142,602).
67. *Where the Sidewalk Ends* 30th anniversary edition by Shel Silverstein. HarperCollins, 2003 (142,476).
68. *Another Monster at the End of This Book* by Jon Stone. Random/Golden, 1999 (141,507).
69. *Twilight* (Twilight Saga No. 1) by Stephenie Meyer. Little, Brown /Tingley, 2006 (139,926).
70. *Go Away, Big Green Monster!* by Ed Emberley. LB Kids, 1993 (139,615).
71. *Walt Disney's Classic Storybook.* Disney, 2009 (138,839).
72. *Gallop!* by Rufus Butler Seder. Workman, 2007 (138,000).
73. *Hop on Pop* (board book) by Dr. Seuss. Random House, 2004 (137,696).
74. *The Alphabet Book* (board book) by P. D. Eastman. Random House, 2000 (133,715).
75. *The Little Red Hen* by J. P. Miller, illustrated by Diane Muldrow. Random/Golden, 2001 (132,017).
76. *Baby Farm Animals* by Garth Williams. Random/Golden, 1993 (129,818).

77. *Thomas and the Great Discovery* by R. Schuyler Hooke, illustrated by Tommy Stubbs. Random/Golden, 2009 (128,300).
78. *Percy Jackson and the Olympians: The Demigod Files* by Rick Riordan. Disney-Hyperion, 2009 (132,268).
79. *New Moon* (Twilight Saga No. 2) by Stephenie Meyer. Little, Brown/ Tingley, 2006 (128,586).
80. *Goldilicious* by Victoria Kann. HarperCollins, 2009 (127,991).
81. *I Can Read with My Eyes Shut!* by Dr. Seuss. Random House, 1978 (126,222).
82. **Blue Hat, Green Hat* (board book) by Sandra Boynton. Little Simon, 1984.
83. *The Lion and the Mouse* by Jerry Pinkney. Little, Brown, 2009 (124,310).
84. *The Saggy Baggy Elephant* by Byron Jackson. Random/Golden, 1999 (123,969).
85. *Disney Christmas Storybook Collection.* Disney, 2009 (123,370).
86. *Thirteen Reasons Why* by Jay Asher. Penguin/Razorbill, 2007 (122,726).
87. *The Lorax* by Dr. Seuss. Random House, 1971 (121,522).
88. *Happy Birthday to You!* by Dr. Seuss. Random House, 1959 (120,094).
89. *Disney/Pixar Cars: Cars* by Ben Smiley, illustrated by Scott Tilley. Golden/Disney, 2006 (119,733).
90. *The Sword Thief* (39 Clues No. 3) by Peter Lerangis. Scholastic, 2009 (118,697).
91. *Ten Apples Up on Top!* by Dr. Seuss. Random House, 1961 (118,612).
92. *Pajama Time* by Sandra Boynton. Workman, 2000 (118,000).
93. *Disney/Pixar Cars: Look Out for Mater!* Golden/Disney, 2009 (117,064).
94. *Scuffy the Tugboat,* illustrated by Tibor Gergely. Random/Golden, 2001 (116,170).
95. *The Sea of Monsters* (Percy Jackson and the Olympians No. 2) by Rick Riordan. Disney-Hyperion, 2006 (115,581).
96. *The Monster at the End of This Book* by Jon Stone, illustrated by Michael Smollin. Random/Golden, 1999 (114,632).
97. *I'm a Big Sister* by Joanna Cole, illustrated by Rosalinda Kightley. HarperFestival, 2009 (113,756).
98. *How to Train Your Dragon* by Cressida Cowell. Little, Brown, 2004 (112,006).
99. *Disney Princess: The Little Mermaid.* Golden/Disney, 2003 (111,372).
100. *Belly Button Book* by Sandra Boynton. Workman, 2005 (111,000).
101. *Oh, the Thinks You Can Think!* (board book) by Dr. Seuss. Random House, 1975 (108,443).
102. *If You Give a Mouse a Cookie* by Laura Numeroff, illustrated by Felicia Bond. HarperCollins, 1985 (108,309).
103. *The Shy Little Kitten* by Cathleen Schurr, illustrated by Gustaf Tenggren. Golden/Disney, 1999 (107,798).

104. *The Night Before Christmas* by Clement C. Moore, illustrated by Mircea Catusanu. Random/Golden, 2001 (107,377).
105. *Disney/Pixar Toy Story: Toy Story 2* by Christopher Nicholas. Golden/Disney, 2006 (107,308).
106. Snow White and the Seven Dwarfs. Golden/Disney, 2003 (106,915).
107. *Put Me in the Zoo* (board book) by Robert Lopshire. Random House, 2001 (106,643).
108. *The Nose Book* (board book) by Al Perkins, illustrated by Joe Mathieu. Random House, 2003 (104,792).
109. *There's a Wocket in My Pocket!* (board book) by Dr. Seuss. Random House, 1996 (104,500).
110. *The Battle of the Labyrinth* (Percy Jackson and the Olympians No. 4) by Rick Riordan. Disney-Hyperion, 2008 (104,495).
111. *Mater's Tall Tales.* Random/Disney, 2009 (104,264).
112. *The Lightning Thief* (Percy Jackson and the Olympians No. 1) by Rick Riordan. Disney-Hyperion, 2005 (103,941).
113. *The Jolly Barnyard* by Annie North Bedford, illustrated by Tibor Gergely. Random/Golden, 2004 (103,806).
114. *Big Red Barn* (board book) by Margaret Wise Brown, illustrated by Felicia Bond. HarperFestival, 1995 (103,313).
115. *Llama Llama Red Pajama* by Anna Dewdney. Viking, 2005 (103,120).
116. *My First Read and Learn Book of Prayers* by Mary Manz Simon. Scholastic/Little Shepherd, 2007 (102,658).
117. *The Titan's Curse* (Percy Jackson and the Olympians No. 3) by Rick Riordan. Disney-Hyperion, 2007 (101,484).
118. *I Love You, Stinky Face* (board book) by Lisa McCourt, illustrated by Cyd Moore. Scholastic/Cartwheel, 2004 (101,022).
119. *Snuggle Puppy* by Sandra Boynton. Workman, 2003 (101,000).
120. *Fancy Nancy* by Jane O'Connor, illustrated by Robin Preiss Glasser. HarperCollins, 2005 (100,510).
121. *Five Little Pumpkins* (board book). Illustrated by Dan Yaccarino. HarperFestival, 1998 (100,354).
122. *Oh, the Thinks You Can Think!* by Dr. Seuss. Random House, 1975 (100,273).

Paperback Frontlist

1,000,000+

1. *Eclipse* (mass market media tie-in edition) by Stephenie Meyer. Little, Brown/Tingley (1,906,658).
2. *Breaking Dawn* by Stephenie Meyer. Little, Brown/Tingley (1,061,395).
3. *The Hunger Games* by Suzanne Collins. Scholastic (1,059,498).

300,000+

4. *Max* (Maximum Ride No. 5) (mass market edition) by James Patterson. Little, Brown (530,367).
5. *Disney/Pixar Toy Story 3: Toy to Toy* (Step into Reading) by Tennant Redbank, illustrated by Caroline Egan. Random House/Disney (483,918).
6. *The Twilight Saga: Eclipse: The Official Illustrated Movie Companion* by Mark Cotta Vaz. Little, Brown (424,606).
7. *Fallen* by Lauren Kate. Delacorte (396,072).
8. *Disney/Pixar Toy Story 3: Toy Trouble* (Pictureback). Random House/Disney (367,000).
9. *Brisingr* (Inheritance Cycle No. 3) by Christopher Paolini. Knopf (358,952).
10. *How to Train Your Dragon* by Cressida Cowell. Little, Brown (358,331).
11. *Disney/Pixar Toy Story: The Great Toy Escape* (Step into Reading) by Kitty Richards. Random House/Disney (344,040).
12. *Vampire Diaries: The Return—Nightfall* by L. J. Smith. HarperTeen (324,308).

200,000+

13. *Pinkalicious: School Rules!* by Victoria Kann. HarperCollins (285,078).
14. *Pinkalicious and the Pink Drink* by Victoria Kann. HarperFestival (250,203).
15. *Witch and Wizard* by James Patterson and Gabrielle Charbonnet. Little, Brown (244,013).
16. *The Fledgling Handbook 101* by P. C. Cast and Kim Doner. St. Martin's Griffin (242,283).
17. **City of Ashes* by Cassandra Clare. Simon & Schuster/McElderry.
18. *Hiccup the Hero* (How to Train Your Dragon) by Catherine Hapka, illustrated by Charles Grosvenor. HarperCollins (221,376).
19. *Disney Tangled: Kingdom of Color* (Step into Reading) by Melissa Lagonegro, illustrated by Jean-Paul Orpinas. Random House/Disney (215,955).
20. *Pinkalicious: Tickled Pink* by Victoria Kahn. HarperFestival (215,853).
21. *Fancy Nancy and the Late, Late, LATE Night* by Jane O'Connor, illustrated by Robin Preiss Glasser. HarperFestival (213,485).
22. *Fancy Nancy and the Delectable Cupcakes* by Jane O'Connor, illustrated by Robin Preiss Glasser. HarperFestival (210,803).
23. **City of Glass* by Cassandra Clare. Simon & Schuster/McElderry.
24. *Barbie: Barbie in a Mermaid Tale* (Step into Reading) by Christy Webster. Random House (206,398).
25. *If I Stay* by Gayle Forman. Penguin/Speak (205,700).
26. *Sweet Little Lies* by Lauren Conrad. HarperTeen (201,201).
27. *Radiance* by Alyson Noël. Macmillan/Square Fish (200,791).

100,000+

28. *Barbie: Fashion Fairytale* (Step into Reading) by Mary Man-Kong. Random House (198,151).
29. *Pinkalicious: Pink Around the Rink* by Victoria Kann. HarperCollins (197,923).
30. *Blood Promise* (Vampire Academy No. 4) by Richelle Mead. Penguin/Razorbill (191,095).
31. *Fancy Nancy and the Sensational Babysitter* by Jane O'Connor, illustrated by Robin Preiss Glasser. HarperFestival (189,992).
32. *Barbie in a Mermaid Tale: A Storybook* (Pictureback) by Mary Man-Kong. Random House (187,587).
33. **The Band Book* by Ilanit Oliver. Simon Spotlight.
34. *The Cat in the Hat Knows a Lot About That!: Show Me the Honey* by Tish Rabe, illustrated by Christopher Moroney. Random House (181,812).
35. *Killer* (Pretty Little Liars No. 6) by Sara Shepard. HarperTeen (177,181).
36. *These Boots Were Made for Stalking* (The Clique No. 12) by Lisi Harrison. Little, Brown/Poppy (176,951).
37. *Barbie: Fashion Fairytale* (Pictureback) by Mary Man-Kong. Random House (175,154).
38. *Meet the Dragons* (How to Train Your Dragon) by Catherine Hapka, illustrated by Charles Grosvenor. HarperCollins (173,458).
39. *Fancy Nancy: My Family History* by Jane O'Connor, illustrated by Robin Preiss Glasser. HarperCollins (172,739).
40. *Iron Man 2: Iron Man's Friends and Foes* by Lisa Shea. LB Kids (171,556).
41. **The Fallen 1* (bind-up) by Thomas E. Sniegoski. Simon Pulse.
42. *Heartless* (PLL No. 7) by Sara Shepard. HarperTeen (169,694).
43. *The Vampire Diaries: Stefan's Diaries No. 1—Origins* by L. J. Smith. HarperTeen (169,339).
44. *Shiver* by Maggie Stiefvater. Scholastic (169,223).
45. **So Many Butterflies!* (Dora the Explorer) by Lara Bergen. Simon Spotlight.
46. *Fancy Nancy: Spectacular Spectacles* by Jane O'Connor, illustrated by Robin Preiss Glasser. HarperCollins (164,988).
47. *Disney Tangled: A Dazzling Day* (Pictureback) by Devin Ann Wooster, illustrated by Britney Lee. Random House/Disney (162,013).
48. *Thomas and Friends: Lost at Sea!* (Pictureback). Illustrated by Tommy Stubbs. Random House (160,847).
49. **Remember Me* (bind-up) by Christopher Pike. Simon Pulse.
50. **The Forbidden Game* (bind-up) by L. J. Smith. Simon Pulse.
51. *Fancy Nancy: Every Day Is Earth Day* by Jane O'Connor, illustrated by Robin Preiss Glasser. HarperCollins (154,612).
52. *Disney/Pixar Toy Story: Toy Story/Toy Story 2* (Pictureback). Random House/Disney (151,633).

53. *Snow Dog Marley* by John Grogan, illustrated by Richard Cowdrey. HarperCollins (151,054).
54. **Dora's Big Birthday Adventure* by Lauryn Silverhardt. Simon Spotlight.
55. **Thirst No. 1* (bind-up) by Christopher Pike. Simon Pulse.
56. *Befriending a Foe* (How to Train Your Dragon) by Devan Aptekar. HarperCollins (148,259).
57. **Thirst No. 3* (bind-up) by Christopher Pike. Simon Pulse.
58. *The Graveyard Book* by Neil Gaiman, illustrated by Dave McKean. HarperCollins (144,347).
59. **Olivia and the Babies* by Jodie Shepherd, illustrated by Jared Osterhold. Simon Spotlight.
60. **Thirst No. 2* (bind-up) by Christopher Pike. Simon Pulse.
61. *How to Be a Pirate* (How to Train Your Dragon No. 2). Cressida Cowell. Little, Brown (140,856).
62. *Magic Tree House: Games and Puzzles for the Tree House* by Mary Pope Osborne, illustrated by Natalie Pope Boyce. Random House (140,255).
63. **Dora's Wizzle World Adventure,* adapted by Leigh Olsen, illustrated by Victoria Miller. Simon Spotlight.
64. *Disney Tangled: Outside My Window* (Step into Reading). Random House/Disney (139,882).
65. *Prom Nights from Hell* by Stephenie Meyer et al. HarperTeen (139,562).
66. **Secrets of the Dragon Sanctuary* (Fablehaven No. 4) by Brandon Mull. Simon & Schuster/Aladdin.
67. *Disney/Pixar Cars: The Spooky Sound* (Step into Reading) by Melissa Lagonegro, illustrated by Ron Cohee. Random House/Disney (134,734).
68. **Hush, Hush* by Becca Fitzpatrick. Simon & Schuster.
69. **Dinner with Olivia,* adapted by Emily Sollinger, illustrated by Guy Wolek. Simon Spotlight.
70. *Disney Princess: A Fairy-Tale Fall* (Step into Reading) by Apple Jordan, illustrated by Francesco Legramandi. Random House/Disney (130,668).
71. *Marley and the Runaway Pumpkin* by John Grogan, illustrated by Richard Cowdrey. HarperCollins (130,556).
72. *Gobber's Guide to Battling Dragons* (How to Train Your Dragon) by Devan Aptekar. HarperCollins (127,599).
73. *Beautiful Creatures* (Caster Chronicles No. 1) by Kami Garcia and Margaret Stohl. Little, Brown (124,373).
74. **The Last Airbender* (movie novelization), adapted by Michael Teitelbaum. Simon Spotlight.
75. **Dora Saves Crystal Kingdom,* adapted by Molly Reisner, illustrated by Dave Aikins. Simon Spotlight.
76. *Toy Story 3 Junior Novelization.* Random House/Disney (122,112).
77. *Percy Jackson and the Olympians: The Lightning Thief, The Graphic Novel* by Rick Riordan. Disney-Hyperion (121,912).

78. *Disney Tangled: Junior Novelization* by Irene Trimble. Random House/Disney (119,278).
79. *My Little Phony* (The Clique No. 13) by Lisi Harrison. Little, Brown/Poppy (118,392).
80. *Ultimate Sticker Book: Toy Story 3*. DK (116,793).
81. *How to Train Your Dragon: The Chapter Book* by J. E. Bright. HarperCollins (115,745).
82. *The Sorceress* (Secrets of the Immortal Nicholas Flamel No. 3) by Michael Scott. Delacorte (115,691).
83. *Disney/Pixar Cars: Off-Road!/Crash Course!* (Pictureback) by Frank Berrios. Random House/Disney (113,955).
84. *Barbie: I Can Be a Pet Vet* (Step into Reading) by Mary Man-Kong, illustrated by Jiyoung An. Random House, 2010 (113,543).
85. **The Fallen 2* (bind-up) by Thomas E. Sniegoski. Simon Pulse.
86. *Haunted Castle on Hallows Eve* (MTH No. 30) by Mary Pope Osborne, illustrated by Sal Murdocca. Random House (111,977).
87. *How to Speak Dragonese* (How to Train Your Dragon No. 3) by Cressida Cowell. Little, Brown (109,675).
88. **Dark Visions* (bind-up) by Elizabeth Chandler. Simon Pulse.
89. *Disney Princess: Ariel's Dolphin Adventure/Snow White's New Friend* by Andrea Posner-Sanchez. Random House/Disney (107,293).
90. *Savvy* by Ingrid Law. Philomel (106,727).
91. **Olivia the Magnificent,* adapted by Sheila Sweeny Higginson, illustrated by Art Mawhinney. Simon Spotlight.
92. *Iron Man 2: The Junior Novel* by Alexander Irvine. Little, Brown (105,377).
93. *Iron Man: Armored Adventures—Whiplash!* (Step into Reading), illustrated by Patrick Spaziante. Random House (105,230).
94. *Justin Bieber: Test Your Super-Fan Status* by Gabrielle Reyes, illustrated by Zoe Quayle. Barron's (105,000).
95. *Strike Three, Marley!* by John Grogan, illustrated by Richard Cowdrey. HarperCollins (104,596).
96. **Dark Secrets 2* (bind-up) by Elizabeth Chandler. Simon Pulse.
97. *The Cat in the Hat Knows a Lot About That!: I Love the Nightlife* by Tish Rabe, illustrated by Aristides Ruiz. Random House (102,533).
98. *Judy Moody and Stink: The Mad, Mad, Mad, Mad Treasure Hunt* by Megan McDonald, illustrated by Peter H. Reynolds. Candlewick (102,321).
99. **Olivia Takes a Trip,* adapted by Ellie O'Ryan, illustrated by Jared Osterhold. Simon Spotlight.
100. *Scat* by Carl Hiaasen. Knopf (101,800).
101. *The Maze Runner* by James Dashner. Delacorte (101,405).
102. **Olivia and the Haunted House,* adapted by Jodie Shepherd, illustrated by Patrick Spaziante. Simon Spotlight.

103. *The Eye of the Fry Cook* (SpongeBob SquarePants) by Erica David, illustrated by Harry Moore. Simon Spotlight.
104. **Nightworld No. 3* (bind-up) by L. J. Smith. Simon Pulse.

Paperback Backlist

1,000,000+

1. *Percy Jackson and the Olympians: The Lightning Thief* (combined editions) by Rick Riordan. Disney-Hyperion, 2006 (1,692,257).
2. *The Sea of Monsters* (Percy Jackson and the Olympians No. 2) by Rick Riordan. Disney-Hyperion, 2007 (1,471,368).
3. *The Titan's Curse* (Percy Jackson and the Olympians No. 3) by Rick Riordan. Disney-Hyperion, 2008 (1,299,039).
4. *The Battle of the Labyrinth* (Percy Jackson and the Olympians No. 4) by Rick Riordan. Disney-Hyperion, 2009 (1,122,192).

300,000+

5. *Twilight* (Twilight Saga No. 1) by Stephenie Meyer. Little, Brown/Tingley, 2006 (969,551).
6. *Eclipse* (Twilight Saga No. 3) by Stephenie Meyer. Little, Brown/Tingley, 2009 (671,688).
7. *Pretty Little Liars* by Sara Shepard. HarperTeen, 2007 (628,894).
8. *Beezus and Ramona* by Beverly Cleary, illustrated by Tracy Dockray. HarperCollins, 1990 (573,955).
9. *New Moon* (Twilight Saga No. 2) by Stephenie Meyer. Little, Brown/Tingley, 2008 (519,094).
10. *Hunted* (House of Night No. 5) by P. C. and Kristin Cast. St. Martin's Griffin, 2010 (511,306).
11. *Flawless* (PLL No. 2) by Sara Shepard. HarperTeen, 2008 (503,188).
12. *Dinosaurs Before Dark* (Magic Tree House No. 1) by Mary Pope Osborne, illustrated by Sal Murdocca. Random House, 1992 (415,290).
13. *The Giver* by Lois Lowry. Laurel Leaf, 2002 (411,680).
14. *The Book Thief* by Markus Zusak. Knopf, 2007 (390,805).
15. *Ultimate Sticker Collection: Lego Minifigure*. DK, 2009 (387,715).
16. *Harry Potter and the Deathly Hallows* by J. K. Rowling, illustrated by Mary GrandPré. Scholastic/Levine, 2009 (368,369).
17. *Harry Potter and the Sorcerer's Stone* by J. K. Rowling, illustrated by Mary GrandPré. Scholastic/Levine, 1999 (346,213).
18. *Marked* (House of Night No. 1) by P. C. and Kristin Cast. St. Martin's Griffin, 2007 (345,459).
19. *Ramona's World* by Beverly Cleary, illustrated by Tracy Dockray. HarperCollins, 2006 (341,772).

20. *The Outsiders* by S. E. Hinton. Speak, 1997 and Puffin, 2006 (335,867).
21. *Where the Wild Things Are* by Maurice Sendak. HarperCollins, 1988 (335,776).
22. *Fancy Nancy Sees Stars* by Jane O'Connor, illustrated by Robin Preiss Glasser. HarperCollins, 2008 (320,190).
23. *The Vampire Diaries: The Awakening* by L. J. Smith. HarperTeen, 2009 (320,086).
24. *L.A. Candy* by Lauren Conrad. HarperTeen, 2009 (317,049).
25. *The Voyage of the Dawn Treader* by C. S. Lewis, illustrated by Pauline Baynes. HarperCollins, 1994 (310,280).
26. *Betrayed* (House of Night No. 2) by P. C. and Kristin Cast. St. Martin's Griffin, 2007 (309,054).
27. *Chosen* (House of Night No. 3) by P. C. and Kristin Cast. St. Martin's Griffin, 2008 (305,394).
28. *Untamed* (House of Night No. 4) by P. C. and Kristin Cast. St. Martin's Griffin, 2008 (303,158).

200,000+

29. *Perfect* (PLL No. 3) by Sara Shepard. HarperTeen, 2008 (297,070).
30. *Disney Princess: What Is a Princess?* illustrated by Jennifer Liberts Weinberg. Random House/Disney. 2004 (288,428).
31. *Fancy Nancy: Pajama Day* by Jane O'Connor, illustrated by Robin Preiss Glasser. HarperCollins, 2009 (287,823).
32. *Fancy Nancy: The Dazzling Book Report* by Jane O'Connor, illustrated by Robin Preiss Glasser. HarperCollins, 2009 (283,181).
33. *The Vampire Diaries: The Fury* by L. J. Smith. HarperTeen, 2007 (278,770).
34. *The Knight at Dawn* (MTH No. 2) by Mary Pope Osborne, illustrated by Sal Murdocca. Random House, 1993 (268,688).
35. *Harry Potter and the Chamber of Secrets* by J. K. Rowling, illustrated by Mary GrandPré. Scholastic/Levine, 2000 (265,813).
36. *Unbelievable* (PLL No. 4) by Sara Shepard. HarperTeen, 2008 (265,200).
37. *Mummies in the Morning* (MTH No. 3) by Mary Pope Osborne, illustrated by Sal Murdocca. Random House, 1993 (264,046).
38. **City of Bones* by Cassandra Clare. Simon & Schuster/McElderry, 2008.
39. *Ramona Quimby, Age 8* by Beverly Cleary, illustrated by Tracy Dockray. HarperCollins, 2006 (255,994).
40. *Alvin and the Chipmunks: The Squeakquel—Meet the "Munks"* by Susan Hill. HarperCollins, 2009 (255,758).
41. *Pirates Past Noon* (MTH No. 4) by Mary Pope Osborne, illustrated by Sal Murdocca. Random House, 1994 (252,945).
42. *The Lion, the Witch and the Wardrobe* by C. S. Lewis, illustrated by Pauline Baynes. HarperCollins, 1994 (250,127).

43. *The Vampire Diaries: The Struggle* by L. J. Smith. HarperTeen, 2009 (245,545).
44. *The Mysterious Benedict Society* by Trenton Lee Stewart. Little, Brown/Tingley, 2008 (245,470).
45. *A Wrinkle in Time* by Madeleine L'Engle. Macmillan/Square Fish, 2007 (244,612).
46. *Ramona the Pest* by Beverly Cleary, illustrated by Tracy Dockray. HarperCollins, 1992 (243,016).
47. *Fancy Nancy: Poison Ivy Expert* by Jane O'Connor, illustrated by Robin Preiss Glasser. HarperCollins, 2008 (239,610).
48. *Ramona the Brave* by Beverly Cleary, illustrated by Tracy Dockray. HarperCollins, 2006 (237,332).
49. *The Care and Keeping of You* by Valorie Schaefer, illustrated by Norm Bendel. American Girl, 1998 (236,493).
50. *Evermore* (Immortals No. 1) by Alyson Noël. St. Martin's Griffin, 2009 (235,484).
51. *Harry Potter and the Prisoner of Azkaban* by J. K. Rowling, illustrated by Mary GrandPré. Scholastic/Levine, 2001 (234,628).
52. *The Vampire Diaries: The Fury and Dark Reunion* by L. J. Smith. HarperTeen, 2007 (233,782).
53. *The Mouse and the Motorcycle* by Beverly Cleary, illustrated by Tracy Dockray. HarperCollins, 2000 (227,121).
54. *Three Cups of Tea* young readers edition by Greg Mortenson. Puffin, 2009 (227,002).
55. *Harry Potter and the Goblet of Fire* by J. K. Rowling, illustrated by Mary GrandPré. Scholastic/Levine, 2002 (225,833).
56. *Harry Potter and the Order of the Phoenix* by J. K. Rowling, illustrated by Mary GrandPré. Scholastic/Levine, 2002 (224,021).
57. *Holes* by Louis Sachar. Yearling, 2000 (219,829).
58. *The Vampire Diaries: The Awakening and the Struggle* by L. J. Smith. HarperTeen, 2007 (217,619).
59. *The Berenstain Bears Forget Their Manners* by Stan Berenstain, illustrated by Jan Berenstain. Random House, 1985 (214,682).
60. *The Absolutely True Diary of a Part-Time Indian* by Sherman Alexie. Little, Brown, 2009 (213,251).
61. *Amelia Bedelia* by Peggy Parish, illustrated by Fritz Siebel. HarperCollins, 1992 (213,131).
62. *Harry Potter and the Half-Blood Prince* by J. K. Rowling, illustrated by Mary GrandPré. Scholastic/Levine, 2002 (212,546).
63. *Junie B. Jones and the Stupid Smelly Bus* (Junie B. Jones No. 1) by Barbara Park, illustrated by Denise Brunkus. Random House, 1992 (212,212).
64. *Fancy Nancy and the Boy from Paris* by Jane O'Connor, illustrated by Robin Preiss Glasser. HarperCollins, 2008 (207,280).

65. *Biscuit* by Alyssa Satin Capucilli, illustrated by Pat Schories. HarperCollins, 1997 (204,679).
66. *The Capture* (Guardians of Ga'Hoole No. 1) by Kathryn Lasky. Scholastic, 2003 (202,638).
67. *Flat Stanley* by Jeff Brown, illustrated by Macky Pamintuan. HarperCollins, 2004 (202,058).
68. *Blue Moon* (Immortals No. 2) by Alyson Noël. St. Martin's Griffin, 2009 (201,569).

125,000+

69. *DC Super Friends: Super Friends Flying High.* Random House, 2008 (199,813).
70. *Night of the Ninjas* (MTH No. 5) by Mary Pope Osborne, illustrated by Sal Murdocca. Random House, 1995 (195,083).
71. *Disney/Pixar Cars: Race Team.* Random House, 2008 (194,161).
72. *Fancy Nancy: Heart to Heart* by Jane O'Connor, illustrated by Robin Preiss Glasser. HarperFestival, 2009 (188,416).
73. *Shadowland* (Immortals No. 3) by Alyson Noël. St. Martin's Griffin, 2010 (187,446).
74. *Disney/Pixar Toy Story: Friends Forever* by Melissa Lagonegro, illustrated by Adrian Molina. Random House, 2009 (186,818).
75. *Frog and Toad Are Friends* by Arnold Lobel. HarperCollins, 1979 (185,747).
76. *Danny and the Dinosaur* by Syd Hoff. HarperCollins, 2008 (183,900).
77. *Alvin and the Chipmunks: The Squeakquel—Battle of the Bands* by Annie Auerbach. HarperCollins, 2009 (183,320).
78. **Hatchet* by Gary Paulsen. Simon & Schuster, 2006.
79. *The Boy in the Striped Pajamas* by John Boyne. Random/Fickling, 2007 (180,562).
80. *Charlotte's Web* by E. B. White, illustrated by Garth Williams. HarperCollins, 1999 (178,622).
81. *Junie B. Jones and a Little Monkey Business* (JBJ No. 2) by Barbara Park, illustrated by Denise Brunkus. Random House, 1993 (178,544).
82. *Afternoon on the Amazon* (MTH No. 6) by Mary Pope Osborne, illustrated by Sal Murdocca. Random House, 1995 (176,407).
83. *Wicked* (PLL No. 5) by Sara Shepard. HarperTeen, 2009 (176,075).
84. *The Cat in the Hat: Cooking with the Cat* by Bonnie Worth, illustrated by Christopher Moroney. Random House, 2003 (175,997).
85. *Little Critter: Just Go to Bed* by Mercer Mayer. Random House, 2001 (173,176).
86. *The Angel Experiment* (Maximum Ride No. 1) by James Patterson. Little, Brown, 2007 (172,641).
87. *Speak* by Laurie Halse Anderson. Penguin/Speak, 2006/2009 (169,856).

88. *Fancy Nancy at the Museum* by Jane O'Connor, illustrated by Robin Preiss Glasser. HarperCollins, 2008 (169,452).
89. *Fancy Nancy: The Show Must Go On* by Jane O'Connor, illustrated by Robin Preiss Glasser. HarperCollins, 2009 (167,376).
90. *Dolphins at Daybreak* (MTH No. 9) by Mary Pope Osborne, illustrated by Sal Murdocca. Random House, 1997 (166,559).
91. *Tales of a Fourth Grade Nothing* by Judy Blume. Puffin, 2007 (164,464).
92. *Disney Princess and the Frog: Kiss the Frog*. Random House/Disney, 2009 (163,802).
93. *The Berenstain Bears Learn About Strangers* by Stan Berenstain, illustrated by Jan Berenstain. Random House, 1985 (163,386).
94. *Judy Moody* by Megan McDonald, illustrated by Peter H. Reynolds. Candlewick, 2002 (162,368).
95. *Fancy Nancy: Halloween . . . or Bust!* by Jane O'Connor, illustrated by Robin Preiss Glasser. HarperFestival, 2009 (160,599).
96. *Junie B. and Her Big Fat Mouth* (JBJ No. 3) by Barbara Park, illustrated by Denise Brunkus. Random House, 1993 (159,368).
97. *Number the Stars* by Lois Lowry. Yearling, 1990 (159,323).
98. *The Adventures of Captain Underpants* by Dav Pilkey. Scholastic, 1997 (159,089).
99. *The Animal Boogie* by Debbie Harter. Barefoot, 2000 (156,894).
100. *Junie B., First Grader: Toothless Wonder* (JBJ No. 20) by Barbara Park, illustrated by Denise Brunkus. Random House, 2003 (156,760).
101. *The Ruins of Gorlan* (Ranger's Apprentice No. 1) by John Flanagan. Puffin, 2006/2010 (156,720).
102. *Maniac Magee* by Jerry Spinelli. Little, Brown, 1999 (156,267).
103. *The Berenstain Bears and Too Much Junk Food* by Stan Berenstain, illustrated by Jan Berenstain. Random House, 1985 (156,038).
104. *Fancy Nancy's Elegant Easter* by Jane O'Connor, illustrated by Robin Preiss Glasser. HarperFestival, 2009 (154,565).
105. *The Name of This Book Is Secret* by Pseudonymous Bosch. Little Brown, 2008 (153,429).
106. *Island of the Blue Dolphins* by Scott O'Dell. Yearling, 1987 (153,057).
107. *Into the Wild* (Warriors No. 1) by Erin Hunter. HarperCollins, 2003 (151,465).
108. *The Cricket in Times Square* by George Selden, illustrated by Garth Williams. Macmillan/Square Fish, 2008 (150,936).
109. *Hoot* by Carl Hiaasen. Yearling, 2005 (150,704).
110. *Because of Winn-Dixie* by Kate DiCamillo. Candlewick, 2001 (150,340).
111. *The Mysterious Benedict Society and the Perilous Journey* by Trenton Lee Stewart and Diana Sudyka. Little, Brown/Tingley, 2009 (150,234).
112. *The Berenstain Bears and the Truth* by Stan Berenstain, illustrated by Jan Berenstain. Random House, 1983 (148,903).

113. *The Berenstain Bears and Too Much TV* by Stan Berenstain, illustrated by Jan Berenstain. Random House, 1984 (147,659).
114. *Alvin and the Chipmunks: The Squeakquel—The Junior Novel* by Perdita Finn. HarperCollins, 2009 (146,312).
115. *Biscuit's Day at the Farm* by Alyssa Satin Capucilli, illustrated by Pat Schories. HarperCollins, 2007 (146,130).
116. *Midnight to the Moon* (MTH No. 8) by Mary Pope Osborne, illustrated by Sal Murdocca. Random House, 1996 (145,709).
117. **Cloudy with a Chance of Meatballs* by Judi Barrett. Atheneum, 1982.
118. **Go Ask Alice* by Anonymous. Simon Pulse, 1982.
119. *Junie B. Jones Has a Monster Under Her Bed* (JBJ No. 8) by Barbara Park, illustrated by Denise Brunkus. Random House, 1997 (144,645).
120. *The Magician's Nephew* by C. S. Lewis, illustrated by Pauline Baynes. HarperCollins, 1994 (144,428).
121. **Frindle* by Andrew Clements. Atheneum, 1998.
122. *The Berenstain Bears and the Messy Room* by Stan Berenstain, illustrated by Jan Berenstain. Random House, 1993 (142,221).
123. *Junie B. Jones and Some Sneaky Peeky Spying* (JBJ No. 4) by Barbara Park, illustrated by Denise Brunkus. Random House, 1994 (142,075).
124. *Vampire Academy* by Richelle Mead. Penguin/Razorbill, 2007 (141,925).
125. *The Alchemyst* (Secrets of the Immortal Nicholas Flamel) by Michael Scott. Delacorte, 2008 (141,514).
126. *Biscuit Goes to School* by Alyssa Satin Capucilli, illustrated by Pat Schories. HarperCollins, 2003 (141,486).
127. *Junie B. Jones and the Yucky Blucky Fruitcake* (JBJ No. 5) by Barbara Park, illustrated by Denise Brunkus. Random House, 1995 (140,331).
128. *Ghost Town at Sundown* (MTH No. 10) by Mary Pope Osborne, illustrated by Sal Murdocca. Random House, 1997 (140,314).
129. **Fablehaven* by Brandon Mull. Aladdin, 2007.
130. *Junie B., First Grader: BOO . . . and I MEAN It!* (JBJ No. 24) by Barbara Park, illustrated by Denise Brunkus. Random House, 2005 (136,847).
131. *Sunset of the Sabertooth* (MTH No. 7) by Mary Pope Osborne, illustrated by Sal Murdocca. Random House, 1996 (136,636).
132. *Ramona and Her Father* by Beverly Cleary, illustrated by Tracy Dockray. HarperCollins, 1990 (136,629).
133. *Hour of the Olympics* (MTH No. 16) by Mary Pope Osborne, illustrated by Sal Murdocca. Random House, 1998 (136,140).
134. *Goodnight Moon* by Margaret Wise Brown, illustrated by Clement Hurd. HarperCollins, 1977 (133,506).
135. *Monster* by Walter Dean Myers. HarperCollins, 2004 (132,741).
136. *Lock and Key* by Sarah Dessen. Penguin/Speak, 2009 (131,723).
137. *Captain Underpants and the Perilous Plot of Professor Poopypants* by Dav Pilkey. Scholastic, 2000 (130,624).

139. *Just Me and My Dad* by Mercer Mayer. Random House, 2001 (129,016).
140. *Superfudge* by Judy Blume. Puffin, 2007 (127,166).
141. *Ramona and Her Mother* by Beverly Cleary, illustrated by Tracy Dockray. HarperCollins, 1990 (127,116).
142. *National Geographic Readers: Sharks!* by Anne Schreiber. National Geographic, 2008 (127,000).
143. *The Berenstain Bears Get the Gimmies* by Stan Berenstain, illustrated by Jan Berenstain. Random House, 1988 (126,728).
144. **Shiloh* by Phyllis Reynolds Naylor. Atheneum, 2000.
145. *Junie B. Jones Is a Party Animal!* (JBJ No. 7). Barbara Park, illustrated by Denise Brunkus. Random House, 1997 (125,234).

E-Books

100,000+

1. *Breaking Dawn* (Twilight Saga No. 4) by Stephenie Meyer. Little, Brown/Tingley (145,568).
2. *The Hunger Games* by Suzanne Collins. Scholastic (128,604).
3. *Eclipse* (Twilight Saga No. 3) by Stephenie Meyer. Little, Brown/Tingley (126,324).
4. *Mockingjay* (Hunger Games No. 3) by Suzanne Collins. Scholastic (124,845).
5. *Twilight* (Twilight Saga No. 1) by Stephenie Meyer. Little, Brown/Tingley (106,853).
6. *Percy Jackson and the Olympians: The Lightning Thief* by Rick Riordan. Disney-Hyperion (102,715).

50,000+

7. *Catching Fire* (Hunger Games No. 2) by Suzanne Collins. Scholastic (98,541).
8. *The Second Life of Bree Tanner: An Eclipse Novella* by Stephenie Meyer. Little, Brown/Tingley (94,095).
9. *New Moon* (Twilight Saga No. 2) by Stephenie Meyer. Little, Brown/Tingley (86,775).
10. *The Sea of Monsters* (Percy Jackson and the Olympians No. 2) by Rick Riordan. Disney-Hyperion (73,419).
11. *The Lost Hero* (Heroes of Olympus No. 1) by Rick Riordan. Disney-Hyperion (71,725).
12. *The Last Olympian* (Percy Jackson and the Olympians No. 5) by Rick Riordan. Disney-Hyperion (70,368).
13. *The Titan's Curse* (Percy Jackson and the Olympians No. 3) by Rick Riordan. Disney-Hyperion (67,005).

14. *The Battle of the Labyrinth* (Percy Jackson and the Olympians No. 4) by Rick Riordan. Disney-Hyperion (64,640).
15. *The Red Pyramid* (Kane Chronicles No. 1) by Rick Riordan. Disney-Hyperion (54,038).

20,000+

16. **The Book Thief* by Marcus Zusak. Knopf.
17. *Witch and Wizard* by James Patterson and Gabrielle Charbonnet. Little, Brown (43,713).
18. *Burned* (House of Night No. 7) by P. C. and Kristin Cast. St. Martin's Griffin (43,205).
19. *Pretty Little Liars* by Sara Shepard. HarperTeen (35,390).
20. *Marked* (House of Night No. 1) by P. C. and Kristin Cast. St. Martin's Griffin (32,236).
21. **Fallen* by Lauren Kate. Delacorte.
22. *Evermore* (Immortals No. 1) by Alyson Noël. St. Martin's Griffin (30,682).
23. *The Twilight Saga Collection* by Stephenie Meyer. Little, Brown/Tingley (27,044).
24. *Tempted* (House of Night No. 6) by P. C. and Kristin Cast. St. Martin's Griffin (26,675).
25. *Fang* (Maximum Ride No. 6) by James Patterson. Little, Brown (24,548).
26. *Flawless* (PLL No. 2) by Sara Shepard. HarperTeen (24,245).
27. **Torment* by Lauren Kate. Delacorte.
28. *Betrayed* (House of Night No. 2) by P. C. and Kristin Cast. St. Martin's Griffin (22,046).
29. *Hunted* (House of Night No. 5) by P. C. and Kristin Cast. St. Martin's Griffin (21,992).
30. *Chosen* (House of Night No. 3) by P. C. and Kristin Cast. St. Martin's Griffin (20,402).
31. *Untamed* (House of Night No. 4) by P. C. and Kristin Cast. St. Martin's Griffin (20,360).
32. **Clockwork Angel* by Cassandra Clare. Simon & Schuster/McElderry.
33. *The Carrie Diaries* by Candace Bushnell. HarperCollins/Balzer & Bray (20,490).
34. *Shiver* by Maggie Stiefvater. Scholastic (20,040).

10,000+

35. *Perfect* (PLL No. 3) by Sara Shepard. HarperTeen (19,950).
36. *Wanted* (PLL No. 8) by Sara Shepard. HarperTeen (18,591).
37. *Unbelievable* (PLL No. 4) by Sara Shepard. HarperTeen (18,430).
38. *Wicked* (PLL No. 5) by Sara Shepard. HarperTeen (17,302).
39. *Heartless* (PLL No. 7) by Sara Shepard. HarperTeen (16,968).

40. *Beautiful Creatures* (Caster Chronicles No. 1) by Kami Garcia and Margaret Stohl. Little, Brown (16,445).
41. **Hush, Hush* by Becca Fitzpatrick. Simon & Schuster.
42. *Killer* (PLL No. 6) by Sara Shepard. HarperTeen (16,045).
43. **City of Bones* by Cassandra Clare. Simon & Schuster/McElderry.
44. **City of Glass* by Cassandra Clare. Simon & Schuster/McElderry.
45. *The Lion, the Witch and the Wardrobe* by C. S. Lewis. HarperCollins (15,401).
46. *Shadowland* (Immortals No. 3) by Alyson Noël. St. Martin's Griffin (15,260).
47. *School's Out—Forever* (Maximum Ride No. 2) by James Patterson. Little, Brown (15,218).
48. *L.A. Candy* by Lauren Conrad. HarperTeen (14,873).
49. *Blue Moon* (Immortals No. 2) by Alyson Noël. St. Martin's Griffin (14,866).
50. *Dark Flame* (Immortals No. 4) by Alyson Noël. St. Martin's Griffin (14,779).
51. **The Necromancer* (Secrets of the Immortal Nicholas Flamel) by Michael Scott. Delacorte.
52. *Sweet Little Lies* by Lauren Conrad. HarperTeen (14,520).
53. **Eragon* by Christopher Paolini. Knopf.
54. **City of Ashes* by Cassandra Clare. Simon & Schuster/McElderry.
55. *Infinity* by Sherrilyn Kenyon. St. Martin's Griffin (13,881).
56. *Linger* by Maggie Stiefvater. Scholastic (13,778).
57. *Percy Jackson and the Olympians: The Demigod Files* by Rick Riordan. Disney-Hyperion (13,570).
58. *The Vampire Diaries: The Return—Shadow Souls* by L. J. Smith. HarperTeen (13,500).
59. *Saving the World and Other Extreme Sports* (Maximum Ride No. 3) by James Patterson. Little, Brown (13,420).
60. *Max* (Maximum Ride No. 5) by James Patterson. Little, Brown (13,051).
61. *The Angel Experiment* (Maximum Ride No. 1) by James Patterson. Little Brown (12,915).
62. **The Maze Runner* by James Dashner. Delacorte.
63. *Sugar and Spice* by Lauren Conrad. HarperTeen (12,599).
64. *The Reckoning* by Kelley Armstrong. HarperCollins (12,551).
65. *The Final Warning* (Maximum Ride No. 4) by James Patterson. Little, Brown (12,243).
66. *Artemis Fowl: The Atlantis Complex* by Eoin Colfer. Disney-Hyperion (12,063).
67. *I Am Number Four* by Pittacus Lore. HarperCollins (11,593).

68. *The Alchemyst* (Secrets of the Immortal Nicholas Flamel) by Michael Scott. Delacorte.
69. *Junie B., First Grader: Jingle Bells, Batman Smells* (JBJ No. 25) by Barbara Park, illustrated by Denise Brunkus. Random House.
70. *Night Star* (Immortals No. 5) by Alyson Noël. St. Martin's Griffin (11,031).
71. *The Sorceress* (Secrets of the Immortal Nicholas Flamel) by Michael Scott. Delacorte.
72. *Brisingr* (deluxe edition) by Christopher Paolini. Knopf.
73. *The Magician* (Secrets of the Immortal Nicholas Flamel) by Michael Scott. Delacorte.
74. *The Graveyard Book* by Neil Gaiman. HarperCollins (10,864).
75. *The Vampire Diaries: The Return—Shadow Souls* by L. J. Smith. HarperTeen (10,716).
76. *The Scorch Trials* by James Dashner. Delacorte.
77. *When You Reach Me* by Rebecca Stead. Random/Lamb.
78. *The Giver* by Lois Lowry. Houghton Mifflin (10,300).
79. *The Boy in the Striped Pajamas* by John Boyne. Random/Fickling.
80. *The Golden Compass* (His Dark Materials) by Philip Pullman. Knopf.
81. *Eldest* (limited edition) by Christopher Paolini. Knopf.
82. *Graceling* by Kristin Cashore. Harcourt (10,034).
83. *Crescendo* by Becca Fitzpatrick. Simon & Schuster.

Note: Penguin declined to share e-book sales for this compilation.

Literary Prizes, 2010

Compiled by the staff of the *Library and Book Trade Almanac*

Jane Addams Children's Book Awards. For children's books that effectively promote the cause of peace, social justice, world community, and equality. *Offered by:* Women's International League for Peace and Freedom and the Jane Addams Peace Association. *Winners:* (younger children) Jeanette Winter for *Nasreen's Secret School: A True Story from Afghanistan* (Beach Lane); (older children) Elizabeth Partridge for *Marching for Freedom: Walk Together, Children, and Don't You Grow Weary* (Viking).

Aesop Prize. For outstanding work in children's folklore, both fiction and nonfiction. *Offered by:* American Folklore Society. *Winners:* Eric A. Kimmel, adapter, and Omar Rayyan, illustrator, for *Joha Makes a Wish: A Middle Eastern Tale* (Marshall Cavendish).

Agatha Awards. For mystery novels written in the method exemplified by author Agatha Christie. *Offered by:* Malice Domestic Ltd. *Winners:* (novel) Louise Penny for *The Brutal Telling* (Minotaur); (first novel) Alan Bradley for *The Sweetness at the Bottom of the Pie* (Delacorte); (nonfiction) Elena Santangelo for *Dame Agatha's Shorts* (Bella Rosa); (short story) Hank Phillippi Ryan for "On the House" in *Quarry: Crime Stories by New England Writers* (Level Best); (children's/young adult) Chris Grabenstein for *The Hanging Hill* (Random); (lifetime achievement) Mary Higgins Clark; (Poirot award, for outstanding contributions to the mystery genre) William Link.

Alex Awards. To the authors of ten books published for adults that have high potential appeal to teenagers. *Sponsor:* Margaret Alexander Edwards Trust and *Booklist*. *Winners:* William Kamkwamba and Bryan Mealer for *The Boy Who Harnessed the Wind: Creating Currents of Electricity and Hope* (HarperCollins); Meg Rosoff for *The Bride's Farewell* (Penguin); Ron Currie, Jr. for *Everything Matters!* (Penguin); David Finkel for *The Good Soldiers* (Farrar, Straus & Giroux); Diana Welch and Liz Welch, with Amanda Welch and Dan Welch, for *The Kids Are All Right: A Memoir* (Random); Lev Grossman for *The Magicians* (Penguin); Peter Rock for *My Abandonment* (Houghton Mifflin Harcourt); Gail Carriger for *Soulless* (Hachette); David Small for *Stitches: A Memoir* (Norton); Kevin Wilson for *Tunneling to the Center of the Earth* (HarperCollins).

Ambassador Book Awards: To honor an exceptional contribution to the interpretation of life and culture in the United States. *Offered by:* English-Speaking Union of the United States. *Winners:* (American studies) James Mann for *The Rebellion of Ronald Reagan: A History of the End of the Cold War* (Viking), Morris Dickstein for *Dancing in the Dark: A Cultural History of the Great Depression* (Norton); (fiction) Colum McCann for *Let the Great World Spin* (Random); (poetry) J. D. McClatchy for *Mercury Dressing* (Knopf); (biography) Melvin Urofsky for *Louis D. Brandeis: A Life* (Pantheon); (biography, special distinction) Robin D. G. Kelley for *Thelonious Monk: The Life and Times of an American Original* (Free Press).

American Academy of Arts and Letters Award of Merit ($10,000). To an American author of novels, poetry, short stories, or drama. *Offered by:* American Academy of Arts and Letters. *Winner:* poet Gerald Stern.

American Academy of Arts and Letters Awards in Literature ($7,500). To honor writers of fiction and nonfiction, poets, dramatists, and translators of exceptional accomplishment. *Offered by:* American Academy of Arts and Letters. *Winners:* Blake Bailey, Peter Cole, Steve Erickson, Peter Everwine, Young Jean Lee, Bruce Smith, Natasha Wimmer.

American Academy of Arts and Letters Rome Fellowships. For a one-year residency at the American Academy in Rome for young writers of promise. *Offered by:*

American Academy of Arts and Letters. *Winners:* Jay Hopler, Heather McGowan.

American Book Awards. For literary achievement by people of various ethnic backgrounds. *Offered by:* Before Columbus Foundation. *Winners:* Amiri Baraka for *Digging: The Afro-American Soul of American Classical Music* (University of California Press); Sherwin Bitsui for *Flood Song* (Copper Canyon); Nancy Carnevale for *A New Language, A New World: Italian Immigrants in the United States, 1890–1945* (University of Illinois Press); Dave Eggers for *Zeitoun* (McSweeney's/Vintage); Sesshu Foster for *World Ball Notebook* (City Lights); Stephen D. Gutierrez for *Live from Fresno y Los* (Bear Star); Victor Lavalle for *The Big Machine* (Spiegel & Grau); François Mandeville for *This Is What They Say,* translated from Chipewyan by Ron Scollon (University of Washington Press); Bich Minh Nguyen for *Short Girls* (Viking); Franklin Rosemont and Robin D. G. Kelley, editors, for *Black, Brown and Beige: Surrealist Writings from Africa and the Diaspora* (University of Texas Press); Jerome Rothenberg and Jeffrey C. Robinson, editors, for *Poems for the Millennium: Volume Three: The University of California Book of Romantic and Postromantic Poetry* (University of California Press); Kathryn Waddell Takara for *Pacific Raven: Hawai'i Poems* (Pacific Raven); Pamela Uschuk for *Crazy Love: New Poems* (Wings); (lifetime achievement) Quincy Troupe, Katha Pollitt.

American Indian Youth Literature Awards. To recognize excellence in books by and about American Indians. *Offered by:* American Indian Library Association. *Winners:* (best picture book) Thomas King and Gary Clement, illustrator, for *A Coyote Solstice Tale* (Groundwood); (best middle school book) Genevieve Simermeyer and Katherine Fogden, photographer, for *Meet Christopher: An Osage Indian Boy from Oklahoma* (Council Oak); (best young adult book) Lurline Wailana McGregor for *Between the Deep Blue Sea and Me* (Kamehameha).

American Poetry Review/Honickman First Book Prize in Poetry ($3,000). To encourage excellence in poetry and to provide a wide readership for a deserving first book of poems. *Winner:* Melissa Stein for *Rough Honey* (American Poetry Review).

Américas Book Award for Children's and Young Adult Literature. To recognize U.S. works of fiction, poetry, folklore, or selected nonfiction that authentically and engagingly portray Latin America, the Caribbean, or Latinos in the United States. *Sponsored by:* Consortium of Latin American Studies Programs (CLASP). *Winners:* Julia Alvarez for *Return to Sender* (Knopf); Carmen Tafolla and Magaly Morales, illustrator, for *What Can You Do With a Paleta?* (Tricycle).

Rudolfo and Patricia Anaya Premio Aztlan Literary Prize ($1,000 and a lectureship). To honor a Chicano or Chicana fiction writer who has published no more than two books. *Offered by:* University of New Mexico. *Winner:* Gloria Zamora for *Sweet Nata: Growing Up in Rural New Mexico* (University of New Mexico Press).

Hans Christian Andersen Awards. Awarded biennially to an author and an illustrator whose body of work has made an important and lasting contribution to children's literature. *Offered by:* International Board on Books for Young People (IBBY). *Sponsor:* Nami Island, Inc. *Winners:* (author) David Almond; (illustrator) Jutta Bauer.

Hans Christian Andersen Literature Award (500,000 Danish kroner, about $92,000). To a writer whose work can be compared with that of Andersen. *Offered by:* Hans Christian Andersen Literary Committee. *Winner:* J. K. Rowling.

Anthony Awards. For superior mystery writing. *Offered by:* Boucheron World Mystery Convention. *Winners:* (novel) Louise Penny for *The Brutal Telling* (Minotaur); (first novel) Sophie Littlefield for *A Bad Day for Sorry* (Minotaur); (paperback original) Bryan Gruley for *Starvation Lake* (Touchstone); (short story) Hank Phillippi Ryan for "On the House" in *Quarry: Crime Stories by New England Writers* (Level Best); (critical nonfiction) P. D. James for *Talking About Detective Fiction* (Knopf).

Asian American Literary Awards. To Asian American writers for excellence in poetry, fiction, and creative nonfiction. *Sponsor:* Asian American Writers' Workshop. *Winners:* (fiction) Paul Yoon for *Once the Shore* (Sarabande); (nonfiction) Minal Hajratwala for *Leaving India: My Family's Journey from Five Villages to Five Continents* (Houghton Mifflin Harcourt); (poetry) Ronaldo V. Wilson for *Poems of the Black Object* (Futurepoem); (members choice award) Jason Koo for *Man on Extremely Small Island* (C&R).

Asian/Pacific American Awards for Literature. For books that promote Asian/Pacific American culture and heritage. *Sponsor:* Asian/Pacific American Librarians Association (APALA). *Winners:* (adult fiction) Jamie Ford for *Hotel on the Corner of Bitter and Sweet* (Ballantine); (adult nonfiction) Bonnie Tsui for *American Chinatown: A People's History of Five Neighborhoods* (Simon & Schuster); (picture book) Dorina K. Lazo Gilmore for *Cora Cooks Pancit*, illustrated by Kristi Valiant (Shen's); (youth literature) Sung Woo for *Everything Asian* (Thomas Dunne).

Audio Publishers Association awards (Audies). To recognize excellence in audiobooks. *Winners:* (audiobook of the year) *Nelson Mandela's Favorite African Folktales* (Hachette Audio); (distinguished achievement in production) *The Help* (Penguin Audiobooks); (fiction) *The Help* (Penguin Audiobooks); (literary fiction) *Wolf Hall* (Macmillan Audio); (mystery) *Devil in a Blue Dress* (Audible); (thriller/suspense) *Darling Jim* (Tantor Media); (romance) *The Untamed Bride* (Harper Audio); (science fiction) *Bellwether* (Blackstone Audio); (inspirational/faith-based fiction) *A Month of Summer* (Recorded Books); (classic) *Great Expectations* (Audio Connoisseur); (nonfiction) *The National Parks* (Random House Audio); (biography/memoir) *Anne Frank Remembered* (Oasis); (history) *Tears in the Darkness: The Story of the Bataan Death March and Its Aftermath* (Tantor Audio); (business/educational) *Rain* (Brilliance Audio); (children's, ages 0–8) *Louise, the Adventures of a Chicken* (Live Oak); children's, ages 8–12) *Operation Yes* (Audible); (teen readers) *Peace, Locomotion* (Brilliance Audio); (inspirational/faith-based nonfiction) *The Word of Promise Audio Bible* (Thomas Nelson); (humor) *Church People: The Lutherans of Lake Wobegon* (High Bridge); (short stories/collections) *Black Mask Audio Magazine, Vol. 1* (Blackstone Audio); (original work) *Tell Me A Story: Women of Wonder* (Listen & Live); (personal development) *Nurtureshock* (Hachette Audio); (best solo narration—female) Jenna Lamia for *The Chosen One* (Macmillian Audio); (best solo narration—male) Charlton Griffin for *Great Expectations* (Audio Connoisseur).

Bad Sex in Fiction Award (United Kingdom). *Sponsor: Literary Review. Winner:* Rowan Somerville for *The Shape of Her* (Weidenfeld & Nicholson).

Bakeless Literary Publication Prizes. For promising new writers. *Offered by:* Bread Loaf Writers' Conference of Middlebury College. *Winners:* (fiction) Shann Ray for *American Masculine: Montana Stories*; (creative nonfiction) Mary Jane Nealon for *Beautiful Unbroken*; (poetry) Dilruba Ahmed for *Dhaka Dust*.

Bancroft Prizes ($10,000). For books of exceptional merit and distinction in American history, American diplomacy, and the international relations of the United States. *Offered by:* Columbia University. *Winners:* Linda Gordon for *Dorothea Lange: A Life Beyond Limits* (Norton); Woody Holton for *Abigail Adams* (Free Press); Margaret D. Jacobs for *White Mother to a Dark Race: Settler Colonialism, Maternalism, and the Removal of Indigenous Children in the American West and Australia, 1880–1940* (University of Nebraska Press).

Barnes & Noble Discover Great New Writers Awards. To honor a first novel and a first work of nonfiction by American authors. *Offered by:* Barnes & Noble. *Winners:* (fiction) Victor Lodato for *Mathilda Savitch* (Picador); (nonfiction) Dave Cullen for *Columbine* (Twelve).

Mildred L. Batchelder Award. For an American publisher of a children's book originally published in a language other than English and subsequently published in

English in the United States. *Offered by:* American Library Association, Association for Library Service to Children. *Winner:* Delacorte Press for *A Faraway Island* by Annika Thor, translated by Linda Schenck.

Beacon of Freedom Award. For the best title introducing American history, from colonial times through the Civil War, to young readers. *Offered by:* Williamsburg (Virginia) Regional Library and the Colonial Williamsburg Foundation. *Winner:* Steve Sheinkin for *Two Miserable Presidents* (Flash Point).

Pura Belpré Awards. To a Latino/Latina writer and illustrator whose work portrays, affirms, and celebrates the Latino cultural experience in an outstanding work of literature for children and youth. *Offered by:* American Library Association, Association for Library Service to Children. *Winners:* (author) Julia Alvarez for *Return to Sender* (Random); (illustrator) Rafael López for *Book Fiesta! Celebrate Children's Day/Book Day; Celebremos El Día de los Niños/El Día de los Libros* by Pat Mora (HarperCollins).

Curtis Benjamin Award. To an outstanding individual within the U.S. publishing industry who has shown exceptional innovation and creativity in the field of publishing. *Offered by:* Association of American Publishers. *Winner:* Not awarded in 2010.

Helen B. Bernstein Award. To a journalist who has written at book length about an issue of contemporary concern. *Offered by:* New York Public Library. *Winner:* David Finkel for *The Good Soldiers* (Farrar, Straus & Giroux).

Black Caucus of the American Library Association (BCALA) Literary Awards. *Winners:* (fiction) Pamela Samuels Young for *Buying Time* (Goldman House); (nonfiction) Gwen Ifill for *The Breakthrough* (Doubleday); (first novelist award) K. C. Marshall for *My Sister's Veil* (XLibris); (outstanding contribution to publishing citation) Henry Louis Gates for *In Search of Our Roots* (Crown).

Irma Simonton Black and James H. Black Award for Excellence in Children's Literature. To a book for young children in which the text and illustrations work together to create an outstanding whole. *Offered by:* Bank Street College of Education. *Winners:* Jon Scieszka and illustrator David Shannon for *Robot Zot* (Simon & Schuster).

James Tait Black Memorial Prize (United Kingdom) (£10,000). To recognize literary excellence in biography and fiction. *Offered by:* University of Edinburgh. *Winners:* (fiction) A. S. Byatt for *The Children's Book* (Vintage); (biography) John Carey for *William Golding: The Man Who Wrote 'Lord of the Flies'* (Free Press).

Rebekah Johnson Bobbitt National Prize for Poetry ($10,000). *Offered by:* Library of Congress. *Winners:* Lucia Perillo for *Inseminating the Elephant* (Copper Canyon).

Bookseller/Diagram Prize for Oddest Title of the Year *Sponsor: The Bookseller* magazine. *Winner: Crocheting Adventures with Hyperbolic Planes* by Daina Taimina (A K Peters Ltd.).

BookSense Book of the Year Awards. See Indies Choice Book Awards.

Booktrust Teenage Prize (United Kingdom) (£2,500). *Offered by:* Booktrust. *Winner:* Gregory Hughes for *Unhooking the Moon* (Quercus).

Borders Original Voices Awards ($5,000). To recognize works by new and emerging writers. *Offered by:* Borders Group, Inc. *Winners:* (fiction) Eugenia Kim for *The Calligrapher's Daughter* (Holt); (nonfiction) Matthew Crawford for *Shop Class as Soulcraft: An Inquiry into the Value of Work* (Penguin); (children/young adult) Amy Efaw for *After* (Penguin).

Boston Globe/Horn Book Awards. For excellence in children's literature. *Winners:* (fiction and poetry) Rebecca Stead for *When You Reach Me* (Random); (nonfiction) Elizabeth Partridge for *Marching for Freedom: Walk Together, Children, and Don't You Grow Weary* (Viking); (picture book) Laurel Croza and Matt James, illustrator, for *I Know Here* (Groundwood).

W. Y. Boyd Literary Award ($5,000). For a military novel that honors the service of American veterans during a time of war. *Offered by:* American Library Association.

Winner: John Hough, Jr. for *Seen the Glory: A Novel of the Battle of Gettysburg* (Simon & Schuster).

Branford Boase Award (United Kingdom). To the author and editor of an outstanding novel for young readers by a first-time writer. *Winners:* Lucy Christopher and Imogen Cooper, editor, for *Stolen* (Chicken House).

Michael Braude Award for Light Verse ($5,000). *Offered biennially by:* American Academy of Arts and Letters. *Winner:* Not awarded in 2010.

Bridport International Creative Writing Prizes (United Kingdom). For poetry and short stories. *Offered by:* Bridport Arts Centre. *Winners:* (short story) (first prize, £5,000) Alison Fisher for "The Woodcutter's Wife"; (second prize, £1,000) Wayne Price for "God's Instruments"; (third prize, £500) Kirsty Logan for "Underskirts"; (poetry) (first prize, £5,000) Esther Morgan for "This Morning"; (second prize, £1,000) Rowland Molony for "Snipe"; (third prize, £500) Jennifer Copley for "There's Another Graveyard."

British Fantasy Awards (United Kingdom). *Offered by:* British Fantasy Society. *Winners:* (novel—August Derleth Fantasy Award) Conrad Williams for *One* (Virgin Horror); (novella) Sarah Pinborough for *The Language of Dying* (PS); (short fiction) Michael Marshall Smith for *What Happens When You Wake Up In The Night* (Nightjar); (collection) Robert Shearman for *Love Songs for the Shy and Cynical* (Big Finish); (anthology) Stephen Jones, editor, for *The Mammoth Book of Best New Horror 20* (Constable & Robinson); (PS Publishing Best Small Press award) David Howe and Stephen James Walker, Telos Publishing; (nonfiction) David Langford for *Ansible*; (artist) Vincent Chong for *The Witnesses Are Gone* (PS) and *The Mammoth Book of Best New Horror 20* (Constable & Robinson); (comic/graphic novel) Neil Gaiman and Andy Kubert for *Whatever Happened to the Caped Crusader?* (DC Comics/Titan Books); (television) Russell T. Davies, head writer, for "Doctor Who"; (film) "Let the Right One In," directed by Tomas Alfredson; (Sydney J. Bounds Award for Best Newcomer) Kari Sperring for *Living With Ghosts* (DAW); (Karl Edward Wagner Award) Robert Holdstock.

Sophie Brody Medal. For the U.S. author of the most distinguished contribution to Jewish literature for adults published in the preceding year. *Donor:* Brodart Foundation. *Offered by:* Reference and User Services Association, American Library Association. *Winner:* Jonathon Keats for *The Book of the Unknown: Tales of the Thirty-Six* (Random).

Cabell First Novelist Award ($5,000). For a first novel published in the previous year. *Offered by:* Virginia Commonwealth University. *Winner:* Victor Lodato for *Mathilda Savitch* (Farrar, Straus & Giroux).

Caine Prize for African Writing (£10,000). For a short story by an African writer, published in English. *Winner:* Olufemi Terry for "Stickfighting Days," published in *Chimurenga*.

Randolph Caldecott Medal. For the artist of the most distinguished picture book. *Offered by:* American Library Association, Association for Library Service to Children. *Winner:* Jerry Pinkney for *The Lion and the Mouse* (Little, Brown).

California Book Awards. To California residents to honor books of fiction, nonfiction, and poetry published in the previous year. *Offered by:* Commonwealth Club of California. *Winners:* (poetry) D. A. Powell for *Chronic* (Graywolf); (nonfiction) Rebecca Solnit for *A Paradise Built in Hell* (Viking); (first fiction) Lori Ostlund for *The Bigness of the World* (University of Georgia Press); (fiction) Yiyun Li for *The Vagrants* (Random); (juvenile) Susan Patron for *Lucky Breaks,* illustrated by Matt Phelan (Simon & Schuster); (young adult) Sherri Smith for *Flygirl* (Putnam); (Californiana) Elaine Elinson and Stan Yogi for *Wherever There's a Fight* (Heyday); (contribution to publishing) Daniel C. Matt for *The Zohar Pritzker Edition, Volume Five* (Stanford University Press).

John W. Campbell Award. For the best new science fiction or fantasy writer whose first work of science fiction or fantasy was published in a professional publication in the previous two years. *Offered by:* Dell Magazines. *Winner:* Seanan McGuire.

John W. Campbell Memorial Award. For science fiction writing. *Offered by:* Center for the Study of Science Fiction. *Winner:* Paolo Bacigalupi for *The Windup Girl* (Night Shade).

Canadian Library Association Book of the Year for Children. *Sponsor:* Library Services Centre. *Winner:* Nancy Hartry for *Watching Jimmy* (Tundra).

Canadian Library Association Amelia Frances Howard-Gibbon Illustrator's Award. *Sponsor:* Library Services Centre. *Winner:* Barbara Reid, writer and illustrator, for *Perfect Snow* (North Winds).

Canadian Library Association Young Adult Canadian Book Award. *Winner:* Lesley Livingston for *Wondrous Strange* (HarperCollins).

Center for Fiction Flaherty-Dunnan First Novel Prize ($10,000). *Offered by:* Center for Fiction, Mercantile Library of New York. *Winner:* Karl Marlantes for *Matterhorn* (Atlantic Monthly).

Chicago Tribune Heartland Prize for Fiction ($7,500). *Offered by: Chicago Tribune. Winner:* E. O. Wilson for *Anthill* (Norton).

Chicago Tribune Heartland Prize for Nonfiction ($7,500). *Offered by: Chicago Tribune. Winner:* Rebecca Skloot for *The Immortal Life of Henrietta Lacks* (Crown).

Chicago Tribune Literary Prize. For a lifetime of literary achievement by an author whose body of work has had great impact on American society. *Offered by: Chicago Tribune. Winner:* Sam Shepard.

Chicago Tribune Nelson Algren Award ($5,000). For unpublished short fiction. *Offered by: Chicago Tribune. Winner:* Baird Harper for "My Thoughts While Cooling Down on the Hotel Veranda."

Chicago Tribune Young Adult Literary Prize. To recognize a distinguished literary career. *Winner:* Walter Dean Myers.

Children's Africana Book Awards. To recognize and encourage excellent children's books about Africa. *Offered by:* Outreach Council of the African Studies Association. *Winners:* (younger readers) David Weitzman for *Pharaoh's Boat* (Houghton Mifflin Harcourt); (older readers) Nelson Mandela Foundation and Umlando Wezithombe for *Nelson Mandela: The Authorized Comic Book* (Norton).

Children's Book Council of Australia Children's Book of the Year Awards. *Winners:* (Eve Pownall Book of the Year) Peter Macinnis for *Australian Backyard Explorer* (National Library of Australia); (picture book) Gregory Rogers for *The Hero of Little Street* (Allen & Unwin); (early childhood) Lisa Shanahan and Emma Quay, illustrator, for *Bear and Chook by the Sea* (Hachette); (younger readers) Odo Hirsch for *Darius Bell and the Glitter Pool* (Allen & Unwin); (older readers) David Metzenthen for *Jarvis 24* (Penguin).

Children's Poet Laureate ($25,000). For lifetime achievement in poetry for children. Honoree holds the title for two years. *Offered by:* The Poetry Foundation. *Winner:* Mary Ann Hoberman (named in 2008).

Cholmondeley Awards for Poets (United Kingdom) (£1,500). For a poet's body of work and contribution to poetry. *Winners:* Gillian Allnutt, Colette Bryce, Gwyneth Lewis, Deryn Rees-Jones.

CILIP Carnegie Medal (United Kingdom). For the outstanding children's book of the year. *Offered by:* CILIP: The Chartered Institute of Library and Information Professionals (formerly the Library Association). *Winner:* Neil Gaiman for *The Graveyard Book* (Bloomsbury).

CILIP Kate Greenaway Medal (United Kingdom). For children's book illustration. *Offered by:* CILIP: The Chartered Institute of Library and Information Professionals. *Winner:* Freya Blackwood for *Harry and Hopper* (Scholastic).

Arthur C. Clarke Award (United Kingdom). For the best science fiction novel published in the United Kingdom. *Offered by:* British Science Fiction Association. *Winner:* China Miéville for *The City and The City* (Macmillan).

David Cohen British Literature Prize (United Kingdom) (£40,000). Awarded biennially to a living British writer, novelist, poet, essayist, or dramatist in recognition of an entire body of work written in the English language. *Offered by:* David Cohen Family Charitable Trust. *Winner:* Not awarded in 2010.

Matt Cohen Award (Canada) (C$20,000). To a Canadian author whose life has been dedicated to writing as a primary pursuit, for a body of work. *Offered by:* Writers' Trust of Canada. *Winner:* Myrna Kostash.

Commonwealth Writers' Prize (United Kingdom). To reward and encourage new Commonwealth fiction and ensure that works of merit reach a wider audience outside their country of origin. *Offered by:* Commonwealth Institute. *Winners:* (best book) (£10,000) Rana Dasgupta, United Kingdom, for *Solo* (Fourth Estate); (best first book) (£5,000) Glenda Guest, Australia, for *Siddon Rock* (Random).

Olive Cook Prize. See Tom-Gallon Trust Award and Olive Cook Prize.

Cork City–Frank O'Connor Short Story Award (€35,000). An international award for a collection of short stories. *Offered by:* Munster Literature Centre, Cork, Ireland. *Sponsor:* Cork City Council. *Winner:* Ron Rash for *Burning Bright* (Ecco).

Costa Book Awards (United Kingdom) (formerly Whitbread Book Awards). For literature of merit that is readable on a wide scale. *Offered by:* Booksellers Association of Great Britain and Costa Coffee (£5,000 plus an additional £25,000 for Book of the Year). *Winners:* (poetry and Book of the Year) Jo Shapcott for *Of Mutability* (Faber); (novel) Maggie O'Farrell for *The Hand That First Held Mine* (Headline Review); (first novel) Kishwar Desai for *Witness the Night* (Beautiful Books); (biography) Edmund de Waal for *The Hare with Amber Eyes* (Chatto & Windus); (children's) Jason Wallace for *Out of Shadows* (Andersen).

Crab Orchard Series in Poetry Open Competition ($3,500 and publication by Southern Illinois University Press). For poetry collections. *Winners:* Brian Barker for *The Black Ocean,* Camille Dungy for *Smith Blue.*

Crime Writers' Association (CWA) Dagger Awards (United Kingdom). *Winners:* (Diamond Dagger, for outstanding achievement in the field of crime writing) Val McDermid; (Gold Dagger, £2,500) Belinda Bauer for *Blacklands* (Corgi); (Ian Fleming Steel Dagger, £2,000) Simon Conway for *A Loyal Spy* (Hodder & Stoughton); (John Creasey New Blood Dagger, £1,000) Ryan David Jahn for *Acts of Violence* (Macmillan); (International Dagger, £1,000 and £500 for the translator) Swedish writer Johan Theorin and translator Marlaine Delargy for *The Darkest Room* (Doubleday); (Gold Dagger for Nonfiction, £1,000) Ruth Dudley Edwards for *Aftermath: The Omagh Bombing and the Families' Pursuit of Justice* (Harvill Secker); (Dagger in the Library, £1,500 to the author, £300 to a participating library's readers' group). To the author of crime fiction whose work is currently giving the greatest enjoyment to library users. Ariana Franklin; (Short Story Dagger, £500) Robert Ferrigno for "Can You Help Me Out Here"; (Debut Dagger, £500) (for an author who has not yet had a novel published commercially) Patrick Eden for *A Place of Dying*; (Ellis Peters Historical Award, £3,000) Rory Clements for *Revenger* (John Murray).

Roald Dahl Funny Prize (United Kingdom) (£2,500). *Offered by:* Booktrust. *Winners:* (ages 6 and under) Louise Yates for *Dog Loves Books* (Knopf); (ages 7 to 14) Louise Rennison for *Withering Tights* (HarperCollins).

Benjamin H. Danks Award ($20,000). To a promising young writer, playwright, or composer, in alternate years. *Offered by:* American Academy of Arts and Letters. *Winner:* (playwright) Jenny Schwartz.

Dartmouth Medal. For creating current reference works of outstanding quality and significance. *Donor:* Dartmouth College. *Winner:* Oxford University Press for *Encyclopedia of Human Rights.*

Derringer Awards. To recognize excellence in short crime and mystery fiction. *Sponsor:* Short Mystery Fiction Society. *Winners:* (flash story, up to 1,000 words) Hamilton Waymire for "And Here's To You, Mrs. Edwardson" in *Big Pulp*; (short story, 1,001 to 4,000 words) Anita Page for "Twas the Night" in *The Gift of Murder*; (long story, 4,001 to 8,000 words) Doug Allyn for "Famous Last Words" in

EQMM; (novelette, 8,001 to 17,500 words) Dave Zeltserman for *Julius Katz* in *EQMM*; (Edward D. Hoch Memorial Golden Derringer Award for Lifetime Achievement) Lawrence Block.

Philip K. Dick Award. For a distinguished science fiction paperback published in the United States. *Sponsor:* Philadelphia Science Fiction Society. *Winner:* C. L. Anderson for *Bitter Angels* (Ballantine).

Dundee International Book Prize (Scotland) (£10,000). For an unpublished novel on any theme, in any genre. *Winner:* Alan Wright for *Act of Murder.*

Dundee Picture Book Award (Scotland) (£1,000). To recognize excellence in storytelling for children. *Winner:* Lizzie Finlay for Dandylion (Barron's Educational Series).

Educational Writers' Award (United Kingdom) (£2,000). For noteworthy educational nonfiction for children. *Offered by:* Authors' Licensing and Collecting Society and Society of Authors. *Winner:* Bill Bryson and Felicia Law, editor, for *A Really Short History of Nearly Everything* (Doubleday).

Margaret A. Edwards Award ($2,000). To an author whose book or books have provided young adults with a window through which they can view their world and which will help them to grow and to understand themselves and their role in society. *Donor: School Library Journal. Winner:* Jim Murphy, author of *An American Plague: The True and Terrifying Story of the Yellow Fever Epidemic of 1793* (Clarion).

Encore Award (United Kingdom) (£10,000). Awarded biennially for the best second novel of the previous two years. *Offered by:* Society of Authors. *Winner:* Not awarded in 2010.

European Union Prize for Literature (€5,000). To recognize outstanding European writing. *Sponsors:* European Commission, European Booksellers Federation, European Writers' Council, Federation of European Publishers. The 2010 round of the competition involved writers from Belgium, Cyprus, Denmark, Estonia, Finland, Germany, Luxembourg, Romania, Slovenia, Spain, and the Former Yugoslav Republic of Macedonia. *Winners:* (Belgium) Peter Terrin for *De Bewaker* (*The Guard*) (De Arbeiderspers); (Cyprus) Myrto Azina Chronides for *To Peirama* (*The Experiment*) (Armida); (Denmark) Adda Djørup for *Den Mindste Modstand* (*The Least Resistance*) (Samleren); (Estonia) Tiit Aleksejev for *Palveränd* (*The Pilgrimage*) (Varrak); (Finland) Riku Korhonen for *Lääkäriromaani* (*Doctor Novel*) (Sammakko); (Germany) Iris Hanika for *Das Eigentliche* (*The Bottom Line*) (Droschl Verlag); (Luxembourg) Jean Back for *Amateur* (Ultimomondo); (Romania) Razvan Radulescu for *Teodosie cel Mic* (*Theodosius the Small*) (Polirom); (Slovenia) Nataša Kramberger for *Nebesa v Robidah: Roman v Zgodbah* (*Heaven in a Blackberry Bush: Novel in Stories*) (Javni Sklad RS za Ljubiteljske Dejavnosti); (Spain) Raquel Martínez-Gómez for *Sombras de Unicornio* (*Shadows of the Unicorn*) (Algaida Editores); (Macedonia) Goce Smilevski for *Sigmund Freud's Sister* (Kultura).

Fairfax Prize ($10,000). For a body of work that has "made significant contributions to American and international culture." *Sponsors:* Fairfax County (Virginia) Public Library Foundation and George Mason University. *Winner:* Ann Patchett.

FIELD Poetry Prize ($1,000). For a book-length poetry collection. *Offered by: FIELD: Contemporary Poetry and Poetics. Winner:* Timothy O'Keefe for *The Goodbye Town* (to be published by Oberlin College Press).

FIL Literary Award in Romance Languages (formerly the Juan Rulfo International Latin American and Caribbean Prize (Mexico) ($150,000). For lifetime achievement in any literary genre. *Offered by:* Juan Rulfo International Latin American and Caribbean Prize Committee. *Winner:* Margo Glantz.

Financial Times/Goldman Sachs Business Book of the Year Award. To recognize books that provide compelling and enjoyable insight into modern business issues. *Winner:* Raghuram G. Rajan for *Fault Lines: How Hidden Fractures Still Threaten the World Economy* (Princeton University Press).

ForeWord Magazine Book of the Year Awards ($1,500). For independently published books. *Offered by: ForeWord* magazine. *Winners:* (fiction) Richard Selzer for *Knife Song Korea* (SUNY Press/Excelsior Editions); (nonfiction) Italian Academy of Cuisine for *La Cucina* (Rizzoli).

E. M. Forster Award. To a young writer from England, Ireland, Scotland, or Wales, for a stay in the United States. *Offered by:* American Academy of Arts and Letters. *Winner:* Dan Rhodes.

Forward Prizes (United Kingdom). For poetry. *Offered by: The Forward. Winners:* (best collection, £10,000) Seamus Heaney for *Human Chain* (Farrar, Straus & Giroux); (best first collection, £5,000) Hilary Menos for *Berg* (Seren); (best single poem, £1,000) Julia Copus for "An Easy Passage."

H. E. Francis Short Story Competition ($1,000). For an unpublished short story no more than 5,000 words in length. *Sponsors:* Ruth Hindman Foundation and English Department, University of Alabama, Huntsville. *Winner:* Karl Luntta for "At Times Like This."

Josette Frank Award (formerly the Children's Book Award). For a work of fiction in which children or young people deal in a positive and realistic way with difficulties in their world and grow emotionally and morally. *Offered by:* Bank Street College of Education and the Florence M. Miller Memorial Fund. *Winners:* Jacqueline Kelly for *The Evolution of Calpurnia Tate* (Holt), Grace Lin for *Where the Mountain Meets the Moon* (Little, Brown).

George Freedley Memorial Award. For the best English-language work about live theater published in the United States. *Offered by:* Theatre Library Association. *Winner:* Andrew McConnell Stott for *The Pantomime Life of Joseph Grimaldi: Laughter, Madness and the Story of Britain's Greatest Comedian* (Canongate); (special jury prize) Marc Robinson for *The American Play: 1787–2000* (Yale University Press).

French-American Foundation Translation Prize ($10,000). For a translation or translations from French into English of a work of fiction and a work of nonfiction. *Offered by:* French-American Foundation. *Winners:* (fiction) John Cullen for his translation of *Brodeck* by Philippe Claudel (Doubleday); (nonfiction) not awarded in 2010.

Frost Medal. To recognize achievement in poetry over a lifetime. *Offered by:* Poetry Society of America. *Winner:* Lucille Clifton.

Lewis Galantière Award. A biennial award for a literary translation into English from any language other than German. *Offered by:* American Translators Association. *Winner:* Margaret Sayers Peden.

Galaxy British Book Awards. *Offered by: Publishing News. Winners:* (Tesco Biography of the Year) Stephen Fry for *The Fry Chronicles* (Penguin); (Tesco Food and Drink Book of the Year) Yotam Ottolenghi for *Plenty* (Random); (National Book Tokens New Writer of the Year) Edmund de Waal for *The Hare with Amber Eyes: A Hidden Inheritance* (Random); (More4 Nonfiction Book of the Year) Andrew Marr for *The Making of Modern Britain: From Queen Victoria to VE Day* (Pan Macmillan); (Sainsbury's Popular Fiction Book of the Year) David Nicholls for *One Day* (Hodder & Stoughton); (Waterstone's United Kingdom Author of the Year) Hilary Mantel for *Wolf Hal* (HarperCollins); (Galaxy International Author of the Year) Jonathan Franzen for *Freedom* (HarperCollins); (WHSmith Children's Book of the Year) Julia Donaldson and Axel Scheffler for *Zog* (Scholastic); (Outstanding Achievement Award) Terry Pratchett, Martin Amis.

Theodor Seuss Geisel Medal. For the best book for beginning readers. *Offered by:* American Library Association, Association for Library Service to Children. *Winner:* Geoffrey Hays for *Benny and Penny in the Big No-No!* (Toon).

David Gemmell Legend Award for Fantasy. For the best full-length fantasy novel published for the first time in English during the year of nomination. *Winner:* Graham McNeill for *Empire* (Time of Legends: Sigmar Trilogy) (Games Workshop).

Giller Prize (Canada). See Scotiabank Giller Prize.

Gival Press Novel Award ($3,000 and publication by Gival Press). *Winner:* Peter Leach for *The Racial Cleansing of Ste. Genevieve.*

Giverny Award. For an outstanding children's science picture book. *Offered by:* 15 Degree Laboratory. *Winner:* Jason Chin for *Redwoods* (Flash Point).

Alexander Gode Medal. To an individual or institution for outstanding service to the translation and interpreting professions. *Offered by:* American Translators Association. *Winner:* Glenn Nordin.

Goldberg Prize for Jewish Fiction by Emerging Writers ($2,500). To highlight new works by contemporary writers exploring Jewish themes. *Offered by:* Foundation for Jewish Culture. *Donor:* Samuel Goldberg and Sons Foundation. *Winner:* Joanna Smith Rakoff for *A Fortunate Age* (Scribner).

Golden Duck Awards for Excellence in Children's Science Fiction Literature. *Sponsored by:* Super-Con-Duck-Tivity. *Winners:* (picture book) Jack Prelutsky and Jimmy Pickering, illustrator, for *Swamps of Sleethe* (Knopf); (Eleanor Cameron Middle Grades Award) Steve Cole for *Zrex* (Penguin); (Hal Clement Young Adult Award) Suzanne Collins for *Catching Fire* (Scholastic); (special award) John Hamilton for *You Write It: Science Fiction* (Abdo).

Golden Kite Awards ($2,500). For children's books. *Offered by:* Society of Children's Book Writers and Illustrators. *Winners:* (fiction) Julia Durango for *Sea of the Dead* (Simon & Schuster); (nonfiction) Ashley Bryan for *Ashley Bryan: Words to My Life's Song* (Simon & Schuster); (picture book text) Marion Dane Bauer for *The Longest Night,* illustrated by Ted Lewin (Holiday House); (picture book illustration) John Parra for *Gracias/Thanks,* written by Pat Mora (Lee & Low).

Governor General's Literary Awards (Canada) (C$25,000, plus C$3,000 to the publisher). For works, in English and in French, of fiction, nonfiction, poetry, drama, and children's literature, and for translation. *Offered by:* Canada Council for the Arts. *Winners:* (fiction, English) Dianne Warren for *Cool Water* (HarperCollins); (nonfiction, English) Allan Casey for *Lakeland: Journeys into the Soul of Canada* (Greystone); (poetry, English) Richard Greene for *Boxing the Compass* (Signal); (drama, English) Robert Chafe for *Afterimage*; (children's literature—text, English) Wendy Phillips for *Fishtailing* (Coteau); (children's literature—illustration, English) Jon Klassen for *Cats' Night Out* (Simon & Schuster); (translation, French to English) Linda Gaboriau for *Forests* by Wajdi Mouawad (Playwrights Canada); (fiction, French) Kim Thúy for *Ru* (Libre Expression); (nonfiction) Michel Lavoie for *C'est Ma Seigneurie que Je Réclame: La Lutte des Hurons de Lorette pour la Seigneurie de Sillery, 1650–1900*; (poetry) Danielle Fournier for *Effleurés de Lumière* (L'Hexagone); (drama) David Paquet for *Porcépic*; (children's literature—text) Élise Turcotte for *Rose: Derrière le Rideau de la Folie*; (children's literature—illustration) Daniel Sylvestre for *Rose: Derrière le Rideau de la Folie*; (translation, English to French) Sophie Voillot for *Le Cafard.*

Dolly Gray Children's Literature Awards. For fiction or biographical children's books with positive portrayals of individuals with developmental disabilities. *Offered by:* Council for Exceptional Children, Division on Autism and Developmental Disabilities. *Winners:* Siobhan Dowd for *The London Eye Mystery* (David Fickling), Clarabelle van Niekerk and Liezl Venter for *Understanding Sam and Asperger Syndrome* (Skeezel).

Eric Gregory Awards (United Kingdom) (£4,000). For a published or unpublished collection by poets under the age of 30. *Winners:* Phil Brown for *OK to Disconnect*; Matthew Gregory for *We Found a Cave*; Sarah Howe for *A Certain Chinese Encyclopaedia*; Abigail Parry for *A Trick of Perspective*; Ahren Warner for *Confer.*

Griffin Poetry Prizes (Canada) (C$200,000 total). To a living Canadian poet or translator and a living poet or translator from any country, which may include Canada.

Offered by: Griffin Trust. *Winners:* (international) Eiléan Ní Chuilleanáin for *The Sun-fish* (Wake Forest University Press); (Canadian) Karen Solie for *Pigeon* (House of Anansi); (lifetime achievement) Adrienne Rich.

Gryphon Award ($1,000). To recognize a noteworthy work of fiction or nonfiction for younger children. *Offered by:* The Center for Children's Books. *Winner:* James Sturm, Andrew Arnold, and Alexis Frederick-Frost for *Adventures in Cartooning* (First Second).

Guardian Children's Fiction Prize (United Kingdom) (£1,500). For an outstanding children's or young adult novel. *Offered by:* The *Guardian*. *Winner:* Michelle Paver for *Ghost Hunter* (Chronicles of Ancient Darkness series) (Katherine Tegen).

Guardian First Book Award (United Kingdom) (£10,000). For recognition of a first book. *Offered by:* The *Guardian*. *Winner:* Alexandra Harris for *Romantic Moderns: English Writers, Artists and the Imagination from Virginia Woolf to John Piper* (Thames & Hudson).

Gumshoe Awards. For crime fiction. *Offered by: Mysterious Ink* online magazine. *Winners:* No longer awarded.

Dashiell Hammett Prize. For a work of literary excellence in the field of crime writing. *Offered by:* North American Branch, International Association of Crime Writers. *Winner:* Jedediah Berry for *The Manual of Detection* (Penguin).

O. B. Hardison, Jr. Poetry Prize ($10,000). To a U.S. poet who has published at least one book in the past five years, and has made important contributions as a teacher, and is committed to furthering the understanding of poetry. *Offered by:* Folger Shakespeare Library. *Winner:* Juliana Spahr.

Harvey Awards. To recognize outstanding work in comics and sequential art. *Winners:* (best writer) Robert Kirkman for *The Walking Dead* (Image Comics); (best artist) Robert Crumb for *Book of Genesis* (Norton); (best cartoonist) Darwyn Cooke for *Richard Stark's Parker: The Hunter* (IDW); (best original graphic publication for younger readers) *The Muppet Show Comic Book* (BOOM! Studios); (best anthology) *Wednesday Comics* (DC Comics); (best syndicated strip or panel) "Mutts" by Patrick McDonnell (King Features Syndicate); (best biographical, historical or journalistic presentation) Denis Kitchen and Paul Buhle for *Art of Harvey Kurtzman: The MAD Genius of Comics* (Abrams ComicArts).

R. R. Hawkins Award. For the outstanding professional/scholarly work of the year. *Offered by:* Association of American Publishers. *Winners:* University of Chicago Press for *Plato's Philosophers: The Coherence of the Dialogues*; John Wiley & Sons, Inc. for *Wiley Interdisciplinary Reviews (WIREs)*.

Anthony Hecht Poetry Prize ($3,000 and publication by Waywiser Press). For an unpublished first or second book-length poetry collection. *Winner:* Matthew Ladd for *The Book of Emblems*.

Robert A. Heinlein Centennial Short Story Contest. For outstanding science fiction writing. *Sponsor:* Heinlein Society. *Winner:* Karl Bunker for "Under the Shouting Sky."

Drue Heinz Literature Prize ($15,000). For short fiction. *Winner:* Tina May Hall for *The Physics of Imaginary Objects* (University of Pittsburgh Press).

O. Henry Awards. See PEN/O. Henry Prize.

William Dean Howells Medal. In recognition of the most distinguished novel published in the preceding five years. *Offered by:* American Academy of Arts and Letters. *Winner:* Peter Matthiessen for *Shadow Country* (Modern Library).

Hugo Awards. For outstanding science fiction writing. *Offered by:* World Science Fiction Convention. *Winners:* (novel) (tie) China Miéville for *The City and The City* (Macmillan); Paolo Bacigalupi for *The Windup Girl* (Night Shade); (novella) Charles Stross for *Palimpsest* in *Wireless* (Ace); (novelette) Peter Watts for *The Island* (Eos); (short story) Will McIntosh for "Bridesicle" in *Asimov's* January 2009; (best related work) Jack Vance for *This is Me, Jack Vance! (Or, More Properly, This is "I")* (Subterranean); (best graphic story) Kaja and Phil Foglio and Cheyenne Wright for *Girl Genius, Volume 9: Agatha Heterodyne and the Heirs of the Storm* (Airship Entertainment); (John W. Campbell Award for Best New Writer) Seanan McGuire.

Hurston/Wright Legacy Awards. To writers of African American descent for a book of fiction, a book of nonfiction, and a book of poetry. *Offered by:* Hurston/Wright Foundation. *Sponsor:* Busboys and Poets. *Winners:* (fiction) Percival Everett for *I Am Not Sidney Poitier* (Graywolf); (nonfiction) Robin Kelley for *Thelonious Monk: The Life and Times of an American Original* (Free Press); (poetry) Haki R. Madhubuti for *Liberation Narratives: New and Collected Poems 1966–2009* (Third World), Rita Dove for *Sonata Mulattica: Poems* (Norton).

Ignatz Awards. To recognize outstanding achievement in comics and cartooning. *Offered by:* Small Press Expo SPX Cartoons and Comic Arts Festival. *Winners:* (outstanding artist) Eddie Campbell for *Alec: The Years Have Pants* (Top Shelf Productions); (outstanding anthology or collection) R. Sikoryak for *Masterpiece Comics* (Drawn & Quarterly); (outstanding graphic novel) James Sturm for *Market Day* (Drawn & Quarterly); (outstanding story) Ken Dahl for "Monsters" (Secret Acres); (promising new talent) Matt Wiegle for *The Orphan Baiter* (Papercutter No. 13) (Tugboat); (outstanding series) Kevin Huizenga for "Ganges" (Fantagraphics); (outstanding comic) *I Want You, Lisa Hanawalt* (Buenaventura); (outstanding mini-comic) Jim Rugg for *Rambo 3.5*; (outstanding online comic) Mike Dawson for *Troop 142.*

IMPAC Dublin Literary Award (Ireland) (€100,000). For a book of high literary merit, written in English or translated into English. *Offered by:* IMPAC Corp. and the City of Dublin. *Winner:* Gerbrand Bakker for *The Twin* (Vintage).

Indies Choice Book Awards (formerly BookSense Book of the Year Awards). Chosen by owners and staff of American Booksellers Association member bookstores. *Winners:* (adult fiction) Abraham Verghese for *Cutting for Stone* (Knopf); (adult nonfiction) David Grann for *The Lost City of Z* (Doubleday); (adult debut) Kathryn Stockett for *The Help* (Putnam); (young adult) Suzanne Collins for *Catching Fire* (Scholastic); (middle reader) Rebecca Stead for *When You Reach Me* (Wendy Lamb); (new picture book) Jerry Pinkney for *The Lion and the Mouse* (Little, Brown); (most engaging author) Kate DiCamillo.

International Prize for Arabic Fiction. To reward excellence in contemporary Arabic creative writing. *Sponsors:* Booker Prize Foundation, Emirates Foundation for Philanthropy. *Winner:* Abdo Khal for *Spewing Sparks as Big as Castles* (Al-Jamal).

Iowa Poetry Prize. For book-length poetry collections by new or established poets. *Sponsor:* University of Iowa Press. *Winners:* Julie Hanson for *Unbeknownst,* L. S. Klatt for *Cloud of Ink.*

IPPY Peacemaker Award. To honor the best book promoting world peace and human tolerance. *Offered by:* Jenkins Group and *Independent Publisher* online. *Winner:* Sheri Snively for *Heaven in the Midst of Hell: A Quaker Chaplain's View of the War in Iraq* (Raven Oaks).

IRA Children's and Young Adult Book Awards. For first or second books in any language published for children or young adults. *Offered by:* International Reading Association. *Winners:* (primary fiction) Liz Garton Scanlon for *All the World* (Beach Lane); (primary nonfiction) Rachel Rodriguez for *Building on Nature: The Life of Antoni Gaudi* (Holt); (intermediate fiction) Michelle Houts for *The Beef Princess of Practical County* (Delacorte), Jacqueline Kelly for *The Evolution of Calpurnia Tate* (Holt); (young adult fiction) Rebecca Stead for *When You Reach Me* (Wendy Lamb).

Rona Jaffe Foundation Writers' Awards ($25,000). To identify and support women writers of exceptional talent in the early stages of their careers. *Offered by:* Rona Jaffe Foundation. *Winners:* Hannah Dela Cruz Abrams, Rachel Aviv, Sara Elizabeth Johnson, Alexandria Marzano-Lesnevich, Laura Newbern, Tiphanie Yanique.

Jerusalem Prize (Israel). Awarded biennially to a writer whose works best express the theme of freedom of the individual in society. *Offered by:* Jerusalem International Book Fair. *Winner:* Not awarded in 2010.

Samuel Johnson Prize for Nonfiction (United Kingdom) (£20,000). For an outstanding work of nonfiction. *Offered by:* British Broadcasting Corporation. *Winner:* Barbara Demick for *Nothing to Envy: Real Lives in North Korea* (Granta).

Sue Kaufman Prize for First Fiction ($5,000). For a first novel or collection of short stories. *Offered by:* American Academy of Arts and Letters. *Winner:* Josh Weil for *The New Valley* (Grove).

Ezra Jack Keats Awards. For children's picture books. *Offered by:* New York Public Library and the Ezra Jack Keats Foundation. *Winners:* (new writer award) Tonya Cherie Hegamin for *Most Loved in All the World,* illustrated by Cozbi Cabrera (Macmillan); (new illustrator award) Taeeun Yoo for *Only a Witch Can Fly,* written by Alison McGhee (Houghton Mifflin Harcourt).

Kerlan Award. To recognize singular attainments in the creation of children's literature and in appreciation for generous donation of unique resources to the Kerlan Collection for the study of children's literature. *Offered by:* Kerlan Children's Literature Research Collections, University of Minnesota. *Winner:* Nancy Carlson.

Coretta Scott King Book Awards ($1,000). To an African American author and illustrator of outstanding books for children and young adults. *Offered by:* American Library Association, Social Responsibilities Roundtable. *Winners:* (author) Vaunda Micheaux Nelson for *Bad News for Outlaws: The Remarkable Life of Bass Reeves, Deputy U.S. Marshall,* illustrated by R. Gregory Christie (Carolrhoda); (illustrator) Charles R. Smith, Jr., for *My People,* written by Langston Hughes (Atheneum).

Coretta Scott King/John Steptoe Award for New Talent. To offer visibility to a writer or illustrator at the beginning of a career. *Sponsor:* Coretta Scott King Book Award Committee. *Winner:* Kekla Magoon for *The Rock and the River* (Aladdin).

Coretta Scott King/Virginia Hamilton Award for Lifetime Achievement. Given in even-numbered years to an African American author, illustrator, or author/illustrator for a body of books for children or young adults. In odd-numbered years, the award honors substantial contributions through active engagement with youth, using award-winning African American literature for children or young adults. *Winner:* Walter Dean Myers.

Kiriyama Pacific Rim Book Prize ($30,000). For a book of fiction or a book of nonfiction that best contributes to a fuller understanding among the nations and peoples of the Pacific Rim. *Offered by:* Pacific Rim Voices. *Winner:* Not awarded in 2010.

Robert Kirsch Award for Lifetime Achievement ($1,000). To a living author whose residence or focus is the American West, and whose contributions to American letters clearly merit body-of-work recognition. *Offered by: Los Angeles Times. Winner:* Evan S. Connell.

Lambda Literary Awards. To honor outstanding lesbian, gay, bisexual, and transgendered (LGBT) literature. *Offered by:* Lambda Literary Foundation. *Winners:* (anthology) Ariel Gore, editor, for *Portland Queer: Tales of the Rose City* (Lit Star); (children's/young adult) Dale Peck for *Sprout* (Bloomsbury USA); (drama) Mart Crowley for *The Collected Plays of Mart Crowley* (Alyson); (nonfiction) James Davidson for *The Greeks and Greek Love* (Random); (fantasy/horror) Catherynne M. Valente for *Palimpsest* (Bantam); (LGBT studies) Margot Canaday for *The Straight State: Sexuality and Citizenship in Twentieth Century America* (Princeton University Press); (bisexual fiction) (tie) Mykola Dementiuk for *Holy Communion* (Synergy), Maria Pallotta-Chiarolli for *Love You Two* (Random); (bisexual nonfiction) Minal Hajratwala for *Leaving India: My Family's Journey from Five Villages to Five Continents* (Houghton Mifflin Harcourt); (transgender) Lynn Breedlove for *Lynnee Breedlove's One Freak Show* (Manic D Press); (lesbian debut fiction) Rhiannon Argo for *The Creamsicle* (Spinsters Ink); (gay debut fiction) Rakesh Satyal for *Blue Boy* (Kensington); (lesbian erotica) Sacchi Green and

Rakelle Valencia, editors, for *Lesbian Cowboys* (Cleis); (gay erotica) Kevin Killian for *Impossible Princess* (City Lights); (lesbian fiction) Jill Malone for *A Field Guide to Deception* (Bywater); (gay fiction) Vestal McIntyre for *Lake Overturn* (HarperCollins); (lesbian memoir/biography) Joan Schenkar for *The Talented Miss Highsmith* (St. Martin's); (gay memoir/biography) Reynolds Price for *Ardent Spirits: Leaving Home, Coming Back* (Scribner); (lesbian mystery) J. M. Redmann for *Death of a Dying Man* (Bold Strokes); (gay mystery) Michael Thomas Ford for *What We Remember* (Kensington); (lesbian poetry) Stacie Cassarino for *Zero at the Bone* (New Issues Poetry and Prose); (gay poetry) Benjamin S. Grossberg for *Sweet Core Orchard* (University of Tampa Press); (lesbian romance) Colette Moody for *The Sublime and Spirited Voyage of Original Sin* (Bold Strokes); (gay romance) Frank Anthony Polito for *Drama Queers* (Kensington).

Harold Morton Landon Translation Award ($1,000). For a book of verse translated into English by a single translator. *Offered by:* Academy of American Poets. *Winner:* Stephen Kessler for *Desolation of the Chimera* by Luis Cernuda (White Pine).

David J. Langum, Sr. Prize in American Historical Fiction ($1,000). To honor a book of historical fiction published in the previous year. *Winner:* Edward Rutherfurd for *New York: The Novel* (Doubleday).

Lannan Foundation Literary Fellowships. To recognize young and mid-career writers of distinctive literary merit who demonstrate potential for continued outstanding work. *Offered by:* Lannan Foundation. *Winners:* Michael McGriff, C. E. Morgan, Malena Mörling.

James Laughlin Award ($5,000). To commend and support a second book of poetry. *Offered by:* Academy of American Poets. *Winner:* Michael Dickman for *Flies* (Copper Canyon).

Claudia Lewis Award. For the year's best poetry book or books for young readers. *Offered by:* Bank Street College of Education and the Florence M. Miller Memorial Fund. *Winners:* Joyce Sidman and Pamela Zagarenski, illustrator, for *Red Sings from Treetops: A Year in Colors* (Houghton Mifflin Harcourt).

Library of Congress Lifetime Achievement Award for the Writing of Fiction. For a distinguished body of work. *Offered by:* Library of Congress. *Winner:* Not awarded in 2010.

Ruth Lilly Fellowships ($15,000). To emerging poets to support their continued study and writing of poetry. *Offered by:* the Poetry Foundation. *Winners:* Brooklyn Copeland, Miriam Bird Greenberg, Nate Klug, Dora Malech, Christopher Shannon.

Ruth Lilly Poetry Prize ($100,000). To a U.S. poet in recognition of lifetime achievement. *Offered by:* the Poetry Foundation. *Winner:* Eleanor Ross Taylor.

Astrid Lindgren Memorial Award (Sweden) (5 million kroner, approximately $744,000). In memory of children's author Astrid Lindgren, to honor outstanding children's literature and efforts to promote it. *Offered by:* Government of Sweden and the Swedish Arts Council. *Winner:* illustrator Kitty Crowther.

Locus Awards. For science fiction writing. *Offered by:* Locus Publications. *Winners:* (best novel) Cherie Priest for *Boneshaker* (Tor); (fantasy novel) China Miéville for *The City and The City* (Macmillan); (first novel) Paolo Bacigalupi for *The Windup Girl* (Night Shade); (young adult book) Scott Westerfeld for *Leviathan* (Simon & Schuster); (novella) Kage Baker for *The Women of Nell Gwynne's* (Subterranean); (novelette) Peter S. Beagle for *By Moonlight* in *We Never Talk About My Brother* (Tachyon); (short story) Neil Gaiman for "An Invocation of Incuriosity" in *Songs of the Dying Earth* (Tor); (anthology) Gardner Dozois and Jonathan Strahan, editors, for *The New Space Opera 2* (HarperCollins); (collection) Gene Wolfe for *The Best of Gene Wolfe* (Tor); (nonfiction book/art book) Ursula K. Le Guin for *Cheek by Jowl* (Aqueduct).

London Book Festival Awards. To honor books worthy of further attention from the international publishing community. *Winner:* (grand prize) Fredrik Stanton for

Great Negotiations: Agreements that Changed the Modern World (Westholme).

Elizabeth Longford Prize for Historical Biography (United Kingdom) (£5,000). *Sponsors:* Flora Fraser and Peter Soros. *Winner:* Tristram Hunt for *The Frock-Coated Communist: The Revolutionary Life of Friedrich Engels* (Penguin).

Los Angeles Times Book Prizes. To honor literary excellence. *Offered by: Los Angeles Times. Winners:* (biography) Linda Gordon for *Dorothea Lange: A Life Beyond Limits* (Norton); (current interest) Dave Eggers for *Zeitoun* (McSweeney's); (fiction) Rafael Yglesias for *A Happy Marriage* (Scribner); (Art Seidenbaum Award for First Fiction) Philipp Meyer for *American Rust* (Spiegel & Grau); (graphic novel) David Mazzucchelli for *Asterios Polyp* (Pantheon); (history) Kevin Starr for *Golden Dreams: California in an Age of Abundance, 1950–1963* (Oxford University Press); (mystery/thriller) Stuart Neville for *The Ghosts of Belfast* (Soho Crime); (poetry) Brenda Hillman for *Practical Water* (Wesleyan University Press); (science and technology) Graham Farmelo for *The Strangest Man: The Hidden Life of Paul Dirac, Mystic of the Atom* (Basic); (young adult) Elizabeth Partridge for *Marching for Freedom: Walk Together Children and Don't You Grow Weary* (Viking); (Robert Kirsch Award) Evan S. Connell; (innovator's award) Dave Eggers.

Amy Lowell Poetry Traveling Scholarship. For one or two U.S. poets to spend one year outside North America in a country the recipients feel will most advance their work. *Offered by:* Amy Lowell Poetry Traveling Scholarship. *Winners:* Elizabeth Arnold, Paula Bohince.

J. Anthony Lukas Awards. For nonfiction writing that demonstrates literary grace, serious research, and concern for an important aspect of American social or political life. *Offered by:* Columbia University Graduate School of Journalism and the Nieman Foundation for Journalism at Harvard. *Winners:* (book prize) ($10,000) David Finkel for *The Good Soldiers* (Farrar, Straus & Giroux); (Mark Lynton History Prize) ($10,000) James Davidson for *The Greeks and Greek Love: A Bold New Exploration of the Ancient World* (Random); (work-in-progress) ($30,000) Jonathan Schuppe for *Ghetto Ball: A Coach, His Team, and the Struggle of an American City* (to be published by Holt).

Macavity Awards. For excellence in mystery writing. *Offered by:* Mystery Readers International. *Winners:* (novel) Ken Bruen and Reed Farrel Coleman for *Tower* (Busted Flush); (best first mystery novel) Alan Bradley for *The Sweetness at the Bottom of the Pie* (Delacorte); (best mystery nonfiction) P. D. James for *Talking about Detective Fiction* (Knopf); (best mystery short story) Hank Phillippi Ryan for "On the House" in *Quarry: Crime Stories by New England Writers* (Level Best); (Sue Feder Historical Mystery) Rebecca Cantrell for *A Trace of Smoke* (Forge).

McKitterick Prize (United Kingdom) (£4,000). To an author over the age of 40 for a first novel, published or unpublished. *Winner:* Raphael Selbourne for *Beauty* (Tindal Street).

James Madison Book Award ($10,000). To honor books representing excellence in bringing knowledge and understanding of American history to children ages 5 to 14. *Offered by:* James Madison Book Award Fund. *Winner:* Award discontinued in 2008.

Man Booker International Prize (United Kingdom) (£60,000). Awarded biennially to a living author for a significant contribution to world literature. *Offered by:* Man Group. *Winner:* To be awarded next in 2011.

Man Booker Prize for Fiction (United Kingdom) (£50,000). For the best novel written in English by a Commonwealth author. *Offered by:* Booktrust and the Man Group. *Winner:* Howard Jacobson for *The Finkler Question* (Bloomsbury).

Lenore Marshall Poetry Prize ($25,000). For an outstanding book of poems published in the United States. *Offered by:* Academy of American Poets. *Winner:* John Koethe for *Ninety-Fifth Street* (HarperCollins).

Mason Award ($10,000). To honor an author whose body of work has made extraordinary contributions to bringing literature to a wide reading public. *Sponsors:* George Mason University and Fall for the Book. *Winner:* Greg Mortenson.

Somerset Maugham Awards (United Kingdom). For works in any genre except drama by a writer under the age of 35, to enable young writers to enrich their work by gaining experience of foreign countries. *Winners:* (£5,000) Jacob Polley for *Talk of the Town* (Picador); (£3,000) Helen Oyeyemi for *White Is for Witching* (Picador); (£2,000) Ben Wilson for *What Price Liberty?* (Faber).

Addison M. Metcalf Award in Literature ($10,000). Awarded biennially to a young writer of great promise. *Offered by:* American Academy of Arts and Letters. *Winner:* Not awarded in 2010.

Vicky Metcalf Award for Children's Literature (Canada) (C$20,000). To a Canadian writer of children's literature for a body of work. *Offered by:* Metcalf Foundation. *Winner:* Polly Horvath.

Midwest Booksellers Choice Awards. *Offered by:* Midwest Booksellers Association. *Winners:* (fiction) Lorrie Moore for *A Gate at the Stairs* (Random); (nonfiction) Jeffrey Zaslow for *The Girls From Ames: A Story of Women and a Forty-Year Friendship* (Penguin); (poetry) Bill Holm for *The Chain Letter of the Soul: New and Selected Poems* (Milkweed); (picture book) Loren Long for *Otis* (Penguin); (children's literature) Maggie Stiefvater for *Shiver* (Scholastic).

William C. Morris YA Debut Award. To honor a debut book published by a first-time author writing for teens and celebrating impressive new voices in young adult literature. *Offered by:* American Library Association, Young Adult Library Services Association. *Donor:* William C. Morris Endowment. *Winner:* L. K. Madigan for *Flash Burnout* (Houghton Mifflin Harcourt).

Gustavus Myers Awards. For outstanding books that extend understanding of the root causes of bigotry. *Offered by:* Gustavus Myers Center for the Study of Bigotry and Human Rights in North America. *Winners:* Not awarded in 2010.

Mythopoeic Fantasy Awards. To recognize fantasy or mythic literature for children and adults that best exemplifies the spirit of the Inklings, a group of fantasy writers that includes J. R. R. Tolkien, C. S. Lewis, and Charles Williams. *Offered by:* Mythopoeic Society. *Winners:* (children's) Grace Lin for *Where the Mountain Meets the Moon* (Little, Brown); (adult) Jo Walton for *Lifelode* (NESFA).

National Book Awards. For the best books of the year published in the United States. *Offered by:* National Book Foundation. *Winners:* (fiction) Jamie Gordon for *Lord of Misrule* (McPherson); (nonfiction) Patti Smith for *Just Kids* (HarperCollins); (poetry) Terrance Hayes for *Lighthead* (Penguin); (young people's literature) Kathryn Erskine for *Mockingbird* (Penguin).

National Book Critics Circle Awards. For literary excellence. *Offered by:* National Book Critics Circle. *Winners:* (fiction) Hilary Mantel for *Wolf Hall* (Holt); (general nonfiction) Richard Holmes for *The Age of Wonder: How the Romantic Generation Discovered the Beauty and Terror of Science* (Pantheon); (autobiography) Diana Athill for *Somewhere Towards the End* (Norton); (biography) Blake Bailey for *Cheever: A Life* (Knopf); (criticism) Eula Biss for *Notes from No Man's Land: American Essays* (Graywolf); (poetry) Rae Armantrout for *Versed* (Wesleyan University Press); (Nona Balakian Citation for Excellence in Reviewing) Joan Acocella; (Ivan Sandrof Lifetime Achievement Award) Joyce Carol Oates.

National Book Festival Award for Creative Achievement. *Offered by:* Center for the Book, Library of Congress. *Winner:* Isabel Allende.

National Book Foundation Literarian Award for Outstanding Service to the American Literary Community. *Offered by:* National Book Foundation. *Winner:* Joan Ganz Cooney.

National Book Foundation Medal for Distinguished Contribution to American Letters ($10,000). To a person who has enriched the nation's literary heritage over a life of service or corpus of work. *Offered by:*

National Book Foundation. *Winner:* Tom Wolfe.

National Translation Awards ($5,000). To honor translators whose work has made a valuable contribution to literary translation into English. *Offered by:* American Literary Translators Association. *Winners:* (National Translation Award) Alex Zucker for *All This Belongs to Me* by Petra Hulová (Northwestern University Press); (Lucien Stryk Asian Translation Prize) Red Pine (Bill Porter) for *In Such Hard Times: The Poetry of Wei Ying-wu* (Copper Canyon).

Nebula Awards. For science fiction writing. *Offered by:* Science Fiction and Fantasy Writers of America (SFWA). *Winners:* (novel) Paolo Bacigalupi for *The Windup Girl* (Nightshade); (novella) Kage Baker for *The Women of Nell Gwynne's* (Subterranean); (novelette) Eugie Foster for *Sinner, Baker, Fabulist, Priest; Red Mask, Black Mask, Gentleman, Beast* (Interzone); (short stories) Kij Johnson for "Spar" (*Clarkesworld* magazine); (Ray Bradbury Award for Outstanding Dramatic Presentation) Neill Blomkamp and Terri Tatchell for "District 9" (Tri-Star); (Andre Norton Award for Young Adult Science Fiction and Fantasy) Catherynne M. Valente for "The Girl Who Circumnavigated Fairyland in a Ship of Her Own Making"; (Damon Knight Grand Master) Joe Haldeman; (author emeritus) Neal Barrett, Jr.

Nestlé Children's Book Prizes (formerly Smarties Book Prizes) (United Kingdom). To encourage high standards and to stimulate interest in books for children. *Offered by:* Nestlé UK Ltd. *Winners:* Award discontinued in 2008.

John Newbery Medal. For the most distinguished contribution to literature for children. *Offered by:* American Library Association, Association for Library Service to Children. *Winner:* Rebecca Stead for *When You Reach Me* (Random).

Nobel Prize in Literature (Sweden). For the total literary output of a distinguished career. *Offered by:* Swedish Academy. *Winner:* Mario Vargas Llosa.

Eli M. Oboler Memorial Award. Biennially, to an author of a published work in English or in English translation dealing with issues, events, questions, or controversies in the area of intellectual freedom. *Offered by:* Intellectual Freedom Round Table, American Library Association. *Winner:* Ernest Freeberg for *Democracy's Prisoner: Eugene V. Debs, the Great War, and the Right to Dissent* (Harvard University Press).

Flannery O'Connor Awards for Short Fiction. For collections of short fiction. *Offered by:* University of Georgia Press. *Winners:* Jessica Treadway for *Please Come Back to Me* (University of Georgia Press), Linda LeGarde Grover for "The Dance Boots" (University of Georgia Press).

Frank O'Connor Short Story Award. See Cork City–Frank O'Connor Short Story Award.

Oddest Book Title of the Year Award. See Bookseller/Diagram Prize for Oddest Title of the Year.

Scott O'Dell Award for Historical Fiction ($5,000). *Offered by: Bulletin of the Center for Children's Books,* University of Chicago. *Winner:* Matt Phelan for *The Storm in the Barn* (Candlewick).

Sean O'Faoláin Short Story Competition (€1,500 and publication in the literary journal *Southword.*) *Offered by:* Munster Literature Centre, Cork, Ireland. *Winner:* Nikita Nelin for "Eddie."

Dayne Ogilvie Grant for an Emerging Gay Writer ($C4,000). *Offered by:* Writers' Trust of Canada. *Sponsor:* Robin Pacific. *Winner:* Nancy Jo Cullen.

Orange Award for New Writers (United Kingdom) (£10,000). For a first novel or short story collection written by a woman and published in the United Kingdom. *Offered by:* Orange plc and Arts Council London. *Winner:* Irene Sabatini for *The Boy Next Door* (Sceptre).

Orange Prize for Fiction (United Kingdom) (£30,000). For the best novel written by a woman and published in the United Kingdom. *Offered by:* Orange plc. *Winner:* Barbara Kingsolver for *The Lacuna* (Faber).

Orbis Pictus Award. For outstanding nonfiction for children. *Offered by:* National Council of Teachers of English. *Winners:* Hester Bass and E. B. Lewis, illustrator, for *The Secret World of Walter Anderson* (Candlewick).

Orion Book Award ($3,000). To recognize books that deepen connection to the natural world, present new ideas about mankind's relationship with nature, and achieve excellence in writing. *Sponsors: Orion Magazine* and the Geraldine R. Dodge Foundation. *Winner:* Charles Bowden for *Some of the Dead Are Still Breathing: Living in the Future* (Houghton Mifflin Harcourt).

PEN Award for Poetry in Translation ($3,000). For a book-length translation of poetry from any language into English and published in the United States. *Offered by:* PEN American Center. *Winner:* Anne Carson for *An Oresteia: Agamemnon by Aiskhylos; Elektra by Sophokles; Orestes by Euripides* (Faber).

PEN/Saul Bellow Award for Achievement in American Fiction ($25,000). Awarded biennially to a distinguished living American author of fiction. *Offered by:* PEN American Center. *Winner:* Don DeLillo.

PEN Beyond Margins Awards. See PEN Open Book Awards.

PEN/Robert Bingham Fellowship ($25,000). To a writer whose first novel or short story collection represents distinguished literary achievement and suggests great promise. *Offered by:* PEN American Center. *Winner:* Paul Harding for *Tinkers* (Bellevue Literary Press).

PEN/Diamonstein-Spielvogel Award for the Art of the Essay ($5,000). For a book of essays by a single author that best exemplifies the dignity and esteem of the essay form. *Winner:* To be awarded in 2011.

PEN/ESPN Lifetime Achievement Award for Sports Writing ($5,000). To a living writer for exceptional contributions to the field of literary sports writing. *Winner:* To be awarded in 2011.

PEN/Faulkner Award for Fiction ($15,000). To honor the best work of fiction published by an American. *Winner:* Sherman Alexie for *War Dances* (Grove).

PEN/John Kenneth Galbraith Award ($10,000). Given biennially for a distinguished book of general nonfiction. *Offered by:* PEN American Center. *Winner:* To be awarded next in 2011.

PEN/Ernest Hemingway Foundation Award. For a distinguished work of first fiction by an American. *Offered by:* PEN New England. *Winner:* Brigid Pasulka for *A Long, Long Time Ago and Essentially True* (Houghton Mifflin Harcourt).

PEN/Malamud Award ($5,000). To an author or authors who have demonstrated long-term excellence in short fiction. *Offered by:* PEN American Center. *Winners:* Edward P. Jones, Nam Le.

PEN/Ralph Manheim Medal for Translation. Given every three years to a translator whose career has demonstrated a commitment to excellence. *Winner:* To be awarded next in 2012.

PEN/Nabokov Award ($20,000). To celebrate the accomplishments of a living author whose body of work, either written in or translated into English, represents achievement in a variety of literary genres. *Winner:* Not awarded in 2010.

PEN/Phyllis Naylor Working Writer Fellowship ($5,000). *Offered by:* PEN American Center. *Winner:* Pat Schmatz.

PEN/O. Henry Prize. To strengthen the art of the short story. *Winners:* Annie Proulx for "Them Old Cowboy Songs" in the *New Yorker*; Kirstin Allio for "Clothed, Female Figure" in *Iowa Review*; Chimamanda Ngozi Adichie for "The Headstrong Historian" in the *New Yorker*; Wendell Berry for "Stand by Me" in *Atlantic Monthly*; Jess Row for "Sheep May Safely Graze" in *Threepenny Review*; Preeta Samarasan for "Birch Memorial" in *A Public Space*; Brad Watson for "Visitation" in the *New Yorker*; William Trevor for "The Woman of the House" in the *New Yorker*; Daniel Alarcón for "The Bridge" in *Granta*; Daniyal Mueenuddin for "A Spoiled Man" in the *New Yorker*; James Lasdun for "Oh, Death" in *Paris Review*; Natalie Bakopoulos for "Fresco, Byzantine" in *Tin House*; Peter Cameron for "The End of My Life in New York" in *Subtropics*; Ted Sanders for "Obit" in *Indiana Review*; Damon Galgut for "The Lover" in *Paris Review*; George Bradley for "An East Egg Update" in *Yale*

Review; Ron Rash for "Into the Gorge" in *Southern Review*; John Edgar Wideman for "Microstories" in *Harper's*; Alice Munro for "Some Women" in the *New Yorker*; Lore Segal for "Making Good" in *American Scholar*.

PEN Open Book Awards (formerly PEN Beyond Margins Awards) ($1,000). For book-length writings by authors of color, published in the United States during the current calendar year. *Offered by:* PEN American Center. *Winners:* Sherwin Bitsui for *Flood Song* (Copper Canyon); Robin D. G. Kelley for *Thelonious Monk: The Life and Times of an American Original* (Free Press); Canyon Sam for *Sky Train: Tibetan Women on the Edge of History* (University of Washington Press).

PEN/Joyce Osterweil Award for Poetry ($5,000). A biennial award to recognize a new and emerging American poet. *Offered by:* PEN American Center. *Winner:* To be awarded next in 2011.

PEN/Laura Pels Foundation Awards for Drama. To recognize a master American dramatist and an American playwright in mid-career. *Offered by:* PEN American Center. *Winners:* (master playwright) David Mamet, (mid-career prize) Theresa Rebeck.

PEN Prison Writing Awards. To provide support and encouragement to prison inmates whose writing shows merit or promise. *Offered by:* PEN American Center. *Winners:* (fiction) Jonathan C. Rosenbloom for "Terremoto"; (essay) Hal Cobb for "The Pursuit of Character"; (poetry) Louis Templeman for "Villanelle to Pio"; (memoir) Arthur Longworth for "Walla Walla IMU"; (drama) Matthew G. Walker for "Not Guilty."

PEN Translation Fund Grants. To support the translation of book-length works of fiction, creative nonfiction, poetry, or drama that have not previously appeared in English or have appeared only in an egregiously flawed translation. *Winners:* Daniel Brunet, Alexander Dawe, Peter Golub, Piotr Gwiazda, David Hull, Akinloye A. Ojo, Angela Rodel, Margo Rosen, Chip Rossetti, Bilal Tanweer, Diane Thiel.

PEN Translation Prize ($3,000). To promote the publication and reception of translated world literature in English. *Winner:* Michael Henry Heim for his translation from Dutch of *Wonder* by Hugo Claus (Archipelago).

PEN/Voelcker Award for Poetry. Given in even-numbered years to an American poet at the height of his or her powers. *Offered by:* PEN American Center. *Winner:* Marilyn Hacker.

PEN/Jacqueline Bograd Weld Award for Biography ($5,000). To the author of a distinguished biography published in the United States during the previous calendar year. *Offered by:* PEN American Center. *Winner:* Michael Scammell for *Koestler: The Literary and Political Odyssey of a Twentieth Century Skeptic* (Random).

PEN/E. O. Wilson Literary Science Writing Award ($10,000). For a book of literary nonfiction on the subject of the physical and biological sciences. *Winner:* To be awarded in 2011.

PEN/L. L. Winship Award. For books of fiction, poetry, or creative nonfiction with a New England subject or written by a New England author. *Offered by:* PEN New England. *Winners:* (fiction) Anne Sanow for *Triple Time* (University of Pittsburgh Press); (poetry) Meg Kearney for *Home By Now* (Four Way); (nonfiction) Elyssa East for *Dogtown* (Free Press).

Maxwell E. Perkins Award. To honor an editor, publisher, or agent who has discovered, nurtured, and championed writers of fiction in the United States. *Offered by:* Center for Fiction, Mercantile Library of New York. *Winner:* Amanda Urban, executive vice president of International Creative Management (ICM).

Phoenix Award. To the author of an English-language children's book that failed to win a major award at the time of its publication 20 years earlier. *Winner:* Rosemary Sutcliff for *The Shining Company* (Farrar, Straus & Giroux, 1990).

Edgar Allan Poe Awards. For outstanding mystery, suspense, and crime writing. *Offered by:* Mystery Writers of America. *Winners:* (novel) John Hart for *The Last Child* (Minotaur); (first novel by an American author) Stefanie Pintoff for *In the Shadow of Gotham* (Minotaur); (paperback original) Marc Strange for *Body Blows* (Dundurn); (critical/biographical) Otto Penzler, editor, for *The Lineup: The World's Greatest Crime Writers Tell the Inside Story of Their Greatest Detectives* (Little, Brown); (fact crime) Dave Cullen for *Columbine* (Twelve); (short story) Luis Alberto Urrea for "Amapola" in *Phoenix Noir* (Akashic); (young adult) Peter Abrahams for *Reality Check* (HarperCollins); (juvenile) Mary Downing Hahn for *Closed for the Season* (Houghton Mifflin Harcourt); (television episode teleplay) Patrick Harbinson for "Place of Execution" (PBS/WGBH Boston); (Robert L. Fish Memorial Award) Dan Warthman for "A Dreadful Day" in *Alfred Hitchcock Mystery Magazine* (Dell); (Simon & Schuster–Mary Higgins Clark Award) S. J. Bolton for *Awakening* (Minotaur); (grand master) Dorothy Gilman.

Poets Out Loud Prize ($1,000 and publication by Fordham University Press). For a book-length poetry collection. *Sponsor:* Fordham University at Lincoln Center. *Winner:* Amy Catanzano for *Multiversal.*

Katherine Anne Porter Award ($20,000). Awarded biennially to a prose writer of demonstrated achievement. *Offered by:* American Academy of Arts and Letters. *Winner:* Tim O'Brien.

Michael L. Printz Award. For excellence in literature for young adults. *Offered by:* American Library Association, Young Adult Library Services Association. *Winner:* Libba Bray for *Going Bovine* (Delacorte).

V. S. Pritchett Memorial Prize (United Kingdom) (£1,000). For a previously unpublished short story. *Offered by:* Royal Society of Literature. *Winner:* Michael Newton for "The Premises."

Pritzker Military Library Literature Award ($100,000). To recognize a living author for a body of work that has profoundly enriched the public understanding of American military history. *Sponsor:* Tawani Foundation. *Winner:* Rick Atkinson.

Prix Aurora Awards (Canada). For science fiction writing. *Winners:* (long-form work in English) Robert J. Sawyer for *Wake* (Penguin); (long-form work in French) Laurent McAllister for *Suprématie* (Bragelonne); (short-form work in English) Eileen Bell for "Pawns Dreaming of Roses" in *Women of the Apocalypse* (Absolute Xpress); (short-form work in French) Alain Bergeron for "Ors Blancs" (Solaris); (work in English, other) *Women of the Apocalypse* (Absolute Xpress); (work in French, other) Joël Champetier, editor, for *Revue* (Solaris).

Prix Goncourt (France). For "the best imaginary prose work of the year." *Offered by:* Société des Gens des Lettres. *Winner:* Michel Houellebecq for *The Map and the Territory* (Flammarion).

Pulitzer Prizes in Letters ($10,000). To honor distinguished work dealing preferably with American themes. *Offered by:* Columbia University Graduate School of Journalism. *Winners:* (fiction) Paul Harding for *Tinkers* by (Bellevue Literary Press); (drama) Brian Yorkey (book and lyrics) and Tom Kitt (music) for "Next to Normal"; (history) Liaquat Ahamed for *Lords of Finance: The Bankers Who Broke the World* (Penguin); (biography/autobiography) T. J. Stiles for *The First Tycoon: The Epic Life of Cornelius Vanderbilt* (Knopf); (poetry) Rae Armantrout for *Versed* (Wesleyan University Press); (general nonfiction) David E. Hoffman for *The Dead Hand: The Untold Story of the Cold War Arms Race and Its Dangerous Legacy* (Anchor).

Quill Awards. To honor excellence in book publishing. *Offered by:* Reed Business Information and the NBC Universal Television Stations. *Winners:* Program suspended in 2008.

Raiziss/De Palchi Translation Award ($5,000 prize and a $25,000 fellowship, awarded in alternate years). For a translation into English of a significant work of modern Italian poetry by a living translator. *Offered by:* Academy of American Poets. *Winner:* (book prize, $5,000) Paul Vangelisti for *The Position of Things: Collected Poems 1961–1992* by Adriano Spatola (Green Integer).

Raven Awards. For outstanding achievement in the mystery field outside the realm of creative writing. *Offered by:* Mystery Writers of America. *Winners:* Mystery Lovers Bookshop, Oakmont, Pennsylvania, and Zev Buffman; (grand master) Dorothy Gilman; (Ellery Queen award) Barbara Peters and Robert Rosenwald of Poisoned Pen Press.

RBC Bronwen Wallace Award for Emerging Writers (Canada) ($5,000). For a writer under the age of 35 who has not yet been published in book form. *Sponsor:* RBC Foundation. *Winner:* Kilby Smith-McGregor for "The Bird in Hand."

Arthur Rense Poetry Prize ($20,000). Awarded triennially to an exceptional poet. *Offered by:* American Academy of Arts and Letters. *Winner:* To be awarded next in 2011.

John Llewellyn Rhys Prize (United Kingdom) (£5,000). For a work of literature by a British or Commonwealth author 35 or younger and published in the United Kingdom. *Offered by:* Booktrust. *Winner:* Amy Sackville for *The Still Point* (Portobello).

Harold U. Ribalow Prize. For Jewish fiction published in English. *Sponsor: Hadassah* magazine. *Winner:* Sara Houghteling for *Pictures at an Exhibition* (Vintage).

Rita Awards. *Offered by:* Romance Writers of America. *Winners:* (first book) Kate Brady for *One Scream Away* (Forever); (contemporary series romance) Beth Andrews for *A Not-So-Perfect Past* (Harlequin); (contemporary series romance: suspense/adventure) Cindy Dees for *The Soldier's Secret Daughter* (Harlequin); (contemporary single title romance) Kristan Higgins for *Too Good To Be True* (Harlequin); (historical romance) Sherry Thomas for *Not Quite A Husband* (Bantam Dell); (inspirational romance) Tamera Alexander for *The Inheritance* (Thomas Nelson); (novel with strong romantic elements) Barbara O'Neal for *The Lost Recipe for Happiness* (Bantam Dell); (paranormal romance) Kresley Cole for *Kiss of a Demon King* (Simon & Schuster); (romance novella) Molly O'Keefe for *The Christmas Eve Promise* in *The Night Before Christmas* (Regency historical romance) Julia Quinn for *What Happens in London* (HarperCollins); (romantic suspense) Laura Griffin for *Whisper of Warning* (Simon & Schuster); (young adult) Simone Elkeles for *Perfect Chemistry* (Bloomsbury).

Rodda Book Award. To recognize a book that exhibits excellence in writing and has contributed significantly to congregational libraries through promotion of spiritual growth. The award is given to books for adults, young adults, and children on a three-year-rotational basis. *Offered by:* Church and Synagogue Library Association. *Winner:* Roseanne Parry for *Heart of a Shepherd* (Random).

Rogers Writers' Trust Fiction Prize (Canada) (C$25,000). To a Canadian author of a novel or short story collection. *Offered by:* Rogers Communications. *Winner:* Emma Donoghue for *Room* (HarperCollins).

Sami Rohr Prize for Jewish Literature ($100,000 first place, $25,000 first runner-up). For emerging writers of Jewish literature. *Offered by:* Family of Sami Rohr. *Winners:* (tie, $62,500 each) Sarah Abrevaya Stein for *Plumes: Ostrich Feathers, Jews, and a Lost World of Global Commerce* (Yale University Press), Kenneth B. Moss for *Jewish Renaissance in the Russian Revolution* (Harvard University Press).

Shamus Awards. To honor mysteries featuring independent private investigators. *Offered by:* Private Eye Writers of America. *Winners:* (hardcover novel) Marcia Muller for *Locked In* (Grand Central); (first novel) Brad Parks for *Faces of the Gone* (Minotaur); (paperback original) Ira Berkowitz for *Sinner's Ball* (Three Rivers); (short story) Dave Zeltserman for "Julius Katz" in *Ellery Queen Mystery Magazine*; (Hammer Award, for creation of a memorable private eye character or a series) Marcia Muller for detective Sharon McCone.

Rosenthal Foundation Award ($5,000). To a young novelist of considerable literary talent. *Offered by:* American Academy of Arts and Letters. *Winner:* Daniyal Mueenuddin for *In Other Rooms, Other Wonders* (Norton).

Royal Society of Literature Jerwood Awards for Nonfiction (United Kingdom). For authors engaged on their first major commissioned works of nonfiction. *Offered by:* Royal Society of Literature. *Winners:* (£10,000) Caspar Henderson for *The Book of Barely Imagined Things*; (£5,000) Miles Hollingworth for *St. Augustine—An Intellectual Biography*; (£5,000) Selina Mills for *Life Unseen—How Blindness Shaped the West*.

Royal Society of Literature Ondaatje Prize (£10,000). For a distinguished work of fiction, nonfiction or poetry evoking the spirit of a place. *Offered by:* Royal Society of Literature. *Winner:* Ian Thomson for *The Dead Yard—Tales of Modern Jamaica* (Faber).

Juan Rulfo International Latin American and Caribbean Prize (Mexico). See FIL Literary Award in Romance Languages.

Carl Sandburg Literary Awards. To honor a significant body of work that has enhanced public awareness of the written word. *Sponsor:* Chicago Public Library Foundation. *Winner:* Toni Morrison.

Schneider Family Book Awards ($5,000). To honor authors and illustrators for books that embody artistic expressions of the disability experience of children and adolescents. *Offered by:* American Library Association. *Donor:* Katherine Schneider. *Winners:* (young readers) Bonnie Christensen for *Django* (Roaring Brook); (middle school readers) Nora Raleigh Baskin for *Anything But Typical* (Simon & Schuster); (teen readers) Francisco X. Stork for *Marcelo in the Real World* (Scholastic).

Scotiabank Giller Prize (Canada) (C$50,000). For the best Canadian novel or short story collection written in English. *Offered by:* Giller Prize Foundation and Scotiabank. *Winner:* Johanna Skibsrud for *The Sentimentalists* (Gaspereau).

Scottish Book of the Year Awards. *Sponsor:* Scottish Arts Council. *Donor:* Scottish Mortgage Investment Trust. *Winner:* (nonfiction, and book of the year) (£30,000) Donald Worster for *A Passion for Nature: The Life of John Muir* (Oxford University Press); (category winners, £5,000) (fiction) John Aberdein for *Strip the Willow* (Polygon); (poetry) Tom Leonard for *Outside the Narrative* (Etruscan); (first book) Sarah Gabriel for *Eating Pomegranates* (Jonathan Cape).

Shelley Memorial Award ($6,000 to $9,000). To a poet or poets living in the United States, chosen on the basis of genius and need. *Offered by:* Poetry Society of America. *Winners:* Kenneth Irby, Eileen Myles.

Shenandoah/Glasgow Prize for Emerging Writers ($2,000). To a writer who has published one book of poetry. *Offered by:* *Shenandoah* literary magazine and Washington and Lee University. *Winner:* Robin Ekiss for *The Mansion of Happiness* (University of Georgia Press).

Robert F. Sibert Medal. For the most distinguished informational book for children. *Offered by:* American Library Association, Association for Library Service to Children. *Winner:* Tanya Lee Stone for *Almost Astronauts: 13 Women Who Dared to Dream* (Candlewick).

Smarties Book Prizes. See Nestlé Children's Book Prizes.

Spur Awards. *Offered by:* Western Writers of America. *Winners:* (long novel) Robert Flynn for *Echoes of Glory* (TCU Press); (short novel) Robert Olmstead for *Far Bright Star* (Algonquin); (original mass market paperback) John D. Nesbitt for *Stranger in Thunder Basin* (Dorchester); (first novel) not awarded in 2010; (western nonfiction biography) David C. Humphrey for *Peg Leg* (Texas State Historical Association); (nonfiction historical) Douglas C. McChristian for *Fort Laramie* (Arthur H. Clark); (nonfiction contemporary) Charles H. Harris III and Louis R. Sadler for *The Secret War in El Paso: Mexican Revolutionary Intrigue, 1906–1920* (University of New Mexico Press); (short story) John D. Nesbitt for "At the End of the Orchard" (*Hardboiled* magazine); (short nonfiction) Roger Di Silvestro for "Teddy's Ride to Recovery" (*Wild West* magazine); (juvenile fiction) Johnny D. Boggs for *Hard Winter* (Gale); (juvenile nonfiction) Nancy Plain for *With One Sky Above Us* (Mondo); (storyteller award) Sandra Day O'Connor and Tom Pohrt for *Find Susie* (Random); (documentary) Candy Moulton for "In Pursuit of a Dream" (Boston Productions); (poem) Paul Zarzyski for "Bob Dylan

Bronc Song" (Two Medicine); (audiobook) Gary McCarthy for *River Thunder* (Books in Motion).

Wallace Stevens Award ($100,000). To recognize outstanding and proven mastery in the art of poetry. *Offered by:* Academy of American Poets. *Winner:* Galway Kinnell.

Bram Stoker Awards. For superior horror writing. *Offered by:* Horror Writers Association. *Winners:* (novel) Sarah Langan for *Audrey's Door* (HarperCollins); (first novel) Hank Schaeble for *Damnable* (Jove), (long fiction) Lisa Morton for *The Lucid Dreaming* (Bad Moon); (short fiction) Norman Prentiss for "In the Porches of my Ears"; (collection) Gene O'Neill for *Taste of Tenderloin* (Apex); (nonfiction) Michael Knost, editor, for *Writers Workshop of Horror* (Woodland); (poetry) Lucy Snyder for *Chimeric Machines* (Creative Guy).

Stonewall Book Awards. *Offered by:* Gay, Lesbian, Bisexual, and Transgendered Round Table, American Library Association. *Winners:* (children's and young adult literature) Nick Burd for *The Vast Fields of Ordinary* (Penguin); (Barbara Gittings Literature Award) David Francis for *Stray Dog Winter* (MacAdam/Cage); (Israel Fishman Nonfiction Award) Nathaniel Frank for *Unfriendly Fire: How the Gay Ban Undermines the Military and Weakens America* (St. Martin's).

Story Prize. For a collection of short fiction. *Offered by: Story* magazine. *Winner:* Daniyal Mueenuddin for *In Other Rooms, Other Wonders* (Norton).

Flora Stieglitz Straus Award. For nonfiction books that serve as an inspiration to young readers. *Offered by:* Bank Street College of Education and the Florence M. Miller Memorial Fund. *Winner:* Tanya Lee Stone for *Almost Astronauts: 13 Women Who Dared to Dream* (Candlewick).

Mildred and Harold Strauss Livings ($50,000 a year for five years). To two writers of English prose literature to enable them to devote their time exclusively to writing. *Winners:* To be awarded next in 2013.

Theodore Sturgeon Memorial Award for the best short science fiction of the year. *Offered by:* Center for the Study of Science Fiction. *Winner:* James Morrow for the novella *Shambling Towards Hiroshima* (Tachyon).

Sunburst Awards for Canadian Literature of the Fantastic (C$1,000). *Winners:* (adult) A. M. Dellamonica for *Indigo Springs* (Tor); (young adult) Hiromi Goto for *Half World* (Puffin).

Charles Taylor Prize for Literary Nonfiction (Canada) ($25,000). To honor a book of creative nonfiction widely available in Canada and written by a Canadian citizen or landed immigrant. *Offered by:* Charles Taylor Foundation. *Winner:* Ian Brown for *The Boy in the Moon: A Father's Search for His Disabled Son* (Random).

Sydney Taylor Children's Book Awards. For a distinguished contribution to Jewish children's literature. *Offered by:* Association of Jewish Libraries. *Winners:* (younger readers) April Halprin Wayland and Stephane Jorisch, illustrator, for *New Year at the Pier: A Rosh Hashanah Story* (Dial); (older readers) Robin Friedman for *The Importance of Wings* (Charlesbridge); (teen readers) Margarita Engle for *Tropical Secrets: Holocaust Refugees in Cuba* (Holt).

Sydney Taylor Manuscript Competition ($1,000). For the best fiction manuscript appropriate for readers ages 8–11, both Jewish and non-Jewish, revealing positive aspects of Jewish life, and written by an unpublished author. *Winner:* Joan Schoettler for "On the Run."

Theatre Library Association Award. See Richard Wall Memorial Award.

Dylan Thomas Prize (£30,000). Awarded biennially for a published or produced literary work in the English language, written by an author under 30. *Offered by:* University of Wales. *Winner:* Elyse Fenton for *Clamor* (Cleveland State University Poetry Center); (Sony Reader Award for Unpublished Writers) (£5,000) *Winner:* Stefan Mohamed for *Bitter Sixteen.*

Thriller Awards. *Offered by:* International Thriller Writers. *Winners:* (hardcover novel) Lisa Gardner for *The Neighbor* (Bantam); (paperback original) Tom Piccirilli for *The Coldest Mile* (Bantam); (first novel) Jamie Freveletti for *Running From the Devil* (Morrow); (short story) Twist Phelan for "A Stab in the Heart" in *Ellery Queen Mystery Magazine*.

Thurber Prize for American Humor ($5,000). For a humorous book of fiction or nonfiction. *Offered by:* Thurber House. *Winner:* Steve Hely for *How I Became a Famous Novelist* (Grove).

Tom-Gallon Trust Award and Olive Cook Prize (£1,000). For a short story. Each is awarded biennially in alternate years. *Winner:* (Olive Cook Prize) Carys Davies for *The Quiet.*

Betty Trask Prize and Award (United Kingdom). To Commonwealth writers under the age of 35 for "romantic or traditional" first novels. *Offered by:* Society of Authors. *Winners:* (Betty Trask Prize, £10,000) Nadifa Mohamed for *Black Mamba Boy* (HarperCollins); (Betty Trask Award, £7,000) Evie Wyld for *After the Fire, a Still Small Voice* (Cape); (£1,500) Jenn Ashworth for *A Kind of Intimacy* (Arcadia); (£1,500) Adaobi Tricia Nwaubani for *I Do Not Come to You By Chance* (Weidenfeld).

Kate Tufts Discovery Award ($10,000). For a first or very early book of poetry by an emerging poet. *Offered by:* Claremont Graduate School. *Winner:* Beth Bachmann for *Temper* (University of Pittsburgh Press).

Kingsley Tufts Poetry Award ($100,000). For a book of poetry by a mid-career poet. *Offered by:* Claremont Graduate School. *Winner:* D. A. Powell for *Chronic* (Graywolf).

21st Century Award. To honor recent achievement in writing by an author with ties to Chicago. *Sponsor:* Chicago Public Library Foundation. *Winner:* Eula Biss.

UKLA Children's Book Awards (United Kingdom). *Sponsor:* United Kingdom Literacy Association. *Winners:* (younger readers) Marcia Williams for *Archie's War* (Walker); (older readers) Siobhan Dowd for *Bog Child* (Random).

Ungar German Translation Award. Awarded biennially for a distinguished literary translation from German into English that has been published in the United States. *Offered by:* American Translators Association. *Winner:* Not awarded in 2010.

Harold D. Vursell Memorial Award ($10,000). To a writer whose work merits recognition for the quality of its prose style. *Offered by* American Academy of Arts and Letters. *Winner:* Peter Schjeldahl.

Amelia Elizabeth Walden Award ($5,000). To honor a book relevant to adolescents that has enjoyed a wide teenage audience. *Sponsor:* Assembly on Literature for Adolescents, National Council of Teachers of English. *Winner:* Kristin Cashore for *Fire* (Dial).

Richard Wall Memorial Award (formerly the Theatre Library Association Award). To honor an English-language book of exceptional scholarship in the field of recorded performance, including motion pictures, television, and radio. *Offered by:* Theatre Library Association. *Winner:* Michel Chion for *Film, A Sound Art,* translated by Claudia Gorbman (Columbia University Press); (special jury prize) Rob King for *The Fun Factory: The Keystone Film Company and the Emergence of Mass Culture* (University of California Press).

Kim Scott Walwyn Prize (United Kingdom) (£3,000). To recognize the professional achievements of women in publishing. *Offered by:* Booktrust. *Winner:* To be awarded next in 2011.

George Washington Book Prize ($50,000). To recognize an important new book about America's founding era. *Offered by:* Washington College and the Gilder Lehrman Institute of American History. *Winner:* Richard Beeman for *Plain, Honest Men: The Making of the American Constitution* (Random).

Carole Weinstein Poetry Prize ($10,000). To poets with strong connections to central Virginia who have made a "significant recent contribution to the art of poetry." *Winner:* Henry Hart.

Whitbread Book Awards. See Costa Book Awards.

E. B. White Read-Aloud Awards. For children's books with particular appeal as read-aloud books. *Offered by:* Association of Booksellers for Children. *Winners:* (picture books) Peter Brown for *The Curious Garden* (Little, Brown); (older readers) Kate Messner for *The Brilliant Fall of Gianna Z* (Walker).

Whiting Writers' Awards ($50,000). For emerging writers of exceptional talent and promise. *Offered by:* Mrs. Giles Whiting Foundation. *Winners:* (fiction) Michael Dahlie, Rattawut Lapcharoensap, Lydia Peelle; (nonfiction) Elif Batuman, Amy Leach, Saïd Sayrafiezadeh; (poetry) Matt Donovan, Jane Springer, LB Thompson; (plays) David Adjmi.

Walt Whitman Award ($5,000). To a U.S. poet who has not published a book of poems in a standard edition. *Offered by:* Academy of American Poets. *Winner:* Carl Adamshick for *Curses and Wishes* (LSU Press).

Richard Wilbur Award ($1,000 and publication by University of Evansville Press). For a book length poetry collection. *Winner:* Marian Shore for *Sand Castle.*

Laura Ingalls Wilder Award. Awarded biennially to an author or illustrator whose books have made a substantial and lasting contribution to children's literature. *Offered by:* American Library Association, Association for Library Service to Children. *Winner:* Not awarded in 2010.

Thornton Wilder Prize for Translation ($20,000). To a practitioner, scholar, or patron who has made a significant contribution to the art of literary translation. *Offered by:* American Academy of Arts and Letters. *Winner:* Not awarded in 2010.

Robert H. Winner Memorial Award ($2,500). To a mid-career poet over 40 who has published no more than one book of poetry. *Offered by:* Poetry Society of America. *Winner:* Leslie Williams.

George Wittenborn Memorial Book Awards. To North American art publications that represent the highest standards of content, documentation, layout, and format. *Offered by:* Art Libraries Society of North America (ARLIS/NA). *Winners:* Michael R. Taylor for *Marcel Duchamp. Étant Donnés* (Philadelphia Museum of Art in association with Yale University Press); Mark Laird and Alicia Weisberg-Roberts, editors, for *Mrs. Delany and Her Circle* (Yale University Press).

Thomas Wolfe Award and Lecture. To honor writers with distinguished bodies of work. *Offered by:* Thomas Wolfe Society and University of North Carolina at Chapel Hill. *Winner:* Lee Smith.

Thomas Wolfe Fiction Prize ($1,000). For a short story that honors Thomas Wolfe. *Offered by:* North Carolina Writers Network. *Winner:* Paul Byall for "Sequestered."

Helen and Kurt Wolff Translator's Prize ($10,000). For an outstanding translation from German into English, published in the United States. *Offered by:* Goethe Institut Inter Nationes, Chicago. *Winner:* Ross Benjamin for his translation of Michael Maar's *Speak, Nabokov* (Verso).

World Fantasy Convention Awards. For outstanding fantasy writing. *Offered by:* World Fantasy Convention. *Winners:* (novel) China Miéville for *The City and The City* (Macmillan); (novella) Margo Lanagan for *Sea-Hearts* in *X6* (Coeur de Lion); (short story) Karen Joy Fowler for "The Pelican Bar" in *Eclipse Three* (Night Shade); (anthology) Peter Straub, editor, for *American Fantastic Tales: Terror and the Uncanny: From Poe to the Pulps/From the 1940s to Now* (Library of America); (collection) (tie) Ludmilla Petrushevskaya for *There Once Lived a Woman Who Tried To Kill Her Neighbor's Baby: Scary Fairy Tales* (Penguin), Gene Wolfe for *The Very Best of Gene Wolfe* (Tor); (artist) Charles Vess; (lifetime achievement) Brian Lumley, Terry Pratchett, Peter Straub.

Writers' Trust Shaughnessy Cohen Prize for Political Writing (Canada) (C$25,000). For a nonfiction book that captures a subject of political interest. *Sponsor:* CTV. *Winner:* John English for *Just Watch Me: The Life of Pierre Elliott Trudeau, 1963–2000* (Knopf).

Writers' Trust Engel/Findley Award (C$25,000). To a Canadian writer predominantly of fiction, for a body of work. *Winner:* Miriam Toews.

Writers' Trust/McClelland & Stewart Journey Prize (Canada) (C$10,000). To a new, developing Canadian author for a short story or an excerpt from a novel in progress. *Offered by:* McClelland & Stewart and James A. Michener. *Winner:* Devon Code for "Uncle Oscar" in *Malahat Review.*

Writers' Trust Nonfiction Prize (Canada) (C$25,000). *Offered by:* Writers' Trust. *Winner:* James FitzGerald for *What Disturbs Our Blood: A Son's Quest to Redeem the Past* (Random House).

Young Lions Fiction Award ($10,000). For a novel or collection of short stories by an American under the age of 35. *Offered by:* Young Lions of the New York Public Library. *Winner:* Wells Tower for *Everything Ravaged, Everything Burned* (Farrar, Straus & Giroux).

Morton Dauwen Zabel Award ($10,000). Awarded biennially to a progressive and experimental writer. *Offered by:* American Academy of Arts and Letters. *Winner:* To be awarded next in 2012.

Zoetrope Short Fiction Prizes. *Offered by: Zoetrope: All-Story. Winners:* (first, $1,000) Joe B. Sills for "Rarities of Unfathomable Worth"; (second, $500) Sarah Donachie for "Hunger"; (third, $250) Sandra Hunter for "30 Below."

Charlotte Zolotow Award. For outstanding writing in a picture book published in the United States in the previous year. *Offered by:* Cooperative Children's Book Center, University of Wisconsin–Madison. *Win-*

Part 6
Directory of Organizations

Directory of Library and Related Organizations

Networks, Consortia, and Other Cooperative Library Organizations

United States

Alabama

Alabama Health Libraries Assn., Inc. (ALHeLa), Lister Hill Lib., Univ. of Alabama, Birmingham 35294-0013. SAN 372-8218. Tel. 205-975-8313, fax 205-934-2230. *Pres.* Lee Vacovich.

Library Management Network, Inc. (LMN), 2132 6th Ave S.E., Suite 106, Decatur 35601. SAN 322-3906. Tel. 256-308-2529, fax 256-308-2533. *Systems Coord.* Charlotte Moncrief.

Marine Environmental Sciences Consortium, Dauphin Island Sea Laboratory, Dauphin Island 36528. SAN 322-0001. Tel. 251-861-2141, fax 251-861-4646, e-mail disl@disl.org. *Coord.* John Dindo.

Network of Alabama Academic Libraries, c/o Alabama Commission on Higher Education, Montgomery 36104. SAN 322-4570. Tel. 334-242-2211, fax 334-242-0270. *Dir.* Ron P. Leonard.

Alaska

Alaska Library Network (ALN), P.O. Box 100585, Anchorage 99501-0585. SAN 371-0688. Tel. 907-269-6587. *Cataloger* Keri Canepa.

Arizona

Maricopa County Community College District/Library Technology Services, 2411 W. 14 St., Tempe 85281-6942. SAN 322-0060. Tel. 480-731-8774, fax 480-731-8787. *Dir. of Technical Services* Thomas Saudargas.

Arkansas

Arkansas Area Health Education Center Consortium (AHEC), Sparks Regional Medical Center, Fort Smith 72917-7006. SAN 329-3734. Tel. 479-441-5337, fax 479-441-5339. *Dir.* Grace Anderson.

Arkansas Independent Colleges and Universities, Firstar Bldg., 1 Riverfront Place, Suite 610, North Little Rock 72114. SAN 322-0079. Tel. 501-378-0843, fax 501-374-1523. *Pres.* Kearney E. Dietz.

Northeast Arkansas Hospital Library Consortium, 223 E. Jackson, Jonesboro 72401. SAN 329-529X. Tel. 870-972-1290, fax 870-931-0839. *Dir.* Karen Crosser.

South Arkansas Film Coop., c/o Malvern-Hot Spring County Lib., Malvern 72104. SAN 321-5938. Tel. 501-332-5441, fax 501-332-6679, e-mail hotspringcountylibrary@yahoo.com. *Dir.* Tammy Carter.

California

49-99 Cooperative Library System, c/o Southern California Lib. Cooperative, Monrovia 91016. SAN 301-6218. Tel. 626-359-6111, fax 626-359-0001. *Dir.* Rosario Garza.

Bay Area Library and Information Network (BayNet), C/o San Francisco Public Lib., San Francisco 94702. SAN 371-0610. Tel. 415-355-2826, e-mail infobay@baynetlibs.org. *Pres.* Linda Suzukie.

Bay Area Library and Information System (BALIS), 2471 Flores St., San Mateo 94403. Tel. 650-349-5538, fax 650-349-5089. *Exec. Dir.* Linda Crowe.

Berkeley Information Network (BIN), Berkeley Public Lib., Berkeley 94704. Tel. 510-981-6166; 510-981-6150, fax 510-981-6246. *Mgr.* Jane Scantlebury.

Califa, 32 W. 25 Ave., Suite 201, San Mateo 94403. Tel. 650-572-2746, fax 650-349-5089, e-mail califa@califa.org. *Exec. Dir.* Linda Crowe.

Central Assn. of Libraries (CAL), 605 N. El Dorado St., Stockton 95202-1999. SAN 322-0125. Tel. 209-937-8649, fax 209-937-8292. *Dir.* Darla Gunning.

Claremont University Consortium (CUC), 150 E. 8 St., Claremont 91711. Tel. 909-621-8026; 909-621-8150, fax 909-621-8681. *CEO* Robert Walton.

Consortium for Open Learning, 333 Sunrise Ave., No. 229, Roseville 95661-3480. SAN 329-4412. Tel. 916-788-0660, fax 916-788-0696. *Operations Mgr.* Sandra Scott-Smith.

Consumer Health Information Program and Services (CHIPS), 12350 Imperial Hwy., Norwalk 90650. SAN 372-8110. Tel. 562-868-4003, fax 562-868-4065, e-mail referenceservices@gw.colapl.org. *Libn.* Amy Beteilho.

Gold Coast Library Network, 3437 Empresa Drive, Suite C, San Luis Obispo 93401-7355. Tel. 805-543-6082, fax 805-543-9487. *Admin. Dir.* Maureen Theobald.

Kaiser Permanente Library System–Southern California Region (KPLS), Health Sciences Lib., Riverside 92505. SAN 372-8153. Tel. 951-353-3659, fax 951-353-3262. *Dir.* William Paringer.

Monterey Bay Area Cooperative Library System (MOBAC), 2471 Flores St., San Mateo 94403. SAN 301-2921. Tel. 650-349-5538, fax 650-349-5089. *Exec. Dir.* Linda Crowe.

Mountain Valley Library System (MVLS), 55 E St., Santa Rosa 95404. Tel. 707-544-0142, fax 707-544-8411 ext. 101. *Exec. Dir.* Annette Milliron.

National Network of Libraries of Medicine–Pacific Southwest Region (NN/LM-PSR), Louise M. Darling Biomedical Lib., Los Angeles 90095-1798. SAN 372-8234. Tel. 310-825-1200, fax 310-825-5389, e-mail psr-nnlm@library.ucla.edu. *Dir.* Judy Consales.

Nevada Medical Library Group (NMLG), Barton Memorial Hospital Lib., South Lake Tahoe 96150. SAN 370-0445. Tel. 530-543-5844, fax 530-541-4697. *Senior Exec. Coord.* Laurie Anton.

Northern California Assn. of Law Libraries (NOCALL), 268 Bush St., No. 4006, San Francisco 94104. SAN 323-5777. E-mail admin@nocall.org. *Pres.* Coral Henning.

Northern California Consortium of Psychology Libraries (NCCPL), Argosy Univ., San Francisco Bay Area Campus, Alameda 94133. SAN 371-9006. Tel. 510-837-3715. *Pres.* Julie Griffith.

Peninsula Libraries Automated Network (PLAN), 2471 Flores St., San Mateo 94403-4000. SAN 371-5035. Tel. 650-349-5538, fax 650-349-5089. *Dir., Information Technology.* Monica Schultz.

San Bernardino, Inyo, Riverside Counties United Library Services (SIRCULS), 3581 Mission Inn Ave., Riverside 92501-3377. SAN 322-0222. Tel. 951-369-7995, fax 951-784-1158, e-mail sirculs@inlandlib.org. *Exec. Dir.* Kathleen F. Aaron.

San Francisco Biomedical Library Network (SFBLN), San Francisco General Hospital UCSF/ Barnett-Briggs Medical Lib., San Francisco 94110. SAN 371-2125. Tel. 415-206-6639, e-mail fishbon@ucsfmedctr.org.

Santa Clarita Interlibrary Network (SCILNET), Powell Lib., Santa Clarita 91321. SAN 371-8964. Tel. 661-259-3540 ext. 3420, fax 661-222-9159. *Libn.* John Stone.

Serra Cooperative Library System, c/o San Diego Public Library, San Diego 92101. SAN 301-3510. Tel. 619-232-1225, fax 619-696-8649, e-mail mad@serralib.org. *Head, ILL* Ralph DeLauro.

Southern California Library Cooperative (SCLC), 248 E. Foothill Blvd., Suite 101, Monrovia 91016-5522. SAN 371-3865. Tel. 626-359-6111, fax 626-359-0001, e-mail sclchq@socallibraries.org. *Dir.* Rosario Garza.

Substance Abuse Librarians and Information Specialists (SALIS), P.O. Box 9513,

Berkeley 94709-0513. SAN 372-4042. Fax 510-985-6459, e-mail salis@salis.org. *Exec. Dir.* Andrea L. Mitchell.

Colorado

Automation System Colorado Consortium (ASCC), c/o Delta Public Lib., Delta 81416. Tel. 970-872-4317. *Technology Consultant* Connie Wolfrom.

BCR (Bibliographical Center for Research), 14394 E. Evans Ave., Aurora 80014-1408. SAN 322-0338. Tel. 303-751-6277, fax 303-751-9787, e-mail info@bcr.org. *Pres. and CEO* Brenda Bailey-Hainer.

Colorado Alliance of Research Libraries, 3801 E. Florida Ave., Suite 515, Denver 80210. SAN 322-3760. Tel. 303-759-3399, fax 303-759-3363. *Exec. Dir.* Alan Charnes.

Colorado Assn. of Law Libraries, P.O. Box 13363, Denver 80201. SAN 322-4325. Tel. 303-492-7535, fax 303-492-2707. *Pres.* Tracy Leming.

Colorado Council of Medical Librarians (CCML), P.O. Box 101058, Denver 80210-1058. SAN 370-0755. Tel. 303-724-2124, fax 303-724-2154. *Pres.* Gene Gardner.

Colorado Library Consortium (CLiC), 770 W. Hampden Ave., Suite 105, Centennial 80112. SAN 371-3970. Tel. 303-422-1150, fax 303-431-9752. *Dir.* Valerie Horton.

Connecticut

Bibliomation, 32 Crest Rd., Middlebury 06762. Tel. 203-577-4070, fax 203-577-4077. *CEO* Mike Simonds.

Capital Area Health Consortium, 270 Farmington Ave., Suite 352, Farmington 06032-1994. SAN 322-0370. Tel. 860-676-1110, fax 860-676-1303. *Pres.* Karen Goodman.

Connecticut Library Consortium, 234 Court St., Middletown 06457-3304. SAN 322-0389. Tel. 860-344-8777, fax 860-344-9199, e-mail clc@ctlibrarians.org. *Exec. Dir.* Christine Bradley.

Council of State Library Agencies in the Northeast (COSLINE), Connecticut State Lib., Hartford 06106. SAN 322-0451. Tel. 860-757-6510, fax 860-757-6503.

CTW Library Consortium, Olin Memorial Lib., Middletown 06459-6065. SAN 329-4587. Tel. 860-685-3889, fax 860-685-2661. *Systems Libn.* Steve Bischof.

Hartford Consortium for Higher Education, 950 Main St., Suite 314, Hartford 06103. SAN 322-0443. Tel. 860-906-5016, fax 860-906-5118. *Exec. Dir.* Rosanne Druckman.

LEAP, 110 Washington Ave., North Haven 06473. SAN 322-4082. Tel. 203-239-1411, fax 203-239-9458. *Exec. Dir.* Diana Sellers.

Libraries Online, Inc. (LION), 100 Riverview Center, Suite 252, Middletown 06457. SAN 322-3922. Tel. 860-347-1704, fax 860-346-3707. *Exec. Dir.* Alan Hagyard.

Library Connection, Inc., 599 Matianuck Ave., Windsor 06095-3567. Tel. 860-298-5322, fax 860-298-5328. *Exec. Dir.* George Christian.

Delaware

Central Delaware Library Consortium, Dover Public Lib., Dover 19901. SAN 329-3696. Tel. 302-736-7030, fax 302-736-5087. *Dir.* Margery Kirby Cyr.

Delaware Library Consortium (DLC), Delaware Academy of Medicine, Newark 19713. SAN 329-3718. Tel. 302-733-1122, fax 302-733-3885, e-mail library@delamed.org. *Dir.* P. J. Grier.

District of Columbia

Computer Sciences Corporation/ERIC Project, 655 15th St. N.W., Suite 500, Washington 20005. SAN 322-161X. Tel. 202-741-4200, fax 202-628-3205. *Dir.* Lawrence Henry.

Council for Christian Colleges and Universities, 321 8th St. N.E., Washington 20002. SAN 322-0524. Tel. 202-546-8713, fax 202-546-8913, e-mail council@cccu.org. *Pres.* Paul R. Corts.

District of Columbia Area Health Science Libraries (DCAHSL), American College of Obstetrics and Gynecology Resource Center, Washington 20024. SAN 323-9918. Tel. 202-863-2518, fax 202-484-1595, e-mail resources@acog.org. *Pres.* Rudine Anderson.

FEDLINK/Federal Library and Information Network, c/o Federal Lib. and Info. Center Committee, Washington 20540-4935. SAN 322-0761. Tel. 202-707-4800, fax 202-707-4818, e-mail flicc@loc.gov. *Exec. Dir.* Roberta I. Shaffer.

Interlibrary Users Assn. (IUA), c/o Urban Institute Lib., Washington 20037. SAN 322-1628. Tel. 202-261-5534, fax 202-223-3043. *Pres.* Nancy L. Minter.

Transportation Research Board, 500 5th St. N.W., Washington 20001. SAN 370-582X. Tel. 202-334-2990, fax 202-334-2527. *Mgr., Info. Services* Barbara Post.

Veterans Affairs Library Network (VALNET), Lib. Programs Office 19E, Washington 20420. SAN 322-0834. *Dir. of Lib. Programs* Ginny DuPont.

Washington Theological Consortium, 487 Michigan Ave. N.E., Washington 20017-1585. SAN 322-0842. Tel. 202-832-2675, fax 202-526-0818, e-mail wtc@washtheocon.org. *Exec. Dir.* John Crossin.

Florida

Central Florida Library Cooperative (CFLC), 431 E. Horatio Ave., Suite 230, Maitland 32751. SAN 371-9014. Tel. 407-644-9050, fax 407-644-7023, e-mail contactus@cflc.net. *Exec. Dir.* Marta Westall.

College Center for Library Automation (CCLA), 1753 W. Paul Dirac Drive, Tallahassee 32310. Tel. 850-922-6044, fax 850-922-4869, e-mail servicedesk@cclaflorida.org. *Exec. Dir.* Richard Madaus.

Consortium of Southeastern Law Libraries (COSELL), Lawton Chiles Legal Information Center, Gainesville 32611. SAN 372-8277. Tel. 352-273-0710, fax 352-392-5093. *Chair* Gordon Russell.

Florida Center for Library Automation (FCLA), 5830 N.W. 39 Ave., Gainesville 32606. Tel. 352-392-9020, fax 352-392-9185, e-mail fclmin@ufl.edu. *Dir.* James Corey.

Florida Library Information Network, R. A. Gray Bldg., Tallahassee 32399-0250. SAN 322-0869. Tel. 850-245-6600, fax 850-245-6744, e-mail library@dos.state.fl.us. *Lending Services Libn.* Linda Pulliam.

Miami Health Sciences Library Consortium (MHSLC), Miami VA Healthcare System, Miami 33125-1624. SAN 371-0734. Tel. 305-575-3187, fax 305-575-3118, e-mail vhamialibrary@va.gov. *Pres.* Devica Samsundar.

Northeast Florida Library Information Network (NEFLIN), 2233 Park Ave., Suite 402, Orange Park 32073. Tel. 904-278-5620, fax 904-278-5625, e-mail office@neflin.org. *Exec. Dir.* Brad Ward.

Panhandle Library Access Network (PLAN), Five Miracle Strip Loop, Suite 8, Panama City Beach 32407-3850. SAN 370-047X. Tel. 850-233-9051, fax 850-235-2286. *Exec. Dir.* William P. Conniff.

SEFLIN/Southeast Florida Library Information Network, Inc, Wimberly Lib., Office 452, Boca Raton 33431. SAN 370-0666. Tel. 561-208-0984, fax 561-208-0995. *Interim Dir.* Jeannette Smithee.

Southwest Florida Library Network (SWFLN), Bldg. III, Unit 7, Fort Myers 33913. Tel. 239-225-4225, fax 239-225-4229, e-mail swfln@fgcu.edu. *Exec. Dir.* Sondra Taylor-Furbee.

Tampa Bay Library Consortium, Inc., 1202 Tech Blvd., Suite 202, Tampa 33619. SAN 322-371X. Tel. 813-740-3963; 813-622-8252, fax 813-628-4425. *Exec. Dir.* Charlie Parker.

Tampa Bay Medical Library Network (TABAMLN), Florida Hospital College of Health Sciences, Orlando 32803-1226. SAN 322-0885. Tel. 407-303-9798, fax 407-303-9408. *Pres.* Deanna Stevens.

Georgia

Assn. of Southeastern Research Libraries (ASERL), c/o LYRASIS, Atlanta 30309-2955. SAN 322-1555. Tel. 404-892-0943, fax 404-892-7879. *Exec. Dir.* John Burger.

Atlanta Health Science Libraries Consortium, Fran Golding Medical Lib. at Scottish Rite, Atlanta 30342-1600. Tel. 404-785-2157, fax 404-785-2155. *Pres.* Kate Daniels.

Atlanta Regional Council for Higher Education (ARCHE), 50 Hurt Plaza, Suite 735, Atlanta 30303-2923. SAN 322-0990. Tel. 404-651-2668, fax 404-880-9816, e-mail arche@atlantahighered.org. *Pres.* Michael Gerber.

Georgia Interactive Network for Medical Information (GAIN), c/o Mercer Univ.

School of Medicine, Macon 31207. SAN 370-0577. Tel. 478-301-2515, fax 478-301-2051, e-mail gain.info@gain.mercer.edu. *Dir.* Jan H. LaBeause.

Georgia Online Database (GOLD), c/o Public Lib. Services, Atlanta 30345-4304. SAN 322-094X. Tel. 404-235-7200, fax 404-235-7201. *Dir., Resource Sharing and Interlibrary Cooperation* Toni Zimmerman.

LYRASIS, 1438 W. Peachtree St. N.W., Suite 200, Atlanta 30309-2955. SAN 322-0974. Tel. 404-892-0943, fax 404-892-7879. *Exec. Dir.* Kate Nevins.

Metro Atlanta Library Assn. (MALA), P.O. Box 14948, Atlanta 30324. SAN 378-2549. Tel. 678-915-7207, fax 678-915-7471, e-mail mala-a@comcast.net. *Pres.* Steven Vincent.

Hawaii

Hawaii Library Consortium (HLC), c/o Hawaii Business Research Lib., Kihei 96753. Tel. 808-875-2408. *Pres.* Sonia I. King.

Hawaii-Pacific Chapter, Medical Library Assn. (HPC-MLA), Health Sciences Lib., Honolulu 96813. SAN 371-3946. Tel. 808-692-0810, fax 808-692-1244. *Chair* A. Lee Adams.

Idaho

Canyon Owyhee Library Group, Ltd. (COLG), 203 E. Owyhee Ave., Homedale 83628. Tel. 208-337-4613, fax 208-337-4933. *Pres.* Bonnie Speas.

Cooperative Information Network (CIN), 8385 N. Government Way, Hayden 83835-9280. SAN 323-7656. Tel. 208-772-5612, fax 208-772-2498, e-mail hay@cin.kcl.org. *Fiscal Agent* John W. Hartung.

Idaho Health Information Assn. (IHIA), c/o Eastern Idaho Regional Medical Center, Idaho Falls 83403. SAN 371-5078. Tel. 208-529-6077, fax 208-529-7014. *Dir.* Kathy Fatkin.

Library Consortium of Eastern Idaho (LCEI), 5210 Stuart Ave., Chubbuck 83202. SAN 323-7699. Tel. 208-237-2192. *Chair* Linda Rasmussen.

LYNX Consortium, c/o Boise Public Lib., Boise 83702-7195. SAN 375-0086. Tel. 208-384-4238, fax 208-384-4025.

Western Council of State Libraries, Inc., c/o Idaho Commission for Libraries, Boise 83702-6055. Tel. 208-334-2150, fax 208-334-4016. *Pres.* Ann Joslin.

Illinois

Alliance Library System, 600 High Point Lane, East Peoria 61611. SAN 371-0637. Tel. 309-694-9200, fax 309-694-9230. *Exec. Dir.* Kitty Pope.

American Theological Library Assn. (ATLA), 300 S. Wacker Drive, Suite 2100, Chicago 60606-5889. SAN 371-9022. Tel. 312-454-5100, fax 312-454-5505, e-mail atla@atla.com. *Exec. Dir.* Dennis A. Norlin.

Areawide Hospital Library Consortium of Southwestern Illinois (AHLC), c/o St. Elizabeth Hospital Health Sciences Lib., Belleville 62222. SAN 322-1016. Tel. 618-234-2120 ext. 2011, fax 618-222-4614.

Assn. of Chicago Theological Schools (ACTS), Univ. of St. Mary of the Lake, Mundelein 60060-1174. SAN 370-0658. Tel. 847-566-6401. *Chair* Thomas Baima.

Capital Area Consortium, 701 N. 1 St., Springfield 62781. *Coord.* Lynne Ferrell.

Center for Research Libraries, 6050 S. Kenwood, Chicago 60637-2804. SAN 322-1032. Tel. 773-955-4545, fax 773-955-4339. *Pres.* Bernard F. Reilly.

Chicago and South Consortium, Jackson Park Hospital and Medical Center, Chicago 60649-3993. SAN 322-1067. Tel. 773-947-7653. *Coord.* Andrew Paradise.

Chicago Area Museum Libraries (CAML), c/o Lib., Field Museum, Chicago 60605-2496. SAN 371-392X. Tel. 312-665-7887, fax 312-665-7893. *Assoc. Libn., Reference and Circulation Services* Christine Giannoni.

Committee on Institutional Cooperation, 1819 S. Neil St., Suite D, Champaign 61820-7271. Tel. 217-333-8475, fax 217-244-7127, e-mail cic@staff.cic.net. *Dir.* Barbara Mcfadden Allen.

Consortium of Academic and Research Libraries in Illinois (CARLI), 100 Trade Center Drive, Suite 303, Champaign 61820.

SAN 322-3736. Tel. 217-244-7593, fax 217-244-7596, e-mail support@carli.illinois.edu. *Exec. Dir.* Susan Singleton.

Council of Directors of State University Libraries in Illinois (CODSULI), Southern Illinois Univ. School of Medicine Lib., Springfield 62702-4910. SAN 322-1083. Tel. 217-545-0994, fax 217-545-0988.

East Central Illinois Consortium, Booth Lib., Eastern Illinois Univ., Charleston 61920. SAN 322-1040. Tel. 217-581-7549, fax 217-581-7534. *Mgr.* Stacey Knight-Davis.

Fox Valley Health Science Library Consortium, c/o Delnor-Community Hospital, Geneva 60134. SAN 329-3831. Tel. 630-208-4299.

Heart of Illinois Library Consortium, 511 N.E. Greenleaf, Peoria 61603. SAN 322-1113. *Chair* Leslie Menz.

Illinois Library and Information Network (ILLINET), c/o Illinois State Lib., Springfield 62701-1796. SAN 322-1148. Tel. 217-782-2994, fax 217-785-4326. *Dir.* Anne Craig.

Illinois Office of Educational Services, 2450 Foundation Drive, Suite 100, Springfield 62703-5464. SAN 371-5108. Tel. 217-786-3010, fax 217-786-3020, e-mail info@ioes.org. *Dir.* Rebecca Woodhull.

LIBRAS, Inc., North Park Univ., Chicago 60625-4895. SAN 322-1172. Tel. 773-244-5584, fax 773-244-4891. *Pres.* Mark Vargas.

Metropolitan Consortium of Chicago, Chicago School of Professional Psychology, Chicago 60610. SAN 322-1180. Tel. 312-329-6633, fax 312-644-6075. *Coord.* Margaret White.

National Network of Libraries of Medicine–Greater Midwest Region (NN/LM-GMR), c/o Lib. of Health Sciences, Univ. of Illinois at Chicago, Chicago 60612-4330. SAN 322-1202. Tel. 312-996-2464, fax 312-996-2226. *Dir.* Kathryn Carpenter.

Network of Illinois Learning Resources in Community Colleges (NILRC), 719 William St., River Forest 60305-1925. Tel. 608-523-4094, fax 608-523-4072. *Exec. Dir.* John W. Berry.

Quad Cities Libraries in Cooperation (QuadLINC), 220 W. 23 Ave., Coal Valley 61240. SAN 373-093X. Tel. 309-799-3155 ext. 3254, fax 309-799-7916.

System Wide Automated Network (SWAN), c/o Metropolitan Lib. System, Burr Ridge 60527-5783. Tel. 630-734-5000, fax 630-734-5050. *Dir.* Aaron Skog.

Indiana

Central Indiana Health Science Libraries Consortium, Indiana Univ. School of Medicine Lib., Indianapolis 46202. SAN 322-1245. Tel. 317-274-8358, fax 317-274-4056. *Officer* Elaine Skopelja.

Collegiate Consortium Western Indiana, c/o Cunningham Memorial Lib., Terre Haute 47809. SAN 329-4439. Tel. 812-237-3700, fax 812-237-3376. *Interim Dean* Alberta Comer.

Consortium of College and University Media Centers (CCUMC), Indiana Univ., Bloomington 47405-1223. SAN 322-1091. Tel. 812-855-6049, fax 812-855-2103, e-mail ccumc@ccumc.org. *Exec. Dir.* Aileen Scales.

Consortium of Foundation Libraries, IUPUI Univ. Lib., Indianapolis 46202. SAN 322-2462. Tel. 317-278-2329. *Chair* Brenda Burk.

Evansville Area Library Consortium, 3700 Washington Ave., Evansville 47750. SAN 322-1261. Tel. 812-485-4151, fax 812-485-7564. *Coord.* Jane Saltzman.

Indiana Cooperative Library Services Authority (INCOLSA), 6202 Morenci Trail, Indianapolis 46268-2536. SAN 322-1296. Tel. 317-298-6570, fax 317-328-2380. *Exec. Dir.* Michael Piper.

Indiana State Data Center, Indiana State Lib., Indianapolis 46202. SAN 322-1318. Tel. 317-232-3733, fax 317-232-3728. *Coord.* Katie Springer.

Northeast Indiana Health Science Libraries Consortium (NEIHSL), Univ. of Saint Francis Vann Lib., Fort Wayne 46808. SAN 373-1383. Tel. 260-399-7700 ext. 6065, fax 260-399-8166. *Coord.* Lauralee Aven.

Northwest Indiana Health Science Library Consortium (NIHSLC), c/o N.W. Center for Medical Education, Gary 46408-1197. SAN 322-1350. Tel. 219-980-6852; 219-

980-6709, fax 219-980-6524; 219-980-6566. *Coord. Lib. Services* Corona Wiley.

Iowa

Consortium of User Libraries (CUL), Lib. for the Blind and Physically Handicapped, Des Moines 50309-2364. Tel. 515-281-1333, fax 515-281-1378; 515-281-1263. *Pres.* Karen Keninger.

Dubuque (Iowa) Area Library Information Consortium, c/o Burton Payne Lib., N.E. Iowa Community College, Peosta 52068. Tel. 563-556-5110 ext. 269, fax 563-557-0340. *Coord.* Deb Seiffert.

Iowa Private Academic Library Consortium (IPAL), c/o Buena Vista Univ. Lib., Storm Lake 50588. SAN 329-5311. Tel. 712-749-2127, 712-749-2203, fax 712-749-2059, e-mail library@bvu.edu. *Univ. Libn.* Jim Kennedy.

Linn County Library Consortium, Russell D. Cole Lib., Mount Vernon 52314-1012. SAN 322-4597. Tel. 319-895-4259. *Pres.* Jason Bengtson.

Polk County Biomedical Consortium, c/o Broadlawns Medical Center Lib., Des Moines 50314. SAN 322-1431. Tel. 515-282-2394, fax 515-282-5634. *Treas.* Elaine Hughes.

Quad City Area Biomedical Consortium, Great River Medical Center Lib., West Burlington 52655. SAN 322-435X. Tel. 319-768-4075, fax 319-768-4080. *Coord.* Judy Hawk.

Sioux City Library Cooperative (SCLC), c/o Sioux City Public Lib., Sioux City 51101-1203. SAN 329-4722. Tel. 712-255-2933 ext. 255, fax 712-279-6432. *Chair* Betsy Thompson.

State of Iowa Libraries Online (SILO), State Lib. of Iowa, Des Moines 50319. SAN 322-1415. Tel. 515-281-4105, fax 515-281-6191. *State Libn.* Mary Wegner.

Kansas

Associated Colleges of Central Kansas (ACCK), 210 S. Main St., McPherson 67460. SAN 322-1474. Tel. 620-241-5150, fax 620-241-5153.

Dodge City Library Consortium, c/o Comanche Intermediate Center, Dodge City 67801. SAN 322-4368. Tel. 620-227-1609, fax 620-227-4862.

Kansas Regents Library Database Consortium (RLDC), c/o Emporia State Univ., Emporia 66801. Tel. 620-341-5480, e-mail rldc@ku.edu. *Chair* Cynthia Akers.

State Library of Kansas/Statewide Resource Sharing Div., 300 S.W. 10 Ave., Room 343 N., Topeka 66612-1593. SAN 329-5621. Tel. 785-296-3875, fax 785-368-7291. *Dir.* Patti Butcher.

Kentucky

Assn. of Independent Kentucky Colleges and Universities (AIKCU), 484 Chenault Rd., Frankfort 40601. SAN 322-1490. Tel. 502-695-5007, fax 502-695-5057. *Pres.* Gary S. Cox.

Eastern Kentucky Health Science Information Network (EKHSIN), c/o Camden-Carroll Lib., Morehead 40351. SAN 370-0631. Tel. 606-783-6860, fax 606-784-2178. *Lib. Dir.* Tammy Jenkins.

Kentuckiana Metroversity, Inc., 109 E. Broadway, Louisville 40202. SAN 322-1504. Tel. 502-897-3374, fax 502-895-1647.

Kentucky Medical Library Assn., VA Medical Center, Lib. Serices 142D, Louisville 40206-1499. SAN 370-0623. Tel. 502-287-6240, fax 502-287-6134. *Head Libn.* Gene M. Haynes.

Kentucky Virtual Library (KVL), 1024 Capital Center Drive, Suite 320, Frankfort 40601. Tel. 502-573-1555, fax 502-573-0222, e-mail kyvl@ky.gov. *Dir.* Enid Wohlstein.

Southeastern Chapter of the American Assn. of Law Libraries (SEAALL), c/o Univ. of Kentucky Law Lib., Lexington 40506-0048. Tel. 859-257-8347, fax 859-323-4906. *Pres.* Amy Osborne.

Theological Education Assn. of Mid America (TEAM-A), Southern Baptist Theological Seminary, Louisville 40280. SAN 377-5038. Tel. 502-897-4807, fax 502-897-4600. *Dir., Info. Resources* Ken Boyd.

Louisiana

Central Louisiana Medical Center Library Consortium (CLMLC), 2495 Shreveport

Hwy., 142D, Alexandria 71306. Tel. 318-619-9102, fax 318-619-9144, e-mail clmlc8784@yahoo.com. *Coord.* Miriam J. Brown.

Health Sciences Library Assn. of Louisiana (HSLAL), LSUHSC Lib., Shreveport 71103. SAN 375-0035. *Pres.* Donna Timm.

Loan SHARK, State Lib. of Louisiana, Baton Rouge 70802. SAN 371-6880. Tel. 225-342-4920, 342-4918, fax 225-219-4725. *Head, Access Services* Kytara A. Gaudin.

LOUIS/Louisiana Library Network, Info. Technology Services, Baton Rouge 70803. *Exec. Dir.* Ralph Boe.

Louisiana Government Information Network (LaGIN), c/o State Lib. of Louisiana, Baton Rouge 70802. SAN 329-5036. Tel. 225-342-4920.

New Orleans Educational Telecommunications Consortium, 2 Canal St., Suite 2038, New Orleans 70130. SAN 329-5214. Tel. 504-524-0350, fax 504-524-0327, e-mail noetc@noetc.org. *Exec. Dir.* Michael Adler.

Maine

Health Science Library Information Consortium (HSLIC), 211 Marginal Way, No 245, Portland 04101. SAN 322-1601. Tel. 207-795-2561, fax 207-795-2569. *Chair* Kathy Brunjes.

Maryland

Maryland Assn. of Health Science Librarians (MAHSL), VA Medical HealthCare System Medical Lib., Baltimore 21201. SAN 377-5070. Tel. 401-605-7093. *Co-Pres.* Brittany Rice.

Maryland Interlibrary Loan Organization (MILO), c/o Enoch Pratt Free Lib., Baltimore 21201-4484. SAN 343-8600. Tel. 410-396-5498, fax 410-396-5837, e-mail milo@prattlibrary.org. *Mgr.* Emma E. Beaven.

National Network of Libraries of Medicine (NN/LM), National Lib. of Medicine, Bethesda 20894. SAN 373-0905. Tel. 301-496-4777, fax 301-480-1467. *Dir.* Angela Ruffin.

National Network of Libraries of Medicine–Southeastern Atlantic Region (NN/LM-SEA), Univ. of Maryland Health Sciences and Human Services Lib., Baltimore 21201-1512. SAN 322-1644. Tel. 410-706-2855, fax 410-706-0099, e-mail hshsl-nlmsea@hshsl.umaryland.edu. *Dir.* Mary J. Tooey.

Regional Alcohol and Drug Abuse Resource Network (RADAR), National Clearinghouse on Alcohol and Drug Info., Rockville 20852. SAN 377-5569. Tel. 301-468-2600, fax 301-468-6433.

U.S. National Library of Medicine (NLM), 8600 Rockville Pike, Bethesda 20894. SAN 322-1652. Tel. 301-594-5983, fax 301-402-1384, e-mail custserv@nlm.nih.gov. *Coord.* Martha Fishel.

Washington Research Library Consortium (WRLC), 901 Commerce Drive, Upper Marlboro 20774. SAN 373-0883. Tel. 301-390-2031, fax 301-390-2020. *Dir. of Lib. Services* Bruce Hulse.

Massachusetts

Boston Biomedical Library Consortium (BBLC), c/o Dana Farber Cancer Trust, Boston 02115. SAN 322-1725. *Pres.* Christine Fleuriel.

Boston Library Consortium, Inc., McKim Bldg., Boston 02117. SAN 322-1733. Tel. 617-262-6244, fax 617-262-0163, e-mail mtrevvett@blc.org. *Exec. Dir.* Melissa Trevvett.

Cape Libraries Automated Materials Sharing Network (CLAMS), 270 Communication Way, Unit 4E, Hyannis 02601. SAN 370-579X. Tel. 508-790-4399, fax 508-771-4533. *Exec. Dir.* Gayle Simundza.

Central and Western Massachusetts Automated Resource Sharing (C/W MARS), 67 Millbrook St., Suite 201, Worcester 01606. SAN 322-3973. Tel. 508-755-3323 ext. 30, fax 508-755-3721. *Exec. Dir.* Joan Kuklinski.

Cooperating Libraries of Greater Springfield (CLGS), Springfield Technical Community College, Springfield 01102. SAN 322-1768. Tel. 413-755-4565, fax 413-755-6315, e-mail lcoakley@stcc.edu. *Coord.* Lynn Coakley.

Fenway Libraries Online, Inc. (FLO), c/o Wentworth Institute of Technology, Boston 02115. SAN 373-9112. Tel. 617-442-

2384, fax 617-442-1519. *Exec. Dir.* Walter Stine.

Massachusetts Health Sciences Libraries Network (MAHSLIN), Brigham and Women''s Hospital Medical Lib., Boston 02115. SAN 372-8293. Tel. 617-632-2489. *Chair* Christine Fleuriel.

Massachusetts Library System, 135 Beaver St., Waltham. 02452. Tel. 781-398-1819, fax 781-398-1821. *Pres.* Sal Genovese.

Merrimack Valley Library Consortium, 1600 Osgood St., North Andover 01845. SAN 322-4384. Tel. 978-557-1050, fax 978-557-8101, e-mail netmail@mvlc.org. *Exec. Dir.* Lawrence Rungren.

Minuteman Library Network, 10 Strathmore Rd., Natick 01760-2419. SAN 322-4252. Tel. 508-655-8008, fax 508-655-1507. *Exec. Dir.* Susan McAlister.

National Network of Libraries of Medicine–New England Region (NN/LM-NER), Univ. of Massachusetts Medical School, Shrewsbury 01545-2732. SAN 372-5448. Tel. 508-856-5979, fax 508-856-5977. *Dir.* Elaine Martin.

North of Boston Library Exchange, Inc. (NOBLE), 26 Cherry Hill Drive, Danvers 01923. SAN 322-4023. Tel. 978-777-8844, fax 978-750-8472. *Exec. Dir.* Ronald A. Gagnon.

Northeast Consortium of Colleges and Universities in Massachusetts (NECCUM), Merrimack College, North Andover 01845. SAN 371-0602. Tel. 978-556-3400, fax 978-556-3738. *Pres.* Richard Santagati.

Northeastern Consortium for Health Information (NECHI), Lowell General Hospital Health Science Lib., Lowell 01854. SAN 322-1857. Tel. 978-937-6247, fax 978-937-6855. *Libn.* Donna Beales.

SAILS, Inc., 547 W. Groves St., Suite 4, Middleboro 02346. SAN 378-0058. Tel. 508-946-8600, fax 508-946-8605. *Pres.* Robin Glasser.

Southeastern Massachusetts Consortium of Health Science Libraries (SEMCO), Youngdahl Lib., Norwood Hospital, Norwood 02062. SAN 322-1873. Tel. 781-278-6243, fax 781-769-9622. *Chair* Denise Corless.

Western Massachusetts Health Information Consortium, Baystate Medical Center Health Sciences Lib., Springfield 01199. SAN 329-4579. Tel. 413-794-1291, fax 413-794-1974. *Pres.* Susan La Forter.

Michigan

Detroit Area Consortium of Catholic Colleges, c/o Sacred Heart Seminary, Detroit 48206. SAN 329-482X. Tel. 313-883-8500, fax 313-883-8594. *Acting Dir.* Chris Spilker.

Detroit Area Library Network (DALNET), 6th Floor SEL, 5048 Gullen Mall, Detroit 48202. Tel. 313-577-6789, fax 313-577-1231. *Dir.* Steven K. Bowers.

Kalamazoo Consortium for Higher Education (KCHE), Kalamazoo College, Kalamazoo 49006. SAN 329-4994. Tel. 269-337-7220, fax 269-337-7219. *Pres.* Eileen B. Wilson-Oyelaran.

Lakeland Library Cooperative, 4138 Three Mile Rd. N.W., Grand Rapids 49534-1134. SAN 308-132X. Tel. 616-559-5253, fax 616-559-4329. *Dir.* Sandra Wilson.

The Library Network (TLN), 13331 Reeck Rd., Southgate 48195-3054. SAN 370-596X. Tel. 734-281-3830, fax 734-281-1905. *Dir.* James Pletz.

Michigan Health Sciences Libraries Assn. (MHSLA), 1407 Rensen St., Suite 4, Lansing 48910. SAN 323-987X. Tel. 517-394-2774, fax 517-394-2675. *Pres.* Sheila Bryant.

Midwest Collaborative for Library Services, 1407 Rensen St., Suite 1, Lansing 48910-3657. Tel. 800-530-9019, fax 517-394-2096. *Exec. Dir.* Randy Dykhuis.

PALnet, 1040 W Bristol Rd., Flint 48507. Tel. 810-766-4070. *Dir.* Stephanie C. John.

Southeastern Michigan League of Libraries (SEMLOL), Lawrence Technological Univ., Southfield 48075. SAN 322-4481. Tel. 248-204-3000, fax 248-204-3005. *Treas.* Gary Cocozzoli.

Southwest Michigan Library Cooperative (SMLC), c/o Niles District Lib., Niles 49120-2620. SAN 371-5027. Tel. 269-683-8545, fax 269-657-4494. *Pres.* Jennifer Ray.

Suburban Library Cooperative (SLC), 44750 Delco Blvd., Sterling Heights 48313. SAN 373-9082. Tel. 586-685-5750, fax 586-

685-3010. *Interim Dir.* Arthur M. Woodford.

Upper Peninsula of Michigan Health Science Library Consortium, c/o Marquette Health System Hospital, Marquette 49855. SAN 329-4803. Tel. 906-225-3429, fax 906-225-3524. *In Charge* Janis Lubenow.

Upper Peninsula Region of Library Cooperation, Inc., 1615 Presque Isle Ave., Marquette 49855. SAN 329-5540. Tel. 906-228-7697, fax 906-228-5627. *Treas.* Suzanne Dees.

Valley Library Consortium, 3210 Davenport Ave., Saginaw 48602-3495. Tel. 989-497-0925, fax 989-497-0918. *Exec. Dir.* Karl R. Steiner.

Minnesota

Capital Area Library Consortium (CALCO), c/o Minnesota Dept. of Transportation, Lib. MS155, Saint Paul 55155. SAN 374-6127. Tel. 651-296-5272, fax 651-297-2354. *Libn.* Shirley Sherkow.

Central Minnesota Libraries Exchange (CMLE), Miller Center, Room 130-D, Saint Cloud 56301-4498. SAN 322-3779. Tel. 320-308-2950, fax 320-654-5131, e-mail cmle@stcloudstate.edu. *Dir.* Patricia A. Post.

Cooperating Libraries in Consortium (CLIC), 1619 Dayton Ave., Suite 204, Saint Paul 55104. SAN 322-1970. Tel. 651-644-3878, fax 651-644-6258. *System Admin.* Deb Bergeron.

Metronet, 1619 Dayton Ave., Suite 314, Saint Paul 55104. SAN 322-1989. Tel. 651-646-0475, fax 651-649-3169, e-mail information@metrolibraries.net. *Exec. Dir.* Ann Walker Smalley.

Metropolitan Library Service Agency (MELSA), 1619 Dayton Ave., No. 314, Saint Paul 55104-6206. SAN 371-5124. Tel. 651-645-5731, fax 651-649-3169, e-mail melsa@melsa.org. *Exec. Dir.* Chris D. Olson.

MINITEX Library Information Network, 15 Andersen Lib., Univ. of Minnesota–Twin Cities, Minneapolis 55455-0439. SAN 322-1997. Tel. 612-624-4002, fax 612-624-4508. *Dir.* William DeJohn.

Minnesota Library Information Network (MnLINK), Univ. of Minnesota–Twin Cities, Minneapolis 55455-0439. Tel. 612-624-8096, fax 612-624-4508. *Info. Specialist* Nick Banitt.

Minnesota Theological Library Assn. (MTLA), Luther Seminary Lib., Saint Paul 55108. SAN 322-1962. Tel. 651-641-3447. *Chair* David Stewart.

North Country Library Cooperative, 5528 Emerald Ave., Mountain Iron 55768-2069. SAN 322-3795. Tel. 218-741-1907, fax 218-741-1908. *Dir.* Linda J. Wadman.

Northern Lights Library Network, 103 Graystone Plaza, Detroit Lakes 56501-3041. SAN 322-2004. Tel. 218-847-2825, fax 218-847-1461, e-mail nloffice@nlln.org. *Dir.* Ruth Solie.

SMILE (Southcentral Minnesota Inter-Library Exchange), 1400 Madison Ave., No. 622, Mankato 56001. SAN 321-3358. Tel. 507-625-7555, fax 507-625-4049, e-mail smile @tds.lib.mn.us. *Dir.* Nancy Katharine Steele.

Southeastern Libraries Cooperating (SELCO), 2600 19th St. N.W., Rochester 55901-0767. SAN 308-7417. Tel. 507-288-5513, fax 507-288-8697. *Exec. Dir.* Ann Hutton.

Southwest Area Multicounty Multitype Interlibrary Exchange (SAMMIE), 109 S. 5 St., Suite 30, Marshall 56258-1240. SAN 322-2039. Tel. 507-532-9013, fax 507-532-2039, e-mail info@sammie.org. *Dir.* Robin Chaney.

Twin Cities Biomedical Consortium (TCBC), c/o Fairview Univ. Medical Center, Minneapolis 55455. SAN 322-2055. Tel. 612-273-6595, fax 612-273-2675. *Mgr.* Colleen Olsen.

Mississippi

Central Mississippi Library Council (CMLC), c/o Millsaps College Lib., Jackson 39210. SAN 372-8250. Tel. 601-974-1070, fax 601-974-1082. *Admin./Treas.* Tom Henderson.

Mississippi Electronic Libraries Online (MELO), Mississippi State Board for Community and Junior Colleges, Jackson 39211. Tel. 601-432-6518, fax 601-432-6363, e-mail melo@colin.edu. *Dir.* Audra Kimball.

Missouri

Greater Western Library Alliance (GWLA), 5109 Cherry St., Kansas City 64110. Tel. 816-926-8765, fax 816-926-8790. *Exec. Dir.* Joni Blake.

Health Sciences Library Network of Kansas City (HSLNKC), Univ. of Missouri–Kansas City Health Sciences Lib., Kansas City 64108-2792. SAN 322-2098. Tel. 816-235-1880, fax 816-235-6570. *Dir.* Peggy Mullaly-Quijas.

Kansas City Library Consortium (KCLC), Kansas City Public Lib., Kansas City 64105-1702. Tel. 816-701-3400 ext. 3520, fax 816-701-3401, e-mail kclcsupport@kclibrary.org. *Coord.* Donna Whitner.

Kansas City Metropolitan Library and Information Network, 15624 E. 24 Hwy., Independence 64050. SAN 322-2101. Tel. 816-521-7257, fax 816-461-0966. *Exec. Dir.* Susan Burton.

Missouri Library Network Corp. (MLNC), 8045 Big Bend Blvd., Suite 202, Saint Louis 63119-2714. SAN 322-466X. Tel. 314-918-7222, fax 314-918-7727, e-mail support@mlnc.org. *Exec. Dir.* Tracy Byerly.

Saint Louis Regional Library Network, 341 Sappington Rd., Saint Louis 63122. SAN 322-2209. Tel. 314-395-1305.

Nebraska

ICON Library Consortium, McGoogan Lib. of Medicine, Univ. of Nebraska, Omaha 68198-6705. Tel. 402-559-7099, fax 402-559-5498.

Southeast Nebraska Library System, 5730 R St., Suite C-1, Lincoln 68505. SAN 322-4732. Tel. 402-467-6188, fax 402-467-6196. *Pres.* Glenda Willnerd.

Nevada

Desert States Law Library Consortium, Wiener-Rogers Law Lib., William S. Boyd School of Law, Las Vegas 89154-1080. Tel. 702-895-2400, fax 702-895-2416. *Collection Development Libn.* Matthew Wright.

Information Nevada, Interlibrary Loan Dept., Nevada State Lib. and Archives, Carson City 89701-4285. SAN 322-2276. Tel. 775-684-3328, fax 775-684-3330. *Asst. Admin., Lib. and Development Services* Karen Starr.

New Hampshire

Carroll County Library Cooperative, c/o Conway Public Lib., P.O. Box 2100, Conway 03818. Tel. 603-447-5552, fax 603-447-6921, e-mail tthomas@conway.lib.nh.us. *Dir.* Tara Thomas.

GMILCS, Inc., 1701B Hooksett Rd., Hooksett 03106. Tel. 603-485-4286, fax 603-485-4246, e-mail helpdesk@gmilcs.org. *Chair* Dianne Hathaway.

Health Sciences Libraries of New Hampshire and Vermont, Breene Memorial Lib., New Hampshire Hospital, Concord 03246. SAN 371-6864. Tel. 603-527-2837, fax 603-527-7197. *Admin. Coord.* Marion Allen.

Librarians of the Upper Valley Coop. (LUV Coop), c/o Hanover Town Lib., Etna 03750. SAN 371-6856. Tel. 603-643-3116. *Coord.* Barbara Prince.

Merri-Hill-Rock Library Cooperative, c/o Manchester City Lib., 405 Pine St., Manchester 03104. Tel. 603-624-6550, fax 603-624-6559, e-mail aletourn@manchesternh.gov. *Chair* Arlene Letourneau.

New England Law Library Consortium, Inc. (NELLCO), 9 Drummer Rd., Keene 03431. SAN 322-4244. Tel. 603-357-3385, fax 603-357-2075. *Exec. Dir.* Tracy L. Thompson.

New Hampshire College and University Council, Three Barrell Court, Suite 100, Concord 03301-8543. SAN 322-2322. Tel. 603-225-4199, fax 603-225-8108. *Pres.* Thomas R. Horgan.

Nubanusit Library Cooperative, c/o Peterborough Town Lib., Peterborough 03458. SAN 322-4600. Tel. 603-924-8040, fax 603-924-8041.

Scrooge and Marley Cooperative, 695 Main St., Laconia 03246. SAN 329-515X. Tel. 603-524-4775. *In Charge* Randy Brough.

New Jersey

Basic Health Sciences Library Network (BHSL), Overlook Hospital Health Science Lib., Summit 07902. SAN 371-4888.

Tel. 908-522-2886, fax 908-522-2274. *Coord.* Pat Regenberg.

Bergen Passaic Health Sciences Library Consortium, c/o Health Sciences Lib., Englewood Hospital and Medical Center, Englewood 07631. SAN 371-0904. Tel. 201-894-3069, fax 201-894-9049. *Coord.* Lia Sabbagh.

Burlington Libraries Information Consortium (BLINC), 5 Pioneer Blvd., Westampton 08060. Tel. 609-267-9660, fax 609-267-4091, e-mail hq@bcls.lib.nj.us. *Coord.* Gale Sweet.

Central Jersey Regional Library Cooperative (CJRLC), 4400 Rte. 9 South, Suite 3400, Freehold 07728-4232. SAN 370-5102. Tel. 732-409-6484, fax 732-409-6492, e-mail carol@cjrlc.org. *Exec. Dir.* Connie S. Paul.

Central New Jersey Health Science Libraries Consortium (CNJHSLA), Saint Francis Medical Center Medical Lib., Trenton 08629. SAN 370-0712. Tel. 609-599-5068, fax 609-599-5773. *Libn.* Donna Barlow.

Cosmopolitan Biomedical Library Consortium (CBLC), Overlook Hospital Medical Lib., Summit 07902. SAN 322-4414. Tel. 908-522-2699, fax 908-522-2274. *Coord.* Pat Regenberg.

Health Sciences Library Assn. of New Jersey (HSLANJ), Saint Michaels Medical Center, Newark 07102. SAN 370-0488. Tel. 973-877-5471, fax 973-877-5378. *Dir.* Peter Cole.

Highlands Regional Library Cooperative, 400 Morris Ave., Suite 202, Denville 07834. SAN 329-4609. Tel. 973-664-1776, fax 973-664-1780. *Exec. Dir.* Joanne P. Roukens.

INFOLINK Statewide Library Cooperative, Inc., 44 Stelton Rd., Suite 330, Piscataway 08854. SAN 371-5116. Tel. 732-752-7720, fax 732-752-7785. *Exec. Dir.* Cheryl O'Connor.

Integrated Information Solutions, 600 Mountain Ave., Room 1B 202, Murray Hill 07974. SAN 329-5400. Tel. 908-582-4840, fax 908-582-3146. *Mgr.* M. E. Brennan.

Libraries of Middlesex Automation Consortium (LMxAC), 1030 Saint Georges Ave., Suite 203, Avenel 07001. SAN 329-448X. Tel. 732-750-2525, fax 732-750-9392. *Exec. Dir.* Eileen Palmer.

Monmouth-Ocean Biomedical Information Consortium (MOBIC), Community Medical Center, Toms River 08755. SAN 329-5389. Tel. 732-557-8117, fax 732-557-8354. *Libn.* Reina Reisler.

Morris Automated Information Network (MAIN), c/o Morris County Lib., 30 East Hanover Ave., Whippany 07981. SAN 322-4058. Tel. 973-631-5353, fax 973-631-5366. *Dir.* Jeremy Jenynak.

Morris-Union Federation, 214 Main St., Chatham 07928. SAN 310-2629. Tel. 973-635-0603, fax 973-635-7827.

New Jersey Health Sciences Library Network (NJHSN), Overlook Hospital Lib., Summit 07902. SAN 371-4829. Tel. 908-522-2886, fax 908-522-2274. *Lib. Mgr.* Patricia Regenberg.

New Jersey Library Network, Lib. Development Bureau, Trenton 08608. SAN 372-8161. Tel. 609-278-2640 ext. 152, fax 609-278-2650. *Assoc. State Libn. for Lib. Development* Kathleen Moeller-Peiffer.

South Jersey Regional Library Cooperative, Paint Works Corporate Center, Gibbsboro 08026. SAN 329-4625. Tel. 856-346-1222, fax 856-346-2839. *Exec. Dir.* Karen Hyman.

Virtual Academic Library Environment (VALE), William Paterson Univ. Lib., Wayne 07470-2103. Tel. 973-720-3179, fax 973-720-3171. *Coord.* Judy Avrin.

New Mexico

Alliance for Innovation in Science and Technology Information (AISTI), 369 Montezuma Ave., No. 237, Santa Fe 87501. *Exec. Dir.* Corinne Lebrunn.

Estacado Library Information Network (ELIN), 509 N. Shipp, Hobby 88240. Tel. 505-397-9328, fax 505-397-1508. *System Admin.* Cristine Adams.

New Mexico Consortium of Academic Libraries, Dean's Office, Albuquerque 87131-0001. SAN 371-6872. *Pres.* Ruben Aragon.

New Mexico Consortium of Biomedical and Hospital Libraries, c/o St. Vincent Hospital, Santa Fe 87505. SAN 322-449X. Tel.

505-820-5218, fax 505-989-6478. *Chair* Albert Robinson.

New York

Academic Libraries of Brooklyn, Long Island Univ. Lib. LLC 517, Brooklyn 11201. SAN 322-2411. Tel. 718-488-1081, fax 718-780-4057.

Associated Colleges of the Saint Lawrence Valley, SUNY Potsdam, Potsdam 13676-2299. SAN 322-242X. Tel. 315-267-3331, fax 315-267-2389. *Exec. Dir.* Anneke J. Larrance.

Capital District Library Council (CDLC), 28 Essex St., Albany 12206. SAN 322-2446. Tel. 518-438-2500, fax 518-438-2872. *Exec. Dir.* Jean K. Sheviak.

Central New York Library Resources Council (CLRC), 6493 Ridings Rd., Syracuse 13206-1195. SAN 322-2454. Tel. 315-446-5446, fax 315-446-5590. *Exec. Dir.* Penelope J. Klein.

Connect NY, Rochester Institute of Technology, Rochester 14623. Tel. 585-475-2050. *Dir. of Technology* Chris Lerch.

Council of Archives and Research Libraries in Jewish Studies (CARLJS), 330 7th Ave., 21st flr., New York 10001. SAN 371-053X. Tel. 212-629-0500, fax 212-629-0508, e-mail fjc@jewishculture.org. *Operations Dir.* Michelle Moskowitz Brown.

Library Assn. of Rockland County (LARC), P.O. Box 917, New City 10956-0917. Tel. 845-359-3877. *Pres.* Sara Nugent.

Library Consortium of Health Institutions in Buffalo (LCHIB), Abbott Hall, SUNY at Buffalo, Buffalo 14214. SAN 329-367X. Tel. 716-829-3900 ext. 143, fax 716-829-2211, e-mail hubnet@buffalo.edu; ulb-lchib@buffalo.edu. *Exec. Dir.* Martin E. Mutka.

Long Island Library Resources Council (LILRC), 627 N. Sunrise Service Rd., Bellport 11713. SAN 322-2489. Tel. 631-675-1570. *Dir.* Herbert Biblo.

Medical and Scientific Libraries of Long Island (MEDLI), c/o Palmer School of Lib. and Info. Science, Brookville 11548. SAN 322-4309. Tel. 516-299-2866, fax 516-299-4168. *Chair* Mary Westermann-Cicio.

Metropolitan New York Library Council (METRO), 57 E. 11 St., 4th flr., New York 10003-4605. SAN 322-2500. Tel. 212-228-2320, fax 212-228-2598. *Exec. Dir.* Dottie Hiebing.

National Network of Libraries of Medicine–Middle Atlantic Region (NN/LM-MAR), NYU Medical Center, New York 10010. E-mail rml@library.med.nyu.edu. *Assoc. Dir.* Kathel Dunn.

New York State Higher Education Initiative (NYSHEI), 22 Corporate Woods Blvd., Albany 12211-2350. Fax 518-432-4346, e-mail nyshei@nyshei.org. *Exec. Dir.* Jason Kramer.

Northeast Foreign Law Libraries Cooperative Group, Columbia Univ. Lib., New York 10027. SAN 375-0000. Tel. 212-854-1411, fax 212-854-3295. *Coord.* Silke Sahl.

Northern New York Library Network, 6721 U.S. Hwy. 11, Potsdam 13676. SAN 322-2527. Tel. 315-265-1119, fax 315-265-1881, e-mail info@nnyln.org. *Exec. Dir.* John J. Hammond.

Nylink, 22 Corporate Woods, 3rd flr., Albany 12211. SAN 322-256X. Tel. 518-443-5444, fax 518-432-4346, e-mail nylink@nylink.org. *Exec. Dir.* David Penniman.

Research Library Assn. of South Manhattan, Bobst Lib., New York Univ., New York 10012. SAN 372-8080. Tel. 212-998-2477, fax 212-995-4366. *Dean of Lib.* Carol Mandel.

Rochester Regional Library Council, 390 Packetts Landing, Fairport 14450. SAN 322-2535. Tel. 585-223-7570, fax 585-223-7712, e-mail rrlc@rrlc.org. *Exec. Dir.* Kathleen M. Miller.

South Central Regional Library Council, Clinton Hall, Ithaca 14850. SAN 322-2543. Tel. 607-273-9106, fax 607-272-0740, e-mail scrlc@lakenet.org. *Exec. Dir.* Mary-Carol Lindbloom.

Southeastern New York Library Resources Council (SENYLRC), 21 S. Elting Corners Rd., Highland 12528-2805. SAN 322-2551. Tel. 845-883-9065, fax 845-883-9483. *Exec. Dir.* John L. Shaloiko.

SUNYConnect, Office of Lib. and Info. Services, Albany 12246. Tel. 518-443-5577, fax 518-443-5358. *Asst. Provost for Lib. and Info. Services* Carey Hatch.

United Nations System Electronic Information Acquisitions Consortium (UNSEIAC), c/o United Nations Lib., New York 10017. SAN 377-855X. Tel. 212-963-2026, fax 212-963-2608, e-mail unseiac@un.org. *Coord.* Noriko Gines.

Western New York Library Resources Council, 4455 Genesee St., Buffalo 14225. SAN 322-2578. Tel. 716-633-0705, fax 716-633-1736. *Exec. Dir.* Sheryl Knab.

North Carolina

Cape Fear Health Sciences Information Consortium, 1601 Owen Drive, Fayetteville 28301. SAN 322-3930. Tel. 910-671-5046, fax 910-671-5337. *Dir.* Katherine Mcginniss.

North Carolina Area Health Education Centers, Univ. of North Carolina Health Sciences Lib., CB 7585, Chapel Hill 27599-7585. SAN 323-9950. Tel. 919-962-0700. *Dir.* Diana McDuffee.

North Carolina Community College System, 200 W. Jones St., Raleigh 27603-1379. SAN 322-2594. Tel. 919-807-7100, fax 919-807-7175; 919-807-7164. *Assoc. V.P. for Learning Technology Systems* Bill Randall.

North Carolina Library and Information Network, State Lib. of North Carolina, Raleigh 27601-2807. SAN 329-3092. Tel. 919-807-7400, fax 919-733-8748. *State Libn.* Mary L. Boone.

Northwest AHEC Library at Hickory, Catawba Medical Center, Hickory 28602. SAN 322-4708. Tel. 828-326-3662, fax 828-326-3484. *Dir.* Karen Lee Martinez.

Northwest AHEC Library at Salisbury, c/o Rowan Regional Medical Center, Salisbury 28144. SAN 322-4589. Tel. 704-210-5069, fax 704-636-5050.

Northwest AHEC Library Information Network, Wake Forest Univ. School of Medicine, Winston-Salem 27157-1060. SAN 322-4716. Tel. 336-713-7700, fax 336-713-7701. *Dir.* Mike Lischke.

Triangle Research Libraries Network, Wilson Lib., Chapel Hill 27514-8890. SAN 329-5362. Tel. 919-962-8022, fax 919-962-4452. *Dir.* Mona C. Couts.

Western North Carolina Library Network (WNCLN), c/o Appalachian State Univ., Boone 28608. SAN 376-7205. Tel. 828-262-2774, fax 828-262-3001. *Libn.* Catherine Wilkinson.

North Dakota

Central Dakota Library Network, Morton Mandan Public Lib., Mandan 58554-3149. SAN 373-1391. Tel. 701-667-5365. *Dir.* Kelly Steckler.

Mid-America Law Library Consortium (MALLCO), UALR Bowen School of Law Lib., 1203 McMath Ave., Little Rock 72202. Tel. 501-324-9980, fax 501-324-9447, e-mail sdgoldner@ualr.edu. *Exec. Dir.* Susan Goldner.

Tri-College University Libraries Consortium, NDSU Downtown Campus, Fargo 58102. SAN 322-2047. Tel. 701-231-8170, fax 701-231-7205. *In Charge* Sonia Hohnadel.

Ohio

Assn. of Christian Librarians (ACL), P.O. Box 4, Cedarville 45314. Tel. 937-766-2255, fax 937-766-5499, e-mail info@acl.org. *Pres.* Linda Poston.

Central Ohio Hospital Library Consortium, 127 S Davis Ave., Columbus 43222. SAN 371-084X. Tel. 614-234-5214, fax 614-234-1257, e-mail library@mchs.com. *Dir.* Stevo Roksandic.

Christian Library Consortium (CLC), c/o ACL, Cedarville 45314. Tel. 937-766-2255, fax 937-766-5499, e-mail info@acl.org. *Coord.* Beth Purtee.

Columbus Area Library and Information Council of Ohio (CALICO), c/o Westerville Public Lib., Westerville 43081. SAN 371-683X. Tel. 614-882-7277, fax 614-882-5369.

Consortium of Popular Culture Collections in the Midwest (CPCCM), c/o Popular Culture Lib., Bowling Green 43403-0600. SAN 370-5811. Tel. 419-372-2450, fax 419-372-7996. *Head Libn.* Nancy Down.

Five Colleges of Ohio, 102 Allen House, Gambier 43022. Tel. 740-427-5377, fax 740-427-5390, e-mail ohiofive@gmail.com. *Exec. Dir.* Susan Palmer.

Northeast Ohio Regional Library System (NEO-RLS), 4445 Mahoning Ave. N.W., Warren 44483. SAN 322-2713. Tel. 330-847-7744, fax 330-847-7704. *Exec. Dir.* William Martino.

Northwest Regional Library System (NORWELD), 181½ S. Main St., Bowling Green 43402. SAN 322-273X. Tel. 419-352-2903, fax 419-353-8310. *Dir.* Allan Gray.

OCLC Online Computer Library Center, Inc., 6565 Kilgour Place, Dublin 43017-3395. SAN 322-2748. Tel. 614-764-6000, fax 614-718-1017, e-mail oclc@oclc.org. *Pres./CEO* Jay Jordan.

Ohio Health Sciences Library Assn. (OHSLA), Medical Lib., South Pointe Hospital, Warrensville Heights 44122. Tel. 216-491-7454, fax 216-491-7650. *Pres.* Michelle Kraft.

Ohio Library and Information Network (OhioLINK), 2455 N. Star Rd., Suite 300, Columbus 43221. SAN 374-8014. Tel. 614-728-3600, fax 614-728-3610, e-mail info@ohiolink.edu. *Interim Exec. Dir.* John Magill.

Ohio Network of American History Research Centers, Ohio Historical Society Archives-Lib., Columbus 43211-2497. SAN 323-9624. Tel. 614-297-2510, fax 614-297-2546, e-mail ohsref@ohiohistory.org; reference@ohiohistory.org. *Research* Louise Jones.

Ohio Public Library Information Network (OPLIN), 2323 W. 5 Ave., Suite 130, Columbus 43204. Tel. 614-728-5252, fax 614-728-5256, e-mail support@oplin.org. *Exec. Dir.* Stephen Hedges.

OHIONET, 1500 W. Lane Ave., Columbus 43221-3975. SAN 322-2764. Tel. 614-486-2966, fax 614-486-1527. *Exec. Officer* Michael P. Butler.

Rural Ohio Valley Health Sciences Library Network (ROVHSLN), Southern State Community College–South, Sardinia 45171. Tel. 937-695-0307 ext. 3681, fax 937-695-1440. *Mgr.* Mary Ayres.

Southeast Regional Library System (SERLS), 252 W. 13 St., Wellston 45692. SAN 322-2756. Tel. 740-384-2103, fax 740-384-2106, e-mail dirserls@oplin.org. *Exec. Dir.* Mary Leffler.

SouthWest Ohio and Neighboring Libraries (SWON), 10815 Indeco Drive, Suite 200, Cincinnati 45241-2926. SAN 322-2675. Tel. 513-751-4422, fax 513-751-0463, e-mail info@swonlibraries.org. *Exec. Dir.* Anne K. Abate.

Southwestern Ohio Council for Higher Education (SOCHE), Miami Valley Research Park, Dayton 45420-4015. SAN 322-2659. Tel. 937-258-8890, fax 937-258-8899, e-mail soche@soche.org.

State Assisted Academic Library Council of Kentucky (SAALCK), c/o SWON Libs., Cincinnati 45241. SAN 371-2222. Tel. 513-751-4422, fax 513-751-0463, e-mail saalck@saalck.org. *Exec. Dir.* Anne Abate.

Theological Consortium of Greater Columbus (TCGC), Trinity Lutheran Seminary, Columbus 43209-2334. Tel. 614-384-4646, fax 614-238-0263. *Lib. Systems Mgr.* Ray Olson.

Oklahoma

Greater Oklahoma Area Health Sciences Library Consortium (GOAL), Resource Center, Mercy Memorial Health Center, Ardmore 73401. SAN 329-3858. Tel. 580-220-6625, fax 580-220-6599. *Pres.* Catherine Ice.

Oklahoma Health Sciences Library Assn. (OHSLA), HSC Bird Health Science Lib., Univ. of Oklahoma, Oklahoma City 73190. SAN 375-0051. Tel. 405-271-2285 ext. 48755, fax 405-271-3297. *Dir.* Clinton M. Thompson.

Oregon

Chemeketa Cooperative Regional Library Service, c/o Chemeketa Community College, Salem 97305-1453. SAN 322-2837. Tel. 503-399-5105, fax 503-399-7316, e-mail cocl@chemeketa.edu. *Coord.* Linda Cochrane.

Coastal Resource Sharing Network (CRSN), c/o Tillamook County Lib., Tillamook 97141. Tel. 503-842-4792, fax 503-815-8194, e-mail webmaster@beachbooks.org. *Pres.* Jill Tierce.

Coos County Library Service District, Tioga, 3rd flr., 1988 Newmark, Coos Bay 97420.

SAN 322-4279. Tel. 541-888-1529, fax 541-888-1529. *Dir.* Mary Jane Fisher.

Gorge LINK Library Consortium, c/o Hood River County Lib., Hood River 97031. Tel. 541-387-4659; 541-386-2535, fax 541-386-3835, e-mail gorgelinklibrary@gorge.net. *System Admin.* Jayne Guidinger.

Library Information Network of Clackamas County, 16239 S.E. McLoughlin Blvd., Suite 208, Oak Grove 97267-4654. SAN 322-2845. Tel. 503-723-4888, fax 503-794-8238, e-mail webmaster@lincc.org. *Mgr.* Joanna Rood.

Orbis Cascade Alliance, 1501 Kincaid, No. 4, Eugene 97401-4540. SAN 377-8096. Tel. 541-346-1832, fax 541-346-1968. *Chair* Lee Lyttle.

Oregon Health Sciences Libraries Assn. (OHSLA), Oregon Health and Science Univ. Lib., Portland 97239-3098. SAN 371-2176. Tel. 503-494-3462, fax 503-494-3322, e-mail library@ohsu.edu.

Portland Area Library System (PORTALS), Port Community College, SYLIB202, Portland 97219. Tel. 503-977-4571, fax 503-977-4977. *Coord.* Roberta Richards.

Southern Oregon Library Federation, c/o Klamath County Lib., Klamath Falls 97601. SAN 322-2861. Tel. 541-882-8894, fax 541-882-6166. *Dir.* Andy Swanson.

Southern Oregon Library Information System (SOLIS), 724 S. Central Ave., Suite 112, Medford 97501. Tel. 541-772-2141, fax 541-772-2144, e-mail solis_97501@yahoo.com. *System Admin.* Marian Stoner.

Washington County Cooperative Library Services, 111 N.E. Lincoln St., MS No. 58, Hillsboro 97124-3036. SAN 322-287X. Tel. 503-846-3222, fax 503-846-3220. *Mgr.* Eva Calcagno.

Pennsylvania

Associated College Libraries of Central Pennsylvania, P.O. Box 39, Grantham 17027. E-mail aclcp@aclcp.org. *Pres.* Gregory Crawford.

Berks County Library Assn. (BCLA), Reading Public Lib., Reading 19602. SAN 371-0866. Tel. 610-478-9035; 610-655-6350. *Pres.* Jennifer Balas.

Central Pennsylvania Consortium (CPC), Dickinson College, Carlisle 17013. SAN 322-2896. Tel. 717-245-1984, fax 717-245-1807, e-mail cpc@dickinson.edu. *Pres.* Katherine Haley Will.

Central Pennsylvania Health Sciences Library Assn. (CPHSLA), Office for Research Protections, Pennsylvania State Univ., University Park 16802. SAN 375-5290. Fax 814-865-1775. *Pres.* Tracie Kahler.

Cooperating Hospital Libraries of the Lehigh Valley Area, Estes Lib., Saint Luke's Hospital, Bethlehem 18015. SAN 371-0858. Tel. 610-954-3407, fax 610-954-4651. *Chair* Sharon Hrabina.

Delaware Valley Information Consortium (DEVIC), St. Mary Medical Center Medical Lib., Langhorne 19047. Tel. 215-710-2012, fax 215-710-4638. *Dir.* Rita Haydar.

Eastern Mennonite Associated Libraries and Archives (EMALA), 2215 Millstream Rd., Lancaster 17602. SAN 372-8226. Tel. 717-393-9745, fax 717-393-8751. *Chair* Edsel Burdge.

Erie Area Health Information Library Cooperative (EAHILC), Nash Lib., Gannon Univ., Erie 16541. SAN 371-0564. Tel. 814-871-7667, fax 814-871-5566. *Chair* Deborah West.

Greater Philadelphia Law Library Assn. (GPLLA), Wolf, Block, Schorr and Solis-Cohen LLP Lib., 25th flr., Philadelphia 19103. SAN 373-1375. *Pres.* Monica Almendarez.

HSLC/Access PA (Health Science Libraries Consortium), 3600 Market St., Suite 550, Philadelphia 19104-2646. SAN 323-9780. Tel. 215-222-1532, fax 215-222-0416, e-mail support@hslc.org. *Exec. Dir.* Joseph C. Scorza.

Interlibrary Delivery Service of Pennsylvania (IDS), c/o Bucks County IU, No. 22, Doylestown 18901. SAN 322-2942. Tel. 215-348-2940 ext. 1620, fax 215-348-8315, e-mail ids@bucksiu.org. *Admin. Dir.* Beverly J. Carey.

Keystone Library Network, Dixon Univ. Center, Harrisburg 17110-1201. Tel. 717-720-4088, fax 717-720-4453. *Coord.* Mary Lou Sowden.

Laurel Highlands Health Science Library Consortium, 361 Sunrise Rd., Dayton

16222. SAN 322-2950. Tel. 814-341-0242, fax 814-266-8230. *Dir.* Rhonda Yeager.

Lehigh Valley Assn. of Independent Colleges, 130 W. Greenwich St., Bethlehem 18018. SAN 322-2969. Tel. 610-625-7888, fax 610-625-7891. *Exec. Dir.* Bonnie Lynch.

Montgomery County Library and Information Network Consortium (MCLINC), 301 Lafayette St., 2nd flr., Conshohocken 19428. Tel. 610-238-0580, fax 610-238-0581, e-mail webmaster@mclinc.org. *Pres.* Carrie L. Turner.

Northeastern Pennsylvania Library Network, c/o Marywood Univ. Lib., Scranton 18509-1598. SAN 322-2993. Tel. 570-348-6260, fax 570-961-4769. *Exec. Dir.* Catherine H. Schappert.

Northwest Interlibrary Cooperative of Pennsylvania (NICOP), Mercyhurst College Lib., Erie 16546. SAN 370-5862. Tel. 814-824-2190, fax 814-824-2219. *Archivist* Earleen Glaser.

Pennsylvania Library Assn., 220 Cumberland Pkwy, Suite 10, Mechanicsburg 17055. Tel. 717-766-7663, fax 717-766-5440. *Exec. Dir.* Glenn R. Miller.

Philadelphia Area Consortium of Special Collections Libraries (PACSCL), P.O. Box 22642, Philadelphia 19110-2642. Tel. 215-985-1445, fax 215-985-1446, email lblanchard@pacscl.org. *Exec. Dir.* Laura Blanchard.

Southeastern Pennsylvania Theological Library Assn. (SEPTLA), c/o Biblical Seminary, Hatfield 19440. SAN 371-0793. Tel. 215-368-5000 ext. 234. *Chair* Daniel LaValla.

State System of Higher Education Library Cooperative (SSHELCO), c/o Bailey Lib., Slippery Rock 16057. Tel. 724-738-2630, fax 724-738-2661. *Dir.* Philip Tramdack.

Susquehanna Library Cooperative (SLC), Stevenson Lib., Lock Haven Univ., Lock Haven 17745. SAN 322-3051. Tel. 570-484-2310, fax 570-484-2506. *Dean of Lib. and Info. Services.* Tara Lynn Fulton.

Tri-State College Library Cooperative (TCLC), c/o Rosemont College Lib., Rosemont 19010-1699. SAN 322-3078. Tel. 610-525-0796, fax 610-525-1939, e-mail office@tclclibs.org. *Coord.* Ellen Gasiewski.

Rhode Island

Library of Rhode Island Network (LORI), c/o Office of Lib. and Info. Services, Providence 02908-5870. SAN 371-6821. Tel. 401-574-9300, fax 401-574-9320. *Lib. Services Dir.* Howard Boksenbaum.

Ocean State Libraries (OSL), 300 Centerville Rd., Suite 103S, Warwick 02886-0226. SAN 329-4560. Tel. 401-738-2200, fax 401-736-8949, e-mail support@oslri.net. *Exec. Dir.* Joan Gillespie.

South Carolina

Charleston Academic Libraries Consortium (CALC), P.O. Box 118067, Charleston 29423-8067. SAN 371-0769. Tel. 843-574-6088, fax 843-574-6484. *Chair* Drucie Gullion.

Columbia Area Medical Librarians' Assn. (CAMLA), School of Medicine Lib., Univ. of South Carolina, Columbia 29209. SAN 372-9400. Tel. 803-733-3361, fax 803-733-1509. *Pres.* Roz Anderson.

Partnership Among South Carolina Academic Libraries (PASCAL), 1333 Main St., Suite 305, Columbia 29201. Tel. 803-734-0900, fax 803-734-0901. *Exec. Dir.* Rick Moul.

South Carolina AHEC, c/o Medical Univ. of South Carolina, Charleston 29425. SAN 329-3998. Tel. 843-792-4431, fax 843-792-4430. *Exec. Dir.* David Garr.

South Carolina State Library/South Carolina Library Network, 1430 and 1500 Senate St., Columbia 29201. SAN 322-4198. Tel. 803-734-8666, fax 803-734-8676, e-mail reference@statelibrary.sc.gov. *Dir. of Lib. and Info. Services.* Mary Morgan.

South Dakota

South Dakota Library Network (SDLN), 1200 University, Unit 9672, Spearfish 57799-9672. SAN 371-2117. Tel. 605-642-6835, fax 605-642-6472, e-mail help@sdln.net. *Dir.* Warren Wilson.

Tennessee

Consortium of Southern Biomedical Libraries (CONBLS), Meharry Medical College, Nashville 37208. SAN 370-7717. Tel. 615-327-6728, fax 615-327-6448. *Chair* Barbara Shearer.

Knoxville Area Health Sciences Library Consortium (KAHSLC), Univ. of Tennessee Preston Medical Lib., Knoxville 37920. SAN 371-0556. Tel. 865-305-9525, fax 865-305-9527. *Pres.* Cynthia Vaughn.

Mid-Tennessee Health Science Librarians Assn., VA Medical Center, Nashville 37212. SAN 329-5028. Tel. 615-327-4751 ext. 5523, fax 615-321-6336.

Tennessee Health Science Library Assn. (THeSLA), Holston Valley Medical Center Health Sciences Lib., Kingsport 37660. SAN 371-0726. Tel. 423-224-6870, fax 423-224-6014. *Coord., Lib. Services* Sharon M. Brown.

Tri-Cities Area Health Sciences Libraries Consortium (TCAHSLC), James H. Quillen College of Medicine, East Tennessee State Univ., Johnson City 37614. SAN 329-4099. Tel. 423-439-6252, fax 423-439-7025. *Dir.* Biddanda Ponnappa.

Wolf River Library Consortium, c/o Germantown Community Lib., Germantown 38138-2815. Tel. 901-757-7323, fax 901-756-9940. *Dir.* Melody Pittman.

Texas

Abilene Library Consortium, 3305 N. 3 St., Suite 301, Abilene 79603. SAN 322-4694. Tel. 325-672-7081, fax 325-672-7082. *Coord.* Edward J. Smith.

Amigos Library Services, Inc., 14400 Midway Rd., Dallas 75244-3509. SAN 322-3191. Tel. 972-851-8000, fax 972-991-6061, e-mail amigos@amigos.org. *Exec. Dir.* Bonnie Juergens.

Council of Research and Academic Libraries (CORAL), P.O. Box 290236, San Antonio 78280-1636. SAN 322-3213. Tel. 210-458-4885. *Coord.* Rosemary Vasquez.

Del Norte Biosciences Library Consortium, El Paso Community College, El Paso 79998. SAN 322-3302. Tel. 915-831-4149, fax 915-831-4639. *Coord.* Becky Perales.

Harrington Library Consortium, 413 E. 4 Ave., Amarillo 79101. SAN 329-546X. Tel. 806-378-6037, fax 806-378-6038. *Dir.* Donna Littlejohn.

Health Libraries Information Network (Health LINE), Univ. of Texas Southwestern Medical Center Lib., Dallas 75390-9049. SAN 322-3299. Tel. 214-648-2626, fax 214-648-2826.

Houston Area Library Automation Network (HALAN), Houston Public Lib., Houston 77002. Tel. 832-393-1411, fax 832-393-1427, e-mail website@hpl.lib.tx.us. *Chief* Judith Hiott.

Houston Area Research Library Consortium (HARLiC), c/o Univ. of Houston Libs., Houston 77204-2000. SAN 322-3329. Tel. 713-743-9807, fax 713-743-9811. *Pres.* Dana Rooks.

National Network of Libraries of Medicine–South Central Region (NN/LM-SCR), c/o HAM-TMC Library, Houston 77030-2809. SAN 322-3353. Tel. 713-799-7880, fax 713-790-7030, e-mail nnlm-scr@exch.library.tmc.edu. *Dir.* L. Maximillian Buja.

Northeast Texas Library System (NETLS), 4845 Broadway Blvd., Garland 75043-7016. SAN 370-5943. Tel. 972-205-2566, fax 972-205-2767. *Major Resource Center Dir.* Claire Bausch.

South Central Academic Medical Libraries Consortium (SCAMeL), c/o Lewis Lib.-UNTHSC, Fort Worth 76107. SAN 372-8269. Tel. 817-735-2380, fax 817-735-5158. *Assoc. V.P. for Info. Resources/Treas.* Bobby Carter.

Texas Council of Academic Libraries (TCAL), VC/UHV Lib., Victoria 77901. SAN 322-337X. Tel. 361-570-4150, fax 361-570-4155. *Chair* Joe Dahlstrom.

Texnet, P.O. Box 12927, Austin 78711. SAN 322-3396. Tel. 512-463-5406, fax 512-936-2306, e-mail ill@tsl.state.tx.us.

Western Council of State Libraries, Inc., Idaho Commission for Libraries, Boise 83702-6055. Tel. 208-334-2150, fax 208-334-4016. *Pres.* Ann Joslin.

Utah

National Network of Libraries of Medicine–MidContinental Region (NN/LM-MCR),

Spencer S. Eccles Health Sciences Lib., Univ. of Utah, Salt Lake City 84112-5890. SAN 322-225X. Tel. 801-587-3412, fax 801-581-3632. *Dir.* Wayne J. Peay.

Utah Academic Library Consortium (UALC), Univ. of Utah, Salt Lake City 84112-0731. SAN 322-3418. Tel. 801-581-3386; 801-581-6594, fax 801-585-3033, e-mail ualcmail@library.utah.edu. *Dir.* Rita Reusch.

Utah Health Sciences Library Consortium, c/o Spencer S. Eccles Health Sciences Lib., Univ. of Utah, Salt Lake City 84112-5890. SAN 376-2246. Tel. 801-585-5743, fax 801-581-3632. *Chair* John Bramble.

Vermont

North Atlantic Health Sciences Libraries, Inc. (NAHSL), Dana Medical Lib., Univ. of Vermont Medical School, Burlington 05405. SAN 371-0599. Tel. 508-656-3483, fax 508-656-0762. *Chair* Susan Warthman.

Vermont Resource Sharing Network, c/o Vermont Dept. of Libs., Montpelier 05609-0601. SAN 322-3426. Tel. 802-828-3261, fax 802-828-1481. *Libn.* Gerrie Denison.

Virgin Islands

Vilinet/Virgin Islands Library and Information Network, c/o Div. of Libs., Archives, and Museums, Saint Thomas 00802. SAN 322-3639. Tel. 340-773-5715, fax 340-773-3257, e-mail info@vilinet.net. *Territorial Dir. of Libs., Archives, and Museums* Ingrid Bough.

Virginia

American Indian Higher Education Consortium (AIHEC), 121 Oronoco St., Alexandria 22314. SAN 329-4056. Tel. 703-838-0400, fax 703-838-0388, e-mail info@aihec.org.

Lynchburg Area Library Cooperative, c/o Sweet Briar College Lib., Sweet Briar 24595. SAN 322-3450. Tel. 434-381-6315, fax 434-381-6173.

Lynchburg Information Online Network (LION), 2315 Memorial Ave., Lynchburg 24503. SAN 374-6097. Tel. 434-381-6311, fax 434-381-6173. *Dir.* John G. Jaffee.

NASA Libraries Information System–NASA Galaxie, NASA Langley Research Center, MS 185-Technical Lib., Hampton 23681-2199. SAN 322-0788. Tel. 757-864-2356, fax 757-864-2375, e-mail tech-library@larc.nasa.gov. *Coord.* Manjula Ambur.

Richmond Academic Library Consortium (RALC), James Branch Cabell Lib., Virginia Commonwealth Univ., Richmond 23284. SAN 322-3469. Tel. 804-828-1110; 804-828-1107, fax 804-828-1105; 804-828-0151. *Univ. Libn.* John E. Ulmschneider.

Southside Virginia Library Network (SVLN), Longwood Univ., Farmville 23909-1897. SAN 372-8242. Tel. 434-395-2431; 434-395-2433, fax 434-395-2453. *Dir.* Wendell Barbour.

Southwestern Virginia Health Information Librarians (SWVAHILI), Carilion Health Sciences Lib., Roanoke 24033. SAN 323-9527. Tel. 540-433-4166, fax 540-433-3106. *Chair* George Curran.

United States Army Training and Doctrine Command (TRADOC)/Lib. Program Office, U.S. Army Hq TRADOC, Fort Monroe 23651. SAN 322-418X. Tel. 757-788-2155, fax 757-788-5544. *Dir.* Amy Loughran.

Virginia Independent College and University Library Assn., c/o Mary Helen Cochran Lib., Sweet Briar 24595. SAN 374-6089. Tel. 434-381-6139, fax 434-381-6173. *Dir.* John Jaffee.

Virginia Tidewater Consortium for Higher Education (VTC), 4900 Powhatan Ave., Norfolk 23529. SAN 329-5486. Tel. 757-683-3183, fax 757-683-4515, e-mail lgdotolo@aol.com. *Pres.* Lawrence G. Dotolo.

Virtual Library of Virginia (VIVA), George Mason Univ., Fairfax 22030. Tel. 703-993-4652, fax 703-993-4662. *Dir.* Katherine Perry.

Washington

Cooperating Libraries in Olympia (CLIO), Evergreen State College Library, L2300, Olympia 98505. SAN 329-4528. Tel. 360-

867-6260, fax 360-867-6790. *Dean, Lib. Services* Lee Lyttle.

Inland NorthWest Health Sciences Libraries (INWHSL), P.O. Box 10283, Spokane 99209-0283. SAN 370-5099. Tel. 509-368-6973, fax 509-358-7928. *Treas.* Robert Pringle.

National Network of Libraries of Medicine–Pacific Northwest Region (NN/LM-PNR), T-344 Health Sciences Bldg., Univ. of Washington, Seattle 98195. SAN 322-3485. Tel. 206-543-8262, fax 206-543-2469, e-mail nnlm@u.washington.edu. *Dir.* Neil Rambo.

Palouse Area Library Information Services (PALIS), c/o Neill Public Lib., Pullman 99163. SAN 375-0132. Tel. 509-334-3595, fax 509-334-6051. *Dir.* Andriette Pieron.

Washington Idaho Network (WIN), Foley Center Lib., Gonzaga Univ., Spokane 99258. Tel. 509-323-6545, fax 509-324-5398, e-mail winsupport@gonzaga.edu. *Pres.* Eileen Bell-Garrison.

West Virginia

Mid-Atlantic Law Library Cooperative (MALLCO), College of Law Lib., Morgantown 26506-6135. SAN 371-0645. Tel. 304-293-7641, fax 304-293-6020. *Lib. Dir.* Camille M. Riley.

Wisconsin

Arrowhead Health Sciences Library Network, Wisconsin Indianhead Technical College, Shell Lake 54817. SAN 322-1954. Tel. 715-468-2815 ext. 2298, fax 715-468-2819. *Coord.* Judy Lyons.

Fox River Valley Area Library Consortium (FRVALC), c/o Polk Lib., Univ. of Wisconsin–Oshkosh, Oshkosh 54901. SAN 322-3531. Tel. 920-424-3348; 920-424-4333, fax 920-424-2175. *Coord.* Jeff Brunner.

Fox Valley Library Council, c/o OWLS, Appleton 54911. SAN 323-9640. Tel. 920-832-6190, fax 920-832-6422. *Pres.* Joy Schwarz.

Library Council of Southeastern Wisconsin, Inc., 814 W. Wisconsin Ave., Milwaukee 53233-2309. SAN 322-354X. Tel. 414-271-8470, fax 414-286-2798. *Exec. Dir.* Susie M. Just.

North East Wisconsin Intertype Libraries, Inc. (NEWIL), 515 Pine St., Green Bay 54301. SAN 322-3574. Tel. 920-448-4412, fax 920-448-4420. *Dir.* Mark Merrifield.

Northwestern Wisconsin Health Science Library Consortium, c/o Gundersen Lutheran Medical Center, Lacrosse 54601. Tel. 608-775-5410, fax 608-775-6343. *Treas.* Eileen Severson.

South Central Wisconsin Health Science Library Consortium, c/o Fort Healthcare Medical Lib., Fort Atkinson 53538. SAN 322-4686. Tel. 920-568-5194, fax 920-568-5195. *Coord.* Carrie Garity.

Southeastern Wisconsin Health Science Library Consortium, Veterans Admin. Center Medical Lib., Milwaukee 53295. SAN 322-3582. Tel. 414-384-2000 ext. 42342, fax 414-382-5334. *Coord.* Janice Curnes.

Southeastern Wisconsin Information Technology Exchange, Inc. (SWITCH), 6801 N. Yates Rd., Milwaukee 53217-3985. SAN 371-3962. Tel. 414-351-2423, fax 414-228-4146. *Coord.* William A. Topritzhofer.

University of Wisconsin System School Library Education Consortium (UWSSLEC), Graduate and Continuing Educ., Univ. of Wisconsin–Whitewater, Whitewater 53190. Tel. 262-472-1463, fax 262-472-5210, e-mail lenchoc@uww.edu. *Co-Dir.* E. Anne Zarinnia.

Wisconsin Library Services (WILS), 728 State St., Room 464, Madison 53706-1494. SAN 322-3612. Tel. 608-265-0580; 608-263-4981; 608-265-4167, fax 608-262-6067; 608-263-3684. *Dir.* Kathryn Schneider Michaelis.

Wisconsin Public Library Consortium (WPLC), c/o South Central Lib. System, Madison 53718. *Dir.* Phyllis Davis.

Wisconsin Valley Library Service (WVLS), 300 N. 1 St., Wausau 54403. SAN 371-3911. Tel. 715-261-7250, fax 715-261-7259. *Dir.* Marla Rae Sepnafski.

WISPALS Library Consortium, c/o Gateway Technical College, Kenosha 53144-1690. Tel. 262-564-2602, fax 262-564-2787.

Wyoming

WYLD Network, c/o Wyoming State Lib., Cheyenne 82002-0060. SAN 371-0661. Tel. 307-777-6339, fax 307-777-6289, e-mail wyldstaff@will.state.wy.us. *State Libn.* Lesley Boughton.

Canada

Alberta

The Alberta Library (TAL), 6-14, 7 Sir Winston Churchill Sq., Edmonton T5J 2V5. Tel. 780-414-0805, fax 780-414-0806, e-mail admin@thealbertalibrary.ab.ca. *CEO* Maureen Woods.

NEOS Library Consortium, Cameron Lib., 5th flr., Edmonton T6G 2J8. Tel. 780-492-0075, fax 780-492-8302. *Mgr.* Margaret Law.

British Columbia

British Columbia Academic Health Council (BCAHC), 402-1770 W. 7 Ave., Vancouver V6J 4Y6. Tel. 604-739-3910 ext. 228, fax 604-739-3931, e-mail info@bcahc.ca. *CEO* George Eisler.

British Columbia Electronic Library Network (BCELN), WAC Bennett Lib., 7th flr., Simon Fraser Univ., Burnaby V5A 1S6. Tel. 778-782-7003, fax 778-782-3023, e-mail office@eln.bc.ca. *Exec. Dir.* Anita Cocchia.

British Columbia College and Institute Library Services, Langara College Lib., Vancouver V5Y 2Z6. SAN 329-6970. Tel. 604-323-5639, fax 604-323-5544, e-mail cils@langara.bc.ca. *Dir.* Mary Anne Epp.

Council of Prairie and Pacific University Libraries (COPPUL), 2005 Sooke Rd., Victoria V9B 5Y2. Tel. 250-391-2554, fax 250-391-2556, e-mail coppul@royalroads.ca. *Exec. Dir.* Alexander Slade.

Electronic Health Library of British Columbia (e-HLbc), c/o Bennett Lib., Burnaby V5A 1S6. Tel. 778-782-5440, fax 778-782-3023, e-mail info@ehlbc.ca. *Coord.* JoAnne Newyear-Ramirez.

Public Library InterLINK, c/o Burnaby Public Lib.–Kingsway Branch, Burnaby V5E 1G3. SAN 318-8272. Tel. 604-517-8441, fax 604-517-8410, e-mail info@interlinklibraries.ca. *Operations Mgr.* Rita Avigdor.

Manitoba

Manitoba Government Libraries Council (MGLC), c/o Instructional Resources Unit, Winnipeg R3G 0T3. SAN 371-6848. Tel. 204-945-7833, fax 204-945-8756. *Chair* John Tooth.

Manitoba Library Consortium, Inc. (MLCI), c/o Lib. Admin., Univ. of Winnipeg, Winnipeg R3B 2E9. SAN 372-820X. Tel. 204-786-9801, fax 204-783-8910. *Chair* Judy Inglis.

Nova Scotia

Maritimes Health Libraries Assn. (MHLA-ABSM), W. K. Kellogg Health Sciences Lib., Halifax B3H 1X5. SAN 370-0836. Tel. 902-494-2483, fax 902-494-3750. *Libn.* Shelley McKibbon.

NOVANET, 1550 Bedford Hwy., No 501, Bedford B4A 1E6. SAN 372-4050. Tel. 902-453-2470, fax 902-453-2369, e-mail office@novanet.ns.ca. *Mgr.* Bill Slauenwhite.

Ontario

Bibliocentre, 31 Scarsdale Rd., North York M3B 2R2. SAN 322-3663. Tel. 647-722-9300, fax 647-722-9301. *Operations Dir.* Andre Paradis.

Canadian Assn. of Research Libraries (Association des Bibliothèques de Recherche du Canada), Morisset Hall, Room 238, Ottawa K1N 9A5. SAN 323-9721. Tel. 613-562-5385, fax 613-562-5297, e-mail carladm@uottawa.ca. *Exec. Dir.* Brent Roe.

Canadian Health Libraries Assn. (CHLA-ABSC), 39 River St., Toronto M5A 3P1. SAN 370-0720. Tel. 416-646-1600, fax 416-646-9460, e-mail info@chla-absc.ca. *Pres.* Susan Powelson.

Canadian Research Knowledge Network (CRKN), Preston Sq., Tower 2, Ottawa K1S IN4. Tel. 613-907-7040, fax 866-903-9094. *Exec. Dir.* Deb deBruijn.

Consortium of Ontario Libraries (COOL), 111 Peter St., Suite 902, Toronto M5V

2H1. Tel. 416-961-1669, fax 416-961-5122. *Dir.* Barbara Franchetto.

Hamilton and District Health Library Network, c/o St Josephs Healthcare Hamilton, Sherman Lib., Room T2305, Hamilton L8N 4A6. SAN 370-5846. Tel. 905-522-1155 ext. 3410, fax 905-540-6504. *Coord.* Jean Maragno.

Health Science Information Consortium of Toronto, c/o Gerstein Science Info. Center, Univ. of Toronto, Toronto M5S 1A5. SAN 370-5080. Tel. 416-978-6359, fax 416-971-2637. *Exec. Dir.* Miriam Ticoll.

Ontario Council of University Libraries (OCUL), 130 Saint George St., Toronto M5S 1A5. Tel. 416-946-0578, fax 416-978-6755. *Exec. Dir.* Kathy Scardellato.

Ontario Health Libraries Assn. (OHLA), c/o Salt Area Hospital Lib., Sault Ste. Marie P6A 2C4. SAN 370-0739. Tel. 705-759-3434, fax 705-759-3640. *Pres.* Kimberley Aslett.

Ontario Library Consortium (OLC), Owen Sound and North Grey Union Public Lib., Owen Sound N4K 4K4. *Pres.* Judy Armstrong.

Parry Sound and Area Access Network, c/o Parry Sound Public Lib., Parry Sound P2A 1E3. Tel. 705-746-9601, fax 705-746-9601, e-mail pspl@vianet.ca. *Chair* Laurine Tremaine.

Perth County Information Network (PCIN), c/o Stratford Public Lib., Stratford N5A 1A2. Tel. 519-271-0220, fax 519-271-3843, e-mail webmaster@pcin.on.ca. *CEO* Sam Coglin.

Shared Library Services (SLS), South Huron Hospital, Exeter N0M 1S2. SAN 323-9500. Tel. 519-235-5168, fax 519-235-4476, e-mail shha.sls@shha.on.ca. *Libn.* Linda Wilcox.

Southwestern Ontario Health Libraries and Information Network (SOHLIN), St. Joseph's Health Care London–Regional Mental Health Staff Libs., St. Thomas N5P 3V9. Tel. 519-631-8510 ext. 49685. *Pres.* Elizabeth Russell.

Toronto Health Libraries Assn. (THLA), 3409 Yonge St., Toronto M4N 2L0. SAN 323-9853. Tel. 416-485-0377, fax 416-485-6877, e-mail medinfoserv@rogers.com. *Pres.* Graziela Alexandria.

Quebec

Assn. des Bibliothèques de la Santé Affiliées a l'Université de Montréal (ABSAUM), c/o Health Lib., Univ. of Montreal, Montreal H3C 3J7. SAN 370-5838. Tel. 514-343-6826, fax 514-343-2350. *Dir.* Monique St-Jean.

Canadian Heritage Information Network (CHIN), 15 Eddy St., 4th flr., Gatineau K1A 0M5. SAN 329-3076. Tel. 819-994-1200, fax 819-994-9555, e-mail service@chin.gc.ca. *CEO* Gabrielle Blais.

National Library and Information-Industry Associations, United States and Canada

American Association of Law Libraries

Executive Director, Kate Hagan
105 W. Adams St., Suite 3300, Chicago, IL 60603
312-939-4764, fax 312-431-1097, e-mail khagan@aall.org
World Wide Web http://www.aallnet.org

Object

The American Association of Law Libraries (AALL) is established for educational and scientific purposes. It shall be conducted as a nonprofit corporation to promote and enhance the value of law libraries to the public, the legal community, and the world; to foster the profession of law librarianship; to provide leadership in the field of legal information; and to foster a spirit of cooperation among the members of the profession. Established 1906.

Membership

Memb. 5,000+. Persons officially connected with a law library or with a law section of a state or general library, separately maintained. Associate membership available for others. Dues (Indiv.) $222; (Associate) $222; (Retired) $56; (Student) $56. Year. July 1–June 30.

Officers

Pres. Joyce Manna Janto, Univ. of Richmond School of Law Lib., 28 Westhampton Way, Richmond, VA 23173-0002. Tel. 804-289-8223, fax 804-289-8683, e-mail jjanto@richmond.edu; *V.P.* Darcy Clark; *Secy.* Ruth J. Hill. E-mail rhill@sulc.edu; *Treas.* Susan J. Lewis; *Past Pres.* Catherine Lemann, Alaska State Court Law Lib., Anchorage, AK 99501. Tel. 907 264 0583, fax 907-264-0599, e-mail clemann@courts.state.ak.us.

Executive Board

Carol Bredemeyer, Lucy Curci-Gonzalez, Christine L Graesser, Janet McKinney, Janet McKinney, Ronald E. Wheeler, Jr., Donna S. Williams.

American Library Association

Executive Director, Keith Michael Fiels
50 E. Huron St., Chicago, IL 60611
800-545-2433, 312-280-1392, fax 312-440-9374
World Wide Web http://www.ala.org

Object

The mission of the American Library Association (ALA) is to provide leadership for the development, promotion, and improvement of library and information services and the profession of librarianship in order to enhance learning and ensure access to information for all. Founded 1876.

Membership

Memb. (Indiv.) 57,933; (Inst.) 3,034; (Corporate) 231; (Total) 61,198 (as of December 2010). Any person, library, or other organization interested in library service and librarians. Dues (Indiv.) 1st year, $65; 2nd year, $98; 3rd year and later, $130; (Trustee and Assoc. Memb.) $59; (Lib. Support Staff) $46; (Student) $33; (Foreign Indiv.) $78; (Other) $46; (Inst.) $110 and up, depending on operating expenses of institution.

Officers (2010–2011)

Pres. Roberta Stevens, Lib. of Congress. E-mail roberta@robertastevens.com; *Pres.-Elect* Molly Raphael, Multnomah County (Oregon) Lib. E-mail mollyr@multcolib.org; *Past Pres.* Camila Alire, Univ. of New Mexico and Colorado State Univ. E-mail calire@att.net; *Treas.* James Neal, Columbia Univ. E-mail jneal@columbia.edu.

Executive Board

Diane R. Chen (2011), Joseph M. Eagan (2011), Patricia M. Hogan (2012), Em Claire Knowles (2011), Charles E. Kratz, Jr. (2010), Stephen L. Matthews (2012), Kevin Reynolds (2013), J. Linda Williams (2013), Courtney L. Young (2012).

Endowment Trustees

Daniel J. Bradbury (chair) (2012), John Vitali (2010), Robert A. Walton (2011); *Exec. Board Liaison* James Neal; *Staff Liaison* Gregory L. Calloway.

Divisions

See the separate entries that follow: American Assn. of School Libns.; Assn. for Lib. Collections and Technical Services; Assn. for Lib. Service to Children; Assn. of College and Research Libs.; Assn. of Lib. Trustees, Advocates, Friends, and Foundations; Assn. of Specialized and Cooperative Lib. Agencies; Lib. Leadership and Management Assn.; Lib. and Info. Technology Assn.; Public Lib. Assn.; Reference and User Services Assn.; Young Adult Lib. Services Assn.

Publications

ALA Handbook of Organization (online).

American Libraries (10 a year; memb.; organizations $70; foreign $80; single copy $7.50).

Booklist (22 a year; U.S. and possessions $109.95; foreign $126.95; single copy $9).

Round Table Chairs

(ALA staff liaison in parentheses)

Continuing Library Education Network and Exchange. Sharon Morris (Darlena Davis).

Ethnic and Multicultural Information Exchange. Homa Naficy (Miguel A. Figueroa).

Exhibits. Gene Shimshock (Amy McGuigan).

Federal and Armed Forces Libraries. Karl E. Debus-López (Rosalind Reynolds).

Gay, Lesbian, Bisexual, Transgendered. Anne Moore, Dale McNeill (Elliot Mandel).

Government Documents. Geoffrey Swindells (Rosalind Reynolds).

Intellectual Freedom. Loida A. Garcia-Febo (Nanette Perez).

International Relations. Patricia Oyler (Michael Dowling).

Library History. Melanie Kimball (Norman Rose).

Library Instruction. Kawanna Bright (Darlena Davis).

Library Research. Linda L. Lillard (Norman Rose).

Library Support Staff Interests. Trish Palluck (Darlena Davis).

Map and Geography. Marcy Bidney (Danielle M. Alderson).

New Members. Deana Groves (Kimberly Sanders).

Social Responsibilities. Mike Marlin (Elliot Mandel).

Staff Organizations. Leon S. Bey (Darlena Davis).

Video. Monique Threatt (Danielle M. Alderson).

Committee Chairs

(ALA staff liaison in parentheses)

Accreditation (Standing). Vicki L. Gregory (Karen L. O'Brien).

American Libraries Advisory (Standing). Andrew K. Pace (Leonard Kniffel).

Appointments (Standing). Molly Raphael (Delores Yates).

Awards (Standing). Andrea R. Lapsley (Cheryl Malden).

Budget Analysis and Review (Standing). James Neal (Gregory L. Calloway).

Chapter Relations (Standing). Annelle R. Huggins (Michael P. Dowling).

Committee on Committees (Elected Council Committee). Jon Michael Grass (Delores Yates).

Conference Committee (Standing). (Amy McGuigan).

Conference Program Coordinating Team. (Amy McGuigan).

Constitution and Bylaws (Standing). Thomas Wilding (JoAnne M. Kempf).

Council Orientation (Standing). Barbara Genco (Lois Ann Gregory-Wood).

Diversity (Standing). Sylvia D. Hall-Ellis (Miguel A. Figueroa).

Education (Standing). Ismail Abdullahi (Lorelle R. Swader).

Election (Standing). Peter D. Hepburn (Eileen Mahoney).

Human Resource Development and Recruitment (Standing). Pat Hawthorne (Lorelle R. Swader).

Information Technology Policy Advisory (Standing). Vivian M. Pisano (Alan Inouye).

Intellectual Freedom (Standing). Barbara K. Stripling (Nanette Perez).

International Relations (Standing). Sha Li Zhang (Michael P. Dowling).

Legislation (Standing). Charles E. Kratz, Jr. (Lynne E. Bradley).

Literacy (Standing). Juliet I. Machie (Dale P. Lipschultz).

Literacy and Outreach Services Advisory (Standing). Dee Holliday (Miguel A. Figueroa).

Membership (Standing). Kay Cassell (John F. Chrastka, Cathleen Bourdon).

Organization (Standing). James R. Rettig. (Delores Yates).

Orientation, Training, and Leadership Development. Therese G. Bigelow (Lorelle Swader).

Policy Monitoring (Standing). John Allyn Moorman (Lois Ann Gregory-Wood).

Professional Ethics (Standing). Marilyn L. Hinshaw (Angela Maycock).

Public and Cultural Programs Advisory (Standing). Carolyn A. Anthony (Deborah Anne Robertson).

Public Awareness (Standing). Rocco Staino (Mark R. Gould).

Publishing (Standing). Gail A. Schlachter (Donald E. Chatham).

Research and Statistics (Standing). Wanda V. Dole (Norman Rose).

Resolutions. Larry Romans (Lois Ann Gregory-Wood).

Rural, Native, and Tribal Libraries of All Kinds. Loriene Roy (Miguel A. Figueroa).

Scholarships and Study Grants. Toni C. Dean (Lorelle R. Swader).

Status of Women in Librarianship (Standing). Lorna Peterson (Lorelle R. Swader).

Web Site Advisory. Aaron W. Dobbs (Sherri L. Vanyek).

American Library Association
American Association of School Librarians

Executive Director, Julie A. Walker
50 E. Huron St., Chicago, IL 60611
312-280-4382, 800-545-2433, ext. 4382, fax 312-280-5276,
e-mail aasl@ala.org, World Wide Web http://www.aasl.org.

Object

The mission of the American Association of School Librarians (AASL) is to advocate excellence, facilitate change, and develop leaders in the school library field. AASL works to ensure that all members of the field collaborate to provide leadership in the total education program; participate as active partners in the teaching/learning process; connect learners with ideas and information; and prepare students for lifelong learning, informed decision making, a love of reading, and the use of information technologies.

Established in 1951 as a separate division of the American Library Association.

Membership

Memb. 8,500+. Open to all libraries, school librarians, interested individuals, and business firms, with requisite membership in ALA.

Officers (2010–2011)

Pres. Nancy Everhart; *Pres.-Elect* Carl Harvey II; *Treas.* Floyd Pentlin; *Past Pres.* Cassandra Barnett.

Board of Directors

Jay Bansbach, Dennis J. LeLoup, Sylvia K. Norton, Ann Perham, Sally Daniels, Cara Cavin, Allison Roberts, Deb Svec, Maribel Garza-Castro, Susan Garvin, Linda Collins, Linda Roberts, Allison G. Kaplan, Dorcas Hand, Bonnie Kelly, Nancy M. Dickinson.

Publications

AASL Hotlinks (mo.; electronic, memb.).

Knowledge Quest (5 a year; $50, $60 outside USA). *Ed.* Markisan Naso. E-mail mnaso @ala.org.

School Library Media Research (electronic, free, at http://www.ala.org/aasl.slmr). *Eds.* Jean Donham. E-mail jean.donham@ uni.edu; Carol L. Tilley. E-mail ctilley@ uiuc.edu.

Committee Chairs

AASL/ACRL Joint Information Literacy Committee. Carla Bosco, Emily Rimland.

AASL/ALSC/YALSA Interdivisional Committee on School/Public Library Cooperation. Mari J. Hardacre.

AASL/ELMSS Executive Committee. Audrey Church.

AASL/ISS Executive Committee. Carla Bosco.

AASL/SPVS Executive Committee. Judith A. Dzikowski.

Advocacy. To be appointed.

Affiliate Assembly. Nancy Dickinson.

Alliance for Association Excellence. Floyd Pentlin.

American University Press Book Selection. Jo Ann Carr.

Annual Conference. Terry Young.

Appointments. Robbie Nickel.

Awards. Terri Kirk.

Best Websites for Teaching and Learning. Pam Berger.
Blog Editorial Board. Patricia Dedicos, Wendy Stephens.
Bylaws and Organization. Dolores D. Gwaltney.
Intellectual Freedom. Helen Adams.
Knowledge Quest Editorial Board. Ann M. Martin.
Legislation. Mirah Dow.
National Conference 2011. Cheryl Steele, Ty Burns.
NCATE Coordinating Committee. Audrey Church.
Nominating. Gail Bush.
Publications. To be appointed.
Research/Statistics. Marcia Mardis.
SLMR Editorial Board. Jean Donham, Carol Tilley.
Web Site Resource Guides Editorial Board. Thomas Adamich.

Task Force Chairs

Common Core Crosswalk. Marcia Mardis.
Educator Pre-Service. Laura Summers.
Leadership Development. To be appointed.
Planned Giving Initiative. J. Linda Williams.
Recruitment to the Profession. Donna Shannon.
Retirees. To be appointed.
Standards and Guidelines Implementation. Susan Ballard.
Urban Schools. Lisa Perez.

Awards Committees and Chairs

ABC-CLIO Leadership Grant. Richard Lord.
Collaborative School Library Award. Leslie Forsman.
Distinguished School Administrator Award. Louis Greco.
Distinguished Service Award. To be appointed.
Frances Henne Award. Margaux DelGuidice.
Information Technology Pathfinder Award. Dawn Nelson.
Innovative Reading Grant. Leslie Preddy.
Intellectual Freedom Award. Bonnie Grimble.
National School Library Program of the Year Award. Elizabeth Marcoux.
AASL Research Grant. Karen Gavigan.

American Library Association
Association for Library Collections and Technical Services

Executive Director, Charles Wilt
50 E. Huron St., Chicago, IL 60611
800-545-2433 ext. 5030, fax 312-280-5033, e-mail cwilt@ala.org
Web http://www.ala.org/alcts

Object

The Association for Library Collections and Technical Services (ALCTS) envisions an environment in which traditional library roles are evolving. New technologies are making information more fluid and raising expectations. The public needs quality information anytime, anyplace. ALCTS provides frameworks to meet these information needs.

ALCTS provides leadership to the library and information communities in developing principles, standards, and best practices for creating, collecting, organizing, delivering, and preserving information resources in all forms. It provides this leadership through its members by fostering educational, research, and professional service opportunities. ALCTS is committed to quality information, universal access, collaboration, and lifelong learning.

Standards—Develop, evaluate, revise, and promote standards for creating, collecting, organizing, delivering, and preserving information resources in all forms.

Best practices—Research, develop, evaluate, and implement best practices for creating, collecting, organizing, delivering, and preserving information resources in all forms.

Education—Assess the need for, sponsor, develop, administer, and promote educational programs and resources for lifelong learning.

Professional development—Provide opportunities for professional development through research, scholarship, publication, and professional service.

Interaction and information exchange—Create opportunities to interact and exchange information with others in the library and information communities.

Association operations—Ensure efficient use of association resources and effective delivery of member services.

Established 1957; renamed 1988.

Membership

Memb. 4,200. Any member of the American Library Association may elect membership in this division according to the provisions of the bylaws.

Officers (2010–2011)

Pres. Cynthia Whitacre, OCLC, 6565 Kilgour Place, Dublin, OH 43017. Tel. 614-764-6183, fax 614-718-7397, email whitacrc@oclc.org; *Pres.-Elect* Betsy Simpson, Smathers Lib., Univ. of Florida, P.O. Box 117004, Gainesville, FL 32611. Tel. 352-273-2730, fax 352-392-7365, e-mail betsys@uflib.ufl.edu; *Past Pres.* Mary M. Case, Univ. of Illinois–Chicago Lib., 801 S. Morgan St., Chicago, IL 60661 Tel. 312-996-2716, fax 312-413-0424, e-mail marycase@uic.edu; *Councilor* Diane Dates Casey, Governors State Univ. Lib., 1 University Pkwy., University Park, IL 60466. Tel. 708-534-4110, fax 708-534-4564, e-mail d-casey@govst.edu.

Address correspondence to the executive director.

Board of Directors

Mary M. Case, Diane Dates Casey, Lauren Corbett, Susan A. Davis, Dina Giambi, Shelby Harken, Tara D. Kennedy, Sara Shatford Layne, Janet Lute, Arthur Miller, Paul Moeller, Rebecca Mugridge, Mary Page, Louise Ratliff, Shilpa Rele, Betsy Simpson, Mary Beth Weber, Cynthia Whitacre, Ginger Williams, Charles Wilt.

Publications

ALCTS Newsletter Online (q.; free; posted at http://www.ala.org/alcts). *Ed.* Mary Beth Weber, Cataloging Dept., Rutgers Univ. Libs., 47 Davidson Rd., Piscataway, NJ 08854. Tel. 732-445-0500, fax 732-445-5888, e-mail mbfecko@rci.rutgers.edu.

Library Resources and Technical Services (q.; nonmemb. $85; international $95). *Ed.* Peggy Johnson, Univ. of Minnesota Libs., 499 Wilson Lib., 309 19th Ave. S., Minneapolis, MN 55455. Tel. 612-624-2312, fax 612-626-9353, e-mail m-john@tc.umn.edu.

Section Chairpersons

Acquisitions. Lauren Corbett.

Cataloging and Classification. Shelby Harken.

Collection Management and Development. Ginger Williams.

Continuing Resources. Paul Moeller.

Preservation and Reformatting. Tara D. Kennedy.

Committee Chairpersons

ALCTS Outstanding Publications Award Jury. Mary Ann Jones.

Hugh C. Atkinson Memorial Award (ALCTS/ACRL/LAMA/LITA). Cheryl Kern-Simirenko.

Ross Atkinson Lifetime Achievement Award Jury. Cynthia Coulter.

Best of *LRTS* Award Jury. Robert Sandusky.

Budget and Finance. Janet Lute.

Continuing Education. Pamela Bluh.

Fund Raising. To be appointed.

International Relations. David Miller.

Leadership Development. Miranda Bennett.

LRTS Editorial Board. Peggy Johnson.

Membership. Deborah Ryszka.

Nominating. Dina Giambi.
Organization and Bylaws. Arthur Miller.
Outstanding Collaboration Citation Jury. Roman Panchyshyn.
Esther J. Piercy Award Jury. Carolynne Myall.
Planning. Sara Shatford Layne.
Program. Joyce McDonough.
Publications. Sion Romaine.

Interest Groups

Authority Control (ALCTS/LITA). Lynnette Fields.
Automated Acquisitions/In-Process Control Systems. Sharon Marshall.
Creative Ideas in Technical Services. Guanxian Fang.
Electronic Resources. Christine Turner.
FRBR. Judy Jeng.
MARC Formats (ALCTS/LITA). Steven R. Kelley.
New Members. Erica Findley, Amy Jackson.
Newspapers. Brian Geiger.
Out of Print. John Riley.
Public Libraries Technical Services. Sally Smith.
Role of the Professional in Academic Research Technical Service Departments. John D. Hall, Wanda Pittman Jazayeri.
Scholarly Communications. Adrian Ho.
Technical Services Directors of Large Research Libraries. Scott Wicks.
Technical Services Managers in Academic Libraries. Joanne Deeken, Linda Lomker.
Technical Services Workflow Efficiency. Dracine Hodges.

American Library Association
Association for Library Service to Children

Executive Director, Aimee Strittmatter
50 E. Huron St., Chicago, IL 60611
312-280-2163, 800-545-2433 ext. 2163, fax 312-280-5271, e-mail alsc@ala.org
World Wide Web http://www.ala.org/alsc

Object

The core purpose of the Association for Library Service to Children (ALSC) is to create a better future for children through libraries. Its primary goal is to lead the way in forging excellent library services for all children. ALSC offers creative programming, information about best practices, continuing education, a prestigious award and media evaluation program, and professional connections. Founded 1901.

Membership

Memb. 4,216. Open to anyone interested in library services to children. For information on dues, see ALA entry.

Address correspondence to the executive director.

Officers

Pres. Julie Corsaro; *V.P./Pres.-Elect* Mary Fellows; *Past Pres.* Thom Barthelmess; *Fiscal Officer* Tali Balas; *Division Councilor* Rhonda Puntney.

Directors

Carolyn S. Brodie, Nina Lindsay, Marge Loch-Wouters, Cecelia McGowan, Leslie Molnar, Elizabeth Orsburn, Jennifer Ralston, Ellen Riordan.

Publications

Children and Libraries: The Journal of the Association for Library Service to Children (q.; memb.; nonmemb. $40; foreign $50).

ALSConnect (q., electronic; memb. Not available by subscription.)

Committee Chairs

AASL/ALSC/YALSA Interdivisional Committee on School/Public Library Cooperation. Elizabeth B. Pollicino.

ALSC/*Booklist*/YALSA Odyssey Award Selection 2012. Lizette Hannegan.

Arbuthnot Honor Lecture 2011. Carol Edwards.

Arbuthnot Honor Lecture 2012. Shawn Brommer.

Mildred L. Batchelder Award 2012. Susan Stan.

Pura Belpré Award 2012. Jamie Campbell Naidoo.

Budget. Heather Rimany.

Randolph Caldecott Award 2012. Steven Herb.

Andrew Carnegie Medal/Notable Children's Videos. Martha Seif Simpson.

Children and Libraries Advisory Committee. Christina Desai.

Children and Technology. Amber Creger.

Distinguished Service Award 2012. Jennifer Brown.

Early Childhood Programs and Services. Kathleen Moore.

Education. Jane Claes.

Theodor Seuss Geisel Award 2012. Carole Fiore.

Grant Administration Committee. Susan Veltfort.

Great Web Sites. Rachel Fryd.

Intellectual Freedom. Bruce Stewart Farrar.

Legislation. Elizabeth Poe.

Liaison with National Organizations. Marna Elliott, Sharon Salluzzo.

Library Service to Special Population Children and Their Caregivers. Erin Ford Nguyen.

Local Arrangements (Washington, D.C.). April Bedford, Meb Norton.

Managing Children's Services. Anitra Steele.

Membership. A. Charlene McKenzie.

John Newbery Award 2012. Viki Ash.

Nominating 2012. Pat Scales.

Notable Children's Books. Kathy Isaacs.

Notable Children's Recordings. Sharon Haupt.

Oral History. Kathleen T. Horning.

Organization and Bylaws. Gene Nelson.

Program Coordinating. Caitlin Dixon.

Public Awareness. Barbara Scotto.

Quicklists Consulting. Natasha J. Forrester, Laura Jenkins.

Charlemae Rollins President's Program 2011. Marian Creamer, Edie Ching.

Scholarships. Ellen Spring.

School Age Programs and Service. Tami L. Chumbley Finley.

Robert F. Sibert Award 2012. Andrew Medlar.

Special Collections and Bechtel Fellowship. Marianne Martens, Ellen Ruffin.

Laura Ingalls Wilder Award 2013. Martha Parravano.

American Library Association
Association of Library Trustees, Advocates, Friends, and Foundations

Executive Director Sally Gardner Reed
109 S. 13 St., Suite 3N, Philadelphia, PA 19107
312-280-2161, fax 215-545-3821, e-mail sreed@ala.org
World Wide Web http://www.ala.org/altaff

Object

The Association for Library Trustees, Advocates, Friends, and Foundations (ALTAFF) was founded in 1890 as the American Library Trustee Association (ALTA). It was the only division of the American Library Association dedicated to promoting and ensuring outstanding library service through educational programs that develop excellence in trusteeship and promote citizen involvement in the support of libraries. In 2008 the members of ALTA voted to expand the division to more aggressively address the needs of friends of libraries and library foundations, and through a merger with Friends of Libraries USA (FOLUSA) became ALTAFF. ALTA had become an ALA division in 1961.

Membership

Memb. 5,200. Open to all interested persons and organizations. For dues and membership year, see ALA entry.

Officers (2010–2011)

Pres. Rodrique Gauvin; *V.P./Pres.-Elect* Donna McDonald; *Councilor* Susan Schmidt; *Past. Pres.* Rose Mosley.

Publications

The Voice for America's Libraries (q.; memb.).

101+ Great Ideas for Libraries and Friends.

Even More Great Ideas for Libraries and Friends.

The Complete Trustee Handbook.

Committee Chairs

ALTAFF Leaders Orientation. Terry Higgins.

Annual Conference Program. Robin Hoklotubbe.

Library Issues. Shirley Bruursema.

Newsletter and Web Site Advisory. To be appointed.

Nominating. Rose Mosley.

PLA Conference Program. Margaret Schuster, Gail Griffin.

American Library Association
Association of College and Research Libraries

Executive Director, Mary Ellen K. Davis
50 E. Huron St., Chicago, IL 60611-2795
312-280-2523, 800-545-2433 ext. 2523, fax 312-280-2520, e-mail acrl@ala.org
World Wide Web http://www.ala.org/acrl

Object

The Association of College and Research Libraries (ACRL) leads academic and research librarians and libraries in advancing learning and scholarship. Founded 1938.

Membership

Memb. 12,126. For information on dues, see ALA entry.

Officers

Pres. Lisa Janicke Hinchliffe, Univ. of Illinois, Urbana, IL 61801-3607. Tel. 217-333-1323, fax 217-244-4358, e-mail ljanicke@illinois.edu; *Pres.-Elect* Joyce L. Ogburn, 327 J. Willard Marriott Lib., Univ. of Utah, Salt Lake City, UT 84103-3322. Tel. 801-585-9775, fax 801-585-7185, e-mail joyce.ogburn@utah.edu; *Past Pres.* Lori Goetsch, 504 Hale Lib., Kansas State Univ., Manhattan, KS 66506. Tel. 785-532-7400, fax 785-532-7415, e-mail lgoetsch@ksu.edu; *Budget and Finance Chair* Janice D. Welburn, Univ. Lib., Marquette Univ., P.O. Box 3141, Milwaukee, WI 53201-3141. Tel. 414-288-7840, fax 414-288-7214, e-mail janice.welburn@marquette.edu; *ACRL Councilor* Maggie Ferrell, Univ. of Wyoming, 1000 E. University Ave., Laramie, WY 82071-2000. Tel. 307-766-3279, fax 307-766-2510, e-mailfarrell@uwyo.edu.

Board of Directors

Officers; Lisabeth A. Chabot, Elizabeth A. Dupuis, Mark Emmons, Linda A. Kopecky, Michael J. LaCroix, John A. Lehner, Ann Campion Riley, Mary Ann Sheble.

Publications

Choice (12 a year; $355; Canada and Mexico $405; other international $475). *Ed.* Irving Rockwood.

Choice Reviews-on-Cards (available only to subscribers of *Choice* and/or *Choice Reviews Online*; $445; Canada and Mexico $495; other international $575).

Choice Reviews Online 2.0; ($495).

College & Research Libraries (*C&RL*) (6 a year; memb.; nonmemb. $75; Canada and other PUAS countries $80; other international $85). *Ed.* Joseph J. Branin.

College & Research Libraries News (*C&RL News*) (11 a year; memb.; nonmemb. $50; Canada and other PUAS countries $55; other international $60). *Ed.* David Free.

Publications in Librarianship (formerly ACRL Monograph Series) (occasional). *Ed.* Craig Gibson.

RBM: A Journal of Rare Books, Manuscripts, and Cultural Heritage (s. ann.; $45; Canada and other PUAS countries $50; other international $60). *Ed.* Beth M. Whittaker.

Committee and Task Force Chairs

AASL/ACRL Information Literacy (interdivisional). Carla Bosco, Emily L. Rimland.

Academic/Research Librarian of the Year Award. Kenley N. Neufeld.

ACRL Academic Library Trends and Statistics Survey. William Miller.

ACRL/LLAMA Interdivisional Committee on Building Resources. Mary Carr.

Annual Conference Programs. Sarah E. Sheehan.

Appointments. Lisa B. German.

Assessment. Irene Hoffman.

Hugh C. Atkinson Memorial Award. Cheryl A. Kern-Simirenko.

Budget and Finance. Janice Welburn.

Choice Editorial Board. Dalia Lapatinskas Corkrum.

Colleagues. Maggie Ferrell, Sara Allison Lowman.

College & Research Libraries Editorial Board. Joseph Branin.

College & Research Libraries News Editorial Board. Gordon Aamot.

Advocacy. Valerie D. Glenn.

Copyright. William C. Welburn.

Doctoral Dissertation Fellowship. Dana M. Sally.

Ethics. Louise S. Sherby.

Excellence in Academic Libraries Award (Nominations). Scott Walter.

Excellence in Academic Libraries Award (Selection). Erika C. Linke.

Friends Fund. Beth McNeil.

Friends Fund Disbursement. Janis Bandelin.

Government Relations. Marilyn Nabua Ochoa.

Immersion Program. Julie Planchon Wolf.

Information Literacy Coordinating. Debra Gilchrist.

Information Literacy Standards. Ellysa Stern Cahoy.

Information Literacy Web Site. Keith E. Gresham.

Intellectual Freedom. Daniel R. Lee.

International Relations. Farzaneh Razzaghi.

E. J. Josey Spectrum Scholar Mentor. Cathleen M. Carney.

Leadership Recruitment and Nomination. Karen Williams.

Liaison Assembly. Kate Corby.

Liaison Coordinating. W. Bede Mitchell.

Liaison Grants. Debbie L. Malone.

Liaisons Training and Development. Kate Corby.

Marketing Academic and Research Libraries. Jennifer Church-Duran.

Membership Coordinating. Susanna D. Boylston.

Membership Promotion. John H. Pollitz.

Membership Recruitment. Melanee Vicedo.

Membership Retention. Meghan Elizabeth Sitar.

Midwinter Preconferences and Annual Workshops. William H. Weare, Jr.

National Conference Coordinating Committee (Philadelphia). Pamela Snelson.

New Publications Advisory. Joan K. Lippincott.

President's Program Planning Committee, 2011. Steven J. Bell, Lisa Janicke Hinchliffe.

President's Program Planning Committee, 2012. To be appointed.

Professional Development Coordinating. Danielle Theiss-White.

Publications Coordinating. Tim Gritten.

Publications in Librarianship Editorial Board. Craig Gibson.

Racial and Ethnic Diversity. Dee Holiday.

RBM Editorial Board. Beth Whittaker.

Research Coordinating. Julie Ann Garrison.

Research Planning and Review. Ryan B. Johnson.

Research Program. Rebecca Jackson.

Resources for College Libraries Editorial Board. Nancy P. O'Brien.

Scholarly Communications. Barbara Jo DeFelice.

Scholarships. Gladys Smiley Bell.

Section Membership. Beth S. Woodard.

Standards and Accreditation. Sharon McCaslin.

Status of Academic Librarians. Connie M. Strittmatter.

Virtual Institutes. Courtney R. Greene.

Discussion Group Chairs

Balancing Baby and Book. Cynthia Dudenhoffer.

Consumer and Family Studies. Lore Guilmartin.

Continuing Education/Professional Development. Elizabeth Avery.

Copyright. Shannon Baird.

Heads of Public Services. Kathryn M. Crowe.

Information Commons. Rudy Leon, Scott B. Mandernack, Michael Whitchurch.

Librarianship in For-Profit Educational Institutions. Catherine J. Sawyer.

Libraries and Information Science Collections. Rebecca Vargha.

Media Resources. Alexa Leigh Pearce.

MLA International Bibliography. Sarah G. Wenzel.

New Members. Allie K. Flanary.

Personnel Administrators and Staff Development Officers. Melissa A. Laning. Philosophical, Religious, and Theological Studies. Joshua Barton.
Popular Cultures. Sarah M. Sogigian.
Regional Campus Libraries. Erica Coe.
Scholarly Communications. Lisa A. Macklin.
Senior Administrators. Charles Gilreath.
Undergraduate Libraries. Carrie J. Kruse.

Interest Group Conveners

Academic Library Services to International Students. Dawn Amsberry.
Health Sciences. Dominique Turnbow.
Image Resources. Joanna Burgess.
Numeric and Geospatial Data Services in Academic Libraries. Hailey Mooney.
Residency Programs. Patricia A. MacDonald.
Universal Accessibility. S. G. Ranti Junus.
Virtual Worlds. Marcia Meister.

Section Chairs

African American Studies Librarians. Joyce K. Thornton.

Anthropology and Sociology. Jennifer Nason Davis.

Arts. Claudia Trevathan Covert.

Asian, African, and Middle Eastern. Triveni S. Kuchi.

College Libraries. Christopher Millson-Martula.

Community and Junior College Libraries. David A. Wright.

Distance Learning. Robin A. Lockerby.

Education and Behavioral Sciences. Stephanie R. Davis-Kahl.

Instruction. Polly D. Boruff-Jones.

Law and Political Science. Christopher Palazzolo.

Literatures in English. Liorah Anne Golomb.

Rare Books and Manuscripts. Henry F. Raine.

Science and Technology. Linda L. Eells.

Slavic and East European. Sandra Levy.

University Libraries. Kim Leeder.

Western European Studies. Brian William Vetruba.

Women's Studies. Jane Nichols.

American Library Association
Association of Specialized and Cooperative Library Agencies

Executive Director, Susan Hornung
50 E. Huron St., Chicago, IL 60611-2795
312-280-4395, 800-545-2433 ext. 4395, fax 312-280-5273
E-mail shornung@ala.org
World Wide Web http://www.ala.org/ascla

Object

The Association of Specialized and Cooperative Library Agencies (ASCLA) enhances the effectiveness of library service by providing networking, enrichment, and educational opportunities for its diverse members, who represent state library agencies, libraries serving special populations, multitype library organizations, and independent librarians. Within the interests of these library organizations, ASCLA has specific responsibility for

1. Development and evaluation of goals and plans for state library agencies, specialized library agencies, and library cooperatives to facilitate the implementation, improvement, and extension of library activities designed to foster improved user services, coordinating such activities with other appropriate units of the American Library Association (ALA)
2. Representation and interpretation of the role, functions, and services of

state library agencies, specialized library agencies, library cooperatives, and independent librarians within and outside the profession, including contact with national organizations and government agencies

3. Development of policies, studies, and activities in matters affecting state library agencies, specialized library agencies, library cooperatives, and independent librarians relating to (a) state and local library legislation, (b) state grants-in-aid and appropriations, and (c) relationships among state, federal, regional, and local governments, coordinating such activities with other appropriate ALA units
4. Establishment, evaluation, and promotion of standards and service guidelines relating to the concerns of this association
5. Identifying the interests and needs of all persons, encouraging the creation of services to meet these needs within the areas of concern of the association, and promoting the use of these services provided by state library agencies, specialized library agencies, library cooperatives, and independent librarians
6. Stimulating the professional growth and promoting the specialized training and continuing education of library personnel at all levels in the areas of concern of this association and encouraging membership participation in appropriate type-of-activity divisions within ALA
7. Assisting in the coordination of activities of other units within ALA that have a bearing on the concerns of this association
8. Granting recognition for outstanding library service within the areas of concern of this association
9. Acting as a clearinghouse for the exchange of information and encouraging the development of materials, publications, and research within the areas of concern of this association

Membership

Memb. 900. For information on dues, see ALA entry.

Officers (2010–2011)

Pres. Diana Reese; *Pres.-Elect* Norma Blake; *Past Pres.* Brenda Bailey-Hainer; *Div. Councilor* Kendall French Wiggin.

Sections

Independent Librarian's Exchange (ILEX); Interlibrary Cooperation and Networking (ICAN); Libraries Serving Special Populations (LSSPS); State Library Agency (SLAS).

Publication

Interface (q.; memb.). *Ed.* Anne Abate. E-mail anne@librarydiscountnetwork.com.

Committees

Accessibility Assembly; Awards; Legislation; Membership; Nominating; Planning and Budget; Publications; Standards Review.

American Library Association
Library Leadership and Management Association

Executive Director, Kerry Ward
50 E. Huron St., Chicago, IL 60611
312-280-5032, 800-545-2433 ext. 5032, fax 312-280-5033
e-mail kward@ala.org
World Wide Web http://www.ala.org/lama

Object

The Library Leadership and Management Association (LLAMA) Strategic Plan sets out the following:

Mission: The Library Leadership and Management Association encourages and nurtures current and future leaders, and develops and promotes outstanding leadership and management practices.

Vision: LLAMA will be the foremost organization developing present and future leaders in library and information services.

Image: LLAMA is a welcoming community where aspiring and experienced leaders from all types of libraries, as well as those who support libraries, come together to gain skills in a quest for excellence in library management, administration, and leadership.

In addition

- LLAMA will be an organization in which value to its members drives decisions.
- LLAMA will expand and strengthen leadership and management expertise at all levels for all libraries.
- LLAMA will facilitate professional development opportunities to enhance leadership and management.
- LLAMA will be the preeminent professional organization that develops and supports library leaders and managers.

Established 1957.

Membership

Memb. 4,800. For information on dues, see ALA entry.

Officers (July 2010–June 2011)

Pres. Gail Kennedy; *V.P.* Janine Golden; *Past Pres.* Gina Millsap.

Address correspondence to the executive director.

Publications

Library Leadership and Management (open access: http://journals.tdl.org/index.php/llm). *Eds.* Wendi Arant Kaspar, Pixey Mosley.

Committee Chairs

Continuing Education. Steven Bowers.
Financial Advancement. Janice Flug.
Leadership Development. Alison Armstrong.
LL&M Advisory. Paul Anderson.
Marketing Communications. Tracy Hull.
Membership. Deb Stansbury Sunday.
Mentoring. Adriana Gonzalez.
Nominating. Melissa Laning.
Program. Philip Tramdack.

American Library Association
Library and Information Technology Association

Executive Director, Mary C. Taylor
50 E. Huron St., Chicago, IL 60611
312-280-4267, 800-545-2433
E-mail mtaylor@@ala.org, World Wide Web http://www.lita.org

Object

As a center of expertise about information technology, the Library and Information Technology Association (LITA) leads in exploring and enabling new technologies to empower libraries. LITA members use the promise of technology to deliver dynamic library collections and services.

LITA educates, serves, and reaches out to its members, other ALA members and divisions, and the entire library and information community through its publications, programs, and other activities designed to promote, develop, and aid in the implementation of library and information technology.

Membership

Memb. 3,352. For information on dues, see ALA entry.

Officers (2010–2011)

Pres. Karen Starr; *V.P./Pres.-Elect* Colleen Cuddy; *Past Pres.* Michelle L. Frisque.

Directors

Mona C. Couts, Aaron Dobbs, Jason Griffey, Colby Riggs, Lorre B. Smith, Cindi Trainor, Maurice York; *Councilor* Adriene Lim; *Bylaws and Organization* Dale Poulter; *Exec. Dir.* Mary C. Taylor.

Publication

Information Technology and Libraries (*ITAL*) (q.; memb.; nonmemb. $65; single copy $30). *Ed.* Marc Truitt. For information or to send manuscripts, contact the editor.

Committee Chairs

Assessment and Research. Bonnie Postlethwaite.
Budget Review. Michelle Frisque.
Bylaws and Organization. Dale Poulter.
Committee Chair Coordinator. Holly Yu.
Education. Danielle Cunniff Plumer, Cody Hanson.
Executive. Karen Starr.
International Relations. Frank Cervone.
ITAL Editorial Board. Marc Truitt.
LITA/Ex Libris Student Writing Award. Danielle Adams.
LITA/Library Hi Tech Award. Erik Mitchell.
LITA/LSSI and LITA/OCLC Minority Scholarships. Ping Fu.
LITA National Forum 2011. Paul Keith.
LITA/OCLC Kilgour Award. Steve McCann.
LITA/Christian Larew Scholarship. Camilla Fulton.
Membership Development. Donald W. Lemke.
Nominating. Mark Beatty.
Program Planning. Ranti Janus.
Publications. Kristin Antelman.
Technology and Access. Elena Soltau.
Top Technology Trends. Jason Vaughan.
Web Coordinating. Matthew Hamilton.

Interest Group Coordinators

Authority Control in the Online Environment (LITA/ALCTS). Amy McNeely.
Blogs, Interactive Media, Groupware, and Wikis. Michelle Jizejewski, Rachel Vacek.
Cloud Computing and Virtualization. Julian Clark.
Digital Library Technologies. Jack Koenig, Mandy Mastrovita.

Distance Learning. Chad Haefele, Lauren Ray.
Drupal4Lib. Nina McHale.
Electronic Resources Management (LITA/ALCTS). Anjana Bhatt, Emma Cryer.
Emerging Technologies. James Hahn.
Heads of Library Technology. Edward Sanchez.
Imagineering. Cara V. W. Kinsey.
Interest Groups Coordinator. Michelle Boule.
Internet Resources and Services. Mary Axford, Sarah Passonneau.
JPEG 2000 in Archives and Libraries. Gretchen Gueguen, Holley Long.
Library Consortia Automated Systems. Jon Mark Bolthouse.
MARC Formats (LITA/ALCTS). Steven Kelley, Chiat Chew.
Mobile Computing. Bohyun Kim, Sara Thompson.
Next Generation Catalog. Suzanne Graham, Michael Kim.
Open Source Systems. Karen G. Schneider.
Public Libraries Technology. Rob Cullin.
RFID Technology. Vicki Terbovich.
Standards. Anne Liebst.
Universal Accessibility. Helen Gbala.
Transliteracy. Bobbi Newman.

American Library Association
Public Library Association

Executive Director, Barbara A. Macikas
50 E. Huron St., Chicago, IL 60611
312-280-5752, 800-545-2433 ext. 5752, fax 312-280-5029, e-mail pla@ala.org
World Wide Web http://www.pla.org

The Public Library Association (PLA) has specific responsibility for

1. Conducting and sponsoring research about how the public library can respond to changing social needs and technical developments
2. Developing and disseminating materials useful to public libraries in interpreting public library services and needs
3. Conducting continuing education for public librarians by programming at national and regional conferences, by publications such as the newsletter, and by other delivery means
4. Establishing, evaluating, and promoting goals, guidelines, and standards for public libraries
5. Maintaining liaison with relevant national agencies and organizations engaged in public administration and human services, such as the National Association of Counties, the Municipal League, and the Commission on Postsecondary Education
6. Maintaining liaison with other divisions and units of ALA and other library organizations, such as the Association for Library and Information Science Education and the Urban Libraries Council
7. Defining the role of the public library in service to a wide range of user and potential user groups
8. Promoting and interpreting the public library to a changing society through legislative programs and other appropriate means
9. Identifying legislation to improve and to equalize support of public libraries

PLA enhances the development and effectiveness of public librarians and public library services. This mission positions PLA to

- Focus its efforts on serving the needs of its members
- Address issues that affect public libraries
- Commit to quality public library services that benefit the general public

The goals of PLA are

- Advocacy and Awareness: PLA is an essential partner in public library advocacy.
- Leadership and Transformation: PLA is the leading source for learning opportunities to advance transformation of public libraries.
- Literate Nation: PLA will be a leader and valued partner of public libraries' initiatives to create a literate nation.
- Organizational Excellence: PLA is positioned to sustain and grow its resources to advance the work of the association.

Membership

Memb. 10,000+. Open to all ALA members interested in the improvement and expansion of public library services to all ages in various types of communities.

Officers (2010–2011)

Pres. Audra L. Caplan, Harford County Public Lib., Belcamp, Maryland (retired). E-mail pla@ala.org; *Pres.-Elect* Marcia Warner, Grand Rapids (Michigan) Public Lib. E-mail mwarner@grpl.org; *Past Pres.* Sari Feldman, Cuyahoga County Public Lib., Parma, Ohio. E-mail sfeldman@cuyahogalibrary.org.

Publication

Public Libraries (bi-mo.; memb.; nonmemb. $65; foreign $75; single copy $10). *Ed.* Kathleen Hughes, PLA, 50 E. Huron St., Chicago, IL 60611. E-mail khughes@ala.org.

Committee Chairs

Annual Conference Program Subcommittee. Alan Harkness.

Baker & Taylor Entertainment Audio Music/Video Product Award. Carol L. Sheffer.

Budget and Finance. Marilyn H. Boria.

Communities of Practice Task Force. Jay Lamar Turner.

Gordon M. Conable Award Jury. Fran Ware.

Continuing Education Advisory Group. Larry P. Neal.

DEMCO New Leaders Travel Grant Jury. Sonia Alcantara-Antoine.

EBSCO Excellence in Small and/or Rural Public Library Service Award. Carol R. Barta.

Highsmith Library Innovation Award Jury. Irmgarde B. Brown.

Intellectual Freedom. Kenton L. Oliver.

Leadership Development Task Force. Luis Herrera.

Legislation and Advocacy. Kathleen S. Reif.

Allie Beth Martin Award Jury. Judy Sasges.

Membership Advisory Group. Jennifer L. Giltrop.

Nominating 2011. Carol L. Sheffer.

Nominating 2012. Sari Feldman.

PLA/ALSC Every Child Ready to Read Evaluation Task Force. Clara Nalli Bohrer.

PLDS Statistical Report Advisory. Ingrid M. Norris.

Polaris Innovation in Technology John Iliff Award. Lynn M. Elam.

Public Libraries Advisory. Sally Decker Smith.

Charlie Robinson Award Jury. Toni A. Garvey.

Romance Writers of America Library Grant Jury. Beth Wheeler-Dean.

National Conference 2012. Karen Danczak-Lyons.

National Conference 2012 Program Subcommittee. Sara Dallas.

American Library Association
Reference and User Services Association

Executive Director, Susan Hornung
50 E. Huron St., Chicago, IL 60611
800-545-2433 ext. 4395, 312-280-4395, fax 312-280-5273
E-mail shornung@ala.org
World Wide Web http://www.ala.org/rusa

Object

The Reference and User Services Association (RUSA) is the foremost organization of reference and information professionals who make the connections between people and the information sources, services, and collection materials they need. Responsible for supporting the delivery of reference/information services to all groups, regardless of age, in all types of libraries, RUSA facilitates the development and conduct of direct service to library users, the development of programs and guidelines for service to meet the needs of these users, and assists libraries in reaching potential users.

The specific responsibilities of RUSA are

1. Conduct of activities and projects within the association's areas of responsibility
2. Encouragement of the development of librarians engaged in these activities and stimulation of participation by members of appropriate type-of-library divisions
3. Synthesis of the activities of all units within the American Library Association that have a bearing on the type of activities represented by the association
4. Representation and interpretation of the association's activities in contacts outside the profession
5. Planning and development of programs of study and research in these areas for the total profession
6. Continuous study and review of the association's activities

Membership

Memb. 4,500+

Officers (2010–2011)

Pres. Barry Trott; *Pres.-Elect* Gary White; *Secy.* Theresa Mudrock; *Past Pres.* Susan J. Beck; *Div. Councilor* M. Kathleen Kern.

Publication

Reference and User Services Quarterly (q.; memb.). *Ed.* Diane M. Zabel, Schreyer Business Lib., 309 Paterno Lib., Pennsylvania State Univ., University Park, PA 16802. E-mail dxz2@psu.edu.

Sections

Business Reference and Services (BRASS); Collection Development and Evaluation (CODES); History (HS); Emerging Technologies in Reference (MARS); Reference Services (RSS); Sharing and Transforming Access to Resources (STARS).

Committees

Access to Information; AFL/CIO Joint Committee on Library Services to Labor Groups; Awards; Budget and Finance; Conference Program; Membership; Nominating; Organization and Planning; Professional Development; Publications and Communications; Standards and Guidelines.

American Library Association
Young Adult Library Services Association

Executive Director, Beth Yoke
50 E. Huron St., Chicago, IL 60611
312-280-4390, 800-545-2433 ext. 4390, fax 312-280-5276
E-mail yalsa@ala.org, World Wide Web http://www.ala.org/yalsa
Blog http://yalsa.ala.org/blog, MySpace http://www.myspace.com/yalsa
Wiki http://wikis.ala.org/yalsa, Twitter http://twitter.com/yalsa, Facebook http://www.facebook.com/YALSA.

Object

In every library in the nation, quality library service to young adults is provided by a staff that understands and respects the unique informational, educational, and recreational needs of teenagers. Equal access to information, services, and materials is recognized as a right, not a privilege. Young adults are actively involved in the library decision making process. The library staff collaborates and cooperates with other youth-serving agencies to provide a holistic, community-wide network of activities and services that support healthy youth development. To ensure that this vision becomes a reality, the Young Adult Library Services Association (YALSA)

1 Advocates extensive and developmentally appropriate library and information services for young adults ages 12 to 18
2. Promotes reading and supports the literacy movement
3. Advocates the use of information and communications technologies to provide effective library service
4. Supports equality of access to the full range of library materials and services, including existing and emerging information and communications technologies, for young adults
5. Provides education and professional development to enable its members to serve as effective advocates for young people
6. Fosters collaboration and partnerships among its individual members with the library community and other groups involved in providing library and information services to young adults
7. Influences public policy by demonstrating the importance of providing library and information services that meet the unique needs and interests of young adults
8. Encourages research and is in the vanguard of new thinking concerning the provision of library and information services for youth

Membership

Memb. 5,600. Open to anyone interested in library services, literature, and technology for young adults. For information on dues, see ALA entry.

Officers

Pres. Kim Patton. E-mail kimpatton@kclibrary.org; *V.P./Pres.-Elect* Sarah Flowers. E-mail sarahflowers@charter.net; *Division Councilor* Nick Buron. E-mail nickburon.ala@gmail.com; *Fiscal Officer* Mary Hastler. E-mail mhastler@bcpl.net; *Secy.* Francisca Goldsmith. E-mail fgoldsmith@gmail.com; *Past Pres.* Linda Braun. E-mail lbraun@leonline.com.

Directors

Jack Martin, Ritchie Momon, Shannon Peterson, Sara Ryan, Chris Shoemaker Stephanie Squicciarini, Gail Tobin.

Publications

Young Adult Library Services (q.) (memb.; nonmemb. $50; foreign $60). *Ed.* Sarah Flowers.

YAttitudes (memb.) *Ed.* Erin Downey Howerton.

AIIM—The Enterprise Content Management Association

President, John F. Mancini
1100 Wayne Ave., Suite 1100, Silver Spring, MD 20910
800-477-2446, 301-587-8202, fax 301-587-2711
E-mail aiim@aiim.org, World Wide Web http://www.aiim.org
European Office: 8 Canalside, Lowesmoor Wharf, Worcester WR1 2RR, England.
44-1905-727613, fax 44-1905-727609, e-mail info@aiim.org.uk

Object

AIIM is an international authority on enterprise content management, the tools and technologies that capture, manage, store, preserve, and deliver content in support of business processes. Founded in 1943 as the Association for Information and Image Management.

Officers

Chair John Chickering, Fidelity Investments; *V. Chair* John Opdyke, Hyland Software; *Treas.* Timothy Elmore, Bank-Fund Staff Federal Credit Union; *Past Chair* Lynn Fraas, Crown Partners.

Publications

Infonomics magazine (bi-mo.; memb., print and online); *Infonomics Weekly eNewsletter.*

American Indian Library Association

President, Jody Gray
World Wide Web http://www.ailanet.org

Objective

To improve library and information services for American Indians. Founded in 1979; affiliated with American Library Association 1985.

Membership

Any person, library, or other organization interested in working to improve library and information services for American Indians may become a member. Dues (Inst.) $30; (Indiv.) $15; (Student) $10.

Officers (July 2010–June 2011)

Pres. Jody Gray. E-mail grayjl@umn.edu; *V.P./Pres.-Elect* Sandy Littletree. E-mail sandy505@email.arizona.edu; *Secy.* Heather Devine. E-mail heather@io.com; *Interim Treas.* Carlene Engstrom. E-mail carleneengstrom@yahoo.com; *Past. Pres.* Liana Juliano, e-mail lj12116@yahoo.com; *Members at Large* Lisa Mitten. E-mail mohawk6nations@yahoo.com; Holly Tomren. E-Mail htomren@uci.edu; David Hurley. E-mail david.hurley@gmail.com.

Publication

AILA Newsletter (q.).

Committee Chairs

Children's Literature Award. Lisa Mitten.
Communications and Publications. Liana Juliano, Heather Devine.
Development and Fund Raising. Richenda Wilkinson.
Distinguished Service Award. Lotsee Patterson.
Nominating. Liana Juliano, Joan Howland.
Programming. Liana Juliano.
Scholarship Review Board. Holly Tomren.
Subject Access and Classification. Mario Klimiades.

American Merchant Marine Library Association

(An affiliate of United Seamen's Service)
Executive Director, Roger T. Korner
635 Fourth Ave., Brooklyn, NY 11232
718-369-3818, e-mail ussammla@ix.netcom.com

Object

Known as "the public library of the high seas," the association provides ship and shore library service for American-flag merchant vessels, and for the Military Sealift Command, the U.S. Coast Guard, and other waterborne operations of the U.S. government. Established 1921.

Officers

Pres. Edward R. Morgan; *V.P.s* Thomas J. Bethel, John M. Bowers, Capt. Timothy A. Brown, James Capo, David Cockroft, Ron Davis, Capt. Remo Di Fiore, Yoji Fujisawa, John Halas, Rene Liocanjie, George E. Murphy, Capt. Gregorio Oca, Michael Sacco, John J. Sweeney; *Secy.* Donald E. Kadlac; *Treas.* William D. Potts; *Gen. Counsel* John L. DeGurse, Jr.; *Exec. Dir.* Roger T. Korner.

American Society for Information Science and Technology

Executive Director, Richard B. Hill
1320 Fenwick Lane, Suite 510, Silver Spring, MD 20910
301-495-0900, fax 301-495-0810, e-mail asis@asis.org
World Wide Web http://www.asis.org

Object

The American Society for Information Science and Technology (ASIS&T) provides a forum for the discussion, publication, and critical analysis of work dealing with the design, management, and use of information, information systems, and information technology.

Membership

Memb. (Indiv.) 3,500; (Student) 800; (Inst.) 250. Dues (Indiv.) $140; (Student) $40; (Inst.) $650 and $800.

Officers

Pres. Linda C. Smith, University of Illinois at Urbana Champaign; *Pres.-Elect* Diane

Sonnenwald, University College, Dublin (Ireland); *Treas.* Vicki Gregory, Univ. of South Florida; *Past Pres.* Gary Marchionini, Univ. of North Carolina

Address correspondence to the executive director.

Board of Directors

Dirs.-at-Large Deborah Barreau, France Bouthillier, Prudence Dalrymple, Elaine Toms.

Publications

ASIS&T Thesaurus of Information Science, Technology, and Librarianship, 3rd edition, ed. by Alice Redmond-Neal and Marjorie M. K. Hlava.

Computerization Movements and Technology Diffusion: From Mainframes to Ubiquitous Computing, ed. by Margaret S. Elliott and Kenneth L. Kraemer.

Covert and Overt: Recollecting and Connecting Intelligence Service and Information Science, ed. by Robert V. Williams and Ben-Ami Lipetz.

Editorial Peer Review: Its Strengths and Weaknesses, by Ann C. Weller.

Electronic Publishing: Applications and Implications, ed. by Elisabeth Logan and Myke Gluck.

Evaluating Networked Information Services: Techniques, Policy and Issues, by Charles R. McClure and John Carlo Bertot.

From Print to Electronic: The Transformation of Scientific Communication, by Susan Y. Crawford, Julie M. Hurd, and Ann C. Weller.

Historical Information Science: An Emerging Unidiscipline, by Lawrence J. McCrank.

Historical Studies in Information Science, ed. by Trudi Bellardo Hahn and Michael Buckland.

The History and Heritage of Scientific and Technological Information Systems, ed. by W. Boyd Rayward and Mary Ellen Bowden.

Information and Emotion: The Emergent Affective Paradigm in Information Behavior Research and Theory, ed. by Diane Nahl and Dania Bilal.

Information Management for the Intelligent Organization: The Art of Environmental Scanning, 3rd edition, by Chun Wei Choo.

Information Representation and Retrieval in the Digital Age, by Heting Chu.

Intelligent Technologies in Library and Information Service Applications, by F. W. Lancaster and Amy Warner.

Introduction to Information Science and Technology, ed. by Charles H. Davis and Debora Shaw.

Introductory Concepts in Information Science, by Melanie J. Norton.

Knowledge Management for the Information Professional, ed. by T. Kanti Srikantaiah and Michael E. D. Koenig.

Knowledge Management in Practice: Connections and Context, ed. by T. Kanti Srikantaiah and Michael E. D. Koenig.

Knowledge Management Lessons Learned: What Works and What Doesn't, ed. by T. Kanti Srikantaiah and Michael E. D. Koenig.

Knowledge Management: The Bibliography, compiled by Paul Burden.

Proceedings of ASIS&T Annual Meetings.

Statistical Methods for the Information Professional, by Liwen Vaughan.

Theories of Information Behavior, ed. by Karen E. Fisher, Sanda Erdelez, and Lynne E. F. McKechnie.

The Web of Knowledge: A Festschrift in Honor of Eugene Garfield, ed. by Blaise Cronin and Helen Barsky Atkins.

The above publications are available from Information Today, Inc., 143 Old Marlton Pike, Medford, NJ 08055.

American Theological Library Association

Executive Director, Brenda Bailey-Hainer
300 S. Wacker Drive, Suite 2100, Chicago, IL 60606-6701
888-665-2852, 312-454-5100, fax 312-454-5505, e-mail atla@atla.com
World Wide Web http://www.atla.com

Mission

The mission of the American Theological Library Association (ATLA) is to foster the study of theology and religion by enhancing the development of theological and religious libraries and librarianship. In pursuit of this mission, the association undertakes

- To foster the professional growth of its members, and to enhance their ability to serve their constituencies as administrators and librarians
- To advance the profession of theological librarianship, and to assist theological librarians in defining and interpreting the proper role and function of libraries in theological education
- To promote quality library and information services in support of teaching, learning, and research in theology, religion, and related disciplines and to create such tools and aids (including publications) as may be helpful in accomplishing this
- To stimulate purposeful collaboration among librarians of theological libraries and religious studies collections, and to develop programmatic solutions to information-related problems common to those librarians and collections

Membership

(Inst.) 252; (International Inst.) 16; (Indiv.) 437; (Student) 67; (Lifetime) 96; (Affiliates) 75.

Officers

Pres. Laura Wood, Andover-Harvard Theological Lib., Harvard Divinity School, 45 Francis Ave., Cambridge, MA 02138. Tel. 617-495-2802, fax 617-496-4111, e-mail lwood@hds.harvard.edu; *V.P.* Eileen Crawford, Jean and Alexander Heard Lib., Vanderbilt Univ., 419 21st Ave. South, Nashville, TN 37240-0007. Tel. 615-343-9880, fax 615-343-2918. e-mail eileen.k.crawford @vanderbilt.edu; *Secy.* Carrie M. Hackney, Howard Univ. School of Divinity Lib.

Directors

H. D. Sandy Ayer, Carisse Mickey Berryhill, Douglas L. Gragg, M. Patrick Graham, William J. Hook, Andrew Keck, Saundra Lipton, Blake Walter, John B. Weaver.

Publications

ATLA Indexes in MARC Format (q.).

ATLA Religion Database, 1949– (q., on EBSCO, OCLC, Ovid).

ATLASerials, 1949– (q., full-text, on EBSCO, OCLC, Ovid).

Catholic Periodical and Literature Index (q., on EBSCO).

Old Testament Abstracts (ann. on EBSCO).

New Testament Abstracts (ann. on EBSCO).

Proceedings (ann.; memb.; nonmemb. $55). *Ed.* Sara Corkery.

Research in Ministry: An Index to Doctor of Ministry Project Reports (ann.) online.

Archivists and Librarians in the History of the Health Sciences

President, Stephen J. Greenberg
E-mail patzere4@gmail.com
World Wide Web http://www.alhhs.org

Object

The association was established exclusively for educational purposes, to serve the professional interests of librarians, archivists, and other specialists actively engaged in the librarianship of the history of the health sciences by promoting the exchange of information and by improving the standards of service.

Membership

Memb. 170. Dues $15 (Americas), $21 (other countries).

Officers

Pres. Stephen J. Greenberg. E-mail patzere4@gmail.com; *Secy.* To be appointed; *Treas.* Arlene Shaner, New York Academy of Medicine, 1216 Fifth Ave., New York, NY 10029. Tel. 212-822-7313, e-mail ashaner@nyam.org; *Membs.-at-Large* Jack Eckert, Dawn McInnis, Jennifer Kane Nieves, Martha Stone; *Past Pres.* Lisa A. Mix. E-mail lisa.mix@library.ucsf.edu.

Publication

Watermark (q.; memb.). *Ed.* Christopher Lyons, Osler Lib. of the History of Medicine, McGill Univ. E-mail christopher.lyons@mcgill.ca.

ARMA International

Executive Director, Marilyn Bier
11880 College Blvd., Suite 450, Overland Park, KS 66210
800-422-2762, 913.341-3808, fax 913.341.3742
World Wide Web http://www.arma.org

Object

To advance the practice of records and information management as a discipline and a profession; to organize and promote programs of research, education, training, and networking within that profession; to support the enhancement of professionalism of the membership; and to promote cooperative endeavors with related professional groups.

Membership

Memb. 11,000. Annual dues $150 for international affiliation (student/retired $25). Chapter dues vary.

Pres. Nicholas De Laurentis, State Farm, 3 State Farm Plaza S, L3, Bloomington, IL 61791-0001. Tel. 309-735-3500; *Pres.-Elect* Galina Datskovsky, Autonomy, 21-00 Rte. 208 S, Fair Lawn, NJ 07410. Tel. 201-475-4734; *Treas.* Fred Pulzello, 26 Holt Court, Glen Rock, NJ 07452. Tel. 201-723-5865; *Past Pres./Chair* Douglas Allen, Global 360, 3103 Sasparilla Cove, Austin, TX 78748. Tel. 512-791-8027.

Directors

Beverly Bishop, Julie J. Colgan, Michael Guentzel, Komal Gulich, William LeFevre,

Samantha Lofton, Susan Lord, Mike Marsh, Brian A. Moriki, Paula Sutton, Sean Tanner, Juana Walker.

Publication

Information Management (*IM*) (bi-mo.).

Art Libraries Society of North America

President, Marilyn Russell
Executive Management, Technical Enterprises, Inc., Scott Sherer, Pres.,
7044 S. 13 St., Oak Creek, WI 53154
414-768-8000, fax 414-768-8001, e-mail sherer@techenterprises.net

Object

The object of the Art Libraries Society of North America (ARLIS/NA) is to foster excellence in art librarianship and visual resources curatorship for the advancement of the visual arts. Established 1972.

Membership

Memb. 1,000+. Dues (Inst./Business Affiliate) $145; (Indiv.) $85; (Student) $45; (Retired/Unemployed) $45; (Sustaining) $250; (Sponsor) $500; (Overseas) $65. Year. Jan. 1–Dec. 31. Membership is open to all those interested in visual librarianship, whether they be professional librarians, students, library assistants, art book publishers, art book dealers, art historians, archivists, architects, slide and photograph curators, or retired associates in these fields.

Officers

Pres. Marilyn Russell, Haskell Indian Nations Univ., 155 Indian Ave., Lawrence, KS 66046. Tel. 785-832-6661, e-mail mrussell@haskell.edu; *V.P./Pres.-Elect* Jon Evans, Hirsch Lib., Museum of Fine Arts—Houston, P.O. Box 6826, Houston, TX 77265-6826. Tel. 713-639-7393, e-mail jevans@mfah.org; *Secy.* V. Heidi Hass, Morgan Lib. and Museum, 225 Madison Ave., New York, NY 10016-3403. Tel. 212-590-0381, fax 212-768-5681, e-mail vhhass@themorgan.org; *Treas.* Tom Riedel, Dayton Memorial Lib., Regis Univ., 3333 Regis Blvd., D-20, Denver, CO 80221. Tel. 303-458-4261, e-mail triedel@regis.edu; *Past Pres.* Amy Lucker, Institute of Fine Arts Lib., 1 E. 78 St., New York, NY 10075. Tel. 212-992-5826, e-mail amy.lucker@nyu.edu.

Address correspondence to Scott Sherer, Technical Enterprises, Inc., 7044 S. 13 St., Oak Creek, WI 53154.

Publications

ARLIS/NA Update (bi-mo.; memb.).
Art Documentation (2 a year; memb., subscription).
Handbook and List of Members (ann.; memb.).
Occasional papers (price varies).
Miscellaneous others (request current list from headquarters).

Committee Chairs

Awards. Jennifer Parker.
Cataloging Advisory. Sherman Clarke.
Communications and Publications. Jonathan Franklin.
Development. Sonja Staum.
Diversity. Laura Haxer, Meredith Kahn.
Finance. Ted Goodman.
International Relations. Kristen Regina.
Membership. Bryan Loar.
Nominating. Leslie Abrams.
Professional Development. Sarah Falls.
Public Policy. Roger Lawson, Carmen Orth-Alfie.
Strategic Planning. Patricia Barnett.

Asian/Pacific American Librarians Association

Executive Director, Gary Colmenar
P.O. Box 1669, Goleta, CA 93116-1669
805-893-8067, e-mail colmenar@library.ucsb.edu
World Wide Web http://www.apalaweb.org

Object

To provide a forum for discussing problems and concerns of Asian/Pacific American librarians; to provide a forum for the exchange of ideas by Asian/Pacific American librarians and other librarians; to support and encourage library services to Asian/Pacific American communities; to recruit and support Asian/Pacific American librarians in the library/information science professions; to seek funding for scholarships in library/information science programs for Asian/Pacific Americans; and to provide a vehicle whereby Asian/Pacific American librarians can cooperate with other associations and organizations having similar or allied interests. Founded in 1980; incorporated 1981; affiliated with American Library Association 1982.

Membership

Open to all librarians and information specialists of Asian/Pacific descent working in U.S. libraries and information centers and other related organizations, and to others who support the goals and purposes of the association. Asian/Pacific Americans are defined as people residing in North America who self-identify as Asian/Pacific American. Dues (Inst.) $60; (Indiv.) $30; (Retiree) $15; (Students/Unemployed Libns.) $10; (life) $350.

Officers (July 2010–June 2011)

Pres. Florante Peter Ibanez, William M. Rains Lib., Loyola Law School, Los Angeles. E-mail florante.ibanez@lls.edu; *V.P./Pres.-Elect* Sandy Wee, San Mateo County Lib., 1 Library Ave., Millbrae, CA 94030. Tel. 650-697-7607, e-mail wee@smcl.org; *Secy.* Liladhar Pendse, Charles E. Young Research Lib., UCLA. E-mail lpendse@library.ucla.edu; *Treas.* Angela Boyd, Davidson Lib., Univ. of California, Santa Barbara. E-mail aboyd@library.ucsb.edu; *Past Pres.* Sherise Kimura, Gleeson Lib., Univ. of San Francisco. E-mail kimura@usfca.edu.

Publication

APALA Newsletter (q.).

Committee Chairs

Constitution and Bylaws. Ben Wakashige.
Literature Awards. Dora Ho.
Membership. Rebecca Kennedy.
Newsletter and Publications. Gary Colmenar.
Nominating. Sherise Kimura.
Program Planning. Eugenia Beh, Sandy Wee.
Publicity. Elnora "Ellie" Tayag.
Research and Travel Awards. Safi Safiullah, Gayatri Singh.
Scholarships. Heawon Paick.
Web. Richard Kong.

Association for Library and Information Science Education

Executive Director, Kathleen Combs
ALISE Headquarters, 65 E. Wacker Place, Suite 1900, Chicago, IL 60601-7246
312-795-0996, fax 312-419-8950, e-mail contact@alise.org
World Wide Web http://www.alise.org

The Association for Library and Information Science Education (ALISE) is an independent nonprofit professional association whose mission is to promote excellence in research, teaching, and service for library and information science (LIS) education through leadership, collaboration, advocacy, and dissemination of research. Its enduring purpose is to promote research that informs the scholarship of teaching and learning for library and information science, enabling members to integrate research into teaching and learning. The association provides a forum in which to share ideas, discuss issues, address challenges, and shape the future of education for library and information science. Founded in 1915 as the Association of American Library Schools, it has had its present name since 1983.

Membership

700+ in four categories: Personal, Institutional, International Affiliate Institutional, and Associate Institutional. Personal membership is open to anyone with an interest in the association's objectives.

Officers (2010–2011)

Pres. Lorna Peterson, Univ. at Buffalo. E-mail lpeterso@buffalo.edu; *V.P./Pres.-Elect* Lynn Horwarth, Univ. of Toronto; *Past Pres.* Linda C. Smith, Univ. of Illinois at Urbana-Champaign; *Secy.-Treas.* Jean Preer, Indiana Univ., Indianapolis; *Dirs.* Susan Roman, Dominican Univ.; Anne Weeks, Univ. of Maryland; Andrew Wertheimer, Univ. of Hawaii.

Publications

Journal of Education for Library and Information Science (*JELIS*) (q.). *Co-Eds.* Michelle Kazmer, Kathleen Burnett. E-mail jeliseditors@gmail.com; *ALISE News* (q.)

Association for Rural and Small Libraries

201 E. Main St., Suite 1405, Lexington, KY 40507
859-514-9178, e-mail szach@amrms.com
World Wide Web http://www.arsl.info

Object

The Association for Rural and Small Libraries (ARSL) was established in 1978 as the Center for Study of Rural Librarianship in the Department of Library Science at Clarion University of Pennsylvania.

ARSL is a network of persons throughout the United States dedicated to the positive growth and development of libraries. ARSL believes in the value of rural and small libraries, and strives to create resources and services that address national, state, and local priorities for libraries situated in rural communities.

Its objectives are

- To organize a network of members concerned about the growth and development of useful library services in rural and small libraries

- To provide opportunities for the continuing education of members
- To provide mechanisms for members to exchange ideas and to meet on a regular basis
- To cultivate the practice of librarianship and to foster a spirit of cooperation among members of the profession, enabling them to act together for mutual goals
- To serve as a source of current information about trends, issues, and strategies
- To partner with other library and nonlibrary groups and organizations serving rural and small library communities
- To collect and disseminate information and resources that are critical to this network
- To advocate for rural and small libraries at the local, state, and national levels

Officers

Pres. Sonja Plummer-Morgan, Turner Memorial Lib., 39 Second St., Presque Isle, ME 04769. Tel. 207-764-2571, e-mail sonjaplummer@presqueisle.lib.me.us; *Past Pres.* Timothy Owens, North Carolina State Lib., 109 E. Jones St., Raleigh, NC 27601. Tel. 909-807-7424, e-mail timothy.owens@ncdrc.gov.

Association of Academic Health Sciences Libraries

Executive Director, Louise S. Miller
2150 N. 107 St., Suite 205, Seattle, WA 98133
206-367-8704, fax 206-367-8777, e-mail aahsl@sbims.com
World Wide Web http://www.aahsl.org

Object

The Association of Academic Health Sciences Libraries (AAHSL) is composed of the directors of libraries of more than 140 accredited U.S. and Canadian medical schools belonging to the Association of American Medical Colleges. Its goals are to promote excellence in academic health science libraries and to ensure that the next generation of health practitioners is trained in information-seeking skills that enhance the quality of health care delivery, education, and research. Founded in 1977.

Membership

Memb. 140+. Regular membership is available to nonprofit educational institutions operating a school of health sciences that has full or provisional accreditation by the Association of American Medical Colleges. Regular members are represented by the chief administrative officer of the member institution's health sciences library. Associate membership (and nonvoting representation) is available to organizations having an interest in the purposes and activities of the association.

Officers (2010–2011)

Pres. Pat Thibodeau, Medical Center Lib., Duke Univ.; *Pres.-Elect* Gary Freiburger, Health Sciences Lib., Univ. of Arizona. Tel. 520-626-6121, e-mail garyf@ahsl.arizona.edu; *Secy./Treas.* Jett McCann, Dahlgren Memorial Lib., Georgetown Univ. Medical Center. Tel. 202-687-1187, e-mail jm594@georgetown.edu; *Past Pres.* Connie Poole, School of Medicine Lib., Southern Illinois Univ. Tel. 217-545-0994, e-mail cpoole@siumed.edu.

Directors

Karen Butter, Univ. of California, San Francisco; M. J. Tooey, Univ. of Maryland, Baltimore; Sandra Franklin, Emory Univ.

Association of Independent Information Professionals

8550 United Plaza Blvd., Suite 1001, Baton Rouge, LA 70809
225-408-4400, fax 225-408-4422, e-mail office@aiip.org
World Wide Web http://www.aiip.org

Object

Members of the Association of Independent Information Professionals (AIIP) are owners of firms providing such information-related services as online and manual research, document delivery, database design, library support, consulting, writing, and publishing. The objectives of the association are

- To advance the knowledge and understanding of the information profession
- To promote and maintain high professional and ethical standards among its members
- To encourage independent information professionals to assemble to discuss common issues
- To promote the interchange of information among independent information professionals and various organizations
- To keep the public informed of the profession and of the responsibilities of the information professional

Membership

Memb. 50+.

Officers (2010–2011)

Pres. Marge King, InfoRich Group. Tel. 484-461-8100; *Pres.-Elect* Cynthia Hetherington, Hetherington Group. Tel. 973-706-7525; *Secy.* Vada Repta, Precision Research Link. Tel. 217-637-0349; *Treas.* Lark Birdsong, Birdsong Information Services. Tel. 303-884-6666; *Past Pres.* Marcy Phelps, Phelps Research. Tel. 303-239-0657.

Publications

AIIP Connections (q.).
Membership Directory (ann.).
Professional papers series.

Association of Jewish Libraries

P.O. Box 1118, Teaneck, NJ 07666
212-725-5359, e-mail ajlibs@osu.edu
World Wide Web http://www.jewishlibraries.org

Object

The Association of Jewish Libraries (AJL) promotes Jewish literacy through enhancement of libraries and library resources and through leadership for the profession and practitioners of Judaica librarianship. The association fosters access to information, learning, teaching, and research relating to Jews, Judaism, the Jewish experience, and Israel.

Goals

- Maintain high professional standards for Judaica librarians and recruit qualified individuals into the profession

- Facilitate communication and exchange of information on a global scale
- Encourage quality publication in the field in all formats and media
- Stimulate publication of high-quality children's literature
- Facilitate and encourage establishment of Judaica library collections
- Enhance information access for all through application of advanced technologies
- Publicize the organization and its activities in all relevant venues
- Stimulate awareness of Judaica library services among the public at large
- Promote recognition of Judaica librarianship within the wider library profession
- Encourage recognition of Judaica library services by other organizations and related professions
- Ensure continuity of the association through sound management, financial security, effective governance, and a dedicated and active membership

Membership

Memb. 1,000+. Dues $50; (Student/Retired) $30. Year. July 1–June 30.

Officers (July 2010–June 2011)

Pres. James P. Rosenbloom. E-mail rosenbloom@brandeis.edu; *V.P./Pres.-Elect* Heidi Estrin. E-mail heidi@cbiboca.org; *V.P. Memb.* Laurie Haas; *V.P. Publications* Deborah Stern; *Recording Secy.* Elana Gensler; *Corresponding Secy.* Rachel Glasser; *Treas.* Sheryl Stahl; *Past Pres.* Susan Dubin.

Address correspondence to the association.

Publications

AJL Newsletter (q.); *Judaica Librarianship* (irreg.).

Division Presidents

Research Libraries, Archives, and Special Libraries. Rachel Leket-Mor.

Synagogue, School, and Center Libraries. Joyce Levine.

Association of Research Libraries

Executive Director, Charles B. Lowry
21 Dupont Circle N.W., Suite 800, Washington, DC 20036
202-296-2296, fax 202-872-0884, e-mail arlhq@arl.org
World Wide Web http://www.arl.org

Object

The Association of Research Libraries (ARL) is a nonprofit organization of 126 research libraries in North America. Its mission is to influence the changing environment of scholarly communication and the public policies that affect research libraries and the diverse communities they serve. ARL pursues this mission by advancing the goals of its member research libraries, providing leadership in public and information policy to the scholarly and higher education communities, fostering the exchange of ideas and expertise, facilitating the emergence of new roles for research libraries, and shaping a future environment that leverages its interests with those of allied organizations.

Membership

Memb. 126. Membership is institutional. Dues: $24,297 for 2011.

Officers

Pres. Carol A. Mandel, New York Univ.; *V.P./Pres.-Elect* Winston Tabb, Johns Hopkins Univ.; *Past Pres.* Brinley Franklin, Univ. of Connecticut.

Board of Directors

Deborah Carver, Univ. of Oregon; Colleen Cook, Texas A&M; Carol Pitts Diedrichs, Univ. of Kentucky; Ernie Engels, Univ. of Alberta; Deborah Jakubs, Duke Univ.; Anne R. Kenney, Cornell Univ.; Wendy Pradt Lougee, Univ. of Minnesota; Charles B. Lowry (ex officio), ARL; Carol A. Mandel, New York Univ.; Carol Moore (ex officio), Univ. of Toronto; James Mullins, Purdue Univ.; Carton Rogers (ex officio), Univ. of Pennsylvania; Winston Tabb, Johns Hopkins Univ.; James F. Williams II (ex officio), Univ. Colorado at Boulder; Sandra Yee, Wayne State Univ.

Publications

Research Library Issues: A Bimonthly Report from ARL, CNI, and SPARC (bi-mo.).
ARL Academic Health Sciences Library Statistics (ann.).
ARL Academic Law Library Statistics (ann.).
ARL Annual Salary Survey (ann.).
ARL Statistics (ann.).
ARL Supplementary Statistics (ann.).
SPEC Kit series (6 a year).

Committee and Working Group Chairs

Diversity and Leadership. Nancy Baker, Univ. of Iowa.
Fair Use and Related Exemptions Working Group. To be announced.
Membership. Paula Kaufman, Univ. of Illinois at Urbana-Champaign.
Influencing Public Policies. James F. Williams II, Univ. of Colorado at Boulder.
Regional Federal Depository Libraries Working Group. To be announced.
Transforming Research Libraries. Carton Rogers, Univ. of Pennsylvania.
Reshaping Scholarly Communication. Carole Moore, Univ. of Toronto.
Special Collections Working Group, Anne Kenney, Cornell Univ.
Statistics and Assessment. William Potter, Univ. of Georgia.

ARL Membership

Nonuniversity Libraries

Boston Public Lib., Canada Inst. for Scientific and Technical Info., Center for Research Libs., Lib. and Archives Canada, Lib. of Congress, National Agricultural Lib., National Archives, National Lib. of Medicine, New York Public Lib., New York State Lib., Smithsonian Institution Libs.

University Libraries

Alabama; Albany (SUNY); Alberta; Arizona; Arizona State; Auburn; Boston College; Boston Univ.; Brigham Young; British Columbia; Brown; Buffalo (SUNY); Calgary; California, Berkeley; California, Davis; California, Irvine; California, Los Angeles; California, Riverside; California, San Diego; California, Santa Barbara; Case Western Reserve; Chicago; Cincinnati; Colorado; Colorado State; Columbia; Connecticut; Cornell; Dartmouth; Delaware; Duke; Emory; Florida; Florida State; George Washington; Georgetown; Georgia; Georgia Inst. of Technology; Guelph; Harvard; Hawaii; Houston; Howard; Illinois, Chicago; Illinois, Urbana-Champaign; Indiana; Iowa; Iowa State; Johns Hopkins; Kansas; Kent State; Kentucky; Laval; Louisiana State; Louisville; McGill; McMaster; Manitoba; Maryland; Massachusetts; Massachusetts Inst. of Technology; Miami (Florida); Michigan; Michigan State; Minnesota; Missouri; Montreal; Nebraska, Lincoln; New Mexico; New York; North Carolina; North Carolina State; Northwestern; Notre Dame; Ohio; Ohio State; Oklahoma;

Oklahoma State; Oregon; Ottawa; Pennsylvania; Pennsylvania State; Pittsburgh; Princeton; Purdue; Queen's (Kingston, Ontario); Rice; Rochester; Rutgers; Saskatchewan; South Carolina; Southern California; Southern Illinois; Stony Brook (SUNY); Syracuse; Temple; Tennessee; Texas; Texas A&M; Texas Tech; Toronto; Tulane; Utah; Vanderbilt; Virginia; Virginia Tech; Washington; Washington (Saint Louis): Washington State; Waterloo; Wayne State; Western Ontario; Wisconsin; Yale; York.

Association of Vision Science Librarians

Chair, 2010–2012, Gale A. Oren, Kellogg Eye Center, Univ. of Michigan,
1000 Wall St., Ann Arbor, MI 48105
734-763-9468, fax 734-936-9050, e-mail goren@umich.edu
World Wide Web http://www.avsl.org

Object

To foster collective and individual acquisition and dissemination of vision science information, to improve services for all persons seeking such information, and to develop standards for libraries to which members are attached. Founded in 1968.

Membership

Memb. (U.S.) 62; (International) 60.

Publications

Core List of Audio-Visual Related Serials.
Guidelines for Vision Science Libraries.
Opening Day Book, Journal and AV Collection—Visual Science.
Publication Considerations in the Age of Electronic Opportunities.
Standards for Vision Science Libraries.
Union List of Vision-Related Serials (irreg.).

Meetings

Annual meeting held in the fall, mid-year mini-meeting with the Medical Library Association.

Beta Phi Mu (International Library and Information Studies Honor Society)

Executive Director, Christie Koontz
College of Communication and Information,
Florida State University, Tallahassee, FL 32306-2100
850-644-3907, fax 850-644-9763, e-mail ckoontz@ci.fsu.edu
World Wide Web http://www.beta-phi-mu.org

Object

To recognize distinguished achievement in and scholarly contributions to librarianship, information studies, or library education, and to sponsor and support appropriate professional and scholarly projects related to these fields. Founded at the University of Illinois in 1948.

Membership

Memb. 36,000. Open to graduates of library school programs accredited by the American Library Association who fulfill the following requirements: complete the course requirements leading to a fifth year or other advanced degree in librarianship with a scholastic average of 3.75 where A equals 4 points (this provision shall also apply to planned programs of advanced study beyond the fifth year that do not culminate in a degree but that require full-time study for one or more academic years) and rank in the top 25 percent of their class; and receive a letter of recommendation from the faculty of their respective library schools attesting to their professional promise.

Officers

Pres. John M. Budd, Univ. of Missouri, 303 Townsend Hall, Columbia, MO 65211; *V.P./Pres.-Elect* Marie L. Radford, Rutgers Univ., 4 Huntington St., New Brunswick, NJ 08901; *Treas.* Bob Branciforte, College of Communication and Info., Florida State Univ., Tallahassee, FL 32306-2100; *Exec. Dir.* Christie Koontz, College of Communication and Info., Florida State Univ., Tallahassee, FL 32306-2100. Tel. 850-644-3907, fax 850-644-9763, e-mail betaphimuinfo@admin.fsu.edu.

Directors

Dirs. Kaye Bray, Daria DeCooman, George Gaumond, Eloise May, Ron Miller, Beth Paskoff, Amanda Ros, Sue Searing, Shannon Tennant, Diana L. Vogelsong.

Publications

Beta Phi Mu Monograph Series. Book-length scholarly works based on original research in subjects of interest to library and information professionals. Available from Greenwood Press, 130 Cremona Drive, Santa Barbara, CA 93117.

Chapbook Series. Limited editions on topics of interest to information professionals. *Ed.* Lorraine J. Haricombe; *Assoc. Ed.* Keith Russell.

The Pipeline (electronic only). *Ed.* John Paul Walters.

Chapters

Alpha. Univ. of Illinois, Grad. School of Lib. and Info. Science; *Gamma.* Florida State Univ., College of Communication and Info.; *Epsilon.* Univ. of North Carolina, School of Info. and Lib. Science; *Theta.* Pratt Inst., Grad. School of Lib. and Info. Science; *Iota.* Catholic Univ. of America, School of Lib. and Info. Science; Univ. of Maryland, College of Info. Studies; *Lambda.* Univ. of Oklahoma, School of Lib. and Info. Studies; *Mu.* Univ. of Michigan, School of Info; *Xi.* Univ. of Hawaii, Grad. School of Lib. and Info. Studies; *Omicron.* Rutgers Univ., Grad. School of Communication, Info. and Lib. Studies; *Pi.* Univ. of Pittsburgh, School of Info. Sciences; *Rho.* Kent State Univ., School of Lib. and Info. Science; *Sigma.* Drexel Univ., College of Info. Science and Technology; *Upsilon.* Univ. of Kentucky, School of Lib. and Info. Science; *Phi.* Univ. of Denver, Grad. School of Lib. and Info. Science; *Chi.* Indiana Univ., School of Lib. and Info. Science; *Psi.* Univ. of Missouri at Columbia, School of Lib. and Info. Science; *Omega.* San Jose State Univ., School of Lib. and Info. Science; *Beta Alpha.* Queens College, City College of New York, Grad. School of Lib. and Info. Studies; *Beta Beta.* Simmons College, Grad. School of Lib. and Info. Science; *Beta Delta.* State Univ. of New York at Buffalo, Dept. of Lib. and Info. Studies; *Beta Epsilon.* Emporia State Univ., School of Lib. and Info. Management; *Beta Zeta.* Louisiana State Univ., Grad. School of Lib. and Info. Science; *Beta Eta.* Univ. of Texas at Austin, Grad. School of Lib. and Info. Science; *Beta Iota.* Univ. of Rhode Island, Grad. School of Lib. and Info. Studies; *Beta Kappa.* Univ. of Alabama, Grad. School of Lib. and Info. Studies; *Beta Lambda.* Texas Woman's Univ., School of Lib. and Info. Sciences; *Beta Mu.* Long Island Univ., Palmer Grad. School of Lib. and Info. Science; *Beta Nu.* Saint John's Univ., Div. of Lib. and Info. Science; *Beta Xi.* North Carolina Central Univ., School of Lib. and Info. Sciences; *Beta Omicron.* Univ. of Tennessee at Knoxville, Grad. School of Info. Sciences; *Beta Pi.* Univ. of Arizona, Grad. School of Info. Resources and Lib. Science; *Beta Rho.* Univ. of Wisconsin at Milwaukee, School of Info.;

Beta Sigma. Clarion Univ. of Pennsylvania, Dept. of Lib. Science; *Beta Tau.* Wayne State Univ., Lib. and Info. Science Program; *Beta Phi.* Univ. of South Florida, Grad. School of Lib. and Info. Science; *Beta Psi.* Univ. of Southern Mississippi, School of Lib. and Info. Science; *Beta Omega.* Univ. of South Carolina, College of Lib. and Info. Science; *Beta Beta Gamma.* Dominican Univ., Grad. School of Lib. and Info. Science; *Beta Beta Epsilon.* Univ. of Wisconsin at Madison, School of Lib. and Info. Studies; *Beta Beta Zeta.* Univ. of North Carolina at Greensboro, Dept. of Lib. and Info. Studies; *Beta Beta Theta.* Univ. of Iowa, School of Lib. and Info. Science; *Beta Beta Iota.* State Univ. of New York, Univ. at Albany, School of Info. Science and Policy; *Beta Beta Kappa.* Univ. of Puerto Rico, Grad. School of Info. Sciences and Technologies; *Pi Lambda Sigma.* Syracuse Univ., School of Info. Studies; *Beta Beta Mu.* Valdosta State Univ., School of Lib. and Info. Science; *Beta Beta Nu.* Univ. of North Texas, College of Info.

Bibliographical Society of America

Executive Secretary, Michèle E. Randall
P.O. Box 1537, Lenox Hill Sta., New York, NY 10021
212-452-2710 (tel./fax), e-mail bsa@bibsocamer.org
World Wide Web http://www.bibsocamer.org

Object

To promote bibliographical research and to issue bibliographical publications. Organized 1904.

Membership

Memb. Dues (Indiv.) $65; (Sustaining) $250; (Contributing) $100; (Student) $20; (Inst.) $100; (Lifetime) $1,250. Year. Jan.–Dec.

Officers

Pres. John Neal Hoover. E-mail jhoover@umsl.edu; *V.P.* Claudia Funke. E-mail claudiafunke@mac.com; *Secy.* Caroline Duroselle-Melish. E-mail cmelish@fas.harvard.edu; *Treas.* G. Scott Clemons. E-mail scott.clemons@bbh.com; *Past Pres.* John Bidwell. E-mail jbidwell@morganlibrary.org.

Council

(2012) David L. Gants, Barbara Shailor, Daniel Slive, David Supino; (2013) Gerald Cloud, Eugene S. Flamm, David Alan Richards, Carolyn L. Smith; (2014) Douglas F. Bauer, John Crichton, Joan Friedman, Gregory A. Pass.

Publication

Papers of the Bibliographical Society of America (q.; memb.). *Ed.* Trevor Howard-Hill, Thomas Cooper Lib., Univ. of South Carolina, Columbia, SC 29208. Tel./fax 803-777-7046, e-mail ralphcrane@msn.com.

Bibliographical Society of Canada (La Société Bibliographique du Canada)

President, Anne Dondertman
P.O. Box 575, Postal Station P, Toronto, ON M5S 2T1
World Wide Web http://www.bsc-sbc.ca/index.html

Object

The Bibliographical Society of Canada is a bilingual (English/French) organization that has as its goal the scholarly study of the history, description, and transmission of texts in all media and formats, with a primary emphasis on Canada, and the fulfillment of this goal through the following objectives:

- To promote the study and practice of bibliography: enumerative, historical, descriptive, analytical, and textual
- To further the study, research, and publication of book history and print culture
- To publish bibliographies and studies of book history and print culture
- To encourage the publication of bibliographies, critical editions, and studies of book history and print culture
- To promote the appropriate preservation and conservation of manuscript, archival, and published materials in various formats
- To encourage the utilization and analysis of relevant manuscript and archival sources as a foundation of bibliographical scholarship and book history
- To promote the interdisciplinary nature of bibliography, and to foster relationships with other relevant organizations nationally and internationally
- To conduct the society without purpose of financial gain for its members, and to ensure that any profits or other accretions to the society shall be used in promoting its goal and objectives

Membership

The society welcomes as members all those who share its aims and wish to support and participate in bibliographical research and publication.

Officers

Pres. Anne Dondertman. E-mail president@bsc-sbc.ca; *Senior V.P.* Janet Friskney; *2nd V.P.* Jeannine Green; *Secy.* Greta Golick. E-mail secretary@bsc-sbc.ca; *Treas.* Tom Vincent.

Publications

Papers of the Bibliographical Society of Canada / Cahiers de la Société Bibliographique du Canada (s. ann).
The Bulletin / Le Bulletin (s. ann).

For a full list of the society's publications, see http://www.library.utoronto.ca/bsc/publicationseng.html.

Committee Chairs

Awards. Julie Frédette.
Scholarships. Linda Quirk.
Publications. Patricia Fleming.

Black Caucus of the American Library Association

President, Jos N. Holman, Tippecanoe County Public Library,
627 South St., Lafayette, IN 47901.
765-429-0118, fax 765-429-0150, e-mail jholman@tcpl.lib.in.us
World Wide Web http://www.bcala.org

Mission

The Black Caucus of the American Library Association (BCALA) serves as an advocate for the development, promotion, and improvement of library services and resources to the nation's African American community and provides leadership for the recruitment and professional development of African American librarians. Founded in 1970.

Membership

Membership is open to any person, institution, or business interested in promoting the development of library and information services for African Americans and other people of African descent and willing to maintain good financial standing with the organization. The membership is currently composed of librarians and other information professionals, library support staff, libraries, publishers, authors, vendors, and other library-related organizations in the United States and abroad. Dues (Corporate) $200; (Institutional) $60; (Regular) $45; (Student) $10.

Officers

Pres. Jos N. Holman. Tel. 765-429-0118, e-mail jholman@ tcpl.lib.in.us; *V.P./Pres.-Elect* Jerome Offord, Jr.; *Secy.* Jannie R. Cobb; *Treas.* Stanton F. Biddle; *Past Pres.* Karolyn S. Thompson.

Executive Board

Jason K. Alston, Gladys Smiley Bell, Vivian Bordeaux, Diane Covington, Anna Marie Ford, D. L. Grant, Emily Guss, Dorothy Guthrie, Sylvia Sprinkle Hamlin, Allene Hayes, Andrew Jackson (Sekou Molefi Baako), Leroy Robinson, Eboni Stokes, Kelvin Watson, Roberta Webb.

Publication

BCALA Newsletter (bi-mo; memb.). *Contact* Makiba J. Foster. E-mail makibaj27@ yahoo.com.

Committee Chairs

Affiliated Chapters. Sylvia Sprinkle-Hamlin, Lainey Westbrooks.

Affirmative Action. Howard F. McGinn, Darren Sweeper.

ALA Relations. Allene Hayes.

Awards. Richard Bradberry, ayo dayo.

Budget/Audit. Bobby Player.

Constitution and Bylaws. D. L. Grant, Gerald Holmes.

Fund Raising. Makiba J. Foster, Kelvin Watson.

History. Sibyl E. Moses.

International Relations. Vivian Bordeaux, Eboni M. Stokes.

E. J. Josey Scholarship. Billy Beal, Joyce E. Jelks.

Literary Awards. Virginia Toliver, Joel White.

Membership. Rudolph Clay, Allison M. Sutton.

Newsletter. Makiba J. Foster.

Nominations/Elections. Wanda K. Brown.

Programs. Jos N. Holman.

Public Relations. Barbara E. Martin.

Recruitment and Professional Development. Andrew P. Jackson (Sekou Molefi Baako).

Services to Children of Families of African Descent. Karen Lemmons.

Smiley Fund. Gladys Smiley Bell.

Technology Advisory. H. Jamane Yeager.

Dr. John C. Tyson Award. Alys Jordan, Esmeralda M. Kale.

Awards

BCALA Literary Awards.
BCALA Trailblazer's Award.
DEMCO/ALA Black Caucus Award for Excellence in Librarianship.

Distinguished Service Award.

E. J. Josey Scholarship Award.

Smiley Student Fund.

John Tyson Award.

Canadian Association for Information Science (L'Association Canadienne des Sciences de l'Information)

President, Nadia Caidi
Faculty of Information, University of Toronto,
45 Willcocks St., No. 335, Toronto, ON M5S 1C7
World Wide Web http://www.cais-acsi.ca

Object

To promote the advancement of information science in Canada and encourage and facilitate the exchange of information relating to the use, access, retrieval, organization, management, and dissemination of information.

Membership

Institutions and individuals interested in information science and involved in the gathering, organization, and dissemination of information (such as information scientists, archivists, librarians, computer scientists, documentalists, economists, educators, journalists, and psychologists) and who support CAIS's objectives can become association members. Dues (Inst.) $109; (Personal) $75; (Student) $49.

Directors

Pres. Nadia Caidi, Univ. of Toronto; *V.P.* Siobhan Stevenson, Univ. of Toronto; *Treas.* Ali Shiri, Univ. of Alberta; *Dir., Communications* Dinesh Rathi, Univ. of Alberta; *Dir., Membership* Heather Hill, Univ. of Western Ontario; *Secy.* Heather O'Brien, Univ. of British Columbia; *Past Pres.* Catherine Johnson, Univ. of Western Ontario.

Publication

Canadian Journal of Information and Library Science. Ed. Clément Arsenault, Univ. de Montréal.

Canadian Association of Research Libraries (Association des Bibliothèques de Recherche du Canada)

Brent Roe, Executive Director
Morisset Hall, 65 University St., Suite 239
University of Ottawa, Ottawa, ON K1N 9A5.
613-562-5385, fax 613.562.5297, e-mail carl@uottawa.ca
World Wide Web http://www.carl-abrc.ca

Membership

The Canadian Association of Research Libraries (CARL), established in 1976, is the leadership organization for the Canadian research library community. The association's members are the 29 major academic research libraries across Canada together with Library and Archives Canada, the Canada Institute for Scientific and Technical Information (CISTI), and the Library of Parliament. Membership is institutional, open primarily to libraries of Canadian universities that have doctoral graduates in both the arts and the sciences. CARL is an associate member of the Association of Universities and Colleges of Canada (AUCC) and is incorporated as a not-for-profit organization under the Canada Corporations Act.

CARL strives to enhance the capacity of Canada's research libraries to partner in research and higher education, seeking effective and sustainable scholarly communication and public policy encouraging research and broad access to scholarly information. CARL's strategic directions for 2010–2012 focus on the continuing transformation of scholarly communication, advocacy for a favorable federal public policy environment, and the strengthening and promotion of Canada's research libraries.

Officers

Pres. (2009–2011) Ernie Ingles, 5-07 Cameron Lib., Univ. of Alberta, Edmonton, AB T6G 2J8; *V.P./Pres.-Elect (2009–2011)* Thomas Hickerson, MacKimmie Lib. Tower, Univ. of Calgary, 2500 University Drive N.W., Calgary, AB T2N 1N4; *Secy. (2009–2011)* Sylvie Belzile, Services des Bibliothèques et Archives, Univ. of Sherbrooke, 2500 Blvd. Université, Sherbrooke QC J1K 2R1; *Treas. (2009–2011)* Lorraine Busby, Queen Elizabeth II Lib., Memorial Univ. of Newfoundland, St. John's, NF A1C 5S7; *Dirs. (2010–2012)*; Karen Adams, Univ. of Manitoba Libs., Winnipeg, MB R3T 2N2; Mark Haslett, Univ. of Waterloo Lib., 200 University Ave. West, Waterloo, ON N2L 3G1.

Member Institutions

Univ. of Alberta, Univ. of British Columbia, Brock Univ., Univ. of Calgary, Carleton Univ., CISTI (Canada Institute for Scientific and Technical Information), Concordia Univ., Dalhousie Univ., Univ. of Guelph, Université Laval, Univ. of Manitoba, Lib. and Archives Canada, Lib. of Parliament, McGill Univ., McMaster Univ., Memorial Univ. of Newfoundland, Université de Montréal, Univ. of New Brunswick, Univ. of Ottawa, Université du Québec à Montréal, Queen's Univ., Univ. of Regina, Ryerson Univ., Univ. of Saskatchewan, Université de Sherbrooke, Simon Fraser Univ., Univ. of Toronto, Univ. of Victoria, Univ. of Waterloo, Univ. of Western Ontario, Univ. of Windsor, York Univ.

Publications

For a full list of publications, see http://www.carl-abrc.ca/publications/publications-e.html.

Canadian Library Association (Association Canadienne des Bibliothèques)

Executive Director, Kelly Moore
1150 Morrison Drive, Suite 400, Ottawa, ON K2H 8S9
613-232-9625 ext. 306, fax 613-563-9895, e-mail kmoore@cla.ca
World Wide Web http://www.cla.ca

Object

The Canadian Library Association (CLA) is its members' advocate and public voice, educator, and network. It builds the Canadian library and information community by promoting, developing, and supporting library and information services and advancing today's information professionals, through cooperation with all who share its values. The association represents Canadian librarianship to the federal government and media, carries on international liaison with other library associations and cultural agencies, offers professional development programs, and supports such core library values as intellectual freedom and access to information, particularly for disadvantaged populations. Founded in 1946, CLA is a not-for-profit voluntary organization governed by an elected executive council.

Membership

Memb. (Indiv.) 1,700; (Inst.) 400. Open to individuals, institutions, library boards, and groups interested in librarianship and in library and information services.

Officers

Pres. Keith Walker, Medicine Hat Community College; *V.P./Pres.-Elect* Karen Adams, University of Manitoba Libraries; *Treas.* Ingrid Langhammer.

Publications

Feliciter: Linking Canada's Information Professionals (6 a year; magazine/journal).

CLA Digest (bi-weekly; electronic newsletter).

Divisions

Canadian Association for School Libraries (CASL).

Canadian Association of College and University Libraries (CACUL).

Canadian Association of Public Libraries (CAPL).

Canadian Association of Special Libraries and Information Services (CASLIS).

Canadian Library Trustees Association (CLTA).

Catholic Library Association

Acting Executive Director, Malachy R. McCarthy
205 W. Monroe St., Suite 314, Chicago, IL 60606
413-443-2252, fax 413-442-2252, e-mail cla@cathla.org
World Wide Web http://www.cathla.org

Object

The promotion and encouragement of Catholic literature and library work through cooperation, publications, education, and information. Founded in 1921.

Membership

Memb. 1,000. Dues $55–$500. Year. July–June.

Officers (2011–2013)

Pres. Malachy R. McCarthy, Claretian Missionaries Archives, 205 W. Monroe St., Chicago, IL 60606; *V.P./Pres.-Elect* Sara B. Baron, Regent Univ. Lib., 1000 Regent University Drive, Virginia Beach, VA 23464; *Past Pres.* Nancy K. Schmidtmann, 174 Theodore Drive, Coram, NY 11727.

Address correspondence to the executive director.

Executive Board

Officers; Jean Elvekrog, 401 Doral Court, Waunakee, WI 53597; Susan B. Finney, St. Mary's Dominican H.S., 7701 Walmsley Ave., New Orleans, LA 70125; Cait C. Kokolus, St. Charles Borromeo Seminary, 100 E. Wynnewood Rd., Wynnewood, PA 19096; Frances O'Dell, OSF, Barry Univ. Lib., 11300 N.E. 2 Ave., Miami Shores, FL 33161; Vincent P. Tinerella, Arkansas Tech Univ., 305 W. Q St., Russellville, AR 72801.

Publications

Catholic Library World (q.; memb.; nonmemb. $100). *General Ed.* Sigrid Kelsey.

Catholic Periodical and Literature Index (*CLPI*). Available as an online subscription (1981–present) through EBSCO. *Ed.* Deborah A. Winarski.

Chief Officers of State Library Agencies

Association Director, Laura Singler-Adams
201 E. Main St., Suite 1405, Lexington, KY 40507
859-514-9151, fax 859-514-9166, e-mail lsingler-adams@amrms.com
World Wide Web http://www.cosla.org

Object

Chief Officers of State Library Agencies (COSLA) is an independent organization of the chief officers of state and territorial agencies designated as the state library administrative agency and responsible for statewide library development. Its purpose is to identify and address issues of common concern and national interest; to further state library agency relationships with federal government and national organizations; and to initiate cooperative action for the improvement of library services to the people of the United States.

COSLA's membership consists solely of these top library officers, variously designated as state librarian, director, commissioner, or executive secretary. The organization provides a continuing mechanism for dealing with the problems and challenges faced by these officers. Its work is carried on through its members, a board of directors, and committees.

Officers (2010–2012)

Pres. Lamar Veatch, State Libn., Georgia Public Lib. Service, 1800 Century Place, Suite 150, Atlanta, GA 30345-4304. Tel. 404-235-7200, e-mail jwalsh@secstate.wa.gov; *V.P./Pres.-Elect* Ann Joslin, State Libn., Idaho Commission for Libs., 325 W. State St., Boise, ID 83702. Tel. 208-334-2150, e-mail ann.joslin@libraries.idaho.gov; *Secy.* Margaret Conroy, State Libn., Missouri State Lib., P.O. Box 387, Jefferson City, MO 65102. Tel. 573-526-4783, e-mail margaret.conroy@sos.mo.gov; *Treas.* David Goble, Dir. and State Libn., South Carolina State Lib., P.O. Box 11469, Columbia, SC 29211. Tel. 803-734-8656, e-mail dgoble@statelibrary.sc.gov; *Past Pres.* Susan McVey, State Libn., Oklahoma Dept. of Libs., 200 N.E. 18 St., Oklahoma City, OK 73105-3298. Tel. 405-521-2502, e-mail smcvey@oltn.odl.state.ok.us; *Dirs.* Jo Budler, State Libn., State Lib. of Kansas, Capitol Bldg., Room 343-N, 300 S.W. 10 Ave., Topeka, KS 66612. Tel. 785-296-5466, e-mail jobudler@kslib.info; Michael York, State Libn., New Hampshire State Lib., 20 Park St., Concord, NH 03301. Tel. 603-271-2397, e-mail michael.york@dcr.nh.gov.

Chinese American Librarians Association

Executive Director, Haipeng Li
E-mail haipeng4cala@gmail.com
World Wide Web http://www.cala-web.org

Object

To enhance communications among Chinese American librarians as well as between Chinese American librarians and other librarians; to serve as a forum for discussion of mutual problems and professional concerns among Chinese American librarians; to promote Sino-American librarianship and library services; and to provide a vehicle whereby Chinese American librarians can cooperate with other associations and organizations having similar or allied interests.

Membership

Memb. 1,400+. Open to anyone who is interested in the association's goals and activities. Dues (Regular) $30; (International/Student/Nonsalaried) $15; (Inst.) $100; (Affiliated) $100; (Life) $300.

Officers

Pres. (2010–2011) Zhijia Shen. E-mail zhijia@u.washington.edu; *V.P./Pres.-Elect (2010–2011)* Min Chou. E-mail minchou.njcu@gmail.com; *V.P./Pres.-Elect (2011–2012)* Esther Lee. E-mail eyw888lee@gmail.com; *Exec. Dir. (2010–2013)* Haipeng Li. E-mail haipeng4cala@gmail.com; *Treas. (2010–2012)* Songqian Lu. E-mail songqian4cala@gmail.com; *Past Pres.* Xudong Jin. E-mail xdjin@owu.edu.

Publications

Journal of Library and Information Science (2 a year; memb.; online). *Ed. (2008–2011)* Min Chou, Congressman Frank J. Guarini Lib., New Jersey City Univ. E-mail minchou.njcu@gmail.com.

Membership Directory (memb.).

Newsletter (2 a year; memb.; online). *Eds.* Priscilla Yu. E-mail pcyu@illinois.edu; Sai Deng. E-mail sai.deng@wichita.edu.

Occasional Paper Series (OPS) (occasional, online). *Ed. (2009–2012)* Xue-Ming Bao. E-mail baoxuemi@shu.edu.

Committee Chairs

Alire Initiative Task Force. Nancy Hershoff, Dora Ho.

Annual Conference, Program Planning (2010–2011). Min Chou.

Annual Conference, Program Planning. (2011–2012). Esther Lee.

Awards. Wenling Liu, Jen-Chien Yu.

Best Book Award. Shuqin Jiao, Hong Cheng.

Constitution and Bylaws. Nancy Hershoff.

Finance. Ruan Lian.

International Relations. Qi Chen, Shuyong Jiang.

Membership. Hong Ma, Li Zhang.

Mentorship Program. Karen Wei, Mengxiong Liu.

Nominating. Xudong Jin.

Public Relations/Fund Raising. Maria Yuen-Hung Fung, Yi Liang.

Publications. Ying Xu, Raymond Wang.

Sally C. Tseng's Professional Development Grant Committee. Elaine Dong, Liana Zhou.

Scholarship Committee. Hong Miao.

Strategic Plan Task Force. Liana Zhou.

Web Committee. Bin Zhang, Vincci Kwong.

Church and Synagogue Library Association

2920 S.W. Dolph Court, Suite 3A, Portland, OR 97219-4055
503-244-6919, 800-542-2752, fax 503-977-3734, e-mail CSLA@worldaccessnet.com
World Wide Web http://www.cslainfo.org

Object

The Church and Synagogue Library Association (CSLA) provides educational guidance in the establishment and maintenance of congregational libraries.

Its purpose is to act as a unifying core for congregational libraries; to provide the opportunity for a mutual sharing of practices and problems; to inspire and encourage a sense of purpose and mission among congregational librarians; to study and guide the development of congregational librarianship toward recognition as a formal branch of the library profession. Founded in 1967.

Membership

Memb. 1,300. Dues (Inst.) $200; (Affiliated) $100; (Church or Synagogue) $70 ($75 foreign); (Indiv.) $50 ($55 foreign).

Officers (July 2010–July 2011)

Pres. Marjorie Smink; *1st V.P./Pres.-Elect* Evelyn Pockrass; *2nd V.P.* Marianne Stowers; *Treas.* Dick Burgduff; *Admin.* Judith Janzen; *Past Pres.* Rusty Tryon; *Ed., Congregational Libraries Today* Jeri Zulli.

Executive Board

Officers; committee chairs.

Publications

Bibliographies (4; price varies).

Congregational Libraries Today (q.; memb.; nonmemb. $50; Canada $60).

CSLA Guides (price varies).

Committee Chairs

Awards. Jeri Baker.
Conference. J. Theodore Anderson.
Finance. Pat Shufeldt.
Nominations and Elections. Jane Hope.
Publications. Dotty Lewis.

Coalition for Networked Information

Executive Director, Clifford A. Lynch
21 Dupont Circle, Suite 800, Washington, DC 20036
202-296-5098, fax 202-872-0884, e-mail info@cni.org
World Wide Web http://www.cni.org

Mission

The Coalition for Networked Information (CNI) is an organization to advance the transformative promise of networked information technology for the advancement of scholarly communication and the enrichment of intellectual productivity.

Membership

Memb. 212. Membership is institutional. Dues $6,700. Year. July–June.

Steering Committee

Daniel Cohen, George Mason Univ.; Jeffrey Horrell, Dartmouth College; Charles B. Lowry, Assn. of Research Libs.; Clifford A. Lynch, CNI; Deanna B. Marcum, Lib. of Congress; Diana G. Oblinger, EDUCAUSE; Patti Orr, Baylor Univ.; Carrie E. Regenstein, Carnegie Mellon Univ.; Sherrie Schmidt, Arizona State Univ.; George O. Strawn, NITRD; Donald J. Waters, Andrew W. Mellon Foundation.

Publication

CNI-Announce (subscribe by e-mail to cni-announce-subscribe@cni.org).

Council on Library and Information Resources

1752 N St. N.W., Suite 800, Washington, DC 20036
202-939-4750, fax 202-939-4765
World Wide Web http://www.clir.org

Object

In 1997 the Council on Library Resources (CLR) and the Commission on Preservation and Access (CPA) merged and became the Council on Library and Information Resources (CLIR). CLIR's mission is to expand access to information, however recorded and preserved, as a public good. CLIR identifies and defines the key emerging issues relating to the welfare of libraries and the constituencies they serve, convenes the leaders who can influence change, and promotes collaboration among the institutions and organizations that can achieve change. The council's interests embrace the entire range of information resources and services from traditional library and archival materials to emerging digital formats. It assumes a particular interest in helping institutions cope with the accelerating pace of change associated with the transition into the digital environment.

CLIR is an independent, nonprofit organization. While maintaining appropriate collaboration and liaison with other institutions and organizations, the council operates independently of any particular institutional or vested interests. Through the composition of its board, it brings the broadest possible perspective to bear upon defining and establishing the priority of the issues with which it is concerned.

Board

CLIR's Board of Directors currently has 15 members.

Officers

Chair Stephen Nichols; *Pres.* Charles Henry. E-mail chenry@clir.org; *V. Chair* Wendy Lougee; *Secy.* Stephen Rhind-Tutt; *Treas.* Joseph King.

Address correspondence to headquarters.

Publications

Annual Report.
CLIR Issues (bi-mo.).
Technical reports.

Council on Library/Media Technicians

Executive Director, Margaret Barron
PMB 168, 28262 Chardon Rd., Willoughby Hills, OH 44092
216-261-0776, e-mail margaretrbarron@aol.com
World Wide Web http://colt.ucr.edu

The Council on Library/Media Technicians (COLT), an affiliate of the American Library Association, is an international organization that works to address the issues and concerns of library and media support staff personnel.

Since 1967 COLT has addressed issues covering such areas as technical education, continuing education, certification, job description uniformity, and the more elusive goals of gaining recognition and respect for the professional work that its members do.

Objectives

COLT's objectives are

- To function as a clearinghouse for information relating to library support staff personnel
- To advance the status, employment, and certification of library staff
- To promote effective communication and cooperation with other organizations whose purposes and objectives are similar to those of COLT

COLT's Web site, http://colt.ucr.edu, provides information on library technician programs, a speaker exchange listing for help in organizing workshops and conferences, bibliographies on needed resources, and jobline resource links.

COLT holds an annual conference, generally immediately preceding the American Library Association Annual Conference.

Membership

Membership is open to all library employees. Dues (Inst.) $70 ($95 foreign); (Indiv.) $45 ($70 foreign); (Student) $35. Year Jan.–Dec.

Officers

Pres. Jackie Hite. Tel. 202-231-3836, fax 202-231-3838, e-mail jmhite0@dia.mil; *V.P./Pres.-Elect.* Chris Egan. E-mail egan@rand.org; *Secy.* Robin Martindill. E-mail rmartind@sdccd.edu; *Treas.* Stan Cieplinski. E-mail stan.cieplinski@domail.maricopa.edu; *Past Pres.* Jackie Lakatos. E-mail jlakatos@lemontlibrary.org.

Federal Library and Information Center Committee

Executive Director, Blane Dessy
Library of Congress, Washington, DC 20540-4935
202-707-4800
World Wide Web http://www.loc.gov/flicc

Object

The Federal Library and Information Center Committee (FLICC) makes recommendations on federal library and information policies, programs, and procedures to federal agencies and to others concerned with libraries and information centers. The committee coordinates cooperative activities and services among federal libraries and information centers and serves as a forum to consider issues and policies that affect federal libraries and information centers, needs and priorities in providing information services to the government and to the nation at large, and efficient and cost-effective use of federal library and information resources and services. Furthermore, the committee promotes improved access to information, continued development and use of the Federal Library and Information Network (FEDLINK), research and development in the application of new technologies to federal libraries and information centers, improvements in the management of federal libraries and information centers, and relevant education opportunities. Founded in 1965.

Membership

Libn. of Congress, Dir. of the National Agricultural Lib., Dir. of the National Lib. of Medicine, Dir. of the National Lib. of Educ., representatives of each of the cabinet-level executive departments, and representatives of each of the following agencies: National Aeronautics and Space Admin., National Science Foundation, Smithsonian Institution, U.S. Supreme Court, National Archives and Records Admin., Admin. Offices of the U.S. Courts, Defense Technical Info. Center, Government Printing Office, National Technical Info. Service (Dept. of Commerce), Office of Scientific and Technical Info. (Dept. of Energy), Exec. Office of the President, Dept. of the Army, Dept. of the Navy, Dept. of the Air Force, and chair of the FEDLINK Advisory Council. Fifteen additional voting member agencies are selected on a rotating basis by the voting members of FEDLINK. These rotating members serve three-year terms. One representative of each of the following agencies is invited as an observer to committee meetings: Government Accountability Office, General Services Admin., Joint Committee on Printing, Office of Mgt. and Budget, Office of Personnel Mgt., and U.S. Copyright Office.

Officers

Chair Deanna Marcum, Assoc. Libn. for Lib. Services, Lib. of Congress; *Co-Chair* Kathryn Mendenhall; *V. Chair* Elaine Cline; *Exec. Dir.* Blane Dessy.

Address correspondence to the executive director.

Medical Library Association

Executive Director, Carla Funk
65 E. Wacker Place, Suite 1900, Chicago, IL 60601-7298
312-419-9094, fax 312-419-8950, e-mail info@mlahq.org
World Wide Web http://www.mlanet.org

Object

The Medical Library Association (MLA) is a nonprofit professional education organization with more than 4,000 health sciences information professional members and partners worldwide. MLA provides lifelong educational opportunities, supports a knowledgebase of health information research, and works with a global network of partners to promote the importance of quality information for improved health to the health care community and the public.

Membership

Memb. (Inst.) 600+; (Indiv.) 3,400+, in 56 countries. Institutional members are medical and allied scientific libraries. Individual members are people who are (or were at the time membership was established) engaged in professional library or bibliographic work in medical and allied scientific libraries or people who are interested in medical or allied scientific libraries. Members can be affiliated with one or more of MLA's more than 20 special-interest sections and its regional chapters.

Officers

Pres. Ruth Holst. E-mail rholst@uic.edu; *Pres-Elect* Gerald Perry. E-mail jerry.perry@ucdenver.edu; *Past Pres.* Connie Schardt. E-mail schar005@mc.duke.edu.

Directors

Jane Blumenthal (2011), Judy Burnham (2011), Marianne Comegys (2013), Cynthia Henderson (2012), Julia Kochi (2011), Ann McKibbon (2012), Beverly Murphy (2011), Rikke Ogawa (2013), Julia Shaw-Kokot (2013).

Publications

Journal of the Medical Library Association (q.; $190).

MLA News (10 a year; $70).

Miscellaneous (request current list from association headquarters).

Music Library Association

8551 Research Way, Suite 180, Middleton, WI 53562
608-836-5825, e-mail mla@areditions.com
World Wide Web http://www.musiclibraryassoc.org

Object

The Music Library Association provides a professional forum for librarians, archivists, and others who support and preserve the world's musical heritage. To achieve this mission, it

- Provides leadership for the collection and preservation of music and information about music in libraries and archives
- Develops and delivers programs that promote continuing education and professional development in music librarianship
- Ensures and enhances intellectual access to music for all by contributing to the development and revision of national and international codes, formats, and other standards for the bibliographic control of music
- Ensures and enhances access to music for all by facilitating best practices for housing, preserving, and providing access to music
- Promotes legislation that strengthens music library services and universal access to music
- Fosters information literacy and lifelong learning by promoting music reference services, library instruction programs, and publications
- Collaborates with other groups in the music and technology industries, government, and librarianship, to promote its mission and values

Membership

Memb. 1,200+. Dues (Inst.) $135; (Indiv.) $100; (Retired or Assoc.) $70; (Paraprofessional) $55; (Student) $45. (Foreign, add $10.) Year. July 1–June 30.

Officers

Pres. Ruthann B. McTyre, 2000 Voxman Music Bldg., Univ. of Iowa, Iowa City, IA 52242-1795. Tel. 319-335-3088, fax 319-335-2637, e-mail ruthann-mctyre@uiowa.edu; *V.P./Pres.-elect* Jerry L. McBride. E-mail jerry.mcbride@stanford.edu; *Rec. Secy.* Pamela Bristah. E-mail pbristah@wellesley.edu; *Treas./Exec. Secy.* Michael Rogan. E-mail michael.rogan@tufts.edu; *Past Pres.* Philip R. Vandermeer, Music Lib., Wilson Lib. CB3906, Univ. of North Carolina at Chapel Hill, Chapel Hill, NC 27514. Tel. 919-966-1113, fax 919-843-0418, e-mail vanderme@email.unc.edu.

Members-at-Large

Members at Large (2009–2011) Linda Fairtile, Stephen Mantz, Jenn Riley; (2010–2012) Susannah Cleveland, Cheryl Taranto, Liza Vick.

Publications

MLA Index and Bibliography Series (irreg.; price varies).

MLA Newsletter (q.; memb.).

MLA Technical Reports (irreg.; price varies).

Music Cataloging Bulletin (mo.; online subscription only, $35).

Notes (q.; indiv. $85; inst. $100).

National Association of Government Archives and Records Administrators

1450 Western Ave., Suite 101, Albany, NY 12203
518-694-8472, e-mail nagara@caphill.com
World Wide Web http://www.nagara.org

Object

Founded in 1984, NAGARA is a growing nationwide association of local, state, and federal archivists and records administrators, and others interested in improved care and management of government records. NAGARA promotes public awareness of government records and archives management programs, encourages interchange of information among government archives and records management agencies, develops and implements professional standards of government records and archival administration, and encourages study and research into records management problems and issues.

Membership

Most NAGARA members are federal, state, and local archival and records management agencies.

Officers

Pres. Paul R. Bergeron, city clerk, 229 Main St., Nashua, NH 03060. Tel. 603-589-3010, fax 603-589-3029, e-mail bergeronp@nashuanh.gov; *V.P.* Daphne DeLeon, administrator, Nevada State Lib. and Archives, 100 N. Stewart St., Carson City, NV 89701-4285. Tel. 775-684-3315, fax 775-684-3311, e-mail ddeleon@nevadaculture.org; *Secy.* Caryn Wojcik, archivist, Records Management Services, Michigan Dept. of Technology, Management, and Budget, 3400 N. Grand River Ave., P.O. Box 30026, Lansing, MI 48909. Tel. 517-335-8222, fax 517-321-3408, e-mail wojcikc@michigan.gov; *Treas.* Nancy Fortna, National Archives and Records Administration, Seventh and Pennsylvania Ave. N.W., Room G-13 NWCC, Washington, DC 20408-0001. Tel. 202-357-5288, e-mail nancy.fortna@nara.gov; *Past Pres.* Tracey Berezansky, Alabama Dept. of Archives and History, P.O. Box 300100, Montgomery, AL 36130-0100. Tel. 334-353-4604, fax 334-353-4321, e-mail tracey.berezansky@archiveds.alabama.gov.

Directors

Jim Corridan, Indiana Commission on Public Records; Bonnie Curtin, Federal Trade Commission; John Paul Deley, Office of Info. Technology; Sandy Hart, McKinney, Texas; Sandra Jaramillo, New Mexico State Records Center and Archives; Douglas K. King, Sedgwick County (Kansas) Government; Val Wood, Records and Licensing Services, King County, Washington.

Publications

Clearinghouse (q.; memb.).
Crossroads (q.; memb.).
Government Records Issues (series).
Preservation Needs in State Archives.
Program Reporting Guidelines for Government Records Programs.

National Church Library Association

Executive Director, Susan Benish
275 S. 3 St., Suite 204, Stillwater, MN 55082
651-430-0770, e-mail info@churchlibraries.org
World Wide Web http://www.churchlibraries.org

Object

The National Church Library Association (NCLA), formerly the Lutheran Church Library Association, is a nonprofit organization that serves the unique needs of congregational libraries and those who manage them. NCLA provides inspiration, solutions, and support to church librarians in the form of printed manuals and guidelines, booklists, the quarterly journal *Libraries ALIVE,* national conferences, a mentoring program, online support, and personal advice. Regional chapters operate throughout the United States.

Membership

Memb. $55. Year. Jan.–Jan.

Officers

Pres. Kathleen Bowman; *Treas.* Moe Conley; *Past Pres.* Charles Mann.

Directors

Gordon Duffy, Bev Etzelmueller, Sandra Neal, Sally Onstad, Sandy Sharps, Kay Smith.

Address correspondence to the executive director.

Publication

Libraries ALIVE (q.; memb.).

National Federation of Advanced Information Services

Executive Director, Bonnie Lawlor
1518 Walnut St., Suite 1004, Philadelphia, PA 19102
215-893-1561, fax 215-893-1564,e-mail nfais@nfais.org
World Wide Web http://www.nfais.org

Object

The National Federation of Advanced Information Services (NFAIS) is an international nonprofit membership organization composed of leading information providers. Its membership includes government agencies, nonprofit scholarly societies, and private sector businesses. NFAIS is committed to promoting the value of authoritative content. It serves all groups that create, aggregate, organize, or facilitate access to such information. In order to improve members' capabilities and to contribute to their ongoing success, NFAIS provides opportunities for education, advocacy, and a forum in which to address common interests. Founded in 1958.

Membership

Memb. 60. Full members are organizations whose main focus is any of the following activities: information creation, organization, aggregation, dissemination, access, or retrieval. Organizations are eligible for associate member status if they do not meet the qualifications for full membership.

Officers (2010–2011)

Pres. Judith Russell, Univ. of Florida; *Pres.-Elect* Keith MacGregor, Thomson Reuters; *Secy.* Barbara Dobbs Mackenzie, *RILM Abstracts of Music Literature*; *Treas.* Suzanne BeDell, Dialog; *Past Pres.* Terence Ford, J. Paul Getty Trust.

Directors

David Brown, Mark Gauthier, David Gillikin, Ellen Herbst, Chris McCue, Judy Salk, Lynn Willis.

Staff

Exec. Dir. Bonnie Lawlor. E-mail blawlor@nfais.org; *Dir., Planning and Communications* Jill O'Neill. E-mail jilloneill@nfais.org; *Customer Service* Margaret Manson. E-mail mmanson@nfais.org.

Publications

For a detailed list of NFAIS publications, see the NFAIS Web site, http://www.nfais.org.

National Information Standards Organization

Managing Director, Todd Carpenter
1 N. Charles Ave., Suite 1905, Baltimore, MD 21201
301-654-2512, fax 410-685-5278, e-mail nisohq@niso.org
World Wide Web http://www.niso.org

Object

NISO, the National Information Standards Organization, a nonprofit association accredited by the American National Standards Institute (ANSI), identifies, develops, maintains, and publishes technical standards to manage information in our changing and ever-more-digital environment. NISO standards apply both traditional and new technologies to the full range of information-related needs, including discovery, retrieval, repurposing, storage, metadata, business information, and preservation.

Experts from the information industry, libraries, systems vendors, and publishing participate in the development of NISO standards. The standards are approved by the consensus body of NISO's voting membership, which consists of more than 80 voting members representing libraries, publishers, vendors, government, associations, and private businesses and organizations. In addition, approximately 30 libraries are NISO Library Standards Alliance members. NISO is supported by its membership and corporate grants. NISO is a nonprofit educational organization. It is accredited by ANSI and serves as the U.S. Technical Advisory Group to ISO/TC 46 Information and Documentation as well as the secretariat for ISO/TC 46/SC 9, Identification and Description.

Membership

Memb. 80+. Open to any organization, association, government agency, or company willing to participate in and having substantial concern for the development of NISO standards. Libraries may support NISO as members of the Library Standards Alliance.

Officers

Chair Janice Fleming, American Psychological Assn., 750 First St. N.E., Washington, DC 20002-4242. Tel. 202-336-5500, e-mail jfleming@apa.org; *V. Chair/Chair-Elect* Bruce Heterick, Ithaka, 149 Fifth Ave., New York, NY 10010. Tel. 212-358-6400, fax

212-358-6499, e-mail bruce.heterick@ithaka.org; *Past Chair* Chuck Koscher, CrossRef, 40 Salem St., Lynnfield, MA 01940. Tel. 781-295-0072 ext. 26, fax 781-295-0077, e-mail ckoscher@crossref.org; *Treas.* Barbara Preece, California State Univ., San Marco, 333 S. Twin Oaks Valley Rd., San Marcos, CA 92096. Tel. 760-750-4350, e-mail bpreece@csusm.edu.

Directors

Nancy Barnes, Nancy Davenport, John Harwood, Charles Lowry, Oliver Pesch, Heather Reid, Bruce Rosenblum, Winston Tabb, Mike Teets.

Publications

Information Standards Quarterly ($130/year, foreign $165, back issues $40).

NISO Newsline (free monthly e-letter released on the first Wednesday of each month. See the NISO Web site for details on subscribing and archived issues).

For other NISO publications, see the article "National Information Standards Organization (NISO) Standards" later in Part 6.

NISO published standards, recommended practices, and technical reports are available free of charge as downloadable pdf files from the NISO Web site (http://www.niso.org). Standards in hard copy are available for sale on the Web site.

Patent and Trademark Depository Library Association

World Wide Web http://www.ptdla.org

Object

The Patent and Trademark Depository Library Association (PTDLA) provides a support structure for the 81 patent and trademark depository libraries (PTDLs) affiliated with the U.S. Patent and Trademark Office (USPTO). The association's mission is to discover the interests, needs, opinions, and goals of the PTDLs and to advise USPTO in these matters for the benefit of PTDLs and their users, and to assist USPTO in planning and implementing appropriate services. Founded in 1983 as the Patent Depository Library Advisory Council; name changed to Patent and Trademark Depository Library Association in 1988; became an American Library Association affiliate in 1996.

Membership

Open to any person employed in a patent and trademark depository library whose responsibilities include the patent collection. Affiliate membership is also available. Dues $25.

Officers (2010–2011)

Pres. Robert Klein. E-mail kleinr@mdpls.org; *V.P./Pres-Elect* Marian Armour Gemmen. E-mail marmour@wvu.edu; *Secy.* Martin Wallace. E-mail martin.wallace@umit.maine.edu; *Treas.* Jim Miller. E-mail jmiller2@umd.edu; *Past Pres.* Andrew Wohrley. E-mail wohrlaj@auburn.edu.

Divisional Representatives

Academic Division

John Meier. E-mail meier@psu.edu; Region 4, Jan Comfort. E-mail comforj@clemson.edu; Suzanne Reinman. E-mail suzanne.reinman@okstate.edu.

Public Division

Michael Strickland. E-mail mstrickland@asl.lib.ar.us; Spruce Fraser. E-mail sfraser@slpl.org; Walt Johnson. E-mail wjohnson@hclib.org.

Publications

PTDLA Newsletter. *Ed.* Suzanne Holcombe. E-mail suzanne.reinman@okstate.edu.

Intellectual Property (*IP*). Electronic at http://www.ptdla.org/ipjournal.html. *Ed.* Michael White.

REFORMA (National Association to Promote Library and Information Services to Latinos and the Spanish-Speaking)

President, Lucía González
National Office Manager, Sandra Rios Balderrama
P.O. Box 4386, Fresno, CA 93744
480-734-4460, e-mail reformaoffice@riosbalderrama.com
World Wide Web http://www.reforma.org

Object

Promoting library services to the Spanish-speaking for nearly 40 years, REFORMA, an affiliate of the American Library Association, works in a number of areas to promote the development of library collections to include Spanish-language and Latino-oriented materials; the recruitment of more bilingual and bicultural professionals and support staff; the development of library services and programs that meet the needs of the Latino community; the establishment of a national network among individuals who share its goals; the education of the U.S. Latino population in regard to the availability and types of library services; and lobbying efforts to preserve existing library resource centers serving the interest of Latinos.

Membership

Memb. 800+. Any person who is supportive of the goals and objectives of REFORMA.

Officers

Pres. Lucía M. González, 16410 Miami Drive, Apt. 404, North Miami Beach, FL 33162. Tel. 305-335-8215, e-mail inotherwordsllc@gmail.com; *Pres.-Elect* Maria Kramer. E-mail mkramer@redwoodcity.org; *Secy./Recorder* Tiffany Herbon. E-mail therbon@slcpl.org; *Treas.* Robin Imperial. E-mail robin.imperial@gmail.com; *Memb.-at-Large* Roberto C. Delgadillo. E-mail rdelgadillo@lib.ucdavis.edu; *Past Pres.* Loida García Febo. E-mail loidagarciafebo@gmail.com.

Committees

Pura Belpré Award. Jaime Campbell Naidoo.
Children's and Young Adult Services. Alma Ramos-McDermott, Jamie Campbell Naidoo.
Education. Siobhan Champ-Blackwell.
Finance. Loida García Febo.
Fund Raising. Sylvia D. Hall-Ellis.
Information Technology. Juan Carlos Rodríguez.
International Relations. Miguel Garcia Colon.
Legislative. Carol Brey-Casiano.
Membership. Daniel Berdaner.
Nominations. Oscar Baeza.
Organizational Development. Yolanda Valentín.
Public Relations. Jessica Hernandez.
Recruitment and Mentoring. To be announced.
Scholarship. Ramona Grijalva.
Translations. Armando Trejo.

Publication

REFORMA Newsletter (s. ann; memb.).

Meetings

General membership and board meetings take place at the American Library Association Midwinter Meeting and Annual Conference.

Society for Scholarly Publishing

Executive Director, Ann Mehan Crosse
10200 W. 44 Ave., Suite 304, Wheat Ridge, CO 80033
303-422-3914, fax 303-422-8894, e-mail info@sspnet.org or amehan@resourcecenter.org
World Wide Web http://www.sspnet.org

Object

To draw together individuals involved in the process of scholarly publishing. This process requires successful interaction of the many functions performed within the scholarly community. The Society for Scholarly Publishing (SSP) provides the leadership for such interaction by creating opportunities for the exchange of information and opinions among scholars, editors, publishers, librarians, printers, booksellers, and all others engaged in scholarly publishing.

Membership

Memb. 900. Open to all with an interest in the scholarly publishing process and dissemination of information. Dues (New Member) $135; (Indiv. Renewal) $150; (Libn.) $75; (Student) $30; (Supporting) $1,350; (Sustaining) $3,275. Year. Jan. 1–Dec. 31.

Executive Committee

Pres. Lois Smith, Human Factors and Ergonomics Society. E-mail lois@hfes.org; *Pres.-Elect* Theresa Van Schaik, American Society of Clinical Oncology. E-mail terry.vanschaik@asco.org; *Secy./Treas.* Mady Tissenbaum, *Journal of Bone and Joint Surgery.* E-mail madyt@jbjs.org; *Past Pres.* Raymond Fastiggi, Rockefeller Univ. Press. E-mail fastigg@rockefeller.edu.

Directors

Michael T. Clarke, Alice Meadows, Carol Anne Meyer, Richard Newman, Anne Orens, Howard Ratner, Alix Vance, William M. Wakeling, Charles Watkinson

Meetings

An annual meeting is held in late May/early June. SSP also conducts a Fall Seminar Series (November), Librarian Focus Group 303-422-3914 (February) and the IN Conference (September).

Society of American Archivists

Executive Director, Nancy Perkin Beaumont
17 N. State St., Suite 1425, Chicago, IL 60602
866-722-7858, 312-606-0722, fax 312-606-0728, e-mail nbeaumont@archivists.org
World Wide Web http://www.archivists.org

Object

Provides leadership to ensure the identification, preservation, and use of records of historical value. Founded in 1936.

Membership

Memb. 5,800. Dues (Indiv.) $77 to $216, graduated according to salary; (Assoc.) $77, domestic; (Student or Bridge) $44; (Inst.) $247; (Sustaining Inst.) $484.

Officers (2010–2011)

Pres. Helen Tibbo, 201 Manning Hall CB 3360, Univ. of North Carolina at Chapel Hill, Chapel Hill, NC 27599-3360. E-mail tibbo@email.unc.edu; *V.P.* Gregor Trinkaus-Randall, Massachusetts Board of Lib. Commissioners, 98 N. Washington St., Suite 401, Boston, MA 02114-1933. E-mail gregor.trinkaus-randall@state.ma.us; *Treas.* Aimee Felker, Univ. of California, Los Angeles, 10920 Wilshire Blvd., Suite 530, Los Angeles, CA 90024.

Staff

Exec. Dir. Nancy Perkin Beaumont; *Dir., Memb. and Technical Services* Brian P. Doyle; *Publishing Dir.* Teresa Brinati; *Educ. Dir.* Solveig DeSutter; *Dir., Finance and Admin.* Thomas Jurczak.

Publications

American Archivist (2 a year; individual print edition, $120; individual online edition, $120; print and online, $145; institutional, $145 print, $145 online, $170 print and online). *Ed.* Mary Jo Pugh; *Reviews Ed.* Amy Cooper Cary.

Archival Outlook (bi-mo.; memb.). *Ed.* Teresa Brinati.

Software and Information Industry Association

1090 Vermont Ave. N.W., Washington, DC 20005
202-289-7442, fax 202-289-7097
World Wide Web http://www.siia.net

Membership

Memb. 520 companies. The Software and Information Industry Association (SIIA) was formed January 1, 1999, through the merger of the Software Publishers Association (SPA) and the Information Industry Association (IIA). Open to companies involved in the creation, distribution, and use of software, information products, services, and technologies. For details on membership and dues, see the SIIA Web site.

Staff

Pres. Kenneth Wasch. E-mail kwasch@siia.net; *V.P. Educ. Div.* Karen Billings; *V.P. Software Div.* Rhianna Collier.

Board of Directors

Suresh Balasubramanian, Adobe Systems, Inc.; Cynthia Braddon, McGraw-Hill; Daniel Burton, Salesforce.com; Alan Davidson, Google, Inc.; Joseph T. FitzGerald, Symantec; Kenneth J. Glueck, Oracle; Kathy Hurley, Pearson School and Pearson Foundation; Steve Manzo, Reed Elsevier; Randy Marcinko, Marcinko Enterprises; Bernard McKay, Intuit; Calvin A. Mitchell, Thomson Reuters; Jim Panos, Houghton Mifflin Harcourt; Tom B. Rabon, Jr., Red Hat; Scott Schulman, Dow Jones; Timothy Sheehy (chair), IBM; Ken Wasch, SIIA.

SPARC

Executive Director, Heather Joseph
21 Dupont Circle, Suite 800, Washington, DC 20036
202-296-2296, fax 202-872-0884
E-mail sparc@arl.org
World Wide Web http://www.arl.org/sparc

SPARC, the Scholarly Publishing and Academic Resources Coalition, is an international alliance of academic and research libraries working to correct imbalances in the scholarly publishing system. Developed by the Association of Research Libraries, SPARC has become a catalyst for change. Its pragmatic focus is to stimulate the emergence of new scholarly communication models that expand the dissemination of scholarly research and reduce financial pressures on libraries. Action by SPARC in collaboration with stakeholders—including authors, publishers, and libraries—builds on the unprecedented opportunities created by the networked digital environment to advance the conduct of scholarship.

SPARC's role in stimulating change focuses on

- Educating stakeholders about the problems facing scholarly communication and the opportunities for them to play a role in achieving positive change
- Advocating policy changes that advance scholarly communication and that explicitly recognize that dissemi-

nation of scholarship is an essential, inseparable component of the research process
- Incubating demonstrations of new publishing and sustainability models that benefit scholarship and academe

SPARC is a visible advocate for changes in scholarly communication that benefit more than the academic community alone. Founded in 1997, SPARC has expanded to represent more than 800 academic and research libraries in North America, Britain, Europe, and Japan.

Membership

SPARC membership is open to North American and international academic and research institutions, organizations, and consortia that share an interest in creating a more open and diverse marketplace for scholarly communication. Dues are scaled by membership type and budget. For more information, visit SPARC's Web site at http://www.arl.org/sparc, SPARC Europe at http://www.sparceurope.org, or SPARC Japan at http://www.nii.ac.jp/sparc.

Steering Committee

Chair David Carlson (Southern Illinois Univ. at Carbondale); Jun Adachi, Japanese National Institute of Informatics (for SPARC Japan); Lars Bjørnshauge, Lund Univ. (for SPARC Europe); Faye Chadwell (Oregon State Univ.); Maggie Farrell (Univ. of Wyoming); Lorraine Harricombe (Univ. of Kansas); Thomas Hickerson (Univ. of Calgary); Paula Kaufman (Univ. of Illinois at Urbana-Champaign); Rick Luce, (Emory Univ.); Jonathan Miller (Rollins College); Patricia Renfro (Columbia Univ.); Lee Van Orsdel (Grand Valley State Univ.); Jean Shipman (Univ. of Utah) and Vicki Williamson (Univ. of Saskatchewan).

Publications

Author Rights (2006), an educational initiative and introduction to the SPARC Author Addendum, a legal form that enables authors of journal articles to modify publishers' copyright transfer agreements and allow authors to keep key rights to their articles

Campus-based publishing partnerships: A guide to critical issues (2009) by Raym Crow.

Income Models for Open Access: An Overview of Current Practice (2009) by Raym Crow.

Greater Reach for Research: Expanding readership through digital repositories (2008), the initiative to educate faculty on the benefits of open repositories and emerging research access policies.

Open Access News Blog, daily updates on the worldwide movement for open access to science and scholarship, written by Peter Suber and cosponsored by SPARC

Publishing Cooperatives: An Alternative for Society Publishers (2006) by Raym Crow.

The Right to Research: The Student Guide to Opening Access to Scholarship (2008), part of a campaign to engage students on the issue of research access.

SPARC e-news, a monthly newsletter featuring SPARC activities, an industry roundup, upcoming workshops and events, and articles relating to developments in scholarly communication.

SPARC Open Access Newsletter, a monthly roundup of developments relating to open access publishing written by Peter Suber.

Sponsorships for Nonprofit Scholarly and Scientific Journals: A Guide to Defining and Negotiating Successful Sponsorships (2005) by Raym Crow.

A more-complete list of SPARC publications, including brochures, articles, and guides, is available at http://www.arl.org/sparc.

Special Libraries Association (SLA)

Chief Executive Officer, Janice R. Lachance
331 S. Patrick St., Alexandria, VA 22314
703-647-4900, fax 703-647-4901, e-mail sla@sla.org
World Wide Web http://www.sla.org

Mission

The Special Libraries Association promotes and strengthens its members through learning, advocacy, and networking initiatives.

Membership

Memb. 10,000. Dues (Organizational) $650; (Indiv.) $99–$200; (Student/Retired/Salary less than $18,000 a year) $40.

Officers (January 2010–December 2011)

Pres. Cindy Romaine, Romainiacs Intelligence Research. E-mail cindy.romaine@romainiacs.com; *Pres.-Elect* Brent Mai, Concordia Univ. E-mail bmai@cu-portland.edu; *Treas.* Dan Trefethen, Boeing. E-mail daniel.b.trefethen@boeing.com; *Chapter Cabinet Chair* Liz Blankson-Hemans, Dialog. E-mail liz.blankson-hemans@dialog.com; *Chapter Cabinet Chair-Elect* Ulla de Stricker, de Stricker Associates. E-mail ulla@destricker.com; *Div. Cabinet Chair* Mary Ellen Bates, Bates Info. Services. E-mail mbates@batesinfo.com; *Div. Cabinet Chair-Elect* Richard Huffine, U.S. Geological Survey. E-mail richardhuffine@yahoo.com.

Directors

Officers; Jill Hurst-Wahl, Daniel Lee, Nettie Seaberry, Sara Tompson.

Publication

Information Outlook (mo.) (memb., nonmemb. $125/yr.)

Theatre Library Association

c/o The New York Public Library for the Performing Arts
40 Lincoln Center Plaza, New York, NY 10023
E-mail info@tla-online.org, World Wide Web http://www.tla-online.org

Object

To further the interests of collecting, preserving, and using theater, cinema, and performing arts materials in libraries, museums, and private collections. Founded in 1937.

Membership

Memb. 297. Dues (Indiv.) $20–$40, (Inst.) $40–$50. Year. Jan. 1–Dec. 31.

Officers

Pres. Kenneth Schlesinger, Lehman College, City Univ. of New York; *V.P.* Nancy Friedland, Columbia Univ.; *Exec. Secy.* David Nochimson, New York Public Lib.; *Treas.* Colleen Reilly, Slippery Rock Univ.

Executive Board

Susan Brady, John Calhoun, Charlotte Cubbage, Phyllis Dircks, John Frick, Stephen Johnson, Beth Kattelman, Diana King, Stephen Kuehler, Francesca Marini, Karen Nickeson, Brook Stowe, Angela Weaver, Sarah Zimmerman; *Honorary* Louis A. Rachow, Marian Seldes; *Legal Counsel* Georgia Harper; *Past Pres.* Martha S. LoMonaco.

Publications

Broadside (3 a year; memb.). *Ed.* Angela Weaver.

Performing Arts Resources (occasional; memb.).

Membership Directory (annual; memb.). *Ed.* David Nochimson.

Committee Chairs

Book Awards. Brook Stowe.
Conference Planning. Nancy Friedland.
Finance and Fund Raising. Colleen Reilly.
Membership. Beth Kerr.
Nominating. Martha S. LoMonaco.
Professional Award. Phyllis Dircks.
Publications. Robert W. Melton.
Strategic Planning. Nancy Friedland.
Web Site. David Nochimson.

Urban Libraries Council

125 S. Wacker Drive, Suite 1050, Chicago, IL 60606
312-676-0999, fax 312-676-0950, e-mail info@urbanlibraries.org
World Wide Web http://www.urbanlibraries.org

Object

Since 1971 the Urban Libraries Council (ULC) has worked to strengthen public libraries as an essential part of urban life. A member organization of North America's leading public library systems, ULC serves as a forum for research widely recognized and used by public and private sector leaders. Its members are dedicated to leadership, innovation, and the continuous transformation of libraries to meet community needs.

As ULC approaches its 40th anniversary, its work focuses on assisting public libraries to identify and utilize skills and strategies that match the challenges of the 21st century.

Membership

Membership is open to public libraries and to corporate partners specializing in library-related materials and services. The organization also offers associate memberships.

Officers (2010–2011)

Chair Melinda Cervantes; *V. Chair/Chair-Elect* Keith B. Simmons; *Secy./Treas.* John F. Szabo; *Past Chair* Raymond Santiago; *Member-at-Large* Joan Prince.

Officers serve one-year terms, members of the executive board two-year terms. New officers are elected and take office at the summer annual meeting of the council.

Executive Board

Susan Adams, Ruth Anna, Jan Harder, Melanie Huggins, Okeima R. Lawrence, Patrick Losinski, Robert S. Martin, Dennis B. Martinez, Dorothy S. Ridings, Rivkah Sass, Rashad Young.

Key Staff

CEO and Pres. Susan Benton; *Media and Marketing* Mary Colleen Bragiel; *Finance and Admin.* Angela Goodrich; *Communications and Member Services* Jodi Lazar; *Membership* Veronda J. Pitchford; *Exec. Assistant to the Pres.* Erika Slaughter.

State, Provincial, and Regional Library Associations

The associations in this section are organized under three headings: United States, Canada, and Regional. Both the United States and Canada are represented under Regional associations.

United States

Alabama

Memb. 1,200. Term of Office. Apr. 2010–Apr. 2011. Publication. *The Alabama Librarian* (q.).

Pres. Jodi Poe, Houston Cole Lib., Jacksonville State Univ., 700 Pelham Rd. N., Jacksonville 36265. Tel. 256-782-8103, e-mail jpoe@jsu.edu; *Pres.-Elect* Steven Yates, Mountain Brook H.S., 3650 Bethune Drive, Brimingham 35223. Tel. 205-826-3303, e-mail yatess@mtnbrook.k12.al.us; *Secy.* Paul O. Blackmon, Trenholm State Technical College, P.O. Box 10048, Montgomery 36108. Tel. 251-575-9222, e-mail pblackmon@trenholmstate.edu; *Treas.* Neil Foulger, Alabama State Univ., 915 S. Jackson St., Montgomery 36101. Tel. 334-356-9422, e-mail nfoulger@alasu.edu; *Past Pres.* Dennis Nichols, Homewood Public Lib., 1721 Oxmoor Rd., Homewood 35209. Tel. 205-332-6620, e-mail dnichols@bham.lib.al.us.

Address correspondence to the association, 9154 Eastchase Pkwy., Suite 418, Montgomery 36117. Tel. 334-414-0113, e-mail administrator@allanet.org.

World Wide Web http://allanet.org.

Alaska

Memb. 450+. Publication. *Newspoke* (q.).

Pres. David Ongley. E-mail david.ongley@tuzzy.org; *Pres.-Elect* Michael Robinson. E-mail afmcr@uaa.alaska.edu; *Secy.* Joyce McCombs. E-mail deltalibrary@wildak.net; *Treas.* Patricia Linville. E-mail ctyrrell@chartercollege.org; *Conference Coord.* M. J. Grande. E-mail mjgrande@juneau.lib.ak.us; *Past Pres.* Mary Jo Joiner. E-mail mjoiner@ci.kenai.ak.us; *Exec. Officer* Mary Jennings. E-mail maryj@gci.net.

Address correspondence to the secretary, Alaska Lib. Assn., P.O. Box 81084, Fairbanks 99708. Fax 877-863-1401, e-mail akla@akla.org.

World Wide Web http://www.akla.org.

Arizona

Memb. 1,000. Term of Office. Nov. 2010–Nov. 2011. Publication. *AzLA Newsletter* (mo.).

Pres. Nancy Ledeboer, Pima County Public Lib., 101 N. Stone Ave., Tucson 85701-1501. Tel. 520-594-5601, fax 520-594-5621, e-mail nancy.ledeboer@pima.gov; *Pres.-Elect* Nancy Deegan, Central Arizona College Lib., 8470 N. Overfield Rd., Coolidge 85228. E-mail nancy.deegan@centralaz.edu; *Secy.* Margaret Espinoza, Prescott Public Lib., Prescott 86303. Tel. 928-777-1500, e-mail margaret.espinoza@prescott-az.gov; *Treas.* Linda Renfro, Blue Ridge Unified School Dist. Tel. 928-368-6119, e-mail lrenfro@brusd.k12.az.us; *Past Pres.* Cynthia Landrum, Glendale Public Lib., 5959 W. Brown St., Glendale 85302. Tel. 623-930-3566, e-mail clandrum@glendaleaz.com; *Exec. Dir.* Debbie J. Hanson. Tel. 480-609-3999, e-mail admin@azla.org.

Address correspondence to the executive director, AzLA, 1030 E. Baseline Rd., Suite 105-1025, Tempe 85283.

World Wide Web http://www.azla.org.

Arkansas

Memb. 600. Term of Office. Jan.–Dec. 2011. Publication. *Arkansas Libraries* (bi-mo.).

Pres. Shawn Pierce, Lonoke/Prairie County Regional Lib., 2504 S. Tyler St., Little Rock 72204. Tel. 501-676-6608, e-mail spierce@lpregional.lib.ar.us; *V.P./Pres.-Elect* Jim Robb, North Arkansas College, 1515 Pioneer Drive, Harrison 72601. Tel. 870-391-

3359, e-mail jrobb@northark.edu; *Secy./Treas.* Michael Strickland, Arkansas State Lib., 900 W. Capitol, Suite 100, Little Rock 72201. Tel. 501-682-2053, e-mail michaels@library.Arkansas.gov; *Past Pres.* Connie Zimmer, Arkansas Tech Univ., 305 W. Q St., Russellville 72801. Tel. 479-968-0434, e-mail czimmer@atu.edu; *Exec. Admin.* Barbara Martin, P.O. Box 958, Benton 72018-0958. Tel. 501-860-7585, fax 501-776-9709, e-mail arlib2@sbcglobal.net.

Address correspondence to the executive administrator.

World Wide Web http://www.arlib.org.

California

Memb. 2,500. Publication. *Clarion* (s. ann.).

Pres. Paymaneh Maghsoudi, Whittier Public Lib. Tel. 562-464-3452, e-mail pmaghsoudi@whittierpl.org; *V.P./Pres.-Elect* Wayne Disher, Hemet Public Lib. Tel. 951-765-2441, e-mail wdisher@cityofhemet.org; *Treas.* Jackie Griffin, Ventura County Lib. Tel. 805-477-7333, e-mail jackie.griffin@ventura.org; *Past Pres.* Kim Bui-Burton, Monterey Public Lib. Tel. 831-646-5601, e-mail buiburto@ci.monterey.ca.us; *Exec. Dir.* Holly Macriss. Tel. 916-233-3298, e-mail hollym@cla-net.org or info@cla-net.org.

Address correspondence to the executive director, California Lib. Assn., 950 Glenn Drive, Suite 150, Folsom 95630.

World Wide Web http://www.cla-net.org.

Colorado

Memb. 1,000+. Publication. *Colorado Libraries* (q.).

Pres. Teri Switzer. E-mail switzer@uccs.edu; *V.P./Pres.-Elect* Linda Conway. E-mail linda.conway@asd20.org; *Secy.* Denise Muniz. E-mail dmuniz@broomfield.org; *Treas.* Chris Brogan. E-mail cgbrogan@msn.com; *Past Pres.* Rochelle Logan. Tel. 303-688-7603, e-mail rlogan@dclibraries.org.

Address correspondence to the president, Colorado Assn. of Libs., 3030 W. 81 Ave., Westminster 80031. Tel. 303-463-6400, fax 303-458-0002.

World Wide Web http://www.cal-webs.org.

Connecticut

Memb. 1,000+. Term of Office. July 2010–June 2011. Publication. *Connecticut Libraries* (11 a year). *Ed.* Kate Sheehan, Bibliomation. Tel. 203-577-4070 ext. 114, fax 203-577-4077, e-mail kate@loosecannonlibrarian.net.

Pres. Debbie Herman, Central Connecticut State Univ. Tel. 860-832-2084, fax 860-832-2118, e-mail hermand@ccsu.edu; *V.P./Pres.-Elect* Betty Anne Reiter, Groton Public Lib. Tel. 860-441-6750, fax 860-448-0363, e-mail breiter@town.groton.ct.us; *Treas.* Alison Wang, Naugatuck Community College, Waterbury. Tel. 203-575-8250, e-mail awang@nvcc.commnet.edu; *Past Pres.* Randi Ashton-Pritting, Univ. of Hartford Libs. Tel. 860-768-4268, fax 860-768-4274, e-mail pritting@hartford.edu; *Coord.* Pam Najarian, Connecticut Lib. Assn., P.O. Box 75, Middletown 06457. Tel. 860-346-2444, fax 860-344-9199, e-mail cla@ctlibrarians.org.

Address correspondence to the coordinator.

World Wide Web http://www.ctlibraryassociation.org.

Delaware

Memb. 150+. Term of Office. Apr. 2010–Apr. 2011. Publication. *DLA Bulletin* (online only).

Pres. Margery Cyr, Dover Public Lib. Tel. 302-736-7032, fax 302-736-5087, e-mail margery.cyr@lib.de.us; *V.P.* Patty Langley, Delaware Div. of Libs., 121 Duke of York St., Dover 19901. Tel. 800-282-8696 (302-739-4748 in Kent County), fax 302-739-6787, e-mail patty.langley@state.de.us; *Secy.* Mary Jane Mallonee, Widener Univ. Law Lib., 4601 Concord Pike, Wilmington 19803. Tel. 302-477-2244, e-mail mmallonee@widener.edu; *Treas.* Pauly Iheanacho, Univ. of Delaware Lib., 181 S. College Ave., Newark 19717-5267. Tel. 302-831-6946, fax 302-831-1631, e-mail pinacho@udel.edu; *Past Pres.* Peggy Dillner. E-mail mpd@udel.edu.

Address correspondence to the association, Box 816, Dover 19903-0816. E-mail dla@dla.lib.de.us.

World Wide Web http://www2.lib.udel.edu/dla.

District of Columbia

Memb. 300+. Term of Office. July 2010–June 2011. Publication. *Capital Librarian* (s. ann.).

Pres. Richard Huffine; *V.P./Pres.-Elect* Megan Sheils; *Secy.* Barbara Conaty; *Treas.* John Williamson; *Past Pres.* Angela Jaffee.

Address correspondence to the association, Box 14177, Benjamin Franklin Sta., Washington 20044. Tel. 202-872-1112.

World Wide Web http://www.dcla.org.

Florida

Memb. (Indiv.) 1,100+. Term of Office. April 2010–May 2011. Publication. *Florida Libraries* (s. ann.). *Ed.* Gloria Colvin, 2505 Blarney Drive, Tallahassee 32309. Tel. 850-645-1680, e-mail gpcolvin@yahoo.com.

Pres. John J. Callahan III, Palm Beach County Lib. System, 3650 Summit Blvd., West Palm Beach 33406-4198, Tel. 561-233-2600, e-mail callahanj@pgclibrary.org; *V.P./Pres.-Elect* Gloria Colvin, 2505 Blarney Drive, Tallahassee 32309. Tel. 850-645-1680, e-mail gpcolvin@yahoo.com; *Secy.* Gladys Roberts, Polk County Lib. Cooperative, 2150 S. Broadway Ave., Bartow 33830-7138. Tel. 863-519-7958; *Treas.* Susan D. Dillinger, New Port Richey Public Lib., 5939 Main St., New Port Richey 34652, Tel. 727-853-1262, e-mail sddillinger@gmail.com; *Past Pres.* Wendy Breeden, Lake County Public Resources Dept., 2401 Woodlea Rd., Tavares 32778. Tel. 352-253-6180, e-mail wbreeden@lakeline.lib.fl.us; *Exec. Dir.* Faye Roberts, P.O. Box 1571, Lake City 32056-1571. Tel. 386-438-5795, e-mail faye.roberts@comcast.net.

Address correspondence to the executive director.

World Wide Web http://www.flalib.org.

Georgia

Memb. 800+. Publication. *Georgia Library Quarterly. Ed.* Susan Cooley, Sara Hightower Regional Lib., 205 Riverside Pkwy., Rome 30161. Tel. 706-236-4609, fax 706-236-4631, e-mail scooley@romelibrary.org.

Pres. Carolyn Fuller, Henry County Public Lib. Tel. 770-954-2806, e-mail cfuller@mail.henry.public.lib.ga.us; *1st V.P./Pres.-Elect* Elizabeth Bagley, McCain Lib., Agnes Scott College, 141 E. College Ave., Decatur 30030. Tel. 404-471-5277, e-mail ebagley@agnesscott.edu; *2nd V.P.* Kim Eccles, Monroe F. Swilley, Jr. Lib., Mercer Univ. Atlanta Campus, 3001 Mercer University Drive, Atlanta 30341. Tel. 678-547-6271, e-mail eccles.kl@mercer.edu; *Secy.* Debbie Holmes, Gould Memorial Lib., College of Coastal Georgia, 3700 Altama Ave., Brunswick 31520. Tel. 912-279-5787, e-mail deholmes@ccga.edu; *Treas.* Cathy Jeffrey, Clayton State Univ. Lib., 2000 Clayton State University Blvd., Morrow 30260. Tel. 678-466-4336, e-mail cathyjeffrey@clayton.edu; *Past Pres.* Carol Stanley, Athens Technical College, 1317 Athens Hwy, Elberton, GA 30635. Tel. 706-213-2116, e-mail cstanley@athenstech.edu.

Address correspondence to the president, Georgia Lib. Assn., P.O. Box 793, Rex 30273-0793.

World Wide Web http://gla.georgialibraries.org.

Hawaii

Memb. 250. Publication. HLA Blog (http://hawaiilibraryassociation.blogspot.com).

Pres. Stewart Chun, Federal Documents Section, Hawaii State Lib. Tel. 808-586-3477, e-mail stewart.chun@imail.librarieshawaii.org; *Secy.* Kimball Boone, Brigham Young Univ. E-mail kimball.boone@byuh.edu; *Treas.* Carrie Young, Pacific Rim Christian College. E-mail youngca2009@yahoo.com; *Past Pres.* Sheryl Lynch, Kapolei Public Lib. Tel. 808-693-7050, e-mail sheryl.lynch@librarieshawaii.org.

Address correspondence to the association at hawaii.library.association@gmail.com.

World Wide Web http://hla.chaminade.edu.

Idaho

Memb. 420. Term of Office. Oct. 2010–Oct. 2011.

Pres. Ben Hunter, Univ. of Idaho Lib., P.O. Box 442350, Moscow 83844-2350. Tel. 208-885-5858, e-mail bhunter@uidaho.edu; *V.P./Pres.-Elect* Gena Marker, Centennial H.S., 12400 W. McMillan Rd., Boise 83713. Tel. 208-855-4261, e-mail marker.gena@meridianschools.org; *Secy.* Phil Homan, Idaho State Univ., 921 S. 8 Ave., Stop 8089, Pocatello 83209-8089. Tel. 208-282-3047, e-mail homaphil@isu.edu; *Treas.* Steve Poppino, College of Southern Idaho, 315 Falls Ave., Twin Falls 83383-1238. Tel. 208-732-6504, fax 208-732-3087, e-mail spoppino@csi.edu; *Past Pres.* Bette Ammon, Coeur d'Alene Public Lib., 702 E. Front, Coeur d'Alene 83814. E-mail bammon@cdalibrary.org.

Address correspondence to the association, P.O. Box 8533, Moscow 83844.

World Wide Web http://www.idaholibraries.org.

Illinois

Memb. 3,600. Term of Office. July 2010–July 2011. Publication. *ILA Reporter* (bi-mo.).

Pres. Gail Bush, Center for Teaching Through Children's Books, National-Louis Univ., 5202 Old Orchard Rd., Suite 300, Skokie 60077. Tel. 224-233-2522, fax 224-233-2522, e-mail gail.bush@nl.edu; *V.P./Pres.-Elect* Lynn Elam, Algonquin Area Public Lib. Dist., 2600 Harnish Drive, Algonquin 60102. Tel. 847-458-6060, fax 847-458-9370, e-mail lynnelam0315@gmail.com; *Treas.* Theodore C. Schwitzner, Milner Lib., Illinois State Univ., Campus Box 8900, Normal 61790-8900. Tel. 309-438-3449, fax 309-438-5132, e-mail redm.andmlibrarian@yahoo.com; *Past Pres.* Carole A. Medal, Gail Borden Public Lib. Dist., 270 N. Grove Ave., Elgin 60120-5505. Tel. 847-429-4699, fax 847-742-0485, e-mail cmedal@gailborden.info; *Exec. Dir.* Robert P. Doyle, Illinois Lib. Assn., 33 W. Grand Ave., Suite 301, Chicago 60654. Tel. 312-644-1896, fax 312-644-1899, e-mail doyle@ila.org or ila@ila.org.

Address correspondence to the executive director.

World Wide Web http://www.ila.org.

Indiana

Memb. 2,000+. Publication. *Indiana Libraries* (s. ann.). *Ed.* Karen Evans, Cunningham Memorial Lib., Indiana State Univ., 650 Sycamore St., Terre Haute 47809. Tel. 812-237-8824, fax 812-237-2567, e-mail karen.evans@indstate.edu.

Pres. John Borneman, Tipton County Public Lib., 10373 W. 650 N., Sharpsville 46068. E-mail johnborneman@gmail.com; *V.P.* Dennis LeLoup, Sycamore Elementary, 3359 Oceanline Drive, Indianapolis 46214. E-mail djleloup@avon-schools.org; *Secy.* Kim Carr. Tel. 765-468-8878, e-mail 01kjcarr@bsu.edu; *Treas.* Jason Hatton, Bartholomew County Public Lib., 536 Fifth St., Columbus 47201. Tel. 812-379-1255, e-mail jhatton@barth.lib.in.us; *Past Pres.* Nancy Dowell, Vigo County Public Lib., 1 Library Sq., Terre Haute 47807. Tel. 812-232-1113, fax 812-235-1439, e-mail ndowell@vigo.lib.in.us; *Exec. Dir.* Susan Akers. Tel. 317-257-2040 ext. 101, e-mail sakers@ilfonline.org.

Address correspondence to Indiana Lib. Federation, 941 E. 86 St., Suite 260, Indianapolis 46240. Tel. 317-257-2040, fax 317-257-1389, e-mail askus@ilfonline.org.

World Wide Web http://www.ilfonline.org.

Iowa

Memb. 1,500. Publication. *The Catalyst* (bi-mo.).

Pres. Dale Vande Haar, Des Moines Public Schools, 1800 grand Ave., Mezzanine 253, Des Moines 50309. Tel. 515-242-7569, fax 515-242-7359, e-mail dale.vandehaar@dmps.k12.ia.us; *V.P./Pres.-Elect* Lorraine Borowski, Decorah Public Lib., 202 Winnebago St., Decorah 52101. Tel. 563-382-3717, e-mail lborowski@decorah.lib.ia.us; *Secy.* Marilyn Murphy, Busse Center Lib., Mount Mercy College, 1330 Elmhurst Drive N.E., Cedar Rapids 52402. Tel. 319-363-8213 ext. 1244, fax 319-363-9060, e-mail mmurphy@mtmercy.edu; *Past Pres.* Ellen Neuhaus, Rod Lib., Univ. of Northern Iowa, Cedar Falls 50613. Tel. 319-273-3729, fax 319-273-2913, e-mail ellen.neuhaus@uni.edu.

Address correspondence to the association, 3636 Westown Pkwy., Suite 202, West Des Moines 50266.

World Wide Web http://www.iowalibrary association.org.

Kansas

Memb. 1,500. Term of Office. July 2010–June 2011. Publication. *KLA Connects* (q.).

Pres. Emily Sitz, Southwest Kansas Lib. System, 100 Military Ave., Suite 210, Dodge City 67801. Tel. 620-225-1231, e-mail esitz @swkls.org; *V.P.* Royce Kitts, Tonganoxie Public Lib., 303 S. Bury, Tonganoxie 66086. Tel. 913-845-3281, fax 913-845-2962, director@tonganoxielibrary.org; *2nd V.P.* Mickey Coalwell, Northeast Kansas Lib. System, 4317 W. Sixth, Lawrence 66049. Tel. 785-838-4090, e-mail mcoalwell@nekls.org; *Secy.* Cindi Hickey, State Lib. of Kansas, 343-N, 300 S.W. 10 Ave., Topeka 66612-1593. Tel. 785-296-3296, e-mail chickey@ kslib.info; *Treas.* Cynthia Berner Harris, Wichita Public Lib., 223 S. Main, Wichita 67202. Tel. 316-261-8520, fax 316-219-6320, e-mail cberner@wichita.gov; *Past Pres.* Denise Smith, Stanton County Lib., 103 E. Sherman, P.O. Box 480, Johnson City 67855. Tel. 620-492-2302, fax 620-492-2203, e-mail dolliesmith@hotmail.com.

Address correspondence to the president, Kansas Lib. Assn., 1020 S.W. Washburn, Topeka 66604. Tel. 785-580-4518, fax 785-580-4595, e-mail kansaslibraryassociation@ yahoo.com.

World Wide Web http://www.kslibassoc.org.

Kentucky

Memb. 1,900. Term of Office. Oct. 2010–Oct. 2011. Publication. *Kentucky Libraries* (q.).

Pres. Leoma Dunn, Thomas More College, 333 Thomas More Pkwy., Crestview Hills 41017. Tel. 859-344-3524, e-mail leoma.dunn@thomasmore.edu; *Pres.-Elect* Terry Buckner, Learning Resource Center, Bluegrass Community and Technical College, 222B Oswald Bldg., 460 Cooper Drive, Lexington 40506. Tel. 859-246-6397, e-mail terry.buckner@kctcs.edu; *Secy.* Lisa Rice, Warren County Public Lib., 1225 State St., Bowling Green 42101. Tel. 270-781-4882 ext. 202, e-mail lisar@warrenpl.org; *Past Pres.* Emmalee Hoover, Dixie Heights H.S., 3010 Dixie Hwy., Edgewood 41017. Tel. 859-341-7650, e-mail emmalee.hoover@ kenton.kyschools.us; *Exec. Secy.* Tom Underwood, 1501 Twilight Trail, Frankfort 40601. Tel. 502-223-5322, fax 502-223-4937, e-mail info@kylibasn.org.

Address correspondence to the executive secretary.

World Wide Web http://www.kylibasn.org.

Louisiana

Memb. 1,100+. Term of Office. July 2010–June 2011. Publication. *Louisiana Libraries* (q.). *Ed.* Vivian Solar. Tel. 225-647-8924, e-mail vsolar@state.lib.la.us.

Pres. Randy Allen DeSoto. Tel. 985-651-6733, e-mail radesoto@stjohn.lib.la.us; *1st V.P./Pres.-Elect* Carla Clark. Tel. 318-797-5382, e-mail carla.clark@lsus.edu; *Secy.* Leslie Carloss. Tel. 337-942-5404 ext. 104, fax 337-942-5922, e-mail vanyar@bellsouth. net; *Past Pres.* Melanie Sims. Tel. 225-578-8815, fax 225-578-5773, e-mail melanie.sims @law.lsu.edu.

Address correspondence to Louisiana Lib. Assn., 8550 United Plaza Blvd., Suite 1001, Baton Rouge 70809. Tel. 225-922-4642, fax 225-408-4422, e-mail office@llaonline.org.

World Wide Web http://www.llaonline.org.

Maine

Memb. 950. Publication. *MLA-to-Z* (q., online).

Pres. Sonja Plummer-Morgan, Mark and Emily Turner Memorial Lib., 39 Second St., Presque Isle 04769. Tel. 207-764-2571, e-mail sonjapmorgan@presqueislelibrary.org; *V.P./Pres.-Elect* Andi Jackson-Darling, Falmouth Memorial Lib., 5 Lunt Rd., Falmouth 04105. Tel. 207-781-2351, e-mail mlatoz newsletter@gmail.com; *Secy.* Lisa Neal-Shaw, Mark and Emily Turner Memorial Lib., 39 Second St., Presque Isle 04769. Tel. 207-764-2571; *Treas.* Mamie Ney, South Berwick Public Lib., P.O. Box 35, South Berwick 03908-0035. Tel. 207-384-3308; *Past Pres.* Molly Larson, Rockport Public Lib., P.O. Box 8, Rockport 04856-0008. Tel. 207-236-3642, e-mail mlarson@rockport.lib. me.us.

Address correspondence to the association, P.O. Box 634, Augusta 04332-0634. Tel. 207-441-1410.

World Wide Web http://mainelibraries.org.

Maryland

Memb. 1,100. Term of Office. July 2009–July 2010. Publications. *Happenings* (mo.); *The Crab* (q.).

Pres. Glennor Shirley, Dept. of Labor, Licensing, and Regulation. Tel. 410-767-9761, e-mail gshirley@dllr.state.md.us; *V.P./Pres.-Elect* Lucy Holman, Univ. of Baltimore. Tel. 410-837-4333, e-mail lholman@ubalt.edu; *Past Pres.* James Fish, Baltimore County Public Lib. Tel. 410-887-6160, e-mail jfish@bcpl.net; *Exec. Dir.* Margaret Carty. E-mail mcarty@carr.org.

Address correspondence to the association, 1401 Hollins St., Baltimore 21223. Tel. 410-947-5090, fax 410-947-5089, e-mail mla@mdlib.org.

World Wide Web http://mdlib.org.

Massachusetts

Memb. (Indiv.) 1,000; (Inst.) 100. Publication. *Bay State Libraries* (4 a year).

Pres. Jacqueline Rafferty, Paul Pratt Memorial Lib., 35 Ripley Rd., Cohasset 02025. Tel. 781-383-1348, e-mail jrafferty@ocln.org; *V.P.* Ruth Urell, Reading Public Lib., 64 Middlesex Ave., Reading 01867. Tel. 781-942-6725, e-mail urell@noblenet.org; *Secy.* Nancy Siegel Dellapenna, West Springfield Public Lib., 200 Park St., West Springfield 01089-3314. Tel. 413-736-4561, email ndellape@cwmars.org; *Treas.* Bernadette D. Rivard, Bellingham Public Lib., 100 Blackstone St., Bellingham 02019. Tel. 508-966-1660, e-mail brivard@bellinghamma.org; *Past Pres.* Susan R. McAlister, Minuteman Lib. Network, 10 Strathmore Rd., Natick 01760. Tel. 508-655-8008 ext. 237, fax 508-655-1507, e-mail smcalister@minlib.net; *Exec. Mgr.* Elizabeth Hacala, Massachusetts Lib. Assn., P.O. Box 535, Bedford 01730. Tel. 781-275-7729, fax 781-998-0393, e-mail mlaoffice@masslib.org.

Address correspondence to the executive manager.

World Wide Web http://www.masslib.org.

Michigan

Memb. (Indiv.) 2,000+. Publications. *Michigan Librarian Newsletter* (6 a year), *Michigan Library Association Forum* (s. ann., online).

Pres. Christine Berro, Portage Dist. Lib.; *Pres.-Elect* Richard Cochran, Central Michigan Univ.; *Secy.* Lee VanOrsdel, Grand Valley State Univ.; *Treas.* Ed Repik, Howell Carnegie Dist. Lib.; *Past Pres.* Larry Neal, Clinton Macomb Public Lib.

Address correspondence to Gretchen Couraud, Exec. Dir., Michigan Lib. Assn., 1407 Rensen St., Suite 2, Lansing 48910. Tel. 517-394-2774 ext. 224, e-mail couraudg@mlcnet.org.

World Wide Web http://www.mla.lib.mi.us.

Minnesota

Memb. 1,100. Term of Office. (Pres., Pres.-Elect) Jan.–Dec. 2011.

Pres. Robin Ewing. E-mail rlewing@stcloudstate.edu; *Pres.-Elect* Carla Urban. E-mail dewey002@umn.edu; *Secy.* Jenny Jepsen. E-mail jjepse@tds.lib.mn.us; *Treas.* Mic Golden. E-mail grrlgolden@yahoo.com; *Past Pres.* Kathleen James. E-mail kathleen@melsa.org.

Address correspondence to the association, 1821 University Ave. W., Suite S256, Saint Paul 55104. Tel. 651-999-5343, fax 651-917-1835, e-mail office@mnlibraryassociation.org.

World Wide Web http://www.mnlibraryassociation.org.

Mississippi

Memb. 650. Term of Office. Jan.–Dec. 2011. Publication. *Mississippi Libraries* (q.).

Pres. Jennifer A. Smith, Warren County–Vicksburg Public Lib. Tel. 601-636-6411, e-mail jensmith@warren.lib.ms.us; *V.P.* Stephen Cunetto, MSU-Mitchell Memorial Lib. Tel. 662-325-8542, e-mail scunetto@library.msstate.edu; *Secy.* Jennifer Brannock, Univ. of Southern Mississippi. Tel. 601-266-4347, e-mail jennifer.brannock@usm.edu; *Treas.* Molly Signs McManus, Millsaps-Wilson College Lib. Tel. 601-974-1086, e-mail signsmj@millsaps.edu; *Past Pres.* Ann Bran ton, Univ. Libs., Univ. of Southern Mississippi. Tel. 601-266-4350, e-mail ann.branton @usm.edu; *Exec. Secy.* Mary Julia Anderson, P.O. Box 13687, Jackson 39236-3687. Tel. 601-981-4586, fax 601-981-4501, e-mail info@misslib.org or marjulia@misslib.org.

Address correspondence to the executive secretary.

World Wide Web http://www.misslib.org.

Missouri

Memb. 800+. Term of Office. Jan.–Dec. 2011. Publication. *MO INFO* (bi-mo.).

Pres. Karen Hicklin, Trails Regional Lib., 432 N. Holden St., Warrensburg 64093. Tel. 660-747-1699, e-mail hicklink@trailslibrary.org; *Pres.-Elect* Glenda Hunt, Adair County Public Lib., 1 Library Lane, Kirksville 63501. Tel. 660-665-6038, e-mail ghunt@adairco.org; *Secy.* Brandy Sanchez, Daniel Boone Regional Lib., P.O. Box 1267, Columbia 65205. Tel. 573-817-7047, e-mail brandysanchez@gmail.com; *Treas.* Neosha Mackey, Duane G. Meyer Lib., Missouri State Univ., Springfield 65897. Tel. 417-836-4525, e-mail neoshamackey@missouristate.edu; *Past Pres.* Sharon McCaslin, Fontbonne Univ., 275 Union Blvd., St. Louis 63108. Tel. 314-889-4567, e-mail smccaslin@fontbonne.edu.

Address correspondence to the president.

World Wide Web http://www.molib.org.

Montana

Memb. 600. Term of Office. July 2010–June 2011. Publication. *Focus* (bi-mo.).

Pres. Samantha Pierson, Lincoln County Public Lib., 220 W. 6 St., Libby 59427. Tel. 406-293-2778, fax 406-293-4235, e-mail spierson@lincolncountylibraries.com; *V.P.* Kim Crowley, Flathead County Lib. System, 247 1st Ave. E., Kalispell 59901. Tel. 406-758-5820, fax 406-758-5868, e-mail kcrowley @flathead.mt.gov; *Secy./Treas.* Sarah Daviau, Lincoln County Public Libs., 220 W 6 St., Libby 59923. Tel. 406-293-2778, fax 406-293-4235, e-mail sdaviau@lincolncountylibraries.com; *Past Pres.* Eva English, Fort Belknap College Lib., P.O. Box 159, Harlem 59526-0159. Tel. 406-353-2607 ext. 262, fax 406-353-2898, e-mail evaenglish@yahoo.com; *Exec. Asst.* Debra Kramer, P.O. Box 1352, Three Forks 59752. Tel. 406-285-3090, fax 406-285-3091, e-mail debkmla@hotmail.com.

Address correspondence to the executive assistant.

World Wide Web http://www.mtlib.org.

Nebraska

Term of Office. Jan.–Dec. 2011.

Pres. Christine Walsh, Kearney Public Lib. E-mail president@nebraskalibraries.org; *V.P./Pres.-Elect* Jan Boyer, UNO. E-mail jboyer@mail.unomaha.edu; *Secy.* Joanne Ferguson Cavanaugh, Omaha Public Lib. E-mail jferguson@omahapubliclibrary.org; *Treas.* Tracy Bicknell-Holmes, UNL. E-mail nlatreasurer@gmail.com; *Past Pres.* Scott Childers, UNL. E-mail schilder1@unl.edu; *Exec. Dir.* Michael Straatmann. E-mail nlaexecutivedirector@gmail.com.

Address correspondence to the executive director.

World Wide Web http://www.nebraskalibraries.org.

Nevada

Memb. 450. Term of Office. Jan.–Dec. 2011. Publication. *Nevada Libraries* (q.).

Pres. Barbara Mathews, Churchill County Lib. E-mail blmathew@clan.lib.nv.us; *V.P./Pres.-Elect* Robbie DeBuff, Las Vegas-Clark County Lib. Dist. E-mail rjdebuff@hotmail.com; *Treas.* Larry Johnson, Las Vegas-Clark County Lib. Dist. E-mail johnsonl@lvccld.org; *Past Pres.* Joan Vaughan, Henderson Libs. E-mail jevaughan@hdpl.org; *Exec. Secy.* Lisa Phelan, Henderson Libs. E-mail lphelan@hdpl.org.

Address correspondence to the executive secretary.

World Wide Web http://www.nevadalibraries.org.

New Hampshire

Memb. 700. Publication. *NHLA News* (q.).

Pres. Mary White, Howe Lib., 13 South St., Hanover 03755. Tel. 603-640-3251, e-mail mary.h.white@thehowe; *V.P./Pres.-*

Elect Lori Fisher, Baker Free Lib., 509 South St., Bow 03304. Tel. 603-224-7113, e-mail bfldirector@comcast.net; *Secy.* Kate Russell, Regina Lib., Rivier College, 420 S. Main St., Nashua 03060. Tel. 603-897-8683, e-mail krussell@rivier.edu; *Treas.* Sean Fleming, Lebanon Public Lib., 9 E. Park St., Lebanon 03766. Tel. 603-448-2459, e-mail sean.fleming@lebcity.com; *Past Pres.* Judith Haskell, Hampton Falls Free Lib., 7 Drinkwater Rd., Hampton Falls 03844. Tel. 603-926-3682766-1711, e-mail judyhaskell@comcast.net.

Address correspondence to the association, c/o LGC, P.O. Box 617, Concord 03302-0617.

World Wide Web http://nhlibrarians.org

New Jersey

Memb. 1,800. Term of Office. July 2010–June 2011. Publication. *New Jersey Libraries Newsletter* (q.).

Pres. Mary Romance, West Orange Public Lib., 46 Mount Pleasant Ave., West Orange 07052. Tel. 973-736-0191, fax 973-324-9817, e-mail mromance@westorangelibrary.org; *V.P.* Susan O'Neal, Middletown Twp. Public Lib., 55 New Monmouth Rd., Middletown 07748. Tel. 732-671-3703, fax 732-671-5839, e-mail soneal@mtpl.org; *2nd V.P.* Allan Kleiman, Montville Twp. Public Lib., 90 Horseneck Rd., Montville 07045. Tel. 973-402-0900, fax 973-402-1174, e-mail kleiman@aol.com; *Secy.* Karen Topham, Bankier Lib., Brookdale Community College, 765 Newman Springs Rd., Lincroft 07738. Tel. 732-224-2479, e-mail ktopham@brookdalecc.edu; *Treas.* Brett Bonfield, Collingswood Public Lib., 771 Haddon Ave., Collingswood 08108. Tel. 856-858-0649, fax 856-858-5016, e-mail bonfield@collingswoodlib.org; *Past Pres.* Susan Briant, Haddonfield Public Lib., 60 Haddon Ave., Haddonfield 08033. Tel. 856-429-1304, fax 856-429-3760, e-mail sbriant@haddonfieldlibrary.org; *Exec. Dir.* Patricia Tumulty, NJLA, P.O. Box 1534, Trenton 08607. Tel. 609-394-8032, fax 609-394-8164, e-mail ptumulty@njla.org.

Address correspondence to the executive director.

World Wide Web http://www.njla.org.

New Mexico

Memb. 580. Term of Office. Apr. 2010–Apr. 2011. Publication. *New Mexico Library Association Newsletter* (6 a year).

Pres. Barbara Lovato-Gassman. E-mail blovatogassman@gmail.com; *V.P.* Mary Tsosie. E-mail mtsosie@unm.edu; *Secy.* Lynette Schurdevin. E-mail lschurdevin@las-cruces.org; *Treas.* Norice Lee. E-mail nlee@nmsu.edu; *Past Pres.* Dan Kammer. E-mail dan.kammer@gmail.com; *Admin.* Lorie Christian. E-mail admin@nmla.org.

Address correspondence to the association, Box 26074, Albuquerque 87125. Tel. 505-400-7309, fax 505-891-5171, e-mail admin@nmla.org.

World Wide Web http://www.nmla.org.

New York

Memb. 4,000. Term of Office. Oct. 2010–Oct. 2011. Publication. *NYLA Bulletin* (4 a year). *Ed.* Michael J. Borges.

Pres. Marcia Eggleston. Tel. 315-250-0352, e-mail megglest@nncsk12.org; *Pres.-Elect* Matthew Bollerman. E-mail mbollerm@suffolk.lib.ny.us; *Treas.* Penelope Klein. Tel. 315-446-5446, e-mail pklein@clrc.org; *Past Pres.* Kathy Miller. Tel. 585-223-7570, e-mail kmiller@rrlc.org; *Exec. Dir.* Michael J. Borges.

Address correspondence to the executive director, New York Lib. Assn., 6021 State Farm Rd., Guilderland 12084. Tel. 800-252-6952 (toll-free), 518-432-6952, fax 518-427-1697, e-mail director@nyla.org.

World Wide Web http://www.nyla.org.

North Carolina

Memb. 1,100. Term of Office. Oct. 2009–Oct. 2011. Publications. *North Carolina Library Association E-news* (bi-mo.). *Ed.* Marilyn Schuster, Local Documents/Special Collections, Univ. of North Carolina–Charlotte. E-mail mbschust@email.uncc.edu; *North Carolina Libraries Online* (2 a year). *Ed.* Ralph Scott, Joyner Lib., East Carolina Univ., Greenville 27858. Tel. 252-328-0265, e-mail scottr@ecu.edu.

Pres. Sherwin Rice, Bladen Community College, P.O. Box 266, Dublin 28332. Tel.

910-879-5641, e-mail srice@bladencc.edu; *V.P./Pres.-Elect* Wanda Brown, Wake Forest Univ., Box 7777 Reynolda Sta., Winston-Salem 27109. Tel. 336-758-5094, e-mail brownw@wfu.edu; *Secy.* Laura Davidson, Meredith College, 3800 Hillsborough St., Raleigh 27607; *Treas.* Andrea Tullos, Orange County Lib., P.O. Box 8181, Hillsboro 27278. E-mail atullos@co.orange.nc.us; *Past Pres.* Phil Barton, Rowan Public Lib., 714 Brookmont Ave., Salisbury 28146-7293. Tel. 704-633-5462, e-mail pbarton2@carolina.rr.com; *Admin. Asst.* Kim Parrott, North Carolina Lib. Assn., 1841 Capital Blvd., Raleigh 27604. Tel. 919-839-6252, fax 919-839-6253, e-mail nclaonline@gmail.com.

Address correspondence to the administrative assistant.

World Wide Web http://www.nclaonline.org.

North Dakota

Memb. (Indiv.) 317; (Inst.) 9. Term of Office. Sept. 2010–Sept. 2011. Publication. *The Good Stuff* (q.). *Ed.* Marlene Anderson, Bismarck State College Lib., Box 5587, Bismarck 58506-5587. Tel. 701-224-5578.

Pres. Rita Ennen, Stoxen Lib., Dickinson State Univ., 291 Campus Drive, Dickinson 58601. Tel. 701-483-2883, fax 701-483-2006, e-mail rita.ennen@dickinsonstate.edu; *Pres.-Elect* Aubrey Madler, Univ. of North Dakota Center for Rural Health, School of Medicine and Health Sciences, Room 4520, 501 N. Columbia Rd., Stop 9037, Grand Forks 58202-9037. Tel. 701-777-6025, e-mail aubrey.madler@med.und.edu; *Secy.* Chandra Hirning, Rasmussen College Lib., 1701 E. Century Ave., Bismarck 58503-0658. Tel. 701-530-9600, fax 701-530-9604, e-mail chandra.hirning@rasmussen.edu; *Treas.* Michael Safratowich, Harley French Lib. of the Health Sciences, Univ. of North Dakota, Box 9002, Grand Forks 58202-9002. Tel. 701-777-2602, fax 701-777-4790, e-mail michael.safratowich@med.und.edu; *Past Pres.* Laurie L. McHenry, Thormodsgard Lib., Univ. of North Dakota, 2968 Second Ave., N Stop 9004, Grand Forks 58202-9004. Tel. 701-777-3475, fax 701-777-4956, e-mail mchenry@law.und.edu.

Address correspondence to the president.

World Wide Web http://www.ndla.info.

Ohio

Memb. 2,700+. Term of Office. Jan.–Dec. 2011. Publication. *Access* (memb., weekly, online only).

Pres. Molly Carver, Bellevue Public Lib., 224 E. Main St., Bellevue 44811-1409. Tel. 419-483-4769 ext. 14, e-mail mcarver@bellevue.lib.oh.us; *V.P./Pres.-Elect* Virginia Sharp March, Perry Public Lib., 3753 Main St., Perry 44081-8501. Tel. 440-259-3300, e-mail marchvi@oplin.org; *Secy./Treas.* David Orlowski, 130 Harbor Point Rd., Rossford 43460-1026. E-mail nodo9584@aol.com; *Past Pres.* Scott Shafer, 1830 Hillcrest Drive, Lima 45805-2618. E-mail shaferexlibris@aol.com; *Exec. Dir.* Douglas S. Evans. E-mail devans@olc.org.

Address correspondence to the executive director, OLC, 1105 Schrock Rd., Suite 440, Columbus 43229-1174. Tel. 614-410-8092, fax 614-410-8098, e-mail olc@olc.org.

World Wide Web http://www.olc.org.

Oklahoma

Memb. (Indiv.) 1,000; (Inst.) 60. Term of Office. July 2010–June 2011. Publication. *Oklahoma Librarian* (bi-mo.).

Pres. Leslie Langley; *V.P./Pres.-Elect* Cheryl Suttles; *Secy.* Stacy DeLano; *Treas.* Lynda Reynolds; *Past Pres.* Charles Brooks; *Exec. Dir.* Kay Boies, 300 Hardy Drive, Edmond 73013. Tel. 405-525-5100, fax 405-525-5103, e-mail kboies@sbcglobal.net.

Address correspondence to the executive director.

World Wide Web http://www.oklibs.org.

Oregon

Memb. (Indiv.) 1,000+. Publications. *OLA Hotline* (bi-w.), *OLA Quarterly.*

Pres. Rob Everett, Springfield Public Lib. E-mail reverett@ci.springfield.or.us; *V.P./Pres.-Elect* Robert Hulshof-Schmidt, Oregon State Lib. E-mail robert.hulshof-schmidt@state.or.us; *Secy.* Emily Papagni, Multnomah County Lib. E-mail emilyp@multcolib.org; *Treas.* Liisa Sjoblom, Deschutes Public Lib. E-mail liisas@dpls.lib.or.us; *Past Pres.* Connie Anderson-Cohoon, Southern Oregon Univ. Lib. E-mail anderson@sou.edu.

Address correspondence to Oregon Lib. Assn., P.O. Box 3067, La Grande 97850. Tel. 541-962-5824, e-mail olaweb@olaweb.org.

World Wide Web http://www.olaweb.org.

Pennsylvania

Memb. 1,900+. Term of Office. Jan.–Dec. 2011. Publication. *PaLA Bulletin* (10 a year).

Pres. Robin Lesher, Adams County Lib. System. Tel. 717 334 5716, e-mail robinl@adamslibrary.org; *1st V.P.* Debbie Malone, DeSales Univ. Tel. 610-282-1100 ext. 253, e-mail debbie.malone@desales.edu; *2nd V.P.* Cindy Whitmoyer, Susquehanna Univ. Tel. 570-372-4459, e-mail whitmoyer@susqu.edu; *3rd V.P.* Carrie Turner, Cheltenham Township Lib. System. Tel. 215-885-0457, e-mail cturner@mclinc.org; *Treas.* Betsey Moylan, Univ. of Scranton. Tel. 570-941-4000, e-mail moylanm1@scranton.edu; *Past Pres.* Margie Stern, Delaware County Lib. System. Tel. 610-891-8622, e-mail mstern@delco.lib.pa.us; *Exec. Dir.* Glenn R. Miller, Pennsylvania Lib. Assn., 220 Cumberland Pkwy., Suite 10, Mechanicsburg 17055. Tel. 717-766-7663, fax 717-766-5440, e-mail glenn@palibraries.org.

Address correspondence to the executive director.

World Wide Web http://www.palibraries.org.

Rhode Island

Memb. (Indiv.) 350+; (Inst.) 50+. Term of Office. June 2009–June 2011. Publication. *RILA Bulletin.*

Pres. Laura Marlane, Providence Community Lib., South Providence Lib., 441 Prairie Ave., Providence 02905. Tel. 401-467-2700 ext. 1610, e-mail president@rilibraryassoc.org; *V.P./Pres.-Elect* Eileen Dyer, Cranston Public Lib., 140 Sockanossett Cross Rd., Cranston 02920. Tel. 401-943-9080 ext. 119, e-mail vicepresident@rilibraryassoc.org; *Secy.* Jenifer Bond, Douglas and Judith Krupp Lib., Bryant Univ., Smithfield 02917. Tel. 401-232-6299, e-mail secretary@rilibraryassoc.org; *Treas.* Cindy Lunghofer, East Providence Public Lib., 41 Grove Ave., East Providence 02914. Tel. 401-434-2453, e-mail treasurer@rilibraryassoc.org; *Past Pres.* Christopher La Roux, Greenville Public Lib., 573 Putnam Pike, Greenville 02828. Tel. 401-949-3630.

Address correspondence to Rhode Island Library Assn., P.O. Box 6765, Providence 02940.

World Wide Web http://www.rilibraries.org.

South Carolina

Memb. 550+. Term of Office. Jan.–Dec. 2011. Publication. *News and Views.*

Pres. Adam Haigh, Jackson Lib., Lander Univ., 320 Stanley Ave., Greenwood 29649. Tel. 864-388-8029, fax 864-388-8816, e-mail ahaigh@lander.edu; *1st V.P./Pres.-Elect* Yvonne Davis, Rogers Lib., Francis Marion Univ., P.O. Box 100547, Florence 29502. Tel. 843-661-1303, e-mail ydavis@fmarion.edu; *2nd V.P.* Jonathan Newton, Sarah Dobey Jones Branch, Greenville Public Lib., 11 N. Hwy. 25 Bypass, Greenville 29617. Tel. 864-246-1695, fax 864-246-1765, e-mail jnewton@greenvillelibrary.org; *Secy.* Todd Rix, Charles W. and Joan S. Coker Lib., 300 E. College Ave., Hartsville 29550. Tel. 843-383-8270, fax 843-383-8129, e-mail trix@coker.edu; *Treas.* Crystal L. Johnson. Richland County Public Lib., 1431 Assembly St., Columbia 29201-3101. Tel. 803-929-3400, fax 803-929-3476, e-mail cjohnson@myRCPL.com; *Past Pres.* Rayburne Turner, Charleston County Public Lib., 2261 Otranto Rd., North Charleston 29406. Tel. 843-572-4094, fax 843-572-4190, e-mail turner@ccpl.org; *Exec. Secy.* Donald Wood, SCLA, P.O. Box 1763, Columbia 29202. Tel. 803-252-1087, fax 803-252-0589. E-mail scla@capconsc.com.

Address correspondence to the executive secretary.

World Wide Web http://www.scla.org.

South Dakota

Memb. (Indiv.) 462; (Inst.) 67. Term of Office. Oct. 2010–Oct. 2011. Publication. *Book Marks* (q.).

Pres. Paula DeMars, Hill City Community Lib., Hill City. E-mail pdemars@hillcitysd.org; *V.P./Pres.-Elect* Annie Brunskill, Haakon

County Public Lib., Phillip. E-mail library@gwtc.net; *Recording Secy.* Kathy Jacobs, Yankton Community Lib. E-mail kjacobs@sdln.net; *Past Pres.* Kay Christensen, Augustana College Lib., Sioux Falls. E-mail kay.christensen@augie.edu; *Exec. Secy./Treas.* Laura G. Olson. E-mail sdla@svtv.com.

Address correspondence to the executive secretary, SDLA, 28363 472nd Ave., Worthing 57077-5722. Tel. 605-372-0235, e-mail sdla@svtv.com.

World Wide Web http://www.sdlibraryassociation.org.

Tennessee

Memb. 600+. Term of Office. July 2010–June 2011. Publications. *Tennessee Librarian* (q.), *TLA Newsletter* (bi-mo.) Both online only at http://www.tnla.org.

Pres. Susan Earl. E-mail susan.earl@nashville.gov; *V.P./Pres.-Elect* Wendy Cornelisen. E-mail wendy.cornelisen@gmail.com; *Recording Secy.* Genny Carter. E-mail genny.carter@tn.gov; *Past Pres.* Kevin Reynolds. E-mail kreynold@sewanee.edu; *Exec. Dir.* Annelle R. Huggins, Tennessee Lib. Assn., Box 241074, Memphis 38124. Tel. 901-485-6952, e-mail arhuggins1@comcast.net

Address correspondence to the executive director.

World Wide Web http://tnla.org.

Texas

Memb. 7,600+. Term of Office. Apr. 2010–Apr. 2011. Publications. *Texas Library Journal* (q.), *TLACast* (9 a year).

Pres. Maribel Castro. E-mail serialreader@gmail.com; *Pres.-Elect* Jerilynn A. Williams, Montgomery County Lib. System. E-mail jeri.williams@countylibrary.org; *Treas.* Jane Clausen, Lubbock Public Lib. E-mail jclausen@mail.ci.lubbock.tx.us; *Past Pres.* Patrick Heath. E-mail patrickheath@windstream.net; *Exec. Dir.* Patricia H. Smith, TXLA, 3355 Bee Cave Rd., Suite 401, Austin 78746-6763. Tel. 512-328-1518, fax 512-328-8852, e-mail pats@txla.org or tla@txla.org.

Address correspondence to the executive director.

World Wide Web http://www.txla.org.

Utah

Memb. 650. Publication. *Utah Libraries News* (bi-mo.) (online at http://www.ula.org/newsletter).

Pres. Andy Spackman, Harold B. Lee Lib., Brigham Young Univ., 1212 HBLL, Provo 84602. Tel. 801-422-3924, e-mail andy_spackman@byu.edu; *V.P./Pres.-Elect* Linda Tillson, Park City Lib., P.O. Box 668, Park City 84060. Tel. 435-615-5605, e-mail ltillson@parkcity.org; *Recording Secy.* Josh Sorensen, 3445 HBLL, Brigham Young Univ., Provo 84602. Tel. 801-422-6447, e-mail joshua_sorensen@byu.edu; *Treas.* Steve Pfeiffer, Anderson-Foothill Lib., 1270 Brandonwood Drive, Murray 84123. Tel. 801-594-8611, e-mail spfeiffer@slcpl.org; *Past Pres.* Ruby Cheesman, Bingham Creek Lib., Salt Lake County Lib. Services, 4834 W. 9000 S., West Jordan 84081. Tel. 801-944-7688, fax 801-282-0943, e-mail rcheesman@slcolibrary.org; *Exec. Dir.* Anna Neatrour, 845 E. 100 S., No. 101, Salt Lake City 84102. Tel. 801-209-3075, e-mail anna.neatrour@gmail.com.

Address correspondence to the executive director.

World Wide Web http://www.ula.org.

Vermont

Memb. 400. Publication. *VLA News* (6 a year).

Pres. Marti Fiske, Dorothy Alling Memorial Lib., 21 Library Lane, Williston 05495. Tel. 802-878-4918, e-mail marti@williston.lib.vt.us; *V.P./Pres.-Elect* Joseph Farara, Johnson State College, Johnson 05656. Tel. 802-635-1272, e-mail joseph.farara@jsc.edu; *Secy.* David Sturges, Hartness Lib. System, Community College of Vermont, 1 Main St., Randolph Center 05061. Tel. 802-728-1231, e-mail dsturges@vtc.edu; *Treas.* Wynne Browne, Downs Rachlin Martin, St. Johnsbury 05819-0099. Tel. 802-473-4216, e-mail wbrowne@drm.com; *Past Pres.* John K. Payne, Saint Michael's College, 1 Winooski Park, Box L, Colchester 05439. Tel. 802-654-2401, e-mail jpayne@smcvt.edu.

Address correspondence to VLA, Box 803, Burlington 05402.

World Wide Web http://www.vermontlibraries.org.

Virginia

Memb. 900+. Term of Office. Oct. 2010–Oct. 2011. Publication. *Virginia Libraries* (q.).

Pres. Matthew Todd, NOVA, 3001 N. Beauregard St., Alexandria 22331. Tel. 703-845-6033, e-mail mtodd@nvcc.edu; *V.P./Pres.-Elect* Connie Gilman, Chinn Park Regional Lib., 13065 Chinn Park Drive, Prince William 22192. Tel. 703-792-6199, e-mail cgilman@pwcgov.org; *2nd V.P.* Diantha McCauley, Augusta County Lib., 1759 Jefferson Hwy., Fisherville 22939. Tel. 540-949-6354, e-mail diantha@augustacountylibrary.org; *Secy.* Diane Adkins, Pittsylvania County Public Lib., 24 Military Drive, Chatham 24531. Tel. 434-432-3271; *Treas.* Elizabeth Tai, Poquoson Public Lib., 500 City Hall Ave., Poquoson 23662. Tel. 757-868-3066, e-mail etai@poquoson-va.gov; *Past Pres.* John A. Moorman, Williamsburg Regional Lib., 7770 Croaker Rd., Williamsburg 23188. Tel. 757-259-7777, e-mail jmoorman@wrl.org; *Exec. Dir.* Linda Hahne, P.O. Box 8277, Norfolk 23503-0277. Tel. 757-583-0041, fax 757-583-5041, e-mail lindahahne@cox.net.

Address correspondence to the executive director.

World Wide Web http://www.vla.org.

Washington

Memb. 1,000+. Term of Office. Apr. 2009–Apr. 2011. Publication. *Alki: The Washington Library Association Journal* (3 a year). *Ed.* Bo Kinney, Seattle Public Lib., 1000 Fourth Ave., Seattle 98104. E-mail alkieditor@wla.org.

Pres. Tim Mallory, Timberland Regional Lib., 415 Tumwater Blvd. S.W., Tumwater 98501. Tel. 360-704-4502, fax 360-586-6838, e-mail tmallory@trlib.org; *V.P./Pres.-Elect* Brian Soneda, Mount Vernon City Lib., 315 Snoqualmie St., Mount Vernon 98273. Tel. 360-336-6209, e-mail brians@ci.mount-vernon.wa.us; *Secy.* Karen Highum, Allen Lib., Univ. of Washington, Box 35290, Seattle 98195-2900. Tel. 206-685-3981, e-mail khighum@msn.com; *Treas.* Priscilla Ice, Spokane County Lib. Dist., 12004 E. Main Ave., Spokane 99206. Tel. 509-893-8451, e-mail pice@scld.org; *Past Pres.* Martha Parsons, WSU Energy Program Lib., 925 Plum St. S.E., Olympia 98501. Tel. 360-956-2159, fax 360-236-2159, e-mail president@wla.org; *Exec. Dir.* Dana Murphy-Love, WLA, 23607 Hwy. 99, Suite 2-C, Edmonds 98026. Tel. 425-967-0739, fax 425-771-9588, e-mail dana@wla.org.

Address correspondence to the executive director.

World Wide Web http://www.wla.org.

West Virginia

Memb. 650+. Publication. *West Virginia Libraries* (6 a year). *Ed.* Pam Coyle, Martinsburg Public Lib., 101 W. King St., Martinsburg 25401. Tel. 304-267-8933, fax 304-267-9720, e-mail pcoyle@martin.lib.wv.us.

Pres. Monica Brooks, 306 Drinko Lib., Marshall Univ., Huntington 25755. Tel. 304-696-6474, e-mail brooks@marshall.edu; *1st V.P./Pres.-Elect* Crystal Hamrick, Bridgeport Public Lib., 1200 Johnson Ave., Bridgeport 26330. Tel. 304-842-8248, e-mail chamrick@bridgeportwv.com; *2nd V.P.* Myra Ziegler, Summers County Public Lib., 201 Temple St., Hinton 25951. Tel. 304-466-4490, e-mail zieglm@mail.mln.lib.wv.us; *Secy.* Barbara LaGodna, WVU Libs., P.O. Box 6105, Morgantown 26506-6105. Tel. 304-293-9748, e-mail blagodna@wvu.edu; *Treas.* Beth Royall, Evansdale Lib., WVU, P.O. Box 6105, Morgantown 26506-6105. Tel. 304-293-9755, e-mail beth.royall@mail.wvu.edu; *Past Pres.* Judy K. Rule, Cabell County Public Lib., 455 Ninth St., Huntington 25701. Tel. 304-528-5700, e-mail jrule@cabell.lib.wv.us.

Address correspondence to the president.

World Wide Web http://www.wvla.org.

Wisconsin

Memb. 1,900. Term of Office. Jan.–Dec. Publication. *WLA Newsletter* (q.).

Pres. Rhonda K. Puntney, Lakeshores Lib. System, 725 Cornerstone Crossing, Suite C, Waterford 53185. E-mail rpuntney@lakeshores.lib.wi.us; *Pres.-Elect* Ronald B.

McCabe, McMillan Memorial Lib., 490 E. Grand Ave., Wisconsin Rapids 54494-4898. E-mail rmccabe@wctc.net; *Secy.* Tasha Saecker, Elisha D. Smith Public Lib., 440 First St., Menasha 54952-3191. E-mail saecker@menashalibrary.org; *Treas.* Jan Berg, DeForest Public Lib., 203 Library St., DeForest 53532. E-mail bergjd@scls.lib.wi.us; *Past Pres.* Alberto Herrera, Jr., Raynor Memorial Libs., Marquette Univ., P.O. Box 3141, Milwaukee 53201-3141. E-mail alberto.herrera@marquette.edu; *Exec. Dir.* Lisa K. Strand, Wisconsin Lib. Assn., 4610 S. Biltmore Lane, Suite 100, Madison 53718-2153. Tel. 608-245-3640, fax 608-245-3646, e-mail strand@scls.lib.wi.us.

Address correspondence to the association.

World Wide Web http://www.wla.lib.wi.us.

Wyoming

Memb. 450+. Term of Office. Oct. 2010–Oct. 2011.

Pres. Sue Knesel, Campbell County Public Lib. System. Tel. 307-687-9229, fax 307-686-4009, e-mail sknesel@will.state.wy.us; *V.P.* Sukey Hohl, Sublette County Lib. Tel. 307-367-4114, fax 307-367-6722, e-mail shohl@sublettecountylibrary.org; *Past Pres.* Jamie Markus, Wyoming State Lib. Tel. 307-777-5914, fax 307-777-6289, e-mail jmarku@state.wy.us; *Exec. Secy.* Laura Grott, Box 1387, Cheyenne 82003. Tel. 307-632-7622, fax 307-638-3469, e-mail grottski@aol.com.

Address correspondence to the executive secretary.

World Wide Web http://www.wyla.org.

Canada

Alberta

Memb. 500. Term of Office. May 2010–Apr. 2011. Publication. *Letter of the LAA* (4 a year).

Pres. Mary Jane Bilsland, Edmonton Public Lib. E-mail mjbilsland@epl.ca: *Past Pres.* Renee Reaume, Univ. of Calgary. E-mail renee.reaume@ucalgary.ca; *2nd V.P.* Linda Williams, Edmonton Public Lib. E-mail lwilliams@epl.ca; *Treas.* Julia Reinhart, Alberta Lib. E-mail jreinhart@thealbertalibrary.ab.ca; *Exec. Dir.* Christine Sheppard, 80 Baker Crescent N.W., Calgary T2L 1R4. Tel. 403-284-5818, fax 403-282-6646, E-mail info@laa.ca.

Address correspondence to the executive director.

World Wide Web http://www.laa.ca.

British Columbia

Memb. 771. Term of Office. April 2010–April 2011. Publication. *BCLA Browser* (online at http://bclabrowser.ca). *Ed.* Sandra Wong.

Pres. Marjorie Mitchell, Univ. of British Columbia, Okanagan, 3333 University Way, Kelowna V1V 1V7. Tel. 250-807-9147, fax 250-807-8057, e-mail marjorie.mitchell@ubc.ca; *V.P./Pres.-Elect* Christopher Kevlahan, Champlain Heights Branch, Vancouver Public Lib., 7110 Kerr St., Vancouver, BC V5S 4W2. Tel. 604-665-3955, e-mail christopher.kevlahan@vpl.ca; *2nd V.P.* Adrienne Wass, Greater Victoria Public Lib., 735 Broughton St., Victoria V8W 3H2. Tel. 250-413-0370, e-mail awass@gvpl.ca; *Treas.* Chris Middlemass, Vancouver Public Lib., 350 W. Georgia St., Vancouver V6B 6B1. E-mail chris.middlemass@vpl.ca; *Past Pres.* Ken Cooley, McPherson Lib., Univ. of Victoria, P.O. Box 1800, STN CSC, Victoria V8W 3H5. E-mail kcooley@uvic.ca; *Exec. Dir.* Errin Morrison. E-mail execdir@bcla.bc.ca.

Address correspondence to the association, 900 Howe St., Suite 150, Vancouver V6Z 2M4. Tel. 604-683-5354, e-mail office@bcla.bc.ca.

World Wide Web http://www.bcla.bc.ca.

Manitoba

Memb. 500+. Term of Office. May 2010–May 2011. Publication. *Newsline* (mo.).

Pres. Sherri Vokey, Neil John Maclean Health Sciences Lib., 770 Bannatyne Ave., Winnipeg R3B 0W3. Tel. 204-789-3344, e-mail sherri_vokey@umanitoba.ca; *V.P.* Emma Hill Kepron, Elizabeth Dafoe Lib., Winnipeg. Tel. 204-474-6710, e-mail emma_kepron@umanitoba.ca; *Secy.* Rebecca

Schramm, Manitoba Infrastructure and Transportation, 1710-215 Garry St., Winnipeg R3C 3Z1. Tel. 204-945-1693, e-mail rebecca.schramm@gov.mb.ca; *Treas.* Kristen Kruse, Univ. of Manitoba Libs., 219 Elizabeth Dafoe Lib., Winnipeg R3T 2N2. Tel. 204-474-7435, e-mail krusek@cc.umanitoba.ca; *Past Pres.* Betty Braaksma, Univ. of Manitoba Libs., E3-362 EITC, Univ. of Manitoba, Winnipeg R3T 2N2. Tel. 204-474-7193, e-mail betty_braaksma@umanitoba.ca.

Address correspondence to the association, 606-100 Arthur St., Winnipeg R3B 1H3. Tel. 204-943-4567, fax 866-202-4567; e-mail manitobalibrary@gmail.com.

World Wide Web http://www.mla.mb.ca.

Ontario

Memb. 5,200+. Publications. *Access* (q.); *Teaching Librarian* (3 a year).

Pres. Tanis Fink, Seneca Libs. E-mail tanis.fink@senecac.on.ca; *V.P./Pres.-Elect* Karen McGrath, Niagara College Libs. and Learning Commons. E-mail kmcgrathniagara@gmail.com; *Treas.* Paul Takala, Hamilton Public Lib. E-mail ptakala@hpl.ca; *Past Pres.* Mary Ann Mavrinac, Hazel McCallion Academic Learning Centre, Univ. of Toronto at Mississauga. E-mail maryann.mavrinac@utoronto.ca; *Exec. Dir.* Shelagh Paterson. E-mail spaterson@accessola.com.

Address correspondence to the association, 50 Wellington St. E., Suite 201, Toronto M5E 1C8. Tel. 416-363-3388, fax 416-941-9581, e-mail info@accessola.com.

World Wide Web http://www.accessola.com.

Quebec

Memb. (Indiv.) 100+. Term of Office. May 2010–April 2011. Publication. *ABQLA Bulletin* (3 a year).

Pres. Anne Wade; *V.P.*Julie-Anne Cardella; *Secy.* Cathy Maxwell; *Exec. Secy./Treas.* Janet Ilavsky, P.O. Box 1095, Pointe-Claire H9S 4H9. Tel. 514-697-0146, e-mail abqla@abqla.qc.ca; *Past Pres.* Maria Luisa Morales.

Address correspondence to the executive secretary.

World Wide Web http://www.abqla.qc.ca.

Saskatchewan

Memb. 200+. Publication. *Forum* (4 a year).

Pres. Jeff Mason, Regina Qu'Appelle Health Region, 0B—Health Sciences Lib., 1440 14th Ave., Regina S4P 0W5. Tel. 306-766-3833, fax 306-766-3839, e-mail jeff_mason@me.com; *V.P.*; Amber Christensen, Prince of Wales Branch, Regina Public Lib., P.O. Box 2311, Regina S4P 3Z5. Tel. 306-777-6140, e-mail achristensen@reginalibrary.ca; *Treas.* Brett Waytuck, Provincial Lib. and Literacy Office, Ministry of Educ., 409A Park St., Regina S4N 5B2. Tel. 306-787-8020, fax 306-787-2029, e-mail brett.waytuck@gov.sk.ca; *Past Pres.* Barbara Kelly, Regina Public Lib., P.O. Box 2311, Regina S4P 3Z5. Tel. 306-777-6004, fax 306-949-7266, e-mail bkelly@reginalibrary.ca; *Exec. Dir.* Caroline Selinger, Saskatchewan Lib. Assn., 2010 Seventh Ave., No. 15, Regina S4R 1C2. Tel. 306-780-9413, fax 306-780-9447, e-mail slaexdir@sasktel.net.

Address correspondence to the executive director.

World Wide Web http://www.saskla.ca.

Regional

Atlantic Provinces: N.B., N.L., N.S., P.E.I.

Memb. (Indiv.) 200+; (Inst.) 26. Publications. *APLA Bulletin* (bi-mo.).

Pres. Sarah Gladwell, Saint John Free Public Lib., Saint John, NB E2L 4Z6. Tel. 506-643-7224, fax 506-643-7225, e-mail sarah.gladwell@gnb.ca; *V.P./Pres.-Elect* Jocelyne Thompson, Univ. of New Brunswick Libs. Tel. 506-458-7053, e-mail jlt@unb.ca; *V.P., Membership* Ann Smith, Vaughan Memorial Lib., Acadia Univ., Wolfville, NS B4P 2R6. Tel. 902-585-1723, fax 902-585-1748, e-mail apla_executive@yahoo.ca; *Secy.* Lori McCay-Peet, Centre for Management Informatics, Dalhousie Univ., Halifax, NS B3H 4R2. Tel. 902-494-8392, e-mail mccay@dal.ca; *Treas.* Bill Slauenwhite, Novanet, 1550 Bedford Hwy., Suite 501, Bedford, NS B4A 1E6. Tel. 902-453-2461, fax 902-453-2369, e-mail bill.slauenwhite@novanet.ns.ca; *Past Pres.* Donald Moses,

Robertson Lib., Univ. of PEI, Charlottetown, PE C1A 4P3. Tel. 902-566-0479, fax 902-628-4305, e-mail dmoses@upei.ca.

Address correspondence to Atlantic Provinces Lib. Assn., c/o School of Info. Mgt., Faculty of Mgt., Kenneth C. Rowe Mgt. Bldg., 6100 University Ave., Halifax, NS B3H 3J5.

World Wide Web http://www.apla.ca.

Mountain Plains: Ariz., Colo., Kan., Mont., Neb., Nev., N.Dak., N.M., Okla., S.Dak., Utah, Wyo.

Memb. 820. Term of Office. May 2010–May 2011. Publications. *MPLA Newsletter* (bi-mo.). *Ed./Advertising Mgr.* Judy Zelenski, 14293 W. Center Drive, Lakewood, CO 80228. Tel. 303-985-7795, e-mail editor@mpla.us.

Pres. Elvita Landau, Brookings Public Lib., 515 Third St., Brookings, SD 57006. Tel. 605-692-9407, fax 605-692-9386, e-mail elandau@sdln.net; *Pres.-Elect* Dana Braccia, Scottsdale Public Lib. System, 3839 N. Drinkwater Blvd., Scottsdale, AZ 85258. Tel. 480-312-7949, fax 480-312-7993, e-mail dbraccia@scottsdaleaz.gov; *Past Pres.* Eileen Wright, Billings Lib., Montana State Univ., 1500 University Drive, Billings, MT 59101. Tel. 406-657-1656, fax 406-657-2037, e-mail ewright@msubillings.edu; *Recording Secy.* Tamara Meredith, Univ. of Wyoming Libs., 1000 E. University Ave., Laramie, WY 82071. Tel. 307-766-2684, e-mail tmeredi3@uwyo.edu; *Exec. Secy.* Judy Zelenski, 14293 W. Center Drive, Lakewood, CO 80228. Tel. 303-985-7795, e-mail execsecretary@mpla.us.

Address correspondence to the executive secretary.

World Wide Web http://www.mpla.us.

New England: Conn., Maine, Mass., N.H., R.I., Vt.

Memb. (Indiv.) 700. Term of Office. Nov. 2010–Oct. 2011. Publication. *NELA News* (online, mo.).

Pres. Jen Alvino Leo, Walker Memorial Lib., 800 Main St., Westbrook, ME 0404092, Tel 207-854-0630, e-mail president@nelib.org; *V.P.* Mary Ann List, Portsmouth Public Lib., 175 Parrott Ave., Portsmouth, NH 03801. Tel 603-766-1719, e-mail vicepresident@nelib.org; *Secy.* Kirsten Corbett, Lane Memorial Lib., 2 Academy Ave., Hampton, NH 03842. Tel. 603-926-3368, fax 603-926-1348, e-mail secretary@nelib.org; *Treas.* Karen Patterson. 83 Elizabeth St., South Windsor, CT 08074. E-mail treasurer@nelib.org; *Past Pres.*Rick Taplin, Minuteman Lib. Network, 10 Strathmore Rd., Natick, MA 01760. Tel. 508-655-8008, e-mail past-president@nelib.org; *Exec. Mgr.* Mary Ann Rupert, 31 Connor Lane, Wilton, NH 03086. Tel. 603-654-3533, fax 603-654-3526, e-mail executivemanager@nelib.org.

Address correspondence to the executive manager.

World Wide Web http://www.nelib.org.

Pacific Northwest: Alaska, Idaho, Mont., Ore., Wash., Alberta, B.C.

Memb. (Active) 172. Term of Office. Aug. 2010–Aug. 2011. Publication. *PNLA Quarterly. Ed.* Mary Bolin, 322B Love Lib., Univ. of Nebraska, P.O. Box 881140, Lincoln, NE 68588-4100. Tel. 402-472-4281, e-mail mbolin2@unlnotes.unl.edu.

Pres. Michael Burris, Public Lib. InterLINK, 7252 Kingsway, Burnaby, BC V5E 1G3. Tel. 604-517-8441, fax 604-517-8410, e-mail michael.burris@interlinklibraries.ca; *1st V.P./Pres.-Elect* Heidi Chittim, Eastern Washington Univ. Libs., 100 LIB, 816 F St., Cheney, WA 99004-2453. Tel. 509-359-2303. fax 509-359-2476, e-mail hchittim@ewu.edu; *2nd V.P.* Jason Openo, Edmonton Public Lib., 145 Whitemud Crossing Shopping Centre, 4211 106th St., Edmonton, AB T6J 6L7. Tel. 780-496-8348, e-mail jopeno@epl.ca; *Secy.* Darlene Hert, Montana State Univ.–Billings. E-mail dhert@msubillings.edu; *Treas.* Katie Cargill, Eastern Washington Univ. Libs., 816 F St., Cheney, WA 99004. Tel. 509-359-2385, fax 509-359-2476, e-mail kcargill@mail.ewu.edu; *Past Pres.* Samantha Hines, Univ. of Montana Mansfield Lib., Missoula, MT 59812. Tel. 406-243-4558, e-mail samantha.hines@umontana.edu.

Address correspondence to the president, Pacific Northwest Lib. Assn.

World Wide Web http://www.pnla.org.

Southeastern: Ala., Ark., Fla., Ga., Ky., La., Miss., N.C., S.C., Tenn., Va., W.Va.

Memb. 500. Publication. *The Southeastern Librarian* (*SELn*) (q.). *Ed.* Perry Bratcher, *SELn* Editor, 503A Steely Lib., Northern Kentucky Univ., Highland Heights, KY 41099. Tel. 859-572-6309, fax 859-572-6181, e-mail bratcher@nku.edu.

Pres. Michael Seigler, Smyrna Public Lib., 100 Village Green Circle, Smyrna, GA 30080. Tel. 770-431-2860, fax 770-431-2862, e-mail m.seigler@ci.Smyrna.ga.us; *V.P.* Gordon N. Baker. E-mail gordonbaker@mail.clayton.edu; *Secy.* Camille McCutcheon. E-mail cmccutcheon@uscupstate.edu; *Treas.* Beverly James. E-mail bjames@greenvillelibrary.org; *Past Pres.* Kathleen R. T. Imhoff, 3617 Gloucester Drive, Lexington, KY 40510. Tel. 859-225-9310, e-mail kathleenrtimhoff@gmail.com.

Address correspondence to Southeastern Lib. Assn., Admin. Services, P.O. Box 950, Rex, GA 30273-0950. Tel. 770-961-3520, fax 770-961-3712.

World Wide Web http://sela.jsu.edu.

State and Provincial Library Agencies

The state library administrative agency in each of the U.S. states will have the latest information on its state plan for the use of federal funds under the Library Services and Technology Act (LSTA). The directors and addresses of these state agencies are listed below.

Alabama

Rebecca Mitchell, Dir., Alabama Public Lib. Service, 6030 Monticello Drive, Montgomery 36130-6000. Tel. 334-213-3901, fax 334-213-3993, e-mail rmitchell@apls.state.al.us. World Wide Web http://statelibrary.alabama.gov/Content/Index.aspx.

Alaska

Linda Thibodeau, State Libn. and Dir., Alaska Dept. of Educ., Div. of Libs., Archives, and Museums, P.O. Box 110571, Juneau 99811. Tel. 907-465-2911, fax 907-465-2151, e-mail linda.thibodeau@alaska.gov. World Wide Web http://library.state.ak.us.

Arizona

GladysAnn Wells, Dir., State Libn., Arizona State Lib., Archives, and Public Records, Rm. 200, 1700 W. Washington, Phoenix 85007. Tel. 602-926-4035, fax 602-256-7983, e-mail gawells@lib.az.us. World Wide Web http://www.lib.az.us.

Arkansas

Carolyn Ashcraft, State Libn., Arkansas State Lib., 900 W. Capitol, Suite 100, Little Rock 72201-3108. Tel. 501-682-1526, fax 501-682-1899, e-mail cashcraft@asl.lib.ar.us. World Wide Web http://www.asl.lib.ar.us.

California

Stacey Aldrich, State Libn., California State Lib., P.O. Box 942837, Sacramento 94237. Tel. 916-654-0188, fax 916-654-0064, e-mail saldrich@library.ca.gov. World Wide Web http://www.library.ca.gov.

Colorado

Eugene Hainer, Dir. and State Libn., Colorado State Lib., Rm. 309, 201 E. Colfax Ave., Denver 80203-1799. Tel. 303-866-6733, fax 303-866-6940, e-mail hainer_g@cde.state.co.us. World Wide Web http://www.cde.state.co.us/cdelib.

Connecticut

Kendall F. Wiggin, State Libn., Connecticut State Lib., 231 Capitol Ave., Hartford 06106. Tel. 860-757-6510, fax 860-757-6503, e-mail kwiggin@cslib.org. World Wide Web http://www.cslib.org.

Delaware

Anne Norman, State Libn. and Dir., Delaware Div. of Libs., 121 Duke of York St., Dover 19901. Tel. 302-739-4748 ext. 5126, fax 302-739-8436, e-mail annie.norman@state.de.us. World Wide Web http://www.state.lib.de.us.

District of Columbia

Ginnie Cooper, Chief Libn., District of Columbia Public Lib., 901 G St. N.W., Suite 400, Washington 20001-4599. Tel. 202-727-1101, fax 202-727-1129, e-mail ginnie.cooper@dc.gov. World Wide Web http://www.dclibrary.org.

Florida

Judith A. Ring, State Libn., Div. of Lib. and Info. Services, R. A. Gray Bldg., 500 S. Bronough St., Tallahassee 32399-0250. Tel. 850-245-6604, fax 850-488-2746, e-mail jring@dos.state.fl.us. World Wide Web http://dlis.dos.state.fl.us/stlib.

Georgia

Lamar Veatch, State Libn., Georgia Public Lib. Services, 1800 Century Place N.E., Suite 150, Atlanta 30345. Tel. 404-235-7120, fax 404-235-7201, e-mail lveatch@georgialibraries.org. World Wide Web http://www.georgialibraries.org.

Hawaii

Richard Burns, State Libn., Hawaii State Public Lib. System, 44 Merchant St., Honolulu 96813. Tel. 808-586-3704, fax 808-586-3715, e-mail stlib@librarieshawaii.org. World Wide Web http://www.librarieshawaii.org.

Idaho

Ann Joslin, State Libn., Idaho Commission for Libs., 325 W. State St., Boise 83713-6072. Tel. 208-334-2150, fax 208-334-4016, e-mail ann.joslin@libraries.idaho.gov. World Wide Web http://libraries.idaho.gov.

Illinois

Anne Craig, Dir., Illinois State Lib., 300 S. 2 St., Springfield 62701-1703. Tel. 217-782-2994, fax 217-785-4326, e-mail acraig@ilsos.net. World Wide Web http://www.cyberdriveillinois.com/departments/library/home.html.

Indiana

Roberta L. Brooker, Dir. and State Libn., Indiana State Lib., 315 W. Ohio St., Indianapolis 46202. Tel. 317-232-3692, fax 317-232-3728, e-mail rbrooker@library.in.gov. World Wide Web http://www.in.gov/library.

Iowa

Mary Wegner, State Libn., State Lib. of Iowa, 1112 E. Grand Ave., Des Moines 50319. Tel. 515-281-4105, fax 515-281-6191, e-mail mary.wegner@lib.state.ia.us. World Wide Web http://www.statelibraryofiowa.org.

Kansas

Jo Budler, State Libn., State Lib. of Kansas, Rm. 168W, 300 S.W. 10 Ave., Topeka 66612-1593. Tel. 785-296-5466, fax 785-296-6650, e-mail jobudler@kslib.org. World Wide Web http://skyways.lib.ks.us/KSL.

Kentucky

Wayne Onkst, State Libn. and Commissioner, Kentucky Dept. for Libs. and Archives, P.O. Box 537, Frankfort 40602-0537. Tel. 502-564-8300 ext. 312, fax 502-564-5773, e-mail wayne.onkst@ky.gov. World Wide Web http://www.kdla.ky.gov.

Louisiana

Rebecca Hamilton, State Libn., State Lib. of Louisiana, 701 N. 4 St., P.O. Box 131, Baton Rouge 70821-0131. Tel. 225-342-4923, fax 225-219-4804, e-mail rhamilton@crt.state.la.us. World Wide Web http://www.state.lib.la.us.

Maine

Linda Lord, State Libn., Maine State Lib., 64 State House Sta., Augusta 04333. Tel. 207-287-5620, fax 207-287-5624, e-mail linda.lord@maine.gov. World Wide Web http://www.maine.gov/msl.

Maryland

Irene Padilla, Asst. State Superintendent for Libs., State of Maryland, 200 W. Baltimore St., Baltimore 21201. Tel. 410-767-0435, fax 410-333-2507, e-mail ipadilla@msde.state.md.us. World Wide Web http://www.marylandpublicschools.org/MSDE/divisions/library.

Massachusetts

Robert Maier, Dir., Massachusetts Board of Lib. Commissioners, 98 N. Washington St., Suite 401, Boston 02114-1933. Tel. 617-725-1860, fax 617-725-0140, e-mail robert.maier@state.ma.us. World Wide Web http://mblc.state.ma.us.

Michigan

Nancy R. Robertson, State Libn., Lib. of Michigan, P.O. Box 30007, Lansing 48909-7507. Tel. 517-373-9464, fax 517-373-5700, e-mail nrobertson@michigan.gov. World Wide Web http://www.michigan.gov/hal.

Minnesota

Nancy K. Walton, Acting State Libn. and Dir., Minnesota Dept. of Educ., 1500 Hwy. 36 W., Roseville 55113-4266. Tel. 651-582-8881, fax 651-582-8752, e-mail nancy.walton@state.mn.us. World Wide Web http://education.state.mn.us/MDE/Learning_Support/Library_Services/index.html.

Mississippi

Sharman Bridges Smith, Exec. Dir., Mississippi Lib. Commission, 3881 Eastwood Drive, Jackson 39211. Tel. 601-432-4039, fax 601-432-4480, e-mail sharman@mlc.lib.ms.us. World Wide Web http://www.mlc.lib.ms.us.

Missouri

Margaret Conroy, State Libn., Missouri State Lib., P.O. Box 387, Jefferson City 65102-0387. Tel. 573-751-2751, fax 573-751-3612, e-mail margaret.conroy@sos.mo.gov. World Wide Web http://www.sos.mo.gov/library.

Montana

Darlene Staffeldt, State Libn., Montana State Lib., 1515 E. 6 Ave., P.O. Box 201800, Helena 59620-1800. Tel. 406-444-3116, fax 406-444-0266, e-mail dstaffeldt@mt.us. World Wide Web http://msl.mt.gov.

Nebraska

Rodney G. Wagner, Dir., Nebraska Lib. Commission, Suite 120, 1200 N St., Lincoln 68508-2023. Tel. 402-471-4001, fax 402-471-2083, e-mail rwagner@nlc.state.ne.us. World Wide Web http://www.nlc.state.ne.us.

Nevada

Daphne DeLeon, State Lib. and Archives Admin., Nevada State Lib. and Archives, 100 N. Stewart St., Carson City 89701-4285. Tel. 775-684-3315, fax 775-684-3311, e-mail ddeleon@nevadaculture.org. World Wide Web http://www.nevadaculture.org/docs/nsla.

New Hampshire

Michael York, State Libn., New Hampshire State Lib., 20 Park St., Concord 03301. Tel. 603-271-2397, fax 603-271-6826, e-mail michael.york@dcr.nh.gov. World Wide Web http://www.nh.gov/nhsl.

New Jersey

Norma E. Blake, State Libn., New Jersey State Lib., P.O. Box 520, Trenton 08625-0520. Tel. 609-278-2640 ext. 101, fax 609-278-2652, e-mail nblake@njstatelib.org. World Wide Web http://www.njstatelib.org.

New Mexico

Susan Oberlander, State Libn., New Mexico State Lib., 1209 Camino Carlos Rey, Santa Fe 87507. Tel. 505-476-9762, fax 505-476-9761, e-mail susan.oberlander@state.nm.us. World Wide Web http://www.nmstatelibrary.org.

New York

Bernard A. Margolis, State Libn. and Asst. Commissioner for Libs., New York State Lib., Empire State Plaza, Albany 12230. Tel. 518-474-5930, fax 518-486-6880, e-mail bmargolis@mail.nysed.gov. World Wide Web http://www.nysl.nysed.gov.

North Carolina

Mary L. Boone, State Libn., State Lib. of North Carolina, 4640 Mail Service Center, Raleigh 27699-4640. Tel. 919-807-7410, fax 919-733-8748, e-mail mary.boone@ncdcrl.net. World Wide Web http://statelibrary.ncdcr.gov.

North Dakota

Doris Ott, State Libn., North Dakota State Lib., 604 E. Boulevard Ave., Bismarck 58505. Tel. 701-328-2492, fax 701-328-

2040, e-mail dott@nd.gov. World Wide Web http://ndsl.lib.state.nd.us.

Ohio

Beverly Cain, Interim State Libn., State Lib. of Ohio, 274 E. 1 Ave., Columbus 43201. Tel. 614-644-6843, fax 614-466-3584, e-mail bcain@library.oh.gov. World Wide Web http://www.library.ohio.gov.

Oklahoma

Susan C. McVey, Dir., Oklahoma Dept. of Libs., 200 N.E. 18 St., Oklahoma City 73105-3298. Tel. 405-522-3173, fax 405-521-1077, e-mail smcvey@oltn.odl.state.ok.us. World Wide Web http://www.odl.state.ok.us.

Oregon

James B. Scheppke, State Libn., Oregon State Lib., 250 Winter St. N.E., Salem 97301. Tel. 503-378-4367, fax 503-585-8059, e-mail jim.b.scheppke@state.or.us. World Wide Web http://www.oregon.gov/OSL.

Pennsylvania

Mary Clare Zales, Deputy Secy. of Educ., Commissioner for Libs., 333 Market St., Harrisburg 17126-1745. Tel. 717-787-2646, fax 717-772-3265, e-mail mzales@state.pa.us. World Wide Web http://www.portal.state.pa.us.

Rhode Island

Howard Boksenbaum, Chief Lib. Officer, Rhode Island Office of Lib. and Info. Services, 1 Capitol Hill, Providence 02908-5803. Tel. 401-574-9301, fax 401-574-9320, e-mail howardbm@olis.ri.gov. World Wide Web http://www.olis.ri.gov.

South Carolina

David S. Goble, Dir. and State Libn., South Carolina State Lib., P.O. Box 11469, Columbia 29211. Tel. 803-734-8626, fax 803-734-8676, e-mail dgoble@statelibrary.sc.gov. World Wide Web http://www.statelibrary.sc.gov.

South Dakota

Dan Siebersma, State Libn., South Dakota State Lib., 800 Governors Drive, Pierre 57501. Tel. 605-773-3131, fax 605-773-6962, e-mail dan.siebersma@state.sd.us. World Wide Web http://library.sd.gov.

Tennessee

Chuck Sherrill, State Libn. and Archivist, Tennessee State Lib. and Archives, 403 Seventh Ave. N., Nashville 37243-0312. Tel. 615-741-7996, fax 615-532-9293, e-mail chuck.sherrill@tn.gov. World Wide Web http://www.tennessee.gov/tsla.

Texas

Peggy D. Rudd, Dir. and Libn., Texas State Lib. and Archives Commission, P.O. Box 12927, Austin 78711-2927. Tel. 512-463-5460, fax 512-463-5436, e-mail peggy.rudd@tsl.state.tx.us. World Wide Web http://www.tsl.state.tx.us.

Utah

Donna Jones Morris, State Libn./Dir., Utah State Lib. Div., Suite A, 250 N. 1950 W., Salt Lake City 84116. Tel. 801-715-6770, fax 801-715-6767, e-mail dmorris@utah.gov. World Wide Web http://library.utah.gov.

Vermont

Martha Reid, State Libn., Vermont Dept. of Libs., 109 State St., Montpelier 05609. Tel. 802-828-3265, fax 802-828-2199, e-mail martha.reid@mail.dol.state.vt.us. World Wide Web http://libraries.vermont.gov.

Virginia

Sandra G. Treadway, Libn. of Virginia, Lib. of Virginia, 800 E. Broad St., Richmond 23219-8000. Tel. 804-692-3535, fax 804-692-3594, e-mail sandra.treadway@lva.virginia.gov. World Wide Web http://www.lva.virginia.gov.

Washington

Rand Simmons, Acting State Libn., Washington State Lib., P.O. Box 42460, Olympia

98504-2460. Tel. 360-704-5253, fax 360-586-7575, e-mail rand.simmons@sos.wa.gov. World Wide Web http://www.secstate.wa.gov/library.

West Virginia

James D. Waggoner, Secy., West Virginia Lib. Commission, Cultural Center, 1900 Kanawha Blvd. E., Charleston 25305-0620. Tel. 304-558-2041, fax 304-558-2044, e-mail waggoner@wvlc.lib.wv.us. World Wide Web http://librarycommission.lib.wv.us.

Wisconsin

Kurt Kiefer, Asst. Superintendent, Wisconsin Div. for Libs., Technology, and Community Learning, Dept. of Public Instruction, P.O. Box 7841, Madison 53707-7841. Tel. 608-266-2205, fax 608-267-9207, e-mail kurt.kiefer@dpi.state.wi.gov. World Wide Web http://dpi.state.wi.us/dltcl.

Wyoming

Lesley Boughton, State Libn., Wyoming State Lib., 2800 Central Ave., Cheyenne 82002. Tel. 307-777-5911, fax 307-777-6289, e-mail lbough@wyo.gov. World Wide Web http://www-wsl.state.wy.us.

American Samoa

Cheryl Morales, Territorial Libn., Government of American Samoa, Feleti Barstow Public Lib., P.O. Box 997687, Pago Pago, AS 96799. Tel. 684-633-5816, fax 684-633-5823, e-mail feletibarstow@yahoo.com. World Wide Web http://fbpl.org.

Federated States of Micronesia

Rufino Mauricio, Secy., National Archives, Culture, and Historic Preservation, P.O. Box PS 175, Palikir, Pohnpei, FM 96941. Tel. 691-320-2643, fax 691-320-5634, e-mail hpo@mail.fm. World Wide Web http://www.fsmgov.org.

Guam

Sandra Stanley, Admin. Officer, Guam Public Lib. System, 254 Martyr St., Hagatna 96910-5141. Tel. 671-475-4765, fax 671-477-0888, e-mail sandra.stanley@gpls.guam.gov. World Wide Web http://gpls.guam.gov.

Northern Mariana Islands

John Oliver Gonzales, Exec. Dir., CNMI Joeten-Kiyu Public Lib., P.O. Box 501092, Saipan, MP 96950-1092. Tel. 670-235-7322, fax 670-235-7550, e-mail jspl.admin@gmail.com. World Wide Web http://www.cnmilibrary.com.

Palau

Mario Katosang, Minister of Educ., Republic of Palau, P.O. Box 189, Koror, PW 96940. Tel. 680-488-2973, fax 680-488-1465, e-mail mariok@palaumoe.net. World Wide Web http://www.palaugov.net/palaugov/executive/ministries/MOE/MOE.htm.

Puerto Rico

Odette Piñeiro, Dir., Lib. and Info. Services Program, Puerto Rico Dept. of Educ., P.O. Box 190759, San Juan, PR 00919-0759. Tel. 787-773-5800, fax 787-250-0275, e-mail opineiro@de.gobierno.pr.

Republic of the Marshall Islands

Wilbur Heine, Secy. of Internal Affairs, Alele Museum and Public Lib., P.O. Box 629, Majuro, MH 96960. Tel. 692-625-8240, fax 692-625-3226, e-mail wilburheine@yahoo.com. World Wide Web http://rmigovernment.org/index.jsp.

Virgin Islands

Ingrid A. Bough, Territorial Dir., Virgin Islands Div. of Libs., Archives, and Museums, 1122 Kings St., Christiansted, St. Croix 00802. Tel. 340-773-5715, fax 340-773-5327, e-mail ingrid.bough@dpnr.gov.vi.

World Wide Web http://www.virginislandspace.org/division%20of%20libraries/dlamhome.htm.

Canada

Alberta

Diana Davidson, Dir., Public Lib. Services Branch, Alberta Municipal Affairs, 803 Standard Life Centre, 10405 Jasper Ave., Edmonton T5J 4R7. Tel. 780-427-4871, fax 780-415-8594, e-mail libraries@gov.ab.cam, World Wide Web http://www.municipalaffairs.alberta.ca/mc_libraries.cfm.

British Columbia

Jacqueline van Dyk, Dir., Public Lib. Services Branch, Ministry of Educ., 605 Robson St., Suite 850, Vancouver V6B 5J3. Tel. 604-660-7343, fax 604-660-0435, e-mail jacqueline.vandyk@gov.bc.ca. World Wide Web http://www.bced.gov.bc.ca/pls.

Manitoba

Trevor Surgenor, Dir., Public Lib. Services, Manitoba Dept. of Culture, Heritage, and Tourism, 300-1011 Rosser Ave., Brandon R7A OL5. Tel. 204-726-6590, e-mail pls@gov.mb.ca. World Wide Web http://www.gov.mb.ca/chc/pls/index.html.

New Brunswick

Sylvie Nadeau, Exec. Dir., New Brunswick Public Lib. Service, Place 2000, 250 King St., P.O. Box 6000, Fredericton E3B 5H1. Tel. 506-453-2354, fax 506-444-4064, e-mail sylvie.nadeau@gnb.ca. World Wide Web http://www.gnb.ca/publiclibraries.

Newfoundland and Labrador

Shawn Tetford, Exec. Dir., Provincial Info. and Lib. Resources Board, 48 St. George's Ave., Stephenville A2N 1K9. Tel. 709-643-0902, fax 709-643-0925, e-mail stetford@nlpl.ca. World Wide Web http://www.nlpl.ca.

Northwest Territories

Alison Hopkins, Territorial Libn., NWT Lib. Services, 75 Woodland Drive, Hay River X0E 1G1. Tel. 867-874-6531, fax 867-874-3321, e-mail alison_hopkins@gov.nt.ca. World Wide Web http://www.nwtpls.gov.nt.ca.

Nova Scotia

Jennifer Evans, Dir., Nova Scotia Provincial Lib., 2021 Brunswick St., P.O. Box 578, Halifax B3J 2S9. Tel. 902-424-2457, fax 902-424-0633, e-mail evansjl@gov.ns.ca. World Wide Web http://www.library.ns.ca.

Nunavut

Ron Knowling, Mgr., Nunavut Public Lib. Services, Box 270, Baker Lake X0C 0A0. Tel. 867-793-3353, fax 867-793-3360, e-mail rknowling@gov.nu.ca. World Wide Web http://www.publiclibraries.nu.ca.

Ontario

Michael Chan, minister, Ontario Government Ministry of Tourism and Culture, Hearst Block, 900 Bay St., Toronto M7A 2E1. Tel. 416-326-9326. World Wide Web http://www.ontario.ca/en/your_government/009887.html. Ontario Lib. Service–North, 334 Regent St., Greater Sudbury P3C 4E2. Tel. 705-675-6467. World Wide Web http://www.olsn.ca. Southern Ontario Lib. Service, 111 Peter St., Suite 902, Toronto M5V 2H1. Tel. 416-961-1669 ext. 5118. World Wide Web http://www.sols.org.

Prince Edward Island

Public Lib. Service of Prince Edward Island, P.O. Box 7500, Morell C0A 1S0. Tel. 902-961-7320, fax 902-961-7322, e-mail plshqat@gov.pe.ca. World Wide Web http://www.library.pe.ca/index.php3?lang=E.

Quebec

Guy Berthiaume, Chair and CEO; Hélène Roussel, Dir. Gen., Lib. Services, Bibliothèque et Archives Nationales du Québec (BAnQ), 2275 rue Holt, Montreal H2G 3H1. Tel. 800-363-9028 or 514-873-1100, fax 514-873-9312, info@banq.qc.ca. World Wide Web http://www.banq.qc.ca/portal/dt/accueil.jsp.

Saskatchewan

Joylene Campbell, Provincial Libn., Provincial Lib. and Literacy Office, Ministry of Educ., 409A Park St., Regina S4N 5B2. Tel. 306-787-2972, fax 306-787-2029, e-mail joylene.campbell@gov.sk.ca. World Wide Web http://www.education.gov.sk.ca/provincial-library.

Yukon Territory

Julie Ourom, Dir., Public Libs., Community Development Div., Dept. of Community Services, Box 2703, Whitehorse Y1A 2C6. Tel. 867-667-5447, fax 867-393-6333, e-mail julie.ourom@gov.yk.ca. World Wide Web http://www.ypl.gov.yk.ca.

State School Library Media Associations

Alabama

Children's and School Libns. Div., Alabama Lib. Assn. Memb. 650. Publication. *The Alabama Librarian* (q.).

Chair Jana Fine, Tuscaloosa Public Lib., 1801 Jack Warner Pkwy., Tuscaloosa 35401. Tel. 205-391-9025, e-mail jfine@tuscaloosa-library.org; *V. Chair/Chair-Elect* Cassie Johnson, Cullman County Public Lib., 910 Third Ave. S.E., Cullman 35055. Tel. 256-734-2720, e-mail johnsonc@ccpls.com; *Secy.* Susan Cordell, Univ. of West Alabama, Sta. 12, Livingston 35470. Tel. 205-652-5421, e-mail scordell@uwa.edu; *Past Chair* Dorothy Hunt, Montgomery Public Schools, 1207 Charnwood Drive, Montgomery 36109. Tel. 334-272-9961, e-mail dorothy.hunt@mps.k12.al.us.

Address correspondence to the association administrator, Alabama Lib. Assn., 9154 Eastchase Pkwy., Suite 418, Montgomery 36117. Tel. 334-414-0113, e-mail administrator@allanet.org.

World Wide Web http://allanet.org.

Alaska

Alaska Assn. of School Libns. Memb. 130. Publication. *The Puffin* (3 a year), online at http://www.akla.org/akasl/puffin/puffinhome.html. *Ed.* Piper Coulter, Ocean View Elementary. E-mail pcoulter@acsalaska.net.

Pres. Ann Morgester, Anchorage. E-mail morgester_ann@asdk12.org; *Pres.-Elect* Robin Turk, Palmer. E-mail rturk@matsuk12.us; *Secy.* Kari Sagel, Sitka. E-mail sagelk@mail.ssd.k12.ak.us; *Co-Treas.* Janet Madsen, West Valley H.S., Fairbanks. E-mail jmadsen@northstar.k12.ak.us; Kerri Geppert, Anchorage. E-mail geppert_kerri@asdk12.org; *Past Pres.* Suzanne Metcalfe, Dimond H.S., Anchorage. E-mail metcalfe_suzanne@asdk12.org.

World Wide Web http://www.akla.org/akasl.

Arizona

Teacher-Libn. Div., Arizona Lib. Assn. Memb. 1,000. Publication. *AZLA Newsletter.*

Co-Chairs Jean Kilker, Maryvale H.S., 3415 N. 59 Ave., Phoenix 85033. Tel. 602-764-2134, e-mail jkilker@phxhs.k12.az.us or jean.kilker@gmail.com; Kerrlita Westrick, Verrado Middle School, 553 Plaza Circle, Litchfield Park 85340. Tel. 623-547-1324 or 623-935-1911, e-mail kerrlita@cox.net or westrick@lesd.k12.az.us; *Past Chair* Sally Roof.

Address correspondence to the chairpersons.

World Wide Web http://www.azla.affiniscape.com.

Arkansas

Arkansas Assn. of Instructional Media. Term of Office. Apr. 2010–Apr. 2011. Publication. *AAIM Journal* (2 a year). Ed. Lori Bush. E-mail lori.bush@lh.k12.ar.us.

Pres. Jana Dixon. Tel. 501-276-8979; *Pres.-Elect* Jil'Lana Heard. Tel. 501-276-8578; *Secy.* Beth Stone. E-mail gjenkins@indian.dsc.k12.ar.us; *Treas.* Devona Pendergrass. E-mail dpendergrass@mtnhome.k12.ar.us; *Past Pres.* Diane Hughes. E-mail dianeallenhughes@gmail.com.

Address correspondence to the president.

World Wide Web http://aaim.k12.ar.us.

California

California School Lib. Assn. Memb. 1,200+. Publications. *CSLA Journal* (2 a year); *CSLA Newsletter* (10 a year).

Pres. (Northern Section) Melanie Lewis, Liberty H.S., 12220 Rd. 36, Madera 93636. Tel. 559-645-3500 ext. 2014, e-mail lhstlmal@gmail.com; (Southern Section) Janice Gilmore-See, 3352 San Carlos Drive, Spring Valley 91978. Tel. 619-668-5700 ext. 6331, e-mail janice.airplane@cox.net; *Pres.-Elect*

(Northern Section) Teresa Lai, A. P. Giannini Middle School, 1675 44th Ave., San Francisco 94122-2932. Tel. 415-465-2133, e-mail infospec@gmail.com; (Southern Section) Kathie Maier, Gilbert H.S., 1800 W. Ball Rd., Anaheim 92804. Tel. 714-999-3738 ext. 350W, e-mail maier_k@auhsd.us; *Exec. Dir.* Deidre Bryant, California School Lib. Assn., 950 Glenn Drive, Suite 150, Folsom 95630. Tel. 916-447-2684, fax 916-447-2695, e-mail diedreb@csla.net.

Address correspondence to the executive director.

World Wide Web http://www.csla.net.

Colorado

Colorado Assn. of School Libns. Memb. 260+. Term of Office. Nov. 2010–Oct. 2012.

Co-Pres. Yvonne Miller, Douglas County Schools. E-mail yvonne.miller@dcsdk12.org; *Pres.-Elect* Becky Johnson, Mesa County Valley School District 51. E-mail rebeccaj@mesa.k12.co.us; *Secy.* Molly Gibney, Mount View Elementary. E-mail mgibney@comcast.net; *Past Pres.* Nancy White, Academy School Dist. 20. E-mail nwhite@asd20.org; Diane Caro, Boulder Valley School Dist. E-mail diane.caro@bvsd.org; *Exec. Dir.* Catherine Spatz, Colorado Assn. of School Libns., 3030 W. 81 Ave., Westminster 80031. Tel. 303-433-4446, fax 303-458-0002, e-mail catherine@imigroup.org.

World Wide Web http://www.cal-webs.org/associations2.html.

Connecticut

Connecticut Assn. of School Libns. (formerly Connecticut Educ. Media Assn.). Memb. 500+. Term of Office. July 2010–June 2011.

Pres. Jacqueline Galante. E-mail jgalante@fairfield.k12.ct.us; *V.P.* Diane Strumello. E-mail dstrumello@milforded.org; *Recording Secy.* Christopher Barlow. E-mail christophbarlow@sbcglobal.net; *Treas.* Martha Djang. E-mail mdjang@hamdenhall.org; *Admin. Secy.* Anne Weimann, 25 Elmwood Ave., Trumbull 06611. Tel. 203-372-2260, e-mail anneweimann@gmail.com.

Address correspondence to the administrative secretary.

World Wide Web http://www.ctcasl.com.

Delaware

Delaware School Lib. Media Assn., Div. of Delaware Lib. Assn. Memb. 100+. Publications. *DSLMA Newsletter* (online; irreg.); column in *DLA Bulletin* (3 a year).

Pres. Marilyn Kulkarni, Brandywine H.S., Wilmington 19810. Tel. 302-479-1600 ext. 5037, e-mail marilyn.kulkarni@bsd.k12.de.us.

Address correspondence to the president.

World Wide Web http://www.udel.edu/erc/dslma.

District of Columbia

District of Columbia Assn. of School Libns. Memb. 8. Publication. *Newsletter* (4 a year).

Pres. André Maria Taylor. E-mail divalibrarian2@aol.com; *V.P.* Vacant.

Address correspondence to André Maria Taylor, 330 10th St. N.E., Washington, DC 20002. Tel. 301-502-4203.

Florida

Florida Assn. for Media in Educ. Memb. 1,400+. Term of Office. Nov. 2010–Oct. 2011. Publication. *Florida Media Quarterly*. *Ed.* Rhoda Cribbs. E-mail rcribbs@pasco.k12.fl.us.

Pres. Pat Dedicos. E-mail dedicosp@duvalschools.org; *Pres.-Elect* Lou Greco. E-mail grecol@stjohns.k12.fl.us; *Secy.* Debbie Rothfield. E-mail coollibrarianchick@gmail.com; *Treas.* Joanne Seale. E-mail seale.joanne@brevardschools.org; *Past Pres.* Cecelia Solomon. E-mail buckysmom@tampabay.rr.com; *Exec. Dir.* Larry E. Bodkin, Jr. Tel. 850-531-8351, fax 850-531-8344, e-mail lbodkin@floridamedia.org.

Address correspondence to FAME, 1876-B Eider Court, Tallahassee 32308. Tel. 850-531-8351, fax 850-531-8344, e-mail info@floridamedia.org.

World Wide Web http://www.floridamedia.org.

Georgia

School Lib. Media Div., Georgia Lib. Assn.

Chair Stephanie Jones, Georgia Southern Univ. College of Education, P.O. Box 8131, Statesboro 30460-8131. Tel. 912-478-5250, e-mail sjones@georgiasouthern.edu; *Chair-*

Elect To be announced; *Past Chair* Tim Wojcik, Our Lady of Mercy Catholic H.S. Tel. 770-461-2202, e-mail wojcikt@bellsouth.net.

Address correspondence to School Lib. Media Div., Georgia Lib. Assn., P.O. Box 793, Rex, GA 30273.

World Wide Web http://gla.georgialibraries.org/div_media.htm.

Georgia Lib. Media Assn. Memb. 700+.

Pres. Valerie Ayer. E-mail valerie_ayer@dekalb.k12.ga.us; *Pres.-Elect* Betsy Razza. E-mail betsy_razza@dekalb.k12.ga.us; *Secy.* Ann Schaub. E-mail schaub@fulton.k12.ga.us; *Treas.* Nan Brown. E-mail brownnt@fulton.k12.ga.us; *Past Pres.* Susan Grigsby. E-mail susan.grigsby@gmail.com.

Address correspondence to GLMA Executive Office, 2711 Irvin Way, Suite 111, Decatur 30030. Tel. 404-299-7700, e-mail glma@jlh-consulting.com.

World Wide Web http://www.glma-inc.org.

Hawaii

Hawaii Assn. of School Libns. Memb. 145. Term of Office. June 2010–May 2011. Publication. *HASL Newsletter* (3 a year).

Pres. Debora Lum. E-mail deblum.haslluvr@rocketmail.com; *V.P., Programming* Susan Clark. E-mail sclark@punahou.edu; *V.P., Membership* Helen Shima. E-mail hmicshima@hawaii.rr.com; *Corresponding Secy.* Cheryl O'Brien. E-mail obrien@damien.edu; *Recording Secy.* Kathleen Nullet. E-mail kislmc@gmail.com; *Treas.* Jo-An Ishida. E-mail jomari@hawaii.rr.com; *Past Pres.* Grace Fujiyoshi. E-mail gracef@hawaii.rr.com.

Address correspondence to the association, P.O. Box 235284, Honolulu 96823.

World Wide Web http://hasl.ws.

Idaho

Educational Media Div., Idaho Lib. Assn. Memb. 44.

Chair Glynda Pflieger, Melba School Dist., 6870 Stokes Lane, P.O. Box 185, Melba 83641. Tel. 208-495-2221, e-mail gpflieger@melbaschools.org.

Address correspondence to the chairperson.

World Wide Web http://www.idaholibraries.org/node/94.

Illinois

Illinois School Lib. Media Assn. Memb. 1,200. Term of Office. July 2010–June 2011. Publications. *ISLMA News* (4 a year); *Linking for Learning: The Illinois School Library Media Program Guidelines* (3rd ed. 2010); *Powerful Libraries Make Powerful Learners: The Illinois Study.*

Pres. Jeremy Dunn, Dept. of Libs. and Info. Services, Medill Technical and Professional Development Center, 1326 W. 14 Place, Chicago 60608. Tel. 773-553-6215, fax 773-553-6211, e-mail jdunn4@cps.k12.il.us; *Pres.-Elect* Sarah Hill, Paris Cooperative H.S., 309 S. Main St., Paris 61944. Tel. 217-466-1175, fax 217-466-1903, e-mail presidentelect@islma.org; *Secy.* Christine Graves, Jefferson Middle School. E-mail secretary@islma.org; *Past Pres.* Gail Janz, Morris Community H.S. E-mail gjanz@mchs.grundy.k12.il.us; *Exec. Secy.* Kay Maynard, ISLMA, P.O. Box 598, Canton 61520. Tel. 390-649-0911, fax 309-649-0916, e-mail islma@islma.org.

World Wide Web http://www.islma.org.

Indiana

Assn. of Indiana School Lib. Educators (AISLE). Publications. *Focus on Indiana Libraries* (mo.); *Indiana Libraries* (q.).

Pres. Lael Dubois, Plainfield H.S., 709 Stafford Rd., Plainfield 46168. Tel. 317-839-7711 ext. 1212, fax 317-838-3682, e-mail ldubois@plainfield.k12.in.us; *Pres.-Elect* Denise Keogh, Tipton Middle School, 3513 Redwood Rd., Anderson 46011. Tel. 765-675-7521 ext. 225, e-mail dkeogh@tcsc.k12.in.us; *Secy.* Susie Highley, Creston Middle School, 10925 E. Prospect, Indianapolis 46239. Tel. 812-532-6806, fax 812-532-6891, e-mail shighley@warren.k12.in.us; *Treas.* Kris Borrelli, Yost Elementary, 100 W. Beam St., Chesterton 46304. Tel. 219-983-3640, e-mail kristen.borrelli@duneland.k12.in.us; *Past Pres.* Vicki Builta, Anderson H.S., 4610 S. Madison Ave., Anderson

46013. Tel. 765-641-2037 ext. 1057, fax 765-641-2041, e-mail vbuilta@yahoo.com.

Address correspondence to the association, c/o Indiana Lib. Federation, 941 E. 86 St., Suite 260, Indianapolis 46240. Tel. 317-257-2040, fax 317-257-1389, e-mail ilf@indy.net.

World Wide Web http://www.ilfonline.org/units/aisle.

Iowa

Iowa Assn. of School Libns., subdivision of the Iowa Lib. Assn. Memb. 180+. Term of Office. Jan.–Jan. Publication. *IASL Journal* (online, 4 a year). *Eds.* Karla Krueger. E-mail karla.krueger@uni.edu; Becky Johnson. E-mail bcjohnson@cr.k12.ia.us.

Pres. Erin Feingold, Marshalltown CSD. E-mail efeingold@marshalltown.k12.ia.us; *V.P./Pres.-Elect* Becky Johnson, Jefferson H.S., Cedar Rapids. E-mail bcjohnson@cr.k12.ia.us; *Secy./Treas.* Tiffany Cooper, Creston Community Schools; *Past Pres.* Karen Lampe. E-mail klampe@ghaea.org.

Address correspondence to the president.

World Wide Web http://www.iasl-ia.org.

Kansas

Kansas Assn. of School Libns. Memb. 600. Publication. *KASL News* (online; q.).

Pres. Debbi Maddy. Tel. 913-422-5121, e-mail maddyd@usd204.net; *Pres.-Elect* Juanita Jameson. Tel. 620-805-8412, e-mail juanitajameson@cox.net; *Secy.* Jane Maresch. Tel. 785-309-4544, e-mail jane.maresch@usd305.com; *Past Pres./Exec. Secy.* Barb Bahm. Tel. 913-845-2627, e-mail bbahm@tong464.org.

Address correspondence to the executive secretary.

World Wide Web http://kasl.typepad.com/kasl.

Kentucky

Kentucky School Media Assn., section of the Kentucky Lib. Assn. Memb. 600+. Publication. *KSMA Newsletter* (q.).

Pres. Melissa Gardner. E-mail melissa.gardner@uky.edu; *Pres.-Elect* Brenda Metzger, Lone Oak H.S., 225 John E. Robinson Ave., Paducah 42003. E-mail brenda.metzger@mccracken.kyschools.us; *Past Pres.* Fred Tilsley, Sandgap Elementary. E-mail fred.tilsley@jackson.kyschools.us.

Address correspondence to the president.

World Wide Web http://www.kysma.org.

Louisiana

Louisiana Assn. of School Libns. Memb. 230. Term of Office. July 2010–June 2011.

Pres. Elizabeth Dumas. Tel. 318-396-9693, e-mail dumas@opsb.net; *1st V.P./Pres.-Elect* Paula Clemmons. Tel. 337-433-5246, e-mail pclemmons@episcopalday school.org; *2nd V.P.* Catherine Smith. Tel. 318-603-6374, e-mail catlib2000@yahoo.com; *Past Pres.* Annie Miers. Tel. 318-387-0567, e-mail miers@opsb.net.

Address correspondence to the association, c/o Louisiana Lib. Assn., 8550 United Plaza Blvd., Suite 1001, Baton Rouge 70809. Tel. 225-922-4642, fax 225-408-4422, e-mail office@llaonline.org.

World Wide Web http://www.llaonline.org/sig/lasl.

Maine

Maine School Lib. Assn. Memb. 230+.

Pres. Peg Becksvoort, Falmouth Middle School. E-mail pbecksvoort@falmouth schools.org; *V.P.* Eileen Broderick. E-mail ebroderick@rus10.org; *Secy.* Kelly Goodfield. E-mail kgoodfield@sad55.org; *Treas.* Dorothy Hall-Riddle. E-mail hall-riddled@rsu5.org; *Exec. Secy.* Edna Comstock. E-mail empoweredna@gwi.net.

Address correspondence to the president.

World Wide Web http://www.maslibraries.org.

Maryland

Maryland Assn. of School Libns. (formerly Maryland Educ. Media Organization). Term of Office. July 2009–June 2011.

Pres. Michele Forney, High Bridge Elementary, Prince Georges County Public Schools. E-mail michele.forney@pgcps.org; *Pres.-Elect* To be announced; *Secy.* Lori M. Carter, Howard County Public Schools. E-mail lori_carter@hcpss.org; *Treas.* Jennifer Harner, Rising Sun Elementary, Cecil County Public Schools. E-mail jharner@ccps.org; *Past Pres.* Elizabeth Napier, North Carroll H.S. E-mail eanapie@k12.carr.org.

Address correspondence to the association, Box 21127, Baltimore 21228.

World Wide Web http://maslmd.org.

Massachusetts

Massachusetts School Lib. Assn. Memb. 800. Term of Office. June 2009–May 2011. Publication. *MSLA Forum* (3 a year, one in print, two online).

Pres. Gerri Fegan, High Plain Elementary School, Andover. Tel. 978-623-8914, e-mail feganpkt@comcast.net; *Pres.-Elect* Valerie Diggs, Chelmsford H.S. Tel. 978-251-5111 ext. 1149; *Secy.* Judi Paradis, Plympton Elementary School, Waltham. Tel. 781-314-5767, e-mail judiparadis@gmail.com; *Treas.* Linda Friel. E-mail lafriel@comcast.net; *Past Pres.* Sandy Kelly, Carlisle School, Carlisle. Tel. 978-369-6550 ext. 3140, e-mail ms.sandyk@gmail.com; *Exec. Dir.* Kathy Lowe, Massachusetts School Lib. Assn., P.O. Box 658, Lunenburg 01462. Tel. 978-582-6967, e-mail klowe@maschoolibraries.org.

Address correspondence to the executive director.

World Wide Web http://www.maschoolibraries.org.

Michigan

Michigan Assn. for Media in Educ. Memb. 1,200. Publications. *Media Spectrum* (2 a year); *MAME Newsletter* (4 a year).

Pres. Rachel Markel, Bangor Public Schools, 309 S. Walnut St., Bangor 49013. Tel. 269-427-6800 ext. 3028, fax 269-427-6893, e-mail rmarkel@bangorvikings.org; *Pres.-Elect* Sue Lay, Birmingham School District, 1300 Derby Rd., Birmingham 48009. Tel. 248-203-5068, e-mail bookwoman0122@sbcglobal.net; *Secy.* Betty Mundy, St. Joseph Public Schools, 2831 W. Garden Lane, St. Joseph 49085. Tel. 269-926-3525, fax 269-926-3503, e-mail bmundy@sjschools.org; *Treas.* Bruce Popejoy, East Jackson Community Schools, 4340 Walz Rd., Jackson 49201. Tel. 517-764-6010, fax 517-764-6081, e-mail mameexhibits@aol.com; *Past Pres.* Lynn Gordon, Clarkston Community Schools, 6850 Hubbard Rd., Clarkston 48348. Tel. 248-623-5513, fax 248-623-5554, e-mail gordonlm@clarkston.k12.mi.us; *Exec. Dir.* Tim Staal, MAME, 1407 Rensen, Suite 3, Lansing 48910. Tel. 517-394-2808, fax 517-394-2096, e-mail tstaal@gmail.com.

Address correspondence to the executive director.

World Wide Web http://www.mame.gen.mi.us.

Minnesota

Minnesota Educ. Media Organization. Memb. 700. Term of Office. July 2010–July 2011. Publication. *MEMOrandum.*

Pres. Tori Jensen, Spring Lake Park H.S., Spring Lake Park 55432. Tel. 763-786-5571, e-mail tjense@district16.org; *Pres.-Elect* Sally Mays, Robbinsdale Spanish Immersion RSI, 8808 Medicine Lake Rd., New Hope 55427. Tel. 763 504 4408, e-mail sally_mays@rdale.org; *Secy.* Mary Mehsikomer, Region 1/NW-LINKS, P.O. Box 1178, 810 Fourth Ave. S., Suite 220, Moorhead 56561. Tel. 218-284-3117, e-mail mary@region1.k12.mn.us; *Treas.* Gina Light, Eagle Creek Elementary, Shakopee 55379. Tel. 952-368-7253, e-mail gmlight@chaska.net; *Past Pres.* Dawn Nelson, Osseo Area Schools, Maple Grove 55369. Tel. 763-391-7163, e-mail nelsond@district279.org; *Admin. Asst.* Deanna Sylte, P.O. Box 130555, Roseville 55113. Tel. 651-771-8672, e-mail admin@memoweb.org.

World Wide Web http://memoweb.org.

Mississippi

School Section, Mississippi Lib. Assn. Memb. 1,300.

Chair Venetia Oglesby; *Exec. Secy.* Mary Julia Anderson.

Address correspondence to School Section, Mississippi Lib. Assn., P.O. Box 13687, Jackson 39236-3687. Tel. 601-981-4586, fax 601-981-4501, e-mail info@misslib.org.

World Wide Web http://www.misslib.org.

Missouri

Missouri Assn. of School Libns. Memb. 1,000. Term of Office. June 2010–June 2011. Publication. *Connections* (q.).

Pres. Patricia Antrim. E-mail antrim@ucmo.edu; *1st V.P./Pres.-Elect* Curtis Clark. E-mail msmediacenter@harrisonville.k12.mo.us; *2nd V.P.* Vickie Howard. E-mail howardv@cape.k12.mo.us; *Secy.* Jane Horsefield. E-mail jhorsefield@stjschools.org; *Treas.* Georganna Krumlinde. E-mail krumling@troy.k12.mo.us; *Past Pres.* Maggie Newbold. E-mail mnewbold@fz.k12.mo.us.

Address correspondence to the association, P.O. Box 2107, Jefferson City 65102. Tel. 573-893-4155, fax 573-635-2858, e-mail info@maslonline.org.

World Wide Web http://www.maslonline.org.

Montana

Montana School Lib. Media Div., Montana Lib. Assn. Memb. 200+. Publication. *FOCUS* (published by Montana Lib. Assn.) (q.).

Chair Nancy Pensa, Russell Elementary, Kalispell 59901. Tel. 406-751-3915; *V. Chair* Kari K. Eliason, P.O. Box 425, Manhattan 59741. Tel. 406-284-3341 ext. 222, fax 406-284-3104; *Exec. Asst., Montana Lib. Assn.* Debra Kramer, P.O. Box 1352, Three Forks 59752. Tel. 406-285-3090, fax 406-285-3091, e-mail debkmla@hotmail.com.

World Wide Web http://www.mtlib.org.

Nebraska

Nebraska Educ. Media Assn. Memb. 370. Term of Office. July 2010–June 2011. Publication. *NEMA News* (q.).

Pres. Betty Meyer. E-mail betty.meyer@thayercentral.org; *Pres.-Elect* Karen Buckley; *Secy.* Beth Kabes; *Treas.* Lynne Wragge; *Past Pres.* Carrie Turner; *Exec. Secy.* Jean Hellwege. E-mail nemacontact@gmail.com.

Address correspondence to the executive secretary.

World Wide Web http://www.schoollibrariesrock.org.

Nevada

Nevada School and Children's Libs. Section, Nevada Lib. Assn. Memb. 120.

Chair Jennifer Jost, Las Vegas-Clark County Lib. Dist. E-mail jostj@lvccld.org; *Exec. Secy.* Lisa Phelan, Henderson Libs. E-mail lphelan@hdpl.org.

Address correspondence to the executive secretary.

World Wide Web http://www.nevadalibraries.org/publications/handbook/nscls.html.

New Hampshire

New Hampshire School Lib. Media Assn. (NHSLMA), Box 418, Concord 03302-0418. Memb. 271. Term of Office. June 2010–June 2011. Publication. *Online News* (winter, spring; online and print).

Pres. Kathy Lane, G. H. Hood Middle School, Derry 03038. E-mail klane@derry.k12.nh.us; *V.P.* Helen Burnham, Lincoln Street School, 25 Lincoln St., Exeter 03833. Tel. 603-775-8851, e-mail hburnham@sau16.org; *Recording Secy.* Melissa Moore, Northwood Elementary, Northwood 03290-6206. Tel. 603-942-5488 ext. 313, e-mail mmoore@northwood.k12.nh.us; *Treas.* Jeff Kent, 43 E. Ridge Rd., Merrimack 03054. E-mail jkent@comcast.net; *Past Pres.* Sharon Silva, Mastricola Upper Elementary, 26 Baboosic Lake Rd., Merrimack 03054. Tel. 603-424-6221, e-mail sharon.silva@merrimack.k12.nh.us.

Address correspondence to the president.

World Wide Web http://www.nhslma.net.

New Jersey

New Jersey Assn. of School Libns. (NJASL). Memb. 1,100. Term of Office. Aug. 2010–July 2011.

Pres. Judith Everitt. E-mail president@njasl.org; *V.P.* April Bunn. E-mail vicepresident@njasl.org; *Pres.-Elect* Fran King. E-mail presidentelect@njasl.org; *Recording Secy.* Pam Gunter. E-mail recordingsecretary@njasl.org; *Corresponding Secy.* Amy Rominiecki. E-mail correspondingsecretary@njasl.org; *Treas.* Michelle Marhefka. E-mail treasurer@njasl.org; *Membs.-at-Large* Karen Brill. E-mail memberatlarge1@njasl.org;

Bosa Mijaljevic E-mail memberatlarge2@njasl.org; *Past Pres.* Pat Massey. E-mail immediatepastpresident@njasl.org.

Address correspondence to Aliah Davis-McHenry, Assn. Mgr., NJASL, Box 610, Trenton 08607. E-mail associationmanager@njasl.org.

World Wide Web http://www.njasl.org.

New York

School Lib. Media Section, New York Lib. Assn., 252 Hudson St., Albany 12210. Tel. 518-432-6952. Memb. 820. Term of Office. Nov. 2010–Oct. 2011. Publications. *SLMS-Gram* (q.); participates in *NYLA Bulletin* (mo. except July and Aug.).

Pres. Fran Roscello. E-mail fran@roscelloassociates.com; *V.P. Conferences* Karen Sperrazza. E-mail ksperrazza@gmail.com; *V.P. Communications* Ellen Rubin. E-mail erubin@wallkillcsd.k12.ny.us; *Pres.-Elect* Pauline Herr. E-mail pherr@acsdny.org; *Secy.* Michelle Miller. E-mail mmiller@mwcsd.org; *Treas.* Patty Martire. E-mail pmartire@mtmorriscsd.org; *Past Pres.* Carole Kupelian. E-mail carolek78@gmail.com.

World Wide Web http://www.nyla.org/slms

North Carolina

North Carolina School Lib. Media Assn. Memb. 1,000+. Term of Office. Nov. 2010–Oct. 2011.

Pres. Deanna Harris, Wake County Public Schools, 1111 S.E. Maynard Rd., Cary 27511. Tel. 919-466-4377, fax 919-466-4388, e-mail ncslma.deanna@gmail.com; *V.P./Pres.-Elect* Sarah Justice, Transylvania County Schools, 749 Pickens Hwy., Rosman 28772. Tel. 828-862-4284, fax 828-885-5572, e-mail sjustice@tcsnc.org; *Secy.* April Dawkins, Union County Public Schools, 2839 Ridge Rd., Indian Trail 28079. Tel. 704-292-7662, fax 704-296-9733, e-mail april.dawkins@ucps.k12.nc.us; *Treas.* Kathy Cadden, Lake Norman Charter School, 21246 Pine Ridge Rd., Cornelius 28031. Tel. 704-756-8735, e-mail kgcadden@gmail.com; *Past Pres.* Kelly Brannock, Dept. of Public Instruction, 6364 Mail Service Center, Raleigh 27699-6364. Tel. 919-807-3267, fax 919-807-3290, e-mail kbrannock@dpi.state.nc.us.

Address correspondence to the president.

World Wide Web http://www.ncslma.org.

North Dakota

School Lib. and Youth Services Section, North Dakota Lib. Assn. Memb. 100. Publication. *The Good Stuff* (q.).

Chair Beth Greff, Mandan Middle School. Tel. 701-663-7491, fax 701-667-0984, e-mail beth.greff@msd1.org.

Address correspondence to the chairperson.

World Wide Web http://ndlaonline.org.

Ohio

Ohio Educ. Lib. Media Assn. Memb. 1,000. Publications. *OELMA News* (3 a year); *Ohio Media Spectrum* (q.).

Pres. Krista Taracuk. E-mail ktaracuk@columbus.rr.com; *V.P.* Sue Subel. E-mail sue.subel@kenstonlocal.org; *Secy.* Sheila Campbell. E-mail librarian@columbuszoo.com; *Treas.* Cynthia DuChane. E-mail duchane@infohio.org; *Past Pres.* Sarah Thornbery. E-mail sthornbery@me.com; *Dir. of Services* Kate Brunswick, 17 S. High St., Suite 200, Columbus 43215. Tel. 614-221-1900, fax 614-221-1989, e-mail kate@assnoffices.com.

Address correspondence to the director of services.

World Wide Web http://www.oelma.org.

Oklahoma

Oklahoma School Libs. Div., Oklahoma Lib. Assn. Memb. 300+. Publication. *Oklahoma Librarian.*

Chair Patty Zody; *Chair-Elect* John Allen; *Secy.* Stephanie Brucks; *Treas.* Tina Ham; *Past Chair* Cathy Carlson. E-mail cjcarlson@okcps.org.

Address correspondence to the chairperson, School Libs. Div., Oklahoma Lib. Assn., 300 Hardy Drive, Edmond 73013. Tel. 405-348-0506.

World Wide Web http://www.ola.oklibs.org/organization/Divisions/oksl.htm.

Oregon

Oregon Assn. of School Libs./Oregon Educ. Media Assn. Memb. 600. Publication. *OEMA Newsletter* (online).

Pres. Ruth Murray. E-mail murrayr@pdx.edu; *Pres.-Elect* Susan Stone. E-mail sstone@pps.k12.or.us; *Secy.* Jenny Takeda. E-mail jenny_takeda@beavton.k12.or.us; *Treas.* Victoria McDonald. E-mail vmcdonald@lshigh.org; *Past Pres.* Carol Dinges. E-mail carol_dinges@lebanon.k12.or.us; *Exec. Dir.* Jim Hayden, 6780 N.W. 25 Lane, Redmond 97756-8168. E-mail j23hayden@aol.com.

Address correspondence to the executive director.

World Wide Web http://www.oasl.info/organization.html.

Pennsylvania

Pennsylvania School Libns. Assn. Memb. 1,400+. Publication. *Learning and Media* (q.).

Pres. Doug Francis. E-mail francisd@lasd.k12.pa.us; *V.P./Pres.-Elect* Eileen Kern; *Secy.* Lindsey Long; *Treas.* Natalie Hawley; *Past Pres.* Nancy Smith Latanision.

Address correspondence to the president.

World Wide Web http://www.psla.org.

Rhode Island

Rhode Island Educ. Media Assn. Memb. 350+.

Pres. Jamie Greene. E-mail greenej@bw.k12.ri.us; *V.P.* Darshell Silva. E-mail ucaplibrarian@verizon.net; *Secy.* Stacey Lyon. E-mail slyon46@cox.net; *Treas.* Jen Simoneau. E-mail jsimoneau4@cox.net; *Past Pres.* Jackie Lamoureux. E-mail jackielam@cox.net.

Address correspondence to the association, Box 470, East Greenwich 02818.

World Wide Web http://riedmedia.org.

South Carolina

South Carolina Assn. of School Libns. Memb. 1,100. Term of Office. June 2010–May 2011. Publication. *Media Center Messenger* (2 print issues a year; 8 online issues a year).

Pres. Joe Myers. E-mail joemyers1961@yahoo.com; *V.P./Pres.-Elect* Kathy Sutusky. E-mail ksutusky@sc.rr.com; *Secy.* Lori June. E-mail junel@sumter17.k12.sc.us; *Treas.* Steve Reed. E-mail screed3103@aol.com; *Past Pres.* Amanda LeBlanc. E-mail aleblanc@greenville.k12.sc.us.

Address correspondence to the president, SCASL, P.O. Box 2442, Columbia 29202. Tel. 864-355-8275.

World Wide Web http://www.scasl.net.

South Dakota

South Dakota School Lib. Media Assn., Section of the South Dakota Lib. Assn. and South Dakota Educ. Assn., 28363 472nd Ave., Worthing 57077. Tel. 605-372-0235. Memb. 140+. Term of Office. Oct. 2010–Oct. 2011.

Chair Muriel Deckert, Milbank Middle/H.S. E-mail muriel.deckert@k12.sd.us.

Tennessee

Tennessee Assn. of School Libns. Memb. 450. Term of Office. Jan.–Dec. 2011. Publication. *Footnotes* (q.).

Pres. Pam Renfrow, St. Agnes Academy-St. Dominic School, 4830 Walnut Grove Rd., Memphis 38117. E-mail prenfrow@ssa-sds.org; *V.P./Pres.-Elect* Hannah Little, Webb School, P.O. Box 488, Bell Buckle 37020. E-mail hlittle@webbschool.com; *Secy.* Alice Bryant, Harpeth Hall School, 3801 Hobbs Rd., Nashville 37215. E-mail awbryant@bellsouth.net; *Treas.* Beth Frerking, Northwest H.S., 800 Lafayette Rd., Clarksville 37042. E-mail beth.frerking@hughes.net; *Past Pres.* Becky Jackman, Northeast H.S., 3701 Trenton Rd., Clarksville 37040. E-mail becky37042@gmail.com.

Address correspondence to the president.

World Wide Web http://www.kornet.org/tasl.

Texas

Texas Assn. of School Libns., Div. of Texas Lib. Assn. Memb. 4,000+. Term of Office. Apr. 2010–Apr. 2011.

Chair Susan Y. Geye, Everman ISD. Tel. 817-568-3560, e-mail sgeye@eisd.org; *Chair-Elect* Naomi M. Bates, Northwest H.S. Tel. 817-215-0203, e-mail nmbates@yahoo.com;

Secy. Faye L. Hagerty, Northside ISD. Tel. 210-397-8199, e-mail faye.hagerty@nisd.net; *Past Chair* Cindy Buchanan, Aldine ISD. Tel. 281-985-7258, e-mail cbuchanan@aldine.k12.tx.us.

Address correspondence to Texas Lib. Assn., 3355 Bee Cave Rd., Suite 401, Austin 78746. Tel. 512-328-1518, fax 512-328-8852, e-mail tla@txla.org.

World Wide Web http://www.txla.org/groups/tasl.

Utah

Utah Educ. Lib. Media Assn. Memb. 500+. Publication. *UELMA Newsletter* (q.).

Pres. Brent Jones, Fremont H.S., 1900 N. 4700 W., Plain City 84404. Tel. 801-453-4034, e-mail bjones@weber.k12.ut.us; *Pres.-Elect* Andrea Woodring, Bonneville H.S., 251 E. Laker Way, Ogden 84405. Tel. 801-452-4405, e-mail http://www.uelma.org/anwoodring@weber.k12.ut.us; *Secy.* Celia Powell, Granite School Dist., Instructional Technology Room D-229, 2500 S. State St., Salt Lake City 84115. Tel. 385-646-4110, e-mail cpowell@graniteschools.org; *Past Pres.* Lanell Rabner, Springville H.S., 1205 E. 900 S., Springville 84663. Tel. 801-489-2870, fax 801-489-2806, e-mail lanell.rabner@nebo.edu; *Exec. Dir.* John L. Smith, High Ridge Media, 714 W. 1900 N., Clinton 84015. Tel. 801-776-6829, fax 801-773-8708, e-mail jlsutah@comcast.net.

Address correspondence to the executive director.

World Wide Web http://www.uelma.org.

Vermont

Vermont School Lib. Assn. (formerly Vermont Educ. Media Assn.). Memb. 220+. Term of Office. May 2010–May 2011. Publication. *VSLA Newsletter Online* (q.).

Pres. Claire Buckley, South Burlington H.S., 550 Dorset St., South Burlington 05403. Tel. 802-652-7085, e-mail cbuckley@sbschools.netl; *Pres.-Elect* Anna Bolognani, Twin Valley H.S., 1 School St., Wilmington 05363. Tel. 802-464-5255 ext. 119, e-mail rebolibrary@hotmail.com; *Secy.* Lindy Sargent, Newport Elementary, 166 Sias Ave., Newport 05855. Tel. 802-334-2455, e-mail sargentl@newportcityelementary.org; *Treas.* Donna Smyth, Proctor Elementary, 14 School St., Proctor 05765. Tel. 802-459-2225 ext. 2005, e-mail smythd@rcsu.org; *Past Pres.* Marsha Middleton, North Country Union H.S., P.O. Box 725, 209 Veterans Ave., Newport 05855. Tel. 802-334-7921 ext. 3040, e-mail mmiddleton@ncuhs.org;

Address correspondence to the president.

World Wide Web http://vsla.info.

Virginia

Virginia Educ. Media Assn. Memb. 1,073. Term of Office. (Pres., Pres.-Elect) Nov. 2010–Nov. 2011 (other officers two years in alternating years). Publication. *Mediagram* (q.).

Pres. Mary Keeling, Newport News Public Schools, Newport News. E-mail mary.keeling@nn.k12.va.us; *Pres.-Elect* Julie Tate, Hanover Public Schools, Hanover. E-mail jtate@hcps4.hanover.k12.va.us; *Secy.* Roxanne Mills, Smithfield. E-mail roxanne.mills@gmail.com; *Treas.* Lori Donovan, Thomas Dale H.S., Chester. E-mail lori_donovan@ccpsnet.net; *Exec. Dir.* Margaret Baker. Tel. 540-416-6109, fax 540-885-6174, e-mail vemaorg@gmail.com.

Address correspondence to the association, P.O. Box 2015, Staunton 24402-2015.

World Wide Web http://www.vemaonline.org.

Washington

Washington Lib. Media Assn. Memb. 1,450+. Term of Office. Oct.–Oct. Publication. *The Medium* (3 a year).

Pres. Steve Coker. E-mail cokers@rainier.wednet.edu; *Pres.-Elect* Craig Seasholes. E-mail seasholes@gmail.com; *V.P.* Gary Simundson. E-mail gsimunds@egreen.wednet.edu; *Secy.* Jeanne Staley. E-mail staleyj54@gmail.com; *Treas.* Kate Pankiewicz. E-mail kate.pankiewicz@shorelineschools.org; *Past Pres.* Linda King. E-mail winesapple@aol.com.

Address correspondence to the association, 10924 Mukilteo Speedway, PMB 142, Mukilteo 98275. E-mail wlma@wlma.org.

World Wide Web http://www.wlma.org.

West Virginia

School Lib. Div., West Virginia Lib. Assn. Memb. 50. Term of Office. Nov.–Nov. Publication. *WVLA School Library News* (5 a year).

Chair Cathy Davis, East Fairmont Junior H.S., 1 Orion Lane, Fairmont 26554. Tel. 304-367-2123, e-mail ctdavis@access.k12.wv.us.

Address correspondence to the chairperson.

World Wide Web http://www.wvla.org.

Wisconsin

Wisconsin Educ. Media and Technology Assn. Memb. 1,100+. Publication. *WEMTA Dispatch* (q.).

Pres. Annette Smith. E-mail arsmith14@gmail.com; *Pres.-Elect* Jo Ann Carr. E-mail carr@education.wisc.edu; *Secy.* Vicki Santacroce. E-mail vsantacroce@ashwaubenon.k12.wi.us; *Treas.* Sandy Heiden. E-mail sheiden@seymour.k12.wi.us; *Assn. Mgr.* Courtney Rounds. Tel. 608-375-6020, e-mail wemamanager@hughes.net.

Address correspondence to WEMA, P.O. Box 206, Boscobel 53805.

World Wide Web http://www.wemaonline.org.

Wyoming

School Lib. Media Personnel Section, Wyoming Lib. Assn. Memb. 90+. Publication. *WLA Newsletter.*

Chair Barb Osborne, Highland Park Elementary. E-mail osborneb@scsd2.com; *Chair-Elect* Christi Hampton, Upton Elementary and H.S. E-mail champton@upton.weston7.k12.wy.us; *Secy.* Sarah Prielipp, Campbell County School Dist. E-mail sprielipp@ccsd.k12.wy.us; *Past Pres.* Peggy Jording, Newcastle Schools. E-mail jordingp@weston1.k12.wy.us.

Address correspondence to the chairperson.

World Wide Web http://www.wyla.org/schools.

International Library Associations

International Association of Agricultural Information Specialists

Barbara Hutchinson, President
E-mail barbara.hutchinson@iaald.org
World Wide Web http://www.iaald.org

Object

The International Association of Agricultural Information Specialists (IAALD) facilitates professional development of and communication among members of the agricultural information community worldwide. Its goal is to enhance access to and use of agriculture-related information resources. To further this mission, IAALD will promote the agricultural information profession, support professional development activities, foster collaboration, and provide a platform for information exchange. Founded 1955.

Membership

Memb. 400+ in 80 countries. Dues (Inst.) US$110; (Indiv.) US$50.

Officers

Pres. Barbara Hutchinson (USA). E-mail barbara.hutchinson@iaald.org; *Pres.-Elect* Edith Hesse (Colombia). E-mail e.hessecgiar.org; *Secy.-Treas.* Toni Greider (USA). P.O. Box 63, Lexington, KY 40588-0063. Tel. 859-254-0752, fax 859-257-8379, e-mail info@iaald.org.

Publication

Agricultural Information Worldwide (q.) (memb.).

International Association of Law Libraries

Petal Kinder, President
High Court of Australia, Canberra, ACT 2600
61-2-6270-6922, fax 61-2-6273-2110, e-mail pkinder@hcourt.gov.au
World Wide Web http://www.iall.org

Object

The International Association of Law Libraries (IALL) is a worldwide organization of librarians, libraries, and other persons or institutions concerned with the acquisition and use of legal information emanating from sources other than their jurisdictions and from multinational and international organizations.

IALL's purpose is to facilitate the work of librarians who acquire, process, organize, and provide access to foreign legal materials. IALL has no local chapters, but maintains liaison with national law library associations in many countries and regions of the world.

Membership

More than 800 members in more than 50 countries on five continents.

Officers

Pres. Petal Kinder, High Court of Australia, Parkes Place, Parkes, Canberra, ACT 2600. Tel. 61-2-6270-6922, fax 61-2-6273-2110, e-mail pkinder@hcourt.gov.au; *1st V.P.* Jeroen Vervliet, Peace Palace Lib., Carnegieplein 2, 2517 KJ The Hague, Netherlands. Tel. 31-70-302-4242, e-mail j.vervliet@ppl.nl; *2nd V.P.* Jennefer Aston, Bar Council of Ireland, P.O. Box 4460, Dublin 7. Tel. 353-1-817-5121, fax 353-1-817-5151, e-mail jaston@lawlibrary.ie; *Secy.* Barbara Garavaglia, Univ. of Michigan Law Lib., Ann Arbor, MI 48109-1210. Tel. 734-764-9338, fax 734-764-5863, e-mail bvaccaro@umich.edu; *Treas.* Xinh Luu, Univ. of Virginia Law Lib., 580 Massie Rd., Charlottesville, VA 22903. E-mail b.xtl5d@Virginia.edu; *Past Pres.* Jules Winterton, Institute of Advanced Legal Studies, Univ. of London, 17 Russell Sq., London WCIB 5DR, England. Tel. 44-20-7862-5884, fax 44-20-7862-5850, e-mail julesw@sas.ac.uk.

Board Members

Ruth Bird, Bodleian Law Lib., Oxford Univ., England; Ligita Gjortlere, Riga Graduate School of Law Lib., Riga, Latvia; Mari Hoffman (ex officio), niv. of California, Berkeley, School of Law Lib.; Mark D. Engsberg (ex officio), MacMillan Law Lib., Emory Univ. School of Law, Atlanta; Janice L. Johnston, Albert E. Jenner, Jr. Memorial Law Lib., Univ. of Illinois; Uma Narayan, Bombay High Court, Mumbai, India; Pedro Padilla-Rosa, Univ. of Puerto Rico Law Lib., San Juan; Anita Soboleva, JURIX (Jurists for Constitutional Rights and Freedoms), Moscow, Russia; Ivo Vogel, Sondersammelgebiet and Virtuellen Fachbibliothek Recht, Berlin, Germany; Bård Tuseth, Dept. of Public and International Law Lib., Oslo, Norway.

Publication

International Journal of Legal Information (3 a year; US$60 indiv.; US$95 institutions).

International Association of Music Libraries, Archives and Documentation Centres

Pia Shekhter, IAML Secretary-General
Gothenburg University Library, P.O. Box 222, SE 405 30 Gothenburg, Sweden
Tel. 46-31-786-4057, cell 46-703-22-62, fax 46-31-786-40-59, e-mail secretary@iaml.info
World Wide Web http://www.iaml.info

Object

The object of the International Association of Music Libraries, Archives, and Documentation Centres (IAML) is to promote the activities of music libraries, archives, and documentation centers and to strengthen the cooperation among them; to promote the availability of all publications and documents relating to music and further their bibliographical control; to encourage the development of standards in all areas that concern the association; and to support the protection and preservation of musical documents of the past and the present.

Membership

Memb. 1,800.

Board Members

Pres. Roger Flury, National Lib. of New Zealand, P.O. Box 1467, Wellington, NZ. Tel. 64-4-474-3039, fax 64-4-474-3035; *Secy.-Gen.* Pia Shekhter, Academy of Music and Drama, Univ. of Gothenburg Lib., Box 210, SE-405 30 Gothenburg, Sweden. Tel. 46-31-786-40-57, fax 46-31-786-40-59; *Treas.* Kathryn Adamson, Libn., Royal Academy of Music, Marylebone Rd., London

NW1 5HT, England. Tel. 44-20-7873-7321; *Past Pres.* Martie Severt, Netherlands Radio Music Lib., Postbus 125, NL-1200 AC Hilversum, Netherlands. Tel. 31-35-6714181, fax 31-35-6714189; *V.P.s* Stanislaw Hrabia, Biblioteka i Fonoteka, Instytut Muzykologii, Uniwersytet Jagiellonski, ul. Westerplatte 10, 31-033 Kraków, Poland. Tel. 48-12-663-1673, fax 48-12-663-1671; Antony Gordon, British Lib. Sound Archive, 96 Euston Rd., London NW1 2DB, England. Tel. 44-20-7412-7412, fax 44-20-7412-7441; Johan Eeckeloo, Koninklijk Conservatorium Brussel, Regentschapsstraat 30, B-1000 Brussels, Belgium. Tel. 32-2-213-41-30; Jutta Lambrecht, WDR D & A / Recherche, Leitung Musik und Notenarchiv, Appellhofplatz 1, D-50667 Köln, Germany. Tel. 49-221-220-3376, fax 49-221-220-9217; *Treas.* Kathryn Adamson, Royal Academy of Music, Marlebone Rd., London NW1 5HT, England. Tel. 44-20-7873-7321; *Past Pres.* Martie Severt, Netherlands Radio Music Lib., Postbus 125, NL-1200 AC Hilversum, Netherlands. Tel. 31-35-6714181, fax 31-35-6714189, e-mail pastpresident@iaml.info.

Publication

Fontes Artis Musicae (4 a year; memb.). *Ed.* Maureen Buja, Hong Kong Gold Coast Block 22, Flat 1-A, 1 Castle Peak Rd., Tuen Mun, NT, Hong Kong. Tel. 852-2146-8047, e-mail mbuja@earthlink.net.

Professional Branches

Archives and Documentation Centres. Marguerite Sablonnière, Bibliothèque Nationale de France, Département de la Musique, 58 rue de Richelieu, 75002 Paris, France.

Broadcasting and Orchestra Libraries. Angela Escott, Royal College of Music, Prince Consort Rd., London SW7 2BS, England.

Libraries in Music Teaching Institutions. Pia Shekhter, Gothenburg Univ. Lib., P.O. Box 222, SE 405 30 Gothenburg, Sweden.

Public Libraries. Hanneke Kuiper, Public Lib., Oosterdoksstraat 143, 1011 DK Amsterdam, Netherlands.

Research Libraries. Stanislaw Hrabia, Uniwersytet Jagiellonski Instytut Muzykologii Biblioteka, ul. Westerplatte 10 31-033 Kraków, Poland.

International Association of School Librarianship

Karen Bonanno, Executive Secretary
P.O. Box 83, Zillmere, Qld. 4034, Australia
Fax 617-3633-0570, e-mail iasl@iasl-online.org
World Wide Web http://www.iasl-online.org

Object

The mission of the International Association of School Librarianship (IASL) is to provide an international forum for those interested in promoting effective school library programs as viable instruments in the educational process. The association provides guidance and advice for the development of school library programs and the school library profession. IASL works in cooperation with other professional associations and agencies.

The objectives of IASL are to advocate the development of school libraries throughout all countries; to encourage the integration of school library programs into the instructional and curriculum development of the school; to promote the professional preparation and continuing education of school library personnel; to foster a sense of community among school librarians in all parts of the world; to foster and extend relationships between school librarians and other professionals connected with children and youth; to foster research in the field of school librarianship and the integration of its conclusions with pertinent knowledge from related fields; to promote the publication and dissemination of information about successful advocacy and program initiatives in school librarianship; to share information about programs and materials for children and youth throughout the international community; and to initiate and coordinate activities, conferences, and other projects in the field of school librarianship and information services. Founded 1971.

Membership

Approximately 600.

Officers and Executive Board

Pres. Diljit Singh, Malaysia; *V.P.s* Barbara Combes, Australia; Lesley Farmer, USA; Lourense Das, Europe; *Treas.* Katy Manck, USA; *Dirs.* Busi Dlamini, Africa–Sub-Sahara; Luisa Marquardt, Europe; Barbara McNeil, Canada; Blanche Woolls, USA; Pat Carmichael, Oceania; Betty Chu Wah Hing, East Asia; Ingrid Skirrow, International Schools; Katharina B. L. Berg, Latin America/Caribbean; Madhu Bhargava, Asia; Ruth Briddock, North Africa/Middle East.

Publications

Selected papers from proceedings of annual conferences (all prices are exclusive of postage):

34th Annual Conference, 2005, Hong Kong. *Information Leadership in a Culture of Change.* US$20.

35th Annual Conference, 2006, Lisbon, Portugal. *The Multiple Faces of Literacy: Reading. Knowing. Doing.* US$20.

36th Annual Conference, 2007, Taipei, Taiwan. *Cyberspace, D-world, E-learning: Giving Libraries and Schools the Cutting Edge.* US$20.

37th Annual Conference, 2008, Berkeley, California. *World Class Learning and Literacy Through School Libraries* US$20.

38th Annual Conference 2009, Abano Terme, Italy. *Preparing Pupils and Students for the Future: School Libraries in the Picture.* US$20.

39th Annual Conference 2010, Brisbane, Australia. *Diversity Challenge Resilience: School Libraries in Action* US$20.

International Association of Scientific and Technological University Libraries

President, Ainslie Dewe, La Trobe University, Victoria, Australia

Object

The object of the International Association of Scientific and Technological University Libraries (IATUL) is to provide a forum where library directors can meet to exchange views on matters of current significance in the libraries of universities of science and technology. Research projects identified as being of sufficient interest may be followed through by working parties or study groups.

Membership

Memb. 239 (in 42 countries); Ordinary, Associate, Sustaining, Honorary. Membership fee 75–150 euros a year, sustaining membership 500 euros a year.

Officers and Executives

Pres. Ainslie Dewe, Univ. Libn., La Trobe University Lib., Victoria, Australia. E-mail a.dewe@latrobe.edu.au; *Secy.* Paul Sheehan, Dublin City Univ. Lib., Dublin 9, Ireland. E-mail paul.sheehan@dcu.ie; *Treas.* Reiner Kallenborn, Munich Technical Univ. Lib., Arcisstrasse 21, Munich 80230, Germany. E-mail kallenborn@ub.tum.de; *Past Pres.* Maria Heijne, Postbus 98, 2600 MG Delft, Netherlands. E-mail m.a.m.heijne@library.tudelft.nl.

Publication

IATUL Proceedings (on IATUL Web site, http://www.iatul.org) (ann.).

International Council on Archives

David Leitch, Secretary-General
60 rue des Francs-Bourgeois, 75003 Paris, France
Tel. 33-1-40-27-63-06, fax 33-1-42-72-20-65, e-mail ica@ica.org
World Wide Web http://www.ica.org

Object

The mission of the International Council on Archives (ICA) is to establish, maintain, and strengthen relations among archivists of all lands, and among all professional and other agencies or institutions concerned with the custody, organization, or administration of archives, public or private, wherever located. Established 1948.

Membership

Memb. Approximately 1,500 (representing about 195 countries and territories).

Officers

Pres. Martin Berendse, National Archivist of the Netherlands; *V.P. Marketing and Promotion* Vi Thi Minh Huong, State Archives of Vietnam; *V.P. Programme* Lewis Bellardo, National Archives and Records Administration, USA; *V.P. Finance* Andreas Kellerhals, Federal Archives, Switzerland; *Past Pres.* Ian E. Wilson, Libn. and Archivist of Canada Emeritus; *Secy.-Gen.* David Leitch.

Publications

Comma (memb.) (CD-ROM only since 2005.)
Flash (3 a year; memb.).
Guide to the Sources of the History of Nations (Latin American Series, 11 vols. pub.; Africa South of the Sahara Series, 20 vols. pub.; North Africa, Asia, and Oceania Series, 15 vols. pub.).
Guide to the Sources of Asian History (English-language series [India, Indonesia, Korea, Nepal, Pakistan, Singapore], 14 vols. pub.; national language series [Indonesia, Korea, Malaysia, Nepal, Thailand], 6 vols. pub.; other guides, 3 vols. pub.).

International Federation of Film Archives (Fédération Internationale des Archives du Film)

Secretariat, 1 rue Defacqz, B-1000 Brussels, Belgium
Tel. 32-2-538-3065, fax 32-2-534-4774, e-mail info@fiafnet.org
World Wide Web http://www.fiafnet.org

Object

Founded in 1938, the International Federation of Film Archives (FIAF) brings together not-for-profit institutions dedicated to rescuing films and any other moving-image elements considered both as cultural heritage and as historical documents.

FIAF is a collaborative association of the world's leading film archives whose purpose has always been to ensure the proper preservation and showing of motion pictures. A total of 151 archives in more than 75 countries collect, restore, and exhibit films and cinema documentation spanning the entire history of film.

FIAF seeks to promote film culture and facilitate historical research, to help create new archives around the world, to foster training and expertise in film preservation, to encourage the collection and preservation of documents and other cinema-related materials, to develop cooperation between archives, and to ensure the international availability of films and cinema documents.

Officers

Pres. Hisashi Okajima; *Secy.-Gen.* Meg Labrum; *Treas.* Patrick Loughney; *Membs.* Vittorio Boarini, Guadalupe Ferrer, Sylvia Frank, Olga Futemma, Luca Giuliani, Lise Gustavson, Eric Le Roy, Michael Loebenstein, Vladimir Opela.

Address correspondence to Christian Dimitriu, Senior Administrator, c/o FIAF Secretariat. E-mail c.dimitriu@fiafnet.org.

Publications

Journal of Film Preservation.

International Index to Film Periodicals.

FIAF International Filmarchive database (OVID).

FIAF International Index to Film Periodicals (ProQuest).

For additional FIAF publications, see http://www.fiafnet.org.

International Federation of Library Associations and Institutions

Jennefer Nicholson, Secretary-General
P.O. Box 95312, 2509 CH The Hague, Netherlands
Tel. 31-70-314-0884, fax 31-70-383-4827
E-mail ifla@ifla.org, World Wide Web http://www.ifla.org

Object

The object of the International Federation of Library Associations and Institutions (IFLA) is to promote international understanding, cooperation, discussion, research, and development in all fields of library activity, including bibliography, information services, and the education of library personnel, and to provide a body through which librarianship can be represented in matters of international interest. IFLA is the leading international body representing the interests of library and information services and their users. It is the global voice of the library and information profession. Founded 1927.

Officers and Governing Board

Pres. Ellen Tise, Univ. of Stellenbosch; *Pres.-Elect* Ingrid Parent, Univ. of British Columbia; *Treas.* Barbara Schleihagen, Deutscher Bibliotheksverband e.v. (DBV); *Governing Board* Helena R. Asamoah-Hassan, Kwame Nkrumah Univ. of Science and Technology; Judith J. Field, Wayne State Univ.; Michael Heaney, Oxford Univ.; Janice Lachance, Special Libs. Assn.; Patrice Landry, Swiss National Lib.; Jesus Lau, Universidad Veracruzana; Pascal Sanz, Bibliothèque Nationale de France; Buhle Mbambo-Thata, UNISA; Danielle Mincio, Bibliothèque Cantonale et Universitaire; Tone Eli Moseid, ABM-Utvikling; Ann Okerson, Yale Univ.; Donna Scheeder, Law Lib., Lib. of Congress; Sinikka Sipilä, Finnish Lib. Assn.; Paul Whitney, Vancouver Public Lib.; Steve W. Witt, Univ. of Illinois at Urbana-Champaign; Qiang Zhu, Peking Univ. Lib.; *Secy.-Gen.* Jennefer Nicholson; *Dir., Professional Programmes* Sjoerd M. J. Koopman.

Publications

IFLA Annual Report.

IFLA Directory (bienn.).

IFLA Journal (4 a year).

IFLA Professional Reports.

IFLA Publications Series.

IFLA Series on Bibliographic Control.

International Cataloguing and Bibliographic Control (q.).

International Preservation News.

American Membership

Associations

American Lib. Assn., Assn. for Lib. and Info. Science Educ., Assn. of Research Libs., Chief Officers of State Lib. Agencies, Medical Lib. Assn., Special Libs. Assn., Urban Libs. Council.

Institutional Members

There are 120 libraries and related institutions that are institutional members or consultative bodies and sponsors of IFLA in the United States (out of a total of 1,150 members globally), and 106 individual affiliates (out of a total of 343 members globally).

International Organization for Standardization

Robert Steele, Secretary-General
ISO Central Secretariat, 1 ch. de la Voie-Creuse, Case postale 56,
CH-1211 Geneva 20, Switzerland
41-22-749-01-11, fax 41-22-733-34-30, e-mail central@iso.org
World Wide Web http://www.iso.org

Object

The International Organization for Standardization (ISO) is a worldwide federation of national standards bodies, founded in 1947, at present comprising 162 members, one in each country. The object of ISO is to promote the development of standardization and related activities in the world with a view to facilitating international exchange of goods and services, and to developing cooperation in the spheres of intellectual, scientific, technological, and economic activity. The scope of ISO covers international standardization in all fields except electrical and electronic engineering standardization, which is the responsibility of the International Electrotechnical Commission (IEC). The results of ISO technical work are published as international standards.

Officers

Pres. Alan Morrison, Australia; *V.P. (Policy)* Sadao Takeda, Japan; *V.P. (Technical Management)* Jacob Holmblad, Denmark.

Technical Work

The technical work of ISO is carried out by 210 technical committees. These include:

ISO/TC 46–Information and documentation (Secretariat, Association Française de Normalization, 11 ave. Francis de Pressensé, 93571 Saint-Denis La Plaine, Cedex, France). Scope: Standardization of practices relating to libraries, documentation and information centers, indexing and abstracting services, archives, information science, and publishing.

ISO/TC 37–Terminology and language and content resources (Secretariat, INFOTERM, Aichholzgasse 6/12, 1120 Vienna, Austria, on behalf of Österreichisches Normungsinstitut). Scope: Standardization of principles, methods, and applications relating to terminology and other language and content resources in the contexts of multilingual communication and cultural diversity.

ISO/IEC JTC 1–Information technology (Secretariat, American National Standards Institute, 25 W. 43 St., 4th fl., New York, NY 10036). Scope: Standardization in the field of information technology.

Publications

ISO Annual Report.

ISO Catalogue on CD-ROM (combined catalog of published standards and technical work program) (ann.).

ISO Focus+ (10 a year).

ISO International Standards.

ISO Memento (ann.).

ISO Online information service on World Wide Web (http://www.iso.org).

Foreign Library Associations

The following is a list of regional and national library associations around the world. A more complete list can be found in *International Literary Market Place* (Information Today, Inc.).

Regional

Africa

Standing Conference of Eastern, Central, and Southern African Lib. and Info. Assns. (SCECSAL), c/o Botswana Lib. Assn., Private Bag 00392, Gaborone, Botswana. Fax 267-391-3501. *Chair* Kgomotso Radijeng. E-mail kgomotsor@bnpc.bw.

The Americas

Asociación de Bibliotecas Universitarias, de Investigación e Institucionales del Caribe (ACURIL) (Assn. of Caribbean Univ., Research, and Institutional Libs.), Box 23317, UPR Sta., San Juan, PR 00931-3317. Tel./fax 787-790-8054, e-mail acurilsec@yahoo.com, World Wide Web http://acuril.uprrp.edu. *Pres.* Carmen Santos-Corrada; *Exec. Secy.* Luisa Vigo Cepeda.

Seminar on the Acquisition of Latin American Lib. Materials (SALALM), c/o *Exec. Secy.* Hortensia Calvo, SALALM Secretariat, Latin American Lib., 422 Howard Tilton Memorial Lib., 7002 Freret St., New Orleans, LA 70118-5549. Tel. 504-247-1366, fax 504-247-1367, e-mail salalm@tulane.edu, World Wide Web http://www.salalm.org. *Pres.* Fernando Acosta-Rodriguez. E-mail facosta@princeton.edu; *Exec. Secy.* Hortensia Calvo.

Asia

Congress of Southeast Asian Libns. (CONSAL), c/o Cultural Affairs Assistant, 7 Lang Ha St., Ba Dinh District, Hanoi, Vietnam. Tel. 90-401-6939, fax 04-3825-3357, World Wide Web http://www.consal.org. *Secy.-Gen.* Nguyen Huy Chuong.

The Commonwealth

Commonwealth Lib. Assn. (COMLA), Learning Resources Center, Univ. of the West Indies, Bridgetown Campus, P.O. Box 144, Mona, Kingston 7, Jamaica. Tel. 876-927-0083, fax 876-927-1926, e-mail nkpodo@uwimonal.edu.jm. *Pres.* Anthony Evans; *Exec. Secy.* Norma Y. Amenu-Kpodo.

Standing Conference on Lib. Materials on Africa (SCOLMA). E-mail scolma@hotmail.com, World Wide Web http://www2.lse.ac.uk/library/scolma. *Chair* Barbara Spina, School of Oriental and African Studies, Univ. of London, Thornhaugh St., Russell Sq., London WC1H 0XG, England. Tel. 020-7898-4157, fax 020-7898-4159, e-mail bs24@soas.ac.uk.

National and State Libs. Australasia, c/o State Lib. of Victoria, 328 Swanston St., Melbourne, Vic. 3000. Tel. 3-8664-7512, fax 3-9639-4737, e-mail nsla@slv.vic.gov.au, World Wide Web http://www.nsla.org.au. *CEO* Anne-Marie Schwirtlich.

Europe

Ligue des Bibliothèques Européennes de Recherche (LIBER) (Assn. of European Research Libs.), Postbus 90407, 2509 LK The Hague, Netherlands. Tel. 070-314-07-67, fax 070-314-01-97, World Wide Web http://www.libereurope.eu. *Pres.* Hans Geleijnse. E-mail hans.geleijnse@uvt.nl; *Exec. Dir.* Wouter Schallier. E-mail wouter.schallier@kb.nl.

National

Argentina

Asociación de Bibliotecarios Graduados de la República Argentina (ABGRA) (Assn. of

Graduate Libns. of Argentina), Parana 918, 2do Piso, C1017AAT Buenos Aires. Tel. 11-4811-0043, fax 11-4816-2234, e-mail info@abgra.org.ar, World Wide Web http://www.abgra.org.ar. *Pres.* Rosa Emma Monfasani.

Australia

Australian Lib. and Info. Assn., Box 6335, Kingston, ACT 2604. Tel. 2-6215-8222, fax 2-6282-2249, e-mail enquiry@alia.org.au, World Wide Web http://www.alia.org.au. *Pres.* Jan Richards. E-mail jan.richards@alia.org.au; *Exec. Dir.* Sue Hutley. E-mail sue.hutley@alia.org.au.

Australian Society of Archivists, P.O. Box 638, Virginia, Qld. 4014. Tel. 800-622-251, e-mail office@archivists.org.au, World Wide Web http://www.archivists.org.au. *Pres.* Jackie Bettington; *V.P.* Pat Jackson; *Secy.-Treas.* Clive Smith.

Austria

Österreichische Gesellschaft für Dokumentation und Information (Austrian Society for Documentation and Info.), c/o OGDI, Wollzeile 1-3, P.O. Box 46, 1010 Vienna. E-mail office@oegdi.at, World Wide Web http://www.oegdi.at. *Chair* Hermann Huemer.

Vereinigung Österreichischer Bibliothekarinnen und Bibliothekare (Assn. of Austrian Libns.), Voralberg State Lib., Fluherstr. 4, 6900 Bregenz. E-mail voeb@mail.uibk.ac.at, World Wide Web http://www.univie.ac.at/voeb/php. *Pres.* Harald Weigel; *Contact* Josef Pauser. E-mail josef.pauser@univie.ac.at.

Bangladesh

Lib. Assn. of Bangladesh, Dhaka Univ. Lib., Shahbagh, Dhaka 1000. Tel. 2-966-190-79, World Wide Web http://www.lab-bd.org; *Pres.* Nasir Uddin Munshi; *Gen. Secy.* Syed Ali Akbor.

Barbados

Lib. Assn. of Barbados, P.O. Box 827E, Bridgetown, Barbados. E-mail milton@uwich.ill.edu.bb. *Pres.* Junior Browne.

Belgium

Archief- en Bibliotheekwezen in België (Belgian Assn. of Archivists and Libns.), Blvd. de l'Empereur 4, 1000 Brussels. Tel. 2-519-5393, fax 2-519-5610. *Pres.* Frank Daelemans. E-mail frank.daelemans@kbr.be.

Association Belge de Documentation/Belgische Vereniging voor Documentatie (Belgian Assn. for Documentation), chaussée de Wavre 1683, B-1160 Brussels. Tel. 2-675-58-62, fax 2-672-74-46, e-mail info@abd-bvd.be, World Wide Web http://www.abd-bvd.be. *Pres.* Vincent Maes; *Secy. Gen.* Christopher Boon.

Association Professionnelle des Bibliothécaires et Documentalistes (Assn. of Libns. and Documentation Specialists), Place de la Wallonie, 15 6140 Fontaine-l'Eveque. Tel. 71-52-31-93, fax 71-52-23-07, e-mail biblio.hainaut@skynet.be, World Wide Web http://www.apbd.be. *Pres.* Laurence Baker; *Secy.* Fabienne Gerard.

Vlaamse Vereniging voor Bibliotheek-, Archief-, en Documentatiewezen (Flemish Assn. of Libns., Archivists, and Documentalists), Statiestraat 179, B-2600 Berchem, Antwerp. Tel. 3-281-44-57, e-mail vvbad@vvbad.be, World Wide Web http://www.vvbad.be. *Exec. Dir.* Marc Storms.

Belize

Belize National Lib. Service and Info. System (BNLSIS), P.O. Box 287, Belize City. Tel. 223-4248, 223-4249, fax 223-4246, e-mail nls@btl.net, World Wide Web http://www.nlsbze.bz. *Chief Libn.* Joy Ysaguirre.

Bolivia

Centro Nacional de Documentacion Cientifica y Tecnologica (National Scientific and Technological Documentation Center), Av. Mariscal Santa Cruz 1175, Esquina c Ayacucho, La Paz. Tel. 02-359-583, fax 02-359-586, e-mail iiicndct@huayna.umsa.edu.bo, World Wide Web http://www.bolivian.com/industrial/cndct. *Contact* Ruben Valle Vera.

Bosnia and Herzegovina

Drustvo Bibliotekara Bosne i Hercegovine (Libns. Society of Bosnia and Herzegovina), Zmaja od Bosne 8B, 71000 Sarajevo. Tel. 33-275-5325, fax 33-212-435, e-mail nubbih@nub.ba, World Wide Web http://www.nub.ba. *Pres.* Nevenka Hajdarovic. E-mail nevenka@nub.ba; *Secy.* Dijana Bilos. E-mail dijana@nub.ba.

Botswana

Botswana Lib. Assn., Box 1310, Gaborone. Tel. 371-750, fax 371-748, World Wide Web http://www.bla.0catch.com. *Chair* Bobana Badisang.

Brazil

Associação dos Arquivistas Brasileiros (Assn. of Brazilian Archivists), Av. Presidente Vargas 1733, Sala 903, 20210-030 Rio de Janiero RJ. Tel. 21-2507-2239, fax 21-3852-2541, e-mail aab@aab.org.br, World Wide Web http://www.aab.org.br. *Pres.* Lucia Maria Velloso de Oliveira.

Brunei Darussalam

Persatuan Perpustakaan Kebangsaan Negara Brunei (National Lib. Assn. of Brunei), Perpustakaan Universiti Brunei Darussalam, Jl. Tungku Link, Gadong BE 1410. Tel. 2-249-001, fax 2-249-504, e-mail chieflib@lib.ubd.edu.bn, World Wide Web http://www.ppknbd.org.bn. *Pres.* Puan Nellie bte Dato Paduka Haji Sunny.

Cameroon

Association des Bibliothécaires, Archivistes, Documentalistes et Muséographes du Cameroun (Assn. of Libns., Archivists, Documentalists, and Museum Curators of Cameroon), B.P. 14077, Yaoundé. Tel. 222-6362, fax 222-4785, e-mail abadcam@yahoo.fr. *Pres.* Jerome Ndjock.

Chile

Colegio de Bibliotecarios de Chile (Chilean Lib. Assn.), Avda. Diagonal Paraguay 383, Torre 11, of. 122, 6510017 Santiago. Tel. 2-222-5652, fax 2-635-5023, e-mail cbc@bibliotecarios.cl, World Wide Web http://www.bibliotecarios.cl. *Pres.* Paola Roncatti Galdames; *Secy.-Gen.* Carlos Pena Mardones.

China

Lib. Society of China, 33 Zhongguancun S, Beijing 100081. Tel. 10-8854-5563, fax 10-6841-7815, e-mail ztxhmsc@nlc.gov.cn, World Wide Web http://www.nlc.gov.cn. *Secy.-Gen.* Gensheng Tang; *Pres.* Zhan Furui.

Colombia

Asociación Colombiana de Bibliotecólogos y Documentalistas (Colombian Assn. of Libns. and Documentalists), Calle 21, No. 6-58, Of. 404, Bogotá. Tel. 1-282-3620, fax 1-282-5487, World Wide Web http://www.ascolbi.org. *Pres.* Edgar Allan Degado.

Congo (Republic of)

Association des Bibliothécaires, Archivistes, Documentalistes et Muséologues du Congo (ABADOM) (Assn. of Librarians, Archivists, Documentalists, and Museologists of Congo), BP 3148, Kinshasa-Gombe. *Pres.* Desire Didier Tengeneza. E-mail didierteng@yahoo.fr.

Costa Rica

Asociación Costarricense de Bibliotecarios (Costa Rican Assn. of Libns.), Apdo. 3308, San José. Tel. 234-9989, e-mail info@cesdepu.com, World Wide Web http://www.cesdepu.com.

Côte d'Ivoire

Direction des Archives Nationales et de la Documentation, BP V 126, Abidjan, Tel. 20-21-74-20, fax 20 21 75 78. *Dir.* Venance Bahi Gouro.

Croatia

Hrvatsko Knjiznicarsko Drustvo (Croatian Lib. Assn.), c/o National and Univ. Lib.,

Hrvatske bratske zajednice 4, 10 000 Zagreb. Tel./fax 385-1-615-93-20, e-mail hkd@nsk.hr, World Wide Web http://www.hkdrustvo.hr. *Pres.* Zdenka Sviben. E-mail z.sviben@kqz.hr.

Cuba

Asociación Cubana de Bibliotecarios (ASCUBI) (Lib. Assn. of Cuba), Biblioteca Nacional Jose Marti, Ave. Independencia 20 de Mayo, Plaza de la Revolucion, Havana. Tel. 7-555-442, fax 7-816-224, e-mail publiweb@bnjm.cu, World Wide Web http://www.bnjm.cu. *Pres.* Margarita Bellas Vilarino.

Cyprus

Kypriakos Synthesmos Vivliothicarion (Lib. Assn. of Cyprus), P.O. Box 1039, 1105 Nicosia. Tel. 22-404-849.

Czech Republic

Svaz Knihovníků a Informačních Pracovníků České Republiky (SKIP) (Assn. of Lib. and Info. Professionals of the Czech Republic), National Lib., Klementinum 190, 110 00 Prague 1. Tel. 221-663-379, fax 221-663-175, e-mail vit.richter@nkp.cz, World Wide Web http://skip.nkp.cz. *Pres.* Vit Richter.

Denmark

Arkivforeningen (Archives Society), c/o Rigsarkivet, Rigsdagsgarden 9, 1218 Copenhagen. Tel. 3392-3310, fax 3315-3239, World Wide Web http://www.arkivarforeningen.no. *Pres.* Christian Larsen. E-mail cla@ra.sa.dk.

Danmarks Biblioteksforening (Danish Lib. Assn.), Farvergade 27D, 1463 Copenhagen. Tel. 3325-0935, fax 3325-7900, e-mail dbf@dbf.dk, World Wide Web http://www.dbf.dk. *Dir.* Vagn Ytte Larsen. E-mail vyl@odsherred.dk.

Danmarks Forskningsbiblioteksforening (Danish Research Lib. Assn.), c/o Statsbiblioteket, Tangen 2, 8200, Arhus N. Tel. 89-46-22-07, e-mail df@statsbiblioteket.dk, World Wide Web http://www.dfdf.dk. *Pres.* Per Steen Hansen; *Secy.* Hanne Dahl.

Dansk Musikbiblioteks Forening (Assn. of Danish Music Libs.), c/o Erling Dujardin, Aspegarden 38, 2670 Count. E-mail sekretariat@iaml.dk, World Wide Web http://www.dmbf.nu. *Pres.* Ole Bisbjerg.

Kommunernes Skolebiblioteksforening (Assn. of Danish School Libs.), Åboulevard 5, 2 th, DK-1635 Copenhagen V. Tel. 33-11-13-91, fax 33-11-13-90, e-mail ksbf@ksbf.dk, World Wide Web http://www.ksbf.dk. *Admin.* Gitte Frausing.

Dominican Republic

Asociación Dominicana de Bibliotecarios (Dominican Assn. of Libns.), c/o Biblioteca Nacional, Cesar Nicolás Penson 91, Plaza de la Cultura, Pichincha, Santo Domingo. Tel. 809-688-4086, fax 809-688-5841.

Ecuador

Asociación Ecuatoriana de Bibliotecarios (Ecuadoran Lib. Assn.), c/o Casa de la Cultura Ecuatoriana, Casilla 87, Quito. Tel. 9832-258-7666, fax 9832-258-8516, e-mail asoebfp@hotmail.com. *Pres.* Amparo Nuñez.

El Salvador

Asociación de Bibliotecarios de El Salvador (ABES) (Assn. of Salvadorian Libns.), Hacienda Gardens Block D, pje. 19 No. 158, City Merliot, Antiguo Cuscatlan, La Libertad, El Salvador. Tel. 503-2241-4464, fax 523-2228-2956, World Wide Web http://www.abes.org.sv. *Pres.* Yensi Vides Ramirez.

Ethiopia

Ye Ethiopia Betemetshaft Serategnoch Mahber (Ethiopian Lib. and Info. Assn.), P.O. Box 30530, Addis Ababa. Tel. 1-511-344, fax 1-533-368.

Finland

Suomen Kirjastoseura (Finnish Lib. Assn.), Vuorikatu 22 A 18, 00100 Helsinki. Tel.

9-6221-340, fax 9-6221-466, e-mail fla@fla.fi, World Wide Web http://www.fla.fi. *Pres.* Sinikka Sipila.

France

Association des Archivistes Français (Assn. of French Archivists), 8 rue Jean-Marie Jego, 75013 Paris. Tel. 1-46-06-39-44, fax 1-46-06-39-52, e-mail secretariat@archivistes.org, World Wide Web http://www.archivistes.org. *Pres.* Xavier de la Selle; *Secy.* Marie-Edith Enderle-Naud.

Association des Bibliothécaires Français (Assn. of French Libns.), 31 rue de Chabrol, F-75010 Paris. Tel. 1-55-33-10-30, fax 1-55-30-10-31, e-mail abf@abf.asso.fr, World Wide Web http://www.abf.asso.fr. *Pres.* Paschal Wagner; *Gen. Secy.* Maite Vanmarque.

Association des Professionnels de l'Information et de la Documentation (Assn. of Info. and Documentation Professionals), 25 rue Claude Tillier, F-75012 Paris. Tel. 1-43-72-25-25, fax 1-43-72-30-41, e-mail adbs@adbs.fr, World Wide Web http://www.adbs.fr. *Pres.* Elisabeth Gayon.

Germany

Arbeitsgemeinschaft der Spezialbibliotheken (Assn. of Special Libs.), c/o Herder-Institute eV, Bibliothek, Gisonenweg 5-7, 35037 Marburg. Tel. 6421-184-151, fax 6421-184-139, e-mail geschaeftsstelle@aspb.de, World Wide Web http://www.aspb.de. *Chair* Juergen Warmbrunn. E-mail warmbrunn@herder-institut.de.

Berufsverband Information Bibliothek (Assn. of Info. and Lib. Professionals), Gartenstr. 18, 72764 Reutlingen. Tel. 7121-3491-0, fax 7121-3004-33, e-mail mail@bib-info.de, World Wide Web http://www.bib-info.de. *Pres.* Susanne Riedel. E-mail susanne.riedel@uni-bielefeld.de.

Deutsche Gesellschaft für Informationswissenschaft und Informationspraxis eV (German Society for Info. Science and Practice), Hanauer Landstr. 151-153, 60314 Frankfurt-am-Main 1. Tel. 69-43-03-13, fax 69-490-90-96, e-mail mail@dgi-info.de, World Wide Web http://www.dgd.de. *Pres.* Stefan Gradmann.

Deutscher Bibliotheksverband eV (German Lib. Assn.), Str. des 17 Juni 114, 10623 Berlin. Tel. 30-644-98-99-10, fax 30-64-49-89-92-9, e-mail dbv@bibliotheksverband.de, World Wide Web http://www.bibliotheksverband.de. *Chair* Gabriele Beger. E-mail beger@dgi-info.de.

VdA—Verband Deutscher Archivarinnen und Archivare (Assn. of German Archivists), Woerthstr. 3, 36037 Fulda. Tel. 661-29-109-72, fax 661-29-109-74, e-mail info@vda.archiv.net, World Wide Web http://www.vda.archiv.net. *Chair* Michael Diefenbacher.

Verein Deutscher Bibliothekare eV (Society of German Libns.), Universitaetsbibliothek Augsburg, Universitaetsstr. 22, 86159 Augsburg. Tel. 821-598-5300, fax 821-598-5354, e-mail sekr@bibliothek.uni-augsburg.de, World Wide Web http://www.vdb-online.org. *Chair* Ulrich Hohoff.

Ghana

Ghana Lib. Assn., c/o INSTI, P.O. Box GP 4105, Accra. Tel. 244-17-4930, e-mail info@librarygla.org, World Wide Web http://gla-net.org. *Pres.* Valentina J. A. Bannerman. E-mail valnin@yahoo.com.

Greece

Enosis Hellinon Bibliothekarion (Greek Lib. Assn.), Skoufa 52, P.O. Box 10672, Athens. Tel./fax 210-330-2128, World Wide Web http://www.eebep.gr. *Pres.* Christina Kyriakopoulou.

Guyana

Guyana Lib. Assn., c/o National Lib., P.O. Box 10240, Georgetown. Tel. 222-486, fax 223-596, e-mail londonh@uog.ed.gy, World Wide Web http://www.natlib.gov.gy. *Pres.* Wendy R. Stephenson, *Secy.* Althea John.

Honduras

Asociación de Bibliotecarios y Archiveros de Honduras (Assn. of Libns. and Archivists of Honduras), 11a Calle, 1a y 2a Avdas., No. 105, Comayagüela DC, Tegucigalpa.

Pres. Francisca de Escoto Espinoza; *Secy.-Gen.* Juan Angel R. Ayes.

Hong Kong

Hong Kong Lib. Assn., GPO Box 10095, Hong Kong. E-mail hkla@hkla.org, World Wide Web http://www.hkla.org. *Pres.* Jim Chang. E-mail jhychang@lcsd.gov.hk,

Hungary

Magyar Könyvtárosok Egyesülete (Assn. of Hungarian Libns.), Budavari Palota F, epulet 439 szoba, Budapest. Tel./fax 1-311-8634, e-mail mke@oszk.hu, World Wide Web http://www.mke.oszk.hu. *Pres.* Klara Bakos; *Secy. Gen.* Nagy Aniko.

Iceland

Upplysing—Felag bokasafns-og upplysingafraeoa (Information—The Icelandic Lib. and Info. Science Assn.), Lygasi 18, 210 Garoabae. Tel. 864-6220, e-mail upplysing@upplysing.is, World Wide Web http://www.upplysing.is. *Chair* Hrafnhildur Hreinsdottir. E-mail hrafnhildur@velvakandi.is; *Secy.* Ingibjorg Osp Ottarsdottir.

India

Indian Assn. of Special Libs. and Info. Centres, P-291, CIT Scheme 6M, Kankurgachi, Kolkata 700054. Tel. 33-2362-9651, e-mail iaslic@vsnl.net. *Pres.* J. N. Satpathi. E-mail satpathijn@rediffmail.com.

Indian Lib. Assn., A/40-41, Flat 201, Ansal Bldg., Dr Mukerjee Nagar, Delhi 110009. Tel./fax 11-2765-1743, e-mail dvs-srcc@rediffmail.com, World Wide Web http://www.ilaindia.net. *Gen. Secy.* R. Chandra.

Indonesia

Ikatan Pustakawan Indonesia (Indonesian Lib. Assn.), Jl. Merdeka Selatan No. 11, 10110 Jakarta, Pusat. Tel./fax 21-385-5729, World Wide Web http://ipi.pnri.go.id. *Pres.* S. Kartosdono.

Ireland

Cumann Leabharlann Na h-Eireann (Lib. Assn. of Ireland), 53 Upper Mount St., Dublin 2. Tel. 1-6120-2193, fax 1-6121-3090, e-mail president@libraryassociation.ie, World Wide Web http://www.libraryassociation.ie. *Pres.* Siobhan Fitzpatrick.

Israel

Israel Libns. and Info. Specialists Assn., 9 Beit Hadfus St., Givaat Shaul, Jerusalem. Tel. 2-658-9515, fax 2-625-1628, e-mail icl@icl.org.il. *Pres.* Benjamin Schachter.

Israeli Center for Libs., P.O. Box 801, 51108 Bnei Brak. Tel. 03-618-0151, fax 3-579-8048, e-mail icl@icl.org.il, World Wide Web http://www.icl.org.il. *Chair* Danny Bustin.

Israeli Society for Libs. and Info. Centers (ASMI), Blum 8, 44253 Kfar Saba. Tel. 77-215-1800, fax 77-434-509, e-mail agudatasmi@gmail.coml; World Wide Web http://www.asmi.org.il. *Chair* Hagafni Shahaf.

Italy

Associazione Italiana Biblioteche (Italian Lib. Assn.), C.P. 2461, 00185 Rome AD. Tel. 6-446-3532, fax 6-444-1139, e-mail aib@aib.it, World Wide Web http://www.aib.it. *Pres.* Mauro Guerrini.

Jamaica

Lib. and Info. Assn. of Jamaica., P.O. Box 125, Kingston 5. Tel./fax 876-927-1614, e-mail liajapresident@yahoo.com, World Wide Web http://www.liaja.org.jm. *Pres.* Paulette Stewart.

Japan

Joho Kagaku Gijutsu Kyokai (Info. Science and Technology Assn.), Sasaki Bldg., 2-5-7 Koisikawa, Bunkyo-ku, Tokyo 112-0002. Tel. 3-3813-3791, fax 3-3813-3793, e-mail infosta@infosta.or.jp, World Wide Web http://www.infosta.or.jp. *Pres.* Onodera Natsuo.

Nihon Toshokan Kyokai (Japan Lib. Assn.), 1-11-14 Shinkawa, Chuo-ku, Tokyo 104

0033. Tel. 3-3523-0811, fax 3-3523-0841, e-mail info@jla.or.jp, World Wide Web http://www.jla.or.jp. *Pres.* Shiomi Noboru.

Senmon Toshokan Kyogikai (Japan Special Libs. Assn.), c/o Japan Lib. Assn., Bldg. F6, 1-11-14 Shinkawa Chuo-ku, Tokyo 104-0033. Tel. 3-3537-8335, fax 3-3537-8336, e-mail jsla@jsla.or.jp, World Wide Web http://www.jsla.or.jp. *Pres.* Kousaku Inaba; *Exec. Dir.* Fumihisa Nakagawa.

Jordan

Arab Archives Institute, P.O. Box 815454, Amman. Tel. 962-6-465-6694, fax 962-6-465-6693, e-mail aainstitute@gmail.com, World Wide Web http://www.alarchef.com. *Dir.* Sa'eda Kilani.

Jordan Lib. Assn., P.O. Box 6289, Amman 11118. Tel./fax 6-462-9412, e-mail info@jorla.org, World Wide Web http://www.jorla.org. *Pres.* Anwar Akroush.

Kenya

Kenya Assn. of Lib. and Info. Professionals (formerly Kenya Lib. Assn.), P.O. Box 46031, 00100 Nairobi. Tel. 20-733-732-799, fax 20-811-455, World Wide Web http://www.klas.or.ke. *Chair* Rosemary Gitachu. E-mail gitachur@yahoo.com.

Korea (Democratic People's Republic of)

Lib. Assn. of the Democratic People's Republic of Korea, c/o Grand People's Study House, P.O. Box 200, Pyongyang. E-mail nsj@co.chesin.com.

Korea (Republic of)

Korean Lib. Assn., San 60-1, Banpo-dong, Seocho-gu, Seoul 137-702. Tel. 2-535-4868, fax 2-535-5616, e-mail license@kla.kr, World Wide Web http://www.korla.or.kr. *Pres.* Ki Nam Shin; *Exec. Dir.* Won Ho Jo.

Laos

Association des Bibliothécaires Laotiens (Lao Lib. Assn.), c/o Direction de la Bibliothèque Nationale, Ministry of Info. and Culture, B.P. 704, Vientiane. Tel. 21-21-2452, fax 21-21-2408, e-mail bailane@laotel.com.

Latvia

Lib. Assn. of Latvia, Terbatas iela 75, Riga LV-1001. Tel./fax 6731-2792, e-mail lbb@lbi.lnb.lv, World Wide Web http://www.lnb.lv.

Lebanon

Lebanese Lib. Assn., P.O. Box 13-5053, Beirut 1102 2801. Tel. 1-786-456, e-mail kjaroudy@lau.edu.lb; World Wide Web http://www.llaweb.org/index.php. *Pres.* Fawz Abdalleh.

Lesotho

Lesotho Lib. Assn., Private Bag A26, Maseru 100. Tel./fax 340-601. *Chair* Celina K. M. Qobo; *Secy.* Makemang Ntsasa.

Lithuania

Lietuvos Bibliotekininku Draugija (Lithuanian Libns. Assn.), Sv Ignoto 6-108, LT-1120 Vilnius. Tel./fax 5-262-55-70, e-mail lbd_sekretore@amb.lt, World Wide Web http://www.lbd.lt. *Pres.* Petras Zurlys.

Luxembourg

Association Luxembourgeoise des Bibliothécaires, Archivistes, et Documentalistes (ALBAD) (Luxembourg Assn. of Libns., Archivists, and Documentalists), c/o National Lib. of Luxembourg, BP 295, L-2012 Luxembourg. Tel. 352-22-97-55-1, fax 352-47-56-72, World Wide Web http://www.albad.lu. *Pres.* Jean-Marie Reding. E-mail jean-marie.reding@bnl.etat.lu; *Secy.-Gen.* Michel Donven. E-mail michel.donven@bnl.etat.lu.

Macedonia

Bibliotekarsko Drustvo na Makedonija (Union of Libns.' Assns. of Macedonia), Blvd. Gotse Delcev 6, 1000 Skopje. E-mail bdm@bdm.org.mk, World Wide Web http://www.bdm.org.mk. *Pres.* Kiril Angelov; *Secy.* Elena Tevcheva.

Malawi

Malawi Lib. Assn., c/o Univ. Libn., P.O. Box 429, Zomba. Tel. 50-522-222, fax 50-523-225.

Malaysia

Persatuan Perpustakaan Malaysia (Lib. Assn. of Malaysia), P.O. Box 12545, 50782 Kuala Lumpur. Tel./fax 3-2694-7390, e-mail ppm55@po.jaring.my.

Mali

Association Malienne des Bibliothécaires, Archivistes et Documentalistes (Mali Assn. of Libns., Archivists, and Documentalists), BP E4473, Bamako. Tel. 20-29-94-23, fax 20-29-93-76, e-mail dnbd@afribone.net.ml. *Pres.* Mamadou Konoba Keita.

Malta

Malta Lib. and Info. Assn. (MaLIA), c/o Univ. of Malta Lib., Msida MSD 2080. E-mail info@malia-malta.org, World Wide Web http://www.malia-malta.org. *Chair* Robert Mizzi.

Mauritania

Association Mauritanienne des Bibliothécaires, Archivistes et Documentalistes (Mauritanian Assn. of Libns., Archivists, and Documentalists), c/o Bibliothèque Nationale, B.P. 20, Nouakchott. Tel. 525-18-62, fax 525-18-68, e-mail bibliotheque-nationale@yahoo.fr.

Mauritius

Mauritius Lib. Assn., Ministry of Educ. Public Lib., Moka Rd., Rose Hill. Tel. 403-0200, fax 454-9553. *Pres.* Abdool Fareed Soogali.

Mexico

Asociación Mexicana de Bibliotecarios (Mexican Assn. of Libns.), Apdo. 12-800, Administración Postal Obreto Mundial, 03001 México DF 06760. Tel. 155-5575-3396, fax 155-5575-1136, e-mail correo@ambac.org.mx, World Wide Web http://www.ambac.org.mx. *Pres.* Jesus Lau; *Secy.* Marisela Castro Moreno.

Myanmar

Myanmar Lib. Assn., c/o National Lib., 85 Thirimingalar Ave., Yangon. Tel. 1-27-2058, fax 01-53-2927.

Nepal

Nepal Lib. Assn., GPO 2773, Kathmandu. Tel. 977-1-441-1318, e-mail info@nla.org.np, World Wide Web http://www.nla.org.np. *Contact* Rudra Prasad Dulal.

The Netherlands

Nederlandse Vereniging voor Beroepsbeoefenaren in de Bibliotheek-Informatie-en Kennissector (Netherlands Assn. of Libns., Documentalists, and Info. Specialists), Hardwareweg 4, 3821 BM Amersfoort. Tel. 30-4546-653, fax 30-4546-666, e-mail nvbinfo@wxs.nl, World Wide Web http://www.nvbonline.nl. *Managing Dir.* Jan van der Burg. E-mail burg@nvbonline.nl.

New Zealand

New Zealand Lib. Assn. (LIANZA), P.O. Box 12-212, Thorndon, Wellington 6144. Tel. 4-473-5834, fax 4-499-1480, e-mail office@lianza.org.nz, World Wide Web http://www.lianza.org.nz. *Exec. Dir.* Alli Smith. E-mail alli@lianza.org.nz.

Nicaragua

Asociación Nicaraguense de Bibliotecarios y Profesionales Afines (ANIBIPA) (Nicaraguan Assn. of Libns.), Bello Horizonte, Tope Sur de la Rotonda 1/2 cuadra abajo, Casa J-11-57, Managua. Tel. 277-4159 ext. 335, e-mail anibipa@hotmail.com.

Pres. Yadira Roque. E-mail r-yardira@hotmail.com.

Nigeria

Nigerian Lib. Assn., c/o National Lib. of Nigeria, Sanusi Dantata House, Central Business District, PMB 1, Abuja GPO 900001. Tel. 803-334-8817, fax 9-234-6773, e-mail info@nla-ng.org, World Wide Web http://www.nla-ng.org. *Pres.* Victoria Okojie; *Secy.* D. D. Bwayili.

Norway

Arkivarforeningen (Assn. of Archivists), Postboks 4013, Ulleval Stadion, 0806 Oslo. Tel. 22-02-26-03, fax 22-23-74-89, e-mail linhol@arkivverket.no, World Wide Web http://www.arkivarforeningen.no. *Chair* Linda Holmans.

Norsk Bibliotekforening (Norwegian Lib. Assn.), Postboks 6540, 0606 Etterstad. Tel. 23-24-34-30, fax 22-67-23-68, e-mail nbf@norskbibliotekforening.no, World Wide Web http://www.norskbibliotekforening.no. *Gen. Secy.* Tore Andersen.

Pakistan

Library Promotion Bureau, Karachi Univ. Campus, P.O. Box 8421, Karachi 75270. Tel./fax 21-3632-1959, e-mail gsabzwari@lpbpk.com.

Panama

Asociación Panameña de Bibliotecarios (Panama Lib. Assn.), c/o Biblioteca Interamericana Simón Bolivar, Estafeta Universitaria, Panama City.

Paraguay

Asociación de Bibliotecarios Graduados del Paraguay (Assn. of Paraguayan Graduate Libns.), Facultad Politecnica, Universidad Nacional de Asunción, 2160 San Lorenzo. Tel. 21-585-588, e-mail abigrap@pol.una.py, World Wide Web http://www.pol.una.py/abigrap. *Pres.* Emilce Noemi Sena Correa.

Peru

Asociación de Archiveros del Perú (Peruvian Assn. of Archivists), Av. Manco Capacc No. 1180, Dpto 201, La Victoria, Lima. Tel. 1-472-8729, fax 1-472-7408, e-mail contactos@adapperu.com. *Pres.* Juan Manuel Serrano Valencia.

Asociación Peruana de Bibliotecarios (Peruvian Assn. of Libns.), Bellavista 561 Miraflores, Apdo. 995, Lima 18. Tel. 1-474-869. *Pres.* Martha Fernandez de Lopez; *Secy.* Luzmila Tello de Medina.

Philippines

Assn. of Special Libs. of the Philippines, Rm. 301, National Lib. Bldg., T. M. Kalaw St., 1000 Ermita, Manila. Tel. 2-740-9625, e-mail aslpboard@yahoo.com.ph, World Wide Web http://aslpboard.multiply.com. *Pres.* Wilhelmina Lopez.

Philippine Libns. Assn., P.O. Box 2926, 1000 Ermita, Manila. Tel./fax 2-525-9401. *Pres.* Lilia F Echiverri. E-mail lily.echiverri@gmail.com.

Poland

Stowarzyszenie Bibliotekarzy Polskich (Polish Libns. Assn.), al Niepodleglosci 213, 02-086 Warsaw. Tel. 22-825-83-74, fax 22-825-53-49, e-mail biurozgsbp@wp.pl, World Wide Web http://ebib.info. *Pres.* Elzbieta Stefanczyk; *Secy.-Gen.* Marzena Przybysz.

Portugal

Associação Portuguesa de Bibliotecários, Arquivistas e Documentalistas (Portuguese Assn. of Libns., Archivists, and Documentalists), Rua Morais Soares, 43C, 1 Dto, 1900-341 Lisbon. Tel. 21-816-19-80, fax 21-815-45-08, e-mail apbad@apbad.pt, World Wide Web http://www.apbad.pt/edicoes/edicoes_cadernos.htm. *Pres.* António José de Pina Falcão.

Puerto Rico

Sociedad de Bibliotecarios de Puerto Rico (Society of Libns. of Puerto Rico), Apdo

22898, San Juan 00931-2898. Tel./fax 787-764-0000, World Wide Web http://www.sociedadbibliotecarios.org. *Pres.* Ivan Calimano. E-mail kalimano@gmail.com.

Russia

Rossiiskaya Bibliotechnaya Assotsiatsiya (Russian Lib. Assn.), 18 Sadovaya St., St. Petersburg 191069. Tel. 812-118-85-36, fax 812-710-58-61, e-mail rba@nlr.ru, World Wide Web http://www.rba.ru. *Pres.* Vladimir Zaitsev; *Exec. Secy.* Elena Tikhonova.

Senegal

Association Sénégalaise des Bibliothécaires, Archivistes et Documentalistes (Senegalese Assn. of Libns., Archivists, and Documentalists), BP 2006, Dakar. Tel. 77-651-00-33, fax 33-824-23-79, e-mail asbad200@hotmail.com, World Wide Web http://www.asbad.org. *Pres.* Adama Aly Pam; *Secy.-Gen.* Alassane Ndiath.

Serbia and Montenegro

Jugoslovenski Bibliografsko Informacijski Institut, Terazije 26, 11000 Belgrade. Tel. 11-2687-836, fax 11-2687-760. *Dir.* Radomir Glavicki.

Sierra Leone

Sierra Leone Assn. of Archivists, Libns., and Info. Scientists, c/o Sierra Leone Lib. Board, Rokel St., Freetown. Tel. 22-22-0758. *Pres.* Oliver Harding.

Singapore

Lib. Assn. of Singapore, National Lib. Board, 100 Victoria St., No. 14-01, Singapore 188064. Tel. 6332-3255, fax 6332-3248, e-mail lassec@las.org.sg, World Wide Web http://www.las.org.sg. *Pres.* Puspa Yeow.

Slovenia

Zveza Bibliotekarskih Druötev Slovenije (Union of Assns. of Slovene Libns.), Turjaöka 1, 1000 Ljubljana. Tel. 01-20-01-193, fax 01-42-57-293, e-mail zbds2010@gmail.com, World Wide Web http://www.zbds-zveza.si. *Pres.* Melita Ambrozic.

South Africa

Lib. and Info. Assn. of South Africa, Dept. of Info. Science, Univ. of South Africa, P.O. Box 392, Pretoria 0003. Tel. 12-328-2010, fax 12-323-1033, e-mail liasa@liasa.org.za, World Wide Web http://www.liasa.org.za. *Pres.* Rachel More; *National Secy.* Judy Henning.

Spain

Federación Española de Archiveros, Bibliotecarios, Museólogos y Documentalistas (ANABAD) (Spanish Assn. of Archivists, Libns., Curators, and Documentalists), Recoletos, 5, 3 izda, 28001 Madrid. Tel. 34-91-575-1727, fax 34-91-578-1615, e-mail anabad@anabad-clm.org, World Wide Web http://www.anabad.org/clm. *Chair* Antonio Casado Poyales.

Sri Lanka

Sri Lanka Lib. Assn., Professional Center, 275/75 Stanley Wijesundara Mawatha, Colombo 7. Tel./fax 11-258-9103, e-mail slla@slltnet.lk, World Wide Web http://www.slla.org.lk. *Pres.* Upali Amarasiri; *Gen. Secy.* Pushpamala Perera.

Swaziland

Swaziland Lib. Assn., P.O. Box 2309, Mbabane H100. Tel. 404-2633, fax 404-3863, e-mail fmkhonta@uniswacc.uniswa.sz, World Wide Web http://www.swala.sz. *Chair* Faith Mkhonta.

Sweden

Svensk Biblioteksförening Kansli (Swedish Lib. Assn.), Box 70380, 107 24 S-Stockholm. Tel. 8-545-132-30, fax 8-545-132-31, e-mail info@biblioteksforeningen.org, World Wide Web http://www.biblioteksforeningen.org. *Secy.-Gen.* Niclas Lindberg.

Svensk Förening för Informationsspecialister (Swedish Assn. for Info. Specialists), Osquars backe 25, SE-100 44 Stockholm. Tel. 8-678-23-20, e-mail kansliet@sfis.nu, World Wide Web http://www.sfis.nu. *Pres.* Peter Almerud. E-mail peter.almerud @gmail.com.

Svenska Arkivsamfundet (Swedish Assn. of Archivists), c/o Swedish Stockholms stadsarkiv, Box 22063, 104 22 Stockholm. Tel. 46-19-70-00, fax 46-19-70-70, e-mail info@arkivsamfundet.se, World Wide Web http://www.arkivsamfundet.se. *Pres.* Sara Naeslund.

Switzerland

Association des Bibliothèques et Bibliothécaires Suisses/Vereinigung Schweizerischer Bibliothekare/Associazione dei Bibliotecari Svizzeri (Assn. of Swiss Libs. and Libns.), Hallestr. 58, CH-3012 Bern. Tel. 31-382-42-40, fax 31-382-46-48, e-mail info@bis.info.

Schweizerische Vereinigung für Dokumentation/Association Suisse de Documentation (Swiss Assn. of Documentation), Hallestr. 58, CH-3012 Bern. Tel. 31-382-42-40, fax 31-382-46-48, e-mail info@bis.info, World Wide Web http://www.svd-asd.org. *Gen. Secy.* Barbara Kraeuchi. E-mail b.kraeuchi @bbs.ch.

Verein Schweizer Archivarinnen und Archivare (Assn. of Swiss Archivists), Schweizerisches Bundesarchiv, Office Pontri GmbH, Strasse 13 Solothurn, CH-3322, Urtenen Schönbühl. Tel. 31-312-26-66, fax 31-312-26-68, e-mail info@vsa-aas.org, World Wide Web http://www.vsa-aas.org. *Pres.* Anna Pia Maissen, Zurich City Archives. E-mail annapia.maissen@ zuerich.ch.

Taiwan

Lib. Assn. of the Republic of China (LAROC), 20 Zhongshan South Rd., Taipei 100. Tel. 2-2331-2675, fax 2-2370-0899, e-mail lac@msg.ncl.edu.tw. *Secy.-Gen.* Teresa Wang Chang.

Tanzania

Tanzania Lib. Assn., P.O. Box 33433, Dar es Salaam. Tel./fax 744-296-134, e-mail tla_tanzania@yahoo.com, World Wide Web http://www.tla.or.tz. *Chair* Alli Mcharazo. E-mail amcharazo@hotmail. com.

Thailand

Thai Lib. Assn., 1346 Akarnsongkrau Rd. 5, Klongchan, Bangkapi, 10240 Bangkok. Tel. 02-734-9022, fax 02-734-9021, e-mail tla2497@yahoo.com, World Wide Web http://tla.or.th. *Pres.* Chutima Sacchanand; *Exec. Secy.* Suwadee Vichetpan.

Trinidad and Tobago

Lib. Assn. of Trinidad and Tobago, P.O. Box 1275, Port of Spain. Tel. 868-687-0194, e-mail info@latt.org.tt, World Wide Web http://www.latt.org.tt.

Tunisia

Association Tunisienne des Documentalistes, Bibliothécaires et Archivistes (Tunisian Assn. of Documentalists, Libns., and Archivists), Centre de Documentation Nationale, 8004 rue Kheredinne Pacha, 1002 Tunis. Tel. 7165-1924.

Turkey

Türk Kütüphaneciler Dernegi (Turkish Libns. Assn.), Necatibey Cad Elgun Sok 8/8, 06440 Kizilay, Ankara. Tel. 312-230-13-25, fax 312-232-04-53, e-mail tkd.dernek @gmail.com, World Wide Web http:// www.kutuphaneci.org.tr. *Pres.* Ali Fuat Kartal; *Secy.* Hakan Anameric.

Uganda

Uganda Lib. and Info. Assn., P.O. Box 8147, Kampala. Tel. 141-256-77-467698. *Pres.* Innocent Rugambwa; *Gen. Secy.* Sarah Kaddu.

Ukraine

Ukrainian Lib. Assn., Lesia Ukrainka Kyiv Public Lib., Turgenivska Str. 83/85, 04050

Kyiv. E-mail pashkovavs@yahoo.com, World Wide Web http://www.uba.org.ua.

United Kingdom

ASLIB, the Assn. for Info. Management, 207 Davina House, 137–149 Goswell Rd., London EC1V 7ET, England. Tel. 20-7253-3349, fax 20-7490-0577, e-mail furtherinformation@aslib.com, World Wide Web http://www.aslib.co.uk.

Bibliographical Society, Institute of English Studies, Rm. 304, Senate House, Malet St., London WC1E 7HU, England. Tel. 20-7611-7244, fax 20-7611-8703, World Wide Web http://www.bibsoc.org.uk/bibsoc.htm. *Pres.* David Pearson.

Chartered Institute of Lib. and Info. Professionals (CILIP) (formerly the Lib. Assn.), 7 Ridgmount St., London WC1E 7AE, England. Tel. 20-7255-0500, fax 20-7255-0501, e-mail info@cilip.org.uk, World Wide Web http://www.cilip.org.uk. *Chief Exec.* Bob McKee.

School Lib. Assn., Unit 2, Lotmead Business Village, Wanborough, Swindon SN4 0UY, England. Tel. 1793-791-787, fax 1793-791-786, e-mail info@sla.org.uk, World Wide Web http://www.sla.org.uk. *Pres.* Miranda McKearney.

Scottish Lib. and Info. Council, 1st fl., Bldg. C, Brandon Gate, Leechlee Rd., Hamilton ML3 6AU, Scotland. Tel. 1698-458-888, fax 1698-283-170, e-mail slic@slainte.org.uk, World Wide Web http://www.slainte.org.uk. *Dir.* Elaine Fulton.

Society of Archivists, Prioryfield House, 20 Canon St., Taunton TA1 1SW, England. Tel. 1823-327-030, fax 1823-371-719, e-mail societyofarchivists@archives.org.uk, World Wide Web http://www.archives.org.uk. *Chair* Peter Emmerson; *Exec. Dir.* John Chambers.

Society of College, National, and Univ. Libs (SCONUL) (formerly Standing Conference of National and Univ. Libs.), 102 Euston St., London NW1 2HA, England. Tel. 20-7387-0317, fax 20-7383-3197, e-mail info@sconul.ac.uk, World Wide Web http://www.sconul.ac.uk. *Chair* Jane Core.

Uruguay

Agrupación Bibliotecológica del Uruguay (Uruguayan Lib. and Archive Science Assn.), Cerro Largo 1666, 11200 Montevideo. Tel. 2-400-57-40. *Pres.* Luis Alberto Musso.

Asociación de Bibliotecólogos del Uruguay, Eduardo V. Haedo 2255, 11200 Montevideo. Tel./fax 2-4099-989, e-mail abu@adinet.com.uy, World Wide Web http://www.abu.net.uy. *Pres.* Alicia Ocaso Ferreira.

Venezuela

Colegio de Bibliotecólogos y Archivólogos de Venezuela (Venezuelan Lib. and Archives Assn.), Apdo. 6283, Caracas. Tel. 212-572-1858.

Vietnam

Hôi Thu-Vien Viet Nam (Vietnamese Lib. Assn.), National Lib. of Vietnam, 31 Trang Thi, 10000 Hanoi. Tel. 4-8254-938, fax 4-8-253-357, e-mail info@nlv.gov.vn, World Wide Web http://www.nlv.gov.vn. *Dir.* Phan Thi Kim Dung.

Zambia

Zambia Lib. Assn., P.O. Box 32379, Lusaka. Tel. 22-277-5411. *Chair* Benson Njobvu. E-mail bensonnjobvu@gmail.com.

Zimbabwe

Zimbabwe Lib. Assn., P.O. Box 3133, Harare. Tel. 4-692-741, e-mail zimlanec@gmail.com. *Chair* Driden Kunaka.

Directory of Book Trade and Related Organizations

Book Trade Associations, United States and Canada

For more extensive information on the associations listed in this section, see the annual edition of *Literary Market Place* (Information Today, Inc.).

AIGA—The Professional Assn. for Design (formerly the American Institute of Graphic Arts), 164 Fifth Ave., New York, NY 10010. Tel. 212-807-1990, fax 212-807-1799, e-mail aiga@aiga.org, World Wide Web http://www.aiga.org. *Pres.* Debbie Millman, Sterling Brands, 350 Fifth Ave., No. 1714, New York, NY 10118. Tel. 212-329-4609, e-mail debbie.m@sterlingbrands.com; *Exec. Dir.* Richard Grefe. E-mail grefe@aiga.org.

American Booksellers Assn., 200 White Plains Rd., Tarrytown, NY 10591. Tel. 800-637-0037, 914-591-2665, fax 914-591-2720, World Wide Web http://www.bookweb.org. *Pres.* Michael Tucker, Books Inc., 1501 Vermont St., San Francisco, CA 94107. Tel. 415-643-3400 ext. 18, fax 415-643-2043, e-mail mtucker@booksinc.net; *V.P./Secy.* Becky Anderson, Anderson's Bookshops, 123 W. Jefferson Ave., Naperville, IL 60540 . Tel. 630-355-2665, fax 630-355-3470, e-mail becky@andersonsbookshop.com; *CEO* Oren Teicher. E-mail oren@bookweb.org.

American Literary Translators Assn. (ALTA), Univ. of Texas at Dallas, 800 W. Campbell Rd., Mail Sta. JO51, Richardson, TX 75080. Tel. 972-883-2092, fax 972-883-6303, World Wide Web http://www.utdallas.edu/alta. *Pres.* Barbara Harshav; *V.P.* Gary Racz; *Secy./Treas.* Russell Valentino; *Contact* Maria Suarez. E-mail maria.suarez@utdallas.edu.

American Medical Publishers Committee (AMPC), c/o Sara Pinto, dir., Professional/Scholarly Publishing Div., Assn. of American Publishers, 71 Fifth Ave., New York, NY 10003-3004. Tel. 212-255-0200 ext. 257, fax 212-255-7007, e-mail spinto@publishers.org.

American Printing History Assn., Box 4519, Grand Central Sta., New York, NY 10163-4519. World Wide Web http://www.printinghistory.org. *Pres.* Paul W. Romaine. *Exec. Secy.* Lyndsi Barnes. E-mail secretary@printinghistory.org.

American Society for Indexing, 10200 W. 44 Ave., Suite 304, Wheat Ridge, CO 80033. Tel. 303-463-2887, fax 303-422-8894, e-mail info@asindexing.org, World Wide Web http://www.asindexing.org. *Pres.* Frances Lennie. E-mail president@asindexing.org; *V.P./Pres.-Elect* Richard Shrout; *Secy.* Lucie Haskins; *Treas.* Janet Perlman; *Past Pres.* Kate Mertes; *Exec. Dir.* Annette Rogers. E-mail arogers@asindexing.org.

American Society of Journalists and Authors, 1501 Broadway, Suite 403, New York, NY 10036. Tel. 212-997-0947, fax 212-937-3215, e-mail director@asja.org, World Wide Web http://www.asja.org. *Pres.* Salley Shannon. E-mail president@asja.org; *Exec. Dir.* Alexandra Owens.

American Society of Media Photographers, 150 N. 2 St., Philadelphia, PA 19106. Tel. 215-451-2767, fax 215-451-0880, e-mail mopsik@asmp.org, World Wide Web http://www.asmp.org. *Pres.* Richard Kelly; *Exec. Dir.* Eugene Mopsik.

American Society of Picture Professionals, 217 Palos Verdes Blvd., No. 700, Redondo Beach, CA 90277. Tel. 424-247-9944, fax 424-247-9844, e-mail director@aspp.com, World Wide Web http://www.aspp.com. *Pres.* Michael Masterson; *Exec. Dir.* Jain Lemos.

American Translators Assn., 225 Reinekers Lane, Suite 590, Alexandria, VA 22314. Tel. 703-683-6100, fax 703-683-6122, e-mail ata@atanet.org, World Wide Web http://www.atanet.org. *Pres.* Nicholas Hartmann; *Pres.-Elect* Dorothee Racette; *Secy.* Virginia Perez-Santalla; *Treas.* Gabe Bokor; *Exec. Dir.* Walter W. Bacak, Jr. E-mail walter@atanet.org.

Antiquarian Booksellers Assn. of America, 20 W. 44 St., No. 507, New York, NY 10036-6604. Tel. 212-944-8291, fax 212-944-8293, e-mail inquiries@abaa.org, World Wide Web http://www.abaa.org. *Pres.* Sarah Baldwin; *V.P./Secy.* John Thomson; *Treas.* Thomas Goldwasser; *Exec. Dir.* Susan Benne. E-sbenne@abaa.org.

Assn. Media and Publishing (formerly Society of National Assn. Publications, or SNAP), 1760 Old Meadow Rd., Suite 500, McLean, VA 22102. Tel. 703-506-3285, fax 703-506-3266, e-mail info@associationmediaandpublishing.org, World Wide Web http://www.associationmediaandpublishing.org. *Pres.* Ryan Johnson; *V.P.* Greg Fine; *Exec. Dir.* Amy Lestition. Tel. 703-506-3285, e-mail alestition@associationmediaandpublishing.org.

Assn. of American Publishers, 71 Fifth Ave., New York, NY 10003. Tel. 212-255-0200, fax 212-255-7007. *Washington Office* 455 Massachusetts Ave. N.W., Suite 700, Washington, DC 20001. Tel. 202-347-3375, fax 202-347-3690. *Pres./CEO* Tom Allen; *V.P.s* Allan R. Adler, Tina Jordan, Andi Sporkin, John Tagler; *Dir., Communications and Public Affairs* Judith Platt; *Exec. Dir., School Div.* Jay Diskey; *Exec. Dir., Higher Education* Bruce Hildebrand; *Exec. Dir., International Copyright Enforcement* M. Luisa Simpson; *Exec. Dir., Digital, Environmental, and Accessibility Affairs* Edward McCoyd.

Assn. of American University Presses, 28 W. 36 St., Suite 602, New York, NY 10018. Tel. 212-989-1010, fax 212-989-0275, e-mail info@aaupnet.org, World Wide Web http://aaupnet.org. *Pres.* Richard Brown, Georgetown; *Pres.-Elect* MaryKatherine Callaway, Louisiana State; *Exec. Dir.* Peter J. Givler. E-mail pgivler@aaupnet.org.

Assn. of Booksellers for Children (ABC). See American Booksellers Assn.

Assn. of Canadian Publishers, 174 Spadina Ave., Suite 306, Toronto, ON M5T 2C2. Tel. 416-487-6116, fax 416-487-8815, World Wide Web http://www.publishers.ca. *Pres.* Margie Wolfe, Second Story Press, 20 Maud St., Suite 401, Toronto, ON M5V 2M5. Tel. 416-537-7850, fax 416-537-0588, e-mail margie@secondstorypress.ca; *V.P.* Bill Harnum, Dept. of Publications, Pontifical Institute of Mediaeval Studies, 59 Queen's Park Crescent E., Toronto, ON M5S 2C4. Tel. 416-926-7144, fax 416-926-7258, e-mail bill.harnum@sympatico.ca; *Exec. Dir.* Carolyn Wood. Tel. 416-487-6116 ext. 222, e-mail carolyn_wood@canbook.org.

Assn. of Catholic Publishers, 11703 Huebner Rd., Suite 106-622, San Antonio, TX 78230. Tel. 210-368-2055, fax 210-368-2601, e-mail cliffk@catholic-publishers.org, World Wide Web http://www.catholic-publishers.org and http://www.catholicsread.org. *Pres.* Jeff Smith; *Exec. Dir.* Cliff Knighten.

Assn. of Educational Publishers (AEP), 300 Martin Luther King Blvd., Suite 200, Wilmington, DE 19801. Tel. 302-295-8350, fax 302-778-1110, e-mail mail@aepweb.org, World Wide Web http://www.aepweb.org. *Pres.* Dan Caton; *Pres.-Elect* Neal Goff; *V.P.* Lee Wilson; *Treas.* Kevin McAliley; *Past Pres.* Suzanne Barchers; *CEO* Charlene F. Gaynor. E-mail cgaynor@aepweb.org.

Authors Guild, 31 E. 32 St., Seventh fl., New York, NY 10016. Tel. 212-563-5904, fax 212-564-5363, e-mail staff@authorsguild.org, World Wide Web http://www.authorsguild.org. *Pres.* Scott Turow.

Book Industry Study Group, 370 Lexington Ave., Suite 900, New York, NY 10017. Tel. 646-336-7141, fax 646-336-6214, e-mail info@bisg.org, World Wide Web http://www.bisg.org. *Chair* Dominique Raccah, Sourcebooks; *Deputy Exec. Dir.* Angela Bole. E-mail angela@bisg.org.

Book Manufacturers' Institute, 2 Armand Beach Drive, Suite 1B, Palm Coast, FL 32137. Tel. 386-986-4552, fax 386-986-4553, e-mail info@bmibook.com, World Wide Web http://www.bmibook.org. *Pres.* James F. Conway III; *V.P./Pres.-Elect* Mike Collinge; *Exec. V.P./Secy.* Daniel M. Bach. Address correspondence to the executive vice president.

Bookbuilders of Boston, 44 Vinal Rd., Scituate, MA 02066. Tel. 781-378-1361, fax 419-821-2171, e-mail office@bbboston.org, World Wide Web http://www.bbboston.org. *Pres.* Kirsten Sims. E-mail kirsten.sims@perason.com; *1st V.P.* Mike Ribaudo. E-mail mike@kaseprinting.com; *2nd V.P.* Michael Mozina. E-mail mmozina@brillusa.com; *Treas.* Scott Payne. E-mail scott_payne@malloy.com; *Clerk* Chris Hartman. E-mail Hartman.cg@gmail.com.

Bookbuilders West, 9328 Elk Grove Blvd., Suite 105, Elk Grove, CA 95624. Tel. 415-670-9564, e-mail operations@bookbuilders.org, World Wide Web http://www.bookbuilders.org. *Pres.* Andrea Helmbolt, McGraw-Hill. E-mail andrea_helmbolt@mcgraw-hill.com; *V.P.* Bill Ralph, Malloy, Inc. E-mail bill_ralph@malloy.com.

Canadian Booksellers Assn., 1255 Bay St., Suite 902, Toronto, ON M5R 2A9. Tel. 866-788-0790, e-mail enquiries@cbabook.org, World Wide Web http://www.cbabook.org. *Pres.* Mark Lefebvre, Titles Bookstore, McMaster Univ., Hamilton, Ontario. E-mail lefebvr@mcmaster.ca; *V.P.* Lee Trentadue, Galiano Island Books, Galiano Island, British Columbia. E-mail lee@galianoislandbooks.com; *Senior Mgr.* Jodi White. Tel. 416-467-7883 ext. 227, e-mail jwhite@cbabook.org.

Canadian ISBN Agency, c/o Published Heritage, Library and Archives Canada, 395 Wellington St., Ottawa, ON K1A 0N4. Tel. 866-578-7777 (toll-free) or 613-996-5115, World Wide Web http://www.collectionscanada.ca/isn/index-e.html.

Canadian Printing Industries Association, 151 Slater St., Suite 1110, Ottawa, ON K1P 5H3. Tel. 613-236-7208, fax 613-232-1334, e-mail belliott@cpia-aci.ca, World Wide Web http://www.cpia-aci.ca. *Pres.* Bob Elliott; *Chair* Dean McElhinney, Unicom Graphics Ltd.

Catholic Book Publishers Assn. See Assn. of Catholic Publishers.

Chicago Book Clinic, 310 W. Lake St., Suite 111, Elmhurst, IL 60126. Tel. 630-833-4220, fax 630-563-9181, e-mail klabounty@apexmanage.com, World Wide Web http://www.chicagobookclinic.org. *Pres.* Eric Platou. E-mail eric_platou@malloy.com; *V.P.* Jason Berg. E-mail jberg@precisiongraphics.com; *Contact* Kimberly LaBounty, Apex Management and Special Events. E-mail klabounty@apexmanage.com or cbc@apexmanage.com.

Children's Book Council, 54 W. 39 St., 14th fl., New York, NY 10018. Tel. 212-966-1990, fax 212-966-2073, e-mail cbc.info@cbcbooks.org, World Wide Web http://www.cbcbooks.org. *Chair* Megan Tingley; *V. Chair* Nancy Feresten; *Secy.* Don Weisberg; *Treas.* Justin Chanda; *Exec. Dir.* Robin Adelson. E-mail robin.adelson@cbcbooks.org.

Copyright Society of the USA, 352 Seventh Ave., Suite 739, New York, NY 10001. World Wide Web http://www.csusa.org. *Pres.* Corey Field; *V.P./Pres.-Elect* Joseph Salvo; *Secy.* Nancy Wolff; *Treas.* Eric Scwartz; *Dir.* Amy Nickerson. E-mail amy@csusa.org.

Council of Literary Magazines and Presses, 154 Christopher St., Suite 3C, New York, NY 10014. Tel. 212-741-9110, fax 212-741-9112, e-mail info@clmp.org, World Wide Web http://www.clmp.org. *Co-chairpersons* Gerald Howard, Nicole Dewey; *Exec. Dir.* Jeffrey Lependorf. E-mail jlependorf@clmp.org.

Educational Book and Media Assn. (formerly Educational Paperback Assn.), P.O. Box 3363, Warrenton, VA 20188. Tel. 540-318-7770, e-mail bgorg@edupaperback.org, World Wide Web http://www.edupaperback.org. *Pres.* Dan Walsh; *V.P.*

Tim Thompson; *Treas.* Gene Bahlman; *Exec. Secy.* Brian Gorg.

Evangelical Christian Publishers Assn., 9633 S. 48 St., Suite 140, Phoenix, AZ 85044. Tel. 480-966-3998, fax 480-966-1944, e-mail info@ecpa.org, World Wide Web http://www.ecpa.org. *Pres./CEO* Mark W. Kuyper; *Chair* Cris Doornbos.

Graphic Artists Guild, 32 Broadway, Suite 1114, New York, NY 10004. Tel. 212-791-3400, fax 212-792-0333, e-mail admin @gag.org, World Wide Web http://www.graphicartistsguild.org. *Pres.* Haydn S. Adams. E-mail president@gag.org; *Exec. Dir.* Patricia McKiernan. E-mail admin@gag.org.

Great Lakes Independent Booksellers Assn., c/o *Exec. Dir.* Deb Leonard, Box 901, 208 Franklin St., Grand Haven, MI 49417. Tel. 800-745-2460, fax 616-842-0051, e-mail deb@gliba.org, World Wide Web http://www.gliba.org. *Pres.* Cynthia Compton. E-mail kidsbooks4@msn.com; *V.P.* Matthew Norcross. E-mail mnorcross@mcleanandeakin.com; *Past Pres.* Sally Bulthuis. E-mail poohs@iserv.net.

Guild of Book Workers, 521 Fifth Ave., New York, NY 10175. Tel. 212-292-4444, e-mail communications@guildofbookworkers.org, World Wide Web http://www.guildofbookworkers.org. *Pres.* Andrew Huot. E-mail president@guildofbookworkers.org; *V.P.* Anna Embree. E-mail vicepresident@guildofbookworkers.org.

Horror Writers Assn., 244 Fifth Ave., Suite 2767, New York, NY 10001. E-mail hwa @horror.org, World Wide Web http://www.horror.org. *Pres.* Rocky Wood. E-mail president@horror.org; *V.P.* Heather Graham. E-mail vp@horror.org; *Secy.* Vince Liaguno. E-mail secretary@horror.org; *Treas.* Lisa Morton. E-mail treasurer @horror.org.

IAPHC—The Graphic Professionals Resource Network (formerly the International Assn. of Printing House Craftsmen), P.O. Box 2549, Maple Grove, MN 55311-7549. Tel. 800-466-4274, 763-560-1620, fax 763-560-1350, e-mail headquarters@iaphc.org, World Wide Web http://www.iaphc.org. *Pres./CEO* Kevin Keane. E-mail headquaters@iaphc.com.

Independent Book Publishers Association (formerly PMA), 627 Aviation Way, Manhattan Beach, CA 90266. Tel. 310-372-2732, fax 310-374-3342, e-mail info@ibpa-online.org, World Wide Web http://www.ibpa-online.org. *Pres.* Florrie Binford Kichler. E-mail florrie@ibpa-online.org; *Exec. Dir.* Terry Nathan. E-mail terry@ibpa-online.org.

International Standard Book Numbering U.S. Agency, 630 Central Ave., New Providence, NJ 07974. Tel. 888-269-5372, fax 908-219-0188, e-mail isbn-san@bowker.com, World Wide Web http://www.isbn.org. *Dir., Identifier Services* Beat Barblan; *Dir.* Louise Timko.

Jewish Book Council, 520 Eighth Ave., Fourth fl., New York, NY 10010. Tel. 212-201-2920, fax 212-532-4952, e-mail jbc@jewishbooks.org, World Wide Web http://www.jewishbookcouncil.org. *Pres.* Lawrence J. Krule; *V.P.s* Harry L. Freund, Judith Lieberman; *Secy.* Mimi S. Frank; *Dir.* Carolyn Starman Hessel.

Library Binding Institute/Hardcover Binders International, 4400 PGA Blvd., Suite 600, Palm Beach Gardens, FL 33410. Tel. 561-745-6821, fax 561-775-0089, e-mail info @lbibinders.org, World Wide Web http://www.lbibinders.org. *Pres.* Mark Hancock, Utah Bookbinding. E-mail mark@utahbookbinding.com; *V.P.* Jack Tolbert, National Lib. Bindery Co. of Georgia. E-mail nlbga@mindspring.com; *Exec. Dir.* Debra Nolan. E-mail dnolan@hardcoverbinders.org.

Midwest Booksellers Association, 2355 Louisiana Ave. N., Suite A, Golden Valley, MN 55427. Tel. 763-544-2993 or 800-784-7522, fax 763-544-2266, e-mail info @midwestbooksellers.org. *Exec. Dir.* Carrie Obry. E-mail carrie@midwestbooksellers.org.

Midwest Independent Publishers Assn., P.O. Box 65686, St. Paul, MN 55165. Tel. 651-917-0021 or 651-797-3801, World Wide Web http://www.mipa.org. *Pres.* Seal Dwyer, North Star Press, P.O. Box 451, St. Cloud, MN 56302. Tel. 320-558-9062, e-mail info@northstarpress.com; *V.P.*

Dorothy Molstad, Molstad Marketing. Tel. 651-342-0447, e-mail dendoor@aol.com; *Secy.* Sheyna Galyan, Yaldah Publishing. Tel. 651-470-3853, e-mail publisher@yaldapublishing.com; *Treas.* Dorie McClelland, Spring Book Design. Tel. 651-457-0258, e-mail +doriem@springbookdesign.com.

Miniature Book Society. *Pres.* Mark Palkovic. E-mail mark.palkovic@uc.edu; *V.P.* Stephen Byrne. E-mail sb@finalscore.demon.co.uk; *Secy.* Edward Hoyenski. E-mail ehoyensk@library.unt.edu; *Treas.* Karen Nyman. E-mail karennyman@cox.net; *Past Pres.* Julian I. Edison. E-mail jiestl@mac.com. World Wide Web http://www.mbs.org.

Minnesota Book Publishers Roundtable. *Pres.* Dan Wallek, Lerner Publishing Group, 241 First Ave. N., Minneapolis 55401. Tel. 612-215-6220, fax 612-332-7615, e-mail dwallek@lernerbooks.com; *V.P.* Ben Barnhart, Milkweed Editions, e-mail ben_barnhart@milkweed.org. World Wide Web http://www.publishersroundtable.org.

Mountains and Plains Independent Booksellers Assn., 8020 Springshire Drive, Park City, UT 84098. Tel. 800-752-0249 or 435-649-6079, fax 435-649-6105, e-mail laura@mountainsplains.org, World Wide Web http://www.mountainsplains.org. *Pres.* Meghan Goel, BookPeople Bookstore, 603 N. Lamar Blvd., Austin, TX 78703. Tel. 512-472-5050, fax 512-482-8495, e-mail kids_buyer@bookpeople.com; *V.P./Secy.* Nicole Magistro, Bookworm of Edwards, 295 Main St., Unit C101, Edwards, CO 81632. Tel. 970-926-7323, fax 970-926-7324, e-mail nicole@bookwormofedwards.com; *Exec. Dir.* Laura Ayrey.

MPA—The Assn. of Magazine Media (formerly Magazine Publishers of America), 810 Seventh Ave., 24th fl., New York, NY 10019. Tel. 212-872-3700, e-mail mpa@magazine.org, World Wide Web http://www.magazine.org. *Pres./CEO* Nina Link. Tel. 212-872-3710, e-mail president@magazine.org.

NAPL (formerly National Assn. for Printing Leadership), 75 W. Century Rd., Suite 100, Paramus, NJ 07652. Tel. 800-642-6275, 201-634-9600, fax 201-634-0324, e-mail info@napl.org, World Wide Web http://www.napl.org. *Pres./CEO* Joseph P. Truncale. E-mail jtruncale@napl.org.

National Assn. of College Stores, 500 E. Lorain St., Oberlin, OH 44074-1294. Tel. 800-622-7498, 440-775-7777, fax 440-775-4769, e-mail info@nacs.org, World Wide Web http://www.nacs.org. *Pres.* Danny A. Key; *Pres.-Elect* Mary Ellen Martin; *CEO* Brian Cartier. E-mail bcartier@nacs.org.

National Coalition Against Censorship (NCAC), 19 Fulton St., Suite 407, New York, NY 10038. Tel. 212-807-6222, fax 212-807-6245, e-mail ncac@ncac.org, World Wide Web http://www.ncac.org. *Exec. Dir.* Joan E. Bertin; *Dirs.* Judy Blume, Susan Clare, Chris Finan, Eric M. Freedman, Stephanie Elizondo Griest, Phil Harvey, George Kannar, Chris Peterson, Larry Siems, Emily Whitfield.

New Atlantic Independent Booksellers Assn. (NAIBA), 2667 Hyacinth St., Westbury, NY 11590. Tel. 516-333-0681, fax 516-333-0689, e-mail info@naiba.com, World Wide Web http://www.newatlanticbooks.com. *Pres.* Lucy Kogler, Talking Leaves, Inc., 951 Elmwood Ave., Buffalo, NY 14222. Tel. 716-884-9524, fax 716-332-3625, e-mail lucyk@tleavesbooks.com; *V.P.* Margot Sage-El, Watchung Booksellers, Watchung Plaza, 54 Fairfield St., Montclair, NJ 07042. Tel. 973-744-7177, fax 973-783-5899, e-mail margot@watchungbooksellers.com; *Exec. Dir.* Eileen Dengler.

New England Independent Booksellers Assn., 297 Broadway, Arlington, MA 02474. Tel. 781-316-8894, fax 781-316-2605, e-mail steve@neba.org, World Wide Web http://www.newenglandbooks.org. *Pres.* Dick Hermans; *V.P.* Annie Philbrick; *Treas.* Lisa Sullivan; *Exec. Dir.* Steve Fischer.

New York Center for Independent Publishing (formerly the Small Press Center), c/o General Society Lib., 20 W. 44 St., New York, NY 10036. Tel. 212-921-1767, fax 212-840-2046, e-mail library@generalsociety.org, World Wide Web http://nycip.wordpress.com.

North American Bookdealers Exchange (NABE), Box 606, Cottage Grove, OR 97424. Tel./fax 541-942-7455, e-mail nabe@bookmarketingprofits.com, World Wide Web http://bookmarketingprofits.com. *Dir.* Al Galasso.

Northern California Independent Booksellers Assn., Presidio National Park, 1007 General Kennedy Ave., P.O. Box 29169, San Francisco, CA 94129. Tel. 415-561-7686, fax 415-561-7685, e-mail office@nciba.com, World Wide Web http://www.nciba.com. *Pres.* Michael Barnard; *V.P.* Calvin Crosby; *Exec. Dir.* Hut Landon.

Pacific Northwest Booksellers Assn., 338 W. 11 Ave., Eugene, OR 97401-3062. Tel. 541-683-4363, fax 541-683-3910, e-mail info@pnba.org, World Wide Web http://www.pnba.org, blog Northwest Book Lovers (http://www.nwbooklovers.org). *Pres.* Sylla McLellan, Third Street Books. E-mail sylla@thirdstreetbooks.com; *Exec. Dir.* Thom Chambliss.

PEN American Center, Div. of International PEN, 588 Broadway, Suite 303, New York, NY 10012. Tel. 212-334-1660, fax 212-334-2181, e-mail pen@pen.org, World Wide Web http://www.pen.org. *Pres.* Kwame Anthony Appiah; *Exec. V.P.* Laurence J. Kirshbaum; *V.P.s* Jessica Hagedorn, Victoria Redel; *Secy.* Roxana Robinson; *Treas.* Maria Campbell; *Exec. Dir.* Steven L. Isenberg. E-mail sisenberg@pen.org.

Periodical and Book Assn. of America, 481 Eighth Ave., Suite 826, New York, NY 10001. Tel. 212-563-6502, fax 212-563-4098, e-mail info@pbaa.net, World Wide Web http://www.pbaa.net. *Pres.* Joe Gallo. E-mail jgallo@ffn.com; *V.P.* Amy Burns. E-mail acbservices@nyc.rr.com; *Chair* William Michalopoulos. E-mail wmichalopoulos@hfmus.com; *Exec. Dir.* Lisa W. Scott. E-mail lscott@pbaa.net or lisawscott@hotmail .com.

Romance Writers of America, 14615 Benfer Rd., Houston, TX 77069. Tel. 832-717-5200, fax 832-717-5201, e-mail info@rwa.org, World Wide Web http://www.rwa.org. *Pres.* Dorien Kelly. E-mail president@rwa.org; *Exec. Dir.* Allison Kelley. E-mail allison.kelley@rwa.org.

Science Fiction and Fantasy Writers of America, P.O. Box 877, Chestertown, MD 21620. E-mail execdir@sfwa.org, World Wide Web http://www.sfwa.org. *Pres.* John Scalzi. E-mail president@sfwa.org; *V.P.* Mary Robinette Kowal. E-mail vp@sfwa.org; *Secy.* Robert J. Howe. E-mail secretary@sfwa.org; *Treas.* Amy Sterling Casil. E-mail treasurer@sfwa.org.

Small Publishers Assn. of North America (SPAN), 1618 W. Colorado Ave., Colorado Springs, CO 80904. Tel. 719-475-1726, e-mail info1@spannet.org, World Wide Web http://www.spannet.org. *Exec. Dir.* Scott Flora.

Society of Children's Book Writers and Illustrators (SCBWI), 8271 Beverly Blvd., Los Angeles, CA 90048. Tel. 323-782-1010, fax 323-782-1892, e-mail scbwi@scbwi.org, World Wide Web http://www.scbwi.org. *Pres.* Stephen Mooser. E-mail stephenmooser@scbwi.org; *Exec. Dir.* Lin Oliver.

Society of Illustrators (SI), 128 E. 63 St., New York, NY 10065. Tel. 212-838-2560, fax 212-838-2561, e-mail info@societyillustrators.org, World Wide Web http://www.societyillustrators.org. *Pres.* Dennis Dittrich; *Exec. V.P.* Tim O'Brien; *V.P.* Victor Juhasz; *Secy.* Joan Chiverton; *Treas.* Scott Bakal; *Assoc. Treas.* David Reuss; *Past Pres.* Richard Berenson.

Southern Independent Booksellers Alliance (SIBA), 3806 Yale Ave., Columbia, SC 29205. Tel. 803-994-9530, fax 309-410-0211, e-mail info@sibaweb.com, World Wide Web http://www.sibaweb.com. *Exec. Dir.* Wanda Jewell.

Technical Assn. of the Pulp and Paper Industry, 15 Technology Pkwy. S., Norcross, GA 30092 (P.O. Box 105113, Atlanta, GA 30348). Tel. 770-446-1400, fax 770-446-6947, World Wide Web http://www.tappi.org. *Pres.* Larry N. Montague. E-mail lmontague@tappi.org; *Chair* Jeffrey J. Siegel; *V. Chair* Norman F. Marsolan.

Western Writers of America, c/o Paul A. Hutton, MSC06 3770, 1 Univ. of New Mexico, Albuquerque, NM 87131-0001. Tel. 505-277-5234, e-mail wwa@unm.edu, World Wide Web http://www.westernwriters.org. *Pres.* Robert J. Conley; *V.P.*

Dusty Richards; *Exec. Dir./Secy.-Treas.* Paul A. Hutton.

Women's National Book Assn., c/o Susannah Greenberg Public Relations, P.O. Box 237, FDR Sta., New York, NY 10150. Tel./fax 212-208-4629, e-mail publicity@bookbuzz.com, World Wide Web http://www.wnba-books.org. *Pres.* Mary Grey James; *V.P./Pres.-Elect* Valerie Tomaselli; *Secy.* Ruth Light; *Treas.* Margaret E. Auer.

International and Foreign Book Trade Associations

For Canadian book trade associations, see the preceding section, "Book Trade Associations, United States and Canada." For a more extensive list of book trade organizations outside the United States and Canada, with more detailed information, consult *International Literary Market Place* (Information Today, Inc.), which also provides extensive lists of major bookstores and publishers in each country.

International

African Publishers' Network, BP 3429, Abidjan 01, Côte d'Ivoire. Tel. 202-11801, fax 202-11803, e-mail apnet@zol.co.zw, World Wide Web http://www.African-publishers.net. *Chair* Mamadou Aliou Sow; *Exec. Secy.* Akin Fasemore.

Afro-Asian Book Council, 4835/24 Ansari Rd., New Delhi 110002, India. Tel. 11-2325-8865, fax 11-2326-7437, e-mail afro@aabcouncil.org, World Wide Web http://www.aabcouncil.org. *Secy.-Gen.* Sukumar Das; *Dir.* Saumya Gupta.

Centro Régional para el Fomento del Libro en América Latina y el Caribe (CERLALC) (Regional Center for Book Promotion in Latin America and the Caribbean), Calle 70, No. 9-52, Bogotá DC, Colombia. Tel. 1-540-2071, fax 1-541-6398, e-mail libro@cerlalc.com, World Wide Web http://www.cerlalc.org. *Dir.* Fernando Zapata Lopez.

Federation of European Publishers, rue Montoyer 31, Boîte 8, 1000 Brussels, Belgium. Tel. 2-770-11-10, fax 2-771-20-71, e-mail info@fep-fee.eu, World Wide Web http://www.fep-fee.be. *Pres.* Frederico Motto; *Dir.-Gen.* Anne Bergman-Tahon.

International Assn. of Scientific, Technical, and Medical Publishers (STM), Prama House, 267 Banbury Rd., Oxford OX2 7HT, England. Tel. 44-1865-339-321, fax 44-1865-339-325, e-mail info@stm-assoc.org, World Wide Web http://www.stm-assoc.org. *Chair* Jerry Cowhig; *CEO* Michael Mabe.

International Board on Books for Young People (IBBY), Nonnenweg 12, 4003 Basel, Switzerland. Tel. 61-272-29-17, fax 61-272-27-57, e-mail ibby@ibby.org, World Wide Web http://www.ibby.org. *Exec. Dir.* Elizabeth Page.

International Booksellers Federation (IBF), rue de la Science 10, 1000 Brussels, Belgium. Tel. 2-223-49-40, fax 2-223-49-38, e-mail ibf.booksellers@skynet.be, World Wide Web http://www.ibf-booksellers.org. *Dir.* Françoise Dubruille.

International League of Antiquarian Booksellers (ILAB), c/o 112 Glebe Point Rd., Sydney, NSW 2037, Australia. Tel. 2-9660-4889, fax 2-9552 2670, World Wide Web http://www.ilab.org. *Pres.* Adrian Harrington; *Gen. Secy.* Paul Feain.

International Publishers Assn. (Union Internationale des Editeurs), ave. de Miremont 3, CH-1206 Geneva, Switzerland. Tel. 22-704-1820, fax 22-704-1821, e-mail secretariat@internationalpublishers.org, World Wide Web http://www.international publishers.org. *Pres.* Y. S. Chi; *Secy.-Gen.* Jens Bammel.

National

Argentina

Cámara Argentina del Libro (Argentine Book Assn.), Av. Belgrano 1580, 4° piso, C1093AAQ Buenos Aires. Tel. 11-4381-8383, fax 11-4381-9253, e-mail cal@editores.org.ar, World Wide Web http://www.editores.org.ar. *Dir.* Norberto J. Pou.

Fundación El Libro (Book Foundation), Hipolito Yrigoyen 1628, 5 piso, C1089AAF Buenos Aires. Tel. 11-4370-0600, fax 11-4370-0607, e-mail fundacion@el-libro.com.ar, World Wide Web http://www.el-libro.com.ar. *Pres.* Horacio Garcia; *Dir.* Marta V. Diaz.

Australia

Australian and New Zealand Assn. of Antiquarian Booksellers, P.O. Box 7127, McMahons Point, NSW 2060. Tel. 2-9966-9925, fax 2-9966-9926, e-mail admin@anzaab.com, World Wide Web http://www.anzaab.com. *Pres.* Peter Tinslay. E-mail peter@antiquebookshop.com.au.

Australian Booksellers Assn., 828 High St., Unit 9, Kew East, Vic. 3102. Tel. 3-9859-7322, fax 3-9859-7344, e-mail mail@aba.org.au, World Wide Web http://www.aba.org.au. *Pres.* Fiona Stager; *CEO* Malcolm Neil.

Australian Publishers Assn., 60/89 Jones St., Ultimo, NSW 2007. Tel. 2-9281-9788, fax 2-9281-1073, e-mail apa@publishers.asn.au, World Wide Web http://www.publishers.asn.au. *CEO* Maree McCaskill.

Austria

Hauptverband des Österreichischen Buchhandels (Austrian Publishers and Booksellers Assn.), Grünangergasse 4, A-1010 Vienna. Tel. 1-512-15-35, fax 1-512-84-82, e-mail sekretariat@hvb.at, World Wide Web http://www.buecher.at. *Mgr.* Inge Kralupper.

Verband der Antiquare Österreichs (Austrian Antiquarian Booksellers Assn.), Grünangergasse 4, A-1010 Vienna. Tel. 1-512-15-35, fax 1-512-84-82, e-mail sekretariat@hvb.at, World Wide Web http://www.antiquare.at. *Pres.* Norbert Donhofer.

Belarus

National Book Chamber of Belarus, 31a V Khoruzhei Str., 220002 Minsk. Tel. 17-289-33-96, fax 17-334-78-47, World Wide Web http://www.natbook.org.by. *Dir.* Elena V. Ivanova.

Belgium

Vlaamse Boekverkopersbond (Flemish Booksellers Assn.), Te Buelaerlei 37, 2140 Borgerhout. Tel. 03-230-89-23, fax 3-281-22-40, World Wide Web http://www.boek.be. *Contact* Luc Tessens.

Bolivia

Cámara Boliviana del Libro (Bolivian Booksellers Assn.), Calle Capitan Ravelo No. 2116, 682 La Paz. Tel. 2-211-3264, e-mail cabolib@entelnet.bo, World Wide Web http://www.cabolib.org.bo. *Gen. Mgr.* Ana Patricia Navarro.

Brazil

Cámara Brasileira do Livro (Brazilian Book Assn.), Rua Cristiano Viana 91, Pinheiros 05411-000 Sao Paulo-SP. Tel./fax 11-3069-1300, e-mail cbl@cbl.org.br, World Wide Web http://www.cbl.org.br. *Pres.* Rosely Boschini.

Sindicato Nacional dos Editores de Livros (Brazilian Publishers Assn.), Rue da Ajuda 35-18 andar, 20040-000 Rio de Janeiro-RJ. Tel. 21-2533-0399, fax 21-2533-0422, e-mail snel@snel.org.br, World Wide Web http://www.snel.org.br. *Pres.* Sonia Machado Jardim.

Chile

Cámara Chilena del Libro AG (Chilean Assn. of Publishers, Distributors, and Booksellers), Av. Libertador Bernardo O'Higgins 1370, Oficina 501, Santiago. Tel. 2-672-0348, fax 2-687-4271, e-mail prolibro@tie.cl, World Wide Web http://www.camlibro.cl. *Pres.* Eduardo Castillo Garcia.

Colombia

Cámara Colombiana del Libro (Colombian Book Assn.), Calle 35, No. 5A 05, Bogotá. Tel. 1-323-01-11, fax 1-285-10-82, e-mail camlibro@camlibro.com.co, World Wide Web http://www.camlibro.com.co. *Pres.* Enrique Gonzalez Villa.

Czech Republic

Svaz českých knihkupců a nakladatelů (Czech Publishers and Booksellers Assn.), P.O. Box 177, 110 01 Prague. Tel. 224-219-944, fax 224-219-942, e-mail sckn@sckn.

cz, World Wide Web http://www.sckn.cz. *Secy.* Ludek Blazek.

Denmark

Danske Boghandlerforening (Danish Booksellers Assn.), Langebrogade 6 opgang J, 1 sal, 1411 Copenhagen K. Tel. 32-54-22-55, fax 32-54-00-41, e-mail ddb@bogpost.dk, World Wide Web http://www.bogguide.dk. *Dir.* Olaf Winslow.

Danske Forlæggerforening (Danish Publishers Assn.), Exchange DK-1217, Copenhagen K. Tel. 33-15-66-88, fax 33-15-65-88, e-mail danishpublishers@danishpublishers.dk, World Wide Web http://www.danskeforlag.dk. *Dir.* Christine Bødtcher-Hansen.

Ecuador

Cámara Ecuatoriana del Libro, Núcleo de Pichincha, Avda. Eloy Alfaro, N29-61 e Inglaterra, Edf. Eloy Alfaro, 9 no. piso, Quito. Tel. 2-553-311, fax 2-222-150, e-mail celnp@uio.satnet.net, World Wide Web http://celibro.org.ec. *Pres.* Fabian Luzuriaga.

Egypt

General Egyptian Book Organization, P.O. Box 235, Cornich El-Nil, Ramlat Boulaq, Cairo 11511. Tel. 2-2577-531, fax 2-5754-213, e-mail info@egyptianbook.org.eg, World Wide Web http://www.egyptianbook.org.eg. *Chair* Nasser Al-Ansary.

Estonia

Estonian Publishers Assn., Roosikrantsi 6, 10119 Tallinn. Tel. 644-9866, fax 617-7550, e-mail kirjastusteliit@eki.ee, World Wide Web http://www.estbook.com. *Dir.* Kaidi Urmet.

Finland

Kirjakauppaliitto Ry (Booksellers Assn. of Finland), Urho Kekkosen Katu 8 C 34b, 00100 Helsinki. Tel. 9-6859-9110, fax 9-6859-9119, e-mail toimisto@kirjakauppaliitto.fi, World Wide Web http://www.kirjakauppaliitto.fi. *Pres.* Tuula Korte; *Managing Dir.* Jarmo Oksaharju.

Suomen Kustannusyhdistys (Finnish Book Publishers Assn.), P.O. Box 177, Lönnrotinkatu 11 A, FIN-00121 Helsinki. Tel. 358-9-228-77-250, fax 358-9-612-1226, World Wide Web http://www.publishers.fi/en. *Pres.* Veli-Pekka Elonen; *Dir.* Sakari Laiho.

France

Bureau International de l'Edition Française (BIEF) (International Bureau of French Publishing), 115 blvd. Saint-Germain, F-75006 Paris. Tel. 01-44-41-13-13, fax 01-46-34-63-83, e-mail accueil_bief@bief.org, World Wide Web http://www.bief.org. *CEO* Jean-Guy Boin. *New York Branch* French Publishers Agency, 853 Broadway, Suite 1509, New York, NY 10003-4703. Tel./fax 212-254-4540, World Wide Web http://frenchpubagency.com.

Cercle de la Librairie (Circle of Professionals of the Book Trade), 35 rue Grégoire-de-Tours, F-75006 Paris. Tel. 01-44-41-28-05, fax 01-44-41-28-19, World Wide Web http://www.electre.com.

Syndicat de la Librairie Française, Hotel de Massa, 38 rue du Faubourg Saint-Jacques, F-75014 Paris. Tel. 01-53-62-23-10, fax 01-53-62-10-45, e-mail contact@union-librarie.fr, World Wide Web http://www.syndicat-librairie.fr. *Pres.* Benoit Bougerol.

Syndicat National de la Librairie Ancienne et Moderne (SLAM) (National Assn. of Antiquarian and Modern Booksellers), 4 rue Gît-le-Coeur, F-75006 Paris. Tel. 1-43-29-46-38, fax 1-43-25-41-63, e-mail slam-livre@wanadoo.fr, World Wide Web http://www.slam-livre.fr. *Pres.* Frederic Castaing.

Syndicat National de l'Edition (SNE) (National Union of Publishers), 115 blvd. Saint-Germain, F-75006 Paris. Tel. 1-44-41-40-50, fax 01-44-41-40-77, World Wide Web http://www.sne.fr. *Pres.* Serge Eyrolles.

Germany

Börsenverein des Deutschen Buchhandels e.V. (Stock Exchange of German Booksellers), Grosser Hirschgraben 17-21, 60311 Frankfurt-am-Main. Tel. 69-13-06-0, fax 069-13-06-201, e-mail info@boev.de, World Wide Web http://www.boersenverein.de.

Verband Deutscher Antiquare e.V. (German Antiquarian Booksellers Assn.), Geschäftsstelle, Seeblick 1, 56459 Elbingen. Tel. 6435-90-91-47, fax 6435-90-91-48, e-mail buch@antiquare.de, World Wide Web http://www.antiquare.de. *Pres.* Eberhard Koestler.

Greece

Hellenic Federation of Publishers and Booksellers, 73 Themistocleous St., 106 83 Athens. Tel. 2103-300-924, fax 2133-301-617, e-mail secretary@poev.gr, World Wide Web http://www.poev.gr. *Pres.* Annie Ragia.

Hungary

Magyar Könyvkiadók és Könyvterjesztök Egyesülése (Assn. of Hungarian Publishers and Booksellers), Postfach 130, 1367 Budapest. Tel. 1-343-2540, fax 1-343-2541, e-mail mkke@mkke.hu, World Wide Web http://www.mkke.hu. *Dir.* Istvan Bart.

Iceland

Félag Islenskra Bókaútgefenda (Icelandic Publishers Assn.), Baronsstig 5, 101 Reykjavik. Tel. 511-8020, fax 511-5020, e-mail baekur@simnet.is, World Wide Web http://www.bokautgafa.is.

India

Federation of Indian Publishers, Federation House, 18/1C Institutional Area, Aruna Asaf Ali Marg, New Delhi 110067. Tel. 11-2696-4847, fax 11-2686-4054, e-mail fip1@satyam.net.in, World Wide Web http://www.fipindia.org. *Pres.* Anand Bhushan.

Indonesia

Ikatan Penerbit Indonesia (Assn. of Indonesian Book Publishers), Jl. Kalipasir 32, Jakarta 10330. Tel. 21-314-1907, fax 21-314-6050, e-mail ikapi@cbn.net.id, World Wide Web http://www.ikapi.org. *Pres.* Dharma Madjid; *Secy.-Gen.* Wanti Syaifullah.

Ireland

Publishing Ireland (formerly CLÉ: The Irish Book Publishers' Assn.), Guinness Enterprise Centre, Taylor's Lane, Dublin 8. Tel. 1-415-1210, e-mail info@publishingireland.com, World Wide Web http://www.publishingireland.com. *Pres.* Alan Hayes.

Israel

Book and Printing Center, Israel Export and International Cooperation Institute, P.O. Box 50084, 61500 Tel Aviv. Tel. 3-514-2855, fax 3-514-2881, e-mail export-institute@export.gov.il, World Wide Web http://www.export.gov.il. *Dir.-Gen.* Avi Hefetz.

Book Publishers' Assn. of Israel, P.O. Box 20123, 61201 Tel Aviv. Tel. 3-561-4121, fax 3-561-1996, e-mail hamol@tbpai.co.il, World Wide Web http://www.tbpai.co.il. *Managing Dir.* Amnon Ben-Shmuel, *Chair* Yaron Sadan.

Italy

Associazione Italiana Editori (Italian Publishers Assn.), Corso di Porta Romana 108, 20122 Milan. Tel. 2-89-28-0800, fax 2-89-28-0860, e-mail aie@aie.it, World Wide Web http://www.aie.it. *Dir.* Ivan Cecchini.

Associazione Librai Antiquari d'Italia (Antiquarian Booksellers Assn. of Italy), Via Cassia 1020, Rome. Tel. 39-347-64-6-9147, fax 39-06-2332-8979, e-mail alai@alai.it, World Wide Web http://www.alai.it. *Pres.* Umberto Pregliasco.

Japan

Antiquarian Booksellers Assn. of Japan, 29 San-ei-cho, Shinjuku-ku, Tokyo 160-0008. Tel. 3-3357-1412, fax 3-3351-5855, e-mail abaj@abaj.gr.jp, World Wide Web http://www.abaj.gr.jp. *Pres.* Takehiko Sakai.

Japan Assn. of International Publications (formerly Japan Book Importers Assn.), c/o UPS, 1-32-5 Higashi-shinagawa, Shinagawa-ku, Toyko 140-0002. Tel. 3-5479-7269, fax 3-5479-7307, e-mail office@jaip.jp, World Wide Web http://www.jaip.gr.jp. *Exec. Dir.* Takashi Yamakawa; *Dir.* Mark Gresham.

Japan Book Publishers Assn., 6 Fukuromachi, Shinjuku-ku, Tokyo 162-0828. Tel. 3-3268-1303, fax 3-3268-1196, e-mail rd@jbpa.or.jp, World Wide Web http://www.jbpa.or.jp. *Pres.* Norio Komine; *Exec. Dir.* Tadashi Yamashita.

Kenya

Kenya Publishers Assn., P.O. Box 42767, Nairobi 00100. Tel. 20-375-2344, fax 20-375-4076, e-mail info@kenyapublishers.org, World Wide Web http://www.kenyapublishers.org. *Chair* Nancy Karimi; *Exec. Officer* James Odhiambo.

Korea (Republic of)

Korean Publishers Assn., 105-2 Sagan-dong, Jongro-gu, Seoul 110-190. Tel. 70-7126-4720, fax 2-738-5414, e-mail webmaster@kpa21.or.kr, World Wide Web http://www.kpa21.or.kr. *Pres.* Sok-Ghee Baek; *Secy.-Gen.* Jon Jin Jung.

Latvia

Latvian Publishers' Assn., K Barona 36-13, LV-1001 Riga. Tel. 67-359-178, fax 67-216-921, e-mail lga@gramatizdeveji.lv, World Wide Web http://www.gramatizdeveji.lv. *Pres.* Janis Leja; *Exec. Dir.* Dace Pugaca.

Lithuania

Lithuanian Publishers Assn., A Jaksto 9-231, LT-01105 Vilnius. Tel./fax 5-261-77-40, e-mail lla@centras.lt, World Wide Web http://www.lla.lt. *Pres.* Lolita Varanaviciene; *Exec. Dir.* Aida Dobkeviciute-Dzioveniene.

Malaysia

Malaysian Book Publishers' Assn., No. 7-6, Block E2, Jalan PJU 1/42A, Dataran Prima, 47301 Petaling Jaya, Selangor. Tel. 603-788-05-840, fax 603-788-05-841, e-mail info@abopa.com.my; World Wide Web http://www.mabopa.com.my. *Pres.* Law King Hui.

Mexico

Cámara Nacional de la Industria Editorial Mexicana (Mexican Publishers' Assn.), Holanda No. 13, CP 04120, Mexico DF. Tel. 155-5605-8784, fax 155-56-04-31-47, e-mail contacto@caniem.com, World Wide Web http://www.caniem.com. *Pres.* Victorico Albores Santiago.

The Netherlands

KVB—Koninklijke Vereeniging van het Boekenvak (formerly Koninklijke Vereeniging ter Bevordering van de Belangen des Boekhandels) (Royal Dutch Book Trade Assn.), Postbus 15007, 1001 MA Amsterdam. Tel. 20-624-02-12, fax 20-620-88-71, e-mail info@kvb.nl, World Wide Web http://www.kvb.nl. *Exec. Dir.* C. Verberne.

Nederlands Uitgeversverbond (Royal Dutch Publishers Assn.), Postbus 12040, 1100 AA Amsterdam. Tel. 20-43-09-150, fax 20-43-09-199, e-mail info@nuv.nl, World Wide Web http://www.nuv.nl. *Pres.* Henk J. L. Vonhoff.

Nederlandsche Vereeniging van Antiquaren (Netherlands Assn. of Antiquarian Booksellers), Prinsengracht 15, 2512 EW The Hague. Tel. 70-364-98-40, fax 70-364-33-40, e-mail kok@xs4all.nl, World Wide Web http://nvva.nl. *Pres.* Ton Kok.

Nederlandse Boekverkopersbond (Dutch Booksellers Assn.), Postbus 32, 3720 AA Bilhoven. Tel. 30-22-87-956, fax 030-22-84-566, e-mail nbb@boekbond.nl, World Wide Web http://www.boekbond.nl. *Chair* Dick Anbeek.

New Zealand

Booksellers New Zealand, P.O. Box 25-033, Wellington 6146. Tel. 4-472-1908, fax 4-472-1912, e-mail info@booksellers.co.nz, World Wide Web http://www.booksellers.co.nz. *CEO* Lincoln Gould.

Nigeria

Nigerian Publishers Assn., GPO Box 2541, Ibadan. Tel. 2-751-5352, e-mail info@nigerianpublishers.org, World Wide Web http://www.nigerianpublishers.org. *Pres.* Samuel Kolawole.

Norway

Norske Bokhandlerforening (Norwegian Booksellers Assn.), Øvre Vollgate 15, 0158 Oslo. Tel. 22-40-45-40, fax 22-41-12-89, e-mail post@bokogsamfunn.no, World Wide Web http://www.bokogsamfunn.no. *Dir.* Randi S. Øgrey.

Norske Forleggerforening (Norwegian Publishers Assn.), Øvre Vollgate 15, 0158 Oslo. Tel. 22-39-68-00, fax 22-39-68-10, e-mail firmapost@bokhandlerforeningen.no, World Wide Web http://www.bokhandlerforeningen.no. *Dir.* Randi S. Øgrey.

Peru

Cámara Peruana del Libro (Peruvian Publishers Assn.), Av. Cuba 427, Jesús María, Apdo. 10253, Lima 11. Tel. 1-472-9516, fax 1-265-0735, e-mail cp-libro@amauta.rcp.net.pe, World Wide Web http://www.cpl.org.pe. *Pres.* Gladys Diaz Carrera.

Philippines

Philippine Educational Publishers Assn., c/o St Mary's Publishing Corp., 1308 P Guevarra St., Santa Cruz, 1308 Manila. Tel. 2-73 4-7790, fax 2-735-0959, e-mail dbuhain@cnl.net, World Wide Web http://nbdb.gov.ph/publindust.htm. *Pres.* Dominador D. Buhain.

Poland

Polskie Towarzystwo Wydawców Książek (Polish Society of Book Editors), ul. Holy Cross 30, lok. 156, 00-116 Warsaw. Tel. 22-407-77-30, fax 22-850-34-76, e-mail ptwk@wp.pl, World Wide Web http://www.wydawca.com.pl. *Pres.* Raphael Skapski; *Secy. Gen.* Maria Kuisz.

Stowarzyszenia Księgarzy Polskich (Assn. of Polish Booksellers), ul. Mazowiecka 2/4, 00-054 Warsaw. Tel./fax 22-827-93-81, e-mail skp@ksiegarze.org.pl, World Wide Web http://www.ksiegarze.org.pl. *Chair* Waldemar Janaszkiewicz.

Portugal

Associação Portuguesa de Editores e Livreiros (Portuguese Assn. of Publishers and Booksellers), Av. dos Estados Unidas da America 97, 6 Esq., 1700-167 Lisbon. Tel. 21-843-51-80, fax 21-848-93-77, e-mail geral@apel.pt, World Wide Web http://www.apel.pt. *Pres.* Graca Didier.

Russia

Assn. of Book Publishers of Russia, ul. B. Nikitskaya 44, 121069 Moscow. Tel. 495-202-1174, fax 495-202-3989, e-mail aski@rol.ru, World Wide Web http://www.aski.ru. *Pres.* Konstantin V. Chechenev.

Rossiiskaya Knizhnaya Palata (Russian Book Chamber), Kremlin nab, 1/9, 119019 Moscow. Tel. 495-688-96-89, fax 495-688-99-91, e-mail bookch@postman.ru, World Wide Web http://www.bookchamber.ru. *Dir. Gen.* Elena Nogina.

Serbia and Montenegro

Assn. of Yugoslav Publishers and Booksellers, Kneza Milosa 25/1, 11000 Belgrade. Tel. 11-642-533, fax 11-686-539, e-mail ognjenl@eunet.yu.

Singapore

Singapore Book Publishers Assn., c/o Cannon International, 86 Marine Parade Central No. 03-213, Singapore 440086. Tel. 6344-7801, fax 6344-0897, e-mail twcsbpa@singnet.com.sg, World Wide Web http://www.publishers-sbpa.org.sg. *Pres.* Triena Ong.

Slovenia

Zdruzenie Zaloznikov in Knjigotrzcev Slovenije Gospodarska Zbornica Slovenije (Assn. of Publishers and Booksellers of Slovenia), Dimičeva 13, SI 1000 Ljubljana. Tel. 1-5898-000, fax 1-5898-100, e-mail info@

gzs.si, World Wide Web http://www.gzs.si. *Pres.* Milan Matos.

South Africa

Publishers Assn. of South Africa (PASA), P.O. Box 106, Green Point 8051. Tel. 21-425-2721, fax 21-421-3270, e-mail pasa@publishsa.co.za, World Wide Web http://www.publishsa.co.za. *Exec. Dir.* Brian Wafawarowa.

South African Booksellers Assn. (formerly Associated Booksellers of Southern Africa), P.O. Box 870, Bellville 7535. Tel. 21-945-1572, fax 21-945-2169, e-mail saba@sabooksellers.com, World Wide Web http://sabooksellers.com. *Chair and Pres.* Guru Redhi.

Spain

Federación de Gremios de Editores de España (Federation of Spanish Publishers Assns.), Cea Bermúdez 44-2 Dcha, 2003 Madrid. Tel. 915-345-195, fax 915-352-625, e-mail fgee@fge.es, World Wide Web http://www.federacioneditores.org. *Pres.* Pedro de Andres; *Exec. Dir.* Antonio María Avila.

Sri Lanka

Sri Lanka Book Publishers Assn., 61 Ven Hikkaduwe Sri Sumangala Nahimi Mawatha, Maradana, Colombo 10. Tel. 74-304-546, fax 1-821-454, e-mail bookpub@sltnet.lk, World Wide Web http://www.bookpublishers.lk. *Gen. Secy.* Upali Wanigasooriya.

Sudan

Sudanese Publishers' Assn., c/o Institute of African and Asian Studies, Khartoum Univ., P.O. Box 321, Khartoum 11115. Tel. 11-77-0022. *Dir.* Al-Amin Abu Manga Mohamed.

Sweden

Svenska Förläggareföreningen (Swedish Publishers Assn.), Drottninggatan 97, S-11360 Stockholm. Tel. 8-736-19-40, fax 8-736-19-44, e-mail info@forlaggare.se, World Wide Web http://www.forlaggare.se. *Dir.* Kristina Ahlinder.

Switzerland

Association Suisse des Éditeurs de Langue Française (ASELF) (Swiss Assn. of French-Language Publishers), 2 ave. Agassiz, 1001 Lausanne. Tel. 21-319-71-11, fax 21-319-79-10, e-mail aself@centrezational.cl, World Wide Web http://www.culturactif.ch/editions/asef1.htm. *Pres.* Francine Bouchet.

Schweizerischer Buchhandler- und Verleger-Verband (Swiss German-Language Booksellers and Publishers Assn.), Alderstr. 40, Postfach, 8034 Zurich. Tel. 044-421-36-00, fax 044-421-36-18, e-mail sbvv@swissbooks.ch, World Wide Web http://www.swissbooks.ch. *Exec. Dir.* Martin Jann.

Thailand

Publishers and Booksellers Assn. of Thailand, 83/156 Soi Chinnakhet 2, Ngam Wong Wan Rd., Thung Song Hong, Lak Si, Bangkok 10210. Tel. 662-954-9560-4, fax 662-954-9565-6, e-mail info@pubat.or.th, World Wide Web http://www.pubat.or.th.

Uganda

Uganda Publishers and Booksellers Assn., P.O. Box 7732, Kampala. Tel. 41-428-6093, fax 41-428-6397, e-mail mbd@infocom.co.ug. *Gen. Secy.* Martin Okia.

United Kingdom

Antiquarian Booksellers Assn., Sackville House, 40 Piccadilly, London W1J 0DR, England. Tel. 20-7439-3118, fax 20-7439-3119, e-mail admin@aba.org.uk, World Wide Web http://www.aba.org.uk. *Admin.* Clare Pedder; *Secy.* John Critchley.

Assn. of Learned and Professional Society Publishers, 1-3 Ship St., Shoreham-by-Sea, West Sussex BN43 5DH, England. Tel. 1275-858-837, World Wide Web http://www.alpsp.org. *Chief Exec.* Ian Russell.

Booktrust, Book House, 45 East Hill, Wandsworth, London SW18 2QZ, England. Tel. 20-8516-2977, fax 20-8516-2978, e-mail query@booktrust.org.uk, World Wide Web http://www.booktrust.org.uk. *CEO* Viv Bird.

Educational Publishers Council, 29B Montague St., London WC1B 5BW, England. Tel. 20-7691-9191, fax 20-7691-9199, e-mail mail@publishers.org.uk, World Wide Web http://www.publishers.org.uk/en/educational. *Chair* Rob Ince; *Dir.* Graham Taylor.

Publishers Assn., 29B Montague St., London WC1B 5BW, England. Tel. 20-7691-9191, fax 20-7691-9199, e-mail mail@publishers.org.uk, World Wide Web http://www.publishers.org.uk. *CEO* Richard Mollet; *Dir.* Graham Taylor.

Scottish Book Trust, Sandeman House, Trunk's Close, 55 High St., Edinburgh EH1 1SR, Scotland. Tel. 131-524-0160, fax 131-524-0161, e-mail info@scottishbooktrust.com, World Wide Web http://www.scottishbooktrust.com. *CEO* Marc Lambert.

Welsh Books Council (Cyngor Llyfrau Cymru), Castell Brychan, Aberystwyth, Ceredigion SY23 2JB, Wales. Tel. 1970-624-151, fax 1970-625-385, e-mail castellbrychan@wbc.org.uk, World Wide Web http://www.cllc.org.uk. *Dir.* Elwyn Jones.

Uruguay

Cámara Uruguaya del Libro (Uruguayan Publishers Assn.), Colon 1476, Apdo. 102, 11 200 Montevideo. Tel. 82-916-93-74, fax 82-916-76-28, e-mail info@camaradellibro.com.uy, World Wide Web http://www.camaradellibro.com.uy. *Pres.* Alvaro Juan Risso Castellanos.

Venezuela

Cámara Venezolana del Libro (Venezuelan Publishers Assn.), Av. Andrés Bello, Centro Andrés Bello, Torre Oeste 11, piso 11, of. 112-0, Caracas 1050. Tel. 212-793-1347, fax 212-793-1368, e-mail unegi@cavelibro.org, World Wide Web http://www.cavelibro.org. *Pres.* Leonardo Ramos.

Zambia

Booksellers Assn. of Zambia, P.O. Box 51109, 10101 Lusaka. Tel./fax 211-255-166, e-mail bpaz@zamtel.zm. *Contact* Enock Mwale.

Zimbabwe

Zimbabwe Book Publishers Assn., P.O. Box 3794, Harare. Tel./fax 4-754-256, e-mail engelbert@collegepress.co.zw.

National Information Standards Organization (NISO) Standards

Information Retrieval

Z39.2-1994 (R2009)	Information Interchange Format
Z39.47-1993 (R2003)	Extended Latin Alphabet Coded Character Set for Bibliographic Use (ANSEL)
Z39.50-2003 (R2009)	Information Retrieval (Z39.50) Application Service Definition and Protocol Specification
Z39.53-2001	Codes for the Representation of Languages for Information Interchange
Z39.64-1989 (R2002)	East Asian Character Code for Bibliographic Use
Z39.76-1996 (R2002)	Data Elements for Binding Library Materials
Z39.84-2005 (R2010)	Syntax for the Digital Object Identifier
Z39.88-2004 (R2010)	The OpenURL Framework for Context-Sensitive Services
Z39.89-2003 (R2009)	The U.S. National Z39.50 Profile for Library Applications

Library Management

Z39.7	Information Services and Use: Metrics and Statistics for Libraries and Information Providers—Data Dictionary
Z39.20-1999	Criteria for Price Indexes for Print Library Materials
Z39.71-2006	Holdings Statements for Bibliographic Items
Z39.73-1994 (R2001)	Single-Tier Steel Bracket Library Shelving
Z39.83-1	NISO Circulation Interchange Part 1: Protocol (NCIP)
Z39.83-2	NISO Circulation Interchange Protocol (NCIP) Part 2: Implementation Profile 1
Z39.93-2007	The Standardized Usage Statistics Harvesting Initiative (SUSHI) Protocol

Preservation and Storage

Z39.32-1996 (R2002)	Information on Microfiche Headers
Z39.48-1992 (R2009)	Permanence of Paper for Publications and Documents in Libraries and Archives
Z39.62-2000	Eye-Legible Information on Microfilm Leaders and Trailers and on Containers of Processed Microfilm on Open Reels
Z39.74-1996 (R2002)	Guides to Accompany Microform Sets

Z39.77-2001	Guidelines for Information About Preservation Products
Z39.78-2000 (R2006)	Library Binding
Z39.79-2001	Environmental Conditions for Exhibiting Library and Archival Materials
Z39.87-2006	Data Dictionary—Technical Metadata for Digital Still Images

Publishing and Information Management

Z39.9-1992 (R2001)	International Standard Serial Numbering (ISSN)
Z39.14-1997 (R2009)	Guidelines for Abstracts
Z39.18-2005 (R2010)	Scientific and Technical Reports—Preparation, Presentation, and Preservation
Z39.19-2005 (R2010)	Guidelines for the Construction, Format, and Management of Monolingual Controlled Vocabularies
Z39.23-1997 (R2009)	Standard Technical Report Number Format and Creation
Z39.26-1997 (R2002)	Micropublishing Product Information
Z39.29-2005 (R2010)	Bibliographic References
Z39.41-1997 (R2009)	Printed Information on Spines
Z39.43-1993 (R2006)	Standard Address Number (SAN) for the Publishing Industry
Z39.56-1996 (R2002)	Serial Item and Contribution Identifier (SICI)
Z39.82-2001	Title Pages for Conference Publications
Z39.85-2001	Dublin Core Metadata Element Set
Z39.86-2005	Specifications for the Digital Talking Book
ANSI/NISO/ISO 12083-1995 (R2002)	Electronic Manuscript Preparation and Markup

In Development/NISO Initiatives

NISO examines new areas for standardization, reports, and best practices on a continuing basis to support its ongoing standards development program. NISO working groups are exploring these areas:

- DAISY Standard (ANSI/NISO Z39.86-2005 Specifications for the Digital Talking Book) Revision
- ERM Data Standards and Best Practices Review
- Establishing Suggested Practices Regarding Single Sign-On (ESPReSSO)
- Improving OpenURLs Through Analytics (IOTA)
- Institutional Identifiers (I2)
- KBART (Knowledge Bases and Related Tools) Phase II (NISO and UKSG)
- Physical Delivery of Library Materials
- Presentation and Identification of E-Journals (PIE-J)
- RFID for Library Applications Revision (NISO RP-6-201x)
- SERU (Shared Electronic Resource Understanding)
- Standardized Markup for Journal Articles

NISO Technical Reports and Recommended Practices

Best Practices for Designing Web Services in the Library Context (NISO RP-2006-01)

Cost of Resource Exchange (CORE) Protocol (NISO RP-10-2010)

Environmental Guidelines for the Storage of Paper Records (NISO TR01-1995), by William K. Wilson

A Framework of Guidance for Building Good Digital Collections, 3rd ed., 2007

Guidelines for Indexes and Related Information Retrieval Devices (NISO TR02-1997), by James D. Anderson

Guidelines for Alphabetical Arrangement of Letters and Sorting of Numerals and Other Symbols (NISO TR03-1999), by Hans H. Wellisch

Journal Article Versions (JAV) (NISO RP-8-2008)

KBART: Knowledge Bases and Related Tools (NISO RP-9-2010)

Networked Reference Services: Question/Answer Transaction Protocol (NISO TR04-2006)

NISO Metasearch XML Gateway Implementers Guide (NISO RP-2006-02)

Ranking of Authentication and Access Methods Available to the Metasearch Environment (NISO RP-2005-01)

RFID in U.S. Libraries (NISO RP-6-2008)

Search and Retrieval Citation Level Data Elements (NISO RP-2005-03)

Search and Retrieval Results Set Metadata (NISO RP-2005-02)

SERU: A Shared Electronic Resource Understanding (NISO RP-7-2008)

Other NISO Publications

The Case for New Economic Models to Support Standardization, by Clifford Lynch

The Exchange of Serials Subscription Information, by Ed Jones

Information Standards Quarterly (*ISQ*) (NISO quarterly open access magazine)

Internet, Interoperability and Standards—Filling the Gaps, by Janifer Gatenby

Issues in Crosswalking Content Metadata Standards, by Margaret St. Pierre and William P. LaPlant

Metadata Demystified: A Guide for Publishers, by Amy Brand, Frank Daly, and Barbara Meyers

The Myth of Free Standards: Giving Away the Farm, by Andrew N. Bank

NISO Newsline (free monthly e-newsletter)

NISO Working Group Connection (free quarterly supplement to *NISO Newsline*)

Patents and Open Standards, by Priscilla Caplan

The RFP Writer's Guide to Standards for Library Systems, by Cynthia Hodgson

Streamlining Book Metadata Workflow, by Judy Luther

Understanding Metadata

Up and Running: Implementing Z39.50—Proceedings of a Symposium Sponsored by the State Library of Iowa, edited by Sara L. Randall

Z39.50: A Primer on the Protocol
Z39.50 Implementation Experiences

NISO standards are available online at http://www.niso.org/standards. Recommended Practices, Technical Reports, White Papers, and other publications are available on the NISO Web site at http://www.niso.org/publications.

For more information, contact NISO, 1 North Charles St., Suite 1905, Baltimore, MD 21201. Telephone 301-654-2512, fax 410-685-5278, e-mail nisohq@niso.org, World Wide Web http://www.niso.org.

Calendar, 2011–2020

The list below contains information on association meetings or promotional events that are, for the most part, national or international in scope. State and regional library association meetings are also included. To confirm the starting or ending date of a meeting, which may change after the *Library and Book Trade Almanac* has gone to press, contact the association directly. Addresses of library and book trade associations are listed in Part 6 of this volume. For information on additional book trade and promotional events, see *Literary Market Place* and *International Literary Market Place,* published by Information Today, Inc., and other library and book trade publications such as *Library Journal, School Library Journal,* and *Publishers Weekly. American Libraries,* published by the American Library Association (ALA), maintains an online calendar at http://www.ala.org/ala/alonline/calendar/calendar.cfm, and ALA keeps a separate calendar at http://www.ala.org/ala/conferencesevents/afficalendar/index.cfm. An Information Today events calendar can be found at http://www.infotoday.com/calendar.shtml.

2011

May

23–26	BookExpo America	New York

June

1–3	Society for Scholarly Publishing	Boston
2–3	Rhode Island Library Assn.	Smithfield
2–4	Assn. of Canadian Archivists	Toronto
2–5	Assn. of American University Presses	Baltimore
2–5	International Book Fair for Small Presses	Mainz, Germany
5–7	Global Information Technology Management Assn.	Las Vegas
6–11	Moscow International Book Fair	Moscow, Russia
7–11	International Conference on Open Repositories	Austin, TX
9–21	Next Library 2011	Aarhus, Denmark
12–15	Special Libraries Assn.	Philadelphia
15–17	Georgia Library Media Assn.	Pine Mountain
15–19	Seoul International Book Fair	Seoul, Korea
16–19	Cape Town Book Fair	Cape Town, South Africa

June 2011 *(cont.)*

19–22	Assn. of Jewish Libraries	Montreal
22–24	International Conference on Electronic Publishing	Istanbul, Turkey
23–28	American Library Assn. Annual Conference	New Orleans
27–29	International Conference on the Information Society	London, England
27–30	Evidence Based Library and Information Practice	Manchester, England
29–7/2	Assn. of European Research Libraries (LIBER)	Barcelona, Spain

July

7–8	European Conference on Information Warfare and Security	Tallinn, Estonia
7–10	Tokyo International Book Fair	Tokyo, Japan
11–13	International Conference on Networked Digital Technologies	Macau, China
12–13	Umbrella 2011 Conference and Exhibition (CILIP)	Hatfield, England
13–16	National Assn. of Government Archives and Records Administrators (NAGARA)	Nashville
19	Library and Information Science Research Coalition	London, England
19–22	Church and Synagogue Library Assn.	Washington, DC
20–26	Hong Kong Book Fair	Hong Kong
23–26	American Assn. of Law Libraries	Philadelphia

August

3–5	Pacific Northwest Library Assn.	Spokane
4–7	Americas Conference on Information Systems	Detroit
11–12	Information Literacy and its Impact on Women (IFLA satellite)	Gurabo, Puerto Rico
13–18	IFLA General Conference and Assembly	San Juan, Puerto Rico
16–19	Scandinavian Conference of Information Systems (SCIS 2011)	Turku, Finland
22–27	Society of American Archivists	Chicago
31–9/4	Beijing International Book Fair	Beijing, China

September

1–11	Rio de Janeiro International Book Fair	Rio de Janeiro, Brazil
14–16	IEEE European Conference on Web Services 2011	Lugano, Switzerland
15–18	REFORMA	Denver
17–24	Colombo International Book Fair	Colombo, Sri Lanka

22–25	Göteborg Book Fair	Gothenburg, Sweden
24–27	Arkansas Library Assn.	Little Rock
28–10/1	Kentucky Library Assn.	Louisville
29–10/2	Library and Information Technology Association (LITA)	St. Louis

October

2–4	New England Library Assn.	Burlington, VT
2–5	Pennsylvania Library Assn.	State College
4–5	Missouri Library Assn.	Kansas City
4–7	North Carolina Library Assn.	Hickory
4–7	West Virginia Library Assn.	Charleston
5–7	Georgia Council of Media Organizations	Athens
5–7	Madrid International Book Fair	Madrid, Spain
5–7	Nebraska Library Assn.	Lincoln
5–7	South Dakota Library Assn.	Spearfish
6–7	Georgia Library Assn.	Athens
7–12	American Society for Information Science & Technology (ASIS&T)	New Orleans
12–14	Iowa Library Assn.	Council Bluffs
12–14	Minnesota Library Assn.	Duluth
12–16	Frankfurt Book Fair	Frankfurt, Germany
13–15	Colorado Assn. of Libraries	Loveland
17–19	Internet Librarian 2011	Monterey, CA
18–19	Streaming Media Europe 2011	London, England
18–21	Illinois Library Assn.	Rosemont
24–27	International Conference on Asia-Pacific Digital Libraries	Beijing, China
26–28	Ohio Library Council	Toledo
27–28	Internet Librarian International 2011	London, England
27–28	Virginia Library Assn.	Portsmouth
27–30	American Assn. of School Librarians	Minneapolis
28–30	Toronto International Antiquarian Book Fair	Toronto

November

1–3	KMWorld 2011	Washington, DC
1–4	Wisconsin Library Assn.	Milwaukee
2–5	New York Library Assn.	Saratoga Springs
8–10	Streaming Media West 2011	Los Angeles
11–14	California Library Association	Pasadena
12–20	Istanbul Book Fair	Istanbul, Turkey
13–20	Miami Book Fair International	Miami
16–21	Montreal Book Fair	Montreal
26–12/4	Guadalajara International Book Fair	Guadalajara, Mexico
27–30	International Conference on Academic Libraries	Hyderabad, India

December 2011

6–8	Sixth International Digital Curation Conference	Chicago

2012

January

4–5	DigCCurr Professional Institute	Chapel Hill, NC
20–24	American Library Assn. Midwinter Meeting	Dallas

February

25–3/4	New Delhi World Book Fair	New Delhi, India

March

13–17	Public Library Assn.	Philadelphia
24–27	Texas Library Association	Houston
25–4/5	Art Libraries Assn. of North America	Toronto

April

24–27	Texas Library Assn.	Houston

May

30–6/1	BookExpo America	New York

June

21–26	American Library Assn. Annual Conference	Anaheim

August

11–16	IFLA General Conference and Assembly	Helsinki, Finland

September

19–23	National Joint Conference of Librarians of Color	Kansas City

October

3–5	South Dakota Library Assn.	Huron
23–26	Wisconsin Library Assn.	La Crosse

November

2–4	YALSA Young Adult Literature Symposium	St. Louis

2013

January

25–29	American Library Assn. Midwinter Meeting	Seattle

April

4–7	Assn. of College and Research Libraries	Indianapolis
8–12	Texas Library Assn.	San Antonio

June

27–7/2	American Library Assn. Annual Conference	Chicago

September

25–27	Mountain Plains Library Assn., North Dakota Library Assn., South Dakota Library Assn.	Sioux Falls

2014

January

24–28	American Library Assn. Midwinter Meeting	Philadelphia

April

8–11	Texas Library Assn.	Dallas

June

26–7/1	American Library Assn. Annual Conference	Las Vegas

October

1–3	South Dakota Library Assn.	Pierre

2015

January

23–27	American Library Assn. Midwinter Meeting	Chicago

April

10–17	Texas Library Assn.	Austin

June

25–30	American Library Assn. Annual Conference	San Francisco

2016

January

22–26	American Library Assn. Midwinter Meeting	Boston

June

23–28	American Library Assn. Annual Conference	Orlando

2017

January

20–24	American Library Assn. Midwinter Meeting	Atlanta

June

22–27	American Library Assn. Annual Conference	Chicago

2018

January

19–23	American Library Assn. Midwinter Meeting	Los Angeles

June

21–26	American Library Assn. Annual Conference	New Orleans

2019

January

25–29	American Library Assn. Midwinter Meeting	Seattle

June

27–7/2	American Library Assn. Annual Conference	New York

2020

January

24–27	American Library Assn. Midwinter Meeting	Philadelphia

June

27–7/2	American Library Assn. Annual Conference	To be announced

Acronyms

A

AALL. American Association of Law Libraries
AAP. Association of American Publishers
AASL. American Association of School Librarians
ABA. American Booksellers Association
ABC. Association of Booksellers for Children
ABFFE. American Booksellers Foundation for Free Expression
AC. Access Copyright
ACRL. Association of College and Research Libraries
AIIP. Association of Independent Information Professionals
AILA. American Indian Library Association
AJL. Association of Jewish Libraries
ALA. American Library Association
ALCTS. Association for Library Collections and Technical Services
ALIC. National Archives and Records Administration, Archives Library Information Center
ALISE. Association for Library and Information Science Education
ALS. National Center for Education Statistics, Academic Library Survey
ALSC. Association for Library Service to Children
ALTAFF. Association of Library Trustees, Advocates, Friends, and Foundations
AMMLA. American Merchant Marine Library Association
APA. Allied Professional Association
APALA. Asian/Pacific American Librarians Association
ARL. Association of Research Libraries
ARLIS/NA. Art Libraries Society of North America
ARSL. Association for Rural and Small Libraries
ASCLA. Association of Specialized and Cooperative Library Agencies
ASIS&T. American Society for Information Science and Technology
ATLA. American Theological Library Association
ATN. Access Text Network

B

BCALA. Black Caucus of the American Library Association
BEA. BookExpo America
BSA. Bibliographical Society of America

C

CACUL. Canadian Association of College and University Libraries
CAIS. Canadian Association for Information Science
CALA. Chinese-American Librarians Association
CAORC. Council for American Overseas Research Centers
CAPL. Canadian Association of Public Libraries
CARL. Canadian Association of Research Libraries
CASLIS. Canadian Association of Special Libraries and Information Services
CCC. Copyright Clearance Center
CDNL. Conference of Directors of National Libraries
CGP. Government Printing Office, *Catalog of Government Publications*
CLA. Canadian Library Association

CLASS. Library of Congress, Center for the Library's Analytical Science Samples
CLIR. Council on Library and Information Resources
CLTA. Canadian Library Trustees Association
CNI. Coalition for Networked Information
CNIB. Canadian National Institute for the Blind
COICA. Combating Online Infringement and Counterfeits Act
COLT. Council on Library/Media Technicians
COSLA. Chief Officers of State Library Agencies
CPSIA. Consumer Product Safety Improvement Act
CRP. Association of American Publishers, Campaign for Reader Privacy
CRS. Congressional Research Service
CSLA. Church and Synagogue Library Association
CUI. Government information, access to, controlled unclassified information

D

DHS. Homeland Security, Department of
DID. Statistics, Digging into Data Challenge
DLF. Digital Library Federation
DMCA. Digital Millennium Copyright Act
DOD. Defense, Department of
DRM. Digital rights management
DTIC. Defense Technical Information Center

E

EAR. National Technical Information Service, Export Administration Regulations
EBL. E-Book Library
ECIP. Library of Congress, Electronic Cataloging in Publication
EDB. National Technical Information Service, Energy Science and Technology Database
EM&PG. Educational Media & Publishing Group
EMIERT. American Library Association, Ethnic and Multicultural Information and Exchange Round Table
ESEA. Elementary and Secondary Education Act

F

FAFLRT. American Library Association, Federal and Armed Forces Librarians Round Table
FAIFE. International Federation of Library Associations and Institutions, Freedom of Access to Information and Freedom of Expression
FBI. Federal Bureau of Investigation
FCC. Federal Communications Commission
FDLP. Government Printing Office, Federal Depository Library Program
FDsys. FDsys (Federal Digital System)
FEDRIP. National Technical Information Service, FEDRIP (Federal Research in Progress Database)
FIAF. International Federation of Film Archives
FISMA. Federal Information Security Management Act
FLICC. Federal Library and Information Center Committee
FOIA. Freedom of Information Act
FRPAA. Federal Research Public Access Act
FTC. Federal Trade Commission

G

GLBT. American Library Association, Gay, Lesbian, Bisexual, and Transgendered Round Table
GLIN. Global Legal Information Network
GODORT. American Library Association, Government Documents Round Table
GPO. Government Printing Office
GSU. Georgia State University

I

IAALD. International Association of Agricultural Information Specialists
IACs. Defense Technical Information Center, Information Analysis Centers
IALL. International Association of Law Libraries
IAML. International Association of Music Libraries, Archives and Documentation Centres
IASL. International Association of School Librarians
ICA. International Council on Archives
ICBS. International Committee of the Blue Shield

IFLA. International Federation of Library Associations and Institutions
IFTP. Association of American Publishers, International Freedom to Publish
IIPA. International Intellectual Property Alliance
ILS. Government Printing Office, Integrated Library System
IMLS. Institute of Museum and Library Services
ISBN. International Standard Book Number
ISO. International Organization for Standardization
ISOO. National Archives and Records Administration, Information Security Oversight Office
ISSN. International Standard Serial Number
IVSL. Iraqi Virtual Science LIbrary

L

LAC. Library and Archives Canada
LC. Library of Congress
LCA. Library Copyright Alliance
LCDP. Association of Research Libraries, Leadership and Career Development Program
LHHS. Labor, Health, and Human Services Appropriations Bill
LHRT. American Library Association, Library History Round Table
LIS. Library/information science; Library of Congress, Legislative Information Service
LITA. Library and Information Technology Association
LJ. Library Journal
LLAMA. Library Leadership and Management Association
LRRT. American Library Association, Library Research Round Table
LSCM. Government Printing Office, Library Services and Content Management
LSP. National Center for Education Statistics, Library Statistics Program
LSTA. Library Services and Technology Act

M

MLA. Medical Library Association; Music Library Association

N

NAGARA. National Association of Government Archives and Records Administrators
NAL. National Agricultural Library
NARA. National Archives and Records Administration
NCAST. National Archives Center for Advanced Systems and Technologies
NCBI. National Center for Biotechnology Information
NCES. National Center for Education Statistics
NCLA. National Church Library Association
NDC. National Archives and Records Administration, National Declassification Center
NDIIPP. National Digital Information Infrastructure and Preservation Program
NDNP. Newspapers, National Digital Newspaper Program
NEA. National Education Association
NEH. National Endowment for the Humanities
NFAIS. National Federation of Advanced Information Services
NHPRC. National Historical Publications and Records Commission
NIH. National Institutes of Health
NISO. National Information Standards Organization
NLE. National Library of Education
NLM. National Library of Medicine
NMRT. American Library Association, New Members Round Table
NSF. National Science Foundation
NTIS. National Technical Information Service
NTRL. National Technical Information Service, National Technical Reports Library

O

ODNI. National Intelligence, office of the Director of
OGIS. Government Information Services, Office of

P

PLA. Public Library Association
PMC. PubMedCentral
PTDLA. Patent and Trademark Depository Library Association
PW. Publishers Weekly

R

RDA. Library of Congress, Resource Description and Access
RL/RC. National Library of Education, Research Library/Reference Center
RUSA. Reference and User Services Association

S

SAA. Society of American Archivists
SAN. Standard Address Number
SASS. National Center for Education Statistics, Schools and Staffing Survey
SBU. Government information, access to, Sensitive But Unclassified
SCI. Scholarly Communication Institute
SIIA. Software and Information Industry Association
SLA. Special Libraries Association
SPARC. SPARC (Scholarly Publishing and Academic Resources Coalition)
SRIM. National Technical Information Service, Selected Research in Microfiche
SRRT. American Library Association, Social Responsibilities Round Table
SSP. Society for Scholarly Publishing
STEM. Education, STEM (science, technology, engineering, and mathematics)
StLA. State libraries and library agencies, IMLS State Library Agencies

T

TLA. Theatre Library Association

U

ULC. Urban Libraries Council

V

VHP. History, Veterans History Project

W

WDL. World Digital Library
WIPO. World Intellectual Property Organization
WNC. World News Connection

Y

YALSA. Young Adult Library Services Association
YPG. Association of American Pubishers, Young to Publishing Group

Index of Organizations

Please note that many cross-references refer to entries in the Subject Index.

B

C

D

V

W

Y

Subject Index

Please note that many cross-references refer to entries in the Index of Organizations.

D

H

I

N

T

U